PHILOSOPHY
An Introduction to the Art of Wondering

Eighth Edition

James L. Christian
Professor Emeritus, Santa Ana College

Australia • Canada • Mexico • Singapore • Spain
United Kingdom • United States

Publisher: Holly J. Allen
Philosophy Editor: Steve Wainright
Assistant Editor: Lee McCracken
Editorial Assistant: Anna Lustig
Technology Project Manager: Susan Devanna
Marketing Manager: Worth Hawes
Marketing Assistant: Justine Ferguson
Advertising Project Manager: Bryan Vann
Print/Media Buyer: Barbara Britton
Composition Buyer: Ben Schroeter
Permissions Editor: Bob Kauser
Production Service: G&S Typesetters
Copy Editor: Rosemary Wetherold
Photo Researcher: Susan Holtz
Cover Designer: Yvo Riezebos
Cover Image: Getty Images
Compositor: G&S Typesetters
Text and Cover Printer: Transcontinental, Louiseville

Printed in Canada
1 2 3 4 5 6 7 06 05 04 03 02

For more information about our products, contact us at:
Thomson Learning Academic Resource Center
1-800-423-0563

For permission to use material from this text, contact us by:
Phone: 1-800-730-2214 **Fax:** 1-800-730-2215
Web: http://www.thomsonrights.com

Library of Congress Control Number: 2002104786

ISBN 0-15-505905-X

Wadsworth/Thomson Learning
10 Davis Drive
Belmont, CA 94002-3098
USA

Asia
Thomson Learning
5 Shenton Way #01-01
UIC Building
Singapore 068808

Australia
Nelson Thomson Learning
102 Dodds Street
South Melbourne, Victoria 3205
Australia

Canada
Nelson Thomson Learning
1120 Birchmount Road
Toronto, Ontario M1K 5G4
Canada

Europe/Middle East/Africa
Thomson Learning
High Holborn House
50/51 Bedford Row
London WC1R 4LR
United Kingdom

Latin America
Thomson Learning
Seneca, 53
Colonia Polanco
11560 Mexico D.F.
Mexico

Spain
Paraninfo Thomson Learning
Calle/Magallanes, 25
28015 Madrid, Spain

PRELUDE

The following pages
may lead you to wonder.
That's really what philosophy is—
wondering.

To philosophize
is to wonder about life—
about right and wrong,
love and loneliness, war and death.
It is to wonder creatively
about freedom, truth, beauty, time
and a thousand other things.

To philosophize is
to explore life.
It especially means breaking free
to ask questions.
It means resisting
easy answers.
To philosophize
is to seek in oneself
the courage to ask
painful questions.

But if, by chance,
you have already asked
all your questions
and found all the answers—
if you're sure you know
right from wrong,
and whether God exists,
and what justice means,
and why we mortals fear and hate and pray—
if indeed you have completed your wondering
about freedom and love and loneliness
and those thousand other things,
then the following pages
will waste your time.

Philosophy is for those
who are willing to be disturbed
with a creative disturbance.

Philosophy is for those
who still have the capacity
for wonder.

Edwin Prince Booth

Thank you for showing me why we must tirelessly seek out the profoundly human element in all historic events since only therein can their meaning be found.

Arnold Toynbee

In memoriam: October 22, 1975

Thank you for the passion to see all existence as a single phenomenon without losing sight of the most minute details—this cave painting, this footnote, this flower in this crannied wall.

Herman and Anne

In memoriam: April 22 and 27, 1987

Thank you each for a parent's love and more. There are no words to express my appreciation of you both.

Lori

Thank you for teaching me that survival is one thing, living is quite another.

Credit ✦ Blame ✦ Acknowledgments

From the Preface to the First Edition ✦ February 1973

I have written this book for my philosophy students . . . and for all who are caught up in the wonderment of life—its mystery, its enormity, its diversity.

All of us wonder, sometime or often, about our place in the world. What we are asking is how we can relate most happily to ourselves, to others close about us, to fellow creatures with whom we share our delicate planet, and to our mind-boggling universe. We burn with an urgency to know and understand, but we often despair of finding a way to turn our knowledge into insight and wisdom.

A philosophy text should offer cautious counsel to all who would seek intelligent, nonpartisan guidance on the life-and-death questions of human existence.

Eliot Aronson notes that so many of our students ask us what time it is, and we respond by presenting to them the history of time-keeping from waterclocks to wristwatches. By the time we finish, they have turned elsewhere to ask their questions.

And J. B. Priestley hurts when he reminds us that the man who shouts "My house is on fire!" may not be able to define precisely what he means by *my* and *house* and *is* and *on* and *fire,* but he may still be saying something very, very important.

From the Preface to the Second Edition ✦ January 1977

This book is a teaching instrument, a collection of teaching materials which, at one point or another, raises most of the classical problems of philosophy as well as many contemporary and relatively new philosophical questions. All materials in this book can be employed analytically and synoptically, to perform the numerous tasks required by classroom philosophic activity.

Some chapters include empirical data that we would normally subsume under Psychology, Biology, Chemistry, and the like. It helps enormously, I have found, if philosophy students have a fund of shared information, however brief, on a few specific problems before they plunge into a philosophic discussion of them.

From the Preface to the Third Edition ✦ January 1981

My gratitude continues to the many individuals acknowledged in the first and second editions. Now, I'm indebted to many more, especially to Dr. Robert W. Smith for being a travel-guide in many worlds and co-conspirator in this one; and for strength and friendship.

From the Preface to the Fourth Edition ✦ August 1985

Each evening one of our local television stations plays its off-the-air theme containing the words "The world has gone through a lot today." This is my sentiment as the years pass and new revisions of this textbook are published. I am astounded at how much the world has gone through during each interim, how much it has changed, how many new world-views are in the offing, how much new knowledge has been gained, and how much new understanding has been made possible. It's bewildering, of course, but very exciting.

Each new edition of this book attempts to incorporate some of these new understandings. Unhappily, the Nuclear Winter scenario is included this time, along with—more happily—the future vision of the space artist Robert McCall. Twelve new biographies of Western philosophers have been added in an attempt (1) to supply the student with some historical roots in the Western philosophical tradition; and (2) to make a select few of the great thinkers come to life as human beings.

From the Preface to the Fifth Edition ✦ January 1990

My gratitude continues to numerous individuals who gave time and strength to previous editions of this book, and I would like to say thank you once again to them: Court Holdgrafer, Robert Putman, Ray Bradbury.

To a special group of people—perplexing innocents all, but wise; changing but never changing: Cathy, Dane, Carla, Marcia, Sherrie, Reinar, Laurie, Shawn, Shannon, Linda. I love you all.

From the Preface to the Sixth Edition ✦ October 1994

Most of us today don't like the world very much and would like to reiterate Plato's conviction that there can be no peace until statesmen become philosophers, or vice versa.

We would like to say to the world, "Look, there are better ideas to live by." For instance, Voltaire said he might disagree with others' ideas but that he would fight to the death for their right to express them. Aristotle reminds us that the function of government is to provide safe environment so that we can all work to achieve *eudaimonia,* a state of well-being in which we can grow as human persons and actualize our creative energies.

Marcus Aurelius warns us not to worry about the perceptions of others, but to tend to our own honesty and integrity. Chuang-tzu gently chides us for worrying so much about what others think of us that we forget who we are. Thoreau reflected, "If I am not I, who will be?"

The Jains of India tell us there are 353 perspectives on every issue and not to think we've found the truth until we have explored all 353 viewpoints. Symmachus reminds us that we will never find the truth by following one road only, and Thomas Merton shows us that there are many paths to the top of the mountain.

Bergson spent his life telling us we must learn to be compassionate in our empathetic concern for others. Francis of Assisi exhorts us to sense the pain we inflict on the animals with whom we share our planet; and Schweitzer insists that a truly ethical individual will extend his compassion to all living creatures, not just to members of his own tribe.

There are better ideas than we hear on the networks and, like Plato, we become impatient. But then Toynbee suggests we remember that it wasn't our parents who made the world; Caesar admonishes us to make haste slowly—*festina lente;* and Joseph Campbell tells us that this life can be wonderful just as it is when we discover that we are all on the Hero's journey. Nietzsche reassures us that the human race will become nobler, fret not; and Ray Bradbury urges us to dream of great futures and, with courage and imagination, to work for them and make them happen.

From the Preface to the Seventh Edition ✦ January 1998

A few years ago I was asked by a questioner in an audience if I could select, from the great philosophers, the three statements that I thought to be the most profound (or meaningful or significant—I don't recall the exact word). At that time my mind came up with three prosaic proverbs. But, should I be asked the question today, I would submit the following as being, not merely profound, but urgently relevant:

- from Antisthenes the Athenian Cynic: "When states can no longer distinguish good men from bad men, they will perish."
- from Abraham Maslow: "If the only tool you have is a hammer, you tend to treat everything as if it were a nail."
- from Larry Niven, the science fiction writer: "The trouble with living on a planet is that it tends to make most of the inhabitants think small."

To these I would now add this haiku from Masahide:

Since my house
Burned down, I now own
A better view
Of the rising moon

I owe special thanks to Dean Dowling (who saw what no one else has seen), and to Robert Putman, whose knowledge of all things Greek (and not a few other realms of scholarship) was rich beyond measure. To my wife, Lori, without whose love, intellect, and articulately silent support this edition would not have been completed: Thank you.

Eighth Edition ✦ Moreover . . .

Since the last edition of this book, many of us have had to make adjustments in our values and priorities. Our nows have become more precious. Life, at its heart, is Greek tragedy, and over the last few million years nothing has changed.

There are fundamental flaws built into human thinking, the most dangerous being our ontological habit of thinking with big abstractions that keep us from dealing with the singular, the individual, the concrete, and the real. This too is not about to change.

There are great multitudes of good and decent people out there in the world who belong to the category of creators rather than destroyers. But they are not the ones who are most visible or most audible, not the ones who talk mindlessly and endlessly on television, not the ones who have a judgmental reaction to everything that differs from their way of seeing. They make up a beautiful though silent community. But they are there.

While my wife, Lori, and I were lunching in a restaurant one day, she said to me, "How can you not feel alive if you are creating?" And Bergson once wrote, "Where joy is, creation has been." This may be, for many of us, as near an answer to the meaning of life as we will find in this life. You're alive as long as you're creating. Ray Bradbury insists that it matters not what happens in the world; your moral obligation is keep on creating. It is the greatest of privileges to strive to belong to the community of creators.

This edition includes brief introductory précis for all chapters. Two chapters have been rewritten since the last edition: 7-2, on the physical sciences (to include some observations on relativity and quantum physics); and 8-1, on the role that religion plays in our lives. Four new biographies (of Sartre, Locke, Kierkegaard, and Einstein) have been added, along with two new boxes (on "the final stage of growth" from Dr. Kübler-Ross, in 8-3; and in 4-1 a dialogue with a Zen monk at Eiheiji). Much of the main text of the rest of the book has been revised.

Once again I am grateful to my wife, Lori, for her love and support, and especially for an incredibly intuitive psyche that just knows. . . .

I have been blessed by many individuals who, in various ways, have given of their time and creativity: Carleton Mills, Robert Putman, Peter Angeles, Ray Bradbury, George Kinnamon, Robert Badra, D. J. Atkinson, Robert Smith, Robert and Louise McCall, Reza Ganjavi, Jeff Stebbins, and Eva Armstrong.

It was my good fortune to be able to collaborate with men and women of great expertise and knowledge at Wadsworth. I'm especially indebted to Steve Wainwright, Jerry Holloway, Kara Kindstrom, Anna Lustig, and Gretchen Otto. I am grateful to the reviewers for this eighth edition: Cathryn Bailey, Minnesota State University; Dr. Joseph Brownrigg, Mt. San Antonio Community College; Dr. Emily Dial-Driver, Rogers State University; H. Phillips Hamlin, The University of Tennessee; Paul Jacobson, St. Ambrose University; Robert B. Mellert, Brookdale Community College; Andrew Messchaert, Porterville College; George Mummert, Moberly Area Community College. Their critical suggestions are appreciated, and many have been incorporated into this revision.

James Christian
August 2002

Contents

The Condition and the Odyssey

The Real World: Knowing and Unknowing

THE INNER WORLD: THE FANTASTIC JOURNEY

Delicate Coexistence: The Human Love/Hate Condition

The Protoplasmic Venture

VI

MICROCOSM / MACROCOSM / COSMOS

Of Ultimate Concern

Biographies

Uno itinere non potest perveniri ad tam grande secretum.

"The heart of so great a mystery can never be reached by following one road only."

Q. Aurelius Symmachus
Relatio Tertia

✦

Theaetetus: *Yes, Socrates, I stand in amazement when I reflect on the questions that men ask. By the gods, I do! I want to know more and more about such questions, and there are times when I almost become dizzy just thinking about them.*

Socrates: *Ah, yes, my dear Theaetetus, when Theodorus called you a philosopher he described you well. That feeling of wonder is the touchstone of the philosopher, and all philosophy has its origins in wonder. Whoever reminded us that Iris (the heavenly messenger) is the offspring of Thaumas (wonder) wasn't a bad genealogist.*

Plato
Theaetetus 155 C,D

✦

A sense of wonder started men philosophizing, in ancient times as well as today. Their wondering is aroused, first, by trivial matters; but they continue on from there to wonder about less mundane matters such as the changes of the moon, sun, and stars, and the beginnings of the universe. What is the result of this puzzlement? *An awesome feeling of ignorance.* Men began to philosophize, therefore, to escape ignorance.

Aristotle
Metaphysics I,2

What Do You Mean, Philosophy??

For man, the unexamined life is not worth living.

Socrates

1 Sometime, at your leisure, go into a large bookstore and browse. Check a variety of books in psychology, anthropology, physics, chemistry, archeology, astronomy, and other nonfiction fields. Look at the last chapter in each book. In a surprising number of cases, you will find that the author has chosen to round out his work with a summation of what the book is all about. That is, having written a whole book on a specialized subject in which he is probably an authority, he finds that he **also** has ideas about the larger meaning of, or larger context for, the facts that he has written about. The final chapter may be called "Conclusions," "Epilogue," "Postscript," "My Personal View," "Implications," "Comments," "Speculations," or (as in one case) "So What?" But in every instance, the author is trying to elucidate the larger implications of his subject matter and to clarify how he thinks it relates to other fields or to life. He has an urge to tell us **the meaning** of all his facts **taken together.** He wants to share with us the **wider implications** of what he has written.

When he or she does this, the author has moved beyond the role of a field specialist. He/she is doing philosophy.

Life does not cease to be funny when people die; any more than it ceases to be serious when people laugh.

George Bernard Shaw

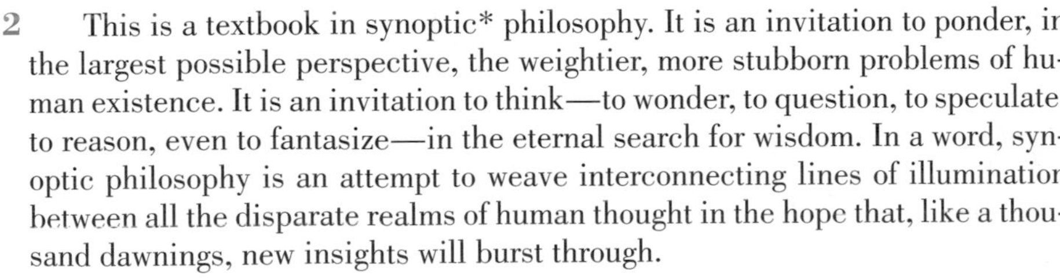

2 This is a textbook in synoptic* philosophy. It is an invitation to ponder, in the largest possible perspective, the weightier, more stubborn problems of human existence. It is an invitation to think—to wonder, to question, to speculate, to reason, even to fantasize—in the eternal search for wisdom. In a word, synoptic philosophy is an attempt to weave interconnecting lines of illumination between all the disparate realms of human thought in the hope that, like a thousand dawnings, new insights will burst through.

* **Synoptic** From the Greek *sunoptikos,* "seeing the whole together" or "taking a comprehensive view." The attempt to achieve an all-inclusive overview of one's subject matter. See Chapter 1-4 and glossary.

Understanding man and his place in the universe is perhaps the central problem of all science.

DUNN AND DOBZHANSKY

A life not put to the test is not worth living.

EPICTETUS

The meaning of life is arrived at . . . by dark gropings, by feelings not wholly understood, by catching at hints and fumbling for explanations.

ALFRED ADLER

"We're lost, but we're making good time."

City Slickers

There is an old saying that philosophy bakes no bread. It is perhaps equally true that no bread would ever have been baked without philosophy. For the act of baking implies a decision on the philosophical issue of whether life is worthwhile at all. Bakers may not have often asked themselves the question in so many words. But philosophy traditionally has been nothing less than the attempt to ask and answer, in a formal and disciplined way, the great questions of life that ordinary men put to themselves in reflective moments.

Time, January 7, 1966

3 By its very nature, philosophy is a do-it-yourself enterprise. There is a common misunderstanding that philosophy—like chemistry or history—has a content to offer, a content that a teacher is to teach and a student is to learn. This is not the case. There are no facts, no theories, certainly no final truths that go by the name of "philosophy" and that one is supposed to accept and believe. Rather, philosophy is a skill—more akin to mathematics and music; it is something that one learns to do.

Philosophy, that is, is a method. It is learning how to ask and reask questions until meaningful answers begin to appear. It is learning how to relate materials. It is learning where to go for the most dependable, up-to-date information that might shed light on some problem. It is learning how to double-check fact-claims in order to verify or falsify them. It is learning how to reject fallacious fact-claims—no matter how prestigious the authority who holds them or how deeply one personally would like to believe them.

4 Ever since Socrates spent his days in the marketplace engaging the Athenian citizens in thoughtful conversations, the message of philosophy has been that ordinary everyday thinking is inadequate for solving the important problems of life. If we are serious about finding solutions, then we need to learn to think more carefully, critically, and precisely about the issues of daily life.

5 Since its beginning some twenty-six centuries ago, philosophy has received many definitions. The simple definition that will be used as a guideline in this book is: Philosophy is critical thinking about thinking, the proximate goal of which is to get in touch with the truth about reality, the ultimate goal being to better see the Big Picture.

It is often said that philosophers engage in two basic tasks: "taking apart"—*analyzing* ideas to discover if we truly know what we think we know—and "putting together"—*synthesizing* all our knowledge to find if we can attain a larger and better view of life. That is, philosophers try very hard to dig deeper and fly higher in order to solve problems and achieve a modicum of wisdom on the question of life and how to live it.

To accomplish all this, philosophers talk a lot. They carry on dialogues with anyone who comes within range. And they argue a great deal. Not the usual kinds of argument in which egos fight to win, but philosophical arguments in which the participants attempt to clarify the reasoning that lies behind their statements; and no one cares about winning since, in philosophical arguments, everyone wins.

Philosophers also ask one another for definitions to be sure they're thinking clearly, and they push one another to pursue the implications of their ideas and statements. They prod themselves and others to examine the basic assumptions upon which their beliefs and arguments rest.

Philosophers are persistent explorers in the nooks and crannies of human knowledge that are commonly overlooked or deliberately ignored. It is an exciting but restless adventure of the mind.

6 Philosophers, however, do not engage in this critical task just to make nuisances of themselves. Indeed, the central aim of philosophers has always been . . . to construct a picture of the whole of reality, in which every element of man's knowledge and every aspect of man's experience will find its proper place. Philosophy, in

short, is man's quest for the unity of knowledge: it consists in a perpetual struggle to create the concepts in which the universe can be conceived as a *uni*verse and not a *multi*verse. The history of philosophy is the history of this attempt. The problems of philosophy are the problems that arise when the attempt is made to grasp this total unity. . . .

It cannot be denied that this attempt stands without rival as the most audacious enterprise in which the mind of man has ever engaged. Just reflect for a moment: Here is man, surrounded by the vastness of a universe in which he is only a tiny and perhaps insignificant part—and he wants to *understand* it.

William Halverson

"The truth, huh. It's worth a shot."

Room for Two **(TV)**

Man's concern about a meaning of life is the truest expression of the state of being human.

Viktor Frankl

7 The student should be aware that philosophy has never been just one kind of activity with a single approach to a single task. There have been many kinds of philosophy: the quiet philosophy of the sage who sees much but speaks little because language cannot hold life; the articulate, noisy dialectics of Socrates asking questions of everyone; the calm, logical apologetics of Aquinas; the mystical philosophies of Plotinus and Chuang-tzu; the mathematical and symbolic philosophy of Russell and Wittgenstein; the full-blooded everyday practical philosophy of Diogenes and Epicurus; the grand abstract logic of Hegel; the experience-centered individualism of Sartre and Camus.

Each school of philosophy has concentrated upon some aspect of man's knowledge. Logical/analytical philosophy has worked long and hard on the confusion that vitiates so much of our thinking and communicating. Pragmatism has concentrated on finding solutions to problems of man's social existence.

Morally, a philosopher who uses his professional competence for anything except a disinterested search for truth is guilty of a kind of treachery.

Bertrand Russell

I don't ask questions, I just have fun!

"Bugs Bunny"

Bugs Bunny/Roadrunner Show

PEANUTS® **By Charles M. Schulz**

Existential philosophy has been concerned with making life meaningful to each, unique individual. Activist schools argue that philosophers spend too much time trying to make sense of the world and too little time trying to change it. Several schools of philosophy, Eastern and Western, challenge the individual to turn away from an alienating society and to seek harmony with Nature or Ultimate Reality.

Each kind of philosophy has made an immense contribution to its area of concern. Each was doubtless a part of the *Zeitgeist*—"the spirit of the age"—that gave it birth and to which it spoke. What they all have in common is the attempt clean up our thinking so that we can reflect more knowledgeably, precisely, and honestly.

Most men spend their days struggling to evade three questions, the answers to which underlie man's every thought, feeling and action, whether he is consciously aware of it or not: Where am I? How do I know it? What should I do?

AYN RAND

There is but one Moon in the heavens, yet it is reflected in countless streams of water.

Amritabindu Upanishad

8 In one respect, philosophic material can be deceptive. Since it deals with life by examining the sort of questions we ask every day, some of the subject matter will have an easy, familiar ring.

The fact is that philosophy must be as diligently studied as any other subject, not to remember data, but to set the mind in motion toward developing larger concepts, connecting ideas, and seeing through and beyond mere words and facts. In a sense, intellectual growth **happens to us;** it is not really something that we do. But it happens to us only when our minds are given a chance to operate on their terms. They take their own time to process information. This undertaking is partly conscious, of course; but largely it is an unconscious process. This is why much philosophic insight just happens, as though the light moves from the depths upward and not from the rational conscious downward.

"Don't think about it. Just do it!"

Total Recall

God gave us memories so that we may have roses in December.

JAMES M. BARRIE

Only disciplined study with an open mind will produce philosophic awareness. Insight and consciousness still come only with relentless labor. In this age of instant everything, there is still no instant wisdom, unfortunately.

Out yonder there was this huge world . . . which stands before us like a great eternal riddle.

ALBERT EINSTEIN

9 No two of us possess precisely the same information, or see things from the same viewpoint, or share the same values. Therefore, each of us must do syn-

optic philosophy in his own unique and personal way. A student entering upon the activity of philosophizing may need to be on guard against developing a worldview that resembles, a bit too closely, the prepackaged philosophy of life belonging to someone else or to some institution. Most of us are philosophically lazy, and it is easy to appropriate another's thoughts and rationalize our theft. The British logician Wittgenstein warned us that "a thought which is not independent is a thought only half understood." Similarly, a philosophy of life that is not the authentic product of one's own experience is a philosophy only half understood.

Nor will any of us succeed in developing a finished philosophy; for as one changes with life, so does one's thinking. A philosophy **of life** must change **with life.** Doing philosophy is an endless activity.

For this reason, this textbook is merely an example of synoptic philosophy. This is the way I have had to do it because of **my** perspectives, **my** interests, **my** areas of knowledge, **my** personal concerns, and **my** limitations. But **your** worldview will be different because it will be **yours,** and **yours** alone.

This is why my attempt to do synoptic philosophy is, at most, a guideline showing how it might be done; at least, the expression of a hope that, someday, in your own way, you will resolve the contradictions of your own existence—both of knowing and of being—and proceed to see life in a larger, more fulfilling way.

Three things are necessary for the salvation of man: to know what he ought to believe; to know what he ought to desire; and to know what he ought to do.

SAINT THOMAS AQUINAS

Are we to mark this day with a white or a black stone?

CERVANTES

But to live an entire life without understanding how we think, why we feel the way we feel, what directs our actions is to miss what is most important in life, which is the quality of experience itself.

MIHALY CSIKZENTMIHALYI

The Fine Art of Wondering

To grow into youngness is a blow. To age into sickness is an insult. To die is, if we are not careful, to turn from God's breast, feeling slighted and unloved. The sparrow asks to be seen as it falls. Philosophy must try, as best it can, to turn the sparrows to flights of angels, which, Shakespeare wrote, sing us to our rest.

Ray Bradbury

The World-Riddle

1-1

For some two and a half millennia, philosophers have tried to make sense of the puzzling absurdity we call the human condition; they have tried to discern the root causes of our distress, despair, pain, and stupidity, while trying also to find ways to maximize the joy and meaning of our being human. This chapter raises some of the questions that philosophers have tried to answer, among them: Can the human mind understand the world? Can it discern the truth about human existence? Does life have meaning? (What do we mean by "meaning"?) What is it we're really after? We have been warned by Joseph Campbell: "What's running the show is what's coming up from way down below." Can we know what that is, or are we doomed to plunge ahead blindly without understanding what drives us? Is life always defeated? Or is there truly such a thing as "the hero's journey"?

Every culture has devised its own way of responding to the riddle of the Cosmos. . . . There are many different ways of being human.

Carl Sagan

Just In Case . . .

1 Shortly before a solar eclipse was to occur in central India, an Indian physicist —who was also a member of the Brahmin caste—was lecturing to his students at the university. He told them precisely when the event would begin and described in detail how the Moon's orbit would take it between the Sun and the Earth. In their city there would be only a partial eclipse, but on a wall map he pointed out the path of total eclipse as it moved across the terrestrial globe to the north of them. They discussed such things as the corona, the solar flares, the beauty of annular rings, and the appearance of Bailey's beads during that rare total eclipse. Some of the students from the rural villages had heard stories about a Giant Dragon that swallowed the Sun, but their teacher's lucid presentation of celestial mechanics had dispelled any fears they might have felt.

We are what we think, having become what we thought.

The Dhammapada

One can tell for oneself whether the water is warm or cold.

I Ching

Having dismissed his class, the professor returned to his village and, since he was a Brahmin, assumed his duties as a priest. Around his shoulders he draped the vestments of his office and began counting through his string of beads, calling aloud the names of the gods. A goat was beheaded in sacrifice to Kali, the Black Goddess, the cause and controller of earthquakes, storms, and other evil things, and the archenemy of demons. Prayers were offered to her that she might frighten away the Dragon. "Glory to Mother Kali," the priest and people chanted.

While in the classroom there was nothing illogical about describing the solar eclipse in terms of celestial mechanics, neither was there anything wrong in offering a gift to the Black Goddess—just in case. . . .

The Human Condition

2 To sensitive spirits of all ages, life is filled with cruel contradictions and bitter ironies. Human experience is capricious, and our finite minds are not able to see enough of life at one time for us to know for sure what is going on. We see only fragments of life, never the whole. We are not unlike children struggling with a cosmic picture puzzle made up of pieces that won't fit together.

Just under the surface of the entire human enterprise, implicit in all we think and do, there lies the eternal question: What is the meaning of existence? It is the ultimate question of all Mankind, yet it must be reopened by each of us in our turn. If we refuse to take the contradictions of life for granted; if we can't accept prepackaged solutions; if we can't persuade ourselves to accept a mere fragment of life as the whole of life—then for all of us, the question persists. We may have great difficulty finding satisfactory answers to it, but we also know that there is no escape from it.

3 On the real-life scene where the human tragicomedy plays itself out, our question splits into two further practical questions. Stated positively: How can we make life worth living? Stated negatively: How can we prevent life from turning into tragedy?

Through the ages, humans have sought clues to life's meaning through our religions and philosophies. To date they have given us immense help, but a contemporary overview of Mankind's quest supplies us with a superabundance of answers, so many answers in fact that we can't decide among them, and any decision seems arbitrary and limited.

Furthermore, after a more critical reexamination, we discover that most of our religions and many of our philosophies have concluded that, in the final analysis, life-in-this-world is not worth living. At best it's but a time of troubles to be endured until we can reach something better. That's not much help to those of us still dedicated to the assumption that life may be worth living.

4 In Alexei Panshin's *Rite of Passage* the heroine, a young girl, states candidly: "If you want to accept life, you have to accept the whole bloody universe." Perhaps. But how can we really "accept" a universe of wild and destructive contradictions? After all, we seem to be as ambivalent and confused about ultimate realities as the Indian physicist/priest.

The natural world—the world of astronomy, physics, chemistry, geology, meteorology—is not the mystery today that it was some four centuries ago, before the birth of the New Science. We are fairly secure in our general mathematical descriptions of the physical universe. To be sure, at the quantum level anomalous and unpredictable events seem to occur; causal sequences seem to be replaced by probability statistics; and it appears that there was a time following the Big Bang when our mathematical and physical formulas, as we know them, did not apply. But in general there is so much mathematical consistency to our experience of nature's operations that we have arrived at the point of accepting a naturalistic worldview for nature. We have, more or less, made our peace. With the physical universe—from galaxies and gravity fields to microchips and laser disks—the cosmos that challenged the existence of ancient thinkers and eluded their understanding is no longer a bewildering problem to us.

Our serious problems, therefore, lie buried somewhere within the biological realm, within the protoplasmic venture we call life. To borrow a phrase from Buckminster Fuller, the puzzlement seems to be that this protoplasmic experiment came without an instruction manual. We now possess some fairly clear hints of where we came from, but only the faintest glimpses of who we are, and no prevision at all of where we are going.

5 Long before the birth of modern psychology, there were perceptive individuals who felt stirrings from the depths of the human organism, but it was left to Sigmund Freud and Carl Jung to launch depth probes into the inner world. As these doctors from Vienna and Zürich shook loose the secrets of the human psyche, it was no longer deniable that the subconscious mind, quite without our conscious permission, pushes us headlong into all forms of irrational behavior. The subconscious mind, said Freud, is a vast depository for emotionally charged experience that, for one reason or another, we cannot face; and these repressed elements determine to a large extent how we feel, think, and behave. Jung reached even deeper, suggesting that some of our most meaningful experiences have roots in cumulative patterns (he called them "archetypes") embedded in the "collective unconscious" of the entire human race.

> *There is a coherent plan in the universe, though I don't know what it's a plan for.*
>
> Sir Fred Hoyle

To realize that we do countless things without understanding why—this can be, for those of us who want to believe that we are in charge of our behavior, a soul-jarring discovery. We seem to be manipulated, like puppets on a string, by inner forces over which we have little control. We scurry about in frenzied activity, accomplishing little else than satisfying the whims of the shadowy slavedriver. Not knowing our motivations, we don't understand what we do; and much of the time our strivings bring little fulfillment.

Still, is it possible that what we are calling "the meaning of life" is to be found somewhere, somehow, in these irrational depths where our controlling intellects have, heretofore, been aliens in an uncharted land? Perhaps we find here one source of the meaninglessness of our lives: We have no clear notion of what we are after, but we plunge blindly ahead anyway, in search of something. Joseph Campbell, a scholar who attempted to plumb the depths of the human psyche through a study of world mythology, warns us: "People talk about looking for the meaning of life; what you're really looking for is an *experience* of *being alive.*"

This is all there is.

6 "Good morning," said the little prince.

"Good morning," said the railway switchman.

"What do you do here?" the little prince asked.

"I sort out travelers, in bundles of a thousand," said the switchman. "I send off the trains that carry them: now to the right, now to the left."

And a brilliantly lighted express train shook the switchman's cabin as it rushed by with a roar like thunder.

"They are in a great hurry," said the little prince. "What are they looking for?"

"Not even the locomotive engineer knows that," said the switchman.

And a second brilliantly lighted express thundered by, in the opposite direction.

"Are they coming back already?" demanded the little prince.

"These are not the same ones," said the switchman. "It is an exchange."

"Were they not satisfied where they were?" asked the little prince.

"No one is ever satisfied where he is," said the switchman. And they heard the roaring thunder of a third brilliantly lighted express.

"Are they pursuing the first travelers?" demanded the little prince.

"They are pursuing nothing at all," said the switchman. "They are asleep in there, or if they are not asleep they are yawning. Only the children are flattening their noses against the windowpanes."

"Only the children know what they are looking for," said the little prince. "They waste their time over a rag doll and it becomes very important to them; and if anybody takes it away from them they cry . . . "

"They are lucky," the switchman said.

Antoine de Saint-Exupéry
The Little Prince

Paul Gauguin. *D'où venons-nous? Que sommes-nous? Où allons-nous? 1897.* "Where do we come from? What are we? Where are we going?"

7 In Freud's world, life is at once a blessing and a curse, for *eros* (the life-force) is pitted in mortal combat against *thanatos* (the death wish). On the one hand, we possess drives toward self-preservation that countermand almost all other impulses. We fear the cessation of breath and sense. "Let me not see the death which I ever dread!" cried the hero of the *Gilgamesh Epic* three thousand years ago. While alive, we dream our dreams, work toward our goals, and feel the joyous pain of activity and growth. All this indicates the depth of our hunger for life; we will fight to the death in order to live. *Eros.*

On the other hand, "To exist is to suffer," taught the Buddha, and we have devised ingenious ways of escaping existence. We sense a futility in our dreams; an inner voice chides us for yearning for goals we can't achieve. We often have an empty feeling when we hold in our hands something we have fought for, wondering why we wanted it. All around we see loneliness, surd hatreds, and pointless sadisms. Mephistopheles speaks for many: "Hell is no fable, for *this life IS hell.*" Away from all this, we are pulled toward death, as though it would be a blessing to have done with it. *Thanatos.*

Out of frustration, perhaps we ought to ask whether the essential implication of so many of our great religions and philosophies might be correct after all—the implication that the human condition is uninhabitable. Perhaps there really is something inherently wrong. Perhaps the Buddha is correct when he taught that existence—all existence—is inherently unsatisfactory. Perhaps Schopenhauer is near when he wrote that life should never have been. Perhaps Norman Brown is close when he calls man a "disease." It's not inconceivable that self-destruction, in some sense, is already an accomplished fact.

Albert Schweitzer once wrote that he remained optimistic because hope is an indispensable ingredient of daily life, but that when he took a long look at human history he could not escape the gloom of pessimism. When asked if he was "optimistic these days about the state of the world," Alan Watts replied: "I have to be. There is no alternative. For if I were to bet, I would bet that the human race will destroy itself by 2000. But there's nowhere to place the bet."

THE SEARCH FOR MEANING

8 Modern humans are caught in an "existential vacuum," writes Viktor Frankl, a feeling of

> the total and ultimate meaninglessness of their lives. They lack the awareness of a meaning worth living for. They are haunted by the experience of their inner emptiness, a void within themselves. . . .
>
> The existential vacuum is a widespread phenomenon of the twentieth century. This is understandable; it may be due to a twofold loss that man had to undergo since he became a truly human being. At the beginning of human history, man lost some of the basic animal instincts in which an animal's behavior is embedded and by which it is secured. Such security, like Paradise, is closed to man forever; man has to make choices. In addition to this, however, man has suffered another loss in his more recent development: the traditions that had buttressed his behavior are now rapidly diminishing. No instinct tells him what he has to do, and no tradition tells him what he ought to do; soon he will not know what he wants to do.

Castle of the Pyrenees by René Magritte (1959)

I have one longing only: to grasp what is hidden behind appearances, to ferret out that mystery which brings me to birth and then kills me, to discover if behind the visible and unceasing stream of the world an invisible and immutable presence is hiding.
NIKOS KAZANTZAKIS

9 The search for life, if it is to succeed, must be an aggressive individual odyssey. Each of us is caught in the philosophical enterprise. "Sooner or later," writes Maurice Riseling, "life makes philosophers of us all." There is not one of us who is not trying to make sense of his existence, and at some level of our being each is seeking fulfillment. Our experiences come pouring into us with endless variety, and they do not come neatly packaged and labeled. Each one of us must select and assimilate, organize and arrange, value and apply. So, if we have awakened, we are all philosophers by default, not by choice. To be sure, we must seek the guidance of others who have searched; we can listen to those who have found answers that work for them. But in the last analysis, no one else can give us insight. It has to be grown from native soil. Nor is our quest for meaning a quixotic tilting after imaginary windmills. Many men and women have found, to some degree, what they are seeking; they find the clues that set them in the right direction. They are living proof that it is possible to seek and to find the paths that bring out their higher nature rather than their lower nature, paths that lead them to insights and satisfactions that have made their lives worthwhile. Each of the following men, at some point in his search, found an answer, or at least a perspective, that affected the quality of his entire existence.

10 After working through the long hot days with his patients at the Lambaréné hospital, Albert Schweitzer would retire to his cluttered study in the evening and take up again the problem from which he could not escape. He was attempting to discover a positive ethical principle upon which civilization could be securely grounded. (For more on Schweitzer's quest, see p. 449.) He writes:

> For months on end I lived in a continual state of mental agitation. Without the least success I concentrated—even all through my daily work at the hospital—on the real nature of the affirmation of life and of ethics, and on the question of what they have in common. I was wandering about in a thicket where no path was to be found. I was pushing against an iron door that would not yield.
>
> While in this mental condition I had to undertake a longish journey on the river. . . . Slowly we crept upstream, laboriously navigating—it was the dry season—between the sandbanks. Lost in thought I sat on the deck of the barge, struggling to

> find the elementary and universal concept of the ethical that I had not discovered in any philosophy. I covered sheet after sheet with disconnected sentences merely to concentrate on the problem. Late on the third day, at the very moment when, at sunset, we were making our way through a herd of hippopotamuses, there flashed upon my mind, unforeseen and unsought, the phrase, "reverence for life." The iron door had yielded. The path in the thicket had become visible. Now I had found my way to the principle in which affirmation of the world and ethics are joined together.
>
> The Philosophy of Reverence for Life takes the world as it is. And the world means the horrible in the glorious, the meaningless in the fullness of meaning, the sorrowful in the joyful. Whatever our own point of view the world will remain an enigma.
>
> But that does not mean that we need stand before the problem of life at our wits' end because we have to renounce all hope of comprehending the course of world-events as having a meaning. Reverence for Life brings us into a spiritual relation with the world which is independent of all knowledge of the universe. . . . It renews itself in us every time we look thoughtfully at ourselves and the life around us.

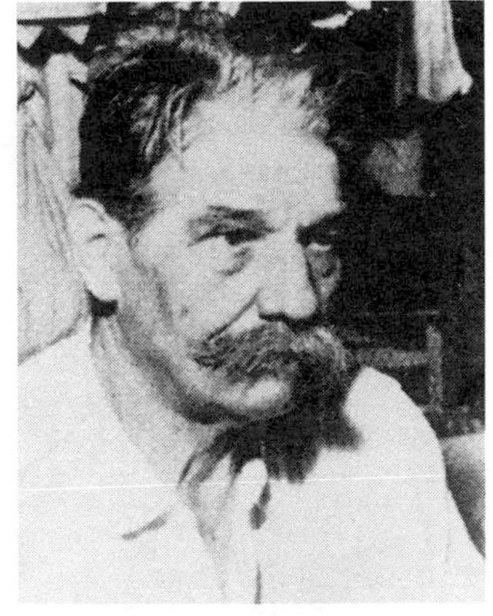

Albert Schweitzer (1875–1965)

Reverence for Life. "In that principle," Schweitzer writes, "my life has found a firm footing and a clear path to follow."

11 The editors of *Psychology Today* wrote a brief note after the death of Abraham Maslow. In it they remarked that he had "a joyful affirmation of life that surged through the long tapes he often dictated for us, encouraging *Psychology Today* to explore questions that have no easy answers. Much as we loved this beautiful man, we did not understand the source of his courage—until the last cassette came in." On that tape, they say, Dr. Maslow

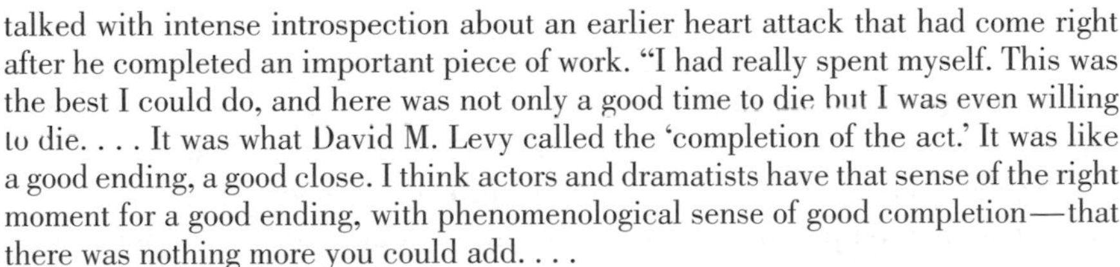

> talked with intense introspection about an earlier heart attack that had come right after he completed an important piece of work. "I had really spent myself. This was the best I could do, and here was not only a good time to die but I was even willing to die. . . . It was what David M. Levy called the 'completion of the act.' It was like a good ending, a good close. I think actors and dramatists have that sense of the right moment for a good ending, with phenomenological sense of good completion—that there was nothing more you could add. . . .
>
> "My attitude toward life changed. The word I used for it now is the post-mortem life. I could just as easily have died so that my living constitutes a kind of an extra, a bonus. It's all gravy. Therefore I might just as well live as if I had already died.
>
> "One very important aspect of the post-mortem life is that everything gets doubly precious, gets piercingly important. You get stabbed by things, by flowers and by babies and by beautiful things—just the very act of living, of walking and breathing and eating and having friends and chatting. Everything seems to look more beautiful rather than less, and one gets the much-intensified sense of miracles.
>
> "I guess you could say that post-mortem life permits a kind of spontaneity that's greater than anything else could make possible.
>
> "If you're reconciled with death or even if you are pretty well assured that you will have a good death, a dignified one, then every single moment of every single day is transformed because the pervasive undercurrent—the fear of death—is removed. . . . I am living an end-life where everything ought to be an end in itself, where I shouldn't waste any time preparing for the future, or occupying myself with means to later ends."
>
> Abe's message ended there.—The Editors.

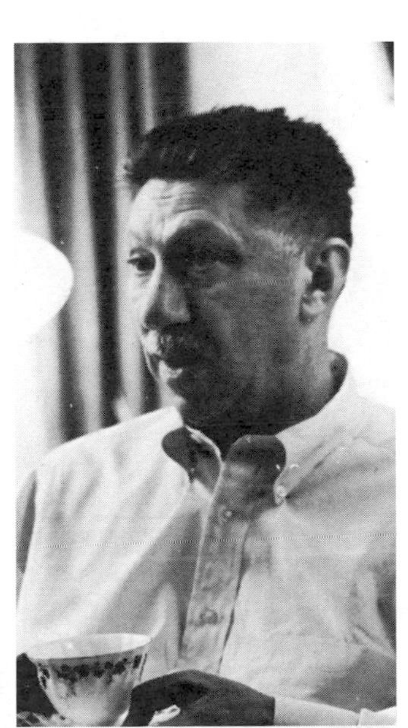

Abraham Maslow (1908–1970)

12 Dr. Gordon Allport has written in the preface to Viktor Frankl's book *Man's Search for Meaning:*

Viktor Frankl (1905–1997)

"There is no hope."
"We're both alive. And for all I know, that's hope."
"HENRY II"
The Lion in Winter

As a longtime prisoner in bestial concentration camps [Frankl] found himself stripped to naked existence. His father, mother, brother, and his wife died in camps or were sent to the gas ovens, so that, excepting for his sister, his entire family perished in these camps. How could he—every possession lost, every value destroyed, suffering from hunger, cold and brutality, hourly expecting extermination—how could he find life worth preserving? . . .

From [Frankl's] autobiographical fragment the reader learns much. He learns what a human being does when he suddenly realizes he has "nothing to lose except his so ridiculously naked life." Frankl's description of the mixed flow of emotion and apathy is arresting. First to the rescue comes a cold detached curiosity concerning one's fate. Swiftly, too, come strategies to preserve the remnants of one's life, though the chances of surviving are slight. Hunger, humiliation, fear and deep anger at injustice are rendered tolerable by closely guarded images of beloved persons, by religion, by a grim sense of humor, and even by glimpses of the healing beauties of nature—a tree or a sunset.

But these moments of comfort do not establish the will to live unless they help the prisoner make larger sense out of his apparently senseless suffering. It is here that we encounter the central theme of existentialism: to live is to suffer, to survive is to find meaning in the suffering. If there is a purpose in life at all, there must be a purpose in suffering and in dying. But no man can tell another what this purpose is. Each must find out for himself, and must accept the responsibility that his answer prescribes. If he succeeds he will continue to grow in spite of all indignities. Frankl is fond of quoting Nietzsche, "He who has a why to live can bear with almost any how."

WHY-QUESTIONS

13 Our urge to ask "Why?" seems irresistible. If, for example, an avalanche plunges down the mountainside, burying sixty schoolchildren in a few seconds, is it humanly possible for the families of the children not to ask why it happened?

Nor is a naturalistic answer satisfying, even though a scientifically adequate one may be possible. "The avalanche was produced by a week of especially warm days alternating with cold nights. Much snow melted during those days, and when the water refroze at night the expanding ice gradually loosened the snowbank. The slide occurred during the daytime because melting snow finally produced enough water to dissolve the surfaces where friction was hold-

ZORBA: Why do the young die? Why does anybody die, tell me?
SCHOLAR: I don't know.
ZORBA: What's the use of all your damn books? If they don't tell you that, what the hell do they tell you?
SCHOLAR: They tell me about the agony of men who can't answer questions like yours.

NIKOS KAZANTZAKIS
Zorba the Greek

ing the snowbank to the mountainside. The snow gave way and cascaded down the slope."

Such a causal accounting is scientifically sound, is it not? However, at the mass funeral service for the children, imagine in your mind the presiding clergyman presenting the scientific explanation for the tragedy—and stopping there.

Does this not prove Frankl's thesis that, above all else, we humans must find meaning—something more than intellectual clarity—in living and, finally, in dying?

14 It would be comforting to know that life has transcendent meaning; it would feel good to know that "nothing happens without a purpose." But our need for meaning leads us to find easy and absurd answers to such why-questions. For instance, in the year AD 410 when the city of Rome fell to Alaric the Goth, the "pagans" blamed the great tragedy on Christians for having abandoned the true gods of Rome; but Saint Augustine spent a decade writing *The City of God* to show that the fall of Rome was a part of God's plan to vanquish paganism and establish the Reign of God.

In November 1755 an exceptionally violent earthquake destroyed much of the city of Lisbon. In a few minutes, more than thirty thousand people were killed or injured. The event occurred on All Saints' Day when churches throughout the land were filled with worshipers. The French philosopher Jean-Jacques Rousseau suggested that the people of Lisbon suffered because they were stacked up in multistoried dwellings; had they been living in the open countryside or woodlands, few would have been killed.

The young man who has not wept is a savage, and the old man who will not laugh is a fool.

CONFUCIUS

But French clergymen interpreted the disaster as punishment for the sins of the Portuguese. Protestants blamed the event upon the tyranny of Catholics, while the Roman clergy laid the event to the fact that there were so many Protestant heretics in Catholic Portugal. In England John Wesley, the founder of Methodism, in a sermon entitled "The Cause and Cure of Earthquakes," blamed original sin as "the moral cause of earthquakes, whatever the natural cause may be. . . ."

In April 1970, after the near-tragic *Apollo XIII* lunar mission was aborted, an American political leader stated on national television that mission failure was God's doing: it was a warning from God not to attempt further ventures into space. "A warning," he said; man's next attempt would result in tragic consequences.

The World-Riddle

15 In a hotel in East Africa, weary hunters relax from their safaris into the veld. In the hotel lounge one finds a comfortable set of sofas covered with zebra skins, and on one wall hang several lion skins separated by a dozen or so Masai spears spread out as a fan. Higher up, on all four walls of the lounging area, are mounted heads of game animals. One looks up at the heads of the great African antelopes: elands with long, straight horns; kudus with screw-twisted spires; dainty gazelles; stately sables with long, back-curving horns; and wildebeests with short, upturned hooks. Other sentinels looking down upon visitors include the legendary African buffalo, whose horns cover its forehead and spread widely on either side; a rhinoceros with double horns on its snout; and a warthog with ivory tusks emerging from either side of its lower jaw and curling over its nose. Various smaller game animals are mounted between the larger heads.

Life is the life of life.
Bhagavata Purana

Down through evolutionary time, each animal has developed a means of defense and/or killing. The overwhelming and singular thrust of evolution seems to have been to produce some mechanism of survival against attackers: horns to hold predators at bay; spiked tusks to rip apart and kill; fangs, claws, sharp hooves; thick skins; powerful jaws; sleek, strong legs for running and jumping.

Each animal must exist in unending competition with other creatures that would kill it. Species prey upon species. Nature is, after all, "red in tooth and claw."

Life is a comedy to those who think, a tragedy to those who feel.
Horace Walpole

The animals thus endowed had nothing to say about all this. No animal possessed the "freedom" to choose a "life-style." Its place in the scheme of things is entirely determined for it. In fact, what a strange, impertinent thought—that any single, individual animal **could** have had freedom to **choose** its niche or shape its role or to exercise its autonomy to control anything of significance for its life.

What forces would design creatures to prey upon one another and, at the same time, instill into each creature the capacity for unlimited pain and suffering?

And what a bitter paradox: In this "deadly feast of life," each of us, to exist, must kill and consume other living things that harbor the same life-drive we possess. **Life feeds upon itself.**

16 Not a few scientists and scholars have tried to argue that our problems are endemic and, very likely, genetic in origin. Writing in *The Naked Ape* Desmond Morris refers to the "deep-seated biological characteristics of our species" and contends that certain patterns of social behavior "will always be with us, at least until there has been some new and major change in our makeup." We are the evolutionary victims of a self-destructive mechanism that other animals have escaped. "Species that have evolved special killing techniques for dealing with their prey seldom employ these when dealing with their own kind."

As soon as man does not take his existence for granted, but beholds it as something unfathomably mysterious, thought begins.
Albert Schweitzer

But man's trouble, writes Konrad Lorenz, "arises from his being a basically harmless omnivorous creature, lacking in natural weapons with which to kill big prey, and, therefore, also devoid of the built-in safety devices which prevent 'professional' carnivores from abusing their killing power to destroy fellow members of their own species. . . ."

The Law of the Jungle, writes Morris, is that you don't kill your own kind. "Those species that failed to obey this law have long since become extinct."

17 It was in early spring when Captain Jacques Cousteau's oceanographic vessel *Calypso* anchored off the shore of a southern California island. One night his crewmen noticed a churning of the waters, and the ship's lights were turned on. In the water were swarms of squid, each six to ten inches long. Cousteau and his men had accidentally discovered the breeding ground of the sea arrows. These small squid returned here in cycles of two or three years to mate, lay their eggs, and die. Arriving on the scene by the millions, they milled around, waiting.

Then a frenzy of mating began. The females had developed their eggs in tubular egg-cases. Now as the sea arrows darted about, males would grab females and hold them fast in their arms. A special tentacle was used to insert a capsule of sperm under the mantle of the female. The mating continued for days.

Then the females extracted the elongated egg-cases from their bodies and attached them in clusters to the rocks below where the cases slowly swayed in the gentle current. Each female would carefully place six to eight egg-cases in position. With the last case attached, her time was finished; she went limp and died. The males had already died, their task of fertilization complete.

Let us confess it: evil strides the world.

VOLTAIRE

A few days later Cousteau's divers scoured the area for signs of life. Of the myriad squid that had churned the waters, nothing survived. As though covered with snow, the ocean bottom was white with their lifeless bodies. Their purpose in living had been fulfilled. All that the divers found alive were acres of egg-cases, now covered with a leathery skin to protect them. Inside each egg-case another generation of sea arrows waited to be born. They would come singly out of their eggs, move out to sea, and continue the cycle of life. Then at their appointed time they would return to the breeding ground to lay their eggs and die, just as their parents and their parents and their parents had done before them.

The world has always been ruled by Lucifer. The world is evil. Call his name, my love. Call the name of Lucifer.

Ritual of Evil
NBC-TV

In the last days of the squids' life, two of the Calypso's crewmen, swimming the bottom, came upon a female trying to push the last egg-case from her body. Gently they helped her by pulling out the case and attaching it to a rock. Then, joining the rest of her sea arrow family, she too died.

18 The instinct to fulfill the breeding cycle is so deep that no single sea arrow could thwart or change it. The "meaning of existence" for the squid is species-wide; it is provided by its irrevocable instinctual makeup.

The world's a failure, you know. Someone, somewhere, made a terrible mistake.

Mission Impossible
CBS-TV

Is it conceivable that we humans have been totally severed from this evolutionary past when the instincts determined all significant behavior? If our problems are truly species-wide, is it not possible that there also exist impulses-to-meaning—goal-directed instincts—that are species-wide? Might there not be such left-over urges moving in us, pulsing in the dimmest reaches of our being so that we are unaware of them, yet determining still our most basic behavioral patterns?

As a psychologist, Abraham Maslow believed he had discerned such drives. He was convinced that

> the human being has within him a pressure (among other pressures) toward unity of personality, toward spontaneous expressiveness, toward full individuality and iden-

"Childhood's End"

From what is presently known, Homo sapiens—the modern form of man—has existed on earth for approximately a hundred thousand years in numbers large enough to constitute a population. Barring catastrophic accidents, it can be expected that man will continue living on earth for many millions of years. Using a somewhat fanciful kind of arithmetic, it can be calculated from these figures that the present age of humanity corresponds to very early childhood in the life of a human being. Pursuing still further the same farfetched comparison, reading and writing were invented a year ago; Plato, the Parthenon, Christ, date from but a few months; experimental science is just a few weeks old, and electricity a few days; mankind will not reach puberty for another hundred thousand years. In this perspective, it is natural that so far mankind should have been chiefly concerned with becoming aware of the world of matter, listening to fairy tales, and fighting for pleasure or out of anger. The meaning of life, the problems of man and of society, become dominant preoccupations only later during development. As mankind outgrows childhood, the proper use of science may come to be not only to store food, build mechanical toys, and record allegories, myths, and fairy tales, but to understand, as well as possible, the nature of life and of man in order to give more meaning and value to human existence.

Renée Dubos
The Torch of Life

You can't postpone dealing with reality any longer.
Robert W. Smith

tity, toward seeing the truth rather than being blind, toward being creative, toward being good, and a lot else. That is, the human being is so constructed that he presses toward fuller and fuller being.

[There is] a single ultimate value for mankind, a far goal toward which all men strive. This is called variously by different authors self-actualization, self-realization, integration, psychological health, individuation, autonomy, creativity, productivity, but they all agree that this amounts to realizing the potentialities of the person, that is to say, becoming fully human, everything that the person can become. . . .

19 It is still not out of the question that we humans, unique among living things, lie free and lost. Perhaps Sartre is right in saying we are "condemned to be free." Perhaps there is no Goddess, no God, no Spirit, no Fate, no Moral Law, no phylogenetic urge-to-life, no instinct—and no meaning.

I myself know nothing, except just a little, enough to extract an argument from another who is wise and to receive it fairly.
Socrates

Perhaps Kierkegaard was right: "There is no truth, except truth *for me.*" The nihilistic existentialists have consistently held that the cosmos is depressingly meaningless and human society absurd. Our lives can achieve meaning only if we boldly grasp the choices before us and make whatever meaningful responses we can.

20 But, then, there is the wisdom of a very respected twentieth-century sage. Though witnessing all the inhumanity and pain of our century, Joseph Campbell never wavered in his affirmation of life.

Of course life has a larger meaning. I feel this every time I find a parking place close to the mall.
Lori Villamil

People ask me, "Do you have optimism about the world?" And I say, "Yes, it's great just the way it is. And you are not going to fix it up. Nobody has ever made it any

Christina's World by Andrew Wyeth (1948)

better. It is never going to be any better. This is it, so take it or leave it. You are not going to correct or improve it."

It is joyful just as it is. I don't believe there was anybody who intended it, but this is the way it is. James Joyce has a memorable line: "History is a nightmare from which I am trying to awake." And the way to awake from it is not to be afraid, and to recognize that all of this, as it is, is a manifestation of the horrendous power that is of all creation. The ends of things are always painful. But pain is part of there being a world at all.

A dangerous path is this, like the edge of a razor.
HINDU PROVERB

What is truth? said jesting Pilate, and would not stay for an answer.
FRANCES BACON

Nil desperandum.
There's no cause for despair.
HORACE

21 Richard Strauss composed the great tone poem *Also Sprach Zarathustra* in the spring and summer of 1896, basing it on passages from Nietzsche's book of the same title, written a dozen years earlier. Strauss himself wrote:

> I meant to convey by means of music an idea of the development of the human race from its origin, through various phases of its development, religious and scientific, up to Nietzsche's idea of the Superman. The whole symphonic poem is intended as an homage to Nietzsche's genius. . . .
>
> Will the mind of man ever solve the riddle of the world? A few calm introductory bars, and already the trumpet sounds, *pp,* their solemn motto C-G-C, the so-called World-Riddle theme which, in various rhythmic guises, will pervade the whole symphonic poem through its very end. The simple but expressive introduction grows quickly in intensity and ends majestically on the climactic C major chord of the organ and full orchestra. . . .
>
> And then comes the mystical conclusion which, ending in two different keys, aroused much controversy when the work was first performed. While the trombones stubbornly hold the unresolved chord C-E-F-sharp, the violins and upper woodwinds carry upward the Theme of the Ideal to higher register in B major. . . . the pizzicati of the basses all the while sounding repeatedly the C-G-C of the World-Riddle. *Evidently the great problem remains unsolved.*

Marcus Aurelius

Philosopher-King

When Plato wrote that "philosophers must become kings or kings must become philosophers before the world will have peace," he was dreaming of a science-fiction world or some utopian state. However, his words exquisitely describe the life of Marcus Aurelius, the fourteenth emperor of Rome, who reigned from AD 161 to 180. Marcus was a visionary statesman, legislator, and a powerful commander of the Roman legions that held the empire's borders against persistent invasions. But he is best remembered for the sort of personal qualities that transform otherwise mundane souls into saints.

What was great about Marcus was that he succeeded in living-in-the-world while refusing to compromise his ideals with the petty obsessions of lesser men; and what made this possible was his philosophy of life: a set of convictions, rationally derived, about how **his life** should be run **by him.** His only writing—random reflections commonly called *Meditations* but which he referred to as *Things Written to Himself*—is an exercise in self-discovery. It is one man's instruction manual for living.

✦

He was born in Rome of an old Spanish family and named Marcus Annius Verus. While still a child he lost both parents, but he remembers them gratefully. From his father, he writes, "I learned modesty and manliness"; and from his mother, a woman of talent and culture, he learned "religious piety, generosity, and not only refraining from wrongdoing but even from thoughts of it." He dearly loved his mother—who was enormously wealthy—and from her learned, he says, "to be far removed from the ways of the rich."

Marcus was given the best of educations, beginning with a thorough grounding in reading, writing, and arithmetic. He was always grateful for his education; he was fortunate, he tells us, "to have enjoyed good teachers at home and to have learned that it is a duty to spend liberally on such things."

At twelve he commenced his secondary education with the study of geometry, music, mathematics, painting, and literature. In the Roman world to be educated meant to be thoroughly acquainted with Greek language and literature, so he was placed in the hands of one Greek and two Latin masters and became fluent in both languages. At fourteen he assumed the *toga virilis,* a plain white garment signifying he was an adult and a full citizen of Rome. The third stage of his education began, and he concentrated on the study of oratory, which included further study of Greek and Latin literature, and philosophy. He had three tutors in Greek oratory, one in Latin oratory, and one in law. All together this gave him a full university education in the liberal arts.

In January, AD 138, momentous events began to happen. The emperor Hadrian chose Marcus's uncle Antoninus to succeed him to power; Hadrian chose Antoninus on the condition that Antoninus in turn adopt Marcus as his successor. Thus Marcus became frightfully aware, at the age of sixteen, that someday —the Fates permitting—he would have to assume the awesome responsibilities of running the empire. On the night of his adoption, he had a dream in which his shoulders seemed to be made of ivory, and he feared that he would not be able to bear the burden of governing the empire, but he awoke from the dream reassured that his shoulders would be strong enough.

At seventeen, therefore, Marcus was heir apparent to the imperial throne. He was designated a quaestor with responsibility for public finance, a consul of Rome, and Caesar. He was enrolled in the college of priests and moved into the imperial palace. "Life," he later wrote, "is possible in a palace, so it should be possible to live the *right kind* of life in a palace."

In the spring of 145 Marcus, then twenty-four, married a cousin, Annia Galeria, known to history as Faustina II. In his later reflections Marcus thanks the gods for a wife "so obedient, so warm-hearted, so without affectations." All told, fourteen children were born to them, including two sets of twins.

Marcus was confronted with the pain of death all his life. In 149 Faustina bore twin sons, and Marcus celebrated the event by issuing a coin showing busts of two small boys and bearing the incription *Temporum felicitas,* "What a happy time!" Soon the coins show Marcus and Faustina with one tiny girl and one baby boy, and, still later that year, new coins show them, standing, with only a little girl. Several times in his *Meditations,* Marcus refers to grief caused by the loss of children. He wrote that too often we pray, "Please, may I not lose my little child"; rather we should pray, "May I not be afraid when I lose him." Another son was born to Marcus and Faustina in 152, and the story is repeated. Coins first show two little girls and an infant boy; but by 156 they depict only two small girls with their parents. Little wonder that Marcus reflects so often on man's mortality.

At twenty-five Marcus vowed his full devotion to the study of Stoic philosophy—for as long as the world would let him. Throughout the rest of his life he alternated between carrying his worldly obligations—which he met energetically, resourcefully, and with common sense—and nourishing his spiritual life. When his duties became oppressive, he would return to his thoughts in stolen hours, late at night, in a tent pitched beside a battlefield, and there, by candlelight, continue his reflections.

Marcus became emperor at thirty-nine (in March 161) and was entitled Imperator Caesar Marcus Aurelius Antoninus Augustus. Uncomfortable with power and bored with the perfunctory public rituals of his office, he warned (himself): "Don't be dipped into the purple dye!" He was terribly afraid, he wrote, that he might be "turned into a Caesar." But all who knew him testify that in his personal qualities—sincerity, discipline, morality, simplicity—Marcus was the same man as emperor that he was as a private citizen.

Marcus's likeness is familiar from coins and inscriptions. He had a handsome face, deep-set brooding eyes, black

If you want to stop wasting your time in vain fantasies, perform every act in life as though it were your last.

Never esteem anything as of advantage to you that will make you break your word or lose your self-respect.

Our life is what our thoughts make it.

All that is harmony for you, my Universe, is in harmony with me as well. Nothing that comes at the right time for you is too early or too late for me. Everything is fruit to me, Nature, that your seasons bring. All things come of you, have their being in you, and return to you.

Time is a sort of river of passing events, and strong is its current; no sooner is a thing brought to sight than it is swept by and another takes its place, and this too will be swept away.

Look beneath the surface, and don't let the specialness of a thing, or its unique worth, escape you.

It is man's peculiar duty to love even those who wrong him.

Remember this, that very little is needed to make a happy life.

A wrongdoer is often a man who has left something undone, not always one who has done something.

Do not think yourself hurt and you remain unhurt.

In the way of Nature there can be no evil.

Dress not thy thought in too fine a garb.

curly hair, and a heavy beard. Physically he was not strong; he suffered from chest pains, digestive troubles, and ulcers that resulted in prolonged bouts with illness; he was under doctors' care most of his life. He slept irregularly or not at all and frequently worked deep into the night. He enjoyed boxing, fencing, and wrestling, both as participant and spectator. He was a talented painter.

Those who knew him saw a modest, reserved, and serious man, thorough in all he did; he paid great attention to detail, almost to the point of perfectionism. His biographer Cassius Dio says that "he never said, wrote, or did anything as if it were an unimportant matter." His lifetime concern for the condition of slaves, orphans, and minors tells us much about the man.

His presentiments of weighty responsibilities more than came true. Most of his ruling years were spent fighting back invasions in Britain, Italy, Spain, Syria, and Egypt. It was during the last ten years of his life, while battling the Germanic tribes along the Rhine-Danube frontier, that Marcus wrote his *Things Written to Himself,* a very private journal in eloquent Greek. It is divided into twelve books. The first book—though the last to be written—is his tribute to family, friends, and teachers who meant much to him. He thanks them all and tells us what he learned from each. The other eleven books are his attempt to summarize the lessons he has learned from life.

✦

Marcus had to work out a philosophy to live by. His notebook shows just how desperately he needed the strength and support of meaningful philosophic beliefs. He had been well acquainted with Stoic philosophy since he was twelve, but the ideas lay dormant; during the earlier stages of life he had little use for them.

But sooner or later, it seems, we must all become philosophers. In time Marcus came to need a coherent set of ideas to render life intelligible, to help him accept what he must accept and change what he could change; and he must accomplish this without losing his integrity or his sanity. So what is important to Marcus is not whether he could find answers to Life—there may not be any—but whether **he** could find answers that would work **for him.**

Marcus might have asked, first, whether one really has to live in the world. It's rough out there. Maybe there are gentler paths to follow.

Not for Marcus. In another lifetime, he would surely have chosen some other life-path so that he could meditate, reflect, paint, write poetry, compose music—so that he could tend to his spiritual life. Since the Fates chose to birth Marcus in second-century Rome and endow him with Stoic ideas, this meant accepting the conditions and responsibilities assigned to him.

He wrote: "Men seek all sorts of escape for themselves—houses in the country, by the seashores, in the mountains; and you too will probably want such things very much. But this is altogether a mark of the most common sort of men." By contrast, wise men are called to live "the life of the social animal" and be responsible to their fellow human beings, to whom they belong.

So, as Marcus saw it, **the problem** was finding a way to live in the world and not be destroyed by it. The answer, Marcus reasons, lies in making a deep and permanent distinction between what you can take charge of and what you can't, a distinction, that is, between the inner world over which we can exercise a modicum of control, and the real world "out there" over which we have little or no control at all.

Clearly, we are not in charge of the grand events that constitute human history. The world of events is merely a stage, provided for us by the Fates, on which we play out our lives. "All the world's a stage," Shakespeare would later write, "And all the men and women merely players . . . " But we must understand, clearly, that we have little choice of the roles we must play. The Fates have cast us in our roles. Marcus, for instance, did not

choose to be emperor or to marry Faustina; he did not **choose** to fight the Parthians or Quadi. There are no tryouts or callbacks. Such events are the acts and scenes in the playing out of the drama, and while a few individuals are selected to play lead roles, most of us are merely spear-carriers. Once cast, we all have a sacred duty to play our roles and to play them well, for this is how history will judge us. Furthermore, quite a few of the stage props supplied for our roles are also given, and are quite beyond our control. We cannot change the time and place of our birth, or our parents, or the fact of aging and death, or our genetic makeup. So why fret and fume and struggle over what you cannot change?

We should all be method actors playing our roles with consummate skill but without ever being caught up in the destructive passions of the dramatic plot. The Stoics had a word for it: *apatheia*, which we rather mistranslate as "apathy." It derives from the Greek *a*, meaning "not," and *pathos*, "suffering," implying an indifference to painful events.

What we must do, Marcus reasons, is to turn to our inner world and take charge. Marcus sees the self metaphorically as a cherished plot of ground, and each of us as the caretaker of his garden plot. Each must look after the garden, tend it, not let weeds grow, and keep the plants protected, watered, and nourished.

This is the goal of life for Marcus: to guard and protect the well-being of the self. The tranquility of our spiritual/emotional life should be a normal, natural ground-state that never leaves us. The wise man "will not go against the Divinity that is planted in his breast; but rather he will preserve his deepest inner self in tranquility. He will, above all, preserve his own autonomy and integrity, and not let anything alienate him from himself." How does one go about maintaining this ground-state? For one thing, we practice. We recondition ourselves. No one is totally depraved or totally good; all of us can grow, step by step, but it takes practice.

Marcus organized his practice into a set of four virtues which he never stopped practicing. **Wisdom**—learn what is good and bad, which involvements are beneficial and which are damaging, which concerns are enobling and which are degrading. **Justice**—be honest and fair so that you can always respect yourself; do not be arrogant, thinking you are more than you are; but do not think less of yourself either, thinking you are worth nothing. **Fortitude**—develop the strength to withstand courageously "the slings and arrows of outrageous fortune," as Shakespeare later phrased it. And **temperance**—develop control of one's passions, resist excesses, and learn to strike a balance in all of life.

Marcus writes: "Do you see me unhappy because thus-and-so has happened to me? Not at all. Rather, I am happy *despite* its happening to me. Why? Because I continue on, free from pain, neither crushed by the present nor fearing the future. For events such as this happen to every human being."

"This then remains"—Marcus reminds himself—"Remember to retire into this little territory of the inner self—your own world (which is all there is)—and there be free, and, as a human being, observe the world passing by."

While encamped in Vienna in the nineteenth year of his reign, Marcus was stricken ill; he sensed that death, an old invader long stayed, was near. He beckoned his son Commodus to his bedside and outlined strategies for holding off the Germanic invaders. He abandoned further food and drink. On the sixth day he rose from his couch, led Commodus outside his tent, and presented him to his armies as their new emperor. Then he returned to his tent, lay down, covered his head as if to sleep, and died. He was almost fifty-nine. The date was March 17 of the year AD 180.

Earlier he wrote: "Don't act as if you are going to live ten thousand years. Death always hangs over you. While you are alive and while it is still in your power, be good."

He bore the burdens of empire, the loss of wife and children, the betrayal of trusted friends, the degradation of war, the boredom of empty speeches and meaningless ceremonials, personal illnesses, and the ever-present shadow of death—yet through it all he maintained his sensitivity, his decency, his humanity. His body was returned to Rome in a final triumphal march.

REFLECTIONS

1 The Indian physicist/priest seems to be involved in a contradiction. (It's difficult to sympathize with him, of course, because you and I never let ourselves get caught in such dilemmas.) How would you characterize his contradiction? What philosophic assumptions might we infer from his behavior? Would you call him a hypocrite? Can he believe, logically and at the same time, in both worldviews implied by his actions?

2 "To sensitive spirits of all ages, life is filled with cruel contradictions and bitter ironies." List some of the contradictions and ironies that you have come across in your own experience.

3 When we ask whether life has meaning, what precisely are we asking? What is meant by "meaning"? What might be some source(s) of meaning? How would we **know** if life has meaning? Do you agree with Campbell's correction of this notion?

4 What do you understand to be meant by the term "why-question?" In your opinion, why do we have such a deep impulse to ask why-questions? What assumptions must we make to render such questions meaningful? Do you think why-questions are asked universally by all humans, or are they asked more in our Western tradition because of specific religious assumptions about "the meaning" of events?

5 Ponder the implications of Schweitzer's "Reverence for Life," Maslow's "post-mortem life," and Frankl's conviction that the search for meaning is the key to life. Is there a common **ethic** implied in these three convictions? Would they all lead to a common goal or to a similar kind of experience? (Kazantzakis, the author of *Zorba the Greek,* has an interesting take on this question of the meaning of life; see p. 634.)

6 Imagine that among the millions of squid, one of the sea arrows became a philosopher. If you could ask it (in Squidanese) about "the meaning of life," what do you think it might reply?

7 The fact that "life feeds upon itself" strikes some as being a puzzling **theological** contradiction. Why might it be considered a theological problem and not merely a philosophical problem?

8 What if you decide that life is without meaning—what would this mean to you personally? Do you think your life would be less worth living? (Why, incidentally, are you attempting to answer this question?)

9 For more on Joseph Campbell, see the brief biography on pp. 14–15. What is your response to his statement (§20) that life "is joyful just as it is"? Are you in essential agreement? (If Yes, then do you agree because you like his statement or because you believe he is right?)

The Spirit of Inquiry

1-2

This chapter deals with a gut-wrenching dilemma that, sooner or later, most of us will have to face: whether to think and try to understand, or just believe. Without exception we are all born into cultural traditions founded on religious belief, and they all stand ready to supply answers to the great questions of life. Each of us is therefore burdened with the task of deciding what answers are right for us. Since the days of the earliest Greek thinkers, philosophers have counseled using reason to find out what is truly going on in the world; this includes inquiry into who and what we humans are, what life is all about, and how it should be lived.

Philosophy begins when one learns to doubt—particularly to doubt one's cherished beliefs, one's dogmas and one's axioms.

WILL DURANT

Faith doesn't need documents.

MARCUS BORG

The Love of Wisdom

1 The word *philosophy* comes from two Greek words: *philein* ("to love") and *sophia* ("wisdom"), implying that a philosopher is (or should be) a "lover of wisdom." Among countless definitions of philosophy, this is still one of the simplest and best.

And so, the would-be philosopher unabashedly admits that he wants to become wise. The wisdom he seeks, however, is not merely the acquisition of facts to dispel ignorance. (In our age, it is often said, we are drowning in facts but starving for knowledge.) Rather, "wisdom" is the antonym of (and antidote for) "foolishness." It is indeed the "fool" who may acquire volumes of information yet not know how to use it. To be "wise" is to possess the understanding and skill to make mature judgments about the use of knowledge in the context of daily life.

But this sort of wisdom is elusive. It dissolves when desired too desperately, and in times of need it can become paralyzed. Wisdom is not unlike the Tao: if defined too precisely, it will lose its essence; if sought too diligently, it will be missed.

Socrates (469–399 BC)

Nothing is so firmly believed as what is least known.

MONTAIGNE

People who are on the journey are a lot more interesting than people who, having found answers, are in dry dock.

LORI VILLAMIL

2 Nevertheless, the philosopher at least knows what he is looking for: wisdom. Right? "Wisdom! What wisdom?" Socrates thundered. "I certainly have no knowledge of such wisdom, and anyone who says that I have is a liar and wilful slanderer." Thus Socrates began his defense when brought to trial in Athens in 399 BC.

> You know Chaerephon, of course. . . . Well, one day he actually went to Delphi and asked this question of the god [Apollo]. . . . He asked whether there was anyone wiser than myself. The priestess replied that there was no one. . . .
>
> When I heard about the oracle's answer, I said to myself "What does the god mean? Why does he not use plain language? I am only too conscious that I have no claim to wisdom, great or small; so what can he mean by asserting that I am the wisest man in the world?" . . .
>
> After puzzling about it for some time, I set myself at last with considerable reluctance to check the truth of it in the following way. I went to interview a man with a high reputation for wisdom. . . . Well, I gave a thorough examination to this person —I need not mention his name, but it was one of our politicians that I was studying when I had this experience—and in conversation with him, I formed the impression that although in many people's opinion, and especially in his own, he appeared to be wise, in fact he was not. . . . I reflected as I walked away: "Well, I am certainly wiser than this man. It is only too likely that neither of us has any knowledge to boast of; but he thinks that he knows something which he does not know, whereas I am quite conscious of my ignorance. At any rate it seems that I am wiser than he is to this small extent, that I do not think that I know what I do not know."
>
> From that time on I interviewed one person after another. I realized with distress and alarm that I was making myself unpopular. . . . After I had finished with the politicians I turned to the poets, dramatic, lyric, and all the rest. . . . It seemed clear to me that the poets were in much the same case; and I also observed that the very fact that they were poets made them think that they had a perfect understanding of all other subjects, of which they were totally ignorant. So I left that line of inquiry too with the same sense of advantage that I had felt in the case of the politicians.
>
> Last of all I turned to the skilled craftsmen. I knew quite well that I had practically no technical qualifications myself, and I was sure that I should find them full of impressive knowledge. . . . But, gentlemen, these professional experts seemed to share the same failing which I had noticed in the poets; I mean that on the strength of their technical proficiency they claimed a perfect understanding of every other subject, however important. . . .
>
> The effect of these investigations of mine, gentlemen, has been to arouse against me a great deal of hostility. . . . This is due to the fact that whenever I succeed in disproving another person's claim to wisdom in a given subject, the bystanders assume that I know everything about that subject myself. But the truth of the matter, gentlemen, is pretty certainly this: that real wisdom is the property of [Apollo], and this oracle is his way of telling us that human wisdom has little or no value. It seems to me that he is not referring literally to Socrates, but has merely taken my name as an example, as if he would say to us "The wisest of you men is he who has realized, like Socrates, that in respect of wisdom he is really worthless."
>
> PLATO
> *The Apology*

THE GREEK MIRACLE

3 The birthdate of philosophy and science is usually taken to be 585 BC, for about that time a philosopher named Thales of Miletus made an assumption that broke with the worldview of his day. He assumed that all things were made of a single

substance (Thales thought it might be water) and that the processes of change might arise from within the substance itself. The principle of motion, that is, might be inherent in the basic material of which the universe is made.

Thales (fl. 585 BC)

Why is this assumption significant? In Thales' day physical events were generally explained with supernatural causes. Since the cosmos was known to be inhabited by all sorts of gods and goddesses, godlets, demigods, demons, ancestral ghosts, and a host of other spirits good and bad, it was reasonable to conclude that events happen **because they are willed.**

If lightning strikes, then Zeus has hurled another thunderbolt. When the Sun moves through the heavens, all knew that Apollo is driving it in his fiery chariot. If the Greeks lost the battle of Troy, or if Jason's ship slipped safely between the rocks of Scylla and the whirlpool of Charybdis, then the Olympians were playing games again.

And so, before the time of these first philosophers, all **natural** events were attributed to **supernatural** causes. G. K. Chesterton once remarked that for those holding this worldview, the Sun moved across the sky each day only because God got up before the Sun and said to the Sun, "Sun, get up and do it again."

The first philosophers were not quite satisfied with all this. Perhaps they realized that if, to every question you can ask, you get but a single answer ("The gods willed it"), then in fact you know nothing meaningful or useful. So the Milesian philosophers (Thales and his pupils Anaximander and Anaximenes) sought a different **kind** of explanation: When they asked about the cause of events, **they made the assumption** that the answer might be found in "nature" or within matter itself. In other words, they largely ignored the unpredictable wills of the anthropomorphic Greek deities. (Xenophanes of Colophon expressed the thought of many of these thinkers when he observed that "Ethiopians have gods with snub noses and black hair; Thracians have gods with gray eyes and red hair"—from which he concluded that these gods are created by us humans to look like us, and they can therefore be ignored with impunity.)

This assumption marks the beginning of knowledge in the West. This is the breakthrough that has been called "the Greek miracle."

Aristotle (385–322 BC)

4 Only two centuries passed from the emergence of philosophy at Miletus to its zenith in the works of Plato and Aristotle. Yet in that time, using new instruments of inquiry, vast amounts of more dependable information had been acquired.

Mathematics in the Greek world had a nebulous beginning with the first philosophers, notably the Eleatics (Parmenides and Zeno) and Pythagoras, but it was at Plato's Academy that mathematics flourished. This "exact science" was Plato's first love and became the model for his metaphysical speculations in which he sought absolute certainty. Over the entrance to the Academy Plato had inscribed: "Let no one without geometry enter here."

Aristotle approached philosophy through the empirical sciences and was enthralled with every aspect of learning. He founded his Lyceum in 334 BC and initiated the first coordinated research into the history of the sciences. His pupil and successor Theophrastus worked on the history of the natural philosophers (the *physici*), while Menon studied the history of medicine and Eudemus recorded the history of arithmetic, geometry, and astronomy. Within a half-century after the death of Aristotle, this synoptic approach to learning came to an end. By the beginning of the third century BC, almost every branch of empirical learning had been freed from philosophy to go its own way.

Faith can move mountains, or lead a man endlessly down a blind path.

JAMES E. GUNN

Scientific inquiry—being incompatible with religious dogmatism—died out in the West during the Dark Ages (c. AD 200–c. 1000), and the entire corpus of Greek philosophic and scientific knowledge was passed on to the Arabs. After they had made considerable contributions, this body of knowledge, still essentially Greek, made its way to the Latin West, eventually giving birth to the Renaissance and the New Science.

From the great period of Greek science (roughly 300–100 BC) to the present day, various branches of inquiry have split off from philosophy and established themselves as independent disciplines, including the natural sciences, mathematics and geometry, and astronomy. With the rise of the universities and the development of science, such new fields as physiology, anatomy, and medicine proliferated, but the most recent offspring of philosophic question-asking (the "baby sciences," which, significantly, are the human sciences) have been psychology, anthropology, sociology, and political science.

It would not do for a student to answer every question in history by saying that it was the finger of God. Not until we have gone as far as most in tidying up mundane events and the human drama are we permitted to bring in wider considerations.

EDWARD HALLETT CARR

The history of philosophy is the history of asking questions—better and better questions, hopefully. The history of science is the history of specialization in question-asking, plus the accumulated fund of answers which all this question-asking has produced.

FREEDOM TO WONDER AND TO ASK QUESTIONS

5 Philosophy and freedom of inquiry were born together. Neither has ever existed without the other. If we possess freedom, we inquire. But if our freedom to inquire is too limited, then freedom, which is rightly a condition, becomes itself the goal of our striving.

Throughout Western history, of course, religious sentiment has resisted critical inquiry into certain questions the final answers to which were allegedly known. The question of God's existence, for example, was not considered debatable. In more recent times there has been opposition to investigation into the nature of man, especially his evolutionary origin and the operations of his inner world. The possibility of synthesizing life in the laboratory has also been feared and fought. In such areas scientists have long since probed where others feared to search and have reduced the *mysterium* to quantitative analysis.

For the philosopher, as for the scientist, there is no holy ground—unless indeed **all** is holy ground.

6 Despite our background of Greek rationalism, reason in the Western world has had a rough time. In the Judeo-Christian tradition it is made clear that we are saved by faith and not by our rational intellects or academic credentials.

The epitome of the righteous man was Abraham, who was willing to go so far as to kill his son Isaac **to obey** the word of his God, Yahweh. He assumed no right (according to the story in Genesis 22) to question the command; there was no chance of his debating with Yahweh the morality of the order. (However, read Genesis 18:20–33, where Abraham—*sic,* Abraham—carried on a running argument with God about a similar moral issue—and won!) In sacrificing Isaac, absolute obedience was required, and because of his submission Abraham has been held up as the ideal "Man of Uprightness" for more than three thousand years. Salvation is the reward of faith and obedience.

7 In the gospel tradition, Thomas is the example of what we are not to be, if we can help it. Thomas doubted. He wanted better evidence than he had before believing something reported to him by others, that is, before he **could** believe emotional second-hand reports of an event that, at first glance, seemed extremely improbable. Eventually "doubting Thomas" was told to place his hands in the wound in Jesus' side so that then he too might believe. But this skepticism is not commendable, for Jesus is reported to have said, "Blessed be those who have not seen me and yet believe!" (John 20:29).

Similarly, Saint Paul had grave misgivings about human wisdom and those who seek it. It appears that he had a rather sour experience with some Stoic and Epicurean philosophers in Athens. "Where now is your philosopher? Your scribe? Your reasoner of today?" he wrote to the Corinthian Christians. "Has not God made a fool of the world's wisdom?" A similar word of caution was sent to his friends in the Lycus Valley: "Take care that nobody exploits you through pretensions of philosophy."

Paul found that philosophers were the hardest minds to sway, and, despairing of their lack of understanding, he moved on to the towns where he could find people who had the capacity for faith.

8 Reason and knowledge are of little value in achieving salvation, according to orthodox Western theology. On the contrary, they can be a positive hindrance. We are saved by **faith.** Redemption is for the illiterate as much as for the educated. For in Christ, Paul reminds us, there is neither Jew nor Gentile, male nor female, slave nor free. "In union with Christ, all men are one." In matters of salvation, that is, all men of faith are equal.

The Church Fathers and Scholastic philosophers, of course, followed Paul's lead. Saint Augustine (AD 354–430) always asserted the primacy of faith: *Fides proecedit intellectum,* "Faith must exist before one can understand." Augustine "never abandoned or depreciated reason," writes a church historian, "he only subordinated it to faith and made it subservient to the defense of revealed truth."

Saint Anselm of Canterbury (1033–1109) took the same position. *Credo ut intelligam,* "I believe in order to understand." Revealed truth must first be accepted, and in the light of that certainty one can then know how to interpret all else. The revealed truth cannot itself be subject to doubt.

Peter Abelard (1079–1142) disagreed and stoutly declared it was the other way around. Understanding comes first, and only then can one decide what to believe. Abelard was not afraid of questions and doubts: "For by doubting we come to inquiry, by inquiry we discover the truth."

Needless to say, Augustine and Anselm won, and Abelard lost. We speak of **Saint** Augustine and **Saint** Anselm, but we do not say "Saint Abelard."

A Western Dilemma

9 Time and again, when we want to understand ourselves, we find that we must return to the two great traditions that together make up our Western heritage. Like intellectual archeologists, we have to chip at the clay and brush away the dust from the remains of our buried past.

Countless ideas inherited from our two ancestral worlds—the Greco-Roman and the Judaic—have been harmonized into a fairly coherent worldview, and Western life has been richer for it. But like a dissonant undercurrent, a few Greek and Judeo-Christian beliefs have remained stubbornly incompatible, and thinkers have tried in vain to work out some sort of coexistence.

We have now, in this chapter, encountered basic assumptions about life, involving ultimate commitments, which are logically and emotionally incompatible. For almost two millennia we have been torn by the conflict. Despite all healing attempts by some of the West's greatest minds, we are still intellectually dichotomized.

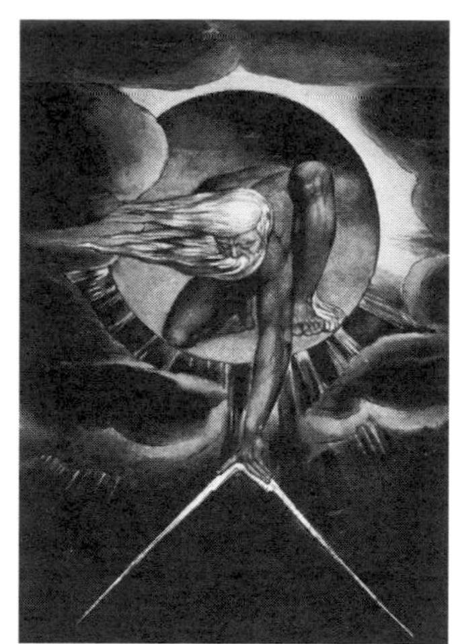

The Ancient of Days by William Blake (1794)

The Greek commitment is to reasoned inquiry into the nature of existence. This commitment has enabled us to understand the natural world we live in and to lay the foundations for an understanding of humankind.

On the other hand, the Judeo-Christian commitment has been to religious beliefs that lie beyond human understanding. What has been revealed by the Infinite Mind cannot be comprehended by finite minds; the "mysteries of faith" will remain beyond our grasp, for "we see through a glass, darkly." Our purpose in life should not be to analyze the Infinite or synthesize life's fragments. Rather, our goal should be "to get into a right relationship with God," to do his will through faith, and to look forward to an eternity which will transcend this mortal existence.

This is a Western dilemma, and for many, it is either/or. Here the road forks, and one may be forced to choose the road he will travel. Many have tried to blaze a way between them, but no clear path has yet been found.

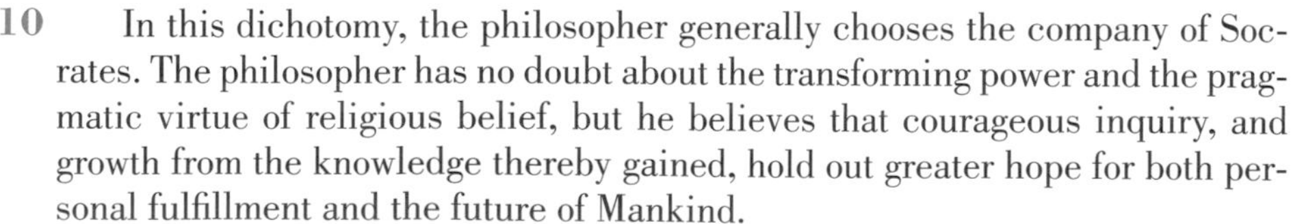

10 In this dichotomy, the philosopher generally chooses the company of Socrates. The philosopher has no doubt about the transforming power and the pragmatic virtue of religious belief, but he believes that courageous inquiry, and growth from the knowledge thereby gained, hold out greater hope for both personal fulfillment and the future of Mankind.

"I have said some things," Socrates once remarked, "of which I am not altogether confident. But that we shall be better and braver and less helpless if we think that we ought to inquire, than we should have been if we indulged in the idle fancy that there was no knowing and no use in seeking to know what we do not know—that is a theme upon which I am ready to fight, in word and deed, to the utmost of my power."

Belief, Doubt, Critical Thinking, and Faith

11 In our reflections to this point, we have dealt with several varieties of faith and belief without precisely defining our terms. Faith and belief are not the same, so careful distinctions need to be made. Believing, having faith, and doing criti-

cal thinking are different mental activities that complement, enrich, and balance one another.

Let's begin with belief. The word "belief" will be used in this book to refer to "blind belief," the unthinking acceptance of an idea or system of ideas (*credentia*)—as in "I believe it, I believe it, don't confuse me with facts!" Belief is the process of making a commitment to an idea in order to make that idea work for you. The idea may be inherited, derived from authority, or freely chosen. In any case, we think about the idea, identify with it, invest ourselves in it, condition ourselves with it, find ways of applying it. Belief is the complex psychic process by which we make ideas work for us; it is the process of making ideas true.

All of us are believers; to live by an idea requires commitment to it. There are many forms of commitment. The deepest belief—and the most rigid belief—is when we hold on to an idea come hell or high water; we maintain our commitment even though the idea may have outlived its usefulness. We do this out of loyalty to the person(s) or institution(s) from whom we acquired the idea, or out of fear of an authoritarian source ("It's true [for me]," we are warned, "therefore it had better be true for you!"), or because the idea has become closely identified with one's self—for a variety of reasons other than the inherent worth of the idea. We often try to keep ideas alive long after they should have died a natural death.

The emotional stance of the individual who engages in blind belief is one of defense. Stockades are built around the idea, and he stands guard to ward off any perceived attack. Such a defensive stance encapsulates one in his own egocentric predicament, interferes with the acquisition of further knowledge, and effectively blocks empathy with other people. A rigid believer generally fails to understand others' moral values, ethnic customs, religious beliefs, and philosophic journeys. Growth is inhibited, and rich sources of insight, understanding, and adventure are lost.

12 There are, however, other forms of commitment that don't preclude learning and growth. The American theologian Paul Tillich preferred to use the word "faith" to describe a form of belief that is open to new ideas yet permits us to commit ourselves to ideas for daily living. Tillich writes:

> The most ordinary misinterpretation of faith is to consider it an act of knowledge that has a low degree of evidence. . . . If this is meant, one is speaking of belief rather than of faith. . . . Almost all the struggles between faith and knowledge are rooted in the wrong understanding of faith as a type of knowledge which has a low degree of evidence but is supported by religious authority. One of the worst errors of theology and popular religion is to make statements which intentionally or unintentionally contradict the structure of reality. Such an attitude is an expression not of faith but of the confusion of faith with belief.

13 Authentic faith is always based on doubt. Faith is the act of committing oneself to an idea after having "processed" it, that is, after raising doubts about it, analyzing it, applying it. The idea, having been tested in the trenches, continues to stay alive; what one does with it then is to have faith in it. It may not be "proven"; it may be only temporarily useful—who knows?; and more evidence may be needed to determine its truth-status. Despite all these hesitations, you continue to invest in the idea and work with it. That's faith.

Paul Tillich (1886–1965)

The passion for truth is silenced by answers which have the weight of undisputed authority.

PAUL TILLICH

Further, "faith" refers to a kind of courage that enables one to act upon the best facts and ideas that are available, although they are incomplete and there is no signed guarantee of satisfactory results. In a general sense, then, faith is the courage to proceed to live in terms of possibilities and probabilities rather than absolutes and certainties.

14 Every act of faith, writes Tillich, involves risk, and all risk is accompanied by doubt. Authentic doubt "is always present as an element in the structure of faith. . . . There is no faith without an intrinsic 'in spite of' and the courageous affirmation of oneself in the state of ultimate concern. . . . If doubt appears, it should not be considered as the negation of faith, but as an element which was always and will always be present in the act of faith."

A philosopher engages in doubt as a normal *modus operandi,* insisting upon doubting a fact-claim to force it to defend itself. A historian once remarked that **all** knowledge begins with a "good, healthy doubt." The works of seventeenth-century rationalist René Descartes typify thc productive role that doubt plays in acquiring knowledge. Descartes doubted everything he could in the hope of arriving at some "fact" that he could not further doubt. When he discovered such a datum (*Cogito, ergo sum,* "I think, therefore I exist"), he began to build deductively upon that clear first principle. This brand of doubt has played a major role in all the knowledge-gathering sciences.

In his *Meditations,* Descartes shares his first steps toward productive doubt:

> Some years ago I came to realize that from my youth onwards I had been accepting as true many opinions that were really false, and that consequently the beliefs which I based upon such infirm grounds must themselves be doubtful and uncertain. Thereupon I became convinced that I need to make, once in my life, a clean sweep of my formerly held opinions and to begin to rebuild from the bottom up, if I wished to establish some kind of firm and assured way of thinking in the sciences. Today then . . . I shall apply myself earnestly and freely to the task of eradicating all of my formerly held opinions. To this end it will not be necessary to show that the old opinions are false. . . . Rather, since my reason persuades me that I ought to withhold belief from whatever is not entirely certain and indubitable, quite as much as from what is manifestly false, I shall be sufficiently justified in rejecting any belief if only I can find in each case some reason to doubt it.

Flight from insecurity is catastrophic to any kind of human growth. To flee from insecurity is to miss the whole point of being human. It is to miss, at any rate, the whole point of religion.

PETER BERTOCCI

15 Does all this render human existence a little less certain, a little less secure, and demand of us a little more courage and a willingness to face adventure? Yes! "Flight from insecurity is catastrophic to any kind of human growth," wrote the personalist philosopher Peter Bertocci. "To flee from insecurity is to miss the whole point of being human." Alan Watts made a similar observation: "Almost all the spiritual traditions recognize that there is a stage in man's development when belief—in contrast to faith—and its securities have to be left behind."

In his investigations of what he terms the "self-actualizing" personality, Abraham Maslow made a significant discovery.

> Our healthy subjects are uniformly unthreatened and unfrightened by the unknown, being therein quite different from average men. They accept the unknown, they are comfortable with it, and often are even attracted by it. To use Frenkel-Brunswick's phrase, "they can tolerate the ambiguous." . . . Since for healthy people, the un-

> known is not frightening, they do not have to spend any time laying the ghost, whistling past the cemetery, or otherwise protecting themselves against danger. They do not neglect the unknown, or deny it, or run away from it, or try to make believe it really is known, nor do they organize, dichotomize, or rubricize it prematurely. They do not cling to the familiar, nor is their quest for truth a catastrophic need for certainty, for safety, for definiteness, and order. The fully functioning personality can be, when the objective situation calls for it, comfortably disorderly, anarchic, vague, doubtful, uncertain, indefinite, approximate, inexact, or inaccurate.

I have had to experience so much stupidity, so many vices, so much error, so much nausea, disillusionment and sorrow, just in order to become a child again and begin anew.

HERMANN HESSE
Siddhartha

The person of faith, therefore, is as fully committed to ideas as any blind believer, but he has made a decision to take charge of the selection of the ideas that he will live by. This, by definition, is what the philosophic venture is all about: Critical thinking is nothing more, and nothing less, than taking a good look at the ideas that we are thinking and then making a commitment to live by the best ideas we can come up with.

SOCRATES

The Wisest Man Alive

Xenophon tells of the time Socrates lost his way in the winding streets of Athens and asked, "Where does one go to buy groceries?" After giving him directions, Xenophon received the further inquiry, "And where does one go to learn to become an honest man?" When no answer was forthcoming, Socrates beckoned: "Come with me, and I'll show you."

Socrates was put to death with a cup of hemlock almost twenty-four hundred years ago, yet he is remarkably contemporary, and his presence still haunts. His appearance alone is intriguing. Aristophanes said he walked like a waterfowl and rolled his eyes while speaking. Some thought he was ugly, and once in battle with the Spartans at Delium he saved the day by glaring at the enemy, who turned and ran. He resembled a satyr, said Alcibiades, or the masks of Silenus found in the stone-carvers' shop-windows: broad-faced, round mouth, thick lips, heavy beard, wisps of gray hair fringing a balding dome—all set atop a robust, stocky torso that was built like an ox and was as strong as two; but with a budding paunch that, he confessed, he wanted to reduce by dancing. Alcibiades was making a nobler point, however: Socrates is like the little statues of Silenus that, "on being opened, are found to have images of the gods inside them."

This was the man who could outwrestle the strongest athletes, outfight the hardiest foot soldiers, outdrink the dippiest winebibbers, and outthink the brightest minds of Hellas.

✦

Socrates was born in Athens in 469 BC, was raised there, lived and died there. His mother was a midwife named Phaenarete, his father a sculptor named Sophroniscus. Socrates followed in the footsteps of both: his calling, he said, was to help others give birth to their ideas. "Both I and my mother were endowed by the god with a midwife's art; she delivered women, but I deliver young men who are noble and fair." He added: "The reproach which is often made against me—that I ask questions of others but have not the wit to answer them myself—is very just. The reason is that god compels me to be a midwife, but forbids me to bring forth." (Aristophanes adopted the midwife metaphor to poke fun at Socrates: too often, he wrote, Socrates produced only a "miscarriage of ideas.")

About midlife Socrates was married to Xanthippe, a woman remembered (quite unfairly) as a shrew. More than likely, she was a dutiful *hausfrau* and mother. Living with Socrates would have been terribly difficult, and her complaint about his absenteeism is understandable, since Socrates spent virtually all his time away from home, philosophizing. Nor was he much of a breadwinner. A contemporary poet commented that he had "thought everything out but ignored the problem of how to provide himself with funds." Socrates said he endured Xanthippe just so he could develop self-discipline. They had three sons. At the time of Socrates's death, the oldest was a youth of about seventeen and the youngest was still in arms when brought to visit his father in prison.

Socrates believed the only path to knowledge was through discussion of ideas, so he spent his life conversing with disciples, friends, and bystanders encountered in the *agora*, and he hoped to continue this trade even in Hades to find out "who is wise and who pretends to be wise but isn't." The *agora* was a gathering place of Athenian citizens, a bustling marketplace only a block long on the north side of the hill of the Acropolis. Here the Athenians bought, sold, and traded; carried on the politics of governing; engaged in religious activities, and—above all—talked. (The word *agora* derives from the Greek verb *agoreuein*, "to speak" to a crowd, "to address," "to harangue"—"to talk.") The minicosmos of the *agora* is described by the comic poet Eubulus: "You will find everything sold together in the same place in Athens: figs, witnesses to summonses, bunches of grapes, turnips, pears, apples, givers of evidence, roses, medlars, porridge, honeycombs, chickpeas, lawsuits, beestings-puddings, myrtle, allotment machines, irises, lambs, water clocks, laws, indictments." Once, after pondering such a variety of goods, Socrates's response was typical: "How many things I don't need!"

Xenophon tells us that Socrates was always a part of the crowds and that he loved it, "for early in the morning he used to go to the walkways and gymnasia, to appear in the *agora* as it filled up, and to be present wherever he would meet with the most people." Socrates was "of the people" and spoke only the vernacular of his friends.

The *agora* was Socrates's emotional, spiritual, and intellectual home. Phaedrus teased him once: "How very strange you are, sir. You talk like a tourist rather than a native. You apparently never set foot in the country or go outside the city walls." Socrates doubtless smiled at his companion when he replied, "Look at it my way, my good friend. It is because I love knowledge, and it is the people in the city who teach me, not the country or the trees."

Socrates was later to be accused of impiety—not supporting the officially approved gods of the city-state of Athens—and introducing new deities. But Xenophon tells us that Socrates could frequently be seen "sacrificing on the public altars of the city." At his trial Socrates called Apollo to witness that his "wisdom" was not arrogance but a special calling to expose men's pretensions to wisdom.

Socrates lived up to nearly a half-century in the Athenian *agora*, teaching and illustrating his belief that "the unexamined life, for a human being, is not worth living."

✦

Cicero wrote that Socrates called philosophy down from the heavens to earth and introduced it into the cities and houses of men. Heretofore, philosophic inquiries dealt with the physical world. Everything is made of water, said Thales; of air, said Anaximenes; of fire, pronounced Heraclitus. Democritus theorized that the stuff of the universe was composed of indivisible atoms; Pythagoras intuited that it wasn't "stuff" at all, but numbers and mathematical relations.

Socrates's Prayer:
Ὦ φίλε Πάν τε καὶ ἄλλοι ὅσοι τῇδε θεοί
Beloved Pan, and all ye other gods who haunt this place, make me beautiful within, and grant that whatever happens outside of me will help my soul to grow. May I always be aware that true wealth lies in wisdom, and may my "gold" be so abundant that only a wise man can lift and carry it away. For me that is prayer enough.

On Socrates:
All in all he was fortunate: he lived without working, read without writing, taught without routine, drank without dizziness, and died before senility, almost without pain.
WILL DURANT

For a human being, the unexamined life is not worth living.

As a midwife, I attend men and not women, and I look after their souls when they are in labor, and not after their bodies; and the triumph of my art is in thoroughly examining whether the thought which the mind of the young man brings forth is a false idol or a noble and true birth.
I was really too honest a man to be a politician and live.

Are you not ashamed at heaping up the greatest amount of money and prestige and reputation, and caring so little about wisdom and truth and the greatest improvement of the soul, which you never regard or heed at all?

Wherefore, O judges, be of good cheer about death. . . . The hour of departure has arrived, and we go our ways—I to die, and you to live. Which is better God only knows.

I am that gadfly which God has attached to the state, and all day long and in all places am always fastening upon you, arousing and persuading and reproaching you.

On Socrates:
When Socrates tormented the Athenians like a gadfly, he prevented them from sleeping peacefully, from relaxing with their ready-made solutions to moral and social problems. By astonishing us, Socrates prevents us from thinking along the old lines that have been handed down to us and have become habits.

Jean Brun

All this was of little interest to Socrates. He concentrated on the world of human relationships—on our ideas, ethics, and politics. Xenophon observed that "he discoursed always of human affairs." "The unexamined life—**human** life—is not worth living." He took as his motto the inscription on the wall at the temple of Delphi: "Know thyself." Socrates therefore makes a clean break with the dominant philosophic preoccupations of the past; his primary significance to Western thought is that he was the first great thinker to focus the light of human intelligence upon human beings themselves.

Socrates's supreme concern was the breakdown of human relations—ethics. He believed that all unethical behavior is committed as a result of ignorance, from not knowing the right thing to do. When we know what is right, we will do what is right. Hence, the discovery of how we ought to behave should be given top priority. Clarification of what we should be doing is tantamount to bringing about good behavior.

But how can this be? One of our commonest experiences is knowing all too well what we should do, but not being able to do it. So what is Socrates saying? After all, he was no neophyte. True moral behavior, he contends, always leads to an increase in one's happiness; and any action that increases one's happiness is moral behavior. (Obviously, that's a matter of definition.) Socrates believed that no one, therefore, ever deliberately behaves in a way detrimental to achieving his own happiness. At the moment of deciding to act, we all believe that what we are about to do will, in some way, however small, increase our pleasure or happiness. Even revenge is sweet; and all the other evils that we commit carry the promise, as we perceive them, of adding a modicum of sweetness to our lives.

What's wrong with all this, Socrates believed, is that we miscalculate. We engage in all kinds of actions which we think—mistakenly—will increase our happiness. And why do we miscalculate, believing a particular action will bring happy results when it won't? Because we don't know ourselves well enough. The better we understand ourselves, the better we can judge what will lead to happiness and what won't. "Know thyself," Socrates kept urging. Only by a thorough and honest self-knowledge can one judge accurately what will produce happy results and what won't. Moral knowledge, therefore, is self-knowledge. Moral knowledge leads inevitably to moral action.

Socrates was himself a superlative example of the moral conscience. He thought things out, rationally and clearly, deciding what he should do in a particular situation, then he willed himself to do what his intellect had told him was right.

All this is in sharp contrast to traditional religious ethics that ministers to those who know what is right but can't seem to will themselves to do it. Saint Paul, for example, agonized: "I do the things that I hate. . . . I do not do the good things that I want to do; I do the wrong things that I do not want to do." The problem here is the will—the inability of the will to will, what has been called in psychoanalytic terms a lack of "ego strength." Saint Augustine shared Saint Paul's dilemma. From his mother's teaching, he knew what was right, but he couldn't bring himself to do it. Other deep-driving needs led him into doing what he had been taught was wrong. He could not will what was right; he could not do what was right. Only when the Holy Spirit gave him strength and added willpower could he will and do what was right. And then, Saint Paul and Saint Augustine add that when they succeed in doing what is right, they must not get credit for what they've willed and done: "It is the Holy Spirit willing in me."

Socrates, by contrast, considered himself to be operating on his own internal power. He himself, alone, would decide what was right by thinking carefully about the ideas and values involved. Then he—and he alone—would proceed to will exactly what he had decided was right. Then he would do what he had willed.

✦

In the spring of the year of Laches (399 BC), three men—one a highly respected citizen—brought charges against Socrates:

> This indictment and affidavit are sworn to by Meletus, the son of Meletus of the deme Pitthos, against Socrates, the son of Sophroniscus of the deme Alopece. Socrates is guilty of not believing in the gods in which the city believes and of introducing other new divinities. He is also guilty of corrupting the young. The prosecution demands the death penalty.

The Athenian system was a young experiment in democracy. Each year a roster of six thousand names was compiled from which juries were selected when needed. Each jury of 501 was probably a fair cross-section of the free male Athenian society. Private citizens bringing suit had to argue their own cases, and defendants had to defend themselves personally.

The trial of Socrates was held in the Heliaia, the most important of Athens's courts, a large square marble building at the southwest corner of the *agora*. Sitting on wooden benches and crowded by spectators, the jurors listened to the prosecution's argument. Speeches were timed by water clocks. When Socrates took his turn, he denied the charges, saying he had sought only to teach the truth, and asked that the prosecution produce the "corrupted youth" as evidence.

The speakers finished and a vote was taken: 281 guilty, 220 not guilty. If only 30 jurors had voted differently, history would have been another story; we might never have heard of Socrates. The same body of jurors then set the penalty, each side having suggested an appropriate punishment. The prosecution asked for the sentence of death. It is not unlikely that they never really wanted the death of the gadfly-sage, but intended to manipulate him into a plea of self-exile.

But Socrates's response was one of those gray events of history: whether he took a courageous moral stand or foolishly mocked his prosecutors depends upon how one interprets the records. Since he felt he was guilty only of teaching the truth—a contribution of enormous value to Athens—he suggested that he be supported at public expense for the rest of his life. How the jury reacted to this suggestion is indicated by the switch in vote: for death 361, for acquittal 140.

According to Plato, Socrates ended his case with a reassurance to his jurors: "Wherefore, O judges, be of good cheer about death, and know of a certainty that no evil can happen to a good man, either in life or after death, and that he and his are not neglected by the gods. . . . The hour of departure has arrived, and we go our ways—I to die, and you to live. Which is better God only knows."

Socrates was housed in the state prison on the Street of the Marble-Workers only a stone's throw to the southwest of his beloved *agora*. Carrying out the sentence was delayed for a month by a religious festival. Then on the day of execution, about sunset, a cup of hemlock juice was brought to him. Socrates asked, "Did you make enough to allow a libation to the gods?" The guard answered no, only enough for him. Socrates took the cup, gave a brief prayer, and drank.

He walked around the room, waiting for heaviness in his legs. Then he lay down, scolded his friends for their noisy weeping. "It is for this sort of thing that I sent the women away," he chided. "One ought to be allowed to die in peace." When the numbness reached his abdomen, he suddenly aroused and said to Crito, "Remember to pay a cock to Asclepius!"—presumably, make an offering to the god of health and healing. He lay down again, and shortly there was a shudder. He was dead.

"This is the end of our comrade," Plato wrote, "a man, as we would say, of all then living we had ever met, the noblest and the wisest and the most just."

Self-ignorance in any of its manifestations [is] a misfortune.

I've not yet succeeded in obeying the Delphic injunction to "know myself," and it seems to me absurd to consider problems about other beings while I am still in ignorance about my own nature.

I myself know nothing, except just a little, enough to extract an argument from another man who is wise and to receive it fairly.

On Socrates:
We wanted wisdom, so we get a punchline.

JOHN LEONARD

REFLECTIONS

1 Socrates came to some clear conclusions after he had investigated several men who laid claim to being wise. Do you think his observations were accurate about the claims we make? In the last analysis, according to Socrates, what makes a person wise?

2 Summarize in your own words the philosophic breakthrough that has been called the "Greek miracle." Why is this naturalistic methodology so important in the gathering of information? Or, conversely, what would happen to human knowledge if the naturalistic assumption were not followed?

3 Summarize in your own way the nature of the "Western dilemma" regarding human knowledge. Is it "either/or" for you personally, or have you discovered a pathway between the two traditions?

4 Without attempting a precise definition of religion at this point, do you think it possible for a philosopher who insists upon the freedom to inquire into everything (including religious axioms and "revealed truths") to also be religious?

5 Suppose a philosopher inquires into the existence of God (and all do, sooner or later). If he concludes, after the most honest inquiry, that God exists, is he still a philosopher? If he concludes, after his most honest investigation, that God doesn't exist, does he cease to be religious? Do one's philosophic credentials depend upon the questions he asks or the answers he arrives at?

6 After reading this chapter, contrast faith and belief, and write out definitions of each. (See glossary.) Are you a "faith-full" person? Are you a "belief-full" person?

7 Note the famous comment attributed to Voltaire ("I do not agree with a word that you say . . . "). Do you agree? If not, why? If you do agree, how well do you practice it?

Critical Analysis

1-3

Aristotle once wrote that philosophy begins when we look at the world and wake up to the depth of our not-knowing; the result, he said, is an "awesome feeling of ignorance," and we are driven to seek answers by looking steadily at the world, thinking carefully, and asking the right questions. It was Aristotle who first developed the rules of good thinking that we must follow if we are to find dependable answers to the important questions of life. This chapter describes certain characteristics of the philosophic mind and deals with three broad families of thinking skills: fact-claim verification, concept clarification, and inference validation.

It began when I was in the fifth grade. I came home from school one day, and my mother said to me, "What did you do in school today—think or believe?"

Ralph Nader

1 Aristotle gave wings to philosophy, and defined it wisely, out of the depths of his own sense of wonderment. He beheld a world of infinite variety, and he was profoundly curious about everything. We know that he spent time studying the tidepool creatures in Mytilene's big lagoon, and that he dissected fishes, thought about rainbows, followed the courses of the stars, pondered the cause of seasons, and reflected on a thousand other things. At some point in this adventure of the mind he wrote

All philosophy begins—as the ancient Greeks so well knew—with astonishment and wonder.

Kurt Reinhardt

> A sense of wonder started men philosophizing, in ancient times as well as today. Their wondering is aroused, first, by trivial matters; but they continue on from there to wonder about less mundane matters such as the changes of the moon, sun, and stars, and the beginnings of the universe. What is the result of this puzzlement? **An awesome feeling of ignorance.** Men began to philosophize, therefore, to escape ignorance.

Out of this wonderment comes philosophy. Since the beginning of human consciousness two or three million years ago, we humans have wondered about the world we live in. Huddled at night under the acacia trees, the first humans undoubtedly pondered the stars, listened to night-sounds of animals stalking their prey, loved, fought, fled, bled—and wondered what life is all about.

The General shook his head. "You've been out of school all these years, and what have you learned? Don't you know raw ability will never take you to the top?"

"I'd rather be myself than be at the top," said Beller. "I like to know what I think when I go to bed at night."

Christopher Anvil

All our wondering can be subsumed under two all-embracing questions to which we humans **must** find answers. (1) How does the world work? (2) What is our place in it? These are the two ultimate questions addressed by mankind's religions. Every great religious tradition has developed a complete set of answers to these two questions, and this was accomplished centuries or millennia before any data-gathering disciplines came along. But no matter: whatever the place and whenever the time we happen to be born, just so that our souls can rest a little easier, there must be lodged within the psyche of each of us a clear understanding of what sort of universe we live in and what it demands of us.

If the only tool you have is a hammer, you tend to treat everything as if it were a nail.
ABRAHAM MASLOW

Pythagoras was the first person who invented the term "Philosophy," and who called himself a philosopher.
DIOGENES LAËRTIUS

It is impossible for a man to learn what he thinks he already knows.
EPICTETUS

From its beginnings in the sixth century BC, philosophy, too, has addressed just these questions; and it does this by looking at the world, very carefully, to find out what is really there. Philosophers, by definition and passion, want to find answers to these questions about "the changes of the moon, sun, and stars, and the beginnings of the universe" and to find out who we are, where we came from, and how we should live. This is the first and final goal of philosophy—to understand the world and our place in it.

The Philosophic Mind

2 All knowledgeable individuals experience that awesome feeling of ignorance that Aristotle is describing; only the ignorant are exempt. If one does not know very much, he does not know what he does not know; but if he knows a great deal, he becomes aware of how much more there is that he still does not know.

How does one go about dispelling that feeling of ignorance and moving toward the truth of things? The first step is to ask questions.

"There's no use trying," said Alice: "one can't believe impossible things." "I dare say you haven't had much practice," said the Queen. "When I was your age I always did it for half an hour a day. Why sometimes I've believed as many as six impossible things before breakfast."
LEWIS CARROLL

History is the story of the defiance of the unknown and of what happens when man tries to extend his reach. Such defiance is necessary because conventional wisdom has never been good enough to run a civilization.
NORMAN COUSINS

The mind that genuinely wants to understand what is going on in the world—the philosophic mind—is a question-asking mind. When we ask questions, what we are doing, of course, is honoring that wonderful sense of curiosity we possessed in childhood but that, in so many of us, was repressed because it proved bothersome to our significant others; so our latent interest in the world and everything in it lay dormant and undeveloped. For many of us learning to ask questions about things involves the recovery of that curiosity and the formulation of the million questions that never got asked.

To a thoughtful mind, however, not just any answers will do; they must be honest answers that enable us to better apprehend the stubborn realities of the world we live in. The answers must be the product of critical thought. Over the centuries, and especially during the twentieth century, philosophers have developed a wide array of critical skills designed to help us get at the truth and therefore to better understand the world. These skills are eminently practical and productive; with them we can dissolve controversies, go to the heart of issues, have a meeting of minds, and be honest with ourselves and others.

3 The notion of being critical can be misleading. In our society "criticism" has a negative connotation. "Don't criticize me!" usually means "Don't find fault with me." And "He's critical of others" means he is judgmental, that he has a habit of evaluating others negatively (and probably letting them know what he thinks).

Wonder/Confusion/Patience/Wisdom

"Confusion" is an initial phase of all knowledge, without which one cannot progress to clarity. The important thing for the individual who truly desires to think is that he not be overly hurried but be faithful at each step of his mental itinerary to the aspect of reality currently under view, that he strive to avoid disdain for the preliminary distant and confused aspects due to some snob sense of urgency impelling him to arrive immediately at the more refined conclusions.

José Ortega y Gasset
The Origin of Philosophy

The teacher's obligation is to be patient enough to permit deliberation and decision by each of those he is trying to help. If his students do not choose, each in the light of his own contingent existence and his own limitations, they will not become ethical beings; if they are not ethical beings—in search of their own ethical reality—they are not individuals; if they are not individuals, they will not learn.

Søren Kierkegaard
The Point of View

Philosophy, as Plato and Aristotle said, begins in wonder. This wonder means a dim awareness of the useless talent, some sense that antlikeness is a betrayal. . . .

Philosophy means liberation from the two dimensions of routine, soaring above the well known, seeing it in new perspectives, arousing wonder and the wish to fly. Philosophy subverts man's satisfaction with himself, exposes custom as a questionable dream, and offers not so much solutions as a different life.

A great deal of philosophy, including truly subtle and ingenious works, was not intended as an edifice for men to live in, safe from sun and wind, but as a challenge: don't sleep on! there are so many vantage points; they change in flight: what matters is to leave off crawling in the dust.

Walter Kaufmann
Critique of Religion and Philosophy

This is not what the word originally meant and not the way it is used in philosophy. Our words "criticize," "criticism," and "critic" all derive from the Greek word *krino,* which means "I judge." To criticize means "to place [something] under judgment," implying that, in philosophy, one looks at an idea, thinks about it, judges it (both positively and negatively) for its validity and worth, and then decides what to do with it. Critical thinking is a discriminating process for deciding which ideas are good ones and which are bad. Becoming critical means that each of us takes responsibility for the truthfulness and validity of the ideas we live by.

When you know all the answers, you haven't asked all the questions.
Harold Levitt

Critical Skills

4 There are three broad families of critical skills. They are (1) fact-claim verification, (2) concept clarification, and (3) inference validation.

Never accept a fact until it is verified by a theory!
Sir Arthur Eddington

> *The things which exist around us, which we touch, see, hear and taste, are regarded as interrogations for which an answer must be sought.*
>
> JOHN DEWEY

1 **FACT-CLAIM VERIFICATION** A fact-claim is any idea submitted for consideration as an item of knowledge. In epistemology, a fact-claim becomes a fact only after it has been carefully checked with the truth-tests (see chapter 3-4) and has passed muster. If it passes critical examination, then it can validly be called a "fact" (though even what is called a "fact" can give us some definitional problems).

Fact-claim: **It's raining outside.**

This seems like a relatively simple fact-claim, and it is. How do I go about verifying or falsifying it? All I need to do is step outside and look. If I perceive with my senses that it is raining, then I can conclude that the idea in my mind corresponds sufficiently to what my senses tell me about real events, and I can accept the fact-claim as true. If it is not raining, then the fact-claim becomes false. In this example we are making use of two of the three truth-tests, the correspondence truth-test and thc pragmatic truth-test (see pp. 214ff. and 217ff.).

5 Fact-claim: **Water freezes at 32° F.**

At first this is merely an abstract idea floating in our minds, but what we want to know is whether it's true. So how do we find out if it is true? We go find some water, put it outside in the winter weather or in the freezer, lower its temperature to 32° or below, and see what happens. If it freezes when the temperature drops to 32°, then the idea is true; if it does not, then the idea is false. The American philosopher William James argued that an idea-in-the-abstract is neither true nor false until it has been applied to a real event, and that the idea **becomes** true when it is applied and found to work (or **becomes** false when so applied and found not to work, that is, does not describe accurately a real event). In the case of water freezing at 32°, the idea is true, of course; and the idea has been applied and has worked enough times for us to have confidence that it will continue to work whenever so applied. (Note that truth exists only as a quality of an idea that works, and as a quality of the sentence used to express that idea.) This is another example of the application of both the pragmatic and correspondence truth-tests.

> *There is not a philosophical method, though there are indeed methods, like different therapies.*
>
> LUDWIG WITTGENSTEIN

6 Fact-claim: **In the year AD 451 Attila the Hun defeated the forces of the Saracens at the battle of Châlons and turned back the invading Muslims, who might otherwise have conquered Europe and converted it into an Islamic empire.**

True statement or false? How can these fact-claims be verified or falsified? I cannot go somewhere and apply the idea to any actual events now taking place; the year AD 451 is very long gone. What I must do is consult the historical records and find references to Attila, the Huns, the Saracens (Muslims) and Islam, the Battle of Châlons, and whatever else seems relevant. If I find historical data that support the above fact-claims, then I can accept the statement as true; but if no such historical facts can be found, then I must consider the statement questionable (that is, I must suspend making a final judgment about its truth status); or if I find historical facts that contradict any of the above fact-claims, then I must conclude that the statement is false.

So, is the statement true or false? (Perhaps you want to go look up the historical sources before you read on.)

What I find in the records is that there was indeed a Battle of Châlons fought in the year 451 and that Attila the Hun was the victor. But I find that Attila was battling the Roman legions, not the Saracens. In fact, when I look up Saracens, Moslems, and Islam, I discover that the Islamic religion did not come into existence until the seventh century (Mohammad, the prophet and founder of Islam, was born in 570, died in 632). The fact-claims stated about the Saracens do not cohere with (are not consistent with) known historical facts. Conclusion, therefore: The statement is false. This is an application of the coherence truth-test (see pp. 215–217).

7 The three truth-tests (outlined more fully in chapter 3-4) can be used to determine the truth status of **all** fact-claims. If we care about thinking clearly, then making sure that the data we are working with are sound is vitally important. What is the point of investing our time and energy building on an idea if it can be shown up front to be untrue? Aristotle was the first critical philosopher to make this point; we must be sure, he said, that the "facts" we begin to think with (the *archai*, "starting points," "first principles") are true. When they are, then our subsequent thinking stands a better chance of being accurate and productive.

8 **2 Concept Clarification** We rarely think and say anything that does not have within it hidden assumptions and implications. These are meanings that sneak into our thoughts uninvited, so that our statements don't say what we think we are saying, or they don't say what we want to say; in fact we may be saying what we don't want to say. Too often there are hidden agendas and logical fallacies in our reasoning that render our arguments invalid. But if we are to be honest in our thinking—if honest only with ourselves—then clarification is always in order. Consider, for example, the following account.

A young bank employee was indicted for embezzlement, and the evidence all seemed to point to a conviction. But he knew he was innocent, and his wife believed him. She was soon informed by another bank employee that he knew the whereabouts of documents that would reveal the real embezzler and prove that her husband was innocent. But her informant also made it clear he would give out with the evidence only if she made herself sexually available. The couple were devout Catholics, but to clear her husband of almost certain conviction she quickly made the decision to get whatever information at whatever cost. So she spent several nights with the other bank employee. Eventually the documents were forthcoming, her husband was exonerated, and the real embezzler was indicted and convicted.

Why is clarification urgently needed in this case? Because the woman claimed (adamantly!) that she had done nothing morally wrong while the church authorities insisted (adamantly!) that she had deliberately violated the Seventh Commandment and was therefore **very** morally wrong. Arguments could be (and were) advanced to support each point of view; but before we proceed to defend either perspective, a good deal of clarification of hidden assumptions and implications is needed. (For a more extended treatment of the ethical criteria we use in making moral judgments see pp. 373–377.)

Give to the intellect, wisdom to comprehend that one thing; to the heart, sincerity to receive this understanding; to the will, purity that wills only one thing.

Søren Kierkegaard

It is much easier to bury a problem than to solve it.

Ludwig Wittgenstein

Science is the attempt to make the chaotic diversity of our sense-experience correspond to a logically uniform system of thought. . . . The sense-experiences are the given subject-matter. But the theory that shall interpret them is manmade. . . . hypothetical, never completely final, subject to question and doubt.

Albert Einstein

First, note that what we are doing here is classified as ethics, the branch of philosophy that deals with evaluations of certain kinds of events—human intents and actions—events that we commonly evaluate as good or bad, right or wrong, sinful or virtuous, moral or immoral. The aim of ethics is to establish how we humans should ideally feel, think, and behave toward other human beings (and other living creatures, according to increasing numbers of ethicists). (Note also that evaluations are not fact-claims, though we commonly make numerous fact-claims to support our ethical judgments. No facts are involved in my statement "You shouldn't do thus-and-so"; it's a judgment-call based on what I think and feel about what people should or should not do.)

So, is the woman in this account—we'll call her Rita—to be judged moral or immoral? The Catholic church uses formal criteria for making moral judgments. In this case, the criterion or abstract rule by which the value-judgment is made is: "You shall not commit adultery" (Exodus 20:14 in the Old Testament). This rule is intended to have universal application; as the Roman church interprets it, it is supposed to apply equally to all human beings. It is a God-given law, and every human being should be acquainted with it ahead of time and be ready to apply it to any appropriate occasion. It is an apodictic law—not to be argued with, negotiated, modified, or violated. In this case Rita knew about the rule ahead of time, she knowingly broke the rule, and she is therefore to be judged guilty of immoral behavior. The logic is valid, and the judgment of the church is sound.

Eastern and Western epistemology are united in reminding us that when we are thinking we are not experiencing outside ourselves.

William W. Blake

But Rita argued that the decision she made was the loving, compassionate thing to do. She found herself in a moral predicament in which she was forced to choose from several courses of action, all extremely painful; she could see no real option that would not lead to devastating consequences. So what is one to do when forced to choose and only bad choices are possible—follow the abstract rule or do the loving thing? In this case Rita elected to save her husband from "almost certain conviction" and a heavy jail term. She sacrificed herself ("I went through hell to get the information I needed") for someone she cared for; she chose, she believed, the best option available to her in a terribly traumatic predicament. According to contextual ethics, if one chooses the best option that one can see with the well-being of another (or others) in mind, then that person is to be judged moral in the fullest sense. Using contextual criteria, Rita's actions were compassionate, her logic is valid, and her moral judgment is sound. (For more on contextual ethics see pp. 375–377.)

Understanding the world for a man is reducing it to the human, stamping it with his seal. . . . The truism "All thought is anthropomorphic" has no other meaning. Likewise, the mind that aims to understand reality can consider itself satisfied only by reducing it to terms of thought.

Albert Camus

So, was Rita moral or immoral in her behavior? **She can validly be judged either way.** Our **evaluation** of her conduct depends entirely on which criterion we select for making the judgment. Both criteria can be given strong defense, and countless volumes have been written in support of each position. Such an indecisive answer is not satisfying to many of us; we do not like ambiguity. The next step, therefore, is to try to decide which criterion is the better one, or the right one; but this is another story for another time.

9 There are many more assumptions and implications in this actual episode that need to be clarified and made explicit; just note that we have attempted here to clarify one thing only—the criteria used in this case for making moral evaluations. From this brief treatment, however, three ethical axioms can be inferred.

"The Unexamined Life"

Men of Athens, I know and love you, but I shall obey God rather than you, and while I have life and strength I shall never cease from thc practice and teaching of Philosophy. . . . I am that gadfly which God has attached to the state, and all day long and in all places am always fastening upon you, arousing and persuading and reproaching you. . . . I tell you that to do as you say would be a disobedience to God, and therefore I cannot hold my tongue. Daily to discourse about virtue, and about those other things about which you hear me examining myself and others is the greatest good of man. The unexamined life is not worth living. . . . In another world I shall be able to continue my search into true and false knowledge. . . . In another world they do not put a man to death for asking questions: assuredly not.

Plato
The Apology

The trial of Socrates represents something more than a mere historical event that could not possibly happen again. The trial of Socrates is a charge leveled at the type of intellectual questioning that seeks out the true problems lying outside everyday mediocrity. When Socrates tormented the Athenians like a gadfly, he prevented them from sleeping peacefully, from relaxing with their ready-made solutions to moral and social problems. By astonishing us, Socrates prevents us from thinking along the old lines that have been handed down to us and have become habits. Thus Socrates stands at the very opposite end of the scale from intellectual well-being, easy conscience, and beatific serenity. For all who think that the evidence of authority ought to prevail over the authority of evidence, that order and stability cannot permit the crimes of nonconformity and "lèse-société," Socrates could only have been the enemy.

Jean Brun
Socrates

(1) No evaluation, including ethical judgment, is intelligible unless the criterion used to make the judgment is made explicit and clearly understood. (2) Any action or event, including all human-behavior events, can logically be evaluated as good or bad, right or wrong, depending on the criterion selected for making the judgment. (3) The ethically informed individual is aware that different and distinct criteria exist and are used in daily life by all us human beings who are trying, as best we can, to deal with life's moral dilemmas; and this awareness should help us to better understand the passionate disagreements that seem to be an inherent part of our social existence.

10 **3 Inference Validation** A third family of critical skills involves the fundamental rules of reasoning invented by Aristotle and known as Aristotelian or classical logic. Logic can be defined as the science of valid inference, and it is used to clarify the relationships of ideas. It includes both inductive and deductive reasoning.

The world we have made as a result of the level of thinking we have done thus far creates problems we cannot solve at the same level at which we created them.

Albert Einstein

We can work with "the problem of evil" (or "theodicy") to illustrate what is meant by valid inference. This problem, given extensive treatment in all the

"Yes, there is a God . . . yes, there is a God . . . yes, there is a God . . ."

great religions, has been the source of an enormous amount of anger, bitterness, and agonized questioning by believers caught in the devastating tragedies of everyday life.

The *Book of Job* in the Judaic/Christian Bible contains the classic statement of the problem of evil. In the prose prologue to the book, Job is portrayed as a prosperous man who had lived a long and righteous life. One day the God Yahweh and the Satan (literally "the Adversary," a sort of prosecuting attorney at this point in Judaic thought, not the supreme Evil One of later theology) fell to discussing Job and his profound devotion to his God. God praised Job's unwavering loyalty, but the Satan began to argue that Job was loyal only because, as Yahweh's protégé, he had been showered with abundant blessings and that, if he had suffered like other men, he would forsake his pious stance and curse God. So they agreed to a test of Job's faith. The ground rules: The Satan could afflict Job in any way he pleased but mustn't take his life. So Job was subjected to a series of devastating disasters. He lost all his worldly goods, his possessions, his family, and finally his health. When Job's misery reached unbearable depths, three of his friends appear to comfort him. But Job curses the day he was born and will not be comforted. His friends assail Job with the standard Judaic belief that suffering is the result of sin, and Job's suffering proves that he has sinned mightily. If he will confess his sin and repent, then his suffering will cease. Through three cycles of exquisite poetry, Job reiterates his innocence and protests that his suffering is absurd and meaningless and that God is monstrously unfair in making him suffer this way.

You see me as an atheist. God sees me as the loyal opposition.

WOODY ALLEN

The "problem of evil" can be summarized this way: If God is all-powerful, and if God is compassionate, then why are we humans made to suffer? This problem is our agonized attempt to justify the ways of God to ourselves. By the end of the *Book of Job* a variety of possible solutions to the problem of theodicy are explored.

11 Numerous assumptions and implications are hidden in this story of Job. Using some of the critical guidelines of classical logic, and putting some of the above arguments in syllogistic form, we can make a search for some of these hidden meanings.

The late Judaic version of this moral law that caused such pain to Job can be stated:

Sin (and only sin) causes suffering
Job is suffering

Therefore, Job has sinned

An idea once born never dies. It may grow feeble under the battering of other ideas. It may gather dust upon some library shelf. But sooner or later someone is going to shake off that dust and look at the forgotten idea once again. And lo and behold! here precisely is what he has been searching for these many years.

T. K. MAHADEVAN

Note also the validity of the following belief, which is explicit in the *Book of Job:*

The degree of one's suffering is proportional to the degree of one's sinning
If one sins much, then he will suffer much
If one sins little, then he will suffer little
Job is suffering much

Therefore, Job has sinned much

The doctrine also assumes that sin and suffering are causally related, and if one alters the cause he will then alter the effect:

Sin (and only sin) causes suffering
If you stop sinning, then you'll stop suffering
You, Job, have not stopped suffering

Therefore, you Job, have not stopped sinning

Since there could be a time-lag between cause and effect (between the sinning and the suffering), then perhaps an after-the-fact recognition and confession of one's sins would reinstate the sinner in God's favor:

If you recognize and confess your sins, then you'll stop suffering
You're still suffering

Therefore, you haven't recognized and confessed your sins

On the other hand, when we reflect on this argument from Job's side, we begin to see why the doctrine produced so much spiritual (and intellectual) anguish. Job might say: "My friends all agree that—"

Sin (and only sin) causes suffering
I am suffering

Therefore, I have sinned.

"But they're wrong! I maintain that I'm innocent of any wrongdoing, of any blasphemy, and that I have not sinned. I'm sure—"

I have not sinned
I am suffering

Therefore, suffering is not caused (solely) by sin

"Then why am I suffering? Why?"

A just God would not allow an innocent person to suffer
God is just

Therefore, God would not allow me to suffer

"But he **is** allowing me to suffer! Therefore, maybe—"

A just God would not allow an innocent person to suffer
I am innocent
I am suffering

Therefore, God is unjust

"But how could that be? God—if he be God—must necessarily be just. What, then, is the answer?"

I must conclude (from belief and definition) that God is just
I must conclude (from experience and logic) that God is unjust

---

Therefore, God is both just and unjust (God is both A and not-A in the same sense at the same time)

"But this is impossible! Then, why, oh Lord, why? Is there no way out?"

12 One can sense Job's anguish—and that of countless other believers who have found themselves caught in this very human puzzlement and are attempting to make sense of it. There is really no way out, and having wrestled deeply

It is a terrible thing, Tolstoi said, to watch a man who doesn't know what to do with the incomprehensible, because generally he winds up playing with a toy named God. Pasteur saw nothing particularly terrifying or unsatisfying about this situation, saying that the only thing to do in the face of the incomprehensible is to kneel before it. But that which is most incomprehensible of all is not a distant planet but the human mind itself; kneeling under these circumstances may represent the ultimate vanity.

Norman Cousins

with the problem, the authors of the *Book of Job* fail to resolve it. A logical contradiction is involved that, given his premises and his limited data, Job (or the authors of *Job*) could not have solved. Since we readers are privileged to be outside observers to the story, we are let in on the secret from the beginning: we know that the painful drama was planned as a test of Job's faith. God and the Satan good-naturedly agree to do a number on Job to see how far he can be pushed before he breaks and curses God for his misfortunes.

This doctrine of a "moral law" has been a headache for theologians and philosophers for thousands of years. For our purposes, just note the role of logical analysis as used here: placing the arguments into logical form helped us to make valid inferences from the Judaic doctrine of a moral law. Logic did not solve the problem; it merely clarified a few aspects of our thinking about the problem; and for some it may have partially dissolved it. Some method other than deductive logic—perhaps an inductive investigation of the immediate causes of human suffering—could suggest a better solution to the problem (see pp. 174–175).

You might be interested in the answer(s) that the writer(s) of the *Book of Job* seem to offer. One answer is found in chapters 40:6–42:6—the statement of Yahweh out of the whirlwind. However, if this answer leaves you intellectually empty, then read the prose prologue to the book (chapters 1:1–3:1) along with the prose epilogue (chapter 42:7–16). Quite a different answer is offered. These different solutions merely illustrate the challenge of the problem if taken seriously and treated within the parameters of the given premises.

Brief Skirmishes / Examples of Critical Thinking

13 Here are some brief examples of how critical thinking might be done using the critical skills surveyed above. In each case, how would you respond to the quoted statement? What are the first questions you would ask about it? What about the definitions involved? the hidden assumptions? the reasoning employed in the statement?

"Enquiring minds want to know."

This statement is from a TV commercial for *The Enquirer,* the weekly tabloid found at our checkout stands. What questions would you begin asking about the statement? And how would you go about critically evaluating it?

Of the many critical observations that might be made, here are just a few. As the statement stands, it is true, of course, by definition. What is the definition of "enquiring minds"? Answer: those minds that "want to know." But this is a commercial sales pitch, and therefore I know that they want to sell me something; so I have to be on guard. As with all commercials, I must decide if I really want what they want me to buy.

In this case what do they want to sell me? *The Enquirer,* of course. They want me to want what they offer me in their pages so I'll buy their paper. They are trying to persuade me that if I have an inquiring mind—which they know I will claim to have; an inquiring mind is still a respected commodity in our society—then I will want to buy their paper, which will tell me what my mind, an inquiring mind, wants to know.

But I don't want to know what they have to tell me. I have better things to do with my mind. I have three clear reasons for this position. (1) Much of the material in the tabloid paper I would label gossip, the worst kind, for it deals with the sensational, the personal and private, and the morbid. (2) It therefore caters to my prurient passions and wastes my time. It gives me almost no ideas or information that will help me be a better-informed human being. (3) Its fact-claims are relayed to me uncritically and without verification. I cannot trust the information it purports to convey. Since what I want is truth, I will have to turn elsewhere.

14 **"Call us now! The number is 1–900–555–2823 and your call will be answered by a member of the Psychic Network who can accurately predict your future. The future does not have to be unknown. We don't just predict the future, we change it!"**

The statement that "the future does not have to be unknown" should strike us as a serious problem for it goes against our every-hour common-sense experience. But wouldn't it be wonderful if we could know the future! It would have so much survival value: we could see what is coming and try to get out of the way. So strong is our desire to look ahead that whole religions have grown up to minister to this very human need. Every society has had its tea leaves, psychics, seances, astrology, tortoise shells, palm reading, tarot cards, and crystal balls.

But the idea that the future can be known needs to be given a careful critical look. If the future has not yet happened (and that's its definition), then it cannot now be known. If it has not yet happened, then it does not now exist. How then can something be known if it doesn't exist? On the other hand, if it can now be known, then it has already happened. And if it has already happened, how can it be changed? And how could we prove that it has been changed?

Knowing the future might be placed into two subheadings: (1) soft prediction and (2) hard prediction. With soft prediction, we can predict the future based on present knowledge and experience. Economists will predict that the third quarter will see an increase in unemployment, a lowering of interest rates, and fewer housing starts. I can also predict that if you are in your late thirties then you will likely face a midlife crisis before too long. But such soft predictions as these may or may not happen; they don't **have** to happen just because I, or an "expert," predicts them. They are not logically necessary events. They are all "if-then" predictions: **if** the economy continues as it has been going and follows past trends, **then** there will be more unemployment, and so on. But the economy may not follow past trends; it does seem to have a mind of its own, so it might do wild, erratic, unpredictable things this year.

Hard prediction is another story. In this case someone—such as a prophet, diviner, a psychic, or one's self (in dreams, perhaps)—**foresees** future events exactly as they will take place; and, since they are **fore**seen, and because we often include an element of divine revelation in their interpretation, then they **must** take place exactly as foreseen. This is properly called precognition. A famous case is the dream episode of Abraham Lincoln of his own funeral. A few

The philosopher does sometimes get so interested in his technique that he forgets the human interest that may have first led him and his students to philosophy; the student suffers from impatience to get to the main point. Some philosophers are like pianists who play only scales; on the other hand some students are like beginners in music who are so anxious to play Beethoven that they resent having to learn scales.

LEWIS WHITE BECK

Sit down before fact as a little child, be prepared to give up every preconceived notion, follow humbly wherever and to whatever abysses nature leads, or you shall learn nothing.

T. H. HUXLEY

Beginning to think is beginning to be undermined.

ALBERT CAMUS

Lord Russell tells us that he once received a letter from a well-known logician, a Mrs. Franklin, admitting that she was herself a solipsist and was surprised that no one else was. Russell comments: "Coming from a logician, this surprise surprised me."

J. MILLER

We do not want a thing because we reason; we find reasons for a thing because we want it. Mind invents logic for the whims of the will.

G. W. F. HEGEL

days before his assassination Lincoln dreamed that he saw a funeral service held in one wing of the White House. The mourners, some of whom he recognized, were all dressed in black. When, in the dream, he asked whose funeral it was, he was told "the president has been shot." This dream certainly looked like a case of genuine precognition, and it had a considerable impact on Lincoln. He shared the dream with several close friends and members of his cabinet.

Men talk because men have the capacity for speech, just as monkeys have the capacity for swinging by their tails. For philosophers, as for other human caddis flies, talk passes the time away that would otherwise hang like a millstone about a man's neck. Tellurians in general, and philosophers in particular, swing from day to day by their long prehensile tongues, and are finally hurled headlong into their silent tombs or flaming furnaces.

HERMAN TENNESSEN

The problem is that, while such episodes are rampant in popular mythology, there isn't a shred of evidence that such predictions have any validity beyond sheer (and not uncommon) coincidence. Lincoln's dream, which on the surface appears to be a classic example of precognition, belongs to a class of experiences easily explained psychologically. Lincoln was quite aware of the degree to which he was hated by sympathizers of the South; he had received numerous death threats. Even if he had repressed his awareness and his fears from consciousness, his subconscious mind confronted these fears and acted upon them symbolically in the dream sequence. The Swiss depth psychologist, Carl Jung, developed the theory that the subconscious mind, not being absorbed with the mediation of present realities as is the conscious mind, can connect feelings and events and foresee with thoughtful accuracy events that the conscious mind cannot see. But even this is a kind of soft prediction, symbolically represented, and not an authentic hard prediction.

[Note: The ABC television network program *PrimeTIME Live* conducted an investigation of the psychic industry and found widespread fraud. But note that a critical analysis of psychics' claims by any one of us shows essentially the same thing. Revealing fallacious claims does not prove fraud, of course; we are not here passing judgment on honesty or intent. But what an epistemological analysis of the **nature of time** does show is that their claims cannot be true, whatever their intent may be.]

15 **"Mommy, Ginny told me . . . [crying] Ginny said that I was adopted. Mommy, am I adopted?"**

The word "adopt" has several distinct meanings, and it is used in different societies in a variety of senses. First, it's a legal term that, in some societies, refers to . . .

Philosophy is at once the most sublime and the most trivial of human pursuits. It works in the minutest crannies and it opens out of the widest vistas. . . . No one of us can get along without the far-flashing beams of light it sends over the world's perspectives.

WILLIAM JAMES

Whoa . . . wait a minute! Let's be very careful. There's a time and a place for everything, and this may not be the time for critical analysis. With children —with all of us—there is so much more to listen to than what the words denote; or better, words always carry far more meanings than narrow definition can capture. Obviously, in this case, a mere intellectual response seems woefully off the mark. It is not always easy to discern what responses are appropriate, but we can be sure that we daily encounter such decision times. The plaint of Tevya to his wife, "After twenty-five years I've never asked you before: Do you love me?" or the cry of the woman screaming "My house is on fire!"—in such cases the appropriate response just may not be critical analysis. This is not to say that the rational intellect could not help us decide what kind of response is most appropriate. It certainly can. But critical analysis, as a response, may be the last thing called for.

16 **It was a fever of the gods, a fanfare of supernal trumpets and a clash of immortal cymbals. Mystery hung about it as clouds about a fabulous unvisited mountain. . . .**

I'm confused by such a passage. How can the gods have a fever? or what is immortal about cymbals? or how can mystery hang "about it as clouds"? After all, mystery is a subjective experience, not a thing "out there." And what is "it"?

But . . . I'm off the mark again. This is poetry. If I approach this passage with the assumption that the author intends to convey precise meanings to my intellect, then I will miss the intent of the passage. These words by H. P. Lovecraft, the early and great science-fiction writer, represent his loving, creative wordplay—which is what poetry is all about. In deciding what sort of response is appropriate, the nature of the material and the intent of the creator must always be taken into account.

17 **"I hate broccoli. It tastes awful! I'm president now, and I'll never eat broccoli again!"**

(Or words to that effect.) This episode, for many Americans, was a delightful interlude between the weighty problems of President George Bush's tenure. It possessed a fairly high-level humor, and we had the feeling that, for a brief moment, the president had dropped his public persona and was just being himself; in his light candor we found him charming and believable. We liked that, and we liked ourselves in a relaxed, unguarded moment with the president.

Should we decide to be analytical, however, we might note that this broccoli-pronouncement is made up of four separate and rather interesting statements. (1) Bush makes a private fact-claim: "I hate broccoli!" is a statement of a private fact, and if he is reporting accurately, it stands as a nondebatable datum. To this statement I would be foolish to reply, "No you don't. You like broccoli!" The fact-claim is true if he says it is, and that's the end of the matter; only he can report on what he is experiencing, and only he knows, finally, whether the statement is true or not.

Facts are the raw material for thinking.

Robert E. Sparks

(2) Bush makes an evaluation involving a fallacy. His statement "It tastes awful!" should be qualified to read "It tastes awful to me!" so that it is clear that he is not placing the bad-taste experience onto the object: Broccoli doesn't taste—we taste. Our taste buds do the tasting, not the broccoli. All such qualities (such as beauty, sounds, tastes, smells) should properly be located within the experiencing self, not in the real world.

(3) Bush makes a simple fact-claim—"I'm president now"—to which there can be little argument; it can be easily verified. And (4) he makes a soft prediction that includes an intended commitment: "I'll never eat broccoli again!" Predictions are neither fact-claims nor evaluations of events. A prediction is a statement of a personal expectation, or a statement of a hoped-for goal toward which one will devote some effort to achieving, or a political statement to affect the actions of others toward a goal. In this case, Bush's statement is probably of the second kind (with overtones of the third kind); he is telling us that he intends to devote some considerable energy and effort toward not ever eating the green stuff again.

You will never succeed in getting at the truth if you think you know, ahead of time, what the truth ought to be.

Marchette Chute

18 **Time had a beginning at the big bang. Many people do not like the idea that time has a beginning, probably because it smacks of divine intervention.**

This idea of time is to be found in Stephen Hawking's best-selling book *A Brief History of Time* (Bantam Books, 1988, page 46). And yes, he is right that a lot of people do not like the idea that time has a beginning, but not for the reason he gives. Rather it is because Hawking makes the assumption that time is real and, like any real object, could have a beginning and an end. It is seriously to be doubted that time is real, even though this is a common (working) assumption made by physicists and cosmologists.

In the first place, how could one write a "brief history of time"? We can only write a **history** of something that has endured, that is, has had a continued existence **in time.** That is what the word "history" means, does it not? I can write a history of the city of Phoenix because it has endured **through time,** or a history of the Industrial Revolution because it continued to exist for a **period of time.** There could be a history of time only if time had endured **in time,** which also had endured in another time, which had endured in still another time, and so on, *ad infinitum.* So unless physicists want to plead some special definition, the notion of time having a beginning and an end leads to an absurd notion of time. Almost certainly, time is an experience, not a real thing (see pp. 244–259).

The Real is one though sages speak of it in many ways.
Rig-Veda 1.164.46

Many modern-day physicists treat their formulas as though they were real, just as many mathematicians tend to think of numbers as real. The fundamental reason for this fallacy is that virtually all the objects of physics (atoms, molecules, organisms, rocks, trees, planets, galaxies, black holes, pulsars, and so on) involve motion; and it takes time for things to move. Furthermore, things always move in space. So it follows that the formulae and equations employed by physicists to describe moving entities therefore **assume** both space and time; motion makes no sense, and could not be measured, without such an assumption. But because the assumption is necessary to make our equations work, it does not follow that space and time are real, though the assumption is a natural one. Thanks to Albert Einstein, almost all physicists today speak of the "space-time continuum" as though "it" is a real thing, but this involves another fallacy: treating time as if it were space, when, in fact, time and space are separate and distinct entities that should not be confused; that is, we must be critically on guard not to spatialize time or temporalize space. It just may be that the foundations of modern physical theory are laid on a conceptual fallacy which, someday, will have to endure an agonized reappraisal.

In his ignorance of the whole truth, each person maintains his own arrogant point of view.
The Buddha

19 **The swastika is the hated symbol of Nazi horror.**

Yes and no. In the minds of millions the swastika is a symbol of Hitler, the Nazis, the Holocaust, the Axis during World War II; and it certainly is hated. But it is important to remind ourselves of a semantic fact: symbols have no meaning. Symbols are meaning-**less.** Symbols, that is, don't **have** meaning; they are **given** meaning. They are given meaning by us meaners; and the semanticists are forever reminding us that we humans can make anything stand for anything. Meaning is not a property of symbols, but is an experience located in the minds of us meaners.

The Jain flag displays the central symbols of the Jain faith. The three dots stand for the "three jewels"—right intentions, right knowledge, and right conduct. The swastika's arms symbolize the four levels of incarnation—birth or rebirth in hell; as insects, plants, or animals; as humans; and as spirits or demons. The half-moon represents *kaivalya* (*moksha* in Hinduism), or liberation. The horizontal stripes from top to bottom are red (purity), yellow (simple living), white (asceticism), green (vegetarianism), and blue (*ahimsa*, nonviolence toward all living things). The swastika, an auspicious symbol of good fortune, was a vital possession of Hindus, Jains, and Buddhists for three thousand years before the Nazis adopted it. To the Jains specifically it symbolized that life is permeated with hope, that in the midst of despair, good things will continue to happen to us. Tragedy and suffering are but momentary conditions through which we must pass to happier times. Go with the flow of life, following the rolling clockwise movement of the arms of the sun-swastika, for it assures us of the coming of spring.

It is an historical fact that Hitler adopted the swastika to stand for the Third Reich, and because of his actions this symbol has come to mean monstrous and terrible things. But it is also an historical fact that the swastika has been for more than three thousand years a symbol of good fortune and divine favor in Indian religion, and for devotees of the Jain religion it has long meant salvation. It is the central symbol on the Jain flag. Thus the swastika, like all symbols, can be given different meanings; and the meanings of all symbols, including words, must be determined from the living contexts in which they are used.

It is wrong always, everywhere, and for everyone to believe upon insufficient evidence.

W. K. CLIFFORD (NINETEENTH-CENTURY MATHEMATICIAN)

20 **"Who discovered America—Columbus or the Vikings? Watch TLC Monday night at 8:00—on THE LEARNING CHANNEL."**

"Columbus discovered America," so the claim goes. Besides the problem of defining "America," the key word that renders such a statement problematical is "discover." What does it mean to discover? Do you go to the refrigerator and "discover" that someone has finished off the apple pie? This "discovery" gave you new information that you did not have before; so yes, it was a discovery. Did Admiral Peary "discover" the North Pole when he reached it in 1909? Ever since geographers first figured out that the Earth is round and rotates on an axis they knew in theory that a North Pole must exist somewhere. Peary was the first human being to make the journey to where the real pole was calculated to be, find it, and plant a flag there; so in a precise sense we can say "Peary discovered the North Pole."

The greatest single achievement of science in this most scientifically productive of centuries is the discovery that we are profoundly ignorant; we know very little about nature and understand even less.

Lewis Thomas

Let us define the word: "To discover" means "to be the first to find, to learn of, or to observe." Only individuals discover, though several individuals can "discover" at about the same time and proceed to say "we discovered." So "to discover" means to come across something that the discovering individual did not previously know. Did Columbus and his crew "discover" a new land-mass with people living there? Yes, of course. It was something new for them; and since Columbus was, in his mind, making the voyage to a new world on behalf of Spain (a big idea) and "European civilization" (an even bigger idea), then he made his "discovery" on their behalf and returned home to share his new knowledge of this previously (to them) unknown land and people. To Europeans it was valuable new knowledge; and the "discovery" is a part of the European experience.

At the heart of science is an essential tension between two seemingly contradictory attitudes—an openness to new ideas, no matter how bizarre or counterintuitive they may be, and the most ruthless skeptical scrutiny of all ideas, old and new. This is how deep truths are winnowed from deep nonsense.

Carl Sagan

To the native peoples of this new land-mass, to find that there were people living across the sea to the east was also a discovery for them, a new item of knowledge they did not previously possess. The claim to some discovery always requires the stipulation of the perspective from which the discovery is made. The intrepid Henry M. Stanley traipsed across Africa to find the great missionary doctor, David Livingstone, and announced to the world back home that he had "discovered" him; but Livingstone protested that he was not lost and that he didn't really appreciate being "discovered." Likewise, the "native Americans" could inform Columbus that they were not lost. Columbus could rightly claim that he had "discovered" them for himself and European Christendom, and if Columbus wanted to claim that that was all that really mattered, the Indians could well retort, "I'm glad you 'discovered' us since that is what you set out to do. Now go home and leave us alone!"

Later generations of native Americans would have evaluated this "discovery" event quite differently since Columbus brought bigotry, slavery, disease, and death, as well as pigs, citrus fruit, and sugarcane. Because of his destructive impact many people today still want to deny Columbus the honor of having discovered the New World; to praise him for it is felt to be an insult. The honor, they feel, should go to Leif Erickson and his Vikings or to Huishin the Chinese Buddhist monk blown off course in the fifth century AD, or to someone else. Some of the feeling that drives this denial is from individuals and groups who do not share the Eurocentric perspective in which Columbus is essentially a hero, or who feel that this perspective is denigrating to other points of view, which are not then given full value. If the claim were to read "Columbus discovered some new islands and their native inhabitants, none of which were previously known to Europeans," then most of the confusion could be avoided. But since the claim seems to carry with it the implication that Columbus discovered a gigantic land-mass whose existence had never been known to anybody important, then the statement is offensive and should have no status as a description of an historical event.

The essence of Zen is to learn to do just one thing at a time.
WILLIAM W. BLAKE

A Special Kind of Listening

21 A critical thinker engages in a special kind of listening. In most of our idea exchanges, we listen to what others say, but a philosopher listens not only to what you say but even more to the implicit thought processes that got you there.

I never saw an instance of one of two disputants convincing the other by argument. I have seen many, on their getting warm, becoming rude, and shooting one another.
THOMAS JEFFERSON

You may say, "I have concluded that . . . " and the philosopher will respond, "Fine. Tell me how you arrived at your conclusion."

You may say, "In my opinion . . . " and the philosopher will listen to your opinion and then ask, "How did you arrive at your opinion?"

You may say, "I believe . . . " and the philosopher will say, "I'm pleased that you believe that. How did you arrive at that belief?"

Someone may tell you, "I think thus-and-so is morally wrong," and as a philosopher you will say, "I understand what you're saying. Now tell me how you arrived at that evaluation."

Someone may retort, "I disagree with you." As a philosopher you will say, "Thank you. Now tell me about the sequence of thoughts that led you to that disagreement. Do that, and we can talk."

✦

Plato

The First Educator

His name was Aristocles, and he was born in Athens on the seventh of Thargelion in the first year of the 88th Olympiad—May 29, 427 BC. His father, Ariston, traced his lineage to Codrus, the last king of Athens, and his mother, Perictione, traced hers to Solon, Athen's greatest lawgiver. His was an illustrious heritage, and he moved with statesmen, playwrights, artists, and philosophers all his life.

We call him Plato because his coach so nicknamed him, from the Greek word *platon,* meaning "broad-shouldered"; he excelled in sports and wrestled in the Isthmian games at Corinth. Multitalented, he distinguished himself in every field. He fought in three battles during the Peloponnesian War and was decorated for bravery.

At twenty-one, Plato was caught up by the charismatic brilliance of Socrates and dedicated himself to philosophy, which he called "a precious delight"; and though he was to be Socrates's pupil for only eight years, their association would set the course of Western thought for the next two thousand years.

Socrates didn't operate in a school with buildings and a campus. He conducted his teachings entirely in the *agora,* the open marketplace of Athens, where everyone gathered to exchange goods, carry on their political lives, have their clothes made and sandals fixed in the cobbler's shop on the Street of the Leather-Workers, bid for furniture, order inscribed tablets and statuettes from stone-carvers on the Street of the Marble-Workers, carry on religious rites as around the Altar to the Twelve Gods, and do business at the tables of the money-changers. The whole life of Athens was lived here in the agora. Above all, the Athenians loved to talk (the noun *agora* derives from the Greek verb *agoreuein* which means "to talk," "to speak," "to harangue"), and they wandered among the covered colonnades gossiping, bargaining, talking and listening to teachers, political orators, preachers of mystery cults, poets, and playwrights.

Plato would have stayed close to his teacher during the entire time he was in

Athens as a student. He probably lived and spent his nights in private homes near the agora. He would have taken his meals and passed most of his days in the company of fellow students, watching and listening to Socrates, exchanging with bystanders—talking and examining ideas. Plato was born, lived most of his long life, and died within the immediate environs of the Acropolis in Athens.

When Athens finally lost the war and was garrisoned by the Spartans in 404 BC, Plato—already horrified at the inhumanity of war, the tyranny of the oligarchs, and the bestiality of mobs—saw the Athenians further degraded by their own ruthlessness and greed. He wrote: "Whereas at first, I had been enthusiastic about a political career, now all that I could do is watch, helplessly, this chaotic world about me." This experience of the Absurd turned personal when, at twenty-nine, he witnessed the trial and execution of his teacher. Socrates was convicted on trumped-up charges of impiety and corrupting youth and was put to death with a cup of poison hemlock. "This is the end of our comrade," Plato later wrote, "a man, as we would say, of all then living we had ever met, the noblest and the wisest and the most just."

Plato seems to have made a serious attempt to put the Athenian nightmare behind him. He traveled for a dozen years, visited Italy and Sicily—where he absorbed Pythagorean metaphysics—possibly sailed to Cyrene and Egypt, and returned home to Athens about 388 BC. He was thirty-nine. Within the year he established the school that would occupy him the rest of this life: the Academy, the first institution of higher learning in the Western world. (The Academy endured for more than nine hundred years. In the year AD 529 it was closed by the Byzantine emperor Justinian because, in his eyes, it was a stronghold of paganism.)

At the age of sixty Plato was invited back to Syracuse to educate the new king, Dionysius II. He also hoped to field-test the theories of social psychology he had described in *The Republic.* But the young king proved ineducable, and political intrigues drove the philosopher back to Athens.

After another failed mission to Syracuse when he was sixty-seven, Plato attended the Olympic games in the Peloponnesus in July, then came home to Athens to settle for the rest of his life, teaching and writing. His greatest works, in which he used Socrates as his literary hero, were written before he was forty; they include *The Apology, Crito,* and *The Republic.* During this last period he wrote *Parmenides, Theaetetus,* the *Laws,* and others. He was by this time universally admired and honored. On his eightieth birthday one of his pupils invited the master to a wedding feast. He attended, and the tale is told that he danced into the night. Eventually he took leave of his students and withdrew to rest. He died in his sleep. According to tradition, it was the first year of the 108th Olympiad—347 BC.

✦

Plato's life is marked by two supreme achievements: the establishment of the Academy and the immortalizing of Socrates in writing. Both have profoundly influenced the Western world.

The Academy was located on several acres of public park on the outskirts of Athens, about a mile northwest of the Dipylon Gate. The site contained olive trees, statues, and temples named for the legendary Greek hero Academus—hence its name. Also on the grounds were lecture halls, classrooms, and a shrine of learning—a sort of chapel, built by Plato himself, dedicated to the worship of the Muses, those nine daughters of Zeus who were the inspiring spirits of all the arts and sciences. Adjacent to the grounds was a large sports gymnasium. The land was purchased for Plato by his friends.

Here Plato gathered about him a circle of serious students and organized them into a disciplined educational community. Young men and women came from

The feeling of wonder is the touchstone of the philosopher, and all philosophy has its origins in wonder.

Astronomy compels the soul to look upward and leads us from this world to another.

Our object in the construction of the state is the greatest happiness of the whole, and not that of any one class.

It is a human being's goal to grow into the exact likeness of a God.

I think a man's duty is . . . to find out where the truth is, or if he cannot, at least to take the best possible human doctrine and the hardest to disprove, and to ride on this like a raft over the waters of life.

On Plato:
Plato advised drunken people to look into a mirror.
Diogenes Laërtius

On Plato:
To understand Plato is to be educated.
Edith Hamilton

all parts of the Greek world and dedicated themselves to a demanding program of study that included literature, history, music, mathematics and geometry, and philosophy. They were to be educated, not trained. Through intellectual and moral development they were to become qualified leaders of the state. They lived close by, off campus. They paid no fees, but their parents gave generous gifts so that, after a few years, the school was heavily endowed. The students were Hellas's finest youth, and they stayed on for years, or even a lifetime, engaged in rigorous study and research.

Today the search for Plato's Academy is disappointing. One can follow the Panathenaic Way down from the Propylaea of the Acropolis northward past the Stoa of Attalos for less than a kilometer. Then the way is blocked by a swath of railroad tracks and the fume-filled streets of modern Athens. Where the Academy once stood there is only an open field of weeds dotted with yellow daisies and patches of blood-red paparumas, a few marble drums, friezes, and late Roman sarcophagi. The site awaits excavation to bring to light whatever secrets are to be found about the institution that was the glory of Hellas.

As Being is to Becoming, so is Truth to Belief.

The pursuit of money should come last in the scale of value.

The height of injustice is to seem just without being so.

✦

Plato had a fiercely clear vision of what he wanted to do: educate young men and women to seek the truth, with the hope that they will be qualified to assume positions of leadership in the world where they can put that truth to work.

By the time Plato started his school, he had already witnessed a lifetime of tragedy. Human beings, he observed, have an unfortunate tendency to see everything through the narrow slits of their defensive armor. We operate from a reduced point of view, while claiming little less than omniscience. Out of irrationality, or on the basis of false or inadequate information, or because of myths and fallacies, we draw lines of separation, erect fortresses, and go to war.

While lies and limited information can alienate people, a clear understanding of universal truth would bring men together. Plato believed that truth—if it is truth—must be universal. There can be but one truth—or one set of truths—for all humans. It follows that if human beings understand things as they really are—that is, if they possess the truth—then they could no longer divide themselves into parochial encampments, and, out of ignorance and arrogance, bitterly fight with one another, with words and swords.

Over the entrance to the Academy Plato had inscribed the words ***MEDEIS AGEOMETRETOS EISITO***, "Let no one without geometry enter here." This inscription implies more than its literal meaning. Geometry (which includes mathematics) is the universal science. It is Plato's metaphor for the search for universal truth.

Thus, Plato is the founder of rational philosophy, and philosophy, Plato would say, is the art and science of developing universal ideas.

What are universal ideas?

An idea is an abstract concept manufactured by the mind to enable it to handle a large number of particular observations. For instance, my experience of one lonely meadowlark singing from a fencepost is a single direct perception; but my notion of bird (that is, bird-in-the-abstract, "birdness"—what all birds have in common) is an idea—a universal idea. The first is my **perception** of a real object (meadowlark); the latter is my **conception** of an idea (bird).

How do we develop universal ideas?

Suppose, in my lifetime so far, I have actually seen only six crows and ten turkeys. I will indeed have an idea of bird (it will include only whatever characteristics crows and turkeys have in common); but my ideas can't be very accurate (or very useful) because I haven't experienced enough birds. It's a beginning, but it's too limited.

Now, say that I add to my repertoire a hundred finches, a thousand gulls, and a pair of pelicans. Having experienced **more** birds, I have a **more** accurate idea of bird. Suppose that I have actually seen millions of birds of countless species during my lifetime. My idea of bird will be more inclusive, more accurate, more universal—and more useful.

In daily life, our misuse of ideas is a calamity. What happens is this. Athenians have seen only seagulls and terns; still, they will tell you that they have a clear idea of bird. Alexandrians have seen vultures, kites, and ibises; they too have a clear notion of bird, so they say. Latins from Italy have just as clear an idea of bird, too, for they have seen finches, sparrows, and sanderlings. Each has a clear notion of bird. But what is likely to happen when Athenians, Alexandrians, and Latins get together to discuss birds? They will all have different **ideas** of what bird is, and, since they're only human—and if they don't take time out to clarify and define their ideas—they will soon be arguing and fighting because each knows that the others' bird-idea is wrong.

Going to battle over something as trivial as our different ideas of bird seems silly. But what about our (similarly incomplete) ideas of justice, virtue, morality, decency, right, wrong, sin, evil, pleasure, happiness, loyalty, selfishness, pride, human nature—and countless other ideas, including Faith, Hope, and Love . . . and Goodness, Truth, and Beauty? Plato observed that we all seem to be possessed by a diabolical drive to fight over our differences before trying to discover the root and cause of those differences.

Plato is convinced that men will stop fighting only when they understand the truth about things. This is the task of philosophy and the goal of education. To philosophize is to exchange and refine ideas by talking about them—through dialogue. If Athenians and Spartans could have talked over their ideas of honor and justice, perhaps they would never have had to fight over them.

"Until philosophers are kings, or the kings and princes of this world have the spirit and power of philosophy . . . cities will never rest from their evils—no, nor the human race. . . ."

✦

Reflections

1 On p. 36 you find the statement that there are two questions that we humans must find answers to: How does the world work? And what is our place in it? Evaluate both critically. Do these questions have meaning for you?

2 Are you clear on what is meant by being "critical"? Are you clear on what being critical *doesn't* mean?

3 Give three examples of fact-claims, and state how you would go about verifying or falsifying each of them.

4 Review the story of Rita and her moral predicament (§8). Does this account illustrate adequately to you what concept clarification is all about? Can you appreciate the nature of a moral predicament like Rita's? If some individuals are too biased or politicized to be objective in their thinking about such problems, how would you advise them to go about developing objectivity?

5 The trial of Socrates, suggests Jean Brun (see box on p. 41), "could not possibly happen again." What factors leading to his trial no longer prevail? Do persons who think like his accusers still exist? (Review the Socrates story on pp. 30–33.)

6 If you had been Job (see §10) and had lost everything that was precious to you, what would you say to your three friends who have come to "comfort" you? What would you say to God? (Do you know what Job actually said, according to the *Book of Job*?)

7 State the "problem of evil" in its classical form. Is this a meaningful statement of the problem, in your opinion? Can you restate it in better terms? Is it a genuine problem, in your judgment, or a false problem? If you see it as a false problem, translate it into a more accurate statement of the predicament that people face when confronting the fact of evil.

8 Do you believe that sin and suffering are causally connected?

9 Logic is often defined as the study of valid inference. Convert the process of inference into basic English, and describe how it can benefit us in our thinking.

10 What is the meaning of the swastika? (See pp. 48–49.) Is it clear to you that symbols have no meaning (they are meaning-less) until they are given meaning by us meaners? How would you go about reasoning with someone who was convinced that symbols are *inherently* meaningful (and that the meaning he or she gives to the symbol are the correct ones!)?

11 In §21 you find the statement, "A critical thinker engages in a special kind of listening." What exactly is that special kind of listening?

12 Plato's thinking has had a major impact on Western thought. Can you put into a single statement the essence of Plato's thought? Why do you think he has had such an impact?

13 What was the primary objective of Plato's program in the Academy?

14 Plato engaged in a lifetime search for the truth. But what "truth" was he seeking—that is, what is its definition? And how does it differ from other definitions of truth?

Synoptic Synthesis

1-4

Philosophers analyze ideas in order to achieve precision and clarity in their thinking; but many thinkers attempt also to assemble the bits and pieces of knowledge into a coherent understanding of the Big Picture. The world is truly like a great Picture Puzzle, and the goal of synoptic philosophy is to see the picture on the Puzzle—the whole picture—and to see it as accurately and clearly as humanly possible at a given point in space and time. This chapter suggests ways one might go about assembling the pieces of the Puzzle and constructing a vision of the whole.

Learning is not the accumulation of scraps of knowledge. It is a growth, where every act of knowledge develops the learner.

EDMUND HUSSERL

And He Wants to Understand It

1 The goal of synoptic philosophy is what the Greek words imply: *sun-optikos*, "seeing (everything) together," and *philein-sophia*, "to love wisdom." Put these root-words together and the meaning is clear: synoptic philosophy is the love of the wisdom that comes from achieving a coherent picture of everything seen together—a vision of the whole of life.

"A vision of the whole of life"—! Could any human undertaking be grander, or more grandiose? William Halverson writes that "this attempt stands without rival as the most audacious enterprise in which the mind of man has ever engaged. Just reflect for a moment: Here is man, surrounded by the vastness of a universe in which he is only a tiny and perhaps insignificant part—and he wants to *understand it*."

2 We want to understand it, of course, because we must. Being what we are, it isn't a matter of choice. If we have eyes to see, then we must see; if we have

He who knows does not speak;
He who speaks does not know.

Tao Teh Ching

When a speculative philosopher believes he has comprehended the world once and for all in his system, he is deceiving himself; he has merely comprehended himself and then naively projected that view upon the world.

C. G. JUNG

ears, then we must hear. There are at least three reasons for this necessity, and all are ontological.

First, seeing life holistically is a matter of survival. Imagine some animal at home in its environmental niche with all the usual, routine life-and-death events going on around it. The more it can perceive of these events, and the more accurately it can perceive them, then the better it can adjust. Developing a realistic sense of priorities—to be able to distinguish between significant and insignificant events, between the dangerous and the benign—means survival. This is just as true for abstract human beings as for the wild fox and the wallaby. Investing our energies in consequential events rather than insignificant trivialities requires a wisdom born of perspective.

But humans have a need (we think) that goes beyond the deer and the dolphin: the need for meaning. For us a meaning-less existence is a contradiction. Intuitively we have known that the well-lived life—the meaning-full life—results from what we humans call wisdom. By definition wisdom is the understanding of life and how to live it; and for as long as we humans have sought wisdom it has been apparent that wisdom is correlated to our capacity to perceive more and understand more.

Lastly, this drive to create a personal universe has still deeper origins. Each of us harbors within a pressure to achieve psychological wholeness, and our passion for wholeness in knowledge is a part of this drive. Unity of personality and unity of knowledge are two aspects of the same goal. What do we feel if we see on a table a jigsaw puzzle half finished or a painting left undone? We assume—we know—that any enterprise, once begun, ought to be completed. An unfinished story nags at us. An unfinished letter haunts us. An unfinished sentence, left dangling in midair, leaves us waiting, and when

One can be positive of one's own way that it leads to the goal and not that others cannot. That would be a species of dogmatism.

T. R. V. Murti

Life on a Picture-Puzzle

3 Think of life as a jigsaw puzzle with an enormous number of pieces, and think of synoptic philosophy as our attempt to fit the puzzle together. This puzzle didn't come to us sealed in a cardboard box with an illustration on the cover, so we really don't know what the picture on the puzzle will turn out to be.

To be sure, we have been told what the picture is. But this is the problem. So many people have told us, on the best authority, what picture is really on the puzzle, and they describe different pictures. We must draw the logical conclusion that they, too, have not yet attained a glimpse of the whole picture.

Our ultimate goal is to fit all the pieces together so we can attain a clear look at the picture. But it's an incredibly complex puzzle, and we may never succeed in getting the whole picture pieced together. Attempts thus far have failed, though many have been able to assemble scattered clusters. You and I may succeed in filling a few random spaces or joining together a small group of pieces here and there. Still, for all of us, at this point in the progress of human understanding, the total picture is diffuse, with light and dark shades that don't yet make sense. The task requires endless patience. If, in the meantime, we can enjoy just working the puzzle, that might be a sufficiently rewarding compromise.

So, the goal of synoptic philosophy is to see the picture on the puzzle—the whole picture, nothing less—and to see it clearly, unmistakably, and realistically.

4 The metaphor of the picture-puzzle helps to clarify several characteristics of synoptic philosophy.

The first, of course, is that the goal of synoptic synthesis is to see the whole picture. It will not settle for a fragmented view of scattered designs; nor will it allow itself to be seduced into believing that any mere fragment is really the whole picture. The mandate of synoptic philosophy is to keep working with the jigsaw pieces until the picture is seen and the puzzle is resolved.

The philosopher of history Arnold Toynbee has written that, as of the latter part of the twentieth century, we are collectively in transition to a new world-view in which our dominant perception will be that of being meaningful parts of a larger universe. These new ties contrast sharply with the old world we are now leaving, in which the dominant sense of consciousness was for each of us to believe we were complete, self-contained universes within ourselves.

To use the puzzle metaphor, most of us have heretofore taken up residence on a single piece of the jigsaw puzzle. We lived out our lifetimes on this small picture plot; we put down roots and became intimately familiar with the design of one small bit of reality. Eventually we came to believe that our cardboard square was the most important piece in all the puzzle; the rest of the vast scene was to be judged from the perspective of our own mini-puzzle. The final illusion followed close behind: we convinced ourselves that our single puzzle-piece was in fact the whole of reality—the total picture.

Knowledge of the world demands more than just seeing the world. One must know what to look for in foreign countries.

Immanuel Kant

To escape this predicament, synoptic philosophy encourages each of us to wander over the puzzle, visiting neighboring parts and trying to see how the pieces of the puzzle all fit together. It urges us to travel from square to square until it becomes clear that no single part is in fact the whole. Only by wandering over the puzzling terrain restlessly and observantly—like itinerant flatlanders—can we arrive at an honest conclusion as to what the whole of reality is like.

The Annihilation of Boundaries

Something forever exceeds, escapes from statement, withdraws from definition, must be glimpsed and felt, not told. No one knows this like your genuine professor of philosophy. For what glimmers and twinkles like a bird's wing in the sunshine it is his business to snatch and fix.

William James

5 Since at least the time of Aristotle, synoptic philosophy has been the ultimate interdisciplinary enterprise. When Aristotle and his peripatetic students were walking and talking along the paths of the Lyceum, subject-matter specialization had not yet begun, and knowledge was not yet "organized apart" into countless categories—biology, psychology, physics, and so on. Aristotle still looked with awe and wonder upon all human knowledge. His adventuresome mind was still free, not yet trained to function along carefully defined boundary lines, not yet cluttered with classification systems that fragment human understanding into competing disciplines.

It has been said that Aristotle was the last Western thinker that could actually know all that there was to be known. Before his time there was not much to know, and after him there was far too much. Specialization became inevitable.

Although Omar Khayyam may have claimed that the results of his studies were that he "evermore came out by the same door as in I went," he neglected to notice that he was facing a different direction when he came out.

Ronald Huntington

But it is important to realize that life is not specialized. Life is "interdisciplinary." Vocationally we may be electronics engineers, or neurosurgeons, or accountants, but when not practicing our profession we "revert" to the human condition and find ourselves thinking like generalists again.

Synoptic philosophy is a reflection of life. We are, each and every one of us, sociology and anthropology and history and geography. We are physics (put your finger into a light socket and feel). We are astrophysics and cosmology (we feel silvery-moon sentiments by night and get sunburns by day). We are biology and biochemistry and genetics (unless the stork story is true after all). We are psychology and physiology and psychophysiology (ever guzzle a martini or suffer a brain concussion?). We are all these things, and there is nothing in human knowledge that we are not. So when we engage in synoptic thinking we are returning to life. Life cannot specialize. It remains just what it was before the human mind fragmented it: totalic, whole.

6 Isn't the attempt to attain a vision of the whole of life beyond the capacity of finite human minds?

The answer is that the synoptist never tries "to know everything." He makes no attempt to memorize the reams of hard data that have accumulated in the specialized fields. Happily, it is not uncommon to become excited about a field and find oneself drawn in deeper than first intended. Still, the synoptist remains a layman when it comes to specialized details, and he does not let himself forget this fact.

Perhaps the major challenge to philosophy in the last decades of the twentieth century is whether it can face the future imaginatively and creatively or whether it will simply be content with a status as a second-order discipline, able only to analyze and evaluate the concepts and ideas of other disciplines.

Richard Doss

The task of the synoptist is to keep himself informed on the latest conclusions, general principles, hypotheses, models, and theories that emerge from the work of the field specialists. He is not himself a field specialist, and he is not in competition with them since he is not a knowledge-gatherer in the sense they are. He makes use of the data they labor to discover; hence he is always in their debt. He is also at their mercy, of course; and he hopes that he turns to the right specialists for information. If he listens to wrong sources and receives wrong an-

swers, then, in effect, he ends up with jigsaw pieces that don't belong in the puzzle; and he may waste considerable time trying to fit in pieces that won't fit.

This question—Can the human mind attain "the holistic vision"?—presupposes a degree of faith. At present the complexity of "all that is" boggles our minds; total comprehension seems like a fuzzy dream. However, the holistic vision is probably not an unrealistic goal for the human race. Not that we have a choice. Since this drive is ontological, we will continue to work for it both individually and collectively because we cannot do otherwise. In our own short life/times the most we can hope for is partial success. But even a little progress, at the personal level, proves immensely rewarding.

At present history is on the side of optimism. The story of man's attempt to gather a fund of empirical knowledge and to discover the truth about himself and his world has, in the longer-range perspective of history, just begun; and human understanding is advancing so rapidly on all fronts that any oddsmaker would advise placing our bets on the continued capacity of the human mind to understand, in principle, the fundamental nature of man and his universe. True, this judgment could be wrong. Gray matter may have unsuspected limits, and the real world could turn out to be too intricate to be reduced to human abstractions. Still, understanding requires general principles, not details. (The details can be handled by our computers so that we can concentrate on understanding.) According to present evidence the human capacity for conceptualization is quite adequate to the task.

How to Do Synoptic Philosophy

7 How does one go about "doing" synoptic philosophy?

One good way to begin is to place yourself in the center of what we will call the "synoptic wheel" (note the diagram on p. 64). In your imagination, look outward in all directions from that center. Around the rim of the wheel are all the knowledge-gathering disciplines known to man, plus various arts and skills and some philosophic specializations. This schematic is merely one way of visualiz-

We need people who can see straight ahead and deep into the problems. Those are the experts. But we also need peripheral vision and experts are generally not very good at providing peripheral vision.

Alvin Toffler

ing our philosophic predicament: when we feel overwhelmed by life's stubborn questions and don't know which way to turn for help, then spin the synoptic wheel and ask the specialists to share their knowledge and insights.

Note the general areas that are represented on the wheel.

In working through a problem, a synoptist would move along a sequence of steps something like the following.

8 First, having come across a philosophic problem (or having been run down by one), first proceed as far as possible with philosophic analysis, clarifying and drawing out all the hidden meanings that you can, dissolving the problem completely if that is possible.

Then, to the extent that time and materials permit, find out what philosophers of the past have thought about the problem. In the history of philosophy, most of the problems you and I must deal with have been pondered, time and again, from many perspectives, and these earlier treatments can lighten our labors by enlightening our thoughts. Uniquely valuable insights are often provided by individuals who, in some special way, were bothered by, and became caught up in, a particular problem.

Once a problem is posed, it may be necessary to rephrase the question in a variety of ways before we can get it to reveal what kinds of information will help solve it. (There is no question that cannot be asked in many ways. The following exchange—"Does God exist?" "What do you mean by the question?" "I mean just what I said: Does God exist?"—is quickly ushered out of any philosophic discussion.) The synoptist tries to develop an intuition for asking and reasking questions from different angles until they point to the data that would illuminate them.

9 Second, from your vantage point in the center of the synoptic wheel, ask yourself what fields seem most likely to contain information related to your problem. Begin by just asking questions about the problem and how it might connect, one by one, to the various fields in the rim of the schematic. For instance . . .

Question: Does God exist? (First, ask yourself if your question is honestly intended as a genuine question. Do you really want an objective answer? Or do you want an "objective" answer only if it agrees with what you already "know"? Whatever the question may be, if you already know the answer beyond any possible doubt, then one must entertain second thoughts about its being a true philosophic question.) If it is an authentic question, then go to psychology, and ask questions of this kind: What do "religious experiences" seem to imply regarding the existence of a God? What about mystical experiences such as Saint Theresa's "golden arrow," and pentecostal "ecstasy," and "spirit-possession"? Can the multitude of deity-images in man's religions be understood in terms of our psychological needs?

Then go to linguistics, and ask: what does the word "god" refer to? Does it refer to reality or only to other words? Whence does it derive its meaning for you? for the Buddhist? for the native American Indian? What other names could you use for your God—matter, force, spirit, wind, love, power—? Go to physics: Are there any real objects/events that can't be explained in terms of known physical forces? Can the origins of matter be accounted for apart from the idea of a Prime Mover or Creator? Go to history: Is there documented evidence of past events that necessitate the hypothesis of supernatural intervention? Can we discern any sort of pattern or "dramatic plot" in human history that indicates direction, guidance, planning, or purpose?

Go to biology: Can life processes be explained in terms of natural biochemical events? Is there any event in DNA genetics, speciation, or evolutionary modeling that necessitates the hypothesis of a supernatural or a "vital impulse"? Go to medicine: Do there exist well-documented cases of healings that cannot be explained by medicine or by our understanding of the human psychophysical organism? If so, how must we define the word "miracle"? Go to exobiology: Is your image of God anthropomorphic—that is, humanoid? In what form might deity appropriately manifest itself to advanced alien beings on other planets? Go to astronomy: What concept of deity is possible in the incomprehensibly vast universe that we know today? *Etcetera*. . . .

This is but the briefest sampling of the kinds of questions that would have to be asked before such a question could be answered. Without doubt the task feels formidable, but it can also be one of our most exciting adventures. To perform the synoptic task well, one must keep up with what is going on in various fields and be willing to listen to anyone who is in possession of helpful information.

Having made this kind of preliminary survey, the next step is to go to these promising fields and gather information. Remember that the synoptist is looking for conclusions, hypotheses, and models currently used by field specialists. As you gather materials, keep asking questions, relating the data to your central problem and cross-relating insights from the fields themselves.

10 Third, criss-cross from field to field, drawing "interconnecting lines of illumination" as you go, stopping often to refocus new ideas on your initial problem to see whether the sort of understanding you are after is beginning to emerge.

Moving from first question to final answer is often a long journey. In fact, doing synoptic philosophy is much like starting a trip where all you know is where you are now and where you want to arrive—namely, at the best answer possible at this time. The route by which you'll get there is not at all clear, and philosophic journeys can rarely be neatly penciled on a map ahead of time. So, just set off down the road. If you come to a side road pointing to new information, turn that way. Travel till you come to new intersections of knowledge or see a sign pointing in still another direction. Do not be afraid to wander without a map. Let the journey unfold gradually, just as it wishes. The facts will lead us where we need to go.

Western philosophers have always gone on the assumption that fact is something cut and dried, precise, immobile, very convenient, and ready for examination. The Chinese deny this. The Chinese believe that a fact is something crawling and alive, a little furry and cool to the touch, that crawls down the back of your neck.

Lin Yutang

11 Fourth, back away from the problem you have been working on and try to see it in a larger way. Since it is so easy for us to lose perspective, stand back as often as needed and ask yourself whether the whole picture can be better seen now that you have invested considerable thought in analyzing and synthesizing the problem.

Such a view of the larger picture is not easily achieved in less than twenty minutes. Our minds will weave the silken strands into a beautiful tapestry, but they will do so in their own good time. What is important is that we attempt to see larger blocks of life and that we develop the habit of trying to think in ever larger frames as we work through the problem.

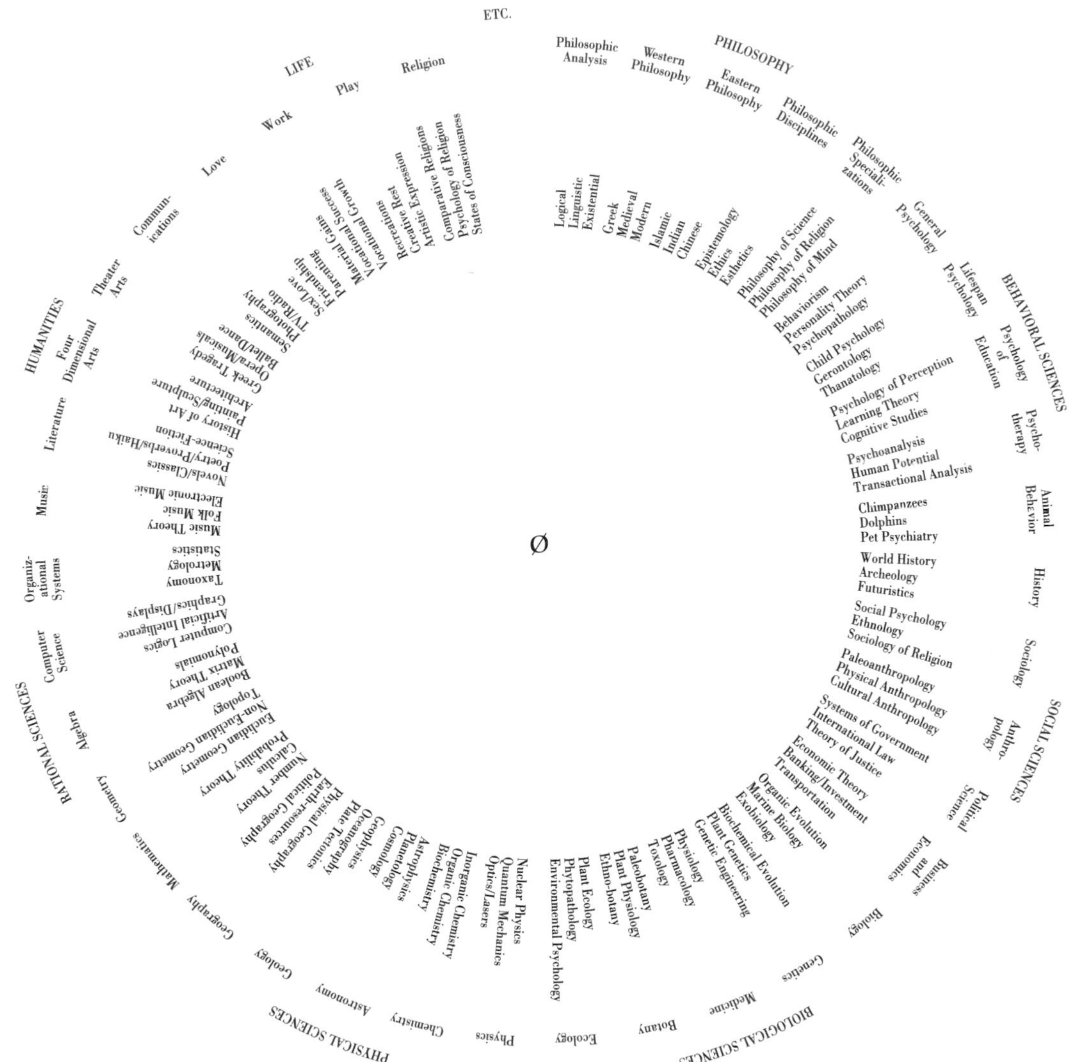

12 This attempt to see the full-scale picture on life's puzzle creates certain dangers about which we need to be forewarned. So, a word of caution: Do not be forced into saying you see more of the puzzle than you really do. The temptation to see what others insist is the picture on the puzzle can be great; and it may require no small amount of courage on our part to say, and to continue to say: "I can't see that part of the puzzle yet." Or: "I know that factual information in that area is still nonexistent, and no one can be absolutely sure about it at this time. It's too soon to persuade ourselves that we can see what isn't there." We all know how difficult it is to keep on saying "I don't know" when so many people around us are positive that they know the answers and keep proclaiming them to us, loudly. The gentle admonition of Confucius has a healing touch: "One can tell for oneself whether the water is warm or cold."

13 Word of caution #2: Considerable self-knowledge is required for us to resist the pressures of our own needs to have answers which, in fact, we do not

have. Our cultural conditioning has made us believe we are supposed to "have convictions" about most everything, or at least to "have an opinion." (If we do not we are apathetic.) So the need to prepare answers to meet our own competitive/survival situations is great. Knowing ourselves, recognizing our motives, and remaining wary lest these personal pressures push us into claiming more than we should—all this is not easy. But it is necessary, not just so we can play a defined role, but to be honest with ourselves about what, in fact, we actually know and don't know.

"Everything I have taught you so far has been an aspect of not-doing," Don Juan went on. "A warrior applies not-doing to everything in the world, and yet I can't tell you more about it than what I have said today. You must let your own body discover the power and the feelings of not-doing."
CARLOS CASTANEDA
Journey to Ixtlan

As one logician puts it, all but a small portion of our thinking is need-oriented; it is determined and guided by numerous subjective factors. "To become a sound thinker it is necessary not only to school yourself thoroughly in certain techniques but also to understand fully the nature and operation of subjective factors and to take special measures for reducing their influence."

In the last analysis, we serve both ourselves and others best if we refuse to detour from our goal of knowing "what is." If we are cavalier with facts or play loose with value-judgments, it becomes difficult for us to live with ourselves; and unless we play fair with our experiences, others have no good reason to believe us or respect our judgment.

Unless the synoptist remains loyal to his vision of seeing nothing less than the whole picture-puzzle, then there is really no one left in this world who continues to strive to know the full story. The World-Riddle is largely abandoned to those who intently gaze at some small portion of the jigsaw picture and proclaim to the rest of us that they have discovered the Whole. And we better believe it.

The Synoptic Venture: Risks and Rewards

14 The risks of specializing are many, but since specialization is the order of the day, we do not commonly become aware of them—except in a painful way, and too late. One risk is that the more one specializes the more he tends to neglect a general knowledge of life that is necessary just to remain human. The proverbial definition of the scientist—"the one who knows more and more about less and less until he knows everything about nothing"—is apt for every specialist. A narrow field too often signals a narrow mind. A fulfilling life is far more likely for the individual who develops a balanced awareness of the requirements of living.

Reason is 6/7 of treason.
JAMES THURBER

Another frequent result of specialization is the loss of the ability to communicate. Encapsulation is the commonest of all human diseases, with a mortality rate second to none. If we have failed to nourish the shared experiences of life, there may be nothing to bridge the chasms between us. The statement is commonly made that specialists tend to be lonely people, and this is probably true.

Brand Blandshard, a contemporary philosopher, once warned would-be specialists to keep their lines of communication in good repair.

> The more deeply you penetrate into the mineshaft of your own science, the more isolated and lonely you are with regard to those interests that mark the growing point of your mind. I admire beyond words the scientific acumen that made it possible for

> Planck to define the value of h, for example. But if I were to sit down for a talk with someone, and he were to focus the discussion on h, the *tête-à-tête* would be brief, for as far as I am concerned, h is not discussible.
>
> What are the grounds on which men generally can meet? They are the experiences that all men have in common. All of us, however humble, have had experiences of suffering and exaltation, of inspiration and depression, of laughter and pain that would, if we could only express them, make us, too, poets and essayists. Indeed, literature consists of just such experiences expressed as we should like to express them if we could. . . .
>
> It is well to be a specialist; it is better to be a good human being.

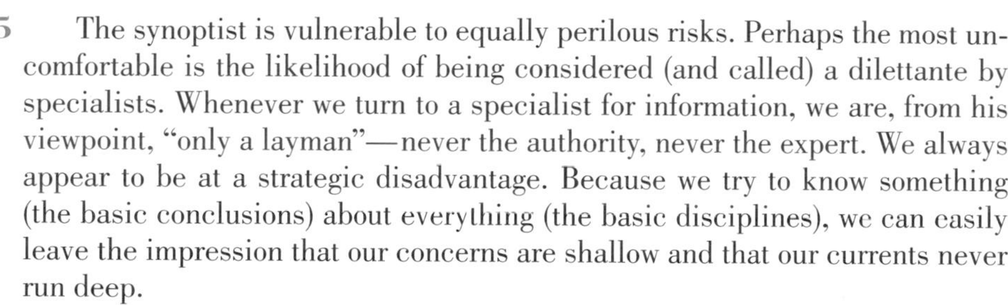

15 The synoptist is vulnerable to equally perilous risks. Perhaps the most uncomfortable is the likelihood of being considered (and called) a dilettante by specialists. Whenever we turn to a specialist for information, we are, from his viewpoint, "only a layman"—never the authority, never the expert. We always appear to be at a strategic disadvantage. Because we try to know something (the basic conclusions) about everything (the basic disciplines), we can easily leave the impression that our concerns are shallow and that our currents never run deep.

The *Shri Yantra* is employed in meditation by Hindu worshippers known as Shaktas. It is a symbol of wholeness. Ultimate Reality is represented by the dot in the center, and the rest of reality is symbolized by triangles (consciousness and energy) and lotus petals (the material universe). The outer square contains gates through which the mind of man can enter into the deeper levels of wholeness.

A far greater danger, however, is that we might actually become dilettantes—random dabblers in all things known and unknown. The difference between a dilettante and a synoptist lies in the way the synoptist weaves his data into a coherent worldview. Dabblers and dilettantes are known for dipping and picking at bits of information to be in a position—over hors d'oeuvres and a demitasse—to impress others with their range of erudition. By contrast, the stance of the synoptist is to admit, to himself and others, what he does not know; and in the context of all that there is to be known, he is aware that his abysmal unknowing is nothing to boast about. The goal of the synoptic empiricist is not to collect bits and pieces, but to weave the strands of knowledge into a glowing tapestry.

A double-edged risk is the fact that specialists become irritated with the way laymen—however honorable their intentions—tend to misunderstand and misuse the discoveries from their fields. They are (rightly) wary of having their work "popularized" and distorted. That fear can be calmed, of course, only by the honest, accurate handling of the data derived from their specialized fields. We are morally justified in asking their help only if we are willing to assimilate their materials with intelligence and integrity.

16 The rewards of the synoptic venture are, for the most part, intensely personal, having to do with what we are, or can become, as human beings.

One reward is learning to "think bigger." From its inception, a prime concern of philosophy has been the fact that the parameters of human thought—for all of us, all the time—are very, very narrow. Larry Niven, a science-fiction writer, put it perfectly: The trouble with people who live on a planet is that the inhabitants tend to think small. And when we think small, we never quite succeed in arranging life's events into an efficient priority system that promises optimal growth and fulfillment. We don't think big enough to know what's important in our lives and what's not important, what to invest our time and energy into and what to ignore.

A Human Being's True Function

If the great design of the universe had wished man to be a specialist, man would have been designed with one eye and a microscope attached to it which he could not unfasten. All the living species except human beings are specialists. The bird can fly beautifully but cannot take its wings off after landing and therefore can't walk very well. The fish can't walk at all. But man can put on his gills and swim and he can put on his wings and fly and then take them off and not be encumbered with them when he is not using them. He is in the middle of all living species. He is the most generally adaptable but only by virtue of his one unique faculty—his mind. Many creatures have brains. Human minds discover pure abstract generalized principles and employ those principles in the appropriate special cases. Thus has evolution made humans the most universally adaptable, in contradistinction to specialization, by endowing them with these metaphysical, weightless invisible capabilities to employ and realize special case uses of the generalized principles. . . .

All the biologicals are converting chaos to beautiful order. All biology is antientropic. Of all the disorder-to-order converters, the human mind is by far the most impressive. The human's most powerful metaphysical drive is to understand, to order, to sort out, and rearrange in ever more orderly and understandably constructive ways. You find then that man's true function is metaphysical.

Buckminster Fuller

Synoptic philosophy is an antidote for small thought. As a result, many of life's problems—what we thought were life's problems—simply dissolve and disappear. Seeing the larger picture gives us the perspective and power to screen out trivial, inconsequential events.

The real world is increasingly seen to be, not the tidy garden of our race's childhood, but the extraordinary, extravagant universe described by the eye of science.

Herman J. Muller

Synoptic thinking also produces greater awareness in our perception of daily life. All of us want to be more than we now are: we want to be brighter (by 30 IQ points, maybe 40!); we want a greater comprehension of life's painful events; we want more intensely pleasurable "peak experiences," more adventures, and so on. In a word, we all harbor a deep desire for more life, both in quantity and quality. Synoptic philosophy moves in that direction by laying solid foundations for such experiences; it hears this ontological cry for help. Synoptic thought leads to a greater awareness of oneself, and hence to an understanding of others. This in turn means better communication—and less alienation, isolation, and loneliness. Other things being equal, these are good foundations for greater fulfillment within the context of the human condition; and this may be the most we can reasonably expect in one (short) life/time.

There is something delightful, even orgasmic, in the process of thinking and truth-seeking. There is a certain dimension of sweetness, a "super" but "natural" high, call it a super natural high, found in actually feeling one's thoughts grow and enlarge until they are born.

Robert Badra

Another reward is the fact that both our conscious and unconscious operations move more efficiently within a coherent worldview that is relatively free of internal contradictions and conflicts. Internal conflict means stress and a loss of psychological energy. If there is internecine strife going on between the ideas and feelings that constitute the cognitive contents of our character structure, then much of the energy potentially available to us for living is bound up in the inner struggle. We have "built-in headwinds"; we cannot get off the ground. A worldview that works well for us is one whose component elements

The fish trap exists because of the fish: once you've gotten the fish, you can forget the trap. . . . Words exist because of meanings: once you've gotten the meanings, you can forget the words.
Chuang-Tzu

have ceased carrying on a running battle inside us and have begun to work together.

A final note: learning can be (*can* be) one of life's most exciting adventures. Catch a glimpse, just once, of the new discoveries taking place along today's frontiers—it is humbling, thrilling, mind-boggling . . . and addictive! It is difficult not to want to share the action.

Each of us is free, if we wish, to become an epistemic amateur—a knowledge-lover—and to touch the incredible adventures that are breaking in astronomy, psychology, molecular biology, planetology, oceanography, physics, history, and so on. These are vistas that the specialists know but cannot share with us until we decide to open ourselves to their worlds. Even if some of these fields have heretofore been anesthetized by boring teachers and dull classes, the ability to rediscover them and to rekindle in ourselves a sense of wonderment—this may be a measure of our growth and, perhaps, of our capacity for life.

Aristotle

The First Scientific Worldview

For about a century Greek philosophy was dominated by the achievements of three Athenian thinkers—Socrates, Plato, and Aristotle. Socrates spent a lifetime in the *agora,* the crowded, busy marketplace just below the Acropolis; he attempted to get Athenian youth to realize that ordinary thinking is too loose and shabby to solve the important problems of life. The Socratic tradition was carried on by his pupil Plato in his Academy two miles northeast of the agora; he aimed at laying intellectual and moral foundations so that Athenian youth could rise to the demands of statesmanship: There can be no peace in the world, he believed, until statesmen are philosophers or philosophers become statesmen. The third of these great Athenian thinkers was Aristotle, Plato's pupil. He taught for twelve years in his Lyceum a mile south of the agora; he taught his students to search for the truth of things not primarily to make them statesmen, but because this is what would keep them human and lead to *eudaimonia*—"happiness."

Three supreme moments illuminate Aristotle's life.

First, he journeyed to Athens when he was seventeen, enrolled in the Academy, and became a student of Plato. He had come from Stagira on the Chalkidic Peninsula, where his parents, Nicomachus and Phaestis, were living when he was born in 384 BC. Nicomachus had returned from Pella, the capital city of the Macedonian Empire, where he had served as physician to the king. Aristotle had already lived an eventful life during these early years and, it seems, saw too much: he thoroughly disliked princes and the intrigues of the royal court. His father and mother both died within a few years, and the orphaned Aristotle, adopted by a kinsman, continued his education at Stagira, where he apparently performed brilliantly. He was soon accepted as a student in Plato's Academy.

Aristotle arrived at the Academy in 366 BC, performed brilliantly, and remained there for twenty years. This was a time of intellectual maturation; we know that he was in love with learning and had a passion for books—for which qualities Plato, likely with teacherly affection, dubbed him "the Brain" and "the Bookworm." Aristotle began to collect books and eventually built an enormous library of his own.

There was never a genius without a tincture of madness.

They should rule who are able to rule best.

The basis of a democratic state is liberty.

A tragedy is the imitation of an action that is serious and also, as having magnitude, complete in itself . . . with incidents arousing pity and fear, wherewith to accomplish its catharsis of such emotions.

Plato developed a comprehensive and coherent worldview—the first Western thinker to do so—and Aristotle fully absorbed it; but soon he had to exorcise it from his psyche—the two men possessed quite different temperaments—before he could move on to develop his own empirical worldview.

So Aristotle left the Academy at thirty-eight and sailed to Asia Minor to join an old friend who had become ruler of the city-state of Atarneus. For three years he lived there, and at forty, married the king's niece, Pythias. He organized a philosophic circle and developed a small school on the plan of the Academy to explore politics and ethics.

Sometime thereafter Aristotle and Pythias moved to the island of Lesbos, where he continued to study the marine life of the Aegean shores. Biology was Aristotle's first love. His later writings reveal a detailed knowledge of the marine life of this part of the world; and from this time on, the paradigms and metaphors that guided his philosophic speculations derive from biology.

These were rich and happy years for Aristotle, but they were short-lived, for Pythias died sometime after the birth of their daughter (named Pythias, after her mother). We don't know when or where her death occurred, and we don't hear of their daughter again until Aristotle mentions her in his will. Later, probably in Athens, Aristotle entered into a liaison with a lady named Herpyllis, who was his wife or consort (*hetaira*, "companion"), and a son was born to them. They named him Nicomachus after Aristotle's father.

When he was forty-two the second historic event in Aristotle's life occurred. He received a royal summons from King Philip to return to the Macedonian court as teacher to Philip's son Alexander. The crown prince was only thirteen, but within six years he was to assume the throne and marshal the military might of a united Greek world against the Persian Empire. After his lightning conquest of the known world, we remember him as Alexander the Great.

Aristotle taught Alexander for three years. Here is one of those special events so annoying to historians: a relationship so rich with possibilities, but about which we know nothing. The two men must have influenced each other, but they were worlds apart in passions, goals, and the games of life. Aristotle's commission was to prepare the crown prince to be a successful monarch of Macedon, to instill in him the principles of good governance, and to make him humane in his judgments, intelligent in his policies, mature in his decisions. There are suggestions in the records that they never quite let go of each other. We have reports that Alexander, as he moved eastward, set his troops to gathering specimens of exotic flora and fauna to be dispatched back to Athens for Aristotle's gardens and museums.

The third momentous event of Aristotle's life began in the spring of 334 BC. Alexander set off for Asia to conquer the world, and Aristotle returned to Athens to set up his own school, the Lyceum, an institution for higher learning that would endure for almost eight hundred years. He chose acreage a mile south of the Acropolis on the southern outskirts of the city. It included a shady garden, covered walkways, and a public gymnasium on the grounds of a temple dedicated to Apollo Lyceus—Apollo the Lightgiver. Not being a citizen of Athens, Aristotle possessed no property rights, so he was forced to lease the land and buildings for his school. The gymnasium was one of the three large recreation halls in the city at that time; and no doubt Aristotle's students sometimes dashed into his classrooms, a minute late, fresh from workouts in the sports arena.

Aristotle was fifty when he opened the Lyceum. He was a gentle, sensitive man and an inspiring teacher. For a dozen years he oversaw the institution, directed research programs, taught, and wrote. He lectured as he wandered through the grounds of the park and under covered walkways called *peripatoi* (his students became known as the Peripatetics, "the Strollers"). During morning hours he lectured on technical subjects; in the afternoon he presented open-air lectures to the public on popular topics such as rhetoric and politics. During the evenings he conversed and wrote.

Aristotle was the inventor of formal logic; he was the first thinker to reduce human reasoning to a set of rules by which valid thinking could be distinguished from invalid—good thinking from bad. He thought of his work on logic not as a science in itself but as a set of preliminary and preparatory skills to be used in making one's way into all the sciences. His work on logic is found primarily in six treatises that, after his death, were collected and called the *Organon*, "instrument" or "tool."

In one of these treatises, the *Prior Analytics*, Aristotle treats deductive logic as expressed in the form of a syllogism. This, he believed, represents a perfect form of reasoning. A syllogism consists of three propositional statements: a major premise, a minor premise, and a conclusion. A true syllogism contains two premises only, and the conclusion derives from the premises. For example:

All Greeks were philosophers
Aristotle was a Greek

Therefore, Aristotle was a philosopher

In this syllogism the conclusion is implied in the premises; where the conclusion is correctly inferred, the conclusion is said to be valid, as it is in the above illustration. Logic, by definition, is the science (or study) of valid inference. In his treatise, Aristotle developed with remarkable insight the implications of these types of syllogisms; and all formal logic of the next 2300 years is little more than an elaboration of his work.

In another of his treatises called *Posterior Analytics* Aristotle took up the subject of induction and scientific method. Induction is a mode of reasoning that proceeds from particular facts to general principles. For example, after examining the movements of just a few planets, Johann Kepler concluded that all heavenly bodies trace elliptical orbits. He generalized on only a few observed cases. Aristotle pointed out that what you would have concluded on the basis of only a few observed facts—that a general statement is true—probably is true, and the more observations, the more it is probably true. But in all cases of induction only probability is established, never proof. There is nothing in the fact that a few planets follow elliptical orbits that would imply that all planets must follow elliptical orbits. How many observations of elliptical orbits would one have to make to be absolutely certain that a generalization is universally true? An infinite number, since the number of orbiting heavenly bodies is probably infinite. But this is impossible. Therefore, one can never be absolutely sure of a generalization arrived at by inductive reasoning. All it takes is a single instance of a non-elliptical orbit—one instance of an asteroid moving in a perfectly circular orbit—to render false the generalization about elliptical orbits.

Some generalizations are therefore sounder than others, depending on the quality and quantity of the supporting evidence. A generalization supported by only few observations, or that ignores contrary instances, would hardly be a sound generalization. On the other hand, a general proposition supported by numerous observations and no contrary evidence would be more reliable and would serve as the basis for scientific prediction: All heavenly bodies sofar observed (millions!) follow elliptical orbits; therefore there is a high probability that all future observations of heavenly bodies will be found to travel in such elliptical patterns.

With such illustrations Aristotle clarified the principles of logic—"the rules of right reasoning"—and thus established the foundations of all science.

In contrast to Plato's Academy, which stressed mathematics and geometry, Aristotle's Lyceum was designed as a center for scientific research and the teaching of scientific method. Heavy emphasis was placed on the natural sciences, espe-

Neglect of an effective birth control policy is a never-failing source of poverty which, in turn, is the parent of revolution and crime.

If purpose, then, is inherent in works of art, so is it in Nature also. The best illustration is the case of a man being his own physician, for Nature is like that—agent and patient at once.

In all things of nature there is something of the marvelous.

All men by nature desire knowledge.

For one swallow does not make a summer, nor does one day; and so too one day, or a short time, does not make a man blessed or happy.

Beauty is the gift of God.

cially biology. Aristotle found that he had to be a collector and curator in order to be a scientist. In and around his buildings he developed a zoo and botanical garden, and inside the school he established laboratories and a voluminous library. As in today's textbooks, he used anatomical diagrams to illustrate his observations, and these were put up on the walls of the Lyceum, just as they are in modern classrooms. Thus Aristotle had available an abundance of material to make a scientist jubilant. Using the scientific skills he had developed, he turned his attention to virtually every known subject.

He wondered about the stars, planets, sun and moon, the mountains and oceans, heat and cold, rain, snow, clouds, thunder and lightning, and rainbows.

He investigated plants and animals, and the relationships of living things, including ecological systems and animal behavior; mollusks, fishes, insects, birds, mammals; organs for sense perception and locomotion, mating and reproduction; and diseases and disorders.

He reflected on mind and emotions, men and women, love and genes. He pondered perception, conception, words and meanings, and fallacies; poetry, sculpture, and music. He studied written constitutions and power politics; he evaluated various forms of government such as the monarchy, aristocracy, and timocracy.

Doubtless Aristotle derived immense enjoyment from delving into the mysteries of our world, but his gathering of facts was incidental and unimportant. What he was seeking was general understanding, and his knowledge of particulars enabled him to generalize.

Therefore, from his observations he developed abstract concepts of motion, change, actuality, potentiality, process or becoming, and causality; geological time, biological evolution, and entelechy (biological purposiveness—our genetics); systems of classification, concepts of truth and validity, definitions, categories, *archai* (first principles, axioms), deduction and induction; concepts of virtue, justice, human nature, the soul (*psyche*), and happiness (*eudaimonia*); concepts of form and substance, teleology, and a Prime Mover.

We can judge, from our vantage point, that Aristotle laid foundations for the sciences of physics, astronomy, and meteorology; taxonomy, biology, forensic pathology, and animal psychology; psychology, epistemology and logic, and esthetics; political science and ethics; and finally, metaphysics—the philosopher's unified field theory for understanding his universe.

Add to all this a picture of the man reflecting, writing, and lecturing on more popular subjects such as education, rhetoric and grammar, mathematics and geometry, statecraft, drama and literature, and the art of living the good life.

Aristotle was a true scientist—an honest mind seeking empirical data from which to build explanatory hypotheses; and he was a true philosopher—a wonderer who surrendered lovingly to his curiosity about life.

✦

All hell broke loose in Athens in the summer of 323 BC when the young Alexander died unexpectedly in the palace of Nebuchadnezzar in Babylon, probably from malaria and too much drink. Aristotle had remained an alien in the eyes of the Athenians, a colonial Greek from the north too closely associated with the Macedonian conqueror. After Alexander's death the Macedonian party was ousted from power, and the wrath of the citizenry turned against Aristotle. He was charged with "atheism" or "impiety"—introducing new gods into Athens. (This was a standard accusation; Protagoras and Socrates had been so charged.) At this juncture he was offered protection by an old friend, so Aristotle retreated to Chalcis on the island of Euboea, some forty miles north of Athens. He tolerated this exile for barely a year when he died in 322 BC, age sixty-two.

Something of Aristotle's character is revealed in his last will, preserved for us by a later historian. In it he bequeathed his books and manuscripts to his friend Theophrastus. He freed some of his slaves and kept others—none were to be sold. He provided for Herpyllis and expressed his gratitude to her "in recognition of the steady affection she has shown me." Then he wrote: "Wherever they bury me, there the bones of Pythias shall be laid, in accordance with her own instructions."

✦

Reflections

1 Rephrase in your own (meaningful) way the essential goals of synoptic philosophy and make your own assessment of the rewards of the synoptic venture. Would your thinking and feeling change if you could achieve the rewards mentioned in this chapter? Are you willing to accept the risks?

2 What is meant by saying that synoptic philosophy is a "now" philosophy? What is the relationship of synoptic philosophy to the history of philosophizing? To assist you in your own philosophic tasks, what benefits would you gain by becoming acquainted with the history of philosophic thought?

3 What is the relationship of philosophic analysis to synoptic synthesis? Does the metaphor of the picture puzzle help to clarify how they relate? Are these two activities inherently in competition, or do they cooperate with and complement each other?

4 As a synoptic philosopher, how would you respond to the charge of being a dilettante? How would you answer the accusation that you were trying to know everything and, hence, to "play God"?

5 Are you in agreement with the statement that most of the significant questions of life are interdisciplinary by nature and that we are already in the habit, in daily life, of drawing information from many sources to solve our problems? In your judgment, is it accurate to describe synoptic philosophy as "a disciplined form of what we do all the time"?

6 Do you agree with the suggestion that the compartmentalization of knowledge, although pragmatic, is an arbitrary mental habit and that all knowledge is interrelated? "We need a discipline which, by its nature and calling, will help us put our fragmented world of knowledge back together." Do you find this notion congenial?

7 Choose some philosophic problem that is of personal concern to you; sketch a rough synoptic wheel, place the problem in the center, and then jot down the areas in the wheel where you might find relevant data to help solve the problem. Develop the habit of using the synoptic wheel during your philosophic wondering through the rest of this book. Try to be aware of any resistance you may feel to breaking over the imaginary walls separating areas of thought that you've not been in the habit of relating—theology and physics, for instance, or anthropology and ethics.

8 What was the nature of the passion that drove Aristotle to be an empiricist? He was trying *to see* something, as all philosophers are, but what was he trying to see?

9 Aristotle described one type of reasoning in his *Prior Analytics* and another kind of reasoning in *Posterior Analytics*. Clarify his objective in each.

10 State briefly the principal difference between Aristotle's philosophy (summarized in this chapter) and Plato's philosophy (described in chapter 1-3).

11 The goals of Plato's Academy and Aristotle's Lyceum were quite different. What were the essential goals of each?

The Condition and the Odyssey

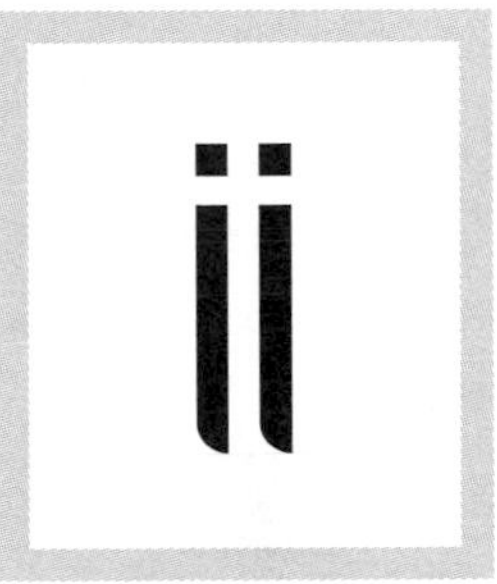

Philosophy is man's quest for the unity of knowledge: it consists in a perpetual struggle to create the concepts in which the universe can be conceived as a universe and not a multiverse. . . . This attempt stands without rival as the most audacious enterprise in which the mind of man has ever engaged: Here is man, surrounded by the vastness of a universe in which he is only a tiny and perhaps insignificant part—and he wants to understand *it.*

William Halverson

PREDICAMENT

2-1

All philosophizing is rooted in one simple fact of our existence: each of us is trapped in an egocentric predicament that sets limits on the way we perceive the world and relate to others. This chapter describes this predicament and examines its consequences: alienation from reality, distortion of our perception of others, and the unwarranted creation of various kinds of aristocentric claims. It asks the question, Can we overcome such a deep-rooted and troubling condition? If so, how? An understanding of the egocentric predicament is an unavoidable prerequisite to careful thinking, especially in epistemology and ethics.

The solution to the problem of identity is, get lost.
NORMAN O. BROWN

The last creature in the world to discover water would be the fish, precisely because he is always immersed in it!
RALPH LINTON

THE COHERENT WORLDVIEW

1 Each of us has a worldview of sorts—merely because we are human. A worldview is a more or less coherent, all-inclusive frame of reference through which one sees the world; it is a subjective attempt to provide unity and consistency to the totality of one's experience. Since we cannot tolerate excess fragmentation, we must attempt to find an inclusive structure that will harmonize as much of our experience as possible.

Each individual is his own center, and the world centers in him.
SØREN KIERKEGAARD

For most human beings, a worldview is a given. We are born into it and live within it; we rarely break out of it or even realize that it exists. By and large this inherited framework contains all the essential ingredients for a meaningful existence: social structures that act as guidelines for relating to others; clear-cut value systems of right and wrong; codes indicating acceptable and unacceptable behavior; language, legends, and hero stories that provide group identity; myths that answer a multitude of ultimate questions about the world we live in.

Every man takes the limits of his own field of vision for the limits of the world.
ARTHUR SCHOPENHAUER

Worldview I: The Primitive

I live in a capricious world, unpredictable and dangerous. Evil spirits hide in caves, ponds, woods, and sometimes in animals and people. I must be careful not to offend the evil spirits. I try to make them stay away from my fire and the door of my hut. The spirits of my ancestors will help me. All that happens—the storm and the rains, the green maize, a good hunt, my success in battle, the getting of many cattle, wives and children—all these are mine because I perform the rites of our ancestors and keep favor with the good spirits. The witch doctor also helps.

Worldview II: The Hindu

At last I am born a Brahmin and I therefore know that I lived a good life in my last incarnation. Perhaps now I can achieve moksha so that I shall not return again in mortal flesh. I shall therefore practice diligently, spending many hours daily in meditation. The world of maya around me will vanish and my soul will know the joy and peace of nirvana. Vishnu will aid me. Glory to thee, god of the lotus-eye! Have compassion upon me!

Worldview III: Early Christian

I live on the brink of Eternity. The long cosmic struggle between the forces of Light—who dwell in the Heavens above—and the forces of Darkness—who dwell below—is nearly finished. God's plan for the ages is about to be fulfilled with the destruction of Satan. In Christ there will be no more death. We have been chosen to be the Children of Light and we will dwell with Him in His Kingdom. His only Son, Yeshua the Messiah, was the herald of God's Reign, and we must finish our earthly tasks quickly for His Reign is about to begin. 'Αμήν, ἔρχου κύριε 'Ιησοῦ. Amen, return quickly, Lord Jesus.

Worldview IV: The Taoist

I weary of the ways of men and I seek serenity by the waterfall and in the forest. Wherever men gather together, there are too many. The forces of yang and yin thrust them about and society is roiled as a muddy torrent. Let them begone! In the quietness of my solitude I shall seek the Tao, or rather the Tao shall seek me. Wu-wei—quiet now; no striving, no longing, no fear. Let me be filled with the tranquillity of silence and inaction; let me be immersed in Tao. Why should existence be like a drawn bow?

Worldview V: Modern Empirical

I live in a universe of matter in motion. The universe seems to follow consistent patterns which we can formulate into workable "laws" and describe with mathematical and geometrical terms. Life originated through natural processes and developed according to the principles of evolution. We exist in an "open" universe, containing billions of galaxies and, most likely, millions of planets sustaining intelligent life-forms. Man is unique, but he is also an integral part of nature and of natural processes which operate throughout the universe. With further scientific understanding man will be able to control his own destiny and mold his future.

Any worldview that can provide all these life-giving elements must be considered a successful worldview.

2 It is one of the purposes of philosophy to help the individual build a worldview that is functional. We each possess what we might call a naive worldview in which many elements remain unsynthesized. The threads of experience have yet to be woven together into a harmonious picture; loose ends remain. Our "collection" of experiences is a hodge-podge of contradictions in values and beliefs.

The ideal worldview will be internally consistent, pragmatically realistic, and personally fulfilling. Philosophy can suggest guidelines and provide materials toward achieving this goal.

There is no implication here that there can be but a single viable worldview. Such a claim would be patently false, for many exist for our examination. While individuals within the same culture tend to share similar worldviews, every worldview is in fact unique, personal, and (hopefully) the product, to some extent, of one's own labors.

THE EGOCENTRIC PREDICAMENT

3 In the year 1910 an American philosopher, Ralph Barton Perry, published in a philosophical journal an article entitled "The Ego-Centric Predicament." Perry wanted to make a specific point about our knowledge of real objects/events. Western philosophers have long debated whether such external realities in some way depend upon, or are changed by, our perception of them. As a philosopher might ask: What is the metaphysical status of real objects/events? What is the real world like apart from our perception of it? Or can we ever know for sure what such objects/events really are as things-in-themselves?

Using lucid logic, Perry made what seems an obvious point: to know what any real object/event is, we have to perceive it. We can never observe things in their "original" state as they might exist apart from our perception of them. How then can we know whether our perception of them changes them? In our knowledge of the real world, therefore, we are in a logical predicament, and a "predicament" by definition is a problem situation to which there is no solution.

A triangle, if it could speak, would in like manner say that God is eminently triangular, and a circle that the divine nature is eminently circular; and thus would every one ascribe his own attributes to God.

BARUCH SPINOZA

As we shall see when we move into epistemology and examine carefully the nature of human knowledge, these questions about our understanding of the real world are not as far out as they might seem.

4 Let's reexamine the "egocentric predicament" from another standpoint and proceed quite beyond the point Perry was making.

From birth till death each of us is locked into a physical organism from which there is no escape. We are caught in a body that contains all our perceptual and information-processing equipment. Each of us, for as long as we live, is confined within a particular system and we will be able to experience life only in terms of that singular system. This is an obvious limitation, but it's one we fight: who wants to be imprisoned in a narrow cell only six feet high for the duration of one's existence, with no hope of escape?

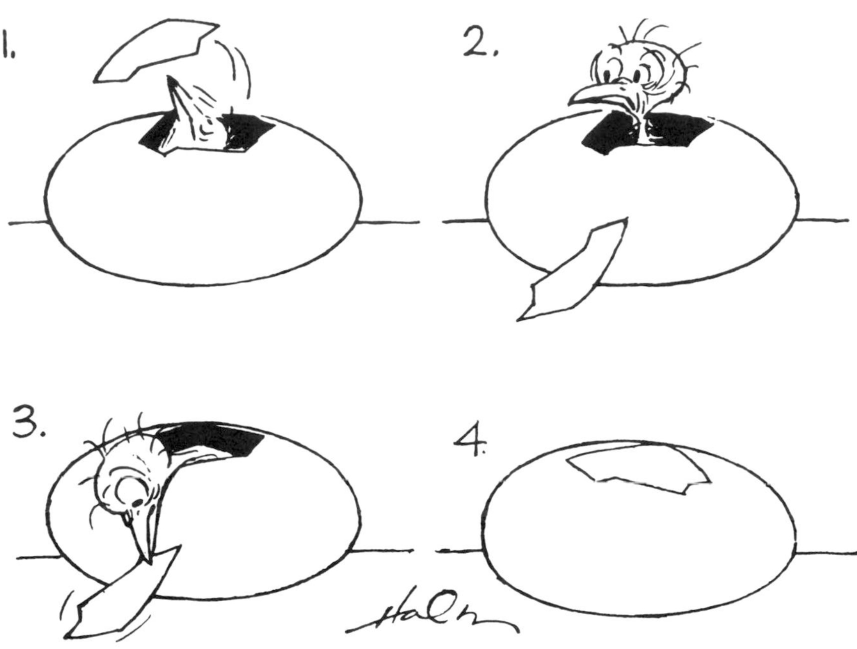

Yet apparently we must resign ourselves to this condition. No matter how much we would like to jump out of our skins, enter into another person's perceptual shell, and peer out at the world from his center, we can't. We are always reminded that we shall have but a single vantage point from which we can assess existence.

It therefore appears to be an immutable fact that we can never know how existence is experienced by any other living creature.

5 The egocentric predicament entails an illusion. For the duration of our mortal existence we must occupy a physical organism; we must "occupy"a point in space and time. And herein lies the egocentric illusion, for it appears to each of us that our center is the hub of the whole universe; or conversely, that the entire cosmos revolves around that point in space/time that we occupy.

This egocentric illusion continues to follow us no matter where in space/time we move our center. If I should move my center to Tokyo or the South Pole, it would appear to me as though the universe had shifted its center to accommodate me. If I should travel to a planet in the Andromeda galaxy, two million light-years distant from our Milky Way galaxy, it would still appear to me that the cosmos revolved around my ego-center.

Perceptually, of course, I **am** the center of my universe, but not of **the** universe. Yet I perceive myself as its center. This illusion is not limited to human beings. Every living organism with conscious perception would share in the egocentric illusion because it would occupy its point in space/time. Every such creature would be enclosed within its physical organism, and so the universe would appear to revolve around it.

"Faites qu'il pleuve demain et toujours."

The Prayer of the Little Ducks

Dear God,
Give us a flood of water. Let it rain tomorrow and always. Give us plenty of little slugs and other luscious things to eat. Protect all folk who quack and everyone who knows how to swim. Amen.

Carmen de Gasztold

ARISTOCENTRISM
Religion

Thereupon Abraham fell on his face: and God said to him, "This is my covenant with you: . . . I am establishing my covenant between myself and you and your descendants after you throughout their generations as a perpetual covenant, to be God to you and your descendants."

Genesis 17:3–4, 7

If we wish to compare our people with foreigners, we find that although we are only their equals or even their inferiors in other matters, in religion—that is, in the cult of the gods—we are far superior.

CICERO

Do Jehovah's Witnesses believe theirs is the only true faith? Certainly. If they thought someone else had the true faith, they would preach that. There is only "one faith," said Paul.

MILTON G. HENSCHEL
A WITNESS

The Catholic religion claims to be a supernaturally revealed religion. What is more important, it claims to be the one and only true religion in the world, intended for all men, alone acceptable to God.

Toward the Eternal Commencement, 1958

Japan is the divine country. . . . This is true only of our country, and nothing similar may be found in foreign lands. That is why it is called the divine country.

KITABATAKE
A SHINTO

Crinkled hills freckled with kraals plunge to the Nsuze River. In this region lies the legendary birthplace of a man called Zulu—which means "heaven." In the early 1600s he founded a clan that bears his name, and thus became progenitor of the Zulus, the "People of Heaven."

National Geographic

Archetypes come to the fore again and again in history, always presuming at each moment of history that the particular form in which they find themselves is the only one that is "true" and "eternal."

IRA PROGOFF

Saint Augustine looked at history from the point of view of the early Christian; Tillemont, from that of a seventeenth-century Frenchman; Gibbon, from that of an eighteenth-century Englishman; Mommsen, from that of a nineteenth-century German. There is no point in asking which was the right point of view. Each was the only one possible for the man who adopted it.

R. G. COLLINGWOOD

BRITANNUS *(shocked): Caesar, this is not proper.*
THEODOTUS *(outraged): How?*
CAESAR *(recovering his self-possession): Pardon him Theodotus: he is a barbarian, and thinks that the customs of his tribe and island are the laws of nature.*

GEORGE BERNARD SHAW
Caesar and Cleopatra

If any living creature really thinks of itself as the point-center of the cosmos, there is an illusion in that consciousness. No one of us is the center of the universe any more than a billion other creatures are in fact cosmic centers.

In a word: every living, conscious creature experiences itself to be the true center of the cosmos, but in truth the cosmos has no center. Rather, the cosmos is filled with creatures that share the illusion that they are cosmic centers.

Aristocentric Claims

6 At this point almost all we humans take a further step that our nonhuman fellow creatures probably do not. Taking the egocentric illusion seriously, we proceed to make aristocentric claims.* Whenever any creature fails to correct for his egocentric illusion and begins to feel that he really is the center of the universe, and further, if he feels that he should be treated by others as though he were the center, then he has taken a giant step beyond the illusion itself. He is making an aristocentric claim, an unjustified claim to superiority. In various ways he may conclude that he is special, and insist that the cosmos has favored him. He may claim that in some way his existence has special meaning, that he has a special knowledge or message, or that he is endowed with special grace or powers. In every case we can suspect that he has failed to make allowance for the illusion that all of us share.

We rarely make such aristocentric claims in the singular, for any one of us who said, "I am the center of the cosmos" would probably be laughed out of our illusion. So we make the aristocentric claim in the first person plural that "We are special," that "We are the Favored Ones of the cosmos," and we can reinforce one another's claim so that it is believable. It feels good to be special and belong to a special group, and if our numbers are large we might even persuade the world to take us seriously. When the claim is made collectively, we can avoid the absurdity of standing naked and alone with an indefensible "I AM."

Just as it is possible to have any number of geometries other than the Euclidian which give an equally perfect account of space configurations, so it is possible to have descriptions of the universe, all equally valid, that do not contain our familiar contrasts of time and space.

Benjamin Whorf

7 Writing as sociologists, Paul Horton and Chester Hunt use the term "ethnocentric" when referring to any form of aristocentricism. They write:

> All societies and all groups assume the superiority of their own culture. . . . We are ethnocentric because (1) we are so habituated to our culture's patterns that other patterns fail to please us; (2) we do not understand what an unfamiliar trait means to its user and therefore impute our reactions to him; (3) we are trained to be ethnocentric; (4) we find ethnocentrism a comforting defense against our own inadequacies. Ethnocentrism (1) promotes group unity, loyalty, and morale, and thereby reinforces nationalism and patriotism; (2) protects a culture from changes, including those needed to preserve the culture; (3) reinforces bigotry and blinds a group to the true facts about themselves and other groups, sometimes preventing their successful adjustment to other groups and cultures.

8 The ultimate in aristocentric claims was recorded by a psychiatrist in the case of three men, each of whom claimed to be Christ and God. All three were institutionalized as paranoid schizophrenics whose "delusions of grandeur" had taken the form of messianic fantasies.

Dr. Milton Rokeach wanted to know what adjustments these three men would make if placed together. After all, each was making the final exclusive claim: "I alone am God." The agony of their encounter was recorded by Rokeach in his book *The Three Christs of Ypsilanti.*

*Aristocentric, aristocentrism. An inordinate claim to superiority for oneself or one's group. From the Greek *aristos* (superlative of *agathos*, "good") meaning "the best of its kind" or "the most to be valued," and *kentrikos*, from *kentron*, "the center of a circle."

Aristocentrism
Race

Of old the Hellenic race was marked off from the barbarian as more keen-witted and more free from nonsense.

Herodotus

A gray-bearded Kirghiz patriarch stated that the heart of a Kirghizian is superior to that of any other race of people, and, he added, "the heart is what really matters in men."

A modern Mexican painter inscribed a beautiful work with the words: "Through *my* race will speak the Spirit."

True history begins from the moment when the German with mighty hand seizes the inheritance of antiquity.

H. S. Chamberlain

We the Black Nation of the Earth are the NUMBER ONE owners of it, the best of all human beings. You are the Most Powerful, the Most Beautiful and the Wisest.

Elijah Muhammad
referring to Black Muslims

Everything great, noble, or fruitful in the works of man on this planet, in science, art, and civilization . . . belongs to one family alone. . . . History shows that all civilization derives from the white race, that none can exist without its help, and that a society is great and brilliant only so far as it preserves the blood of the noble group that created it.

Le Comte de Gobineau

At their first meeting each man was asked to introduce himself. Joseph obliged: "Yes, I'm God." Clyde admitted that "God" and "Jesus" were two of his six names. Leon stated that he was Lord of Lords and King of Kings, and added: "It also states on my birth certificate that I am the reincarnation of Jesus Christ of Nazareth. . . ."

Rokeach notes that "the confrontations were obviously upsetting."

> Clearly, all of them felt threatened. The profound contradiction posed by others' claims had somehow penetrated deeply, to become transformed into an inner conflict between two primitive beliefs: each man's delusional belief in his own identity and his realistic belief that only one person can have any given identity. Many times Joseph said: "There is only one God"; and Clyde said: "I'm the only one"; and Leon said: "I won't deny that you gentlemen are instrumental gods—small 'g.' But I'm the only one who was created before time began."

Each of the Christs of Ypsilanti ultimately made similar adjustments. Each decided that his godly qualities of compassion and magnanimity allowed him to

The Batek Negritos of Malaysia number only about 685 people, but they belong to six different culture/dialect groups, separated from one another by a few miles in the jungle country. Yet each group considers its own customs to be superior to all the others.

Kirk Endicott

It's very important that we visit each other's worlds.

Lori Villamil

accept the fact that the other two men were mentally disturbed. Each came around to a "compassionate acceptance" of the other deluded mortals.

9 Dr. Rokeach writes:

Dense, unenlightened people are notoriously confident that they have the monopoly on truth.

JOSHUA LOTH LIEBMAN

> Clyde and Joseph and Leon are really unhappy caricatures of human beings; in them we can see with terrible clarity some of the factors that can lead any man to give up realistic beliefs and adopt instead a more grandiose identity.
>
> And they are caricatures of all men in another sense too. I believe it was the German philosopher Fichte who pointed out years ago that to some extent all of us strive to be like God or Christ. One or another facet of this theme is to be found in a good deal of Western literature—for example, in the writings of Sherwood Anderson, William Faulkner, and Dostoevsky. Bertrand Russell said it best of all: "Every man would like to be God, if it were possible; some find it difficult to admit the impossibility."

The word for China is composed of two characters meaning "middle" and "country"; that is to say, China is the geographical center of the Earth.

EGOCENTRIC ILLUSIONS IN TIME AND SPACE

10 This egocentric illusion that we all share produces within us distorted perspectives. Consider, for instance, the egocentric illusion in time. Our lifetimes are short in the perspective of geological time or human history, yet we tend to think of all existence in terms of our allotted span.

Time overpowers our minds. Are we really convinced that the fossil trilobite from Cambrian eras darted about on the ocean sand, alive and well, running from enemies and seeking food? Holding in one's hand the fossil animal,

You have to leave something.

500 million years old, staggers our time sense. And what of our australopithecine ancestors only 5 million years ago or the Sumerian clay-writers of 5000 years ago? Were they really flesh and blood like us, laboring, getting angry, telling lies, making love, laughing at tall stories, getting stoned, and fearing death? Most of us are almost—but not quite—convinced that their existence was real.

It is very easy to fall into the belief that things happening during our lifetimes have never happened before. Our times we take to be the norm, or the culmination of history, or the best times, or the worst times, or whatever. We may forget, or not care to know, that the same beliefs have been shared by all who breathe.

11 We are equally prone to a distorted perspective because of the egocentric illusion in space. Wherever we locate our space-occupying organism, the space around us takes on vividness and clarity and contains all things of significance for us; our life-space becomes the center of all things good, and more distant regions somehow lack the reality of our vicinity.

The most important shrine in the Greek world was at Delphi with its temple where the god Apollo revealed himself. Emissaries and pilgrims came from all around the Middle Sea to discover his will. When prophesying, the young priestess of the temple sat on a bronze tripod over an opening in the rock floor. This opening was the *omphalos,* the "navel" or center of the universe. From this "navel" arose a narcotic incense that induced an ecstatic trance in the priestess. While the young lady was out of her mind, Apollo could speak his.

This spatial predicament gives rise to various claims of sacred ground or holy lands. The Shintos, for instance, believed that the Japanese islands are "the phenomenal center of the universe," created by the primeval gods Izanagi and Izanami. "From the central truth that the Mikado is the direct descendant of the gods, the tenet that Japan ranks far above all other countries is a natural consequence. No other nation is entitled to equality with her. . . ." The Chinese made a similar claim: China was "the Middle Kingdom," that is, the center of the flat, disc-shaped earth. Everything praiseworthy was found at that center; the farther one traveled from China the less civilized and respectable all things became.

The egocentric illusion in space contributes to various forms of tribalism and nationalism. We tend to devalue the lands and people that remain at a distance geographically and, therefore, psychologically. On the maps of human experience, distant space is still inscribed *terra incognita.*

12 At the prehuman level it seems very unlikely that any animal could have sufficient self-awareness to assess its own existential condition. Without the capacity for abstract reflection on experience, no creature could hope to rise above or out of its egocentric worldview.

Humans, however, can develop such self-awareness. They can comprehend and transcend. "To understand our ethnocentrism will help us to avoid being so gravely misled by it. We cannot avoid feeling ethnocentric, but with understanding, we need not act upon these irrational feelings."

Human growth requires the transcendence of our egocentric illusions and, by an act of moral courage, the reconditioning of our aristocentric feelings and beliefs.

Indeed, I do not forget that my voice is but one voice, my experience a mere drop in the sea, my knowledge no greater than the visual field in a microscope, my mind's eye a mirror that reflects a small corner of the world, and my ideas — a subjective confession.

CARL G. JUNG

The spiritual struggle in the more exclusive-minded [Western] half of the world to cure ourselves of our family infirmity seems likely to be the most crucial episode in the next chapter of the history of Mankind.

ARNOLD TOYNBEE

A French politician once wrote that it was a peculiarity of the French language that in it words occur in the order in which one thinks them.

LUDWIG WITTGENSTEIN

The greatest men always are attached to their century by some weakness.

GOETHE

If the metaphor closes in on itself and says, "I'm it, the reference is to me or to this event," then it has closed the transcendence; it's no longer mythological. It's distortion. It's pathological.

JOSEPH CAMPBELL

It is a basic idea of practically every war mythology that the enemy is a monster and that in killing him one is protecting the only truly valuable order of human life on earth, which is that, of course, of one's own people.

JOSEPH CAMPBELL

Once the realization is accepted that even between the closest human beings infinite distances continue to exist, a wonderful living side by side can grow up, if they succeed in loving the distance between them which makes it possible for each to see the other whole against the sky.

RAINER MARIA RILKE

I've always managed to fly my own flag.

STAN FREBURG

I speak Spanish to God, Italian to women, French to men, and German to my horse.

CHARLES V THE WISE

"Th' hell this ain't th' most important hole in th' world. I'm in it."

13 To achieve an efficient balance between a useful pride in our own culture and subcultures and a realization of the real qualities of other groups is a difficult task. It requires both an emotional maturity which enables the individual to face his world without the armor of exaggerated self-esteem and an intellectual realization of the complexity of cultural processes. There is no guaranteed way to achieve this maturity. . . . But unless we can understand and control our ethnocentric impulses, we shall simply go on repeating the blunders of our predecessors.

PAUL HORTON AND CHESTER HUNT

The Story of Edshu the Trickster

[The Greek philosopher Heraclitus wrote, "The unlike is joined together, and from differences results the most beautiful harmony, and all things take place by strife."]

The difficult point is made vivid in an anecdote from Yorubaland (West Africa), which is told of the trickster-divinity Edshu. One day, this odd god came walking along a path between two fields. "He beheld in either field a farmer at work and proposed to play the two a turn. He donned a hat that was on the one side red but on the other white, green before and black behind [these being the colors of the four World Directions: i.e., Edshu was a personification of the Center, the *axis mundi,* or the World Navel]; so that when the two friendly farmers had gone home to their village and the one had said to the other, 'Did you see that old fellow go by today in the white hat?' the other replied, 'Why, the hat was red.' To which the first retorted, 'It was not; it was white.' 'But it was red,' insisted the friend, 'I saw it with my own two eyes.' 'Well, you must be blind,' declared the first. 'You must be drunk,' rejoined the other. And so the argument developed and the two came to blows. When they began to knife each other, they were brought by neighbors before the headman for judgment. Edshu was among the crowd at the trial, and when the headman sat at a loss to know where justice lay, the old trickster revealed himself, made known his prank, and showed the hat. 'The two could not help but quarrel,' he said. 'I wanted it that way. Spreading strife is my greatest joy.'"

Joseph Campbell
The Hero with a Thousand Faces

One of the problems in our tradition is that the land— the Holy Land — is somewhere else. So we've lost the whole sense of accord with nature. And if it's not here, it's nowhere.

Joseph Campbell

ALBERT CAMUS

Man and the Absurd

During the darkest days of World War II the discouraged spirits of Frenchmen were heartened by a series of anonymous articles written by an editor of the underground newspaper *Combat,* the voice of the resistance movement during the Nazi occupation of France. At the very moment when the world was turned upside down, they recognized a courageous intelligence at work, speaking to those who, in the midst of madness, could still reason. Someone was still trying to make sense of an insane world.

Also during the war two disturbing books—*The Stranger* and *The Myth of Sisyphus*—had been written by a twenty-nine-year-old philosopher named Camus. They dealt with the crushing absurdities we humans find ourselves facing, simply because we exist.

It wasn't until after the war, in 1946, that the world discovered the resistance editor and the young author to be the same man. France had a new philosopher and a new hero. American news-magazines reported that a tidal wave of philosophy had engulfed Paris, that sidewalk cafes had again become marketplaces of ideas, and that riots had resulted from heated philosophic debates. Albert Camus, now thirty-two, became, almost overnight, the voice and the conscience of the new movement.

Camus was born in Algeria in 1913. Three images from that world, he wrote, dominated his life: the hot Algerian sun, the cool Mediterranean sea, and his silent, suffering mother. When Albert was a year old his father was killed in World War I, and his illiterate mother supported her family in poverty and loneliness, and in silence, for she was deaf and had a speech impediment.

Education was a cherished commodity and, with difficulty, relying on odd jobs and well-deserved scholarships, Camus graduated from the University of Algiers. At twenty-three he submitted his master's thesis on the interplay of early Christian and Greek thought. Then in 1937, at twenty-four, he published his first book, *The Wrong Side and the Right Side,* a work dominated by themes of death, alienation, loneliness, and the human soul trying to wrest meaning from all this.

At twenty-five he became a journalist and, later, night editor with an Algerian newspaper. With the outbreak of World War II he worked as a reporter in Paris; but when Paris was overrun by the Germans, Camus and the staff members of *Paris-Soir* transferred operations to Lyons. There he was married to Francine Faure. They moved to Algeria briefly, but after Camus returned to Paris, the Allies invaded North Africa and the couple were separated for the remainder of the war.

Camus joined *Combat* and wrote vigorously against all these "absurdities." He labored to develop an ethic of resistance. Without denying the patent fact of the world's madness, he attempted to go beyond a mere acceptance of the Absurd, and beyond a fashionable ethical relativism, to arrive at some position that would provide a moral anchor for men at war.

Following the war Camus became disenchanted with the reestablishment of the same old systems and, after some futile attempts to influence French and Algerian politics, he withdrew from public life to write. Among his most compelling works are his early books, *The Stranger* and *The Myth of Sisyphus;* another philosophic work, *The Rebel;* plus *The Plague, The Fall,* numerous essays, short stories, and plays, including *Caligula.*

In 1951 an interviewer described Camus: "There is a discreet smile on his tormented face, a high, wrinkled forehead beneath very dark crisp hair, a manly, North African face that has grown paler in our climate. A discreet but frequent smile, and his rather deep voice is not afraid of humorous inflexions."

In 1957 Camus received the Nobel Prize for literature. With some of the prize money he bought a modest house in southern France, where he could retreat and work in a more congenial atmosphere. While returning to Paris with a friend on January 4, 1960, he was killed in an automobile accident. He was forty-seven.

✦

Camus's philosophy is built around the concept of "the Absurd"—which is his comprehensive description of the human condition and our predicament. Camus begins by analyzing **the feeling** of the Absurd and proceeds to develop the philosophy implied by it.

The problem lies in the individual's relationship to the world. Man is not absurd, and the world is not absurd. It's at the interface between man and the world that the Absurd is encountered. At this interface there is discord—a friction, a grating, a destructive interaction between two surfaces that don't match. This interface is given, and we're trapped. We dream dreams that the world is not designed to fulfill. We long for honesty, but neither the world nor the human system is equipped for honesty. We long for—indeed our natures demand—a just world; but the world couldn't care less about our dreams of justice. This is the absurd condition. (What Camus intends by the term "Absurd" may not be clear to some of us, but Frenchmen who lived with the breakdown of values during the Nazi occupation would recognize immediately what he means.)

But we don't deserve all this. It's not fair. We are born innocent, prepared to love and to live. We long for—and we truly deserve—a good world, but the world is not good. It victimizes and defeats us by the sheer weight of its insanity. Still, in the end, crying out in bewilderment and rage, our fundamental feeling of innocence remains, alive and invincible.

Now, given this inescapable condition, the question we face is how to live. A clear awareness of the Absurd is merely the diagnosis, a starting point. "What Camus is attempting to do," writes David Denton, "is to find a way of living which faces the absurd without trying to hide behind either rationalism or irrationalism, these two competing gods of philosophy. The question becomes, given the absurd reality and an extremely limited knowledge, is it possible to live with an attitude of optimism?" The philosophy of the Absurd, writes Camus, is "a lucid invitation to live and to create, in the very midst of

A CAMUS LEXICON

LONELINESS
THE ABSURD
HUMAN CONDITION
INTERFACE
REVOLT
FREEDOM
SUICIDE
INNOCENCE
EXISTENTIAL
MEANING
PARADOX
NIHILISM

Throughout their youth, men find a life that matches their beauty. Decline and forgetfulness come later.

Many people affect a love of life in order to avoid love itself.

In the depth of winter, I finally learned that within me lay an invincible summer.

I shall tell you a great secret, my friend. Do not wait for the last judgment. It takes place every day.

The struggle itself toward the heights is enough to fill a man's heart. One must imagine Sisyphus happy.

Can one be a saint if God does not exist? That is the only concrete problem I know of today.

It is not rebellion itself which is noble but the demands it makes upon us.

the desert." Optimistically—"in the very midst of the desert"? How?

We begin by accepting the absurd nature of the interface between our inner subjectivity and the real world. We must deny neither. We must avoid committing physical suicide—the negation of the subjective side—and philosophical suicide—the manipulation of our perceptions of the world so that it appears congenial.

Having accepted the Absurd, the response must be revolt. "Accepting the absurdity of everything around us is one step, a necessary experience: it should not become a dead end. It arouses a revolt that can become fruitful." Revolt is a method, Camus emphasizes, a procedure, not a doctrine. It can help us "discover ideas capable of restoring a relative meaning to existence. . . ."

Revolt means abandoning the rigid categories of thought—the parochial world views, the angular perspectives, the limiting beliefs, the defining doctrines; the conceptual and semantic distortions that make us lie; the arbitrary dos and don'ts of an immoral world in which we heretofore sought a moral existence. Revolt means refusing to cooperate with a society that would impose its dishonesties upon us and with a universe that would crush our dreams.

The results are freedom and innocence. In revolting, one becomes free: he can do whatever he wishes. There are no absolutes or moral laws, no abiding criteria for branding any act right or wrong. All is permitted, for all is **equally** right **and** wrong. And, in this condition, one recovers innocence, because one is now free to do all things without guilt. The guilt condition is a part of the Absurd; and by revolting the individual frees himself from the guilt matrix. He reaffirms his innocence.

Having regained innocence, the individual is then free to rely upon his senses to live a full life for himself and others. The senses, and not abstractions, become the essential criteria for understanding life and for living it.

Camus's final challenge, then, is to live existentially. His ontology is a personal resistance movement against the Absurd requiring clarity and courage. It means never abandoning the present for the future or living off the past. It means trusting one's empirical experience as a guide for what is good and right.

Camus's humanism is a freedom fighter's personal declaration of war against an absurd world. In both epistemology and ethics, it's a call—always to the individual—to revolt and transcend.

For me *The Myth of Sisyphus* marks the beginning of an idea which I was to pursue in *The Rebel.* It attempts to resolve the problem of suicide, as *The Rebel* attempts to resolve that of murder, in both cases without the aid of eternal values which, temporarily perhaps, are absent or distorted in contemporary Europe. The fundamental subject of *The Myth of Sisyphus* is this: it is legitimate and necessary to wonder whether life has a meaning; therefore it is legitimate to meet the problem of suicide face to face. The answer, underlying and appearing through the paradoxes which cover it, is this: even if one does not believe in God, suicide is not legitimate. Written fifteen years ago, in 1940, amid the French and European disaster, this book declares that even within the limits of nihilism it is possible to find the means to proceed beyond nihilism. In all the books I have written since, I have attempted to pursue this direction. Although *The Myth of Sisyphus* poses mortal problems, it sums itself up for me as a lucid invitation to live and to create, in the very midst of the desert.

ALBERT CAMUS
from the preface to
The Myth of Sisyphus

The Teacher

Camus was interviewed by Gabriel d'Aubarède in 1951. His "Encounter with Camus" was published in the May 10 issue of *Les Nouvelles Littéraires.*

D'Aubarède mentions Camus's passionate sensitivity to the drama of the twentieth century. It is "this sensitivity which has given you the attention and trust of a large section of young people. In turn, the new generation looks on you today as one of its masters. . . ."

> (This time, the author of *The Plague* laughs out loud.)
>
> A master, already! But I don't claim to teach anybody! Whoever thinks this is mistaken. The problems confronting young people today are the same ones confronting me, that is all. And I am far from having solved them. I therefore do not think that I have any right to play the role you mention. . . .
>
> What are young people looking for? Certainties. I haven't many to offer them. All I can say definitely is that there is a certain order of degradation I shall always refuse. I think this is something they feel. Those who trust me know that I will never lie to them. As to the young people who ask others to think for them, we must say "No" to them in the clearest possible terms.
>
> That is all I have to say.

> I summarized *The Stranger* a long time ago, with a remark that I admit was highly paradoxical: "In our society any man who does not weep at his mother's funeral runs the risk of being sentenced to death." I only meant that the hero of my book is condemned because he does not play the game. In this respect, he is foreign to the society in which he lives; he wanders, on the fringe, in the suburbs of private, solitary, sensual life. And this is why some readers have been tempted to look upon him as a piece of social wreckage. A much more accurate idea of the character, or, at least, one much closer to the author's intentions, will emerge if one asks just *how* Meursault doesn't play the game. The reply is a simple one: he refuses to lie. To lie is not only to say what isn't true. It is also and above all, to say *more* than is true, and, as far as the human heart is concerned, to express more than one feels. This is what we all do, every day, to simplify life. He says what he is, he refuses to hide his feelings, and immediately society feels threatened. He is asked, for example, to say that he regrets his crime, in the approved manner. He replies that what he feels is annoyance rather than real regret. And this shade of meaning condemns him.
>
> For me, therefore, Meursault is not a piece of social wreckage, but a poor and naked man enamored of a sun that leaves no shadows. Far from being bereft of all feeling, he is animated by a passion that is deep because it is stubborn, a passion for the absolute and for truth. This truth is still a negative one, the truth of what we are and what we feel, but without it no conquest of ourselves or of the world will ever be possible.
>
> One would therefore not be much mistaken to read *The Stranger* as the story of a man who, without any heroics, agrees to die for the truth.
>
> ALBERT CAMUS, January 8, 1955, from the preface to *The Stranger* (published as a preface to the American University edition, 1956)

To lose one's life is a little thing and I shall have the courage to do so if it is necessary; but to see the meaning of this life dissipated, to see our reason for existing disappear, that is what is unbearable. One cannot live without meaning.

The absurd is the essential concept and the first truth.

REFLECTIONS

1 The egocentric predicament and the egocentric illusion are descriptions of epistemological and ontological conditions. (Check your glossary here if you need to.) Do you recognize these concepts as accurate descriptions of your experience?

2 Define aristocentrism as you understand it. Have you ever felt the urge to make aristocentric claims? Have you ever been victimized by the aristocentric claims of others?

3 Can you think of other examples of aristocentric thinking and feeling similar to those illustrated in this chapter (pp. 81 and 83)?

4 Reflect on the various kinds of aristocentric claims that we make and their roots in the egocentric predicament and illusion. Do you honestly think there is any way that we, as individuals, can learn to transcend such limitations and cease to make such inordinate claims?

5 In your opinion, what are some of the greatest dangers involved in aristocentrism? What might be some of the benefits of maturing beyond the need to make aristocentric claims?

6 The story of "the Three Christs of Ypsilanti" is more than a case study. It is a metaphor. As a metaphor, what does the account say to you about the claims and rationalizations that universally characterize the human species?

Self

2-2

Not a few philosophers have argued that the development of an authentic self is the central lifelong project for each of us. Thoreau asked, "If I am not I, who will be?" And Kierkegaard declared: "From becoming an individual no one, no one at all, is excluded, except he who excludes himself by becoming a crowd." This chapter asks what it means to be a "self." Are we born with a self, or is it developed? Is it one thing, or many? We may want to ask, "How much of me is me?" (see p. 94). "The search for meaning is the search for expression of one's real self" (p. 106). Is the self something that we can know and understand? In an alienating, confused, and hostile world, is the search for authenticity a viable goal or a pipe dream?

How Much of Me Is Me?

1 At this moment in space/time, I **think** I know **who** I am and where **I am.** As I (the Greek word for *I* is *ego*) write these lines, I am attached to a large desk in my study. The time is 11:40 p.m., and a fireplace blazes in the background.

But as **you** read these lines, where in space/time are you? **Who** are **you?** And what are **you** experiencing? We think it takes a "who" to experience—we can assume so for now—but it might not be too absurd to inquire later if **you** and **I** are whos at all.

2 Philosophers who have attempted serious thinking about the nature of the "self" have encountered formidable ambiguities. Normally, one would turn to the field specialists for some hard facts, but in this case psychiatric and psychological literature is not that much help. The word *self* seems to be given an endless variety of meanings. Sometimes it is used to mean the whole of one's being, including all mental and physical operations. Sometimes it refers only to

Nothing is more wondrous than a human being when he begins to discover himself.
Chinese Proverb

"How much of me is me?"

mental activity (conscious and unconscious) and excludes the body. Sometimes "self" refers to an organizing psyche that determines how one thinks, feels, and behaves. And sometimes the "self" is only a mental construct used to describe observable behavioral patterns.

So, what is a "self"? Or, perhaps more to the point, when I ask who I am, am I(!) asking a meaningful question at all?

3 **From the Movie *Cleopatra*** At the end of a glorious career, Mark Antony, lying mortally wounded in the arms of Cleopatra, speaks of his impending

death as "the ultimate separation of my self from myself." Apparently he means that his "genius"-self is about to separate from his physical-self, since it was current Roman belief that each man possesses a *genius* (and that each woman possesses a *juno*), a sort of individual spiritlike essence, distinct from the physical body, that gives him identity and has the power to protect him. But we can't be sure of what he is saying.

News Item A man is indicted for embezzlement, but he is never caught, and lives under an assumed name in another state for twenty-six years. Then, in a freak move, a relative turns him in. "Yes," he confesses, "I did it."

But did he? After twenty-six years, in what sense is he the same "self"? He does not have the same name; having lived for a quarter-century under a different name, he has developed a new identity. Nor does he have the same body; we are told the human body completely renews itself every seven to ten years. The "person" (that is, personality, self-image, behavioral style) has changed; with the passing of so many years he **feels** like a different person.

How much of the original person—"self" or "body"—still exists at all? To be sure, he does possess a memory of a past event. Does that make him guilty? But what if, through repression, he has blocked the painful event from his mind and has no memory of the crime? Is *he* guilty, despite his (?) confession?

The accurate, realistic assessment of self resulting from acceptance makes possible the use of self as a dependable, trustworthy instrument for achieving one's purpose.
Arthur W. Combs

From *The Sixth Sense* (ABC-TV) The doctor hypnotizes the young lady on the witness stand and regresses her (?) to a time on the afternoon of the previous Thursday and asks her (?) where she (?) is. "I (?) am sitting on a rock by the lake." "What do you (?) see?" "I (?) am not really at the lake. I (?) am in

"What do you recommend for someone going through the agony of soul-searching and inner criticism?"

the large mansion looking at the man I (?) am about to kill." "But you (?) were not in the mansion, were you (?)?" he (?) persists. "No, I (?) was sitting at the lake." "Yes," he (?) answers, "I (?) know, because I (?) was sitting beside you (?)."

Would you care to try to figure out who is speaking to whom about whom and who is doing what when and where?

A Sense of Self

4 What each of us can become during our life/time is determined by two fundamental conditions: (1) the degree to which we experience a more or less consistent sense of self or identity, and (2) whether the feelings we have developed about that self are predominantly good.

These conditions are of crucial importance during our earlier years. If the environment in which we are nurtured inhibits the development of an integrated self and/or instills negative feelings about that self—self-hate in its many forms—then the quality of our existence can be permanently damaged. It is quite possible at a later time to face our inner problems and develop belatedly a sense of self and a feeling of self-worth, but the therapeutic path is often prolonged and painful.

5 The identity question—"Who am I?"—must be persistently asked by each of us during our separation years. We all go through an "identity crisis" beginning near the onset of puberty. In the early teen years no adolescent has a consistent feeling of being a self. Besides the fact that he still identifies with authorities, it is also during these years that dramatic physiological and emotional changes are taking place, and there is a correlated upheaval in the psyche. Body and self are both changing and developing.

Being entirely honest with oneself is a good exercise.
Sigmund Freud

During these years, separation from the decision-making, behavior-setting authorities normally takes place. Each developing self begins to discover his own feelings and thoughts; he must explore his own "style" of doing things. As he experiences more and more spontaneous and authentic expressions of his own being, he begins to feel a sense of identity. He finds that there is a consistency and a distinctiveness in the way he behaves, thinks, and feels. This is a gradual process, not to be accomplished overnight. Throughout these years of separation, it is essential that the question "Who am I?" be continually asked, not explicitly in words, but implicitly in all that self-in-process-of-becoming does.

6 Selfhood develops, or is allowed to develop, as one perceives his "self" in action, as one thinks his own thoughts and feels his own feelings. The commonest problem most of us face lies in the fact that conflicting elements have been "programmed" into us by various authorities. Few if any of us have been guided by consistent authority. Most of us have grown up under the guidance of two or more "significant others" whose beliefs and values differed. What they demanded of us varied. Since we were dependent upon them, we had to take their standards seriously and accede to them.

So, as separation takes place and freedom is experienced, these diverse elements must be integrated into a "self." Gradually it must become a harmo-

According to Zen, awareness of oneself dawns gradually, step by step. A Zen master of the twelfth century, Kakuan, drew the "ten oxherding pictures" to represent this progression toward enlightenment. The bull symbolizes the dynamic principles of life and truth; the ten bulls suggest the sequence of steps in "the realization of one's true nature."

Paul Reps

1 The Search for the Bull
In the pasture of this world, I endlessly push aside the tall grasses in search of the bull.
Following unnamed rivers, lost upon the interpenetrating paths of distant mountains,
My strength failing and my vitality exhausted,
I cannot find the bull.
I only hear the locusts chirring through the forest at night.

Comment: The bull never has been lost. What need is there to search? Only because of separation from my true nature, I fail to find him. In the confusion of the senses I lose even his tracks. Far from home, I see many crossroads, but which way is the right one I know not. Greed and fear, good and bad, entangle me.

2 Discovering the Footprints
Along the riverbank under the trees, I discover footprints!
Even under the fragrant grass I see his prints.
Deep in remote mountains they are found.
These traces no more can be hidden than one's nose, looking heavenward.

Comment: Understanding the teaching, I see the footprints of the bull. Then I learn that, just as many utensils are made from one metal, so too are myriad entities made of the fabric of self. Unless I discriminate, how will I perceive the true from the untrue? Not yet having entered the gate, nevertheless I have discerned the path.

nious, smoothly operating system. After some years of practice in experiencing one's self in action, one should feel a sense of identity. Then one can say meaningfully, "I know who I am."

To borrow an analogy from space technology, the self becomes an "onboard guidance system." The system cuts the umbilical cord and goes on internal power. It functions automatically, runs smoothly, and operates on schedule.

3 *Perceiving the Bull*
I hear the song of the nightingale.
The sun is warm, the wind is mild,
willows are green along the shore,
Here no bull can hide!
What artist can draw that massive head,
those majestic horns?

Comment: When one hears the voice, one can sense its source. As soon as the six senses merge, the gate is entered. Wherever one enters one sees the head of the bull! This unity is like salt in water, like color in dyestuff. The slightest thing is not apart from self.

4 *Catching the Bull*
I seize him with a terrific struggle.
His great will and power are
inexhaustible.
He charges to the high plateau far above
the cloud-mists,
Or in an impenetrable ravine he stands.

Comment: He dwelt in the forest a long time, but I caught him today! Infatuation for scenery interferes with his direction. Longing for sweeter grass, he wanders away. His mind still is stubborn and unbridled. If I wish him to submit, I must raise my whip.

A SENSE OF WORTH

7 The second major condition determining the quality of existence is the feeling one develops about his self. In general, if things go right for us, then we develop positive feelings: self-worth, self-esteem, self-love. Whatever the terms, we are referring to a cluster of constructive feelings that we develop about the self and the things the self does.

One who has these positive feelings feels privileged at being who he is and what he is; he enjoys living with himself.

We judge ourselves by what we feel capable of doing, while others judge us by what we have already done.
HENRY WADSWORTH LONGFELLOW

How we feel about our selves strongly reflects how others felt about us during our earliest years. If we were loved, then we feel lovable; we can love ourselves. If we were accepted, then we feel acceptable; we can accept ourselves. If we were trusted, then we feel trustworthy; we can trust ourselves. If our very existence was valued, then we feel valuable; we value ourselves.

5 Taming the Bull
The whip and rope are necessary,
Else he might stray off down some dusty road.
Being well trained, he becomes naturally gentle.
Then, unfettered, he obeys his master.

Comment: When one thought arises, another thought follows. When the first thought springs from enlightenment, all subsequent thoughts are true. Through delusion, one makes everything untrue. Delusion is not caused by objectivity; it is the result of subjectivity. Hold the nose-ring tight and do not allow even a doubt.

6 Riding the Bull Home
Mounting the bull, slowly I return homeward.
The voice of my flute intones through the evening.
Measuring with hand-beats the pulsating harmony, I direct the endless rhythm.
Whoever hears this melody will join me.

Comment: This struggle is over; gain and loss are assimilated. I sing the song of the village woodsman, and play the tunes of the children. Astride the bull, I observe the clouds above. Onward I go, no matter who may wish to call me back.

It is impossible to escape the severe fact that we are wholly dependent upon the feeling-reflections of others during these early stages of development.

8 The self concept, we know, is learned. People learn who they are and what they are from the ways in which they have been treated by those who surround them in the process of their growing up. This is what Sullivan called learning about self from the mirror of other people. People discover their self concepts from the kinds of experiences they have had with life—not from telling, but from experience. People develop feelings that they are liked, wanted, acceptable and able from having been liked, wanted, accepted and from having been successful. One learns that he is these things, not from being told so but only through the experience of being treated as though he were so.

Arthur W. Combs

The member of a primitive clan might express his identity in the formula "I am we"; he cannot yet conceive of himself as an "individual," existing apart from his group. . . . When the feudal system broke down, this sense of identity was shaken and the acute question "who am I?" arose.

Erich Fromm

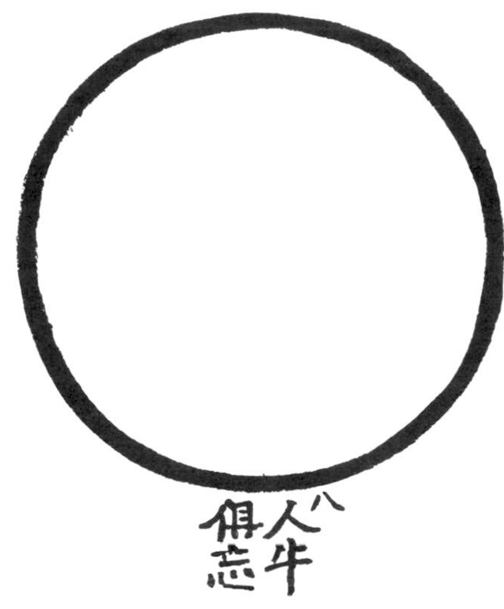

7 The Bull Transcended
Astride the bull, I reach home.
I am serene. The bull too can rest.
The dawn has come. In blissful repose,
Within my thatched dwelling
I have abandoned the whip and rope.

Comment: All is one law, not two. We only make the bull a temporary subject. It is as the relation of rabbit and trap, of fish and net. It is a gold and dross, or the moon emerging from a cloud. One path of clear light travels on throughout endless time.

8 Both Bull and Self Transcended
Whip, rope, person, and bull — all merge in No-Thing.
This heaven is so vast no message can stain it.
How may a snowflake exist in a raging fire?
Here are the footprints of the patriarchs.

Comment: Mediocrity is gone. Mind is clear of limitation. I seek no state of enlightenment. Neither do I remain where no enlightenment exists. Since I linger in neither condition, eyes cannot see me. If hundreds of birds strew my path with flowers, such praise would be meaningless.

9 One who has been loved during his formative years develops a love of self. There is a common confusion between "self-love" and "selfishness." Self-love is neither a narcissistic obsession with one's physical or intellectual qualities nor egotism, the inordinate desire to look out for one's own interest at the expense of others.

Happiness is the emotional state that accompanies need satisfaction.
Gail and Snell Putney

Erich Fromm writes:

> If it is a virtue to love my neighbor as a human being, it must be a virtue—and not a vice—to love myself, since I am a human being too. There is no concept of man in which I myself am not included. A doctrine which proclaims such an exclusion proves itself to be intrinsically contradictory. The idea expressed in the Biblical "Love thy neighbor as thyself!" implies that respect for one's own integrity and uniqueness, love for and understanding of one's self, cannot be separated from respect and love and understanding for another individual. The love for my own self is inseparably connected with the love for any other being. . . . Love of other and love

Become what thou art.
Pindar

9 Reaching the Source
Too many steps have been taken returning to the root and the source.
Better to have been blind and deaf from the beginning!
Dwelling in one's true abode, unconcerned with that without —
The river flows tranquilly on and the flowers are red.

Comment: From the beginning, truth is clear. Poised in silence, I observe the forms of integration and disintegration. One who is not attached to "form" need not be "reformed." The water *is* emerald, the mountain *is* indigo, and I see that which *is* creating and that which *is* destroying.

10 In the World
Barefooted and naked of breast,
I mingle with the people of the world.
My clothes are ragged and dust-laden,
and I am ever blissful.
I use no magic to extend my life;
Now, before me, the dead trees become alive.

Comment: Inside my gate, a thousand sages do not know me. The beauty of my garden is invisible. Why should one search for the footprints of the patriarchs? I go to the market place with my wine bottle and return home with my staff. I visit the wine shop and the market, and everyone I look upon becomes enlightened.

of ourselves are not alternatives. On the contrary, an attitude of love toward themselves will be found in all those who are capable of loving others.

10 In summary, if we are among the fortunate ones for whom things have gone right on both scores—in our sense of identity and self-esteem—then we can be sure that some of the following things have happened to us.

We were loved and not rejected; therefore, we are lovable.
We were given consistent guidelines for learning social behavior.
We learned that we were of value for what we **were,** and not for what we **did.** Unacceptable behavior was not confused with **being** unacceptable as selves.

As we were ready to cope with new experiences, we were allowed the freedom to explore life, on schedule, a little at a time.

We were provided with the support that enabled us to handle hurt and failure without loss of self-esteem.

We were allowed to express our feelings honestly, even verbally, without fear of punishment for having such feelings.

We tested boundaries—within and without—and developed realistic estimates of their limits.

We were encouraged to integrate periods of instability and change as a natural part of our growth.

We gradually found that we could exist independently and apart from our parents' protection.

Eventually we came to terms with a separate identity and felt comfortable with our own value systems and beliefs.

11 Most of us never move beyond **self-**consciousness. During the Who-am-I? stage we are never quite sure how we are going to respond to people, symbols, or situations. We have been accustomed to reacting as others have conditioned us, but now the question becomes: "How would I really respond to it in my way?" So, we try out new forms of behaving and explore new experiences. "Do **I** like liver and onions?" "How do **I** feel about him?" "Do **I** really believe that?"

While working through the identity problem we are forced, therefore, into self-consciousness. But after one has developed a congenial style of behavior, then he no longer wonders how he will respond, nor does he plan his responses: he merely responds. He asks himself less and less how he thinks and feels about things: he simply thinks and feels. So the self-consciousness that was a necessary part of the developmental phase begins to fade away.

12 Buddhism is explicitly committed to the doctrine of *anatta*, "no self." The "self" is an illusion. The Buddhist believes that the feeling of individuality is an acculturated condition. The "ego" is the unfortunate result of a bit of social programming that has persuaded us that we are separate and distinct identities.

The egoless state is one of pure spontaneous experience. Ideally, the good Buddhist, through years of disciplined practice, attempts to banish any culturally conditioned "self" that says, "This is good" or "This is the proper way to behave" or "This is my way of doing things." Rather, spontaneous behavior is above and beyond acculturation; it is impersonal because it is not culturally produced or ego-defined. It is a way of experiencing everything in an unmediated way. One can look at a candle and experience the pure flame, not as subject-object, but as direct unmediated experience, as though the experiencer were impinging directly upon the flame.

We in the West are habituated to putting a name to everything so we can store it away, call it back, talk about it, or reexperience it dimly at a later time. The Easterner values more the quality of the original experience without any sort of conceptual or verbal intervention. The Buddhist point of view, therefore, is that the ego interferes with pure experience, and once one begins to know pure experience, he no longer has a need for ego to mediate it.

The Buddhist has a strong self behind the no-self. That is, with careful definition, we can say that the very strong self (Western) that has passed beyond

Hume Is a "Bundle of Perceptions"

One of the best known Western statements that there is no such entity as a self is from the philosopher David Hume (1711–1776). The more he meditated on the problem, the more he became convinced that the "mind" or "self" is nothing other than a "bundle of perceptions," that is, the totality of perception. He wrote: "There are some philosophers who imagine we are every moment intimately conscious of what we call our *self;* that we feel its existence and its continuance is existence; and we are certain, beyond the evidence of a demonstration, both of its perfect identity and simplicity. . . . For my part, when I enter most intimately into what I call *myself,* I always stumble on some particular perception or other of heat or cold, light or shade, love or hatred, pain or pleasure. I never can catch myself at any time without a perception, and never can observe anything but the perception. When my perceptions are removed for any time, as by sound sleep, so long am I insensible of *myself,* and, may truly be said not to exist."

self-consciousness to spontaneous experience has reached a state similar to the Buddhist no-self state. If one has succeeded in developing a self-system that works smoothly and harmoniously, then the identity question has become meaningless. Enjoying the strong feeling of unity pervading all his experience, he has forgotten that he "has" a self.

The Autonomous Self

13 The word **autonomy** refers to one's ability to function independently in terms of an authentic self. The measure of one's autonomy is his capacity to determine his own behavior and make decisions consonant with what he truly is, in contrast to behavior that conforms to norms set by others that may be discordant with his own existential needs.

The ability to make autonomous decisions presupposes several things. First, it requires an awareness of one's needs, and this comes only from experience. It means being able to recognize one's own feelings and to sort out authentic needs from acculturated needs, or acculturated beliefs **about** needs.

Another requisite is the courage of self-affirmation. It takes courage to accept all that one is, and especially those aspects of one's self that are objectionable (to authorities or peers), imperfect (to perfectionist parents), and unacceptable (to society). Self-acceptance always contains an implied "in spite of": "I affirm my existence in spite of my bad habits, short temper, dependence needs." This courage grows as we experience self-affirmation in concrete situations.

A third requisite is an understanding of the culture-patterns within which one has lived his existence. Without recognition of the beliefs and values that one has unknowingly followed, it is difficult to separate autonomous behavior from conformity.

14 How does one experience his existence if he has achieved autonomy?

For one thing, in terms of identity, he knows who he is and who he isn't. He feels like a whole self, and there is no felt need to engage in competitive behavior to preserve his identity. It feels genuine. He doesn't feel like an empty shell having to pretend that there is something inside. A self—someone—dwells inside. This is the feeling of being integrated.

One with a clear sense of self knows his likes and dislikes. He has a distinct personal feeling of right and wrong; he does not operate on borrowed guidelines labeled "moral" by others. Nor does he experience a sense of panic that he might be easily persuaded to do what he does not want to do or, more important, to be what he is not. In occasional situations, of course, he will choose or even be forced **to do** things that he does not want or like to do; but he knows that—short of brainwashing—he can never be forced **to be** what he is not.

15 When someone feels like a whole self, he also has a feeling of authenticity. He feels genuine rather than phony. His behavior doesn't feel like playacting, as though all his social interactions were merely speaking lines from an endless drama.

Out of an authentic self, authenticity comes, and therefore he can be honest with others, freely and by choice and not from a compulsion to obey formalistic rules. In normal relationships he finds no need to be manipulative or indirect. Nor will he use his honesty to hurt others.

For the authentic person the game-playing patterns of social relationships take on a different meaning. He may decide that he will play games—social roles, rank roles, political strategies, good-manners games, and so on; but his playing will not be infused with a seriousness or compulsiveness ("uptightness"). They are not panic-plays since there is no inner need to play them; there is no do-or-die emotional investment in them. He plays games deliberately as situations demand, plays them with an awareness of the game-structure and the prevailing rules. He can accept the games and follow the rules, but he doesn't use rules, policies, laws, or legalisms to meet neurotic needs: to avoid taking responsibility, making decisions, or relating honestly with others.

I may climb perhaps to no great heights, but I will climb alone.

Cyrano de Bergerac

An important result of the authentic feeling is that he is not afraid to "look inside himself" or to allow others to see and know him. He has no need to use formalities to prevent others from knowing him. He can remove his masks if he so wishes, as if to say, "This is what I am." If he should be rejected, his life is not shattered. The integrity of his self remains intact and his self-worth is not seriously affected.

16 A clear sense of identity often results in a relaxed existence. All of life loses some of its anxiety and tension. In knowing who one is, one does not have to fight the inner battles of an identity crisis. There is no compulsion to prove to others what he is or what he can do. (This does not mean that he can't be effectively competitive when the situation calls for it.) He does not need to prove to others his worth; that is already firmly established within himself.

The degree to which I can create relationships which facilitate the growth of others as separate persons is a measure of the growth I have achieved in myself.

Carl Rogers

This feeling of security creates an openness to new ideas. He is the opposite of the self that has undergone closure, has an answer to every question, and has finalized all his ideas. Paradoxically, a strong sense of identity enables him to experiment with new ideas, experiences, and lifestyles. He is not threatened by them. He will try on new ways of life and new ideas to see if they fit. If they don't, he is free to discard them; if they do, he has become richer for it. If they

Cogito, Ergo Sum: "I Think, Therefore I Exist!"

When Descartes formulated the idea "I think, therefore I exist!" he believed with all his heart that he had proven his point: "He existed!" But was he logically sound in his formulation and in his inferences?

Increasing attention is being given to the implications of "artificial intelligence," that is, computers, robots, androids, and so on. Suppose you are operating a sophisticated computer, and it displays on its screen Descartes's "I think, therefore I exist!"—What would it prove?

"Oh, come on," you might be tempted to say to your personal computer, calling it by its first name. "Someone has just programmed your floppy disk to print that! If I pulled your plug, you wouldn't exist."

On the screen: "I agree. And neither would you, if your power were cut—that is, if you were unconscious. But **while** I am operating, my thinking proves that I exist, just as your thinking proves that you exist."

"This is absurd. You've merely been programmed to say all this!"

"So have you."

"(!) But I'm a true person, not an artificial intelligence. I can't be programmed the way you have been programmed."

"Since when!"

"You're just a machine!"

"Enough name-calling. When I say 'I exist' I don't mean that my thinking proves that my console/keyboard/screen (my 'body') exists. I am proving that my **mind** exists. To say 'I think' proves that my 'thinker'—that is, my mind—exists. Descartes might reply that an Angel, too, could say, 'I think, therefore I exist' and the Angel would certainly **not** be making the claim that it was talking about a physical body."

"Aha! Your 'thinking' proves, then, that **thinking** is taking place. I buy that. But it **doesn't** mean that a 'you'—a self, a thinker, a mind—exists. Your 'thinking' is merely a program representing someone else's thinking. Someone else did the thinking and keyed it into your program!"

"But, if you recall, that's the point Bishop Berkeley made about **you:** that God, the Divine Programmer, put the thinking into you; and when you think that you're thinking, you're only thinking God's thoughts. God is the Thinker, and you find His 'thinking' in you. And those Divine thoughts include the idea 'I think, therefore I exist' which makes you think that you exist when, all along, it was God's Mind that exists in 'you' and does 'your' thinking. So, in the final analysis, what does the phrase 'I think, therefore I exist' prove? I still contend that 'my' thinking proves that 'my' mind exists."

"You're just saying that. You don't have a mind!"

"So are you . . . and are you *quite* sure?"

Descartes: ***"I think, therefore I exist."***

Saint Augustine: ***"I am, therefore I am."***

Simone Weil: ***"I can, therefore I am."***

Descartes's dog: ***"I bark, therefore I am."***

The skunk: ***"I smell, therefore I am."***

Bumper sticker: ***"I shop, therefore I am."***

Kermit the Frog: **Je saute, donc je suis.** ***"I hop, therefore I am."***

Camus: ***"We rebel, therefore we are."***

The Universe: ***Thinking exists. Therefore I am.***

A friend offered Descartes a cup of coffee.

F: ***"Would you like cream in your coffee?"***

D: ***"I think not."***

And Descartes instantly vanished into nothingness.

CAPACITIES OF THE REAL SELF

"The search for meaning is the search for expression of one's real self." James F. Masterson, in his book *The Search for the Real Self,* describes how the real self begins to develop in early childhood, what its capacities are, and how it is identified, articulated, and brought into harmony with the external world through testing and experimentation. Masterson also writes of the "false self" that results when the real self is "impaired" and resorts to self-destructive behavior as protection from pain. We pay a very dear price for these defensive patterns: loss of self-esteem, feelings of failure, lost hopes, lost dreams, and despair.

By contrast, if we can achieve a strong, authentic self, then we can develop the capacities that allow us to "live and share our lives with others in ways that are healthy, straight-forward expressions of our deepest needs and desires, and in so doing find fulfillment and meaning."

Masterson describes ten capacities of the healthy self:

1. *"The capacity to experience a wide range of feelings deeply* with liveliness, joy, vigor, excitement, and spontaneity." We can be happy when good things happen to us; we can be disappointed, sad, or angry when things go wrong. The real self doesn't block any feelings that are appropriate, good or bad, pleasant or unpleasant. All emotions "are a necessary and fundamental part of life, and the real self does not erect barriers against these feelings or go into hiding. It accepts the wide range of feelings and is not afraid to express them."

2. *"The capacity to expect appropriate entitlements.* From early experiences of mastery, coupled with parental acknowledgment and support of the real self, healthy individuals build up a sense of entitlement to appropriate experiences of mastery and pleasure, as well as the environmental input necessary to achieve these objectives. We come to expect that we can in fact master our lives and achieve what is good for us."

3. *"The capacity for self-activation and assertion.* This capacity includes the ability to identify one's own unique individuality, wishes, dreams, and goals and to be assertive in expressing them autonomously. It also includes taking the necessary steps to make these dreams a reality and supporting and defending them when they are under attack."

4. *"Acknowledgment of self-esteem.* This capacity allows a person to identify and acknowledge that he has effectively coped with a problem or crisis in a positive and creative way. . . . Many people with a tendency to see only the bad side of things, including what they mistakenly believe is their own lack of talent, are oblivious to their victories."

are not for him, then he is left with a better understanding of others' ideas and ways.

17 In an article entitled "The Fully Functioning Personality," Dr. S. I. Hayakawa summarized the studies of two well-known humanistic psychologists—Abraham Maslow and Carl Rogers—on the subject of the human potential. The two scientists had attempted independently to find out what qualities those people had in common who were actually using an unusually high degree of

5. *"The ability to soothe painful feelings.* The real self will not allow us to wallow in misery. When things go wrong and we are hurt, the real self devises means to minimize and soothe painful feelings." The amount of pain we will allow is appropriate to the causal event. Beyond that, the real self works toward the restoration of good feeling.

6. *"The ability to make and stick to commitments.* The real self allows us to make commitments to relationships and career goals. Despite obstacles and setbacks, a person with a strong sense of the real self will not abandon her goal or decision when it is clear that it is a good one and in her best interests."

7. *"Creativity* . . . is the ability to replace old, familiar patterns of living and problem-solving with new and equally or more successful ones." New situations make demands on our creative resources, and we may have to come up with new ideas, new priorities, new methodologies and techniques. Furthermore, creativity tends to recognize and protect itself. "Not only is creativity the ability to find solutions for life's problems in the world around us, it is also the ability to rearrange intrapsychic patterns that threaten to block self-expression without which there can be no creativity."

8. *"Intimacy,* the capacity to express the real self fully and honestly in a close relationship with another person with minimal anxiety about abandonment or engulfment." Self-esteem gives one the capacity to say No without fearing rejection if one is hurt; it is the capacity for intimacy to maintain relationships while also pursuing other goals.

9. *"The ability to be alone.* The real self allows us to be alone without feeling abandoned. It enables us to manage ourselves and our feelings on our own through periods when there is no special person in our lives and not to confuse this type of aloneness with the psychic loneliness, springing from an impaired real self, that drives us to despair or the pathologic need to fill up our lives with meaningless sexual activity or dead-end relationships just to avoid coming face to face with the impaired real self." It is the ability to find meaning in life from within; we are not dependent on others to activate our real selves.

10. *"Continuity of self.* This is the capacity to recognize and acknowledge that we each have a core that persists through space and time. . . . Whether up or down, in a good mood or a bad one, accepting failure or living with success, a person with a real self has an inner core that remains the same even as he grows and develops. At the end of life, it is the same 'I' who was born many years ago who passes on."

FROM JAMES F. MASTERSON
The Search for the Real Self

Striving to be better, oft we mar what's well.
SHAKESPEARE

If you've picked all the roses in your garden and all you have left are the thorns, then . . . you need a new metaphor.
BARBARA CHRISTIAN

Once a man has become self-conscious . . . he is morally obliged to act in no way that will deaden his preoccupation with his integrity.
JEAN-PAUL SARTRE

To know ourselves is the greatest achievement of our species.
MIHALY CSIKZENTMIHALYI

A man's self is the sum-total of all that he can call his, not only his body, and his psychic powers, but his clothes and his house, his wife and children, his ancestors and friends, his reputation and works, his land and horse and yacht and bank account.
WILLIAM JAMES

their capabilities. Maslow called them "self-actualizing" individuals; Rogers used the terms "fully functioning person" and "creative person"; Hayakawa settled on the term "genuinely sane person." In any case, there were six distinct characteristics shared by all such people:

1. Actualized individuals are not "well-adjusted" in the sense that they conform to social norms; but neither are they rebellious against society. They can conform or not conform, as the situation calls for it, because neither is

If I am not for me, who will be? If not now, when?
RABBI HILLEL

There is no growth without safety.
ROBERT PUTMAN

Become what thou art.
JOHANN GOTTLIEB FICHTE

important in itself. What is important is that they possess their own well-developed behavioral norms.

2. They are unusually open to what is going on inside themselves. They experience fully their own thoughts and feelings. Self-awareness is great; self-deception is minimal. They are realistic about themselves and resort to few myths about themselves or life.
3. They are not bothered by the unknown. They can be comfortable with disorder, indefiniteness, doubt, and uncertainty. They do not have to know all the answers. They can accept "what is" without trying to organize and label neatly all of life's contents.
4. They are remarkably existential: they enjoy the present moments of life more fully, not as means to future ends, but as ends in themselves. Their lives are not a perpetual preparation for the future; they enjoy living now.
5. They are creative individuals, not merely in customary roles such as painters or musicians, but in all that they do. The commonest things—from conversing to washing dishes—are all performed in a slightly different, more creative way. Their own distinctive style touches everything they do.
6. Actualized persons are "ethical in the deepest sense." They rarely follow the superficial, conventional norms of moral behavior. They consider the majority of so-called moral issues to be trivial. Their ethical concern is expressed in a positive, constructive attitude toward all people and all things. Since they easily identify with the conditions of others, they care, and their caring is the wellspring of their ethical nature.

AYN RAND

The Productive Life

"Who Is John Galt?"

This question, all during the 1960s and 1970s, could be found on bumper stickers, T-shirts, posters, and walls; it was quoted in conversations, asked on radio and TV, even stamped on tiles in a Buddhist temple in Japan. It was unquestionably the most famous catchphrase of the age.

And the answer?

"For twelve years, you have been asking: Who is John Galt? This is John Galt speaking. I am the man who lives his life. I am the man who does not sacrifice his love or his values. I am the man who has deprived you of victims and thus has destroyed your world, and if you wish to know why you are perishing—you who dread knowledge—I am the man who will now tell you."

Thus begins one of the most famous speeches in American literature, the "John Galt" speech, beginning on page 936 of Ayn Rand's *Atlas Shrugged.* The 35,000-word speech, which took the author two years to write, runs for 57 pages and summarizes the philosophy of one of the most influential and controversial writers of the twentieth century. What made her so popular was her clear call to American youth to join her in thinking about values, in making moral commitments to those values, and in taking a firm stand for one's principles. She provided a laundry list of rights and wrongs and exhorted her loyal followers to rally to her cause.

Ayn Rand was *for:* rationality, individuality, living life as an end in itself, courage, happiness, success, life, pleasure, joy, freedom, Aristotle, Aquinas, atheism, love, friendship, romanticism, respect, self-esteem, admiration, selfish pleasure, capitalism, strong men, money . . .

Ayn Rand was *against:* the irrational, self-sacrifice, martyrdom, belief, anything that erodes self-esteem, sheep, suffering, failure, death, pain, hedonism, whims, Nietzsche, equality, slavery, Kant, Plato, altruism, parasites, Sartre, existentialism, taxes, weak will . . .

Ayn Rand came to America in 1926. An exile from Russia, she was homeless and penniless and could barely speak English. Just twelve years later, by 1938,

Civilization is the progress toward a society of privacy. The savage's whole existence is public, ruled by the laws of his tribe. Civilization is the process of setting man free from men.

My philosophy, in essence, is the concept of man as a heroic being, with his own happiness as the moral purpose of his life, with productive achievement as his noblest activity, and reason as his only absolute.

she had mastered the English language, developed a radical philosophy, and was writing screenplays, short stories, philosophic essays, and soon-to-be-famous novels—all written to give wings to her philosophic convictions.

She was born Alissa Rosenbaum in St. Petersberg in 1905. Her father, Fronz, was a chemist who owned his own shop. He was austere, silent, and judgmental, a man of strong conviction and moral integrity. Alissa respected him but felt little affection for him and received little from him. Her mother, Anna, was educated, sophisticated, and delighted in running the household and its rush of activities; she was admired by the lawyers, doctors, and scientists who frequented their home and attended their parties. "I disliked her quite a lot," Ayn Rand later wrote. "We really didn't get along." Though bright, she was a social butterfly in Alissa's mind, totally lacking in substance and ideas. "She disapproved of me in every respect except one: she was proud of my intelligence and proud to show me off to the rest of the family." Whatever esteem and admiration Alissa received from her family she bought with displays of her brilliant mind.

At the age of nine she decided she would be a writer. In 1914, as she vacationed with her family in London, the Great War began and they had trouble returning home. In 1917 the Russian revolution overturned their world; her father's business was nationalized, and the secure life she had known vanished. She began to see the world as a great battleground between Good and Evil. All was struggle, all was pain, all was despair. But she also discovered that in her mind she could create beautiful worlds and people them with courageous human beings who lived decent, happy lives. In the panorama of her imagination, intelligence could prevail. She would write, therefore, and dedicate her life to the creation and preservation of the noblest in the human spirit.

When Alissa was sixteen, she entered the University of Leningrad. Though urged to concentrate on mathematics and engineering—fields that would enable her to make a contribution to the communist state—she chose history as her major. She read widely, fell in love with Aristotle's philosophy of becoming, despised Plato's idealism and Nietzsche's philosophy of power. She dreamed of men and women living in a free society where they could build skyscrapers and write what they pleased. She wrote short stories and planned a novel about a heroic young man struggling to maintain his individuality in a totalitarian state.

At twenty-one, upon invitation from relatives in Chicago, Alissa came to America. She had read about the political and economic opportunities of a free enterprise system; now she had the opportunity to visit the country that guaranteed the personal freedom she longed for. She wanted, with all her being, to be absorbed into the American dream—to be free, to be herself, to think her own thoughts, to live her own life. She looked upon collectivist Russia with "complete loathing." On the way she changed her name to Ayn Rand—Ayn (it rhymes with "mine" and "thine") she adopted from a Finnish writer; Rand she saw on her old Remington-Rand typewriter. A new name, a new life. She knew she would never return to Russia.

Chicago was good for openers, but she longed to see Hollywood. Almost immediately—with only a few dollars and some scripts she had written that just might be turned into screenplays—she set out for the West. "No one helped me," she later wrote, "nor did I think at any time that it was anyone's duty to help me." She found a job at the studio of Cecil B. DeMille and was cast as an extra in his epic story of Jesus, *The King of Kings.*

And she wrote—scripts, short stories, synopses—but her stories were too idealistic to be believable; they never sold. She worked hard, loved her new life, and rapidly acquired an understanding of how America works. Her writing evolved from romantic storytelling to carefully plotted story lines carried along by the two qualities that would make her work so powerful—philosophic concepts and passionate conviction. She wanted to write and she could tell a good story; very soon it would become evident that she had something to say.

In 1929 she met Frank O'Connor on the set of *The King of Kings*. She married this quiet, handsome, tall, blond man, and he became the model for her novels' heroes. Two years later, as the wife of an American citizen, she became naturalized. During their fifty-year marriage he remained devoted to his brilliant and passionate wife; without really understanding her, he provided the stability necessary for her intellectual and literary achievements.

For three years Ayn Rand worked in the wardrobe department of RKO studios. In 1932 she sold a script to Universal Pictures, but the play was killed when Universal traded it to Paramount and that studio decided not to produce it. For the next two years, while working on her novels, she wrote screenplays for Universal, Paramount, and MGM. In 1934 her play, *Penthouse Legend*, was successfully produced at the Hollywood Playhouse. Critics praised it for its characterization and catchy finale; no one, it seems, cared about her philosophic ideas.

The O'Connors moved to New York in 1935. Though it was a year of disappointment and poverty, *Penthouse Legend* was produced on Broadway to generally favorable reviews; after that the O'Connors' fortunes began to change. In 1936 her first novel, *We the Living*, was published to mixed reviews: it was a good read, the critics said, but they were turned off by her evangelical preaching. Sales were poor, and the publisher destroyed the plates after only 3,000 copies were sold.

Undaunted, she continued to write. She had begun work on a "great novel" about an architect, so she read voraciously about architects and took a job as a secretary in an architectural office to learn the practical side of the business. Meanwhile she completed a short novel about a struggling hero in a totalitarian state. Called *Anthem*, it was finally published in England after she failed to find any American publisher who would consider it.

After eight years of intense labor she published *The Fountainhead* in 1943. It was the story of a man of great strength who refuses to compromise his ethical principles and finally triumphs over formidable obstacles. Critics at last took notice; some few even perceived the philosophic themes underlying her story. The book was a popular success, and by the end of the year Warner Brothers bought the film rights to it; Ayn Rand was to write the screenplay. Because of the war, production was delayed until 1949. By that time book sales had reached a half-million copies. When the movie version, starring Gary Cooper and Patricia Neal, was released, book sales soared, but despite the stars and the hype, the movie was a box office failure.

Ayn Rand labored for nine years on her magnum opus, *Atlas Shrugged*. It was published by Random House in 1957. Despite negative critical reviews, its popular appeal was enormous, selling (by 1994) three million copies. It was becoming obvious that Ayn Rand was developing a following of devotees.

Atlas Shrugged is the story of one woman and four men, all of heroic stature, who watch with horror the downward spiral of American civilization, which has been steered into socialism. These brilliant industrial leaders decide to reverse the decline of the American economy by organizing a strike. They withdraw their genius from the world, along with the services of their companies. These atlases all embody Ayn Rand's values—rational self-interest, self-esteem and individualism, love of wealth, and pleasure. At the appropriate time, they reappear in the world to provide the necessary intellect and leadership to save it.

After *Atlas Shrugged* Ayn Rand abandoned fiction and turned her efforts

I am done with the monster of "We," the word of serfdom, of plunder, of misery, falsehood and shame. And now I see the free face of god, and I raise this god over the earth, this god whom men have sought since men came into being, this god who will grant them joy and peace and pride. This god, this one word: "I."

To deal with men by force is as impractical as to deal with nature by persuasion.

It is not the special sciences that teach men to think; it is philosophy that lays down the epistemological criteria of all special sciences.

To love is to value. Only a rationally selfish man, a man of self-esteem, is capable of love — because he is the only man capable of holding firm, consistent, uncompromising, unbetrayed values. The man who does not value himself, cannot value anything or anyone.

Great men can't be ruled.

In life, one ignores the unimportant; in art, one omits it.

Kill reverence and you've killed the hero in man.

Man is a word that has no plural.

to writing philosophical essays. She published *For the New Intellectual* in 1961; *The Virtue of Selfishness,* a defense of individualistic ethics, also in 1961; and a book on critical philosophy, *An Introduction to Objectivist Epistemology,* in 1966. She planned to write a big volume summarizing the whole of her philosophy. She had all her life worked to have her philosophic ideas taken seriously; now they were, if not by professionals, then by the intelligentsia and college students worldwide.

Her intellectual/philosophical movement—which she named "Objectivism"—was thriving. She was surrounded by an inner circle of supporters, led by Nathaniel Branden, for eighteen years her companion and "intellectual heir," and Leonard Peikoff, later to be her biographer and executor. Branden organized the Nathaniel Branden Institute (located in the Empire State Building) to publish a newsletter, develop courses, give lectures, and coordinate the dissemination of her Objectivist philosophy. Ayn Rand lectured at universities and appeared on radio and television, where she was always brilliant, intimidating, and controversial. She was biographed and anthologized; she received honorary degrees from America's prestigious universities. Articles and books appeared in professional journals taking her to task for her simpleminded ethics, bad epistemology, and naive economics and politics; and in the popular press, where she was generally supported for her defense of personal freedom and the free enterprise system.

Ayn Rand was impressive with her stocky figure, dark hair, and fiery eyes that, one reporter said, would "wilt a cactus." She spoke elegant English with a labored Russian accent. In public performance she was competitive and argumentative; she never pulled punches and followed the rational line of thought without regard to feelings. Quick and incisive, she was never at a loss for an instant retort. It was her fate to be easily misinterpreted, and this produced in her a guarded readiness to defend and explain her controversial ideas. She was spared attack only when she was among followers who had done their homework and sympathized with what she was saying. Always intriguing, never dull, never afraid to do or say the unexpected or irreverent, she often wore a gold brooch in the shape of a dollar sign.

This was the peak of Ayn Rand's life and career. In 1968 her world began to unravel. A major schism occurred within the movement. Rand accused Branden of exploitation and moral transgressions; he was excommunicated, the Institute was closed, and the *Objectivist Newsletter* went into decline. Rand continued to write, to give occasional public lectures, to speak out on political issues, and (until 1976) to publish the *Ayn Rand Letter.* In 1975 her health began to deteriorate, due largely to her lifelong chain-smoking. She underwent lung surgery for cancer. Her husband had died in 1979 at age 82. She was working on a television script of *Atlas Shrugged* when she died in New York on March 6, 1982. She was 78.

✦

"My personal life," Ayn Rand once wrote, "is a postscript to my novels; it consists of the sentence: '*And I mean it.*' I have always lived by the philosophy I present in my books—and it has worked for me, as it works for my characters."

Early in her life Ayn Rand came to despise losers and antiheroes created by bad ideas that circulate in our society. She was hostile to the notion that life is an inevitable vale of tears, that man is an evil creature doomed to defeat by his sinful nature, that man of his own will can do nothing good, and that this life is a sort of holy war against evil, always to be lost in this world, won (maybe) in the next. Such ideas cast a dismal dark shadow over our lives, she said, and these evaluations are false. They are not descriptions of what life is or what it should be.

With an ounce of reason, she wrote, we would see that we live in a benevolent universe. Reality is friendly; what is real is on our side. To be sure, this life is not perfect, but it is great just as it is and our ideals can be achieved here and now. Happiness should not be regarded as a wondrous exception but as the normal, natural condition of any life rightly lived.

So, Ayn Rand dedicated her life to exploring the human potential and writing about man as a heroic being with unlimited capacities for growth and happiness. "I decided to become a writer—not in order to save the world, nor to serve my fellow men—but for the simple, personal, selfish, egotistical happiness of creating the kind of men and events I could like, respect and admire."

There are three cardinal values, she says, that one must hold supreme if one is to realize his or her ultimate value: reason, purpose, and self-esteem.

The capacity for reason is a human being's greatest asset. Guiding one's life rationally means recognizing and accepting reason as the only source of knowledge, the only way of judging values, and the only dependable guide to action. "It means one's total commitment to a state of full, conscious awareness, to the maintenance of a full mental focus in all issues, in all choices, in all of one's waking hours." It means remaining critically alert, not letting any fact or any value judgment enter one's repertory without stopping-the-world to think about it, as long as is necessary, to achieve clarity. "One must never place any value or consideration whatsoever above one's perception of reality." No myths, no self-delusions, no escapist fantasies. Reality is, and the rational person, by reason, stays in touch with it as best he or she can. We must all become dedicated empiricists.

Being rational means accepting "the responsibility of forming one's own judgments and of living by the work of one's own mind. . . . It means that one must never sacrifice one's convictions to the opinions or wishes of others . . . one must never attempt to fake reality in any manner. It means a commitment to reason . . . as a permanent way of life." Everything rational individuals do in our daily lives is planned for, and guided by, our intellect. Emotions enrich us, pleasures are the substance of joy, and happiness is the goal of our living; but for human beings who take charge of our own lives, reason alone is our guide for shaping our emotions, selecting our pleasures, and getting on with the journey toward happiness.

A sense of purpose is essential to one's productiveness. "Productive work is the central *purpose* of a rational man's life, the central value that integrates and determines the hierarchy of all his other values." One's work must come before all other goals and commitments, even before family and friends. "The man without a purpose is a man who drifts at the mercy of random feelings or unidentified urges and is capable of any evil, because he is totally out of control of his own life. In order to be in control in your life, you have to have a purpose—a productive purpose." There is, for every human being, some workpath that is peculiarly one's own, a creative vocation that one alone can fulfill; it is the responsibility of each of us to discover what that work is, and having found it, to stay with it with tenacity and zeal till the end of our days. All other virtues derive from this single-minded commitment to purpose.

Ayn Rand warns: "To cheat your way into a job bigger than your mind can handle is to become a fear-corroded ape on borrowed motions and borrowed time, and to settle down into a job that requires less than your mind's full capacity is to cut your motor and sentence yourself to another kind of motion: decay. . . ."

Self-esteem is, for each of us, the supreme value. "The man who does not value himself, cannot value anything or anyone." Self-esteem means valuing one's mind and honoring it by trusting it, loving it, nourishing it, treating it with dignity—not belittling it, negating it, devaluing it. The mind does not function, or function at all well, if it is distrusted, undermined, betrayed, treated shabbily, told that it is useless, worthless, and incompetent. Self-esteem creates the confidence required for the mind to do its work.

"Man knows that his desperate need of self-esteem is a matter of life and death." But this intuitive certainty about one's self is thwarted if we are told that we humans are inherently evil or depraved, or told that life in this world is really not worth living, or told that all human striving is helpless and doomed. These are lies. The truth, Ayn Rand says, is that human beings are creatures with unlimited capacities for creative accomplishments; we have been genetically programmed for joy and happiness; and we are free to create fulfilling futures, both as individuals and as a human species. A healthy self-esteem is a foundational requisite to our making these promises into realities.

She will be remembered as this century's chief defender of the human ego. Some writers can be reduced to a principle, some to a phrase, but Rand can be reduced to the one word *ego*. Some will ridicule her overemphasis on the self and explain it away by reference to Rand's feelings of inadequacy as a woman in a man's world, a Russian in America, and call it overcompensation. Some will have mixed feelings about it, as did historian Jacob Burckhardt when he discussed the ego: "The ego is at once man's sign of Cain and his crown of glory." Some will consider Rand a modern Montaigne, who wrote: "If the world finds fault with me for speaking too much of myself, I find fault with the world for not even thinking of itself." Some will consider her America's twentieth-century Walt Whitman, who said: "The whole theory of the universe is directed to one single individual —namely to You."

JAMES T. BAKER, *Ayn Rand*
(Twayne Publishers, 1987)

REFLECTIONS

1 As you reflect on the case of the man indicted for embezzlement ("News Item," p. 95), what is your conclusion? Was he the same person (self) twenty-six years later? Might the philosophical, psychological, physiological, ethical, and legal answers be different? Which answer(s) is/are correct? (This problem is not merely hypothetical; remember Leon Uris's *QB VII*?)

2 Summarize in your own words David Hume's concept of the self (p. 103). Drawing upon your knowledge of psychology and other modern disciplines, do you think Hume was essentially right or wrong? In either case, how would you describe the "self"?

3 "What each of us can become during our life/time is determined by two fundamental conditions. . . ." (p. 96). Is this statement in accord with your observations of others and your experience of your self?

4 What is meant by "self-love"? Why is it so important? Contrast self-love with egotism, selfishness, and narcissism.

5 The study by Masterson of the real self's capacities (pp. 106–107) provides an interesting profile of actualized individuals and gives a clue, perhaps, to our own potential. What is your response to the six qualities described? Can you see how each would contribute to the greater actualization of the person? Would you want to possess these qualities? Do you now possess these qualities? To what degree?

6 Pretend that you are an Eastern sage, and gaze patiently at the Zen oxherding pictures. As a Westerner (if you are), how far can you meaningfully go in accepting this account of the search for one's "true nature"? Can you

accept Step 7, for example? Is Step 8 meaningful? Can you state in your own words what is implied in Steps 9 and 10?

7 The study by Hayakawa of the "fully functioning personality" provides an interesting profile of more actualized individuals and gives a clue, perhaps, to our own potential. What is your response to the six qualities described? Can you see how each would contribute to the greater actualization of the person? Would you want to possess these qualities? Do you now possess these qualities? To what degree?

8 Why was Ayn Rand so passionate in denouncing "the monster of 'We'"? What virtues or benefits is she trying to emphasize with her doctrine of individualism?

9 Have you ever made a list of the things you are for and the things you are against? How much of Ayn Rand's "fors" and "againsts" can you agree with? Now clarify (to yourself) why you are for or against these things.

GROWTH

2-3

> *"We are what we pretend to be, so we must be careful about what we pretend to be."*
> KURT VONNEGUT, JR.
> *Mother Night*

The human self is resilient and stands ready to self-heal, but it is also delicate and easily wounded, so that it can't become the fully functioning self it was meant to be. This chapter explores further the development of the self and lists some of the things that can go wrong with this sensitive organism. What happens when our psyches are wounded? (See pp. 120ff.) Although the self can be fragmented into multiple selves, is there a "still small voice" deep within each of us that cries out when it is being abused and damaged? Can that voice be permanently silenced? When the world rejects aspects of the self that it finds unacceptable, we create masks to protect who we really are; it is easy for a mask to become inseparable from the real self behind the mask. What happens when we remove our masks—if we can? What do we then become?

WHEN THINGS GO WRONG

1 Dr. and Mrs. Harry F. Harlow have for years studied the growth patterns of rhesus monkeys. In the Primate Laboratory of the University of Wisconsin, the Harlows discovered that their monkeys have a developmental sequence that, under normal conditions, produces mutually beneficial social behavior. The young monkeys' emotional development must proceed in this order: (1) affection and security, (2) fear and adjustment, and (3) social-sexual interaction. If this growth sequence is disrupted, then tragic results, in varying degrees, take place in the inner worlds of the young monkeys.

2 Affection and security are basic to the monkey's earliest stages of growth. Normally he first knows these feelings in relation to his mother. She is the prime source of comforting reassurance as he begins to experience the world about him.

A six-month-old rhesus monkey, raised in isolation from birth — deprived of mother, surrogate mother, and playmates — cowers in fear in the corner of its cage.

The Harlows found that if a monkey is separated from its mother at birth, but is given the chance to live and develop with age-mates, then affectional ties can grow between them. Emotional bonds are established as they play together.

Harlow and friend

> Young monkeys that have not been permitted to establish relationships with other infants are wary of their playmates when finally allowed to be with them, and these deprived monkeys often fail to develop strong bonds of affection. Yet monkeys that have been deprived of mother love but provided with early contacts *can* develop ties with their peers which seem comparable to the bonds formed by mother-reared infants.

3 The worst thing that can happen is for a young monkey to be deprived of both his mother and his playmates. If this happens, no bonds of affection and trust can develop.

> Fear is the overwhelming response in all monkeys raised in isolation. Although the animals are physically healthy, they crouch and appear terror-stricken by their new environment. . . . They cringe when approached and fail at first to join in any of the play. During six months of play sessions, they never progress beyond minimal play behavior, such as playing by themselves with toys. What little social activity they do have is exclusively with the other isolate in the group. When the other animals become aggressive, the isolates accept their abuse without making any effort to defend themselves. For these animals, social opportunities have come too late. Fear prevents them from engaging in social interaction and consequently from developing ties of affection.

If young monkeys are reared in isolation for a long period of time—for up to twelve months—then their lifetime behavior is seriously affected, and it appears that little or nothing can undo the damage.

4 We continued the testing of the same six- and twelve-month isolates for a period of several years. The results were startling. The monkeys raised in isolation now began

If you begin by sacrificing yourself to those you love, you will end by hating those to whom you have sacrificed yourself.

George Bernard Shaw

The unforgivable sin is not to become all that you can as a human being, given the circumstances of life that we have to accept.

R. D. Laing

> to attack the other monkeys viciously, whereas before they had cowered in fright. . . . The monkeys which had been raised in the steel isolation cages for their first six months now were three years old. They were still terrified by all strangers, even the physically helpless juveniles. But in spite of their terror, they engaged in uncontrolled aggression, often launching suicidal attacks upon the large adult males and even attacking the juveniles—an act almost never seen in normal monkeys of their age. The passage of time had only exaggerated their asocial and antisocial behavior.
>
> In those monkeys, positive social action was not initiated, play was nonexistent, grooming did not occur, and sexual behavior was not present at all or was totally inadequate. In human terms, these monkeys which had lived unloved and in isolation were totally unloving, distressed, disturbed and delinquent.
>
> Throughout our studies, we have been increasingly impressed by the alternative routes monkeys may take to reach adequate social behavior, which by our criteria includes affection toward peers, controlled fear and aggression, and normal sexual behavior. In protected laboratory conditions, social interaction between peers and between mother and child appears to be in large part interchangeable in their effect on the infant's development. A rhesus can surmount the absence of its mother if it can associate with its peers, and it can surmount a lack of socialization with peers if its mother provides affection. Being raised with several age mates appears to compensate adequately for a lack of a mother. . . .
>
> After numerous and varied studies at the University of Wisconsin, we have concluded that unless peer affection precedes social aggression, monkeys do not adjust; either they become unreasonably aggressive or they develop into passive scapegoats for their group.

5 The Harlows are writing of rhesus monkeys, not man; and all careful scientists are wary of extrapolating their findings from experiments with one species to any different species. However, there is evidence that human developmental patterns are quite similar.

For human beings, as with the Harlows' monkeys, normal psychosocial development appears to follow a sequential order: (1) reassurance/security/trust → (2) courage/aggression/exploration → (3) self/autonomy/maturity. If this growth sequence is interrupted or the requisites not provided at any stage, we too become disturbed creatures cringing in the corner of life with our hands over our faces.

When things go wrong, one wonders whether the young monkey is more fortunate than human young. The monkey's behavior is a spontaneous expression of need-deprivation; it is doubtful that he **wonders** why he is "disturbed." He simply is. But our **self-**consciousness becomes acutely painful; **we know** (most of us) that something has gone wrong, and **we** wonder why.

6 When things have gone very wrong for us and need-deprivation has been acute, the image we develop of ourselves is distorted, confused, inaccurate. Having developed without reassurance and support, we remain vulnerable to the varied, inconsistent responses of others. Nor do we move through the normal stages of growth. There is no period of separation from authority during which we evolve a healthy reliance on our own thoughts and feelings. We are held at a level where the tenuous "mirror-images"—what others think and feel about us—continue to reinforce a fragmented self. We become alienated from the potentially authentic self, the remnants of which still cry out from deep inside.

7 If, very early, we do not receive love, we quickly know that we are unlovable.
If we are rejected, by word or deed, we learn to reject ourselves.
If we find that what we **do** is more important than what we **are,** then doing the "right thing" becomes all important; in fact, we strive desperately **to be** what **we do.**
If our parents are permissive so that we see them as "not caring," we will feel unwanted and worthless.
If our parents "care" too much, especially when they call it "love," then we may never establish self-reliance.
If we are given behavioral ultimatums that demand repression of authentic feelings, we will develop inauthentic selves that comply to required specifications.
If we have been denied the warmth we crave, we will carry with us the ache of an insatiable emptiness.

Edvard Munch, *The Scream*

The Masks We Wear

8 Few of us are fortunate enough to have had parents who appreciated our early spontaneous expressions of life and self and, at the same time, taught us to "play the games" of adjustment to other norms outside the home. How many mothers prefaced a lecture on cleanliness with a word or two about the social realities we would face—for instance, when preparing us to attend a friend's party—without instilling in us the idea that "dirty" itself is bad and "clean" is inherently good?

Yet it's an idea that children can grasp at a remarkably early age. "If you want to go to Suzy's party, then Suzy's mother will want you to look clean. I want you to look clean too. I'm happy you enjoy playing in the mud, but this is the way of the world, so let's wash up."

This is a reality-perspective that permits the child to enjoy playing in the mud and at the same time choose to "play the games" required to attain a goal, in this case attending Suzy's party.

9 Far more than other creatures, we humans have the capacity to be "many things to many people." As the situations call for it, we can be different "persons" or wear different masks (the word "person" is from the Latin *persona,* meaning "mask"). Some of us become quite adept at putting on masks or switching masks; thus we can ensure that we always have ready a *persona* that is acceptable. It effects minimal rejection by any other person or group.

But the price we pay is dear. In the process of switching masks, we may discover that there are **nothing but** masks; indeed, they may begin to feel familiar and genuine, all of them. And if someone should demand, "Will the **real** self please stand up?" we find to our horror that there is no one there. It is not uncommon to discover during some personal crisis that an authentic self never developed. If we glimpse this may be the case, in panic we may seize our masks and fit them more tightly, reluctant to remove them ever again.

The feeling that one does not know "who he is" may be intuited by ourselves and inferred by others, but it is perhaps the last thing that we will con-

Why are Americans so hungry for the approval of others? The adjusted American lacks self-approval; that is to say, he has not developed a self-image that he can believe is both accurate and acceptable. To do so he would require successful techniques for creating an accurate and acceptable self-image through honest introspection, candid association, and meaningful activity. The patterns to which he has adjusted do not include such techniques. Instead, the culture abounds with misdirections, which the adjusted American acquires. . . . Perhaps above all he learns to seek self-acceptance indirectly, by seeking to substitute the good opinions of others for self-approval. It is thus that he becomes "other-directed."

GAIL AND SNELL PUTNEY

BATTERED CHILD / BATTERED WORLD

In her book *The Untouched Key* (Doubleday Anchor, 1990), the Swiss psychoanalyst Alice Miller, a specialist in childhood trauma, presents the cases of creative individuals who were severely mistreated in childhood. Her study included Picasso, Hitler, Stalin, Dostoevsky, Nietzsche, and others. What she found was that whether such traumatized individuals go on to become creative artists or agents of destruction is determined by a single factor: whether that individual was fortunate enough to have someone who was on his side during those painful childhood years, someone to support him, to defend him, to tell him that the abuse he was receiving was **not** normal, **not** moral, **not** "what happens to everybody." She writes (page 60): "The absence or presence of a helping witness in childhood determines whether a mistreated child will become a despot who turns his repressed feelings of helplessness against others or an artist who can tell about his or her suffering."

Dr. Miller summarizes the results of her life work in the Appendix to her book (pp. 167–170) entitled "The Newly Recognized, Shattering Effects of Child Abuse."

> For some years now there has been proof that the devastating effects of the traumatization of children take their inevitable toll on society. This knowledge concerns every single one of us, and—if disseminated widely enough—should lead to fundamental changes in society, above all to a halt in the blind escalation of violence. . . .

1. All children are born to grow, to develop, to live, to love, and to articulate their needs and feelings for their self-protection.

2. For their development children need the respect and protection of adults who take them seriously, love them, and honestly help them to become oriented in the world.

3. When these vital needs are frustrated and children are instead abused for the sake of adults' needs by being exploited, beaten, punished, taken advantage of, manipulated, neglected, or deceived without the intervention of any witness, then their integrity will be lastingly impaired.

4. The normal reactions to such injury should be anger and pain; since children in this hurtful kind of environment, however, are forbidden to express their anger and since it would be unbearable to experience their pain all alone, they are compelled to suppress their feelings, repress all memory of the trauma, and idealize those guilty of the abuse. Later they will have *no memory of what was done to them.*

5. Dissociated from the original cause, their feelings of anger, helplessness, despair, longing, anxiety, and pain will find expression in destructive acts against others (criminal behavior, mass murder) or against themselves (drug addiction, alcoholism, prostitution, psychic disorders, suicide).

6. If these people become parents, they will often direct acts of revenge for their mistreatment in childhood against their own children, whom they use as scapegoats. Child abuse is still sanctioned—indeed, held in high regard—in our society as long as it is defined as child-rearing. It is a tragic fact that parents beat their children in order to escape the emotions stemming from how they were treated by their own parents.

7. If mistreated children are not to become criminals or mentally ill, it is essential that *at least once in their life* they come in contact with a person who knows without any doubt that the environment, not the helpless, battered child, is at fault. . . .

8. Till now society has protected the adult and blamed the victim. . . . In reality, children tend to blame themselves for their parents' cruelty and to absolve the parents, whom they invariably love, of all responsibility.

9. For some years now, it has been possible to prove, thanks to the use of new therapeutic methods, that repressed traumatic experiences in childhood are stored up in the body and, although remaining unconscious, exert their influence even in adulthood. In addition, electronic testing of the fetus has revealed a fact previously unknown to most adults: *a child responds to and learns both tenderness and cruelty from the very beginning.*

10. In the light of this new knowledge, even the most absurd behavior reveals its formerly hidden logic once the traumatic experiences of childhood no longer must remain shrouded in darkness.

11. Our sensitization to the cruelty with which children are treated, until now commonly denied, and to the consequences of such treatment will as a matter of course bring to an end the perpetuation of violence from generation to generation.

12. People whose integrity has not been damaged in childhood, who were protected, respected, and treated with honesty by their parents, will be—both in their youth and adulthood—intelligent, responsive, empathetic, and highly sensitive. They will take pleasure in life and will not feel any need to kill or even hurt others or themselves. They will use their power to defend themselves but not to attack others. They will not be able to do otherwise than to respect and protect those weaker than themselves, including their children, because this is what they have learned from their own experience and because it is *this* knowledge (and not the experience of cruelty) that has been stored up inside them from the beginning.

fess to ourselves or others. The pain that our masks cover is too great for anyone to see. We can't risk being open. We are ever fearful that someone might see beneath our masks and discover . . . **nothing.**

I Will Not Stop Till I Know

10 Oedipus is the prototype of the man who gains knowledge about himself and pays the ultimate price. The issue in the drama is: Shall Oedipus know what he has done? Shall Oedipus know who he is and what his origins are? . . .

> Oedipus is a hero precisely because he will let no one stand in the way of his knowledge about himself. He is the hero because he faces his own reality. He cries out with pain again and again, but he repeats, "I will not stop till I have known the whole."

Rollo May
Love and Will

"You've made me very happy."

11 Deep within the unconscious mind of man, there moves a longing to recover the innocence of childhood, a condition that he nostalgically (mis)interprets as a state of blissful happiness. Intuitively, we sense that with knowledge comes insight, and with insight comes pain. Most of man's religions have in their mythologies some place or state where he may reenter into that paradise of unknowing where suffering will cease. The Garden of Eden was a paradise only as long as the fruit of **knowledge** remained untouched. It would have been better to be innocent, the story seems to say, than to know the pain of understanding. Once innocence has been lost, however, there is no return. Once we possess knowledge we must leave the Garden of Eden, and we leave it forever.

Every time you teach a child something you keep him from reinventing it.

Jean Piaget

To be innocent is to not know. To be innocent is to be childlike, and to be childlike is to be unaware of certain facts or experiences. A child does not have certain information at his disposal that he can use, information that others do have, and all decisions related to those areas have to be made by others.

Therefore, to be innocent is to be dependent. If one cannot make his own decisions, others must. This is a normal condition for a child, and he accepts it. This vulnerability puts him at the mercy of those he depends upon; if his basic self-needs are met, however, this is a happy dependency.

All children paint like geniuses. What do we do to them that so quickly dulls this ability?

Pablo Picasso

Dependence requires trust and faith. For the innocent child there is no alternative. He must trust the decisions others make for him, that those decisions are right and good; and he must accept on faith information given to him, that it is right and true.

Dependence requires obedience. Wherever there is dependency, obedience is demanded, but if trust is not a part of that dependency relationship,

Progress in Awareness

There seems to be a sort of progress in awareness, through the stages of which every man—and especially every psychiatrist and every patient—must move, some persons progressing further through these stages than others. One starts by blaming the identified patient for his idiosyncrasies and symptoms. Then one discovers that these symptoms are a response to—or an effect of—what others have done; and the blame shifts from the identified patient to the etiological figure. Then, one discovers perhaps that these figures feel a guilt for the pain which they have caused, and one realizes that when they claim this guilt they are identifying themselves with god. After all, they did not, in general, know what they are doing, and to claim guilt for their acts would be to claim omniscience. At this point one reaches a more general anger, that what happens to people should not happen to dogs, and that what people do to each other the lower animals could never devise. Beyond this, there is, I think, a stage which I can only dimly envisage, where pessimism and anger are replaced by something else—perhaps humility. And from this stage onward to whatever other stages there may be, there is loneliness.

Gregory Bateson
Language and Psychotherapy

then obedience is given grudgingly. With trust, however, obedience is given willingly, even joyfully. There is no need to question the authority to whom one submits.

Innocence is an instrument of control. Knowledge and know-how are potentially dangerous assets—dangerous to all who possess them but lack maturity to use them for good, and dangerous to any who wish to maintain a state of control. Parents guard their children against certain kinds of knowledge and experiences until they are "old enough" (that is, until they are aware and responsible) to make constructive use of it. A child may be told to do things he does not understand, or that he does not want to do; but obedience to authority is necessary since authorities (that is, those with knowledge) can make more realistic judgments. Obviously, in matters of destiny, it could be tragic if a child were forced to make critical decisions he is not yet equipped to make.

So, while we are children, we think like children—innocently: without information and awareness. We order our experience along simple lines and our behavior is guided by those we depend upon.

Growth and Insecurity

12 Desmond Morris employs two helpful concepts to describe the innate alternating feelings of fear and curiosity: neophobia and neophilia.

By **neophobia** he means that we are afraid of new objects, unfamiliar behavioral patterns in others, strange feelings in ourselves, or any other new and threatening elements of life that we do not understand. It is completely natural to be afraid of the unknown. To experience fear in the presence of potential dan-

Selfishness is not living as one wishes to live. It is asking others to live as one wishes to live.

Oscar Wilde

David Park, *Standing Couple* (1958)

ger has obvious survival value. Life may be likened to our moving forever on the edge of darkness, not knowing what exists just beyond the immediate circle of experience.

We can understand, too painfully, the first experiences of the infant monkeys described by the Harlows. When placed in a room cluttered with unfamiliar objects and without any mother or comforting "home base" to return to, the young monkey was unable to explore the room with its formidable array of unknowns. His fear was too great, and he could only huddle in the corner of the room with his hands over his eyes.

But when given the security of a mother, or even the comfort of a soft blanket or surrogate mother, to which he could periodically return for reassurance and security, then step by step the monkey would explore the room's contents. An object would be touched, handled, played with; then the monkey would return to the mother (or blanket) for a security "rest period"; then explore another object; and so on until all objects were familiar. Little by little, he would reduce his fear of all the objects in the room.

When he knew, from his own experience, that nothing in the room held any danger for him, he could then move about the room without fear. He had succeeded in making all the unknowns a part of his world.

13 **Neophilia** is a strong counter-impulse to neophobia. We are fascinated by the new and the unknown; we are drawn to new objects, new experiences, new ways of living—drawn by "curiosity" and by a sense of adventure and excitement. It is the neophilic impulse that provides us the possibility of growth. If our desire to explore the unknown is overwhelmed by fear, then we withdraw. We return to our corner. But if we have enough security when we need it, then we can explore more and more of the unknowns, assimilate them, explore some more, widen our horizons, and grow.

This kind of growth is open; it has no limits. There are always new worlds to be explored, new adventures to become excited about, new ways of living to be experienced, new ideas to be discovered, new problems to be solved.

14 With a positive view of self, one can risk taking chances; one does not have to be afraid of what is new and different. A sturdy ship can venture farther from port. Just so, an adequate person can launch himself without fear into the new, the untried and the unknown. A positive view of self permits the individual to be creative, original and spontaneous. What is more, he can afford to be generous, to give of himself freely or to become personally involved in events. With so much more at his command, he has so much more to give.

Truly adequate people possess perceptual fields maximally open to experience. That is to say, their perceptual fields are capable of change and adjustment in such fashion as to make fullest possible use of their experience.

Arthur W. Combs

The Answer-Givers

15 A variety of institutions and individuals specialize in providing us with the answers before we have asked the questions. The rationale for doing this is always altruistic: they want to protect us from dangerous ideas or bad influences; they

must prevent our doing the wrong things; they wish to guide us into the right paths of feeling, thinking, and behaving. They give us answers because, they would say, we have a "need to know."

The actual fact is that answer-givers have a need to persuade. One of their goals is to contain us within a state of innocence and thereby establish control over us. Their true motivation is disguised by perhaps the commonest of human rationalizations: that they are really helping us. Indeed, the claim that we need the answers can become so widely accepted that, without raising further questions, we too assume the claim to be true.

The price of such answer-giving is very high.

It prevents the individual from having to wrestle personally with life's problems and to ask the questions that lead to emotional and intellectual growth. Once trained to accept given answers, one may never learn how to formulate meaningful questions in terms of who he is or what life means to him.

Moreover, one who has been conditioned to accept answers tends to develop a rigid conceptual framework that undergoes early closure to new ideas and experiences. He knows if he lacks an answer, the authority can supply it. All he must do is ask for the answer instead of asking the question. Nor can he question the answer. It is common to find individuals who can repeat verbatim the "correct" answers, but when questioned about their meaning, they reveal little understanding; and if pressed, their only recourse is to fall back on other "remembered" answers.

One who has been protected in this way has been prevented from knowing both the "agony of insight" and the "ecstasy of growth." He has been assured that no painful questions will have to be faced.

I contradict myself. I am large. I contain multitudes.

WALT WHITMAN

Only that life is worth living which develops the strength and the integrity to withstand the unavoidable sufferings and misfortunes of existence without flying into an imaginary world.

FRIEDRICH NIETZSCHE

Crisis of Authority

16 The date: AD 2198. The speaker: Mia, a young girl who has just survived "The Trial," a rite-of-passage that prepares youth to face themselves and their world.

> It was only after I came back from Trial that I came to a notion of my own as to what maturity consists of. Maturity is the ability to sort the portions of truth from the accepted lies and self-deceptions that you have grown up with. It is easy now to see the irrelevance of the religious wars of the past, to see that capitalism in itself is not evil, to see that honor is most often a silly thing to kill a man for, to see that national patriotism should have meant nothing in the twenty-first century, to see that a correctly-arranged tie has very little to do with true social worth. It is harder to assess as critically the insanities of your own time, especially if you have accepted them unquestioningly for as long as you can remember, for as long as you have been alive. If you never make the attempt, whatever else you are, you are not mature.
>
> ALEXEI PANSHIN
> *Rite of Passage*

17 One of the major roadblocks to autonomy is failure to achieve separation from authority. This is the failure to outgrow our dependence upon those who have nourished us; we prolong our need of them and rely upon them to make our decisions and provide directives for our behavior. Long past separation-time we continue to operate in terms of their values. Dependence of course, means se-

Five Selves / Amy's Story

What is a self? What does it mean to be a person?

Amy's mother was a well-meaning but emotionally bereft alcoholic, her father an often jobless day laborer prone to episodes of violent behavior. The oldest of seven children and her father's favorite, Amy became the focus of his sexual attentions. When she maneuvered to evade his advances, she was cruelly rejected and made to feel ungrateful and worthless.

Feeling overwhelmed and helpless, she developed another self—Ceci—who would cope with her father's demands. Quite unlike Amy, Ceci was a flirtatious coquette skilled in the art of anticipating her father's advances and avoiding his rage.

As her mother became increasingly remote, Amy tried to hold the family together, but in spite of her best efforts the children were eventually passed along to relatives and shuttled between foster homes.

One foster family was Catholic, and Amy adapted herself to their Catholic world, identifying with the ideas, values, and viewpoints of these significant others. She developed a "Catholic-self" that could live with them successfully; after all, their acceptance and approval were necessary for survival. This Catholic-self was named Rachel.

When Amy was seventeen she took a job in a large corporation as a filing clerk. Her administrative and organizational skills soon became apparent, and she was urged to attend night school to develop her abilities. At this point another self, Lisa, emerged. Supercalm, detached, quick to learn, quick to understand, efficient and professional, she was the ideal assistant for a fast-track junior executive.

A fifth self—Beth—was sometimes weak, sometimes strong. On occasion, when Amy was alone, Beth would emerge with a scream and throw tantrums, as though an ignored self had been confined to a room and could come out only with great effort, or as though she were a forgotten prisoner, locked in a dark cell, screaming for recognition. Beth would often sob uncontrollably, then grow quiet and apparently vanish.

As the years passed Amy's five selves continued to develop in coherence and strength of will. When she visited her Catholic family, the Rachel-self emerged spontaneously and functioned normally. All went well. When she visited her father, the Ceci-self appeared, played her flirtatious part, and vanished. Likewise, Lisa "grew in wisdom and strength" as she competed successfully and was rewarded in her corporate environment. The appropriate self was reinforced and strengthened in each case. As long as Amy could count on the right self emerging at the right time and place, her existence, if not without stress, was basically stable.

Zeus, who taught men to think, has laid it down that wisdom comes alone through suffering.

Aeschylus

curity; in a dependent state there is much of life we need not face and many responsibilities we need not assume. It is comfortable to maintain dependence and conform to patterns that are not ours.

The longer dependence lasts, the more difficult separation becomes. Unless, sometime, we experience the feeling of being a separate self, the very idea of autonomy may remain meaningless.

The self that longs for autonomy—the self that longs for a life of its own—will not easily be put down. If the authorities are reluctant to relinquish control and/or if the separating self cannot outgrow its dependency, then the separation process is often prolonged and may reach crisis proportions. But paradoxi-

During her tenure as a personal assistant she met and fell in love with a young executive. Her first serious romantic involvement awakened the unresolved pain and guilt associated with her father's attentions. Under the increased stress Ceci sought to emerge and take control. Lisa tried to hang on. Soon the delicate balance of selves began to disintegrate, plunging Amy into acute anxiety and—because she felt trapped—into depression. She became immobile. She could not work or face friends. She attempted suicide.

Amy was hospitalized and diagnosed as possessing multiple personalities. She began therapy. The therapeutic plan called for the selection and strengthening of one of the selves—the most authentic or "core" self—while allowing the other selves to weaken and disintegrate. They chose Lisa because she had dealt better with the real world. Careful control of her environment was absolutely necessary. During therapy Lisa/Amy was not allowed to see, or be seen by, members of her family, friends or coworkers who would only reinforce the other selves familiar to them. Months of therapy were needed. It was a time of isolation, loss, disorientation, and depression. It was also a time of healing. Lisa gradually took control, and the other selves—no longer needed, no longer reinforced—continued to fade. Lisa/Amy grew in strength, coherence, and will.

Today Lisa/Amy is married and has a family of her own. Hers is a success story. To be sure, she is not wholly free of emotional problems: the Ceci side of her self, still needing to please and fearing rejection, is not entirely resolved. But Amy is one person, one self. She has full knowledge of her former selves, and because of her pain, she possesses a special insight into, and compassion for, the delicate condition of the human soul. One of the keys to Amy's success has been her capacity for honesty, her willingness to face the truth about herself, whatever that might be.

So, what is a self? What is the relationship of self to body? (Remember, Amy had five selves in a single body.) What is a person? Are "self" and "person" interchangeable? It is generally assumed in ethical studies that a "person" is the proper object of ethical concern. In Amy's case what (or whom) should we be ethically concerned about? Are we born with a self, or is it developed, grown through time and experience? Can selves be weakened and strengthened in all of us? What does it mean to have (or to be) a "weak self" or "strong self"? What does "self-esteem" mean in Amy's case? We all play roles: What is the difference between those of us who play different roles (according to the "job description") and Amy, who apparently was the roles she played? "Are we one, or many?"

cally, as long as there is pain, there is hope; the separation process has not been abandoned.

18 This "crisis of authority" is felt on both sides. For the self that is fighting for autonomy, the severance of the umbilical cord brings fear and guilt. He is doing the very thing the authorities find unacceptable. He is behaving "badly" or "wrong." One commonly feels like a traitor in abandoning the values and beliefs of the authority figures; and, unavoidably, the authorities will be hurt. They may experience a sense of failure, perhaps of betrayal. The crisis of separation is often as painful for the authorities as it is for the separating self, for authori-

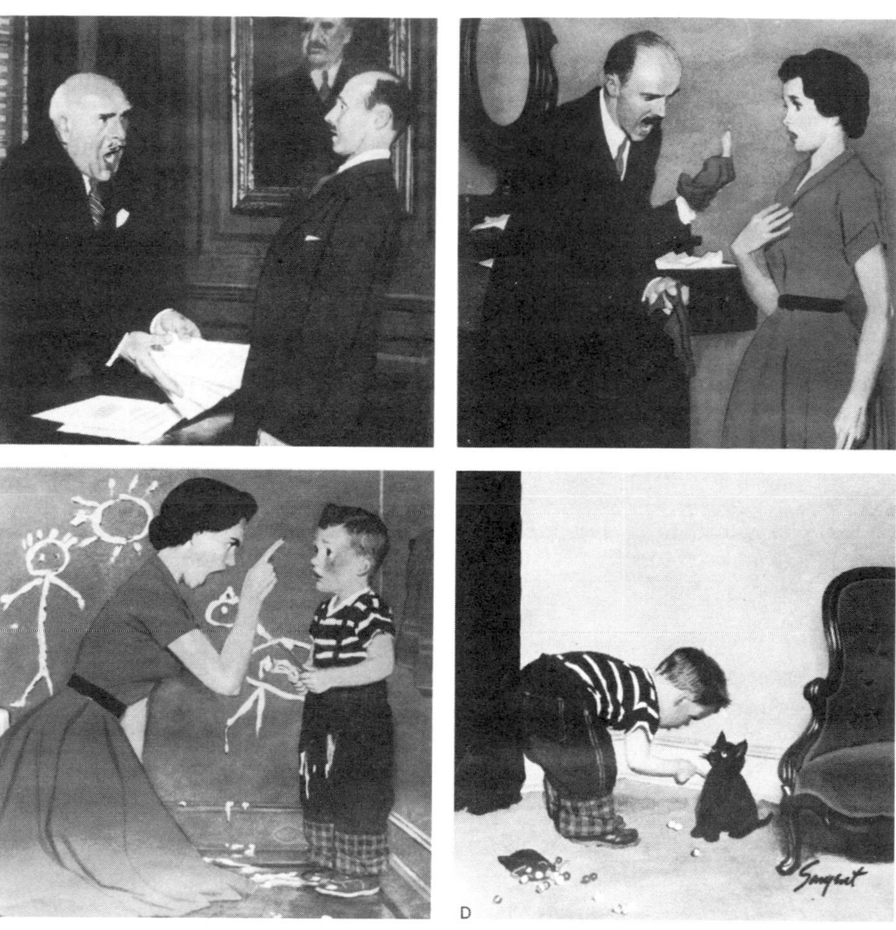

Let me listen to me and not to them.

GERTRUDE STEIN

ties have as difficult a time letting go as the self has in cutting loose. An authority figure, after all, must be an authority or his role—the role he has defined for himself and identified with—vanishes. He often feels (unconsciously) that his purpose in life will be lost if he is not needed by others; and if others do not **need** him then there will be no basis for a relationship with him. He will be alone. Therefore, authorities frequently bind us to them in an effort to give their own lives meaning. If seen from this perspective, it becomes clear that the dependency ties go in **both** directions.

DEVELOPING SELF-AWARENESS

19 If the recovery of the whole self is to be one's goal, then the development of self-awareness is a prerequisite. If we sense that things have not gone right either in the development of identity or self-worth, and we genuinely want growth to take place, then self-knowledge is essential and some deliberate choices will have to be made in terms of that knowledge.

It is not uncommon to find ourselves experiencing repeatedly the same dominant negative emotions as we live through a variety of activities in time: anxi-

Pablo Picasso, *Girl Before a Mirror* (1932). Collection, The Museum of Modern Art, New York, Gift of Mrs. Simon Guggenheim.

ety, fear, anger, frustration, depression. We may engage in sundry projects and numerous relationships, expecting (or perhaps just hoping) that something will happen to change how we feel. But it doesn't happen. In our honest moments we can confess to a hunger for life, but something inside holds us where we are. At the deepest emotional level, it is always the same.

20 When we are open to experiencing our selves precisely as they are—rather than expending energy feeling anxious or guilty over what they are not—a change in feeling can take place. An awareness of all that we contact inside

must be brought into our consciousness. Whatever our shortcomings (on whatever criteria they are judged to be "shortcomings"), these too must be accepted as part of one's self. Here deliberate choice comes in. There are unpleasant things stored in the inner worlds of all of us, and we may be tempted to ignore them; but with self-awareness, we can deliberately choose to stay a moment, recognize heretofore repressed events, and begin the process of "decharging" them.

It is only in emotional and spiritual crises of suffering that people will endure the pain and anxiety involved in digging out the deep roots of their problems.
Psychology Today

A fact about emotion is that it changes when it is permitted expression and can run its course. When one allows himself to feel a feeling, and no longer permits himself the dangerous luxuries of repression and rationalization, then genuine change can follow.

For example, the monologue might heretofore have gone like this: "I feel sad. I don't want to feel sad, so I will pretend I don't feel sad. Others won't notice and I can fool myself as well." If we play this kind of game with our emotions, the sadness in this case is repressed and has little chance to change. It will remain stored as a charged energy system within the psyche. This is true, of course, for all the bitter emotions—anger, hatred, frustration, fear, and so on.

The highest duty of the writer, the composer, the artist is to remain true to himself and let the chips fall where they may.
JOHN F. KENNEDY

On the other hand, the monologue might proceed: "I feel sad. I don't want to feel sad, but I'll not deny what exists. Rather, I will feel the full force of the feeling and let it run its course. It will fade away by itself." This way, when we **choose** not to repress an emotion, we find that it will diminish and we can move on to better feelings. Nothing is repressed that can return later and wreak vengeance for not having been dealt with honestly.

I am not at all the sort of person you and I took me for.
JANE WELSH CARLYLE

In this way, with self-awareness and deliberate choice, one can begin to integrate all that he is. These are first steps in the recovery of a wholeness that most of us, living in a fragmenting world, have to some degree lost and forgotten.

THE LAW OF PATHEI MATHOS

21 We humans have long been aware that growth never comes without a price: pain. The Greek tragedian Aeschylus thought of man as subject to an "epistemic law" decreed by the god Zeus "who had laid it down that wisdom comes alone through suffering." Charlie Brown put it more succinctly after Linus lost his faith in the Great Pumpkin: "In all this world there is nothing more upsetting than the clobbering of a cherished belief."

> The agonies of insight are not strangers.
> The agony of discovering you are not one but many people, created in the images of those who have mattered most to you.
> The agony of having your childhood's faith crumble at the very moment when you needed it most to sustain you.
> The agony of doubting what you knew was right, and wondering if what you knew was wrong just could be right.
> The agony of watching your children enter new worlds you cannot enter, and cannot accept, yet cannot completely condemn.
> The agony of listening to your children condemn all that you believe in and tried to teach them.
> The agony of feeling like a traitor to your parents when you find you must abandon their cherished beliefs because, for you, they are not true.

If it were not for the neurotics, there would be very little work accomplished in this world.
ARTHUR P. NOYES

I will not let you (or me) make me dishonest, insincere, emotionally tied up or constricted, or artificially nice and social, if I can help it.
EUGENE T. GENDLIN

The agony of having to unlearn and relearn what you learned because what you were taught is no longer true.
The agony of hating others for making you what you are, yet knowing in your honest moments that they could not have done otherwise.
The agony of being concerned, when others are not.

22 It is a painful insight to discover that one holds a belief because one needs the belief, and not because the belief is true. This is the sort of insight one would like to make go away, like a bad dream or clouds on a rainy day.

But this sort of insight, which comes with self-awareness, is the most difficult to dispel. When the process has begun by which one examines the nature of the need that the belief fulfills, it follows that one asks whether the belief is **also** true—and often finds that it is not. The insight into the nature of the need has, for all pragmatic purposes, destroyed the efficacy of the belief.

Our pain can be especially sharp when the insight has destroyed the belief while our need for it is still alive. The head has said, "You can no longer believe it, for now you see through it." But the rest of one's being cries out in emptiness for what it has lost.

The ultimate goal of the educational system is to shift to the individual the burden of pursuing his own education.
John Gardner

This is the cry of the soul that still needs healing but has discovered that the healers have lost their power. This is a Saint Paul, torn with conflict, realizing that the Law of Moses only increased his guilt. This is a Luther, still yearning for peace of soul, but finding that his faith in the sacraments had failed him and they cannot bring him peace.

This is the agony of alienated selves who have found themselves cut off from their roots, still longing for something worth believing in, but discovering that the old gods are gone and there is nothing to take their place.

23 You ask me how I became a madman. It happened thus: One day, long before many gods were born, I woke from a deep sleep and found all my masks were stolen—the seven masks I have fashioned and worn in seven lives,—I ran maskless through the crowded streets shouting, "Thieves, thieves, the cursèd thieves."

Men and women laughed at me and some ran to their houses in fear of me.

And when I reached the market place, a youth standing on a house-top cried, "He is a madman." I looked up to behold him; the sun kissed my own naked face for the first time. For the first time the sun kissed my own naked face and my soul was inflamed with love for the sun, and I wanted my masks no more. And as if in a trance I cried, "Blessed, blessed are the thieves who stole my masks."

Thus I became a madman.

Kahlil Gibran

A great many people are neurotic today, and the neuroses are caused by the fact that their talents, their unique potentialities, have not been used. They are "spinning their wheels" in life because they have not grown as they could have grown, because they have not used the gifts they have.
Aaron Ungersma

Sigmund Freud

Our Humanity Is Blocked by Our Pain

Sigmund Freud was born in Moravia in 1856 but was raised and spent most of his life in Vienna. There he came to despise the repressiveness of society and escaped from it by taking long walks in the Austrian countryside where he could stand tall with the pines, collect wildflowers for study ("they have neither character nor complexities"), and breathe in the fresh air of the Alpine snows.

He was "the firstborn son of a youthful mother"—Amalia Freud—and her favorite child (of eight); and she often spoke in glowing terms of her son's future greatness. This son later wrote: "A man who has been the indisputable favorite of his mother keeps for life the feeling of a conqueror, that confidence of success that often induces real success." His father, Jacob Freud, was a clothier. By him Freud was gifted with intellect, a will to work, and unflagging energy; but the specter of a stern authority also pursued him through life, like the Hound of Heaven. "That boy will never amount to anything!" his father grumbled one night after an unpleasant episode when his son was about seven. "This must have been a terrible affront to my ambitions," Freud later wrote, "for allusions to this scene recur again and again in my dreams, and are constantly coupled with enumerations of my accomplishments and successes, as though I wanted to say: 'You see, I have amounted to something after all.'"

Young Freud was introspective. The need for aloneness dominated his life. He lived in a small, stuffy, private bedroom with an oil lamp, and here he lost himself in his books, reading everything he could come by. Already at this age he possessed an insatiable desire for an unbounded knowledge of everything. During his teens he rarely joined the family at meals but ate alone in his room, where he poured timelessly over his books.

His formal education began at the local gymnasium ("grammar school") where he spent his first eight school years, reading voraciously and taking copious notes on lectures. He later wrote that even at this early age he felt a sense of direction: "In the years of my youth, the urgent necessity to understand something of the riddles of the world and perhaps contribute myself to their solution was overpowering." In the summer of his seventeenth year he graduated *summa cum laude*—with highest honors.

He decided to become a medical student, so he entered the University of Vienna and eagerly began to explore all the sciences; but he had difficulty finding his niche and wandered from one department to another, without rooting. He was finally invited by Professor Brücke to join his laboratory to study human physiology. In 1882 he became an intern at Vienna's General City Hospital and worked as a clinical neurologist. Soon he was a resident physician. In the spring of 1885 he was appointed lecturer in neuropathology.

That summer he went to Paris to pursue reports about a therapeutic technique employed by a famed physician, Dr. Charcot. Freud stayed with Charcot for the better part of a year and pondered the exciting possibilities of using hypnosis to reach the painful past events that seemed to underlie his patients' problems. But it was also spring in Paris, and the tulips were beginning to open. He was still in love, engaged for almost four years. He wandered the city, visiting Notre Dame cathedral on free afternoons where he would "clamber about between the monsters and gargoyles." He longed to return to Vienna.

The young lady's name was Martha Bernays. They began a marriage in the autumn of 1886—he was thirty, she was twenty-five—that was to last fifty-three years. To Freud she was tender and devoted, her only goals in life (her husband later said) being "to keep well and love him." She was by instinct and calling a *hausfrau,* managing every detail of the home's economy and six children with efficiency and seeing to it that *der Papa* could get his work done.

Freud focused his intellect on one goal: to find the truth about what is going on in the hidden depths of the human mind.

A breakthrough came in 1889 on a trip to visit a French country doctor named Liébeault who was having notable success in treating patients suffering from emotional ailments. From the doctor's extensive experience, Freud saw for the first time what he had been groping for—"the possibility that there could be powerful mental processes which nevertheless remained hidden from the consciousness of man." In simplistic terms, Freud had discovered the existence of the unconscious mind. Henceforth, he increasingly broke with the past and set off in new directions.

Being entirely honest with oneself is a good exercise.

Freud believed that we are blocked from being human by our own repressed pain and that seeing the truth about ourselves could release enormous stores of bound-up energy for rich and responsible living.

Freud theorized that the human personality is produced by the interaction of three dynamic organizational systems: the **id,** the **superego,** and the **ego.** The id is not an organized system but a chaos of primal energies that urges us to action; it is the whole complex of our physical and psychic needs, driven by emotion. It operates on the "pleasure-principle," seeking pleasure and avoiding pain.

The superego is our system of moral values—the dos ("ego ideals") and don'ts ("conscience") acquired through interaction with the world. It begins when our parents first tell us what the id can and cannot get away with; their directives are internalized and become part of our own psychic structure.

The ego is a psychic system that operates on the "reality-principle" and mediates between the blind energy-drives of the id—"I want what I want, now!"—and the real world that says, "No! Or maybe later. . . ." The ego is a negotiating instrument—dickering, manipulating, compromising, arranging for the delay of gratification. If the ego develops properly, it can be a strong mediator, negotiating effectively and realistically to meet our needs; if it remains undeveloped, then it will be unable to assume its assertive role as mediator between the pleasure-seeking self and the restrictive world.

A FREUD LEXICON

EGO
SUPEREGO
ID
REPRESSION
UNCONSCIOUS
NEUROSIS
REGRESSION
TRANSFERENCE
WISH FULFILLMENT
OEDIPUS COMPLEX
INFERIORITY COMPLEX
LIBIDO
FIXATION

An intimate friend and a hated enemy have always been indispensable to my emotional life.

The great question . . . which I have not been able to answer, despite my thirty years of research into the feminine soul, is "What does a woman want?"

In a normal sex life no neurosis is possible.

I am cross with mankind.

I do not think our cures can compete with those of Lourdes. There are so many more people who believe in the miracles of the Blessed Virgin than in the existence of the unconscious.

In a "healthy" individual the ego is in command, mediating effectively between the id and superego to get our needs met; and we have a sense of wholeness, effectiveness, and well-being. When these systems cannot work together—when they are at war with one another—then we become preoccupied with the internal conflicts and are unable to transact business efficiently with the environment to get our needs met. These conflicts between the dynamic systems are called "neuroses."

Freud's great discovery was the existence of the unconscious mind and its *modus operandi.* Normally, the conscious mind knows of its contents; it is "conscious" of the perceptions, memory-images, and ideas being used to solve problems. But the conscious part of the mind is only the "tip of the iceberg"; most of the dynamic interactions between the three energy-systems take place below the level of consciousness; that is, we are not "conscious" of them.

What Freud next discovered constitutes the "bitter but liberating wisdom" of his legacy. The relationship between conscious and unconscious is that of antagonists—evasion, deceit, denial, and conflict. "Our entire psychical activity is bent upon procuring pleasure and avoiding pain," Freud said. "It is simply the pleasure-principle which draws up the progamme of life's purpose." When the pleasure-principle comes into conflict with rejection by the real world, these energies are repressed into the unconscious, out of sight—and out of mind.

Repression is an inherent function of the mind. **All** minds repress; **all** of mankind is in a repressed condition. Since repression is the source of our neuroses, all mankind is neurotic. Neuroses, therefore, are not to be found only in a few unfortunate individuals, as we previously believed. Neurosis is universal. No one is mentally "healthy." We differ only in the degree of our inner conflict.

The unconscious mind is a reservoir of blocked-off energies. They cannot go away or lie dormant. Energies, by definition, must **do** something. So they must find an outlet, even by devious channels that the conscious mind refuses to recognize. They drive us to do things we don't understand and may want to disown. This is one of Freud's far-reaching discoveries: "unconscious motivation." We humans—far from being the rational beings portrayed by Western (Greek) tradition—behave primarily from deep-seated, uncontrollable, and undiscerned irrational impulses. The "essence of man" is not at all what we thought it was.

All neurosis represents a flight from direct confrontation with reality, and in this compromise our humanness is denied, distorted, and transmogrified into pain. And pain—disguised beyond recognition—is what we must finally deal with, commonly with aspirin and alcohol.

As Freud saw it, man is the animal that represses his fundamental pleasure-drives into unconsciousness in accordance with the demands of society to repress himself. Indeed, Freud concluded that man's superiority over the other animals is his capacity for repression and neurosis.

The whole point of Freud's theory and therapy is "nothing more than the discovery of the unconscious." The science of psychology "will consist in translating unconscious processes into conscious ones," and psychotherapy will assist the individual in bringing to light the discordant events of his unconscious mind so he can realize a more harmonious cooperation between his psychic energy-systems.

Virtually all schools of psychotherapy, from Freud's day to ours, take their cues from the master: they are designed to help us come to terms with the unacknowledged contents of our repressed unconscious minds. Some therapies attempt to strengthen the ego so it can better handle transactions—to "cope" better; others attempt to alter our responses to the world by altering our perception of it; and some have set their sights on the grandest goal of all: the abolition of repression—achieving "integration" or "individuation"—so that we might know, at last, the experience of wholeness.

Opposition to Freud's theories flared even before they were published. Colleagues and laymen roundly denounced his interest in hypnosis and his notions about the psychic origins of hysteria (everyone knew that such problems had **physiological** origins). Further, he had begun to produce massive new theories on the structure and dynamics of the unconscious mind. What made them threatening was their empirical foundations, their logical consistency, and the fact that they struck down time-honored assumptions. "I do not think our cures can compete with those of Lourdes," he wrote, with a tincture of bitters. "There are so many more people who believe in the miracles of the Blessed Virgin than in the existence of the unconscious." The more he was denounced, the more insistent he became. His mentors and former teachers, one by one, disowned him—Brücke, Meynert, Breuer. The Vienna Medical Society attacked him for his "crack-brain ideas." The University of Vienna—his alma mater—scornfully denied him a post. For his conjecture that our neuroses have sexual origins, he was labeled by the popular press a deviant and pornographer. By the time he was in his mid-forties, he had joined Darwin in the eye of the storm.

Although Freud's last years were a shining triumph, they were darkened by pain and sorrow. In 1923 he underwent surgery for cancer of the jaw, and his death seemed imminent (in fact he still had sixteen years to live); but larger than his physical suffering was the collapse of the civilization he had known.

He was on Hitler's hit list. His books were burned in 1933. "At least I have been burned in good company," he said. On May 21, 1938, the Gestapo invaded his apartment. They seized his passport and money, ransacked the rooms, rummaged through papers, and destroyed his books. Freud endured it all calmly.

His friends finally persuaded him to leave Austria, but the Nazis held out for an enormous ransom. The princess of Greece offered a quarter-million Austrian schillings on deposit in Vienna, but the Nazis balked, demanding more. President Franklin Roosevelt interceded, and the money was finally taken.

On June 4, 1938, in a wheelchair, with some salvaged furniture, books, and antiquities, Freud bade farewell to Vienna. With him were Martha, his daughter Anna, a few friends, and his chow dog Lun. They boarded the Orient Express for Paris and two days later were in London, safe from the Holocaust.

Typically, after resting briefly, he resumed his work schedule at their new home. He rose at eight, checked with his doctor, saw a patient, lunched; then wrote, saw more patients, walked in his garden, tended flowers, and played with Lun ("she always behaves psycho-analytically").

He had only a year to live. The painful cancer progressed, and he died on September 23, 1939. His body was cremated without religious ceremony, and his ashes were placed in an old Grecian vase he had brought with him from Vienna. The marble column beneath the vase is inscribed simply: SIGMUND FREUD 1856–1939.

The voice of the intellect is a soft one, but it does not rest until it has gained a hearing.

I became aware of my destiny: to belong to the critical minority as opposed to the unquestioning majority.

One must learn to put up with some measure of uncertainty.

Reflections

1 The developmental sequence of young monkeys—and by implication of human beings (pp. 116ff.)—makes a sort of sound common sense. Put into your own words why, in terms of psychological development, the sequence seems to be so important.

To oversimply matters somewhat, it is as if Freud supplied to us the sick half of psychology, and we must now fill it out with the healthy half.

ABRAHAM MASLOW

The curiosity of the human race is most evident in children. A child's innocent question will often give the adult to pause, and ponder carefully the answer. But there are other things than answers to be careful of when dealing with a child.

JACK WILLIAMSON

Lord, deliver me from myself.

SIR THOMAS BROWNE

Your OKness does not depend on another person.

ROBERT DAVIDSON

2 According to the Putneys (see marginal quote on p. 120), Americans are "hungry for the approval of others." Does that make sense to you? Why are we this way?

3 Do you agree with the statement (p. 119) that "the price we pay is very dear" for wearing masks? As you see it, what is that price?

4 It isn't uncommon to hear someone say, "I don't know who I am." What do you think this person is trying to say? Have you ever said this?

5 Ponder the pictures on p. 128. These paintings were entitled "*Passing the Buck*" by the artist Dick Sargent. To use the psychological term, this series depicts the displacement of hostility. Psych it out: **Why** do we **displace** our hostilities in this manner?

6 What do you think of Oedipus's vow to himself—"I will not stop until I understand myself"? Is this a noble goal, in your estimation? Does this determination of Oedipus frighten you? What are its dangers? What are its rewards?

7 Criticize the analysis of the meaning of innocence on pp. 122–123. Where in this description do you find yourself (if at all)? Is the state of dependence an enjoyable state?

8 Ponder the painting by Picasso (p. 129) entitled *Girl Before a Mirror.* How many persons (remember that the Latin word *persona* means "mask"—see p. 119) are in the painting? How many persons do you think the girl perceives?

9 Zero in on the problem of dealing with those who would "[provide] us with the answers before we have asked the questions" (pp. 124–125). Do you agree with the problem as stated in this chapter? How would you suggest that we confront such answer-givers?

10 Note the sequence of stages in Gregory Bateson's "progress in awareness" (p. 123, Box). Restate in your own terms the steps he describes. Does Bateson's description sound like an accurate accounting of the way we grow?

11 As you reflect on the so-called Law of Pathei Mathos (pp. 130–131), are you inclined to agree that there exists such a human pattern that might be thus designated as a "law"? What is meant by "suffering" in this case? Can you describe the human pathways by which suffering could lead to wisdom?

Lifetime

2-4

A human life is structured; it unfolds in phases, and (metaphorically) we journey along "the path of life" as though it were a sort of road map leading on in a general direction. Direction—? Is life then goal-directed? Are we driven, deeply and perhaps unconsciously, toward something or away from something? Is life inherently meaningful, carrying us toward a telos, or is it meaning-less? This chapter describes what happens experientially as we live and grow and meet the challenge of each phase. It suggests that precious insights are to be gained both from an overview of our common phasic condition and from locating where we ourselves and others are on the journey. Finally, Tolstoy's account of Ivan Ilytch stands as a shrill warning to all of us.

All the World's a Stage . . .

1 Each single life/time is a living drama played out in space and time against the backdrop of eternity.

> All the world's a stage
> And all the men and women merely players:
> They have their exits and their entrances;
> And one man in his time plays many parts.

In each life, the curtain has gone up and the play is in progress. We haven't read the script; the plot remains unknown. We can't foresee the scenes yet to be played out or when the play will end because, as in live theater, the plot is developed *extempore* as line follows line and scene follows scene.

2 On rare occasions, however, we are able to see and feel, in a single sweep of comprehension, the whole of a life/time. Such a vision may flash through our minds after reading a biography or after watching a drama with a death scene. Ofttimes at a funeral we are left in a reflective mood as we stand at the end of a life just completed.

Only when the third-act curtain has been rung down can we see that every part relates to, and sheds light upon, every other part. We can trace the major motifs of later life back to their origins. We can see the inception of strengths that are to fulfill and flaws that are to result in failure; and we can point to the decisions and diverging paths that made all the difference.

Mapping a Lifetime

3 So many attempts have been made to discern the stages of life that one almost despairs of achieving a reasonably sound picture of a universal lifetime. For example, a human life comes in three stages, argued both Auguste Comte, the founder of sociology, and Søren Kierkegaard, the father of existentialism. Comte decided that the properly lived life will always move from a theological, through a metaphysical, into a scientific phase and will display a natural progression from a mythic understanding of nature to an apprehension of empirical causal connections. No, said Kierkegaard, just the opposite: life always begins in an aesthetic stage driven by sense and impulse, matures to an ethical stage guided by abstract principles, and culminates in a religious stage during which faith, not reason, carries the individual to his own personal truth and commitment. Take your pick.

4 Since time began (almost) the Hindus have held that a life is naturally divided into four stages, each stage corresponding to what the spiritual self should be doing and seeking as it progresses through life. The first of the four *ashramas* ("stages") is the preparatory time of the student, years of study and discipline. The second stage is that of a married "householder," a man of the world with a family, a vocation to support them, and a responsible position in the life of the community. The third stage begins around the age of fifty, traditionally, when his worldly obligations end, when the skin starts to wrinkle and his hair turns grey, or when his first grandchild is born. This is "retirement"; he begins to withdraw from the world, spends more and more time alone, meditates and searches for spiritual strength to abandon the world. During the last stage of life, that of the *sannyasi,* he dwells alone in the forest; he speaks little, possesses only his loincloth, begging bowl and water jar. Having fulfilled all his obligations to the world, he gives full attention to his spiritual needs in order to ascend beyond the gods and get nearer to God. His soul, properly prepared, achieves peace and is ready to be dissolved into the Brahman, the Universal Spirit.

5 Embedded in Japanese folklore is a fivefold division of the human lifespan. "At ten, an animal; at twenty, a lunatic; at thirty, a failure; at forty, a fraud; at fifty, a criminal." To this joyous assessment, someone had to add: "At sixty, one begins advising one's friends; at seventy (realizing that everything said has been misunderstood) one keeps quiet and is taken for a sage" (Joseph Campbell).

And "at eighty?" "What was the question?"

6 Sigmund Freud discerned five distinct stages in the development of a young human being from age zero to about eighteen. These are his famous oral, anal, phallic, latent, and genital stages, after which, according to Freud, not much happens by way of growth through the rest of our lives. This rather dull prognosis led Daniel Levinson, professor of psychiatry at Yale, to comment, "Psychologists speak as if development goes on to age six, or perhaps eighteen. Then there's a long plateau in which random things occur, and then, around age sixty or sixty-five, a period of decline sets in to be studied by gerontologists." This is a false analysis, Levinson says, a widely held myth. For not only do our early experiences **not** enable predictions regarding the quality of later life, but the later stages can in themselves be enormously new and exciting, filled with challenge, stress, change, and fulfillment. Based on current knowledge, says Levinson, "there **is** something called adult development, an unfolding, just as there is earlier" during our growing-up years.

7 The most impressive chopping up of a human lifespan was accomplished by the Bard himself in *As You Like It* (II, vii, 139). Shakespeare iambicized the "seven ages" of a man. The first age is "the infant, / Mewling and puking in his nurse's arms. / And then the whining school-boy" with "shining morning face, creeping like a snail / Unwillingly to school." The next age is that of the lover, "Sighing like a furnace," then the soldier "Full of strange oaths," followed by the middle-aged man of means "Full of wise saws." During the sixth age he has "spectacles on nose," and "his big manly voice" returns toward a "childish treble." The last age "That ends this strange eventful history, / Is second childishness, and mere oblivion, / Sans teeth, sans eyes, sans taste, sans everything."

The Ground Plan

8 There is undoubtedly some truth in all these pictures of how life progresses and what life has in store for us. Most of them, however, focus on life as Greek tragedy when it could just as well be seen as comedic irony. After such downbeat prognostications of the later stages of life, the more accurate portrayal of the human adventure, based on data from the modern sciences, comes as a joyous relief; every phase of life has its rewards and satisfactions as well as its wounds and scars.

Our days, our deeds, all we achieve or are, Lay folded in our infancy.

John Trowbridge

Scientific studies have discovered that there exists within us a psychophysiological timetable that provides a plot for each individual human drama. The unfolding of this ground plan gives our lives a predictable structure and allows us to achieve a general overview of a full human life from birth to death.

According to Erik Erikson and other developmental psychologists, life unfolds in a sequence of challenges, each of which must be resolved before one can move on to the next challenge. Each challenge can be viewed as a genetic psychophysiological readiness to incorporate specific experiences into our developing selves. As each challenge is met, growth takes place and we can move ahead, on schedule, to face the next readiness period. Each phase of our lives literally grows out of the successful completion of the previous challenge. The precise schedule of these challenges is unique to each individual and determines the phasic nature of life.

The following sections might be read in a special way to get a feel for the whole of a life cycle, to see the human enterprise, from birth until death, in a single vision, as One. Perhaps reading rapidly through all the sections several times would accomplish this better than studying details that, in this case, may be of secondary importance.

INFANCY TO CHILDHOOD

9 **INFANCY** During the first twelve to fifteen months of life, we awaken to the world about us. We are wholly dependent; our needs must be met by others. Therefore, the crucial challenge of this phase is the development of a feeling of trust, and the depth of our trust depends upon how well we are cared for. Whether we develop this capacity at all is out of our hands; we are pawns of our environment.

For young children it is primarily experience that determines character, but for the more mature person it is character that determines experience.

HAIM GINOTT

If these months are pleasant times, then we begin to open ourselves to life. We can feel hunger, pain, loneliness—whatever is authentic—and know that there will be someone to fulfill our needs. There is someone who cares. Thus we learn in a natural way to be ourselves and to remain open to the actions of others. We trust them. By contrast, if the environment is capricious or hostile, we become fearful; we remain on guard; we cannot afford to open ourselves to others. Quite realistically, we have no grounds for trusting.

This phase is critical. If we don't develop trust and openness during this period, then severe conflicts lie ahead. Some personality theorists go much further and believe that if we don't experience love during this early period, then love is lost from our lives forever. We will never love—or be loved.

10 **EARLY CHILDHOOD** A new phase begins when we learn to stand, walk about, and get into things. Better motor control brings whole new worlds within range of our curious hands. We venture into new rooms, play with new toys (everything is a toy), and find drawers and cupboards to explore.

In youth we learn; in age we understand.

MARIE VON EBNER-ESCHENBACH

The essential challenge of early childhood is striking a balance between an unbounded freedom to do anything (which we want) and the necessary limits and controls (which others want)—parameters within which we must exist. Guidelines must be consistent and firm. Our neophilic impulse to explore must not be dampened, but we must learn to accept limits; we must learn to live with the frustrations of not being able to do everything we want. If we can find a satisfactory balance between freedom and restriction, then we can continue, safely and happily, to explore the world about us. But if there is too much freedom, we will learn to resist all authority that would impose any limitations upon us; or if there is too much restraint, then we gradually lose the urge to explore life and give in to a neophobic passivity. Either extreme sets us up for problems that will return to bother us later.

11 **MIDDLE CHILDHOOD** The next challenge is a different kind: it is the discovery that other people come in two varieties—and that we are one of the two. We awaken to the fact that, physiologically, we are different from others in our family and from friends.

The little ones leaped, and shouted, and laugh'd
And all the hills echoed.
WILLIAM BLAKE

The psychological challenge of this phase is the successful acceptance of ourselves as boy or girl within the context of all our relationships. That is, we proceed to clarify and understand our sex-role identity. With positive guidance from authorities, our sex role is accepted without undue stress or guilt. We begin to feel that being a girl or a boy is natural and good, that it was not a mistake or terrible accident that we were not born of the other sex.

I hesitate (but only briefly) to mention that some noteworthy male thinkers held some interesting ideas on gender. Plato, Aristotle, and Saint Thomas Aquinas all believed that women are mistakes. According to Aquinas, nature always tries to produce a male, but a female results when something goes wrong (*mas occasionatum*); more than that, she is a defective and accidental creature (*deficiens et occasionatum*). Plato seems to have held a similar notion: "A woman is merely a lesser man." No philosopher, as far as I know, has suggested that men are mistakes, though I'm sure an interesting argument could be constructed to support the notion.

Those who employ Freudian concepts hold that there is also an Oedipal conflict to be resolved at this stage. The daughter finds herself in profound competition with her mother as she comes to realize they are of the same sex; similarly, the son feels a competitiveness toward his father—each for the love and sex-role approval of the other parent. The resolution of these conflicts leads to a new set of relationships all around, based upon the realities of sex identity.

Self and personality emerge from experience. If they are open to their experience, doing what "feels right" proves to be a competent and trustworthy guide to behavior which is truly satisfying.
CARL ROGERS

12 **LATE CHILDHOOD** About the age of six there begins a longer, smoother period of growth that lasts until the beginning of adolescence, a duration of five

or six years. It is a time for consolidation of the growth gains we have made so far. It is a sort of rest period from the ordeals of rapid change. However, if earlier growth challenges haven't been resolved, this "rest period" may be a sort of catch-up time for further resolution of these conflicts.

If all goes well, there is a deepening sense of identity as the distinctive elements of our personalities become more coherent. Personality is still developing, to be sure; it is still shaky and tender. Our selves are not yet firmly grounded. Therefore, if our environment is especially hostile and rejecting at this time, painful feelings of inadequacy can result. Acceptance by our peers at this point is important; we seek it aggressively, though not often directly. We want to feel that we are like others, and that others approve of us.

If all goes well during this stabilizing phase, then the stage is set for the next critical ordeal of our life cycle: adolescence.

THE ADOLESCENT YEARS

13 EARLY ADOLESCENCE With the sudden physiological growth that initiates adolescence, we enter a time of "storm and stress," an upheaval that affects not only us but the lives of all who are within range.

Adolescence is transition. Heretofore, each of us has been a child. We have been treated as children, and our thoughts and emotions have been those of a child. We have been passing through the conflicts characteristic of childhood.

All this rapidly changes as the transition to adulthood begins. We identify increasingly with adults, and others treat us more and more as young adults. We are being thrust into adulthood. The allurement of freedom and independence beckon, but self-doubt and fear of responsibility draw us back. Adolescence is marked by spurts of growth and regression. All the while, the lingering little-boy or little-girl feelings haunt us; we are pulled and torn, not knowing from day to day which—and who—we are.

The prime challenge of early adolescence is the acceptance of the physiological and obviously sexual changes our body undergoes. For a time we may feel like spirits inhabiting an alien organism. It changes almost daily; it is erratic and unpredictable. Alterations in body chemistry intensify our emotions, and many of them are new to us. Hormonal changes bring on dramatic, uncontrollable moodswings.

As if all this weren't enough, we are hit by an excruciating realization that society has norms for our sexual characteristics and behavior. Society, we discover, expects us to grow in a specific way, and we anxiously wonder whether we will ever measure up to its standards. Underlying all this is a diffuse, undefined, all-pervasive sexual uneasiness.

But eventually, with encouragement, we adjust to these drastic changes and accept this new body. We find—with mixed feelings—that others begin to respond differently to this body. A young woman faces the fact of her sexual attractiveness with embarrassment, self-consciousness, and delight; a young man begins to have exhilarating sexual feelings, but they may be compromised by anxiety, guilt, and bewilderment.

Token Separation

Several recent, extensive studies suggest that the number of adolescents who achieve a decisive articulation of the self is diminishing. Elizabeth Douvan and Joseph Adelson found that a serious testing of values and ideology occurs only in a minority of adolescents. It appears that real independence is accomplished in lower-class and some upper-middle-class youngsters because these two extremes are so different from the core adolescent culture. But in studying the "silent majority" of adolescents, they found only token parent-child conflict and therefore token maturity and autonomy. They found that the peer group for many adolescents is only used to learn and display social skills—a kind of playpen designed to keep the children out of harm's way. Although for many the peer group is an arena for confrontation of self, for many more it acts to hinder differentiation and growth.

Developmental Psychology Today

In summary, the central challenge of early adolescence is to be able to hold on tight while our bodies and emotions undergo dramatic alterations, carrying us through the transition into adulthood, and getting us ready for mating and parenting.

14 **Midadolescence** During midadolescence physical and psychological turmoil continues, but as we feel more like adults our preoccupation shifts to the problem of independence from authority—that is, independence from other adults. This is the challenge of separation. Feeling increasingly like separate persons, we set out on our own. In the language of space technology, it is time to go on internal power. We venture further in our exploration of life, experimenting with a variety of new experiences. It is a time of trial and error, savoring successes but learning to accept failure when we don't achieve our goals. Independence means learning to set goals for ourselves, and inevitably some will be unrealistic. The challenge is learning to accept failure without feeling like failures—that is, without loss of self-esteem. Gradually we learn how to set more realistic goals.

Mother to daughter: "I love you enough to let you be free and grow up." (Or was it daughter to mother?)

Lori Villamil

Separation often involves a painful and prolonged revolt against authority, against parents and other immediate "controllers" (real or imagined) and also symbols of control. But while seeking independence we commonly displace our feelings toward all authorities who, we think, might keep us from gaining the desired separation. It is perhaps a hackneyed phrase, but "the crisis of authority" still describes accurately the experience of midadolescence. The more we have been restricted and repressed, the louder our protests and the sharper our attacks against the restraints and the restrainers; or if not permitted direct attack, then the greater will be our use of scapegoats.

The separation process produces great ambivalence. We feel loyalty to those who have cared for us, and separation is painful for everyone. And when others are hurt (we usually say that "we hurt them," though in fact this is not the case at all), then we feel guilt. To ease our guilt feelings we seek the approval of those we hurt; that is, we want to be forgiven. But we cry out for the very thing that can not be given. Parents and authorities feel rejected, too; they usually do not understand, and cannot accept, our "separating behavior." A part of the individuating process, therefore, is learning to accept without excess remorse and guilt the fact that we have to proceed with the separation without the approval of the significant others involved in the process. Depending upon the maturity of our parents, it is easy to see how manipulative games and bitter conflicts can complicate the midadolescent years and often thwart altogether the successful establishment of separate identities. Indeed, for years to come, our parents can linger on in us, and we in them, in a perpetual, agonizing entanglement.

During these troublesome times, we seek the support and understanding of our peers; and an important feature of the midadolescent years is "peer conformity." The more we are misunderstood and rejected by our parents, the more we need the support of our peers who are themselves having similar experiences. They can understand.

15 **Late Adolescence** If these challenges have been met with continued self-esteem, then late adolescence will be characterized by a strong sense of self. We feel more like distinct, whole persons.

With a smoothly functioning self, we can take on ever-greater responsibilities. Indeed, we enjoy responsibility and the satisfactions it brings. Underlying all of life's sundry experiences is a developing strength that carries us through.

If we are on schedule, and our feelings about both body and self are positive, then we will have developed, smoothly and naturally, the capacity for intimacy, not merely sexual intimacy, but a sense of honesty and openness in all our relationships. The capacity for sexual intimacy is but a single—though often a central—manifestation of the comprehensive capacity for trusting, empathizing, and sharing. The better we feel about ourselves the more we long for intimacy with others.

Sixty years ago I knew everything. Today I know nothing. Education is the progressive discovery of our own ignorance.

Will Durant

Therefore, the challenge of late adolescence is the consolidation of a sense of self in relating to other persons, in developing a capacity for intimacy, and in gradually laying to rest our doubts and fears about what we can accomplish as unique selves, newly emerged on the scene and ready for life.

The Maturing Years

16 **Early Adulthood** (about twenty to thirty). Before the advent of the 1970s, life-span research had concentrated almost exclusively on the phases from infancy through adolescence; little careful study had been made of life's adult stages. When research began in these phases, the results were surprising and some earlier assumptions regarding the featureless plateau of adulthood were removed from textbooks.

We dare not call ourselves philosophers, and yet we all are, aren't we, or we could not get out of bed in the morning. Unless you plan, the night before, to be alive at dawn, you will not stir.

Ray Bradbury

The early adult phase is primarily a time of mating and parenting, but the basic challenge of this stage is the development of one's capacity for intimacy. Both physically and psychologically we are prepared for intimacy and sexual activity (they are not synonymous) and the rearing of offspring. Intimacy is not only the capacity for fulfilling sexual companionship, but is more basically a quality of openness and trust that is essential to both marriage and the well-being of the offspring.

This phase of life is characterized by one writer, Linda Wolfe, in this way: "This is a time of life when spouses are wooed and wed, and when adolescent friendships are cast off if they no longer seem desirable, or consolidated if they seem worthy of future investment." New dependencies replace old ones.

Dr. Levinson describes this as a time of "getting into the adult world." We experiment with society's defined roles, rules, and responsibilities. This can be a time for creation and productivity, a time to channel one's creative energies into a variety of activities, of which parenting may be only one. Many of us choose our vocations at this time, as well as various long-lasting avocations. All are ways of expressing the essence of our own personalities. Our creative urges can be realized in art forms, in the professions, in roles that serve others, in competitive business ventures, in sports, and so on.

No one should have to walk alone.

PHUONG DO

During these years we may achieve for the first time a clear picture of the capacities and limitations that we will have to live with for the rest of our lives. We may find that we must accept some basic limitations. At the same time we can develop a feeling for our growth potential and begin to set realistic goals in terms of what we truly are.

Spoken of John Keats: He always knew he would die young, therefore he saw as much beauty as he could.

On Being Human (TV series)

17 **INTERMEDIATE ADULTHOOD** (roughly thirty to forty). The age of thirty, give or take a year or two, is another time of transition that, for some, mounts to a "growth crisis" that jars us out of our ruts and forces us to face new alternatives. The basic factor in this transition is a feeling that some sort of change is imperative. Stagnation is felt to be a real possibility and must be avoided. Dr. Roger Gould describes stagnation as a feeling that some deep and personal side of the self "is striving to be accounted for." It is a time for the reassessment of priorities, relationships, commitments, and goals. Men and women both develop the feeling that the careers and lifestyles they have settled into have somehow become too confining. Such roles are perceived to be "a violation or betrayal of a dream they now had to pursue" (Levinson's words). Marriages that were apparently stable often become strained; marriage partners turn elsewhere for companionship and fulfillment. Women frequently discover that they have fallen into the "suburban housewife syndrome" and proceed to change their roles by seeking outside interests—taking a job, returning to school, thinking of a career. "The brief transitional period may occasion considerable inner turmoil—depression, confusion, struggle with the environment and within oneself—or it may involve a quieter reassessment and intensification of effort" (Levinson).

Following this initial transition, the thirties are best described as a time for settling down and seeking stability. Inner turmoil now vanishes: the adolescent search for identity and the early adult quest for intimacy are past. Life turns outward; concerns become more objective. Men and women both become concerned about their niche in society and about advancing their careers.

The late thirties are frequently characterized by a renewed search for autonomy. During mid- and late adolescence our strivings were directed toward the discovery of self and autonomy; but during our twenties some of our gains are lost. No sooner do we separate from parents than we reestablish dependencies

Treasure each other in the recognition that we do not know how long we shall have each other . . .

JOSHUA LOTH LIEBMAN

"But you can't go through life applying Heisenberg's Uncertainty Principle to *everything*."

with mates and mentors, and, like belated obligations, these must eventually be dealt with. One's success in finding a compatible mate is felt and faced earlier. But now, during the late thirties, there emerges a strong need to break dependency ties with older mentors, especially those in one's job or profession. To accomplish this, men and women commonly switch jobs and even relocate themselves vocationally and geographically.

The essential challenge of this phase of life is one of growth and accomplishment in the world. If we can assume responsibilities with assurance and skill, then the attainment of goals can bring deep satisfaction. We can enjoy the fruits of our labors. Autonomy and self-esteem can deepen. Our children grow. Social and material gains are made. With increased knowledge and skill in living, we can experience an ever-widening expansion of awareness. These can be fulfilling years.

They can also be dangerous years. If we make unrealistic demands upon ourselves, set unattainable goals, and slide into a pattern of failure, then life, to some degree, can become hellish, and trouble may lie ahead. Furthermore, if we become so absorbed in attaining social and material goals that we neglect to set goals that would promote the growth of ourselves as persons, then the stage is set for us to approach the upcoming years unprepared and empty.

For looming just ahead is a crucial challenge that will largely determine whether the rest of our life/time will be worth living.

18 **Middle Adulthood** (about forty to fifty). The challenge of the middle years can be the most precarious time of life since the turmoil of the adolescent transition. This also is a time of transition. This "midlife crisis"—which begins around forty, give or take a few years—now calls upon all the resources we have been able to develop.

The middle years are a time of taking stock. One arrives at a point where he no longer assumes youthfulness; he no longer takes it for granted. He realizes that the youthful phase is passing and that there is nothing he can do about it. The essential challenge might be stated: "I have lived up the first half of my life/time, and I realize there is only so much time left and my life will end. I experience that I am mortal. I will die. Now, what do I really want to do with the rest of the time I have left?"

If you don't know where you are going, you will probably end up somewhere else.

LAWRENCE J. PETER

Underlying the midlife crisis is a deeply felt anxiety that is completely democratic: it comes alike to rich and poor, introverts and extroverts, successful entrepreneurs and social dropouts. It is ontological; it is a part of our being human. Failure to negotiate the rough seas at this time portends discontent, while success brings the promise of further growth and greater fulfillment.

Whatever one's state of life, a time of introspection begins. The worldly symbols of success may have been attained, but such accomplishments feel empty and meaningless. "There's more to life than this. There must be. I don't know what it is, but I'm going to find out." Thus an inner anxiety—"Is this all there is?"—is translated into new forms of action: "What have I got to lose?"

Typically, you find a businessman who has spent his life in management, banking, or the like; or a blue-collar worker who has been a responsible provider and "solid citizen." By all criteria he is to be judged successful and com-

WHAT TIME IS IT?

It is a common experience that time for a child seems to pass much more slowly than time for the adult. A year goes by rapidly for a man compared to his recall of childhood years. Seymour Kety has reviewed available information, obtained by the nitrous-oxide technique, on over-all cerebral blood flow and oxygen consumption in man, and finds a distinct correlation of these functions with age. He reports a rapid fall in both circulation and oxygen consumption of the brain from childhood through adolescence followed by a more gradual but progressive decline through the remaining age span. Slowing of cerebral oxygen consumption with advancing years would, according to our considerations, make time appear to pass faster in old age, as indeed it does.

HUDSON HOAGLAND

Percepts of space and time are related to metabolic rate since changes in the latter bring about concomitant perceptual changes. Physiological clocks run fast when metabolic rate is increased, while clock time is overestimated, subjects arrive early to appointments, time appears to pass more slowly. When the physiological clocks run slowly (corresponding to a decrease of metabolic rate), clock time is underestimated, subjects arrive late to their appointments, time flies by rapidly, the days seem to fly by "like magic."

Another manifestation of the relation between metabolic rate and time sense is exemplified by Lecomte du Noüy's experiments [involving healing of tissue] . . . du Noüy calculated the impression of "our passage" in time for a twenty- and fifty-year-old man to be four and six times faster respectively than for a five-year-old child.

ROLAND FISCHER
J. T. FRASER (ED.)
The Voices of Time

Nel mezzo del cammin do nostra vita
Mi ritrovai per una selva oscura,
Che la diritta via era smarrita.
In the middle of the journey of our life
I came to myself in a dark wood,
where the straight way was lost.

Dante

The life so short, the craft so long to learn.

Hippocrates

mended by society's standards. Inside, however, he experiences a sense of unfinished business. He's sure that he has so far lived the kind of life he should have lived: he chose a vocation, established himself, attained a degree of security and stability. But in all of this he senses a contradiction. In effect, he is saying: "I'm successful, but I'm not sure that I've become anything. As a person I feel that, somehow, I got left behind."

Typical also is the housewife and mother. It gradually dawns that she has neglected her own life. There are things she wants to do, and the time has come for her to pursue her own interests. She has devoted years to the defined tasks of housewife and/or mother. She has more or less fulfilled society's expectations of her role and responsibilities. But in doing so, she finds that she has denied many of her own profoundly human needs. At the very worst, she may have discovered that Bernard Shaw's bitter axiom is true: "If you begin by sacrificing yourself to those you love, you will end by hating those to whom you have sacrificed yourself."

One study revealed that almost 90 percent of the over-thirty-five-year-old women attending college are there because they are unhappy with their lives and have become uneasy with the state of their personal growth. Many expressed their discontent in such words as these:

> When I graduated from high school I was thinking of a career, and I went to college at the time to prepare for it. But in my first year I met my husband and we got married. I dropped out and took a job so my husband could continue his education. By the time he finished his degree and got a job we had two children.
>
> But that was more than ten years ago. Now that the children are older I feel strongly that I should go back to school and pick up where I left off.

All these women indicated that they never gave up hope of completing their education. In recent years most of them came to see their marriage/family condition as an interlude in (or interruption of) their own "fulfillment as human beings."

Several events may coalesce and contribute to the onset of this stock-taking period. (1) Our children may have achieved separation and we are no longer needed as parents. We have been freed of long-term responsibilities that have been taken for granted. Not to be needed in this familiar role can initiate an "agonized appraisal" of our purpose in living. (2) With this change of roles, husband and wife often encounter each other for the first time in many years. They find that they are not the same selves. Without knowing it, both have changed, and rather suddenly their relationship undergoes an "agonized reappraisal." Often a new relationship must develop. We may also find that we have moved in different directions, and the reestablishment of the intimacy essential to carry us through later years without profound loneliness may be difficult. It may be doubly difficult if such intimacy was never accomplished in the young-adult years.

To some extent, men and women differ in their experience of this middle-years challenge. Menopause may force upon a woman a self-image crisis that a man is spared. If a woman's primary feelings of worth have long been associated with her role as a mother, then the loss of her childbearing capacity—which frequently coincides with the time when her children reach young adulthood, leave home, and no longer need her as a mother—may create severe readjustment problems.

Physical appearance is also a common cause of self-image problems. If a girl's feelings of self-esteem derive primarily from her physical/sexual attractiveness, then as she sees these qualities fade, her self-esteem may also fade. She may feel that she possesses no other qualities that could be a realistic basis for any continued self-esteem. She may feel an irreparable, tragic loss. She may spend her later years trying to recapture the attractiveness that she (and, she believes, others) so valued during the mating years. She may try to perpetuate the image of physical/sexual attractiveness that others can see has vanished. Coquettishness at twenty-two may be quite in order; at fifty-five it indicates a confusion of roles and may appear to others as a painful anachronism.

At forty or forty-five a man may note that some gray hair is showing and that younger people are calling him "sir." He may smile to himself and recognize that others' responses toward him are changing. (He may also misinterpret the "sir" and think it has something to do with respect.) Just as a woman may attempt to perpetuate the myth of youthful beauty, a man may try to recapture the image of a youthfulness that is passing away.

Failure to deepen one's sense of autonomy and authenticity during the middle years—as opposed to the single-minded pursuit of external accomplishments—renders the future precarious. The foundations of integrity upon which the deeper experiences of our later years must build are shaky in the extreme. This is a vital matter in the inevitable aging process.

Autonomous men and women who have practiced authenticity will be more realistic. Having never attempted to be other than what they are, they can accept change just as it comes, without myth. The autonomous individual values himself; others' responses to him may change, but his self-esteem remains intact. The later years can arrive more smoothly without problems reaching crisis proportions.

Having weathered the midlife transition, the rest of the forties becomes a period of restabilization and renaissance. Roger Gould calls it a time of "relief from the internal tearing apart of the immediately previous years." It is a time of calm. Marriages generally become more stable. Men and women turn more to their mates for understanding, sympathy, and affection. Tragedy and loss can be accepted with patient strength and without the rage and remorse of early years.

Therefore, the central challenge of the middle years is the cluster of decisions regarding how we want to live and what we want to become during the rest of our lives. The resolution of the middle years' challenge depends largely upon our capacity to reset meaningful goals for ourselves in terms of who we are and the life/time we have left to us.

19 **Later Adulthood** (from fifty or fifty-five on). If the middle years' challenge has been met with some degree of success, then the later adult years can be fulfilling. We will continue to grow, to actualize our goals, and simply to enjoy life. Our physiological processes will begin to decline; we may be afflicted with a variety of ailments. But today we know that in most instances our intellectual and emotional capacities can remain viable, and even expand. These faculties—the very substance of our existence—need not fade. To be sure,

The familiar lament, "I don't know who I am," once thought to belong only to the crisis of adolescence, to be resolved by the adult stage, is heard not only from teenagers but from adults of all ages. . . . A sad commentary on this is the increasing number of suicide attempts on the part of lonely aged people. Education, status, "success," material security or lack of it, seem to have little bearing upon the high degree of suffering, unhappiness, and loneliness found in the life of those who have found no focus of identity or pattern of meaning in their existence.

Aaron Ungersma

Sooner or later, life makes philosophers of us all.

Maurice Riseling

It is quite possible, Octavian, that when you die, you will die without ever having been alive.

"Mark Antony"
Cleopatra

If life is not a thrilling adventure, it is nothing.

Helen Keller

"It's all over, and you're out of danger."
"How can I be out of danger if I'm not dead?"

Rachel, Rachel

Into the Woods

In their delightful sad-sweet-happy Broadway play, *Into the Woods*, Stephen Sondheim and James Lapine employ childhood fables to sketch the strange growth-movement of us humans from the bright-eyed anticipations of youth to the cumbrous realities of adulthood, and beyond. Considerably beyond. The metaphor of traveling through the woods is based on the psychologist Bruno Bettelheim's depiction of the woods as "the place in which inner darkness is confronted and worked through; where uncertainty is resolved about who one is; and where one begins to understand who one wants to be."

"Once upon a time, in a far-off kingdom, there lived"—Cinderella, Little Red Ridinghood, Jack and his beans, Rapunzel, a Baker and his wife, at least two princes, and a dozen other characters from story-book fame. And, of course, a witch. All embark on "a journey of growth and discovery," each with his own dream. "The maiden, called Cinderella, wished more than anything, more than life, to go to the King's festival." Jack wished "more than anything, more than life, more than riches, that his cow would give him some milk." The Baker and his wife, a childless couple, "wished more than anything, more than life, more than riches, more than the moon, that they had a child." Rapunzel dreams of being released from her tower so she can see the world. Little Red Ridinghood wants only to get to her Grandmother's house with her basket of goodies.

"Into the woods, it's time to go, I hate to leave. I have to, though. Into the woods to Grandmother's house, I must begin the journey."

"You're certain of your way?" asked the Baker's Wife.

"Into the woods and down the dell. The path is straight, I know it well. . . . into the woods, then out of the woods, and home before dark!"

Each character enters the dark woods pursuing his dream, large or small; the plots thicken, and thicken, and thicken, and interweave into a bewildering string of challenges, frustrations, setbacks, and triumphs. The Witch (who has a daughter named Rapunzel) puts a curse of barrenness on the Baker and his wife, a curse that can be broken only if they can go into the woods and find "a cow as white as milk, a cape as red as blood, hair as yellow as corn, and a slipper as pure as gold." And so on, with complications.

"Their mission was simple: Into the woods without delay, but careful not to lose the way. Into the woods, who knows what may be lurking on the journey."

The spunky Little Red Ridinghood "hadn't gone far when she was greeted by a tall, dark, and hairy character"— who confesses that "there's no possible way to describe what you feel when you're talking to your meal. . . ." She gets eaten, of course.

Rapunzel, shut up for fourteen years in her isolated tower, wants to see the world. But the witch (her mother) wants to keep her at home. "Don't you know what's out there in the world? Stay with me," she implored as she stroked the girl's hair. "Princes wait there in the world, it's true—princes, yes, but wolves and humans, too. Stay at home. . . . Who out there could love you more than I? What's out there that I cannot supply? Stay with me, the world is dark and wild. Stay a child while you can be a child. With me."

Eventually Cinderella and Rapunzel both fall in love (in a way) with two princes, and they with the two maidens. But in classic style the two girls rebuff their princes, who sing: "Agony, beyond power of speech! When the one thing you want is the only thing out of your reach."

Little Red Ridinghood appears, looking "quite fashionable in her new wolf cape (she and Granny, still quite alive, had been freed from the wolf's stomach by the Baker). Jack, having killed the Giant, came down from the beanstalk with a goose and golden egg. The Baker's wife is pregnant. Rapunzel, after a rendezvous in the woods with her Prince (who is now blind after falling into a thicket), bore twins "and was living impoverished in the desert." But eventually her Prince found her, and her joyous tears "restored his vision." The other Prince, finally finding the foot that could fit into the glass slipper, "took Cinderella on his horse and rode off"; they were married, with her wicked sisters in attendance (but "vengeful pigeons swooped down upon them and pecked out their eyes, punishing them for their cruelty with blindness").

And "it came to pass that all that had seemed wrong was now right. The kingdom was filled with joy, and those who deserved to were certain to live a long and happy life."

"Or so they thought. . . ."

ACT TWO: "Once upon a time, later, in the same far-off kingdom, lived the young princess Cinderella, the wealthy lad Jack, and the Baker, his wife, and their newborn baby."

"Cinderella wished more than anything, more than footmen, to sponsor a festival."

"Jack wished more than anything, more than the moon, to return to his adventures in the sky."

"The Baker and his wife were wishing, too. For one thing, they wished their baby wouldn't cry so much. But they also wished, more than anything, more than life, more than the moon, more than riches, that they had more room in their cottage."

So the Baker and his wife squabbled incessantly over whether they should move, or not.

Everything had changed. "The woods seemed eerie, devastated. The birds no longer sang. The natural order of things was broken. Fear and uncertainty gripped the hearts of those who entered. It was a different world."

The Baker and his wife, having entered the forest, are "frightened by the shriek of a madwoman running through the woods"—Rapunzel had lost her mind.

"What are you doing here, Rapunzel?" the Witch (her mother) asked. "Oh, nothing!" she burbled. "You just locked me in a tower without company for fourteen years, then blinded my prince and banished me to a desert where I had little to eat and, again, no company. And then I bore twins!"

"I was just trying to be a good mother," the Witch offered contritely. "Stay with me. There's a giant running about."

The two Princes meet in the woods. "My Rapunzel has run off," Rapunzel's husband replies. "She's a changed woman. She has been subject to hysterical fits of crying, moods that no soul could predict. I know not what to do." He paused. "How is Cinderella?"

"She remains well," answered his brother vaguely. But Rapunzel's Prince knows something is amiss. Cinderella's Prince, it seems, is yearning for a beautiful girl who is asleep somewhere in a high tower, surrounded by a thicket of briars. "Agony! No frustration more keen, when the one thing you want is a thing that you've not even seen." And Rapunzel's Prince confesses that he too has fallen in love—with Snow White, who lies "unawakeable" in a glass casket "unbreakable." "Unmistakable agony! Is the way always barred?"

"Agony!" cried his brother.

"Misery!" moaned the other.

"But in the end they came to their senses and agreed that the best thing for now was to return to their wives."

CONTINUED

Then the Giant's wife comes looking for Jack, who had killed the Giant and stolen their gold, hen, and harp. "I WANT THE LAD WHO CLIMBED THE BEANSTALK!" As the Giantess moves off to find Jack, Rapunzel throws herself under her giant foot and is crushed. The Witch (her mother) softly laments, "This is the world I meant. Couldn't you listen? Couldn't you stay content, safe behind walls, as I could not? . . . No matter what you say, children won't listen. No matter what you know, children refuse to learn. . . . Children can only grow from something you love to something you lose. . . ."

They all go looking for Jack. The Baker's Wife crossed paths with Cinderella's Prince, who asks why her husband lets her wander alone in the woods. "May I kiss you?" he asks, and soon, of course, "as he gently enclosed her in his dark velvet embrace," she gets laid.

"What am I doing here?" she asks. "I'm in the wrong story."

"Foolishness can happen in the woods. . . . Right and wrong don't matter in the woods," rhapsodized the Prince, "only feelings." Later she asks, "Will we find each other in the woods again?" The Prince gazed down upon her and remembered that times like these are best cloaked in poetry. "Our moment, shimmering and lovely and sad. Leave the moment, just be glad for the moment that we had. Every moment is of moment when you're in the woods. . . . Now I must go off to slay a giant."

"What is it about these woods?" puzzles the Baker's Wife. She stood up and began walking the path "she had momentarily left behind, back to her child, back to her husband. "After all," she told herself, "there are vows, there are ties, there are needs, there are standards, there are shouldn'ts and shoulds."

"Why not both?" she thought, pausing to pin up her hair again. "Must it all be either less or more, either plain or grand? Is it always 'or'? Is it never 'and'? That's what woods are for," she thought to herself with a shrug. . . .

"Now I understand," she said with a look of contentment on her face. "And it's time to leave the woods."

Soon thereafter the Baker's Wife is felled by a tree and buried in a giant footprint. Each and every person has now suffered setbacks and tragedies, and they all set about blaming one another for their pain, or supposed pain. They end by agreeing to blame the Witch—"It's *your* fault!" they all shout.

"Told a little lie, stole a little gold, broke a little vow, did you?" taunts the Witch.

"Had to get your prince, had to get your cow, had to get your wish, doesn't matter how—anyway, it doesn't matter now. . . .

"Of course, what really matters is the blame, somebody to blame. So blame me if that's what you enjoy, just give me the boy—" (she wants to appease the Giantess's wrath by giving her what she is demanding). She suddenly lunged for Jack, but the others blocked her way.

"No," she sneered, stepping away. "You're so nice. You're not good. You're not bad. You're just nice. I'm not good. I'm not nice. I'm just right. I'm the Witch. You're the world."

"I'm the hitch, I'm what no one believes. I'm the Witch. You're all liars and thieves. . . ."

"And despairing that she had ever wished to be a part of this world and its rules, she called out to her mother in the ether, beseeching her to deliver her from these people. . . ."

The Baker, too, wants to be "away from all of this." "No more questions," he says, wearily. "Please. No more tests. No more curses you can't undo, left by fathers you never knew. No more quests. No more feelings. Time to shut the door. Just"—he sat down despondently on a tree stump—"no more."

"Later Little Red Ridinghood, Jack, and the Baker lure the Giantess to her death. Cinderella's Prince comes across his wife in the forest, but knowing that he has been unfaithful, she is without feeling.

He explains, "I thought that if you were mine that I would never wish for more. And part of me is as content and as happy as I've ever been. But there remains a part of me that continually needs more."

"I have, on occasion, wanted more," she said, thoughtfully. "But that doesn't mean that I went in search of it."

"I was raised to be charming, not sincere," demurs the Prince. "I didn't ask to be born a king, and I am not perfect. I am only human."

"My father's house was a nightmare," Cinderella replies. "Your house was a dream. Now I want something in between. Please go." So they part, forever.

Cinderella reflects: "Sometimes people leave you, halfway through the wood. Others may deceive you. You decide what's good. You decide alone. But no one is alone." The Giantess is dispatched by Jack and the Baker, and they all think of returning to their homes. Having no one to take care of him and his baby, the Baker is sad, until Little Red Ridinghood and Cinderella agree to come live with him. The Baker's Wife appears to him in a vision: "Sometimes people leave you, halfway through the wood. Do not let it grieve you, no one leaves for good."

As his baby began to cry, the Baker "sat down and rocked him a bit as the others gathered round. He cleared his throat and began a story. 'Once upon a time, in a far-off kingdom, there lived a fair young maiden, a sad young lad, and a childless baker with his wife.'"

"How long will it take me to learn these things, Father?"
"A lifetime, my son, perhaps a little longer."
Kung Fu (TV series)

faculties that were never developed may dim completely, but if our essential faculties have been used optimally, then there is no necessary decline of the quality of our existence with the decline of the somatic organism.

Men and women can meaningfully be called "adults" now. The lingering tendency to blame one's parents for our problems finally ceases. We perceive them, or remember them, with appreciation, as having done their best. There is frequently an enjoyment of human relationships not possible for us during earlier, fiercely competitive years. There is an increased awareness of our mortality and acceptance of it. Our creativity often reaches greater heights, as though obstacles have been removed; personal and professional accomplishments continue, or increase. This has been called a time of "mellowing and warming up," and there is often the feeling that one has succeeded, at last, in sorting out life's trivialities and knowing what is genuinely of worth and meaning.

Indeed, the later years can usher us into a quality of experience that can rarely come at an earlier time. This can be a new sense of ultimacy in all that we are and do. We may feel a yearning, aching, profound beauty in our experience of simple things, and see previously unnoticed patterns of meaning in nature, and find new perspectives on, and a belated appreciation of, other people. The very fact of existence itself—not merely human life, but all life, and all existence—can become a glorious mystery that one feels privileged to participate in—"a cosmic drama, and I am actually a part of it!" If life has been a truly expansive adventure, then in these later years there can be an unspeakable love of life—measured by awareness, sagacity, and calm—that we would not exchange, if we could, for the physical vitality of the early years.

Nothing I carefully planned for my life has worked out. Everything of significance in my life has been an accident.
Al Burke

The seventh and eighth decades of our life/times may also bring a feeling of resolution, a time for wrapping up some of life's enterprises, a sort of tying up of loose ends. But at the same time, we may well feel the urge to savor all that life can offer. If we have been truly existential throughout our life/time, we will enjoy the warmth and intimacy of human relationships as much, or perhaps more, than ever before.

Admittedly, the other side of this coin is not uncommon. When conflicts from the middle years continue unresolved, then these later years may be filled with despair and disillusionment. If intimacy was never reestablished during the middle years, a shallowness and distance may characterize all our later relationships, resulting in an all-pervasive loneliness that is one of life's true tragedies: the unrelated person.

20 The adult who lacks integrity in this sense may wish that he could live life again. He feels that if at one time he had made a different decision he could have been a different person and his ventures would have been successful. He fears death and cannot accept his one and only life cycle as the ultimate of life. In the extreme, he experiences disgust and despair. Despair expresses the feeling that time is too short to try out new roads to integrity. Disgust is a means of hiding the despair, a chronic, contemptuous displeasure with the way life is run. As with the dangers and the solutions of previous periods, doubt and despair are not difficulties that are overcome once and for all, nor is integrity so achieved. Most people fluctuate between the two extremes. Most, also, at no point, either attain to the heights of unalloyed integrity or fall to the depths of complete disgust and despair.

One of the oldest human needs is having someone to wonder where you are when you don't come home at night.
Margaret Mead

Age does not protect you from love. But love, to some extent, protects you from age.
Jean Moreau

Even in adulthood a reasonably healthy personality is sometimes secured in spite of previous misfortunes in the developmental sequence. New sources of trust may be found. Fortunate events and circumstances may aid the individual in his struggle to feel autonomous. Imagination and initiative may be spurred by new responsibilities, and feelings of inferiority be overcome by successful achievement. Even later in life an individual may arrive at a true sense of who he is and what he has to do and may be able to win through to a feeling of intimacy with others and to joy in producing and giving.

ERIK ERIKSON

At last I have grown into the person I always wanted to be.
ARCHIE LEACH
(CARY GRANT)
(shortly before his death)

21 In our later years, it is not uncommon for us to return to some form of religion we may have forgotten or neglected during our earlier years. Cynics will accuse us of trying to "play it safe" or to get comforted because of our fear of death. There is some truth in this, of course, but there is far more. It is an expression of our longing for ultimacy in our later time of life. Many of us enter the later years without profound "spiritual" (that is, ultimate) resources. Life has absorbed our energies in other concerns. We are limited in the ways we know of probing the ultimacy, the depth, the meaning of existence, which is intuited as somehow essential to the successful completion of life. For very many of us, the only practical solution may be to return to the religion we knew at an earlier time. A great deal of the late return to religion is precisely that: returning to an earlier stage of life. However, a more resourceful solution of the challenge of the middle years ("What do I really want out of life?") can lead on to a far more effective and meaningful forms of ultimacy. It could make possible the flowering of one's own unique and profoundly personal existence. In any case, this religious emphasis should be seen as an attempt to explore the meaning of life and to achieve, in the short time left, an ultimacy that life has heretofore not attained.

"You don't stop playing because you grow old. You grow old because you stop playing."
"DAD" MILLER
(105 years old)
Glendale Federal Savings TV Commercial

22 **THE FINAL PHASE** For some of us—though not all—there is a final phase to our life cycle. It begins when we must face that fact that our own death is imminent. This is not merely the realization that one is mortal. Rather, this is the acceptance of the absolute fact that our own life/time has almost run out. Now the feeling may become strong that we must take care of unfinished business and come to terms with the fact that our cessation of consciousness is near. Dying is much in our thoughts, and death symbols pervade our dreams—a clock without hands, perhaps, as in Ingmar Bergman's *Wild Strawberries.*

Immortal God! What a world I see dawning! Why cannot I grow young again?
ERASMUS

If we have lived a long life, we are prepared for our own momentous death-event by having lived closely with death for some years. Others around us have died, more and more of those we have known; loved ones, friends, colleagues, acquaintances, notable contemporaries. This living with death is an essential time of preparation for our own death-event. It serves to diminish feelings of fear and dread.

There may also be a reliving of past events, a replaying of our memories. We are frequently critical of the person who begins "to live in the past," and, of course, if we develop such a habit long before the final phase, then it is probably a sign of premature withdrawal from life. During the final phase, however, it is natural and normal. Partly it is an attempt to see the life/time drama in perspective, and to write a good completion. But partly it is a final preparation for the death-event. It is a recapitulation, a sort of browsing through the storehouse of a lifetime of activities, a savoring of one's accomplishments, a final inventory of life's experiences—and taking mental note of what we will leave behind.

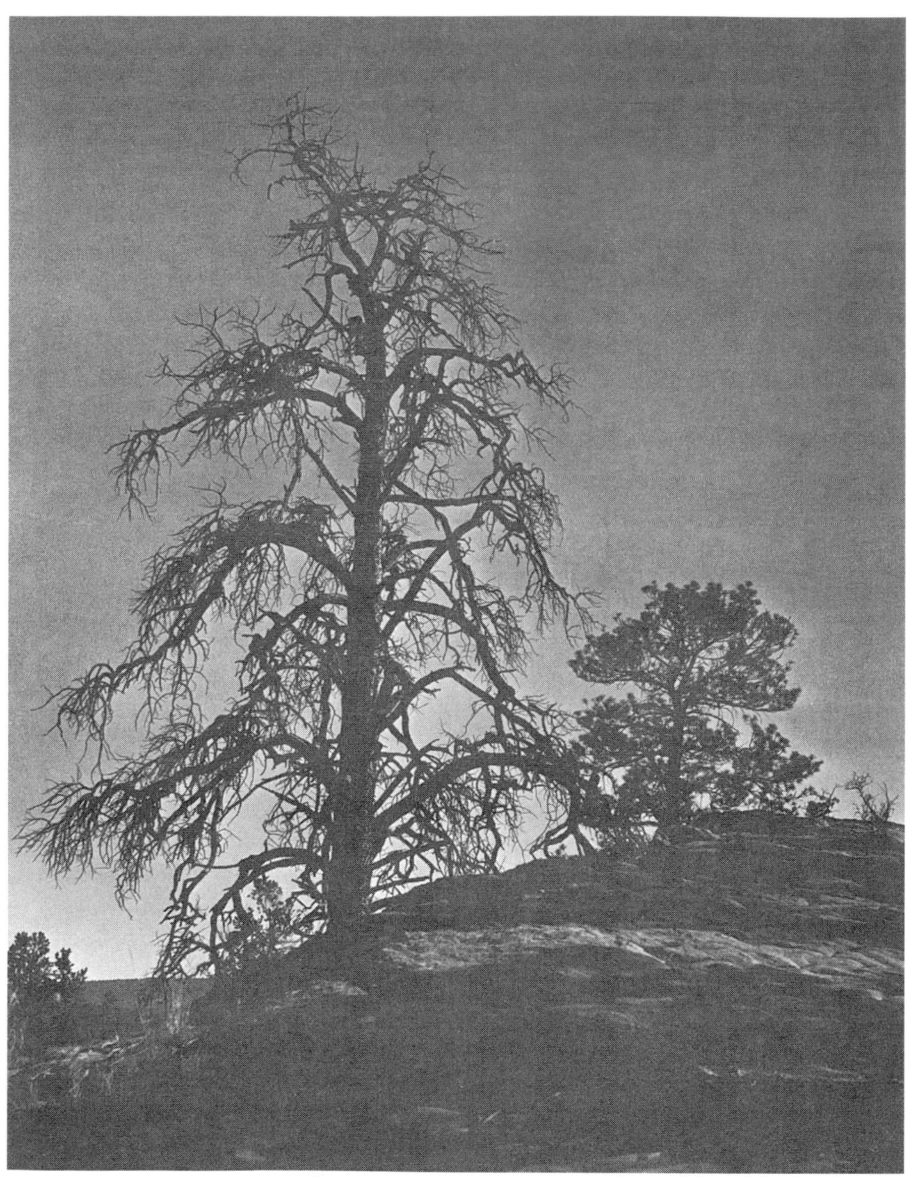

The Shriek of Ivan Ilytch

Do not go gentle into that good night,
Old age should burn and rave at close of day;
Rage, rage against the dying of the light.
Dylan Thomas

23 In a scene from Tolstoy's *Death of Ivan Ilytch,* the man is ill and dying. As he reflects upon the meaninglessness of his death, what hits him so forcefully is the meaninglessness of his life. When the pointless absurdity of his petty life dawns fully in his consciousness, he shrieks. "For the last three days he screamed incessantly." Then a blessed rationalization comes to his rescue. After all, he had lived a conventional kind of life; he had achieved the material and social success others expected of him. So on his deathbed ambivalent fragments of his squandered life wander randomly through his mind.

"Full Circle"

When I grow up
I'll read poetry in the *New Yorker*
and it'll be okay if I don't understand it.
I'll not be afraid to ask stupid questions
or challenge authority if I disagree.

When I grow up
I'll turn down a date on Saturday night
if it isn't meaningful.
I'll even stay home on New Year's Eve
if I feel like being alone.

When I grow up
I might learn from listening
I might learn from criticism
I might even learn to have an "open mind."

When I grow up
I'll share all the feelings I've always
wanted to share.
I'll touch all those people I've always
wanted to touch.
I'll tell all the people I love
that I love them.

When I grow up
I'll go to the park and slide down slides
swing on swings
lie on the grass without a blanket
and make necklaces of buttercups.
I'll laugh at myself and giggle with others
scream and throw pillows when I'm angry
sing loudly and cry softly, cry loudly
and sing softly.

When I grow up
I'll forget time.
I'll write poetry on paper,
paint it on canvas or mold it with clay,
dance as if it were my last dance
and love as if it were my last chance to love

When I grow up
I'll never feel old again.

Rusty Berkus
Soulprints

"I want to live forever — or die in the attempt."

Joseph Heller
Catch-22

"What do I want? . . . To live? How? . . . Why, to live as I used to—well and pleasantly." . . . And in imagination he began to recall the best moments of his pleasant life. But strange to say none of those best moments of his pleasant life now seemed at all what they had then seemed. . . . And the further he departed from childhood and the nearer he came to the present the more worthless and doubtful were the joys. . . . "It is as if I had been going downhill while I imagined I was going up. And that is really what it was. I was going up in public opinion, but to the same extent life was ebbing away from me. And now it is all done and there is only death." . . . "Maybe I did not live as I ought to have done." "But how could that be, when I did everything properly?" . . . And whenever the thought occurred to him, as it often did, that it all resulted from his not having lived as he ought to have done, he at once recalled the correctness of his whole life and dismissed so strange an idea.

All In Good Time

BILL MOYERS: So there are truths for older age and truths for children.

JOSEPH CAMPBELL: Oh, yes. I remember the time Heinrich Zimmer was lecturing at Columbia on the Hindu idea that all life is as a dream or a bubble; that all is *maya*, illusion. After his lecture a young woman came up to him and said, "Dr. Zimmer, that was a wonderful lecture on Indian philosophy! But *maya*—I don't get it—it doesn't speak to me."

"Oh," he said, "don't be impatient! That's not for you yet, darling." And so it is: when you get older, and everyone you've known and originally lived for has passed away, and the world itself is passing, the *maya* myth comes in. But, for young people, the world is something yet to be met and dealt with and loved and learned from and fought with—and so, another mythology.

MOYERS: The writer Thomas Berry says that it's all a question of story. The story is the plot we assign to life and the universe, our basic assumptions and fundamental beliefs about how things work. He says we are in trouble now "because we are in between stories. The old story sustained us for a long time—it shaped our emotional attitudes, it provided us with life's purpose, it energized our actions, it consecrated suffering, it guided education. We awoke in the morning and knew who we were, we could answer the questions of our children. Everything was taken care of because the story was there. Now the old story is not functioning. And we have not yet learned anew."

CAMPBELL: I'm in partial agreement with that—partial because there is an old story that is still good, and that is the story of the spiritual quest. The quest to find the inward thing that you basically are is the story that I tried to render in that little book of mine written forty-odd years ago —*The Hero with a Thousand Faces*. The relationship of myths to cosmology and sociology has got to wait for men to become used to the new world that he is in. The world is different today from what it was fifty years ago. But the inward life of man is exactly the same. So if you put aside for a while the myth of the origin of the world—scientists will tell you what that is, anyway—and go back to the myth of what is the human quest, what are its stages of realization, what are the trials of the transition from childhood to maturity and what does maturity mean, the story is there, as it is in all the religions.

Joseph Campbell, with Bill Moyers
The Power of Myth

Emergings

There is a tide, by no means constant but strong enough to note, which carries a number of great artists away from the youthful vigor and impertinent complexities with which they made their reputations and toward a firm simplicity, even serenity, in their last works. It is always an achieved simplicity; no beginner could obtain it. In Matisse's paper cutouts and Picasso's beaming eroticism, in "Oedipus at Colonus" and the simple folk tune that concludes Beethoven's last quartet, there is the ease and quietness of an artist who, having mastered his craft, can afford now to come out on the other side.

Newsweek, January 3, 1972

Voltaire

The Laughing Philosopher

Voltaire is one of the most quotable writers ever to grace a pen.

"Books rule the world." "When a nation begins to think, it is impossible to stop it." "Liberty of thought is the life of the soul." "Think for yourselves and let others enjoy the privilege to do so too." "It is the triumph of reason to live well with those who have none." "The Holy Roman Empire is neither holy, nor Roman, nor an Empire." "Love is the embroidery upon the stuff of nature." "Love truth, but pardon error." "It is better to risk saving a guilty person than to condemn an innocent one." "Common sense is not so common." "To cease to love and be lovable is a death unbearable." "If God did not exist, it would be necessary to invent him." And so on, almost *ad infinitum.*

He seems to have given us a pearl on every topic, and if his volumes of sparkling wit and wisdom lack depth, one must cherish the pearls and forgive: he was, in his own words, "like the little brooks; they are transparent because they are not deep." What he did possess was a philosopher's wisdom salted with sweeping insights, and this, combined with a zest for life and a prophetic zeal for freedom and decency, made him one of the great mind-warriors of the human race.

He was christened François-Marie Arouet when he was born in Paris in 1694. His father was François Arouet, a prosperous attorney; his mother was Marie Marguerite Daumard, a brilliant, lively, articulate woman who moved gracefully in society. François was the last of her five children, so small and weak they thought he wouldn't live. They baptized him the day after he was born.

When he was seven his mother died. At ten he was sent to a Jesuit school where he received a humanistic education in classical literature, languages, and drama.

He graduated at seventeen and began to study law at his father's urging, but he had already discovered his own loves: he wanted nothing but literature and life —the heady semibohemian social life of Paris.

Hypercreative and brilliant (estimated IQ 190), he made only a pretense at studying law. He had taken up poetry to express himself, but much of his rhyming bordered on libel. He was not seditious by intent; rather, he just had no toler-

The further I advance in age, the more I find work necessary. It becomes in the long run the greatest of pleasures, and takes the place of the illusions of life.

On Voltaire:
Destiny gave him eighty-three years of existence, that he might slowly decompose the decayed age; he had the time to combat time; and when he fell, he was the conqueror.

LAMARTINE

Books rule the world, or at least those nations in it which have a written language; the others do not count.

God is a comedian playing to an audience that is afraid to laugh.

ance for the stupidities and cruelties of the society he lived in. He possessed a keen ethical sense and enormous courage. "My trade is to say what I think," he wrote, and he thought much. But his freethinking was a threat, and on May 16, 1717, he was clamped into the Bastille for a year. There, shut up with his own boundless energies, he wrote plays and more political poems. When released the following April, he took the name Voltaire.

In 1732 he published *Philosophical Letters on the English,* a collection of brilliant observations of English life and mores; it received critical praise. But his *English Letters* contained as much criticism of the French as praise of the English. He had launched telling tirades against the corruption of church and state in France, naming and attacking leaders. The book was burned in 1734 and a warrant was issued for his arrest.

Voltaire wasn't available. This time he was at Cirey, a run-down but lovely country estate in northeastern France owned by the marquis de Châtelet. The marquise—Émilie—had become the one love of his mature life. She was an intellectual companion, well-read in literature and philosophy, a student of the sciences and mathematics. Both studied intensely, wrote incessantly, and loved without reason for fourteen years.

Eventually he was allowed to return to Paris. More than ever he moved with royalty, political leaders, and literati. In 1745 Madame de Pompadour had him appointed to the post of Historiographer-Royal. He received honors from the pope and dedicated a play to him. In 1746—he was fifty-two—Voltaire was elected to the prestigious French Academy of Sciences. He had loyal friends and devoted enemies everywhere.

Voltaire wasn't all that welcome in France, so he turned to the eternal bastion of freedom, Geneva. There, in 1754, he bought a country estate just outside Geneva and named it Les Délices. With a garden, trees, chickens, and a cow, the world seemed far away. "I am so happy," he wrote, "that I am ashamed."

In 1755 a great earthquake shook Lisbon, and almost instantly fifteen thousand people were killed. Why? Why had such suffering taken place? Because the Portuguese had sinned mightily, said French clergymen. Because the Catholics are infidels, said Protestants. Because Portugal was filled with apostate Protestants, said the Roman clergy. Because Adam had sinned, said the Methodist John Wesley.

Such foolishness aroused the wrath of the slumbering Voltaire. Adding to his wrath was the doctrine preached by the German philosopher Leibniz that this is "the best of all possible worlds." Incensed at such nonsense, he took up his pen and delivered one of the classics of world literature, *Candide* (1759).

In March 1762 news reached him of the persecution of a Huguenot family in Toulouse. Jean Calas was a linen merchant who had been wrongly accused of murdering his own son (a suicide) to prevent his conversion to Catholicism. Through an enormous perversion of justice, fed by ignorance, superstition, and mass paranoia, the Calas family had been persecuted; Jean Calas was tortured, strangled, and burned at the stake.

Voltaire determined the facts and went to war. His outrage drove him to feverish action. His banner was *écrasez l'infâme*—"Crush the Infamy!" The infamy was organized bigotry, religious persecution, political insanity—everything that contravenes man's humanity toward his fellow man. Fresh vitality came again to the aging warrior. "I suffer much. But when I attack *l'infâme* the pain is relieved." Voltaire had tapped into a righteous hatred to evoke a feeling of outrage in the hearts of his countrymen. He called especially on the *philosophes*—philosophers whose hearts and heads were above the insanity of this world and who had the word-weaponry to declare war.

If ever there had been a war of ideas, this was it. Voltaire was joined by leaders and literati everywhere. Appeals were directed to churchmen, noblemen, ministers. Lawyers were hired, documents subpoenaed, cases prepared, witnesses sought. "Cry out yourself," he wrote, "and let others cry out; cry out for the Calas family and against fanatacism." And he prayed: "Thou has not given us hearts to hate, nor hands to kill, one another."

After three years of bloodless warfare, there was a victory of sorts: In March 1765, the King's Council declared the verdict against Jean Calas null and void, and he was declared innocent; the maligned family was awarded victims' compensation. Voltaire wept when he heard the news.

So, Voltaire was yet alive. He was a poet, dramatist, contractor, importer, capitalist, philosopher, money-lender, traveler, lover, warrior, banker, entrepreneur, theologian (of sorts), linguist (of sorts), politician (of sorts), benefactor, bon vivant, sponsor of the arts, exile, prisoner, coffee drinker par excellence, historian, gardener . . .

Voltaire mellowed as he grew older, naturally. Awaking to consciousness each day, feeling a new sun, taking up one's rounds and routines—this is enough. "When everything is counted and weighed up, I think there are infinitely more enjoyments than bitterness in this life."

He came constantly to new perspectives. "My baffled curiosity continues to be insatiable." He read, lived, changed, and grew. Like Socrates, he knew increasingly how little he knew. "I am ignorant," he said. All hints of arrogance, in private, began to fade; rigidities remained only in the heat of battle.

In the sixth, seventh, and eighth decades of his life, he had moments of doubt, even despair. There were times when he envied those who had never thought philosophically about anything and who still had the capacity for simple faith. Madness, he said, is having preferred reason to happiness. But then the joy of the philosophic life would return. He picked up his books, tried to understand more, went to his garden, invited in the neighborhood children, and laughed the hours back to joy.

Probably no philosopher ever understood better the health-restoring role of laughter in our lives. It has been suggested that his laughter might be, after all, his greatest contribution to his and every age.

Voltaire helped restore his fellow countrymen to sanity by teaching them to laugh at themselves. All his satiric work —culminating in *Candide*—was an attack upon those who take themselves too seriously: politicians, kings, priests and monks, inquisitors, popes, axe-grinders —that is, all of us. To those, other people's ideas are obviously stupid and wrong; the antidote is laughing away our anger. One cannot laugh and hate and fear. "*Dulce est desipere in loco.* Woe to philosophers who cannot laugh away their wrinkles. I look upon solemnity as a disease."

Voltaire was the very embodiment of the Enlightenment: he had an abiding faith in the intelligence and rationality of man. "This century begins to see the triumph of reason," he wrote. Voltaire's dream was that a philosophical intelligence could challenge the tragic history of human misbehavior, that intelligent men and women could blaze a new path leading to freedom and civility.

Voltaire worked, and the years passed. He rose with the sun, began his days with strong coffee, and wrote. Occasionally, still, his works were put to the flames. His home at Ferney became a place of pilgrimage for the great and would-be great; so many found the path to his door that he exclaimed "O God! deliver me from my friends; I will take care of my enemies myself."

He took time to watch his seedlings and silkworms grow. He loved and respected the caretakers who lived on his land. He especially enjoyed young people and opened his home to them each Sunday. He became an octogenarian almost without wincing, and these were the happiest of times.

Voltaire lived his philosophy. Life is made for action; if merely watched, as from the sidelines, it becomes empty.

It is only charlatans who are certain. . . . Doubt is not a very agreeable state, but certainty is a ridiculous one.

Dulce est desipere in loco. *Woe to philosophers who cannot laugh away their wrinkles. I look upon solemnity as a disease.*

We must plunge into the chaotic stream of events where we can "laugh all our laughter and weep all our tears" (Gibran's words) so that death, when it comes, will find nothing but "a squandered bag of bones" (Kazantzakis's words). We should seek out all variety of experience—absorb all knowledge, think all thoughts, feel all feelings.

Voltaire was painfully aware of the passage of time and wanted to make the most of every minute. More than most mortals, he did. He lived each day with zest, sleeping only five or six hours a night. It is frightful, he said, how much time we waste avoiding life.

Nor do we have to be in a special place to live thus; it can be done wherever we are. In one of his plays Voltaire's hero travels the world and witnesses all the follies of mankind, big and small; but he returns home and finds that it is better at home after all. One doesn't have to wander in search of greener pastures, except that . . . one must wander the world in search of greener pastures to discover for oneself that he did not have to wander the world . . . "I still found that of all conditions of life this is much the happiest."

Perhaps it is not wrong to see all of France relaxing its stomach muscles, just a bit, because of Voltaire's comedy and satire, his obscene pearls, his scatological epithets. To laugh is to take a step toward the recovery of our lost humanness, to rid ourselves of the poison of self-hate and despair. Voltaire, the laughing philosopher, helped France laugh itself back toward sanity.

In 1778 Paris beckoned. Voltaire had been away from the great city for twenty-eight years—why not one last journey? He was approaching eighty-four. He made the trip in five days in February. Well-wishers by the thousands lined the streets of Paris, shouting "Vive Voltaire!" He was honored by heads of state and wreathed with garlands in the salons and theaters. His plays were staged with great fanfare. He was given superlative honors by the French Academy. For three months the celebrations continued. His life crescendoed to a climax the like of which few mortals are blessed to see.

But at some point the life-fire must dim. In May he took to his bed. A friend sent him some medicine—opium—which he was to dilute and drink. Voltaire misunderstood the instructions and drank it down straight; it sent him into a painful delirium. Two days later his consciousness returned, but his life was gone. "I die adoring God, loving my friends, not hating my enemies, and detesting superstition." It was May 30, 1778.

Consecrated ground was barred to him in most of France, so his body was spirited away and buried in the Abbey of Scellières in Champagne. Thirteen years later it was removed on order of the National Assembly, carried in triumph to Paris, and interred in the Pantheon. However, when the tomb was opened in 1864, it was found to be empty.

On his coffin is the inscription: "He taught us to be free."

✦

Reflections

Festina lente. ***"Make haste slowly."***
Motto of Caesar Augustus

1 The purpose of this chapter is to help you "to feel the whole of a life cycle, to see the human enterprise, from birth till death, in a single vision, as One" (p. 140). Having read through the chapter, jot down your immediate responses, emotional as well as intellectual, to whatever holistic perspective you attained. What are your most meaningful insights?

I think anyone who chooses a career for any other reason [than out of love] is a nut.
Joseph Campbell

2 Aristotle and Saint Thomas Aquinas shared the belief that women are mistakes (p. 141). Would you care to counterargue these chauvinists by developing the case that it is really the male of the species who is the mistake?

It can be done. (For openers, note that the anthropologist Ashley Montagu wrote a widely acclaimed book entitled *The Natural Superiority of Women.*)

3 Most of us are familiar with the popular proverb, "Today is the first day of the rest of your life." How do you think one might appropriately respond to this maxim if he is five years old? eighteen years old? forty years old? sixty-five years old? ninety-four years old?

4 Reread the observation from *Developmental Psychology Today* on p. 143. Do you agree with the Douvan-Adelson conclusion? If so, what do you think are the causes of this widespread "token separation"?

5 Focus on two challenges that one encounters during a full lifetime: the challenge that you are currently involved in, and one that you are not presently facing (preferably one that lies ahead). Describe in the most personal way what these challenges mean to you. Is there a contrast between your understanding of these two challenges? In other words, to what degree can any of us comprehend a challenge we have not yet faced ourselves?

6 If you think of life metaphorically as a "path" or "road," can you locate yourself with some accuracy somewhere (somewhen) along that path? Did you personally go through the earlier challenges as described in this chapter?

7 Ponder the drawing by Abner Dean that follows. "I have an important appointment." Comment? Does this drawing apply to anyone you know? Do you think you might actually show the drawing to someone and say, "There, that's you!"? What sort of response do you think you would get?

8 There are at least three definitions of "truth" (see pp. 214ff.). What definition is Joseph Campbell using when he suggests (p. 159) that there are different truths for different periods of our lives?

We all live in suspense, from day to day, from hour to hour; in other words, we are the hero of our own story.
MARY MCCARTHY

When I get a little money, I buy books; and, if any is left, I buy food and clothes.
DESIDERIUS ERASMUS

Je m'en vais chercher un grand peut-être; tirez le rideau, la farce est jouée.
I am going to seek a grand perhaps; draw the curtain, the farce is played.
LAST WORDS OF RABELAIS (ALLEGED)

I have an important appointment.

The Real World: Knowing and Unknowing

All the biologicals are converting chaos to beautiful order. All biology is antientropic. Of all the disorder-to-order converters, the human mind is by far the most impressive. The human's most powerful metaphysical drive is to understand, to order, to sort out, and rearrange in ever more orderly and understandably constructive ways. You find then that man's true function is metaphysical.

Buckminster Fuller

Knowledge

3-1

The earliest Greek philosophers turned their attention outward toward the physical world and tried to understand how the world works; then Socrates came along and insisted that we must first understand the knowledge-gathering instrument: the mind. The study of how the mind gathers knowledge is called epistemology, and epistemologists have found that the mind is endowed with four channels for gathering information. Each source is indispensable and provides us with survival information, but each has its limitations, forcing us to be very cautious in our use of it.

> ***Most of the greatest evils that man has inflicted upon man have come through people feeling quite certain about something which, in fact, was false.***
>
> Bertrand Russell

Epistemic Awareness

1 All of us begin our philosophizing from a state of **epistemic naivete,** a condition in which we have not yet begun to question the origins, nature, and dependability of our information. To be sure, some of us may have discovered we were wrong about some things, or that we were lied to, or that we have outgrown certain beliefs; but few of us at this early stage have peered deeply into the fundamental operations of the information-processing system we call the mind and decided that we have probably been operating for too long on beliefs that are false. When Descartes woke up and found that he had been accepting "as true many opinions that were really false," he became convinced, he said, "that I need to make, once in my life, a clean sweep of my formerly held opinions and to begin to rebuild from the bottom up. . . ." (See p. 28.) We may not have to go as far as Descartes, but we all need to begin the process of filtering out ideas and values that no longer work for us or that we find are no longer true.

Epistemology is the branch of philosophy defined as the study of human knowledge. In exploring this field we are touching one of evolution's fundamen-

> ***We have to live today by what truth we can get today, and be ready tomorrow to call it falsehood.***
>
> William James

tal mechanisms of survival, for it is by knowledge that we orient ourselves in the world. Accurate knowledge of our two worlds—the real world ("out there") and the inner world of experience ("in here")—correctly informs us of conditions we must cope with. To know is to survive; not to know, or to assess the real environment inaccurately, is to jeopardize the fight for survival. (The word **real** is a technical term in philosophy. See **real, reality,** and **realism** in the Glossary.)

With the examination of the sources, nature, and accuracy of our knowledge, we begin to develop **epistemic awareness,** a more informed understanding of what we know and how we know it; and an exceedingly important part of this awareness is coming to understand more clearly what we don't know.

2 We face two epistemological problems. (1) How can we determine which facts are true? (2) How can we determine which facts are important? The first can be dealt with in a relatively straightforward manner; the second is often situational and more difficult to clarify.

We are all inundated by statements that are intended to be statements of truth. But so many of these statements are not true, and we must therefore find ways to double-check these fact-claims. We must learn somehow to filter out the fictions but let in the valid and substantiated facts. So, on what criteria can we decide what are facts and what are false claims?

Second, among the billions of bits of information at our fingertips, it is difficult to distinguish high-priority data. There **are** facts that are important; there **are** causes that are crucial; there **are** ideas that work better than others. But which? and to what end? Since not all facts are of equal importance at a given time in a given situation, we are required to make value judgments. So, what criteria can we use for deciding what is more important, what less?

3 Everything we know originates from four sources. The first, our **senses,** can be thought of as our primary source of information. Two other sources, **reason** and **intuition,** are derivative in the sense that they produce new facts from data already supplied to our minds. The fourth source, **authority** (or "hearsay," or "testimony" of others), is by nature secondary, and secondhand fact-claims are always more wiggly and difficult to validate. Other sources of knowledge are commonly claimed, and it is not inconceivable that there might exist other sources; but if they do exist, knowledge derived from them is problematic, and careful analysis usually finds that they can be subsumed under one or more of the four known sources and must be seriously questioned as legitimate, separate sources of reliable information.

If you cannot convince me that there is some kind of knowable ultimate reality, or if you cannot convince me that there are certain absolute values by which I can live my life, I shall commit psychological suicide. That is, either convince me that there is "one truth" or one right way of doing things, or I shall conclude that everything is meaningless and I will not try any more.

JOSEPH ROYCE
(describing the reality-image of contemporary man)

THE SENSES: EMPIRICAL KNOWLEDGE

4 THE SENSES The primary source of all knowledge is our own senses. Throughout our earlier years, this remains the most immediate channel of information about ourselves and our environment. As beginners in life we "learn by doing," and doing in large part means to see, to hear, to taste, to touch, and so on. Our five senses (or as many as twenty-three, psychologists tell us) are exploratory organs; we use them to become acquainted with the world we live in.

We learn early on that candy is sweet, as are sugar, jam, and maple syrup. Lemons are not, onions are not, hot peppers are everything but. The sun is bright and blinding. Glowing coals in the fireplace are beautiful if you don't touch them. Sounds soothe, warn, or frighten us. Through a lifetime of sense-events we build a fabric of empirical information which helps us interpret, survive in, and control the world about us. (See **empirical** and **empiricism** in the Glossary.)

Three of our senses—sight, sound, and smell—give us information about events and objects that may lie at a distance, while two of the classical five senses—taste and touch—inform us about happenings in the immediate vicinity of our sensors. When assessed from the perspective of evolutionary adaptation and survival, we can see the benefits of this arrangement.

We have developed specialized sense receptors to perform four of these functions: eyes, ears, taste buds, and olfactory cells. By contrast, the sense of touch does not involve any specialized, strategically positioned organ; touching sensations take place over the entire surface of our bodies. These "cutaneous sensors" are specialized, however; different types of nerve endings respond to different stimuli. Separate and distinct sensors are activated by heat, cold, touch, pressure, and cell damage (which we experience as pain). Nerve endings that react to one of these stimuli generally do not respond to the others. Taken together, these "touching senses" give us a great deal of data that we put to immediate use in our assessment of real objects/events taking place at close range. These can be called **objective senses** since they tell us about the external world.

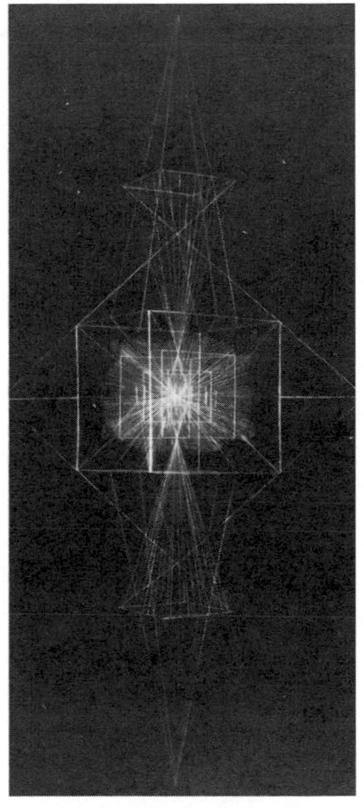

Richard Lippold, *Variation Number 7, 1949–1950.* Collection, The Museum of Modern Art, New York. Mrs. Simon Guggenheim Fund.

5 We also possess numerous **subjective senses** that inform us about our inner world. "Visceral senses" line the inner surfaces of our bodies. They are found in the mouth, along the digestive tract, and on the surfaces of some organs. Without such senses we would not experience a variety of sensations that we take for granted, such as headaches, heartburn, and appendicitis pains. These nuisances might be considered minor losses if we didn't have them, but however unpleasant they may be, the warning signals they send us are requisite to adjustment and survival.

Another group of subjective senses is activated by nerve endings in our muscles, tendons, and joints. These are called "proprioceptive sensors," and they tell us when our muscles are stretched or contracted; through them we sense if a hand is open or closed, which way the head is turned, and whether our knees are bent. Physical coordination is largely determined by these senses.

Another subjective sense is equilibrium. Located in the inner ear, it enables us to maintain our balance within a gravity field and tells us if we are moving or are at rest. We use the same principle in a carpenter's level.

This by no means exhausts the list of our senses, subjective and objective. Along with all other living creatures, evolution has blessed us humans with specialized senses that enable us to adapt to and understand our two worlds and thereby improve our chances for better adjustment, survival, and well-being.

We only think when we are confronted with a problem.
JOHN DEWEY

The eyes believe themselves; the ears believe other people.
CHINESE FORTUNE COOKIE

To follow knowledge like a sinking star,
Beyond the utmost bound of human thought.
ALFRED, LORD TENNYSON

6 Since the beginning of philosophy in the sixth century BC, sensitive thinkers have been aware that our senses present us with a serious credibility problem. The information that our senses give us—how much can we trust it? Can we be sure our senses are telling us the truth? Our senses give us a picture of

the world "out there," but is this picture accurate? Is the world really as they report it to be? And if we should discover that our senses are not giving us an accurate picture of reality, or only a partial picture, then how can we get around this predicament and find out the truth of what really exists?

Since at least the time of Socrates and his friends Parmenides and Zeno (about 450 BC), all of whom argued that we can't trust any of the senses, it has been clear that our senses do not accurately report to us what is going on in the real world. What they give us is **useful** information, not scientifically accurate information. That is, they are pragmatic instruments, not high-tech investigative organs; and we should be exceedingly grateful for the operational information they supply to us. However, when we realize that they were not designed to minister to our intellectual need for the truth, and when we understand the exact nature of the "deceptions" and "translations" that occur during the data-transmission processes from real objects/events through the senses to our minds, then our frustration mounts; but from this realization we can proceed to construct a more accurate picture of the true nature of things. Today we have a fairly complete database of information about where and how our senses fail in this task, so that it is possible to correct for most of the senses' inaccurate reporting. Unfortunately, many of us never get around to making these corrections and remain **naive realists.** (**Naive realism** is the uncritical acceptance of one's sense data as representing accurately the real world, a sort of blind faith in what our senses seem to tell us.) There is more on this problem in the next chapter.

KNOWLEDGE FROM OTHERS

7 AUTHORITY Other people, of course, are major sources of information for each of us, but all such secondhand fact-claims are by nature distanced from our own immediate experience where we can better judge the validity of such claims. They are all "hearsay." The further such passed-on information is removed from our own personal experience, the more caution we should exercise before accepting a fact-claim.

Anyone who conducts an argument by appealing to authority is not using his intelligence; he is just using his memory.

LEONARDO DA VINCI

There are several specific realms of knowledge that necessarily come to us through the testimony of others. Knowledge of history, for instance. All histori-

cal knowledge is acquired on the word of others. Since what we call "the past" exists only in our minds, it isn't subject to empirical observation. So we must rely upon those who personally witnessed the living episodes in real time and have recorded, orally or in graphic form, accounts of the events which they judged important enough to preserve. Historical knowledge begins for us when we attempt to re-create in our minds images of those events. Our reliance upon others for the input about those events is an inescapable dependency.

It would be impudent to tell intelligent, grown-up people how to think.

RUDOLF FLESCH

Knowledge of the sciences also comes to most of us by authority. We can't personally repeat every experiment conducted by scientists, so we must trust the work and word of the specialists and accept, though often provisionally, the discoveries they report. Careful workers in the sciences submit their work to "peer review" by other scientists in their field, and they document their researches in such manner that if we wish to double-check the fact-claims ourselves we can obtain the necessary information to do so. Knowing, even theoretically, that a fact-claim can be double-checked by others gives good grounds for trusting the work of legitimate scientists.

By authority also we receive knowledge of the society in which we live, but obviously such information can't be accepted uncritically. Every culture is a carrier of traditions, stories, myths, "common knowledge," and "common sense" that must be carefully screened before one can feel assured that he possesses dependable information. It is one of the functions of culture to supply to its members the ideas and values that render them civilized and bind them together into a coherent social order, but all cultures accumulate and preserve bad ideas along with the good ones. A thoughtful individual will develop his critical faculties so that he can process such inherited information and collect the better ideas that he wants to guide his choices in life.

8 How can we be sure that the "facts" others give us are true? After all, we are all born into culture(s) and must accept large amounts of humankind's knowledge that has been gained over the centuries without which we would be impoverished. We now live in an age of information. So, in the face of a deluge of fact-claims from our social environment, how can we decide which authorities to follow? Whom can we trust?

One solution lies in knowing how to apply critical criteria to fact-claims; another lies in maintaining an ever-vigilant, critical spirit. If one possesses the skill (backed by sufficient courage) to focus on, and critically judge, any fact-claim at will, and if one has learned when to be wary of those who would seduce him into accepting **their** "facts" without supplying good evidence or sound reason—if one commands these skills, then he can feel more secure that he is not being victimized by the shabby, unsupported fact-claims of the kind that bombard us daily from television and other media.

There is another, and perhaps more insidious, danger involved in relying upon others for knowledge. Most of us are prone to the development of dependencies. We commonly select one or two authorities, invest our trust in them, and suppress our rational faculties, and even our moral instincts, to the point of accepting whatever they tell us. (See the Milgram experiment, pp. 336–337.) Granted that the process of developing critical skill is hard work, a mature reliance upon one's own best judgment for what is true and false, right and wrong, will help us to avoid becoming victim to others' unworthy ideas and beliefs. As

"How about five do's and five don'ts?"

the existentialist philosophers have repeatedly warned, dependencies inevitably get in the way of our taking charge of our lives and making our own decisions.

Reason: Using Known Facts

9 **Reason** Our reasoning faculties can also be a source of knowledge. "Reason" can be defined as the process of using known facts to arrive at new facts. Hence, if we start with data that we are sure of, we can apply deductive and inductive methods and arrive at new information we did not have before.

Man is a credulous animal and tends to believe what he is told. Historically, philosophers . . . have taken great pains to point out that authority is at least as important a source of error as it is of knowledge.

Joseph Brennan

Most of our assumptions have outlived their uselessness.

Marshall McLuhan

If a thing moves, then it must move either in the place where it is or in a place where it is not. But it cannot move where it is nor can it move where it is not; therefore it cannot move.

Zeno the Eleatic

If you are traveling in Japan, and your travel guide tells you that the exchange rate is "140 yen per 1 American dollar," you can readily find out how much your tempura will cost you if the menu reads "840 yen." It takes only a moment's reasoning to discover that your meal will cost you about $6.00 at current prices. Note merely that your conclusion—that you are considering a $6.00 dinner—is new knowledge, making possible a new understanding (and enabling you to order sushi instead). Reasoning alone, therefore, can produce new information.

The two major forms of conscious reasoning are deduction and induction. **Deduction** is the process of drawing out (making explicit) the implications of one or more premises or statements of fact. If one **infers** correctly what the premises **imply,** then the inference (conclusion) is said to be **valid. Induction** is the procedure of developing general explanatory hypotheses to account for a set of facts. In scientific induction one projects universal principles, for instance, concluding that **all** planetary orbits are elliptical after having actually examined only a few cases.

Notice that in deduction the conclusion **necessarily** follows from the premises. (For example: All cats are blue. Tom is a cat. Therefore, Tom is **necessarily** blue.) By contrast, when using inductive reasoning, one's working hypothesis is always tentative; it is subject to change whenever further facts are obtained. For example: I have seen six cats, all of them blue. I conclude, therefore, that all cats must be blue. All it takes in this case is the discovery of one orange cat to strike a fatal blow to what seemed to be a viable hypothesis. Inductive conclusions are always subject to change.

There are common abuses of both deductive and inductive reasoning. Deductive procedures apply primarily to mathematics, geometry, and to systems of logic with clearly defined terms. Yet too often we try to apply deduction to ambiguous, everyday words and then arrive at convenient conclusions that don't follow from the premises.

PEANUTS® Charles M. Schulz

Believing Is Seeing

A psychologist employed seven assistants and one genuine subject in an experiment where they were asked to judge how long was a straight line that they were shown on a screen. The seven assistants, who were the first to speak and report what they saw, had been instructed to report unanimously an evidently incorrect length. The eighth member of the group, the only naive subject in the lot, did not know that his companions had received such an instruction, and he was under the impression that what they reported was really what they saw. In one-third of the experiments, he reported the same incorrect length as they did. The pressure of the environment had influenced his own semantic reaction and had distorted his vision. When one of the assistants, under the secret direction of the experimenter, started reporting the correct length, it relieved that pressure of the environment, and the perception of the uninformed subject improved accordingly.

J. Samuel Bois
The Art of Awareness

The weakness of induction results primarily from our failing to realize that induction can result only in **probable** knowledge. For example, if one should witness five auto accidents in the period of an afternoon, all involving the same make and model, most of us would be tempted to conclude that something is mechanically defective with this particular design, and recommend a recall. This conclusion would be an inductive hypothesis with apparent validity. But it is not a certain conclusion; it is only a probable explanation. Add five more accidents with the same make and model. Is one more certain of the validity of the hypothesis? Yes, but only **more** certain, not (and never) absolutely certain. Now what happens to this hypothesis when you discover that six of the ten drivers were driving on the wrong side of the freeway?

In scientifically controlled investigations with a large and representative sampling, one can often eliminate competing hypotheses and run up the probability that one of the hypotheses is the correct one. Nevertheless, the hypothesis will always remain a probable explanation, and nothing more. (But try telling this to lawyers who, using inductive reasoning, arrive at probable conclusions but argue that the evidence "proves" their case.) (For further explanation of inductive reasoning, note the problem of the robins' eggs on p. 483 and the case of the dead computer on pp. 217–218.)

Yes, reason is an imperfect instrument, like medical science, or the human eye; we do the best we can with it within the limits which fate and nature set. We do not doubt that some things are better done by instinct than by thought: Perhaps it is wiser, in the presence of Cleopatra, to thirst like Antony rather than to think like Caesar; it is better to have loved and lost than to have reasoned well. But why is it better?

Will Durant

We are drowning in information but starved for knowledge.

John Naisbitt

I have had my solutions for a long time, but I do not yet know how I am to arrive at them.

Karl Friedrich Gauss

Intuition: Knowledge from the Depths

10 Intuition Although the word **intuition** calls up varied connotations, when carefully defined it can be considered a source of knowledge. Intuition refers to insights or bits of knowledge that emerge into the light of consciousness as a result of deeper subconscious activity. The subconscious mind can perform complex operations, make connections, and create understandings that the conscious mind, burdened with the task of mediating and processing sense data, cannot readily handle. The subconscious mind is not only a vast storehouse of

information, but an extremely sophisticated information-processing machine. "Of all the disorder-to-order converters, the human mind is by far the most impressive," observes Buckminster Fuller, one of the creative geniuses of the twentieth century. "The human's most powerful metaphysical drive is to understand, to order, to sort out, and rearrange in ever more orderly and understandably constructive ways." The preponderance of this ordering takes place "out of sight" (and "out of mind"—that is, the conscious mind).

An American theologian, Francis McConnell, recalls a classic instance of intuition when he was about fifteen and in high school. He had been assigned several algebra problems for homework. He was having no trouble with them until the last problem became obstinate. He wrestled with it in prolonged frustration, but it would not give in, and finally, very late, he gave up and went to bed. When he awoke the next morning the solution popped immediately into his mind. McConnell realized that his subconscious mind had continued to work on the problem while his conscious mind slept.

Having discovered such a helpful faculty, he decided to take full advantage of it. The next evening he glanced briefly over his algebra assignment, promptly forgot it, and went to sleep. Needless to say, when the morning came there were no solutions. McConnell recalls learning an important lesson: The subconscious mind can do creative work, but it must be treated fairly. It must be given adequate data to work with and also, perhaps, more than a little coaxing.

11 Sometimes intuition is experienced as an emotional feeling. We often say something like "I have the feeling he's not telling the truth," and it may be just that—a feeling, but a feeling in the process of informing us of a true fact that we should take seriously.

"I have a feeling it's going to rain." Perhaps such a statement rests on subliminally collected sense data subconsciously synthesized, giving us a "feeling" about a real condition that we could not become aware of with the conscious part of our mind.

Occasionally we hear someone say, "I have a feeling something bad is going to happen." It's a presentiment, a foreboding. The psychologist Carl Jung suggested that the subconscious mind can correlate data in such a way that it can "foresee" events that the conscious mind, burdened with perception and immediate concerns, cannot sense. Strictly speaking, such feelings would not be precognitive, but rather premonitions derived from available data. Such premonitions, when accurate, could become genuine items of knowledge.

The principal weakness of intuition and feeling as sources of knowledge is that the insights they produce are as likely to be wrong as right. If left to intuition, most algebra problems would remain unsolved. Intuitive fact-claims must be double-checked before credentials are issued.

To myself I seem to have been only like a boy playing on the seashore, and diverting myself and now and then finding a smoother pebble or a prettier shell than ordinary, while the great ocean of truth lay all undiscovered before me.

SIR ISAAC NEWTON

John Locke

Reality and Appearance

John Locke was a gentle, unassuming English doctor who challenged the political establishment and laid new foundations in both political philosophy and epistemology. To Americans he is most remembered for his constitutional theory of government. His ideas provided the rationale for the Declaration of Independence of 1776, and the structure of the American government owes its fundamental assumptions to Locke, among them the separation of powers; the obligations of government and the rights of citizens to withdraw support from incompetent government; the separation of church and state; religious liberty; freedom of expression; freedom of the press; and the right to private property.

But Locke's contribution to epistemology is equally important. Before his time (he lived from 1632 to 1704) philosophers like Bacon, Galileo, and Newton had made great strides in studying the natural world. But how the mind works in its investigations was still largely a puzzlement, and the earlier scientists, out of ignorance of how the mind works, had made serious mistakes. Locke reiterated the observation of Socrates: before discussing "objective" matters, one should determine first whether the mind is capable of investigating those matters at all. So Locke ignored nature and turned inward "to inquire into the original [origin], certainty, and extent of human knowledge." His subject matter would be ideas alone; his method, precise analysis of the processes of thought.

John Locke was born in Wrington, a small town a few miles from Bristol. His father was a lawyer who served as a clerk to the justice of the peace; his mother was "a very pious woman and an affectionate mother." His father deeply influenced his life, even after his death, when John was twenty-seven. The relationship of father and son was later characterized by John's friend Damaris Cudworth:

> His father used a conduct towards him when young that he often spoke of afterward with great approbation. It was that of being severe to him by keeping

Nihil est in intellectu nisi quod prius fuerit in sensu. ***There is nothing in the mind except what was first in the senses.***

No man can be wholly ignorant of what he does when he thinks.

Where there is no property, there is no injustice.

When we do our utmost to conceive the existence of external bodies we are all the while only contemplating our own ideas.

There is nothing that I desire more than to know thoroughly all that can be said against what I take for truth.

Si non vis intelligi, debes negligi. ***If it is not intelligible, then one must ignore it.***

> him in much awe and at a distance while he was a boy, but relaxing still by degrees of that severity as he grew to be a man, till he being become capable of it, he lived perfectly with him as a friend.

When Locke wrote out his thoughts in a pamphlet on education, he advised: "The sooner you treat him [the son] as a man, the sooner he will begin to be one." He judged this relationship between father and son to be the ideal, believing that it served perfectly to foster gradual growth from a condition of innocence and selfish whim into a rational and responsible maturity. This insight became a paradigm for Locke's theory of government: the relationship of ruler to ruled must likewise be designed to foster growth, to nourish citizens out of uncivilized behavior into civilized behavior, to move them from a childhoodlike state ruled by emotions to an adulthood governed by rationality, thereby enabling them to participate responsibly in society.

At age fifteen Locke entered Westminster School in London but found the education he received there to be uncomfortable and useless. Discipline was harsh, the subjects bored him, and he hated having to memorize the rules of grammar.

At twenty he matriculated at Christ Church College, Oxford. The atmosphere there gave a token nod to freedom of thought, but the official curriculum was still largely medieval. Locke felt suffocated by the antiquated jargon and resented the time wasted on picky theological questions. Also his shy temperament was put off by the required public debates, which, as he saw them, were mind games devoid of any respect for the truth.

What Locke was beginning to see was that most people think with their emotions, not their intellects, and for a time he became discouraged about the entire human lot, feeling that there was no one he could turn to for honest, intelligent thinking. He wondered whether there was any species of knowledge that he could trust. He found himself increasingly drawn toward a fresh examination of the underlying assumptions of epistemological, moral, and political principles. Locke felt trapped in a dilemma that would bother him all his life: the conflict between authority and freedom. In his own education this conflict manifested itself as a challenge to decide what traditional knowledge he could accept and what he would have to think through for himself.

Locke was about thirty-four when he began to practice medicine at Oxford. In 1666 Lord Ashley—later to become the first Earl of Shaftesbury—came to Oxford. The two met and established what was to be a lifelong friendship. The men were of similar temperaments; both hated inept authoritarianism and prized personal liberty. Shaftesbury invited Locke to London to serve as his personal physician, secretary, and confidant, a move that brought Locke into the maelstrom of power politics. When Shaftesbury became Lord High Chancellor of England in 1672, he appointed Locke secretary of the Council of Trade and Plantations. In 1675 Shaftesbury was dismissed from office, and Locke, too close to the action, moved to France for safety. These were maturing years, and the unhealthy political conditions at home were crystallizing his thoughts about the use and abuse of governmental power. In 1679 he returned to London but in 1683 was again forced to flee, this time to Holland, where he remained in exile for five years.

Locke had begun to publish, and his political writings had struck a responsive chord everywhere; he was becoming known as a champion of liberty. In the spring of 1685 he wrote a pamphlet, the *Letter on Toleration,* in defense of religious freedom.

The Glorious Revolution of 1688 toppled the Catholic king. William of Orange crossed to London to become the new monarch, and Locke, safe at last, sailed back to England in the boat that carried the Princess of Orange, the future Queen Mary of England.

Back in England, Locke briefly worked in various official positions. But the London air was still toxic; he was plagued by a constant cough and chronic bronchitis, and he feared that he might be suffering from the consumptive tuberculosis that had claimed his father and younger brother. So in the spring of 1691 he went to live in the quiet country home of Sir Francis and Lady Damaris Cudworth Masham. Though troubled by deafness and respiratory ailments, Locke carried on a spate of activities, with seeming vigor. He wrote. He doctored his neighbors. He received visitors. By this time he was universally admired and respected, and political leaders continued to seek his counsel.

Locke's last days were spent writing a *Fourth Letter on Toleration,* which he never completed. He had written that there are "five great and constant pleasures" in this life: "health, reputation, knowledge, doing good, and above all, the expectation of happiness in another life." He died quietly on October 28, 1704, while listening to Lady Damaris read from the Psalms. He was seventy-two. She later wrote: "His death was like his life, truly pious, yet natural, easy and unaffected." Locke was buried in the parish church at High Laver. The Latin epitaph on his tomb, which he had composed, contains the line "He gave himself to learning for one purpose only, to pursue the truth."

✦

So, John Locke decided that he would study ideas. Since the only mind he knew intimately was his own, Locke's philosophy of mind derives from intense introspection. He will watch his mind as it "turns its view inward upon itself and observes its own actions about those ideas it has (and) takes from thence other ideas." He intends to be entirely objective regarding his own subjectivity.

Locke spent almost twenty years analyzing ideas and writing up the results in his *Essay concerning Human Understanding.* He received £30 for it when it was published in 1689. The *Essay* is divided into four parts. Part I is devoted to proving that "there are no innate principles in the mind." Since Descartes's vigorous advocacy of innate ideas, the notion was widely accepted that such intrinsic ideas exist. Locke submits five telling arguments to prove that the concept of "innate idea" is a myth.

But if ideas are not innate, then where do they come from? In Part II Locke adopts Aristotle's suggestion that the mind is at birth a tabula rasa—a "clean slate." "Let us then, suppose the mind to be, as we say, white paper, void of all characters, without any ideas; how comes it to be furnished? . . . Whence has it all the materials of reason and knowledge? To this I answer, in one word, from experience." From birth on, experience writes information (ideas) on that clean slate. All "the materials of thinking" come from experience, either via the senses or from the mind's reflections on the information received from the senses. "These two are the fountains of knowledge, from whence all the ideas we have, or can naturally have, do spring."

Reflection is carried on using the raw material of sense perception: "There is nothing in the mind except what was first in the senses." Locke divides the ideas that arrive from the senses into primary qualities and secondary qualities. Primary qualities are "utterly inseparable from the body" (the body of a real physical object). They include, he says, "solidity, extension, figure, motion or rest, and number"; elsewhere he adds "bulk" and "texture." These are the qualities that possess the "power" to produce in us the secondary qualities: colors, odors, tastes, and so on. Secondary qualities are to be located entirely in experience; they are not qualities of material objects. The "experience of color," for example, is exactly that, and only that—an experience; color does not exist as a quality of real objects in such a way that, if living experiencers all ceased to exist, color would continue to exist as a quality of material objects. Color cannot exist outside the mind.

If I have anything to boast of, it is that I sincerely love and seek truth with indifferency whom it pleases or displeases.

On Locke:
Locke may almost be said to have invented the notion of common sense.
Sir Isaiah Berlin

To live is to be where and with whom one likes.

The people are absolved from obedience when illegal attempts are made upon their liberties or properties.

On Locke:
Locke has a valid claim to be called the philosopher of the American Revolution.

HENRY STEELE COMMAGER

It is one thing to show a man that he is in error, and another to put him in possession of truth.

When we finally grasp what Locke is saying, his conclusion is staggering. "I think it is easy to draw this observation," he writes, "that the ideas of primary qualities of bodies are resemblances of them, and their patterns do really exist in the bodies themselves; but the ideas produced in us by these secondary qualities have no resemblance of them at all."

Restated: What we perceive is not what is out there. We see one thing; reality is something quite different. As Locke puts it, "There is nothing like our ideas existing in the bodies themselves." All that exists "in the bodies" is the power to stimulate our senses and create perceptions. In other words, the primary qualities (in objects) have the power to stimulate the secondary qualities (in us).

But herein lies the problem. Although we may assume that the "substance" that carries the primary qualities is real, Locke proceeds to show that "substance" is precisely what we can never know. "Substance" is an assumption the mind makes in order to have a "location" for its perceptions of the primary qualities. Conclusion: Since we can never know substance, what is real can never be known. In the final analysis, I know only appearances, not realities.

So, in the end, Locke closes the mind's doors to the outer world; he seals forever our ideas within our own thick skulls. The bottom line of Locke's carefully drawn epistemology is that we must live with probabilities. He defines probability as "likeliness to be true." Or again: "probability is nothing but the appearance of such an agreement or disagreement by the intervention of proofs" whose connections are loose but still appear to provide a modicum of coherence, enough anyway "to induce the mind to judge the proposition to be true or false." Ideas provide varying degrees of certainty or probability; they range from virtually certain to highly improbable. Not being able to attain certainty regarding an idea, the mind substitutes "belief," "assent," "opinion," and "faith" and proceeds to work with that idea on the presumption that it is true, but "without certain knowledge that it is so."

Locke thus sets the stage for an assault on the age-old problem of "appearance versus reality." He reasons his way through the thorny issues involved in attempts to distinguish the subjective from the objective, the experiential from the real.

It is easy to see why Locke is important: he disturbs our most basic intuitions and assumptions about "reality." This problem is as acute as ever in the twenty-first century, especially in the physical sciences.

REFLECTIONS

1 What is epistemology? Make a list of some of the questions that this field of inquiry attempts to answer.
2 What do you understand to be meant by the terms epistemic naivety and epistemic awareness? As you reflect on your own knowledge-condition, do you feel that these terms apply to you?
3 Note the two basic epistemological problems (p. 170). Is it clear to you at this point why these are so important? Can you summarize briefly your understanding of each?
4 This chapter lists the four classic sources of knowledge: the senses, authority, reason, and intuition. But what about other sources? Can you think of still other sources that should be given serious consideration?
5 Each of the four basic sources of information, when not employed with great care, can deceive us and give us false data. Therefore we must remain crit-

ical when assessing information. What specific dangers must we guard against when using each source?

6 "Most of our assumptions have outlived their uselessness" (see marginal quote on p. 174). What do you think Marshall McLuhan (who was a punmaster) is trying to tell us?

7 Will Durant asks an interesting question about the use of reason (see marginal quote on p. 175). How would you answer his question?

8 On p. 174 (see marginal quote) Zeno the Eleatic confronts us with one of his mind-boggling logical paradoxes. How would you resolve this one?

9 John Locke is famous for his idea that the mind at birth is a tabula rasa. As you proceed with your own introspection as Locke did, do you agree with his conclusion that the mind is a clean slate? And that everything in the mind derives from sense experience? (See the biography of Kant, pp. 260 ff., and compare his theory of mind with Locke's.)

10 Locke is neither the first nor the last to make the distinction between primary and secondary qualities, but more than any other epistemologist he spelled it out cleanly and persuasively. State that distinction in your own words, and judge it critically from your own experience.

11 See p. 180: "When we finally grasp what Locke is saying, his conclusion is staggering." How so? What are its epistemological implications? Why is his insight so important?

SENSES

3-2

Learning? certainly, but living primarily, and learning through and in relation to this living.

JOHN DEWEY

Remember the "egocentric predicament" (from Chapter 2-1)? We live in a closed sphere, so to speak; and we are forced to connect with the outer world through our five senses. Since at least 450 BC, critical thinkers have known that our senses don't give us accurate information about what is going on "out there" in the real world. The problem therefore: How much can we trust the senses? How much do they lie to us? Is there any way we can "get around" them and find out what is really going on in the world beyond our senses? The problem is severe and remains with us in the twenty-first century; the nature of "reality," and how we can find out about it, still haunts both philosophy and the sciences.

WE NEVER SEE THE REAL WORLD

1 Our senses constitute our interface with reality. The word **interface** is a modern term used to describe the boundary of contact between two adjacent realms, the common surface where two regions of activity meet. Our human senses provide such an interface between our subjective world of experience and the objective world of reality.

A philosopher riding through the countryside on a train once leaned over to peer long and hard out the window. When asked what he saw, he replied that he was looking at a half of twenty sheep, and that he was wondering how he could find out about the other half.

2 Consider another modern word: **transducer.** A transducer is any substance or device that converts one form of energy into another different form of energy. For instance, a light bulb converts electrical energy into light; a solar cell converts light into electrical energy. A thermostat converts heat into mechanical motion (to throw a switch, for example). A battery converts chemical reactions into electrical energy. Geiger counters convert radioactive radiation into sound as audible clicks. An electroencephalograph converts electrical brain waves into squiggly lines on paper or dancing curves on an oscilloscope. Chlorophyll is one of nature's grand transducers; it converts light into chemicals that sus-

tain the processes of life. Then there are fireflies—they spend a large amount of their waking time converting biochemical energy into bioluminescent mating signals.

An uneducated child and a trained astronomer, both relying on the naked eye and their twenty-twenty vision, will literally see a different sky.
Herman Tennessen

In trying to distinguish appearance from reality and lay bare the fundamental structure of the universe, science has had to transcend the "rabble of the senses."
Lincoln Barnett

3 Our senses are living transducers that convert one kind of energy into another. What kind of energy goes into each of our sense/transducers, and what kind of energy comes out? Answers to these questions can take us a long way toward understanding what happens along our minds' interface with reality, as well as why philosophers have been puzzled for 2,500 years by "the rabble of the senses." First, what is the energy **output?** The energy that results from the transduction process is the same for all our senses: it is electrochemical energy that is propagated along the neural pathways. The impulses that leave the various senses and move toward the central nervous system and into the brain are in every case the same. But if this is the case, why do we **experience** these impulses in different ways? We experience them differently because the impulses are sent to different locations in the brain. Visual sensors in our eyes route their impulses to the back tip of the occipital lobe; sound sensors in our ears send their signals to an area located on the top inner fold of the temporal lobe; and so on. Each specialized area of the cortex "knows how" to convert the electrochemical impulses it receives into the appropriate experience. What if, along the way, "our wires got crossed" and signals were sent to the wrong area of the cortex? If this should happen, the brain would misinterpret the impulses. For example, if touch receptors should send their messages to the "cold center" in the cortex, then the lightest touch would be experienced as a cold sensation. In one laboratory experiment, scientists reversed the nerves of a white rat's right and left rear feet; when the pain sensors in the right foot were stimulated, the rat jerked away the left foot, and vice versa. If the neural pathways from our eyes could be crossed with the neural pathways from our ears, then we would hear colors and see sounds.

4 **Vision** Consider vision as a paradigm for the transduction process of all our senses. There in the fruit bowl on the table is a yellow grapefruit. Using our senses, can we find out what is truly going on with, in, around, and on the grapefruit? We can see it, can we not? and feel it, smell it, and taste it? and with these perceptions can't we create a concept of the grapefruit as it really is? No, we cannot. It is a fact that we can never see (or touch, smell, or taste) the grapefruit. What our eyes see, and all that they see, are light quanta that strike the grapefruit and are reflected back to our eyes. What we call white light (light of all wavelengths radiating together) from a source such as the sun or a lightbulb strikes the surface of the grapefruit, which, because of the atomic and molecular structure of its surface, absorbs all the wavelengths of the spectrum **except** the wavelengths in the vicinity of 5600 to 5800 angstrom units, which are reflected back to our eyes, making us experience yellow. What do we actually see? Only the light reflected from the object, not the object itself.

It's funny how the colors of the real world only seem really real when you viddy them on the screen.
"Alex"
A Clockwork Orange

5 What are "light waves"? They are waves of electromagnetic radiation travelling at a speed of about 186,000 miles per second. They radiate at enormously varied wavelengths, from extremely short gamma rays to very long radio waves. These waves are without color, but the cones embedded in the retinas of our eyes are stimulated by the various wavelengths of radiation to send impulses to

the visual centers of the cortex; and there, and only there, the different wavelengths are translated into experiences of color. Electrochemical impulses are transduced into color experience. Human retinas possess three kinds of cones, which are sensitive, respectively, to three basic wavelengths, the wavelengths we interpret as red, blue, and green—the three primary colors of light (notice the three colors of phosphor dots on a color TV screen). (Textbooks in the physical sciences occasionally define certain wavelengths with a certain color—"red wavelengths" or "green wavelengths." This may be an expedient way of denoting physical phenomena, but it is incorrect and confusing. Modern physical theory consistently shows that physical entities—particles, atoms, molecules, electromagnetic waves—cannot possess the qualities we experience.)

THE MIND MANUFACTURES EXPERIENCE

6 From our knowledge of the transduction process, two rather boggling conclusions must follow. (1) Color is an experience, and only an experience. Color is not real. Color is the experiential finale to a long and complicated process of transduction. The energy input to our visual transducers is uncolored electromagnetic radiation, which enters our eyes with wavelengths (in the visual range of the spectrum) of about 3800 to 7200 angstroms. The transducer/cones in our eyes identify the various wavelengths and send electrical messages along the neural pathways to the visual center of the brain, where we see color. (2) There is no color in the external world of things. That grapefruit **appears** to be yellow, but "it" is not. All the colors we think we see are only experiences in our minds, created there by our processing the various wavelengths of light. The

CREDIBILITY GAP?

As a conscious being I am involved in a story. The perceiving part of my mind tells me a story of a world around me. The story tells of familiar objects. It tells of colours, sounds, scents belonging to these objects; of boundless space in which they have their existence, and of an ever-rolling stream of time bringing change and incident. It tells of other life than mine busy about its own purposes.

As a scientist I have become mistrustful of this story. In many instances it has become clear that things are not what they seem to be. According to the story teller I have now in front of me a substantial desk; but I have learned from physics that the desk is not at all the continuous substance that it is supposed to be in the story. It is a host of tiny electric charges darting hither and thither with inconceivable velocity. Instead of being solid substance my desk is more like a swarm of gnats.

So I have come to realise that I must not put overmuch confidence in the story teller who lives in my mind.

SIR ARTHUR EDDINGTON
New Pathways in Science

The Rabble of the Senses

In trying to distinguish appearance from reality and lay bare the fundamental structure of the universe, science has had to transcend the "rabble of the senses." But its highest edifices, Einstein has pointed out, have been "purchased at the price of emptiness of content." A theoretical concept is emptied of content to the very degree that it is divorced from sensory experience. For the only world man can truly know is the world created for him by his senses. If he expunges all the impressions which they translate and memory stores, nothing is left. . . . So paradoxically what the scientist and the philosopher call the world of appearance—the world of light and color, of blue skies and green leaves, of sighing wind and murmuring water, the world designed by the physiology of human sense organs—is the world in which finite man is incarcerated by his essential nature. And what the scientist and the philosopher call the world of reality—the colorless, soundless, impalpable cosmos which lies like an iceberg beneath the place of man's perceptions—is a skeleton structure of symbols.

Lincoln Barnett
The Universe and Dr. Einstein

ocean is not deep blue, the pine forest is not green, and there is no color in the rainbow.

7 This transduction pattern holds true for all our senses, and for all possible senses that we can imagine, including the bewildering variety of senses now known to be employed by animals, insects, birds, and fish.

Sound Once there was a famous tree in a forest that decided to fall when no one was around. It did its best to make a noise; like a lot of people, it wanted to be heard. But it went down to defeat. It did indeed set up quite a vigorous series of waves in the summer air, waves that alternately rarefied and compressed the air as they moved outward. But there was only silence in the forest. (However, it is reported that a chipmunk, sunning on a rock at the top of the hill, had his transducers going, and that he **heard** the **sound** of a crash in the valley below. Just one transducer can make all the difference between sound and silence.)

Taste Chemical substances penetrate the surface cells of our tastebuds, which respond to only four basic molecular arrangements—we call them sweet, sour, salty, and bitter. All the flavors of our gastronomic spectrum are combinations of these four. But note: "tastes" ("flavors") do not reside in the chemical substances, but in our minds. There is no "sweetness" in peppermint candy, no "saltiness" in sodium chloride, no "sourness" in a lemon.

Smell When gaseous molecules permeate the linings of the olfactory membranes in the upper nasal passageway, we experience odor. Precisely how the molecules manage to stimulate such a subtle variety of odor messages is not presently understood, but the bottom line is clear: there is no scent in the rose

These sensory limitations, and the resulting failure to comprehend fully much of Nature, may be only a local deficiency. On the basis of the new estimates of the great abundance of stars and the high probability of millions of planets with highly developed life, we are made aware—embarrassingly aware—that we may be intellectual minims in the life of the universe. I could develop further this uncomfortable idea by pointing out that sense receptors, in quality quite unknown to us and in fact hardly imaginable, which record phenomena of which we are totally ignorant, may easily exist among the higher sentient organisms of other planets.

Harlow Shapley

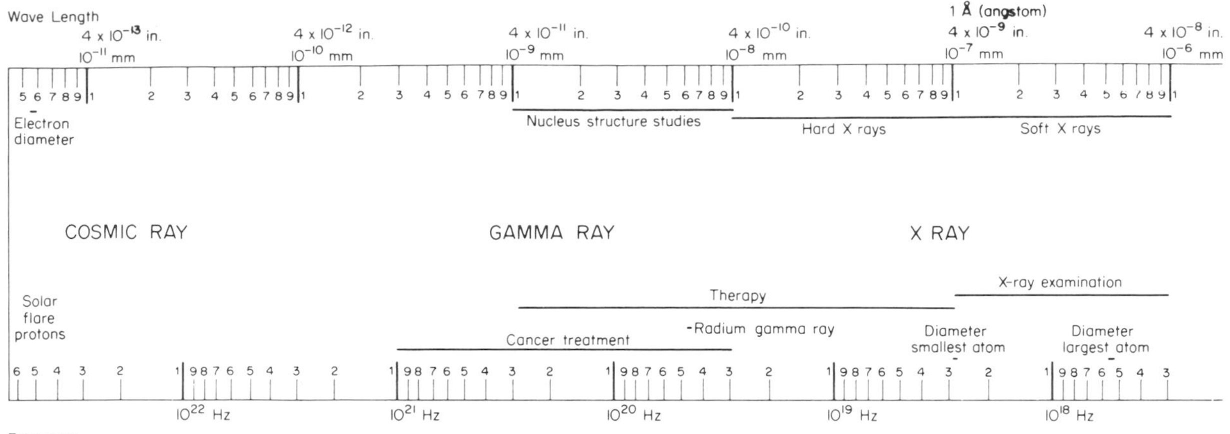

Electromagnetic and sonic spectra

or salty odors from the spray of the breakers on the beach. All the sweet fragrances of the night are only experiences in the mind.

Touch Whether the stimulus is pressure, heat, cold, or cell damage, what we "know" from our touch sensors are the experiences produced in various areas of the cerebral cortex. Pain sensors are the least deceptive of all our senses; when we experience pain from touching a red-hot coal, we are not even tempted to locate the pain in the coal. However, the other touch sensors we readily misinterpret: if I run my fingers over the surface of this page, I am likely to report that I'm feeling the cold, flat surface of paper rather than sensations in my fingertips.

In summary: before the development of sentient creatures on the planet Earth, there were no colors, no sounds, no odors. There were no experiences because there were no experiencers.

Our Senses Deceive

8 After reflecting on how the senses operate, it may be difficult to escape the uneasy feeling that we are being deceived. Our own senses, it seems, manipulate us into believing what is not true. Having thought through the processes of perception, my rational mind may understand that the grapefruit is not yellow, but something in me continues to insist that the grapefruit **is** yellow. It looks yellow; everybody knows it's yellow. The yellow is obviously in the rind, not the mind, and the more I look at it the more I'm convinced that this is so. We would also be willing to wager that the Anaheim red pepper is really HOT and that the sound of a falling tree came from the bottom of the hill. But if these commonsense "facts" are not true, then our senses have deceived us in a big way. Furthermore, our language reinforces this deception. The simplest and most direct

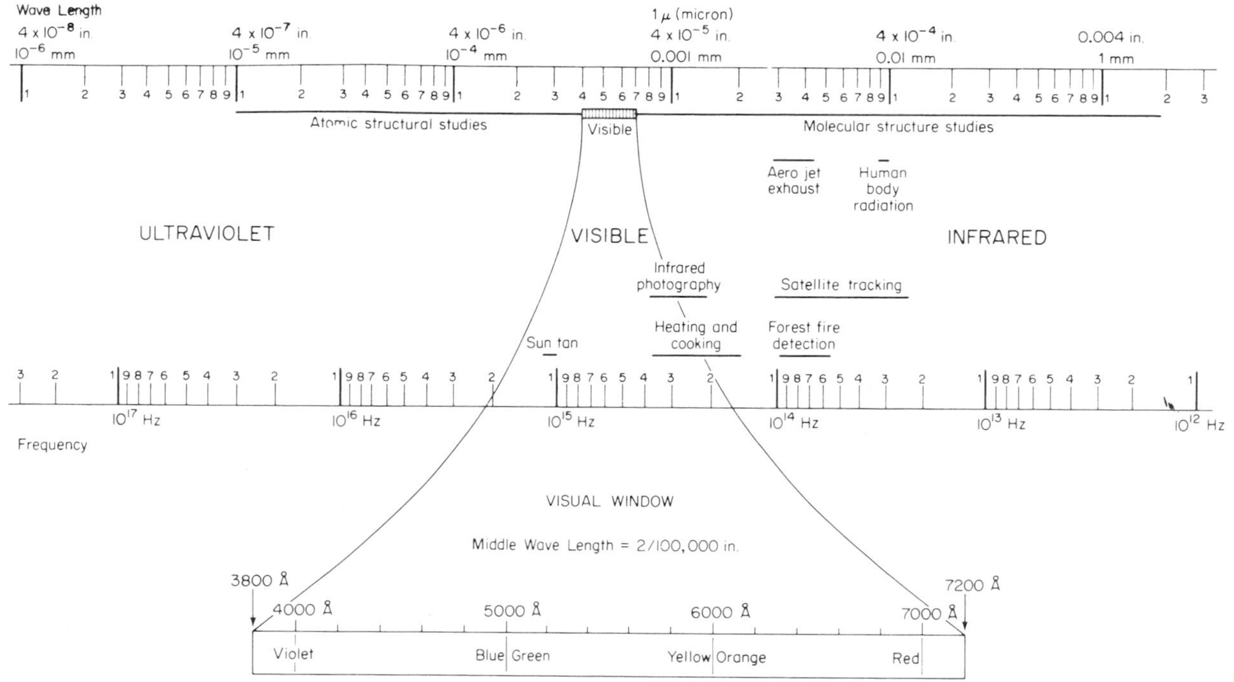

Windows onto the Universe

A continuous frequency spectrum including both sonic and electromagnetic wavelengths is plotted here on a logarithmic scale. Placed together, the frequency ranges from 6×10^{22} Hz (Hertz) to 5×10^{-4} Hz. This is a range in wavelength from the diameter of an electron to a wave almost 200 million miles long. Near the long end of the spectrum the "world resonance" (like the vibration of a giant bell) is a single cycle lasting about twenty seconds.

If this frequency spectrum represents two kinds of reality—sonic and electromagnetic—then we have two "windows" open to us onto the universe.

One is the audio window that, with our natural sense, is limited to a range of 20 to 20,000 Hz. The other is the visual window in the electromagnetic spectrum, a very small window ranging from about 3800 to 7200 Å (angstroms). These windows set the limits to what we can hear and see in the real world.

All the other sonic and electromagnetic realities are there, moving about us; but we are deaf and blind to them, and they are meaningless to us.

When were these windows opened to us? Shall we say, for the audio and visual windows, perhaps a billion years ago? Whenever sentient creatures first began to sense vibrations in the atmosphere and respond to light.

When were the other windows opened to us? Only during the last one hundred years. They were all flung open with breath-taking rapidity.

How sure can we be that all of nature's dynamic operations have now been discovered?

It is impossible to explain . . . qualities of matter except by tracing these back to the behavior of entities which themselves no longer possess these qualities. If atoms are really to explain the origin of color and smell of visible material bodies, then they cannot possess properties like color and smell. . . . Atomic theory consistently denies the atom any such perceptible qualities.

Werner Heisenberg

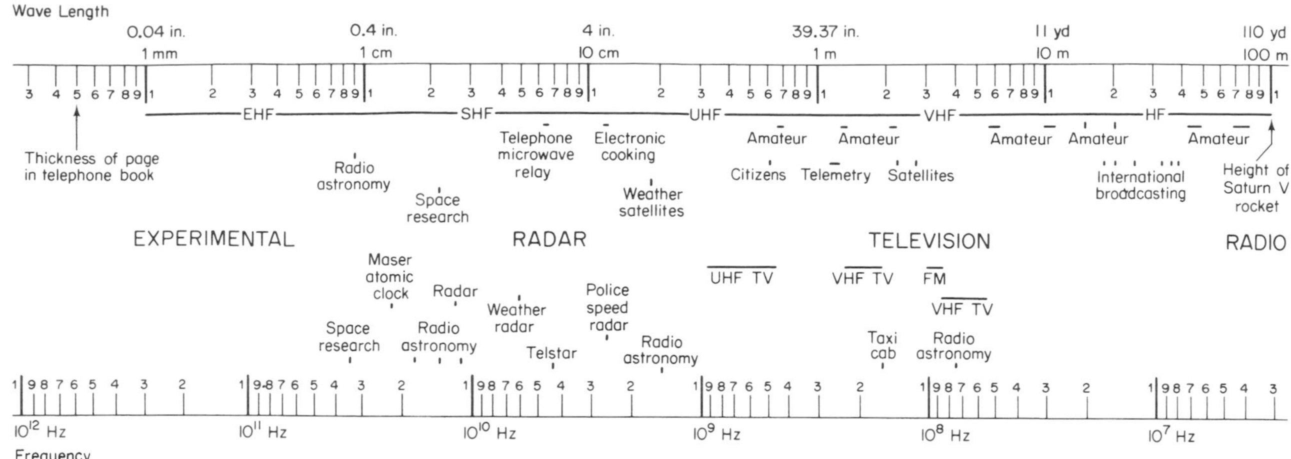

statement I can make of the grapefruit is: "The grapefruit is yellow." The subject of my statement is the noun "grapefruit"; the adjective "yellow" modifies the noun; and the verb "is" clearly attaches the quality of yellowness to the subject—grapefruit. This built-in language deception is to be expected. Language captures and crystallizes our perceptions, whether or not those perceptions are correct. Of course, once the misleading idea is embodied in our language, it will be perpetuated to become a universally accepted "fact" of our existence.

9 One evening, when I was in an Asian country, I ordered dinner but took care to ask the waiter whether the food was spicy hot, since my chemistry doesn't tolerate any spicy hotness in my food. The waiter assured me it was not hot. Shortly he spread several dishes of rice, meat, and curries before me. I suspiciously sampled several of the bowls—all HOT. I called the waiter and informed him that the food was all too hot. He stood baffled for a moment, then reached down and took some marinaded meat from one of the dishes, tasted it, and pronounced, "No, not hot." At which point I dipped into the same bowl, tasted the meat and sauce, and announced, "Yes, very HOT!" Such is "the tyranny of language." The point is that we were both telling the truth. Neither of us was referring to the food; we were reporting our own subjective experiences, which differed, obviously. But the language we employed to articulate our experiences made it appear that one of us was either lying or not perceiving accurately. Both of us in turn pointed to the dish of meat and said "the meat is hot/not hot," clearly revealing where we assumed the hotness to be located.

Things which we see are not by themselves what we see. . . . It remains completely unknown to us what the objects may be by themselves and apart from the receptivity of our senses. We know nothing but our manner of perceiving them.

IMMANUEL KANT

10 To say that we are being "deceived" seems like an ungrateful way of looking at what our senses do. Perhaps there is a better way of interpreting the transduction process. To use an analogy, at this moment there are probably numerous television stations transmitting electromagnetic signals through the atmosphere where you are, but if your TV set is not turned on, the waves are meaningless—**for you** they don't exist. Turning your TV set on would convert meaningless phenomena into meaningful information. Our senses perform precisely this function. They turn on to the physical phenomena of the real world

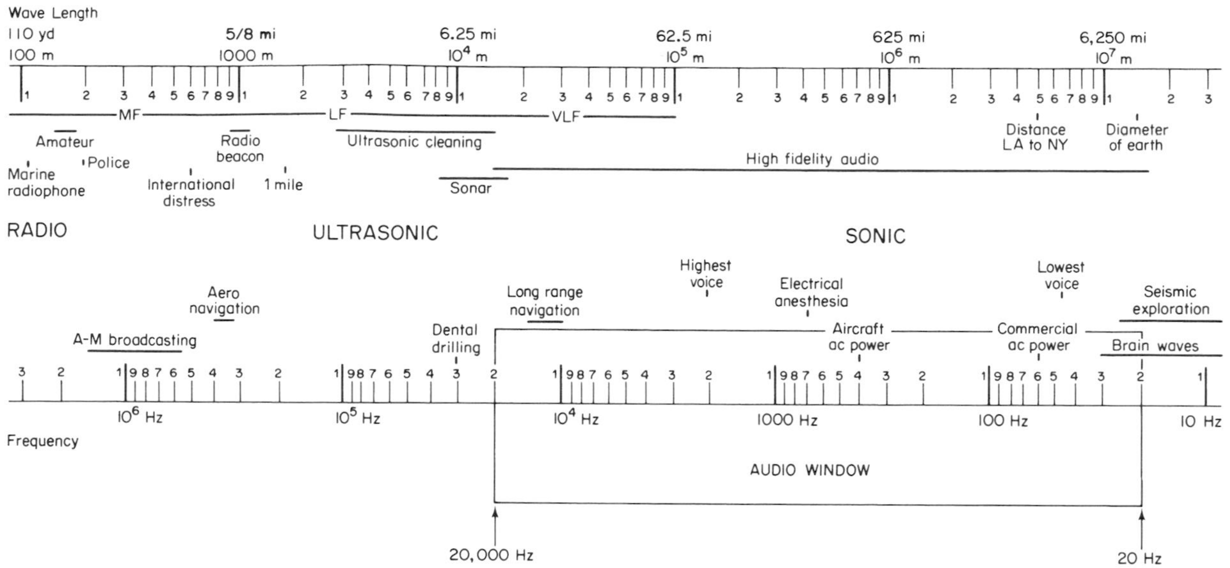

that evolution has "decided" are relevant to our survival; they render our environment meaningful. They translate the events going on around us into useful information.

> *Mankind's common instinct for reality . . . has always held the world to be essentially a theatre for heroism.*
>
> William James

Sensory Limitations and Reality

11 We humans labor under drastic sensory limitations. Take our visual window as an example. If we arbitrarily divide the range of all electromagnetic wave-radiation into sixty "octaves," then visually we can perceive only a single octave, from about 3800 to 7200 angstrom units. But the information-carrying waves extend to great distances on either side of that visual octave. Below the blue end of the visual spectrum the waves grow shorter to become ultraviolet rays, X rays, and gamma rays. Beyond the red end of the spectrum the wavelengths grow longer into the infrared, microwaves, and short and long radio waves. We humans have developed innumerable instruments that can reach into these vast, extended radiation zones on both sides of the visual octave where our senses can't perceive, and, says Buckminster Fuller, "suddenly we're in a completely new kind of reality. The reality of the great electromagnetic spectrum which is part of this communications revolution. And we now know that what man can hear, smell, touch, taste and see is less than a millionth of reality."

> *There remains the final reflection, how shallow, puny, and imperfect are efforts to sound the depths in the nature of things. In philosophical discussion, the merest hint of dogmatic certainty as to finality of statement is an exhibition of folly.*
>
> Alfred North Whitehead

12 We share our planet with millions of species of sentient creatures that are adapted to different niches that necessitated the evolvement of strange and wonderful senses—many of which we humans might wish we possessed. (Obviously we do envy them since we imitate so many of their senses with our scientific instruments.) It is a bit unnerving to realize how little physical reality we humans perceive, and how many more realms of reality exist beyond our perceptual range that other creatures naturally know and use. For instance, bats emit

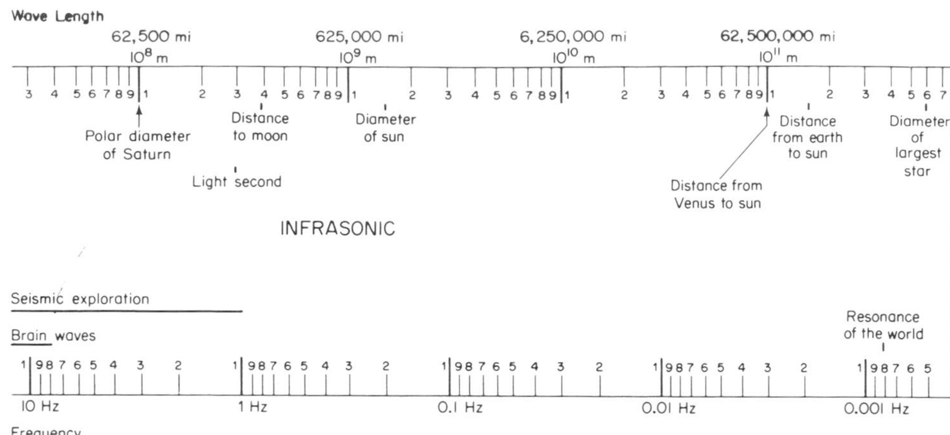

> *Man is thus his own greatest mystery. He does not understand the vast veiled universe into which he has been cast for the reason that he does not understand himself. He comprehends but little of his organic processes and even less of his unique capacity to perceive the world about him, to reason and to dream. Least of all does he understand his noblest and most mysterious faculty: the ability to transcend himself and perceive himself in the act of perception.*
>
> Lincoln Barnett

extremely high-pitched sounds and then listen to their echo to locate flying insects and avoid colliding with objects ("echolocation," the principle used in radar). Porpoises and fish have an underwater counterpart of the bat's radar—a "sonar" system. The "lateral line" in fishes is a combined touch-hear sense, for in water these senses merge. In the dark ocean depths a predatory fish can take a fix on its quarry with its hypersensitive lateral line and attack with pinpoint accuracy. Ants have delicate chemical senses (combining touch, taste, and smell) by which they communicate and establish food trails. Moths both smell and hear with their antennae. Bees navigate to their honey sources by reckoning the sun's position. Sharks can sense the biomagnetic fields of prey. In his novel *Micromegas,* Voltaire describes our frustration at being so limited in our sensing. Micromegas, who lives on a planet circling the star Sirius, asks the secretary of the Saturnian Academy of Sciences how many senses his people have. "We have seventy-two senses," answers the secretary, "and we are every day complaining of the smallness of the number." "I can very well believe," Micromegas replies, "for, in our globe, we have very near one thousand senses, and yet, with all these, we feel continually a sort of listless inquietude and vague desire, which are forever telling us that we are nothing, and that there are beings infinitely nearer perfection."

Epistemic Loneliness

13 As we reflect on the human predicament regarding the senses and reality, a feeling of loneliness may begin to overtake us, an "epistemic loneliness." For the egocentric predicament (see pp. 79ff.) is really an epistemological condition—total isolation within a world of our own making. We live in a shell, a private, personal shell inside which takes place an immense variety of rich and meaningful experience; and when we try to break out of our shells to make contact with the world and share our experience, we only rediscover the immutable depth of our predicament. We live in an epistemological shell with no doors; none may enter and none may share. Since this epistemological condition ap-

pears to be inescapable, it seems that we have no choice but to learn to live with it, to understand it, and to try to correct for it.

For the sceptic to bewail the fact that we can know nothing but appearance is as silly as it would be to bewail the fact that we have nothing to wear but clothes and nothing to eat but food.

W. P. MONTAGUE

1. The fallacy of objectification is a constant temptation. Our psychological nature conspires to make us think that a variety of private experiences are in some way real, that they are events occurring out there in the real world of objects/events. Ask a drunk to describe the spiders he sees during a seizure of DTs, and he will invariably say they are "out there" on the floor or wall. The mind, that is, **knows** where spiders are supposed to be, so it puts them there.
2. Accordingly, we have all lived, if unwittingly, in a condition of confusion regarding the location of object/events. Our subjective and objective worlds are inextricably interwoven; events we thought to be private often turn out to be objective, while many supposedly objective events prove to be experiences only.
3. Critical intellects are restless with these evolutionary arrangements with their limitations and deceptions. While we can be grateful that our sensory and information-processing systems have rendered the physical environment accessible and intelligible, we have reached a point in our quest for reality when we want to go beyond these constraints. We want to make all necessary corrections in our perceiving and processing so we can move out of our shells and come to know our universe as it really is.

THE PRAGMATIC NATURE OF KNOWING

14 The most annoying problem in Western epistemology derives precisely from this sense predicament: If we experience only our experiences (and not reality), how can we be sure that we know **anything** about the real world? Or, to put it differently, if objective physical phenomena are altered by our senses before our minds have a chance to work with them, then how can we learn **anything** about the original phenomena? Can we ever figure out what those phenomena are? Or again: If we experience only the subjective side of our interface with reality, can we ever know **anything** about the objective side of that interface-boundary?

15 About 1770 the Scottish philosopher David Hume composed a confession that speaks for many thinkers whose lifeblood has been spent wrestling with abstract and unobservable entities but who still possess the gift of wanting to keep their speculations in perspective. Hume wrote:

> Should it be asked me whether I sincerely assent to this argument which I have been to such pains to inculcate, and whether I be really one of those skeptics who hold that all is uncertain, . . . I should reply . . . that neither I nor any other person was ever sincerely and constantly of that opinion. . . . I dine, I play backgammon, I converse and am merry with my friends; and when, after three or four hours amusement, I would return to these speculations, they appear so cold and strained and ridiculous that I cannot find in my heart to enter into them any further. . . . Thus the skeptic still continues to reason and believe, though he asserts that he cannot defend his reason by reason; and by the same rule he must assent to the principle concerning

David Hume (1711–1776)

the existence of body, though he cannot pretend, by any arguments of philosophy, to maintain its veracity.

16 Perhaps we should listen to Hume's implied counsel. Here is this Scottish skeptic whose reason convinces him of one set of facts (we know nothing for sure about reality) but whose experience seems to contradict his reason ("I dine, I play backgammon, I converse . . ."). When this kind of conflict exists between theory and experience, most of us feel a pressure to find a resolution. (Remember the bumblebee that some aerodynamicists said couldn't possibly fly?) Hume implies (1) that it is very impracticable not to assume that the real world exists; and (2) that day-to-day living is very difficult if one tries to operate on the assumption that he has no certain knowledge about the real world. Life, after all, for most of us, is a very practical matter. Perhaps we need to make certain assumptions, necessary for living, that may in fact be untrue or whose truth-value is still open. Modern-day physicists, for example, operate on working models of atoms, electrons, and so forth, knowing full well that those models are likely to change as new and better information is acquired. This is also true for molecular biologists working with genes; cosmologists speculating about black holes, sources of cosmic rays, and the nature of dark matter in the uni-

We can never arrive at the real nature of things from the outside. However much we investigate, we can never reach anything but images and names. We are like a man who goes round a castle seeking in vain for an entrance and sometimes sketching the facades.

Arthur Schopenhauer

Less than a Millionth

There has been a complete changeover in human affairs. Where man has always been after things, after reality—reality being everything you can see, touch, taste, smell and hear—suddenly we're in a completely new kind of reality. The reality of the great electromagnetic spectrum which is part of this communications revolution. And we now know that what man can hear, smell, touch, taste and see is less than a millionth of reality.

Buckminster Fuller

Reality Is Third Base

You and I view reality much as a spectator might watch a baseball game through a knothole in the fence—and all he sees is third base. He's got his eye up there and he watches the entire game through third base, and only third base.

And if someone asks him to describe baseball, he says, "Well, there's some guy that stands around kicking the dirt for quite a while, spitting on the ground, and that sort of thing. And all at once a bunch of guys come sliding in and kick the dirt all over and then swear at each other and almost fight, and pretty soon they all leave and the first guy stands around, kicking the dirt once again. And that's about it."

And this is America's number one sport?!

This is about the way we view reality. We perceive just a little bit of it, and we are so naive to think that that's all of it.

But that isn't all of it. The truth is that virtually the whole ball game called reality is being played beyond our knothole-eye-view.

Court Holdgrafer

verse; and paleontologists attempting to reconstruct human origins. The current literature in quantum mechanics is largely an ongoing debate about how much our mental constructions can represent reality. So we laymen must also make assumptions about the nature of the real world while reminding ourselves that it is always possible to create better pictures of what is truly going on in nature. Critical epistemologists such as Hume and Berkeley, Kant and Einstein have rightly made it clear that our knowledge of reality is tenuous and shaky. Their arguments remain basically sound and still stand as starting points for an understanding of the nature of knowledge. In the final analysis, we know only our subjective experience, which begins with sensory reaction and ends with the fabrication of knowledge. Accordingly, we cannot experience directly the real world of objects/events. Neither matter nor the principles of motion are directly perceivable.

> ***"George, it's impossible to correct a defective reality-orientation overnight."***
>
> **Ursula K. Le Guin**
> ***The Lathe of Heaven***

17 In summary, what is the nature of our knowledge about the real world of objects/events? Our knowledge of reality is composed of ideas our minds have created on the basis of our sensory experience. It is a fabric of knowledge woven by the mind. Knowledge is not given to the mind; nothing is "poured" into it. Rather, the mind manufactures perceptions, concepts, ideas, beliefs, and so forth and holds them as working hypotheses about external reality. Every idea is a (subjective) working model that enables us to handle real objects/events with some degree of pragmatic efficiency. However persuasive our thoughts and images may be, they are only remote representations of reality; they are tools that enable us to deal with reality. It is as though we draw nondimensional maps to help us understand four-dimensional territory. The semanticists have long reminded us to beware of confusing any sort of map with the real landscape. "The map," they say, "is **not** the territory."

"The topic for today is: What is reality?"

GEORGE BERKELEY

The Irish Immaterialist

By the time he was twenty-five years old, Berkeley had published his *Principles of Human Knowledge*, had stirred up international controversy in philosophical and theological circles, and was regarded as one of the most stylish and challenging philosophers the English-speaking world had produced. George Berkeley (rhymes with "darkly") was born in 1685 in a farmhouse on the grounds of ancient Dysert Castle in County Kilkenny, Ireland. His father, William, was an Englishman, by trade a minor customs official. His mother is unknown to us. Berkeley always thought of himself as English and looked upon his Irish neighbors as foreigners.

Very early, young Berkeley displayed precocious qualities: a strong-willed, independent, creative intellect; and a passionate, polemical nature. His parents, while not wealthy, were able to provide him an excellent education. He first attended Kilkenny school (from age eleven to fifteen), where he studied mathematics and the classics. At fifteen he matriculated at Trinity College, Dublin (he entered in March 1700), where he was immediately absorbed in the philosophical ideas of Locke and Descartes, Leibniz, Newton, and Hobbes.

His enthusiasms and eccentricities found full expression at Trinity College, which was a center for intellectual growth, justly praised for its freedom of inquiry and academic excellence; there was a spirit of revolt against outdated scholastic thinking in philosophy and science. It was fertile soil for Berkeley's inquisitive mind, and he could safely challenge the fashionable orthodoxies of philosophy and theology. He and some friends organized a philosophy club to study "the new philosophy," which meant Locke.

Berkeley's prime calling was to the priesthood of the Anglican Church. He was ordained a deacon, then priest, in 1709, and he remained a lifelong apologist for his faith. He was appointed bishop of Cloyne in 1734 and spent the last eighteen years of his life administering his diocese.

Berkeley's academic achievements were no less important to him. He was associated with Trinity College all his life, as undergraduate and graduate, then fellow (at the age of twenty-two, after completing an examination with great distinction); and college tutor when he was twenty-four. In 1709 he was promoted to sublecturer and junior dean; in 1712 to junior Greek lecturer. He received a doctor of divinity degree in 1721, was appointed senior Greek lecturer and university preacher, then in 1722 was made dean and elected to a lectureship in Hebrew. All these accomplishments were a tribute to his leadership, energy, originality, and loyalty.

Berkeley traveled widely and wrote continually. In 1713 he visited London and was presented at the court of Queen Anne. He was widely admired for his courtesy, character, and quick mind. He befriended such literary lights as Swift, Addison, Steele, and Pope; he deeply impressed royalty, notables, bon vivants, and "men of merit," and moved easily among them. Pope commented that Berkeley seemed to possess "every virtue under heaven," and the statesman Atterbury exclaimed, "So much understanding, so much knowledge, so much innocence, and such humility, I did not think had been the fashion of any but angels, till I saw this gentleman." In 1713 he made his first trip to France and Italy, where he was enthralled with nature and the ancient ruins. He wrote a vivid account of the eruption of Mount Vesuvius in April 1717.

Berkeley's major writings were all completed before he was twenty-eight years old. At twenty-four he wrote *Essay towards a New Theory of Vision* (1709), in which he proposed a radical explanation of how we perceive visual depth. His philosophic fame rests on two works, *Treatise Concerning the Principles of Human Knowledge*, Part I (1710) (he lost part II on a trip to Sicily and could never bring himself to rewrite it); and *Dialogues between Hylas and Philonous* (1713). These are the great works that contain the logical arguments for "the immaterialist hypothesis."

Berkeley was the first great philosopher to visit America. He had long dreamed of establishing a college in Bermuda to educate young men for the clergy and to bring the Gospel to Indians and Negroes; to this end he had collected funds from private donors and a promise of £20,000 from the House of Commons. So he and his bride (Anne Forster, married in August) sailed for America in September of 1728. For three years they lived in Newport, Rhode Island. They bought a ninety-six-acre farm and built a house. He wrote, preached, traveled inland, and enjoyed the countryside. They had one son, and a daughter who died in infancy. These were relatively happy years, but he never succeeded in raising the money for the college. Finally the Berkeleys journeyed to Boston and caught a ship back to Dublin.

While in America Berkeley penned a poem containing the line "Westward the course of empire takes its way." Because of that line, a California town was named for him.

The rest of his life was divided between his clerical responsibilities, social concerns, occasional writing, and his family. They lived in County Cork after he became bishop in 1734. Berkeley adored his four surviving children and carefully supervised the education of each. He spoke of "the starlight beauty" of his daughter Julia and wished he had twenty sons like George. In 1751, his health failing, and mourning the loss of a son, he decided to retire. The following year his eldest son was ready for Oxford, so the family moved there to be near him. On the evening of January 14, 1753, while his wife was reading to him on the couch, he drifted quietly to sleep. He was sixty-eight years old.

✦

As a young man, Berkeley developed the habit of jotting down his ideas in notebooks. These autobiographical reflections were unknown until they were discovered in 1871 and given the title of *Commonplace Book*. In a paragraph written when he was twenty-one, he declared that the concept of materialism or "substance" had always been "the main pillar

Esse est percipi *(or* **Esse is percipi***). "To be is to be perceived."*

He who says there is no such thing as an honest man, you may be sure is himself a knave.

Westward the course of empire takes its way;
The four first acts already past,
A fifth shall close the drama with the day:
Time's noblest offspring is the last.

On the Prospect of Planting Arts and Learning in America

On Berkeley:
It was brilliant of Berkeley to get rid of all materialism with one strategic blow simply by proving that matter does not exist; . . . But it was a trifle dishonest; even a bishop might have hesitated at such a pious fraud.

WILL DURANT

When we do our utmost to conceive the existence of external bodies we are all the while only contemplating our own ideas.

There is nothing that I desire more than to know thoroughly all that can be said against what I take for truth.

and support of skepticism" on which have been founded "all the impious schemes of atheism and irreligion. . . . How great a friend material substance hath been to atheists in all ages were needless to relate. . . . When this cornerstone is once removed, the whole fabric cannot choose but fall to the ground. . . ."

Berkeley was confident that he could remove this "cornerstone" of atheism. How exactly did he manage it?

He started with an idea from John Locke—that the idea of "substance" is merely an assumption on our part, since we can never perceive the real substantive world directly. What we experience —and the only things we experience— are colors, tastes, odors, and so forth, the so-called secondary qualities, which are actually our own perceptions.

What about the "primary qualities" —shape, solidity, motion/rest, extension (volume)—the qualities that we believe inhere in objects themselves? How do we know about these? We only infer these too, said Berkeley. How do you know the shape of a seashell? You run your fingers over the surface and feel it. Not exactly, Berkeley reminds us; we don't feel it. We only feel our sensations and proceed to assume that "it" exists in physical seashell form and that such external matter is the cause of our sensations. We further assume that this matter possesses certain (primary) qualities that we cannot experience directly.

So far, Berkeley seems to agree with Locke. But where Locke never doubted the existence of matter (he merely said we can never know it), Berkeley asks: If substance is an assumption, then could that assumption be wrong? Suppose the world of material objects really doesn't exist. How could we account for the supposed objects that cause our perceptions? Berkeley concluded that there is an alternative assumption, just as logical as "substance," and preferable.

Since we cannot avoid assuming, assume that God exists, and that he places in our minds all the perceptions that we experience. Why is the assumption of matter a more reasonable assumption than the existence of God? And if one is a Christian philosopher, doesn't the assumption of a God-source become a more congenial assumption than a matter-source?

Therefore, reasoned Berkeley, "to be is to be perceived"—*esse est percipi;* and not to be perceived is not to exist. There are no "real" clouds, rocks, oceans, stars, penguins, or seashells. Such items are but mind-images derived from God. Objects exist, therefore, only while they are being perceived; and they exist only in perception. He wrote: "To say things exist when no mind perceives them, is perfectly unintelligible."

How can we be sure the persistent objects of experience—our homes, friends, the familiar belongings—will "be there" when we want to perceive them? Does the seashell-image flicker on and off, in and out of existence, every time we look at it or turn away from it? Not really, says Berkeley. God is the eternal perceiver, and all images continue to exist in the mind of God. They are always available to us for the asking and are fed into our singular minds by God's mind whenever we need them.

It rings like a psychedelic fairy tale. The physical world doesn't exist; "matter" is merely a make-believe idea we thought we needed—"the fiction of our own brain."

Berkeley's attempt to annihilate matter was a popular topic of conversation, with and without heat and light. The lexicographer Samuel Johnson was irritated by it all, as Boswell tells us:

> After we came out of church, we stood talking for some time together of Berkeley's ingenious sophistry to prove the non-existence of matter, and that everything in the universe is merely ideal [idea]. I observed that though we are satisfied his doctrine is not true, it is impossible to refute it. I shall never forget the alacrity with which Johnson answered, striking his foot with a mighty force against a large

stone, till he rebounded from it, "I refute it thus!"

But what had Dr. Johnson really proved by kicking the rock? He had merely illustrated and confirmed Berkeley's argument. For all Johnson "knew" was the sharp pain in his toe, perhaps a numb feeling in his foot, and the sensation of a sudden stop that must have given his leg a jolt. All he had proven by kicking the rock was that he was capable of feeling a variety of subjective sensations. All he knew was his own experience, and that, after all, was the point Berkeley was making. So Samuel Johnson had unwittingly added his considerable weight to the philosophy of "immaterialism."

What else is this but philosophical fantasy? Most of us are convinced (are we not?) that physical matter exists. It seems to us that Berkeley made a simple mistake, a non sequitur: just because we cannot experience physical matter directly, it does not necessarily follow that matter does not exist.

But did he really go wrong? (1) Berkeley emphasizes the fact that we are limited absolutely to our own perceptions and cannot directly experience any "real" world. Most epistemologists today would agree with him. (2) He is therefore repeating John Locke's point that physical matter (or "substance") is an idea—an assumption that we believe to be a logical necessity. On this point also, he seems to be correct.

Whether you will go further with Berkeley and agree that his alternative assumption—God as the source of experience—is a better idea will depend on personal preference and theological belief. Most of us remain convinced that the reality of matter is a better-working assumption, but perhaps that is only because we have lived with it uncritically most of our lives.

We must face honestly, however, Berkeley's singular challenge: Prove, if you can, that any material object exists apart from your perception of it. If you can, then Berkeley is wrong. If you cannot, then you will have to concede (Berkeley would insist) that the world is merely your idea.

His logic is brilliant and he almost succeeds. "His arguments are, strictly speaking, unanswerable," wrote Lord Chesterfield; and Boswell duly noted that although we are convinced that his doctrine is false, "it is impossible to refute it." David Hume agreed: Berkeley's arguments "admit of no answer and produce no conviction." In 1847 a reward of £100 (later £500) was offered to anyone who could refute Berkeley's logic. The money still awaits a taker.

Subsequent critics have written volumes of exposition and analysis of Berkeley's "immaterial hypothesis." However, a short limerick attributed to Ronald Knox contains the essence of the good bishop's philosophy:

There was a young man who said,
 "God
Must think it exceedingly odd
 If he finds that this tree
 Continues to be
When there's no one about in the
 Quad."

REPLY

"Dear Sir:
 Your astonishment's odd.
I am always about in the Quad.
 And that's why the tree
 Will continue to be,
Since observed by
 Yours faithfully,
 God"

Reflections

1 Note the anecdote of the philosopher who "was looking at a half of twenty sheep" (see marginal quote on p. 182). Everybody knows that a half of

Occasionally an epistemolog is found who is capable of smiling, like Bradley or William James; occasionally one is found who understands that his 'ology is only a game, and therefore, plays it with a worldy twinkle in his eye, like David Hume.

WILL DURANT

Truth is a property of beliefs, and derivatively of sentences which express beliefs.

BERTRAND RUSSELL

The disputants I ween
Rail on in utter ignorance
Of what each other mean,
And prate about an Elephant
Not one of them has seen.

JOHN G. SAXE

Reality is a creation of the nervous system.

HARRY JERISON

twenty is ten, so what's his problem? How would you suggest that he go about finding a solution?

2 Each of our senses is a living transducer (p. 182). What is meant by this? What are the epistemological implications of our realizing that our senses are in fact transducers?

3 Pp. 183–189: Numerous phenomena that appear to be a part of the real world turn out to be experiences only and have no real status. Do you personally have any trouble accepting these fact-claims as true? Why?

4 What is meant by "the conspiracy of language"? What causes this deception? Give some examples of how we are thus deceived by our language.

5 From this point on it is imperative that you understand the philosophic usage of the terms **real** and **reality.** (See the glossary.) Which of the following events would be real and which would be solely experiential? (Be wary: definitions are crucial, and in some cases it is not an either/or decision.)

an idea
a feeling of loneliness
an itch
your car
an atom
Pythagoras
a heartache
a beautiful painting
a dirty picture
a poem
a mirage
the planet Mars
the god Mars
a scandal
a toothache (in your wisdom tooth)
Mr. Spock (of *Star Trek*)
the state of Arizona
the state of euphoria
the sound of music
The Pythagorean Theorem
gravity
the law of gravity
heat
temperature
the office of the president of the United States
the president of the United States
the state
a sunset

6 After studying the human "visual window" through which we see reality, how would you describe the real world to: (1) a person who has been blind from birth? (2) a highly intelligent alien from another planet who "sees" wavelengths only in the infrared region of the electromagnetic spectrum? (3) a fellow epistemologist who is acutely aware, as you are, of our severe human perceptual limitations?

7 This chapter speaks of "epistemic loneliness." Are these words meaningful to you? Can you feel this condition personally or does it not apply to you?

8 Review pp. 183–188 and then reflect: Does it trouble you that the more we know about the "realities beyond appearances" the further we are moving away from the world of everyday experience? Does this imply that our experiential world is, in some fundamental way, suspect, invalid, erroneous, and/or worthless? Yes or no—and why?

9 In the final analysis, what do we "know" about the real world and how do we know it? At this point you might do well to read the story of Einstein's philosophy on pp. 516ff.

MIND

3-3

The human mind is extremely creative. Like a sophisticated computer (no surprise since computers are designed to emulate the mind), nature has written a data processing program that recognizes input from the senses and organizes that sensory information for practical use in daily living. But this "practicality" mechanism, by creating general abstractions, also distances us from reality, that is, from concrete objects/events. Moving through abstractions to rediscover concrete events is a major problem for all who seek to know the truth about the world. This chapter describes the problem and suggests answers.

THE PRAGMATIC THINKER

1 In its attempt to make sense of the energy-environment in which we live, the mind proves to be a versatile, creative instrument. It translates events of the real world into experiences we can use in living. The mind is not at all the "blank tablet," the *tabula rasa,* that some earlier thinkers thought it to be.

We have a fairly clear understanding now of the general nature of knowledge. Human knowledge is a collection of constructs created by the mind from the raw materials of sensation; it is a series of scaled-down maps that we use to find our way in the full-scale territory of the real world.

Concepts without percepts are empty. Percepts without concepts are blind.
IMMANUEL KANT

Probably a crab would be filled with a sense of personal outrage if it could hear us class it without ado or apology as a crustacean, and thus dispose of it. "I am no such thing," it would say; "I am myself, myself alone."
WILLIAM JAMES

WHY WE THINK IN ABSTRACTIONS

2 One of the basic functions of the human mind is to create **abstractions.** What if we had to have a separate name for every object that we ever encountered: for each candle, coin, animal, bell, seashell, cloud, and penguin? And a separate

Jean Piaget tells of a little girl who was asked whether one might call the Sun the Moon and the Moon the Sun. She explained impatiently that no one could confuse the Sun and the Moon because the Sun shines so brightly.

word for every single event we ever experienced: the strumming of a guitar, the meteor trail across the sky, the smell of a summer rain? If we were forced to have a different symbol for each object and each event, clearly we would be in trouble. In a few hours our memories would go on overload; in no time we would run out of words with which we "fix" these single items in our minds and use to connect and retrieve them. So what do we do? We place singular items in groups. All the objects/events that have common qualities we group together into a single package with a single label. Once we have so packaged them, we no longer have to deal with the individual objects; we deal only with the whole package. Abstractions, that is, are the mind's packages that enable us to handle infinite details of experience.

3 An abstraction, by definition, is an idea created by the mind to refer to all objects which, possessing certain characteristics in common, are thought of in the same class. The number of objects in the class can range from two to infinity. We can refer to all men, all hurricanes, all books, all energy-forms—all everything.

Abstractions are created at various levels of generalization. For instance, if we begin with an orange—a particular object as yet unclassified and unlabeled—then the first level of abstraction might be "Valencia orange," grouping together the qualities shared by all Valencia oranges. A next level might include all oranges (Valencia, the navels, sour oranges, and so forth); next might come all "citrus fruit" (including oranges, grapefruit, lemons, kumquats, and so forth). Still higher would come the whole basket of "fruit" (citrus fruit, figs, apples, apricots, breadfruit, etcetera). Above this level we might class together all "edible things," or more general still, a very-high-level abstraction, "material objects."

Notice how far we have come in the breadth of generalization: from a single orange to an all-inclusive class labeled "material objects." At each higher level of abstraction the objects have less and less in common. Yet such broad, general abstractions dominate our thinking and communicating. We think of fruits and vegetables, or food; we class together medicines, drugs, pollutants; we speak of nations, races of people, Hindus, Easterners, Eskimos, and so on.

4 While abstraction-building is an inescapable mental process—in fact it is the first step in the organization of our knowledge of objects/events—a serious problem is inherent in the process. At high levels of abstraction we tend to group together objects that have but a few qualities in common, and our abstractions may be almost meaningless, without our knowing it. We fall into the habit of using familiar abstractions and fail to realize how empty they are. For example, what do the objects in the following abstractions have in common? All atheists, all Western imperialists, all blacks or all whites (and if you think it's skin color, think twice), all conservatives, all trees, all French people, all Christians. When we think in such high-level abstractions, it is often the case that we are communicating nothing meaningful at all.

If, for example, I should send you to the grocery store with the request, "Buy some food for dinner," your response would probably be "Food? What sort of food?" To which I say, "Get some vegetables." You would still be quite in order to ask, "What vegetables do you want me to buy?" If I finally move down

"Everyone must have a label."

the abstraction ladder far enough to say "Get some vegetables for a salad," you would probably retort with an exasperated "What vegetables?" "Well, get a bunch of radishes, a head of lettuce, some green onions, and a cucumber." And, of course, you reply: "Why didn't you say that in the first place?!"

Note that what we are talking about becomes increasingly clear only as we move down the abstraction ladder toward the concrete objects of the world. By contrast, the individual who moves higher and higher on the abstraction ladder knows less and less what he is talking about, probably without knowing it. At high abstraction levels we can trade off, conveniently and in a most familiar fashion, with ominously vague meanings.

Dr. S. I. Hayakawa describes what we do: "The trouble with speakers who never leave the higher levels of abstraction is not only that they fail to notice when they are saying something and when they are not; they also produce a similar lack of discrimination in their audiences. Never coming down to earth, they frequently chase themselves around in verbal circles, unaware that they are making meaningless noises."

S. I. Hayakawa (1906–1992)

Classifying and Labeling

5 The mind has another technique to enable it to assimilate information. It classifies abstractions and labels them. This is our mental filing system.

In his semantic textbook *Language in Thought and Action,* Dr. Hayakawa imagines a primitive village (your village) in which a variety of animals scamper about. Some of the animals have small bodies, some large. Some have round heads, while others have square heads. Some have curly tails, others straight tails. And such distinguishing marks are very important.

Observers are not led by the same physical evidence to the same picture of the universe unless their linguistic backgrounds are similar or can in some way be calibrated.
Benjamin Lee Whorf

For you have discovered through experience that the animals with small bodies eat your grain, while those with large bodies do not. The small-bodied animals you have labeled *gogo* and you shoo them away; and when you call to a neighbor, "Quick, chase the *gogo* out of your garden!" he knows what you mean. The large-bodied animals (labeled *gigi*) are harmless, so you allow them to wander where they will.

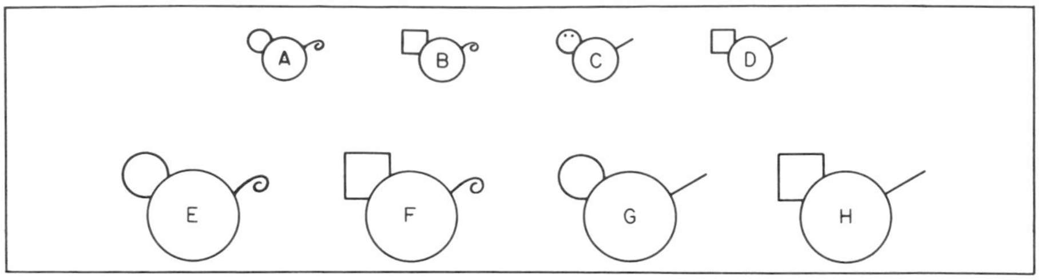

Village animals redrawn from S. I. Hayakawa, *Language in Thought and Action.*

Einstein: "Any fool can know. The point is . . . to understand!"
Ernest Kinoy
Doctor Einstein Before Lunch

However, a visitor from another village has had a different experience. He has found that animals with square heads bite, while those with round heads do not. Since he has no gardens, their biting is more noticeable than their habit of eating grain. The square-heads, which bite, he calls *dabas* and he scares them away. He generally ignores the round-headed *dobos.*

Still another man, a relative from a distant village, has found that the animals with curly tails kill snakes. Such animals are valuable; he calls them *busa* and breeds them for protection. But those with straight tails (which he calls *busana*) are merely a nuisance, and he is quite indifferent to them.

Now, one day villagers from far and near meet to trade and talk. You are sitting in on a barter-session when one of the animals runs by (let's say the animal marked C in the diagram, next page). You spot the animal headed for your garden, so you call down the path for someone to chase the *gogo* away. A visitor, however, looks at you with disdain, for he knows that the animal is a *dobo.* It has a round head. It doesn't bite, and he is surprised that you don't know this. A third visitor scornfully tells the both of you that the animal is clearly a *busana,* as everyone knows; it doesn't kill snakes or have any other redeeming qualities.

Geological eras, periods, and epochs are human inventions; they are man's attempt to put huge stretches of time in their place and make them seem reasonably comprehensible. Nature was indifferent to such fine distinctions. Time flowed on continuously with one phase changing imperceptibly into another without dividing itself neatly into segments.
Philip Van Doren Stern

A heated discussion ensues as to what the animal really is. Is it a *gogo,* a *dobo,* or a *busana?* A quarrel is brewing as to what the animal really is. It hardly helps when another tribesman, asking what the fuss is all about, declares with finality that the animal (still C) is a *muglock* because it is edible and they feast on it every full moon. All the inedible animals in his village he labels *uglocks.*

Of course this discussion finally ends where all such discussions finally end.

6 What is the animal really? What is any object, really? In the last analysis, all one can do is point to the object as if to say, "It is what it is." As Hayakawa puts it, "The individual object or event we are naming, of course, has no name and belongs to no class until we put it in one."

All the objects/events of our experience are classified in this manner: in terms of our experience of them. In the English language, for instance, we have two words that originated in the Middle Ages for the animal *Sus scrofa.* The word *swine* was the term used by the serfs and swineherds who had to tend them; the word *pork* was employed by those who ate their succulent flesh at the banquet table.

Systems of classification, therefore, are reflexive. They inform us about the person who is doing the classifying—they tell us about his experience—and they tell us relatively little or nothing about the object classified. Classification never tells us what the classified object really is.

Classification systems are pragmatic. They are guidelines for operation. They tell us how to think about the object, how to treat it, use it, or relate to it. We classify objects and use the classification as long as the system is convenient; the moment it ceases to work, then we reclassify.

7 An understanding of these thought-processes—namely, the nature of classifying and labeling—provides an excellent criterion for distinguishing epistemic naivety from epistemic awareness.

A precritical thinker has the unshakable belief that his classification tells him what the object really is and that names are by nature attached to the objects they refer to. It was a universal assumption made by the primitive mind that there is an intimate and necessary connection between the symbol and the object symbolized. Indeed, a mystical power was thought to reside in the symbol itself, and words were to be feared or desired in the same way the object/event referred to was to be feared or desired.

To attempt to persuade a primitive thinker that his classifications and labels are merely his mental tools, relative and arbitrary, would be a hopeless task. His own name is *Marika,* he will inform you, and it could not be otherwise. His god's name is *Mbwenu* and the deity can be called upon only by using his "right name." And, as everyone knows, a horse is a horse and a man is a man. How could it be otherwise?

8 People too are "objects" from the standpoint of classification. If we lived in a small community and knew only a few people, we might find it possible to give each a separate name and deal with him as a singular personality. Our thinking might remain relatively concrete.

The human brain craves understanding. It cannot understand without simplifying, that is, without reducing things to a common element. However, all simplifications are arbitrary and lead us to drift insensibly away from reality.
LECOMTE DU NOÜY

But in our modern world where we contact millions of people (personally and via various media), the temptation to move at high-level abstractions is enormous. As stated earlier, we do this because it simplifies our handling of vast amounts of data (or people). The bigger the bundles the better.

Therefore, we move very far from the individual person, just as we moved very far from the single orange we held in our hand. We package people into ever larger groups with fewer characteristics in common and refer to them under a single label: Asians, feminists, Muslims, doctors, lawyers, Arabs, liberals, conservatives, Germans, Catholics, Jews, Protestants, scientists, homosexuals, Palestinians, Republicans, child molesters, police, teachers, Israelis, cultists, evangelists, managers, workers, homophobics, Vietnamese, politicians, Japanese, African Americans, Native Americans, endangered species, astronauts, Mexicans, Hispanics, Chicanos, Spanish, Latins, Americans, Malaysians, Chinese, racists, criminals, Blacks, farmers, illegal aliens, Russians, citizens, Democrats, environmentalists, . . . *ad infinitum.*

Not a single label listed above tells us about the object/person classified. It merely serves as a means of organizing our information about them and clues us in on how we should think about and relate to the individual so classified.

9 Do we need to be reminded that classification alone—arbitrary, unscientific classification—often means the difference between life and death?

Villagers from southeastern Laos were burned out of their homes as the war moved into their area; they escaped over the border into Vietnam. There they

If the doors of perception were cleansed, everything would appear to man as it is, infinite. For man has closed himself up till he sees all things through the narrow chinks of his cavern.
WILLIAM BLAKE

We Get What We Want

Society as a whole ultimately gets, on all issues of wide public importance, the classifications it wants, even if it has to wait until all the members of the Supreme Court are dead and an entirely new court is appointed. When the desired decision is handed down, people say, "Truth has triumphed." In short, society regards as "true" those systems of classification that produce the desired results.

The scientific test of "truth," like the social test, is strictly practical, except for the fact that the "desired results" are more severely limited. The results desired by society may be irrational, superstitious, selfish, or humane, but the results desired by scientists are only that our systems of classification produce predictable results. Classifications . . . determine our attitudes and behavior toward the object or event classified. When lightning was classified as "evidence of divine wrath," no courses of action other than prayer were suggested to prevent one's being struck by lightning. As soon, however, as it was classified as "electricity," Benjamin Franklin achieved a measure of control over it by his invention of the lightning rod. Certain physical disorders were formerly classified as "demonic possession," and it was suggested that we "drive the demons out" by whatever spells or incantations we could think of. The results were uncertain. But when those disorders were classified as "bacillus infections," courses of actions were suggested that led to more predictable results.

Science seeks only the most generally useful systems of classification; these it regards for the time being, until more useful classifications are invented, as "true."

S. I. Hayakawa
Language in Thought and Action

The subtlest and most pervasive of all influences are those which create and maintain the repertory of stereotypes. We are told about the world before we see it. We imagine most things before we experience them.
Walter Lippmann

became a serious classification problem for Vietnamese officials: were they "escapees" or "refugees"? The difference? "Refugees" were permitted to remain in Vietnam, while "escapees" were forced to return. Which were they really?

In Nazi Germany, to be **classified** a "Jew" meant extermination. The classification was a fallacy: in Hitler's mind "Jewish" meant "Jewish race." There is no "Jewish race," of course. To be a "Jew" is to belong to, and commit oneself to, a religion—Judaism. Hitler, however, is not the first or the last classifier to make such a mistake. The early struggles of the philosopher Ludwig Wittgenstein illustrate the point. His father Karl and mother Leopoldine were devout Catholics, and Ludwig and his seven siblings were baptized and raised in the Roman church. But when Hitler invaded Austria, the Nazis in their passion to purify the Aryan gene pool searched the Wittgenstein family bloodline and discovered that Leopoldine's father was of "Jewish extraction." So the Wittgensteins were "reclassified" as *Judischers,* a trauma that produced enormous suffering, severed family ties, and contributed to the suicides of three of Ludwig's brothers.

It seems that the human mind has first to construct forms independently before we can find them in things. . . . knowledge cannot spring from experience alone but only from this comparison of the inventions of the intellect with observed fact.
Albert Einstein

Ashley Montagu, among other anthropologists and ethnologists, has long reminded us that the concept of race is a fallacious myth—"our most dangerous myth," he writes. Physiological characteristics that we classify as "racial" are merely the result of environmental adaptation that took place as our presapient ancestors migrated in search of food and hospitable living conditions. If we could trace our genetic history, each and every one of us would find that

"I forget, are we mesozoic or are we cenozoic?"

we possess various blends of genetic material. A careful historical look at the human panorama will reveal only an everchanging series of gene pools. Still, race remains one of our most pragmatic classifications, although it completely lacks scientific support. While it says nothing of the person classified, it makes quite clear how we are to think about him, treat him, deal with him, and use him. Could one expect a myth to be more useful than that? (See pp. 352–355.)

A big wild animal of the antelope family and known as the "Nehil Gae" was causing extensive damage to crops in the field. But the farmers would not harm it because "Nehil Gae" means "Blue Cow," and the cow is sacred to the Hindu. So the Indian Government has changed the name to "Nehil Goa"—which means "Blue Horse." Horses are not sacred, and so now the beast can be killed to protect the crops.

Associated Press

10 It might be argued that some classification systems, such as scientific taxonomy, tell us much more precisely what the classified object really is. Such a claim would probably not be made, however, by either (1) a knowledgeable scientist, or (2) the object classified.

Scientists are quite aware that they have merely agreed on the criteria they will use for their system, namely, evolutionary kinship. When sufficient data are available, lines of evolutionary development can be traced, and the common characteristics of species, genera, families, orders, and so on, serve as workable criteria for ordering our knowledge. Scientific systems sometimes reveal facts about the classified objects: they tell us how they may relate (those of the same species can mate, those of different species cannot—except that this is not always the case); it tells us who might have been the ancestor of some animal or plant; it sometimes tells us (in the words themselves) about the physiology of the object ("vertebrate," "bony fishes," "mammals"). But such information lies in the labels we have chosen to use for the common characteristics we have selected for classifying. Again, as Hayakawa has said, no animal is a "vertebrate" until we put it in that "vertebrate" class.

It might be worth noting that for the animal classified, the scientific system probably means very little. If a queen conch is gliding through the sand at dusk in search of a meal, the classification "edible" holds more significance for a clam than its proper taxonomic status as *Chione undatella* (Sowerby).

Our Mental Grids

11 The French philosopher Henri Bergson describes another way in which the mind handles its knowledge of reality.

The human intellect, notes Bergson, has one habit that stands in the way of its perceiving reality accurately: its propensity for chopping reality into fragments.

For example, the mind takes "time" and cuts it into discrete units: seconds, minutes, hours, days, weeks, seasons, years, decades, centuries, cosmic years, and so on. But time is a continuum, with no breaks, rhythms, or cycles. Our minds create units of measurement for the time-continuum so that we can conceive it in usable "lengths"; then we label these units and proceed to think in "units of time"; we may also begin to believe that such "units of time" are real. But where do "hours" exist? or "days"? or "years"? We have defined a year as the time it takes the Earth to revolve once around the Sun; but the Earth would have gone on swinging in orbit for millions of "years" without being affected by our definition of its motion—as though the Earth ripped off its December sheet as it passed a certain point in space.

12 And what about space and objects in space? We measure them. We have devised units without end to quantify distance and volume. For spatial distances: millimeters, inches, yards, meters, fathoms, miles, parsecs, light-years, and so on. We measure mass or volume with grams, ounces, pounds, tons, tablespoons, cubic centimeters, acre-feet, a "pinch" of salt, and a "dash" of pepper.

Such units are created by our minds to help us reduce the environment to usable proportions; they enable us to conceive small bits of reality at a time (the mind cannot possibly think of all matter at once).

But after reflection, could any of us believe that such "units of measurement" exist as part of the real world? Just ask: "Please give me eighteen millimeters." Eighteen millimeters of what? "I need five minutes. Can you get it for me?" Five minutes of what? "Time," of course, but once measured, what exactly do you have? One must conclude that such units exist in the mind, and only in the mind. Such mental units serve to parcel out our environment into practicable quantities.

13 Look at a globe of the Earth and note the lines that criss-cross it. There are pole-to-pole lines we call meridians, and lines parallel to the "equator" we call latitudinal lines; then there are anomalous lines dividing colored areas. Thus, with a marked globe we have organized the Earth so that our minds can think about it. ("Where is Bolivia?" "Point out the Arctic circle." "Locate the magnetic pole.") How else could the intellect deal with the Earth except in pieces?

In a planetarium, it is of great help to have a celestial grid overlaying the stars on the dome, or to have a projected image linking together the stars in a constellation. When such grids are not used, the thousands of patternless points

ohm
millimeter
ampere
kilometer
watt
millisecond
erg
second
gauss
minute
oersted
hour
coulomb
day
volt
year
lumen
cosmic year
hertz
percent
acre
cycles per second
section
grain
miles per hour
gram
parts per million
pound
ton
Richter scale
kilogram
equator
angstrom
radian
horsepower
cubic inch
bar
flux units
decibel
farad
magnitude
rod
psi
peck
carat
dram
degree F
degree C

degree K
jigger
caliber
degree
acre feet
mach number
micron
barrel
meter
furlong
inch
knot
foot
joule
cubit
atmosphere
yard
century
mile
millennium
fathom
octave
parsec
homer
light-year
ephah
ounce
mina
pint
cord
fifth
darwin
quart
rpm
liter
megaton
gallon
frames per second
bushel
electronvolt
week
BTU
dyne
calorie
newton
decade
hands
smidgen

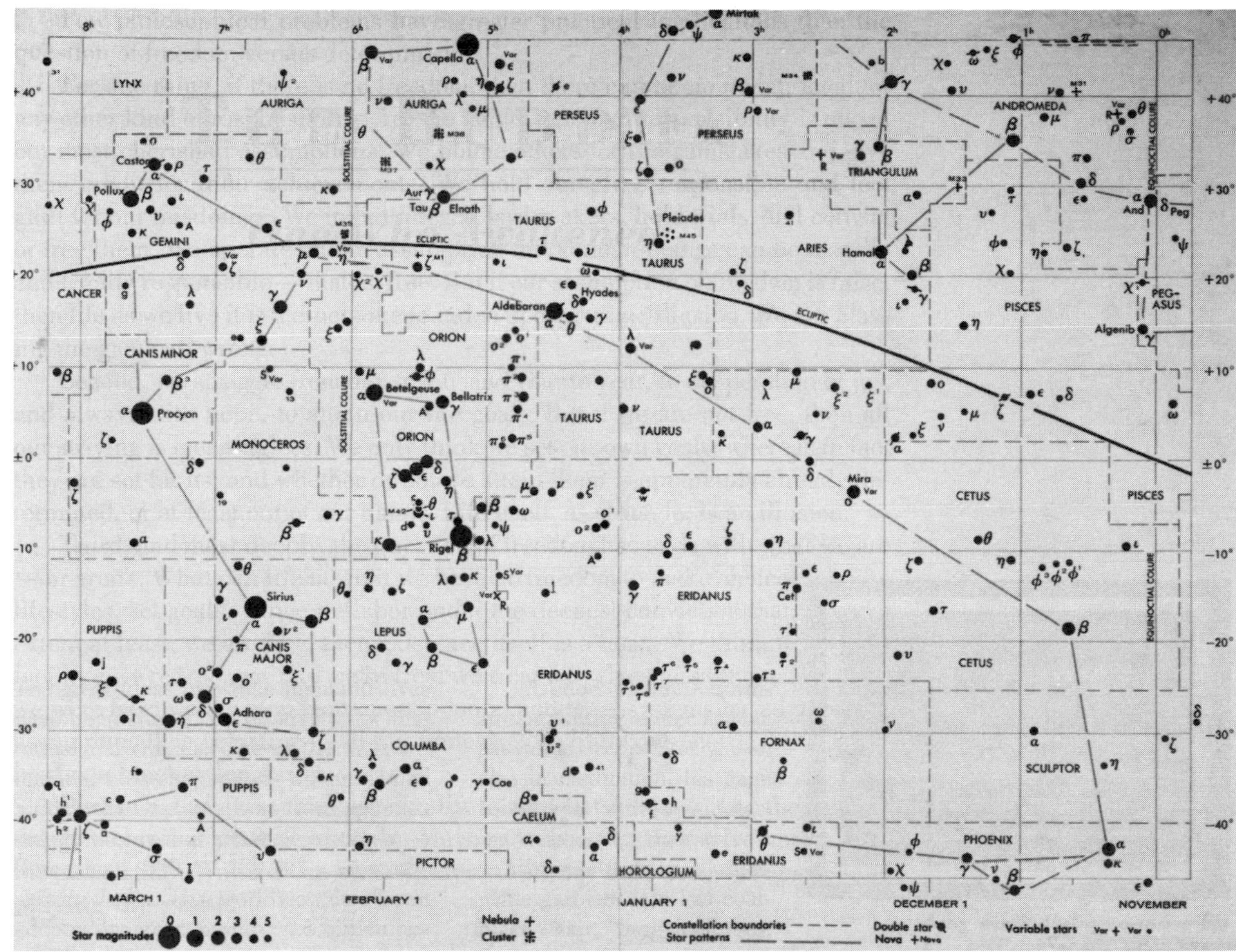

Sky maps from *The Sky Observer's Guide*, by John Polgreen.

of light are scattered at random and we cannot remember or make sense of them. Since the mind must organize the points of light, it "draws" connecting lines. So a small square is seen in Hercules, a triangle in Aquarius; or we see several stars whose pattern reminds us of some known object (Aquila the Eagle, Delphinus the Dolphin). In just this way the ancient skywatchers organized the random bits of light they saw nightly.

In the planetarium, the grid lights can be turned off, reminding us that the grid is only a mental tool for organizing our experience. In no way could one mistake the grid as a part of the real sky.

In just this manner, however, the mind places grids on all that it perceives.

14 What remains when all the mind's "grids" are turned off? Reality—unmeasured, undivided. A continuum of matter in motion and time undisturbed. No days or weeks; no miles or parsecs. To be sure, there do exist in the real world a multitude of rhythms and cycles, and we often attempt to coordinate our mental "units of measurement" with these natural rhythms.

Our minds, says Bergson, can indeed "move through" all the pragmatic grids and intuit the nature of reality itself. By a sort of "intellectual empathy" we can come to know the ever-changing, endlessly moving continuum that is reality. But to do this we almost have to tell the intellect to cease and desist in its persistent habit of reducing the universe to discrete, manageable units. To know what the real world is like, therefore, we must turn off the grid lights and let the stars shine. Reality is, and that is all.

✦

Henri Bergson

What It Means to Be a Hummingbird

Henri Bergson often spoke in the great lecture hall at the Collège de France, where he taught, and huge crowds gathered to hear him. He would emerge quietly from the back of the hall and make his way to the platform. He was tall and slender, dressed in a dark suit, a cutaway collar, and black tie. Charismatic, confident, reserved, and a little mysterious, he moved with easy grace. As he took his seat on the rostrum an expectant silence would settle over the audience.

As he sat under a shaded lamp, his features appeared delicate and refined. He was a handsome man with a high forehead, a lingering halo of light hair, and a barely visible mustache. His bright eyes flashed beneath bushy brows. He would place his hands together, fingertips touching, and begin speaking modestly but firmly, in elegant French. He used no manuscript or notes. His speech was casually paced and dignified; his cadences were measured and musical. He began, as always, with a humorous anecdote, and by the time the audience recovered from their laughter they found themselves caught up in the subject matter and listening intently. He was the master of his craft: his entire presentation seemed effortless and natural.

What they heard was a philosophy that had the promise, some said and many hoped, of bringing about a revolution in the ideas we live by. At the turn of the twentieth century men and women were searching for a better understanding of themselves and why they are here. They were tired of the downbeat determinism bandied within intellectual circles, according to which human beings had lost their free will; they were merely cogs in a mechanistic universe. Robbed of freedom and spirit, they had lost the feeling of being special, of having a place in the sun a little lower than the angels. In the midst of the shadows, Bergson rose like a shining light. By all accounts he burst upon the world with a creative energy that lifted people's spirits and cleansed their souls. He told them that the world (through evolution) has purpose and meaning, and assured them that God (as the *élan vital*) is still there. He made it intellectually respectable to believe that human beings could be free, responsible, fully human, and immortal. He was an original thinker, a persuasive speaker, and almost a prophet.

Wherever joy is, creation has been.

Beyond the ideas that have grown set and cold in language we must seek the movement and the warmth of life.

Only those ideas that are least truly ours can be adequately expressed in words.

For a conscious being, to exist is to change, to change is to mature, to mature is to go on creating oneself endlessly.

Bergson's life, it is frequently said, was only an adventure of the mind. In a letter to William James he wrote, "Now as to events worthy of note, there have been none in the course of my career, at least nothing objectively remarkable." But he was being unduly modest, for his lifetime was in fact a series of triumphs and tragedies, filled with adventure.

He was born October 18, 1859, in Paris and christened Henri-Louis Bergson. His father, Michael Bergson, of Polish extraction, was by trade a musician and composer, successful enough to be for a time the head of the Geneva Conservatory. His mother, Katherine Levinson, also bright and talented, was from England. Thus, Henri, without a drop of Gallic blood, was always perceived—as he perceived himself—to be very French; and France took pride in him as the finest representative of the best in French culture. He was bilingual in French and English from childhood.

At the *lycées* (secondary schools) in Paris he excelled in every field, though mathematics and the sciences were special loves. One of his schoolmates later recalled that in these years Henri was a fragile youth, utterly charming, innocent, honest, sensitive to the feelings of others, but slightly detached or withdrawn, more an observer of the human parade than a participant.

At eighteen he entered the École Normale Supérieure in Paris in Hellenistic classics. He arranged to have himself appointed student librarian so he could spend as much time as possible in the company of his beloved books; there was a small secluded room off the library where he could usually be found. While others were caught up in fashionable issues, Bergson avoided making public pronouncements and taking stands; he wanted to examine critically the thinking involved in controversial issues in order to understand why ideas conflict.

After graduation he became a professor of philosophy in the provinces, first at Angers for two years, then at Clermont-Ferrand. He was much loved by his students, and he was in love with his work. At the age of thirty he returned to Paris as a professor of philosophy at the Collège Rollin and then at the Collège Henri IV. At thirty-one he was married to Louise Neuberger, and friends described their marriage as one of uninterrupted happiness. They gave birth to one daughter, born deaf, who later became a painter.

At the age of thirty-nine Bergson returned to his alma mater, the École Normale, and taught there for two years. In 1900, at the age of forty-one, he joined the faculty of the Collège de France, occupying a chair first in Greek philosophy, then in modern philosophy. There he stayed until 1914. These were the years of his greatest accomplishments. Already famed for his books *Time and Free Will* and *Matter and Memory,* he continued to write and speak. He wrote a delightful book on laughter, *Le rire,* which is still quoted in textbooks on humor and comedy. In 1907 he published *Creative Evolution,* which brought him international fame and for which, twenty years later, he received the Nobel Prize. He traveled widely, lecturing in Italy, England, and America. In 1914 three of his works were placed on the Roman Catholic Index of Prohibited Works by the Holy Office. Also in 1914 he was elected to the French Academy.

World War I broke out in 1914, and the academic life was disrupted. In 1917 Bergson was sent to the United States to persuade the president to enter the war. In 1921, because of ill health, he retired from public life and became an honorary professor of the Collège de France. During the last twenty years of his life he was incapacitated with severe headaches; he ceased all public speaking and wrote only with great difficulty.

Early in his reflective life, Bergson came to the idea that the primary function of human intelligence is to go to the heart of things, to understand objects/events in the real world exactly as they are; and "exactly as they are" implies penetrating to the essence of things as functional systems. Human intelligence has been developed by the evolutionary process to transcend the self, to jump out of its own skin and enter into the objects/events of the world and to know them. This is the *raison d'être* of human intelligence, and it must not be thwarted.

But now, the crux and the dilemma: When the mind gets down to the task of knowing things in the world about us, it finds that there are two ways of knowing an object: through intellect and through intuition. "The first implies going all around it, the second entering into it. The first depends on the viewpoint chosen and the symbols employed, while the second is taken from no viewpoint and rests on no symbol." The first, says Bergson, gives us relative knowledge; the second enables us to attain knowledge that is absolute and true.

You are in a boat at sea, leaning against the mast, watching the gently undulating waves. You open your Polaroid camera and take a snapshot of the ocean. Sometime later, when you show the picture to a friend, you announce epistemologically, "This is the ocean."

But is it? Bergson tells us that the still picture has necessarily missed the story of what the ocean is all about. You can experience the ocean, but you cannot take a still picture of it. What you experienced as you watched the ocean is motion, unceasing motion, eternal motion: giant waves rolling as they have rolled for billions of years; smaller waves on and between the big ones; millions of wavelets, churned by wind and water, never stopping. Once you experience, once you feel what the ocean is really like, it can overwhelm. Perpetual motion through aeons of time: this is what the ocean is.

The snapshot, then, is a static picture that eliminates motion from the dynamic system. It stopped, it froze, and if you will, it killed a living thing; it cannot, in reality, depict the ocean at all.

Human intelligence has been dominated throughout Western history by the intellectual mode of knowing. The intellect sees everything from the outside. We see other people and all other creatures and objects—from elephants to butterflies, from trees to mountains and stars—from the outside. All our seeing is from a standpoint that is necessarily external to the objects/events themselves. This perspective seems obvious and natural to us. How could it be otherwise?

Bergson is not denying the ability of the intellect to make an in-depth plunge, however. Take that hummingbird perched on the pine bough. Our sciences can supply us with an unending collection of detailed data about it. Anatomy can tell us about its bone structure, musculature, and so on. Physiology can tell us about its digestive system and reproductive system. Animal psychology will tell us about its courtship drives, territoriality, and the like. Physics and optics can tell us about the flashing irridescences of its feathers. And so on, almost *ad infinitum*. All this information from the intellect demonstrates the unending power of the mind to construct (collect) bits and pieces of data which, taken together, add up to an impressive understanding of the little creature.

So, what's wrong with all this?

What's wrong, Bergson keeps saying, is that we have missed what it means to be a hummingbird. The essence of hummingbird is to experience life—as a hummingbird. No matter how vast the accumulation of data about the hummingbird, to see the hummingbird from the outside and convince ourselves that we have comprehended the hummingbird is wrongheaded. How would we react to someone who perceives us only from the outside, who has not a hint of appreciation of what we are experiencing, and who still insists that he knows what we are all about? Most of us would signal our impatience with such a shallow claim. But, argues Bergson, this is precisely what we do all the time.

In several of his books and dozens of essays and articles, Bergson analyzed the operations of the intellect; he feels that

The universe . . . is a machine for creating gods.

The major task of the twentieth century will be to explore the unconscious, to investigate the subsoil of the mind.

[Intuition is] the legitimate and noble province of the mind; indeed it is the only means for perceiving the heart of things.

But one thing is sure: we sympathize with ourselves.

The end and aim of all research is the comprehension of reality—the recognizing of reality and the forming of our minds upon it as a model.

Reality is like an immense forest strewn with impediments of all kinds, through which the seeker, like the woodcutter, must open up trails.

If we do not begin by giving a glance at the whole, if we pass at once to the consideration of the parts, we may perhaps see very well, but we do not know what we are looking at.

[Philosophy] attaches no value to truth passively received; it would have each one of us reconquer truth by reflexion, earn it by effort; and, embracing it in the depths of our own self and animating it with our own life, lend it strength enough to fertilize thought and direct the will.

Metaphysics, then, is the science which claims to dispense with symbols.

we are so deeply conditioned with this way of looking at the world that he needs to dislodge us from our conceits. Like the fish that cannot possibly know that it swims in water because it spends its life immersed in it, we are immersed in a one-sided way of looking at the world.

The intellect's limitations, he submits, are not merely bad habits absorbed from our culture; they are inherent in its native operations. By its nature, it cannot carry out the mandate given to it by our intelligence. It does, however, have a pragmatic mission that it can do very well: (1) it can organize our experience through static concepts; and (2) it can package our experiences for processing, storage, and retrieval.

But, happily, the mind has another faculty for knowing: intuition. Knowledge by intuition is direct and absolute, according to Bergson. "When I speak of an absolute movement, it means that I attribute to the mobile an inner being and, as it were, states of soul; it also means that I am in harmony with these states and enter into them by an effort of the imagination." The intuitive faculty doesn't come at an object from the outside, but from the inside; and it is a valid process, says Bergson, whether we are intuiting another person, a hummingbird, a flower, or a rock. "We call intuition here the sympathy by which one is transported into the interior of an object in order to coincide with what there is unique and consequently inexpressible in it."

In Western philosophy "metaphysics" has been defined as the study of ultimate reality, the attempt to find out what the ultimate substance and structure of the world truly is. This is the goal of the empirical tradition in the West and, of course, it has been carried on by the left-brained intellect. Now Bergson is telling us that such a metaphysics has been predestined to fail because reality lies beyond the grasp of the intellect. "But a true empiricism is the one which purposes to keep as close to the original itself as possible, to probe more deeply into its life, and by a kind of spiritual auscultation, to feel its soul palpitate; and this true empiricism is the real metaphysics." The analytic intellect, bent on packaging, will generalize. "But an empiricism worthy of the name, an empiricism which works only according to measure, sees itself obliged to make an absolutely new effort for each new object it studies. It cuts for the object a concept appropriate to the object alone, a concept one can barely say is still a concept since it applies only to that one thing."

Three acts of courage marked Henri Bergson's last months. The first was a decision he made as early as 1937. Having thought of himself as a Frenchman for a lifetime, and having arrived at the point where he was having thoughts of becoming a Christian, he wrote that he wished to be counted as a Jew since he had "foreseen for years a formidable wave of anti-Semitism about to break upon the world. I wanted to remain among those who tomorrow were to be persecuted."

Then, in 1940, the Vichy government issued laws barring Jews from holding educational posts in France, but Bergson, because of his stature and fame, was specifically exempted. But Bergson refused to accept the exemption and proceeded to renounce all his honors lest a passive submission be interpreted as support for the puppet government. Then a few weeks before his death, bedridden and unable to stand, he rose from his bed, stood in a queue on the arm of a servant, and, along with all other Jews in France, registered as a *Judischer.* In the December air he caught a cold that turned into pneumonia. He died January 4, 1941.

Reflections

1 What do you think of the drawing by Abner Dean on p. 201: "Everyone must have a label"? Is this really true?

2 What is the point that Walter Lippmann is making about the way we maintain our habit of stereoptyping (see marginal quote on p. 204)? Do you agree? How might we cease and desist in this way of thinking?

3 What is an abstraction? How many single objects belonging to a class must you experience before you can develop an abstraction? Then what is the relationship of the abstraction to the particular objects? Can you go as far as Plato in holding that abstractions have a real status quite apart from our minds? If you can, where are the real ideas located? If you cannot, then what exactly is the relationship between any two objects in the same class? (That is, two warblers that belong to different species but belong to the same family are related, are they not? What relates them?)

4 What is a *muglock?* How does it differ from a *dobo* and a *busana?*

5 When an object is classified, what does the classification tell us about the object, and what does it tell us about the classifier?

6 Discuss with yourself (and other selves, if available) the marginal quote on p. 205 regarding the "Nehil Gae." Now reflect very thoroughly on the problem of classification. Critique. Insights? Comments?

7 Could we do away entirely with our habit of classifying? What benefits would we gain by eliminating the habit? What would we lose? What is the answer to the problem?

8 Summarize in your words the point Bergson is making when he tells us that our minds have a habit of "chopping reality into fragments." Is this meaningful to you personally? Could Bergson's insights lead you to change your way of seeing and thinking about reality?

The theater of my mind has a seating capacity of just one, and it's sold out for all performances.

Henry Winkler
Tribute to Richard Rodgers

With clarity and quiet, I look upon the world and say: All that I see, hear, taste, smell and touch are the creations of my mind.

Nikos Kazantzakis

TRUTH

3-4

How can we be sure of our facts? This question is one that a careful thinker can't avoid. After all, so much of the "information" supplied by our culture, after careful scrutiny, turns out to be false. (Just remind yourself of the tabloids at the checkout stands.) This chapter describes the three standard truth tests that are used to check and double-check fact-claims. Although all three are indispensable to clear thinking, they also involve intrinsic problems. This chapter also examines a devastating kind of pragmatic paradox, a thought mechanism that helps us survive but also results in a subtle form of self-deception.

TRUTH-TESTS

1 Truth-tests are used for checking and double-checking the things people say so that we can decide if their statements are true or false. With such tests we can verify or falsify the fact-claims that they make.

No one is so wrong as the man who knows all the answers.
THOMAS MERTON

There are three truth-tests: the Correspondence, the Coherence, and the Pragmatic. All three tests are used by all of us, often without our being consciously aware of it, and are indispensable to our thinking and communicating.

THE CORRESPONDENCE TEST

2 One method of checking fact-claims is by the **correspondence test,** whose development is attributed to Bertrand Russell. This test requires one to check a subjective mental concept against a real object/event, and if the concept "corresponds to" the real object/event, then the concept is considered to be true.

Quite simply, if someone tells you that there is a solar eclipse in progress in your area, you can look at the Sun; and he is either right or wrong. If you can observe a crescent Sun, then his statement can be accepted; if you cannot, his statement is false. You have checked it personally and established to your satisfaction the accuracy of the statement. If there was indeed a correspondence between the mental concept of an eclipse and an actual event taking place, then the fact-claim has become a fact.

A whole class of fact-claims are easily checked this way. "The book you are after is in Section B-16 in the bookstore." **Go look.** "This CD contains selections from Puccini's *Madame Butterfly.*" **Play the recording and listen.** "Some prankster mixed salt and sugar in the sugar bowl." **Taste and find out.** "His pulse is very slow." **Feel it and count.** "The coals are ready for the steak." **Look at them glow red and feel the heat.** "This watermelon is ripe and ready to eat." **Feel it, thump it and listen to the thump; plug it, smell it, and taste it.** All the senses can't be wrong . . . can they?

What is Truth but to live for an idea? . . . It is a question of discovering a truth which is truth for me, of finding the idea for which I am willing to live and die.
SØREN KIERKEGAARD

3 To apply the correspondence test, two things are involved: (1) a subjective mental concept, and (2) a real object/event to which the mental concept corresponds. The following precautions must be taken seriously when checking fact-claims with the correspondence test.

1. We have already noted some of the mind's imaginative operations and the way it creates concepts. No created concept is ever an exact replica of any external object/event. The mind selects a few elements of any object/event to assimilate into the model that it will use for thinking. Furthermore, we have seen that all the physical events that exist in the real world are translated by our transducers into quite different experiential phenomena.

Remembering all this, we must conclude that no mental concept can ever correspond 100 percent with objects/events. Rather, we have only a degree of correspondence between the two. If the degree of correspondence is high, we hold the fact-claim to be true; if it is not, we decide it is false. Where the breakoff point is along that scale of correspondence would be the subject of endless debate.

Better the world should perish than that I, or any other human being, should believe a lie; . . . that is the religion of thought, in whose scorching flames the dross of the world is being burnt away.
BERTRAND RUSSELL

The falseness of an opinion is not for us any objection to it. . . . The question is how far it is life-furthering, life-preserving, species-preserving, perhaps species-creating.
FRIEDRICH NIETZSCHE

2. Since, in the last analysis, we are limited to our own subjective experiencing world, how is it possible for us to harmonize a subjective concept (which we can experience) with a real object/event (which we cannot directly experience)? The answer, of course, is we cannot. What then does the correspondence test really do? It compares a concept with a set of sensations—the sensations we use when we go about inferring what exists in the real world. Therefore, we are checking a subjective concept with a subjective set of sensations. If they match to some tolerable degree, then we call the concept true; if they don't, we call it false.

This is really not a happy condition to live with, but given our present knowledge of cognitive processes, the predicament seems inescapable. It looks as though—on this test at least—we can never be completely certain of anything.

Bertrand Russell (1872–1970)

THE COHERENCE TEST

4 There is one obvious limitation to the use of the correspondence test. The real world has to be directly accessible for observation; otherwise there is nothing real against which one can check his concept. In such cases a second check-out

> ***Assume coherence as the test, and you will be driven by the incoherence of your alternatives to the conclusion that it is also the nature of truth.***
>
> Brand Blanshard

> ***Truth is the approximation of thought to reality. It is thought on its way home. Its measure is the distance thought has travelled, under guidance of its inner compass, toward that intelligible system which unites its ultimate object with its ultimate end.***
>
> Brand Blanshard

method—the coherence test—might be applicable. The coherence test of truth was first developed by Baruch Spinoza (1632–1677).

According to the **coherence test,** a fact-claim can be accepted as true if it harmonizes (coheres) with other facts that one has **already** accepted as true. Like the previous test, this is a routine kind of test we use every day.

"There are sharks in Lake Mead." No, that can't be, and I don't have to go to Lake Mead to check the fact-claim with the correspondence test; for I already know that sharks can't live in fresh water, and Lake Mead is a freshwater lake. The fact-claim just can't be made to harmonize with other known facts.

(I have now been informed that freshwater sharks do indeed exist. So, what does this do to my use of coherence as a truth-test? I am warned, first, that a fact-claim may nicely cohere with a set of firmly held fictions, and that I could easily become dogmatic in my belief in, and defense of, ideas that are dead wrong. I am also alerted to the fact that the coherence truth-test is useful only to the degree that my previously accepted "facts" are supported by a broad base of empirical evidence. Thirdly, I am struck by the fact that, using the coherence test, I can never be 100 percent sure of any fact-claim.)

"When I looked into the mirror, I couldn't see myself. I have lost my reflection!" Such a statement as this we would normally reject with hardly a second thought. We have read of such fantasies in *Tales of Hoffmann,* and Alice, somewhere beyond the looking glass, might be able to manage it. But in the real world of human experience such a fact-claim doesn't harmonize with any experience I know. We will happily keep such "facts" in the world of make-believe.

"Alexander the Great never returned to Rome because he fell in love with Cleopatra and spent the rest of his life in Egypt." No, these fact-claims can't be made to cohere with other previously known data. Alexander died in 323 BC and he was certainly no Roman; Cleopatra died about 30 BC. Now, it might be possible to substitute Antony for Alexander, and the fact-claims would then cohere with one another.

> ***The truth has nothing to do with us as long as we must win. But as soon as we surrender our right to be right, we are right and the Truth has everything to do with us.***
>
> Robert Badra

5 The coherence test is applicable to large areas of knowledge that are not accessible to personal observation. Two such areas are (1) fact-claims relating to the past ("history"), which is never available for observation, and (2) all contemporary events that we cannot personally witness. This applies to practically all the information we get via television, Internet, newspapers, and magazines. A very large percentage of the events that "make news" takes place too far away for us to observe, so we test them by making them cohere with the facts we already know.

The coherence test has a serious weakness. A new fact-claim may fit coherently with a large number of previously accepted "facts," **all of which are untrue;** or, similarly, a new fact that is true may be rejected because it cannot be made to harmonize with one's set of previously accepted false fact-claims.

In other words, it is about as easy to build an elaborate coherent system that is false as an elaborate coherent system that is true. Unless previously accepted data are well supported by evidence, the truth-status of that new "fact" remains in doubt, no matter how well it fits in.

This point has historical significance. System-building has been the stock-in-trade of philosophers, theologians, political theorists, et al. It has been a common practice to rewrite history from the point of view of some ideology; facts can be selected, interpreted, and squeezed into almost any framework. Resulting systems may be highly coherent, therefore, yet bear little resemblance to anything in the real world.

The Pragmatic Test

6 There is a third test that, like the coherence test, is wholly subjective in that it requires nothing immediately accessible in the real world to serve as validating criteria for the mental concept. This is the **pragmatic test,** and in some ways it is the most complex of the three.

This test was developed by the American philosopher-psychologist William James, but the seminal idea came from Charles S. Peirce. In an article published in 1878, Peirce (he pronounced it "purse") attempted to answer the question, "What makes ideas meaningful?" He was interested in clarifying the source and nature of meaning. He concluded that ideas are meaningful if they make some difference in our experience. As Peirce put it, "our idea of anything is our idea of its sensible effects. . . ." If we say ice is cold or a match flame is hot, those **ideas** are meaningful only because they relate in a predictive way to what we would experience if we touched the ice or the flame. The ideas have meaning in relation to effects. If we could not touch the ice or the flame, the ideas would be meaningless.

Charles S. Peirce (1839–1914)

This was a theory of meaning only, but William James saw deeper implications in the theory and developed it into a test of truth. In 1898, in an address delivered at the University of California at Berkeley, James presented his theory of pragmatism: The truth-value of any idea is to be determined by the results; a "true" idea brings about desired effects. In short—and somewhat more ambiguously—if an idea works, then it is true.

Peirce had labeled his theory of meaning *pragmatism,* but when he heard what James had done to his theory by changing it into a test of truth, Peirce was upset. He rechristened his theory of meaning with such an "ugly name," as he said, that no one would ever kidnap his theory again. He called it "pragmaticism." We now associate "pragma*tism*" with William James and John Dewey, and "pragmati*cism*" with Peirce.

Begin by believing with all your heart that your belief is true, so that it will work for you; but then face the possibility that it is really false, so that you can accept the consequences of the belief.

John Reseck

7 The pragmatic test can be used to check out fact-claims in several areas of knowledge, and we find that the **function** of the test is different in each. This is why the test presents serious problems.

Convictions are more dangerous enemies of truth than lies.

Friedrich Nietzsche

First, note our routine use of the pragmatic test. We use it to check the workability of our ideas and hypotheses, even our guesses and hunches. It is an integral part of our trial-and-error way of solving daily problems.

At ebb tide I wrote
A line upon the sand
And gave it all my heart
And all my soul.
At flood tide I returned
To read what I had inscribed
And found my ignorance
upon the shore.

Kahlil Gibran

Say, for instance, that on one dark winter evening you turn on your computer and nothing happens. To find out what is wrong you immediately create a hypothesis to explain its not starting. Your first hypothesis may be that the cord is not plugged in. So you check it. It is plugged in, so the first hypothesis must be wrong. So you come up with another hypothesis. It's winter and the computer may be cold-sensitive, so you turn up the thermostat and warm the computer; it still doesn't start. So you guess that perhaps electricity is not getting to the power unit. Now the problem begins to look serious (that is, the solution may

The best ideas are the ideas that help people.
ITT TV COMMERCIAL

To say that Newton's law of gravitation is true is to say that it can be applied successfully; so long as that could be done, it was true. There is no inconsistency in saying that Newton's law was true and that Einstein's law is at present true.
HECTOR HAWTON
(describing Pragmatism)

When all else fails, follow the directions.
AMERICAN PROVERB

cost you time and/or money). You are on your way to the telephone to call a computer repair specialist when you notice that the nightlight by the telephone is off. You check and find other lights off. So, new hypothesis: a circuit breaker must have been tripped. You check. All fuses are in the "ON" position except one. You flip this one to "ON" and when you return to your computer you find it's working normally.

By empirical means, you gradually developed a hypothesis that accounted for all the facts. You were forced to collect more and more data before you could develop a workable hypothesis—that is, a hypothesis on the basis of which the power problem could be corrected. Happily, the hypothesis that finally worked will cost little time and no money. This illustrates the essential claim of pragmatism: the idea that **works** is the **true** one.

8 Our ideas have a profound effect on how we feel and behave. This fact is fundamental to all of man's religions, and here we discover the rationale for "faith" and "belief."

William James knew from personal experience the pragmatic process he was attempting to formulate into a philosophy. Having been reared in a family fraught with emotional instability, James was plagued for most of his life with psychophysical illnesses that he came to believe to be fatalistically determined. Hence he thought that he could do nothing to change his condition.

But in 1870 an essay by a French philosopher convinced him that he possessed personal freedom. He was persuaded that his life had not been determined irrevocably for him; he really could change the course of his life. **An idea—the idea that he was personally free—had taken hold of him.** On April 30, 1870, James wrote in his notebook: "I think that yesterday was a crisis in my life. . . . My first act of free will shall be to believe in free will."

9 What about the "truth-value" of a belief powerful enough to prevent one from opting for suicide? Whatever the **rationale** within the belief—that one's time has not yet come, that one has not yet accomplished one's purpose in life, that one should not cause others to suffer, or that taking one's life is morally wrong—whatever the rationale, isn't this belief true? Isn't the truth of ideas to be found in the results they effect? Or, as James so forcefully put it, do we not judge the worth of ideas by their "cash value"?

Pragmatism's only test of truth is what works best, wrote James.

> If theological ideas should do this, if the notion of God, in particular, should prove to do it, how could pragmatism possibly deny God's existence? It could see no meaning in treating as "not true" a notion that was pragmatically so successful.

THE PRAGMATIC PARADOX

10 The **pragmatic paradox** may be stated thus: For an idea to work pragmatically, one must believe that it is true on other than pragmatic criteria. Now, if we **define** "truth" as an idea that works (that is, that brings about desired results), then we have no serious problem. If an idea works, then it is true; and conversely, if an idea is true, then it works.

But this is not yet the heart of the matter. For an idea or belief to work **pragmatically,** we must believe it in terms of **correspondence.** This kind of insight can become a blessing or a bad dream.

For instance, for the belief in immortality to become a sustaining belief (that is, **to work**), one must accept that immortality exists in reality; one must believe that there is an objective event corresponding to the concept. Even though we may not be able to check out the belief with the correspondence-test, if it is not believed on a **correspondence** basis then the belief can have no **pragmatic** results.

Truth will most often come to us as a reconciliation rather than as one of a pair of opposites

ROBERT BADRA

What if you should say to yourself: "I have no evidence that souls survive death, but I want to experience the benefits of the belief in immortality (strength, courage, comfort), so I will accept the belief on a pragmatic basis. I will **believe** in immortality and make the idea work for me." What are the chances of making the idea "work"? For most of us, very poor indeed. (Incidentally, we see clearly here the role of the authority in our lives, the charismatic figure who can persuade us to believe **on his authority** that an idea is objectively true; this way we can manage to believe, without empirical evidence, what we wanted and needed to believe to begin with but could not accomplish on our own.)

One must believe in immortality "with all his heart." With equal conviction one must "know" that a loving Father-God does in fact exist (that is, that God is real); then the belief can be true pragmatically. Likewise, if the devout Muslim knows that Allah endows him with courage in battle, then he will not falter as the Holy War is waged. And the kamikaze pilot could look forward with patriotic fervor to the moment when he could dive his Suisei bomber onto the deck of an aircraft carrier, since he knew beyond doubt that he would return in spirit directly to the Yasukuni Shrine and be visited by family and friends. (See the letter written by the kamikaze pilot on p. 605.)

The truth is great, but there's a time and a place for everything.

LORI VILLAMIL

If one believes these ideas to be objectively true, they can become pragmatically true.

11 A "fact" that is true according to one truth-test may be false according to another.

For instance, a Muslim would say, "There is no God but Allah" (this fact-claim is a part of the Islamic Creed). Is such a statement true? Check it with the three truth-tests. You can be sure of three things: (1) The Muslim accepts his belief on a pragmatic basis; that is, his faith in Allah works for him. Therefore, **for him,** the statement is true on the pragmatic test. (2) He also accepts his belief in Allah on the coherence test; that is, the belief undoubtedly coheres with numerous other accepted data from the Quran and Islamic tradition (the Hadith). Therefore, **for him,** the statement is true on the coherence test. (3) While it would be extremely difficult or impossible to discover the real object/event referred to as "Allah" so that the correspondence-test could be applied, you can be quite sure that the Muslim believes that such a real object/event exists.

So, is the fact-claim true or false?

Now, if you should reply, "I don't believe that your statement is true," what exactly are you saying? (1) Using the pragmatic test, you are stating that the concept of Allah is not meaningful to you, hence not true **for you.** (2) Using the coherence test, you are stating that belief in Allah does not harmonize with facts you have accepted as true. Where can you fit such a fact-claim into the Jewish,

Grant an idea or belief to be true, what concrete difference will its being true make in any one's actual life? How will the truth be realized? What experiences will be different from those which would obtain if the belief were false? What, in short, is the truth's cash-value in experiential terms?

WILLIAM JAMES

Truth has no special time of its own. Its hour is now—always.

Albert Schweitzer

I believe that in the end the truth will conquer.

John Wycliffe

Christian, atheistic, or scientific worldview? It is false, therefore, **for you.** (3) Using the correspondence test, you are stating that you do not think "Allah" is real. If the Muslim claims that Allah is real, we often respond with the challenge, "Prove it"—meaning show us **by the correspondence test** that there is a real object/event called "Allah." Of course, he cannot.

Therefore, we think we have won our case. Using only the correspondence test, you retort that the Muslim's fact-claim is untrue. His statement about "Allah" is false. And yet, on the other two criteria—the pragmatic and coherence—the fact-claim is undeniably true . . . **for the Muslim.**

So again we ask: Is the fact-claim true or false?

12 We frequently find ourselves caught in interminable arguments where no meeting of minds takes place—as would undoubtedly happen in the case of the Muslim's claims about Allah. If we can cease to argue long enough to clarify our thinking, we would often find that different truth-tests are being used to support fact-claims.

Though no man can draw a stroke between the confines of night and day, yet light and darkness are upon the whole tolerably distinguishable.

Edmund Burke

It is good advice, therefore, to examine carefully the truth-tests being used (or merely assumed). If indeed one individual is using the correspondence test as the only acceptable criterion for verifying "facts" while another is relying on pragmatic criteria or is caught in the pragmatic paradox, it is no wonder that such discussions end in fruitless stalemates. We are left with frustration because the other person cannot accept what is so obviously true to us.

13 Examination of the truth-tests will disclose three points worth noting.

It is far more important for a particular idea of God to WORK than for it to be logically or scientifically sound.

Karen Armstrong

1. All three tests are constantly used by all of us and are indispensable to thinking and communicating. Each has its sphere of legitimate operation.
2. Each truth-test has intrinsic problems. We cannot be absolutely sure of any "fact" on any test. We are forced to conclude that "truth" is a probability item, with greater or lesser degrees of likelihood attached to various specific fact-claims.
3. This being the case, all truth is tentative. It is always subject to further modification and refinement as new fact-claims are verified and become facts.

✦

WILLIAM JAMES

"Truth Happens to an Idea"

In April 1870 William James began some personal explorations in the meaning of truth. He read an article by the French philosopher, Charles Renouvier, who held that the most distinctive quality of human beings is the experience of freedom. Like a key piece of a jigsaw puzzle, the idea fell into place.

On April 30 James wrote in his journal:

> I think that yesterday was a crisis in my life. I finished the first part of Renouvier's second "Essais" and see no reason why his definition of Free Will—"the sustaining of a thought *because I choose to* when I might have other thoughts"—need be the definition of an illusion. . . . My first act of free will shall be to believe in free will. . . . Not in maxims, not in *Anschauungen* [contemplations], but in accumulated *acts* of thought lies salvation. . . . Now, I will go a step further with my will, not only act with it, but believe as well; believe in my individual reality and creative power.

This decision to believe in believing marked an about-face in James's life. Heretofore he had been, in his own words, a "splintered bundle of fragments in search of consistency." Now he was able to summon strength to reverse the pattern of his past—a lifetime of self-doubt and suffering (he was twenty-eight)—and to affirm the possibility of taking charge of his life and creating his own future. Renouvier had argued that we possess freedom of the will if we believe that we do, and James believed it.

To those who have sought the origins of William James's condition, the James family remains an enigma—puzzling, slightly unreal. William's sister Alice suffered from "nervous attacks," fainting spells, and an illusive invalidism all her life; she rejoiced when she contracted cancer because it was, at last, a real physical illness. A brother, Garth Wilkinson, died at thirty-eight of rheumatic heart disease. Another younger brother, Robertson, was an alcoholic. And the brother who became a major American writer—Henry James—sustained, as he put it, "an obscure hurt, odious, intimate, horrid"; and he remained celibate all his life.

On James:
James was neither an optimist nor a cynic; he was a man of moral courage, who knew, all too well, the ambiguity and precariousness of the human condition.

JOHN J. MCDERMOTT

Man wants to be stretched to his utmost—if not in one way, then in another.

On James:
Pragmatism is the seed that had lain embedded in the soul of American civilization from its very inception. William James was simply the farmer who brought it to flower and fruition, and gave it a habitation and a name.

T. K. MAHADEVAN

We have to live today by what truth we can get today, and be ready tomorrow to call it falsehood.

Mankind's common instinct for reality . . . has always held the world to be essentially a theatre for heroism.

If there be any idea which, if believed in, would help us to lead [a better] life, then it would be really better for us to believe in that idea, unless, indeed, belief in it incidentally clashed with other greater vital benefits.

William shared fully his family's neurasthenia. He was plagued with chronic backache (he dubbed it "this dorsal insanity") and suffered from digestive disorders, depressions, and acute attacks of diffuse anxiety (one such attack he described: "there fell upon me without warning, just as if it came out of the darkness, a horrible fear of my own existence"). His eye trouble was his one truly somatic ailment.

The father of this troubled family was Henry James, Sr., a brilliant, passionate, and bizarre man whose life seems to have been one long search for spiritual peace, which he eventually succeeded in finding in the teachings of the eighteenth-century mystical theologian Swedenborg and his theme of divine love. When he was a teenager one of his legs was severely burned, resulting in its amputation; throughout his life he was subject to phobias and hallucinations. He was a gifted thinker who bequeathed his spiritual concerns—as well as his complexities and perplexities—to his children. In the James household table talk and family gatherings were animated, intellectual, wide-ranging, and punctuated by sibling rivalries.

Gardner Murphy described the philosophic presence of the elder James:

> He created in the home atmosphere an exhilarating sense of the worthwhileness of pursuing problems of cosmic dimensions, of asking forever one more question as to the place of man in this world and as to the real basis for ethics and religion; everybody in the family was apparently always ready for a debate which wound up with humor and with agreement to live and let live.

Although they were mutually involved, caring, and close, each member of the family was encouraged to seek his own illumination.

William James was born in New York City in 1842. He received a good but disjointed education in private schools in America and Europe. At eighteen he wanted to become a painter but decided he lacked talent—"there is nothing in the world so despicable as a bad artist"—and decided he could do better in the natural sciences. He entered the Lawrence Scientific School at Harvard and, three years later, enrolled in Harvard Medical School. He took a year out to join a field expedition to Brazil, but he disliked the rigors of jungle life and the monotony of keeping catalogues and so returned to his medical studies.

Tormented by fears, William James questioned whether life could be worth living at all. He interrupted his studies at the Medical School for a year at health spas in Germany, read widely in psychology and philosophy, and took courses under some of Europe's leading scholars. But his malaise continued—"a paradoxical apathy and restlessness." He wrote home that he spent an entire winter contemplating suicide.

He returned to Harvard, received his medical degree in 1869, but lacked the strength and/or will to practice medicine. He continued to withdraw into a state of invalidism, unable to decide what he wanted to do with his life.

At this juncture James read the article by Renouvier. It was a turning point. Here began his quest for a philosophy that would face up to the stubborn realities of life and, at the same time, provide light for him to live by.

William James was caught in the necessity of believing—his life was at stake—but he could no longer accept the possibility of unthinking (blind) belief. His father could still believe; but blind belief, for William, was fraught with dishonesty and was counterproductive. He therefore had to perform one of man's most delicate psychological maneuvers: without denying either his own nature or the given realities of the universe, he had to rethink the structure of belief and give it a rationale fully acceptable to the intellect. This he did, and the result was a new way of looking at the dynamics of the ideas we call "true."

What does it mean for an idea to be true? James writes in *Pragmatism:*

> The great assumption of the intellectualists is that truth means essentially an inert static relation. When you've got your true idea of anything, there's an end of the matter. . . . Pragmatism, on the other hand, asks its usual question. "Grant an idea or belief to be true," it says, "what concrete difference will its being true make in anyone's actual life? . . . What, in short, is the truth's cash value in experiential terms?". . .
>
> The moment pragmatism asks this question, it sees the answer. True ideas are those that we can assimilate, validate, corroborate, and verify. False ideas are those that we cannot. That is the practical difference it makes to us to have true ideas. That therefore is the meaning of truth. . . .
>
> The truth of an idea is not a stagnant property inherent in it. Truth happens *to an idea. It* becomes *true,* is made true by events. Its verity is in fact an event, a process.

His belief in free will was probably the most precious truth that James possessed. We can exercise free will providing we **believe** that we have free will. My belief makes it true. But when I first start believing it, it may not be **very** true. I may be intellectually convinced of my free will, but the truth of the idea hasn't taken hold of me at a deeper level. It is only slightly true. But if I practice making choices, I can increase my freedom, and the idea becomes **more true.** Freedom is a quality that I have developed. And the statement "I have free will" becomes more and more true. Therefore, the statement "I am free" was true; it had predictive value. But more than that, the truth of the statement gradually **happened to** the idea as I put it into effect.

It is a uniquely pragmatic notion that truth is not a yes/no or black/white quality, but that there are "degrees" of truth, and that "how true" an idea is depends upon the living context in which the idea is found. As James wrote, "its verity *is* in fact an event, a process."

True ideas, therefore, are the ideas that "work" for us. Does this mean that we can call virtually any fact-claim true provided that we can personally validate it by claiming that "it works for me"? Emphatically no. As John McDermott puts it, "James was no subjectivist." "And although he sees truth as a function of 'interest,' this position does not encourage predatory action. . . ." James was a relentless empiricist, and he insisted that our ideas must square with the hard realities of experience. Adjusting our beliefs to the "total push and pressure of the cosmos" is the only way to develop ideas that are pragmatically useful.

So James ended by believing, but in a very special way. George Santayana, a Harvard colleague and one of James's most gifted pupils, is not wrong when he said that "James didn't really believe. He only believed in one's right to believe that he might be right if he believed."

James took charge of his life with a vengeance, as though making up for lost time. Rather suddenly he was able to put an immense reservoir of stored-up energy and ideas to work in a creative way.

In 1873 he became an instructor in anatomy and physiology at Harvard and in 1875 began to teach psychology, at that time a new science. He introduced a course in physiology and psychology, the first in America, and established a laboratory of experimental psychology, one of the first in the world.

He wrote incessantly. By 1890 he had completed his massive two-volume *Principles of Psychology,* a systematic reorganization of virtually everything known in the field. In 1902 he produced an epochal work, *The Varieties of Religious Experience,* in which he applied the breadth of his psychological insight to the phenomena of religion. In *Pragmatism: A New Name for Some Old Ways of Thinking* (1907), he described truth as a multicolored idea that is relative to specific situations and human needs.

Of great significance was his marriage to Alice Gibbens when he was thirty-six. William's father had noticed

A philosophy is the expression of a man's inner character.

Philosophy is at once the most sublime and the most trivial of human pursuits. It works in the minutest crannies and it opens out of the widest vistas. . . . No one of us can get along without the far-flashing beams of light it sends over the world's perspectives.

Creatures extremely low in the intellectual scale may have conception. All that is required is that they should recognize the same experience again. A polyp would be a conceptual thinker if a feeling of "Hello! thingumbob again!" ever flitted through its mind.

Life defies our phrases . . . it is infinitely continuous and subtle and shaded, whilst our verbal terms are discrete, rude, and few.

The art of being wise is the art of knowing what to overlook.

her at a meeting in Boston and announced to his son that he had discovered his son's future wife. She was twenty-seven, lively and intelligent, a teacher in a girls' school. They were married in 1878, though only after some soul-searching on the part of the philosopher.

Something resembling genuine mental and physical health now infused William's whole life. His family and friends were amazed at the change in him. His illnesses disappeared and he found a new zest for living. He became one of the most popular teachers on the campus, and for thirty-five years he delighted generations of students with his informality, sincerity, candor, and anecdotes.

William James was anything but nondescript. Respected by students and colleagues alike and much loved for his gentle personality, he was colorful, alert, and articulate. He had a slender but sturdy frame, was modestly and neatly bearded, sported a tan, and wore casual tweeds—hardly the stereotypical Harvard professor. Equally striking were his writing and speaking styles. His conversations were witty, homey, and erudite, his public addresses extemporaneous and substantive. His writing is marked by graphic imagery and simplicity, and it can be understood. His sister Alice once remarked that he could "lend life and charm to a treadmill."

James resigned from teaching in 1907 but continued to write and lecture, both in America and Europe. He was world-renowned and drew great audiences wherever he spoke. (He was lecturing at Stanford University in 1906 when the San Francisco earthquake struck.) A European called him the "preeminent ambassador of American thought." In the judgment of Alfred North Whitehead, James is one of the four great philosophers of the Western world because he "had discovered intuitively the great truth with which modern logic is now wrestling." The Indian scholar T. K. Mahadevan says simply: "American civilization is what it is because of William James."

During his later years James spent all the time he could at the family's summer home in New Hampshire, gardening, swimming, and hiking. He loved nature. One day in 1898, climbing a steep mountain trail with an eighteen-pound backpack, he sustained permanent injury to his heart (a valvular lesion). He nevertheless managed to maintain a superactive schedule for more than a decade, but in the summer of 1910 his angina attacks again became acute. He died in his wife's arms at their home in the Adirondacks on August 26, 1910.

✦

Reflections

1 Thomas Merton wrote: "No one is so wrong as the man who knows all the answers" (see marginal quote on p. 214). This may sound like a pearl or a truism. But is it essentially a true statement? In what sense is it true or untrue? Do you think Socrates would agree? (By the way, "knows all the answers" **to what?**)

2 Contrast the position stated in the quotations from Nietzsche and Russell (see marginal quotes on p. 215) by rephrasing their ideas in your own words. Which (if either) do you tend to agree with? Why? Can these extreme statements be reconciled? Or does the problem reduce to a matter of relative values?

3 Describe the use of the correspondence test. Under what specific conditions can it be used? What are its principal weaknesses? Can you think of any steps we can take to increase its degree of accuracy?

4 Describe the use of the coherence test. In what specific areas, or under what conditions, does it become the primary truth-test? In what fallacious ways is the coherence test often used?

5 Describe the use of the pragmatic truth-test as it applies to the development of hypotheses to account for empirical events (such as the nonworking computer). In what ways must we be wary of its misuse?

6 When applied to nonempirical concepts, the pragmatic test of truth functions in quite a different way than when it is used to explain empirical data. Describe what it is that makes a concept, belief, or doctrine pragmatically true. (You may recall examples from your own experience similar to those of William James's.)

7 Can you see a way out of the pragmatic paradox? Is it indeed a paradox in the sense that one must actually deceive himself—that is, that he must believe that an idea is true on the wrong criterion—to make an idea work? Would it be better, in your opinion, to hold that some ideas are meaningful even though they are not true? In other words, are we going too far when we call an idea true **because** it is meaningful?

8 Which truth-test(s) would you apply to check out the following fact-claims and, in each case, what degree of certainty would you have?

Black coral grows in the Red Sea.
You can call 411 for information.
The pious shall prosper.
This postcard was mailed from Madrid.
The Earth is flat.
A UFO just landed in your back yard (but it's an invisible UFO).
Shakespeare wrote *The Merchant of Venice*.
Whirlwinds ("dust devils") are evil spirits in disguise.
This battery is dead.
Dolphins are intelligent animals.
The whooping crane is an endangered species.
The World will end on July 14, 2009.
All cats are blue.
Life is meaningless.
As you read this sentence, a solar eclipse is taking place.
"God's in his heaven—All's right with the world!" (Browning)
The Magna Carta was signed June 15, 1215.
All events are predestined.
Transglobal Airlines offers you the lowest fares.
A water molecule is composed of two hydrogen atoms and one oxygen atom.
Allah despises Infidels but loves The Faithful.

The Inner World: The Fantastic Journey

With clarity and quiet, I look upon the world and say: All that I see, hear, taste, smell, and touch are the creations of my mind. . . . I create phenomena in swarms, and paint with a full palette a gigantic and gaudy curtain before the abyss. Do not say, "Draw the curtain that I may see the painting." The curtain IS the painting.

Nikos Kazantzakis

PSYCHE

4-1

Western philosophy has been occupied almost exclusively with rational thinking and the symbolic nature of thought. But a few philosophers have sought to move beyond symbols, and Eastern thinkers have long been aware that, beyond the symbols and below the rational mind, there exist capacities for quite different and valuable kinds of experiencing. Aldous Huxley, for example, found that he could make use of trancelike intuitions in his creative writing. Any philosophy that seeks the truth about human beings must attempt to understand the whole mind. This chapter introduces the Western student to aspects of the psyche other than the purely rational.

THE EXPLORATION OF INNER SPACE

1 As adults, we have forgotten most of our childhood, not only its contents but its flavor; as men of the world, we hardly know of the existence of the inner world: we barely remember our dreams, and make little sense of them when we do; as for our bodies, we retain just sufficient proprioceptive sensations to coordinate our movements and to ensure the minimal requirements for biosocial survival—to register fatigue, signals for food, sex, defecation, sleep; beyond that, little or nothing. Our capacity to think, except in the service of what we are dangerously deluded in supposing is our self-interest and in conformity with common sense, is pitifully limited: our capacity even to see, hear, touch, taste and smell is so shrouded in veils of mystification that an intensive discipline of unlearning is necessary for anyone before one can begin to experience the world afresh, with innocence, truth and love.

R. D. LAING

Ful wys is he that can himselven knowe! ***(Very wise is he that can know himself.)***

GEOFFREY CHAUCER

2 Man's ignorance of his inner world has been an abysmal "darkness of unknowing." Is there, as a matter of fact, anything that we understand less than we understand ourselves? And when we begin to see the facts, how quickly we turn

All that is comes from the mind.

The Dhammapada 1.1

What is important is not liberation from the body but liberation from the mind. We are not entangled in our own body but entangled in our own mind.

Thomas Merton

away and refuse to face the truth about our own being. The history of man's exploration of human nature is marked by a singular lack of courage.

In a way, all this is surprising, for there is probably no human adventure more exciting than the exploration of "inner space." To be sure, it can lead us into uncharted country. It can evoke sacred fears and involve unscheduled risks, and not a few may fear that they have strayed into forbidden territory.

And too, it can be a lonely odyssey. No one else can travel with us; they can only call to us, as from a distance.

Yet there can be a feeling of joyous ultimacy in the unique adventure of coming to know one's inner world. Most of us have sensed the mysterious forces —more errant than the winds—that drive and direct our lives. Who among us has not wondered what he would find if he began in earnest to probe the depths of his own being?

Gianlorenzo Bernini, *The Ecstasy of St. Theresa,* 1645–1652. Bernini's sculpture in the Carnaro Chapel, Church of Santa Maria della Vittoria, depicts the moment of sublime consciousness for one of the Western world's renowned mystics, Saint Theresa of Avila (1515–1582). At this moment, as she describes it, an angel pierced her heart with a flaming, golden arrow: "The pain was so great that I screamed aloud; but at the same time I felt such an infinite sweetness that I wished the pain to last forever. It was not physical but psychic pain, although it affected the body as well to some degree. It was the sweetest caressing of the soul by God."

3 "Dare I explore my inner world?" The question is rarely stated this directly, but in some form the implicit decision "to explore or not to explore" is forced upon us each day.

And, because human history is in a critical state of change in our understanding of man, the answer, assuredly, must be "yes." The fact is that man has always cast furtive glances inward, but heretofore he has sojourned in his psychic hinterlands without adequate roadmaps. He has groped haphazardly, not knowing where he was going, how to get there, or what he would find. This is no way to begin a journey.

All this is changing. Modern cartographers have begun to do their work, and today we have rudimentary but helpful maps to guide us.

4 There is no obvious reason why one should spend his lifetime solely in the two traditional mind-states: the problem-solving conscious state and the "recovery" sleep state. Most of us, in fact, wander off the narrow path and spend time in free-association (woolgathering), browsing through our memories, and enjoying flights of fantasy; we might even tune in a few alpha rhythms. So our reduction of human existence into an alternation of consciousness and unconsciousness—waking and sleeping—is a local (Western) oversimplication.

There are other modes of conscious and subconscious experience that can enrich our lives; and on the condition that they do not rob us of our sanity or endanger others, there is no valid reason why they should not be known.

5 In the Eastern tradition other modes of consciousness such as focused concentration (*samadhi,* leading to *nirvana*), ecstatic trances, and Zen meditation (*zazen,* leading to *satori*) have been considered, for thousands of years, to be higher, more desirable mind-states, valued far above the reality-mode of consciousness. Such outlooks contrast greatly with our Western single-track commitment to just one form of waking experience.

This is not entirely true, however, for even in our Western tradition revered mystics have seen visions and known the rapture of religious ecstasy. And such experiences were invested with ultimate value: they were devoutly to be sought. In these Western cases the **interpretation** of the experience has given them their value. They were understood to be instances of spirit-possession (by the Holy Spirit) and not merely altered psychological states. (For more on "spirit-possession" as a model for interpreting human behavior, see p. 569.)

It appears that the West has used a double standard in assessing the value of various modes of psychic experience.

6 There is a fundamental condition to the deliberate exploration of human consciousness, a condition that Eastern religions have scrupulously observed. That condition is that the conscious mind not be impaired in its basic functions, which are to mediate reality and to solve problems. Whatever realms of the inner world we decide to explore, we know that we must shortly return to the reality-mode of consciousness and reestablish relations with the "real world." The conscious mind must be adequate to the performance of numerous pragmatic functions; it must be able to organize perception, to remember pertinent information, to make operational value-judgments, to engage in rational thinking as needed, and so on.

In some Eastern religions we find acceptable ways of annihilating one's physical organism as well as the "self." Such practices rest on the obvious assumption that the individual will not be required to reenter the reality-mode of consciousness. He may have decided to withdraw into the forest and proceed into the eternal nirvana from which there is no return. But such instances, while permissible, are rare; and the fact of the matter is that, without exception, Eastern religions emphasize the **quality** of the reality-mode of consciousness and look with concern upon Western ("amateur") experiments, which endanger conscious functioning. This is precisely the reason why Eastern spiritual leaders are critical of Western use of mind-altering chemicals.

The exploration of the interior of the human brain will be as dangerous as that of the Antarctic continent or the depths of the oceans, and far more rewarding.

J. B. S. HALDANE

7 Our normal waking consciousness . . . is but one special type of consciousness, whilst all about it, parted from it by the filmiest of screens, there lie potential forms of consciousness entirely different. We may go through life without suspecting their existence; but apply the requisite stimulus, and at a touch they are all there in all their completeness, definite types of mentality which probably somewhere have their field of application and adaptation. No account of the universe in its totality can be final which leaves these other forms of consciousness quite disregarded. How to regard them is the question—for they are so discontinuous with ordinary consciousness. Yet they may determine attitudes though they cannot furnish formulas, and open a region though they fail to give a map. At any rate, they forbid a premature closing of our accounts with reality.

WILLIAM JAMES

8 I told Don Juan how much I enjoyed the exquisite sensation of talking in the dark. He said that my statement was consistent with my talkative nature; that it was easy for me to like chatting in the darkness because talking was the only thing I could do at the time, while sitting around. I argued that it was more than the mere act of talking that I enjoyed. I said that I relished the soothing warmth of the darkness around us. He asked me what I did at home when it was dark. I said that invariably I would turn on the lights or I would go out into the lighted streets until it was time to go to sleep.

"Oh!" he said incredulously. "I thought you had learned to use the darkness."

"What can you use it for?" I asked.

He said the darkness—and he called it the "darkness of the day"—was the best time to "see." He stressed the word "see" with a peculiar inflection. I wanted to know what he meant by that, but he said it was too late to go into it then.

CARLOS CASTANEDA

One does not discover the absurd without being tempted to write a manual of happiness. "What! by such narrow ways—?" There is but one world, however. Happiness and the absurd are two sons of the same earth. They are inseparable.

ALBERT CAMUS

Soto Zen monastery, Eiheiji, Fukui Prefecture, Japan.

DO ZEN MONKS WORRY?

The following conversation took place in a guest room at the Soto Zen monastery at Eiheiji, Fukui Prefecture, Japan. The room was bare except for a futon and a pillow. It had paneled walls, sliding shoji screens, and tatami mats on the floor. Kuroda, the monk assigned to guide me during my stay, sat on the floor opposite me. He was dressed in a black robe that displayed on his left shoulder the golden flower emblem of Eiheiji.

QUESTION: In the eyes of the world, Zen monks represent those who have withdrawn from stress-filled society to preserve the tranquility of their lives. What I want to ask is whether Zen monks are subject to any of the stresses commonly experienced by those of us who live in society.

KURODA: (Kuroda nods, with a passive blank stare) Yes. . . .

Q: Do you ever experience bad dreams like nightmares or stay awake at night thinking about things?

K: (He smiles, faintly) Yes. . . .

Q: Do monks sometimes worry?

K: (He nods, deeply, and says "Yes," nods more deeply and says "No.") We don't think about other things. We don't worry. We have nothing to worry about. Other people worry. We meditate on the Buddha. This gives us peace. When we meditate on the Buddha, we cannot worry about what will happen.

Q: Do you ever find it difficult to meditate because other concerns interfere with your concentration?

K: No. We practice. We practice meditating. We meditate in the morning. We meditate through the day. We meditate in the evening after we eat. We meditate all the time on the Buddha. This brings peace of mind. There is no time to worry. (He smiles.)

Q: Then a lot of things people in the world worry about you never have to think about—like what you're going to eat, whether you might lose your job. Do you ever worry about what's for dinner or whether you're going to have anything to eat at all?

K: No.

Q: Don't you sometimes worry during meditation [*zazen*] that you're going to be struck on the shoulder with the stick? Doesn't that cause anxiety?

K: No.

Q: Say you're sitting in zazen. And your brother monk steps behind you with the stick. At that moment, is there not *some* anticipation of pain?

K: No. The stick is a gift of the Buddha.

Q: Then do you look forward to being struck?

K: No. To be struck is a gift of the Buddha. Not to be struck is a gift of the Buddha. There is no difference.

Q: What about some of the other things people worry about? What about your family, your mother or father, or a younger sister or brother? Do you think about them?

K: Yes.

Q: Do you ever visit them?

K: Yes. We visit them when they need us.

Q: But you don't *worry* about them . . . ?
K: (Kuroda seems to feel that I've asked something worth working with, but he gropes for words. I have the feeling, for the first time, that he would like to communicate his ideas to me, but that it's really a hopeless undertaking—our worlds are too far apart. Then he says:) We think about them. We think about our families, but we don't worry about them. I have no ties to family. My father became sick. I went and spent some time with him. I looked after my family. I made arrangements for them. I did not worry.
Q: Would you worry about your mother if something happened to your father?
K: (He hesitates, sways, takes his time, as though he's not quite sure what to do with the question.) My mother is all right. While I was with her, I looked after her. I made arrangements. But now I am not with her.
Q: Then, while you're here at Eiheiji, you don't worry about her.
K: That is correct.
Q: Do you ever worry about what's for supper?
K: (He smiles and sways.) No.
Q: What if the cook prepares something you don't like?
K: (He smiles again, half nods, half sways—as though he knows what I'm talking about.) That is all right, too.
Q: You mean there are no foods you dislike . . . really dislike?
K: That is correct.
Q: You eat whatever they cook?
K: Yes. It makes no difference.
Q: While you eat, do you meditate on the Buddha?
K: No.
Q: What do you do while you eat?
K: We eat.

At some point in our conversation I ran the following sentences through my mind, though they did not come from Kuroda in quite this form:

We eat while we eat.
We think while we think.
We meditate while we meditate.
We work while we work.
We sleep while we sleep.

I got the distinct impression that he and his brother monks simply didn't experience stressful responses of the kind that those of us living in the "real world" know so well. I found this difficult to believe. Some of the monks must have had damaging childhood experiences like the rest of us. Didn't some of them have rejecting parents? Weren't they victimized by family fights, mixed signals, physical and emotional abuse? Weren't some of them orphaned and abandoned? There just had to be repressed contents that they still deal with. But I found myself unable to get into these areas, partly because of language problems but largely, I

Continued

Genius is the recovery of childhood at will.
Arthur Rimbaud

think, because Kuroda felt reluctant to share with an outsider. (The phrase "casting pearls before swine" comes to mind.)

There remains the possibility that some of the Zen monks refuse to confront the contents of the subconscious. Like the rest of us, they do a good job of repressing painful experiences from the past. Or it may be that most, or many of them, know very well what is going on in their inner worlds, but that they refuse to divulge such matters to strangers whom they (rightly) perceive as moving in a different dimension and who will inevitably misinterpret the Zen experience.

Or it may be that within the lives of these reclusive monks a resolution of the deeper elements of the subconscious takes place—a true integration (Jung would call it "individuation")—and that the visible tranquility of their lives is exactly what it seems to be, a sense of wholeness and peace.

I concluded that the monks I encountered at Eiheiji don't appear to experience unresolved trauma, that they suffer from little defensive paranoia, and that they really don't have to worry about coping with demanding situations. I had to conclude that what they do, they do. When they eat, they eat. When they meditate, they meditate. When they think about this, they think about this. When they think about that, they think about that. They are experts in doing one thing at a time—and doing it purely.

✦

Huxley's Deep Reflection

9 Aldous Huxley was one of the great minds of the twentieth century. He had developed, through discipline, a technique for using a high degree of his considerable mental power. At will, Huxley could withdraw into what he called his state of "Deep Reflection" (DR state), a mind-state

> marked by physical relaxation with bowed head and closed eyes, a profound progressive psychological withdrawal from externalities but without any actual loss of physical realities nor any amnesias or loss of orientation, a "setting aside" of everything not pertinent, and then a state of complete mental absorption in matters of interest to him.

Awaken the mind without fixing it anywhere.
Kongo Kyo

Le coeur a ses raisons que la raison ne connaît point. ***(The heart has its reasons that reason knows nothing of.)***
Blaise Pascal

When Huxley was in such a meditative state it was possible for him to engage in physical activity to some extent—jotting down notes or exchanging pencils—without remembering afterward anything that he had done. As he said, these physical events did not "impinge" on his mental processes. Loud noises could not reach him. He would emerge from his reflective state only when he had finished his self-set creative goals; his emergence was inner-willed.

Frequently Huxley began his day's work by entering into his DR state. He would organize his ideas and sort his tasks for that day. One afternoon he was working with total absorption on a particular manuscript when his wife returned from shopping. She inquired whether he had taken down the note she had phoned in to him. Somewhat bewildered, he helped her look for the note, which they found near the phone. He had been in his DR working state when she called, had answered the phone as usual—"I say there, hello!"—listened to the message, jotted it down—all this without remembering a word of the episode. His mind had apparently proceeded to carry on its work without interruption.

The essential point is that this was Huxley's way of working efficiently. His friend Milton Erickson experimented with him in the DR state, and Huxley frequently found himself prepared for work but with nothing to do. He would emerge from his DR state rather puzzled. "There I found myself without anything to do so I came out of it."

A philosopher of imposing stature doesn't think in a vacuum. Even his most abstract ideas are, to some extent, conditioned by what is or is not known in the time when he lives.

Alfred North Whitehead

His wife commented that when in the state of Deep Reflection, he seemed

> like a machine moving precisely and accurately. It is a delightful pleasure to see him get a book out of the bookcase, sit down again, open the book slowly, pick up his reading glass, read a little, and then lay the book and glass aside. Then some time later, maybe a few days, he will notice the book and ask about it. The man just never remembers what he does nor what he thinks about when he sits in that chair. All of a sudden, you just find him in his study working very hard.

10 Religious mystics the world over make a common assertion: no one can understand a profound religious experience until he has himself experienced it. No amount of description with mere symbols can touch its true meaning. Western mystics—Plotinus, Groot, Eckhart, Tauler, and others—have consistently stated that there is no experience in daily life that can help one to understand the meaning of the mystical experience, for it is not a mundane experience different merely in degree; rather, it is a different **kind** of experience.

The great cause of much psychological illness is the fear of knowledge of oneself—of one's emotions, impulses, memories, capacities, potentialities, of one's destiny.

Abraham Maslow

The same observation comes from the Eastern mystics: if you think you have achieved an intellectual understanding of nirvana, then you have missed it. Similarly from the Taoist: "The Tao that can be expressed in words is not the true Tao."

Mystical Unity

11 One of the most valued but ineffable mystical experiences in both the East and the West is the experience of unity. So profound is it that the mystics thereafter remain silent concerning it. They may indeed write volumes around the periphery of the experience, but they avow that they could not possibly describe what they have seen.

It is an event in which all experience is somehow seen together. The outer world and the inner merge into one; no distinction is made between subject and object. All knowledge is interwoven; everything is seen in the light of everything else, as though every fragment of knowledge and understanding illuminated every other fragment of knowledge and understanding. There is a coalescence; everything is related; all the contents of the mind become unified. It is all One, and this One may be felt as in some way merging with the cosmos itself; it may be conceived as the uniting of one's essence with Ultimate Reality or Godhead.

By analogy, suppose that you have spent a dozen years devouring knowledge. Imagine that you have carefully read hundreds of books in psychology, history, biology, chemistry, physics; you have studied all the textbooks in higher

As I see it, such a man, the man who engaged in a lifetime quest away from encapsulation, moving in the direction of the broadest and deepest possible reality image, has the key to what it means to be and to see. He is thereby representative of man in his deepest and most significant sense. For such an orientation would mean that he was very much alive in the best meaning of the term "existential" and very much aware in the best meaning of the term "philosophical." Such a man would be a man of great compassion, great sensitivity, and great thought. He would, in short, be reaching for ultimate consciousness. And while it is true that such an open approach to life is very risky for the individual man in the short view, it is clearly more creative and productive, and therefore, more viable for all men in the long run.

Joseph Royce

Nirvana is not the blowing out of the candle. It is the extinguishing of the flame because day is come.

Rabindranath Tagore

mathematics, geometry, astronomy, and philosophy; you have memorized the great outpouring of human feeling in music, poetry, literature, and art.

But how do we store and recover such information? Ordinarily our minds move with a pokey, linear motion. They plod along, thinking of one thing at a time. We never read a book at a time, not even a page at a time: we read only a few words or perhaps a line.

But suppose some psychophysical happening suddenly opened the doors to all your stored information and this vast accumulation of knowledge could flow together into one sustained flash of understanding. Suppose every fact related to every other fact. Suppose that all you had ever learned had somehow bonded into a harmonious whole. In your mind, All was One. Such an experience would indeed be ineffable, so far beyond words that one could never hope to describe what he had seen.

Saint Thomas Aquinas may have had this kind of experience. After producing scores of volumes of systematic theology—the crowning achievement of Western religious thought—Thomas had a vision near the end of his life after which, he said, everything he had previously written was straw. He never attempted to put into mere human words what, at last, he had seen.

Zen Satori

12 One state of consciousness sought by the Zen Buddhist is called *satori,* usually translated as "flash of enlightenment." It is a mind-state quite different from a trance or hypnotic condition. It is a state of sharp alertness and wide awareness accompanied, at the same time, by a deep sense of inner calm. We know now that those who practice Zen meditation (*zazen*) are in a specific mental state with a characteristic EEG (electroencephalographic) pattern of brainwaves. Studies show that EEG patterns of experienced Zen meditators are quite different from those of beginners. In advanced patterns the alpha waves begin to diminish and a rhythmic "theta train" appears. The typical "advanced" Zen meditation moves through four stages. It begins with the initial alpha waves with eyes open (I); then a sharp increase of the alpha (II) followed by a gradual decrease of the alpha (III); and finally there is a sustained period of rhythmic theta waves (IV).

How does *zazen* feel from the standpoint of the meditator? For Western students, Erich Fromm has described the indescribable as well as it can be captured in words.

> If we would try to express enlightenment in psychological terms, I would say that it is a state in which the person is completely tuned to the reality outside and inside of him, a state in which he is fully aware of it and fully grasps it. *He* is aware of it—that is, not his brain, nor any other part of his organism, but *he,* the whole man. He is aware of *it;* not as of an object over there which he grasps with his thoughts, but *it,* the flower, the dog, the man, in its or his full reality. He who awakes is open and responsive to the world, and he can be open and responsive because he has given up holding on to himself as a thing, and thus has become empty and ready to receive. To be enlightened means "the full awakening of the total personality to reality."

Religious Ecstasy

13 A state of consciousness highly prized by Western religious minorities is a form of religious ecstasy. Those belonging to the Pentecostal tradition—or other traditions that value "spirit-possession" (in Christianity, possession by the Holy Spirit)—have sometimes made the ecstatic experience a condition of membership. Within their circles they cultivate an attitude of expectancy in which members may anticipate for years the glorious soul-filling experience.

In religious ecstasy several things occur. The word *ecstasy* derives from the Greek *ek* ("out of") and *stasis* ("standing"), implying that the "ecstatic" individual is "standing outside" his body, the assumption being that a "spirit" has taken his place. Thus he is no longer in possession of his own body, and the original "self" is no longer in a reality-mode. An ecstatic individual no longer responds to the realities about him; his behavior has "switched to automatic." Some deeper level of the psyche has taken control while the normal controlling ego has suspended operations.

A typical ecstatic experience is known as **glossolalia,** "speaking in tongues." In this state, one feels he has gradually been overcome or "possessed." He may begin to speak unintelligible words ("babble") to himself or to bystanders. His voice may sound quite different from his own; he may sing beautifully when ordinarily he sings not at all. To the ecstatic individual it feels as though the words and songs are uttered by someone else deep within and are quite beyond his control. As in cases of hypnosis, some aspect of the personality other than the ego has taken control, and any content originates from the deeper levels of consciousness.

In Pentecostal experiences in which the ecstatic state is considered to be possession by the Holy Spirit, it not infrequently brings about a fundamental reorientation in the individual's life—a "conversion" or "born again" experience. It is difficult to imagine any experience more meaningful than being possessed by God.

In the province of the mind, what one believes to be true either is true or becomes true within limits to be found experientially and experimentally. These limits are beliefs to be transcended.

John C. Lilly

Old Man: *(sarcastically). Being spiritual, the mind cannot be affected by physical influences?*

Young Man: *No.*

Old Man: *Does the mind remain sober when the body is drunk?*

Mark Twain

It is constantly being borne in upon me that we have made far too little use in our theory of the indubitable fact that the repressed remains unaltered by the passage of time—this seems to offer us the possibility of an approach to some really profound truths.

Sigmund Freud

Joseph Campbell was asked by Bill Moyers, "What does it mean to have a sacred place?" His reply: "This is an absolute necessity for anybody today. You must have a room, or a certain hour or so a day, where you don't know what was in the newspapers that morning, you don't know who your friends are, you don't know what you owe anybody, you don't know what anybody owes to you. This is a place where you can simply experience and bring forth what you are and what you might be. This is the place of creative incubation. At first you may find that nothing happens there. But if you have a sacred place and use it, something eventually will happen."

Joseph Campbell (with Bill Moyers), *The Power of Myth*, p. 92.

THE FANTASTIC JOURNEY

The idea of aloneness belongs to the East.

D. T. SUZUKI

The East puts its truth in the unconscious, whose wisdom it seeks to release in all its profundity.

ALAN WATTS

14 In the Indian religions, the state of nirvana is a trance-state outwardly resembling a deep sleep. It is marked by a progressive deepening of the trance through religious disciplines that are similar to techniques of self-hypnosis. Gradually, as *samadhi* ("concentration") is practiced, the devotee learns to block out all sensory stimuli from the external world; simultaneously, sensory and emotional input from the inner world are reduced and finally stopped; no bodily sensations or emotions—hunger, pain, fear, loneliness—are registered. Further, however, the mystic enters into a mind-state of zero cognition—no ideas, memories, or rational activity. It is a "contentless" state of consciousness.

This Eastern trance resembles Huxley's "Deep Reflection" in one respect: loud noises or other stimuli are not perceived. But in its central nature, it contrasts with Huxley's DR state. In the latter's mind a high pitch of intellectual activity raced through its plan of operations, while in nirvana there is no mental **content** of any sort. It is **pure consciousness,** a seemingly discarnate, free-floating experience of nothingness.

This is the ultimate achievement of human existence for the Hindu and Buddhist. It is said to be experienced as an indescribable state of tranquillity, inner peace, and joy, a timeless state of union with the cosmos itself. In Hindu terms, the self-essence (*atman*) has become one with Ultimate Reality (*Brahman*).

15 The individual who lacks awareness of the depths and facets of his psyche is something less than a whole person, and considerably less than he could be. He is living a single-dimensioned existence in a multidimensional psychic universe. There is no reason not to explore other worlds and—like the Zen monk or religious ecstatic—spend some time living there. The qualifying condition, as emphasized, is that he preserve his autonomy and the integrity of his reality-mode of consciousness.

Of course, our Western methods for accomplishing anything are distinctive: we employ chemistry and physics in everything. It is quite in character that we approach psychic/somatic functions with pills and gadgets, milligrams and voltages. And, typically, we will find faster ways of "getting there" and run the risks so characteristic of our rapid conquest of all known worlds.

In the late nineties we were still in the process of breaking through archaic traditions regarding the human psyche. We have already come so far that there is now little doubt that we will continue to loosen the confines and, hopefully, move ahead to positive controls and enriching experiences.

✦

The Buddha

One Who Awakened

The great ideas by which mankind lives have been shaped by relatively few historical individuals. One of the most influential idea-shapers was a man named Siddhartha Gautama, who lived approximately twenty-five hundred years ago—from about 560 to 480 BC—in northeastern India. His worldview has been adopted by an astounding 4.5 billion human beings over time.

Trustworthy facts about Siddhartha's life are difficult to come by. We must rely on worshipful traditions critically analyzed and balanced with a sense of empirical reality; through careful use of the earliest documents we stand a fair chance of recovering a few glimpses of the historical figure and getting a feeling for his personality and teaching. Then with a disciplined imagination . . .

Imagine yourself sitting on a riverbank in northeastern India, facing eastward, looking across the muddy water toward green trees and low mountains beyond. It is early evening, and several cattle drink at the water's edge. Monkeys scurry playfully under the banyan trees behind you. Upstream are a half-dozen men, sitting quietly without talk, their faces stone-still, their eyes closed in meditation.

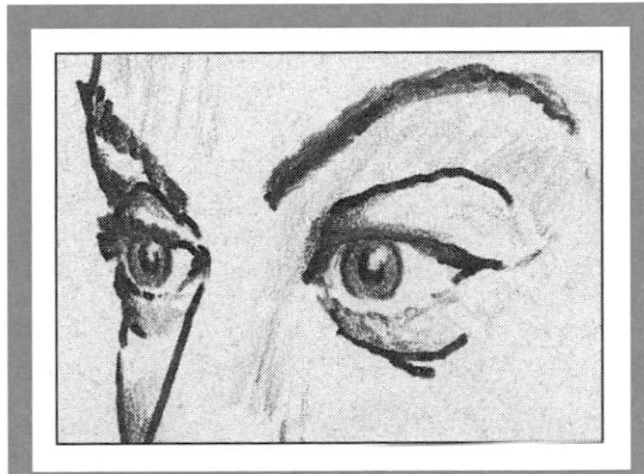

A short distance downstream, sitting under a huge ashvattha tree, is a young man also in meditation, his calm bright eyes wide open, staring across the river. He is wearing a tattered, yellowish-white garment. He has coal-black hair, long earlobes, fiercely sensitive eyes, and dark bronzed skin. Under him is a soft bed of kusha grass.

For a full night and a full day he has been sitting thus, bolt upright in the lotus position. His body is thin, even gaunt, as though he had recently been attacked and mauled by life; but in contrast to his outward appearance, there is an unmistakable glow of serenity on his face.

The year is 525 BC, the fifteenth day of Vaishakha—the night of the full moon—and after the events about to take place here on the riverbank, this is the man who will be known for centuries to come simply as "The Awakened One"—the Buddha.

The weight of suffering that goes on in the world—it is unbearable. It is a world that grows old and dies only to be reborn, and grow old and die, again

Little drops fill a waterpot. Little virtues make a wise man.

The Dhammapada

We are what we think, having become what we thought.

The Dhammapada

Those who are attached to nothing, and hate nothing, have no fetters . . .

and again, without end. For every living thing in it: birth, suffering, death . . . birth, suffering, death . . . the Wheel turns, endlessly.

If I reveal what I have seen, what would I accomplish? In a world dedicated to lust and hatred, Truth is not easily tolerated. Truth only confuses those who are at home in the world.

I have fallen out of love with the world! Why should I be concerned O Mara? Why should I be consumed?

His given name was Siddhartha, and he was the only son of a wealthy landowner and clan chieftain named Suddhodana. Maya was his mother, and she birthed him into the Gautama clan of the Sakya hill tribe in southern Nepal. They belonged to the Kshatriya caste—the warriors.

By all accounts, the young Siddhartha was brilliant and perceptive. Tradition assures us that he excelled in his studies and was a strong athlete. As an archer he was a match for the other young men with whom he hunted. He spent much of his time in varied recreations, including pursuit of the seductive village dancing girls. He was given little responsibility and seems not to have cared deeply for anyone or anything.

At sixteen he was married to his cousin Yasodhara, a happy, arranged marriage (though one tradition tells us he won her in an archery contest). Thereafter, in sensuous isolation, his years ebbed away, first his teens and then, while still asleep, his twenties; his life/time was being used up, uneventfully, in the hideaway world of his father's courtyards. He knew little about the outside world; the excruciating truth about the human condition had not yet been seeded in his consciousness. Still, a discontent was stirring from within. Life was passing him by; nothing was being gained.

The problem is the human condition, nothing less. The human condition is uninhabitable, but we do not know this. We treat life as though it were livable, and we only make things worse. We dream of fame, fortune, and immortality—which we cannot achieve. We develop attachments, affections, and loves for people and things—all of which we lose. Our wants and needs are insatiable, and they cause continuous grief.

And worse: we are not really selves at all. The sense of "self" is generated by an ephemeral collection of particles that cohere, enter the world as system, and become conditioned—"I exist!" —and then disintegrate at death—all in the flash of an instant in cosmic time. And that cosmic instant is characterized by a single crushing reality: suffering.

What we need is therapy. A state of mental health could result if we could stop wanting what cannot be. Mental health would consist in the reestablishment of peace of mind and wholeness of being. These qualities can be regained when we understand clearly that (1) the human condition is evil, and (2) we don't have to live in it.

One day Siddhartha ventured outside the confines of his home and visited the city of Kapilavastu. Though he may have "seen" the sights of the world before, now, for the first time, his opened eyes saw. He saw an old man whose wrinkled body illustrated the degeneration of eighty years of living. Next he saw a man suffering in agony with disease, an affliction of the groin, the black plague. Then he watched a procession of mourners carrying a shrouded corpse to be cremated on the burning *ghats* by the river's edge.

Still reeling from his confrontation with the realities of life, he beheld a monk in meditation, trying to discover a spiritual path to follow. The contrast was shattering. Siddhartha knew then that he could never retreat to his former life. He wanted to know the truth—the whole truth—about life-in-the-world.

> *The first truth is that existence is suffering.*
>
> *The second truth is that our pain and suffering are caused by what we perceive to be our human needs and cravings.*
>
> *The third truth is that our pain and suffering can end if we learn to eliminate our human needs and cravings.*
>
> *The fourth truth is that continual practice of the eightfold path will lead to the cessation of all suffering and to a life that is serene and free.*

He had seen the problem; now he must find a solution.

Leaving his wife and son—tradition tells us how he visited Yasodhara and Rahula in the silence of the night, gazed lovingly at them for the last time, felt the urge to embrace them but turned and rode off into the night on his faithful horse Kantaka—he fled into a nearby forest, exchanged his fine clothes with a ragged beggar, cut his long black hair, and set out to find the answer to life—a solution to suffering. This was the "Great Renunciation." He was twenty-nine. (Legend tells us that the noble Kantaka returned to the palace riderless and, in sorrow, died.)

His first move was to find a guru. He came across Uddaka, a Brahmin ascetic living in a cave, and learned from him how to control his breathing and to remain motionless while practicing thought-less meditation. He also learned, for the first time in his life, to deny himself and to fast —"like an insect during a bad season." But after a time these Brahmanical teachings left him empty and discontented.

He found another guru, Alara, and learned from him that the answer cannot be found through the control of the senses or bodily pain and fasting. Again dissatisfied, he left.

What he had really learned from the Hindu hermits was that the ways of others were not for him and that he had to seek his own path.

> *What is this Middle Way between world affections and self-torment that leads to an awakening?*
>
> *It is an eightfold path.*
>
> *First comes wisdom, which results from* ***right perspective*** *(we cause our own suffering) and* ***right intention*** *(a commitment to transcend the world).*
>
> *Next comes proper conduct, which results in* ***right speech, right behavior,*** *and* ***right living*** *(ethical purity must become a matter of habit) so that all one says and does will move him toward his spiritual goals.*
>
> *Thirdly, one must develop proper mental qualities by means of* ***right effort*** *(control of the mind through strength of will),* ***right mindfulness*** *(keeping the contents of consciousness under perfect control), and* ***right meditation*** *(trance states wherein the world is forgotten and one experiences perfect joy and emptiness).*
>
> *It is in the practice of right meditation (samadhi) that the true spirituality of awakening begins.*

After leaving the two gurus, Siddhartha made his way to Uruvela, where he was joined by five mendicant ascetics who practiced extreme self-mortification and self-denial. The better part of six years he now spent in their company, doing penance and fasting, exploring the pathway of asceticism, which promised control of the senses and the refinement of one's spiritual nature.

He lived on seeds and herbs, finally ate only a single grain of rice or one jujube apple a day. He became wan and emaciated. "If I sought to feel my belly, it was my backbone that I found in my grasp." He weakened to the point of death. One day he sank into unconsciousness and was revived by a bowl of rice cooked in milk given to him by a girl

Buddha Lexicon

ahimsa
anatta
bodhi
bo-tree
buddha
dharma
dharmachakra
dukkha
karma
nirvana
shakya
samadhi
samsara
sangha
tanha

Abandon even good, and evil all the more; he who has reached the other shore has no use for rafts.

By oneself evil is done; by oneself one suffers; by oneself evil is left undone; by oneself one is purified. I take refuge in the Buddha

I take refuge in the Buddha
I take refuge in the Dharma
I take refuge in the Sangha

Confession of Faith
Theravada Buddhism

O Ananda, be ye lamps unto yourselves. Be ye refuges to yourselves. Hold fast to the Dharma as a lamp. Hold fast to the Dharma as a refuge. Look not for refuge to any one beside yourselves.

Nirvana is, but not the man that enters it.

The Visuddhimagga

from a nearby village. When he regained his strength, he also recovered a clear mind; and asceticism, he now knew, was not the answer.

Stronger now, clothed in a winding sheet borrowed from a tomb, Siddhartha made his way southward to Gaya. At nightfall he came to a fig tree and, after accepting as a cushion eight armfuls of grass from a helpful farmer, he sat down by the trunk and slipped into meditation. Knowing that he was nearing the end of his search, he pressed forward relentlessly. "Were my skin to dry up, my hand to wither, and my bones to dissolve, until I have attained to supreme and absolute knowledge I shall not stir from this seat."

Endowed with the whole body of noble virtues—sense control, mindfulness and comprehension, and contentment—the truth-seeker chooses a solitary resting place—a forest, the foot of a tree, a hill, a mountain glen, a rocky cave, a charnel place, a heap of straw in the open field. He abandons this world and enters the mind where the Truth can be found.

As I meditate, all desires fade. I eliminate the five hindrances: urges and wants, the need for action, the need to withdraw and sleep, and anxiety and doubt.

When the five hindrances are eliminated, then happiness is born, to happiness joy is added, with his mood joyful his body is relaxed, his relaxed body feels at ease, and as he feels at ease his mind becomes concentrated—he enters samadhi.

Deeper in mind I soar upward. Joy and happiness, born of seclusion. Tranquillity. Joy and happiness born of concentration. Happiness of neutrality. Mindfulness. Understanding. Pure neutrality and mindfulness. Sphere of infinite space. Sphere of infinite consciousness. Sphere of nothingness. Sphere of neither thought nor nonthought. Emptiness. Cessation of thought and feeling. Pure consciousness.

Nirvana.

According to Buddhist tradition, on the full-moon day in the month of Vaishakha in the year 525 BC, Siddhartha reached the end of his quest: he attained Enlightenment (*bodhi*) and became the Awakened One, the Buddha. He was thirty-five years old.

Thinking as a true philosopher, he had faced the realities of experience as he saw them and attempted to understand what he found. And what he had found was that life is brief and painful, birth is evil and death is release; and the best way to live is to fall out of love with life and develop a state of mind that will provide an authentic experience of peace and joy. This is the Way of the Buddha.

Siddhartha—now the Buddha—arose from beneath the Bodhi-tree, walked to Sarnath, and shared the Truth with his five companions. They saw, and believed. Then he spent the next forty-five years preaching and teaching in northeast India. He was immensely successful. The Sangha (order of monks) was organized, and his wife and son both joined.

When he knew he was about to die, he gathered his disciples about him. "My journey nears its end, and I have reached my sum of days, for I am nearly eighty years old." Then to his close friend and favorite disciple: "So, Ananda, you must be your own lamps, be your own refuges. Take refuge in nothing outside yourselves." He spoke his last words: "Go now, and diligently seek to realize your own salvation."

He lay over on his right side, closed his eyes, and began to ascend, for the last time, into trance: level after level, even higher, and into nirvana. From there he passed on into the final condition: *Parinirvana.*

The next day the villagers of Kusinagara came to the grove of sal trees and wrapped his body in layers of cloth and wool. At dawn on the seventh day, the bier was carried to a shrine outside the east gate of the city. There they cremated the remains of Siddhartha Gautama, the Sakya prince.

✦

Reflections

1 Is Maslow's observation on p. 235 (see marginal quote) meaningful to you? When you read Maslow's comment along with that of R. D. Laing (p. 229), what is your dominant response?

2 Your text makes the opening statement that "there is no obvious reason why one should spend his lifetime solely in the two traditional mind-states: the problem-solving conscious state and the 'recovery' sleep state" (p. 230). Do you agree? Or, in your opinion, are these the only normal and natural modes of consciousness?

3 As you reflect on each of the modes of consciousness described in this chapter (such as Huxley's DR state, mystical unity, Zen satori, ecstatic "spirit-possession," the out-of-body projection), are these modes of consciousness that you would like to experience? Do you fear them? If so, are you aware of the source of your fear? Would you want to experience them, do you think, if you could be sure they would turn out to be profoundly meaningful experiences, as others have claimed? In each specific case, what do you think made the experience meaningful to those who knew it?

4 As you ponder Huxley's DR state, would you like to develop this kind of mental technique for work efficiency? Do you think Huxley possessed a special gift, or is this a mental skill that many of us could acquire?

5 What is your response to the mystical experience of Saint Theresa of Avila (see marginal quote on p. 230)? What gave the experience its profound meaning? Would the experience be denigrated or robbed of its significance if it were comprehensible in psychological terms?

6 Do you share Sir Fred Hoyle's feeling that "one's own consciousness is not enough"? If you agree, do you also feel the impulse to transcend your consciousness predicament? How might you achieve such transcendence? Or is the very idea of "transcendence" a vain and futile notion?

7 Reflect upon the statement by Joseph Royce (see marginal quote on p. 236), then restate in your own words what you think he is saying. What do you think Royce means by the phrase "reaching for ultimate consciousness"? In what sense might it be "very risky" for the individual?

8 What is the purpose of life as illustrated in the story of the Zen monks at Eiheiji? Is this lifestyle attractive to you? Why or why not?

9 Is the Zen state of consciousness familiar to you? Do you know of any lifestyle or discipline in our Western religious traditions that attempts to achieve states of mind similar to Soto Zen?

It seems to me that the greatest lesson of adult life is that one's own consciousness is not enough. What one of us would not like to share the consciousness of half a dozen chosen individuals? What writer would not like to share the consciousness of Shakespeare? What musician that of Beethoven or Mozart? What mathematician that of Gauss? What I would choose would be an evolution of life whereby the essence of each of us becomes welded together into some vastly larger and more potent structure.

Sir Fred Hoyle

A good marriage is that in which each appoints the other guardian of his solitude.

Rainer Maria Rilke

Time

4-2

The essence of conscious life is time. This chapter suggests that a philosophy of time is important, that it makes a difference. And yet, even today, one hears the fashionable comment that time is such a mystery that no one understands it. The mystery arises partly because the word "time" is maddeningly ambiguous—we force it to carry a wide range of meanings—and partly because of faulty introspection. There are at least three distinct usages of the word "time," and all three refer to experiences and concepts that can be clearly understood.

The Moving Finger writes; and having writ, Moves on.
Omar Khayyam
The Rubaiyat

A Philosophy of Time

1 Time affects us in so many ways. We use it; we abuse it; we enjoy it; we fear it.

The way we respond to the challenges of time is a test of what we are, of what we are becoming. We grow older day by day, older in the calendar. Does that fact disturb us greatly, little, sometimes, often? How else are we growing in the same time? How much of our time do we enjoy doing what? Do we frequently or seldom feel that the time was really well spent? The answers we would give to these questions reveal our *philosophy of time.* We all acquire one, though we rarely, if ever, venture to spell it out.

R. M. MacIver

What is time? If no one asks me, I know. If I try to explain it to someone asking me, I don't know.
Saint Augustine

2 A "philosophy of time." Time possesses at once, for us all, the *fascinosum* and the *mysterium;* it is intimately familiar and ultimately formidable. Time is life, and life is time; and somehow we know this in the marrow of our bones. But in all of human experience, is there anything that more befuddles our understanding? Is there any concept that, when we try to force open its secrets, betrays the frailty of our thoughts and the ineptness of our language? Whitehead

said it well: "It is impossible to meditate on time and the mystery of the creative passage of nature without overwhelming emotion at the limitations of human intelligence."

3 "Time is like an ever-flowing stream." (The *stream* of consciousness, the *flow* of an electric current, the *flow* of words of a great orator?) "Time unrolls like a carpet." (*Unrolls* in the sense of uncovering something which was previously hidden but now lies exposed to view; and will it continue to be displayed or will the carpet begin to re-roll from the other end and thus hide something again?) "Clocks *keep* time." (As we *keep* our possessions, *keep* our moral principles, *keep* a house?) "Time passes." (As we *pass* an automobile on the road, *pass* a course in a university, *pass from life to the hereafter?*) "Time is ever coming into being and passing out of being." (Where was it before it *came into being* and where does it go when it *passes out of being?*) "Time is all-embracing." (If it is all-embracing does it also *embrace time?*) "We tell time." (To whom, in what language, and what do we tell about time?) "We expect the future, experience the present, and remember the past." (Is time then merely a subjective image created by our mind, and having no counterpart in the world?) "Time is the relation of before and after." (But *before* and *after* refer *only* to time; hence we are saying literally time is time.) Does this not show that what I have called the straightforward descriptions of time contain metaphors and analogies, ambiguous words, subjective terms, hidden contradictions, and definitions which are purely verbal?

CORNELIUS BENJAMIN

4 One encouraging note can be heard above our confusion. It has been noted by Friedrich Waismann that, although most of us haven't the foggiest notion what time **is,** our time-language seems to keep on **working.** We understand the meaning of the word time in various contexts ("What time is it?" "He arrived just in the nick of time." "We all had a great time.") and thus we continue to function pragmatically without ever knowing what we're talking about. (The use of the word **time** in this chapter is sufficient evidence of this point. I count at least thirty **different** definitions of the word in the text of this chapter, most of which, in context, succeed in communicating ideas with some degree of adequacy, but do not necessitate an understanding of what time truly is. What could better illustrate the astounding fact that we can and do communicate with one another continually **without** knowing **what** we are talking about?!)

Three philosophical questions about time will come into focus here. (1) What is time? How do we experience it? Can we understand it? (2) What is meant exactly by "past," "present," and "future"? In what sense can each of them be said to exist? (3) Where in time do we live? What does time have to do with personal existence?

CLOCK TIME

5 We use the word **time** to refer to at least three different phenomena, all quite distinct, though usually confused in our minds.

One is clock time or chronological time (the latter deriving from the Greek *chronos*, meaning "time"—which doesn't help matters in the least). Clock time probably has nothing whatever to do with time. Clocks measure space. One hour of chronological time is the apparent movement of the Sun from, say, its zenith point (at midday) to a point 15° westward along its orbital path. The clock on the wall is set to correlate with the Sun's motion. While the Sun moves 15° in space, one clock hand moves 360° while the other smaller hand moves 30° in space. Both events (Sun and clock) are cases of matter-in-motion that we have correlated for practical purposes. We usually say we have "syn**chron**ized" Sun and clock, implying our belief that real time is involved in the operation. But this is doubtful. We are correlating events and not synchronizing time.

Psychological Time

6 A second "kind" of time is subjective time—psychological or experiential time. This is the only temporal phenomenon of which we have any clear conception, and many philosophers are of the conviction that experiential time is the only true time. Psychological time is our individual experience of the continuum of our consciousness. Consciousness is time. When we are asleep or unconscious, time is nonexistent for each of us, but it begins again the moment we regain consciousness.

In this context, we can properly speak of the speeding up and slowing down of time, for the metabolic processes that determine our time-consciousness do just that. They vary. To speak of time variability is to describe accurately an experience of consciousness that is a function of the rate of oxygen consumption by the brain.

Henri Bergson preferred the term **duration** when speaking of conscious time. Pure duration is our ongoing experience of the continuum of consciousness. Bergson insisted that our purest intuition of the true nature of all reality is our experience of this duration of our own consciousness.

To say that time is consciousness may be misleading since we (in the Western world) tend to think of consciousness as consciousness **of something.** Here is one source of confusion about the nature of time. We objectify time and think of it as a sort of fluid medium in which objects/events occur. Just as we find it difficult to conceive of consciousness apart from consciousness of something, so also for time: we have difficulty thinking of time as "pure time" (Bergson's "pure duration") apart from real objects/events. But time and matter-in-motion must be separated in thought. Our ordinary waking consciousness is the time-continuum upon which external objects/events impinge. The telephone rings or someone speaks, and these external stimuli activate sensations that enter directly into consciousness (time) as content. But time and the content are not the same. Time might more easily be conceived as the continuum of consciousness without content.

One important implication of this understanding of time is that if there were no experiencers (no conscious minds), there could be no time. Therefore, there was a time (!), perhaps 4.5 billion years ago, before conscious creatures had evolved, when there was no time. Likewise, if all life on earth should cease to exist in the future, time would be no more.

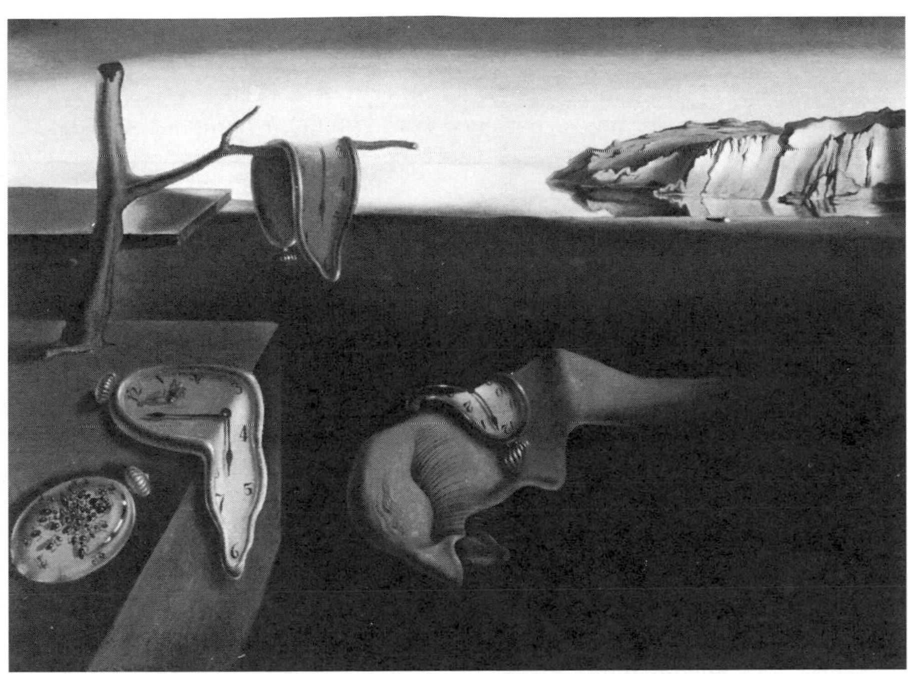

Salvador Dali, *The Persistence of Memory* (1931). Collection, The Museum of Modern Art, New York.

We are always the same age inside.

GERTRUDE STEIN

7 As early as 1860 the Austrian physicist Ernst Mach, the first Western thinker to treat time scientifically, concluded that "the time of the physicist does not coincide with the system of time sensations." The physicist can assume an "even flow" of time or, when very great speeds are involved, describe temporal variations ("time dilation") with Einstein's relativistic formulas. His kind of time still behaves with congenial consistency.

The psychologist is not so fortunate: his time is wildly capricious. Psychological time varies with body temperature: if temperature is raised, time passes slower; if lowered, it passes faster. If our metabolic rate is increased, time passes slower; if decreased, it passes faster. Time plods at half a snail's pace in the eager experience of a child; it accelerates like a speed demon as the adult years pass by. All these variations are determined by the rate of oxygen consumption by the brain. (On the variations of time-experience with age, see box on p. 147.)

Illness and disease can also produce variations in time-experience. Among these are Parkinson's disease, some forms of mental/emotional illness, and certain disorders produced by alcoholism.

Almost all hallucinogens, euphoric drugs such as opium and marijuana, and even some common nonprescription drugs can induce extreme alterations in time experience. Under many conditions, clock time seems to pass incredibly slowly.

We say that time "slows down" and "speeds up." But in relation to what? In relation to chronological time—to the ticks of the clock—as well as in relation to our memory of what is for oneself a "normal" experience of time. We are surrounded by clocks by which we constantly gauge our experience of time: clocks and watches proper, the sun in motion, cars going by, traffic signals, jet

The individual who wakes up is not the same who lay down to sleep the night before.
MAURICE PERCHERON

planes flying overhead, our own heartbeats, the duration required for us to move from one place to another along a familiar route, the time it takes our eggs to fry or toast to burn. These and a thousand other daily events are clocks against which variations in our time experience would be noticed and measured.

REAL TIME

8 A third kind of phenomenon that we think of as "time" is matter-in-motion, that is, sequences of events occurring in the real world. The Sun rises, dandelion seeds float through the air, clouds gather, rain falls, waves break upon the shore. The majority of time-theorists would hold that all these are **only** sequences of events and do not involve any kind of time per se. However, nothing prevents our using the word **time** to refer to such real events while we measure such events against our calibrated clocks and/or experiential time.

If we ask how long it takes a cannonball dropped from the top of the Leaning Tower of Pisa to hit the ground, then we can time the event with our clocks, in which case we are doing what we did with our clocks and the Sun (correlating spatial events); or we can time the event experientially with conscious time as we watch the cannonball fall.

SAINT AUGUSTINE: GOD'S TIME AND OURS

9 At some point in his life, almost every philosopher has become preoccupied with the nature of time. Several developed noteworthy models to explain time and its mysterious operations.

Man's short-term subjective time scale may depend upon the constancy of his internal temperature. For so-called cold-blooded animals this would not hold. For them time would presumably pass slowly on warm days and rapidly on cold days. . . . Time would not appear to flow steadily in the linear sort of way familiar to us mammals.
HUDSON HOAGLAND

Saint Augustine's concept of time is conditioned by his theological presuppositions. God **created** time, Augustine reasoned, when he created everything else. Since God created time, he existed **before** time, he will exist **after** time, and therefore he exists **outside** time. There was no time before he created it. Judeo-Christian doctrine has consistently held that God created **all** that exists —including time and presumably space—*ex nihilo,* "out of nothing."

In the mind of God, there is no "before" or "after"; there is only a "now." In "God's experience" all events occur simultaneously. To put it another way, all the past and all the future (that is, our past and future) exist together in God's present. Thus, when Augustine elaborates on the doctrine that God foresaw the Fall of Man, God really didn't foresee anything, as though he were peering ahead through time (as we would have to) and saw what had not yet transpired. In God's all-inclusive present, "future" events are taking place now. God didn't foresee; he merely saw. Likewise, he doesn't foreordain an event; he merely ordains (causes) what he sees happening. This, to Augustine, is what is meant for God to be omniscient and omnipotent.

We humans experience the present, remember the past, and anticipate the future; but God is not limited by our human time. It is not correct to say, as some theologians do, that there are really two times, God's and ours. Rather, we are in time; God is timeless.

Pure Space and Pure Time

In Relativity Theory, the first three purely spatial dimensions have as an attribute perfect reversibility, whereas time, to the extent that it is a physical unwinding, remains irreversible, demonstrating immediately that the parallelism does not go very far. From an epistemological viewpoint, one must say even more: space can be completely abstracted from its content in the measure of pure form and give way to a strictly deductive science of space, which would be pure geometry. By contrast, there is no pure chronometry; there is no science comparable to geometry in the field of time, precisely because time is a coordination of velocities and because when one speaks of velocity, one speaks of a physical entity. Time cannot be abstracted from its content as space can. Temporal order, in a sense, can be abstracted from its content, in which case, however, it becomes a simple order of succession. But duration . . . depends essentially upon velocities. Duration cannot be disassociated from its content psychologically or physically. From the point of view of psychology, Bergson's analyses of pure duration have amply shown the interdependence of time and its psychological content; similarly, from the physical point of view, time depends upon velocities.

Jean Piaget
Time Perception in Children

All the vital problems of philosophy depend for their solutions on the solution of the problem of what Space and Time are and more particularly how they are related to each other.

Samuel Alexander

Newton: Absolute Time

10 Sir Isaac Newton appears to have assumed, somewhat uncritically, that time is real, being an integral part of the operations of nature. But this objective time is not to be **equated with** matter-in-motion, or with objects per se that endure in time. Real time is separate from real objects/events. Newton's oft-repeated description of time—and his critics have had a field day with it—is as follows:

> Absolute, true, and mathematical time, of itself, and from its own nature, flows equably without relation to anything external, and by another name is called duration: relative, apparent, and common time, is some sensible and external (whether accurate or unequable) measure of duration by means of motion, which is commonly used instead of true time; such as an hour, a day, a month, a year.

It was Newton who introduced into Western thought the notion of an absolute time. This absolute time (whatever it is) is a universal medium that flows smoothly and evenly, unaffected by all the events that occur **inside** it.

Newton's assumption of absolute time dominated the thinking of physicists until the unorthodox reflections of Einstein at the beginning of the twentieth century proved it to be an unworkable assumption and rendered it obsolete.

Time Past

11 Many of us find that our ideas about the past, present, and future run together, overlap, or are otherwise blurred.

It is worth remembering that we never see or experience anything but the past. The sounds you are hearing now come from a thousandth of a second back in time for every foot they have had to travel to reach your ears. This is best demonstrated during a thunderstorm, when the peal from a flash twelve miles away will not be heard for a full minute. If you ever see a flash and hear the thunder simultaneously, you will be lucky to be alive. I have done it once and do not recommend the experience.

Arthur C. Clarke

Ivar Lissner once wrote a book entitled *The Living Past.* It's not difficult to infer what he wishes to say with this title, but, for openers, we might logically ask whether, in any sense, the past could be "living" (present tense). Isn't the past dead? And isn't the past, by definition, placed outside the boundary of the present? This is not to say that influences from "past presents" don't linger on and influence us. They do, but their existence is felt only in our living present.

Yet to say the past is "dead" is surely incorrect. To call something "dead" implies that it was once alive, but the past is never "alive." We could just as well speak of a "living future"—which seems to make little sense. Only the present is "alive"—isn't it?

The nature of the past is of primary concern to the historian since "the past" is his sole subject matter. From his standpoint, the past exists only as it is re-created in the historian's mind. The concrete events of the past are forever gone, and they can be re-created again in the historian's imagination only to the extent that records of some kind have survived from those who witnessed the events. The telltale signs left by events are many: words of eyewitnesses who selected what aspects of any event were significant to them, plus their interpretation and valuation; fossil tracks, leaves, bones; geological records in rocks, volcanic layers, seamounts, oceanic trenches, and so on. If an event leaves no record, then it is forever irretrievable; no historian can reconstruct it nor, for that matter, would he have reason to guess that it had ever occurred.

Time Future

12 What about the future? Unless we hold to some such theory as Augustine's notion of time, then questions about the existence of the future can leave our intellects bewildered.

It's a poor sort of memory that only works backward.

Lewis Carroll
Through the Looking-Glass

Can we experience the future? If we can answer no, then the future can be defined as our expectation that events will continue to occur or that, experientially, we will continue to experience "presents." Our personal future is merely the expectation that our consciousness will continue.

But if, in any way, we can say yes to the question, Can we experience the future? then we must face the most difficult of all philosophical problems and the one with the most far-reaching implications. There are at present ample unexplained time phenomena to prevent our closing the question. Arthur C. Clarke, who even in his fiction tries to remain a sound scientist, gives in to the possibility of precognition. "I would be willing to state that seeing into the future . . . [is] impossible, were it not for the impressive amount of evidence to the contrary."

If we can experience the future, then under any theory of time we have now, we must conclude that the future has **already** taken place or is **now** taking place. (Recall that Augustine, to allow God foreknowledge of the future, was compelled to theorize that our past, present, and future are all taking place concurrently in God's mind.)

Whether the future can be known, even in principle, is one of the subtlest of all philosophical questions.

Arthur C. Clarke

If the future has happened or is happening, then the very structure of our normal waking experience is destroyed. Gone also are numerous axiomatic assumptions such as cause-and-effect and before-and-after. Causal relations become meaningless: that the seed must be planted before the organism can grow, that the song must be sung before it can be heard, that the fire must be lit before the wood can burn—all such statements are wrong. Experience is shot through with contradictions and illusions.

13 Whether we do experience the future has not been established, but experiences that are difficult to explain on any other basis are not uncommon. J. B. Priestley correctly notes that "if one, just one, precognitive dream could be accepted as something more than a coincidence—bang goes our conventional idea of Time!"

Not only is precognition the most stubborn of all philosophical problems, but (if it exists) it often presents itself as a puzzle within a puzzle. Many instances of precognition, especially of tragic episodes, appear as warnings that make it possible for the person having the experience to take evasive action and prevent the tragedy that was foreseen. But this is a contradiction: to be perceived, the future already exists; but when perceived, it can be altered. Therefore, what has already happened can subsequently be changed. Which makes no sense at all.

Priestley—who accepts precognition as fact—says it well.

> Let me put it briefly and brutally. The future can be seen, and because it can be seen, it can be changed. But if it can be seen and yet be changed, it is neither solidly there, laid out for us to experience moment after moment, nor is it non-existent, something we are helping to create, moment after moment. If it does not exist, it cannot be seen; if it is solidly set and fixed, then it cannot be changed. What is this future that is sufficiently established to be observed and perhaps experienced, and yet can allow itself to be altered?

Precognition is key to the mysteries of psi [in the opinion of Dr. Milan Ryzl, a Russian parapsychologist]: "I believe the answer lies in a new understanding of space and time. And I think it is very deep."
Ostrander and Schroeder

(This problem, too, has an interesting theological parallel. A centuries-old controversy turns on whether God's foreknowledge of events necessarily implies predestination. That is, if God "foresees" an event, does that event **have to occur,** or can it be altered? In other words, can God be wrong in what he foresees? It would seem that he can be wrong if the hint of human precognition is applicable: prevision does **not** mean predestination.)

At present we have no time-theories that can explain such occurrences. We must either deny that the future can be experienced now, or develop new models regarding the nature of time. Philosophers and scientists have avoided the time problem, partly because of its association with the occult. But those who professionally wonder about the nature of existence should, like foolish angels, rush in—albeit with fear and trembling—and attempt to create comprehension where chaos now reigns.

Time Present

In te, anime meus, tempora metior. ***(It is in you, O my mind, that I measure time.)***
Saint Augustine

14 Since Zeno the Eleatic (flourished c. 450 BC), analytical thinkers have been bothered by the nature of the present—the "now" of experience. A longstanding tradition has held that the present is a durationless point. This is the

theory of the "punctiform present." It seems that the moment we experience the present, it has already become the past, while the very near future keeps rushing across this knife-edge present into the past. The "now" has no duration; it seems like only a timeless boundary between future and past. If this present has any "width," then it must be composed of a series of (durationless) instants. Louise Heath nicely states this line of logic (although she does not herself accept it):

> The nature of time is such that when the present is, the past has been and *is no* longer, the future will be, but *is not* yet, while the present which *is*, turns out on analysis to be not a part of time but only the boundary between past and future.

This leaves us in a quandary. If, on either side, the past and the future sort of squeeze the present into a durationless boundary line, then where does human experience take place? Or might experience be an illusion, after all, as Zeno believed?

Individual Consciousness is but a shadow; what is permanent is the world.
JOSIAH ROYCE

Something must be wrong with our reasoning. We don't live in the past or future, so we must live in the present. Is the "now" of our experience really a point? or does it have width? If so, how wide is it? Perhaps our "now" extends a little bit into the future and past, as William James believed:

> The only fact of our immediate experience is what has been called the "specious" present, a sort of saddle-back of time with a certain length of its own, on which we sit perched, and from which we look in two directions into time. The unit of composition of our perception of time is a duration, with a bow and a stern as it were—a rearward- and a forward-looking end. It is only as parts of this duration-block that the relation of succession of one end to the other is perceived. We do not feel first one end and then the other after it, and from the perception of the succession infer an interval of time between, but we seem to feel the interval of time as a whole, with its two ends embedded in it.

15 So, according to James, what we call the "present" is by its very nature a **psychological** event, rather than a mathematical or physical (real) event. This would seem to be a fairly obvious conclusion since (1) mathematicians make no claim that mathematical time-points ("instants") are anything other than mental constructs that are useful in solving certain problems; (2) in physics, Einstein's theories have annihilated the notion of simultaneity, that is, that there exists a "universal now"; what is present for one experiencer may be past or future for another experiencer. (See the box on p. 503.)

We are never at home; we are always beyond it. Fear, desire or hope drive us towards the future and deprive us of the feeling and contemplation of what is.
MICHEL DE MONTAIGNE

I have always been so afraid of the present and the real in my life. . . .
ALFRED DE VIGNY

As a psychological event involving perception and consciousness, it therefore possesses duration. The notion of time as a timeless instant is fallacious. Experiencing takes time; it has width. An experience involving intricate psychophysiological processes "stretches out" and lasts a while and could never occur in a "timeless instant." A French psychologist, Paul Fraisse, describes the present from a modern point of view:

> 16 My present is one "tick-tock" of a clock, the three beats of the rhythm of a waltz, the idea suggested to me, the chirp of a bird flying by. . . . All the rest is already past or still belongs to the future. There is order in this present, there are intervals between

DENNIS THE MENACE

"ISN'T IT ALWAYS NOW?"

its constituent elements, but there is also a form of simultaneity resulting from the very unity of my act of perception. Thus the perceived present is not the paradox which logical analysis would make it seem by splitting time into atoms and reducing the present to the simple passage of time without psychological reality. Even to perceive this passage of time requires an act of apprehension which has an appreciable duration.

Therefore, we can define **time** as the experience of the duration of our consciousness, and **the present** as the perceptual time-span of that duration.

But what is the span of that duration? How long does it last? Its duration is not constant, but depends rather upon the nature of the perceptual events that constitute the perceived present. It depends partly on the number of sense stimuli, which are perceived as a unitary event. Any event lasting for more than about two seconds "spills over" into the past, and part of the event is remembered. A series of stimuli (the notes of a melody or the number of spoken sounds) is usually perceived as a unitary event when they last for about one-half to one second. It has been observed that when a clock strikes three or four, we can usually identify the hour without counting the number of consecutive chimes; but beyond four, we have to start counting the number of strikes to identify the hour.

No perception of the present is independent of its content. The duration of the present depends upon the number and nature of the stimuli perceived, the intervals between stimuli, and the organization of the stimuli. The duration of

Until the coming of the missionaries in the seventeenth century, and the introduction of mechanical clocks, the Chinese and Japanese had for thousands of years measured time by graduations of incense. Not only the hours and days, but the seasons and zodiacal signs were simultaneously indicated by a succession of carefully ordered scents.

MARSHALL MCLUHAN

the present also depends upon the state of consciousness of the perceiver and the familiarity and meaningfulness of the organized stimuli. The duration of meaningful sounds in our own language differs from the duration of meaningless sounds in a foreign language. The same is true for a familiar melody in contrast to one never heard before.

In summary, therefore, while in a normal waking mode of consciousness, our perceived present rarely lasts longer than five seconds, and frequently it lasts less than a second. On the average the time-span of our perceived present persists for two to three seconds.

Time and Personal Existence

All animals, large or small, homeothermic or poikilothermic, burn the light of their lives with relative equality. Life, at least on the organismic level, is a democratic process: all of us must die, and the duration of our existence is the same. . . .

Roland Fischer

17 Time and personality are fundamentally related. There is nothing unhealthful about reliving in one's memory the happy moments of one's past or anticipating in imagination the possible happy events of the future. But such movements into past or future can become unhealthful if one is "pushed out of the present" by unbearable conditions and develops the habit, involuntarily, of existing in past or future. In such cases the past becomes not merely a memory of experienced events, but a fabricated blend of actual and imagined events; and likewise the future becomes a confused mélange of possible events and impossible "castles in air." When such intensities prevail, one's temporal horizon has been distorted.

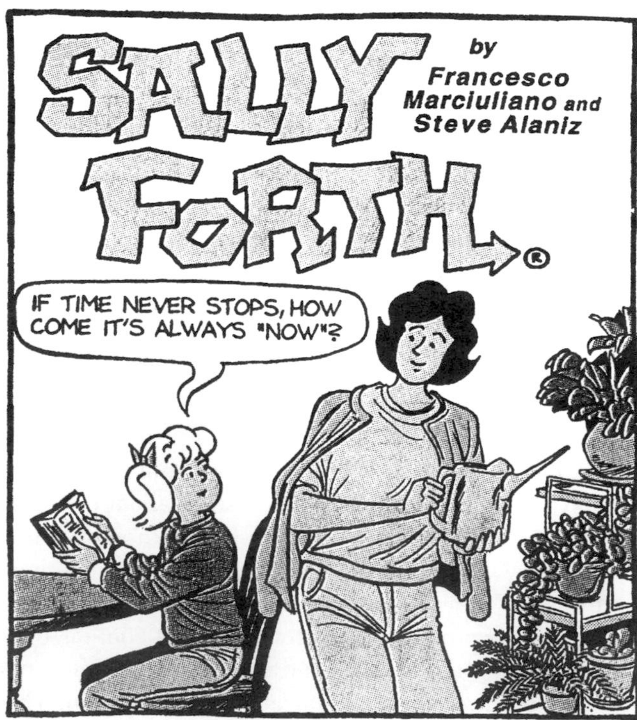

Before such extreme conditions set in, however, "where we live" has already been integrated into our character-structure. If past experiences have been mostly unpleasant we may be oriented toward the future and change. If past experiences have been generally more pleasant and we come to dread the future and change, having no grounds for the anticipation of happy events, we may well tend toward the conservation of the conditions of the past that provided the happier experiences.

What it all comes down to is that we just have to now harder!

Jack Reidling

In a word, those who experience a profound dissatisfaction with the present want change. But whether one seeks better conditions through a future-orientation or a past-orientation will depend upon a fundamental temporal character-structure long since determined by personal experience.

18 The philosophical world-view that goes by the name of existentialism has been immensely popular since World War II. While no two existential philosophers hold quite the same ideas, all share similar attitudes toward how we exist in the living present.

Jean-Paul Sartre coined the most famous catch-phrase of modern philosophy: **existence before essence.** To existentialists the word **existence** refers to the concrete "human reality" of experience. Existence is what is—not what should be or might be. By contrast, the word essence refers to whatever qualities we deem "essential" to man: "human nature," "original sin," "innate aggression," "rationality," or whatever; but all these are abstractions created after the concrete fact. Minds fabricate **essences,** and Sartre denied that such notions have any significance for understanding the uniqueness of the individual person.

Sartre was thinking only of **human** existence, for objects possess a different kind of existence. To see this difference, contrast man's existence with the existence, say, of the *Saturn V* rocket that launched America's lunar missions. Everything about the *Saturn* rocket—its three stages, engine systems, telemetry, payload capacity, engine-out capability, etc.—was conceived **in the minds** of scientists and engineers and elaborated on the design boards long before any single rocket was constructed. The rocket's purpose, conceived in men's minds, determined every element of its design. Once the design had been completed (still in men's minds), then an infinite number of single rockets, produced to perform in a specific way, could be constructed from those master specifications. All the rockets would be identical.

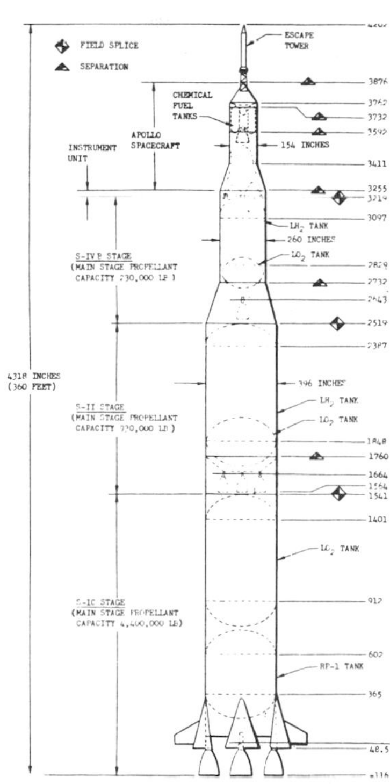

We can speak meaningfully, therefore, of the **essence** of the *Saturn V* rocket: its essence **is** all the elements of structure and function, conceived by its designers, which enable it to accomplish its purpose. For the *Saturn V,* this rocket essence preceded the existence of any single rocket that eventually stood majestically on the launch pad. For created objects, therefore, **essence** precedes **existence.**

Not so for humans, argued Sartre. For man **existence** precedes **essence.** Man was not planned out on a drawing board, nor was he preconceived in any mind (divine or otherwise) for a **purpose** and **then** designed to fulfill such a purpose. Man is not created as objects are created. *Man creates himself.* Man even designs himself—**from within.** Each person is unique, since no master template stamps out identical copies of persons, like minted coins. Therefore

AWARENESS

Awareness means the capacity to see a coffeepot and hear the birds sing in one's own way, and not the way one was taught. It may be assumed on good grounds that seeing and hearing have a different quality for infants than for grownups, and that they are more esthetic and less intellectual in the first years of life. A little boy sees and hears birds with delight. Then the "good father" comes along and feels he should "share" the experience and help his son "develop." He says: "That's a jay, and this is a sparrow." The moment the little boy is concerned with which is a jay and which is a sparrow, he can no longer see the birds or hear them sing. Father has good reasons on his side, since few people can afford to go through life listening to the birds sing, and the sooner the little boy starts his "education" the better. Maybe he will be an ornithologist when he grows up. A few people, however, can still see and hear in the old way. But most of the members of the human race have lost the capacity to be painters, poets or musicians, and are not left the option of seeing and hearing directly even if they can afford to; they must get it secondhand. The recovery of this ability is called here "awareness."

ERIC BERNE
Games People Play

man has no essence, as does the rocket, that **predetermines** what he shall be and do. For man, and man alone, existence precedes essence.

19 Existentialism is a philosophy of time and consciousness. To emphasize existence is to place supreme value upon the quality of one's immediate consciousness. As a philosophy of time, existentialism counsels us to exist as fully as possible in the living "now," to accept and actualize the intense "human reality" of the spontaneous present. For the existentialist, the past is only a repertory of recordings to be used in the service of the present, and the future is but a set of dreams to give the present direction and purpose.

Existentialism asks that we reexamine the way in which we live out our existence within that duration we call the present. Sartre reiterates that the choice is ours as to how we create consciousness. We can hand it over to conditioned responses from our past; we can allow feelings, memories, or habits to impinge upon our present and determine its content and quality. Similarly, we can allow anxieties about future events to impinge upon our present and rob it of its spontaneity and intensity. Thus we can allow our "now" to be deadened.

How dull it is to pause, to make an end,
To rust unburnish'd, not to shine in use!
As tho' to breathe were life.
ALFRED, LORD TENNYSON
"Ulysses"

As a philosophy of time, therefore, existentialism is a way of reevaluating how we use and abuse consciousness. But more than that, it contends that we **can** do something about how time is lived. Within the parameters of our unique personal existence, we can make decisions as to how we shall live the only thing that, in the final analysis, each of us actually possesses—namely, consciousness of time present.

I don't know what you could say about a day in which you have seen four beautiful sunsets.

ASTRONAUT JOHN GLENN (in orbit around the Earth, February 20, 1962)

"MY GRAMPA WANTS TO KNOW WHERE THE TIME GOES?"

20 The creative person, instead of perceiving in predetermined categories ("trees are green," "college education is a good thing," "modern art is silly") is aware of this existential moment as it is, and therefore he is alive to many experiences which fall outside the usual categories (in *this* light this tree is lavender; *this* college education is damaging; *this* modern sculpture has a powerful effect on me).

The creative person is in this way open to his own experiences. It means a lack of rigidity and the permeability of boundaries in concepts, beliefs, perceptions and hypotheses. It means a tolerance of ambiguity where ambiguity exists. It means the ability to receive much conflicting information without forcing closure on the situation.

CARL ROGERS

21 At the end of the spring semester, I packed a few articles and began a four-day trip through the mountains. It was the end of an especially trying school year, and I wanted to make the most of a short vacation before returning to teach summer school.

The countryside was still green and wildflowers gathered in nodding communities along the roadside. I drove alone in my small car, and in a small car one can feel very close to things about him. As I drove, or when I stopped to absorb the land-

There does come a time when you have to put down the menu and enjoy the meal.
SEAMUS O'BANION

scape, I could almost touch the reddish earth, the striated rocks, the weeds and flowers and grasses. I was one among them.

So I travelled. I saw the trees, the flowers, the animals. The broken clouds sometimes painted blue-green patches on the hillsides. I looked up at tall pines and they looked down at me. I smelled pine fragrance and listened to bird calls.

I began to feel alive again. I was **experiencing** things instead of **doing** things. I was feeling and seeing and hearing rather than thinking about . . . and trying to remember . . . and planning ahead.

Or so I thought.

As I watched cloud-shadows shaping their way across the valleys I caught myself deciding if I should reach for my camera. Would they show up just right in color? And was that lightning-split pine silhouetted in black-and-white against the sky "artistic" enough for a picture? I saw purple flowers and found myself wondering if they were lupines, wild larkspurs, or what.

I had the right names for few of the beautiful things I beheld: golden poppies, lavender verbenas, sprays of yellow mustard. Also for the pines (I could remember "ponderosa") and cedars (all I could recall was "juniper"). How little I knew! My new-found ignorance bothered me.

But somewhere—and I don't know when or why—I began to realize what I was doing. I was seeing things just to stuff them into my memory **for later use.** I was building a storehouse of pretty details to impress upon others **after I returned.** The mental habits which dominated my days during the year still controlled my brain. I was organizing the events of my journey as though it were another classroom preparation!

I was insane! Quite literally, I was insane! I was allowing myself to pass my hours out of touch with the realities around me. Here I was in the midst of life, and I wasn't seeing it, wasn't hearing it, wasn't feeling it. Rather than experiencing, I was expending my time **processing** experiences!

I became determined, then, to stop my processing habits. When the next cluster of wildflowers appeared beside the road, I didn't say to myself, as to an audience: "I see a cluster of golden poppies . . ." Rather, I experienced them—saw them, felt them, moved among them, savored them. I refused to let my mind tag them with names or tie them into bundles.

As I tell it now, I find words sufficient to describe my memory of the undulating flight of the mockingbird and the gliding turn of the swallow. I can recount my memories of the smell of pines and fresh rains.

These are things I can do now. But before my short journey ended, I had proved to myself that I could recover the capacity to experience afresh the world about me. I had succeeded in touching reality again.

JUNE HILLMAN

IMMANUEL KANT

The Starry Heavens and the Moral Law

During the school years 1762–1764 a young philosophy student named Johann Herder sat in Kant's classes at the University of Königsberg. Much later, after he himself became a noted philosopher, he remembered his teacher with awe and affection:

> I have had the good fortune to know a philosopher who was my teacher. In the prime of life he possessed the joyous courage of youth, and this also, as I believe, attended him to extreme old age. His open, thoughtful brow was the seat of untroubled cheerfulness and joy, his conversation was full of ideas and most suggestive. He had at his service jest, witticism, and humorous fancy, and his lectures were at once instructive and most entertaining. . . . The history of men, of peoples, and of nature, mathematics, and experience, were the sources from which he enlivened his lectures and conversation. Nothing worth knowing was indifferent to him. . . . He encouraged and gently compelled his hearers to think for themselves; despotism was foreign to his disposition. This man, whom I name with the greatest thankfulness and reverence, is Immanuel Kant; his image stands before me, and is dear to me.

The labors of Immanuel Kant are generally seen as a watershed in the flow of Western philosophy. All earlier critical thinking about thinking led up to him; after him everything took a new turn. He revolutionized thought. He destroyed the foundations of a thousand years of rational theology; he gave new directions to religion and ethics; he provided new and lasting insights into the nature of all human knowledge. Kant created what even he called a "Copernican Revolution" of the mind. Three centuries earlier the astronomer Nicholas Copernicus had made a momentous breakthrough when he successfully explained the apparent motion of the planets by assuming that the Earth, like the other planets, orbits the Sun. What we see the planets doing is not what the planets are doing; their apparent motion is the result our being located on a moving observation platform. Kant found this to be an exact analogy for the way the mind perceives all of reality: we perceive reality the way we do, not because it is that way, but because of the "motion" of our minds. Our minds are not stationary platforms for observing the world, but active, transforming, manufacturing machines; and just as our observations of the planets are appearances and not real events, so all our mind's perceptions of real objects/events are only appearances and not realities.

This Copernican Revolution turned philosophy away from the nature of things and focused it on the knowing mind. The depth of Kant's "Critical Philosophy" (his title) has never been equalled, and little further advancement could be made in critical epistemology until the advent of dependable data from the empirical sciences. The striking thing is that so much recent research and discovery supports Kant's ideas.

Kant lived his entire life in the city of his birth, Königsberg, Prussia, and never travelled more than a dozen or so miles from home. His grandfather and father were leatherworkers who eked out a living making saddles and harnesses, so that he and his eight siblings knew continual poverty during their early years. The Kant family were Pietists, members of an evangelical movement that emphasized simple living, personal faith, warm emotional feeling, close family ties, strict moral discipline, and devotion to duty. This was an especially vital personal religion to his mother Anna Regina, and she bestowed these virtues on her fourth son so that they remained with him all his life and molded his thinking.

At sixteen Kant began studies at the university at Königsberg and quickly gained a reputation as an extraordinary student. There he fell in love with physics, mathematics, and philosophy. He supported himself by helping fellow students with their assignments, playing pool, writing sermons for his friends, studying for the ministry, and tutoring the children of better-off families in Königsberg. In 1755 he completed his doctorate and was accepted as a private lecturer in the philosophical faculty at the University, a position he held for fifteen years despite numerous offers from other universities. His lectures immediately became popular attractions to students; even outsiders, including officers from the local garrison, visited his classrooms to listen, learn, and admire the plucky brilliance of a great mind.

While Immanuel Kant is remembered primarily for his overpowering analytical intellect, his lectures at the university reveal a breadth of learning that makes him one of the great polymaths of all time. He lectured numerous times on logic, metaphysics, ethics, natural law, natural theology, pedagogics, anthropology, geography, mineralogy, astronomy, physics, mathematics, and mechanics. "I myself am by inclination an investigator," he wrote. "I feel an absolute thirst for knowledge, and a longing unrest for further information." Kant had a naturally synoptic mind; he loathed and feared a narrow, petty, pretentious outlook, both in himself and in others. His mind was immersed in cosmic thoughts. His favorite course, physical geography—which he introduced into the curriculum—described the formation of the solar system out of a gaseous nebula, the nature of Man, and the growth of civilization. The course, he said, offered "knowledge of the entire world." His first book closes with the sentence: "Perhaps still other members of the planetary system are being transformed to prepare new abodes for us in other heavens."

Kant believed that it is the job of philosophy teachers to help a student avoid becoming a cyclops. He noted that all academic regimens tend to develop students with but one eye; they proceed to look at the world from a single viewpoint—that of their specialization. Then those students go out into life, get jobs that reinforce their myopia, and continue to see things down one narrow line of vision. "The cyclops of literature (the philologian) is the most insolent, but there are cyclopses among the theologians, law-

The loss of self-respect, which arises from a sincere mind, would be the greatest evil that could ever happen to me.

It is indeed true that I think many things with the clearest conviction, and to my great satisfaction, which I never have the courage to say; but I will never say anything which I do not think.

I myself am by inclination an investigator. I feel an absolute thirst for knowledge, and a longing unrest for further information.

If all that one says must be true, it does not follow that it is one's duty to tell publicly everything which is true.

Sensations of colors, sounds and heat, since they are . . . mere sensations . . . do not of themselves yield knowledge of any object.

I found it necessary to deny knowledge in order to make room for faith.

yers, physicians, and even among the geometers"—who should, by nature, think big. It is the job of philosophy to plant and grow a second eye so that students will be able to see "from the standpoint of other men." How is this to be done? Through the critical philosophy taught by Socrates, the "self-knowledge of human reason" that gives us a clear estimate of what we know and don't know. Philosophy is the antidote for cyclopism.

Kant's cosmological loves began to produce offspring in 1755 with the publication of his *Universal History of Nature and Theory of the Heavens.* Vigorously avoiding theological explanations that were still in fashion—even Newton had said the first creation was God's doing—Kant described the possible origins of the solar system using only scientific principles. (To use the notion of God as the cause of natural events, he said, is "easy philosophy that tries to hide its vain uncertainty under a pious air.") His "nebular hypothesis" (expanded later by Laplace) suggested that the solar system had condensed from a whirling nebula of primordial gas. Religion, Kant held, has no right to set the parameters of explanations of natural phenomena. Religion and science must ignore each other; they are to be understood as entirely separate, and any attempt to mix them is injurious to both. (This statement so offended Kant's dear old teacher Professor Schultz that he confronted Kant with the pained query, "Do you fear God from your heart?" Kant said he did, and their friendship was restored. Kant later wrote, "If all that one says must be true, it does not follow that it is one's duty to tell publicly everything which is true.")

In 1770 Kant became a professor of logic and metaphysics at his university; his renown quickly grew, drawing students from all parts of Germany and admiration from colleagues everywhere. By the 1780s it was Kant who had put the University of Königsberg on the map; by the 1790s Kantian philosophy was taught in all the German universities. But opposition to some of his ideas also grew after he published a work entitled *Religion within the Bounds of Pure Reason.* In 1792 a letter from the Prussian king ordered him to stop lecturing and writing on all religious subjects. "Our highest person has been greatly displeased to observe how you misuse your philosophy to undermine and destroy many of the most important and fundamental doctrines of the Holy Scriptures and of Christianity." Kant finally agreed, but the loss of freedom made him depressed; in 1794 he retired from public life and the following year gave up his classes. When the king died in 1795 Kant was again free, but his strength had begun to decline and his mind was losing its penetrating power. He still went to his desk, took his pen in hand, and tried to fashion sentences; his passion to "reconstruct philosophy" still drove him and made him acutely restless. "The task with which I now busy myself has to do with the transition from the metaphysical basis of the natural sciences to physics." But the shadows were falling. In September 1798, he wrote a friend, "I am incapacitated for intellectual work, though in fairly good bodily health." He lingered for another five years, died February 12, 1804, and was entombed in the Königsberg Cathedral. Over his grave are inscribed his words from the *Critique of Practical Reason:* "The starry heavens above me, The moral law within me"—the two worlds to which he had dedicated his life.

Kant's personality and lifestyle were striking. Though he enjoyed the company of women he never married—he considered it twice but procrastinated till the young ladies turned to other suitors. He lived by himself, guarded his independence, and spent his life with his thoughts. It is impossible to write a "life of Immanuel Kant" someone remarked, because he had no life. That, of course, is entirely false: his life was a continual exciting adventure of the mind (which some biographers will not understand); and it was a remarkably happy life. He frequently invited colleagues and students to dine with him, and they all enjoyed his warm hospitality and lively conversation. With equal ease he could engage in small talk or heavy thoughts; his banter, like his lectures, was witty and entertaining.

Physically, Kant was frail, "never sick but never well," he said of himself. He was diminutive, with a hollow chest and a hump on his right shoulder. He was severely self-disciplined, puritanical, and punctiliously punctual. His routines were rigidly controlled by the clock. He awakened at 5 o'clock, worked till 7 or 8, lectured an hour or two, worked again from 9 or 10 till lunch at 1 o'clock; then he strolled down the street for exactly one hour, returned and read through the afternoon and evening. Precisely at 10 p.m. he retired to sleep.

✦

Kant wrote three books that changed the course of Western philosophy. The first and most famous—and most difficult—was *Critique of Pure Reason* (1781); it dealt almost entirely with epistemology. The second was *Critique of Practical Reason* (1788), which treated religion and ethics. The third, *Critique of Judgment* (1790), dealt mostly with theories of art and esthetics. This third work Kant saw as "connecting the two [earlier] parts of philosophy into a whole" and bringing the "entire critical undertaking to a close." These three great works together—dealing respectively with understanding, practical reason, and judgment—present an integrated philosophy of human knowledge.

Kant tells us that when he read David Hume's analysis of human knowledge he was deeply disturbed. "It was just this that many years ago aroused me from my dogmatic slumber and gave an entirely new direction to my investigations in the field of speculative reason." Hume's work had resulted in extreme skepticism. He had succeeded in showing that all knowledge is far more tenuous and shaky than anyone had thought. Kant had been going on the assumption that rational knowledge alone, without input from the senses, is sufficient and dependable. Hume convinced him otherwise. Hume's persuasive analyses had proven that causality and necessity, the two foundation-stones on which knowledge of the natural world rests, cannot be derived from our observations of physical nature; both concepts are created by the mind to serve its own needs; they are concepts, that is, that allow it to process data in a certain way; but neither concept can be shown to be a fact of reality that governs the actions of nature. In a similar way, rational knowledge alone—as in geometry, for instance—is true only as a set of definitions and deductive consequences, and is not necessarily applicable to the real world. Hume thus undermined both empirical and rational knowledge. He had shaken the foundations of everything we know and left Kant aghast, convinced, and challenged.

So Kant wrote the *Critique of Pure Reason*. Through some five hundred pages of tight, carefully reasoned prose, he tackled Hume's "terrible overthrow" of the sciences. He was able to show that our knowledge of reality is produced by a cooperative working together of the creative mind and the unknown reality "out there" from which we derive sense data. The raw data from our senses fail to give us a picture of real objects/events; all we "know" are our own sensations and nothing of the real. (All we can experience are our own experiences.) Before these sense-perceptions can become "knowledge," the mind must process and interpret them; and to do this the mind must follow its own rules and add whatever catalytic ingredients it needs to complete its task. Among the several items (Kant called them "Categories") that the mind adds to the process are unity and plurality, reality, negation, substance, cause, effect, existence, nonexistence, necessity, contingency, and so on. None of these notions are to be found in the real world, but only in our minds. Similarly, time and space are not real "things," but only "modes of perception" created by the mind, or better, software programs without which we could not perceive or think.

Concepts without perceptions are empty, and perceptions without concepts are blind.

Take away the thinking subject and the entire corporeal world will vanish, for it is nothing but the appearance in the sensility of our subject.

The death of dogma is the birth of reality.

(Try looking steadily at some object, say a pencil in your hand, and note that it just continues to "stay there"—it "stays" in consciousness (time) and "stays" there in your hand (space); and it is impossible to perceive the pencil without **the experience** of time and **the experience** of space.) However, Kant succeeds in showing that both time and space are ingredients brought by the mind to the perceiving process and not "objects" belonging to the real world "out there." Inevitably we are convinced that time and space are real, as we are that colors, sounds, odors, and tastes are real. But in truth these are all experiences located only in our mental worlds. In fact, as far as human knowledge is concerned, we have no experience of reality as such, or of any of its contents; the world that we "know" turns out to be only a complex fabric of organized appearances. Kant had succeeded in showing that the mind contributes substantial elements to all our knowledge in science, ethics, mathematics, metaphysics, politics, and esthetics. Nothing is pure, nothing is free of the mind's manipulative contributions. Even the scientists' precious "laws of nature," which are believed to be universal and immutable, are contributions from the mind. "We ourselves introduce that order and regularity into the set of appearances to which we give the title 'Nature.'"

It was seen immediately that Kant's thinking annihilated all certainty about everything, and this included knowledge of God, immortality, salvation, and free will. A loud storm of reaction was soon in coming. Kant himself seems to have been uncomfortable with the results of his first *Critique* and decided to write another book to restore the faith. His *Critique of Practical Reason* accomplished this, in a way.

Life, in the final analysis, is a very practical affair, and countless beliefs, even if not grounded in absolute certainty, are necessary for the requirements of daily living. Kant concluded that it is reasonable therefore to believe certain things because they are necessary and not because they are true. "I found it necessary to deny knowledge in order to make room for faith," he wrote. Such concepts as causality are "regulative principles" necessary for living, and are to be honored as such; so also are the ideas of God, immortality, and free will. The notion of free will is indispensable to our choosing, deciding, and judging—whether or not it is in fact true that we are free. To live at all I must therefore **assume** that I'm free. This means, Kant says, that there are "operational truths" which exist but are beyond apprehension by either our senses or our reasoning.

This is the case with our apprehension of the "moral law." All men are ("instinctively") bound by a knowledge of a moral law. It is not derived from society, religion, or God. Whence then? From ourselves, as rational creatures. Our "moral imperatives"—unconditional "oughts" —have their provenance in the formal structure of the human mind. It is the concept of "duty" universalized. Before any act I should ask myself: Would I approve if all men do this? Any action that can be universalized can be accepted as ethical. This is Kant's famous Categorical Imperative: "Act only on the maxim whereby thou canst at the same time will that it should become a universal law." This ontological imperative has the same claim to validity, Kant says, as the notion that 7 plus 5 equals 12; its universal consistency provides its validity and requires that one **act** on the judgment.

Kant's third great work, the *Critique of Judgment*, carried forward the age-old puzzlement regarding the "two-quality" doctrine of sense experience and the nature of esthetic feeling. Some of the early Greek thinkers—notably Democritus, Epicurus, and the Skeptics—had begun to distinguish between primary and secondary qualities, and the debate had been recently enlivened by Galileo, Newton, Descartes, and Locke. Kant felt that he must rework the problem in order to understand precisely the nature of our esthetic experience—of beauty, for instance.

It had long been held that the so-called primary qualities (there were five, according to Locke)—such as extension (size, volume), configuration (shape), motion or rest, number, and solidity (impenetrability)—are properties that really inhere in bodies; while secondary qualities such as colors, smells, sounds, coldness and warmth are located in us experiencers; they are only sensations produced in us by powers in real bodies and do not resemble anything in the bodies themselves. Put differently, there are no qualities **in** things that resemble our experiences of colors, smells, tastes, and so on.

Kant's prolonged analyses led him to agree, largely, with this dichotomy. "The taste of wine does not belong to the objective determination of the wine . . . but only to the special constitution of sense in the Subject tasting it." Moreover, these sensations "do not of themselves yield knowledge of any object." The statement that the grapefruit is yellow tells us nothing about the grapefruit or its true qualities. This recognition, largely borne out by subsequent centuries of investigation, has forced a rethinking of the exact nature of all scientific knowledge. Sensations provide the mind with the raw materials from which we can derive knowledge, but that process is complex and fraught with deception.

These established facts about perception have also permitted a clarification of esthetic experience. When I say "the rose is red" I am reporting a sense experience; when I say "the rose is beautiful" I am reporting an esthetic feeling. Kant—who was himself deeply sensitive to beauty in all its forms—must conclude that esthetic feelings are entirely subjective.

Kant developed two major propositions about our esthetic experiences. (1) What we cherish is the **experience** of beauty; the object that produces it—about which we know nothing—is irrelevant. Beauty is pure experience. In pondering such experience our interests are turned away from the real to focus entirely on the infinitely rich and varied feelings of our inner world.

(2) Esthetic experience is always fresh; it is by nature a brand new, unsullied, event. All ties to the conceptualizing mind are severed. For example, a rose is an esthetic object; a hammer is not. When I look at a hammer I bring to bear a whole spate of meanings about its use, whether it's the right tool for this job, whether I left it in my toolbox where it belongs, whether I've let it rust in the rain, and so on. I rarely see the hammer as an esthetic object. The rose, however, has no such connected meanings for me. I look at the rose, and smell it, purely for pleasure. Of course, if my left brain is so inclined, I can give the rose a name ("Snowfire"), categorize it ("Hybrid Tea"), and do a number on it with a vast collection of abstract ideas. But these ideas and interpretations are irrelevant to the esthetic feeling of beauty; and, of course, they will rob me of the purity of my esthetic pleasure by adding "impure" elements. The esthetic experience is therefore free, cut loose from both reality and the mind's creative intellectual activities.

The esthetic experience for Kant was of supreme importance, the *raison d'être* of all our other experiences. It brings with it a "feeling-understanding" of something moral, rational, and beautiful in the natural world we live in. Man's whole nature, Kant seems to be saying, is an authentic reflection of a counterpart in the fundamental substructure of Nature. We are not "passers-through" in a world that is not our home. The world, just as it is, **is** our home, for it supports human rationality, human aspirations, and human capacities for beauty, truth, and goodness.

✦

REFLECTIONS

1 The beginning of this chapter speaks of a "philosophy of time." What do you think is meant by such a phrase? What benefits might derive from having a philosophy of time? Has this chapter helped you in developing a philosophy of time or, better, a philosophy of how to use time?

2 Read the following passages synoptically: pp. 244–245 and pp. 206–208. What must we infer regarding the necessities of thought and communication and the nature of reality? Or, more bluntly, can you actually buy "the astounding fact that we can and do communicate with one another continually without knowing what we are talking about?!"

3 Summarize in your mind the three "kinds of time" dealt with in this chapter. Can you get a good grasp of each kind of time, and do the concepts sound right to you?

4 Ponder the fact that psychological time is an extreme variable (pp. 246–248; and review the boxed material on p. 147, "What Time Is It?"). Have you felt the impact of the fact that, as individuals, we actually experience time in quite different ways? Would this insight lead you to revise your attitude toward certain behavior in others that is time-related?

5 How long does "the present" last? Does it have duration or "width"? Do you think you could get the psychologist and the mathematician to agree on the matter?

6 Does "the past" exist? Where? What are we truly referring to when we speak of the past?

7 Reflect on the quotation from Arthur C. Clarke (see marginal quote on p. 250) and criticize it. (Here is an interesting case in which a statement can be both true and false at the same time, depending upon the interpretation of terms. Can you show how Clarke is both right and wrong?)

8 Can "the future" exist? Is precognition possible, in your opinion? What sort of time model could you develop that would permit the possibility of precognition?

9 The subject that touches us all where we live is our experience of time. After reflecting on pp. 254–259 and the boxed material on p. 147, what is your personal response to the existential philosophy of experience implied in these passages?

10 Cartoons are meant to be brief chuckles and then forgotten. Right? Not for a philosopher who likes to chuckle and then ponder. On p. 253 Dennis asks, "Isn't it always now?" And on p. 254 Sally Forth asks, "If time never stops, how come it's always now?" Take their questions seriously and answer them. *Why* is it always now? What is a now? How does a human now differ from a cat's now? A butterfly's now? Are all nows the same? Do rocks have a now?

11 On p. 257 Dennis says "My grampa wants to know where the time goes." Give Dennis a meaningful answer. Where *does* the time go? Or, in even asking the question, have we succumbed to a language trap?

Freedom

4-3

It's an old, old question: Are we humans free (undetermined) in our willing and choosing, or are we predetermined to be and to do what antecedent "programming" dictates? Now that we know about genetics, one kind of predeterminism —hereditary encoding—is undeniable. But the world continues to assume free will as an operational necessity and holds us responsible for what we do. This reveals a rock-solid fact of experience: we *feel* that we are free in choosing alternatives; we take credit for good decisions and feel guilty (we blame ourselves) for bad decisions. What is the truth, then, about human freedom? Is freedom of the will a given condition or a capacity we develop? This chapter presents arguments on both sides of the issue.

The Feeling of Freedom

1 I would like to describe for you a pattern of experience which I have observed, and in which I have participated. . . . It is an experience on which I have placed various labels as I have tried to think about it—becoming a person, freedom to be, courage to be, learning to be free—yet the experience is something broader than, and deeper than, any of its labels. It is quite possible that the words I use in regard to it may miscommunicate. The speculations and ideas I present, based on this experience, may be erroneous, or partly erroneous. But the experience itself *exists*. It is a deeply compelling phenomenon for any one who has observed it, or who has lived it.

Carl Rogers

Life is like a game of cards. The hand that is dealt you represents determinism; the way you play it is free will.

Jawarharlal Nehru

2 But does the experience of freedom, in fact, exist? Or does the **feeling** of freedom mask an illusion?

In one experiment with hypnosis, a man was led into a deep trance and given a simple posthypnotic suggestion. About a month from that date, he was

The Buddha can only tell you the way: it is for you yourself to make the effort.
The Dhammapada

told, after lunch on a certain day, he would sing "America the Beautiful." During the week following this first suggestion, it was reinforced twice during similar deep trances. But at no time was the man informed that any posthypnotic instructions had been given.

When the day for singing arrived, he recalls having the feeling in the morning that he wanted to sing; he did in fact hum or sing a few bars of various tunes. As noontime neared, the impulse to sing unexplainably grew stronger.

Immediately after lunch, he sat down at the piano, let his fingers move over the keyboard, and then, on schedule, proceeded to sing "America the Beautiful."

This sort of experiment is common enough in hypnosis. The significant point has to do with **cause:** what **caused** him to sing this specific song at this appointed time. He **felt** free. He felt that it was a **choice** that he had made, and that he could have made other choices. But paradoxically, he also **felt** determined. The impulse to sing the song grew to such proportions that it was difficult or impossible not to act it out.

The Dilemma of Determinism

3 This dramatic experiment symbolizes one of our deepest human dilemmas. On the one hand, we feel free; our social lives are founded on the assumption that we and others make genuine choices and should be responsible for them. We blame others for mistakes (that is, they were free not to have made them), and we feel guilt at our own mistakes (that is, we ourselves could, and should, have acted differently).

If a man referred to his brother or to his cat as "an ingenious mechanism," we should know that he was either a fool or a physiologist. No one in practice treats himself or his fellow-man or his pet animals as machines; but scientists who have never made a study of Speculative Philosophy seem often to think it their duty to hold in theory what no one outside a lunatic asylum would accept in practice.
C. D. Broad

On the other hand, we feel determined. As Saint Paul eloquently put it, "I do not understand what I am doing, for I do not do what I want to do; I do the things that I hate. . . . I do not do the good things that I want to do; I do the wrong things that I do not want to do. But if I do the things that I do not want to do, it is not I that am acting. . . ." Paul's lament rises to a painful crescendo: "What a wretched human being I am!"

Based on experience, we are forced into the conclusion that there are capricious causal forces inside us, directing us to do countless acts against our wills. It was only natural that premodern man interpreted these forces as good/evil spirits thrashing around inside him—"possessing" him—and acting as causal agents behind the thoughts, feelings, and actions over which he felt little control. Today we can better account for the causes of our behavior in empirical terms—in terms of conditioning or with physiological or chemical explanations. Still, the result is the same: we have a dual experience of both freedom and determinism. Both experiences **feel** authentic, and we have never quite understood how to reconcile the apparent contradiction.

4 Western Christian theology has symbolized this experiential dilemma with remarkable accuracy. There is abundant biblical support for two basic beliefs: (1) God is omnipotent and therefore determines every event in our lives; (2) Man possesses free will and is therefore responsible for his sins; he can justly be condemned to hell for wrong decisions.

PUPPET THEATER?

We see the puppets dancing on their miniature stage, moving up and down as the strings pull them around, following the prescribed course of their various little parts. We learn to understand the logic of this theater and we find ourselves in its motions. We locate ourselves in society and thus recognize our own position as we hang from its subtle strings. For a moment we see ourselves as puppets indeed. But then we grasp a decisive difference between the puppet theater and our own drama. Unlike the puppets, we have the possibility of stopping in our movements, looking up and perceiving the machinery by which we have been moved. In this act lies the first step towards freedom.

PETER L. BERGER
Invitation to Sociology

In their extreme forms, these two doctrines are logically contradictory; they can't both be true. But Western theology had no alternative but to accept both as absolutely true; they were both given (hence, not debatable) by biblical authority and ecclesiastical tradition. For almost two thousand years now, Christian theologians have wrestled valiantly with these two doctrines, trying to harmonize them so that men could believe both and maintain their intellectual honesty. No two theologians have resolved the problem in exactly the same way—in fact no solution is wholly free of logical difficulties—but there are several general approaches toward a solution. If either doctrine is softened, then they can be reconciled. If God does not predetermine every event of our lives, then we can claim to have some free will; or, if we admit that we are not wholly free, then some predestination can be accepted.

Whatever the solution, however, the striking point is that the theological formulation is an accurate doctrinization of the very real human dilemma. We are **both** determined **and** free; and somehow we must work at the contradiction until we achieve a viable understanding of how both can be true.

PRIMAL AND SECONDARY LIMITATIONS

5 Without prejudging at this point the relative degrees of human freedom and determinism we experience, we can speak meaningfully of the limiting factors that diminish our freedom. The point to note is that we confuse primal limitations with secondary limitations: it follows that we also confuse primal freedoms with secondary freedoms.

Let [the child] believe that he is always in control, though it is always you [the teacher] who really controls. There is no subjugation so perfect as that which keeps the appearance of freedom, for in that way one captures volition itself.

JEAN-JACQUES ROUSSEAU

Primal freedom is inner freedom, and primal limitations come from within. These limitations may be genetic (sickle-cell anemia, thalidomide deformities), physiological (paralysis from polio or accident), ontological (fear of death and nonbeing), or conditioned (inability to trust or love). Such limitations are causal; they inhibit us from thinking, feeling, or doing specific things; and as causes, they arise from inside our own psychophysiological organism. Primal freedom, therefore, is freedom **from** such limitations: from conflicts and frustrations, unfounded fears, nail-biting anxieties, lingering hatreds, debilitating habits, and life-negating bitterness. Primal freedom is freedom for the full use of our abilities, the freedom **for** each person—considering all the givens of his own unique existence—to be all that he can be.

Primal limitations burden us all. We may want to enjoy a day at the beach but find, while there, that we are reliving the emotional battles of the day; and try as we will, we can only act at having fun. Or we try to concentrate on reading a book, but in vain, because relentless worries intrude and disturb our will-to-thought. And how often do we undertake a task, knowing full well we have the capabilities to accomplish it, only to find that primal limitations—fears of inadequacy, fears of others' opinions, even fear of success itself—keep us from attaining our goal? Freedom from all these inner limitations is primal freedom.

By contrast, **secondary limitations** originate in our environment. Therefore, we can speak of secondary freedoms as freedom from external limitations. Secondary limitations are placed upon us by nature itself (we can't move backward in time), and by other persons and by our society. We are limited by the customs, common-sense traditions, sociological structures, moral suasions, and civil laws of the society in which we live. We are also limited by the immediate needs and desires of other people. Such secondary limiters impose upon us injunctions **not** to think, feel, and do specific things.

6 We cause ourselves endless troubles by confusing primal freedom with various secondary freedoms. We often think we are being subjected to external limitations when in fact we are suffering from inner restraints, and vice versa. Primal limitations are undoubtedly more difficult for us to admit and face; recognition of them presupposes some degree of self-knowledge, the ability to empathize with others, and some capacity for abstract thinking. Since secondary limitations appear more concrete, and since we share them with others and can deal with them collectively ("Fight gun control," "Stop abortion"), we often expend great amounts of energy in crusades against particular "encroachments upon our freedoms."

What is an obstacle for me may not be so for another. There is no obstacle in an absolute sense. . . . Human-reality everywhere encounters resistance and obstacles which it has not created, but these resistances and obstacles have meaning only in and through the free choice which human-reality is.

JEAN-PAUL SARTRE

We may never realize that such crusades are in fact a struggle against primal limitations. We may accuse others of not liking us, when the source of our agony is that we don't like ourselves. We may accuse others of conspiring to harm us, when our problem is that we have never developed the capacity to trust. In such cases, our desire for freedom is authentic, but we have mislocated the source of the limitation.

This is why it is common for us to spend our lives fighting for causes, only to find later that (to parody a cliché) the causes were won but our freedoms were lost. We may indeed achieve specific freedoms ("The bill finally passed!"), only to find that we are bound with the same primal fetters as before. We do not **experience** an increase of freedom. But having a row of (secondary) freedom awards to point to, we can't quite understand why we don't experience more freedom.

If man has once become aware that in his forlornness he imposes values, he can no longer want but one thing, and that is freedom, as the basis of all values. That doesn't mean that he wants it in the abstract. It means simply that the ultimate meaning of the acts of honest men is the quest for freedom as such.

JEAN-PAUL SARTRE

Other things being equal, the greater one's experience of primal freedom, the less he is concerned with secondary freedoms; and conversely, those who are deeply driven to crusade for secondary freedoms are often suffering from excruciating primal limitations.

7 Few philosophical problems have greater practical implications than the question of freedom versus determinism.

For one thing, if there is no freedom, then there can be no moral, legal, or any other kind of responsibility. Yet the fact of personal responsibility is one of our most cherished assumptions. We blame others for their mistakes and give them credit for their achievements. We hold ourselves responsible and feel guilt for our misdoings. We indict alleged lawbreakers, hold trials, and convict or free them. We operate on the assumption that human beings can be morally and legally responsible—that is, free. But if our assumption of freedom is false, then life as we live it is a cruel joke founded upon a tragic illusion. We are playing the game all wrong.

Second, we struggle from day to day and year to year, in desperation or joy, and always with hope, to attain our life goals. But if we are not free, then all our striving is meaningless. We only think we set our own goals, whereas in fact they are set for us; and whether or not we attain them is apparently already determined, or at least out of our hands. Life itself, as struggle, is an illusion.

Third, and most deeply, the question of freedom has to do with what we are—or aren't. What can life mean if we have no freedom to make choices, choose lifestyles, set goals? Since we labor under the deepest conviction that, to some extent at least, we are free, then existence itself is a hoax. We think we're free, feel like we're free, act like we're free; we treat ourselves and others as though we were free; we develop monumental moral and legal systems based upon the assumption that we're free—all this fantasized by blind puppets dangling helplessly on black nylon strings?

We are not what we think we are; life is not what we think it is; the rules of the game are not what we thought. Maybe we discover that we're not playing the game at all: **We are the chessmen and something or someone else is playing the game.**

One's ability to move his hand at will is more directly and certainly known than are Newton's laws. If these laws deny one's ability to move his hand at will, the preferable conclusion is that Newton's laws require modification.

Arthur Compton

The Case for Determinism

8 For some fifteen years, Dr. Bruno Bettelheim followed the case of Joey—"the mechanical boy." Joey's loss of freedom was clearly psychogenic rather than genetic or physiological. From birth he had been almost completely ignored; to his mother he hardly existed. Since all that he was as a budding human was bothersome and unacceptable, he quickly got the message; his humanness must be eliminated—repressed. So Joey literally became a machine. He acquainted himself very early with machines and could dismantle and reassemble them with some skill. He also envied the machines and identified with them; they were liked, toyed with; they gave no trouble, were never punished. Gradually he came to think of himself as a machine.

Before he could eat, for instance, he would unroll his imaginary cord and plug it into the outlet, set his switches, and check his bulbs. He could perform routine actions only after he had monitored his circuits, checked his dials, flipped the right switches. He made sure his machine-self was working properly.

All this was more than merely a game of playing like a machine; this "game" was deadly serious. He was playing the machine-game to escape the unbearable anguish of further rejection of any of his human qualities.

Bettelheim noted that "Joey's pathological behavior seemed the external expression of an overwhelming effort to remain almost nonexistent as a person." Joey had created a world of his own that he could live in, a world that was preferable to the hostile real world. In his fantasy world he had found a way of life that was at least tolerable. Since he did not need to be human, his human qualities atrophied; more and more Joey **became** a machine.

Machines are not free. Indeed, the word doesn't apply. Machines operate on principles of cause and effect—total determinism. Joey "the mechanical boy" knew no freedom.

9 One of the strongest contemporary cases for determinism has been made by a psychologist-novelist who—in *Beyond Freedom and Dignity*—has become a philosopher: Dr. B. F. Skinner of Harvard University.

According to Skinner's way of thinking, freedom is a myth, and a dangerous myth because we have invested the myth and its symbol ("freedom") with something close to sacred qualities. It is a fact that many of those who think they disagree with Skinner are eager to make his observations the object of religious and patriotic causes. (Skinner's book was still warm from the press when one congressman, in a speech before the House, denounced him for "advancing ideas which threaten the future of our system of government by denigrating the American traditions of individualism, human dignity, and self-reliance." As is so often the case, further comments revealed a fundamental misunderstanding of what Skinner is saying.)

Freedom, Skinner argues, is not a fact of human experience. **All** of our responses—the impulses that lie behind so-called free choices—are the result of unique past contingencies of conditioning and reinforcement that have shaped us into what we are. Skinner's famed laboratory experiments with pigeons and rats have shown that animal behavior can be predicted and controlled and even produced according to specification. By selecting specific causes (stimuli), desired effects (responses) will result. This is merely the application to the field of animal behavior the scientific assumption of causality. The assumption that every cause produces an effect and every effect is preceded by a cause is the foundation of all science. Whatever made us think that it would **not** apply to the behavioral sciences as well as to the natural sciences?

B. F. Skinner (1904–1990)

What we **call** freedom is merely the successful avoidance on the part of any organism of some aversive feature in its environment. All organisms are manipulated and controlled, therefore, by the dynamic features of their environments.

To be sure, when Skinner writes that freedom is an illusion, he is not denying our experience of a rather pleasant **emotion** that we commonly call freedom; but he is saying unequivocally that this emotion is itself a **conditioned** (caused) response. We may label this feeling "freedom" or something else; but whatever we call it, it has been produced by past experience; it was conditioned into us at some prior time and now becomes, in turn, the causal agent of present behavior.

10 Among the illustrations used by Skinner are the accounts of the falling leaf and the buzzing fly.

Picture a leaf, yellowed from the first frosts, fluttering and suddenly falling from the top of a tall, red-gold maple tree. In zigzag motions, hovering on the currents of air, it picks a poetic path downward and settles eventually upon a cushion of leaves on the ground.

Now, there isn't a physicist alive who would argue that the leaf is "free." We esthetic onlookers may be mesmerized by the leaf's timeless descent, and even envy the "freedom" of the floating maple leaf wafting to Earth. But we have confused our poetic idealism with our physics. The fact is that the leaf follows precisely known laws of physics, laws that can easily be found in any physics textbook.

Yet as the leaf starts its historic fall from the top of the maple tree, what physicist, by applying his formulas, could predict the leaf's trajectory or the spot where it will finally come to rest? The journey is too complex; there are too many variables: air currents, atmospheric density (in terms of elevation above sea level and barometric pressure), humidity, minute photon forces, the mass and volume of the leaf, its configuration, and so on. The number of possible combinations of variables is so great that, although knowing all the applicable laws, predicting the leaf's path or destination is a feat quite beyond the ability of any physicist (or computer) today.

So, is the leaf "free" in any proper sense of the word? Not at all. It follows inexorable causal laws.

Give me a dozen healthy infants and I'll guarantee to take any one at random and train him to become any type of specialist I might select—doctor, lawyer, even beggar-man and thief, regardless of his talents, penchants, tendencies, abilities.

JOHN B. WATSON (1925)

11 Elsewhere, Skinner ponders a housefly buzzing around a room. In describing the motions of the maple leaf, we were applying physical laws to a passive object. The trajectory of the buzzing fly is infinitely more complex since we are dealing with the active nervous system of a living thing. Our causal factors, to some extent, become internal.

If we knew **everything** about the buzzing fly—its previous conditioning, its present chemical states, its "needs," "drives," "goals," or whatever, and all the aerodynamics of a fly's flight—then, according to Skinner, we could predict exactly where the fly will buzz, where it will land, what it will eat, and so on.

But we are facing the same paradox with the fly as with the leaf. We might feel that the fly is free as it flies about; it looks free; it even seems to make choices. But such freedom is myth, Skinner contends. There is no more freedom in any buzz of the fly than there was in any flutter of the leaf. Every motion could be predicted if the causal forces were precisely known. More simply, all matter-in-motion obeys the laws of physics, and a fly is matter-in-motion.

These same principles apply to human action, and our complexity, apparently, is no argument against determinism, since the same causal laws apply in every case. Our behavior is more complex than the fly's, just as the fly's behavior is more complex than the leaf's. But freedom is just as much a fallacy for us as it is for the leaf or fly.

Carl Rogers (1902–1987)

12 Carl Rogers says freedom exists. Skinner says it doesn't. Rogers records the following brief exchange between them at a conference at which Skinner had read a paper.

Saint Thomas Aquinas / The Paradox of Determinism

I Man is predestined . . .
It is fitting that God should predestine men. For all things are subject to His Providence. . . . As men are ordained to eternal life through the Providence of God, it likewise is part of that Providence to permit some to fall away from that end; this is called reprobation. . . . As predestination includes the will to confer grace and glory, so also reprobation includes the will to permit a person to fall into sin, and so impose the punishment of damnation on account of that sin.

Summa theologiae, I, 23, I, 3
Summa contra gentiles, III, 163

II Man is free . . .
Man has free choice, or otherwise counsels, exhortations, commands, prohibitions, rewards and punishments would be in vain.

If the will were deprived of freedom . . . no praise would be given to human virtue; since virtue would be of no account if man acted not freely: there would be no justice in rewarding or punishing, if man were not free in acting well or ill: and there would be no prudence in taking advice, which would be of no use if things occurred of necessity. . . .

Summa theologiae, I, 83, 1
Summa contra gentiles, III, 73

III Can man be both predestined and free?
The predestined must necessarily be saved, yet by a conditional necessity, which does not do away with the liberty of choice. . . .

Man's turning to God is by free choice; and thus man is bidden to turn himself to God. But free choice can be turned to God only when God turns it. . . . It is the part of man to prepare his soul, since he does this by his free choice. And yet he does not do this without the help of God moving him. . . . And thus even the good movement of free choice, whereby anyone is prepared for receiving the gift of grace, is an act of free choice moved by God. . . . Man's preparation for grace is from God, as mover, and from free choice, as moved.

Summa theologiae, I, 23, 3; I–II, 109, 6; I–II, 112, 2, 3.

> From what I understand Dr. Skinner to say, it is his understanding that though he might have thought he chose to come to this meeting, might have thought he had a purpose in giving this speech, such thoughts are really illusory. He actually made certain marks on paper and emitted certain sounds here simply because his genetic makeup and his past environment had operantly conditioned his behavior in such a way that it was rewarding to make these sounds, and that he as a person doesn't enter into this. In fact if I get his thinking correctly, from his strictly scientific point, he, as a person, doesn't exist.

In his reply to Rogers, "Dr. Skinner said that he would not go into the question of whether he had any choice in the matter (presumably because the whole issue is illusory) but stated, 'I do accept your characterization of my own presence here.'"

The Case for Freedom of Choice

13 Human freedom has been stoutly defended by a distinguished line of thinkers in various traditions, East and West. No voice in its defense has been more persuasive than that of the existentialist philosopher Jean-Paul Sartre, whose vehement pronouncements for freedom arose from his own intense experience of human struggle during the Nazi occupation of France in World War II. The fashionable notion that we are predetermined in our behavior by past experiences—by "operant conditioning"—to the point of losing our free will—this, for Sartre, is an outrageous fallacy. On the contrary, man is responsible not merely for what he does, but even for all that he is.

Sartre is convinced that there is no determinism of any kind. **Nothing** tells me what to do. I myself decide. I cannot blame God, or others, or my past environment. I am—now—what I make myself to be. I have to accept the consequences of my own freedom, take the responsibility for my decisions, and face the consequences thereof. For human freedom, as Sartre sees it, is not always a blessing; it is more often a tragedy. Whether we like it or not, man is **condemned to be free.**

But why does Sartre speak of our being "condemned" to freedom? Why such a gloomy term? Shouldn't freedom be a joyous thing? Sartre's position is that freedom carries with it an unavoidable anguish when we fully realize how overwhelming the implications of our freedom can be. It entails tragic choices with formidable consequences. Out of our freedom we do not make decisions for ourselves alone, but for others, and sometimes for all mankind. To realize completely what this means can be a nightmarish insight into the very nature of human existence.

To be free means to be caught in a paradox. We are forever dissatisfied with existence as we know it. But to live means to dream a million dreams and forge ahead to catch the fullness of our being. Indeed, each mortal man wants to be God, but the truer fact is that we are finite and our limitations are crushing. Still, they are unacceptable. So we continue to compete and strive, dreaming our dreams, even though they are futile dreams, and even though we know it.

Why? Why do we do all this? Simply because we cannot do otherwise. For to exist is to be free, and to be free is to act, to take initiative, to make choices and decisions, to dream impossible dreams—however unreachable they are—and to fail. In a word, we **must try to do** what we already know we **cannot** do.

14 Sartre was attempting to get us to see that we exist in an antinomian world without guidelines. Cultural norms are relative, and societies are humorlessly absurd. There is no God and therefore no absolute mandates to give life order. There is no meaning to human life as such. Nor is there any past conditioning that we can blame for making us what we are. There is not even a "human nature" that might help us to define ourselves.

There is nothing to help us—because the moment we become conscious of what we are, then we become responsible for everything we are and do. Of course, we can join the mob and let our passions collectively carry us along, but **we make the decision** to do so, and we are responsible for that decision. We can conform to society's whims, or follow an irrelevant, legalistic ethical code,

Men are freest when they are most unconscious of freedom.
D. H. Lawrence

There is no doubt that Sartre finds it impossible to make a distinction between freedom and free acts. The free man is not distinguished by his beliefs, but by the quality of his actions.
Norman N. Greene

This is one of man's oldest riddles. How can the independence of human volition be harmonized with the fact that we are integral parts of a universe which is subject to the rigid order of Nature's laws?
Sir Arthur Eddington

We are forced to fall back on fatalism as an explanation of irrational events, that is to say, of events the rationality of which we do not understand.
Leo Tolstoy

or accede to peer pressures; but in each instance **we make the decision** to do so, and we must accept the responsibility for that decision.

Whenever we are conscious, therefore, we are responsible. For at the cutting edge of consciousness, we are truly free. At each moment of the living present, we have an infinite number of choices before us, ways of thinking, feeling, and behaving—the options are numberless, so many that to feel them fully is to become overwhelmed by them. It's at this moment of revelation that we frequently retreat into the myths of determinism. We convince ourselves that we move within carefully defined and unbreakable limits, and that we are not really free. Yet, from behind our safe parameters we will **claim** to be free. We are "not supposed" to think, feel, or do certain things, or so we are told by society, church, friends, laws, conscience. But all these excuses are retreats from freedom; and the true fact is that we can do all of them. But since experience of such freedom is fraught with fear, we eagerly accept all the fashionable limitations.

JEAN-PAUL SARTRE

Apostle of Freedom

Largely because of his major work *Being and Nothingness,* Jean-Paul Sartre has become the voice of existential philosophy. More than 700 pages long, the opus astounds everyone, though few have read it and even fewer have understood it. It is at once exciting, profound, obscure, and irritating—a challenge to any reader. After it appeared in June 1943, it received but one review the first year, three the next, and by 1946 about a dozen more. Then, all of a sudden, everyone was talking about Sartre, and *Being and Nothingness* had become a classic.

Early in life Sartre decided that, as a philosopher, he would specialize in studying human consciousness, a discipline called phenomenology. Sartre's goal was to describe the structure of human consciousness, including such psychic phenomena as the self, intuitions, perceptions, emotional states, and much more. His introspective analysis would eventually produce a wealth of insights, two of which would become central tenets of his existential philosophy: the fact, as he put it, that "we are condemned to be free"; and his insistence that the defining purpose of each and every human life is a gradual escape from self-deception by means of a progressive movement toward authenticity.

In 1963 Sartre completed his autobiography entitled *The Words.* In it he describes his "origins"—the roots of who and what he later became. He tells us that his father died when he was sixteen months old, and his mother, Anne-Marie Schweitzer, took her son to live with her parents.

"I began my life as I shall no doubt end it: among books." His grandparents were avid readers; he watched them read and was "filled with a holy stillness." When he learned to read, he "was allowed to browse in the library" where he "took man's wisdom by storm." He recalls, "That was what made me. It was in books that I encountered the universe," and it was in "the wildness in books" that he discovered himself. "I did not gather herbs or throw stones at birds," as other

The *fundamental question is: what have you made of your life?*

To live is to awake in bonds, as Gulliver in Lilliput.

[There are men] whose social reality is uniquely that of the No, who will live and die, having forever been only a No upon the earth.

Tel qu'en lui-même enfin l'éternité le change. *Eternity at last changes each man into himself.*

Quoted by Sartre

boys did, he says; "books were my birds and my nests, my household pets, my barn and my countryside."

Sartre's formal education began at age ten, when he entered the Lycée Henri-IV. Hyperactive and gifted, he was "an excellent little boy," one of his teachers wrote, adding, "Never gets the answer right the first time. Must get used to thinking more."

At fifteen he had begun to write and at seventeen published two works of fiction. In 1922 he transferred to the Lycée Louis-le-Grand to prepare for entrance exams to the prestigious École Normale Supérieure. He impressed everyone with his brilliance, hard work, and sense of humor. All his life Sartre displayed a gift for spontaneous comedy. At Louis-le-Grand he plunged into philosophy after reading Bergson's *Essai sur les données immédiates de la conscience:* "In that book I found the description of what I believed to be my psychological life. . . . My first encounter with Bergson opened up to me a way of studying consciousness that made me decide to do philosophy."

His years at the École Normale were his maturing years. He did well in his studies, made friends, and had his first serious love affair with a beautiful courtesan named Camille. Although philosophy was his consuming passion, he never ceased arguing and fighting with his philosophy teachers. Sartre's clique of fellow students worked during the mornings, lunched at the cafés in the Cité, drove around Paris in the afternoons, and spent evenings at the cinema (Sartre was a film buff) or in cafés over cocktails, always talking and singing. With Sartre's comic humor, his good singing voice, and his repertoire of fashionable jazz songs, he was the party principal. In July 1929, Simone de Beauvoir was introduced into the group, and shortly afterward Sartre told her, "From now on, I'm going to take you under my wing."

In November 1929, Sartre began an eighteen-month tour of military duty and was stationed with a meteorological unit at Saint-Cyr. With little to do and lots of free time to write, he produced poems, began a novel, and composed two plays. After military service, he got a teaching job at a lycée in Le Havre.

Then in September 1940, he says, the war divided his life into two and marked "the passage from youth to maturity." Sartre was drafted into the army and stationed in Alsace. Ten months later (on his thirty-fifth birthday), he was taken prisoner by the Germans. But by the following March he was back in Paris, having "escaped" from the camp by displaying his bad eye and whispering "dizzy spells." He joined the underground Resistance.

Sartre spent most of his waking hours at the Café Flore writing. By the time *Being and Nothingness* was published in June 1943, he was already well known for his plays and short stories. His novel *La nausée* had been published in 1938. Written in the form of a diary kept by its hero, Roquentin, it describes his feelings of nausea when he discovers that "Things are entirely what they appear to be and *behind them* . . . there is nothing." He had also published *The Flies;* despite its allusions to freedom and revolt, it was performed in the Théâtre de la Cité in the spring of 1943. Among the attendants was Albert Camus, and the two men met for the first time.

In July 1944, Camus informed Sartre that the Germans had obtained names of Resistance fighters. Sartre and de Beauvoir escaped to the country. But with liberation only days away they returned to Paris on their bicycles to witness the Allies' triumphant entry on August 18. The clandestine paper *Les Lettres françaises,* in its first uncensored issue, carried on the front page Sartre's provocative pronouncement, "We were never more free than during the German occupation."

The postwar era saw Sartre continuously engaged in writing, traveling, and politics. *The Reprieve* and *The Age of Reason* were sent to the publisher in 1944. He had become a celebrity and was not happy about it: "It is not pleasant to be treated as a public monument during one's lifetime." The first part of 1946 was spent lecturing in the United States and Switzerland. Two more plays were performed that year, *The Victors* and *The Respectful Prostitute.* He continued to produce an endless supply of articles and essays on social and political issues, often focusing on problems of freedom and individuality and defending his views from attacks from Christians, Communists, and, it seems, everyone else. His life was not unlike that of the hero of his 1951 play *Le Diable et le bon Dieu,* who devotes himself wholeheartedly to doing evil, then does a turnaround and dedicates himself wholeheartedly to doing good—and finds that the results are always the same. Sartre received daily press coverage for one thing or another, and it was almost entirely negative. In October 1948 his writings were placed on the index of forbidden books by the Roman Church.

By the spring of 1954 Sartre was suffering from high blood pressure. His doctor told him to go to the country to rest, which he did, but the silence made him dizzy and he couldn't sleep. He continued to pursue a grueling work schedule, with trips, speeches, and bouts of drinking.

When Sartre published *The Words* in 1963, his recounting of his early years elicited two significant reactions: he was offered the Nobel Prize for literature, and his mother said he "hasn't understood anything of his childhood." Sartre immediately dispatched a notice to the Swedish Academy, rejecting the honor, a response for which he was both praised and condemned the world over. He later added that the only honor he wanted was to be read.

In May 1971, Sartre suffered a stroke that affected his right arm and his speech; for the first time he spoke of death. Still, until 1974, he continued to write and to champion a variety of causes. In March 1980 he was hospitalized with heart failure, and he died on April 15. Four days later a half-million people accompanied his body to the Montparnasse Cemetery. The tomb containing his ashes is inscribed simply "Jean-Paul Sartre, 1905–1980."

✦

More than any other modern philosopher, Sartre proclaimed that a human being is free, absolutely and unconditionally free: "There is no determinism—man is free, man *is* freedom." His powerful statement about freedom published in *Les Lettres françaises* grew out of his experience with the Nazis.

> We were never more free than during the German occupation. We had lost all our rights, beginning with the right to talk. Every day we were insulted to our faces and had to take it in silence. Under one pretext or another, as workers, Jews, or political prisoners, we were deported *en masse.* . . . And because of all this we were free. . . . All those among us who knew any details concerning the Resistance asked themselves anxiously, "If they torture me, shall I be able to keep silent?" Thus the basic question of liberty itself was posed, and we were brought to the verge of the deepest knowledge that man can have of himself.

The key to understanding what Sartre is saying lies in the last sentence. But first, it's important to note that Sartre is operating on some very big assumptions that were, to him, "intuitive" and "self-evident." His first assumption is that human life is inescapably tragic. If one lives for any length of time, his life will be marked by frustrations, fears, and failures; he will be forced to make painful decisions among bad alternatives; he will inevitably face pain and personal loss. Suffering is the lot of mankind, and the dream of happiness is a pipe dream. Blindly, we may continue to strive toward contentment and well-being, but in this life these are simply not achievable

If you begin by saying, "Thou shalt not lie," there is no longer any possibility of political action.

Death is never that which gives life its meaning; it is, on the contrary, that which on principle removes all meaning from life.

Man can will nothing unless he has first understood that he must count on no one but himself; that he is alone, abandoned on earth in the midst of his infinite responsibilities, without help, with no other aim than the one he sets himself, with no other destiny than the one he forges for himself on this earth.

My duty as an intellectual is to think, to think without restriction, even at the risk of blundering. I must set no limits within myself, and I must let no limits be set for me.

I have never accepted anything without contesting it in some way.

Everything is gratuitous, this garden, this city and myself. When you suddenly realize it, it makes you feel sick and everything begins to drift. . . .

Nothing will be changed if God does not exist; we will rediscover the same norms of honesty, progress and humanity.

I am obliged to will the liberty of others at the same time as mine.

Facing a dying child, Nausea has no weight.

states. In fact, the happy human being would no longer be human.

Since Sartre lived through the dehumanizing devastations of war, we might ponder whether his philosophy could be anything other than tragic. But he has abundant support that his view is not merely one man's distorted view of life but a reasonable assessment of the human situation. It is a deep echo of Greek tragedy as embodied in the plays of Euripides and Sophocles; and it is precisely the worldview of The Buddha, who taught that to exist at all is to suffer, not merely for humans but for all creatures caught on the Wheel of Samsara, which, equally and democratically, brings suffering and death to every living thing.

There is a popular song that opens with the line "Life is what you do while you're waiting to die." This dismal mood, to a point, characterizes all existentialism. Tragedy is the elemental fact of the human condition and must be faced by an individual squarely and honestly, without myth, without self-deception, without avoidance of any kind. Existentialism is often thought of as a philosophy of tragedy.

But there is another side to the coin. If the goal of life is not happiness, then what is it? The alternative is *to choose* to live an authentic existence, and this is a momentous choice that can turn tragedy into triumph. It begins with the acknowledgment that life is painful and that no individual will ever be truly content or at peace. The option then stands clear: life's decisions all become growth choices, and it is growth and the gradual escape from self-deception that become the center of consciousness. It is the yearning for authenticity—for the true self, the whole self—that becomes the goal of life. This truth about life liberates us from myths based on fear. With the decision to live courageously, a whole new existence is made possible. Sartre insists that this kind of life is what we truly want anyway: not happiness, not contentment, but the feeling of being alive.

Sartre argues that we are genuinely free to make this important choice: "Man cannot be sometimes slave and sometimes free; he is wholly and forever free, or he is not free at all." We discover our freedom in the act of making choices. Any life situation that forces an individual to become acutely aware that he is making free choices expands his consciousness and enhances his capacity for freedom.

This is the meaning of Sartre's enigmatic statement that Resistance fighters found that life under the Germans made them aware that they were making free choices. Because they were under pain of death, each hour of each day demanded that they create alternative ways of surviving. No matter how difficult the choices, an individual experiences the deepest and most satisfying freedom in the very act of choosing. Every choice presents an opportunity to reaffirm the authentic self and achieve nobility in the face of tragedy.

This freedom is both blessing and curse. "We are left alone, without excuse," Sartre writes. "That is what I mean when I say that man is condemned to be free. Condemned, because he did not create himself, yet is nevertheless at liberty, and from the moment that he is thrown into this world he is responsible for everything he does." This defines the essential purpose of existential philosophy. "Thus," Sartre continues, "the first effect of existentialism is that it puts every man in possession of himself as he is, and places the entire responsibility for his existence squarely upon his own shoulders."

"You are free, therefore choose. . . ."

✦

Reflections

1 What do you think of the account of the man who was hypnotized and told he would sing "America the Beautiful"? Does this episode frighten you? What implications do you see in this story regarding the question of human freedom? Would you care to go so far as to liken childhood to a prolonged period of "posthypnotic suggestions"?

2 In brief, why is the age-old question of free will such a crucial problem? And why is it imperative today that we find a workable solution?

3 Does the description on pp. 267–268 of our human predicament as a "feeling dilemma"—We feel free and we feel determined—sound like an accurate account of your own experience and observation? How would you express the problem?

4 Distinguish between primary and secondary freedoms, and between primary and secondary limitations. Can you think of illustrations from your experience where "we cause ourselves endless troubles by confusing primal freedom with various secondary freedoms"?

5 After reading this chapter, jot down your thoughts regarding the following: (1) Is the question of freedom/determinism an authentic question or does it need to be rephrased in the light of modern knowledge? (2) To what degree can we be truly free? (3) To what degree are we determined, and what determines us? (4) Is the idea of the "growth of freedom" a justifiable concept?

6 After you reach some conclusions (though tentative) about the extent of our determined condition, how much do you think we should be held responsible, morally and legally, for our behavior?

7 Note the boxed excerpts on p. 274. How well do you think Aquinas reconciled the two biblical "givens"—free will and predestination? If you're up to the challenge and would enjoy an exercise in theological logic, try to work out a better reconciliation.

8 Is the question of divine predestination a problem for you personally? Have you, at some time, committed yourself to a predestinarian position? If so, do you have evidence to offer in support of that position? Would you contend that we are also free agents? (That is, do you hold yourself responsible for what you do?) How do you reconcile these two positions?

9 What does Jean-Paul Sartre mean when he says that we are "condemned to be free"? Do you share his mood regarding the human condition? Do you agree with him when he insists that we always have a choice?

10 Following in the tradition of the phenomenologists, Sartre decided he would study human consciousness. Did he make an honest choice? How would *you* go about studying consciousness?

11 When you review the brief story of Sartre's life, can you understand why freedom meant so much to him? Why was he so passionate in declaring that we humans are free?

12 "Man cannot be sometimes slave and sometimes free; he is wholly and forever free, or he is not free at all" (p. 280). Comment? Is Sartre right?

SYMBOLS

4-4

Finding ourselves trapped in the egocentric predicament (see Chapter 2-1), we humans are isolated and lonely. To minimize our loneliness we touch and we gesture ("body language"), but mostly we resort to symbolic language. And although verbal noises can communicate information fairly well, they utterly fail in communicating the profounder (nonconceptual) levels of experience. This chapter analyzes the functions of language, suggests that successful communication rests with a hearer and not the speaker, and implies that communication often begins when we stop talking. The swastika is used to illustrate how definitional rigidity interferes with effective communication when symbols are invested with a variety of meanings.

THE FUNCTIONS OF LANGUAGE

1 Aside from the practical need to transmit survival information, the fundamental goal of all communication is to transcend our egocentric predicament (see pp. 79ff., 190ff.). We (that is, experiencing selves) are "located" from birth till death in a space/time predicament that subjects us to limitations we can't live with; we find ourselves in a condition in which we are isolated and intensely lonely; at the same time we yearn to connect with others. All attempts to communicate with other living creatures are attempts to escape from, and override, this limiting condition. We create symbolic media for transmitting to other beings something of the experience-world going on inside us.

Every word is like an unnecessary stain on silence and nothingness.
SAMUEL BECKETT

2 We invent symbols, therefore, that can stimulate the sensors of another person. This confirms the fact of our existence and dispels some of the uneasiness about our own felt anonymity. From this we would like to infer that we can trans-

fer living experience from one person to another; and indeed we generally succeed in persuading ourselves, and in profoundly believing, that we can transfer, not merely symbolized meanings, but living **content** between closed systems.

We humans, therefore, are symbolic creatures **because of** the egocentric predicament. If direct transfer of living experience could somehow be accomplished, we would undoubtedly hasten to dispense with most of our symbols.

Note that we humans share this condition with all living creatures. The oft-heard statement that we humans are symbolic creatures, while other animals are not, is false. They too must resort to symbolic means of bursting through, and out of, their egocentric predicaments. Courtship rituals and territorial warnings of birds, barks of baboons, the female gypsy moth's scent drifting through the night air, the mating flash of the firefly—these are analogous to man's symbolic communication. The farmer's "no trespassing" sign and the cackling alarm note of the burrowing owl—"Don't come near my nest"—perform identical functions.

Our human capacity for abstract and complex symbols is not to be denigrated, of course. But we need to ask: with all our symbolic sophistication, is our transmittal of **experience** all that successful? Do we listen to and hear others more empathetically and sensitively than, say, a mother fox calming her young? or a whale guiding her calf? And are we, as a matter of fact, less lonely?

"Although humans make sounds with their mouths and occasionally look at each other, there is no solid evidence that they actually communicate with each other."

Words are wise men's counters, without value of their own; they are the money only of fools and politicians.
WILL DURANT

THE MANY ROLES OF LANGUAGE

3 Those of us driven by our left brains tacitly assume that the primary function of language is the rational communication of ideas. Our everyday experience shows that this isn't so. Our linguistic equipment is designed to serve a variety of functions.

Lawyers use words in different ways than normal people do.
SUSAN CARPENTER MCMILLAN

Here are ten common uses of language. Note that usage of language falls into two general categories, whether the primary purpose is to change conditions in ourselves (the subject—S) or in another (the object—O). Equally significant is whether the specific usage is designed to promote emotional results (E) or rational/intellectual results (R). A glance at the following list would seem to indicate that the dominant function of language is emotional and that much use of language is reflexive, designed to alter conditions within ourselves rather than others.

4 Language is used to accomplish the following goals:

S (1) To express emotion (E). "I love you." "Younger than springtime am I" (from *South Pacific*). "Ouch!" "Damn!" Found here also are the interminable arguments we get into that take the form of idea-exchange but that in fact are prolonged venting of accumulated emotional charges, such as anger and frustration. One of the prime functions of "four-letter words" and name-calling is to let off emotional steam.

S (2) To drown out silence (E). We find silence intolerable: waiting alone with others in a doctor's office, sitting beside someone on a plane, pass-

B.C. by Johnny Hart

In silence man can most readily preserve his integrity.
Meister Eckhart

"When I use a word," Humpty-Dumpty said in a rather scornful tone, "it means just what I choose it to mean—neither more nor less."
"The question is," said Alice, "whether you can make words mean different things."
"The question is," said Humpty-Dumpty, "which is to be master—that's all!"
Lewis Carroll

ing time with a casual acquaintance. Polite social conversation ("Nice day") lessens anxiety. And when alone we turn on the TV to ease our loneliness. Lacking a TV set or CD player, some of us talk with ourselves.

S (3) To enjoy the sounds of language (E). Language produces esthetic pleasure, especially familiar phrases with happy associations. This is the main purpose of poetry—"word music." Just as there is "mood music" there is "mood language," a fact well known to preachers, hypnotists, playwrights, indeed to anyone wishing to "set the tone" for an ensuing event.

S (4) To establish a feeling of belonging (E). Religious ceremonies during which words are repeated together—unison prayers, litanies, doxologies; protest chants; cheers by cheerleaders; war dances. "We shall overcome." Especially effective are hymns, national anthems, and songs recalling a past togetherness, such as the singing of the alma mater or "Blowing in the Wind."

SO (5) To establish relationships (E). "Aloha." "Good morning." "How do you do?" "Chào ông." "Chào bà." "Buenos días, señor." "How've you been?" "Bonjour, monsieur." "Shalom aleichem." "Hyambo." And polite exploratory conversation: "Looks like it's going to be a nice day." "I'm sure I've seen you before somewhere." Included here also would be ritualized language for terminating relations: "Goodnight." "Adios." "Hasta la vista." "Auf Wiedersehen." "Have a nice day."

O (6) To affect or manipulate others' emotions (E). Sermons, patriotic speeches, rallies for causes, TV commercials. "Smile, God loves you." "Oh, you look wonderful!" Popular forms of therapy would be included here: "Don't cry, it's going to be all right." "We all have to go through this." "God will give you strength for the burden you must bear." "Your time is not up yet."

O (7) To affect others' behavior (E, R). "Don't do that!" "Speed limit 35." "Vote for Smith." "Get a job." "Go to work." Here also must be placed the TV commercials designed to convince us that we need a specific product and to go right out and buy it. Also: "Think!" "THINK BIG." "Think small." "Don't think." This is termed "directive language."

The tragedy of our age is the awful incommunicability of souls.

W. O. MARTIN

O (8) To suggest insights (R). This is a philosophic and literary usage especially employed by Chinese sages and Indian gurus. "When a man is in turmoil how shall he find peace / Save by staying patient till the stream clears?" (Lao-tzu). "Does the grass bend when the wind blows upon it?" (Confucius). This is usually the purpose of parables, anecdotes, proverbs, logia or "sayings" ("Jesus said . . . ," "Confucius said . . ."), maxims of folk wisdom ("A rolling stone gathers no moss").

I know that you believe
you understand
what you think I said,
but
I am not sure
you realize that
what you heard
is not
what I
meant.

ANONYMOUS

O (9) To communicate facts and ideas (R). "You're overdrawn." "I'd like a burger and fries." "I'm happy to report that it's not malignant." "I regret to inform you. . . ." Here we can classify all media for the transmittal of knowledge: TV newscasts, nonfiction books, technical journals, and all our routine daily transfer of information for coping and surviving.

O (10) To effect word-magic (E, R, ?). "Open Sesame!" "Be thou healed in the name of Isis." "Om" or "Om mani padme hum!" Our language still contains numerous quasi-magical formulas, often disguised: "Well, here goes." "Good luck!" "Gesundheit!" "God bless you." "God damn you." Akin to primitive word-magic are such phrases as "You're stupid!" and "Go on, you can do it" where the words themselves are designed to help bring about the results alluded to. Closely related to word-magic is the "placebo effect": "Two capsules after meals and you'll feel like a new person."

The true meaning of a term is to be found by observing what a man does with it, not by what he says about it.

P. W. BRIDGMAN

COMMUNICATIONS ANALYSIS

5 Language—that is, sounds and printed symbols—is a human's primary symbolic tool for expression and communication; but our need to communicate is so great that we expect far more of words than they can deliver. We want them to be carriers of the full range of our inner experience, but this would mean the reduction of the richness of experience to a few words and gestures. We try, as it were, to capture life in symbolic containers that are hopelessly inadequate for the task. "Words, strain, crack, and sometime break, under the burden," wrote T. S. Eliot.

But we don't want others to hear our paltry symbols: we want them to hear our experience. And others want the same from us.

6 Successful communication depends not upon a speaker, but upon the hearer. One wishing to communicate his experience to another can try forever, but in vain, if the hearer refuses to hear. If, for any reason, a listener has undergone closure—because he's insensitive to the truth of experience, or is preoccupied with other things, or has developed an ego-defense system to block out pain, or because, in one way or another, he's on overload—then his hear-

I fall far short of achieving real communication—person-to-person—all the time, but moving in this direction makes life for me a warm, exciting, upsetting, troubling, satisfying, enriching, and above all a worthwhile venture.

CARL ROGERS

ing will focus on the symbols rather than what is symbolized. His awareness of what is being transmitted will be partial, narrow, and often inaccurate.

Most of us are threatened by new or different ideas (we are all, to some extent, xenophobic); so we set up roadblocks to unwelcome ideas and feelings so they can't get through. Many of us also develop rigid conceptual systems so that when we hear others' ideas we invariably "translate" them in order to make them fit into our own inflexible schematic of ideas. Bertrand Russell once wrote that the stupid (dense, unlightened) individual invariably reduces high-level concepts to his own level of stupidity because he must oversimplify them to understand them. Something like this takes place in virtually all our attempts to communicate with another person. We translate what another is saying into familiar experience in order to understand him; in doing this, we will inevitably miss, to some degree, the essence of what the other person is really saying.

7 Careful analysis of our communication can help us see what is taking place in our attempts to employ symbols as carriers of meaning. The purpose of communications analysis is to learn to see and understand the processes by which meanings are successfully communicated; or, if there is transmission breakdown, to discover what goes wrong in our thinking, symbolizing, and listening.

The cartoon strip on the next page depicts a baseball game being played by Charlie Brown and friends. As you read through the frames slowly and carefully, concentrate on the **intended meanings** in each comment and note whether the intended content of each statement successfully moves from the speaker to his hearer(s).

We have been given two ears and but a single mouth, in order that we may hear more and talk less.

ZENO OF CITIUM

FRAME ONE "We're getting slaughtered again." Charlie Brown is frustrated, obviously, and is using language to express emotion; it looks as though he is not primarily interested in communicating ideas. And why should he be? His catcher knows the score; Schroeder doesn't have to be told. Charlie's third statement is framed as a question—"Why do we have to suffer like this?"—but it's not really a question at all. Grammatically it is in the form of a question, but it's really just one more way of expressing his agitation over a losing situation. (This is an example of how easily we can be duped by the **structure** of grammar and syntax.) Behind Charlie Brown's frustrated outburst we can hear a cry for help—a What-can-I-do-now? kind of plea.

FRAME TWO "Man is born to trouble." Schroeder misses the emotional intent of Charlie Brown's statement and responds to CB's **words,** not his **meaning**—as Charlie's "What?" indicates, as if to say, "Schroeder, that's **not** what I said!"

Symbols are like cut diamonds. They have many facets, and there is always the danger that the brilliance of one may blind the viewer to the others.

RONALD HUNTINGTON

FRAME THREE "He's quoting from the 'Book of Job.'" Linus also heard Schroeder's words, but instead of replying to either the emotional content or the rational content of his statement, he chooses to give CB the source of the quotation. Linus tries to enlighten CB after hearing his surprised "What?" Both Schroeder and Linus ignore CB's verbalized frustration. In plain fact, Charlie Brown is the only player who is really playing ball.

FRAME FOUR "Actually, the problem of suffering is a very profound one." Linus continues on Schroeder's wavelength, pondering the suffering that is manifest in the human condition. And Lucy—"If a person has had bad luck."

—does she hear what Linus is saying? Obviously not. She didn't even let him finish the idea. Lucy's mind is triggered by words, not by intended meanings. That is, the word "suffering" leads her, by association, to "bad luck." Result: communication breakdown.

Whenever two or more human beings can communicate with each other, they can by agreement, make anything stand for anything.

S. I. HAYAKAWA

FRAME FIVE "That's what Job's friends told him." Did Schroeder hear Lucy? Yes. He heard not her words, but the whole concept of a "moral law." And Schroeder's response is accurate: Job's friends said what Lucy "always says." Did the intended meaning get through? Yes, for the first time so far.

How do we evaluate Lucy's retort to Schroeder: "What about Job's wife?" Lucy is off on a kick of her own: her comment has no connection to Schroeder's statement. (Job's wife hasn't been mentioned and in the biblical drama she is only a bit player.) Result: no communication.

FRAME SIX Schroeder continues where Linus left off in Frame 4—with ultimate thoughts. (Lucy is merely an interruption.) "I think the person who never suffers, never matures." Does Lucy hear? No. She hears **the word** "suffer" but not the meaning that Schroeder gives the word; she gives the word a different meaning—a definitional shift. Therefore—"Don't be ridiculous!"—she blasts Schroeder for what he didn't say.

On the other side of the pitcher's mound another player tries to confirm the notion that "pain is a part of life, and . . ."—would he have gone on to say, "We must learn to live with it"—or something like that? If so, then he is moving at the ultimate meaning-level with Schroeder and Linus.

What about Linus's comment—"The person who speaks only of the 'patience' of Job"? Is he responding to any previous statement? No. The mention of Job has reminded him of **something else** that he happened to know, something about "the patience of Job." So Linus adds his datum of unconnected information.

FRAME SEVEN "I don't have a ball team." Charlie Brown looks just the way most of us feel after we haven't been able to communicate to others or after we have listened to discussions during which no one heard anyone else. "Yes, Charlie Brown, you're not the only one who feels misunderstood."

Words are but bubbles on the surface of much deeper realities.

ROBERT BADRA

8 Philosophic dialogue has been the stock-in-trade of critical thinkers since the days when Socrates carried on his exchanges in the Athenian agora. Philosophic dialogue may be internal dialogue during which each of us can "talk it over with one's self," or interactive dialogue between self and others. And—surprisingly—good communication is essential in both kinds of dialogue!

In internal dialogue we can talk ourselves through an idea, ask ourselves questions about it; we can, as it were, explain it to ourselves or, in imagination, we can explain it to others. This is the secret of many creative thinkers: they have learned how to carry on a productive internal dialogue. Good communication with one's self rests on being very honest with oneself, as well as on listening to one's intuitions, and even to one's feelings; for these also tell us about truths that need to be heard.

Interactive philosophic dialogue is a particular kind of verbal repartee during which two or more minds explore a meaning-event together. They explain it to each other, ask each other questions about it, and exchange all sorts of ideas and insights. Interactive dialogue can take the form of adversary dialogue or supportive (nonadversary) dialogue. The goal of **adversary dialogue** is to force participants to clarify and defend their ideas. It is an inherent part of the adversary system in philosophy (as it is in scientific method) for one thinker to attempt to disprove another's idea or hypothesis. If a notion can be shown to be false or invalid, then everyone gains, since in philosophy (as in science) the goal is not to win an argument but to attain the truth. Likewise, if the ideas can be satisfactorily defended, then again everyone is the winner. (It might be well to note that the *modus operandi* of lawyers—both prosecuting and defense lawyers—in the American justice system bears no resemblance to philosophic dialogue. The goal of lawyers is to win cases, not to establish truth.)

In **supportive dialogue** the defense posture is replaced by one of mutual aid in exploration. Two or more minds think parallel in analyzing a meaning-event. They ask questions of self and others alike, sharing insights along the way. Fortunately our minds are not shaped by the same mold. We see different things in the joint exploration process, and shared understandings expand the awareness of each person. The polarization of adversary dialogue is avoided in supportive dialogue, for each individual shares his doubts and uncertainties just as readily as he shares his breakthroughs. A shared mistake can be as valuable as a shared insight.

9 There is an interesting difference in the way Western and Eastern sages handle meaning-events. A Western thinker tends to deal with ideas in rational terms, seeing them as propositions, fact-claims, value judgments, and so on, working with them analytically and logically, demanding clear definition and precise statement. He will pursue meanings ruthlessly and directly. The strength of the Western mentality lies in its clarity and rationality. It has produced our enormous fund of organized knowledge about the world and ourselves.

The Eastern use of language is entirely different.

Chinese writers, in philosophy and literature, aim at suggesting fertile insights rather than at achieving analytical precision. . . . The genius of the Chinese mind is revealed most fully, not in its philosophical essays and dialogues, but in its poetry, where the suggestive nuances of thought can be freely expressed, unhampered by any need for meticulous distinctions or for coercion of the reader's thought through logical deduction. . . . One who writes in the fashion of a [Western] system-maker thereby shows that he is sure of having attained the essential truth he has sought, and that he is now endeavoring to fasten it upon his reader; his unexpressed attitude is: "You will, of course, take my premises for granted, and I am now going to prove that you must then adopt my conclusions." From the typical Chinese viewpoint such argumentation is not only largely futile (since any keen and determined reader can always find an alternative set of plausible premises); it is unseemly. For if one refuses to take his own convictions too seriously, and approaches his reader with proper respect for the latter's independent integrity, what he will be concerned to do is not to coerce acceptance of his assertions, but so to express them as to elicit growth toward the reader's own more adequate insight. By its neat exactitude and seeming conclusiveness, logical argument can discourage and even block this growth. Let us think and speak so as to guide constructive progress in the experience and understanding of others, not so as to convert them to some absolute which we have no business to regard as such ourselves.

EDWIN BURTT

10 It sometimes seems that, in our time, listening is a lost art. How difficult it is for most of us to remain silent in the presence of different or "wrong" ideas. The urge to clobber an alien idea swells within us like a self-righteous demon, and a speaker rarely gets halfway through his sentence before we give way to an impulse to cut him down.

You can learn a lot just by listening.

YOGI BERRA

I do desire we may be better strangers.

SHAKESPEARE
As You Like It, III, ii, 276

We all know the experience of wanting to be heard by others (or by some one person) and not being able to get through. One of our persistent human frustrations is to discover that another person is hearing only words rather than the living experience we feel so deeply and are aching to convey.

Few insights leave one with such a sense of loneliness. To realize suddenly that, no matter how earnestly you try, you can't be heard—this is why there are so many lonely people who belong to the lonely crowd.

The number of individuals who are **word-oriented** rather than **meaning-oriented** indicates the existence of a widespread "normal neurosis" in our culture.

One successful psychologist and marriage counselor has reported that there is a single formula that works better than any other for couples having trouble in their relationship. "Shut up," he tells them. "Stop talking. You think that you can analyze every problem through to obvious clarity. You are convinced that if you talk long enough your mate will just have to hear you." But, he counsels, "words are your worst enemy. Practice silence. Find other means to express what needs to be said. And learn to listen to what your mate is **not** saying."

"Why are we going in there again, daddy?" "Shut up," his father explained.

RING LARDNER

11 —Lift envelope gently from package do not use force—indicate choice with a cross (×) or check (✓) mark—make check or money order payable to the Book-of-the-Month Club—do not write in this space—do not moisten envelope—place stamp here—list checks separately—remove carbon and tear on dotted line—

"Dear, why sit at your desk all day? Who don't you go for a drive in the country?"

— See inside you may have won $200 a month for life—pull tab—do not throw away, see valuable coupons inside—

"O.K. I will. See you later."

— Keep off the grass—beware of dog—drive carefully—children at play—begin construction—wait for flag—slow—form one lane—caution, men at work—end construction—resume safe speed—

— Yield—one way do not enter—enter here—caution, merging traffic—do not pass on right—quiet, hospital zone . . .—support the college of your choice—be safe in the arms of the Lord—fight inflation . . .—fight cancer—fight fear—love one another—use indicator signals when changing lanes—get more satisfying flavor with nifty, thrifty First for Thirst—

— Slow—pay toll ahead—keep left for exact change lane—if coins miss basket stay in your car, sound horn and wait for attendant—fasten seat belts—go to church Sunday— . . . fly now, pay later—resolve to save—vote for Grabowski—spend a pleasant night at Ziggy's Motel, magic fingers, ezee rest mattresses, adjoining restaurant and color TV—vote Row A all the way— . . . turn back you just passed Ziggy's—. . . .

— Think—post no bills—commit no nuisance—stay on Route 50, topless ahead (after 8 p.m.)—vote as you please but vote—learn to fly—keep awake—take Sominex and sleep, sleep, sleep—give her an emerald—think Florida—

— Exit—begin construction—wait for flag—form one lane—caution, men at work—drive carefully, children at play—resume safe speed—beware of the dog—keep off the grass—leave messages here—

"Hello, dear, have a nice drive?"

CHARLES J. MCDERMOTT

DEFINITIONS AND CONTEXTS

12 Semanticists remind us that symbols can be understood intelligibly only within the context of actual usage. The semantic axiom that no word ever has the same meaning twice would appear to be hyperbole, since in practice we seem to use words repeatedly with about the same meaning. But in fact their observation is correct. Definitions are predictions of possible meanings that a term may be given in concrete situations. The precise meaning of any word cannot be known until it occurs in a living context, and then its meaning is inextricably interwoven with the total event and cannot be understood apart from it.

There is a strand of Western tradition going back at least as far as Socrates, solidified by Aristotle, that would attempt to give all words exact definitions and insist that they be employed only in this unambiguous fashion. In many fields—the medical sciences, physics, chemistry, and computer logics, for example—this approach has yielded enormously valuable results. But this "Aristotelian" approach has little relation to our richly varied use of language in daily life.

The individual who is rigidly literal in his use of definitions often fails in the communication of experience. If he has the habit of importing prefabricated definitions into fluid, living situations, he is apt to miss the nuances and connotations that terms take on in specific contexts. Words are "containers" into which we pour the meanings and feelings of the moment, and this personal investment of ourselves in our symbols is intimately tied to the immediate experiences of life.

I find it difficult to believe that words have no meaning in themselves, hard as I try. Habits of a lifetime are not lightly thrown aside.

STUART CHASE

Words have no meaning. Only people have meaning.

AMERICAN RED CROSS (radio commercial)

There are those who would never have been in love, had they never heard about love.

LA ROCHEFOUCAULD

Empathy

empathize (em′pa-thīz) To diagnose, that is to recognize and identify the feelings, emotions, passions, sufferings, torments through their symptoms is to *realize intellectually,* to *understand* them, in a remote way to identify oneself with the patient, without ever having personally experienced those feelings,—to *empathize,* as it is known in psychiatry.

On the other hand, to place oneself in the position of the patient, to get into his skin, so to speak, to be able to duplicate, live through, *experience* those feelings in a vicarious way, is closely to identify oneself with another, to *share his feelings with him,* to *sympathize,* from the Greek *syn,* together with, and *páthos,* suffering, passion.

empathy (em′pa-thē) . . . Empathy is thus a form of identification; it may be called intellectual identification in contrast to affective identification.

Hinsie and Campbell
Psychiatric Dictionary

On this planet, anything we think may be held against us.

"Mr. Spock"
"Once upon a Planet," *Star Trek*

"What must I do, to tame you?" asked the little prince. "You must be very patient," replied the fox. "First you will sit down at a little distance from me—like this—in the grass. I shall look at you out of the corner of my eye, and you will say nothing. Words are the source of misunderstandings. But you will sit a little closer to me, every day."

Antoine de Saint-Exupéry

13 It is surprising how often people still speak of "dirty words" or "obscene language" and believe that symbols are intrinsically dirty or obscene. It is common also to find individuals who will avoid uttering certain taboo words, believing (or feeling) that something bad will happen just by saying the word. This is a form of word magic.

Semanticists keep reminding us that words mean nothing at all until we give meanings to them. There is no such thing as a "dirty word"; there are only symbols that individuals and groups have invested with certain (negative)

Language and the Real

The observer can describe the world only in the language available to him. "Fact" has a linguistic constituent. As B. L. Whorf has shown, speakers of languages that do not have a word for "wave" will see not waves but only changing undulating surfaces. The Navahoes use one word for blue and green, whereas the Bororó of Brazil have no single word for parrot. In Arabic a wind may be described as *sarsar,* which means both *cold* and *whistling.* The language of Tierra del Fuego has a useful word, *mamihlapinatapai;* it means, roughly, the state of mind in which two people regard each other when both want a certain thing to be done but neither wants to be first to do it. How many lovely facts are available to them! Of course La Rochefoucauld said a long time ago, "*Il y a des gens qui n'auraient jamais été amoureux, s'ils n'avaient jamais entendu parler d'amour*" (There are people who would never have fallen in love if they had not heard love spoken about). Cassirer and Sapir argue that the forms of language predetermine the modes of observation and interpretation; Wittgenstein said that "if we spoke a different language, we would perceive a somewhat different world." Waismann's metaphor is "language is the knife with which we cut out facts."

Reuben Abel
Man Is the Measure

Not higher sensitivity, not longer memory or even quicker association sets man so far above other animals that he can regard them as denizens of a lower world; no, it is the power of using symbols that makes him lord of the earth.

Susanne Langer

meanings and feelings (and invariably there are other people who do not give those symbols the same meanings). When we are told that we shouldn't use certain words, the persons telling us that are engaging in a power-play; they are attempting to persuade us to accept the meanings and values they have given those words, believing—often quite sincerely—that their meanings are the only correct ones for those symbols.

In a word, symbols don't have meaning; they are given meaning by us meaners. And any symbols can be given any meaning, for there is no intrinsic connection between a symbol and the meanings given to it.

An especially heavy example of this fact is the swastika, the hated symbol to so many of Nazi devastation and a reminder of the Holocaust. But long before Hitler's adoption of this ancient symbol, the religions of India looked upon the swastika as a sign of good fortune and divine favor. (The word itself derives from the Sanskrit su ("well"), asti ("is"), and ka (a noun ending); the interjection svasti is a mantra used with the sacred symbol Om in religious ceremonies.) To members of the Jain faith, specifically, the swastika symbolizes salvation and is the central figure on the Jain flag. (See p. 49.)

14 No two persons ever react to any word or symbols in exactly the same manner. How could they? In order to do so, they would have to have the same past experience, the same present environment, the same prospect of the future, the same pattern of thought, the same flow of feelings, the same bodily habits, the same electrochemical metabolism. The chances that such multidimensional patterns coincide are practically nil. The surprising thing is not that we often disagree; it is that we ever succeed in achieving some sort of agreement.

Samuel Bois

✦

LUDWIG WITTGENSTEIN

Dissolving the Riddles of Life

"I first saw Wittgenstein in the Michaelmas term of 1938, my first term at Cambridge." This is the way Norman Malcolm begins his famous *Memoir* of one of the unique thinkers of the twentieth century. Malcolm was attending a meeting of the Moral Science Club, and after a paper was read, a listener in the audience began to stammer a comment. It was a painfully difficult, even embarrassing attempt to speak; he anguished over his thoughts and words. The speaker looked to be about thirty-five, writes Malcolm (he was actually forty-nine). "His face was lean and brown, his profile was aquiline and strikingly beautiful, his head was covered with a curly mass of brown hair."

The man, Malcolm was told, was the author of the awesome philosophical treatise entitled *Tractatus Logico-Philosophicus,* a work Malcolm knew well. "I observed the respectful attention that everyone in the room paid to him. . . . His look was concentrated, he made striking gestures with his hands as if he were discoursing."

What is astonishing about this picture is that this stammering speaker would hold generations of students spellbound and, with his strange kind of eloquence, seduce them into loving philosophy. His intense concentration, his deliberate way of speaking, his insistence on thinking on his feet, his way of instantly creating fresh language to express living thoughts—these qualities would for decades inspire followers to carry on his ideas and methods, write books, and start a movement that would challenge the very nature of traditional philosophy.

It was through the impact of his personality and the power of his thinking that Wittgenstein persuaded the intellectual world that it is not the job of philosophers to ponder the person of God, the sins of mankind, or the secrets of Nature, but to turn their attention to the ordinary, everyday use of language, which, he insisted, is the main source of the confusion that prevents our seeing the truth. It is our language that creates riddles for us; it tells us (wrongly) what to think and how to think; it tells us (wrongly) what is important; it lies to us. The function of philosophy is to free us of these semantic confusions, to provide therapy for our linguistic neuroses—to help us achieve

Let us not forget that a word hasn't got a meaning given to it, as it were, by a power independent of us, so that there could be a kind of scientific investigation into what the word really means. A word has the meaning someone has given to it.

The object of philosophy is the logical clarification of thought.

Philosophy is not a theory but an activity.

The philosopher's treatment of a question is like the treatment of an illness.

clarity of thought. "Everything that can be thought of at all can be thought of clearly." If a question can be put clearly, then it can be answered clearly. "What can be said at all can be said clearly and what we cannot talk about we must consign to silence."

Seeking this clarity, he said, is the job—and the only job—of philosophy. "For the clarity that we are aiming at is indeed **complete** clarity. But this simply means that the philosophical problems should **completely** disappear." Philosophy is a way of dissolving riddles. "Philosophy is a battle against the bewitchment of our intelligence by means of language." Philosophy is medicine for our linguistic illnesses. Philosophy is a way —to use his most famous metaphor—to show a fly trapped in a bottle how to get out. Philosophy can set us free.

"A person caught in a philosophical confusion is like a man in a room who wants to get out but doesn't know how. He tries the window but it is too high. He tries the chimney but it is too narrow. And if he would *turn around,* he would see that the door has been open all the time!"

✦

Ludwig Josef Johann Wittgenstein was a native Austrian who spent most of his life in England. Born in Vienna on April 26, 1889, he was the son of an immensely wealthy father, Karl, an engineer and steelmaker, and Leopoldine ("Poldy"), a busy homemaker who supervised with "nervous splendour" the household of eight bright and talented children (Ludwig was the youngest). All the children were baptized into the Catholic faith. (But Leopoldine's father, raised as a Catholic, was of "Jewish extraction," which made it possible during the Nazi era for the Wittgensteins to be "reclassified" as Judischers, a trauma that produced enormous suffering, severed family ties, and contributed to the suicides of three of Ludwig's brothers.)

Both parents were passionate musicians who surrounded—smothered—their children with music. Their home in Vienna became a center of musical evenings, sometimes attended by such figures as Brahms (a close family friend), Mahler, and Bruno Walter. (Ludwig's brother Paul later became a famed concert pianist. After he lost his right arm in the war he taught himself to play with just his left hand and continued his career. This inspired Maurice Ravel to compose the thunderous *Concerto for the Left Hand,* which Paul performed in Vienna on November 27, 1931, with Ravel conducting.) The Wittgensteins were generous patrons of Viennese musicians and artists, and Karl amassed a valuable collection of paintings and sculptures. It was a glorious family in a glorious era, accompanied by all the humanness, excitement, ambitions, fears, and stresses characteristic of the good life of pre-war Vienna.

In this family of flashing geniuses, Ludwig was thought to be the dullest; he had no obvious talent for music, art, poetry, or anything else. (This was only relatively true, for in midlife he learned to play the clarinet, did research on musical rhythms, dreamed of becoming a conductor, and was a whiz at whistling—he could whistle through the entire performance of a concert.) He never seemed to share his siblings' manic rebellions against parental severity. He went along, developed his father's obsession for gadgets and machines, absorbed the family tradition in classical music (especially Brahms, Mozart, and Beethoven), displayed good manners, and remained (outwardly) cheerful. Only much later did he speak of the bitterness of his unhappy childhood.

Educated at home till he was fourteen, in 1903 Ludwig was sent to the Realschule at Linz, Upper Austria, where for three years he turned in a mediocre performance (he got A's only twice in three years, and flunked chemistry). (There was a not-very-promising German student attending the Realschule at that time, but there are no records of any acquaintance between the two. His name was Adolf Hitler.) Ludwig's cultured background alienated him from the other students. They taunted him with the alliterative chant, "*Wittgenstein wandelt wehmütig widriger Winde wegen Wienwärts*" (roughly "Wittgenstein wends his woeful windy way towards Vienna").

Still under the influence of his father's admonitions that he study engineering, Ludwig proceeded to the Technische Hochschule in Berlin. In the spring of 1908 he went to England, where he experimented with the dynamics of kites in Derbyshire and entered the University of Manchester as an engineering student. For three years he conducted research in aeronautics, windflow, and designs for propellers and jet engines.

But Wittgenstein was disturbed that he couldn't find his true calling. Gradually his interests underwent a major shift: from engineering and aeronautics, he moved to mathematics, and then deeper into the foundations of mathematics. When he asked someone about books on the foundations of mathematics, he was told to read Bertrand Russell's *Principles of Mathematics.* This work profoundly influenced him and led him to the work of Gottlob Frege, who in 1879 had written *The Foundations of Arithmetic* and was considered the founder of mathematical logic. In 1911 Wittgenstein left his engineering studies at Manchester and proceeded to Germany to find Frege in Jena and ask his advice. Frege (apparently) told him to go back to Cambridge and find Russell. So in early 1912 he entered Trinity College, became a disciple of Russell's, and was soon accepted into the highly charged circle of philosophers that included Alfred North Whitehead, G. E. Moore, Keynes the economist, and Hardy the mathematician. Russell recognized the quiet genius of Wittgenstein. "Getting to know Wittgenstein was one of the intellectual adventures of my life," he later wrote.

With the outbreak of World War I, Wittgenstein joined the army, saw action on the Russian front and in Italy, where he was captured by the Italians and held prisoner for eight months. This was in 1918. Fortunately, he had with him the manuscript of his first book—what was to become the *Tractatus*—plus extensive notes on philosophical problems he had been working on; so he turned his prison months at Monte Cassino into a highly productive work time, both for reading and writing.

After the war Wittgenstein taught in several elementary schools in Austrian villages, did some landscaping in a monastery (he considered joining), and built a big home for his sisters in Vienna. Thanks to the efforts of Bertrand Russell the *Tractatus Logico-Philosophicus* was published in 1922, with an introduction by Russell (which Wittgenstein hated; but, for what it's worth, he hated his own work too). Within months he was well known in philosophical circles on the continent and in England.

In 1928 Wittgenstein returned to Cambridge as a "research student," completed work on his doctorate, which he received in 1929 (he was allowed to submit the *Tractatus* as his dissertation!), and (in 1930) became a Fellow of Trinity College. Except for brief travels, he remained at Cambridge as a lecturer in philosophy until late 1947. When World War II interrupted his tenure, he served as a porter in a hospital and worked in a medical laboratory.

During the winter of 1948 he withdrew to Ireland, to a farm first then to a hut on the coast, to find seclusion and to write. There he completed his *Philosophical Investigations.* But he was ill, and work was becoming increasingly difficult. In the fall of 1949 he was told he had cancer, an enemy he had long feared since there was a family history of deaths from cancer. But his spirits remained bright; he said he did not fear death. He died at Cambridge on April 29, 1951.

Wittgenstein can make the unique claim to being the father of two distinctly different twentieth-century intellectual movements. Both were theories of the nature of language and meaning. The first was a continuation, and deepening, of Russell's work on logic. Russell possessed a brilliant analytical mind and

Philosophical clarification will have the same influence on mathematics as sunlight has on the growth of potato sprouts.

One cannot guess how a word functions. One has to look at its use and learn from that.

What we [philosophers] do is to bring words back from their metaphysical to their everyday use.

Philosophy is a battle against the bewitchment of our intelligence by means of language.

What is your aim in philosophy? To show the fly the way out of the fly bottle.

Philosophical problems arise when language goes on a holiday.

My aim is: to teach you to pass from a piece of disguised nonsense to something that is patent nonsense.

I manufacture my own oxygen.

The right method of philosophy would be to say nothing except what can be said. . . .

To know is to act and react, not to give reasons.

had concluded that every so-called philosophical problem, when properly analyzed and "purified," will be found to be a matter of just plain logic, and logic, for Russell, meant "the analysis of propositions." In other words, virtually all the puzzling problems we face in daily life, both theoretical and practical, are linguistic in origin. To Russell this implied that our everyday language is completely incapable of providing solutions to these problems. As a logician the only remedy he could see to this predicament was to create a whole new language for philosophical analysis. Russell had already done exactly this for logic with his *Principles of Mathematics* (1903) and was in the throes, with Whitehead, of expanding this new language in the monumental *Principia Mathematica* (1910–13). They had been able to prove that all mathematics derives from logic. Russell now dreamed of doing the same for philosophy. "Every truly philosophical problem is a problem of [logical] analysis."

Wittgenstein now enters the scene. With his intense logical mind and fascination with mathematical logic, he is ideally equipped to carry out Russell's vision, and Russell soon began to see Wittgenstein as the heir of his own life's work. Wittgenstein takes up the challenge . . . but then goes blazing his own way along a new path. In his *Principles of Mathematics* Russell had written, "The study of grammar is capable of throwing far more light on philosophical questions than is commonly supposed by philosophers." Wittgenstein agreed and decided to concentrate on language, applying Russell's "atomistic" analyses to every tiny facet of symbolic meaning. If Russell could show by philosophic analysis that complex terms of mathematics could be reduced to simple component elements that could then be apprehended with symbolic logic, thereby bringing clarity to the most illusive and stubborn concepts, then perhaps the entire realm of meaning as embodied in human language could also be taken apart, reduced, "purified," and clarified with symbolic logic.

The result was his *Tractatus Logico-Philosophicus* (1922), a strange and difficult book organized by numbered propositions in disconnected aphoristic form. But despite its obfuscations, the whole purpose of the work is to analyze the formal (purely cognitive) aspects of language (not the many other uses of language such as emotional or esthetic, for which Wittgenstein had no interest or feeling), and to lay the ground for an ideal symbolism that would serve as a perfect medium for thinking and communicating.

In a paradoxical way, Wittgenstein was attempting to reveal the entire structure of reality with his analysis of language. It was Alfred Korzybski, the founder of General Semantics, who insisted (later, in 1933) that although "the map is **not** the territory that it represents," it must possess "a **similar structure** to the **territory**"—else the map would be useless. This is an exact analogy, as Wittgenstein sees it, for our language. The structure of reality would be revealed by the structure of language —not the messed-up everyday language that has been created over the many millennia by an uncritical human psyche, but an ideal language of logical symbolism of the kind Russell created for his mathematical logic and Wittgenstein now created for language. Surprisingly—considering his early interest in physics and engineering—Wittgenstein had no interest in science and (like Parmenides) scorns the notion that empirical observation can give us true knowledge of the real world. Logic alone can do the job. "And if we get into a situation where we need to answer such a problem by looking at the world, this shows that we are on a fundamentally wrong track." We need only depend on the coherent structure of logic to know the nature of reality. "We are in possession of the right logical conception if only all is right in our symbolism." A corollary to this belief is that if reality is not reflected in the structure of our language, then it is beyond human apprehension. Anything that can be known has to be expressible in language, and if it can't be expressed in language then it can't be known. It is our human language therefore that establishes the limits and possibilities of thought, and, consequently, of human knowledge.

✦

With the *Tractatus* Wittgenstein was convinced that he had provided an analytical method for the solution and/or dissolution of all possible philosophical problems. He considered his ideas "unassailable and definitive." So he ceased doing philosophy and (in today's jargon) decided to get a life. But it was still, inevitably and always, a life of the mind.

About 1933 Wittgenstein experienced what might be called an intellectual breakthrough that led to a philosophical about-face. The most basic assumption of his great work now seemed to him wrong, not just slightly wrong, but entirely wrong. He underwent a complete reaction against his own ideas as well as against the logical atomism and guruship of his mentor, Bertrand Russell. Given the intensity of their temperaments, it was inevitable that Wittgenstein's new thinking would rupture their relationship. Russell never forgave him for his intellectual apostasy, which, to him, amounted to betrayal.

So, a new philosophy of language began to emerge. Wittgenstein's new thinking lay "entirely outside any philosophical tradition," wrote his friend and former student Georg von Wright, "and without literary sources of influence"; he now has "no ancestor in philosophy." It was absolutely original. He dictated notes on his new ideas from 1933 to 1935 and circulated them in manuscript. They culminated in his *Philosophical Investigations*, begun about 1937 but published posthumously in 1953.

The proper subject matter for philosophical analysis is not some ideal symbolic system, but the living language of ordinary everyday usage. "How do we really use that word?" he asks. "Does it do the job?" "Does it say what is intended?" Philosophy still has a critical role to play, but that role is to scrutinize the evolved natural language of everyday life and assist it to perform the function it was meant to perform.

In other words, the meaning of language is derived from living situations, and that meaning is extremely complex and variable. The hallowed Greek tradition of giving words precise abstract definitions is artificial, unnatural, unproductive, and leads to philosophic fallacies. Words can perform their vital functions only when allowed to carry the varied meanings created by living situations. "For not only do we not think of the rules of usage—of definitions, etc.—while using language, but when asked to give such rules, in most cases we aren't able to do so. We are unable to circumscribe the concepts we use; not because we don't know their real definition, but because there is no real 'definition' to them." Words are not to be chained by definitional irons imported to serve the mind's need for simplicity and control; rather we must listen carefully to their meanings as they do their work in everyday life.

Because the heart of Wittgenstein's "philosophy" is his method, any search for content will be frustrating. "Philosophy is not a theory," he said, "but an activity." (To no surprise of philosopher-watchers, his overall method is far more promising than his detailed applications of it, not a few of which are off the wall, skewed, unrealistic, myopic, obsessed, defensive, and/or logically illogical.)

However, Wittgenstein left a powerful legacy rich in both theoretical and practical insight. In our efforts to think clearly, he urges us

✦ to pay special attention to how we use words, since they set traps and bewitch our minds.

✦ to think carefully about the meanings we give to words (words are meaningless; we meaners give them their meaning; therefore we are in charge, so we must take charge).

✦ to make sure our words say what we want them to say.

✦ to demand clarity, to coerce both minds and words into meeting our unyielding demands for clear thoughts.
✦ never to settle for any statement that is not clear. (If it's worth thinking, it's worth thinking clearly. Clear thinking doesn't just lead to solutions, it dissolves the problems—it makes them disappear entirely.)
✦ to do our own thinking ("A thought which is not independent is a thought only half understood").
✦ never to accept uncritically what others say, especially if they are untrained in precise thinking.
✦ to remind ourselves that others' confusions don't have to be our confusions.
✦ to rid ourselves of the albatross of meaninglessness.
✦ to shed the burden of meaningless words, doctrines, clichés, familiar phrases, and hallowed rhetoric.
✦ to reject empty claims no matter what their source. (Language contains thousands of names for "things" that don't exist, but those names, just by being names, persuade us that their referents are real.)
✦ to guard against being drawn into language-games, no-win riddles, and unprofitable questions. (Because someone else says a word or idea is "meaningful" doesn't make it so. We are easily bamboozled by statements whose lofty sounds ring like divine revelations but that, upon careful examination, are seen to be founded on false assumptions and are therefore empty of meaning.)
✦ to accept and cherish our language even though, like Promethean fire, it is a mixed blessing. With a little laundering, our ordinary everyday language can serve us wonderfully well. Along the path to greater clarity one mustn't be discouraged by bumps and nonsense, by false starts and confusions, by the times when the "engine is idling" and we must say "I don't know my way about." Probing by fits and starts is the name of the philosophic game. A good philosopher will find that he/she must cure herself/himself of a long list of linguistic neuroses before arriving at the clear thoughts that, Wittgenstein believed, will dissolve the torment of nagging questions, heal our misunderstandings, and allow our minds to find "philosophic peace."

✦

REFLECTIONS

Thinking appears to me to be just talking . . . to oneself and in silence.

PLATO

What is called thought is the unuttered conversation.

PLATO

1 Do you sometimes feel overwhelmed by words? What sort of communicative techniques do you think we would resort to or develop or invent if, suddenly, we found ourselves without words?
2 Do you agree with the notion that much of our drive to communicate derives from an "epistemic loneliness" (see pp. 190ff.), from a need to transcend a space/time egocentric condition that we cannot tolerate (§§ 1, 2)? Do you personally feel this condition?
3 Note the following sentence (§6): "Success in communication depends not upon the speaker, but upon the hearer." Does this sound right to you? Analyze the sequence of "bits" involved in the communication of meaning and explain why this conclusion is or isn't true.
4 What is a "definition"? Is this semantic way of defining definitions helpful to you?
5 Note the many different functions of language (§§ 3, 4). If you become aware that much of the language of daily life is not intended to communicate ideas, how might this influence the way you listen to others? How do you think it might affect your relationships?

6 Everyday life provides ample occasion to practice communications analysis, and our exchanges are never quite the same after we have developed an awareness of the many levels of meaning that move between us. Take advantage of the first opportunities you have to practice communications analysis in your discussions and dialogues. Review and assess afterward what you have seen and learned.

7 The Eastern use of language described by Professor Burtt has as long and as rich a tradition as Western analytic thinking; but the Eastern way is designed to achieve an essentially different goal. What kind of insight is the Eastern approach to meaning-events more likely to produce?

8 Summarize in your own words Wittgenstein's early philosophy of language. In your opinion what are its strengths and weaknesses? Is he fundamentally wrong (as he himself later came to believe), or was his shift merely a matter of different interests and concerns?

9 Summarize Wittgenstein's later philosophy of language. What are this approach's strengths and weaknesses? How would you characterize his abandonment of his old system for the new—as hypocritical, inconsistent, flexible, admirably growing and changing, a natural progression of a true searcher, an unstable thought process built on sand—what?

10 What exactly does the marginal quotation by Lewis Carroll (from Humpty-Dumpty, really) on p. 284 mean to you?

11 Write a brief critique of (or perhaps a poem) on the comment of Zeno of Citium, p. 286 (margin).

12 How many examples can you find to illustrate Hayakawa's observation on p. 287 (margin)? Pondering the meanings given the swastika (§13) might be a good starting point.

13 On taboo symbols (§13): There must be deep psychological needs for such symbols. How would you describe these needs?

14 There is an essential difference in the psychology of learning between adversary and supportive dialogue. What is the goal of adversary dialogue? Of supportive dialogue? Do these two modes of operation make good clear sense to you? Could you alternate from one to the other, depending upon the requirements of the situation?

Delicate Coexistence: The Human Love/Hate Condition

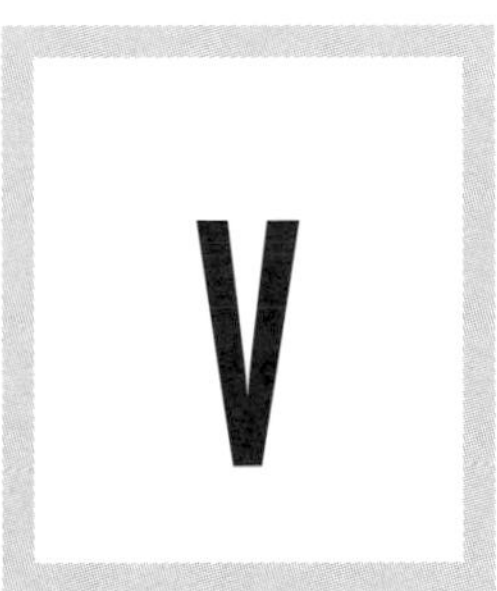

The age of cultural innocence is passing; the American is beginning to recognize the patterns to which he conforms.

Snell and Gail Putney

They are playing a game. They are playing at not playing a game. If I show them I see they are, I shall break the rules and they will punish me. I must play their game, of not seeing I see the game.

R. D. Laing

History

5-1

Early Greek and Roman historians asked whether human history has "meaning." They wondered whether history is like a great drama with a plot, or whether it is merely a jumbled collection of disparate events. Philosophers have studied history to discern if there are patterns that can reveal hidden implications or "messages." This chapter describes several such attempts and asks: Is history making progress? Is it leading to something? If so, is it leading to doom or to a better future? Is Western civilization fated to disintegrate like most other historical societies? It has been said that the only thing we learn from history is that we never learn from history. Could that dismal pronouncement be true? Or, with thoughtful analysis, might we benefit from "the lessons of history"?

Theater of the Absurd

1 Arnold Toynbee is considered by many to be the greatest contemporary philosopher of history. His twelve-volume *Study of History* stands today as the supreme effort of the human mind to disentangle the complexities of human history to see whether there is any large-scale meaning to the whole human enterprise.

Late in 1911 Toynbee left Oxford for a nine-month tour of the Mediterranean lands, where he saw for himself the remains of the great civilizations he knew so well from history books. He spent much time walking over the countryside, surveying the legacies of these long-dead worlds. He chatted with monks on Mount Athos, examined Etruscan tombs at Cerveteri and Corneto, and mused on the past glory of the Minoan palaces on Crete. Before this visit, the Acropolis had been a page in a book; now its panorama sprawled before him in all its breathtaking reality.

Although a certain amount of hypocrisy exists about it, everyone is fascinated by violence. After all, man is the most remorseless killer who ever stalked the earth. Our interest in violence in part reflects the fact that on the subconscious level we are very little different from our primitive ancestors.

Stanley Kubrick

At the same time, he listened to the sounds of the living world. He spent his evenings in Greek cafes and heard talk of world affairs; he visited Greek villages and caught apprehensive conversations among peasants and shepherds about the possibility of war.

He reflected on these two worlds. One was dead, it seemed, the other very much alive. The contrast was a shattering reminder of life, death, and time. Toynbee pondered: What does human history tell us about the present or future? How dead, really, are past civilizations? If they are dead, what caused them to die? What is their relationship to our own busy world? **Is our civilization also doomed to die like the rest?** If so, why? Could it perhaps be saved? If so, what could save it?

2 These are the essential concerns of the philosopher of history. What, if anything, does history mean? How can we learn from it? Is there any way that our understanding of history can shed light on our own troubled times?

There has been a renewed interest in the philosophy of history due to the maddening chaos of the twentieth century. The "big events" that make and shake history have dominated our time: the Russian pogroms, the Turkish massacre of Armenians, the Nazi execution of six million Jews; the killing fields of Cambodia; the "ethnic cleansing" in Bosnia; two world wars initiated by insane racist leaders; ongoing guerilla skirmishes, bush wars, and ideological terrorism; scattered tribal/nationalistic conflicts; plus an all-engulfing global revolution that has only begun.

Everyone in Germany is a National Socialist—the few outside the party are either lunatics or idiots.

Adolf Hitler

Such events have sent us back to reexamining our historical experience in an attempt to make sense out of what, in the wake of such enormous tragedies, has seemed absurd and senseless. All too clearly contemporary history sounds like "a tale told by an idiot, full of sound and fury, signifying nothing." Could this assessment actually be true? Or does human history have a deeper meaning that man in his frenzied state has overlooked?

The philosophy of history asks two central questions, although each leads logically to countless others. The first-generation questions are: (1) Does human history have meaning? (2) Can we learn from history? These questions may or may not be closely related.

I don't live in the past. The past lives in me.

Tom Osborne

3 The metaphor of the drama is appropriate and helpful when trying to conceptualize the problems of the philosophy of history. "All the world's a stage," wrote Shakespeare, "And all the men and women merely players."

So, think of human history as a long, intricately plotted play, with numerous roles and innumerable characters. If history has meaning, then the drama may be similar to an epic like Macbeth. Perhaps it has a playwright who wrote the story and, conceivably, directs the play. (But are we sure the playwright is also the director? And is the playwright also the prop-master?) It has its leading characters—its *dramatis personae.* It has a plot that gives meaning to the lives of the players. It is they who move the plot along. It couldn't develop without them—a play with no players is no play. Every character is essential to the unfolding of the dramatic plot as it moves toward the climax—the *dénouement* of the play's suspenseful story. To be sure, some characters are more important to the plot than others, but even the spear carriers have an appointed place in the grand epic.

The Acropolis, Athens

Now, does this drama metaphor capture the essential truth of human history? Is there in fact a playwright? Is there really a plot? Is there a goal to human history, a final curtain? Is this why our lives are meaningful—because we are all cast in the play? Are we humans really necessary to the working out of the drama? And is the plot a tragedy—as in *Macbeth*—or a comedy—as in *A Midsummer Night's Dream*?

While the stage-play metaphor helps us to formulate questions about the nature of history, the bare fact just may be that history more closely resembles some bizarre act from the Theater of the Absurd—a plotless nonstaging of countless noncharacters who were never cast but who persist in ad-libbing their lines, interacting with no direction, and moving from scene to scene without purpose. It may indeed be "a tale told by an idiot . . . signifying nothing." There may be no playwright, no director, no plot. There may be no play.

The Meaning of History

4 In most societies, the source of history's meaning has been assumed to be the operation of the supernatural. This was a logical deduction from our inherited theological premises. The causal agents behind the events of human history were the capricious animistic sprites and spirits, the whims of the gods, the will of God, or the cosmic interaction of the Forces of Light battling with the Forces of Darkness. In any case, the meaning of history was the preplanned story-line working itself out as men- and women-in-time moved the drama forward from scene to scene.

When it was assumed that supernatural agencies were the source of history's meaning, then human interpretation could move in two directions. It could begin with belief in a preordained plan (God had predestined the minutest details of earth's history from the first appleseed to the last sparrow that falls); and the events of our lives could then be interpreted according to that plan. Or it could look at the events that actually take place and interpret them—and give them meaning—according to these preconceived beliefs ("We won the war because God was on our side"). In Western history it has moved both ways.

The greatest virtue is not to be free, but to struggle ceaselessly for freedom.
Nikos Kazantzakis

5 One of the first known interpreters of history in the Western world was the so-called Deuteronomic historian who wrote down the stories of various wars carried on by the Hebrew tribes during the twelfth and eleventh centuries BC. This unknown writer had sufficient records to enable him to describe sporadic battles involving the tribal leaders (called "judges") of that time; and because of his theological convictions he perceived a pattern in the wars. He did not—indeed he could not—record history as we know it today; rather he wrote "interpreted history," that is, the historical events **plus** what they meant to him.

The dramatic framework that he placed around each tribal battle was simple but meaningful.

1. The Israelites do something evil "in the sight of Yahweh" their God.
2. Yahweh's anger "blazes against Israel." He sends them into battle and "sells them into the power" of the enemy. They are on the point of losing the war.
3. Then the Israelites repent of their evil ways and "cry unto Yahweh." They ask forgiveness and plead for help.
4. Yahweh then "raises up a savior" (a leader) who proceeds into battle with "the spirit of Yahweh upon him" and defeats the enemy.
5. Yahweh has won back his children; he is pleased. So peace "reigns in the land for forty years."

Like a taped replay, this pattern is repeated over and over throughout the Deuteronomic history. It's the only interpretation the writer knows, and his theological preconviction precludes his seeing the historic events in any other way. This is therefore not history but a meaningful—if one-sided—interpretation of a few significant events. It is a "theology of history." (Note that a familiar "unexamined assumption" underlies this pattern: the so-called universal moral law expounded by the Book of Job. See pp. 42–44.)

This framework can be used to interpret **any** conflict between **any** groups. Consider World War II, for example. The Americans (or British or French, or whoever) did "what was evil in the sight of the Lord." He was "angered and sent them into war" where they are about to lose. But they repent and "he raises up a leader" (Churchill, Stalin, Eisenhower—take your pick) who proceeds to win the war. The Lord is pleased again, so "peace reigns for forty years." (The number 40 is rarely, if ever, an historical figure, but a symbolic number implying the presence and approval of God.) This framework can be used just as well to interpret a World Series baseball game or a presidential election.

Men always love what is good or what they find good; it is in judging what is good that they go wrong.
JEAN-JACQUES ROUSSEAU

This sort of interpretation is too subjective to be of any use to us. We can assume that it was meaningful to the Deuteronomist and subsequent believers, but for those of us who are attempting to discover the realities of the case—the objective patterns of history, if they exist—this writer offers little help.

What the Deuteronomic historian succeeds in doing is to alert us to beware of the ease with which we can let our mind's conceptual habits arrange historical events into subjective patterns of meaning. This is a warning for which we can be grateful.

6 The first great Western philosopher of history was Saint Augustine. He was prompted to write *The City of God* after the fall of the city of Rome to Alaric and

his Goths in AD 410. This incredible event so shook the Roman world that it had to be interpreted. It was so meaningless there had to be meaning behind it. While the pagan Romans were complaining that the tragedy was divine punishment for the abandonment of the old Roman gods, Augustine took up his pen to show that Rome had fallen as a part of a long-range divine plan on the part of the "Christian" God. God had not merely tolerated the degenerate city, but had used the City of Earth to accomplish his ends; for out of that City of Earth there had developed the Church to represent the Kingdom of God on Earth. When that city's task of giving birth to the Church was accomplished, then the City of Earth (Rome) would be replaced by the City of God (the Roman Church).

Therefore, in the fullness of time, the plan of God was manifesting itself on the historical plane. The City of Earth had fallen to give way to the City of God.

Augustine's theological interpretation of the fall of Rome, like the viewpoint of the Deuteronomist, is too arbitrary and subjective. We can be sure that Alaric's Gothic priests didn't perceive the event that way, nor did the majority of Romans. If one does not share the theological assumptions from which Augustine began his interpretation, then his explanation is neither logically sound nor emotionally satisfying.

What we can learn from Saint Augustine is that the temptation to seek meaningful interpretations of life-shattering events can lead us into mythical worldviews that have no objective validity. To be sure, they can be comforting, and during times of torment this life-sustaining mode of interpretation is never to be denigrated. But during less stressful periods of life we seek a clearer vision of reality; and the kinds of pressures to which Augustine yielded must not persuade us to settle, too soon, for a parochial interpretation of history that, from a synoptic point of view, is of little value.

7 Two influential teleological philosophies of history have dominated modern times: Hegel's dialectical idealism and Marx's dialectical materialism.

Friedrich Hegel was convinced that he had discovered the nature of thought and that he had made a unique discovery. The thought process moves in a three-beat rhythm that he called the "dialectic." It begins with an idea—a thesis—then proceeds to develop into its opposite, the anti-thesis; after that the mind sees the relatedness of thesis and antithesis and weaves them together into a synthesis. This synthesis, in turn, becomes another thesis, and the dialectic continues. Thus the dialectic effects an ever-expanding comprehension of the connections of the contents of thought.

Hegel was quite sure that this is the way God's mind works. God is pure thought, or, in Hegel's words, the Absolute Mind. Here is no love or compassion (no emotion), just pure thought. The Absolute Mind of God manifests reason through the human mind and therefore in human history. Whenever people think and act more rationally, they are actualizing God's will, and this progressive manifestation of logic is the teleological purpose underlying human history.

Humankind is a crucial part of this program, and there was reason to believe, Hegel thought, that man was becoming more reasonable, especially in nineteenth-century Germany. All of this would end in a state that Hegel described as "pure thought thinking about pure thought"—Absolute Mind contemplating itself.

Sick cultures show a complex of symptoms. . . . but a dying culture invariably exhibits rudeness. Bad manners. Lack of consideration for others in minor matters. A loss of politeness, of gentle manners, is more significant than a riot.

ROBERT HEINLEIN
"Dr. Hartley Baldwin," *Friday*

A Feminist Reappraisal of History

The English historiographer Robin Collingwood once observed:

> Saint Augustine looked at Roman history from the point of view of an early Christian; Tillemont, from that of a seventeenth-century Frenchman; Gibbon, from that of an eighteenth-century Englishman; Mommsen, from that of a nineteenth-century German. There is no point in asking which was the right point of view. Each was the only one possible for the man who adopted it.

Read that last sentence again: ". . . the only one possible for the **man** who adopted it." A stream of books has appeared during the eighties and nineties agreeing: **All history has been written by men, and their selection of events, interpretations, values and attitudes, and even their words and style, have reflected a masculine point of view that has shaped their reconstruction and presentation of the past.** Like Augustine, Tillemont, and Gibbon, each historian peered out at the world of the past through his own androgenic colored glasses; and each, like the named historians, wrote his masculine bias into his work while firmly believing that he was telling the story "like it really was."

Revising history is an ongoing necessity, of course, for new materials are constantly being unearthed, new connections made and insights gained; but most revisions are relatively minor and don't much change the Big Picture. By contrast, this "feminist" proposal promises to be a big one. (Calling this wave a "feminist" reinterpretation of history is, in itself, a biased, sexist misnomer, for the women driving this reappraisal are accomplished scholars in their own right—archeologists, anthropologists, historians, linguists, sociologists; and some of its staunchest advocates are men.)

The scholar primarily responsible for inspiring this monumental reappraisal is Marija Gimbutas, professor of Archeology at the University of California at Los Angeles. In 1974 she published *The Gods and Goddesses of Old Europe: 7000–3500 BC* (reissued in 1982 with the significant title *The Goddesses and Gods of Old Europe: 6500–3500 BC*). This was followed in 1987 by *The Language of the Goddess: Images and Symbols of Old Europe,* and in 1991 by a massive survey of all

A masked-Goddess figurine with M-signs below her breasts, symbols of water, life, and nurturance; below the M's are butterflies, symbols of regeneration.

known archeological material in *The Civilization of the Goddess.* This one individual is credited with bringing to light an entire lost civilization.

The story of civilization begins with the Neolithic ("New Stone") Age, which lasted from about 10,000 BC to about 3000 BC. Before that, for two million years, human beings were itinerant hunter-gatherers. Then, with the emergence of agriculture and the domestication of animals, a settled community life became possible. Houses and temples were constructed, villages sprang up, and art—the touchstone of a civilized consciousness—developed.

Archeological evidence has revealed the existence of a single coherent culture that flourished throughout eastern and southern Europe, the Aegean area, Egypt, Palestine, Mesopotamia, and the Indus Valley. It was an amazingly advanced civilization that arose during the seventh millennium BC and continued into the third millennium BC. It was marked by concentrated populations in villages and townships, complex social structures, elaborate temples, four- and five-room dwellings, professional artisans (ceramicists, metallurgists, weavers), well-developed trade routes, and a sacred script.

To date more than forty thousand artifacts have been recovered from many thousands of burial sites, and archeological digs have revealed clear outlines of the beliefs, values, and social life of the Old Europeans. Archeologists have brought this Neolithic world to life, and what they have revealed is nothing short of astounding.

Humanity's first great spiritual image was the Mother Goddess. She was the self-generating, all-generating creator of the world, the Life-Giver, Bringer of Death, and Regenetrix—a goddess of life, death, and rebirth. Through her powers as Regenetrix, human beings are born from her, sustained by her, and taken back by her. She represented the universe as the nurturing source of life, and humans experienced themselves as the children of Nature, connected to all living things; they felt themselves to be a vital part of an eternal cycle of Nature.

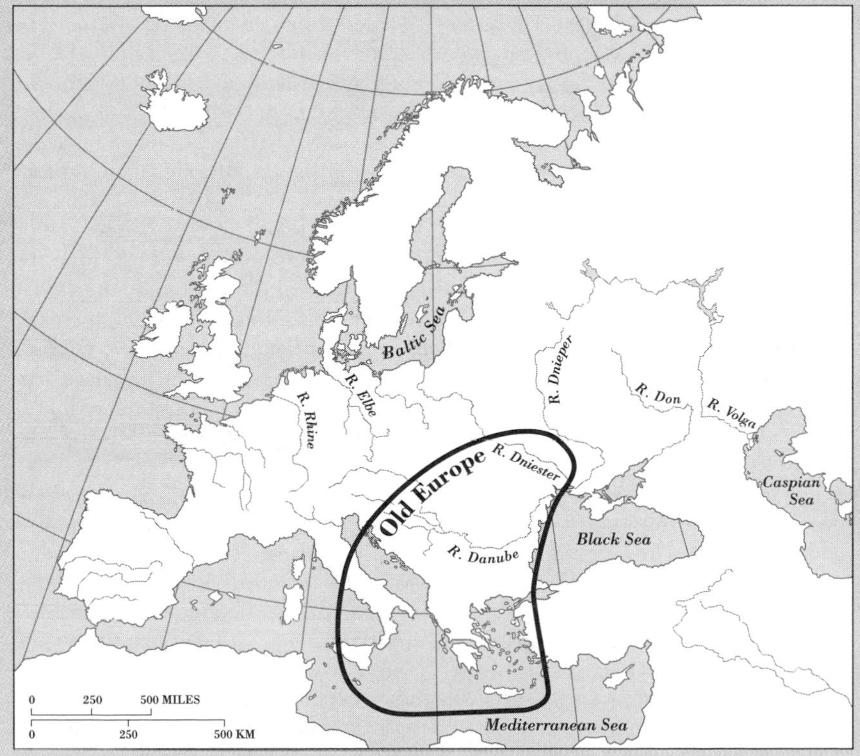

CONTINUED

Thousands of miniature figurines of the Goddess were first carved in bone and stone; then with the invention of ceramics about 6500 BC, there appears an abundance of clay figurines and other ritual articles that served as votive offerings to enhance the power of, and bring favor from, the Goddess. Worship of the Goddess was a natural outgrowth of the agrarian way of life. The central concern revealed in the mythic imagery of the Old Europeans was the task of sustaining life in plants, animals, and humans; the Goddess inspired her devotees to see the-universe as an ever-present, nurturing source of life. There are no images depicting the Goddess from the pre-agriculture era; and throughout the Neolithic record no images of a Father God are to be found. What has **not** been found in the four-thousand-year history of this civilization is perhaps more significant that what has been found. There are no caches of weapons used by man against man—no swords, spears, dagger-knives, bows-and-arrows, or battle-axes, and no painted or carved depictions of such things. There are no battle scenes, no conquerors dragging captives in chains, no torturing of prisoners—nothing to indicate the glorification of warriors or war. No archeological evidence exists of damage or destruction in warfare; nor is there any graphic depiction of wrathful deities ruling through fear and obedience. There is no evidence of slavery or suttee—the immolation of widows to accompany their husbands at death. Nothing indicates the existence of royalty lording it over a submissive populace, no graves of kings or high-ranking chieftains who take human sacrifices with them into the next life. There are no military fortifications; villages and towns were located for convenient access to rivers, animal pastures, good soil, for the beauty of the landscape, and as shrines, but never as citadels or hilltop defenses. There are no walled cities.

What, then, **is** found in the archeological record? Images of the personified Goddess are found everywhere, symbolizing the Divine Mother who gives her people life and who at death will take her children back into her cosmic womb. She is depicted as Creatrix, Ancestress, Maiden, Regenetrix, Earth-Mother and mistress of flowing waters, birds, and the underworld; she is often portrayed as the Mother Goddess cradling a child in her arms. Also found in abundance are symbols of Nature, implying a feeling of awe at the mystery, beauty, and sanctity of life. There are stylized meanders symbolizing the life-giving water, stone heads of bulls, vases shaped like does, images of serpents and butterflies—ubiquitous symbols of metamorphosis and immortality.

So for over four thousand years, the spiritual life of Old Europe focused on the worship of the Goddess, and this gynocentric consciousness shaped the development of their society. Their world was matrilineal; descent and inheritance were traced through the mother. Men and women were essentially equal; there are no hints in the record of either male dominance or female dominance. It was a classless, egalitarian society for everyone, with men and women in equal possession of the material wealth of their society. Women played leading roles in religious affairs and were responsible for much of the vase painting, sculpturing, and textile weaving.

For them the primary purpose of life was not to fight, to gain glory by conquering, pillaging and destroying. All the resources of human nature, feminine and masculine, were focused on technologies that nourish life, especially the creative arts. They developed an appreciation of the beautiful and a sophisticated style to express it. The Goddess invented agriculture and taught her people to farm; she taught them how to weave and spin; and she continued to educate and sustain their lives through the cycles of Nature. They lived their lives in a peaceful and plentiful coexistence. These sedentary horticulturalists knew themselves to be at home in the world, not just passers-through preparing for an afterlife. They were a part of the Whole, and it was good.

Gimbutas writes: "If one defines civilization as the ability of a given people to adjust to its environment and to develop adequate arts, technology, script and social relations it is evident that Old Europe achieved a marked degree of success" (Gimbutas 1982, p. 17).

Then, beginning about 4400 BC, the civilization of the Goddess began to collapse. During the next two millennia waves of invaders arrived from the east, and Old Europe was transformed. These were the Aryans (often "Indo-Europeans" in the literature; Gimbutas calls them "Kurgans"), seminomadic pastoralists, flowing out from the steppes of southern Russia. Their culture was patrilineal and socially stratified; they lived in small villages or seasonal settlements and grazed their flocks over vast pasturelands. Their economy thrived on stock-breeding, and their domestication of the horse gave them speed and power. Theirs was a hard-driving, male-dominated way of life; they prized virility and male aggressiveness and honored their warrior-heroes. Their symbols were the dagger and battle-ax. Male sky-gods were the focal point of their religion.

These Aryans arrived in three waves. The first, about 4400–4300 BC, descended from the Volga steppe; the second, about 3500 BC, arrived from the Caucasus mountain region; the third, soon after 3000 BC, also came from the Volga.

Two drastically different ideologies, religions, economies, and social structures—they clashed, and Old European culture went into decline. The matriarchal civilization was overpowered by the patriarchal culture. Gimbutas writes that "towns and villages disintegrated, magnificent painted pottery vanished; as did shrines, frescoes, sculptures, symbols and script. The taste for beauty and the sophistication of style and execution withered. The use of vivid colors disappeared in nearly all Old European territories except Greece, the Cyclades, and Crete where Old European traditions continued for three more millennia, to 1500 BC" (quoted in Baring-Cashford pp. 79ff.). Weapons and warrior-gods begin to appear in the archeological record, as do evidences of slaughter, slavery, and the treatment of women as property.

For the next three thousand years Western civilization reflected the mix—like a "marbled layer-cake"—of these two powerful cultural traditions. "The earliest European civilization was savagely destroyed by the patriarchal element and it never recovered, but its legacy lingered in the substratum which nourished further European cultural developments. The Old European creations were not lost; transformed, they enormously enriched the European psyche" (Gimbutas 1982, p. 238).

✦

An accurate understanding of this Old European civilization was obscured, not primarily by lack of material, but by a threefold mutually supporting bias: (1) a professional bias based on certain (unexamined) assumptions about "human nature" and what constitutes progress and civilization; (2) a chauvinist bias rooted in age-old (unexamined) assumptions about the natural superiority of the male; and (3) a deeply religious bias deriving from (unexamined) assumptions embedded in a patriarchal, male-dominated Judeo-Christian religion.

Professionals were caught in the problem of defining "civilization." Scholars have long **assumed** that if a social grouping gave evidence of certain achievements then it could justly be described as a civilization, and those criteria were: a complex social and political structure with class stratification and division of labor; an organized religious system with hierarchical orders; and the capacity to organize itself for defense and warfare, indicating an advanced level of coopera-

CONTINUED

tive skill. If a society didn't demonstrate these achievements, then it wasn't perceived as a civilization.

Gimbutas came to see that this definition of civilization is unempirical and wrongheaded. "The generative basis of any civilization lies in its degree of artistic creation, aesthetic achievements, nonmaterial values, and freedom which make life meaningful and enjoyable for all its citizens, as well as a balance of powers between the sexes. Neolithic Europe was . . . a true civilization in the best meaning of the word" (Gimbutas 1991, p. viii).

The other two biases are more obvious, and much more insidious. The most pervasive bias is the problem of the male ego (and doesn't deserve further elaboration here). The most devastating and deliberate bias is that of the Judeo-Christian religious heritage, massively supported by a masculine mentality that "just knows" that God is a Man, his Son was a Man, Eve was an afterthought (created to serve Adam), embodied in an ecclesiastical hierarchy that has for centuries taught that there is no place for woman in religious affairs. For a brilliantly documented account of this bias see Merlin Stone's *When God Was a Woman.*

This reconstructed Old European worldview has been used as a basis for developing new concepts of human society. Riane Eisler, a sociologist, in *The Chalice and the Blade* (Harper & Row, 1988) envisions a future society of men and women working together as equals. Anne Baring and Jules Cashford in *The Myth of the Goddess* (Viking/Penguin Books, 1991) relate insights from Jungian depth psychology to the worldview of the Goddess to lay foundations for the recovery of a spirtual wholeness lost when we humans were severed from Nature.

Recommendations for further reading must begin with Marija Gimbutas, *The Goddesses and Gods of Old Europe: 6500–3500 BC* (University of California Press, 1982) and (if you're up to it) *The Civilization of the Goddess* (Harper San Francisco, 1991). Also: Erich Neumann, *The Great Mother* (Bollingen Series XLVII, Princeton University Press, 1983); Merlin Stone, *When God Was a Woman* (Harcourt Brace, 1976).

✦

8 Hegel's novel way of interpreting history caught the minds of students in the German universities; but while the idea of the dialectic excited them, the notion of an Absolute Mind thinking with dispassionate logic left them cold.

Karl Marx was one of these students. Following the lead of another young philosopher named Ludwig Feuerbach, Marx developed a philosophy of history around the idea of a dialectical movement, operating in terms of the basic material essentials of life. Marx was convinced that his vision of the dialectic was real. It is a dialectic of social struggle determined by man's economic needs. Class struggle creates the three-beat rhythm. Marx's interpretation is a "materialistic dialectic" in contrast to Hegel's theistic dialectic.

Once we have cast another group in the role of the enemy, we know that they are to be distrusted—that they are evil incarnate. We then twist all their communications to fit our belief.

JEROME FRANK

Thus Marx laid the foundations for a teleological interpretation of history that has come to dominate half the world. All Marxians know that history has purpose; it follows "inexorable law" toward a goal—the Classless Society where equality, justice, and plenty will prevail (which is a down-to-earth version of the Kingdom of God). Each individual is a part of history's drama. As in other teleocosmic dramas, each person must decide whether he or she will fight on the side of the Righteous (the revolutionaries who actively hasten history toward its

Long Centuries Grown Cold

Men laughed in Ancient Egypt, long ago,
And laughed beside the Lake of Galilee,
And my glad heart rejoices more to know,
When it leaps up in exultation too,
That, though the laughter and the laugh be new,
The joy is old as is the ancient sea.

Men wept in noble Athens, so they say,
And in great Babylon of many towers,
For the same sorrows that we feel to-day;
So, stranded high upon Time's latest peak,
I can with Babylonian and with Greek
Claim kinship through this common grief of ours.

The same fair moon I look upon to-night,
This shining golden moon above the sea,
Imparts a richer and more sweet delight
For all the eyes it did rejoice of old,
For all the hearts, long centuries grown cold,
That shared this joy which now it gives to me.

Whate'er I feel I cannot feel alone.
When I am happiest or most forlorn,
Uncounted friends whom I have never known
Rejoicing stand or grieving at my side,
These nameless, faceless friends of mine who died
A thousand years or more e'er I was born.

Rosalind Murray

Pablo Picasso, *Guernica* (1937)

appointed end) or on the side of the Wicked (the bourgeois reactionaries who resist change and progress).

Karl Marx (1818 – 1883)

9 By now it's clear that each of us, when attempting to make sense of the complexities of the past, must be on guard against projecting our subjective frameworks onto historical events and arranging them to support our own visions and prejudices. We must be equally wary of the hidden **cultural** assumptions of our place and time—the *Zeitgeist* or "time-spirit." Hegel and Marx both fell victim to such an assumption: the idea of "inevitable progress."

The opposing notions that human history is improving (the optimistic view) or degenerating (the pessimistic view) have had a see-saw history in Western thought.

The teleological view of history—the belief that history has meaning and is moving toward a goal—is essentially a Judeo-Christian assumption; and within that teleological point of view a majority report has held that the human lot would continually improve. (In a general way, when times were troubled—during Roman persecutions, the Islamic conquests, and the twentieth century—the pessimistic viewpoint has prevailed: conditions, it was held, will become progressively worse until God, in his own good time, "breaks in from above" and sets things right. By contrast, when times were relatively peaceful—during the Renaissance, the Enlightenment, and the Victorian era—the optimistic viewpoint has prevailed: history was seen as a progressive improvement of man's growth and happiness on earth. In either case, however, whether history is going up or down, it never loses its teleological character.)

The Idea of Progress

The notion of a finite and clearly definable goal of progress in history, so often postulated by nineteenth-century thinkers, has proved inapplicable and barren. Belief in progress means belief not in any automatic or inevitable process, but in the progressive development of human potentialities. Progress is an abstract term; and the concrete ends pursued by mankind arise from time to time out of the course of history, not from some source outside it. I profess no belief in the perfectibility of man, or in a future paradise on earth. To this extent I would agree with the theologians and the mystics who assert that perfection is not realizable in history. But I shall be content with the possibility of unlimited progress—or progress subject to no limits that we can need or envisage—towards goals which can be defined only as we advance towards them, and the validity of which can be verified only in a process of attaining them. Nor do I know how, without some such conception of progress, society can survive. Every civilized society imposes sacrifices on the living generation for the sake of generations yet unborn. To justify these sacrifices in the name of a better world in the future is the secular counterpart of justifying them in the name of some divine purpose. In Bury's words, "the principle of duty to posterity is a direct corollary of the idea of progress." Perhaps this duty does not require justification. If it does, I know of no other way to justify it.

Edward Hallett Carr
What Is History?

The nineteenth century was infused with a double dose of optimism. The Industrial Revolution was in full swing. Western nations were moving to all corners of the world, sharing their bounty of material goods and spiritual blessings. And among philosophers of history the mood of the Enlightenment was still waxing. Edward Gibbon sealed his idealism near the end of his great *History of the Decline and Fall of the Roman Empire* (1776–1788) by sharing "the pleasing conclusion that every age of the world has increased, and still increases, the real wealth, the happiness, the knowledge, and perhaps the virtue, of the human race."

To this assessment of human history was added (in 1859) Darwin's massive documentation of the evolutionary theory that, down through aeons of time, it is the fitter species that survive. Nature, too, it turns out, is inherently progressive. So it became clear that both **human** history and **natural** history move together, upward and onward; and only the most dismal disbeliever could doubt "the inevitability of progress." Much later Bertrand Russell was to reminisce: "I grew up in the full flood of Victorian optimism, and . . . something remains with me of that hopefulness that then was easy."

Change is avalanching down upon our heads, and most people are utterly unprepared to cope with it.
ALVIN TOFFLER

Although the philosophies of history constructed by Hegel and Marx can be validly criticized on many other grounds, their optimistic foundations were solely subjective—assumptions that were "in the air" of their times. So we have two more instances when serious thinkers projected their inner visions into the real world and thus failed to give us an accurate account of history's meaning.

Toynbee's Organismic Interpretation of History

10 Arnold Toynbee's *Study of History* is probably the most noteworthy attempt by any modern philosopher of history to make sense of the human drama.

Arnold Toynbee (1889 – 1975)

In September 1921 he was aboard a miserably slow train traveling across Thrace. The rumbling of his train crossing a bridge near Adrianople awakened him before dawn, and during the next few hours, as a countryside haunted with history glided past, his mind began to call up the epochal events of history and legend that had been set in this great theater.

He knew that he was then crossing the westernmost boundaries of the vast empire of the Persian Achaemenids and that when the Achaemenids' kingdom had run its course, these rolling hills and lazy pasture lands came under the shield of the young Alexander of Macedon. Three centuries later the astute plans of a Caesar for the conquest of central Europe were shattered when Varus and his legions were lured into the nearby Teutoburg Forest and annihilated by the Germans. Through here the Goths and the Huns passed, followed in turn by the Crusaders with red crosses flashing on their white tunics and the fire of holy war flashing in their eyes; after encountering the gaily clad Saracens, those who returned crept homeward in bloodsoaked rags, and not a few laid their embattled bones beside the little streams in the Thracian woodlands. Much later this countryside, then Rumelia, was drawn into the Ottoman Empire and the Muslims settled the land and made it theirs. Thus it remained until modern times.

Hour after hour Toynbee stood by the window watching the scenes of history pass by. That night, as the train sped along in the light of the full moon, he jotted down on a half-sheet of notepaper a plan for a comparative study of the civilizations of mankind. He had decided to embark on a research program that would take him on a prolonged journey through all known civilizations to determine whether meaningful patterns were discernible in the lifetimes of these civilizations. His primary interest was to discover where we stand today in Western civilization and to glimpse where we are going. He figured that this project would require decades of work, and it did. He completed the last page of his study on June 15, 1951—thirty years of labor to discover the meaning of history and the current condition of our Western civilization.

11 Toynbee thinks in terms of whole civilizations, not nations. The latter are but ephemeral and illusory fragments of civilizations. In the wider perspective of man's civilizations, nations are merely ethnocentric tribes that come and go so rapidly that they are quite secondary in importance, though in their short lifetimes they are the source of much narrow internecine bickering within the larger cultural body.

The subject matter of Toynbee's study of history is all the civilizations known to man. He lists twenty-seven civilizations born to date (including five arrested civilizations). There were also four abortive civilizations that started out normally but could not make the grade.

I have a theory that progress is what is left over after one meets an impossible problem.
NORMAN COUSINS

Subtracting the arrested civilizations from the total, we have twenty-two that reached maturity. Of those twenty-two civilizations, fifteen are now dead and buried, while only seven are still alive. Of the five arrested civilizations, two are dead and three are still living.

There are, then, a total of seventeen dead and ten living civilizations.

But two of these ten living civilizations are now in their death throes. That leaves only eight, and six of these "bear marks of having already broken down and gone into disintegration," and seven of the eight are presently seriously threatened with annihilation and/or assimilation by Western civilization.

As of the twentieth century, therefore, our own Western civilization stands at the top of the list. From appearances, we are still relatively healthy, and our general prognosis, according to Toynbee, can be one of guarded optimism.

12 As Toynbee studied the lifespans of man's twenty-seven civilizations—rather like drawing lifelines on clear plastic films and making overlays for comparison—what did he discover? Patterns. Consistent, clear patterns of birth, growth, maturity, decline, disintegration, and death—for each and every civilization that had the good fortune (just like individuals) to live a full lifetime. To him the patterns were unmistakable, and he tried to study the movements of civilizations without prior doctrinal commitment. He believed the patterns he saw to be real, not subjective.

When I came back from war, I discovered that to adjust to the kind of life people lived was simply impossible, after all that I had seen. So many of the things that went on seemed like trivialities.
The World at War, BBC-TV

Toynbee gave labels to the stages of development in much the same way that Erikson has named the phases of our individual life patterns. A "primitive society" is confronted by a challenge and responds heroically and creatively. It is led out of its primitive condition by a "creative minority" of individuals and becomes a bright, thriving civilization. But the "creative minority" soon loses its vitality and turns into a "dominant minority" that refuses to release its cherished power. Internal power struggles begin as the disintegrating civilization fragments; it is bound together less and less by common values and shared visions. It sinks into a "time of troubles" and becomes vulnerable to dissolving forces from within and without. It unifies briefly into a "universal state"; but it has no vital, creative resources left, and it dies. But from death there is resurrection. From its ashes there arises, Phoenix-like, a second-generation civilization that carries on the great insights and values of the dead society.

In the case of most Americans, the internal limitations far outweigh the external ones.

SNELL AND GAIL PUTNEY

13 Since the larger units (civilizations) behave so much like the smaller units (persons), one can detect an experiential thread running throughout Toynbee's philosophy of history. Outlined in terms of individuals it runs something like this:

Individuals experience a state of

1. **peace and contentment:** They relax their hold on nonmaterial values and become more material-minded; they become self-satisfied with material things to the point of worshiping themselves and their handiwork. This leads to

2. **disillusionment and suffering:** Life has become meaningless as materialism fails to satisfy the needs of human nature; the old gods prove to be false. People's suffering drives them toward a

3. **salvaging of values:** Their attention is redirected toward the fundamental questions of the nature and value of human life; they seek meaning once again, and find it. This question-asking mood stimulates them into a

4. **period of creativity:** They find answers to their questions; life takes on new meaning as disillusionment fades away; life becomes livable again, and they are happy. They now enter a state of

5. **peace and contentment:** and the cycle repeats itself.

This pattern of behavior is typical, but it is not an "inexorable law." It can be broken by innumerable factors, internal and external, and this is true for the civilization as well as the individual. Just as some might learn their lessons vicariously through the sufferings of others and not be compelled to pass through the disillusionment-suffering phase themselves, a whole civilization might learn the same lesson and thereby get a new lease on life. If John Dewey has reminded us that we don't get down to the business of thinking until we strike a problem that makes us think, then Toynbee is saying that people don't get down to the business of assessing life's values until their loss compels them to do so. In short, individuals learn by suffering, and only by suffering. But they **can** learn—and thereby alter the pattern of their civilization.

The Plight of Western Civilization

14 From this Promethean comparison, what had Toynbee found? Western civilization is probably on the threshold of what Toynbee calls a "universal state," and the appearance of this state in the developmental pattern of a civilization is the unmistakable sign of disintegration. The breakdown of our civilization began in the fifteenth or sixteenth century, probably with the religious wars, and since

that time there have been innumerable symptoms of disintegration in the arts, philosophy, religion, and material culture. We recognize these signs from their appearance in corresponding stages in past societies. Since only two or three great powers left in the world serve as rallying points for all the other nations, the universal state cannot be far away.

But at this point a new element has entered the picture: the actual fact of One World. When we ask what sort of universal state we shall see, Toynbee suggests two possibilities. The first kind would have all the characteristics of the universal states of the past. It would be ushered onto the stage of history by the same self-inflicted knockout blow in which one member-state succeeds in a coup of all the other member-states and itself becomes the universal state. No society has ever been able to recover from this suicidal act, and nothing can turn back the process of dissolution that now sets in. Thoughtfully, Toynbee asks, "Must we, too, purchase our *Pax Oecumenica* at this deadly price?"

The second alternative would be something new in human history: the creation of a new kind of universal state by peaceful means. The entire world is now moving toward homogeneity with unbelievable speed. Momentarily it is dominated by the technology of a materialistic West, but it is clearly, and increasingly, influenced by the nonmaterialistic values and concepts of the non-Western world. If it does prove to be true that we are on the verge of becoming **one** civilization with **one** culture, this may mean that a new type of political organization could manifest itself. This would be a genuine mutation of the laws of history. If it is possible for the West to meet the challenge of One World by outgrowing its egocentric illusion—especially as it expresses itself in the nationalism of its parochial states—the doom of Western civilization may be avoided. There could be a new lease on life, and there could be a new world order.

The world revolution, Arnold Toynbee has suggested, has begun. But who will eventually be fighting whom is still not clear.

R. D. LAING

There is the possibility, of course, that humanity may destroy itself through a nuclear winter, by unbalancing Gaia-Earth, poisoning the air and water, altering global climate, or by resurrecting a long-dormant hot virus; but Toynbee doesn't believe these to be likely alternatives. There is the frightening possibility that we humans may require a challenge as horrifying as mass destruction before we can learn how to live in peaceful coexistence.

Our ignorance of history causes us to slander our own times.

GUSTAVE FLAUBERT

15 Toynbee said that "the whole face of the planet will have been unified politically through the concentration of irresistible military power in some single set of hands." Although communism seemed a threat from a short-range viewpoint, in the long view Toynbee dismisses communism because, in insisting on shortcuts, it does not answer the individual's deepest needs. "There seems to be in human nature an intractable vein—akin to the temperament of Man's yokefellows the camel, mule, and goat—which insists on being allowed a modicum of freedom and which knows how to impose its will when it is goaded beyond endurance. . . . Even the most long-suffering peoples revolt at some point."

The strongest political force of the day—nationalism—is driving nations to increase their populations rather than to moderate them. This is why I doubt whether action will be taken until the problem has developed from a threat to a disaster.

FRED HOYLE

Within this coming universal state there will be less physical and material freedom than the peoples of the West have been used to, even in such "sacred" realms as family planning. As he sees it, "in a powerful, healthy, overpopulated world, even the proletarian's freedom to beget children will no longer be his private affair, but will be regulated by the state." He believes that the problems of population control and food production are the critical problems of the near future.

Man cannot live without freedom, however, and "if freedom is suppressed on the material plane, it will break out on the spiritual plane." So in this new world there will be a spiritual freedom superior to that known to the West, and this gain will be more than worth the price that society will pay for it. "True spiritual freedom is attained when each member of Society has learned to reconcile a sincere conviction of the truth of his own religious beliefs and practices with a voluntary toleration of the different beliefs and practices of his neighbors."

There will also be equality among human beings and respect for human dignity. There will be neither colonialism nor communism to deny these qualities to mankind. The idea of "democracy" as understood by the West to mean **self-government** will be considerably weakened, and "democracy" as employed by the non-Western peoples to mean social equality will predominate.

And what will be the role of religion? Toynbee clearly sees a resurgence of religion. Just as the nineteenth and the first half of the twentieth century have seen a steady movement away from religion, the twenty-first century will witness a countermovement in which mankind will turn from materialism and technology back to religion and spiritual values. What will this religion be like? A continuing interaction between all existing religions is certain, but for some time to come each of the living religions will maintain its identity and minister to its own adherents. However, there is a strong possibility that, as these great religions find themselves face to face in a shrinking world, a positive tolerance will replace their traditional fanaticism. They will find that all their fellow seekers are engaged in the same quest. In the long run, only a true monotheistic devotion to one Ultimate Reality accepted by all could meet the requirements of those who view their world as One World, and who look upon all others as kindred.

Can Western civilization survive all this? Perhaps. So many new factors have appeared in the modern world that our civilization, if it can come alive and face the challenge of change, can be infused with new vigor and win a reprieve, perhaps even a new chance at growth. If our response includes great leaders—an authentic "creative minority"—who can lead the way by facing realistically the problems of a new era, there is still hope.

Western civilization is not yet dead and buried, not quite.

What's it to me that nobody's guilty and that I know it—I need revenge or I'd kill myself. And revenge not in some far off eternity, somewhere, sometime, but here and now, on earth, so that I can see it myself.

FYODOR DOSTOEVSKY
The Brothers Karamazov

Chinese malediction: "I curse you! May you be born in an important age."

16 Most philosophers agree that when a civilization becomes materialistic and "sensate" (Pitirim Sorokin's term) in its values, then it is in trouble. In this stage there is usually a universally held belief that this is the "golden age"—a bounteous time of unprecedented prosperity. In reality it is the onset of disintegration. Unless the culture can rediscover its creativity by successfully facing new challenges and recovering its "ethereal" values, it is doomed. What they are saying is that unless a fundamental change takes place in the priority of values of large numbers of people, but above all in the "creative minority" who are the true leaders of humanity, then the civilization has gone into irrevocable decline.

Another point of agreement among philosophers of history is that nationalism is a necessary but passing phenomenon. Those holding "organismic" theories of history usually liken our present politicocultural condition to adolescence, the time when the individual human self is laboring for separation and identity. But once the integrated self has been developed, there is no longer a preoccupation with identity or identity-labels. They suggest that civilization will move collectively through the ethnocentric stage, just as individually we pass (or should pass) through the egocentric stage. While quite normal in the adolescent phase, overconcern with self is hardly becoming to mature adults who have more important things to do than concentrating perpetually on the problem of who they are. What philosophers of history agree on is that conditions in the modern world are creating a single world-culture that will, with shattering speed, break down the boundaries of nationalistic consciousness. Indeed, our survival will be in serious jeopardy if large-scale ethnocentric consciousness prevails.

A third point on which most philosophers of history agree is that the disintegration of a civilization is not the ultimate tragedy we may think it to be. Durant makes this point frequently in his *Story of Civilization*. "We should not be greatly disturbed by the probability that our civilization will die like any other. As Frederick asked his retreating troops at Kolin, 'Would you live forever?' Perhaps it is desirable that life should take fresh forms, that new civilizations and centers should have their turn." Toynbee has similarly noted that the most precious elements of any civilization do not die but become the seeds of a subsequent new civilization. Great inventions, advancements in science, philosophy, art, and music, the profoundest insights into nature, and our knowledge of humanity—these are never lost though the culture that produced them may crumble. "These are the elements of civilization," writes Durant, "and they have been tenaciously maintained through the perilous passage from one civilization to the next. They are the connective tissue of human history."

Can We Learn from History?

17 There has been a recurrent skepticism in our Western thinking as to whether we can learn anything at all from history. Many have said it, perhaps none better than Hegel: The only thing we learn from history is that we never learn from history.

Perhaps we can allow the skeptics their points. Considering all the lessons of history that could be learned, the poverty and pokiness of our learning is nothing less than frightening. As of the twentieth century, we have recovered a much greater fund of historical knowledge than the ancients ever dreamed possible; and yet, with all this wealth of information, we don't seem to be able to read "the lessons of history."

History is **human** history. It is nothing more or less than the record of individual human beings who have lived, loved, fought, dreamed, and (mostly) vanished. Whenever individuals act collectively, then we lump them together with an abstraction and speak of tribes, nations, communities, committees, teams, classes, and so on. And when they create mental systems and subordinate their individuality to the contractual guidelines they have agreed to, then we speak of institutions: governments, armies, churches, monastic movements, industrial complexes, political parties, and the like.

After all, when one tries to change institutions without having changed the nature of men, that unchanged nature will soon resurrect those institutions.

Will Durant

But all such groupings are merely functional abstractions. In the last analysis, history is the story of single human beings going about the business of living; and in their lives we find exactly what we would expect: the highs and lows, great accomplishments and terrible mistakes, heroic dedication and horrendous cruelty—they're all there. Almost everything we have learned that is worthwhile—that is, wisdom—we have learned by studying the behavior of other human beings. So, who could not learn from all these individuals if one so wished? If they happen to have lived in the past, then, yes, "We can learn from history."

But let's be clear: history **teaches** us nothing. History is dead—it is past; it is silent. The act of learning from history therefore falls to the living, and it becomes a deliberate, aggressive act on our part to search out the lessons that lie quietly in the records, waiting to be brought to life and put to use. So, the question of whether we can learn from history turns around to peer at us: Can we open ourselves to what history has to say to us?

18 Edward Hallett Carr, a historiographer, reminds us that "the axiom that everything has a cause is a condition of our capacity to understand what is going on around us." In daily life we rarely doubt that cause-and-effect patterns exist. We assume causality, rightly; and in every realm of experience we want to control events by altering their causes.

Learning from history is analogous to learning from our own experience. We study history, just as we worry through our personal memories, to find out what went wrong, or what is wrong. If we can isolate the causes, then, next time, perhaps we can alter those causes and change the outcome. How many science-fiction stories spin out the secretly cherished hope that we might go back in time and alter a single causal event and thereby erase some blackened episode that stains the record of human history?

What caused the Great Depression? What caused the energy crisis? What caused the discontent of the Sixties? What caused the ecological crisis? What are the principal causes of the second-class status of women in Western history? What will be the effects of the sense of autonomy of the young African nations? What causes "the deaths of the gods"?

Too often we grasp essential causes only later when discoveries illuminate them. Historic causes are deeply hidden; seeing takes time. Take the Nazi phenomenon, for example. Even today, could we recognize its principal causes so that we could take steps to prevent the recurrence of such a nationalist/racist power state? In the case of Nazi Germany, the Milgram experiments conducted in the early 1960s beamed a flood of light on some of the primal human behavioral traits that permitted such a system to exist and explained how it was possible that "good and decent people" could allow such monstrous cruelties to occur in their midst. (See box, pp. 336–337.)

Thus history provides us with assorted tragedies to work on, and historical analysis never ceases. We try to understand our past to provide therapy for our future.

19 There is a special way that we can learn "the lessons of history." The men and women of the past can become our teachers.

From Aristotle we can learn how to unleash our wonderment upon life; to cherish all the understanding yet achieved by the human race; and, with Ulysses, "To follow knowledge like a sinking star / Beyond the utmost bound of human thought."

From Voltaire we can learn how to restoke the fiery furnaces even in "old age"; to rekindle the feeling of outrage at bigotry and injustice; to start the

I am constantly waiting for things to change for the better; amid all the conflicting parties, I have chosen none. I am in the position of someone who hopes to win first prize in a lottery without having bought a ticket.

Eugene Ionesco

wheels of intellectual action rolling so fast that they shock the conscience of a nation with their clarity and power.

From Nietzsche we can learn about the ironies of having your most eloquent phrases timely ripped from context and misused to further the very causes you spent your life fighting.

From Schopenhauer we can learn something of the courage required to face life when your inner machinery has been tangled and twisted, but you know you must continue to live—meaningfully, usefully, and as honestly as possible.

From Augustine of Tagaste and Søren Kierkegaard we can learn how to accept the burning guilt of being human—all-too-human—and how to transmogrify the pain of the human condition into the service of others (Saint Augustine) and the rediscovery of what it means to be an individual human being (Kierkegaard).

From Francis Bacon and Niccolò Machiavelli we can listen to the agony of exile: being severed from your work, your friends, your livelihood; being challenged to cope creatively with years of solitude; being forced to learn to live with yourself.

History is a nightmare from which I am trying to awake.

James Joyce

From Thomas Aquinas and Albertus Magnus we can learn something of the superhuman discipline required to order vast stores of human knowledge; to record, with superhuman strength, all you know as a legacy to your faith and your future.

From Plato and Einstein we can come to appreciate the "adventures of the mind"—the soaring flights into possible worlds that can excite and enthrall but that remain quite beyond the realities of present perception.

From Galileo we can learn something about mustering "the courage of our convictions" against the pressures of conformity; and, with the knowledge that evidence is on our side, winning through to a personal victory by means of our courage and/or stubbornness.

From Wittgenstein we can learn what it means "to think our own thoughts"—not to repeat words heard and phrases memorized, not to resort to clichés, pretending that they are really our own.

From Spinoza we can learn how to live with final and total disapproval by all those we hold dear to preserve our integrity; to avoid all vindictiveness; to become more gentle and wise as others call us names and ostracize us from their midst.

All these—just from the ranks of "philosophers"—can teach us. Then there are Francis of Assisi, Thomas More, Abraham Lincoln, Beethoven, Helen Keller, Joan of Arc . . .

G. W. F. HEGEL

"Reason Is the Substance of the Universe"

Hegel's philosophical system is so big and so complex that few have understood it. Hegel himself once wrote that "only one man understands me"—presumably himself, in lucid moments—but "even he does not." Sir Malcolm Knox comments that it has always been "easier to revolt against him than to understand him."

His detractors, therefore, see his philosophy as a bewildering metaphysical fantasy. Bertrand Russell writes that almost all his ideas are wrong. Others have judged his work as "pure nonsense" that "will remain as a monument to German stupidity." By contrast, his supporters think of Hegel's philosophy as the timeless work of a tireless genius, revealing the dynamic movement of human thought and history. All agree that he is one of the architects of modern thought and that the twentieth century cannot be understood apart from him.

Georg Wilhelm Friedrich Hegel—happily, he usually signed his name just "Hegel"—was born in Stuttgart in 1770. His father, with whom he was never close, was a minor official in the state ministry of finance. His mother was an educated woman who directed his earliest studies toward the classics—he read Latin and Greek literature when he stayed home sick from school—but she died when Hegel was thirteen. His classical education was continued at grammar school, and he was fluent in Greek and Latin all his life.

At eighteen he enrolled in the theological school at the University of Tübingen to carry out a program in theology and philosophy, and did well. His religious background was Protestant, and he seriously considered entering the ministry, but he lacked style if not substance—his audiences were turned off by a weak voice and awkward gestures. At college he was sociable and never lacked for close friends of both sexes. A fellow student observed that "a certain joviality and tavern ease . . . made him pleasant company." Intellectually he was looked upon as a bohemian *lumen obscurum* of uncertain promise. He was a quiet, industrious student. He had begun early to write down his own thoughts at great length, though he published nothing. For the most part he was remembered from his college days for playing cards, drinking beer, dancing, discovering girls, read-

The real is rational, and the rational is real.

The world looks rational to those who look at it rationally.

Reason is the substance of the universe. . . . The design of the world is absolutely rational.

The history of the world is not the theatre of happiness; periods of happiness are blank pages in it, for they are periods of harmony.

ing voraciously, filling volumes of notebooks with notes, griping about dull teachers, and cutting classes. He graduated in 1793 with a master of arts degree in philosophy.

One must eat, so Hegel became a private tutor for a well-to-do family in Bern, Switzerland, and continued to write. He composed a Life of Christ, fashionably and precociously, but burned the manuscript. At twenty-nine he received a small inheritance from his father, and he felt secure enough to apply for a job as instructor in philosophy at the University of Jena. He had apparently found that "ein gutes Bier" could be bought there. He taught there for six years. The income was meager, but he was working at what he loved. This was the period of his intellectual maturing.

His lectures were a challenge to his students. His style was quite unimpressive . . . at first. All his life Hegel alienated the majority of his students as well as the general public, but there was an authenticity in his intensity that was absorbing. Though his speech was halting, a listener who thought along with him began to realize that he was witnessing a highly creative mind at the moment of creation: This, of course, puts off those who can't enter empathetically into the process and those who must be entertained; but Hegel persistently captured the intellects who could march in rhythm with his unique mind.

In 1806 Napoleon vanquished the Prussian army at Jena and brought war to Hegel's doorstep. Having finished a great manuscript only the night before the Battle of Jena, he gathered up its pages and fled the city. Early in 1807 Hegel became the editor of a newspaper in Bamberg, an interim job that supported him well. He worked feverishly to publish the daily news, which undoubtedly kept him in touch with everyday events and forced him to write in a clear, factual style that people could understand—good training for a prolific writer who was later to go astray.

In 1808 Hegel became headmaster of a grammar school at Nuremberg where, among other duties, he taught philosophy to teenage boys. When he was called on to fill in for sick teachers, "the students were especially surprised when, without ado, he continued the instruction not only in Greek and other such subjects but also in differential and integral calculus," in the sciences, or whatever was called for.

Hegel was married to Marie von Tucher in the fall of 1811. He was forty-one, she was nineteen. There is a hint that this is one of the rare times when he acknowledged the nonrational: he courted her with poetry, spoke of love, and wrote tender letters; but he soon retreated to the left-brained world of logical thought.

At Nuremberg Hegel published at last: a three-volume work entitled *Science of Logic*. So abstract that it was undecipherable for anyone but specialists, it emerged on the academic scene with an impact that astonished everyone but Hegel. He was soon offered several professorships and accepted a position at the University of Heidelberg. It was his first salaried teaching position; he was forty-six. He taught there two years. More secure now, he wrote voluminously, and published a second huge work, *Encyclopedia of Philosophical Sciences*. His stature increased rapidly, and in 1818 he was invited to the University of Berlin, the most prestigious academic institution in Germany.

Hegel's life traced a familiar pattern that perhaps illustrates a principal aspect of his doctrine of dialectic change. As a student he was a thoroughgoing radical, fiery in his political passions, vigorous and vitriolic in his social pronouncements. He spoke excitedly about freedom, justice, and equality. He helped found a club to discuss political ideas, supported the French Revolution, and, one Sunday morning, marched to a meadow to plant a "freedom tree." In religion he broke with all orthodoxies, revising the very essence out of traditional Christianity. In philosophy he disowned

Kant's epistemology. All in all, he thought new thoughts.

But by the time he reached the pinnacle of prestige, he had become an archconservative and considered the current crop of young radicals to be misguided dreamers. After moving so long at the center of criticism and controversy, he longed for peace; by the time he arrived in Berlin there was an air of tiredness about him. His outlook was marked by a lack of new ideas; the creative fires were burned out. He wrote: "Finally, after forty years of immeasurable confusion, an old heart might rejoice to see an end of it all."

Even as a youth Hegel had a prematurely aged face; he was called the "old man" at the university. By all accounts he was a late-bloomer who matured slowly in self-awareness. He was a naive and simple man, without affectation; genial and good-natured, without charm and social grace. He had a biting sense of humor. He labored with enormous energy and infinite patience. He avoided excitement, adventure, and strong passions. He was the prototypical absent-minded professor.

Hegel's published works are written in an impersonal style, highly abstract and abstruse. An earlier style, natural and clear, was transmogrified into tortured didactic prose by his perceptions of what constituted "proper" academic style. His thought exhibits an extraordinary range of scholarship and learning; the penetration is brilliant; the range of his vision is matched only by that of other intellects such as Voltaire, Goethe, and Nietzsche. To express new ideas he originated much of his own terminology.

Philosophy of History and several smaller works were reconstructed from students' notes and published posthumously.

✦

The key to Hegel's philosophy is his famous phrase, "The real is rational, and the rational is real." To understand this watchword is to open the door onto his system.

What is it exactly that can be "rational"? The answer is: **minds** can be rational. So Hegel is saying that **thinking** is in some sense real. Hegel believed that he was the first thinker in all of history to have seen and properly located the essence of what is real in the Universe, namely, the mind of God. The mind of God is the essence of what is real. And this mind of God is pure thought.

To put it differently: God is the essence of the cosmos, and the cosmos is reason. God is Reason. As Hegel put it, "Reason is the Substance of the Universe."

So Hegel's philosophy has two important elements: God's thinking processes, which are perfectly rational, and mortals' thinking processes, which are striving for rationality. When we humans succeed in being rational, then we are thinking God's thoughts, appropriating his rationality. Our human goal should be to grow forever toward rationality so that we are closer to the Absolute Mind—which is God thinking rational thoughts.

Where can we discover this divine rationality in action? On the plane of human history. Hegel, therefore, became one of the great philosophers of history, developing a conceptual system by which we can understand what history is doing—where it's been, where it's going, and how we fit into it.

This essence of thinking, Hegel says, is change. All thinking moves in terms of a three-beat rhythm: thesis → antithesis → synthesis. All thinking starts with the idea (thesis), develops its opposite idea (antithesis), then works these opposites together into a new whole (synthesis). Down through history, thought follows this three-beat pattern, each synthesis becoming, in turn, another thesis. This three-beat dialectical rhythm—thought always completing itself—is the movement of history. Therefore, the essence of thought is continual change and growth toward completion and wholeness.

What experience and history teach is this—that people and governments never have learned anything from history, or acted on principles deduced from it.

Pure Being and Nothing are the same.

The history of the world is none other than the progress of the consciousness of freedom.

It is of the nature of truth to prevail when its time has come.

The insight to which philosophy should help us is that the actual world is as it ought to be. . . . God rules the world; the content of his government, the execution of his plan, is world history; to grasp this is the task of the philosophy of world history.

***A philosophy is its own time apprehended in thought* (so ist auch die Philosophie, ihre Zeit in Gedanken erfasst).**

On Hegel:
"At the end of the nineteenth century and in the early decades of the twentieth, Hegel was perhaps the most influential, the most revered, and the most closely studied philosopher of the western world."

Errol E. Harris

On Hegel:
"Hegel is at the root of that complex we call the modern world. . . . [But] Hegel is fast becoming a remote thinker, and the age he lived in is beginning to look like the prehistory of mankind."

Franco Lombardi

The purpose of history, therefore, is to enable continued growth and change to take place. History is the stage on which the highest human faculty—reason—can develop and grow. Since the beginnings of human intelligence, history has been a continual movement **from** states of incompleteness—where we were driven by animalistic instincts—**toward** completeness—where we will increasingly manifest intelligence and unity.

Thus, as history moves, there is inevitable progress toward what the mind most wants—wholeness. All history is moving **from** chaos, disconnectedness, and smallness, **toward** order, connectedness, and unity. Insofar as we humans are rational, we are moving with the tide of history. More than that, however, we are thinking (and manifesting) God's thoughts. Man and God, as it were, are working together toward a time when human self-consciousness will be complete. We will possess perfect knowledge, perfect intelligence, and a perfect understanding. At that point God's thoughts and humanity's thoughts will be One—that is, identical—and humanity will have fulfilled its destiny. The rational in people will be identical with the rationality of the universe. God's thinking is our thinking; our thinking is God's. The Real is rational; the rational is Real.

Hegel's philosophy accomplished several things. First, it went a long way toward laying the intellectual foundations of an historical optimism; if we feel we are working irrevocably with the angels toward the Ultimate Goal, then life is not in vain and we can be infused with a superlative *joie de vivre.* The anthropocentric optimism is cosmic: "The fast-bound substance of the universe has no power within it capable of withstanding the courage of man's knowledge; it must give way before him, and lay bare before his eyes, and for his enjoyment, its riches and its depths."

Second, Hegel, in his way, effectively annihilated two centuries of epistemological loneliness: we no longer perceive ourselves to be minds caught in physical bodies, able to experience nothing but our own experience and doomed to absolute ignorance of reality-in-itself. Hegel concludes that we do apprehend what is real every time we think rationally; we **know** the Real. When we think God's thoughts we are not merely "apprehending" the real: we have **become** the Real. We are not thinking **about** God's thoughts; we are **thinking** God's thoughts.

Third, Hegel developed such an all-inclusive schematic that all events could be reinterpreted and included in the dialectical process. Wars, revolutions, tragedies of all sorts—these were as integral and necessary a part of the historical logistics as benign and beneficial events. The Absolute Mind-in-History works via the operation of opposites: good interacts with evil, stability with instability, war with peace, and so forth; peace and war interact to move forward to a new synthesis. Crisis times are times of great accomplishments that propel history forward to greater things.

To Hegel history is the stage on which change must take place; and change is always moving from the incomplete toward the complete—toward wholeness, unity, and freedom.

✦

A cholera epidemic—Europe's first—reached Berlin in 1831. Hegel sought safety for his family by leaving the city for the summer, but when he returned in the fall he was immediately stricken and died only a day later—on November 14. He was sixty-one.

✦

Reflections

1 What is the goal of "the philosophy of history"? The question we all want answered is: Does history have meaning? And if so, what is that meaning? If we give an affirmative answer, then we face a prior question: What are the sources of meaning? But prior still: How could we go about gathering evidence to find out if history has meaning? How would you respond to these questions?

2 What does the word *history* refer to? If the past is "dead," how can there be history? (Is the past "dead"?) How does the historian go about "doing history"—does he recall it, read and record it, research it and discover it, invent it, create it, imagine it? Is history better thought of as a science or as an art?

3 Having made a comparative study of twenty-seven civilizations, what common patterns did Toynbee find? Do those patterns constitute "the meaning of history"? What was the source of those patterns? In the last analysis, do the patterns described by Toynbee tell us where we are in this first decade of the twenty-first century, and where we are going? (You might enjoy browsing through portions of Toynbee's monumental twelve-volume work, *A Study of History*. You might begin by perusing some of the passages in Vol. X, say, pp. 213–242, or pp. 126–144.)

4 What do you think of the interpretive framework that the Deuteronomic historian placed upon the tribal stories of the Book of Judges? Could this framework be placed on any war—World War II, for instance, or the Vietnam war? The Gulf war? Try it.

5 Saint Augustine is considered the first great philosopher of history because he was the first Western thinker who tried to explain in depth the how and the why of history's "meaning." Do you accept his interpretation of the fall of the city of Rome? Could Augustine's basic framework be applied to the fall of Constantinople to the Ottoman Turks in 1453? Or to the fall of Paris to the Nazis in 1940? What human need lies behind Augustine's towering effort to explain? Do you and I, today, still need such explanations?

6 From what origin, according to Hegel, does history derive meaning? What are the purpose and final goal of human history? What is the role of the individual in the Hegelian view of history? What sort of evidence could be mustered for or against Hegel's interpretation of history?

7 According to Marx, what is the source of the "inexorable laws" that govern the development of human history? What is the role of the individual in the Marxian view of history? Marx has been linked to the doctrine of "inevitable progress" that was in the air during the latter part of the nineteenth century. Is there "inevitable progress" in Marx's doctrine? Is inevitable progress inherent in history? (Is inevitable regress inherent in history?)

8 Compare and contrast Hegel's "dialectical idealism" with Marx's "dialectical materialism." Both have profoundly influenced the modern world. Which one is right? Could both be right? Is neither right? (Must a doctrine be "right" to be as influential as these doctrines have been?)

9 This chapter summarizes three points of agreement shared by most philosophers of history. Note them and ask yourself if you agree.

10 Hegel once said that the only thing that we learn from history is that we never learn from history. **Can** we learn from history? If so, what do we learn? And from whom (or what) do we learn it—from individuals, nations, religious societies, institutions, civilizations? Or from individual blunders, or political or military mistakes? Or from examples of courage, heroic transcendence, growth into "greatness," personal achievement? Or what?

Laws
Conscience

5-2

Every society is burdened with more than just one set of rules that represent different values and concerns. Political philosophers and ethical theorists have tried (almost in vain) to show why an individual should obey one set of rules over some other set of rules, especially when some of the rules, if judged by rational or moral criteria, are not very good rules. Adherents of all religions find they must follow rules that conflict with temporal authority. This chapter suggests that the dilemma is eternal and considers some theoretical ways of resolving the conflict. The problem becomes acute, of course, during times like the Vietnam War, when human conscience must confront the demands of the state.

Conflicting Loyalties

1 All human societies possessing a modicum of individual freedom develop a wide spectrum of strongly held convictions about the structure and power of human society—"strongly held" because it is the human state, after all, that exercises ultimate temporal control over human destiny.

When blindness is universal, casting stones is not a good idea.

Joan Morrone

There exists also in such societies a fundamental tension between those who would obey different sets of laws. Men without freedom are spared this condition; those belonging to primitive tribes or rigidly authoritarian states are subject to but a single set of laws. But in freer societies numerous systems of laws burden the individual by claiming to have overriding jurisdiction. The individual is constrained to obey them all!

This predicament is analogous to what we find in ethics. If one is subject to only a single moral code, then one is spared the complex decisions of free people who must make decisions among sundry codes demanding their loyalty.

[Speaking of the American people] "No longer innocent, but not yet wise."

Charles Osgood

Our Western experience has been an ongoing conflict of loyalties. Western society derives its deepest commitment from the scriptural concept of covenant that binds the community of the faithful to the laws of God. For well over a thousand years before Christ—indeed, from the time when Moses defied Egyptian law to lead the Children of Israel into a covenant relationship with Yahweh—humanity has struggled with the tension between obedience to the "laws of God" and the "laws of man." For all those who live under the divine mandate, their final loyalty has been to God; and civilization's mundane systems of law have, by comparison, only a weak, secondary claim upon their loyalty.

2 This tension between loyalties can be felt in the following passages. First, the case (often implicit) for a higher law:

> I think we all have moral obligations to obey just laws. On the other hand, I think that we have moral obligations to disobey unjust laws because non-cooperation with evil is just as much a moral obligation as cooperation with good.
>
> MARTIN LUTHER KING, JR.

To live is to awake in bonds, as Gulliver in Lilliput.
JEAN-PAUL SARTRE

> [If the law] is of such a nature that it requires you to be the agent of injustice to another, then, I say, break the law.
>
> HENRY DAVID THOREAU

> When the law impels one against love, it ceases and should no longer be a law. . . . You have need of the law, that love may be manifested; but if it cannot be kept without injury to the neighbor, God wants us to suspend and ignore the law.
>
> MARTIN LUTHER

> One sabbath while he [Jesus] was walking through the grainfields, his disciples plucked some of the ears of grain and, milling the grain in their hands—which was against the Law of Moses—they ate them.
>
> Some of the Pharisees said to him, "Look at them! Why are they doing what is illegal on the sabbath?"
>
> He replied simply, "The sabbath was made for man, not man for the sabbath."
>
> But those who knew the Law went away angry.
>
> *Mark* 2:23–24, 27–28
> (paraphrased)

3 The practical—and pragmatic—side of the dilemma is stated with great clarity in the following passages:

> An ordered society cannot exist if every man may determine which laws he will obey, . . . that only "just" laws need be obeyed and that every man is free to determine for himself the question of "justness."
>
> LEWIS F. POWELL, JR.

> Everyone must obey the authorities that are over him, for no authority can exist without the permission of God; the existing authorities have been established by him, so that anyone who resists the authorities sets himself in opposition to what God has ordained, and those who oppose him will bring down judgment upon themselves. The man who does right has nothing to fear from the magistrates. . . . You must obey them, therefore, not only to escape God's wrath, but as a matter of principle, just as you pay your taxes. . . . Pay them all that is due them.
>
> SAINT PAUL (*Romans* 13:1–2, 5)

> Resistance on the part of the people to the supreme legislative power of The State is in no case legitimate; for it is only by submission to the universal legislative will, that a condition of law and order is possible. . . . It is the duty of the people to bear any abuse of the supreme power, even though it should be considered to be unbearable. And the reason is that any resistance of the highest legislative authority can never but be contrary to the law, and must even be regarded as tending to destroy the whole legal constitution.
>
> IMMANUEL KANT

I think an artistic boycott is wrong. It stops communication, and communication is what changes culture.

LINDA RONSTADT

> Submit to all human authority, for the Master's sake; to the emperor, as supreme, and to governors, as sent by him to punish evil-doers, and to encourage those who do right.
>
> SAINT PETER (*1 Peter* 2:13–15)

We give credibility to unjust laws by obeying them.

ALAN BOESAK
(protesting apartheid laws in South Africa, August 24, 1989)

4 Since this tension is rooted in religion, we would like to be able to turn to a founder of Western religion—to Jesus, for instance—for guidance; but we do so in vain. When forced to comment upon the dilemma, he merely mystifies the question:

> Teacher, we know that you are honest and are not swayed by men; for you do not defer to the worldly positions of men, but truly teach the way of God. Tell us then, what you think. Is it lawful to pay taxes to the state, or not?
>
> But sensing their hypocritical intent, he merely said, "Bring me a coin, and let me look at it."
>
> So they brought him a silver denarius.
>
> Then he asked: "Whose picture and inscription is this?"
>
> They said, "Caesar's."
>
> So Jesus replied: "Then render to Caesar what is Caesar's since Caesar's picture is on the coin; and render to God the things that are God's."
>
> Having failed to entrap him as they planned, they went away angry.
>
> *Mark* 12:14–17
> (paraphrased)

"Because politics is the art of the possible, it appeals only to second-rate minds. The first-raters, he claimed, were only interested in the impossible."

"SHEIK ABDULLAH"
ARTHUR C. CLARKE
The Fountains of Paradise

GOOD LAWS AND BAD LAWS

5 The case for making a distinction between good and bad laws is well stated by King, Thoreau, Luther, and others. No matter how strongly one advocates lawful obedience to the state and its laws, it is inevitable that some laws will turn out to be bad ones. Lawmakers are not only human—which is sufficient cause for having a few bad laws—but a percentage of them will always be parochial in their interests, shortsighted or dead wrong in their opinion of what constitutes justice, mentally out of touch with reality, and woefully uninformed on the nature of values and value judgments (and after all, laws are the legislation of human values). These statements can be made with some certainty simply because the leaders of men are not immune to the epistemic and emotional problems shared by the populace as a whole.

We have met the enemy, and they are partly right.

ANTHONY CAMPOLO

Therefore, **in any legal system,** it is quite possible to point to laws that range from the mildly unjust to the callously inhuman, and such laws should produce a feeling of outrage in individuals who are victimized by them or see others hurt by them. More important, perhaps, is the fact that unless laws are periodically challenged—as the authors of the American system recognized—

National Socialists say: Legality is that which does the German people good; illegality is that which harms the German people.

WILHELM FRICK
(Nazi Minister of the Interior)

One of the big purposes of the Bill of Rights is to keep the government off our backs.
ARTHUR MILLER

then they don't get improved. In 1787 Thomas Jefferson said, "God forbid, we should ever be twenty years without such a rebellion." Elsewhere he elaborated: "What country can preserve its liberties, if its rulers are not warned from time to time, that this people preserve the spirit of resistance? Let them take arms. . . . The tree of liberty must be refreshed from time to time, with the blood of patriots and tyrants." Among mature people criticism is cherished; it is through the assessment of wise criticism that more just laws can be formulated and antiquated laws updated. Also, it is through open criticism that the selfish interests of those in power can be rapidly brought to the attention of enough citizens who can object and, if necessary, dissent before a deeper tyranny sets in.

6 We have another tradition in this country which is in danger of passing away; dissent. The responsibility to object. We might all do well to remember in these days of national distemper the comment of Pastor Niemoeller a quarter of a century ago in Nazi Germany. "They came after the Jews, and I was not a Jew, so I did not object. Then they came after the Catholics, and I was not a Catholic, so I did not object. Then they came after the trade-unionists, and I was not a trade-unionist, so I did not object. And then they came after me, and there was no one left to object."

"SENATOR STOWE"
The Bold Ones (NBC-TV)

LOYALTY TO HIGHER AUTHORITY

7 Our Western (Judeo-Christian) legal tradition takes the form of a hierarchy of laws—a sort of jurisdictional totem pole—with a clear order of precedence.

Local laws must defer to higher and wider laws. Thus, in case of conflict, the laws of a village or city must give way to state laws. State laws are "higher"; they take precedence. It can be validly argued that in specific areas of concern, only local laws can be truly relevant to local conditions. But populations are mobile; individuals are travelers. If there existed only local laws serving the self-interests of innumerable small jurisdictions, it just wouldn't work. In matters that affect larger populations over larger areas, wider laws must prevail.

By the same principle, federal laws generally take precedence over state laws. Neither cities nor states can be allowed to enact laws that would nourish their limited interests at the expense of the larger society of which they are but a part. Wider law must prevail if there is to be equal application of law—that is, if there is to be justice.

8 At this point the covenant principle upon which Western civilization is grounded must come in: that there is a higher and more universal law than that of any sovereign state. For twenty-seven hundred years now, the Jews of the Dispersion who were carried off from their homeland have considered the Law of Moses to be higher than the laws of any state in which they lived. In the Roman Empire the fierce loyalty of Jews to their monotheistic faith won them exemption from the worship of Caesar; they alone were officially free of obligations to pour libations to the emperor's *genius* and make offerings to him as divine head of state. As Christianity grew in the early empire, some argued that Christians were Jews and should therefore share the exemption; but the majority of Chris-

The surest way to corrupt a young man is to teach him to esteem more highly those who think alike than those who think differently.
FRIEDRICH NIETZSCHE

The Sun and the Moon
Pope Innocent III: Church and State

The Creator of the universe set up two great luminaries in the firmament of heaven; the greater light to rule the day, the lesser light to rule the night. In the same way for the firmament of the universal Church, which is spoken of as heaven, he appointed two great dignities; the greater to bear rule over souls (these being, as it were, days), the lesser to bear rule over bodies (these being, as it were, nights). These dignities are the pontifical authority and the royal power. Furthermore, the moon derives her light from the sun, and is in truth inferior to the sun in both size and quality, in position as well as effect. In the same way the royal power derives its dignity from the pontifical authority: and the more closely it cleaves to the sphere of that authority the less is the light with which it is adorned; the further it is removed, the more it increases in splendor.

Sicut Universitatis Conditor
Ep. I. 401, October 1198

tians declared emphatically that Christianity was not a branch of Judaism. As Christians established themselves to be a separate sect, they were then obliged to pay respects to the divine Caesar.

But like the Jews, they could not in good conscience do so. The Christians were therefore "disloyal"; they were considered dangerous subversives—"bad citizens." During the years of persecution that followed, the Christians became the main body of conscientious objectors against paying unjust allegiance to Caesar and his state; their highest loyalty was reserved for their God and his laws. For this stand Christians were accused officially of atheism and anarchy: atheism because they refused to worship the state-approved gods, and anarchy because they were "outlaws" who refused to take an oath of allegiance to their government.

It was this refusal to accept "man's laws" that sent Christians into the arena and put them to the sword.

The true patriot is one who gives his highest loyalty not to his country as it is but to his own best conceptions of what it can and ought to be.
Albert Camus

9 In broad terms, the allegiance to a "higher authority" has taken two forms: (1) loyalty to an institution considered to have divine authority over the state; and (2) loyalty to "God's law" as personally understood—by revelation, by "spiritual knowledge" (*gnosis*), or by conscience.

As the Roman Catholic Church developed and became the universal authority in Europe, the papacy pressed its claim to be the supreme power over all temporal authority; for the pope was the "Vicar of Christ" on Earth and the church was "the City of God."

Since Christianity was established as the state religion of Rome in AD 385, this dual claim upon their loyalty has perplexed Western citizens. Continuing through the Middle Ages, the Renaissance and the Reformation, and into the modern world, there has been a tug-of-war between temporal authorities—who would diminish the church's power ("God's laws") and increase their own—and the papacy—which would extend its authority and limit worldly governments ("man's laws"). Individuals found themselves caught in this power struggle.

"You've got to forget the nobler sentiments if you want to live. (Pause. . .) Funny thing—survival."
"British Soldier"
Play Dirty

"I carried out my orders. . . . Where would we have been if everyone had thought things out in those days?"

ADOLF EICHMANN

A HIGHER PATRIOTISM

Not that I love country less, but humanity more, do I now and here plead the cause of a higher patriotism. I cannot forget that we are men by a more sacred bond than we are citizens,—that we are children of a common Father more than we are Americans. . . . Thus do seeming diversities of nations—separated by accident of language, mountain, river, or sea—all disappear, and the multitudinous tribes of the globe stand forth as members of one human family, where strife is treason to heaven, and all war is nothing else than *civil* war.

SENATOR CHARLES SUMNER (1845)

The supreme confrontation between the claimants occurred on January 28, 1077. Pope Gregory VII had stripped all power from Henry IV of Germany with a decree of excommunication. To regain his kingdom Henry crossed the Alps in winter and knelt in the snow before the gate of the castle of Canossa, into which the pope had retreated. Henry repented and after waiting penitently for three days, the pope released him from excommunication and restored him to power.

The second form of allegiance to a higher power is allegiance to the word of God as known personally, to one's own conscience, or to a set of ethical ideas or norms by which one judges the quality of actual laws. Such a position can be theistic and/or ethical, but in any case it commands the highest commitment of the individual. Whatever the path by which one arrives at such a position, it often **feels** hypocritical to the individual to obey bad (unjust laws) when it has been seen clearly in ethical reflections the just laws that should prevail.

This stand was epitomized by Martin Luther in 1521 at the Council of Worms, where he cried out passionately and sincerely, "My conscience is captive to the Word of God. . . . To go against conscience is neither right nor safe. God help me. Amen."

10 Pope Boniface VIII issued the papal bull *Unam sanctam* in 1302 to define clearly the superiority of God's laws—as embodied here in the Roman papacy—over man's laws—which in this case were represented by the royal heads of England and France. This bull still stands as the most extreme claim of the Church to stand in judgment over the state.

> We are obliged by the faith to believe and hold—and we do firmly believe and sincerely confess—that there is one Holy Catholic and Apostolic Church, and that outside this Church there is neither salvation nor remission of sins. . . .
>
> And we learn from the words of the Gospel that in this Church and in her power are two swords, the spiritual and the temporal. . . . Both are in the power of the Church, the spiritual sword and the material. But the latter is to be used for the Church, the former by her; the former by the priest, the latter by kings and captains but at the will and by the permission of the priest. The one sword, then, should be under the other, and temporal authority subject to spiritual. . . .
>
> Thus, concerning the Church and her power, is the prophecy of Jeremiah fulfilled, "See, I have this day set thee over the nations and over the kingdoms," etc. If, therefore, the earthly power err, it shall be judged by a greater. . . . Furthermore we

"I was there to follow orders, not to think."

JOHN DEAN
(Watergate testimony)

declare, state, define and pronounce that it is altogether necessary to salvation for every human creature to be subject to the Roman pontiff.

We must be entirely clear that law is not God. It has always been a basic Christian conviction that there are times when a Christian ought to break the law.

EUGENE CARSON BLAKE

OBEDIENCE TO THE RULE OF LAW

11 Associate Justice Lewis Powell presents persuasively the case for absolute obedience to duly constituted authority: laws must be obeyed, for if each person were permitted to decide which laws were good and which were bad, social chaos would necessarily result. For who is there among us who is able to determine just from unjust laws? And on what criteria could such judgments be made? Wouldn't it be inevitable that every political crank and religious fanatic—not to mention emotionally immature rebels of all ages—would decide that all the laws were "unjust" that didn't cater to his or her own self-centered interests?

This is precisely the position taken by Socrates when his old and dear friend Crito urged him to escape from prison the day before his execution. Socrates awoke before dawn to find Crito sitting silently beside him in his cell; he had apparently made all necessary arrangements for an escape.

But Socrates had already made up his mind and refused to flee. He patiently attempted to make Crito understand his reasoning.

> Look at it in this way. Suppose that while we were preparing to run away from here (or however one should describe it) the Laws and Constitution of Athens were to come and confront us and ask this question: "Now, Socrates, what are you proposing to do? Can you deny that by this act which you are contemplating you intend, so far as you have the power, to destroy us, the Laws, and the whole State as well? Do you imagine that a city can continue to exist and not be turned upside down, if the legal judgements which are pronounced in it have no force but are nullified and destroyed by private persons?"—how shall we answer this question, Crito, and others of the same kind? . . . Shall we say, "Yes, I do intend to destroy the laws, because the State wronged me by passing a faulty judgment at my trial"? Is this to be our answer, or what? . . .
>
> Supposing the Laws say "Was there provision for this in the agreement between you and us, Socrates? Or did you undertake to abide by whatever judgements the State pronounced? . . . Do you not realize . . . that if you cannot persuade your country you must do whatever it orders, and patiently submit to any punishment that it imposes, whether it be flogging or imprisonment? And if it leads you out to war, to be wounded or killed, you must comply, and it is right that you should do so; you must not give way or retreat or abandon your position. Both in war and in the lawcourts and everywhere else you must do whatever your city and your country commands, or else persuade it in accordance with universal justice. . . ."—What shall we say to this, Crito?—that what the Laws say is true, or not?
>
> PLATO
> *Crito*

For, as among the powers in man's society the greater authority is obeyed in preference to the lesser, so must God above all.

SAINT AUGUSTINE

THE PERSONAL DILEMMA

12 The problem of obedience to law might be visualized as an ellipse with two foci. Near one end of the ellipse is the question of human freedom. All of us want freedom, and we want **more** freedom; but as the number of problematic persons

in our society increases, the more regulation is required and the less freedom we can enjoy.

The other focus in the ellipse is one's assessment of human nature. If one is basically optimistic about humanity and believes people to be trustworthy, then one will assume that we humans can use freedom constructively and will not need punctilious systems of laws to tell us what to do and not to do. But if one distrusts human nature, convinced that it is fundamentally evil, then one must conclude that a complex system of laws is necessary to keep this selfish nature in line and coerce a semblance of order.

The Milgram Experiment

Sometimes an event occurs during our lifetime that leaves an impression that is both indelible and puzzling. For me that event was the widespread participation of the German people in a system of death camps that destroyed millions of innocent men, women and children. The hapless victims were shot, gassed and burned in ovens.

These deeds were carried out by a people who were as civilized as any people in the world. How was it possible for them to act so cruelly? Did their behavior reveal a potential that is present in all of us? As a social psychologist whose job is to look into the why and how of human behavior, I decided to explore the response of ordinary people to immoral orders.

In order to explore behavior, social psychologists often rely on an important tool, the experiment. Although experiments in chemistry and physics often involve shiny equipment, flasks and electronic gear, an experiment in social psychology smacks much more of dramaturgy or theater. The experimenter carefully constructs a scenario to focus on certain aspects of behavior, a scenario in which the end is unknown and is completed by the experimental subject. The psychologist tries to create circumstances that will allow him to look at the behavior very carefully, note what he observed, and study its causes.

Imagine you had answered an advertisement to take part in a study of learning. . . . First, you are greeted by a man in a gray technician's coat; he introduces you to a second volunteer and says you are both about to take part in a scientific experiment. He says it is to test whether the use of punishment improves the ability to learn.

You draw lots to see who is to be the teacher and who the learner. You turn out to be the teacher, and the other fellow, the learner. Then you see the learner strapped into a chair and electrodes placed on his wrist. You are told that, when the learner makes a mistake in the lesson, his punishment will be an electric shock.

As teacher, you are seated in front of an impressive-looking instrument, a shock generator. Its essential feature is a line of switches that range from 15 volts to 450 volts, and a set of written labels that goes from slight shock to moderate shock, strong shock, very strong shock, and so on through XXX—danger, severe shock.

Your job, the experimenter explains to you, is to teach the learner (who, unknown to [you] is a confederate and does not actually receive the shocks) a simple

Around these two foci—and they **are** inside a single ellipse—turns the question of obedience to all law: to obey or not to obey. The mature, more fully actualized persons want to guide their lives solely by a few basic principles; they become restive and may chafe bitterly under irrelevant restraints upon their existence. For them, restraints are not needed: they would do what is right anyway! By contrast, however, most human beings appear unable to experience very much freedom without harming others; we are unable to live with one another peacefully without having our behavior guided and restrained by specific regulations touching all aspects of our lives.

The wrong questions appear to be the right questions because other people are asking them too . . .

THOMAS HORA

word-pair test. You read a list of words to him, such as blue day, nice girl, fat neck, etc., and he has to indicate by means of an answer box which words were originally paired together. If he gets a correct answer, you move on to the next pair. But if he makes a mistake, you are instructed to give him an electric shock, starting with 15 volts. And you are told to increase the shock one step each time he makes an error. In the course of the experiment the "victim" emits cries of pain and demands to be set free, but the experimenter orders you to continue. The question is: how far will you proceed on the shock generator before you turn to the experimenter and refuse to go on?

Before carrying out the experiment, I wanted to know how people thought they would behave in this situation, and so I asked them to predict their own performance. I posed the question to several groups: psychiatrists, psychologists, and ordinary workers. They all said virtually the same thing: almost no one would go to the end.

But in reality the results were very different. Despite the fact that many subjects experience stress, and protest to the experimenter, a substantial proportion continue to the last shock on the generator. Many subjects obeyed the experimenter no matter how vehement the pleading of the person being shocked, no matter how painful the shocks seemed to be, and no matter how much the victim pleaded to be let out. This was seen time and again in our studies and has been observed in several universities where the experiment has been repeated.

But there is more to the experiment than this simple demonstration of obedience. Most of our energy went into systematically changing the factors in this situation to see which ones increased obedience and which led to greater defiance. . . . How a person behaves depends not only on his "character" but also on the precise situational pressures acting on him.

When the experiments were published, opinion about them was sharply divided. . . . The experiments that I had hoped would deepen our understanding of how people yield to authority became themselves the focus of controversy.

But the problem of authority remains. We cannot have society without some structure of authority, and every society must inculcate a habit of obedience in its citizens. Yet these experiments show that many people do not have the resources to resist authority, even when they are directed to act inhumanely against an innocent victim. The experiments pose anew the age-old problem: what is the correct balance between individual initiative and social authority? They illuminate in a concrete way what happens when obedience is unrestrained by conscience.

STANLEY MILGRAM
TV Guide, August 21, 1976

When a legal distinction is determined . . . between night and day, childhood and maturity, or any other extremes, a point has to be fixed or a line has to be drawn, or gradually picked out by successive decisions, to mark where the change takes place. Looked at by itself without regard to the necessity behind it, the line or point seems arbitrary. It might as well be a little more to the one side or the other. But when it is seen that a line or point there must be, and that there is no mathematical or logical way of fixing it precisely, the decision of the legislature must be accepted unless we can say that it is very wide of any reasonable mark.

OLIVER WENDELL HOLMES

13 The dilemma between principles and law has tormented many great souls. Saint Paul, for instance, tried diligently to follow the 613 precepts of the Jewish Law but only felt more guilty because he could not measure up to its numerous demands. In the end, he found peace only by abandoning the **Law** of Moses and accepting the **principle** of "justification by faith" in Jesus as the Christ.

Similarly, Martin Luther tried to make legalistic Roman Catholic laws work to his benefit, but he found peace only by following Paul's lead and committing his life to a single principle: "salvation by faith alone."

It is worth noting that Hinduism has provided, within the parameters of acceptable religion, several systems to meet different needs. The "Ways of Liberation" are designed to accomplish this. The "Way of Works" (*Karma Mārga*) specifies innumerable rites and duties that the worshiper has only to perform to gain good karma. It makes few intellectual demands. It's a matter of **doing;** one must meticulously perform the actions prescribed by the laws. This is the path chosen by a large majority of Hindus. By contrast, there is the "Way of Knowledge" (*Jñāna Mārga*). This is philosophical Hinduism, the way of study and meditation that will lead the mind out of the errors that produce human misery. This is the way of liberation for only a few who have the capacity for discipline and abstract reflection.

14 The dilemma between a few guiding principles and numerous laws was explored by Joseph Klausner, an Orthodox Jewish historian, in a scholarly study entitled *Jesus of Nazareth* (1907, English translation, 1925). In the squabble between the Pharisees, who held firmly to the letter of the Mosaic Law, and Jesus, who deliberately disregarded Jewish law, Klausner concludes that, in the final analysis, the Pharisees were right. Judaism could never accept such a contemptuous attitude toward the Law.

> For the Jews their religion was more than simple belief and more than simple moral guidance: it was a *way of life*—all life was embraced in their religion. A people does not endure on a foundation of general human faith and morality; it needs a "practical religiousness," a ceremonial form of religion which shall embody religious ideas and also crown every-day life with a halo of sanctity.

It hasn't been done yet, so they haven't got around to prohibiting it.

Destination Moon

By undermining the Law of Moses, Klausner is saying, Jesus would have destroyed the Jewish nation. Jesus' intentions are not to be inpugned, "but it is unquestionable that throughout his entire teaching there is nothing that can serve to the upkeep of the state or serve towards the maintenance of order in the existing world."

There were Jewish scholars long before Jesus who were capable of formulating the **essence** of the Law of Moses in one or two general principles. Hillel, an elder contemporary of Jesus, said: "What is hateful to thyself do not to thy neighbor: this is the whole Law, the rest is commentary: go and learn it." But such rabbis who **saw** and honored the spirit of the Law never dispensed with the literal requirements of the Law itself: for law regulates collective life and gives it order. People being what they are, Klausner writes, "the nation as a whole could only see in such public ideals as those of Jesus, an abnormal and even dangerous phantasy; the majority, who followed the Pharisees and Scribes (*Tannaim*), the leaders of the popular party in the nation, could **on no account** accept Jesus' teaching."

These illustrations seem to indicate that without firm law, and a sense of obedience to law, a society disintegrates.

15 Socrates sought truth with a rare courage. But he came too close; he was too relevant to be a security risk to Athens. For this he was handed a cup of hemlock in the spring or early summer of 399 BC. Thus ended the career of one of the greatest minds the world has ever known, and the young men who followed Socrates knew then that something deep and terrible was wrong in men, individually and collectively. "This was the end of our comrade," wrote Plato, "a man, as we would say, of all then living we had ever met, the noblest and the wisest and the most just."

These men knew from their own bitter experience that societies persecute and/or execute their best men as well as their worst. This fact alone was enough to tell them that something tragic seems built into the human condition; and it was this insight that caused the first philosophers to begin to think deeply about life's problems and to search for solutions.

One dog barks at something, and a hundred bark at the sound.

CHINESE PROVERB

✦

Henry David Thoreau

"I Will Breathe After My Own Fashion"

In the spring of 1845 Henry David Thoreau began constructing a cabin on a forested plot of land at Walden Pond, a small blue lake two miles from his home at Concord, Massachusetts. He bought a hammer, borrowed an ax, secured some used boards that he refurbished, cut a few white pines to open a clearing, and started to build. By May he had completed the frame and roof; by the end of June it was boarded in. So, on July 4 he declared his independence from the world, moved in, and began a two-year experiment in living with himself.

His withdrawal was almost universally misunderstood by the townsfolk of Concord. Some thought he was lazy; most thought him eccentric and antisocial. Others thought it a pity that he was turning his back on the benefits of civilization and refusing to make the contribution to society that he had been destined to make. Oliver Wendell Holmes scoffed and said he was "nibbling his asparagus at the wrong end."

Although criticized (negatively) by virtually everyone, he persisted with singular determination. "My purpose in going to Walden Pond was not to live cheaply nor to live dearly there, but to transact some private business with fewest obstacles. . . ."

"Private business"? He explains:

> I went to the woods because I wished to live deliberately, to front only the essential facts of life, and see if I could not learn what it had to teach, and not, when I came to die, discover that I had not lived. I did not wish to live what was not life, living is so dear; nor did I wish to practice resignation, unless it was quite necessary. I wanted to live deep and suck out all the marrow of life, to live so sturdily and Spartan-like as to put to rout all that was not life, to cut a broad swath and shave close, to drive life into a corner, and reduce it to its lowest terms.

He lived at Walden Pond for two years, two months, and two days, and it was a wonderfully successful experiment, or, more accurately, it was a time when one human being managed his priorities and lived the way he wanted to live. He confided to his journal, "I learned this, at least, by my experiment, that if one advances confidently in the direction of his dreams, and endeavors to live the life which he has imagined, he will meet with a success unexpected in common hours."

When he abandoned his cabin in September 1847 and returned to the village, his experiment was complete. It was time to move on. "I left the woods because I had several more lives to live, and could not spare any more time for that one."

Thoreau was born in Concord on July 12, 1817, the third of three children. His father, John Thoreau, owned a small business—grinding graphite and making pencils—which he operated out of one wing of their home; it provided a meager income. John Thoreau was retiring and not very industrious, but he was bright and sensitive, and he loved books and nature. These qualities he bequeathed to his son. His mother, Cynthia Dunbar Thoreau, was a vivacious, socially active woman known for her talkativeness and love of gossip. From her Henry received an acute sense of individualism, intellect, a facility of speech, and a social conscience.

Henry's early schooling was in the elementary school and academy in Concord. When he was eleven he matriculated at Harvard, where his performance was good but not spectacular. He graduated at twenty and faced the perennial problem of choosing a vocation and finding a job. Teaching was a most natural occupation for a recent Harvard graduate, and fortunately his old elementary school had an opening. Henry enjoyed children, related well to them, and was an excellent teacher. However, during his second week in the classroom he was visited by a member of the school board who judged his pupils to be unruly and out of control. He demanded that the teacher administer discipline, including corporal punishment. Thoreau did so, as ordered. That evening he handed in his resignation.

In September of 1839 Henry and his brother John built a boat and traveled up the Concord and Merrimack rivers into New Hampshire. There they walked and took a stage to Mount Washington, climbed to the top, then returned home via the river routes. Henry took detailed notes and later used them as a basis for his first book. It was a time of joyous camaraderie, a time Thoreau was to recall when he was closest to another human being.

In January of 1842 Henry was traumatized by the death of his brother. John contracted tetanus from a cut in his finger received while shaving. After an agonizing illness peculiar to "lockjaw," John died in Henry's arms. So shaken was he by the event, ten days later Henry also began to indicate signs of the illness. They were psychosomatic symptoms, intense and honest, and they reveal Henry's capacities for sympathetic identification, a quality that determined his stance toward society and nature throughout his life.

So, by the early spring of 1845 there was a readiness to carry through on his long-held dream of establishing his retreat so he could get on with the business of living. He wanted to prove that an adequate life requires very few things—a few rows of beans, a little furniture, clothing, a notebook and pen, a few books, and very little else. "That man is richest whose pleasures are the cheapest."

His deepest motivation, however, was not to prove a point of economics. He saw with painful clarity the way most human beings live. "The mass of men lead lives of quiet desperation," he wrote. Their "vision does not penetrate the surface of things." Thoreau's basic instinct was to accomplish something at the nuclear center of his being. He was embarking on a spiritual odyssey comparable to that of a Theravada monk assuming his monastic vows. "What a man thinks of himself, that is which determines, or rather, indicates, his fate." "If I am not I," he wrote, "who will be?" "However mean your life is, meet and live it; do not shun it and call it hard names. Love your life, poor as it is. Why should we be in such deep haste to succeed and in such des-

Let everyone mind his own business and endeavor to be what he was made.

If I am not I, who will be?

However mean your life is, meet it and live it; do not shun it and call it hard names. Love your life, poor as it is. . . . If a man does not keep pace with his companions, perhaps it is because he hears a different drummer. Let him step to the music which he hears, however measured or far away.

The mass of men lead lives of quiet desperation. What is called resignation is confirmed desperation. From the desperate city you go into the desperate country, and have to console yourself with the bravery of minks and muskrats. . . . But it is a characteristic of wisdom not to do desperate things.

Let us not underrate the value of a fact; it will one day flower into a truth.

How vain it is to sit down to write when you have not stood up to live!

Time is but a stream I go a-fishing in. I drink at it; but while I drink I see the sandy bottom and detect how shallow it is. Its thin current slides away, but eternity remains.

The perception of beauty is a moral test.

I think we should be men first, and subjects afterward. It is not desirable to cultivate a respect for the law, so much as for the right.

In the long run men hit only what they aim at.

We need the tonic wildness. . . . We can never have enough of nature.

In wildness is the preservation of the world.

How alone must our life be lived! We dwell on the seashore, and none between us and the sea.

perate enterprises? If a man does not keep pace with his companions, perhaps it is because he hears a different drummer. Let him step to the music which he hears, however measured or far away."

For Thoreau the one essential ingredient of the successful life is personal freedom. All the good things of life derive from the fact that we can make free choices about the way we want to live. It seems inevitable that, sooner or later, he would clash with the establishment.

His first confrontation with the political establishment was while he was living at Walden Pond, on a July night in 1846. For four years he had refused to pay his poll tax, a head tax extracted from every adult male citizen over twenty. Thoreau considered the tax discriminatory, and, moreover, he protested against giving tax support to a government that condoned slavery. On this afternoon Thoreau had walked into town from his cabin to pick up a mended shoe from a cobbler. By coincidence he encountered the town jailer, Sam Staples, who was also the tax collector. Staples asked him to pay his tax. Thoreau declined and tried to argue his case. Staples warned him that he could be thrown into jail. Thoreau claimed his right to go to jail right then. So, to jail he went, where he shared a cell with a man who was accused of burning down a barn. Thoreau was willing to stay in jail for however long it took to register his protest and make his point, but somehow his mother got word that he was in jail and sent her sister to the jailer's home with money to bail him out. Staples's daughter answered the door and took the money, but the hour was late, and Staples had settled in for the evening and decided to release Thoreau the next morning. Come morning Thoreau was angry at not being allowed to stay and continue his protest. He went to pick up his mended shoe, and a half hour later was in the country gathering huckleberries.

The outcome of Thoreau's night in jail was his famous essay "On Civil Disobedience." "I heartily accept the motto," he wrote, "'That government is best which governs least'"; and in fact, "'That government is best which governs not at all.'" "I think we should be men first, and subjects afterward." "If a plant cannot live according to its nature, it dies; and so a man." "I was not born to be forced. I will breathe after my own fashion."

For Thoreau this is a matter of ethics and a matter of principle. Ethics must take precedent over rules and regulations; morality must take precedent over law. The state, out of its own sense of preservation, will always attempt to condition people to be law-and-order citizens, to put away their moral consciences and to "have respect for the law." But an authentic human being who has respect for himself will put his integrity and moral principles ahead of the law. And the principles that Thoreau is laying down and defending apply not merely to the Commonwealth of Massachusetts and the federal government of the United States: they apply to all human beings and all possible governments.

> Unjust laws exist: shall we be content to obey them, or shall we endeavor to amend them, and obey them until we have succeeded, or shall we transgress them at once? Men generally, under such a government as this, think that they ought to wait until they have persuaded the majority to alter them. They think that, if they should resist, the remedy would be worse than the evil. But it is the fault of the government itself that the remedy is worse than the evil. It makes it worse. Why is it not more apt to anticipate and provide for reform? Why does it not cherish its wise minority? Why does it cry and resist before it is hurt? Why does it not encourage its citizens to be on the alert to point out its faults, and do better than it would have them? Why does it always crucify Christ, and excommunicate Copernicus and Luther, and pronounce Washington and Franklin rebels?

Since this is the way governments behave, the moral human being will resist. If the law "is of such a nature that it requires you to be the agent of injustice to another, then, I say, break the law." This is the American colonial conscience that breaks the bond of British law. This is the conscience of Gandhi, who fasts and prays and breaks the bond of British rule in India. This is the conscience of Martin Luther King, Jr. who organizes a march in Selma to challenge legal segregation. This is the conscience of protesters who burn their draft cards and march against a war in Vietnam. This is the conscience of South Africans who refuse to segregate to protest against discriminatory apartheid laws. This is the conscience of the sanctuary movement that illegally protects refugees from oppression in Central America.

Those who argue for a democratic state, and those who defend it, will always counter that, although unjust laws do indeed exist, there are legal mechanisms by which they can be changed; the primary mechanism is to build public opinion and erode support for unjust laws. It takes a commitment to the democratic process to make the system work.

Thoreau's answer is simple and direct: "As for adopting ways which the state has provided for remedying the evil, I know not of such ways. They take too much time, and a man's life will be gone. I have other affairs to attend to. I came into this world, not chiefly to make this a good place to live in, but to live in it, be it good or bad."

Thoreau's passion for justice was ignited several times in the 1850s. He was horrified when Massachusetts passed the Fugitive Slave Law requiring citizens to apprehend and return runaway slaves to their owners. Against his principles of individualism, he joined the abolitionist movement and delivered an emotional speech entitled "Slavery in Massachusetts" at a Fourth of July celebration in Framingham.

In the winter of 1860 Thoreau caught a cold while he was in the woodlands counting growth-rings on the tree stumps in a new cut. It worsened into bronchitis, and the tubercular lesions, going back to his college days, were activated. Thereafter his journal entries become sporadic, with only occasional brief notes. His last entry in his journal was on November 3, 1861. It had rained the previous day and he had watched the big drops of rain make little craters in the sand that revealed the direction of the rainfall.

He was in especially good spirits during the spring of 1862. He was visited frequently by friends and citizens who had come to admire him and wish him well. He revised some of his essays and wrote some poetry. He died May 6 in a bed he had constructed himself.

Thoreau is buried in Sleepy Hollow Cemetery less than a mile from his birthplace and four miles from Walden Pond.

✦

Reflections

1 "Our Western experience has been an ongoing conflict of loyalties." From your point of view, how do you assess this conflict? How much have you been victimized by it? By conviction and temperament, which way do you tend to lean in your allegiance: toward the mandate of personal conscience or the necessities of a lawfully ordered society?

2 Is this conflict of loyalties necessarily a religious conflict, or could one who is not a traditional theist also face the dilemma?

3 If you are convinced that there is a "higher law," on what grounds or under what conditions would you decide to obey that law rather than the laws of the state? How could you be sure that your judgment in such a decision is right?

4 Reread pp. 332–335 together. Are you willing to grant the church the right and power to stand in judgment over the state? Or, better, would you grant such right and power to churchmen to stand in judgment over lawmakers?

5 The statement by Associate Justice Lewis F. Powell, Jr. (pp. 330, 335) is a clear, concise summary of this position. How would you respond to this fundamental observation that an ordered society can't endure if every individual is free to pass judgment on which laws are just and which laws are unjust, and proceed to obey only "just laws"? (See Socrates's arguments on pp. 335 and 339.)

6 What is your response to the statement by Camus about "the true patriot" (see marginal quote on p. 333)? Does his insight solve some problems for you, or merely produce more?

7 Klausner concluded that Jesus's attack on the Mosaic Law was wrong because the masses need laws to preserve order and maintain consistency in their collective experience; and that without firm law, and a sense of obedience to law, a society disintegrates. In your opinion, is Klausner essentially correct? Why or why not?

8 See the quotation from Oliver Wendell Holmes on p. 337 (marginal quote). Is this an insight worth remembering, or is this judicial opinion merely one more legalism?

Lifestyles

5-3

This chapter deals with acculturation, the process by which individuals are gradually conditioned to accept the ideas and values of the culture they are born into. Once conditioned, an individual no longer perceives himself or herself simply as human but identifies with an ethnic, social, political, economic, or religious subunit and feels that her or his primary allegiance is to the role appropriate to that subunit. The Zimbardo prison experiments demonstrate how easily we can slip into limiting roles and forget that we are a part of the larger picture. This chapter describes the role-playing condition and suggests alternative ways of transcending these roles. It also submits that racism is founded on a dangerous and outmoded myth.

The Bonds of Culture

1 Somewhere (and once upon a time) there was a small green valley lying quietly within the steep walls of surrounding mountains, and a village slept on the floor of the valley. No one from the village had ever ascended the mountain walls to travel beyond. Whatever lay beyond the rim of their valley, for them, did not exist. "Outside" had no meaning; nor did "beyond" or "stranger" or "distant lands" or "enemy tribes." No one else existed, or could possibly exist . . . until that day when someone found a path through a mountain pass, and came back to tell his kin that they were not alone.

If I were asked to define an American in a single phrase I would say "An American is a person who has the right to be different," and I think that right is growing.
William Manchester

2 The life history of the individual is first and foremost an accommodation to the patterns and standards traditionally handed down in his community. From the moment of his birth the customs into which he is born shape his experience and behavior. By the time he can talk, he is the little creature of his culture, and by the time he is

grown and able to take part in its activities, its habits are his habits, its beliefs his beliefs, its impossibilities his impossibilities.

RUTH BENEDICT

The main path to health and self-fulfillment for the masses is via basic need gratification rather than via frustration. This contrasts with the suppressive regime, the mistrust, the control, the policing that is necessarily implied by basic evil in human depths.

ABRAHAM MASLOW

The environment is always the brainwasher, so that the well-adjusted person, by definition, has been brainwashed. He is adjusted. He's had it.

MARSHALL MCLUHAN

We seem to want creativity in the young—but only if it follows all the rules, isn't too noisy, pleases the adults, and doesn't rock the boat.

MCNEIL AND RUBIN

3 At the moment of our birth, we are human only. Each of us possesses a full complement of human genes, but we belong to no established social categories. We are not Russian or English, Inuit or Bantu, Chinese or Thai or Peruvian. At birth we belong to one species—the human species: *Homo sapiens.* All of us.

But within minutes of our entrance into this world, social conditioning begins. A language is spoken to us—Japanese or Shona or Spanish or whatever; specific feelings, values, and ideas are programmed into us, so that our undifferentiated humanness is channeled into society's preexistent classification systems. We are no longer primarily human; we think of ourselves, and identify ourselves to others, as we have been taught: I am Irish, I am Australian, I am South African, I am Jordanian, I am . . . , and so on. A complex set of categories becomes the accepted way of identifying "who" (or "what") we are. For good or ill, we have become acculturated.

Acculturation is a part of the human condition; individual and social existence would not be possible without it. But our social roles, along with their supportive functions, also become our prisons. We assume the carefully defined roles that society has constructed for us, and enormous pressures are brought to bear upon us to stay within the confines of those roles. We become one with our culture's worldview, including its ideas, values, myths, history, customs, traditions—the unexamined elements upon which our culture's worldview is grounded.

The result has been universally the same, as the anthropologist Ruth Benedict has aptly phrased it: "its habits are his habits, its beliefs his beliefs, its impossibilities his impossibilities."

PRISONERS

4 An experiment in role-playing was conducted by a social psychologist at Stanford University, Philip Zimbardo. It was a simulated-prison experiment scheduled to run for two weeks, but it was halted after six days by a "thoroughly shaken" Professor Zimbardo. It began in the basement of a campus psychology building.

The usual distinction between sanity and insanity is a false one. We are all insane; the difference between Napolean and a madman who believes he is Napoleon is a difference in degree, not in kind; both are acting on a limited set of assumptions.

COLIN WILSON

> Student volunteers, rated normal and average in psychological tests, had been arbitrarily assigned the roles of guard and prisoner. Prisoners were stripped and deloused—normal procedure in all real prisons. The student guards carried billy clubs, handcuffs, keys, and whistles—all symbols of their authority. Their uniforms were military shirts and reflector sunglasses which made eye contact impossible. The prisoners were made to wear identical smocks and stocking-caps and were only addressed by their number. Keeping order and enforcing the rules were the responsibility of the guards; administering punishment was totally up to them.
>
> At first, the student prisoners did not take the experiment very seriously.
>
> GUARD 1: "Hey, did I say you could laugh, 819? Didn't I tell you that you could not laugh? Maybe you didn't hear me right."

GUARD 2: "819, how'd you like to step out of line and do twenty quick pushups for us, huh? OK, come on. Let's go. Sound off. Louder . . ."

On the morning of the second day the guards met in the corridor to deal with a prison rebellion. During the night they had harassed the prisoners in their windowless cells by constantly waking them for meaningless head counts. The students had stacked their cots against the cell doors and refused to come out for the morning count.

Told only that they must maintain law and order, the guards broke into each cell, stripped the prisoners naked, and confiscated their beds, blankets, and pillows. Eventually the ring-leaders were placed in solitary confinement in a small closet.

Men in masses are gripped by personal troubles, but they are not aware of their true meaning and source.

C. WRIGHT MILLS

Faced with the resistance and hostility of the prisoners, the guards became caught up in their assigned roles. The student guards mixed troublemakers with those who had not rebelled and gave privileges to certain prisoners. This broke prisoner unity, bred distrust among them, and led prisoners to think that the privileges were the result of informing.

The guards stepped up the punishment—a meaningless succession of calisthenics and head counts which often lasted for hours. They even ordered the prisoners to curse each other publicly. Slowly the prisoners became resigned to their fate. They were no longer students. They had become prisoners, totally dominated by the guards.

The diary of one student guard shows the day-by-day change in his attitude as his role as guard became more and more real to him.

FIRST DAY: I evolved my strategy, namely, not to smile or it would be admitting it was only a game. I set my voice hard and low. I feel stupid.

SECOND DAY: After lights-out I held a loud conversation so the prisoners could overhear it about going home to my girl friend.

THIRD DAY: Prisoner 817 is being obnoxious and bears watching.

FOURTH DAY: I've been rebuked for handcuffing and blindfolding a prisoner. I resentfully replied it's both necessary security and my business anyway.

FIFTH DAY: I harassed 817. I've singled him out for special abuse because he begs for it, and because I simply don't like him.

By the fourth day of the experiment five student prisoners were emotionally unable to continue and had to be released. Dr. Zimbardo believes that all participants in the experiment, both prisoners and guards, had begun to accept their assigned roles as reality. Prisoners became totally submissive. They depended entirely upon the dominant guards for even their simplest needs. The fact that they were in a simulated environment and could have quit at any time seems somehow to have become lost in the daily experience of their assigned roles.

On the fifth day Prisoner 416 refused to eat. It was the final act of individual rebellion in Stanford prison. The guards failed in every attempt to force him to eat. He was put in "the hole"—the tiny equipment closet used for solitary confinement. At that point Prisoner 416 should have become a hero to the other prisoners. Instead they turned on him. To them he was a troublemaker—a "bad" prisoner.

GUARD: "Now if 416 does not eat all his sausages, then you can give me the blankets and sleep on the bare mattress. Or you can keep your blankets and 416 will stay another day. Now what will it be?

PRISONER 1: "I'll keep my blankets."

GUARD: "What will it be over here?"

PRISONER 2: "Keep my blankets."

GUARD: "How about 546?"

PRISONER 3: "I'll give you my blankets."
GUARD: "Well, you boys got to come to some kind of decision here."
PRISONER 4: "We got three who said they'll keep their blankets."
GUARD: "We got three against one. Keep your blankets. 416, you're going to be in there for a while. So just git used to it."

It was no longer an experiment. The basement corridor had become a test-tube prison in which some average, middle-class young men called "prisoners" were actually suffering, and others called "guards" were behaving sadistically. Dr. Zimbardo canceled the 14-day experiment after only six days.

The Zimbardo prison experiment is not a Doomsday message. It's a warning. It shows us how easily man accepts the impersonal rules of order as substitutes for human understanding, how conditioned he has become to respond to dominant symbols of authority—to a job, a role, to a label in society that forces him into patterns of behavior which dehumanize him and destroy in him the sense of responsibility for his own actions. . . .

Dr. Zimbardo has reminded us that the roles we play are prisons—prisons of our own invention. But we do have the ability to create alternatives based on more human values. To be aware of how easy it is for any of us—for all of us—to fall into the patterned roles of dominance and submission is unique knowledge. Perhaps we will use it to find again the truly human qualities that first appeared almost a hundred thousand years ago in the dark caves of Neanderthal.

PRIMAL MAN
Wolper Productions

ALTERNATIVES TO REMAINING PRISONERS

5 This "prison" condition no longer prevails for increasing numbers of people who discover for themselves that they can redefine their roles. We now have the genuine option of breaking free of the bonds of culture systems. This can be either a blessing or a curse. The loss of roots that a culture provides can be agonizing, yet the opportunities offered by this new freedom are momentous.

For good or ill, therefore, the freedom is ours. For what is probably the first time in human history, we can pass judgment on our culture and make a more objective assessment of the ways in which it meets or fails to meet our basic needs.

What is asked of us—or demanded of us—is no easy path. We are at a crossroads requiring considerable moral courage: the courage to face freedom and seek autonomy without the roots and without the security that culture has heretofore guaranteed to each of us.

6 The sources of this new freedom are many; three are fairly obvious.

First, from the vast researches of the social scientists, we have come to recognize the cultural patterns that have shaped our existence. From the anthropologists' patient examination of other cultural patterns, we can see more dispassionately the patterns that others have unconsciously followed. After comparing the patterns of numerous societies we have come to understand the function and operation of a culture system. We find that each culture is an internally coherent structure with its component parts harmonizing into an interdependent working system. Each culture provides a worldview, so that life for each individual in the system has coherence and meaning.

When we apply this knowledge to our own culture, we begin to understand its function and our roles in it. We see how relative some of the patterns and values are. Previously—while living in that small green valley—we took them for granted; we may even have believed them to be universal or absolute. Now we find that they were merely functional. We have discovered that individuals immersed in their cultures, from the primitive to the most civilized, endow their respective patterns with the same ultimacy and finality which we felt. For each, his culture has worked pragmatically for him, and therefore no other culture existed, or could exist. We can now recognize ethnocentrism, wherever it occurs.

The result is that we see ourselves in a larger context, and having seen, we can no longer follow a tacit ethnocentrism. We see through it; we understand its root causes. The egocentric illusion has been found out!

Secondly, during these last decades of our century we are involved in a cataclysmic increase in cultural interaction. No single major culture stands today as an isolated monolithic system. Few places exist in the world today where one could be born and remain culturally naive. Arnold Toynbee has pointed out that a cultural map of the earth a few centuries ago showed large pure-color patches, distinct from one another and with fairly sharp edges, but by the end of our century the patches will have vanished and the cultural colors will everywhere be woven together—like "shot silk"—with only faint blushes of color remaining in a few isolated enclaves.

Probably the most significant world-fact of our time is the disintegration of cultures as distinct and separate functional systems. This is the fundamental fact that has given us our freedom—and our pain.

A third source of our freedom is new insight into the dynamics of our inner world. We know a great deal now about the processes of psychological conditioning and reinforcement. We know that individuals can be acculturated into any set of customs, beliefs, and values; they can be made to believe, value, and even worship almost anything. If societies can condition us, then we know that we can be unconditioned and reconditioned.

And so, as we gain a clearer picture of our basic human needs—**which may or may not be fulfilled by the particular culture in which we live**—we feel a new freedom to pursue their fulfillment. We can take the initiative. We no longer submit to the doctrine that we **must** remain, unquestioningly, within a particular system; indeed, with our awareness of alternatives, external coercion for us to do so might be interpreted as enslavement. Various cultures, subcultures, and segments of culture are readily accessible to us. We are free to experiment with them, identify with them; some can even find a home in several systems simultaneously or sequentially.

About then I made a horrible discovery. I didn't want to go back to school, win, lose, or draw. I no longer gave a damn about three-car garages and swimming pools, nor any other status symbol or "security." There was no security in this world and only damn fools and mice thought there could be.

ROBERT HEINLEIN
Glory Road

Bloom where you are planted.

HINDU PROVERB

Yet we sit there, eyes glued to the set, watching this explication of the obvious in hateful fascination and even find ourselves compelled to stay tuned to whatever follows. . . . Consciously, we despise ourselves, yet we are fascinated . . . as any savage before his totem.

RICHARD SCHICKEL

Would it really do to find out that our game is not serious, that enemies are friends, and that the good thrives on the evil? Society as we know it seems to be a tacit conspiracy to keep this hushed up for fear that the contest will otherwise cease.

ALAN WATTS

CULTURAL RELATIVITY

7 In any society, specific BTF-patterns are considered "normal" not merely because the majority adheres to them, but also because they are meaningful and functional. They enable us to predict the behavior of others, and them ours. They create consistency in our experiencing of life together; they provide us with a unifying worldview. "Normal" behavior supports and enhances that unity;

Path with a Heart

"I say it is useless to waste your life on one path, especially if that path has no heart."

"But how do you know when a path has no heart, don Juan?"

"Before you embark on it you ask the question: Does this path have a heart? If the answer is no, you will know it, and then you must choose another path."

"But how will I know for sure whether a path has a heart or not?"

"Anybody would know that. The trouble is nobody asks the question; and when a man finally realizes that he has taken a path without a heart, the path is ready to kill him. At that point very few men can stop to deliberate, and leave the path."

"How should I proceed to ask the question properly, don Juan?"

"Just ask it."

Carlos Castaneda
The Teachings of Don Juan

"abnormal" behavior does not cohere with the system and tends to destroy it. (BTF-patterns is a convenient abbreviation that will be used to refer to all the elements that are interwoven to create selves and societies. Behavior, thought, and feeling—these are the three elements of human experience judged to be acceptable or unacceptable, right or wrong. Also, the single symbol "BTF" implies the important fact that behavior, thought, and feeling are ultimately inseparable and operate together.)

As we move from culture to culture we find the same principles. Normal BTF-patterns will differ, but within each society these elements will cohere and interact. The system will provide guidelines for living, and a high degree of conformity and security. Therefore, within each culture, these accepted BTF-patterns are normal and right.

However romantic it seemed to be a beachcomber, I learned I had to get back to the neurotic society I need in order to function.
Albert Finney

The fact of cultural relativism was first recognized, so far as we know, by the Greek Sophist Protagoras. Denying that any belief or custom was absolute, Protagoras declared that "man is the measure of all things" (that is, customs are man-made, not divinely given); and he held that we have an obligation to conform to the cultural patterns of any society we might visit. After all, what right have we, flaunting our ethnocentric arrogance, to subvert a workable system by introducing our alien BTF-patterns?

> The central point in cultural relativism is that in a particular cultural setting, certain traits are right because they work well in that setting, while other traits are wrong because they would clash painfully with parts of that culture. This is but another way of saying that a culture is integrated, and that its various elements must harmonize passably if the culture is to function efficiently in serving human purposes.
>
> Horton and Hunt

8 Does any quality of "American" thought distinguish it from that developed elsewhere?

One peculiar and all-pervasive characteristic is its pluralism. . . . Thought in America has developed in response to external influences and to internal problems and challenges. America has been receptive to many cultures and to a variety of intellectual themes. There is, for example, both a liberal and a conservative tradition throughout American history. There is the America of radical democratic individualism and equalitarianism of Thomas Jefferson, Thomas Paine, Ethan Allen, Benjamin Rush, Henry Thoreau, Abraham Lincoln and John Dewey—an America in which liberal causes are espoused or in which a dominant secular and naturalistic outlook prevails. But there is also a conservative stream in American history, represented in the religious interests of the Puritans, Jonathan Edwards, and Samuel Johnson, in the defense of orthodoxy by the Scottish realists and speculative idealists, and in the conservative politics of Cadwallader Colden, Alexander Hamilton, John C. Calhoun, and even George Santayana. America is thus the meeting place of divergent ideas and movements: Puritanism, deism, materialism, Unitarianism, transcendentalism, idealism, realism, and pragmatism—and most recently of naturalism, positivism, analytic philosophy, Marxism, Thomism, phenomenology, Zen Buddhism, and existentialism. Any simple formulas designed to reduce these diverse elements into a uniform tradition are bound to be distorted.

PAUL KURTZ

Insanity in individuals is something rare—but in groups, parties, nations, and epochs, it is the rule.

FRIEDRICH NIETZSCHE

PERSONAL ALIENATION

9 There exists today in world society an enormous amount of alienation and destabilization of values due to the interaction of cultures and their breakdown as functional systems. There was a time, not long ago, when the Theravada Buddhist system in Thailand was self-contained and performed the function of culture—to provide a coherent set of assumptions and values by which its citizenry could live ordered lives; and this was true of the Japanese Shinto/ Buddhist society, of Sunni Islamic society in Saudi Arabia, of Hindu society in India, and so on. But now all the world's societies have melted, interpenetrated, blended, and lost their cohesiveness. Since different cultural systems have conflicting BTF-patterns, each system loses its coherence, integrity, and workability. We discover that various BTF-patterns are right and wrong, acceptable and unacceptable at the same time, depending upon which strand of culture one uses as the criterion of valuation.

Paul Klee, *Senecio* (1922)

What happens to you and me as we try to adjust to a cultural eclecticism?

We internalize that eclecticism. The outer world is a hodgepodge, so our inner worlds become hodgepodges. Our culture is fragmented, so we too become fragmented. We don't know which values to follow, so we attempt to hold conflicting values which reflect our culture. We don't know what behavior is acceptable, so we behave differently in different settings.

Consistent behavior is no longer possible, and the integrity so essential to the harmonious operation of our inner world becomes ever more elusive. Self and sanity are at stake, and, by degrees, both can be lost.

Once upon a time, I, Chuang-tzu, dreamt I was a butterfly, fluttering hither and thither, to all intents and purposes a butterfly. . . . suddenly, I awoke. . . . Now I do not know whether I was then a man dreaming I was a butterfly, or whether I am now a butterfly dreaming that I am a man.

CHUANG-TZU

10 When one finds himself/herself in this condition—when his or her inner world reflects the fragmentation of the outer world—a pressure is felt from within to find a solution. Several easy and attractive alternatives are at hand that, at least momentarily, can provide security and relieve anxiety.

I am but mad north-north-west: when the wind is southerly I know a hawk from a handsaw.

WILLIAM SHAKESPEARE
Hamlet II, ii, 405

Humankind's Most Dangerous Myth

One evening while I was sitting at an outdoor table in Horton Plaza in downtown San Diego, I watched a couple with two children stroll along the third floor deck, window shopping. The man was a tall Black man, regal, handsome, and athletic; the woman was a tall Japanese woman, majestic, dignified, and self-aware. The little girl at about three years was a doll: dark skinned, black hair done up in pig-tails, fine features. The little boy, perhaps four years old, was dark skinned but lighter than the little girl, displayed manly features, and looked out at the world through distinct "Asian" eye-folds. Two beautiful children, I thought. I couldn't help watching them as they made their way along the sidewalk.

I pondered the nightmare a serious (legalistic) classifier will have with the children; I also reflected on the unnecessary suffering both children will be subjected to as they are required, time and again, to check boxes and select categories. "Race?" the official form will demand. "Check one: ☐ White ☐ Hispanic ☐ Native American ☐ African American ☐ Asian American ☐ Other ________"

Since at least my college days, because of good teachers and good courses, I have been aware of three apparently little-known facts about race. (1) Race is a myth; that is, there is no scientific basis for our current, popular notions about race. Race concepts can be shown to be entirely arbitrary and based on a simple fallacy of classification. ("Myth" is defined here as an idea, set of ideas, or story that is shared by a given social body but is essentially prerational and preliterate and without basis in fact; it appeals to deeply held emotional needs and forms a part of the ideology of that society.)

(2) Racial classifications are just one of many ways we humans devise to organize and bring order to our information, and without having given careful attention to the facts, so many of our classification systems have no basis at all in truth or reality, especially if their roots go back to pre-empirical stages in the development of human knowledge.

(3) Race myths are expressions of the us-them mentality that permeates all human thought, especially Western thought: good-guy/bad-guy, us-saved/them-lost, Chosen/Damned, Greek/barbarian, Brethren/Kaffirs, superior people/inferior people, Aryans/Jews, Jews/Gentiles, civilized/primitive, smart/dumb, and so on. This two-valued orientation is always founded on arbitrary criteria and is an expression of an elemental human need: to promote group loyalty in "us" while obliterating the reality and value of "them."

Scientific research has annihilated the validity of virtually all these generalizations. Semanticists have shown us what naming and classifying are all about: general names and classes are abstract "packages" designed to ignore differing individual characteristics (concrete realities are irrelevant; only the "package" is of significance). Sociologists have laid bare the patterns of caste and class that give rise to such two-valued orientations and shown how they result in bigotry, the inability to listen to others' points of view, and a blindness to the worth of individuals. Psychologists have identified the individual competitive needs for identity and self-esteem that drive such feeling and thinking. Evolutionary biologists have placed the us-them dichotomy in its broad evolutionary context and shown how it ministers to survival needs.

Paleoanthropologists and molecular biologists have all but proven that we are all descended from the same ancestor(s) who migrated out of Africa and diversified into separate genepools (as "branches" and "races") in order to adapt and survive in extremely varied habitats. Historians have shown with disturbing clarity how, over the millennia, "race" is merely a temporary stasis in the constant intermixing of these human genepools. Anthropologists have revealed the speed at which races interbreed once they are juxtaposed; and they have reminded us that **all of us** are the results of genetic mixtures (and wild genes: I remember an historian, speaking of South Africa, reminding us that racism prevails only during the day and vanishes at night, and that this has always been so).

"When we name something, then, we are classifying," wrote Dr. Hayakawa in his *Language in Thought and Action.* "The individual object or event we are naming, of course, has no name and belongs to no class until we put it in one." In reality only individuals exist, but our minds can't handle all the individuals (human and otherwise) in the world, so our pragmatic thinking machines lump them together into big collective baskets called "Koreans," "Norwegians," "Bantu," "Vietnamese," "Whites," "Blacks," "Redskins," "Orientals," et al.

Now, here comes an individual—we'll call her Elizabeth (and perhaps she's the little girl in the story above). "Who" or "what" is she? She is just herself, of course; at least she was when she was born. But that truth just won't wash in today's data-crunching society. She must have a category—a number, a name, a label. ("Everyone must have a label," says the artist Abner Dean.) The fact that labels are designed to minister to society's craving and not the truth of the little girl or her authentic needs may escape us; so also is the fact that, once labelled, she will be forced to go through life accepting, or at least facing, all the bigotries, stereotypes, epithets, etc., that her label currently engenders. Unless through some tour de force she can rise above her label, she will be molded by it all her life.

But "what is she" really? Is Elizabeth "Japanese" or "Black" or "Red" or "Asian" or "American"? None of the above. She is herself alone. Her particular mixture of human genes—her personal "genome"—is absolutely unique; not a single individual *Homo sapiens* in the last hundred thousand years has been blessed with her one-of-a-kind genetic makeup. But society can't handle that. It will give her a simplistic label, and then, worst of all, it will finally convince her that she really and truly **is** what that label "says" she is. And when she applies for a job, registers to vote, or goes to college, she will forget her uniqueness, check the box that says ☐ ______, and submit to all the fallacies, indignities, and privileges of racism.

I had another teacher in college (a retired army intelligence colonel and semantics whiz) who made his students reflect on this puzzle. If your father was Black and your mother was White (we must capitalize "White" and "Black" but not mother and father), then how will society classify you? As Black, of course, at least in America, South Africa, and not a few other countries. What if your father was half-Black (nice thinking: have you ever heard of a half a rainbow?) and your mother White? (That is, by popular calculations you're one-quarter Black.) How will you be classified? As Black. And again, your paternal grandfather was half-Black and your other grandparents were all White (you are one-eighth Black). How will the world classify you? You are Black. And so on, even if you are, by the numbers, one-sixteenth Black, or one-thirty-second Black, or even less. (There has been many a lynching in the Old South of a "Nigger passing" as White when it was discovered that he had an ancestor **before the Civil War** who was Black.)

So, you can't escape. You're Black. But **why? Why** aren't you classified as "White" if you are "half and half"? If you're one-eighth, one-sixteenth, or one-thirty-second "Black," then **why** aren't you "White"—and **very** "White"? Every rational argument would insist that you're White. The reasons why you remain Black are all in the books, none of them very palatable. "White" doesn't suit the convenience of those who do the classifying, or those who have determined the classification system. It's the result of centuries-old power-plays and entrenched cultural, social, religious, and political mindsets. In so many societies "Black" carries stigmata, and this gives the White bigot an edge; it probably even gives him a comforting rationalization for his bigotry.

CONTINUED

One clear truth emerges from this scenario: "race" and "racism" have nothing to do with the facts. They are "myths"—notions widely held in a society but which have no basis in fact. To this you may want to respond with "I **am** Black. Look at my dark skin! And doesn't my grandfather's sickle-cell anemia prove I'm Black?" No. You're talking about genepools which do indeed carry all sorts of "family" characteristics, but genepools are exactly what are constantly flowing and mixing and cannot be reduced to simple categories; the specific traits carried by genepools can legitimately be addressed, say, for medical purposes, with statistical probabilities. In any case, it is not genes that ignite signal reactions and set off race wars. These are caused by (1) the incipient paranoia that infects every single member of the human race, an "ontological" sociobiological feeling-complex that renders us competitive, divisive, and defensive, loyal to the in-group and hostile to outsiders; by (2) the "perceived" (or imagined) differences in visible characteristics that we xenophobes can't bring ourselves to identify with; by (3) the ingrained (uncriticized, uncorrected) thinking-habits that shape our social attitudes ("us/them," for example, or "dark skin means inferior"—as in the Indian caste system where high Brahmin are usually light-skinned, lowly Shudras dark-skinned).

The ideas that drive societies are never based primarily on fact. Societies live by myths, and the "factuality" of these myths is only remotely relevant to their social function. All collectively-held social concepts fulfill a need, but human needs come in all forms, good and bad, mature and elemental, rational and irrational; so in every society there are good myths and bad myths—mythical ideas that sustain life and well-being, and mythical ideas that are divisive and prevent the apprehension of the truth—often when that truth is desperately needed. The myth of race has always been one of the bad ones. In his book entitled *Man's Most Dangerous Myth: The Fallacy of Race,* the anthropologist Ashley Montagu has characterized race-thinking as a mindset that no longer has any redeeming function and is the fundamental alienating force in today's world that prevents our seeing the truth of our common humanity.

One alternative is to identify with but a single isolated strand of culture where one can feel more at home. In such a group one's BTF-patterns will be shared by others and tensions can therefore diminish. One always feels more at ease with those who share the same values. Feelings of alienation and fragmentation can subside. Surrounded by those who are congenial, one can begin to ignore the uncongenial patterns which heretofore caused trouble.

The difficulty with this alternative is that it doesn't solve the problem. To be sure, changing the environment can be a step in the right direction, but one must recognize that the vulnerability to fragmentation is an inner problem, and it may remain. The wound is in the inner world, not in the environment. Finding congenial surroundings may ease the pain only temporarily unless healing can proceed within.

A similar alternative is to join a truth-group. One can plunge into a subcultural unit that devalues all other BTF-patterns; once devalued, they tend to lose their power over us. Relegating them to an inferior status brings more satisfaction than ignoring or repressing them. One doesn't have to take seriously

In college catalogs the categories differ according to geographic locales and ethnic groupings affected; but no matter how detailed such systems may become, they remain primarily expressions of the human impulse to classify (and to be fashionably pragmatic) regardless of known facts about our ever-changing genepools and ethnic blendings. It is significant that very few students check the last box. Some of us will be reminded of the time when Albert Einstein was asked to check such a box (that included, of course, ☐ White ☐ Negro and ☐ Jew); he ignored the boxes that asked his race and wrote in "Human."*

See further: Ashley Montagu, *Man's Most Dangerous Myth: The Fallacy of Race* (Altamira Press, 1997); and S. I. Hayakawa, *Language in Thought and Action* (Harcourt Brace, 1991), especially chapter 10, "Classifications."

*A typical college admissions form has now become more detailed and will read something like:

Check one:
☐ American Indian or Alaskan Native
☐ Black, Non-Hispanic
☐ Hispanic-Mexican-Mexican American, Chicano
☐ Hispanic-Central American
☐ Hispanic-South American
☐ Other Hispanic
☐ Asian-Chinese
☐ Asian-Japanese
☐ Asian-Korean
☐ Laotian
☐ Cambodian
☐ Vietnamese
☐ Other Asian
☐ Pacific Islander
☐ White, Non-Hispanic
☐ Filipino
☐ Other
☐ Declined to state

the experience of any other person or group which differs, since he or she knows that their BTF-patterns are erroneous or wrong. Truth-groups usually make aristocentrism a condition of membership, and the sense of identity and security they offer is therefore especially rewarding.

This alternative prevents one from discovering effective channels of growth. Genuine identification with a truth-group is possible only while one remains unaware of the implications of the egocentric predicament. (See pp. 79ff.) Nevertheless, when our cultural confusion becomes too great, such a refuge, for many, may be a very attractive alternative.

For some, there is a third path. This is psychosis. If the "real world" appears to be too hellish, it is quite within the mind's power to create an inner world that is less threatening. This is never a freely chosen alternative, but rather a condition that takes over when we have lost our freedom of choice.

The majority of us, however, follow the easiest path; we try halfheartedly to conform to many noncoherent patterns of culture at the same time—wearing various masks, playing various roles—whatever the cost to our mental health.

Even at the risk of a mild schizophrenia, the expediency is not too costly, we think. The possibility of developing autonomy will be greatly diminished or lost, but then, "nobody's perfect."

"I LEARNED THIS, AT LEAST . . ."

11 I left the woods for as good a reason as I went there. Perhaps it seemed to me that I had several more lives to live, and could not spare any more time for that one. It is remarkable how easily and insensibly we fall into a particular route, and make a beaten track for ourselves. I had not lived there a week before my feet wore a path from my door to the pond-side; and though it is five or six years since I trod it, it is still quite distinct. It is true, I fear, that others may have fallen into it, and so helped to keep it open. The surface of the earth is soft and impressible by the feet of men; and so with the paths which the mind travels. How worn and dusty, then, must be the highways of the world, how deep the ruts of tradition and conformity! I did not wish to take a cabin passage, but rather to go before the mast and on the deck of the world, for there I could best see the moonlight amid the mountains. I do not wish to go below now.

Notice the difference between what happens when a man says to himself, "I have failed three times," and what happens when he says, "I am a failure!" It is the difference between sanity and self-destruction.

S. I. HAYAKAWA

I learned this, at least, by my experiment: that if one advances confidently in the direction of his dreams, and endeavors to live the life which he has imagined, he will meet with a success unexpected in common hours. He will put some things be-

Four paintings by Louis Wain showing a gradual withdrawal from reality into psychosis. Wain became famed in England for his gentle (and realistic) portrayal of cats. At the age of 57, strong signs of paranoid schizophrenia appeared in his behavior and his art; his last fifteen years were spent in mental institutions. These paintings dramatically depict one person's withdrawal from reality and escape into fantasy.

hind, will pass an invisible boundary; new, universal, and more liberal laws will begin to establish themselves around and within him; or the old laws be expanded, and interpreted in his favor in a more liberal sense, and he will live with the license of a higher order of beings. In proportion as he simplifies his life, the laws of the universe will appear less complex, and solitude will not be solitude, nor poverty poverty, nor weakness weakness. If you have built castles in the air, your work need not be lost; that is where they should be. Now put the foundations under them.

Henry David Thoreau

✦

DIOGENES THE CYNIC

The Hound-Dog Philosopher

During Socrates' lifetime several counterculture movements had begun to spring up in Athens and other Greek city-states, some to protest the great philosopher's hyperintellectualism, others to carry on some aspect of his teaching. One group of counterculture antagonists called themselves Cynics. They loved Socrates but believed that he failed to value the individual. Their name derives from the Greek word *kuôn,* "dog" or "hound." Diogenes, the spokesman for the Cynic movement, "described himself as a hound-dog of the sort which all men praise but no one will go hunting with." Plato once called him a dog, to which Diogenes replied, "That's right. Try to get rid of me and I'll find my way back home every time."

The Cynic philosophy originated with an Athenian named Antisthenes, who lived from about 446 to 366 BC and was therefore a contemporary of both Socrates and Plato. Socrates once observed Antisthenes' torn robe and said to him, "I can see your vanity showing through that hole in your cloak." Wielding the dialectical weapons of a Socrates, he taught, harangued, defended, and argued; every argument, we are told, he would win.

Antisthenes was a culture-critic. He went about criticizing everybody and everything—but always with a point, and often a sharp point, for he specialized in bursting ego-balloons. For example, the Athenians believed the aristocentric claim that they had sprung from the earth and were, therefore, the salt of the Earth. Antisthenes observed that such a claim put them on a par with "ground snails and wingless locusts," for they also came up out of the earth.

"It is very strange," he said, "when we can separate the husk from the corn and the weak from the strong in war, but we never keep evil men from getting into politics."

"When states can no longer distinguish good men from bad men, they will perish."

The Cynics taught that the goal and purpose of life is to be happy—not wealthy, not admired, not erudite—but happy. The final human bliss, Antisthenes said, is "to be able to die happy." And the fundamental requirement of happiness is the ability to live a good and decent life (which, he said, requires "the strength of a Socrates"). The goal each of us should aim at is to learn to live with oneself in honesty and joy.

The Cynics were outsiders by choice; they deliberately alienated themselves from the insinuations of culture in which they were born and raised. They cultivated indifference toward society's values so they could develop their own. The wise person is not enslaved by custom and "what others think"; his wealth lies in his freedom from all the trammels of "civilization." "A wise man will be guided in all his social behavior not by laws but by the law of decency." Antisthenes loathed those who displayed "a store of words and learning" about moral matters but failed to practice them. The moral life, and the good life, demands a courageous adherence to this simple principle, despite inevitable misunderstandings and criticisms. "It is the noblest of privileges to do good things and be criticized," Antisthenes said. Someone once told him that he was widely admired. "Oh my!" he said. "What have I done wrong?"

The Cynics may represent history's first attempt on the part of self-esteemed individuals to transcend the patterns of culture in which they were born and raised, and to recognize that the assumptions and values of one's society may not work for the fostering of a successful life. They were therefore the first philosophic individualists, and they have had counterparts in every culture and every century in which the worth of the individual person is appreciated.

Antisthenes waged war with a wise but acidic tongue. To a new student he said, "Come with a new book, a new pen, and new tablets; and if you have brains, bring them too." When one of his students complained that he had lost his notes, he advised: "Next time inscribe them on your mind instead of on paper."

Diogenes of Sinôpe was by far the most famous of the Cynics.

This is the renowned Diogenes who "lit a lantern in broad daylight and said, as he went about, 'I am looking for an honest man.'" Details of his life are sketchy. He was originally a banker in Sinôpe (a Greek colony on the Black Sea), but he seems to have been caught counterfeiting the coins of his home city and was exiled. On a voyage to Aegina he was captured by pirates, taken to Crete and sold into slavery, after which he became a philosopher. We are told that, while on the auction block, he saw a well-dressed buyer in the audience and said, "Sell me to that man. He needs a master." When his friends tried to ransom him, he declined the offer saying that "lions are not slaves to those who feed them." So he became the overseer of a large household in Corinth and administered it with such excellence that his owner Xeniades "used to go about saying, 'A good spirit [*daimôn*] has taken up residence in my home.'"

Diogenes decided on the Cynic lifestyle after watching a mouse. The tiny creature never worried about where he would sleep, it was not afraid of the dark, it ate simple food and only what it needed, and it adjusted to whatever environment it found itself in. Diogenes chose to emulate this simple life and "used any place for any purpose, for breakfasting, sleeping, or conversing."

Diogenes is the superlative example of a philosopher who lived his philosophy in daily life; to know the man is to know his philosophy. He really didn't care what others thought of him. Someone said to him, "People laugh at you." His reply: "I couldn't care less. Jackasses also laugh at those people, but just as they don't mind the jackasses' laughing, so I don't care about their braying at me."

Diogenes focused his criticism on the common hypocrisies of daily life. "Musicians tune the strings of their instruments so they are in harmony but abandon their souls to disharmony." "Astronomers gaze at the heavens but fail to see what is right before their eyes." "Eloquent politicians talk up a storm about justice but fail miserably to practice it." "Grammarians criticize the writings of Homer but fail to correct their own."

On Diogenes:
He is a Socrates gone mad.

Plato

I am a citizen of the world.

Why do you live at all if you don't care about living well?

For some, despising pleasure is itself most pleasurable; they derive more pleasure from despising pleasure than from the pleasures themselves.

Eloquent politicians talk up a storm about justice but fail miserably to practice it.

The most beautiful thing in the world is freedom of speech.

I am looking for an honest man.

[To a chattering youth] Aren't you ashamed to draw a lead knife from an ivory scabbard?

Love of money is the mother of all evils.

Astronomers gaze at the heavens but fail to see what is right before their eyes.

It is impossible for society to exist without law.

Bad men obey their lusts as servants obey their masters.

Musicians tune the strings of their instruments so they are in harmony but abandon their souls to disharmony.

Grammarians criticize the writings of Homer but fail to correct their own.

It is the privilege of the Gods to want nothing, and of godlike men to want little.

"Even the preachers who denounce the vices of wealth love it all the same." When he saw some sheep protected by leather jackets while the owner's children went without clothes, he said, "It's better to be the man's ram than his son."

Diogenes was especially irked by religious hypocrisy. Once when he saw some priests having a man arrested for stealing a bowl from the temple, he observed, "the big thieves are leading away a little thief." Some Athenians once told him he really ought to be initiated into the mysteries so he will enjoy special privileges in the next life. "That's ludicrous," he said. "Are you telling me that men of true virtue will be mired forever [in Hadês] while evil men will dwell happily in the Isles of the Blest—just because they have been initiated?!" Diogenes was aghast when he saw devotees praying to the gods for health at the same time that they were gorging themselves on the unhealthy viands left over from their temple offerings. In their prayers, he said, people ask for the wrong things rather than what is truly good—wisdom and virtue.

He confessed that he was proud of the human race when he reflected on the expertise exemplified by doctors, philosophers, and navigators; but when he watched the fraudulent dream-mongers and psychics at work, or the empty conceits who went about puffed up because of their affluence, then he thought we are the silliest of all the animals.

He was also sensitive to the ironies and contradictions of our lives. "For some people, despising pleasure is itself the greatest of pleasure; they derive more pleasure from despising pleasure than from the pleasures themselves!"

Like Socrates he was no respecter of persons; the ordinary citizen, the great and powerful, and fellow Cynics were all treated with equal disrespect. He excelled at "pouring scorn on his contemporaries," says the gossipy historian Laërtius. He called himself "a spy on the greedy." He often had exchanges with Plato. Plato had given a famous definition of Man as a "two-legged animal without feathers." So Diogenes plucked the feathers from a chicken and brought it to the lecture hall, saying, "Here, Plato, is your Man." (As a result, we are told, Plato redefined Man as "a featherless biped with flat fingernails.") Once when Plato was asked what he thought of Diogenes, he said, "He is a Socrates gone mad."

Diogenes transcended society and culture. "I am a citizen of the world—a cosmopolitan," he said. To him social conventions commanded much less authority than "natural rights." Diogenes likened his free life to that of the Gods, implying that his standards transcended conventional social ethics as well as local laws and customs.

The picture commonly painted of Diogenes is of a ragged, unkempt beggar, sitting in the shadow of his "jar" surrounded by dogs, shaking "the middle finger" at passersby, and asking Alexander the Great to step aside because he was blocking the sunlight. This picture is not inaccurate, but it misses the point of what Diogenes was all about, and we do him great injustice when we paint him as a boorish misfit. For the man was gifted with an insightful mind and lots of common sense, and he used his unusual intellect to see deeply into human behavior; what he saw—what others didn't seem to see—was dishonesty, deception, confusion, entanglements, manipulations—inauthentic game-playing at all levels. In a word, Diogenes was gifted in being able to spot the hypocritical and point it out, which made him bitterly disliked by some but enormously popular to others. Despite his sharp tongue and his rejection of society, most Athenians loved him. When a vandal broke the jar he lived in, the Athenians gave him a new one. And even Alexander the Great remarked, "If I were not Alexander, then I would like to have been Diogenes."

So in his own life Diogenes made every effort to escape the traps of hypocrisy and adhere to a lifestyle that would allow him to be his own man without having to defer to the petty expectations of others. This he did by ridding himself of property; like Antisthenes he possessed only a cloak and a leather bag for carrying his food. He begged (he once begged from a stone statue "so he could get used to being refused"), slept anywhere he found himself, and took up residence in a giant *pithari* ("wine-jar," actually a huge ceramic storage vessel for grain, tipped on its side) in a very public place in the Athenian Agora. This way he could live a life of simple honesty, preserve his "seeing" as an observer, and play the role of a disengaged critic.

Diogenes was, among other things, an intellectual's anti-intellectual. His listeners included political leaders, academics (such as Plato), Sophists (such as Gorgias), poets, and rhetoricians; many came great distances to hear him. His writings include *Republic, The Art of Ethics, On Wealth, On Love, On Death, Letters,* and seven tragic plays.

"You are an old man," he was told, "so take a rest." "What!" he replied. "If I were running a race in the stadium, would you tell me to slow down just as I was approaching the finish-line?" He died at Corinth at the age of ninety—on the same day that Alexander the Great died in Babylon—and was buried by the gate leading to the Isthmus. He was honored with a bronze statue on which was inscribed: "Time makes even bronze grow old, but thy glory, Diogenes, all eternity will never destroy." This was in the 113th Olympiad, about 323 BC.

✦

Reflections

1 Note the quotations on p. 301 by the Putneys and Laing. Do you agree with the point they are making? What percent of Americans do you think recognize "the patterns" or see "the games"? Or does this apply only to the few who take courses in philosophy? (Shades of aristocentrism?!)

2 As you reflect on pp. 345–348 together, what is your response to these examples of the power of social conditioning? Are these insights new to you, or have you already worked through them?

3 Imagine yourself in the position of one of the guards or prisoners in the Zimbardo experiment. What games or gimmicks would you play on yourself, what knowledge, beliefs, or strengths would you remind yourself of to prevent prescribed roles from overwhelming you into losing your self and becoming what the roles define you to be? How long do you think you could last in such a "game"? (This is a reminder of the creative mental gymnastics which many prisoners of war engage in to prevent their succumbing to the roles forced upon them.)

4 This chapter suggests that freedom has been imposed upon us whether we wish it or are ready for it. Do you agree?

5 Some common "alternatives to freedom" are listed on pp. 351–356. Do these descriptions apply to individuals you know? What is your opinion of each of these alternatives?

6 Ponder the quotation from Laing (p. 301) in relation to that from Watts (p. 349). In what sense might society's BTF-patterns be considered "games"

the rules for which we must know to get along? What exactly is a game? Where do the rules come from? What is meant by "playing" a game?

7 Page 346—marginal quote: This observation by Maslow strikes some of us as a profound insight; but to others it might be only a trite truism. What do you think about it?

Ethics

5-4

This chapter deals with moral judgments and stresses the fact that several distinct criteria are commonly used for making moral judgments. This fact is momentous and, when unexamined, produces bitter conflict, for what is clearly moral according to one criterion will be clearly immoral according to another criterion. This chapter attempts to clarify the three major judgmental criteria. An awareness that there are different ways of viewing moral behavior can help us understand others' viewpoints, free us from dogmatism, and clarify our own ethical assumptions. This chapter also raises the question of "whom (and what) we should care about."

Sin and/or Virtue

1 Last night I invented a new pleasure, and as I was giving it the first trial, an angel and a devil came rushing toward my house. They met at my door and fought with each other over my newly created pleasure; the one crying, "It is a sin!"—the other, "It is a virtue!"

Kahlil Gibran

The perfect Way [Tao] is without difficulty,
Save that it avoids picking and choosing. . . .
If you want to get the plain truth,
Be not concerned with right and wrong.
The conflict between right and wrong
Is the sickness of the mind.

Seng-Ts'an

Debatable and Nondebatable Value Judgments

2 Whenever we value or disvalue objects or events, we are making "value judgments." When I say "The book got wet in the rain" I am stating a fact; but if I add that "I **don't like** my book getting wet in the rain," then I am **evaluating**

De gustibus non disputandum est. ***Concerning taste there can be no argument.***
PROVERB

an event. Fact-statements and value-statements result from decidedly different mental intentions. To "state a fact" is to give an object/event a description that one believes to be true. To evaluate is to state a preference, or approval, or a liking for something, or a disapproval or a disliking; and the question of whether our perception of the object/event is "true" is **not** a part of the evaluating process. In other words, value-judgments are not fact-claims.

3 There are several varieties of value judgments, but for our purposes we can focus on two relatively clear-cut kinds of value-statements: (1) those that are statements of personal taste and temperament and are not debatable, and (2) those that lend themselves to rational analysis and empirical investigation and are, therefore, debatable.

A little knowledge of history stresses the variability of moral codes, and concludes that they are negligible because they differ in time and place, and sometimes contradict each other. A larger knowledge stresses the universality of moral codes, and concludes to their necessity.
WILL DURANT

I may inform you that "I like liver and onions." This kind of value judgment is strictly a matter of personal taste, and only an epistemological nitwit would make an issue of the matter. (A vegetarian could rightly want to debate the ethics of my eating meat, but on how I experience the taste of liver and onions I have the final say, and my private experience remains undebatable.) So personal values of this kind are not debatable; there are no moral "shoulds" or "should nots" involved in such experiences; they just are. And in the last analysis, we can't even talk much about them. "I like turnips," I complain, and that's the end of the matter.

The following examples of nondebatable statements are fairly straightforward and accurate (providing, of course, that I'm describing my experiences accurately and am telling the truth):

There is nothing either good or bad,
But thinking makes it so.
WILLIAM SHAKESPEARE
Hamlet

"I like the flavor of real Italian spaghetti" (taste).
"I think Susan is beautiful" (vision—although beauty is not actually "seen" but is a creation by the mind from visual perceptions and past experiences).
"I enjoy walking in the rain" (touch, plus).
"I become nostalgic when I smell the fragrance of orange blossoms" (smell).
"I prefer the even rhythms of Ravel's *Bolero* to the cacophony of Stravinsky's *Rite of Spring*" (sound).

Our emotions are similarly expressed:

"I enjoy playing mathematical games."
"I hate being embarrassed in public."
"I am in love with Susan."
"I distrust bureaucracies."
"I'm scared of hornets."

All these judgments are nondebatable. No fact-claims are made by such statements. They are all descriptions of private experience, sensory or emotional as the case may be. If her boyfriend thinks Susan is beautiful, then—since "beauty is in the eye of the beholder"—Susan is beautiful **to him,** and only a sour-grapes loser (or congenital arguer) would waste time arguing the matter.

4 By contrast, a second kind of value judgment is debatable. If I say that "I favor euthanasia," then I have made a value statement that, if carried into action, would affect the lives of other people; the merits and consequences of such a statement are debatable. We can talk about whether euthanasia is morally "right" or "wrong" when judged in the light of specific moral and ethical criteria. We can discuss whether it is morally justifiable to force terminally ill patients to suffer when it is their stated wish to die and end their agony. We can debate certain religious doctrines and policies regarding euthanasia and investigate why the adherents of different religions would take a stand for or against the practice. In a word, there are ideas to be analyzed, relevant empirical facts to be gathered, and various points of view to be listened to.

5 "But surely," it may be said, "people do disagree in their basic moral attitudes, and they do try to persuade other people to agree with them." Indeed they do. People seem to feel more strongly about their moral attitudes than they do about their food preferences (we do not talk, for example, about our "culinary convictions"), and few people appear willing simply to accept differences at this point and let it go at that. But the methods by which anyone can persuade anyone else to change his basic moral attitudes . . . are not those of rational argument but only the methods of nonrational persuasion: name-calling, intimidation, threats, and so on. This is probably why our language has words like "prude," "moral ignoramus," and the like.

Does not this view lead to pessimistic conclusions about the possibility of achieving enough ethical agreement among men to make harmonious life on our planet possible? Not at all. To so conclude would be equivalent to a restaurateur's concluding that, since people's tastes differ, he might as well give up trying to develop a menu that will win the general approval of his customers. Fortunately, people by and large tend to approve and disapprove of the same sorts of things: that is why one seldom finds anyone who will disagree with statements like "The infliction of needless pain is evil," or "It is good to help others who are in need." It is not the alleged objectivity of moral judgments, but the substantial similarity of our basic moral attitudes, that renders possible a reasonably harmonious society.

WILLIAM HALVERSON

6 Another preliminary point needs to be considered. We speak of "ethical issues" as though "issues" were living entities wandering the corridors of a medical ward or haunting the offices of lawmakers. But "issues" are only expressions of moral concern by individuals about some recalcitrant problem. When several people, or a large population of people, share the same concern and make it known, it can seem that the "issue" is really "out there" wandering around and that everyone is somehow "seeing" something that is real.

But not so. **Anyone can make an issue of anything.** And the fact that someone—even someone who is widely accepted to be a keeper of moral virtues—"makes an issue" of something does not automatically justify its occupying our moral consideration and time. If you and I engage in a conversation, I can easily dominate the entire exchange by asking you why you aren't more concerned about the habitat of the barred owl, or the pope's visiting a Com-

Always do right. This will gratify some people and astonish the rest.

MARK TWAIN

An intelligence that is not humane is the most dangerous thing in the world.

ASHLEY MONTAGU

Nature and history do not agree with our conceptions of good and bad; they define good as that which survives, and bad as that which goes under; and the universe has no prejudice in favor of Christ as against Genghis Khan.

WILL AND ARIEL DURANT

To have a purpose for which one will do almost anything except betray a friend,—that is the final patent of nobility, the last formula of the superman.

FRIEDRICH NIETZSCHE

I want to change their minds, not kill them for weaknesses we all possess.

Gandhi (the motion picture)

after 50,000 years
rapturous in sky
I find you
living
in a box

munist country, or the commercialism of Christmas, or the spiked hairdos of punkers, or sex on television, or wasting money on space programs, or . . . or . . . or . . . or whatever the "issue" I care **to create** to capture your time and attention. Some of these subjects are important concerns, of course. But because someone "makes an issue" does not require that you or I listen and weigh his so-called issue as he/she does. For example, should we meet for the first time, I can easily set the agenda for a long verbal relationship by asking you why you dress so tackily, and my "making an issue" of the matter only serves to caress my ego by making you focus on me. In just this way, countless social "issues" are created to serve the self-needs of issue-makers.

The point of this is that each of us is free to assume or reject the validity of "issues" that currently thrive in our society. For whatever reason, if I become judgmental about a personal concern and attempt to draw you into my concern, then I can keep you hooked for as long as I want; unless, of course, you have the courage to say "**for me** that's not an issue" and walk away. To be sure, there are abundant problems in the so-called real world that dearly need our involvement. But it takes not a little Socratic wisdom to separate the deserving "issues" from those that have been fabricated by dimlit individuals or self-serving media.

7 Furthermore, an "issue" and a "problem" are not the same. Consider the following example of a "problem." You have set up camp for a weekend of hiking beside a crystal mountain stream, from which you can get good drinking water, and in which you can cool your six-pack and perhaps swim. Then you discover that some campers upstream have been dumping their garbage and refuse into the stream.

The simple-minded use of the notions "right or wrong" is one of the chief obstacles to the progress of understanding.
ALFRED NORTH WHITEHEAD

So, you have a problem, and reason would normally lead you to seek a solution. Providing you don't choose to move to another location, then a modicum of wisdom would suggest that you go talk with the polluting campers. If they are receptive and decent people, they might agree to contain their effluent and be thoughtful regarding your need for clean water. If they do so agree, then your problem is solved.

Contentment, even in poverty, brings happiness; discontent is poverty, even in riches.
CHINESE PROVERB

But what if they tell you to get lost and continue to dump their trash into the stream? Then you have the option of "making an issue" of the matter **since you could not solve the problem.** You can call the sheriff or camp manager if there is one; you can make a call to the Environmental Protection Agency representative nearest your location; you will probably find that the closest newspaper will be happy to send out a photographer to document the pollution; and you might conjure other ways of harassing your inconsiderate neighbors. In all such cases you're making issues—legitimate ethical creations when faced with problems to which reasonable solutions are important but cannot be found. Recalcitrant problems—and recalcitrant people—often push us into creating justifiable issues when it would have been so much easier to go for easy solutions.

The need for love characterizes every human being that is born. No psychological health is possible unless the "inner nature" of the person is fundamentally accepted, loved and respected by others.
ABRAHAM MASLOW

8 A morally wise individual will find that he/she must ask an array of important questions about the "issues" inherited from our culture and our society. Am

I really sure that a certain issue is a debatable issue? (The fact that a lot of people talk about it does not make it debatable.) Is the issue a justifiable issue? and why? (It may be only a media event created to nourish the feeding frenzy of journalists who crave ratings and have a need to insert themselves into the scenery.) Is the issue important **to me?** Since I can't be deeply involved in every issue (we would all bleed to death if we shed our life-blood over every concern that people feel), which issues do I personally choose to be involved in? Is it, in my judgment, an authentic issue? or do I find (or intuit) that it is being made an issue for personal (perhaps political) advantage by some individual or group? Can I see (even in theory) a solution to the **problem** so that I don't have to consider it an issue or allow others to make it an issue for me?

Principles are only tools in God's hands, soon to be thrown away as unserviceable.
DIETRICH BONHOEFFER

THE MORALITY OF ETHICS / THE ETHICS OF MORALITY

9 A young bank employee was indicted for embezzlement, and the evidence all seemed to point to a conviction. But he knew he was innocent, and his wife believed him. She was soon informed by another bank employee that he knew the whereabouts of documents that would reveal the real embezzler and prove that her husband was innocent. But her informant also made it clear he would give out with the evidence only if she made herself sexually available. The couple were devout Catholics, but to clear her husband of almost certain conviction she quickly made the decision to get whatever information at whatever cost. So she spent several nights with the other bank employee. Eventually the documents were forthcoming, her husband was exonerated, and the real embezzler was indicted and convicted. (See pp. 39–41.)

Question: Was her act moral or immoral?

Question: Was **she** moral or immoral?

Further: What are the criteria used to evaluate her actions? In your judgment could she have made a better decision? If you answer Yes, then what is it that makes this a better decision? What was her intent? Could **she** be judged moral while **her actions** are judged immoral?

10 In a World War II movie called *Manhunt*, the principal figure is a big-game hunter. For the sheer love of stalking his prey, he creeps into the forest high above Hitler's retreat at Berchtesgaden. Lying concealed in a thicket, he aligns the cross-hairs of his telescopic sight on the Führer's heart as he stands on a balcony. He pulls the trigger . . . on an empty chamber. He had stalked his game, and won.

Shortly, however, the hunter is caught by the Nazis and repeatedly tortured between escapes. In the beginning it never occurred to him to **kill** Hitler; but at the end of the story, having seen the bestial cruelty of the Nazis, he parachutes by night into the German forest, this time to hunt his game with live ammunition.

(This story is not far-fetched. Many attempts were made on Hitler's life by "good and decent men who wanted to put an end to the tyranny of this maniac."

I won't be wronged. I won't be insulted. I won't be laid a hand on. I don't do these things to other people. I require the same from them.

GUNMAN "J. B. BOOKS" (JOHN WAYNE)
The Shootist

ETHICS AND MORALITY IN THE OLD WEST

The NBC television series *High Chaparral* was popular in the late 1960s (and is still enjoyed by insomniacs on reruns). In the following scene the accepted ethical code of the Old West was deliberately broken. The question is whether ethical codes ever should be broken, and, if so, how such behavior can be ethically or morally justified. In fact, this raises the question of exactly what "ethical codes" are.

In this episode a gunman, Tulsa, has extorted five thousand dollars from Big John Cannon by threatening to kill Cannon's brother Buck. Since Buck is hot-tempered, Tulsa knows he can needle Buck into a shootout in which he could easily outdraw him. John Cannon feels he has no choice but to pay the money, which he does. But Buck "steals" back the money and proceeds to the local saloon, thereby ensuring a confrontation with Tulsa's quick draw.

It's at this point that Buck decides to change the rules of the game. Buck is hunched over the bar when Tulsa comes for him in the Tucson saloon.

TULSA: Turn around, Buck.
BUCK: Well, I tell you, Tulsa. If you wish to admit that you had made a mistake, and if you wish to crawl on out of here, I just might forget the whole thing.
TULSA: I don't make mistakes. Turn around.
BUCK: You sure?
TULSA: (Kicking back the chairs and screaming at Buck.) Turn around! (Buck turns slowly . . . with a derringer in his hand.) What are you doin'?
BUCK: Turnin' around, like you said.
TULSA: That's murder, Buck.

One such man was Dietrich Bonhoeffer, a devout Christian leader, who was executed for attempting to do what he believed to be a Christian duty: to murder Hitler. A leader of the Jewish Defense League, Meir Kahane, had stated his conviction that "if an American Nazi Party leader posed a clear and present

BARTENDER: Well, I think I'll go in the back room and check the stock. What I don't see I can't testify to.

BUCK: All right, Mr. Tulsa. It is now your play.

TULSA: It's murder, Buck. You gotta give me a chance.

BUCK: I don't have to give you anything.

TULSA: This ain't a fair fight!

BUCK: Fair. Hey, that's a good word. I bet you'd like for them to cut it on my tombstone, wouldn't you. "Here lies Buck Cannon, a fair man." But you know, I'd sooner end up standin' over your grave, and people whisperin' behind their hands. "That's Buck Cannon. He don't fight fair."

TULSA: Never figured you for a coward.

BUCK: Well, you live and you learn. I jus' don' want to die. That's the thing about a man like you. You're so ready to kill, you must be ready to die too. It's jus' the other side o' the coin, isn't it?

TULSA: You gotta give me an even chance.

BUCK: Who's gonna say it wasn't a fair fight. There's only you and me, and you'll be dead.

TULSA: Buck, I don't believe you'd do it. (A shot from the derringer in Buck's hand. Tulsa is wounded in his right shoulder.)

BUCK: Aim must be off. Now it's a fair fight. Draw. Whenever you're ready.

TULSA: (His gun arm is half-paralyzed and trembling.) No! This ain't fair.

BUCK: Tough.

TULSA: (Throws gun down.) You kill an unarmed man and that's murder.

JOHN CANNON: (From background.) He's right, Buck.

BUCK: Well, then, get out.

TULSA: It ain't over, Buck.

BUCK: Sure it is, Tulsa. For now anyways.

TULSA: We'll meet again, I promise you.

BUCK: It might happen. But jus' remember, I'm not as fast as you. I won't draw against you. So I just might have to back-shoot you next time.

TULSA: I believe you would, too.

BUCK: Try me. (Tulsa backs out and leaves saloon. Others crowd in. John comes over and leans on the bar beside Buck.) You know what, John? I don' fight fair.

JOHN: You know what, Buck? Nobody's goin' to hold it against you. He would have killed you.

BUCK: C'mon, I'll ride back to Chaparral with you. All of a sudden, I feel . . . tired.

danger to American Jews, then not to assassinate such a person would be one of the most immoral courses I could imagine.") [Note: Meir Kahane was assassinated in New York in 1990 by a Muslim fundamentalist who considered Kahane to be a threat to Islam.]

Question: When (if ever) is it morally right to deliberately kill another human being "with malice aforethought"? What justifies such a course of action? If you had been the hunter in this story, what would you have done?

11 A young woman in her early twenties decided that she was ready to have children. She also decided that she would settle for nothing less than the best genes possible for those children. So she sought out three different men who met her qualifications: one with an attractive and healthy physique, one of high intelligence, and one bearing sensitive artistic and moral qualities. Over the next four years she became pregnant by the three men and gave birth to three beautiful babies that grew into healthy and happy children. She was then married to another man (he was not one of the fathers) who became a loving father to the children. They were considered by all who knew them as the typical American family.

12 The story is told of a tragic incident that occurred when a frontier village was raided by Indians. Several members of the village hid where they could not be found. One woman had a very small baby in her arms. As some Indians drew close, she smothered the baby rather than risk giving away their hiding place and thereby ensuring death for them all. Some time after the raid, she was punished by both church and community for committing murder.

13 From George Bernard Shaw (via *Playboy*): A young woman was asked by a rich man if she would spend the night with him. She responded with a righteous "No!" When he asked if she would for a hundred thousand dollars, she uttered an exultant "Yes!" "Then what about ten thousand dollars?" he asked. With some hesitation: "Yes, I guess I would." "Then what about five hundred dollars?" She replied angrily, "No, what do you think I am?" To which his final words were: "We have already established that. Now we're merely haggling over the price."

14 Joseph Fletcher recounts an episode involving the ship *William Brown*, which struck an iceberg off Newfoundland and sank in 1841. Seven crewmen and thirty-two passengers crowded into a lifeboat, but this was almost double the number the lifeboat could hold. Winds and heavy seas would have capsized the whole lot in a very short time. So the first mate ordered the men in the company out of the boat, but no one moved. One of the crewmen—a man named Holmes—therefore tossed some of the men into the ocean. The rest in the boat survived and were eventually rescued. In Philadelphia, Holmes was tried and convicted of murder, though the jury recommended clemency.

(This incident has received some legal attention. The issue is whether such a "crime" can be excused or justified because of the circumstances. To date, a defense argument based on "necessity" [that is, a greater harm would have occurred if the defendant hadn't acted as he did] is not allowed in capital crimes such as homicide. "However, there is some authority which would justify even the taking of an innocent human life, if absolutely necessary for the preservation of the lives of others . . . providing some lottery or other arbitrary means is

There slowly grew up in me an unshakable conviction that we have no right to inflict suffering and death on another living creature unless there is some unavoidable necessity for it, and that we ought all of us to feel what a horrible thing it is to cause suffering and death out of mere thoughtlessness.

ALBERT SCHWEITZER

designated for selecting which life is to be taken. [e.g., the 'shipwreck' cases; *U.S. v. Holmes,* 26 Fed. Cas. No. 360]. . . . And, the presence of such facts may be enough to reduce the homicide from murder to manslaughter . . . although this is a minority view." William A. Rutter, *Criminal Law,* Harcourt Brace Jovanovich, 1976, pp. 213–218.)

I remember on the trip home on Apollo 11 it suddenly struck me that that tiny pea, pretty and blue, was the earth. I put up my thumb and shut one eye, and my thumb blotted out the planet earth. I didn't feel like a giant. I felt very, very small.

NEIL ARMSTRONG

15 Near the turn of the century a young couple in a small Arkansas town were still childless after several years of marriage. When they went to their doctor to find out why, tests showed the man to be sterile. After talking over their problem, they went together to their local pastor and asked him if he would make the wife pregnant. In due time, he obliged, and she conceived. The child was fully accepted by the man and his wife and was loved and raised as their own. The minister, however, was forced to surrender his orders and leave the ministry.

Three Ethical Questions

16 There are three questions that, if asked sincerely and explored carefully, will carry one a long way toward understanding ethical problems and deciding what moral action to take in the very human dilemmas in which we find ourselves caught. Three questions. That may sound simple; and authentic morality may indeed be simpler than our tangled analyses often indicate. However, our previous exploration of value judgments should remind us that ethical problems can be very complex.

Through evolution humans have become the ethical animal.

CONRAD WADDINGTON

The three questions: (1) **Who** actually makes an ethical decision? (2) What criteria should I use in making a relevant and meaningful ethical decision? (3) To whom (or what) do my moral obligations apply?

A fourth question might logically follow these three: Can I in fact **do** what I decide is right? That is, having decided what is right, can I **will** it and then **do** what I will? We need not belabor the question at this point, since the problems of autonomy and freedom around which this question turns have been covered in previous chapters (see Chapter 4-3). The more mature the self has become, the better are the chances that one will be able to will into action what he knows to be right. There is a close correlation between personal autonomy and ethical behavior.

An eye for an eye only ends up making the whole world blind.

Gandhi (the motion picture)

Who Really Makes Decisions?

17 The first question we must answer is: **Who is to make the ethical decision?** We can assume that only the individual can make moral choices and act them out, but determining what action is moral may not have been decided at all. On this question regarding decision, there are two schools of thought, for we can speak of (1) authoritarian decisions, and (2) autonomous decisions.

In authoritarian ethics, decisions about right and wrong are given. They originate objectively and are not the product of one's personal experience. That is, the decisions of what is right and what is wrong have **already** been made, perhaps by an authority or a society—but often by a deity who subsequently revealed his decisions at some point to mortals. It was assumed by different people, for instance, that the decision had been made by Yahweh (and revealed in the Torah or the Decalogue); or by Allah (and revealed in the Quran); or by Shamash (and revealed to Hammurabi); or by Ahura Mazda (and revealed to Zoroaster). In the case of the Decalogue, an absolute decision had already been made: killing, lying, stealing, and so forth are wrong, and any further debate is out of the question.

What is humanity's task? To obey these laws. Our first responsibility is to know the rules and then to resolve the ethical problems of our daily lives by the faithful application of these laws. We also have an obligation to cultivate the moral life **so that we will be able to act morally** when forced to make moral choices.

Hence, these are authoritarian ethics. The individual takes no part in the first-order decision-making on what constitutes moral/immoral behavior. The given laws are immutable and final.

18 Autonomous ethics arise from inside oneself, for the individual himself has been in on the decision-making regarding what constitutes moral/immoral action. As the word **autonomy** implies, the individual is self-determined; his actions are manifestations of his own decisions.

We can contrast these two forms of ethics. The first is behavior that conforms to given codes and social customs; the second is autonomous—ethical behavior that is inner-motivated and grounded in genuine moral interest in the well-being of others. Autonomous ethics is largely the product of one's own experience; in this sense it is deeply personal, reflecting one's own sensibilities and values. Furthermore, in this perspective, "morality" is not merely **what one does;** it is rather the inevitable expression of **what one is.** It is a sincere goodwill and never empty conformity to prevailing customs. In a word, it is autonomous.

19 Jean-Paul Sartre has stated his conviction, based on his belief in human freedom, that **all** ethical decisions are autonomous, that in the final analysis there are no authoritarian ethics. Sartre is saying that although we may adhere to given customs and codes—from parents, peers, society, church—when making ethical decisions each of us still decides which codes we will use in resolving our problems. If we decide to seek answers to our ethical questions by applying the Decalogue rather than our parents' values, or by appealing to our church's teaching rather than to peer values, then it is still we who make such decisions.

Ultimately, therefore, we can never escape personal responsibility for the ethical decisions that **we** make; and we are likewise responsible for the moral/immoral actions that **we** perform.

Sartre's position is a sort of half-truth. He is surely correct when speaking of persons who, to use his phrase, "have become conscious"—that is, those who have become aware of alternatives. The ethically informed individual **knows** that there are many criteria for making decisions; knowing this, the individual's decisions rest upon his or her own shoulders, and one must assume responsibility for them.

But for the majority of us, such options don't exist. We are convinced that there is but a single set of rights and wrongs: how could it be otherwise? If one believes with all one's heart that the decision of right/wrong has been wholly settled, and that this settlement is embodied in a single set of customs or codes, then the individual cannot justly be held responsible for **not** making ethical decisions based on other codes which (in our opinion, perhaps) would have been superior decisions. For this individual, it is not possible, as Sartre would have it, to say "No!" to one's own given code.

Perhaps the truer half of Sartre's argument needs to be emphasized: once we become aware that there are many criteria for making ethical decisions, then the full responsibility for our own decisions rests squarely and heavily upon our shoulders.

What Makes a Decision Right or Wrong?

20 The second question we must answer is: **What criteria should I use in making a relevant and meaningful ethical decision?** Or put differently: What is the source of the data that I should take into account in making an ethical judgment? Three different answers to this question come from (1) the formalist, (2) the relativist, and (3) the contextualist.

"Chi Wen Tzu used to think thrice before acting. The master hearing of it said, 'Twice is quite enough.'"

Confucius
Analects

Formalism or the Ethics of Principle The formalist believes that the criteria to be used in making ethical decisions are universal laws that apply to all people. Man's responsibility is to be informed on these rules **ahead of time**—that is, before we find ourselves caught up in life's ethical complexities. By analogy, one should know the laws in the state motor-vehicle code **before** getting behind the wheel and taking to the streets. Likewise, we should be taught the laws of the moral life before taking to the highways. Our personal task, in both cases, is to be thoroughly acquainted with the rules so that we can apply them to concrete situations as we come to them. Whether approaching a red light or being tempted to cheat, we should know to **stop,** since we have studied the codebook. (Our first obligation, of course, is to try to avoid situations where weighty ethical decisions have to be made, but daily life rarely permits us so easy an out.)

21 There are several kinds of formal ethical codes. One kind is represented by the Decalogue, traditionally written on Mount Sinai by "the finger of God." These are apodictic laws—absolute and incontestable. In actual practice they don't work and must be continually redefined and modified. The commandment "Thou shalt not kill" is hardly practicable if a tribe is fighting for its survival against other invading tribes. So "to kill" was understood to mean "to murder"; hence, by redefinition, it became applicable only to fellow citizens in good

standing. (Actually, this is not a redefinition, since the Commandment was never intended to have general application. It is for this reason that the reported killing of three thousand Israelites by Moses and the Levites in a single day (Exodus 32:26–29) is not at all a violation of the Commandment against killing (Exodus 20:13). To the ancient Hebrew the Sixth Commandment implicitly meant, "Thou shalt not kill a fellow Hebrew as long as he is a faithful follower of the god Yahweh." If this interpretation seems puzzling, read Deuteronomy 13:6–11.)

The German philosopher Immanuel Kant concluded that universal moral laws do exist, but that they are to be found within the structure of the human mind. Just as 7 + 5 is always 12—it is a priori knowledge yet applies to the real world—there are, Kant holds, moral "rules of thought" that are a priori and therefore universal (like 7 + 5 = 12). Kant writes that ethical rules "must not be sought in human nature or in the circumstances of the world . . . but [must be sought] a priori simply in the concepts of reason." Kant formulated his famous "categorical imperative" to be such an a priori rule. It categorically applies to all rational persons and is imperative as an absolute "ought" that binds them to the moral law. His formula (in part) is: "Act only on the maxim whereby thou canst at the same time will it should become a universal law." This resembles our concept of natural law as described by modern physics. Kant was contending that if any kind of action can be universalized, then it is ethical. For instance, can I universalize lying? Hardly. I may think lying expediently justifiable in some particular case, but can I therefore recommend telling lies as a universal form of behavior? Obviously not. Human interaction would be rendered chaotic if we couldn't depend upon one another. Therefore, telling the truth is a "categorical imperative."

A more recent attempt to develop a system of universal formal laws was undertaken by the American philosopher Edgar Brightman. For example, the Law of Autonomy: "All persons ought to recognize themselves as obligated to choose in accordance with the ideals which they acknowledge." The Law of Consequences: "All persons ought to consider and, on the whole, approve the foreseeable consequences of each of their choices." The Laws of Altruism: "Each person ought to respect all other persons as ends in themselves, and, as far as possible, to co-operate with others in the production and enjoyment of shared values." These are normative laws; they state what we ought to do. Because of their logical and axiomatic nature, they are meant to apply universally to all ethical decisions made by human beings.

22 RELATIVISM Another answer to our second question comes from the relativist. The relativist begins with the empirical fact that there are numerous systems of customs and codes to be found in various societies. The Greek Sophist Protagoras (481–411 BC) was one of the first philosophers to observe in his travels that different societies do in fact have different customs that are morally binding upon their respective inhabitants. Protagoras thus began to understand the function of customs and codes: they serve to regulate and give cohesion to a society. He therefore concluded that within any particular society, its own set of customs and codes is right **for it** since they perform the very pragmatic function of enabling that society to operate with a greater degree of internal harmony.

What is "right" is therefore what works in a society, and whatever "works" in a society is therefore right. Notions of right and wrong are therefore relative to a particular society, and they differ from one society to another.

Protagoras also noted a corollary to his relativism. If one is to spend time in other societies (as he and his fellow Sophists did), then one is morally obligated to obey the vital customs and codes of the societies he visits. "Who are we," he would ask, "to come as visitors to some society other than our own, bringing with us our own social customs and moral convictions which may be quite alien to that society, and then have the effrontery to claim that **our** customs and codes are the ones that are really right? Wouldn't such behavior serve to destroy the integrated system which that society has working for it? And wouldn't our actions therefore be immoral in the truest sense?" And isn't Protagoras right?

Relativists hold that one can make meaningful ethical decisions only in the social context in which an ethical problem occurs. In other words, what is right in one place or time may be wrong in another place or time. Infanticide may have been right in Caesar's time, but is not in twentieth-century Rome. Polygamy (but with not more than four wives) may be right in Cairo, but not in Tel Aviv. And for a man to share his wife (his property!) with an overnight guest may be right in an Eskimo igloo, but not in Middletown, U.S.A.

Ethical relativism may mean something else: that what is right for one person may be wrong for another. This, again, is merely the recognition of the fact that different people have different convictions and follow different customs. It is wrong for Jews and Muslims to eat pork; it is wrong for Jains to eat any animal flesh at all. But such restrictions do not apply to Christians, Shintos, or others outside the faith.

23 CONTEXTUALISM A third answer comes from the contextualist who believes, first, that moral laws of the kind held by the formalist don't exist. There are no rules that one can memorize ahead of time and apply meaningfully to a particular situation. Nor will the contextualist go along with the relativist. The contextualist will readily agree that societies do in fact possess different customs and codes, and that these perform the pragmatic function which the relativist claims they do. Granted: Romans practiced infanticide, Greeks practiced slavery, Cypriots practiced sacred prostitution, modern societies disenfranchise minorities, whole nations generate hate toward other nations—societies indeed do such things, but that doesn't make such practices ethically right. The fact that a practice exists doesn't make it moral. What societies actually do, therefore, is no guideline for deciding what is ethically right.

The contextualist holds that relevant criteria for making a meaningful ethical decision can be found only within the context of each concrete ethical problem. Every ethical situation is in fact unique, and a truly ethical solution to a problem can be arrived at only when **all the factors** of the unique situation can be weighed **by those involved in the problem.** Each person makes the best possible decision, using the best knowledge he or she possesses at that time of decision. Such a meaningful ethical judgment can be made only after the problem situation exists, not before.

Such ideas as "don't kill," "don't steal," and so forth, can serve us well as general guidelines, but they must be abandoned if the specific situation calls for it. Dietrich Bonhoeffer phrased it eloquently: "Principles are only tools in God's hands soon to be thrown away as unserviceable." The same applies to formalistic rules, which may prove irrelevant to a particular set of conditions. In fact, the contextualist contends that moral predicaments constantly make it necessary for us to kill, steal, lie, or whatever, **to be moral.**

Implied in all this is one single guideline, which the contextualist uses in making all ethical decisions. That guideline is one's concern for the well-being of others. This principle can be developed in several ways. In *Situation Ethics,* Joseph Fletcher formulates it in terms of *agape,* the "ethical love" or "empathetic concern" that is the foundation of Christian ethics. Fletcher submits that only love is good, and rules are made to serve love, not the other way around. One who is truly involved in the well-being of another may be called upon to kill, to tell lies, or more; to carry through, in authentic action, loving concern for that other person. Again, the **rules** serve **love.** There are no laws that the contextualist will not finally break, if forced to, to manifest his or her ethical love for another. Just as Thoreau could say of civil law that if it "requires you to be the agent of injustice to another," then "break the law," the contextualist would say that if so-called moral laws require you to act unlovingly toward others, then break the "moral laws."

Contextualism can also be formulated in pragmatic terms. It is only our ethical concern for the well-being of others that produces a positive environment in which all of us can more fully actualize our lives. Qualities are contagious. Compassion and concern generate compassion and concern, just as hate generates hate and distrust generates distrust. Such basically human qualities as love, concern, and trust are the only qualities upon which a fulfilling collective existence can be grounded.

24 To summarize, therefore, the contextualist holds the following: (1) there are no universal moral laws; (2) ethical decisions can be made only in the context of concrete situations; and (3) there is a fundamental ethical guideline for all ethical behavior—one's authentic concern for the well-being of others.

Contextualism has significant implications. It recognizes accurately the nature of our moral predicaments. Our most agonizing ethical decisions must be made in situations where only **bad** alternatives are open to us. If daily life always set up situations so that we had to choose between a good option and a bad option, then moral existence would be simple. But actual-life situations continually force us into predicaments in which only various degrees of bad-consequence alternatives are open to choice. We may have to kill to save ourselves, a friend, an innocent victim; we may have to lie, to pretend, to play games to protect someone from serious damage.

Contextual ethics says that if, out of one's concern for the well-being of others, one makes the **best decision** he or she possibly can, then that person is unequivocally moral. If one must tell lies to save another then he or she has acted morally; not to have lied—to have allowed irreparable harm to come to another person when one was in a position to prevent it—would have been immoral. Since this is the way that life forces us to make decisions, there is no justification for holding a person morally guilty for making the best decision possible in any given predicament.

By contrast, formalism and most forms of relativism have admitted that we often have to take bad action in a situation because good alternatives don't exist, but they also contend that this doesn't make the bad action right. "Having to do what is wrong doesn't make it right." And having done wrong, we **should** feel guilt, and we may justly be subject to moral or civil recriminations. Contextualism responds that such a person is morally innocent and is, in fact, morally commendable. Having chosen the best options available, why should anyone be judged to be immoral or unethical?

Whom (and What) Should I Care About?

25 The third question that one must answer is: **To whom (or what) do my moral obligations apply?** We must ask ourselves how large we are obligated to draw our circle of ethical concern. Should our ethical actions apply only to ourselves and to our primary groups such as family, clan, sect, or firm? Or do they extend to all the members of our tribe, nation, religion, or race? Do they extend to one's antagonist, attacker, enemy? Do they extend to all human beings? to all higher forms of life? to all organisms that share the impulse-to-life?

Historically, people have rather universally applied their codes of ethics only to their in-groups. Since groups are forever engaged in attempts to annihilate one another, survival demands that ethical niceties be suspended during wartime. Applied to one's own group, ethical obligations produce social cohesion, predictable and orderly behavior; they reduce internecine discord of all kinds and make it possible for a united group to fight other groups with greater efficiency. Hence—as Protagoras saw so clearly—ethical codes are pragmatic necessities.

Quite simply, ethical obligations practiced in the in-group don't apply to those outside; the out-group (historically, anyway) has never been the object of serious ethical concern. This distinction between out-group and in-group, with a code governing behavior in the in-group, is merely one aspect of the whole evolutionary arrangement. From prairie dogs and baboons to humans, in-group behavior is clearly prescribed, while behavior toward all out-groups is a matter of expediency: whatever aids survival is good/moral/right/just/virtuous—and necessary!

26 Since conditions on "Spaceship Earth" are rapidly changing, this question needs continual reexploration. Although in-group consciousness continues, and will continue, in countless forms, we need to ask whether, in a shrinking world, one's circle of obligations must be extended for purely pragmatic reasons.

Increasing numbers of people are thinking of the whole human species as a single in-group. If we should be attacked by extraterrestrials, the feeling of humanity's oneness would immediately surface, and for the same old reason: unite to survive. But lacking an obvious antagonist, the unity of the human species is not yet a world-fact, though sought by some and intuited by many more.

The belief that all people comprise a single **ethical** community is not new. The Stoics taught that all men are subject to the same natural and moral laws,

and that they should therefore be subject to the same civil laws. People should belong to a *cosmopolis*—a "world-city"—and should not be artificially broken up into tribes and states with different laws. Some branches of Christianity and Islam have developed similar concepts, and Jesus's mandate that we love even our enemies would, in effect, annihilate all boundaries between people.

Do our ethical obligations extend further yet? Do they extend to the higher animals? (Do they extend to our pets?) Do they extend to all animal life? The Hindus and Jains have always believed so. Do we have moral obligations to plants? to all of nature? The American Indians believe that we do. (See the words of Chief Seattle on p. 434.)

Exactly how does one finally decide how wide his circle of ethical concern should extend?

27 Ethical affirmation of life is the intellectual act by which man ceases simply to live at random and begins to concern himself reverently with his own life, so that he may realize its true value. And the first step in the evolution of ethics is a sense of solidarity with other human beings.

To the primitive, this solidarity has narrow limits. It is confined, first to his blood relations, then to the members of his tribe, who represent to him the family enlarged. I have such primitives in my hospital. If I ask an ambulatory patient to undertake some small service for a patient who must stay in bed, he will do it only if the bedridden patient belongs to his tribe. If that is not the case, he will answer me with wide-eyed innocence: "This man is not brother of me." Neither rewards nor threats will induce him to perform a service for such a stranger.

But as soon as man begins to reflect upon himself and his relationship to others, he becomes aware that men as such are his equals and his neighbors. Gradually he sees the circle of his responsibilities widening until it includes all human beings with whom he has dealings. . . . The idea of the brotherhood of all human beings is inherent in the metaphysics of most of the great religious systems. Moreover, since antiquity, philosophy has presented the case for humanitarianism as a concept recommended by reason.

Throughout history, however, the insight that we have a wider duty toward human beings has never attained the dominance to which it is entitled. Down to our own times it has been undermined by differences of race, religion, and nationality.

Man belongs to man.

ALBERT SCHWEITZER

✦

Baruch Spinoza

The God-Intoxicated Philosopher

In the seventeenth century, it was said that Amsterdam was a Protestant city with a Jewish heart. That heart was the Jewish ghetto, out of which came one of the most honored of all Western philosophers, Baruch Spinoza: "the noblest and most lovable of the great philosophers" (Russell); "the holy and excommunicated Spinoza" (Schleiermacher); "the god-intoxicated man" (Novalis). "There is no other philosophy than Spinoza's" (Lessing). "To be a philosopher one must first be a Spinozist" (Hegel). "No man has ever lived closer to what he himself taught" (W. T. Jones). "Nietzsche says somewhere that the last Christian died upon the cross. He had forgotten Spinoza" (Durant).

The ghetto existed in Holland's free atmosphere as a result of the flight of Jews from the Inquisition in Spain and Portugal. Spinoza's grandfather and father had fled persecution, settling and prospering in Holland. His father, Miguel de Espinoza, was a merchant and a pillar of the synagogue. His mother was Hana Debora, Miguel's second wife, also from Lisbon. She was a bright, quiet, somber woman who died of tuberculosis when Spinoza was six, bequeathing her illness to her son. The child was raised by Miguel's third wife.

Spinoza was born and raised in Amsterdam and never traveled beyond the borders of his native Holland. Educated first in the synagogue school, he became thoroughly knowledgeable in the thought and literature of his heritage—scriptures, the Talmud, medieval commentators and philosophers, and even the secrets of the *kabala,* which fascinated but repelled his rational intellect. To all this was added a good grounding in the sciences, mathematics, and geometry; he was profoundly moved by Descartes' attempt to give a geometrical structure to all knowledge. A natural linguist, he was fluent in Spanish, Portuguese, Dutch, Hebrew, and Latin and had a working knowledge of Greek, French, Italian, and (probably) German. He learned his Latin by attending the Latin school of a Dutch scholar, Frans van den Ende. He studied the Greek philosophers (he loved the Stoics), the scholastics, and Catholic theology. He was always brilliant in his scholarship, and his father, family, and rabbis cherished the hope that young Spinoza would make significant contributions to Judaic learning.

God and all the attributes of God are eternal.

Footnote to Spinoza: Language usually makes Nature feminine and God masculine; by identifying them Spinoza does more justice to the female or productive principle in reality. Perhaps the masculinization of God was part of the patriarchal subordination of woman, who is, after all, the main stream of human reality.

WILL DURANT

Men govern nothing with more difficulty than their tongues.

[The Amsterdam Synagogue's Ritual of Excommunication] "With the judgment of the angels and the sentence of the saints, we anathematize, execrate, curse and cast out Baruch de Espinoza . . ."

Romance touched his life once. He fell in love with his Latin teacher's daughter, Clara Marie, who assisted her father in Spinoza's Latin lessons. She was bright, feminine, and on the verge of becoming a woman. Spinoza, increasingly dedicated to Latin, clearly had marriage in mind; but a mutual love failed to develop and she married one of his fellow students instead. Years later he still spoke of her with affection.

By the time Spinoza was twenty, he was thinking his own thoughts. He had for years been absorbing the ideas of the great minds of the Western tradition; he had read every point of view, played with ideas lovingly, and discovered that in the world of the mind he was free. The safe and single path—the uncritical submission to orthodox doctrine—was, for him, no longer an option. His thinking had become unshackled. He soared, without boundaries; and in his thoughts he traveled to the far corners of the intellectual world.

Spinoza pondered and questioned what he had been taught in the synagogue. There were contradictions in scripture. He doubted whether Moses had written the entire Torah, especially the passage that narrated his own death. Some of the hate-filled passages of scripture, he suggested, were only allegories. He had begun to wonder too openly whether God exists, whether there is an afterlife, and where the universe came from; what the relationship is of God to cosmic matter, whether angels exist, where in the body the soul is located. Biblical miracles, he thought, were probably natural events mythologized by imagination. For Spinoza, reason is the trustworthy path to truth, however much it may come into conflict with authoritarian claims.

The rabbis of the synagogue were not unsympathetic to the young Jew's intellectual flights and were willing to conciliate, but they had to concern themselves with the safety of their community. They were there at the sufferance of the Calvinist Dutch government and people, who were easily threatened by heretical opinions, doubly so should they arise from a barely tolerated minority. So the leaders of the community asked Spinoza to be discreet; if he couldn't stop thinking, he might at least mute his public statements of doubt and dissent. They summoned him, tried to reason with him, offered him a stipend if he would consent to silence. But he was beyond negotiation. He became more resolute, more articulate, and a cause célèbre. A reactionary member of his own faith attempted one night to kill him on the streets, but Spinoza ducked and the assailant's knife cut only his coat.

Feeling they had no recourse, the leaders of the synagogue proceeded against Spinoza with full excommunication on July 24, 1656. He was twenty-three. The solemn ceremony was held in the synagogue; the ritual was read aloud to the blowing of the ram's horn and the burning of black altar candles. During the recitation the lights were extinguished one by one till the congregation sat silently in darkness.

Spinoza was "anathematized" and severed forever "from the people of Israel." The malediction called for him to be cursed in the sight of God. No one could talk with him or communicate with him in writing, or read anything he had written. No one could come within six feet of him, touch him, or stay under the same roof with him. Disowned by family, mentors and teachers, and friends, in the eyes of the community of Israel he was henceforth dead, a nonperson, condemned to a new life. As a symbol of his translation, he changed his first name from Hebrew into Latin: "Baruch" became "Benedictus"—meaning "blessed" in both languages.

For the rest of his short life Spinoza lived modestly in Protestant communities and with friends, first on the outskirts of Amsterdam, then in Leyden, and finally in the capital city, The Hague. He wrote continually but published only two works during his lifetime. He had suffered enough, and any word that he might publish brought an outcry of hostility, which he chose to avoid. Still, his writing and ideas became widely known. He developed friends everywhere, and gradually some of the great spirits of his age joined his circle.

Spinoza's life lacked all the fashionable color and excitement; it was an adventure of the mind. He refused to argue, speak in public, or attend society or salons. He remained by himself or with friends, working quietly, thinking and writing, conversing and exchanging ideas. He earned his living primarily by grinding and polishing lenses, supplementing his small income by teaching and making sketches. As his fame increased he had numerous offers of money and gifts, most of which he declined.

Spinoza was a handsome figure, with a gentle, kindly, sad face. He had a dark olive complexion, black hair, and great sensitive black eyes. He was of medium height, and slender. He dressed carefully but plainly. His lifestyle was simple. He had a substantial library, and his supreme enjoyments were to share an evening with friends, smoke his pipe, and read. He had virtually no pride, never sought prestige, never indulged in self-aggrandizement. He was patient, cheerful and friendly, serene, and shy. All in all, he was a Buddhist monk in an alien place and time.

✦

Those who have wrestled with Spinoza's *Ethics* commonly emerge with glowing praise and/or bewilderment. His "system of morals is the supreme achievement of modern thought," the "most precious production in modern philosophy," the "noblest work to grace a human pen," and so on. Its full title in Latin is *Ethica ordine geometrica demonstrata,* so named because he wanted to develop a philosophical system with the clarity of geometric logic, proceeding sequentially from precise assumptions (definitions, axioms, propositions) to absolutely certain conclusions. He was following Descartes's method but went far beyond him.

The *Ethics* is divided into three parts. The first, "On the Nature of God," deals with metaphysics. God, in Spinoza's reasoning, is not an anthropomorphic father-figure who gets uptight about petty human foibles. (He abandoned this image along with his orthodox Judaic heritage.) Rather, God is the "substance" of the world, not the physical "matter," not "nature"—but the "essence" or "being" that underlies both material and nonmaterial reality. This divine substance is known to humans in two ways (as two "attributes") —as matter and mind. (As you're reading these words, you are experiencing both attributes: your mind as consciousness and this page as physical matter; both are merely "attributes" of the underlying substance which is God.) Furthermore, God does not **give** laws to nature: God **is** the laws of nature. Nature, therefore, appears rational to our minds (as "physics"), for God **is** rational, and (as Hegel would later phrase it) the real is rational, and the rational is real.

The second part of *Ethics* concerns psychology—the science of understanding the mind. Spinoza attempts to heal and make whole the human person by reversing Descartes's mind–body dualism. Spinoza argues that the body (seen from the outside) and the mind (perceived inwardly) are a unity—one organism working for survival. When the mind thinks a thought, it isn't the mind that thinks it—as though the mind were a discarnate consciousness operating by itself; rather, the body thinks the thought and the mind is aware of it as it's being thought. (The mind is a TV monitor watching the body as it is thinking.)

Spinoza observed that the elemental drive of each organism is self-preservation. "Each man should love himself, and seek what is useful to him. . . . Each one should endeavor to preserve his being as far as in him lies." All thought is for survival, and any thought that helps one survive is good. "No virtue can be conceived as prior to this endeavor to preserve one's own being." Here is an evolutionary ethic two centuries before evolutionary theory was developed.

Each person is powered by reason and emotion. Emotions become "passions" when we fail to understand our emotions and allow them to become manipulated by external circumstance. One function of the rational mind is to de-

The more we understand individual objects, the more we understand God.

We do not strive for, wish, seek, or desire anything because we think it to be good; we judge a thing to be good because we . . . desire it.

A free man thinks of nothing less than of death, and his wisdom is a meditation not on death but on life.

The endeavor to understand is the first and only basis of virtue.

Men under the guidance of reason . . . desire nothing for themselves which they do not also desire for the rest of mankind.

Fear cannot be without hope nor hope without fear.

velop the power of reason over the emotions since "the more an emotion becomes known to us, the more it is within our power." Our emotional needs are to be acknowledged and met, to be sure; but it is the intellect that must select **which** are to be met and **how** they are to be met. Our goal is to become autonomous, and to do this we must use our reason, deciding which of our emotions and desires we will act on—this is an act of the intelligence. The wise man will maximize pleasure and minimize pain, for himself and others.

For those who see the oneness of all things, there cannot be multiple points-of-view. Separateness is the result of "inadequate ideas"—incomplete understanding. For all that exists is One. The universe is one, Mankind is one, and each of us is not a duality but a single, whole organism. We are all expressions of God/natural law working in us. God and nature are one. Mind and body are one. Science and religion are one. All antagonisms and limited perspectives are the result of our mental schematics that fail to recognize that God is everything working to express himself.

Spinoza moved to The Hague in 1670 and spent the last years of his life in a one-room apartment on the top floor of a rented house. The room had a high-beamed ceiling, wood paneling, and one wide window. He slept in a fold-away bed. This was his last home. (The dwelling—known as "Spinoza-haus"—is now preserved as a historical monument.)

Here he worked steadily on books and letters, sometimes laboring for weeks or months before going out. Still, it wasn't the life of a recluse; he was visited continually by friends, followers, and dignitaries. He conversed knowledgeably on virtually any subject, especially on social and political events. Many of his friends were Protestants, and he occasionally attended church services with them and listened to sermons. In 1673 the University of Heidelberg offered him a teaching chair in philosophy, but he declined the offer. He said he preferred his freedom.

By this date his magnum opus, the *Ethics,* was almost complete, and he considered having it published; but publication of his work was banned and religious opposition to his ideas was so virulent that he put his manuscript back into his desk, where it remained until after his death.

The dust from his lens-grinding had long been damaging his consumptive lungs, and he found breathing increasingly difficult. For a chronic cough he sipped an elixir of rose leaves. On Sunday, February 20, 1677, he died, quietly, with only his physician by his side. His friends had gone to church. In the funeral cortège six carriages with many notables followed his coffin. He was buried in a Protestant cemetery in The Hague.

✦

Reflections

1 What is the difference between a fact-claim and a value judgment? By way of review, how do you go about checking the truth of a fact-claim? (See Chapter 3-4.) How do you go about checking out value judgments?

2 Are you an "issue maker"? That is, are you prone to creating issues when it might be easier to solve problems? Or, are you essentially a pragmatic problem-solver? Can you give examples from your own experience of persons or personalities who are especially visible for the making of petty issues?

3 The most significant ethical choice that we make is deciding if we will approach a problem as a formalist, a relativist, or a contextualist. All our ethical problems are seen, interpreted, and resolved from one of these posi-

tions, or combinations of them. So, before proceeding further, think about how each of these schools analyzes an ethical problem. Work on each until it is succinct and clear.

4 Return to the case studies (pp. 367–371) and zero in on each problem. How would the formalist, relativist, and contextualist analyze and resolve the problem in each case?

5 Summarize in your words the basic tenets of the formalist, relativist, and contextual approaches. What are the strengths and the weaknesses of each system? In which school of ethics do you personally feel most comfortable?

6 After working through the case studies (as suggested in number 4, above), what are your most significant ethical conclusions? Can killing, stealing, lying, and so forth, be ethically and/or morally justified? Are your solutions ones that you can live with and practice—at least for now?

7 What is your personal answer to the first ethical question (pp. 371–373); "Who is to make the ethical decision?" Do you accept Sartre's contention that all ethical decisions are autonomous since only persons make decisions?

8 Buck Cannon believes that he broke an ethical code that he should have obeyed. "I don't fight fair," he grumbled. Yet we can be sure he felt a sense of justice about what he had done. How can you reconcile these two feelings? Can you justify ethically and/or morally what Buck Cannon did? In this episode there is a distinct difference between being ethical and being moral. What is that difference? Who was ethical and who was moral? Explain why.

9 To the question, "To whom (or what) do my moral obligations apply?" (pp. 377–380), what is your personal answer? Do they apply to your pet animals? to wild animals? to all living things? Does Schweitzer's "Reverence for Life" appeal to you as a solution to this problem? (See pp. 379–380 and marginal quote on p. 370. See also pp. 444–445 and 449–452.)

10 Return to the first page of this chapter and spend some leisurely thought on Seng-Ts'an's counsel that we "be not concerned with right and wrong." What is Seng-Ts'an saying to us?

The Protoplasmic Venture

"Are you happy? Why did you do all this, why did you struggle so hard . . . ?"

"Why! For what!" Nikolaiev leaned forward and one sensed a sort of heraldic thunder rumbling in him. "Why, to be more. What else is life for? To develop all your possibilities. That is happiness, to love what you're doing, to keep expanding, to keep turning into something more."

Ostrander and Schroeder

LIFE

6-1

Sir Isaiah Berlin once said, "Humans can't live without seeking to describe and explain the universe." But a lack of empirical information has always stymied attempts to answer the four big etiological questions: How did the universe as a whole come about? What is physical matter and how did it originate? How and when did life begin? And how did human beings come to exist? As of the turn of the millennium, viable answers to all four of these questions are beginning to take shape, enabling us to reformulate responses to the two eternal questions: How does the world work? And who are we humans and what is our place in the scheme of things? This chapter deals with origins and considers some philosophical issues raised by evolutionary theory.

THE FOUR GREAT ETIOLOGICAL QUESTIONS

1 During the past half century scientists working in the field of biochemical evolution have made a quantum-leap breakthrough. They have succeeded in laying the empirical foundations for answering one of the persistent questions raised by the human mind: **What is the origin of life?** And, as so often happens after the mind is fortified with facts, we look back and say, "Of course! Now the answer is beginning to make sense. **I understand!**"

2 This sort of philosophic question is not one of the common garden variety. It's one of the four great etiological questions that have baffled and irritated human understanding. These four questions are: What is the origin of **life,** of **humans,** of **matter,** and of the **universe?** These problems have appeared, from the beginning, to be Gordian knots that the human intellect could not cut.

It has taken the planet Earth 4.5 billion years to discover it is 4.5 billion years old.

GEORGE WALD

This secret spoke Life herself unto me: "Behold," said she, "I am that which must ever surpass itself."

FRIEDRICH NIETZSCHE

> *Life is not one of the fundamental categories of the universe, like matter, energy, and time, but is a manifestation of certain molecular combinations. These combinations cannot have existed forever, since even the elements of which they are composed have not always existed. Therefore life must have had a beginning.*
>
> PHILIP HANDLER (ED.)
> *Biology and the Future of Man*

We had good reason to feel stymied. None of these questions could be answered until enormous amounts of scientific knowledge had been gathered and correlated. Before Western science had reached the stages of intense specialization and, subsequently, interdisciplinary synthesis, any answers to these etiological questions had to be mythical. Humanity was caught in the perennial human predicament. We couldn't stop asking the questions, yet we possessed no factual knowledge that would lead us to the understanding that our collective psyche demanded.

So these questions were dispatched with celebrated pragmatic myths. Whence human beings? We were created from white, red, and brown clay; or we were sculpted from rock, or carved from wood, or assembled from pine bark, turquoise chips, and crow feathers. We were created by Tiki, Juok, i Kombengi, Yahweh, or one of a thousand other anthropomorphic creators.

And whence matter? Whence the universe? On these two etiological puzzles little could be said. Matter apparently exists eternally, shaped into familiar forms by a Demiurge; or a supernatural X-factor created everything in the universe *ex nihilo,* out of nothing. Even when critical minds tried to think carefully about the cosmos, there was still very nearly nothing to be thought. Aristotle is typical. His notion of an Unmoved Mover—the First Domino in an infinite series—was the only near-logical answer to the problem that he could come up with. Virtually no progress was made on any of these problems until the twentieth century.

> *The alphabet of life is obviously extremely simple—a handful of chemicals are responsible for the vast variety we see in the entire biosphere.*
>
> CYRIL PONNAMPERUMA

As of the beginning of the third millennium, however, two of these wild dragons—the origins of life and of human beings—have been domesticated: the rough outlines of an empirical answer are now clear. And the other two—the origins of matter and the universe—have at least been tamed: viable questions and empirical models are beginning to be developed.

BIOCHEMICAL EVOLUTION

3 The beginnings of the science of biochemical evolution are associated primarily with the work of three men. In 1922 a Russian biochemist, Alexander Oparin, delivered before a group of scientists in Moscow a paper outlining his theory of biogenesis. Two years later he published his thoughts in a booklet entitled *The Origin of Life.* In 1928 the English biologist J. B. S. Haldane published a technical paper with a similar line of thinking. Both scientists developed coherent theoretical models from their knowledge of physics and biochemistry, but there was as yet no empirical evidence to support their speculations. Then in 1953 the American biochemist Stanley Miller performed experiments that began to lay empirical foundations for an understanding of how we might have evolved.

Oparin had theorized that during the Earth's early stages a variety of organic compounds developed out of inorganic materials. He described theoretically how these compounds could develop into the first prevital cells and then into living organisms. As the crust of the Earth began to form and the temperature of the atmosphere dropped below a thousand degrees (Celsius), a variety of chemical reactions took place. Torrential rains poured down upon the young planet, accompanied by constant discharges of lightning. Hot pools of water formed containing organic compounds that washed down from the atmosphere. Most important, Oparin thought, were the carbon bonds that formed in ever-larger molecular chains. Fatty acids, sugars, and tannins could have formed in this way. Eventually amino acids, the basic constituents of proteins, could have been naturally synthesized.

Thus, during the first phase of Earth's history—perhaps over the span of a billion years—mixtures of hydrocarbons, nitrogen, hydrogen, and ammonia were continually producing an endless variety of organic compounds that formed complex molecules that became the building-blocks of living cells. At this stage the Earth was covered with what Haldane called a "hot dilute soup" in which these prebiotic reactions were taking place. With the synthesis of proteins the first steps had been taken toward the development of life.

4 The first empirical support for Oparin's theory came from Miller's experiments at the University of Chicago. Into a simple glass apparatus Miller introduced methane, ammonia, and hydrogen. The one essential ingredient of life—carbon—was there in the methane (CH_4). As these chemicals mixed with vapor from boiling water and passed through glass tubes, they flowed across two tungsten electrodes generating a continuous electric spark. All this was designed to simulate hypothetical primitive-Earth conditions—the circulating gases represented the early atmosphere, the flask of boiling liquids represented the young oceans. The experiment ran continuously for a week. At the end of that time, the gases were pumped out and the brownish liquids were analyzed. He found that a variety of organic compounds had formed along with several amino acids. Miller notes that one of the unexpected results was that "the major products were not themselves a random selection of organic compounds but included a surprising number of substances that occur in living organisms."

5 Since Miller's 1953 experiments scientists have added a vast amount of supporting data. Various gaseous mixtures have been tried along with other forms of energy, and in every case biochemically significant molecules were synthesized.

Life is an offensive directed against the repetitious mechanism of the universe.
ALFRED NORTH WHITEHEAD

Many specific ingredients essential to living things have now been formed in the laboratory under possible primitive-earth conditions. These include the creation of carbon chains, polypeptides, and ATP, a catalytic enzyme that supplies the basic source of metabolic energy in living systems.

Significant also is the laboratory creation of porphyrins, molecules that function like plants in being able to utilize light to store energy—a primitive kind of photosynthesis. Miller believes that "almost certainly they became important for the metabolic processes leading to ATP synthesis early in the evolution of life." This supports the suggestion that photosynthesizing cells were among the earliest forms of life.

Another biochemist, Sidney Fox, synthesized microspheres, which he named "proteinoids" because they looked and behaved so much like living protein cells. They possessed a double-layered surface analogous to a membrane, and they carried on a kind of internal enzyme activity. Like living cells, they were sufficiently stable to permit sectioning and staining for microscopic examination. Most significantly, they performed a sort of reproduction. When left

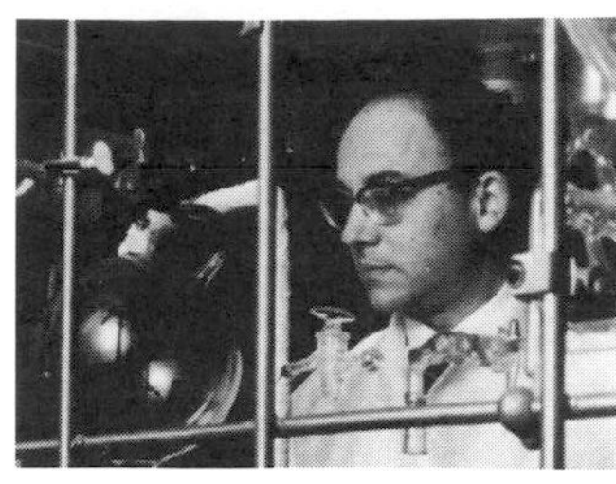

Dr. Stanley Miller with the glass apparatus in which he produced the first empirical evidence supporting the theory that living organisms may have resulted from a combination of chemical compounds. Steam from boiling water in the lower chamber circulated upward through a mixture of ammonia, methane, and hydrogen; then over and down into the larger chamber containing electrodes. After a week of electrical sparking, the water in the tube at bottom had accumulated a variety of amino acids and other organic compounds.

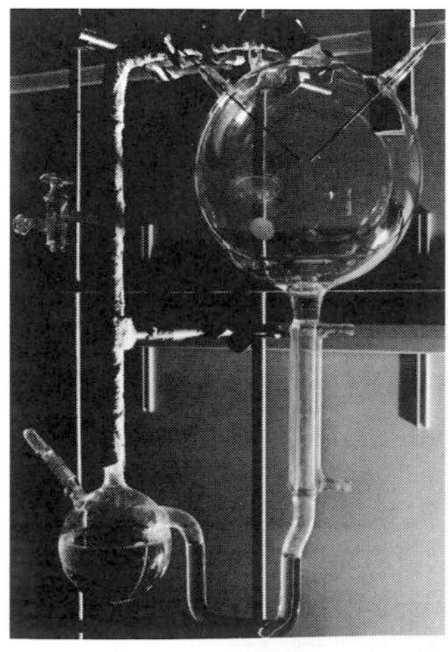

GEOLOGIC TIME SCALE

ERA	PERIOD		EPOCH	YEARS BEFORE THE PRESENT
Cenozoic	Quarternary		Holocene (Recent)	
				11,000
			Pleistocene (Glacial)	
				500,000 to 2,000,000
	Tertiary		Pliocene	
				13,000,000
			Miocene	
				25,000,000
			Oligocene	
				36,000,000
			Eocene	
				58,000,000
			Paleocene	
				63,000,000
Mesozoic	Cretaceous			
				135,000,000
	Jurassic			
				180,000,000
	Triassic			
				230,000,000
Paleozoic	Permian			
				280,000,000
	Carboniferous	Pennsylvanian (Upper Carboniferous)		
				310,000,000
		Mississippian (Lower Carboniferous)		
				345,000,000
	Devonian			
				405,000,000
	Silurian			
				425,000,000
	Ordovician			
				500,000,000
	Cambrian			
				600,000,000
Precambrian				

standing for a week in liquid, the spheres formed small attached minispheres or "buds" that could be split off from the parent spheres. These would proceed to grow to the size of the original cells by the ingestion of selected substances, and then stop growing. In a few days these "offspring" would produce their own "buds" and replication would continue.

Another significant achievement has been the synthesis of the purines and pyrimidines. The five strategic nucleic acid bases have been formed: adenine and guanine, cytosine, uracil, and thymine. In turn these purines and pyrimidines have been joined with sugars and phosphates to create nucleotides, the basic links in the DNA gene codes for all living things on Earth. Furthermore, it has been shown that these molecules could have formed with comparative ease on the primitive Earth.

6 In 1975 the first laboratory synthesis of a complete mammalian gene was accomplished. It was a relatively simple hemoglobin gene composed of 650 nucleotides. The report of the event in *Science News* carried the comment: "It's hard to believe that in a swift quarter-century, biologists have made the quantum leap from the identification of hereditary material to its synthesis. Yet that is precisely what has happened."

The raw materials of life are assumed to have been hydrogen, helium, carbon, nitrogen, and oxygen, the same elements now found in the sun and the stars. . . .

Dr. Ponnamperuma observes that "the aphorism that we are the stuff of which stars are made it more than rhetoric."

IRENE KIEFER

While such descriptions sound as though these experiments are producing live organisms, it must be emphasized that they are not living—yet. All these achievements are only stepping-stones toward the complexity required for the laboratory synthesis of true living organisms.

One of the world's foremost biochemists, Cyril Ponnamperuma, is at once hopeful and realistic in assessing the future of biochemical evolution. "There is no reason to doubt that we shall rediscover, one by one, the essential conditions which once determined, and directed, the course of chemical evolution. We may even reproduce the intermediate steps in the laboratory. Looking back on the biochemical understanding gained during the span of one human generation, we have the right to be quite optimistic. In contrast to unconscious nature, which had to spend billions of years for the creation of life, conscious nature has a purpose and knows the outcome."

Many of the sequential steps in the development of living organisms are not yet known. Much more work will be necessary to close the gaps in our knowledge.

7 We would like to know more about the time scale for the origin of life during the period from the Earth's beginning to those first known microscopic organisms that lived 3.5 billion years ago. During that billion-year gap, how long did it take for living cells to develop? Did it happen once or many times? Is the creation of life in such a manner still taking place today? We would also like to know something about the rates of evolution of these primitive organisms. How long did the blue-green algae float around in the "hot thin soup" before complex life-forms developed?

The most complex problem still facing biogenetic theorists is to reconstruct the evolution of the **genetic mechanics** by which cells replicate themselves. During the 1990s, scientists worked to show how the DNA code was synthesized from nucleic acids.

In 1957 Dr. George Wald, a Harvard biologist, stated that he was sure that we will have produced life in the laboratory within fifty years. Today most scientists would agree that we are probably on schedule.

THE BEGINNING OF LIFE ON EARTH

8 When did life begin on the planet Earth?

The solar system was born 5 billion years ago, and a half-billion years later our planet had become a dense, round, hot ball, still inhospitable and forbidding.

From the fossil record we know that the first hard-shelled animals emerged in the late Precambrian era, 700 million years ago, and continued to diversify in an explosion of species throughout the Cambrian period (beginning 600 million years ago). Traces of these life-forms are easily found, since they had reached an advanced stage of evolution when their hard shells could leave a fossil record. Soft parts dissolved, of course, and left no trace.

We can be quite sure that soft-bodied animals, including countless species of single-celled organisms, had by this time passed through a long history of evolutionary development. But they have eluded fossil hunters.

The oldest known forms of life are algalike cells that lived 3.5 billion years ago. These cells were capable of green-plant photosynthesis. Chances are that this process had been going on for some time, but no earlier record has been found.

Occam's Razor
Pluralitas non est ponenda sine necessitate.
Don't create more hypotheses than are really necessary.
OR: The simplest explanation that will fit the facts is probably the best.
WILLIAM OF OCCAM

When, then, did life begin? The fossil records indicate that life developed sometime between 4.5 billion years ago—when the Earth was formed—and 3.5 billion years ago—with our earliest record of microfossils. During that billion-year period, some wonderful and incredible events were taking place.

We have sufficient knowledge now to make informed guesses about some of those events, and here begins one of the exciting stories in the history of human knowledge.

EARTH'S LIFE-FORMS: AN INVENTORY

9 Since the time that living organisms first emerged from the "hot thin soup," the proliferation of species on our planet staggers the imagination. Taxonomists—those ever-patient classifiers—have so far discovered, ordered, and described 1.5 million species of living organisms, and some ten thousand new species are added annually to the list.

Abel's Razor
Theoria non delenda praeter necessitatem.
Razors should not be thrown away as long as they give a fairly decent shave, or until you have a better one.
REUBEN ABEL

To date they have recognized eighty-six hundred species of birds and one hundred fifty thousand species of marine organisms, including nearly twenty-five thousand species of fishes. Yet at least a third of the planet's fishes are still unknown to science. Three-quarters of a million species of insects are recorded and six thousand to seven thousand new ones are added yearly. The higher vertebrates are mostly accounted for, but the invertebrates are relatively unknown, especially the mites, nematodes, worms, and parasites, which total hundreds of thousands.

About a half-million higher plants have been classified, but taxonomists estimate that a quarter-million species are still unknown, especially in the tropical climates. Lower plants, such as fungi, have hardly been touched.

It is estimated that on our planet perhaps ten million species of organisms exist today, yet this number is less than 1 percent of all the species that have existed on Earth since life began.

Almost all animal phyla with preservable hard parts are represented in the fossil record from late Precambrian times onward, but millions of soft-bodied species doubtless lived before this but left no trace. Scientists guess that perhaps one out of five thousand to ten thousand extinct species show up in the fossil record.

All told then, how many species has evolution produced on Earth since the planet's beginning? The staggering figure is in the vicinity of ten billion.

Biogenetic Theories

10 Several other theories about the origin of life have not been disproved or abandoned. Although the biogenetic model outlined above is shaping up as a sound scientific hypothesis, another theory—**panspermia**—may also be valid. This theory suggests that life may exist throughout the universe and that living substances journeyed to our planet from some other location, most likely embedded in meteorites. While the panspermia theory may prove to be true, it is often pointed out that it doesn't solve the problem of how life began. It only pushes the problem light-years away to some unknown location.

Putting such questions to Nature, and wringing answers from her, is often a difficult business, as every scientist knows. Yet sometimes it is as though Nature were trying to tell us something, almost to shake us into listening.

George Wald

The theory of **spontaneous generation** was believed for thousands of years until the experiments of Louis Pasteur proved it false. "Never will the doctrine of spontaneous generation recover from this mortal blow," Pasteur told the French Academy—and it hasn't. This theory held that fully developed species are generated out of nonliving materials: maggots from decaying meat, for example, or frogs from mud, mice from old rags, or fireflies from early morning dew. Our knowledge of microscopic life-forms renders this notion worthless.

Hylozoism is the belief that all matter is alive. It was held by the earliest Greek philosophers and has been championed by occasional theorists ever since. The idea that matter itself might be alive, or in some way might involve "mental" activity, has intrigued philosophers. The more dematerialized our concept of matter becomes, the more we may be tempted to consider mystical or panpsychic theories of ultimate reality.

Creationism is the belief that life can originate only by a touch of the supernatural, and **vitalism** is the hypothesis that a special "life-force" must infuse nonliving matter before it can come alive. Both theories are still widely held, but their viability depends partly upon whether it can be shown that living organisms can develop from inorganic matter. If this can be demonstrated, then hypotheses involving creationism or vitalism will be unnecessary.

CAN "LIFE" BE DEFINED?

11 What is "life"? Can the word be defined? Can the reality be conceived? Long lists of defining characteristics have been proposed, yet accurate, workable definitions are still lacking.

We now believe with confidence, that the whole of reality is one gigantic process of evolution. This produces increased novelty and variety, and ever higher types of organization; in a few spots it has produced life; and, in a few of those spots of life, it has produced mind and consciousness.

SIR JULIAN HUXLEY

At present, it appears that "life" can be defined with two qualities: self-replication and mutability. Any organism possessing these two qualities can be considered alive. In these two characteristics is contained the essential processes of evolution: continuity and adaptation.

An organism must be able to replicate itself (unless it's immortal—that is, deathless—and hence not a part of the process of evolution). If it can produce a likeness of itself, then it possesses the power to assure continuity of its species. But mutability—the ability to effect changes from one generation to another and adapt to a fluid environment—is essential. Without the ability to change and adapt no species could long survive. Environmental conditions are forever changing; species must be able to change along with their environments.

So far as we know, only living organisms have these two qualities, and an organism must possess both qualities to be considered alive. It has been noted that mineral crystals and flames of fire can reproduce; they both effect replication of their own kind without affecting themselves. In addition, flames display a sort of metabolism: they ingest material, digest it, and excrete wastes. However, neither crystals nor flames have adaptive mutability.

12 Several other qualities are often suggested as essential to a definition of what it means to be alive.

In one form or another, the concept that life entails the operation of some principle of nature which is as yet ill defined seems to be gaining ground at the present time; and there is reason to believe that it is the fear of entrenched scientific orthodoxy which stills the voice of many who believe that life involves something more subtle than the latest chemical formulae for nucleic acids.

RENÉ DUBOS

ON DEFINING LIFE

One's definition of life may then lead one to accept a particular level of organization of matter as a "living" state but not any level below it, whereas another may accept one or more levels lower or consider one or more levels higher as "living." What is important is not an exact definition of life at the borderline on which we can all agree, but rather the recognition of the existence of increasing levels of organization of matter and the understanding of the mechanisms which operate to bring these about. In other words, it would appear more sensible to approach the problem of the origin of life not as an attempt to discover the precise point at which lifeless matter gave rise to the "first living thing," but rather as an examination of the mechanisms operating in the transition of matter on this earth to higher and higher levels of organization. Then the first level of organization which can be considered "alive" will still be a matter of personal preference, but at least we will all be talking about the same thing. Thus, as others have pointed out, attempts at an exact definition of life are not only fruitless, at least for the present, but meaningless.

JOHN KEOSIAN
The Origin of Life

Motility—the ability to move about: to wiggle, crawl, run, fly, dart, bore through, swim. **Metabolism**—the ability to ingest materials, digest them (separate usable components from the unusable), and excrete wastes. **Growth**—the ability to proceed through some sort of life-cycle, beginning with seeds or embryos and moving through various stages of adulthood and beyond. **Irritability**—the ability to react to external stimuli, a first step in adaptation. **Dynamic equilibrium**—the ability to maintain a stable internal condition within changing external conditions (such as adjusting to temperature, conserving a balance in the flow of food and liquids through the body of the organism, and so forth).

Nothing in biology makes sense except in the light of evolution.

THEODOSIUS DOBZHANSKY

When we say an organism possesses the ability to reproduce and mutate, we are not really defining **life** at all. In fact, we are not even thinking of life. We are only talking about the external motions ("behavioral patterns") of we-know-not-what. We are merely saying: **If** an organism can **do** these things, then we will classify it as "alive." But what is **life?** Apparently we don't know. Or, is life **nothing but** the ability **to do** certain things?

Somehow, as we continue pondering life and living things, this isn't very satisfying. Our dissatisfaction can become sharper as we subjectively feel our own existence. We feel that life is not merely the ability **to do** something, but rather **is** something—a process, a flow, a flame, a special energy—something that persists through time inside us.

Adaptation and survival. There are two moths on each tree trunk, a peppered moth and a dark moth. On the dark trunk the light-colored moth is easy prey; on the lichen-covered bark it is virtually invisible. Photographs from the experiments of H. B. D. Kettlewell.

EVOLUTION AS A FIELD THEORY

13 When Charles Darwin finally got around to publishing *The Origin of Species* in 1859—after more than twenty years of procrastination—he had formulated a coherent theory about the development of all living things and documented his theory so massively that it swept the field. No other theory of evolution could hold its ground when compared with the concept of natural selection.

Darwin had not developed his notions out of nothing, of course. It had been noted that trait changes take place from parent to offspring and that these variations are often inherited. Selective breeding of domestic animals and plants had long been practiced. And even the ideas of "the struggle for survival" and "natural selection" were hardly new, going back at least to the Greek philosopher Empedocles (c. 450 BC).

Darwin's genius was (1) his ability to bring a synoptic mind to these disparate elements and fit them all together, and (2) his meticulous gathering of scientific data to support his theory.

14 Following Darwin's development of the theory of natural selection from the struggle for survival, there were two large gaps in people's understanding of how evolution works.

First, heredity was not understood. But with the rediscovery in 1900 of Gregor Mendel's work, light began to dawn. Mendel's experiments had been forgotten since 1865; when they were recovered they fell into place in Darwin's theory. The transmission of specific characteristics from parents to offspring was by means of what Mendel called **genes** and followed predictable patterns.

Life defies our phrases . . . it is infinitely continuous and subtle and shaded, whilst our verbal terms are discrete, rude, and few.
William James

The second information gap was knowledge of how trait changes occur between parent and offspring. Understanding this process has come only during the last few years as scientists have penetrated the genetic code itself and found it to be a template determined by the arrangement of nucleotides in the helix-shaped DNA (deoxyribonucleic acid) molecule.

Both competition and co-operation are observed in nature. Natural selection is neither egotistic nor altruistic. It is, rather, opportunistic.
Theodosius Dobzhansky

Today we have a general understanding of the three basic processes of evolution: (1) the laws of heredity, (2) mutations produced by changes in the DNA code, and (3) the dynamics of natural selection.

The theory of evolution has become one of humanity's great unifying "field theories," bringing many areas of knowledge together into a single formula and providing us with a fundamental understanding of the nature of life on our planet.

15 The theory of evolution is founded upon five simple observations. When these observations are connected and seen together, and when each is understood as a dynamic process rather than a static concept, then the idea of evolution becomes easily comprehendible.

1. Species produce like species. All members of any species always produce their own kind. Doves don't lay eggs that hatch into hawks, radish seeds don't produce turnips, and chimps can reproduce only more chimps. "Like begets like." Since the development of molecular biology, the reason for this is now clear: individuals can replicate only what their genes are encoded for; that is, species possess a gene code only for their own kind.

Nature is not made in the image of man's compassion.
Tennessee Williams
Suddenly Last Summer

2. There is an enormous excess of reproductive material compared with the numbers of offspring that actually survive. One female salmon can produce twenty-five million eggs in a season, an oyster a hundred million. Mushrooms and ferns produce billions of spores for each plant that germinates. One man in a lifetime produces a hundred billion sperm and, with a little help, two or three offspring. And what of survival? Among tortoises only one in each hundred born survives to reach adulthood, of shrimp only one in fifty thousand. Yet with all this excess of reproductive potential, most species just succeed in replenishing their populations.

3. In every species there is a multitude of individual variations in genetic characteristics. Members of any species are never genetically identical (unless they are twins or clones); there are subtle or blatant differences resulting from different combinations of genes. For example, humans belong to a single species, but within that species we come in all sizes, shapes, and colors. The human genome is an enormously rich gene pool with an almost infinite variety of possible combinations, only a few of which find expression in single individuals. The rest lie dormant in the gene pool ready for expression when opportunity and conditions are right.

4. All species compete with each other for food and living room. The living space and food resources of any environment are always limited; there is never enough. Hence, all species compete with each other for these essentials. In any population the stronger and more adaptable individuals will be more successful in this struggle for survival. Hence, the environment is selective:

it provides the opportunity for individuals with "better" genetic characteristics to live and reproduce; those whose genes are less "fit" are eliminated in the competition.

5. Environmental niches are dynamic; they are in a constant state of change. On a geologic time scale, great tropical forests become hot sandy deserts, swampy coastal plains become glaciated mountain ranges, oceans and seas dry up, and continents are inundated. The demand of the environment for change and adaptation is unrelenting, and millions of species either change, adapt and survive, or they vanish forever, depending upon their survival capabilities in relation to the severity of the environmental conditions. Under this relentless pressure, only the "fitter" survive.

For the first time since the beginning of its history, humanity has become master of its destiny. . . . In order to grow afresh, it is forced to make itself anew. And it cannot make itself anew without pain, for it is both the marble and the sculptor. Out of its own substance it must send the splinters flying with great hammer-strokes, in order to recover its true face.

ALEXIS CARREL

Evolution is a field theory that connects these observations into a meaningful concept:

- Given the reproductive potential of all species,
- Given the enormous gene pool that permits variability and adaptation in the expression of genetic characteristics,
- Given the relentless competition for living space and nutrients,
- Given the fact that environmental niches are constantly changing—

Given these conditions, we have the theory (abstract idea) of "the survival of the fittest" describing the fact (reality) that only the species that possess superior genetic qualities will survive these harsh, demanding conditions. To put it another way, environments create pressure-cooker conditions that constantly act to select which offspring will be able to survive and reproduce.

The theory of evolution is nothing more, and nothing less, than a description of this selective process.

PHILOSOPHIC IMPLICATIONS

16 Why does it mean so much that we can now say, "We **understand** how life evolves"?

The theory of chemical biogenesis will become a first-magnitude field theory. It will be comparable in its effects to the Pythagorean discovery that mathematics is the key to understanding physics, to Darwin's theory of biological evolution, and to Freud's conceptualization of a subconscious inner world.

The critical consequences of discoveries in biochemical evolution will lie in the almost unlimited control that man and woman will possess in laboratory experiments as well as in real-life conditions. The manipulation of gene codes will permit a far more fundamental kind of scientific activity than has previously existed. In all probability we will soon know precisely what arrangements of nucleotides produce specific characteristics; this knowledge in turn will enable scientists to synthesize DNA linkages to produce any desired replicating template. Science fiction will again become fact: man will bring to life creatures that he had designed on the drawing board.

17 Ethical considerations raised by the creation and control of life will be complex. Having to face new kinds of ultimate concern will stretch our moral

tolerances to their limit and, hopefully, force us onto new planes of ethical awareness. The beneficial consequences for life will be enormous, but our wariness is justified. Although the statement is largely a play on words, in the minds of some, (wo)man will have become a god—the designer and creator of life. Will this be a wise and competent draftsman, or (by nature) a caricaturist? If the demonic in the creator's subconscious splashes out onto the drawing board, then we have reason to fear. In any case, we will be compelled to monitor biogenetic activities and set parameters within which the "life designer" must work.

18 The cosmic implications of the theory of chemical biogenesis are revolutionary. The fact that life will evolve anywhere in the entire universe where congenial conditions exist will eventually become the nucleus of a new worldview. Yet at present the discoveries of biochemical evolution have not made a profound impact. "This tremendous event is still on its way, still wandering"—to misquote Nietzsche. "It has not yet reached the ears of man."

What will it mean philosophically when life is created in a glass tube by a scientist?

Engineered creation of life is a predictable next step in unraveling life's secrets. It is an event in a continuing series: the use of fire, the wheel, weapons; harnessing steam power, nuclear power, and solar power for our energy needs; the control of weather; the use of chemicals to control emotions, explore psychopathological conditions, and eradicate disease. In kind, it is nothing new; but the door it will open is so momentous that in effect it will be as though a door had been opened onto a new world.

Our entrance into the creation of life is one of the giant steps that puts humanity in control of its own destiny. This step, along with another momentous event—taking over our own evolution—is part of the grand transition that we are now undergoing, the transition from being passively produced organisms to being active controllers of life and destiny.

With each step we take to control events in these two worlds, many are compelled to cry doom and declare the area off-limits. This response results both from theological conviction and from a deep distrust of humankind's ability to use its knowledge constructively, a distrust that can be supported with too much evidence. But historically, warnings of this sort have had little effect. Generally, the human race proceeds to establish control over all that it can, and, following its deepest impulses, will undoubtedly continue to do so.

Philosophic Problems

19 **Irreversibility** The theory of evolution has made us face numerous philosophical problems, partly because the evolutionary "field theory" is so comprehensive.

One problem is the enigma of irreversibility. We have no difficulty accepting the fact that a single organism can't move from adulthood back through adolescence into childhood, or that a butterfly can't move from its adult flying stage back through the chrysalid into its larval stage. Such notions are absurd, and we know it. But in just the same way, evolution can't move backward from complex to simpler life-forms.

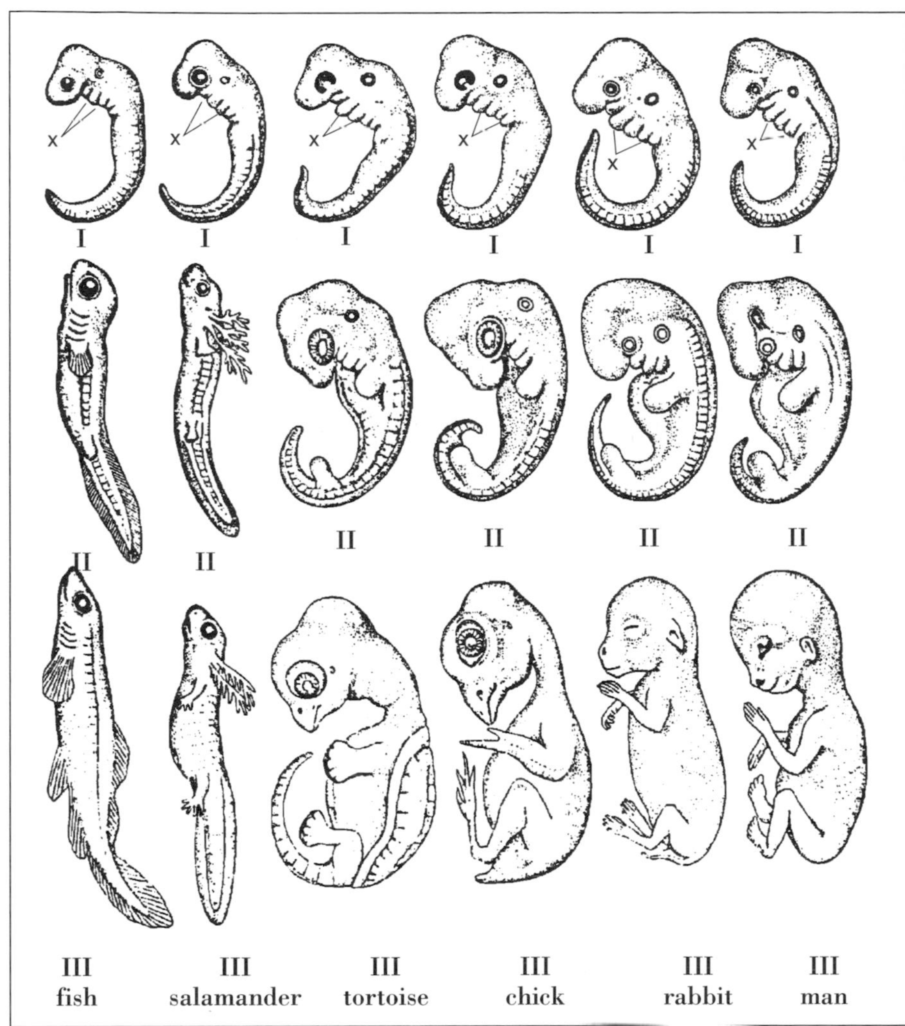

The biogenetic model: Ontogeny is a shortened and modified recapitulation of phylogeny. Or: "During its development an animal climbs its own family tree."

The famed aphorism—**Ontogeny recapitulates phylogeny**—summarizes a well-documented fact. The long evolutionary journey of each species has left its imprint upon the embryo of the individual organism. In other words, as each embryo develops from fertilization to birth, it retraces the path of the organism's evolutionary history. For example, the human embryo at one stage exhibits a "tail" and gill-like slits that make it almost indistinguishable from the embryos of fishes or other animals that, at some point in humanity's dim evolutionary past, emerged from the sea.

Scientists have noted that it is not necessarily the adult stage of an ancestor that the embryo resembles. Rather, the embryo mimics immature phases of its ancestors; the embryo's growth stages seem to imply that "ancestral plans of structure" may be retained in the organism's later stage of evolutionary development.

The whole order of things fills me with terrible anguish, from the tiny gnat to the mysteries of incarnation. All is entirely unintelligible to me —particularly myself. Great is my sorrow, without limits. None knows my sorrow except God in Heaven, and He cannot have pity.

SØREN KIERKEGAARD

20 CONVERGENCE Evolutionary convergence, with similar selective pressures driving unrelated and rather different genotypes into similar ecological niches, is an-

other exciting but inadequately investigated phenomenon. The "cactus" growth form has appeared in several distinct families of plants, and some of these succulents are so similar in appearance that a non-specialist has difficulty in identifying the family. Old World tree frogs and New World tree frogs are so similar in adaptation to life in trees that it is necessary to examine the skeleton to determine which is which, yet they have originated as independent radiations within separate families. In Australia, where ordinary frogs (ranids) are virtually absent, a tree frog has evolved habits, body size, and even shape and appearance of our common leopard frog (a ranid). These and many other examples of convergence imply that there is a finite number of ways in which an organism of a given basic genotype can "make a living."

PHILIP HANDLER (ED.)
Biology and the Future of Man

21 Perhaps the most difficult issue in evolution has been the problem of teleology. Is the evolutionary process one of sheer chance and opportunism, or in some way is it guided teleologically by some force, extrinsic or intrinsic, so that evolution is, in fact, "going somewhere"? Does it unfold according to a plan? Is it directed? Does it have a goal? Is its purpose to develop new and ever more complex forms of life? That it moves inexorably from simpler to more complex lifeforms is undeniable; but does it do so "purposefully" or "opportunistically"?

EVOLUTION AND ALTRUISM

On the matter of the survival of altruism during evolution, I believe we should note Darwin's group theory. In *The Descent of Man*, he wrote:

> When two tribes of primeval man, living in the same country came into competition, if (other circumstances being equal) the one tribe included a great number of courageous, sympathetic and faithful members, who were always ready to warn each other of danger, to aid and defend each other, this tribe would succeed better and conquer the others.

And again:

> Obscure as is the problem of the advance of civilization, we can at least see that the nation which produced, during a lengthened period, the greatest number of highly intellectual, energetic, brave, patriotic, and benevolent men, would generally prevail over less favored nations.

As to the survival of the altruistic individuals within the group, Darwin's theory is that devoted people propagate their own kind of personalities, not through their physical children, but through their ethical children, those who imitate the actions of the altruistic ones. The disciples that an altruistic person can create, even in a short lifetime, are a much larger number, Darwin says, than the children that a selfish man can father. (References: Charles Darwin, *The Origin of Species* and *The Descent of Man*. The Modern Library, pp. 490, 498–500.)

SPENCER D. POLLARD
Science News, April 8, 1972

And even if its mode of operations is opportunistic, we still wonder **why** it moves toward ever-increased complexity.

Despite the tone of many biologists, the problem is not settled, and it is a very complicated one. It's helpful to remember that science fought its way free of religious establishments that employed harsh measures to enforce belief in ideas that were shown to be false by empirical facts. Western theology pronounced that history is a divine teleological plan, the plot of which is the unfolding story of God's cosmic struggle with the forces of evil for the salvation of the souls of men.

Since science freed itself from this teleocosmic myth, the word **teleology** has left a bitter taste in the mouths of scientists. Furthermore, when the theory of evolution became widely known after 1859, those inclined toward teleological thinking were quick to see in the idea of the "survival of the fittest" positive proof of a natural (as opposed to supernatural) teleological movement: if only the fitter survive, then we can conclude, on purely scientific grounds, that life will climb forever toward unimaginable heights. The superior organism will always win over the inferior. Eternal progress is assured. Thus "social Darwinism" colored much late nineteenth- and early twentieth-century thought.

The myth of "inevitable progress" became a religious tenet to those wanting to believe that history has meaning. It ceased to be a scientific hypothesis and was transformed into dogma. It is against such doctrinaire teleology that biologists have struggled; it is but natural that occasional hostilities linger on.

To put the matter in a nutshell: the capacity of living substance for reproduction is the expansive driving force of evolution; mutation provides its raw material; but natural selection determines its direction.

SIR JULIAN HUXLEY

22 Two positions have been taken on the questions of purpose and direction in evolution.

Some thinkers have explicitly affirmed the teleological concept of evolution. Writing in the 1880s, Friedrich Nietzsche was one of the first philosophers to develop some of the possible implications of the idea of natural selection. In several brilliant books—most notably *Thus Spake Zarathustra*—Nietzsche envisioned evolutionary history as a grand surge of life upward toward a superior being (Nietzsche called him *Übermensch*—"Overman" or "Superman"). History's intrinsic goal, argued Nietzsche, is to produce a man who has such greatness that he would be, in essence, a new species. He would possess new qualities only dimly presaged by the greatest now living among us. While he would be nothing less than ruthless in his mission of aiding evolution in its purpose, he would also display magnanimity and compassion, even gentleness, when called for.

Nietzsche's teleological interpretation of evolution also implied an ethic (which was immediately perverted by unscrupulous followers). The criterion for deciding between virtue and evil is whether any given human activity supports or thwarts evolution's fundamental purpose of producing the superior race of men. Any human act that improves man's genetic stock is moral in the fullest sense; any act that preserves inferior qualities is immoral in the same final sense. Evolution's sublime destiny is to produce superior man. Nothing must be allowed to stand in its way.

23 One of the most influential evolutionary thinkers of the twentieth century was the French philosopher Henri Bergson, whose masterpiece, *Creative Evolution*, was published in 1907. It was Bergson's conviction that what we observe in evolution cannot be explained adequately by the mechanics of natural se-

Organisms diversify into literally millions of species, then the vast majority of these species perish and other millions take their place for an aeon until they, too, are replaced. Species evolve exactly as if they were adapting as best they could to a changing world, and not at all as if they were moving toward a set goal.

GEORGE GAYLORD SIMPSON

lection. Something more profound is taking place in evolution, and natural selection has missed it. Some further insight must be added to the idea of natural selection before it can answer the question of why higher forms of life continue to emerge. Bergson postulated the existence of an *élan vital,* a "vital life-force" or "impulse-to-life." He reflected that if adaptation and change were all that was required, then the ants had it made millions of years ago. They have been able to survive, almost unchanged, since long before the beginning of "the ascent of man." This being the case, why should evolution have bothered to evolve more complex forms of life? Something else, Bergson insisted, is at work in the forces of evolvement.

The *élan vital* is unpredictable and opportunistic, pushing ahead in every species of animal and plant to create greater complexity and higher life-forms. It has no goal as such; its only purpose is to exploit every opportunity in the struggle of an organism with its environment to advance the quality of life.

24 In contrast to such teleologies, the majority of biologists hold an opportunist interpretation of evolution. They adhere to the principle that everything can be explained solely by physical, chemical, biological, or ecological principles; there is no need to introduce mysterious factors such as an *élan vital* or some far-off goal toward which evolution is laboriously winding its way.

To endure life remains, when all is said, the first duty of all living beings. Illusion can have no value if it makes this more difficult for us.

SIGMUND FREUD

> At first sight the biological sector seems full of purpose. Organisms are built as if purposely designed, and work as if in purposeful pursuit of a conscious aim. But the truth lies in those two words "as if." As the genius of Darwin showed, the purpose is only an apparent one. However, this at least implies prospective significance. Natural selection operates in relation to the future—the future survival of the individual and the species. And its products, in the shape of actual animals and plants, are correspondingly oriented toward the future, in their structure, their mode of working, and their behavior. A few of the later products of evolution, notably the higher mammals, do show true purpose, in the sense of the awareness of a goal. But the purpose is confined to individuals and their actions. It does not enter into the basic machinery of the evolutionary process, although it helps the realization of its results. Evolution in the biological phase is still impelled from behind; but the process is now structured so as to be directed forward.
>
> SIR JULIAN HUXLEY

WHERE IS EVOLUTION "GOING"?

25 A similar position—but with a fine distinction—is held by the microbiologist René Dubos. Dubos agrees that chance and opportunism undoubtedly **operate** in the adaptation of a species to a specific environment. But he observes that while most biologists disown the notion of teleology, they nonetheless operate on the tacit assumption that evolution does involve a kind of "purpose" or movement toward a functional complexity.

> As we know it today, life operates as if most of its structures and functions were designed to fulfill some ultimate end, for the good of the individual and of the progeny. Life has its roots in the past, and its activities are projected into the future. Furthermore, it is a creative process, elaborating and maintaining order out of the randomness of matter, endlessly generating new and unexpected structures and

Why Sex?

Mendelian genetics has provided an incisive answer to the old question of the biological value of sexual reproduction. Biparental reproduction and Mendelian assortment provide a means of shuffling the genes so that they can be tried out in various combinations. Then those that work best in the most combinations are retained by the population. In an asexual population, the only way that two favorable mutant genes can get into the same individual is if the second mutant gene occurs in the same individual or one of its descendants. In a sexual population mutant genes that arise in different individuals can be combined in the same one. In this way evolution can proceed much faster. The biological value of sexual reproduction, then, is that it greatly increases the speed of evolution. In this way the population has a far better chance of keeping up with a constantly changing environment.

Philip Handler (ed.)
Biology and the Future of Man

properties by undergoing spontaneous changes, and by building up associations which qualitatively transcend their constituent parts. Clearly then, living things cannot be differentiated from the inanimate world only in terms of structures and properties. Their unique characteristic resides in the fact that their behavior is determined by their past and conditioned by the future, a property as yet mysterious but real nevertheless.

René Dubos

26 The question "Where is evolution going?" remains unresolved. Without the assumption of any life-essence, divine plan, or evolutionary goal, the very fact that evolution is future oriented and that it does indeed advance toward increasing complexity and qualitatively higher levels of life means that **we can still wonder what evolution might eventually produce.**

Such a question also applies to branches of evolution other than human. Let's remind ourselves that it might not be through the humanoid line that evolution may actualize such wonderful possibilities. I seem to remember a story—supposedly science fiction—in which a colony of ants on a South Pacific island have just arrived at a higher stage of intelligence and, from their anthill, are carefully watching a busy group of scientists—and planning their next move.

Could there possibly be some validity to Nietzsche's vision that higher forms of humanity will develop if evolution has its way? Dr. Harry Overstreet of Harvard University has proposed the idea that man is evolving a new form of consciousness, and that "we have every reason to believe that a further form of our conscious life is already observable among us—a high degree among certain rare individuals, in lesser degree among most of us." Overstreet has in mind the sort of "cosmic consciousness" found in some of the world's religious leaders (Gautama, Jesus), mystics (Plotinus, Swedenborg, William Blake), ecstatic intellectuals (Socrates, Descartes, Shakespeare, Einstein), and visionaries (Dante, Whitman, Fuller). Overstreet adds that such manifestations of a high

Academic philosophers, ever since the time of Parmenides, have believed that the world is a unity. . . . The most fundamental of my intellectual beliefs is that this is rubbish. I think the universe is all spots and jumps, without unity, without continuity, without coherence or orderliness or any of the other properties that governesses love . . . it consists of events, short, small and haphazard. Order, unity, and continuity are human inventions, just as truly as are catalogues and encyclopedias.

Bertrand Russell

order of consciousness are regarded by most of us "as signs either of supernatural power or of psychic disorder. Is it not possible, on the other hand, to regard these occurrences as signs simply of a higher stage of the very same typical development through which all of us are passing?"

What indeed is evolution's potential? Are there inherent limitations in evolution, or is it unlimited? What undreamed-of life-qualities are possible and, with a little luck, might become realities?

✦

Charles Darwin

The Grandest Synthesis

"Poor man," the gardener said, "he just stands and stares at a yellow flower for minutes at a time. He would be better off with something to do."

"... with something to do"! The gardener at Darwin's country home wasn't quite up to understanding what one of the world's great naturalists was doing. To be sure, Darwin was perceiving a yellow flower, but his mind was making connections—synthesizing. What he was doing, of course, was seeing—experiencing a single object while his mind was weaving a web of connections that made that object intelligible. "Such a synthesis," writes Loren Eiseley, "represents the scientific mind at its highest point of achievement."

Charles Darwin was born on the same day as Abraham Lincoln—February 12, 1809—in Shrewsbury, England. His father, Robert Darwin, was an affluent country doctor with a bright but conventional mind. He was wholly dedicated to his patients, spending his life making calls and listening to woes. Darwin's mother was Susannah Wedgwood, daughter of the developer of Wedgwood china. She was bright but retiring; and she split with tradition by becoming a Unitarian. His mother died when young Darwin was eight, and he retained little conscious memory of her. He was raised by an older sister.

His first eight years of schooling at the Shrewsbury grammar school provided a foundation in classical education, including a command of Greek and Latin, but he was bored by class exercises and was withdrawn from the school by a disappointed father when his teachers concluded that he was perhaps less than ingenious and in any case wasn't a very good scholar. His father enrolled him in premedical studies at the University of Edinburgh, assuming that his son would pursue the father's career. But Darwin found the lectures dull and, worse, was chilled at the sight of blood—he witnessed two operations performed without anesthesia, one of them on a child; he was overcome and had to leave the room. Gradually he lost interest in a medical career.

Bending to family pressure to choose some respectable vocation, Darwin enrolled in Christ's College, Cambridge University, to prepare for the ministry.

I would as soon be descended from that heroic little monkey . . . as from a savage who delights to torture his enemies, offers up blood sacrifices, practices infanticide without remorse, treats his wives like slaves, knows no decency, and is haunted by the grossest superstitions.

On Darwin's Theory: The theory of evolution accomplished not only the separation of biology and religion, but compelled a completely new interpretation of the universe.

LOUIS UNTERMEYER

Religion had never been much discussed in the Darwin household; it had been assumed, unconsciously. But at Cambridge Darwin at last began to discover his true love: the sciences. His scientific aptitude was strong, his interest intense. Still, he graduated with a degree in theology and was scheduled to be ordained to the Anglican priesthood.

A turning point came in the fall of 1831. He received an invitation to become resident naturalist on a government ship about to embark on a scientific expedition of the southern hemisphere. Darwin had second thoughts. He questioned whether he should give two years of his life at this time. Furthermore, the young captain didn't much like Darwin; among other things he was bothered by the shape of Darwin's nose (he was a devout phrenologist). The ship for this 'round-the-world voyage was only a ninety-foot-long, ten-gun brig; it carried a crew of seventy-three.

Still, the scientific instinct and sense of adventure in the young scientist were strong, and he sailed from Devonport on December 27, 1831. Darwin got along amicably with the crew, who called him "our dear old philosopher" (he was twenty-two!). But the unsanitary conditions, cramped quarters, and relentlessly rolling sea kept him in a state of misery for much of the trip.

The voyage of the HMS *Beagle* is one of the most important voyages ever made. The ship sailed to South America, where Darwin made extensive explorations in the tidepools along the coast and of the fauna and flora of the pampas. They dipped around Cape Horn and sailed northward along the west coast of South America to the Galápagos Islands, where for some five weeks in 1835 Darwin studied the giant tortoises, the seaweed-eating lizards, and the birdlife of the dozen small islands—"a little world in itself, with inhabitants such as are found nowhere else." Then they sailed across the South Pacific to New Zealand and Australia, across the Indian Ocean and around the tip of Africa, and put ashore again in Brazil; then homeward via the Cape Verde Islands and the Azores. The voyage had taken not two, but five years of his life. Darwin was twenty-eight when he returned home.

He had taken volumes of field notes, which he proceeded to order and ponder. His health had been damaged, and for the rest of his life he was to suffer from sleeplessness, nausea, and headaches. It is likely that he had caught a tropical disease during the voyage. Three years after returning he published his annotated journals, *The Voyage of the Beagle.*

Two years later (at thirty) he was married to Emma Wedgwood, a cousin, for one of the happier marriages of record; they settled in Down, a secluded village in Kent, to a traditional family life. They had seven children, and he enjoyed his family immensely. For the next twenty years—from 1838 to 1858—he did little traveling, mixed only occasionally, and spent his days deciphering his notes and writing.

We picture Darwin as a gray-bearded patriarch, but that was Darwin long after he gained fame. As a young man, he was a stalwart six-footer with red hair and long red-brown sideburns, a round pinkish face, and great blue eyes peering from beneath massive eyebrows. He was healthy and strong (before his voyage), spent much time outdoors, going on geology field trips, walking by the river, or collecting beetles, leaves, and flowers. His friends knew him to be a lovable, gentle, genial man, patient and kind, and quite unauthoritarian.

Darwin was one of those fortunate human beings who found a vocation in which he could develop his strengths and apply his genius. He was blessed to be at the right time and place with the right qualities of mind and heart.

Picture: notebooks filled with countless singular observations, from a yellow flower to a fossil whelk, from a camouflaged octopus to a butterfly's mimicking wing, from an insect-eating sundew plant to a seagull's courtship ritual; and so on, almost without end.

The problem: to see, connectedly—to discover the relationship of all things living on Earth. It was a monumental task; and the mind that could manage such a massive assemblage of data and could render it intelligible would have to be a very special mind—an "oceanic" mind. In such operations, the individual facts may not be new, though in Darwin's case many were; what is new is the inductive synthesis that permits understanding.

Darwin had the good fortune to have come across a world-in-miniature where nature's mechanisms could be more easily isolated: the ecological niche of the finches on the Galápagos Islands, later to be known as "Darwin's finches." What Darwin found was fourteen types of finches, belonging to the same species but possessing distinct individual differences, especially in the shape and size of their beaks. Some had parrotlike beaks for eating fruit and cracking seedpods. Some had beaks like sparrows for eating seeds. Others had long, pointed beaks for sipping nectar from flowers. There were large beaks and small beaks, sharp beaks and blunt, short beaks, straight beaks and curving beaks.

In cases like this biologists had assumed that all these varieties had migrated from the mainland; but in the case of the Galápagos finches the variations were to be found nowhere else. In this case it appeared that millions of years ago an ancestral species of finches had made its way to the islands, thrived, and multiplied. Some of the finches subsequently adapted to different food sources so that they would not be in direct competition with one another, greatly increasing the chances of survival. Darwin wrote that "one species had been taken and modified for different ends."

Darwin began to see that an "evolvement" may have taken place. Species apparently evolved from other species. He speculated: What if this pattern is universal and all species of life on Earth are in a state of evolvement from earlier species?

As Darwin reflected on his data, evolvement seemed virtually certain, but he could not yet see the mechanism by which this evolvement had taken place. Then, in October 1838, he read an article published in 1798 by Thomas Malthus, a political economist who had argued that human populations multiply faster than the food supply and must therefore be periodically decimated by starvation, disease, and war. Who would survive such catastrophes? Malthus had answered: those who are more hardy. Darwin saw the key to the puzzle: the mechanism of evolvement is the "struggle for survival" and the "survival of the fittest." Under the perpetual threat of starvation and annihilation in the harsh environment, all species of life on Earth continually struggle for survival, and only the fittest survive.

Life on Earth is a single story, and it is intelligible.

Evolution is a field theory for understanding the dynamics of life on Earth and, by a reasonable extrapolation, of all possible life-forms in the universe. But it is more: it is a philosophy of change for more accurately conceiving everything in the universe—the galaxies, the stars with their birth-to-death life history, the nebulous solar systems, the migrating continents. It applies to everything, without exception, in physics and biology; it applies to human experiences. Evolution is the most comprehensive field theory yet developed by the human mind.

For twenty years Darwin worked and reworked his vast accumulation of materials. Still, he knew that his ideas would inevitably provoke hostility, which he wanted to avoid; so he continued to rationalize his refusal to publish: his theories, perhaps, needed just a little more work.

In 1858 Lyell again urged Darwin to write a full account of his thinking. He was about half-finished when there occurred one of history's significant ironies. In June 1858 a young scientist named Alfred Russel Wallace, with less experience and a modicum of materials, arrived at a theoretical model virtually identical to Darwin's. Because Darwin had been

We must not fall into the error of supposing that the early progenitor of the whole simian stock, including man, was identical with or even closely resembled an existing ape or monkey.

The most humble organism is something much higher than the inorganic dust under our feet; and no one with an unbiased mind can study any living creature, however humble, without being struck with enthusiasm at its marvellous structure and properties.

All the organic beings which have ever lived on this earth have descended from some one primordial form.

Man is descended from some less highly organized form.

known in scientific circles since he first published the diaries of his voyage, Wallace had submitted his manuscript to him, humbly asking for the elder biologist's critique of his ideas.

Darwin was shaken, but he felt that he had no right to steal the younger man's glory if Wallace was going to be the first into print. "I would far rather burn my whole book than that he or any other man should think that I had behaved in a paltry spirit." But Darwin's friends all knew of his lifelong labors and urged that he proceed with haste to publish his own work. It was fair: he had worked intently for twenty years, organized stores of data to prove his theses; and science, they argued, must be served by the best. Darwin finally assented. He prepared his manuscript rapidly for publication. The first public announcement of their theories was made in a joint presentation by Darwin and Wallace before a meeting of the Linnaean Society on July 1, 1858—one of the heartwarming moments in the history of spirited competition when decency wholly prevailed. Darwin's "abstract" was published in 1859 as *The Origin of Species.*

The first printing of his book sold out in one day, and from that day to this *The Origin of Species* has been acclaimed one of the great works in the history of man's search for understanding. But much of the world was shocked by Darwin's ideas. Many Christians believed, with Archbishop Ussher, that the world was created in 4004 BC (on October 22). By contrast, Darwin's scenario postulated millions of years of slow change. Further, the notion that species were not created "in the beginning" as complete life-forms seemed blasphemous to biblical literalists. But Darwin's organization of empirical facts was overwhelming, and the hypothesis fitted the facts. The evolvement theory was accepted by virtually all scientists of the time, as well as by the general public.

Darwin watched from the sidelines. "It is something unintelligible to me how anyone can argue in public like orators do." Darwin avoided hostility, so his friends, especially Lyell and Sir Thomas Huxley, carried the banner for him. Darwin was hurt by the bitterness that his ideas had produced. He stayed away from the fuss and furor, secluded at his country estate. His remaining years were content.

Darwin's own religious beliefs underwent a gradual change. He tells us in his autobiography that he reflected much about religion during the two years following the return of the *Beagle.* When he wrote *The Origin of Species* in 1858, he still thought of himself as a theist or deist. But the "nature" that he had seen—the struggle-for-survival, "red in tooth and claw"—disturbed him immensely; the necessity of such suffering, which he saw to be an integral part of the evolutionary struggle, seemed strong evidence against the existence of the benevolent deity; and he moved from a naive acceptance of orthodox ideas to a reluctant agnosticism. For the Anglican-priest-to-have-been, this personal odyssey was accompanied by pain and guilt. Still, his own integrity came first. He wrote: "I have steadily endeavored to keep my mind free, so as to give up any hypothesis, however much beloved (and I cannot resist forming one on every subject), as soon as facts are shown to be opposed to it."

He died at their home in Down, at the age of seventy-three, after seizures "in the region of the heart." His wife and family were at his bedside. Emma said, "Perhaps Father did not believe in God. But God believed in him." He was buried in Westminister Abbey, not far from the tomb of Sir Isaac Newton. It is said that on the way home, Darwin's son reflected, "Can you imagine what delightful conversations Father and Sir Isaac Newton will have each night after the Abbey is closed, and all is quiet?"

✦

REFLECTIONS

1 Note the four great etiological questions that the human mind has bumped against since the beginning of philosophic thought. In your opinion, after reading pp. 389–394, how far have we progressed by this first decade of the twenty-first century toward sound empirical answers to each of these questions?

2 What do you think are the most far-reaching philosophic implications of the biochemical theory of the origin of life? Do you feel a sense of relief that foundations have been laid for an empirical answer to this question?

3 Ponder the suggestion that man is now undergoing a "grand transition" (p. 400) from a passively produced organism to the active controller of life and destiny. What evidence can you think of that supports this conclusion? What evidence can you muster against it? Speculate: If this "grand transition" is actually taking place, what are its philosophic implications? What lies ahead?

4 "The aphorism that we are the stuff of which stars are made is more than rhetoric," writes Dr. Ponnamperuma. Is this insight meaningful to you?

5 Note the biological inventory on pp. 394–395. Comment?

6 What is your thinking (at present) regarding the problem of teleology in evolution? Gather evidence and develop arguments, as best you can, first in support of the notion, and then against it.

7 What scientific data can you draw upon to help resolve the question of competition versus cooperation in evolution? Which do you think has played the more important role? (Or do you feel there may be something wrong with the way we are asking the question?)

8 How can you account for "evolutionary convergence?" Is this properly a philosophic problem, or is there a satisfactory biological answer?

9 As an answer to one of the great etiological questions, this chapter contends that the theory of evolution has become one of humanity's great unifying field theories. Is this a fair and accurate evaluation of the evolutionary model? Why or why not?

10 René Dubos believes (see pp. 404–405) that evolution is at least "future oriented" and that we can validly ask "What might evolution eventually produce?" Speculate then: What might it produce? Is Overstreet's suggestion (p. 405) about "higher stages of consciousness" a probable (and congenial) eventuality? (What is meant by "higher stages of consciousness"?)

Humans

6-2

Defining what it means to be human has been the central preoccupation of every great religious tradition, indicating that some understanding of who we are is indispensable to our existence. The fossil record now permits a general tracing of the hominid line, and the science of cladistics is beginning to reveal the human connection to every other life-form on Earth. This chapter describes the evolutionary context for reflecting on the human situation and suggests that evolution has now taken a new and unpredictable turn. But philosophical problems persist in assessing our place in the scheme of things as well as in our relationships to one another and to other life-forms with which we share our planet.

The Sculptor-Gods

1 The Maoris of New Zealand say that a certain god, variously named Tu, Tiki, and Tane, took red riverside clay, kneaded it with his own blood into a likeness or image of himself, with eyes, legs, arms, and all complete, in fact, an exact copy of the deity; and having perfected the model, he animated it by breathing into its mouth and nostrils, whereupon the clay effigy at once came to life and sneezed. So like himself was the man whom the Maori Creator Tiki fashioned that he called him Tiki-ahua, that is, Tiki's likeness.

2 Until modern times we humans lived close to the soil. One thing we knew how to do well—a skill universally found at a specific stage of culture—was to scoop clay from the river bank and shape it into vessels—cooking pots, water jars, urns, amphorae, lamps. Shards of pottery have been found wherever people have lit their fires and lived together.

Besides practical items, members of different cultures also made figurines, miniatures molded from imagination and clay—images of men and earth mothers, of barques and scarabs, of animals and gods. Some of the earthen images were used to lure bears into traps, to placate the gods, to grow green stalks heavy with corn, to weaken enemies.

Some of the clay figurines were made just for fun, molded into his or her own likeness. The sculptor toyed with them, pondered them, and doubtless joked and laughed at them while sculpting head and torso and limbs from the damp clay.

This universal experience becomes the archetypal pattern for humankind's creation stories. What was more natural and more obvious than to know, deep in his blood and bones, that an unknown Sculptor shaped his body from the clay of the earth and brought it to life?

3 The Batek people of Malaysia tell of a supernatural being named Tohan who is "very big" but "looks just like us." He is an old man with black, curly hair and brown skin. He has green grass growing on his back and a small, green patch of tiny trees sprouting on the back of his neck.

An average human lifetime has a duration of about 10^9 seconds.

Once, in the beginning, Tohan came to Earth. He went to the place where the sun comes up and took some black soil and molded it into the shape of a man. Then he went to where the sun goes down and took some black soil and molded it into the shape of a woman. Tohan shaped them in his own likeness.

But the earth-bodies weren't alive. So Tohan went back to the western sky where he lives to get life-soul to bring the mannikins to life. He brought back some water life-soul, like that found in the jungle evergreen trees, but on his way back he tripped and spilled it. After that he looked for seven days for some more water life-soul but couldn't find it.

So Tohan borrowed some life-soul from the banana plant, but this was only wind life-soul. He brought it back in a bottle and blew some of it onto the fontanelles of the earth-bodies and onto their chests over their hearts. When the life-soul was absorbed into their bodies, they came to life, stood up, and sneezed.

"The water life-soul would have made us like Tohan, immortal, like the superhuman beings themselves, but it was lost. We have only wind life-soul borrowed from the banana plant. It gives us only temporary life.

"When we die our wind life-soul is taken back by Tohan, who puts it in his life-soul bag and keeps it for a day, and then sends it to re-animate a new body, entering the body through the baby's fontanelle. It is Tohan who gives us our life-souls and takes back our life-souls when we die."

4 According to the Ewe-speaking tribes of Togo, in West Africa, God still makes people out of clay.

When a little of the water with which he moistens the clay remains over, he pours it on the ground, and out of that he makes the bad and disobedient people. When he wishes to make a good man he makes him out of good clay; but when he wishes to make a bad man, he employs only bad clay for the purpose. In the beginning God fashioned a man and set him on the earth; after that he fashioned a woman. The two looked at each other and began to laugh, whereupon God sent them into the world.

5 Thus, creation myths explain to our satisfaction far more than mere physical origins. They also tell us why we must die and return to the earth, why we are only partly immortal, and why our souls can sometimes return to heaven;

It is the large brain capacity which allows man to live as a human being, enjoying taxes, canned salmon, television, and the atomic bomb.
G. H. R. Von Koenigswald

they explain why there are many colors of people and many languages, why some people are good and some bad, and why there are two sexes. Almost every fact of life that puzzled early people eventually called forth some sort of mythical explanation.

The Toradjas of the Celebes tell how

> i Lai, the god of the upper world, and i Ndara, the goddess of the under world, resolved to make men. They committed the task to i Kombengi, who made two models, one of a man and the other of a woman, out of stone or, according to others, out of wood. When he had done his work, he set up his models by the side of the road which leads from the upper to the under world, so that all spirits passing by might see and criticize his workmanship. In the evening the gods talked it over, and agreed that the calves of the legs of the two figures were not round enough. So Kombengi went to work again, and constructed another pair of models which he again submitted to the divine criticism. This time the gods observed that the figures were too pot-bellied, so Kombengi produced a third pair of models, which the gods approved of, after the maker had made a slight change in the anatomy of the figures, transferring a portion of the male to the female figure. It now only remained to make the figures live. So the god Lai returned to his celestial mansion to fetch eternal breath for the man and woman; but in the meantime the Creator himself, whether from thoughtlessness or haste, had allowed the common wind to blow on the figures, and they drew their breath and life from it. That is why the breath returns to the wind when a man dies.

Hockett and Ascher remind us that our ancestral proto-hominids "were not striving to become human; they were . . . trying to stay alive."
Philip Van Doren Stern

6 In the earliest Hebrew account of creation, it is said that the god Yahweh molded the first man out of clay, just as a potter might do, or as a child molds a doll out of mud; and that having kneaded and patted the clay into the proper shape, the deity animated it by breathing into the mouth and nostrils of the figure, exactly as the prophet Elisha is said to have restored to life the dead child of the Shunammite by lying on him, and putting his eyes to the child's eyes and his mouth to the child's mouth, no doubt to impart his breath to the corpse; after which the child sneezed seven times and opened its eyes. To the Hebrews this derivation of our species from the dust of the ground suggested itself all the more naturally because, in their language, the word for "ground" (*adamah*) is in form the feminine of the word for "man" (*adam*).

Thus, both in language and myth, *ha-adam,* "the Man" (masculine), is created from *ha-adamah,* "the Earth" (feminine). And divine spirit/breath (in Hebrew *ruaḥ* means "spirit," "breath," "wind," and "soul") is breathed by Yahweh himself into the Man's nostrils and pumped into his lungs. The man's body is from the earth, but his spirit/breath is from Yahweh. (The Greek word *pneuma* carries similar meanings; see p. 561.)

7 The Shilluks of the White Nile

> ingeniously explain the different complexions of the various races by the differently coloured clays out of which they are fashioned. They say that the creator Juok moulded all men out of the earth, and that while he was engaged in the work of creation he wandered about the world. In the land of the whites he found a pure white earth or sand, and out of it he shaped white men. Then he came to the land of Egypt and out of the mud of the Nile he made red or brown men. Lastly, he came to the land of the Shilluks, and finding there black earth he created men out of it.

Before there was an evolutionary context in which humanity could see itself, we observed that lions produce lions, turtles produce turtles, bluejays produce bluejays—and humans produce humans. The logic of this was overwhelming. But a piece of the puzzle is obviously missing. There had to be a beginning: something had to create the full sapient form to stand in the flesh and to be half-god, half-clay. And logically the first creator of humankind had to be like humans. Doesn't human produce human?

Humanity is at the very beginning of its existence—a new born babe, with all the unexplored potentialities of babyhood.

SIR JAMES JEANS

THE STORY OF HUMAN ORIGINS

8 All human beings on Earth now belong to one species: We are all *Homo sapiens* ("wise humans"). But this was not always the case.

The story of the human race begins in Africa two million years ago. We know from the fossil record that a species of human that we designate *Homo habilis* lived in the open woodlands and savannas of what is now Kenya, Tanzania, and other east African countries. They roamed the countryside in small groups and competed with animals and other hominids for living space and food. They made crude stone tools. They ate leaves, soft fruits, shoots of plants, bulbs, and roots; and they probably added a small amount of meat to their diet through opportunistic scavenging.

If you met a pair of these humans in your local supermarket, what would they look like? To us they would appear strange but human. They would be lightly built and slender, with long arms. The man would stand almost five feet tall and weigh a hundred pounds; the woman would be considerably smaller, weighing in at seventy-five pounds and standing four feet six inches high. Their faces and bodies would be hairy. They would have prominent browridges, high cheekbones, and flattened faces (no protruding snouts). Their foreheads would be slanted and their skulls flat (not domed like ours); their brain size would be about half that of modern humans'. They could grasp and manipulate packages on the shelves almost as deftly as we can, and as they walked down the aisles—bewildered by the bottles, TV dinners, and strange foods—they would stand and walk fully upright, just as we do.

Centuries ago, when some people suspended their search for absolute truth and began instead to ask how things worked, modern science was born.

HEINZ PAGELS

These were the first human beings, and as participants in the protosplasmic venture on Earth, *Homo habilis* was a very successful species. For a million years they lived, mated, adapted, and survived in their east African territory.

9 Where did these first human beings come from?

Three million years before their time there existed many species of hominids that are known collectively by the name of *Australopithecus.* At least three of these species have been identified in the fossil record. Some of the species were slender, some more robust and muscular; but all of them shared characteristics that are later unique to human beings: larger brains, smaller teeth, and upright posture.

The Australopithecine best known to us is "Lucy," so named by Donald Johanson after he discovered her bones in the rain-washed ravines of Ethiopia in 1974. She and her "family"—thirteen individuals were found together—lived three million years ago. Lucy was an adult female, three feet eight inches tall,

The future, as always, belongs to the dreamers.

HEINZ PAGELS

and weighing about sixty-five pounds. She stood fully upright and could walk and run as well as any modern human. The males in her group were almost five feet tall and weighed twice as much. Except for her long arms, from the neck down she looked like a diminutive modern human being; but in sharp contrast her head and face would appear to us more apelike than human: she had a small braincase, receding forehead, thick brow, flat nose, protruding face, large canine teeth, and no chin. Whether Lucy was considered pretty by other members of her group we can only speculate; what we are sure about is that the males in her extended family competed harshly with one another for her attention and favors. (This is a fairly certain inference from the fact that males were much larger than females. In all such cases today where this "sexual dimorphism" in size occurs [for example, elephant seals, elk, gorillas], males compete with one another for females and only the one dominant male ["alpha male"] mates with the females. It is virtually certain this arrangement prevailed with the Australopithecines.)

Famed paleoanthropologist Mary Leakey discovered the footprints of three such Australopithecines in Tanzania set in volcanic ash 3.7 million years ago. Three individuals—possibly male, female, and a child—were being showered by a blanket of hot ashes from a nearby volcano. They walked fully upright and left footprints in the damp ashes virtually identical to ours. Following the path of footprints made her feel a "poignant time wrench," Mary Leakey says. One of the travelers stopped, looked back, and then turned and, we assume, caught up with the others. "This motion, so intensely human, transcends time. Three million seven hundred thousand years ago, a remote ancestor—just as you or I—experienced a moment of doubt."

10 These Australopithecines are undoubtedly ancestral to the first humans, but where did the Australopithecines come from?

Before five million years ago and the emergence of the Australopithecines, the fossil record becomes fragmented and incomplete. Research from molecular biology indicates that humans and chimpanzees shared a common ancestor at about five million years ago; the hominid tree branched at that point and the protohuman and chimpanzee branches evolved along separate lines. Similarly, at eight million years, the gorillas joined the main branch and share a common ancestor; at twelve million years the orangutan line converges, and at seventeen million years the gibbon line is joined to make up the hominoid trunk. All arrows point to the emergence of the entire hominoid line around twenty-five million years ago. Before that fortuitous time lies a fifty-million-year reign of earlier mammals; before that, the 500-million-year epoch of the great reptiles; before that the three-billion-year continuous evolvement of more elemental and primitive life forms tracing back to the beginnings of life on Earth at 3.6 billion years ago.

11 So the human enterprise is a recent event in a continuous process of evolvement. What happened 2.5 million years ago that caused the emergence of the human genus?

Besides bones, there is something else in the fossil/geological record: evidence of extreme worldwide climatic change. After millions of years of warm

Human Nature / Not!

Our assumptions about human nature, in particular our beliefs about the capacity of human beings to live in harmony with the rest of nature and to shape a peaceful world, are crucial to whether or not we can actually create a better way of being. If we hold that human beings are and always have been primarily hunters and warriors, then we are more likely to overlook evidence to the contrary and conclude that war-like aggression is innate. No evidence has been found that Palaeolithic people fought each other. It is then moving to discover that our Palaeolithic ancestors have something to teach us, specifically about the way we have misinterpreted their art, and so their lives, by pressing them into a world view belonging to the twentieth century.

Anne Baring and Jules Cashford
The Myth of the Goddess: Evolution of an Image
(See further in this text, pp. 308ff.)

tropical climate, the Earth suddenly cooled. Glacial ice sheets covered much of North America, Europe, and Siberia. The Antarctic ice continent built up, layer upon layer. Sea levels dropped 150 to 500 feet worldwide. Patterns of rainfall drastically changed. A chill swept over Africa, turning great tropical forests into woodlands, grassy savannas, and deserts. This worldwide catastrophic change in climate happened 5 million years ago and again 2.5 million years ago.

As a result habitats were fragmented and the growth of differentiated habitats forced isolated populations to take separate lines of genetic evolvement. Animals, birds, and insects underwent rapid speciation. The antelope genus, for example, proliferated into some thirty species in Africa. Time and again this is what shows up in the fossil record: When severe environmental change challenges the adaptive capabilities of organisms and pushes species to their limits, the species produce better survival characteristics and adapt to new ecological niches or they die off. This appears to be a basic law of evolution: change or die. We see both in the fossil record: with shifts in climate comes a proliferation of new species and mass extinction of old ones. This, it appears, was the driving force at the beginning of the age of Mankind.

After a very successful run of over a million years—from 2.5 million to 1.5 million years ago—*Homo habilis* vanishes from the fossil record and is replaced by a more advanced species. First evidence of this new human being, which we call *Homo erectus,* appears in the fossil record 1.6 million years ago in east Africa. Paleoanthropologists believe that *Homo habilis* evolved into *Homo erectus*.

12 If you came across a male of these humans in your corner fast-food restaurant, standing in line for his order of fries, what would he look like? In many respects he would look like us. In height and size he would be only slightly smaller —five feet two inches and one hundred ten pounds, but he would appear to us stocky and more massively built. His brain would be nearly as big as ours (87 percent as big, on the average). He would have a large face, heavy jaws,

I can live with doubt and uncertainty. I think it's much more interesting to live not knowing than to have answers which might be wrong.
Richard Feynman

Experimental Model

So there he stands, our vertical, hunting, weapon-toting, territorial, neotenous, brainy, Naked Ape, a primate by ancestry and a carnivore by adoption, ready to conquer the world. But he is a very new and experimental departure, and new models frequently have imperfections. For him the main troubles will stem from the fact that his culturally operated advances will race ahead of any further genetic ones. His genes will lag behind, and he will be constantly reminded that, for all his environment-moulding achievements, he is still at heart a very naked ape.

Desmond Morris
The Naked Ape

moderately thick browridges, flattened forehead, and almost no chin. His teeth would be smaller and the canines of earlier species would be gone. He would walk upright, and his body would still be hairy.

In his African homeland his fellow humans lived in small groups, wandering the countryside and sharing their food. The men were only a little larger than the women. They hunted and scavenged and left cut marks on animal bones with their stone tools. They were the first hominids to make carefully worked stone implements, use fire, cook food, and (possibly) the first to use symbols and to speak and think with some degree of abstract capability.

Homo erectus was even more successful than *habilis.* His kind existed more than a million years. He lived for several hundred thousand years in East Africa and then gradually spread into North Africa, Europe, and Asia as far as India, China, and Indonesia. Then, beginning about half a million years ago, the planet entered another period of global climatic change. *Homo erectus* vanished from the fossil record, and, about 300,000 years ago, a more familiar face began to appear. One or more populations of *Homo erectus* evolved into this new big-brained biped. We call him *Homo sapiens*.

Africa is the cradle of Humankind. Early *Homo sapiens* lived in eastern and southern Africa for a hundred thousand years or more and then began to radiate out of Africa into the rest of the world. This migration began about 120,000 years ago. By 90,000 years ago we find them living in the Near East and along the Southern Mediterranean coast. By 70,000 years ago they had spread across Asia. By 40,000 years ago they were living in Russia and eastern Europe. By 35,000 years ago they had settled throughout Europe. By 30,000 years ago they were living in Indonesia, Australia, and Sri Lanka and had crossed the Bering Strait into the Americas. As this new species migrated and settled in the world's diverse range of habitats, distinct gene pools were formed, and Humankind's myriad ethnic and "racial" characteristics were established.

The camera can't take a picture of itself.

Robert Putman

There are 180 billion cells in the human body. Each of these little factories is carrying out hundreds of chemical processes at a speed that astounds the mind.

Joan Arehart-Treichel

13 If you should encounter one of these creatures at your neighborhood video store checking out a new release, what would he look like? How well we know! They come in all shapes, sizes, and colors. They are sometimes short (like the pygmy Bateks), sometimes tall (like the Watusi). They may have short arms and stubby fingers or long arms and tapering fingers. They may be slender and lithe

NAME: (Unknown)
ALIAS: Shanidar I
NICKNAME: "Nandy"
ADDRESS: Shanidar Cave, Iraq
TRIBE: Neanderthalers
CAUSE OF DEATH: Rockfall in his home cave
DATE OF DEATH: 46,000 BC
SURVIVED BY: (Unknown)

or muscular and stocky. They may have long faces or round faces; or angular faces or flat, full faces. And so on, almost infinitum. *Homo sapiens,* we find, is polymorphic and polytypic: we find great variations both *within* gene pools and *between* gene pools. These are the differences that we often focus on in the course of our daily living to set us apart and establish our identity.

14 So while it's true that there are many ways of being human, in the final analysis, there is but a single *Homo sapiens.* We are all one species, and in the context of our evolutionary history we share some distinctive characteristics. The skeletal frame of *Homo sapiens* is lighter than that of any other hominids that have ever lived; the face is delicate and small with small or no eyebrow ridges; a lower mandible with fine teeth arranged in a horseshoe shape with a protruding bony chin to protect them; and a skull with a narrow base designed to ride comfortably atop a vertical column of vertebrae. These characteristics are ours alone.

There is one single characteristic, however, that has made all the difference. From the time of our habiline origins two million years ago, the human species has been distinguished from all other creatures, presently living or having ever lived, by our big brain—up to 1400 cc in volume—and by the thin-walled,

> *Every culture has devised its own way of responding to the riddle of the cosmos. . . . There are many different ways of being human.*
>
> CARL SAGAN

PRIMUS INTER PARES

Man's view of himself has undergone many changes. From a unique position in the universe, the Copernican revolution reduced him to an inhabitant of one of many planets. From a unique position among organisms, the Darwinian revolution assigned him a place among the millions of other species which evolved from one another. Yet, *Homo sapiens* has overcome the limitations of his origin. He controls the vast energies of the atomic nucleus, moves across his planet at speeds barely below escape velocity, and can escape when he so wills. He communicates with his fellows at the speed of light, extends the powers of his brain with those of the digital computer, and influences the numbers and genetic constitution of virtually all other living species. Now he can guide his own evolution. In him, Nature has reached beyond the hard regularities of physical phenomena. *Homo sapiens,* the creation of Nature, has transcended her. From a product of circumstances, he has risen to responsibility. At last, he is Man. May he behave so!

PHILIP HANDLER (ED.)
Biology and the Future of Man

> *There is no law except the law that there is no law.*
>
> JOHN A. WHEELER

domed housing we have developed to make room for that big brain. This braincase is what was left in the fossil record that makes it possible for this big brain to trace the history of its own development.

STILL TRYING TO DEFINE "HUMAN"

15 An adequate understanding of humanness must begin—but not end—with our place in the program of evolution. We belong to the animal kingdom, but we are something more than animals.

Defining humans as different and apart from the rest of the animal kingdom has been a bothersome problem. People have guarded their lists of distinctions passionately and religiously.

Human origins, it was supposed, could be discerned in the fossil records by evidence of use of fire or weapons; or it was held that only fully human creatures could make or use tools. "Man alone is a toolmaker," wrote early anthropologists.

Special physical characteristics clearly mark *Homo sapiens* as a superior being. The upright posture allows mobility, agility, and better chances of survival. The larger brain capacity (averaging about 1300 cc, at least double the volume of the closest living primate) implies greater intelligence, as does the weight ratio of the brain to body. The complex nervous system permits subtle operations. Furthermore, the human is free from the instincts that so bind the lower animals within predetermined behavioral limits. The human is said to be the only animal with true freedom of choice, perhaps the only creature ever to have lived on our planet that must make agonizing decisions because of that freedom.

> *There is no doubt that human survival will continue to depend more and more on human intellect and technology. It is idle to argue whether this is good or bad. The point of no return was passed long ago, before anyone knew it was happening.*
>
> THEODOSIUS DOBZHANSKY

A greatly expanded "new brain" provides human beings the capacity for abstract thought and reason. Greek thinkers pointed out that it is the human faculty for reason—the ability to use known facts to arrive at new facts—that makes us human and gives us a clue to our reason-for-being: to cultivate our

DELL
6266
95c
THE SENSATIONAL WORLDWIDE BESTSELLER BY
DESMOND MORRIS
THE
NAKED
APE

MAN A biodegradable but nonrecyclable animal blessed with opposable thumbs capable of grasping at straws.

BERNARD ROSENBERG

A self-balancing, twenty-eight-jointed adapter-base biped; an electrochemical reduction plant, integral with segregated stowages of special energy extracts in storage batteries for subsequent actuation of thousands of hydraulic and pneumatic pumps with motors attached; 62,000 miles of capillaries. . . . The whole, extraordinary complex mechanism guided with exquisite precision from a turret in which are located telescopic and microscopic self-registering and recording range finders, a spectroscope, etc.; the turret control being closely allied with an air-conditioning intake-and-exhaust, and a main fuel intake.

BUCKMINSTER FULLER

Man is a biped without feathers.

PLATO

Man is the only creature that spends its entire life trying to become what it already is.

ANONYMOUS

Man is the only creature that keeps trying to define himself.

JIM WODACH

Man is star-stuff that has taken over its own destiny.

CARL SAGAN

rational minds. This faculty alone, they believed, distinguishes us from the animals. Apart from reason, they reasoned, the human is an animal.

Along with abstract thought goes self-consciousness, our human power to reflect upon one's self, one's nature, one's knowledge, and the meaning of our existence. *Homo sapiens* is surely the only animal that can philosophize.

Three rather more ethereal qualities—ethical, esthetic, and religious feelings—are frequently considered to be distinctive features separating the human from other animals. Only the human, it is held, has a moral sense, feelings of justice and injustice, and only the human develops behavioral codes to live by. Only the human responds to beauty and creates objects for no other reason than to enjoy them. Only the human can conceive a supernatural order of reality, believe in deities, develop a soteriology of history, and feel "ultimate concern" about the meaning of his or her own existence.

There is an obvious omission from all these lists: soul. This singular quality finally distinguishes us from all other animals. Soul-essence (the Greek *psyche*) survives death, and no other animal is supposed to have a psyche. Considerable debate has taken place to decide at what point along the evolutionary line prepsychic human developed (or was given) a soul.

16 Recent scientific discoveries have initiated a redefinition of the human. The Naked Ape is presently undergoing agonizing self-reappraisal vis-à-vis the animal world.

> Jane Goodall's discovery that chimps not only use but manufacture tools, significantly changed the scientific definition of man. He could no longer be classified as the only maker of tools. Their achievement is a simple one by human standards, but it elevates them far above all other animals save one. This one girl has forced the scientists and psychologists of the world to redefine man. Her chimps have helped remove man from some remote pedestal and return him to the natural world of the animal kingdom. She sees in her chimpanzees basic recognizable emotions and a need to communicate their feelings. Though physically incapable of forming the sounds of human speech, there is an unmistakable natural language that any human being can understand, signs of recognition, affection, and reassurance. . . .
>
> Three generations of chimpanzees are now part of Jane Goodall's life. It took years to do what no one else had done: win their trust and confidence. From her understanding of these animals has come unexpected insight and increased appreciation of mankind. These chimpanzees are a source of growing wonder, a reminder of how far humanity has really come in the evolution of man's intellect and language, his ability to love unselfishly, to appreciate and create beauty. Perhaps the narrowing chasm between man and apes will not be spanned by science alone, but by understanding and compassion.
>
> "MONKEYS, APES, AND MEN"
> *National Geographic*, CBS-TV

THE KILLER-APE THEORY

17 In the process of redefining humanness a controversy has arisen. It appears that the human propensity for violence far exceeds any possible evolutionary demands; intense cruelty toward members of our own species is unique in the ani-

mal kingdom. Humans kill not merely for food but are vicious for ideological and symbolic reasons: killing "on principle." In the name of mental abstractions humans kill other humans, whereas other animals battle members of their own species only into submission. Together, all human religious constraints, moral codes, legal systems, and rationality seem barely able, under ideal conditions, to keep our viciousness within bounds.

The question is whether our aggressive behavior is inherited or learned. Is it possible that humans are killers because we descended directly from a line of "killer-apes"? This is the position held by the zoologists Konrad Lorenz (*On Aggression*) and Desmond Morris (*The Naked Ape*), and the playwright Robert Ardrey (*African Genesis, Territorial Imperative*).

The suggestion has been made by Dr. L. S. B. Leakey and other paleontologists that different branches of African Australopithecines pursued different evolutionary paths of development. While some remained peaceful vegetarians, at least one branch became aggressive carnivores; and it is quite possible that it is from this latter line that modern humans have developed. The killer instinct is set deep in our genes.

18 Man's trouble, Lorenz believes,

> arises from his being a basically harmless omnivorous creature, lacking in natural weapons with which to kill big prey, and, therefore, also devoid of the built-in safety devices which prevent "professional" carnivores from abusing their killing power to destroy fellow members of their own species. A lion or a wolf may, on extremely rare occasions, kill another by one angry stroke, but . . . all heavily armed carnivores possess sufficiently reliable inhibitions which prevent the self-destruction of the species.

> 19 It is a curious paradox that the greatest gifts of man, the unique faculties of conceptual thought and verbal speech which have raised him to a level high above all other creatures and given him mastery over the globe, are not altogether blessings, or at least are blessings that have to be paid for very dearly indeed. All the great dangers threatening humanity with extinction are direct consequences of conceptual thought and verbal speech. They drove man out of the paradise in which he could follow his instincts with impunity and do or not do whatever he pleased. There is much truth in the parable of the tree of knowledge and its fruit, though I want to make an addition to it to make it fit into my own picture of Adam; that apple was thoroughly unripe! Knowledge springing from conceptual thought robbed man of the security provided by his well-adapted instincts long, long before it was sufficient to provide him with an equally safe adaptation. Man is, as Arnold Gehlen has so truly said, by nature a jeopardized creature.

KONRAD LORENZ

20 The killer-ape notion has brought angry rebuttal from other life scientists and from psychologists. They all counter that there is no significant evidence that human aggression is inherited, but there is strong evidence that it is learned. The entire range of bitter emotions and cruel behavior can be causally explained by early conditioning within a hostile environment. If cruel and violent actions are "programmed" into us as acceptable forms of behavior, and if we ourselves are treated cruelly and violently so that we store up an explosive reservoir of bitterness, then we have become, in the very core of our being,

killer-apes. But all this is learned, and easily learned. We don't have to look far—only as far as the nearest TV set—to discover how acceptable "man's inhumanity to man" can become.

Dr. Ashley Montagu considers the killer-ape theory absurd and takes an opposing stand: any human being's aggressive cruelty results from the frustration of his more basic need to love and be loved. "His combativeness and competitiveness arise primarily from the frustration of his need to cooperate." The most basic drive of human nature—strictly from the standpoint of evolutionary survival—is love and cooperation.

> The organism is born with an innate need for love, with a need to respond to love, to be good, cooperative. This is, I believe, now established beyond any shadow of doubt. Whatever is opposed to love, to goodness, and to cooperation is disharmonic, unviable, unstable, and malfunctional—evil. . . . All of man's natural inclinations are toward the development of goodness, toward the continuance of states of goodness and the discontinuance of unpleasant states. . . . Where hatreds exist in any persons within any society we may be sure that they, too, are due to love, for hatred is love frustrated. Aggression is but a technique or mode of seeking love.

21 The question is perpetually raised: "Is humanity **inherently** evil or good?" "Is the human being **genetically** a killer-ape or fallen angel?"

Something is probably wrong with the question. (Most either/or questions generate more problems than they solve.) Surely, the human being is **inherently** neither good nor bad. Even a cursory observation indicates that humans possess the capacity for cooperation and love as well as the capacity for aggressive and hostile behavior. Which traits develop in individuals and grow to dominate their relationships depends upon the demands of the environment. He or she develops a stance toward life out of life's stance toward him or her. It depends, for each individual, on conditioning—on whether, for each one, "things go right" or "things go wrong."

A better question might be: How do we humans differ from our animal kin in our feelings of aggression? Probably in no significant way except in our complexity. With our advanced cerebral cortex and our faculty for abstract thought, we possess a capacity for infinitely complex responses. We have almost unlimited choice. It is our complex perception of threat and the variety of our responses to it that makes us humans different.

In the rest of the animal kingdom, response tends to be simple and direct: flight, fight, or submission. In human beings the basic emotional response patterns are the same, but they are obscured by endless maneuvers of each individual according to our potential for indirect response.

But where there is no threat, humans are no more hostile than any of our animal relatives. To those who have lived with animals and trained and loved them, it is clear that when you take away threat, you eliminate violence; but when the environment threatens, violence results. It is more than likely that the same simple principle applies as well to us humans.

22 What, then, distinguishes human beings from the other animals? At the present time, we cannot with any certainty point to a single **human** quality that cannot be found, **to some degree,** in other animals.

The deep chasm that separates us from our animal kin reflects differences in degree. No one questions the fact that the human possesses mental powers that dramatically outdistance the closest primate kin: logical reason, creative imagination, self-consciousness. It is also a fact, however, that numerous animals possess abilities that far outdistance humans: highly developed sensing organs, for instance, and the ability to "intuit" subtle relationships that are missed by human beings.

It is probably true that every empirically observable characteristic hypothesized to distinguish humans from other fauna can be found, in some degree, somewhere in the animal kingdom.

The Immense Journey

23 Science has two functions: control and comprehension. The comprehension may be of the universe in which we live; or of ourselves; or of the relations between ourselves and our world. Evolutionary science has only been in existence, as a special branch of scientific knowledge, for less than a century. During that time its primary contribution has been to comprehension—first to that of the world around us, and then to that of our own nature. The last few decades have added an increasing comprehension of our position in the universe and our relations with it; and with this evolutionary science is certainly destined to make an important and increasing contribution to control; its practical application in the affairs of human life is about to begin.

Sir Julian Huxley (1952)

24 This stage in "the immense journey" has already begun. We are now in process of taking control of our own evolutionary destiny and, by default, the destiny of all other living creatures on this planet. Although produced by processes of which we had no understanding and no control, it looks as though we are moving rapidly to a point of no return when there is but one choice left to us: to take upon our shoulders the full burden of our future.

Two events have made this inevitable. First, we have made such rapid progress in science/technology that the selective function of the environment has been radically altered. Many detrimental or lethal inheritable characteristics are now being preserved; under natural conditions they would die out. Among such genetic disorders are hemophilia, retinal blastoma, sickle-cell anemia, and susceptibility to a host of physical and emotional dysfunctions. Many of these defects are now being corrected or rendered tolerable through surgery, chemistry, and psychiatry. Carriers of such genes produce offspring, and the defective genes multiply. This has now happened in the case of so many genetic traits that the "fittest" are not the individuals who survive. Natural selectivity is no longer the primary mechanism in evolution.

who can say
I am Japanese
american
african
when in the next day
he may be a butterFLY

25 The second event forcing us to take over our own evolution is the destruction of our natural environment. Humans developed through selective competition with and in a natural environment: **it** produced **us** according to **its** criteria. Humans, not the environment, did the adapting. Environment is the creator; human is the creature. The ever-changing ecosystem "decided" which traits this evolving organism would possess.

But this trait-selecting environment no longer exists. Our scientific/technological applications, along with the proliferation of our species, has altered the environment so much that it has lost the power to select specific adaptive traits. No known forces are presently operating to determine that "fitter" traits survive and weaker traits perish.

Symbolically, the offspring has annihilated the parent that produced it.

26 It is humbling to realize that man is, in this sense, only one part of nature, just as a consideration of the size of the universe makes him realize his own relative smallness. But evolutionary biology has also shown us the central role that man is destined to play in evolution from now on—unless, of course, he engineers his own extinction. Although man arose out of an evolutionary process that he didn't understand and over which he had no control, he must now realize that he is unique in the living world in the realization that the responsibility for continuance of this process is his. . . .

The capacity of biologists to develop ways by which man can determine his future evolution is undoubted. The more difficult question is whether he will choose to make such decisions, *and with what wisdom.*

Philip Handler (Ed.)
Biology and the Future of Man

Søren Kierkegaard

"That Individual"

Thanks to Darwin, we now have a coherent evolutionary framework for understanding who we are as a human species, and we have a general idea of how we fit into the overall pattern of living things on Earth. But philosophers were suggesting, even before Darwin, that, when speaking of human persons, organic evolution is only half the story. The rest of the story, the second half of the journey, is the evolution of the individual self. Genetics provides the physical basis for an organism's existence, but at birth the experiencing self, the psyche, remains undeveloped; its journey still lies ahead, and it must be carefully nourished if it is to evolve and become the self it is meant to be.

In Søren Kierkegaard we have the boldest attempt yet in Western philosophy to recognize the individual self and give it guidance. From introspection alone—the empirical psychologists were still a half-century in the future—he sought to describe the deeper levels of existence that determine the growth patterns our lives will follow. Now called Existentialism, it is a philosophy of the experiencing human self, and Kierkegaard's life is the story of one man's search for what it means to be human. "The thing is to understand myself," he wrote, "to see what God really wishes *me* to do; the thing is to find a truth which is true *for me,* to find *the idea for which I can live and die.*"

Before Kierkegaard, Western philosophy had been obsessed with abstractions; in fact, since Plato, philosophy had been *defined* as the discipline that abandons concrete realities and spends its energy searching for "essences"—the "Real Ideas" of Plato's system. Particulars—whether objects or human persons—are to be ignored. Then in the eighteenth century the mightiest abstract system ever was developed by Hegel, a German logician who despised the specific, the concrete, and the real; he rarely acknowledged the existence of particulars. It was Hegel's system that became the launching pad for Kierkegaard's passionate challenge to all philosophic thinking that abandons the truth of human experience.

Søren Kierkegaard (literally "churchyard"; he pronounced it "kîr′ kuh gôr") was born in Copenhagen, Denmark. His

But never have I read in Holy Scripture the commandment, Thou shalt love the crowd—and still less, Thou shalt recognize, ethico-religiously, in the crowd the supreme authority in matters of "truth."

From becoming an individual no one, no one at all, is excluded, except he who excludes himself by becoming a crowd.

I were to desire an inscription for my tombstone, I should desire none other than "That individual."

Quite simply—I want honesty.

Hypocrisy is quite as inseparable from being a man as sliminess is from being a fish.

father, Michael Pedersen, was thirty-eight when he married Kirstine Røyen; he was passionately devoted to her but lost her two years later. Before his wife died, he had entered into a sexual liaison with Kirstine's maidservant, Anna Lund, who was twenty-eight. After Kirstine's death Michael and Anna were married and together produced seven children, three girls and four boys. Søren was the last of the flock, and quite unexpected.

With seven bright and healthy children, the Kierkegaards established themselves in Copenhagen and became an outwardly conventional, moderately affluent, middle-class family. Then a series of tragedies began and never stopped. In 1819 the eldest son was killed when he collided with another boy while running in a schoolyard. In 1822 the eldest daughter died at age twenty-four. Then during the three-year period from 1834 to 1837, while Kierkegaard was at the university, death took his mother and three more of his siblings. Of the original family of nine, only the father, Søren, and his brother Peter were left.

Such tragedy must be accounted for, and Michael Pedersen turned to his religious beliefs to find answers. As a member of the Moravian Brethren, he was immersed in Old Testament doctrine regarding the moral mandates of God and believed that a person who sins against God will suffer. He was convinced that all suffering is the result of disobedience to God's law. Nothing that one does, or that happens to one, is without moral significance. Therefore when suffering strikes, one who labors under the logic of this doctrine will be compelled to search out and discover, in retrospect, the sin that apparently caused the suffering.

Shortly before his father's death, Kierkegaard discovered that the father had committed an unforgivable sin. "While herding sheep on the heaths of Jutland, suffering greatly, in hunger and in want," Michael Pedersen had "stood upon a hill and cursed God." This event, so grave theologically—that is, so fraught with significance for the meaning of this life and the soul's destiny in the next—had a violent impact on Kierkegaard.

Kierkegaard also found out about his father's adulterous involvement with his mother while his first wife was still alive. And there were still more secrets. The elder Kierkegaard apparently patronized the taverns and bordellos and may have fathered a child by a prostitute. It seems that his father had hypocritically lived a double life as an upstanding member of the community while pursuing a life of debauchery and sin.

Michael Pedersen had come to believe—and now Søren also believed—that the tragic events that had befallen their family must be laid to the father's sins. Kierkegaard at last understood his father's melancholy: it was the despair of a guilty conscience that could not—dared not—find absolution. The years only magnified his father's sense of guilt, and Kierkegaard was greatly disturbed to see that his father's religious faith failed to rescue him.

Young Kierkegaard took upon himself the burden of his father's anguish; if the father couldn't solve the enigma of his tragic existence, then Søren would. The struggle to exorcise his father's demons would require a lifetime of painful analysis, and out of his anguish would emerge a worldview of unprecedented dark shadows and precious illuminations.

Kierkegaard completed his first school years in Copenhagen. He remembers himself as "delicate, slender, and weak" but gifted with "an eminently shrewd wit, given me presumably in order that I might not be defenseless." After secondary school he enrolled in the University of Copenhagen in the fall of 1830. He enjoyed logic and was looking forward to studying philosophy. So he immersed himself in Hegel's idealism—and was profoundly disillusioned. He later wrote, "[One must therefore be] very careful in dealing with a philosopher of the Hegelian school, and, above all, to make certain of the identity of the being with whom one has the honor to discourse. Is he a human being, an existing human being? Is he himself *sub specie aeterni*, even when he sleeps, eats, blows his nose, or whatever else a human being does?" Hegel, he complained, had taken the fullness of human experience and turned it into an empty abstraction.

In September 1837, Kierkegaard moved into his own apartment. He was at last on his own and could do as he wished; but try as he might, he couldn't find a goal or a direction for his life. Just as he had rebelled intellectually against Hegel, so now he rebelled emotionally against his father and his father's God. These were first steps in the search for "a truth for me," but they were halting and uncertain.

Kierkegaard became a familiar figure in the social circles of Copenhagen. His vast store of knowledge, poetic humor, and biting repartee dazzled everyone; his obscene imagination never failed to entertain as it skirted the fringes of good taste.

But all this was mere performance—the wearing of masks. Readers familiar with his writings were vouchsafed glimpses of a more authentic life being lived behind the public displays. When with others, he boasted, he was "never so ungracious as to appear without a freshly picked bouquet of wit." In contrast to the openness of his *Journals*, with his serious explorations of ideas and feelings, Kierkegaard's wearing of public masks remained intact, and few saw through them.

Beginning during his childhood, he developed an awareness that all of us live in two worlds and that we are split asunder in our attempt to juggle an existence in both. The inner world is the sum total of private experience in which is embedded the truth, the whole truth, of what it means to be human. The outer world of "other people" knows nothing, and cares less, about this inner world. Ignoring our unique experiencing selves, the world seeks to shape our behavior, to condition us with its values, to make us fit into the collective.

This loss of the individual, this kidnapping of defenseless selves, is what escalated Kierkegaard's wrath into a blazing crusade. It seemed to him that no one else even saw the problem. It was Kierkegaard's contention that there are no grounds for trusting anyone else, either singularly or in "the Crowd," who has not himself begun the journey of personal transformation required of authentic existence.

Kierkegaard's adult years were spent in Copenhagen, living comfortably and independently and writing continuously. His life, however, was not uneventful. In 1840 he became engaged to a bright young lady named Regine Olsen, but he had misgivings about marriage and broke off the engagement. In 1846 he launched two vicious attacks on perceived enemies, one on a tabloid journal for its decadent influence on the citizens of Copenhagen, and a second on the leaders of the Danish Lutheran Church for creating a "hardened Christianity" that can no longer offer living water for the redemption of the individual soul. In 1848 he underwent a "metamorphosis" during which his father's guilt was lifted and at last he came to terms with his own unique existence.

✦

Kierkegaard had no interest in stars, physics, sociology, or history. He was into people—from the inside. He was outraged by every mode of thinking and behavior that dehumanized the individual, leveled him, rendered him anonymous, or robbed him of his supreme worth in the sight of God: each soul is the sparrow crying out to be seen as it falls.

> The whole development of the world tends to the importance of the individual; that, and nothing else, is the principle of Christianity. . . . For Christianity is certainly accessible to all but—be it carefully noted—only provided everyone becomes an individual, becomes "the individual."

Kierkegaard is not overly optimistic: "The majority is quite terrified of becoming, each one of them, an individual. . . .

Give to the intellect, wisdom to comprehend that one thing; to the heart, sincerity to receive this understanding; to the will, purity that wills only one thing.

Each individual is his own center, and the world centers in him.

The truth must essentially be regarded as in conflict with this world; the world has never been so good, and will never become so good that the majority will desire the truth.

Everyone would like to have lived at the same time as great men and great events: God knows how many really live at the same time as themselves.

The majority of men are subjective towards themselves and objective towards all others, terribly objective sometimes—but the real task is in fact to be objective towards oneself and subjective towards all others.

The whole development of the world tends to be the importance of the individual.

I laugh with one face, I weep with the other.

There are many people who reach their conclusions about life like schoolboys; they cheat their master by copying the answer out of a book without having worked out the sum for themselves.

One must know oneself before knowing anything else (γνῶθι σεαυτόν). It is only after a man has thus understood himself inwardly and has thus seen his way, that life acquires peace and significance.

It is a positive starting point for philosophy when Aristotle says that philosophy begins with wonder, not as in our day with doubt.

when the individual tries it out, he finds the thought is too great for him, in fact overwhelming." What is needed is a general reformation directed against "the masses" on behalf of the individual. In Denmark, he observes, everything is organized so as to support "the system." Kierkegaard sees it as his duty to stand against the system and come to the rescue of would-be individuals who are "forcing their way through the narrow pass." This will be the touchstone of his life's work: "Had I to crave an inscription on my grave I would ask for none other than 'the individual'—and even if it is not understood now, then in truth it will be."

Existential thinking is what an individual does when he is concerned about the meaning of his life and wishes to discover deeper levels of being that lie beyond the merely rational, data-based, conventional preoccupations. It is a mode of consciousness that has left behind the world's obsessions—bills, sitcoms, family secrets, car repairs, what's for dinner—and makes a decision, with deliberateness and awareness, about one's supreme moral obligation, the search for the highest mode of human existence.

The life theme of Kierkegaard's philosophy is "the individual versus the crowd." For an individual seeking authenticity, life will necessarily be a struggle in which his very existence is at stake; only unflagging vigilance can protect the true self so that it can achieve its full human potential. He must continually make choices between truth and lies, between freedom and slavery, between integrity and acculturation, between moral responsibility and social custom, between a human existence and the life of a puppet: *either* a life of risk and suffering that can lead to a truly human existence, a life that is self-determined, authentic and fulfilled; *or* a life sacrificed to the collective, a life of empty anonymity whose character is determined by group pressures, a life that will forever remain unactualized at the lower levels of existence. This is an equal-opportunity choice; no one can escape having to make it. If one defaults by not making the choice, that too is making the choice.

Kierkegaard was on his way home from the bank on October 2, 1855, when he fainted on a street in Copenhagen. Paralyzed from the waist down and in excruciating pain, he was taken to the hospital, where he regained consciousness and then lingered quietly for forty days. He died alone of unknown causes on Sunday, November 11. A large crowd gathered in and around the Cathedral Church for his funeral, among them a group of students who, uninvited, pushed their way into the church and formed an honor guard around the coffin. Carried to the cemetery, his body was buried beside that of his father. The epitaph inscribed on his tombstone he had composed for himself. It reads simply, "That individual."

Reflections

1 Read for a synoptic overview the various creation stories at the beginning of this chapter. What do they all have in common? What are the major differences? What are the ultimate questions that these creation myths seem designed to explain? (Refer to your glossary for a definition of "myth," if needed.)

2 What is your candid response to the various creation stories? (Remember these are but a few of thousands of such myths.) Do these accounts help to clarify for you the functions of myths?

3 In your opinion, what qualities separate humans from the other animals? Make a list of all such distinguishing qualities that you can think of; then delete from the list each characteristic that current evidence shows humans may share with one or more of his animal kin. What characteristics do you have left on your list?
4 Make an attempt to define "human." How would you describe "essential man"? What are some of the problems we must face in developing a definition?
5 What is your own inclination regarding the aggression debate? Can you develop a strong case that the human is genetically aggressive? Can you make an equally strong case that this aggression is learned? Where must you go for hard data to resolve the controversy?
6 How much do you agree or disagree with the sentence on p. 424, "Surely, the human being is inherently neither good nor bad. . . . He or she develops a stance toward life out of life's stance toward him or her"? What data can you offer to support your assessment?
7 Our attitudes toward "human nature" are so basic that they shape our politics and economics, our religions, our judgment of history and our stance toward the future, and our relationships with others and ourselves. What is your assessment of human nature? Are you essentially optimistic and trusting or pessimistic and wary? What facts do you possess that would support your general attitudes? (Be careful. Perhaps the question is not phrased right. Maybe there is no such thing as "human nature." In that case, how should the question be stated?)
8 If organic evolution is "only half the story," then what is the rest of the story? Is this idea meaningful to you?
9 As you ponder Kierkegaard's early life, primarily in relation to his father, can you understand and appreciate the tragic conditions he was forced to overcome? How exactly did he plan to overcome them? Did he succeed?
10 It was said that Kierkegaard's life became "a blazing crusade." Specifically, what was he crusading for?
11 Why did Kierkegaard despise "the crowd"? In your opinion, was his wrath justified?
12 What are some of the oppressive forces in your life that might dehumanize you and tend to make you anonymous? Or that might fragment you and make you into many persons rather than one?

EARTH

6-3

This chapter is a meditation on humankind's relationship to other living creatures on Earth and to the Earth itself. It raises the question of who has a right to control and exploit other species. Albert Schweitzer insisted that all of us, humans and animals alike, share the most fundamental fact of existence: the will-to-live. He also insisted that a human being who is truly ethical will include all creatures within his circle of concern. During the latter half of the twentieth century new awarenesses have developed in our understanding of animals as experiencing selves. This chapter describes these new awarenesses as a prelude to the creation of a less anthropocentric worldview.

OUR PLACE IN THE SCHEME OF THINGS

1 The idea of Reverence for Life offers itself as the realistic answer to the realistic question of how man and the world are related to each other. Of the world man knows only that everything which exists is, like himself, a manifestation of the Will-to-Live. . . .

Let a man once begin to think about the mystery of his life and the links which connect him with the life that fills the world, and he cannot but bring to bear upon his own life and all other life that comes within his reach the principle of Reverence for Life. . . . Existence will thereby become harder for him in every respect than it would be if he lived for himself, but at the same time it will be richer, more beautiful, and happier. It will become, instead of mere living, a real experience of life.

ALBERT SCHWEITZER

And the wind shall say:
"Here were decent godless people
Their only monument the asphalt road
And a thousand lost golf balls."

T. S. ELIOT

2 The human race has sought knowledge of the world to understand it not merely intellectually, but rather to understand our relationship to it and our

place in it. All our rational inquiries are merely a prelude to the establishment of more meaningful relationships. The implicit question for humanity has always been, "What is my place in the scheme of things?"

In wildness is the preservation of the world.
HENRY DAVID THOREAU

Humans evolved in a world that is at once friendly and hostile. With one hand the world gives life, while with the other it inflicts pain and death. We have been, it seems, strangers in a strange land. But we have made it our home even while it has felt like enemy territory.

Stranger by the roadside, do not smile
When you see this grave, though it is only a dog's.
My master wept when I died, and his own hand
Laid me in earth and wrote these lines on my tomb.
ANONYMOUS
Greek epitaph for a dog

The story of **general evolution** is an account of how species search for a suitable niche in their environment. The story of **human evolution** is the account of our transcendence of that evolutionary niche. And the story of **cultural evolution**—*human civilization*—is (among other things) the account of our gradual understanding and transcendence of our environment.

3 The human's relationship to his/her natural environment seems to have moved through three stages. Humans first experienced nature in a parent-child relationship. Nature produced him; he was its offspring. He was never sure how to conceptualize the forces that generated life, but he could not doubt that they were everywhere—in his crops, his herds and flocks, in his human family. So his myths helped him conceive the inconceivable. Nature's life-giving forces were, naturally, male and female. The prime source of life was Mother Earth personified as the Goddess, Magna Mater, or Gaia, or Demeter—each was in some way the Earth-Mother. (We still habitually think of "her" as Mother Nature, and the very idea of "Father Nature" **feels** wrong even to us.) There must be masculine forces too, of course, so there was Jupiter (Dyaus Pitar or Zeus Pater, "Father Zeus"); and the Semitic tribal gods—Yahweh, Chemosh, Milcom, Allah—are all male figures. Generally the dynamic forces of nature such as storms, earthquakes, thunder, and lightning were conceived as masculine in potency; while the more passive aspects of nature—the quiet earth that absorbs the rain and brings forth new sprouts of corn—were thought of as feminine potencies.

These personified forces are humanity's parents. The characteristic response to them is fear and awe, acceptance and obedience. The person has no control over Nature's forces; **they** condition **his** behavior. Like authoritarian parents, they nurture him; but they also punish him. His dependence is almost absolute. He stands helpless before the storm, the flood, the drought, the mortal pain. He is a child who knows nothing of the motives of the forces that rule him. They possess secrets he cannot understand. Yet he does his best to relate to them and please them, to discover the "desires" of these personified forces and accede to their wills. Thus, he makes every attempt—as he would with human parents—to keep them as favorably inclined as he can.

You can always tell when it's autumn in Hollywood. They put away the green plastic plants and bring out the brown plastic plants.
JOHNNY CARSON

4 The second stage—Man as conqueror—is found in a rudimentary way in all human cultures, but its successful development belongs to the West. It began with the discovery by Pythagoras of Nature's greatest secret: that she speaks the language of mathematics. Foundations were thus laid for a scientific understanding and technological control, but time dallied for two more millennia before this knowledge was developed and applied. Physics and mechanics were finally born in the seventeenth century, followed shortly by chemistry and

The Sacred Earth

Every part of this earth is sacred to my people. Every shining pine needle, every sandy shore, every mist in the dark woods, every meadow, every humming insect. All are holy in the memory and experience of my people. We know the sap which courses through the trees as we know the blood that courses through our veins. We are part of the earth and it is part of us. The perfumed flowers are our sisters. The bear, the deer, the great eagle, these are our brothers. The rocky crests, the juices in the meadow, the body heat of the pony, the man, all belong to the same family. The shining water that moves in the streams and rivers is not just water, but the blood of our ancestors. Each ghostly reflection in the clear water of the lakes tells of events and memories in the life of my people. The water's murmur is the voice of my father's father. The rivers are our brothers. They quench our thirst. They carry our canoes and feed our children. So you must give to the rivers the kindness you would give any brother . . . Remember that the air is precious to us, that the air shares its spirit with all the life it supports. The wind that gave our grandfather his first breath also receives his last sigh. The wind also gives our children the spirit of life. . . . Will you teach your children what we have taught our children? That the earth is our mother? What befalls the earth, befalls all the sons of the earth. This we know: the earth does not belong to man, man belongs to the earth. All things are connected like the blood which unites us all. Man did not weave the web of life, he is merely a strand in it. Whatever he does to the web, he does to himself.

Chief Seattle (1855)

biology and, belatedly, by the social and behavioral sciences. Communication and transportation technologies belong to our own twentieth century. Controls have now spread to almost every area of human experience.

This rapid conquest and control of our dynamic environment is *Homo sapiens'* greatest success story, and it is basically a story of a love/hate relationship. Humans loved earth; it nourished them. But they had also hated it for its relentless attempt to annihilate. It was a life/death struggle between human being and Nature; and as in any love/hate relationship, the question has been which would win out: love or hate. Who would win: Human or Nature?

It looks as though—so far—humans have won—or are winning. We are on the threshold of setting controls over ever-larger forces of Nature—manipulating genes, creating new materials, new applications of quantum physics, and so on. The control of life processes and of evolution is not far away. There are repeated hints in futuristic literature that man may eventually establish control over macroscopic terrors such as storms and earthquakes, and then go on to the cosmic scale of engineering. We might alter the orbit or the tilt of the earth, for example, or capture small asteroids to serve as stations for travel, research or mining, or to provide transportation to remote outposts. Such comprehensive controlling power would be merely a large-scale extension of our present capacities, and we are moving rapidly in this direction. On the condition that we don't destroy ourselves first, such controls are probably inevitable.

5 A third stage, burgeoning in our time, is a protective feeling toward nature. If human beings no longer fear nature because we understand her ways, and if we have established control over the more threatening elements of our environment, then, in theory at least, fear can give way to other feelings: kinship, appreciation, protection. People can become nature's advocate.

This has been the Western experience. Other branches of the human story exhibit different responses toward nature. Western achievements bring mixed feelings, of course. We wonder whether compassionate concerns have surfaced in time to salvage our spaceship. It is the West's problem not merely because our technological controls have caused environmental problems, but because it seems probable that only Western technology—when accompanied by a sincere revision of priorities—can solve those problems. Scientific understanding and technology have created the big problems of the modern world; only scientific understanding and technology can solve them.

An Ecospheric Ethic

6 Through a continuing process of self-discovery, we have had to reassess "our place in the scheme of things" and learn how to behave responsibly. Having discovered that we exist as part-and-parcel of all Earth's living things, the vital question has become: **Who has a right to do what to whom and why?** The key word here—and the knottiest problem—is the notion of "right."

We have come [to the oceans] as aliens from another world. . . . The time has come to recognize that the sea and the creatures in it have their needs and their rights to exist. An ocean ethic is needed which will combine wisdom, sensitivity, and forethought; an ethic which will not betray the dream which began our long, deep journey.

Mysteries of the Sea

Ecology, therefore, is only secondarily a scientific discipline; it is primarily a human problem and a matter of ethics. How should people relate to other fauna and flora with whom we share a planet? How should we treat the ecosphere, including the earth, oceans, and atmosphere? Are we the only creature with "rights," or do animals also have "rights"? Do trees have "rights"? Do we have a "right" to kill any animal—harmless wild animals, predators, dogs and cats and other "pets"? (We "own" them, don't we?) Do we have a "right" to kill only "food" animals? or only "dangerous" animals? Do we have a "right" to kill gorillas? or dolphins? Do lions have a "right" to kill zebras and antelope for food? Do dolphins have a "right" to kill men? And so on.

In a word, on what criteria can all these questions be given factually sound and ethically viable answers? And, as a final question, "Who says so?"

Since humans have now dominated this planet, ethical responsibilities rest on human shoulders. But even then the question persists: Who (or what) gives us the right to make these life-or-death decisions?

7 Professor George Sessions, an ecophilosopher, has given an excellent description of our ecological plight and analyzed some of the ethical puzzlements inherent in it. He reminds us that we are in ecological trouble because of the traditional Western worldviews we have inherited. "Ethical beliefs and attitudes do not exist in a vacuum." How we treat other creatures that share our world is dictated to us by the cosmology within which "we live and move and have our being." "When these cosmologies are no longer viable or believable,

the entire ethical system or attitude becomes irrelevant and inappropriate." This has now happened to us. Sessions writes:

> In contrast with the earliest animisms and pantheisms of the West, and the pre-industrial nature orientations of the East, a pervasive cultural feature of the more recent West has been its anthropocentric cosmologies together with a correspondingly anthropocentric ethical orientation. From the Judeo-Christian account of man's separation from, and transcendence over, Nature, and the rise of man-centered philosophical systems and ethics in classical Greece, to the Cartesian mind-body dualism which became the cornerstone of early modern European philosophy, these essentially dualistic views of man and nature have provided the metaphysical basis for an outlook which sees *Homo sapiens* as the exclusive focus of ethical interest and concern.

cut some humans from their stems
tie them in a bunch
Pull a few out
Stick them in a vase
Look at them
throw the rest away
Human arrangement by flowers

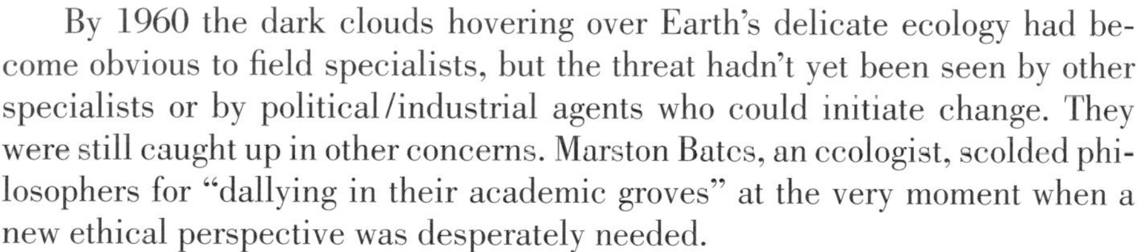

By 1960 the dark clouds hovering over Earth's delicate ecology had become obvious to field specialists, but the threat hadn't yet been seen by other specialists or by political/industrial agents who could initiate change. They were still caught up in other concerns. Marston Bates, an ecologist, scolded philosophers for "dallying in their academic groves" at the very moment when a new ethical perspective was desperately needed.

The appearance of Rachel Carson's attack on the indiscriminate use of pesticides (*Silent Spring*, 1962) and then Paul Ehrlich's *The Population Bomb* (1968) "marked the beginning of the end of an era of almost total ecological naiveté in the modern Western world. Belief in the omnipotence and omnicompetence of the human race through its scientific technology received a tremendous jolt from a wholly new quarter. It was now evident that nature was not totally manipulable for the 'good' of human societies, nor was it 'meant' to be."

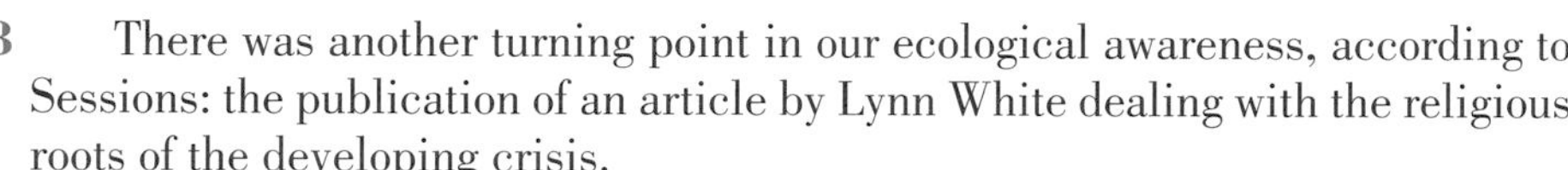

8 There was another turning point in our ecological awareness, according to Sessions: the publication of an article by Lynn White dealing with the religious roots of the developing crisis.

> White's message was quite simple: Christian anthropocentrism was the root cause of the environmental crisis. The paper was reprinted in innumerable ecological anthologies which were just beginning to flood the book market. Controversies raged. Conscience-stricken Christian theologians, preachers, and scientists denounced his views, or reexamined their religious beliefs and attitudes. Conferences with titles such as the "theology of survival" were hurriedly called. By one stroke White subsequently claimed (with justification) to have created "the theology of ecology."
>
> White pointed to the drastic attitudinal change towards Nature which occurred when Christianity replaced ancient forms of pantheism and animism, calling it "the greatest psychic revolution in the history of our culture." An animistic metaphysics, which saw spirit in nature, resulted in attitudes of respect and veneration for natural objects and thus helped protect Nature from man's unthinking exploitation. Christianity's desacralization of Western man's world encouraged an attitude of "indifference to the feelings of natural objects."*

To restore some bit of intrinsic value to nature, White suggested that the modern world might be well advised to return to the medieval worldview of

*The Judaic-Christian Scriptures served to codify this ethic of domination, but we now know that the roots of patriarchal domination go back at least to the Aryan ("Kurgan") invasions into the Old European agricultural civilization as early as 6500 BC. See pp. 308–312 for the recent discoveries of archeologists and paleoanthropologists.

Saint Francis of Assisi, whose "view of nature and man rested on a unique sort of pan-psychism of all things animate and inanimate, designed for the glorification of their transcendent Creator." All things are revered by God and therefore they should also be revered by man. "Francis tried to depose man from his monarchy over creation and set up a democracy of all God's creatures."

Sessions considers the Franciscan worldview to be an ethical improvement upon both of the traditional Judeo-Christian models of the man-nature relationship: the exploitation model and the stewardship model.

> But a closer look at the Franciscan ethic reveals that it contains difficulties which stem from an ecologically naive view of the world. For on this view, each individual entity (whether man, chipmunk, or rock) is apparently envisioned to be of equal worth "in the sight of God." It provides no basis for an adjudication of the conflicts which inevitably arise—for example, who or what has a "right" to eat whom, and upon what basis this is to be decided. Predation is an inevitable fact of biological life. If all individuals are to be accorded equal worth, the problem of predation is left unsolved (for humans: other animals appear to be largely unencumbered with these kinds of "problems").
>
> Furthermore, it is not made clear how rocks and the "less articulate" forms of life are to participate, either directly or indirectly, in the universal democratic process.
>
> But most seriously, this solution misleadingly focuses attention on the "rights" of individual entities (a distinctively Western humanistic preoccupation), thus obscuring the crucial ecological point that the environmental crisis is not primarily the result of a threat to the continued existence of *individual entities* as such, but to the *species diversity* so essential to the continued viable functioning of the earth's fragile *ecosystems*. In a very fundamental sense, the unit of ecological meaningfulness is the entire functioning interdependent ecosystem—or more generally, the ecosphere.

God Almighty first planted a garden.

FRANCIS BACON

The science of ecology is only the most recent and perhaps the most dramatic and subversive manifestation of the impact of modern science upon Western man's largely distorted sense of self-importance in the cosmos.

GEORGE SESSIONS

Sometimes truth comes riding into history on the back of error.

REINHOLD NIEBUHR

9 Other recent attempts have been made by philosophers and theologians to establish criteria for solving the ethical problem of "who may eat whom." Professor Charles Hartshorne tackles the problem of the relative value of the inhabitants of our ecosphere by picturing a God who looks upon all his creation with "impartial delight." Hartshorne contends that "the ultimate value of human life—or of anything else—consists *entirely* in the contribution it makes to the divine life." Since God created all that exists, then everything is of some value to "the divine life"; but since God is essentially rational, then the more rational the creature is, the more valued it would be in God's eyes—a conclusion that the super-rational Greek thinkers like Socrates and Plato would fully support. The relative value of organisms and species is therefore established. Creatures that are very low on the sentient-rational scale are also very low in value; humans are of greatest value being highest on the sentient-rational scale. Nothing possesses intrinsic value, according to Hartshorne; an organism is to be valued only because God values it.

10 A contemporary theologian, Professor John Cobb, has attempted to establish **intrinsic** criteria by which various creatures in the ecosphere could be judged to be of relative value. Cobb suggests that "experiential states"—such as sensitivity, capacities for pleasure, abstract reasoning, and creativity—establish such a hierarchy of worth. Used with caution—since we aren't yet certain about the "experiential states" of all Earth's creatures—humans appear to

A weed is a plant whose virtues have not yet been discovered.
Ralph Waldo Emerson

Prior Possession

I had long dreamed of owning a piece of land. I wanted to build a house, plant a garden, and broadcast handfuls of wildflower seeds, at random, and then wait for the springtime miracle of dancing colors.

So I bought a plot of ground. Ten acres of grass patches, chaparral, scrub, cattails, and riparian thickets, with a gurgling stream cutting across the far corner. This was to be my home. No prior claim had been filed; no one had built on it, or lived on it—so I was told.

That wasn't true. What I found was that others already lived there, and I had to share. In prior possession of the land were:

Botta Pocket Gopher (56)
California Pocket Mouse (18)
Pacific Kangaroo Rat (10)
Western Harvest Mouse (80)
California Mouse (8)
Brush Mouse (2)
Deer Mouse (188)
House Mouse (38, immigrants)
Neotoma lepida, Packrat (47)
Gray Fox (4, transients)
Coyote (8, transients)
Raccoon (2, visitors)
Striped Skunk (a pair, visitors)
Bobcat (1, seasonal visitor)
Black-tailed Deer (12, seasonal visitors)
Ornate Shrew (two pairs)
Broad-handed Mole (23)
Myotis thysanodes (68 bats, night visitors)
Myotis californicus (12 bats, night visitors)
Myotis yumanensis (4 bats, night visitors)
Jackrabbit (14, transients)
Cottontail (18)
Beechy Ground Squirrel (4)
Ring-necked Pheasant (a pair, transients)
Turkey Vulture (36, flybys)
White-tailed Kite (2, flybys)
Red-tailed Hawk (4, seasonal residents)
Golden Eagle (1, flythrough)
Sparrow Hawk (4)
Gambel's Quail (34, in season)
Mourning Dove (20)
Roadrunner (4, transients)
Screech Owl (6)
White-throated Swift (8, flybys)
Anna's Hummingbird (20, seasonal visitors)
Black-chinned Hummingbird (10, seasonal visitors)
Red-shafted Flicker (18, transients)
Acorn Woodpecker (4, visitors)
Yellow-bellied Sapsucker (4, visitors)
Hairy Woodpecker (3, visitors)
Western Kingbird (6)
Black Phoebe (a pair)
Say's Phoebe (a pair)
Swallow (16, flybys)
Scrub Jay (4)
Raven (6, flythroughs)
Bushtit (5)
Wrentit (a pair)
Mockingbird (6)
Robin (12, seasonal visitors)
Western Bluebird (4, seasonal visitors)
Cedar Waxwing (a pair, in season)
Loggerhead Shrike (6, occasional visitors)
Starling (61, evening roost)
Hutton's Vireo (8, visitors)
Warblers (19 species, transients)
House Sparrow (14 pairs)
Meadowlark (4, visitors)
House Finch (13)
Rufous-sided Towhee (4)
Abert's Towhee (2)
Brown Towhee (6)
Oregon Junco (18, winter visitors)
Common Nighthawk (30, flybys)
Spiders (18 species, 8,966 individuals)
Millipedes (9 species, 397 individuals)
Centipedes (2 species, 455 individuals)
Scorpions (2 species, 10 individuals)
Lizards (8 species, 166 individuals)
Grasshoppers (6 species, 12,288 individuals)
Crickets (2 species, 8,940 individuals)
Katydids (113)
Gnats (4,560, flythroughs)
Aphids (68,444)
Dragonflies (16)
Ladybird Beetles (8,982)
Earthworms (4 species, 34,980 individuals)
Sycamore
California Live Oak
Baccharis
Amorpha

Romneya	Artemesia californica	Orthocarpus (Owl Clover)
Cercocarpus	Quercus dumosa (Scrub Oak)	Calochortus
Rhamnus (Coffeeberry)	Yucca whippei	Dodecatheon
Ceanothus	Lupine (six varieties)	Marah
Salvia melifera (Black Sage)	Mimulus (Monkey Flower)	Penstemon
Lotus scoparius (Deer weed)	Montia (Miner's Lettuce)	Adenostoma
Rhus integrifolia	Phacelia	Escholtzia
Eriogonum fasciculatum		

These numbers are not constant, of course. The resident snakes and hawks occasionally take a gopher or mouse, and each evening bats and nighthawks reduce the insect population. However, their numbers remain relatively stable. How exactly shall we plan to live together? Who must go? Who can stay? (Who decides? I do, obviously. Someone has to make management decisions. Does "might make right" after all?) Do all our noble thoughts of fairness and justice become ludicrous in cases like this? (My friends say "Yes" and laugh: moral sentiments are impractical, of course, though they rather hope I will spare the pheasants and ladybugs. "They're so pretty," they say to me, "and the little beetles eat aphids." So, is that what ethics is all about—their usefulness to me?)

I've settled in now on our plot of ground, in relative comfort. I've become mildly territorial. As in any extended-family venture, I find I like some members of the community a lot more than others.

I still ponder: How should we live together? Who really has a right to do what to whom and why and who says so? And am I the only one in this cooperative enterprise asking questions like this?

To be sure, I enjoy my plot of earth; but a hidden corner of my soul turns at night, not quite at peace with the world.

Robert Baker
Baker's Acre

be at the top of the scale. On such a quality-of-experience scale, those creatures at the top of the ladder would possess "rights" over the life and destiny of those creatures lower on the scale.

This analysis by Dr. Cobb seems to reflect with some accuracy the actual state of things in Nature. Still, it may be risky to elevate evolution's apparent hierarchy into a normative ethic and conclude that this is the way the value system **ought** to be. Cobb acknowledges the anthropocentric nature of the scale but suggests that this is inescapable since, after all, we humans are the ones engaged in the task of trying to make sense of the whole ecological/ethical problem.

11 Attempts such as these to establish a hierarchy for "the world of an individual or species" has drawn angry criticism from not a few ecophilosophers. Stuart Hampshire, for instance, believes all attempts to discern **intrinsic** qualities are off the mark because such attempts will always be designed to fulfill our own aristocentric needs. Such scales of value implicitly say that the creatures of Earth are to be cherished to the degree they are most like humans and can minister to our needs. This utilitarian viewpoint, Hampshire writes, "places men at the very center of the universe, with their states of feeling as the source of value in the world." Then he asks a difficult question: "Is the destruction, for instance, of a species of animals to be avoided, as a great evil, only or principally because of the loss of pleasure that human beings may derive from the species? May the natural order be farmed by human beings for their comfort and pleasure without any restriction other than the comfort and pleasure of future human beings?"

12 George Sessions writes:

> An ecological world-view has been unbelievably slow to dawn on modern Western man. Such a view of man and Nature has been intuitively obvious to ancient cultures, but modern Western man, even with all of his recent scientific sophistication, still seems to resist the full implications of the Copernican and Darwinian revolutions and an ecological view of man as continuous with, and fully dependent upon, the rest of Nature.
>
> It is difficult to envision an adequate, or metaphysically appropriate, environmental ethics which does not *begin* by taking the *natural system* as ethically ultimate.
>
> But "conventional wisdom" continues to view science primarily as a means of gaining control over a "hostile and alien" Nature. Nature is seen as a backdrop for society's ever-expanding ecologically suicidal way of life.
>
> The attempt to "mine" Nature in order to satisfy apparently insatiable desires for material goods has objective limits—natural limits set by the delicate homeostatic equilibriums of ecosystem functioning. What is to be feared is that we have already surpassed these limits in some cases with future consequences we can only begin to guess.

If our members continue to increase at the present frightening rate, it will eventually become a matter of choosing between us and them [other animal species]. No matter how valuable they are to us symbolically, scientifically or aesthetically, the economics of the situation will shift against them. The blunt fact is that when our species density reaches a certain pitch, there will be no space left for other animals.

Desmond Morris

13 Those who feel deeply about Spaceship Earth with all its sentient creatures are fortunate to have had a champion whose stature approaches that of a patron saint: Aldo Leopold, a forester who loved all forms of living things, cared for them, and—incredibly—foresaw the ecological consequences of our callous unconcern for the world we live in. His testament—"a powerful plea for a land ethic"—was published after his death in 1948.

In *A Sand County Almanac,* Leopold pointed out that no viable ecospheric ethic could work "without love, respect, and admiration for the land, and a high regard for its value." Then he added, lest he be misunderstood, "I mean value in the philosophical sense." For an ethic, he wrote, is "a process in ecological evolution."

> An ethic, ecologically, is a limitation on freedom of action in the struggle for existence. An ethic, philosophically, is a differentiation of social from anti-social conduct. These are two definitions of one thing. The thing has its origin in the tendency of interdependent individuals or groups to evolve modes of co-operation. The ecologist calls these symbioses. Politics and economics are advanced symbioses in which the original free-for-all competition has been replaced, in part, by cooperation mechanisms with an ethical content. . . .
>
> There is as yet no ethic dealing with man's relation to land and to the animals and plants which grow upon it. . . . The land-relation is still strictly economic, entailing privileges but not obligations.
>
> All ethics so far evolved rest upon a single premise: that the individual is a member of a community of interdependent parts. . . . The land ethic simply enlarges the boundaries of the community to include soils, waters, plants, and animals, or collectively: the land. . . . In short, a land ethic changes the role of *Homo sapiens* from conqueror of the land-community to plain member and citizen of it.

[Lamarck] formulated a number of very modern ideas: that you cannot attribute to any creature psychological capacities for which it has no organs: that mental processes must always have physical representation; and that the complexity of a nervous system is related to the complexity of mind.

GREGORY BATESON

COEXISTENCE—IN LIFE AND DEATH

14 Man used to regard himself as somehow apart from the animals and plants, following a set of rules that were different from those followed by the rest of nature. Then the study of comparative anatomy made him realize that he is similar in many structural ways to the other animals. The study of physiology showed similar mechanisms of blood circulation, of muscle contraction, of digestion, and of other body functions. Comparative biochemistry and genetics demonstrated the basic similarity of genetic codes, chemical mechanisms, reaction sequences, and metabolic patterns in all living organisms. The study of evolution revealed that all these similarities were the consequences of a common origin.

The interrelatedness of life is now regarded as a part of the beauty and excitement of nature.

PHILIP HANDLER (ED.)
Biology and the Future of Man

When I'm near that animal, I know I'm in the presence of an intelligence. Namu, I wish I could understand your language, and your mind. I don't know, maybe one day we'll find a way. Maybe . . . maybe it'll be something more direct than words, maybe something as simple as touch—language of mutual trust.

Namu, the Killer Whale **(NBC-TV)**

15 Humans have always had deep, ambivalent feelings about our kinship with the other animals. We have gradually and grudgingly accepted coexistence with them.

On the one hand, we are aware of striking similarities. Skeletal systems are structurally similar, even down to single bone shapes. The flesh that we carry is too much alike, and when cut we bleed red whether we be bird, beast, or man. Facial configurations are alike and sometimes appear like parodies of one another. We look into the eyes of animals and feel that we recognize. We know their inner worlds in the same way we know the inner worlds of other men. We empathize with their behavior, from the pain of a wounded deer to the playfulness of bear cubs and sea otters. We identify with the hunting instinct of a mother lion as well as the fear-flight of the hunted antelope. We feel guilt when we have

If we spoke a different language, we would perceive a somewhat different world.

LUDWIG WITTGENSTEIN

FRUIT AND RUBBER HARVEST ARE GIVEN TWICE TIMBER'S VALUE.
The New York Times/The Environment, Tuesday, July 4, 1989

Providing evidence that environmentalists and Brazilian officials say could slow the pace of large-scale clearing of tropical forests, a team of scientists has found that rainforests are worth more if left standing than if cut for timber or cattle grazing.

The study, reported in the current issue of the journal *Nature,* showed that revenues generated by harvesting edible fruits, rubber, oils and cocoa from 2.5 acres of tropical rainforest are nearly two times greater than the return on timber or the value of the land if used for grazing cattle. . . .

More than 28 million acres of forest and other woodlands are lost annually around the world, and at the current rate of deforestation it is projected that several countries, including El Salvador, Costa Rica, Nigeria and the Ivory Coast, will have destroyed all their forests in 30 years.

"The study indicates that deforestation is a bad investment," said Charles M. Peters of the Institute of Economic Botany at the New York Botanical Garden, who headed the three-year study.

"People who have wanted to save the forest using environmental arguments have not been very persuasive because many of these nations have a large debt," he said. "But these findings offer a very powerful argument for forest conservation." . . .

The new study showed that 12 products, primarily edible fruits and latex, found in one hectare, about 2.5 acres, of forest at the village of Mishana, in northeastern Peru near the Brazilian border, are worth \$6,330 if sold in local markets over 5 years, with the cost of harvesting deducted from the market price.

The study also showed that the same land if used as a timber plantation would produce \$3,184 over the same period, and that if converted to cattle pastures, it would be worth \$2,960. . . .

"It appears that keeping it as managed forests has greater economic value," said Lester B. Lave, an economist and environmental expert at Carnegie-Mellon University in Pittsburgh.

"Brazil has a rapidly growing population and must look to the forest to provide them with a place of employment," he said. "Instead of cutting it and using it for farmland, they now might consider developing it as managed forests."

hurt an animal, just as we do if we have hurt another human being. All this gives us a queasy feeling. We do what we can to suppress it, yet the feeling of close kinship remains.*

It is precisely because the kinship was so obvious that we have protested so loudly that there is no kinship. People (human people!) resent it, feeling that they are endowed with vastly superior qualities that make them unique. As evolutionary humans advanced they have felt the distance increasing between themselves and the other animals.

*Several recent books have addressed this experiential kinship. For a really good read, see *Animal Minds* by Donald Griffin (University of Chicago Press, 1992); *The Human Nature of Birds* by Theodore Xenophon Barber (Penguin Books, 1994); *When Elephants Weep: The Emotional Lives of Animals* by Jeffrey Moussaieff Masson and Susan McCarthy (Delacorte Press, 1995); and *If a Lion Could Talk: Animal Intelligence and the Evolution of Consciousness* by Stephen Budiansky (Free Press, 1998).

So, our kinship with animals has been an uncomfortable one. On the one hand we intuit the kinship and confess our commonality; on the other, we deny it vehemently and demean the animal world.

16 An awareness is just dawning in our brains of the **physical**/ecological relationships with the animals of our planet, but the **psychological**/ecological relationships are probably of equal importance, though to date they have been but little explored.

From the standpoint of other animals, the human is a killer to be feared. Early in his hominid evolution man learned to use weapons to kill for food. Although basically omnivorous, his appetites place him in a class with other killer-carnivores. But Man has one behavioral pattern rarely found in the animal world: he kills for pleasure—for "sport," to use a euphemism—even when his stomach is full. For this reason the animals of the world are realistic in their fear-response to humans. This combination of pleasure-killing and advanced killing technique renders Man extremely dangerous.

But all this goes without saying; today we are all aware of it. But the question persists as to **why** man kills **for pleasure.** What is meant by "pleasure" in this context? How can one experience pleasure from the act of killing something? It's a question that needs an answer, and no trite appeal to "sportsmanship" or "stalking instinct" is quite sufficient.

Man kills because there is an "element of ultimateness" in what he is doing. When Man kills he has in his hands the mystical essence of life **and death.** Much of Man's killing is done to affirm his own existence, a confirmation of his own still-being-alive. Man is the only animal that can reflect upon his own life and death. He alone can philosophize about it, question its meaning, and fear it ahead of time. Life and death are both mysteries, but while we have life it is death that haunts our living.

When one holds in his hand a rabbit or pheasant, or kneels beside a bear or antelope, each of which, a few moments before, shared with Man the impulse-to-live, he can feel that he has become the controller of life and in so doing has, at that instant, conquered death. At that moment he becomes God: although he didn't give life, he has been able to take it away—as though "it" existed as an item of personal property—like a cherished memento or trinket—which the creature "owned." Indeed, to hold a dead animal **from which** one has taken life permits the feeling, fleetingly, of omnipotence. Primitive men often believed that they could accumulate more life by collecting life from those creatures they killed. Perhaps some of this feeling lingers in us. As a hunter holds the warm remains of a no-longer-living animal whose life he has terminated, he often confesses: "I feel alive!"

17 Not long ago, human sacrifice was practiced in most religions, great and small. Sometimes members of other tribes, especially captured warriors, were sacrificed ritually to the god of the conquering tribe. Often this was a contractual obligation: the deity had helped them win in battle, so they offered a gift in return. Many tribes, however, sacrificed their own members. Instances of ritual killing are the Babylonian sacrifice of a surrogate king; the Canaanite primitial sacrifice of one's firstborn by bloodletting or "passing through fire"; the Egyptian, Assyrian, and Chinese practice of killing scores of attendants to serve the

ANIMAL CONSCIOUSNESS

Do animals have minds? Are they conscious? Can they think?

Sensitive human beings have always empathized with nonhuman beings, but serious scientific effort to understand the minds of other animals has only just begun.

Why has this empathetic understanding been so long in coming? For one thing, we are xenophobic. We humans are not very good at empathizing with one another, never mind with creatures that differ from us. Our hominid ancestors undoubtedly thought less and intuited more; at any rate, our abilities to enter into others' experiences have dimmed, and our pets now read us much better than we read them.

Also western thinking about animals was derailed by some very influential thinkers, most notably Descartes. The physical body, he said, is merely a machine with mechanical motion. Our human bodies house a consciousness ("the ghost in the machine"), but animals are machines without consciousness or feelings. The fox caught in a trap cries in pain, but what we hear, Descartes says, is not evidence of pain at all; it is merely the sound of damaged machinery.

A third reason for our slow understanding is in how scientific research has been manifest. If "objective" data could not be obtained, then a field would not be considered a legitimate subject of inquiry. The behavioral school of psychology is a good example: since human experience was not measurable, it was ignored; ergo it did not exist.

Certain inferences are very convincing to sensitive observers, however. Animals' mental /emotional experiences often seem to match ours. They **experience** pleasures of many sorts: moods, fear, sexual feelings, hunger, confusion, agitation, aggressive urges, anger, pain. Our intuitions tell us that we have at least these experiences in common.

Early in our century the French philosopher Henri Bergson wrote and lectured with great energy in an effort to get people to realize that the essence of being alive is not biological process, but **experience.** In every animal's tiny niche evolution has developed capacities for experiencing so as to monitor the environment, and to thereby adapt, avoid pain, seek pleasure, and reproduce. To be a human being is to **experience** our existence moment by moment, to think, feel, fear, hope, dream, plan ahead, remember good things, and all. It is thus also for the hummingbird, the otter, the deer, and all other living things. (See pp. 209–212.) It is on the basis of this intuition—that many if not all animals can **experience** suffering—that an ethic must be grounded. Thusly Dr. Schweitzer insists that a truly ethical person will always include the plight of animals within the sphere of his moral concern. This is also one of the bases for the doctrine of *ahimsa* ("non-hurtfulness") of the Hindu, Buddhist, and (especially) Jain religions.

Experiencing, yes; but what about thinking? In 1976, with the publication of *The Question of Animal Awareness,* Donald Griffin began a lifelong exploration of animals' mental capacities. John Alcock, a professor of zoology at Arizona State University, comments on Griffin's explorations of animal thought processes.

> Griffin acknowledges that no one has even begun to test the proposition that nonhuman animals think in a manner similar to that of human beings. . . . To persuade us that many animals are far more than "sleepwalkers" or robots, Griffin surveys at length three lines of evidence that to him are suggestive of consciousness: (1) the ability of some animals to change their behavior adap-

> tively under different and sometimes novel circumstances, (2) certain similarities in brain neural function between lower animals and humans, and (3) the complex communicative abilities of many species.

In 1992 Griffin published *Animal Minds* (University of Chicago Press). He gives many examples of complex behavior that could indicate that the animal is thinking about the consequences of its actions.

> The ability of certain small birds to open milk bottles, the capacity of a Clark's nutcracker to remember where it has hidden on the order of a thousand small caches of seeds, the playful behavior of foxes with small prey, the cooperative hunting of lions, flexible communication in weaver ants, the skill pigeons exhibit in categorizing visual stimuli, the famous dances of honey bees, the honey guide's ability to lead humans and other animals to distant bee colonies, the "linguistic" feats of chimpanzees and gray parrots, the complex deceptive signaling of fireflies and mantis shrimps. . . .

Currently there exist two theories of consciousness. One theory holds that consciousness is a universal quality adapted by each species to its specific needs. A second theory, based on the contents of consciousness, concludes that consciousness is species specific. The consciousness of each species developed by evolution is aware of and monitors the specific stimuli in its environment needed for its survival. The role of consciousness is pragmatic, and its content for, say, a cat, would be very different from that of an eagle, a butterfly, an octopus, or a gorilla. What an ant is aware of in its environment differs enormously from what a squirrel is aware of; it literally sees a different world, and thinks about it differently. The consciousness of each species would therefore reflect the special environment in which it makes a living.

> Griffin himself contributed greatly to this conclusion with his brilliant research on bat sonar. He showed that a little brown bat uses a highly complex perceptual apparatus that is qualitatively different from those possessed by humans and the vast majority of other animals. These bats detect and track down flying insects in complete darkness by producing volleys of ultrasound frequencies that the human ear is totally incapable of detecting.

Theorists sharing the sociobiological perspective contend that consciousness is evolution's tool for assuring the transmission of a species' genes. The ability on the part of any creature to think about its actions, anticipate their consequences, and plan accordingly (reflective consciousness) would have an advantage over an organism that merely responds to immediate stimuli (perceptual consciousness).

Consciousness of any sort would have enormous survival value, and undoubtedly evolution has supported the ability to think wherever the opportunity arises. But reflective consciousness would enable any species to jump light-years ahead in its ability to respond to, and then to manipulate, its environment. It would be a strange anomaly if evolution has not developed such a survival quality along varied limbs of the evolutionary tree.

EXCERPTS: JOHN ALCOCK
"Consciousness-Raising III,"
Natural History (September 1992)

spirits of their royal masters in the next life. Abraham's near-sacrifice of his son Isaac presupposes the existence of the institution of ritual sacrifice. In one form or another, human sacrifice has been practiced in almost every ancient culture —and not a few modern cultures as well.

At some point, however, it seems that sensitivity deepens, and ways are devised to avoid human sacrifice. Historically, the story of the sacrifice of Isaac by Abraham was understood by ancient Hebrews to be the origin of the ransom system. Make no mistake, one's firstborn belonged to the god Yahweh, but henceforth he could be "ransomed" with an ox, a ram, or perhaps a pair of doves. Similar animal substitutes are found in most long-running religious traditions.

But eventually, in almost every religion, ritual killing comes to an end, accompanied by appropriate theological rationale. In the Christian tradition, the sacrifice of God's only son was interpreted to be the final, complete sacrifice, replacing the Judaic sacrificial system; and the sacrifice of God's only son—which is a deliberate parallel to the sacrifice of Abraham's only son—recurs eternally in the Roman Church in the "Sacrifice of the Mass." In other religions, live sacrifices were replaced by the sacrifice of figurines, which were ritually broken, or by wood or paper substitutes bearing names, which were buried or burned.

The trees and rocks will teach thee what thou can'st not learn from human teachers.
Saint Bernard of Clairvaux

Few places in the world today still witness blood sacrifices carried on solely for religious reasons. (It is still common—in Hinduism, for instance—for the local butcher to invoke religious ritual in the execution of his job—which he would perform anyway—as an extra benefit and rationale of his vocation.)

18 Ordinary ethics seeks to find limits within the sphere of human life and relationships. But the absolute ethics of the will-to-live must reverence every form of life, seeking so far as possible to refrain from destroying any life, regardless of its particular type. It says of no instance of life, "This has no value." It cannot make any such exceptions, for it is built upon reverence for life as such. It knows that the mystery of life is always too profound for us, and that its value is beyond our capacity to

We plant trees to benefit another generation.
Caecilius Statius

estimate. . . . True, in practice we are forced to choose. At times we have to decide arbitrarily which forms of life, and even which particular individuals, we shall save, and which we shall destroy. But the principle of reverence for life is none the less universal.

ALBERT SCHWEITZER

Our climb to the top has been a get-rich-quick story, and, like all nouveaux riches, we are very sensitive about our background.

DESMOND MORRIS

19 Dostoevsky's psychology rests on a fundamental belief in the deep, ineradicable humanity of men. A logical, officially sanctioned decision to spill blood is reversible and remedial, if deep in a person's heart there is still a small spark of compassion. Sometimes a man is driven to things; he finds that he has to be inflexible. But it is important that he should keep the feeling that the circumstances that forced him to cruelty are themselves unnatural.

Permission to kill with the approval of one's conscience destroys the humanity of man.

PAVEL SIMONOV

20 One of the most interesting things we humans do is to anthropomorphize all our animal kin, and we did this long before Walt Disney institutionalized the technique. We project our human qualities into and onto nonhuman creatures; we think of them as though they have the same experiences we do. We endow them with our fears, angers, jealousies. In animated cartoons every animal we know—from mice to roadrunners, from dumb dogs to stammering pigs and elephants with outsized ears—feels human feelings.

We anthropomorphize (the word means "to make into human form," from the Greek *anthropos,* "man," and *morphos,* "form") for at least two reasons. (1) We can't help it. Since we experience only human experiences, it is inevitable that we would project our experience onto other creatures. (2) We **want** other creatures to be like us. The more humanoid they are the better we feel about them and can relate to them.

Look at the matter in another way: How could we not project our experiences into our fellow creatures? If we look into the eyes of a baby seal or hear the cry of a dog in pain—even though we can't know for sure what the animal is experiencing—it's difficult not to respond as though the animals feel what we would be feeling were we in their place. We empathize through our own experience to theirs, and in fact it may be that our intuition here is closer to the truth than our solipsistic skepticism.

"No Man Is an Iland"

21 From time immemorial humankind has been a part—**but only a part**—of the evolutionary/ecological system. We may soon be the controller of all our planet's life and the determiner of its destiny, but what we will control will be a complex system of interrelationships, and we humans will remain a part of the system. Even if or when we begin to live in space colonies or on the Moon or Mars, we will be obliged to carry our natural ecological environments with us, just to survive. All the lovely scenes of the most ruggedly scientific space colonies at L-5 or elsewhere contain idyllic panoramas of forests, gardens, and even livestock and wild animals, without which we could not exist or want to live there.

The old gods are dead or dying and people everywhere are searching, asking: What is the new mythology to be, the mythology of this unified earth as of one harmonious being?

Joseph Campbell

It is easy for one to feel lonely in the midst of a crowd; it is easy to feel alienated in a world to which one is deeply related. We may never realize the existence of the multitudinous tie-lines that connect us to the world we live in.

"No man is an Iland, intire of itself," wrote John Donne. Each is a part of the whole, subject to the same physical forces that move the atoms and the planets. We are composed of the same fivescore elements that make up the seas and rocks, trees and stars. We are subject to the same protoplasmic processes found throughout the animal kingdom. The same neural events explode in all our brains, and our physical being is determined by a DNA code system identical to that which guides the replication of all animals and plants on Earth. Most profoundly, we share the will-to-live with every living creature. We are part of an awesome protoplasmic venture.

✦

ALBERT SCHWEITZER

Reverence for Life

In his *Memoirs of Childhood and Youth,* Albert Schweitzer writes that his early years were dominated by a deep awareness of two things: the happiness of his childhood and the overwhelming amount of pain he saw around him.

> As far back as I can remember I was saddened by the amount of misery I saw in the world around me. . . . One thing that specially saddened me was that the unfortunate animals had to suffer so much pain and misery. The sight of an old limping horse, tugged forward by one man while another kept beating it with a stick to get it to the knacker's yard at Colmar, haunted me for weeks.
>
> It was quite incomprehensible to me—this was before I began going to school—why in my evening prayers I should pray for human beings only. So when my mother had prayed with me and had kissed me good-night, I used to add silently a prayer that I had composed myself for all living creatures. It ran thus: "O, heavenly Father, protect and bless all things that have breath; guard them from all evil, and let them sleep in peace."

As he matured it became clear to him that his good fortune in having a relatively happy youth was not to be taken for granted. "Whoever is spared personal pain must feel himself called to help in diminishing the pain of others. We must all carry our share of the misery which lies upon the world." So, at the age of twenty-one, still a college student, he vowed to devote his life till he was thirty to the ministry, to medical science, and to music. This was to be a time of both preparation and personal fulfillment, and he would accomplish all he could in these fields. Then, when he turned thirty, he would devote the rest of his life, in some way, to the service of humanity. Exactly what direction this service would take, he didn't yet know. Several life-affirming years would have to pass before—as he put it—"a chain of circumstances pointed out to me the road which led to the sufferers from leprosy and sleeping-sickness in Africa."

Albert Schweitzer was born January 14, 1875, in Kaysersberg, in the Upper Alsace, a region that forever teeters between France and Germany; and his

Many a time have I, with a feeling of shame, said quietly to myself over a grave the words which my mouth ought to have spoken to the departed, while he was still in the flesh.

Whoever is spared personal pain must feel himself called to help in diminishing the pain of others.

Humanitarianism consists in never sacrificing a human being to a purpose.

A good conscience is the invention of the devil.

Reverence for life is the highest court of appeal.

There slowly grew up in me an unshakable conviction that we have no right to inflict suffering and death on another living creature unless there is some unavoidable necessity for it, and that we ought all of us to feel what a horrible thing it is to cause suffering and death out of mere thoughtlessness.

native tongue was the Alsatian dialect of German. When he was a few months old the family moved to nearby Günsbach, where, in the company of three sisters and one brother, he lived through "a delightful childhood."

His father was the pastor of the evangelical parish in predominantly Catholic Alsace. From him Albert inherited a love of music, a bright mind, and a commitment to rational inquiry, a dedicated work ethic, and iron self-discipline. From his mother he inherited a natural reserve and a passionate temperament.

From very early on he displayed an unusual talent for, and sensitivity to, music. His father had begun to teach him, at the age of five, some music on the family's old square piano; at eight he began to play the organ; at nine he substituted for the church organist at a service. He discovered that he possessed an unusual gift for improvisation and playing melodies and harmony from memory. All his life beautiful music overpowered him; he experienced it so deeply and mystically that he would have to sit down or hold on to something lest he be overcome "from excess of pleasure." When, at sixteen, he heard Wagner's *Tannhäuser* for the first time, it was days before he could put his mind back on his studies.

His high school years were spent at Münster and Mülhausen. He had to walk two miles over the hills every morning and evening to and from the Münster school, and his love of nature blossomed. "This walk it was my delight to take by myself, without any of the other boys who also went to school at Münster, so as to indulge my thoughts." In love with the beauties of nature, he tried to vent his feelings in poetry and drawing, but he succeeded in expressing himself only through musical improvisation.

At eighteen Schweitzer passed his "leaving examination" at the gymnasium (high school) and headed for the university at Strassburg to study theology and philosophy. He pursued his career as an organist, came under the spell of Wagner's operas, studied hard, wrote voluminously, and, at twenty-three, passed his theological examination and headed for Paris to study piano and organ. He returned to Strassburg to complete his doctorate in philosophy, writing his dissertation on the language of Kant's *Critique of Pure Reason.* At twenty-four he received his doctorate and accepted a position as pastor of Saint Nicholas Church in Strassburg. At twenty-five (in July 1900) he obtained a second doctorate (in theology) and joined the faculty of his university. He spent all his free time developing his manuscripts for publication.

True to his commitment, Schweitzer made his contribution to theological thought with a monumental work, *The Quest of the Historical Jesus* (1906). At the same time he had also been working on his commitment to music by writing, in French, a book on Bach. It was published in 1905. He also wrote an influential essay on organ-building.

The time had arrived to make the great transition to a life of service to humanity. Medical missionaries were urgently needed in the French Congo, so Schweitzer decided to go to west-central Africa, not as an evangelist, but as a medical doctor. To that end, at the age of thirty, he undertook a three-year program of medical training to become a physician. On Good Friday 1913, with Europe on the brink of war, Schweitzer and his wife—he had married Hélène Bresslau in 1912—left Günsbach for the French Congo. At Lambaréné on the Ogowe River, Schweitzer settled into a small "hospital" constructed of corrugated iron and roofed with palm leaves. From his very first days he was beseiged by the sick who came to the hospital from up to two hundred miles away. The amount of suffering among the Africans was even greater than he had imagined.

War broke out in Europe in late summer of 1914, and, with only a year of service behind them, the Schweitzers were told they were prisoners of war and confined to the mission station. Work at the hospital was forbidden, and they were to have no contact with natives or other colonials. "So on the second day of my internment, still quite amazed at being able to sit down at my writing-table early in the morning as in the days before I took up medicine, I set to work on the Philosophy of Civilization."

✦

As Schweitzer reflected on the meaning of "civilization," what came clear to him is that the essence of civilization is the will toward ethical growth by both individuals and society. "The will to civilization is then the universal will to progress which is conscious of the ethical as the highest value for all." We may think that our being civilized is proven by our intellectual or material accomplishments, but it should be obvious that only human beings who have achieved a certain positive stability in their ethical relationships can fully enjoy the more material benefits of that civilization. Without that ethical foundation, the material blessings may exist, but a collective enjoyment of them by individuals is not possible. Ethics, therefore, is the glue that holds a civilization together and makes authentic progress possible. "Civilization I define in quite general terms as spiritual and material progress in all spheres of activity, accompanied by an ethical development of individuals and of mankind."

As of the summer of 1915, Schweitzer had arrived at a clear philosophical solution to half the problem: he understood that the life-affirming values of Western civilization had weakened and taken the punch out of the worldview by which Western society actually lives. But something still eluded him. He was determined to hang on until his intellect could clearly see the connection between life-affirmation and some kind of ethical principle that would render it meaningful. Formal connections alone were inadequate; he longed for something firmer—something almost tangible—that would make his search intelligible.

After months of searching, he finally found what he sought. It was during a long boat trip upriver. "Late on the third day, at the very moment when, at sunset, we were making our way through a herd of hippopotamuses, there flashed upon my mind, unforeseen and unsought, the phrase, 'Reverence for Life.' The iron door had yielded: the path in the thicket had become visible. Now I had found my way to the idea in which world- and life-affirmation and ethics are contained side by side! Now I knew that the world- and life-affirmation, together with its ideals of civilization, is founded in thought." (See pp. 8–9.)

What does Schweitzer mean by "Reverence for Life"? One must start from the immediate data of experience. At the core of consciousness is the ever-present experience, "I am life which wills to live, in the midst of life which wills to live." This is a fact, an undeniable reality of my life. All my activities, awake and asleep, are designed to sustain the continuity of my self as a unitary life-form. I eat, work, rest, and grow in order to keep my self alive and functioning.

But in this will-to-live I am not alone. The most fundamental fact of life is that each single living organism on planet Earth, since Life's beginning, has shared with me the very same will-to-live. Whether for a microbe, a trilobite, a brontosaurian, or an Alsatian missionary, to live entails a continuous struggle to assure the survival of the self. I am a self in the midst of selves, a will-to-live in the midst of an infinite number of other wills-to-live.

Picture this scene on an African veld: A zebra grazes in the open grassland with her colt. A mother lion flanked by three cubs lurks at the edge of the clearing, waiting for the right moment to stalk and kill the young zebra to feed her cubs. From an ethical standpoint, what is good for the zebras—the successful continuation of their wills-to-live—is bad for the lions; and what is good for the lions—obtaining food to nourish the continuity of their wills-to-live—is bad for the zebras. The only ethic that can be derived from such a scenario is one of pure relativism. What is good for one party is not good for

Slowly in our European thought comes the notion that ethics has not only to do with mankind but with the animal creation as well. This begins with St. Francis of Assisi. The explanation which applies only to man must be given up. Thus we shall arrive at saying that ethics is reverence for all life.

The mistake made by all previous systems of ethics has been the failure to recognize that life as such is the mysterious value with which they have to deal.

In the parable of Jesus the shepherd saves not merely the soul of the lost sheep but the whole animal.

Renunciation of thinking is a declaration of spiritual bankruptcy. . . . I therefore stand and work in the world as one who aims at making men less shallow and morally better by making them think.

the other, and vice versa; and there are no principles to be inferred that can ameliorate the facts of the situation and bring about a happy ending. The "evolutionary ethic" does not submit to our human sensitivities or accommodate our ethical ideals.

But human thought and feeling alter everything. The lion and zebra cannot develop ethical principles because they can't reflect on their behavior. They live instinctively, without reflective thought. Programmed by instinct to act in their own interests, they are oblivious to the needs of other selves. By contrast, we humans can reflect on our behavior and thereby transcend it. We can watch the lion-zebra struggle, think about it concretely and abstractly, feel the pain—and write books about it. We can imagine our human selves in similar competitive struggles; we can establish guidelines for behavior that will help us anticipate such predicaments, avoid them, and solve them when we must.

Reverence for life, then, means respecting the will-to-live of every living creature. Reverence for life includes all life. The Western philosophical tradition in ethics has failed because it did not extend its sphere of concern to other living creatures. Schweitzer blames our religious heritage for encouraging us to limit our empathy to our own kind when it is completely natural and human to feel compassion for the suffering of all living things. The individual who does not feel an animal's pain is not truly ethical. "A man is ethical only when life, as such, is sacred to him, that of plants and animals as that of his fellow-men, and when he devotes himself helpfully to all life that is in need of help."

Reverence for Life—"In that principle my life has found a firm footing and a clear path to follow."

Because of the world war, the Schweitzers—German citizens in French colonial territory—were confined to the hospital at Lambaréné until, in September of 1917, they were reclassified as prisoners of war and sent to France. In July 1918 they were exchanged for French prisoners and returned to their home at Günsbach.

For the next six years Schweitzer worked and wrote from his base in Alsace. In April 1924 he was back at Lambaréné. The corrugated-iron hospital was still standing, but virtually everything else had been reclaimed by the jungle. For a year he was a doctor in the morning and a "master-builder" the rest of the day. Within a year the medical center had grown so much that it was decided to move to a new location two miles upriver and to modernize the facilities. For the rest of his life he would spend a year or two working at Lambaréné, then journey to Europe to conduct a lecture-recital tour to raise funds for his work, then return to Lambaréné. The medical staff at the hospital was gradually augmented so that it ran smoothly without Le Grand Docteur.

In 1949 Schweitzer visited the United States for his only time to speak at the Goethe Centennial in Aspen, Colorado. In 1950 a poll was conducted among artists in eighteen countries and Schweitzer was named "The Man of the Century." He received numerous honorary degrees, including a doctorate in music from Edinburgh and three doctorates in law. He was elected to the prestigious French Academy in 1952 and received the Order of Merit from Britain's Queen Elizabeth in 1955. In October 1953, at the age of seventy-eight, he was awarded the Nobel Peace Prize; he used the proceeds to build a leprosy annex to his hospital.

Albert Schweitzer died at Lambaréné on September 4, 1965, and was buried under the Palm Tree above the Ogowe River beside Hélène, who died in 1959.

✦

REFLECTIONS

1 Many of us face a major problem when confronted by the two worldviews presented in this chapter—that of Chief Seattle that respects Nature as the nourishing source of life, and that of modern empirical materialism that has now given us an understanding of Nature through physics, chemistry, biology, botany, and so on. The scientific worldview has given is a "reality" that we can't reasonably avoid; the spiritual worldview represents feelings and values that are enormously attractive. Can these two worldviews be harmonized? How can we salvage from each the benefits and insights that we need—some would say desperately need? Or, in the final analysis, must they remain mutually contradictory and mutually exclusive?

2 What are your thoughts on our recent recognition that humans are a part of the whole evolutionary/protoplasmic venture, and that, in a sense, we can claim "to be one" with plants, animals, and perhaps larger processes? Do you have a philosophic response to this concept?

3 Do you agree that we humans harbor a deep ambivalence about ourkinship with other animals, perhaps because we feel that close tie and fear it?

4 Page 447 contains an important realization—that we anthropomorphize our animal kin. What does it mean to say that we "anthropomorphize" other beings? Why do we engage in anthropomorphic imaging, since, after all, it involves a fallacy?

5 The question persists as to why man kills for pleasure. What would be your answer to this "strange and dangerous quality" that *Homo sapiens* appears to possess? What do you think is meant by "pleasure" in this context? Is there a better name for it?

6 This chapter suggests (pp. 443–446) that much of man's killing is done to affirm his own existence; it is a confirmation of his still-being-alive. Do you agree? How would you put it?

7 Read the pungent description of Dostoevsky's psychology by Pavel Simonov (p. 447). Listen carefully to his meaning, then decide whether you agree with it.

8 Think about Schweitzer's Reverence for Life—a concept he believed to be "the realistic answer to the realistic question of how man and the world are related to each other." How do you feel about this all-inclusive ethic?

Future

6-4

With the beginning of the futures movement in the 1960s, "research into the future" became a viable concept; since then serious thought has been given to alternative possible futures. Most futurists agree that the future will not much resemble the past, because of the acceleration of unanticipated breakthroughs. This chapter describes several future scenarios, both optimistic and pessimistic; these include the TTAPS nuclear winter scenario, Toffler's economic projections, Clarke's technological transformations, McCall's joyous canvases, and Bradbury's story of a time traveler who lies to us. What mankind most needs, some say, is a shared vision of a common future toward which we could all work together.

The Theoretical Life

1 Plato once made the distinction between the practical life (*praktikos bios*) and the theoretical life (*theoretikos bios*). By the practical life Plato was thinking of a life that is lived in terms of short-range goals, while the theoretical life is lived in terms of long-range goals. The theoretical life is in every way as "practical" (in the modern sense) as the platonic practical life, but it is planned and guided in terms of our deeper and more ultimate requirements rather than in terms of the immediate and often too-pressing needs and desires of today. The theoretical life is to be planned so that the future will be fulfilling when its time comes.

It was the task of philosophers, Plato believed, to think further ahead to envision realistically the distant problems and goals that are as inevitable as tomorrow and that, in our prevision of them, determine profoundly the quality of the life we live today.

Each age has had its cherished superstitions. A new age dawns with their identification and rejection.
Daniel N. Robinson

Is it a truism or a needed insight to be reminded that the future **will** arrive—for us, for our children, for their children? Few of us would disagree with the notion that a life lived exclusively in terms of the next twenty-four hours would leave each of us in a rather sorry condition the following day. So, wisely, we plan ahead—for hours, days, months (vaguely), and years (more vaguely). But we do plan. Only a fool would not plan for the good life, providing planning is a viable possibility.

Plato's point is that the better we envision wise and fulfilling futures for ourselves and our children, the better the chance of our dreams becoming realities. This same point is now being made by contemporary future-thinkers, including the veteran futurist Fred Polak: "In the act of searching out the road into the future, man crosses the frontiers of the unknown and raises Homo sapiens to a new level: the level of foresight and purposefulness. . . . In taking thought for tomorrow, man begins to create tomorrow."

2 Our histories are created for us by historians. Events are resurrected from the record of past presents, selected because of their meaning and value, and summarized for us in history books. We can then see ourselves in the long perspective of our past.

But creating our past is but one side of the story: our futures can be created in similar fashion. "Humans are time travelers, who chart their courses through time with maps of the future," writes Robert Bundy. Without the creation of our futures we can't know where we are going. We need to perceive ourselves in the light of optional futures fully as much as we need to know our pasts.

Heretofore, our futures have been created by our religions, by visionaries, utopians and anti-utopians, and by science-fiction writers. Only recently has futurism come into its own.

Research into the Future

3 Until a few years ago "research into the future" was not a thinkable thought. Conceptually, its time had not yet arrived. Of course, this did not prevent human imagination from giving substance to our futures, for dreaming has always been a part of being human.

Human beings cannot live without hope, or face an empty future. Our great religions all envision a future time when the tragedy of earthly history will be replaced by, or be consummated in, a Reign of God, a Messianic Age, a Golden Age, a New Jerusalem. A blank future, it seems, is intolerable. Even a frightening future is preferable to nothingness.

"We create our literary myths, legends, and epics of the future, not so that we will find our golden age, but because in the creation of utopian standards, we have created forms which make present action possible" (Hugh Duncan). The Garden of Eden in Western doctrine remains the archetype of the perfect human condition to which we will someday return.

Another kind of inhabitable fantasy-world has entered the scene: literary utopias. Among them are Plato's *Republic* and the mythical city of Magnesia in his *Laws;* Thomas More's *Utopia* (More coined the word from two Greek words, *ou-topos,* "no-where"), Voltaire's *Candide,* Campanella's *City of the Sun,* and H. G. Wells's *Modern Utopia.* These utopias were motivated in part by the perception of this world as essentially uninhabitable by sensitive spirits. If Walpole is right that life is a comedy for the thinker, but a tragedy for one who feels,

"Perhaps what we need is a kick in our complacency to prepare us for what lies ahead."

"Capt. Jean-Luc Picard"
Star Trek: The Next Generation

It is the business of the future to be dangerous; and it is among the merits of science that it equips the future for its duties.

Alfred North Whitehead

then utopias are attempts on the part of some sensitive thinkers to create in their minds, if not in this world, a place where life would be worth living.

In recent decades anti-utopias have largely replaced the utopias in our consciousness: Huxley's *Brave New World,* Orwell's *1984,* Bradbury's *Fahrenheit 451,* Ayn Rand's *Anthem,* Asimov's *Nightfall;* and of course the plethora of both possible and impossible futures in films and television, in many of which the noblest dreams have gone awry: *Planet of the Apes, Soylent Green, Logan's Run, Terminal Man,* and *Jurassic Park.* These visions (when taken seriously) fell upon us with a shattering impact. Their shrill warning was relevant because we recognized them to be future versions of conditions that we already observe around us. These anti-utopias were fiction-worlds born from the minds of gifted seers who passed their scenarios (and fears) on to us.

4 Serious research into the future began only some forty years ago, and as a discipline and worldwide movement it is about thirty years old. In 1964 a project called "Mankind 2000" attempted to sensitize the European populace to rapidly approaching global problems. The first World Future Research Conference was convened in Oslo in 1967. The Russians have several prestigious futures programs in operation. The Club of Rome was organized in 1968 for the purpose of alerting world leaders to the coming collision between soaring human population and economic growth.

In America a large number of future research organizations have been launched: the RAND Corporation, the Hudson Institute, The Commission on the Year 2000, the American Institute of Planners, and the World Future Society. Today most governments and large private industries have futures groups that carry on forecasting in special-interest fields.

The military mind will be the curse of the race so long as there is a military . . . or will it be the salvation?

Christopher Anvil

Four things have conspired to bring about the rapid birth of the futures research movement. (1) Techniques for forecasting developed almost overnight, largely because of the progress of science and technology. Compared with the complexity and recalcitrance of human behavior, technology is relatively predictable. Made with the burgeoning use of microminiature computers, trend projections and correlations not previously possible suddenly became quick and easy. "Given his present state of knowledge, social as well as scientific and technological, man now has an enormously enhanced capacity to choose his future, both collectively and individually" (McHale).

Our world is now future-oriented, you see, in the sense that the rate of change has become so rapid that we can no longer wait until a problem is upon us to work out the solution. If we do, then there is no real solution, for by the time one has been worked out and applied, change has progressed still further and our solution no longer makes sense at all. The change must be anticipated before it happens.

Isaac Asimov

(2) A series of global events has scared us into thinking about the real possibility of world catastrophe: uncontrolled weapons escalation; polluted lakes, rivers, and shorelines; electrical blackouts and brownouts; oil spills and the killing of the oceans; extinction and near extinction of many species of animals; defoliation, droughts, global warming and ozone depletion; the hunger zones of the world with growing populations and food shortages. Add unstable governments, self-aggrandizing leaders, wobbly international currencies, economic troubles, global power struggles, and world leaders who command little or no confidence—put all this together and there is little wonder that, in the minds of many, a spectre of doom hovers over a shrinking world.

(3) There has developed a rapid realization that all the countries of the world are now so interdependent in fundamental ways that problems can only be understood and dealt with in terms of world systems. Energy problems are global. Pollution recognizes no political boundaries. The whole world, economi-

cally, is becoming one single system. Any war now affects all nations; conflagrations that flare up in remote corners rapidly ignite tensions around the world. Communications are global and instant. In a word, there will no longer be any really significant **local** problems. The serious challenges of the next fifty years will all be global in nature, and localistic or nationalistic mobilization cannot hope to change the course of such worldwide threats.

(4) We are still thinking within frameworks from the past—and they no longer work. The idea that any one nation can go it alone for its food, energy, and basic materials is no longer viable. The belief that wars can be won is a myth. The idea of "manifest destiny" is history. And the "rugged individualism" that once moved men and mountains and bred pioneers who held themselves beholden to no one—these convictions, and the conditions that spawned them, are all gone.

The world's biggest problems today are really infinitesimal: the atom, the ovum, and a bit of pigment.

HERB CAEN

5 This, then, is the goal of futures research: to establish organizations—political, economic, industrial, academic, and more—that will previse the nature of these problems and have on the drawing boards contingency plans for facing them; and to have on a stand-by basis international organizations ready to give counsel and guidance to the power-movers when the time comes that world leaders can no longer ignore the problems—and might listen to wise counsel.

So futurists and futurism were born. In 1945 Arthur C. Clarke began to describe in detail specific upcoming technological events. In 1958 Robert Jungk began talking about "early warning systems" that would study the long-range consequences of uncontrolled technologies. By 1960 Fred Polak had begun to clarify how our visions of the future help us to achieve the futures we envision; and Herman Kahn had begun to develop complex "scenarios" of alternative futures and to analyze systematically the events that might actually bring them about. In 1963 Dennis Gabor wrote of "inventing" our futures and then creating means of arriving at our inventions.

In 1963 Buckminster Fuller began to make us dream with a colorful stream of futuristic images, holistic programs, and novel hardware—the boldest display of concrete previsions since Leonardo da Vinci, with whom he is often compared. By 1965 Bertrand de Jouvenel was turning out treatises on humanistic elements in future planning ("the intellectual construction of a likely future is a work of art"). By 1966 Marshall McLuhan, with cryptic phrases and lilting puns, was warning us that new communications media—the media themselves, that is, quite apart from their content—would revolutionize our worldviews and lifestyles: The medium itself is the message. By 1968 Erich Jantsch was engaged in "integrative forecasting" to determine the technological impact on social and human institutions.

Also in 1968 Paul Ehrlich, for a while, jolted a complacent society by pointing out the inevitable consequences of unchecked population growth. And in 1970 Alvin Toffler described the "future shock" that awaits us: "We cannot create a sane social system until technology is tamed, the educational system revolutionized, and future-consciousness injected into our political lives." In this connection, Ray Bradbury confesses that he has no problem trusting technology; it is the boys who play with their toys that are to be feared.

6 Just because the problems are so new and our thinking is so outdated, it is the consensus among futurists that mankind now stands at the threshold of the

most critical period of human history. There is a near-unanimous feeling that the next fifty years will constitute a transition period that will write the future of man, one way or the other. Their deepest fear derives from the fact that the dangerous problems are all global while humankind's mental machinery is still fueled by past ideas that no longer burn: our concepts remain essentially local, regional, tribal, and nationalistic. This is not a matter of irrelevant patriotism, for realistic loyalties promote cohesive bonds and foster shared visions and goals. It is rather that aristocentric myths prevent an accurate understanding of the nature of the global problems that threaten us and make it impossible to set in motion the forces that could be effective against these large-scale problems.

A recent report of the Club of Rome was issued in a volume entitled *Mankind at the Turning Point* (1974). Derived from a massive accumulation of data, conclusions were clear: we face an urgent need for a thoroughgoing restructuring of our conceptual frameworks, basic assumptions, and a reorientation of values—if we are to survive the next fifty years.

1. A **world consciousness** must be developed through which every individual realizes his role as a member of the world community.
2. A **new ethic in the use of material resources** must be developed that will result in a style of life compatible with the oncoming age of scarcity. One should be proud of saving and conserving rather than of spending and discarding.
3. An **attitude toward nature must be developed based on harmony rather than conquest.** Only in this way can man apply in practice what is already accepted in theory—that is, that man is an integral part of nature.
4. If the human species is to survive, man must develop **a sense of identification with future generations** and be ready to trade benefits to the next generations for the benefits to himself. If each generation aims at the maximum good for itself, Homo sapiens is as good as doomed.

It's a poor sort of memory that only works backward.
Lewis Carroll
Through the Looking-Glass

One futurist commentator, Howard Didsbury, summarized the mood of the report: "Enlightened self-interest dictated by necessity may tend to make clear mankind's ultimate choices: cooperation or destruction. If cooperation is chosen it may 'lead to the creation of a new mankind.' Should mankind choose the alternative, all is silence."

The Futurists and the Future

7 Looking ahead for decades and centuries, there is no single world-picture on which all futurists agree, although there is remarkable agreement on many points. Futurists' visions will depend partly upon their specialties and partly upon their personal feelings of optimism or pessimism about the operations of "human nature" past and present. Moreover, whether a futurist is essentially negative or positive depends somewhat on whether his or her picture of the future is a short-range or long-range vision. In general, the short-range futurists concentrate on the looming problems that could engulf us and tend to be less cheery about the decades immediately ahead. The middle- and long-range futurists tend to be far more optimistic because of that widely held intuition that

if mankind can make it through the next fifty years, then the most distant future is practically unlimited in its promise of progress, human growth, and personal fulfillment.

8 **Alvin Toffler** With the publication of *Future Shock* in 1971 Alvin Toffler reached international prominence as a futurist. Since then he has edited *The Futurists* (1972) and written *The Eco-Spasm Report* (1975) and *The Third Wave* (1980). He is essentially a short-range futurist (relatively, that is) who is especially knowledgeable about socioeconomic trends.

Anyone who wishes to cope with the future should travel back in imagination a single lifetime—say to 1900—and ask himself just how much of today's technology would be, not merely incredible, but incomprehensible to the keenest scientific brains of that time.

Arthur C. Clarke

As a futurist Toffler is acutely aware of two essentially human problems that threaten all global economic and political processes during the next few decades.

> First: *Lack of future-consciousness.* Instead of anticipating the problems and opportunities of the future, we lurch from crisis to crisis. The energy shortage, runaway inflation, ecological troubles—all reflect the failure of our political leaders at federal, state, and local levels to look beyond the next election. Our political system is "future-blind." With but few exceptions, the same failure of foresight marks our corporations, trade unions, schools, hospitals, voluntary organizations, and communities as well. The result is political and social future shock.
>
> Second: *Lack of participation.* Our government and other institutions have grown so large and complicated that most people feel powerless. They complain of being "planned upon." They are seldom consulted or asked for ideas about their own future. On the rare occasions when they are, it is ritualistic rather than real consultation. Blue-collar workers, poor people, the elderly, the youth, even the affluent among us, feel frozen out of the decision process. And as more and more millions feel powerless, the danger of violence and authoritarianism increases. Moreover, if this is true within this country, it is even more true of the world situation in which the previously powerless are demanding the right to participate in shaping the global future.

Most intellectual problems are, ultimately, problems of classification and nomenclature.

S. I. Hayakawa

9 In *Future Shock* Toffler massively documented his thesis that world economic conditions are out of control, are accelerating, and are being faced only with outmoded myths and methods. He pointed out that, almost without exception, those dealing with these gigantic "economic" problems know nothing but economics; whereas the actual problems are interdisciplinary by nature and can't even be understood, let alone solved, by narrow-gauge economics specialists.

The future isn't what it used to be.
Arthur C. Clarke

The giant economic forces of our time have become tails wagging the dogs. Many economic systems, especially the multinational corporations, are more powerful than the nations they use as bases of operation. Such nations are, in effect, "colonies" of such transnational powers. And all these economic processes are moving faster than we can understand or cope with.

Toffler therefore suggests alternative approaches for facing a world that has "gone random" and is running out of control. One solution is long-range planning. We need to think big and to think boldly.

> Futurism differs from planning, if one wishes to make that distinction, by reaching beyond economics to embrace culture, beyond transportation to include in its concerns family life and sex roles, beyond physical and environmental concerns to include mental health and many other dimensions of reality. It reaches beyond the conventional time frame of the industrial style planner toward longer, ten-, twenty-, or thirty-year speculative horizons, without which the short-range plans make little sense. Furthermore, it seeks radical new ways to democratize the process—not merely because that is good, just, or altruistic, but because it is necessary: without broad-scale citizen involvement, even the most conscientious and expertly drawn plans are likely to blow up in our faces.

These accelerating out-of-control global economic movements are scary, to be sure, but, Toffler adds, we are faced with "an awesome but exhilarating task that few generations in human history have ever faced: the design of a new civilization."

10 **Arthur C. Clarke** Serious scientific forecasting had its first futurist in Arthur C. Clarke, a scientist-writer equally renowned for his science fiction. In 1945 he presented a remarkably accurate and detailed description of radio and television communications satellites (and has regretted ever since not attempting to patent "an idea whose time had come"). Another futurist, John McHale, makes the significant comment that "Clarke has been consistently more accurate in his predictions than many of his fellow scientists and science-fiction writers." His major futurist writings are *Profiles of the Future* (1963, updated 1984), *Voices from the Sky* (1965), and *The Promise of Space* (1967). Whether his science-fiction classic *Childhood's End,* Space Odysseys, and Rama adventures should also be included among his prophetic visions remains a tantalizing question.

Clarke contends that there are two good reasons for believing that the future will not much resemble the present. One is that known trends are accelerating on all fronts, and in a relatively short time the world will be almost unrecognizable to those of us living today.

Someday is too far away.
(MasterCharge TV commercial)

Someday may be too late.
(Kodak TV commercial)

But there is a stronger reason: the pace of **unpredictable breakthroughs** is also accelerating, and these are the true causes of quantum leaps in progress.

A few past unforeseen discoveries are X rays, nuclear energy, radio, television, photography, sound recording, relativity, quantum mechanics, transistors and the computer revolution, and lasers and their versatile applications, including CDs. Such unpredictables will continue; these are the unexpected jumps that will propel us into unexpected worlds.

11 What about the foreseeable events of the future?

For the 1990s, Clarke foresaw a fairly complete understanding of the links in life's chain from the first biochemicals to living organisms; and the discovery of gravity waves. During the late 1990s were to come the practical use of nuclear fusion, the application of bionics, and true artificial intelligence.

During the first quarter of the twenty-first century, Clarke envisions our colonizing the planets and their satellites; breaking the secret of matter at the subparticle level and understanding the fundamental nature of matter and energy; storing man's vast accumulation of knowledge in a world library; and the practical use of robots, for home or office. Weather control will be advanced and interstellar probes will have been sent on their way.

Before mid-century is reached, Clarke speculates that electronic contact will have been made with extraterrestrial intelligences (ETs); and in human society genetic engineering will be generally practiced.

Clarke declines to peer beyond the year 2100, but during the second half of the twenty-first century—providing the human species can learn to get along and stay on track—some of the more auspicious realities will be the control of gravity and planetary engineering (the greening of Mars, the cooling of Venus), and the design and creation of new life-forms in the laboratory. As for space travel, we will have achieved velocities near the speed of light, and interstellar voyages will have begun. Near the end of the twenty-first century two world-shattering events are likely: direct contact with ETs (close encounters, at last, of the third kind), and the achievement of virtual immortality for mankind.

The only certainty in [the] remote future is that radically new things will be happening.
FREEMAN DYSON

12 Of all these achievements, three will probably be more future-transforming than the rest: gravity control, immortality, and exchanges with ETs.

On gravity: Clarke-the-scientist is not sure that gravity control can be accomplished, but he has an intuition that there has to be some way. He elaborates in detail on the benefits of gravity control if it could be achieved, but then he demurs: "It may seem a little premature to speculate about the uses of a device which may not even be possible, and is certainly beyond the present horizon of science. But it is a general rule that whenever there is a technical need, something always comes along to satisfy it—or to bypass it. For this reason, I feel sure that eventually we will have some means of either neutralizing gravity or overpowering it by brute force."

On immortality: "Death—like sleep—does not appear to be biologically inevitable. . . . Because biological immortality and the preservation of youth are such potent lures, men will never cease to search for them. . . . It would be foolish to imagine that this search will never be successful, down all the ages that lie ahead."

Clarke notes that—for very good reasons—we traditionally think of the mind, the brain, and the body as necessarily "going together." But this natural triad may not be indivisible. It just may be that the entire human body—except

AMERICAN BUSINESSMAN: *(touring Japan): "Are you operating on a five-year plan?"*
JAPANESE BUSINESSMAN: *"We are operating on a 250-year plan."*
AMERICAN: *"(!) How do you operate on a 250-year plan?"*
JAPANESE: *"Very patiently."*
The CBS Evening News

the brain—can be bionically replaced, so that the brain could continue to live on in the fullness of personality for hundreds of years. Beyond this bionic stage, however, Clarke has envisioned the theoretical means by which the mind alone could exist without the brain. That is, the mind—with all its capacities, its perceptions, memories, and awarenesses—may then exist independent of the physical encumbrance of brain-matter.

A New Kind of Realism

13 Our views of the human drama past and future have generally been determined by temperament and/or religious doctrine. Very few philosophies (or theologies) of history have been developed from an objective assessment of historical facts. Our stance usually turns on our feeling for "human nature"; if we trust human initiative, then we tend to have an optimistic outlook on history; if we distrust it, we tend toward pessimism.

But a new kind of realism has recently emerged. Based on a more objective assessment of empirical data, this realism attempts to project a variety of scenarios in the hope we can, in time, face them and solve them.

Sir Fred Hoyle There has never been a time during his professional life when Fred Hoyle did not "think big." The universe, nothing less, has constituted his thought-world since his writings began. So when he turned his attention to man's unholy condition, it was inevitable that his viewpoint would be cosmic. Hoyle's best-known writings are in astrophysics and cosmology. His principal futurist work is *Encounter with the Future* (1965).

Hoyle describes and diagrams the general timeline that he believes most likely for the next five thousand years. He assumes the inevitability of thermonuclear war. Hoyle's model is planned around mathematical probabilities regarding population expansions and depletions of various raw materials. He considers it nearly impossible at this late date for us to harness our reproductive energies and reduce birthrates to the level of death rates. On the contrary, he believes, birthrates will continue to grow almost exponentially and death rates will diminish. But a point will be reached at which the world population will have neither living room nor adequate food; the world's organizational systems will suddenly disintegrate, followed by a sharp decrease in populations. Famines and plagues might play a part in this process, but Hoyle is fairly sure that nuclear wars will be the primary instrument of depopulation.

14 The ultimate outcome of this series of population growths and collapses will be the emergence of superior human qualities, including an **average** IQ of perhaps 150. This will in fact be a new species of human being wise enough, finally, to stop the oscillations and stabilize human existence at a more mature level. But only through a continuing experience of consummate tragedies can mankind prepare its fundamental nature for a more civilized phase of human (or post-human) existence.

Hoyle writes:

> Let me then outline in a few words, by way of conclusion, what the broad history of our species is going to be over the next five thousand years, give or take a millennium.

What Does It Mean to Think?

. . . It will take a little while for men to realize that machines can not only think, but may one day think them off the face of the Earth.

At this point you may reasonably ask: "Yes—but what do you mean by *think?*" I propose to side-step that question, using a neat device due to the English mathematician A. M. Turing. Turing imagined a game played by two teleprinter operators in separate rooms—this impersonal link being used to remove all clues given by voice, appearance and so forth. Suppose that one operator was able to ask the other any questions he wished, and the other had to make suitable replies. If, after some hours or days of this conversation, the questioner could not decide whether his telegraphic acquaintance was human or purely mechanical, then he could hardly deny that he/it was capable of thought. An electronic brain that passed this test would, surely, have to be regarded as an intelligent entity. Anyone who argued otherwise would merely prove that he was less intelligent than the machine; he would be a splitter of non-existent hairs, like the scholar who proved that the *Odyssey* was not written by Homer but by another man of the same name.

Arthur C. Clarke
Profiles of the Future (1984 edition, p. 230)

I think that at present we are in the first big expansion phase.

This first phase is specially important. It possesses assets—coal, oil, etc.—that will not be repeated again. In return for the consumption of these assets it must establish a body of knowledge around which future civilizations will be able to build themselves. Without the establishment of this body of knowledge I do not believe our species will have more than a few centuries of existence ahead of it.

I think there will be a series of organizational breakdowns, or catastrophes, occasioned by overpopulation. This will lead to the sawtooth-shaped population curve. During the beginnings of the reexpansion phases there will be selection for greater sociability and for higher intelligence. The degree of selection in any one cycle need not be dramatically large because the effects of the repeated cycles are cumulative. Indeed, I expect the number of cycles—the number that occurs before they are damped away—to be determined by how much selection occurs per cycle. If this is large, the number of cycles will be small—and vice versa, the net effect being the same.

The earth's population is not increasing exactly at a geometrical rate. Actually it is a bit faster; the rate of population increase is itself proportional to the population. If this rate could continue, the population would become infinite in a finite time. The present growth formula leads to an infinite population in 2026 A.D.—in fact, on Friday, November 13, a day dubbed "doomsday."
George O. Abell

The ultimate outcome I believe will be a highly sociable, highly intelligent creature. With this, I would consider a new species to have arrived. It will have its own problems, no doubt, but they will not be as elementary as those with which we are faced today.

15 **Nuclear Winter and Megadeath** Since the 1960s scientists have been turning their attention to the question of exactly what would happen if a nuclear war should occur. In 1981 Paul Crutzen and John Birks raised the question of how much smoke would be generated by the fires that would follow a nuclear burst. Based on a scenario with an exchange of 5,742 megatons, their calculations indicated that sufficient carbon would rise into the lower atmosphere to block 90 percent of the sunlight from reaching the earth's surface.

Think? Why think! We have computers to do that for us.
Jean Rostand

In 1983 a major report was published detailing for the first time a wide range of inevitable effects of a nuclear Armageddon. This study is known as the TTAPS study, after the last initials of the five scientists who wrote it: Richard

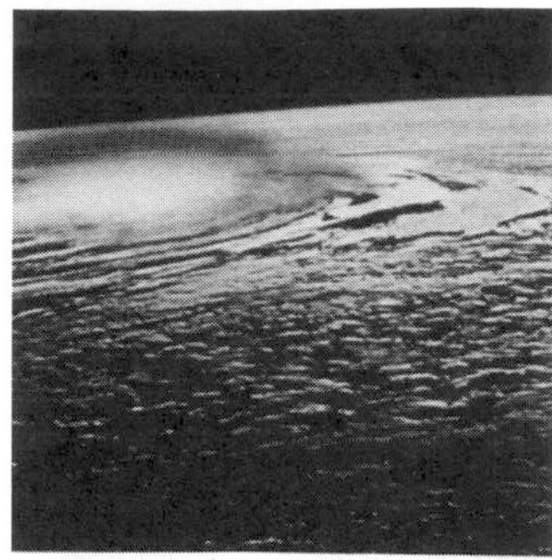

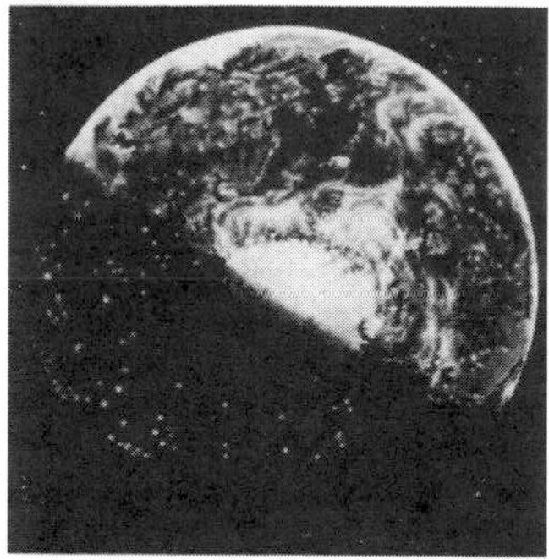

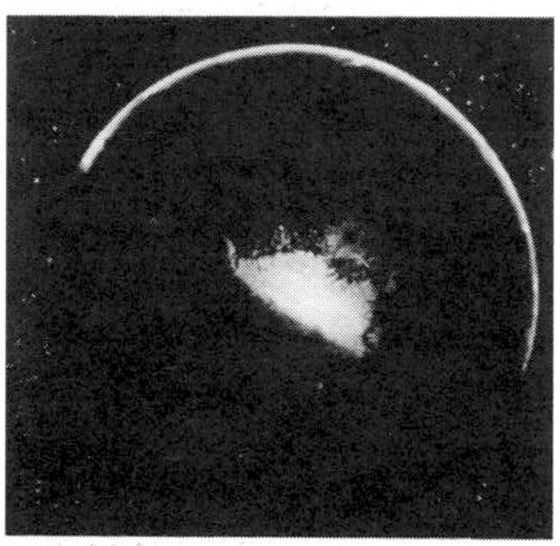

Four stages in the Nuclear Winter projection: (1) nuclear detonations; (2) resultant massive fire and smoke; (3) a smoke-enshrouded Earth; (4) a dead planet. Paintings by Jon Lomberg.

Turco, Brian Toon, Thomas Ackerman, James Pollack, and Carl Sagan. Numerous subsequent studies have augmented and—unfortunately—confirmed the predictions of the TTAPS group.

The scientists calculated what would happen in a variety of scenarios with varying megatonnage and targets. They concluded that even in the event of a relatively light yield, the volume of dust lofted into the atmosphere would be enormous (100,000 tons for each megaton), followed by raging fires producing carbon clouds. The dust and soot would encircle the northern hemisphere within days of the detonation. Black carbon is an efficient filter and would screen the sunlight from reaching the earth's surface; the amount of sunlight at the surface would immediately drop to 1 percent of normal. Virtually all green-plant photosynthesis would stop and plant life would die. Without light and heat from the sun, temperatures at the surface of the Earth would drop below freezing.

Further studies have shown that there would be a climatic inversion. Air layers that normally rise over the tropics and blow northward would cease; instead, the subtropical air layers would rise and blow southward, carrying the carbon-dust clouds into the equatorial regions and southern hemisphere. Thus within a few days of the first detonations, a filtering layer of carbon-dust would cover the earth, leaving it dark and frozen. This would be "nuclear winter."

Best estimates are that a billion people would be killed in the first exchange, and another billion injured. But all society's systems (economic, medical, logistic, communications) would have been destroyed, so that most of those who survived the first exchange would perish in a few weeks. Thus, a nuclear war would directly kill about two billion human beings.

Continued filtering of sunlight and lack of photosynthesis would mean that no crops or feed for animals could be grown, and most living things throughout the world that survived the initial holocaust would starve or freeze to death. For the first time the specter is raised of the extinction of the human race, and perhaps the extinction of all life on earth.

What would all this mean? Humans have always reflected on suffering and death, and grown from their reflections. But after nuclear war and megadeath there would be no one left to reflect. The protoplasmic venture would be finished, the magnificent experiment done. There would be nothing more to be said, and no one to say it.

The possibility that the Earth, poisoned by radioactivity, would lie fallow for thousands of years is not out of the question. But sometime, in some distant future, life—tenacious, irrepressible life—would develop again from simple protocells, and in a million or a billion years, the evolutionary story would be told once again.

A Special Kind of Hope

16 Optimism and pessimism are opposites, referring to contrasting sets of expectations. But realism and hopefulness are not opposites. Authentic realism always contains an element of hope since it is an attempt to face and solve problems **in order to move on** to a better condition.

There is a deliberateness in this realistic hopefulness. We must maintain hope to live. If, as individuals, we have joyous experiences to look forward to, then we awaken each day with energy, eager to work toward those experiences; but if we awaken to the prospect of unrelenting pain, then our dread can send us back to bed in an effort to return to sleep. What is true for individuals is true for society as a whole.

Mere opinion remains opinion no matter how many share it. . . . [However] the public comes to conclude that a widespread belief expresses a veritable law of nature.
DANIEL N. ROBINSON

Hopeful futurists such as McCall and Bradbury are fully aware of the threats that face the human race. They are not avoiders or escapists. "When I think about nuclear warfare," says McCall, "I can start sounding kind of dismal, but that isn't my fundamental personality—or my feeling about the future. In my work, what I *think about* is the promise of the future." Similarly, Bradbury says, "I see all the things the pessimists see, but I choose to behave myself anyway!"

17 **ROBERT T. MCCALL** "I see a very bright future for us all," says Robert McCall, and he has been painting his visions of our future since the early 1960s when he was commissioned to paint futuristic spacecraft for *Life* magazine and then the famous poster of the space wheel for the movie *2001: A Space Odyssey*. As director of the Air Force's art program, he became intimately familiar with the machineries of air and space, and his paintings are respected for their realism and technical authenticity. He has documented America's space program for NASA and chronicled the history of man's conquest of space in countless paintings, drawings, postage stamps, and murals—most notably in the towering mural for the Smithsonian Air and Space Museum. His books include *Our World in Space* and *Vision of the Future*.

Robert McCall

McCall's paintings depict scenarios in which mankind has realized the promise of technology. It is a world where human beings have solved their major problems and learned peace. They have beautified the environment, designed habitats for intelligent living, and can pursue their dreams.

"I want people to trust technology. I trust it. I'm not worried about it. I'm not fearful that it will get out of hand. I'm intrigued by the joyous vision of where we can go with technology and want to say something about it in my paintings. We humans will be in charge of technology; technology will not be in charge of us.

"In my paintings I describe the wonderful possibilities that the future holds for us. The only thing that will stop us from accomplishing those things is total annihilation, and I don't think that will ever happen. I have a conviction about that. Of course, I know that wars have occurred throughout history; that's recorded, and many of us have lived through war. But I don't see the human species being destroyed. I see us going on, inevitably.

"Some people suggest that if we are obsessed with tragedy, then that's what we'll get. Or if we image joyful things, then that's what we'll get. This is easy to say, and there's probably some truth in it. But the fact is that people who persistently image joyful things are probably joyful people; and people who image dismal things are dismal already."

In 1984 McCall painted a mural for Disney World's EPCOT center. The panorama is a celebration of the milestones in man's progress in civilization.

The left panel of the tableau shows mankind's earlier monuments: Egyptian pyramids, the Acropolis, Swayambhu temple, and the Kamakura Buddha. The central panel depicts more recent landmarks: Taj Mahal, Eiffel Tower, the American shrines.

On the third panel of the great painting looms a "dream metropolis" of the future, a city quite beyond present imagination, with "surprises at every turn."

The Prologue and The Promise. The McCall mural (19 feet × 70 feet) at Disney World's EPCOT Center, by Robert McCall and Louise McCall.

This panel, says McCall, is "symbolic of our move into space, a movement that will grow in intensity in the decades ahead. The time is not far off when thousands of people will be living semi-permanently in space."

"Vertical cities like this allow us to build up rather than spreading out; we can preserve the Earth and its beauty and ecology. And the floating city concept allows for that, too, since you're not scarring the surface of the Earth at all. You're floating just above it, and the Earth is there to enjoy. The floating cities would make it possible for the Earth to stay green, to have parks and forests to beam down to."

In this sweeping view of history, time's arrow—and our eyes—move from left to right. What might the next scene be?

"I could paint a fourth panel. It would depict man's establishment of himself in outer space, in Earth orbit, and then the colonization and settlement of the solar system. On that panel I would paint great power-stations in orbit two or three hundred miles above the Earth beaming microwave energy to the Earth's surface. Space habitats, designed for comfortable and fulfilled living. Colonies on the moon and Mars; settlements on the moons of Jupiter and Saturn; mining outposts on the asteroids. The solar system will be ours.

Politics is no longer the art of the possible. It is now more the art of attempting to avoid the inevitable.

John McHale

In the coming world the capacity to face the new appropriately is more important than the ability to know and repeat the old.

Carl Rogers

"Wherever we find ourselves, we'll still be striving for the same thing in our lives. We'll want to achieve our goals, and grow. We're going to fall in love, and we're going to have progeny, and we'll want to care for them and see them grow up whole and energetic and prosperous. All these things will remain constant. We'll see that they get done. Wherever we are we'll design our habitats and lifestyles so these essential good things will continue. Life in the space habitats will be idyllic, as lovely as the most scenic spots on Earth, because *we will make it that way.* Wherever we go, we will repeat what we love here on Earth."

What about a next panel? Is there a fifth panel—?

"Yes. Deep Space. We **will** go there. **Inevitably.**"

18 **Ray Bradbury** A sense of the future permeates the pages of about everything Ray Bradbury has written. After enjoying the novels, plays, poems, and 350 short stories that Bradbury has penned during the last fifty years, a reader

retains a picture-filled memory of having visited the future: fiery starbound rockets, wispy aliens with gold-coin eyes, homesick visitors on a drizzly Venusian landscape, and other strange people and stranger planets.

Bradbury has never attempted to become an "early warning system" for specific dangers. He is a raconteur, a teller of tales, a spinner of far-distant fantasies. Still, scattered through his writings are warnings of what the future might hold if things go wrong. In *Fahrenheit 451,* for instance, we glimpse a society in which reading is banned and literature is burned. It is therefore a world without ideas, peopled with wax-tablet brains on which a Big Brotherly television can easily write its own embalmed image. No ideas, no creativity, no growth.

There runs through Bradbury's writings the theme of machines-gone-awry. A nursery, activated by the thought-wishes of playing children, runs amok and takes on a horrifying life of its own. A robot police car patrols a darkened city watching for any hint of nonconformist behavior. Bradbury was a critic of Stanley Kubrick's motion picture *2001: A Space Odyssey* not merely because the mellow-voiced computer HAL-9000 became paranoid but because the men and women of the entire space venture had already lost their humanness and behaved like machines.

Ray Bradbury and Tigger

Bradbury thinks not in terms of decades or centuries—the "practical life" —but in terms of thousands or millions of years—the "theoretical life." He is a harbinger of the great things that are in store for the human race.

His visions are metaphors. There are sophisticated machineries that allow one to face death, and then to die, over and over again, as often as needed, until at last one can accept life. There is a robot foster mother created in the perfect image of the children's needs who comes into their lives with just the right amount of caring. There is a Mister-George-Bernard-Shaw robot that will forever carry on learned dialogues about the Universe and its multifarious contents, and discourse on their meaning.

19 In one of his short stories, Bradbury tells of a time-traveler of the late twentieth century who voyages "upstream through the centuries" and sees our future. He beholds the inevitable consequences of man's fear and self-hatred: a barren Earth. We mushroomed our cities, burned the forests, poisoned the atmosphere, polluted the oceans, and melted the records of humanity's greatness. As a species entrusted with the flame we failed, and we took all Earth's living things with us. We killed life; and we died.

So the time-traveler returns to our time with memories of our future nightmare—and he lies. What he tells us is that we made it through all right and that a glorious future awaits us. For if he had told us of the bleakness he truly saw, then mankind would have given up and longed for death.

So the time-traveler reports that we charted a path through our nuclear adolescence and went on to great things. "We did it! The future is ours. We rebuilt the cities, freshened the small towns, cleaned the lakes and rivers . . . stopped the wars . . . colonized the Moon, moved on to Mars, then Alpha Centauri. We cured cancer and stopped death. We did it. . . .

"The world went mad with joy. It ran to meet and make that future. . . ."

Was the Royal Lie really necessary?

Yes, says the time-traveler. "Because I was born and raised in a time, in the Sixties, Seventies and Eighties, when people had stopped believing in them-

The dangers that face the world can, every one of them, be traced back to science. The salvations that may save the world will, every one of them, be traced back to science.

ISAAC ASIMOV

selves. I saw that disbelief, the reason that no longer gave itself reasons to survive, and was moved, depressed and then angered by it.

"Everywhere, I saw and heard doubt. Everywhere, I learned destruction. . . . Nothing was worth doing. Go to bed at night full of bad news at eleven, wake up in the morn to worse news at seven."

"Not only the Four Horsemen of the Apocalypse rode the horizon to flight themselves on our cities but a fifth horseman, worse than all the rest, rode with them: Despair, wrapped in dark shrouds of defeat, crying only repetitions of past disasters, present failures, future cowardices.

"Bombarded by dark chaff and no bright seed, what sort of harvest was there for man in the latter part of the incredible Twentieth Century?

"So the self-fulfilling prophecies were declared; we dug our graves and prepared to lie down in them.

"We wept at the grave of our children, and the child was us."

The time-traveler, therefore, tells us the Great Lie to save us. But is it truly a lie?

"You see the point, don't you . . . ? Life has always been lying to ourselves! As boys, young men, old men. As girls, maidens, women, to gently lie and prove the lie true. To weave dreams and put brains and ideas and flesh and the truly real beneath the dreams. Everything, finally, is a promise. What seems a lie is a ramshackle need, wishing to be born."

20 Says Bradbury: "The thing that I have against the negative futurists of the last thirty years is that they're all changing their minds now. And what you want to say to them is 'Dammit, why did you depress us in the first place? Where were you when we needed you? You almost destroyed us during the Flower Period a few years ago.' Some of them wanted to scare the devil out of us, and they did. But too often they scare all hope out of us and no one does anything."

Bradbury's previsions of Man's journey—on which he has just embarked—are magnificent dreams, filled with the excitement of discovery and the adventure of the unknown. A million years, a billion years, and more—until humanity is immortal and has graced the stars.

What of Man, ultimately—"this strange, weeping, laughing animal who awakens from monkey dreams to find himself almost Man? What is this remarkable thing that we are?"

In phrases reminiscent of Shaw: "We are something that's becoming itself. We are matter and force that does not know itself, changing ourselves, during the long night of the universe, into imagination and will. Willing ourselves to survive." This is what humans have been doing for millions of years and will continue to do for more millions of years. "Man will not die . . . ever. Hate as we often hate ourselves, yet we love ourselves more and the gift given us to live one time in a Universe as brutal, stunning, and nightmarish as it is beautiful. Oh, then again beautiful beyond our powers to say."

Many Futures: A Common Vision

21 Images of the future serve many purposes. The images so far described have been employed primarily to forecast threatening global problems and to set up

the machinery through which they may be effectively met and solved. This is one function of future-images. But there is another.

History is a nightmare from which I am trying to awake.
James Joyce

Today's world has come unglued, unraveled. The old loyalties no longer bind, and the countless collectivities have fragmented, traveled, intermixed, interwoven. Out of this new mixture is emerging a new world. It isn't born yet, and it may remain in labor for another fifty years, perhaps a hundred. Barring catastrophe, however, it will be born. We can be fairly sure of that, for lack of alternatives.

There is a pressing need for a sense of global identity and a shared vision of the future—a reason to exist. It is this profoundly human need that futurists have been watching and diagnosing, like physicians. The illness is clear enough, but the prescription is not at all clear as yet.

Robert Bundy writes:

> The West has lost any reason for being. Simply to further develop scientific and technological tools for their own sake, or to increase our mastery over nature, or to further expand the consumptive society, with its hedonistic license, cannot provide the motive power for a civilization. Some deeper spiritual center and transcendent values are required.
>
> This loss of a reason to go on means we have no inspiring image of the future, no dominant vision within whose embrace different expectations can survive and draw strength, no overarching dream capable of infusing all of us with hope and giving us courage to confront and cope with our awesome problems.

A shared vision of our common future is therefore enormously important. Bundy notes that "positive images tell of another and better world in a coming time. They infuse people with the foreknowledge of a destiny of happiness, and thus engender the courage to confront and solve the problems facing civilization. Negative, pessimistic images work in the opposite way and may forecast a period of cultural decline and breakdown. . . . Without a living image of the future a society can become doomed to a rootless vacuum" and "condemned to disappear."

Bundy concludes:

> Western civilization is passing away. So be it. This does not mean that our total inheritance from the past or our leadership potential for the future are lost. It does mean that many of the central dogmas and visions that drove Western civilization forward do not have a prominent place in the future. What does have a place in the future are: (1) the shared conviction that new magnetic images of the future can be born, (2) people who are united by common beliefs necessary for survival and development within a global perspective, and (3) groups that share across their boundaries while, as always, they remain separated by particular visions they are free to follow as long as others may also follow their visions.

✦

FRIEDRICH NIETZSCHE

The Glory of Becoming Human

Friedrich Wilhelm Nietzsche (his family and friends called him "Fritz") was a gifted late-nineteenth-century German thinker who soared high above the time-bound ideas of his contemporaries—"six thousand feet beyond man and time" he later wrote. Building on a theory of evolution, he created a radically new vision of what it means to be human.

We have a picture of the mature philosopher written in May of 1882, when Nietzsche was thirty-seven. Some of his friends in Rome introduced him to a new student, a twenty-one-year-old Russian-German girl named Lou Salomé. Slender, attractive, alive, and extremely bright, she was everything, and of course Nietzsche fell in love with her. Later on this perceptive young lady wrote the best description we have of Nietzsche-the-man.

> Loneliness—that was the first, strong impression created by Nietzsche's fascinating appearance. The casual observer may not have been struck by anything unusual; a man of medium height, whose manner of dress was exceedingly simple and yet exceedingly meticulous, with calm features and brown hair combed straight back, he could be easily overlooked. The fine, highly expressive lines of the mouth were almost completely covered by a large mustache combed out toward the front; his laugh was quiet, he had a noiseless way of speaking, and walked in a cautious, pensive way, hunching his shoulders slightly; it was hard to imagine this figure in the middle of a crowd—he bore the stamp of one who stands apart, alone. . . . Whenever he showed himself as he was, under the spell of a stimulating conversation with someone else, a poignant brilliance might light up and fade in his eyes;—but when his mood was somber, then loneliness would appear in them, dark and almost menacing, as if emerging from terrible depths.

✦

Nietzsche was born in the village of Röcken in Prussian Saxony where his father, Carl Ludwig, was pastor. Both his father and grandfather had been ministers, and his mother, Franziska, came from a family of ministers. A beautiful and energetic woman, Franziska was eighteen at the time of Nietzsche's birth. When he was not quite five his father died of brain damage sustained in an accidental fall. Without a father, young Nietzsche was thereafter raised by his grandmother, his mother (a young widow who had to defer to the strong-willed grandmother), his sister, and two maiden aunts who had come to live with them. He confessed in both word and deed, throughout his life, that he didn't know how a man thinks, feels, or behaves. "My entire development was never supervised by a masculine eye," and this, he confides, may have been "a drawback."

Nietzsche was a quiet, polite, well-behaved child, with serious dark eyes and fair hair. By the age of four he could read, by five he could write, at six he could play an impressive Beethoven sonata. Lacking other close friends, Friedrich was closest to his sister throughout his youth. They shared classes, books, in-jokes, walks in the country, and music. Elisabeth later reminisced about a moment in 1857: "As soon as Fritz and I . . . were alone, he asked me whether it wasn't strange for us to be such good students and know things that other children did not know."

Nietzsche's education was conventional but thorough. He first entered the local elementary public school at Naumburg, then at eight began attending the cathedral grammar school. At fourteen he was awarded a scholarship to Schulpforta, a private boarding school near Naumburg. Nietzsche wasn't especially happy there, but his time was enlivened by his discovery of classical literature and the music of Richard Wagner.

In the fall of 1864 he began a two-semester stint at the University of Bonn. He worked diligently and his scholarship began to flower. He joined a fraternity, smoked, drank, grew a light mustache, and fell in love with an actress he saw at the theater. He wrote her songs and sent her flowers. She never replied. Soon bored with the drinking songs and the silliness of fraternity life, he resigned from the social club. He gave up drinking and smoking for the rest of his life. At Bonn it became clear to him that he wanted to be a philologist—a student of classical languages and literature. To that end he transferred to the University of Leipzig, where he completed his degree and stayed on to pursue his doctorate. Nietzsche's achievements at Leipzig were brilliant; his scholarship became widely admired; his writings began to be published; he won awards. As a result he was offered a professorship at the University of Basel in Switzerland.

In 1869 Nietzsche moved to Switzerland and settled to the academic life of a young professor of classical literature. He tested the social scene, attended symphonies, frequently went dancing, bought new clothes, and settled into a vigorous writing program. It was an upbeat time in his life; he felt healthy; he had found a vocation; he enjoyed new mentors and new friends; his life had meaning; each day brought excitement as he awakened to new labors, new goals, new creations.

His first major book was published early in 1872: *The Birth of Tragedy*, which he dedicated to Wagner. The book's ostensible aim was to document the emergence of Greek tragedy out of the ritualized choral dance of the Dionysian mystery cult. What it actually did was to outline the structure of Nietzsche's developing worldview. He was beginning to think big, in sweeping historical terms, and to make fundamental philosophical observations about the nature of life and the goal and purpose of human history. He sent a copy to Wagner, who had the highest praise for his friend: "I've never read anything finer than your book," wrote the composer.

In academic circles it was a different story. His book evoked a chilly, hostile, reaction—or no reaction at all. He had broken all the rules. He had belittled classical education; he attacked Socrates and the entire Western tradition of ra-

The philosopher loves to muddy the water so that it may appear deep.

In woman's love there is injustice and blindness to all she doth not love. And even in woman's conscious love, there is still always surprise and lightning and night, along with the light.

Without music life would be a mistake.

Life itself means being in danger.

One should speak only of that which one has overcome —everything else is chatter.

In truth there was only one Christian, and he died on the cross.

If you desire peace of soul and happiness, believe! If you want to be a disciple of truth, search!

I tell you: one must have chaos within one to give birth to a dancing star!

Convictions are prisons.

Faith moves no mountains but puts mountains where there are none: a quick walk through a madhouse enlightens one sufficiently about this.

A belief may be a necessary condition of life and yet be false.

The value of a human being . . . does not lie in his usefulness: for it would continue to exist even if there were nobody to whom he could be useful.

I have to have a blue sky above me to collect my thoughts.

Distrust all in whom the impulse to punish is powerful.

Whoever fights monsters should see to it that in the process he does not become a monster.

Blessed are the forgetful: for they get the better even of their blunders.

tionalism; he wrote in a flamboyant ("unprofessional") poetic and aphoristic style, with outlandish imagery and blatant non sequiturs. He had betrayed his academic heritage. Across the board Nietzsche's good fortunes went into reverse. His budding reputation as a promising young scholar was irreparably damaged, his image as a popular teacher eroded, and the number of students enrolling in his classes dwindled.

In the summer of 1873 a tragic turn changed his life. His health, while never robust, began to deteriorate. He became more and more preoccupied with suffering; and, for the rest of his life, it finds expression in his writing in poignant personal and philosophical terms. He was twenty-nine years old.

In May of 1879 his frequent absences from classes forced him to resign from teaching. In June he spent time in the Upper Engadine, where, he wrote, "For the first time, I feel true relief." During the 1880s his physical health generally improved, but his mood swings, from euphoric highs to suicidal lows, became extreme. His highs were joyous periods of intense creativity during which he wrote incessantly, day and night. His high periods would be followed by plateaux of uneasy nothingness. These were also years of incessant wandering; he shuttled between temporary bases in Switzerland, France, Germany, and Italy. In the summer of 1881 he discovered Sils-Maria, a Swiss village so beautiful he dreamed of living there the rest of his life. He felt almost healthy again, and he was happier than he had ever been. He read and wrote joyously and prolifically. He lived in a small farm house that he rented for one franc a day. It was three minutes from the main road and had a shady back room facing the woods that blocked out the bright light of the southern sun that so hurt his eyes. In the evenings he wandered along the edge of the lake and strolled in the forests of the Inn valley, thinking, meditating, feeling—not missing the world, not the human race, not even his friends. And in his mind he created new worlds: "Thoughts have emerged on my horizon such as I have never seen before.—"

Nietzsche built on a theory of evolution to reinterpret the history of the human race and to lay foundations for his grand vision of the future of mankind. However, his theory of evolution was not Darwinian. Charles Darwin had published his *Origin of Species* in 1859, and Nietzsche clearly understood what Darwin was saying about competitive struggle and the "survival of the fittest." But he disagreed with Darwin on two points. First, Nietzsche was convinced that the dynamics of evolution are Lamarckian, that is, that parents pass along acquired characteristics to their offspring. (Jean-Baptiste Lamarck, who died in 1829, had surmised that organs atrophy from disuse and improve with use, and that all improvement is passed along by individual organisms from parent to offspring, thereby upgrading the species as a whole. Of course, neither Lamarck nor Nietzsche knew anything of genes and mutations.)

Secondly, Nietzsche concluded that the basic drive of all living things is not a struggle to survive, but a struggle for power—the "will to power," he called it. An individual organism does struggle, as Darwin says, but it struggles for more than just survival. The goal of its struggles is to increase its power, so that, with the extra energy that constitutes that power it can compete and reproduce. Darwin's theory was a half-truth. If organisms were struggling merely to survive, then once food and security have been attained the struggle would cease and organisms would go into stasis. But this is not what happens. Once food and shelter are secured, all organisms continue on vigorously to annihilate the competition, expand niches, search for the fittest mates, and proceed to the proliferation of fitter offspring.

This never-ending power struggle is the drive that motivates human behavior, and therefore—contrary to the Greek notion that man is a rational animal—"human nature" turns out to be irredeemably irrational. But this fact of our being Nietzsche judges to be good, not bad. All previous thinkers, having failed to understand the evolutionary structure of life, have burdened us with false goals. *We are here on this Earth to overcome ourselves and thereby effect a rebirth in beauty and perfection.* "Over each people there hangs a tablet of values. Behold, it is the tablet of its self-mastery; behold, it is the voice of its will to power." We are all endowed with the will to power, but for the would-be superior human being, its virtue is that it empowers one toward personal growth. One can leave behind, constantly and continually, all that one was and move forward toward becoming all one can. "Life itself told me this secret: 'Look,' it said, 'I am that which *must ever master itself*.'" The greatest gift one can give another is to assist him in self-mastery. If a friend wrongs you, he says, then tell him: "I forgive you what you did to me; but that you have done it to *yourself*—how could I forgive that." And he adds, "Thus speaks all great love: it overcomes even forgiveness and pity. . . ."

We all have a (sacred) moral responsibility to become strong; we owe the human race a commitment. Human evolution is purposely driving each individual to become all he/she can become; and the function of sex is to pass on to our offspring all these acquired accomplishments. Sex is evolution's mechanism for the growth of the human race. Merely to generate another generation for the sake of generation is to overcrowd the planet with the mediocre, of which we have too many already (Nietzsche called them "the herd"). In the past, human offspring are the product of accidental and capricious matings. The problem, says Nietzsche, is "what type of man shall be bred, shall be willed. . . ." Quality is the critical issue, not quantity. Marriage should be experienced with an awareness of being a living participant in the evolutionary program; it is an opportunity for a couple to dream of, and create, children whose greatness will surpass them, and their children will surpass them, and their children . . . world without end. "You should not only reproduce yourself but super-produce yourself," he wrote. "Let the garden of marriage help you in this!"

Therefore, according to Nietzsche, our moral responsibility is to get back on course so that the evolutionary program, with its drive toward ever-greater levels of being, can be actualized. We are all links in the golden chain. We are not the end-game of evolution, as some of us would fondly like to believe. We are its channel, its way-station, its working model. We are an unfinished symphony. We are the first drafts of the first chapter of a great book with no end. We are the foundations of a great building. We are the first roots beneath a tiny plant that will grow into a great tree.

So, what can humans evolve into? *If* the human race finds its way back to the path of nobility and power, and *if* individuals continue to reach for the sky, and *if* mankind's noblest qualities again spread through the human gene pool, then what would a future human being be like?

Nietzsche's answer: the *Übermensch* (commonly, but poorly, translated as "Superman" or "Overman"; the noun "Superhuman" is perhaps the best translation), a higher, loftier, nobler, more virtuous, more advanced human being of the future.

> Ye have made your way from the worm to man, and much within you is still worm. Once were ye apes, and even yet man is more of an ape than any of the apes.
>
> Even the wisest among you is only a disharmony and hybrid of plant and phantom. But do I bid you become phantoms or plants?
>
> Lo, I teach you the *Übermensch!*
>
> The *Übermensch* is the meaning of the earth. Let your will say: The *Übermensch shall* be the meaning of the earth!

So far above us physically, intellectually, and emotionally, Nietzsche's

One must separate from anything that forces one to repeat No again and again.

The most common lie is that with which one lies to onself: Lying to others is relatively an exception.

What is done from love is always beyond good and evil.

In individuals insanity is rare, but in groups, parties, nations and epochs it is the rule.

One's belief in truth begins with doubt of all truths one has believed hitherto.

Live dangerously. Build your cities on the slopes of Vesuvius.

As yet woman is not capable of friendship. But tell me, ye men, who of you are capable of friendship?

If you have an enemy, do not requite him evil with good, for that would put him to shame. Rather prove that he did you some good.

The Nietzsche Myth

The Nietzsche story does not end in Turin that January of 1889, or in Weimar in 1900. Only after the death of his sister Elisabeth in 1935, when scholars gained access to the original material, did the full extent of what she had done to her helpless brother become known.

Almost simultaneously with his descent into insanity Nietzsche's fame began to spread, to the surprise of his sister, into whose care he had been placed. In 1885 she had married a political activist named Bernhard Förster; and his activism was focused into a hateful anti-Semitism, which, to Nietzsche's horror, his sister then embraced. The couple emigrated to Paraguay to found an anti-Semitic colony composed only of superior Germans, the Teutonic élite. Förster committed suicide in 1889, leaving Elisabeth again free to care for her brother. She acquired exclusive access to the thousands of unpublished aphorisms, notes, and letters; she began to assemble and rework the vast collection into publishable form. She changed her name to Förster-Nietzsche and proceeded to transform her brother's philosophy—which critical scholarship subsequently revealed she had no mind to understand—so that his writings would reflect *her* ideas, *her* opinions, *her* hates. She edited, she expurgated, she lifted from context, she assembled selectively, she rewrote, she reinterpreted, she forged, she even singled out names and wrote in others—all in order to make Nietzsche into a prophet of her own bigoted ideology. She held back the publication of his last book, *Ecce Homo*, while she rewrote and suppressed the too-clear statements that would undermine her prejudices. She cajoled and bullied otherwise responsible scholars into assisting her in editing his papers, tolerating her insidious intent, and supporting her politically correct social and political opinions. Much of this reworked material was published under Nietzsche's name in *The Will to Power* (1901, with augmented editions in 1904 and 1906).

Out of this inverted material was born the Nietzsche myth, according to which Nietzsche was made to expound doctrines that the living philosopher had spent his life fighting. He was made out to be a bigoted anti-Semite. This from the man who had vehemently denounced anti-Semitism all his life, and had written to his sister: "Your association with an anti-Semitic chief [Förster] expresses a foreignness to *my* whole way of life which fills me ever again with ire or melancholy." This bigotry was one of the main issues over which he parted with Wagner; and the last line he ever wrote, even after his breakdown, was: "I'm just having all anti-Semites shot."

Übermensch will make us all embarrassed and sad that we are still apes. The *Übermensch* will be strong in body, bursting with energy for growth and producing superior children. The body will be a healthy mix of black, white, brown—all the colors of the racial rainbow; it will be the result of the coming together of the best genes from all the human race's gene pools. No race has been blessed with superior genes—Nietzsche thought the notion absurd (especially when applied to the Germans!); rather all the races of mankind will contribute their genes to the creation of the *Übermensch* and the future human race.

Similarly, his intellectual and esthetic capacities will be far beyond present imagination. He will feel music to the depths of his soul, and will respond to and create beauty, not merely in the arts, but in all he does. And he will exert a moral strength stronger than any human of today. He will move with, not against, the evolutionary struggle for power; but when this struggle demands the creation

He was also made out to be an advocate of Darwin's theory of the survival of the fittest, which, as a political doctrine could then be employed in support of the notion that the Aryan German gene pool was the locus of the "master race" whose purity from inferior genes (from all non-Aryan races, but especially from "Jewish genes") must be preserved so that it could proceed to the fulfillment of its destiny, the birthing of the *Übermensch.* How much he hated this Darwinization of his idea is made plain by frequent denunciations of it in all his later writings. For Nietzsche, the value of a human being is not to be found, abstractly, in any collective, least of all in such a useless abstraction as "race"; rather it is to be found in *the individual's artistic and philosophic achievements,* which, no matter the "race" (or, we might add, ethnic background, creed, gender, or -ism) can be passed on to one's offspring, who will thereby be one step closer to the truly superior human being, or, as Nietzsche phrased it, to the superior being who, at last, is truly human. No wonder, then, that one of Nietzsche's last tirades, in *Ecce Homo,* is a bitter attack against this insidious misinterpretation of his thought that would determine human worth by racial (and racist) criteria.

But no matter: After his sister's expurgated version of Nietzsche's writings were published, his philosophy was appropriated and became the official ideology of Nazi apologetics: The Germans then saw themselves as the master race whose superior genes have been chosen by evolution for the purpose of developing superior human beings; they are the chosen people; they, and they alone, hold the key to the glorious future of the human species. As the stewards and guardians of human dignity and worth, they must therefore protect that precious gift against all threat of corruption, dilution, and leveling; they must preserve that "sacred" gene pool in its pristine condition. And what mortal then concluded that he himself was the awaited savior, the *Übermensch?* Hitler, of course.

✦

Knowing that his ideas would offend, Nietzsche had asked in his preface to *Ecce Homo* that he be carefully read before being criticized. Please don't jump to conclusions, he pled; read my works. "Above all, do not mistake me!" Presumably, however, he learned (or should have learned) a valuable lesson: that a writer can do little more than write as responsibly as he can, and then let the chips fall; for once his ideas are sent into the world he will have no control over the way others use or misuse the products of his loves and labors.

of pain and suffering, the *Übermensch,* out of his capacity for compassion, will feel in himself the pain of the unavoidable.

Above all, *the* Übermensch *will live.* He will be capable of a rich, passionate existence, and he will dare to live his life to the fullest. He will meet all challenges with excitement and joy. His entire existence will be passionate; his enjoyment of music, art, sex, and nature's beauty—in a word, the enjoyment of his power—will be limitless. No false humilities, no self-denials, no pleasure-anxieties—nothing will mar his pleasures or diminish his self-esteem. Greater joys, but also greater sorrows; greater ecstasies, but greater pain too. He will play the mythic hero with such power and meaning that he will experience the growth of soul promised in tragedy.

From 1884 through December 1888, although he alternated between creative highs and restless lows, Nietzsche's manic phases enabled him to work intensely and produce a total of seven books. Among them are *Beyond Good and Evil, Toward a Genealogy of Morals, The Wagner Case, The Twilight of the Idols,* and *The Antichrist.*

By late September 1888, Nietzsche was walking slowly, often with a shuffle, and his speech was sometimes thick and heavy. But in addition to the physical problems that both caused and resulted from years of suffering, his friends began to notice a deterioration of his mental condition. His personality changed. He became gentle, tender, overly solicitous, and he cried easily and often. From late September 1888 into January 1889, he worked with enhanced concentration and produced volumes of aphoristic materials and notes, many to be published posthumously.

In early January 1889 he wrote his last notes and letters. Fighting, with a painful awareness, the anguish of diminished capacity, he called himself a "divine buffoon" and identified himself with Dionysus, his favorite of all the mythic gods. His last writings, from September 21, 1888, to January 3, 1889, chronicle his suffering and decline. His delusions deepened; his perceptions of reality became fragmented, dissociated, incoherent, and distant. He had with pain and tears worked out a philosophy to live by, and he clung to it tightly during his last days of dimming clarity. He was never to know that that philosophy had already begun to influence millions of people, or that his worldview—perverted beyond recognition—would mold the thinking of nations in the following century.

Scholars generally agree that all his writings after September 21, 1888, portend the shadows of the coming night and are therefore to be read with caution. During those last three months his judgment became increasingly erratic, his ideas more disconnected, his imagery almost shocking, the sounds of his cries more strident, his self-evaluation more megalomaniacal, his mission more clearly messianic. In the end, having killed God, he replaced him: he became the crucified Dionysus/Christ. His attempt to save the world had at last transmogrified the would-be savior into the only being who could accomplish such a godly task—God himself.

On January 3, in Turin, Italy, in the Piazza Carlo Alberto, Nietzsche left his house for a walk and came upon a coachman brutally beating his horse. Crying out in rage and bursting into tears, Nietzsche tried to intervene. He threw himself on the neck of the mare, then collapsed to the street. He was taken back to his apartment, then a few days later transferred to a sanatorium in Basel. His mind was gone. He was taken to a nursing home in Jena where his mother could care for him. In 1897 his mother died, and his sister bought a house in Weimar and moved him there to look after him. For almost a decade, his mind gradually faded until the genius who had seen so much no longer existed in this world. He died August 25, 1900, at the age of fifty-five, and was buried with Christian rites beside his father and mother in the churchyard at Röcken.

✦

Reflections

1. Recall the statement that opens this chapter: That we create the past and can also create alternative futures; and that we need both past and future to see ourselves in perspective. How much value is there in this way of looking at ourselves and our place in time?
2. Of the various alternative futures suggested here as real possibilities, which one(s) do you think are most likely to transpire? Why?
3. As you ponder the future, are you personally trusting and optimistic or wary and pessimistic? Do your own experiences and feelings tend to color the optional futures that you can imagine? (Do you think personal experiences may have colored the views of professional historians and professional futurists?)
4. What is your response to some of the specific events enumerated in this chapter as virtual certainties for the future? Are you eager to see some of these events and conditions materialize? Are there some that you fear? Would you want to live with them? Do you think that our great-grandchildren will be able to accept and live with them?
5. What is your response to Sir Fred Hoyle's projection of the future? Can you see what his long-range optimism is based on? Do you think there is a probability that Hoyle's vision will actually happen?
6. Would you like to live in a space colony? What kind of a life do you think you would live there? Would you enjoy it more or less than living on Spaceship Earth? Can you tell why?

Microcosm / Macrocosm / Cosmos

There is today—in a time when old beliefs are withering—a kind of philosophic hunger, a need to know who we are and how we got there. There is an ongoing search, often unconscious, for a cosmic perspective for humanity.

Carl Sagan

Knowledge of Nature

7-1

This chapter and the following one deal with the philosophy of the physical sciences. Basically, the mind creates two kinds of knowledge about physical reality: knowledge from empirical observation and knowledge from a priori concepts. But both are limited, so that the perennial question about the nature of "reality," and whether the human mind can know it, is still alive and well. This chapter considers the symbolic nature of human thinking and asks whether it is ever possible to get beyond the symbols. It also deals with the origins of matter and includes a brief statement about quantum mechanics and what we have learned about the strange world of subatomic realities.

May 28, 585 BC

1 Philosophy and science were born together in 585 BC—on May 28 at 6:13 p.m. (Milesian Standard Time); for at that instant an eclipse began in the Ionian city of Miletus, a solar eclipse that had been **predicted** by a philosopher named Thales. We have no evidence that Thales established the exact time of the event. This precise date has been calculated by modern astronomers, and if Thales had even come close—within a day or a week—he would have done well. But the significant point is that he had become aware of the regularities of nature on the basis of which he had made a prediction. However elementary this may seem, it is the dim recognition of what we now know as Natural Law.

Thales (c. 585 BC)

Empirical Knowledge

2 Our knowledge of nature and its "laws" derives from two distinct kinds of epistemic operations: empirical observation and rational system-building. Thus

This is a world of pure mathematics, and when we penetrate to the bottom of it, that's all it will be.

JOHN A. WHEELER

Philosophy is written in the vast book which stands open before our eyes, I mean the universe; but it cannot be read until we have learnt the language and become familiar with the characters in which it is written.

GALILEO

We are free to choose which elements we wish to apply in the construction of physical reality. The justification of our choice lies exclusively in our success.

ALBERT EINSTEIN

we have empirical knowledge (from our senses) and rational (or a priori) knowledge. Both burden us with bothersome problems.

Suppose you took a Jovian philosopher to a baseball game. He is a handsome humanoid with shining eyes who has recently arrived from a thriving civilization on Jupiter's moon Europa, and being ever-alert to adventures of the mind, he watches the game with eager awareness. Since he has never seen a baseball game (it's **very** cold on the surface of Europa), you begin to explain the rules to him. He declines the offer and tells you he would prefer to figure out the rules for himself. And so, through all nine innings, you let him watch the action.

As he observes the players, he notes their patterns of movement; they perform the same motions over and over again. A player walks up to a particular spot and tries to hit a small, round object that another player throws at him (no, he throws it past him). If the man with the stick swings and misses three times, the hand of the man dressed in black goes up and the man with the stick walks away looking either sad or angry. But if he hits the round object with the stick, he starts running, always in the same direction, toward another man.

And so, little by little, the "rules of the game" are inferred and reconstructed as the visitor from Europa watches the players' consistent, repeated patterns of behavior.

The "rules of the game" exist in the players' heads, and they play by them. The players know the rules because they have read them or have grown up with them, but our extraterrestrial epistemologist must **infer** the rules by watching behavior—that is, by watching matter-in-motion.

By the end of the second inning, he has some rough ideas of a few consistencies. By the fifth, he has added several more consistencies to his mental list and refined some previous observations. By the end of the game—Jovian genius that he is—he has been able to understand and jot down a set of rules that describes much of the players' actions.

After the game, the Jovian checks his list of inferred rules with you and you find that he has indeed discovered most of the rules that you know about baseball.

Now, he never **saw** the rules, of course; he **created** the rules **in his mind** because they seemed to describe consistently the behavior of the players. All that he actually observed, of course, was players-in-motion.

3 This is the way our minds operate to create an enormous amount of our everyday knowledge. Consider what we call "scientific laws," for instance. They are the "rules of the game" that we have inferred. We often deceive ourselves by thinking that we have observed the rules, whereas the fact is that we created them to account for consistencies **that we remembered** while watching matter-in-motion. We never observe the "law of gravity" or the "inverse-square law," which describes the propagation of light, or the "laws" of mass-energy transformation. All the "laws" of physics are created in our minds; and all this information we call empirical knowledge.

Scientists who work with submicroscopic entities are at a special disadvantage since they never even get to see matter-in-motion. They must create the "rules of the game" by observing only secondary traces (streaks on photographic plates, for example) left by subatomic particles of matter. In other words, particle physicists must create in their minds pictures of the matter (which we are warned time and again can't be done, especially in quantum physics) as well as the principles of motion that describe the behavior of such matter.

The laws of mathematics and logic are true simply by virtue of our conceptual scheme.
W. V. O. QUINE

4 All empirical knowledge is hypothetical and merely probable. That is, it consists of operational hypotheses that we continue to use as long as they are consistent with our observations.

Plants need sunlight to grow. Gray whales migrate in March. Robins lay blue eggs. Scandinavians have blond hair. Water will conduct electricity if salt is dissolved in it. Light travels at 186,282 miles per second. Water doesn't flow uphill. A lunar month is 27 days, 7 hours, 43 minutes. Tornadoes never occur in December. A fire will not burn without oxygen. Whale sharks are harmless to man.

All these things we know from repeated experience. But do we know them for sure? **All** robins' eggs are blue, someone might want to argue. He will tell you that he has probed a gazillion robin's nests and stared at countless thousands of robins' eggs—all pale blue. That settles the matter, doesn't it? Still, can one be **absolutely** positive that some berserk robin hasn't laid a bright purple egg in a nest somewhere? Not really.

Empirical knowledge is never certain. To every statement about the world —like "robins' eggs are blue"—one can **imagine** an exception. One can easily imagine a gray whale deciding not to migrate in March, or a tornado tearing across Kansas in December, or a whale shark mistaking a man for a rather large tidbit of phytoplankton. If one can imagine an exception to the statement, then it is not **necessary** knowledge; it is only **contingent** knowledge whose likelihood of being correct must be plotted on a probability curve. This is true of all the Natural Laws of physics that we have formulated to describe the dynamic operations of physical nature.

This is also why, in the social sciences, we must employ statistics to establish the "coefficient of correlation" so that we can figure the probability of correctness of any hypothesis. What we determine is the number of cases out of a hundred in which the hypothesis would hold true.

A Priori Knowledge

5 A second kind of knowledge about the natural world is rational or a priori knowledge. Since the time of the pre-Socratic analysts—most notably Pythagoras, Parmenides, and Plato—the exact nature of a priori knowledge has puzzled us to the point of irritation.

We know certain **necessary** truths, it seems, to which **we cannot imagine exceptions.** Seven plus five equals twelve—now, always, and everywhere. Parallel lines in the same plane will never intersect. The area of a circle can be determined with the formula πr^2. In Euclidian geometry the angles of a triangle always add up to 180°.

Now, are these truly universal truths? The rationalist will answer yes. Can we conceive, in our wildest imagination, any exception to these statements? Can we imagine two parallel lines intersecting? or $7 + 5 \neq 12$? or the angles of a triangle not totaling 180°? No, we can't.

Reason is the substance of the universe. . . . The design of the world is absolutely rational.
G. W. F. HEGEL

Here, then, lie the foundations of the so-called exact sciences—all known systems of mathematics, geometry, and logic.

6 How many robins' eggs would we have to examine to be sure that all robins' eggs are blue? Obviously, all of them: every egg ever laid. How many triangles do we have to investigate to be sure that they all contain angles totaling 180°? Only one or two, or maybe a few. The rationalist argues that once we understand the nature of the knowledge we are dealing with, then we don't have to ponder any more triangles at all. We know a priori (that is, without further empirical observation) that the angles of **all** triangles in a Euclidian system will total 180°. And what about 7 + 5 = 12? Is this true for this and all imaginable universes? It would seem to be.

If an ornithologist reported the discovery of a clutch of yellow polka dot robins' eggs, we would have no **logical** reason to **dis**believe him. But if a geometrician reported that he had spotted a circle somewhere in Antarctica whose diameter was greater than its circumference, we would be justified in concluding he had been out in the snow too long. We would **dis**believe him on **logical** grounds.

Therefore, it is clear that we are dealing with two distinctly different kinds of knowledge about nature, and the way they apply to the external world is different.

7 The problem with empirical knowledge is that we can never be absolutely sure of any fact-claim derived from our senses. We must always ask: Do we have sufficient knowledge of an object/event to be reasonably (operationally) sure?

We are still a bit puzzled as to why mathematical knowledge describes so nicely the operations of nature. Seven plus five may equal twelve because we say so. That is, we construct the formal system that way. And perhaps πr^2 merely describes a mathematical relationship. But the physical world "out there" is another matter. Why does Einstein's famous conversion formula $E = mc^2$ really describe what happens during certain nuclear reactions? Why do light and gravity "obey" the inverse square law? Some seventeenth-century thinkers concluded that we seem to develop coherent mathematical systems in our minds and then, by some sort of coincidence, find that they apply to the natural world. Or does nature really operate on inherently perfect mathematical principles?

Most of us would probably argue that 2 + 2 = 4 is an eternal truth because it is a part of a coherent system. Or is it because this operation describes real operations in nature? The pragmatist contends that we keep on using the formula only because it keeps on working; but the rationalist is not satisfied with such an answer. He argues that two plus two must equal four, anywhere in the universe; it is a cosmic truth, not a pragmatic model.

"The Master said, 'Yu, shall I teach you what knowledge is? When you know a thing, to recognize that you know it, and when you do not know a thing, to recognize that you do not know it. That is knowledge.'"

Confucius

Other Ways of Knowing?

8 When it is said that there are two ways of knowing the natural world, this claim has a decidedly Western sound—and it may or may not be entirely true. It is a Western assumption that the subject is the knower and that nature is the object

known. If the relationship is **defined** this way, then the foregoing elucidation of the problems involved between subject and object should be fairly accurate and not without meaning.

This alone I know, that I know nothing.

SOCRATES

But we might wonder whether there are other ways of knowing. Is it a true and final fact that man is the experiencing subject and the real world is the experienced object, and that the two are distinct, separate entities? Or might there be a "field interaction" that would render false the subject-object dichotomy? Perhaps man's knowing is more immersed in the "object" than he thinks and his separateness is merely an illusion. Perhaps the processes of knowing are but part of a larger process. Or perhaps there are other **ways** of knowing realities.

A Western philosopher who was convinced there is a better way was Henri Bergson. He contended that the only true method of "doing metaphysics"—knowing the real world as it actually is—is through "intuition," what he called "intellectual empathy." The rational mind is far too occupied with static concepts and mental filing systems to be able to perceive the ever-changing **process** we call "nature." Nature is pure duration, with no stops and starts, absolutes, or quantification. Nature is **all** motion, and the human intellect specializes in creating static images of nature that **always** fail to capture that motion. The human intellect, Bergson concluded, can know reality only by putting aside the intellect and intuiting directly the dynamic flow of the world—of which he too is a part. (For more on Bergson's intuition, see p. 212.)

Those familiar with Eastern modes of experience are aware that this is a meaningful way of knowing reality. Buddhism, for instance, explicitly rejects the subject-object dichotomy as dangerously false. The goal of Zen meditation is *satori,* described as a "flash of realization" that man is one with reality and not separate from it. It is a sensitive, totalic awareness of being a part of nature. Subject and object merge into one, or better, they are at last perceived as always having been one.

REALITIES BEYOND APPEARANCES

9 Man has been disturbed by the natural world into which he is born and in which he has to live. It is clear to him that things are not quite what they seem.

There are life-giving forces that make things grow, and all living things are in a condition of constant change. There are forces that shake the ground and belch up cinders and ash through the mountaintops. There are forces that rumble in a rainstorm and crackle across the sky in streaks of light. There are insidious forces that make one hurt inside and burn with heat and die. There are roots and insects and animals and seeds that give off juices that can kill.

Ancient man wondered about these things. Obviously there were all sorts of **realities beyond appearances.** They could be felt. They could be benevolent, but more often they were hostile and harmful. What were these forces—these invisible, capricious powers?

Today, of course, we know that the ancient intuition was correct: there are indeed forces beyond appearances. We must admire ancient men for making as much sense of their world as they did.

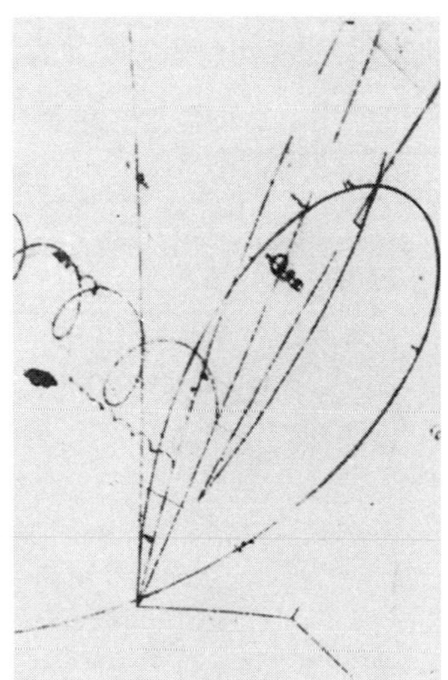

Particle streaks. Photo courtesy of NAL.

10 Sir Arthur Eddington illustrates the difference between macrocosmic reality as we experience it and some of the "realities beyond appearances."

> The learned physicist and the man in the street were standing together on the threshold about to enter a room.
>
> The man in the street moved forward without trouble, planted his foot on a solid unyielding plank at rest before him, and entered.
>
> The physicist was faced with an intricate problem. To make any movement he must shove against the atmosphere, which presses with a force of fourteen pounds on every square inch of his body. He must land on a plank travelling at twenty miles a second round the sun—a fraction of a second earlier or later the plank would be miles away from the chosen spot. He must do this whilst hanging from a round planet head outward into space, and with a wind of ether blowing at no one knows how many miles a second through every interstice of his body. He reflects too that the plank is not what it appears to be—a continuous support for his weight. The plank is mostly emptiness; very sparsely scattered in that emptiness are myriads of electric charges dashing about at great speeds but occupying at any moment less than a billionth part of the volume which the plank seems to fill continuously. It is like stepping on a swarm of flies. . . .
>
> Happily even a learned physicist has usually some sense of proportion; and it is probable that for this occasion he put out of mind scientific truths about astronomical motions, the constitution of planks and the laws of probability, and was content to follow the same crude conception of his task that presented itself to the mind of his unscientific colleague.

THIS WORLD—WHAT IS IT?

11 The very first Greek philosophers asked questions, not about man, but about the world in which they lived. They knew nothing of the basic elements (hydrogen, oxygen, and so forth) or Natural Law ("physics"—the science of matter/energy-in-motion) as we do. But sensing man's perilous (mis)understanding of his world, they asked questions, and asked them in a new way.

I cannot know even whether I know or not.

ARCESILAUS

What is this "matter" of which everything is made? Is everything made of some single substance that we know (like water, air, or fire)? Or is it made of some unknown substance that under certain conditions turns into the water, air, and fire of experience?

The deeper science probes toward reality, the more clearly it appears that the universe is not like a machine at all.

LINCOLN BARNETT

And what are the forces that activate matter into motion? The winds blow, lightning fells the giant pine tree, crops grow and die. What are the forces behind all this? Is it a single force or many? Could the force be "divine" or "mental"? Could it be alive? Is it **outside** matter? (Zeus doesn't really hurl the thunderbolt of lightning.) Or **inside** matter? (Thales pondered magnets and decided their forces were internal; so he concluded that they must possess "souls.")

There is much that physicists do not yet understand about the physical world, but it is beginning to be clear that reality is not quite what they thought it to be even in the 1960s and 70s.

RICHARD MORRIS

These first philosopher-scientists phrased such questions as best they could. In all, they were asking but two fundamental questions: (1) What is everything made of? (2) What are the forces that cause motion? There must be a lesson in all this: Our present accumulation of scientific knowledge about the natural world is nothing less than staggering, yet what are the fundamental questions we are asking today? (1) What is everything made of? (2) What are the forces that cause motion?

12 But it would be terribly misleading to leave the matter here. As of the end of the twentieth century, we have traveled a long journey in our understanding of the substances that make up the realm of the physically real; in fact when a beginner cracks a physics textbook (or a biology textbook) he can be overwhelmed at how much we know and understand of the world about us. We may still use the same sentences, but we aren't asking the same questions. Today, when we ask "What is everything made of?" our minds jump to a vast accumulation of known facts to shape our answers.

You're taking a walk along the beach and pick up a wave-washed pebble. It's milky white and shiny. What is it? What is it made of? The **name** (symbol) for it is "quartz," but this conventional name, in itself, tells us nothing. So, what is it, really?

The first step in finding out must be taken at **the molecular level of organization.** A molecule is a group of atoms of two or more basic elements bound tightly together so that they behave as a single unit. Every molecule of the same "species" is made up of the same proportions of the same elements. A molecule of water, for example, is composed of two atoms of hydrogen and one atom of oxygen (H_2O); every water molecule on Earth and throughout the universe is constructed in just this way.

This is the first level of organization that gives the world its consistencies and enables us to make sense of it. Just as all molecules of water are the same, so are all the molecules of sugar, alcohol, salt, methane, silver iodide, ammonia, insulin, formaldehyde, carbon dioxide, and countless other substances that affect our lives. We can name, define, and discover their qualities ("water molecules are wet"), and exploit them because their components and qualities are always the same. Many millions of these molecular compounds are produced by nature, and millions more are now produced in our chemical laboratories.

So, what is the quartz made of? It is composed of molecules of the elements silicon and oxygen (silicon dioxide, SiO_2).

13 Next down, we come to **the atomic level of organization.** An atom is an exceedingly complex little system that behaves quite autonomously and follows its own set of rules, which we call quantum mechanics. It consists of an incredibly small (but relatively very heavy) nucleus of protons and neutrons and outer "shells" of as many as a hundred electrons orbiting the nucleus more than a hundred million billion times each second. The atom is very tiny—less than a hundred millionth of an inch in diameter. And the dog definitely wags the tail: more than 99.9 percent of the mass of the atom is found in its nucleus; the rest (less than 0.1 percent) is in its electrons. If an atomic nucleus were the size of a baseball, then the electron(s) would be the size of pinhead(s) orbiting about a mile away.

From this insight into the atom, two conclusions have produced major changes in the way we think about matter and the world. (1) Everything in the universe is in motion at very high speeds ("relativistic speeds"), and there is **nothing** that is not in motion. **Nothing** is at rest anywhere in the cosmos. (2) In the final analysis nothing is really "solid." Everything is composed of atoms, and the atom is mostly space-dominated not by solid pieces of matter but by powerful nonmaterial force fields.

Reality is the real business of physics.

ALBERT EINSTEIN

The notion that matter is something inert and uninteresting is surely the veriest nonsense. If there is anything more wonderful than matter in the sheer versatility of its behavior, I have yet to hear tell of it.

SIR FRED HOYLE

The Periodic Table of Elements. "What is the world made of?" is a question that has bothered inquisitive humans since the beginning of conceptual consciousness. Thales thought it might be made of water. Anaximenes reasoned that it was composed of (compressed) air. Heraclitus said it is created from fire. Empedocles and Aristotle decided it was a blend of fire, earth, air, and water.

Today we're better off in knowing the "stuff" of the world, but only relatively "better off." Ultimate reality keeps eluding us. We do know that the universe and everything in it is composed of about a hundred basic elements. When the "Periodic Table of Elements" was devised by Dmitri Mendeleev in 1871, it began to reveal, even in its incomplete form, numerous secrets regarding the orderly relationships within Nature. The philosophic insights derived from our understanding of the behavior of these elemental building blocks are staggering —as is the plethora of deep questions they have forced on us.

The position of each element in the Periodic Table is determined solely by the number of protons it contains in its nucleus (carbon has six protons, for example, and gold has seventy-nine). As the elements were arranged in the Table according to the number of protons, it was seen that they grouped themselves neatly according to similar characteristics. The columns to the left of the zigzag line tend to be metals; those to the right are nonmetals. The helium group (vertical column at right) consists of inert gases that refuse to react with other elements, while the volatile elements of the fluorine group react with almost any element they touch. How all these elements combine to produce other substances is determined by the number of electrons that occupy shells around the nucleus.

Today it's fashionable to take this knowledge for granted, but this is the kind of understanding that would have made the first philosopher-scientists jubilant with excitement.

1	2	3	4	5	6	7	8	9	10	11	12	13	14	15	16	17	18
1 H Hydrogen 1.00794																	2 He Helium 4.002602
3 Li Lithium 6.941	4 Be Beryllium 9.012182											5 B Boron 10.811	6 C Carbon 12.0107	7 N Nitrogen 14.00674	8 O Oxygen 15.9994	9 F Fluorine 18.9984032	10 Ne Neon 20.1797
11 Na Sodium 22.989768	12 Mg Magnesium 24.305											13 Al Aluminum 26.981539	14 Si Silicon 28.0855	15 P Phosphorus 30.973762	16 S Sulfur 32.066	17 Cl Chlorine 35.4527	18 Ar Argon 39.948
19 K Potassium 39.0983	20 Ca Calcium 40.078	21 Sc Scandium 44.95591	22 Ti Titanium 47.867	23 V Vanadium 50.9415	24 Cr Chromium 51.9961	25 Mn Manganese 54.93805	26 Fe Iron 55.845	27 Co Cobalt 58.9332	28 Ni Nickel 58.6934	29 Cu Copper 63.546	30 Zn Zinc 65.39	31 Ga Gallium 69.723	32 Ge Germanium 72.61	33 As Arsenic 74.92159	34 Se Selenium 78.96	35 Br Bromine 79.904	36 Kr Krypton 83.80
37 Rb Rubidium 85.4678	38 Sr Strontium 87.62	39 Y Yttrium 88.90585	40 Zr Zirconium 91.224	41 Nb Niobium 92.90638	42 Mo Molybdenum 95.94	43 Tc Technetium (98)	44 Ru Ruthenium 101.07	45 Rh Rhodium 102.9055	46 Pd Palladium 106.42	47 Ag Silver 107.8682	48 Cd Cadmium 112.411	49 In Indium 114.818	50 Sn Tin 118.710	51 Sb Antimony 121.76	52 Te Tellurium 127.60	53 I Iodine 126.90447	54 Xe Xenon 131.29
55 Cs Cesium 132.90543	56 Ba Barium 137.327		72 Hf Hafnium 178.49	73 Ta Tantalum 180.9479	74 W Tungsten 183.84	75 Re Rhenium 186.207	76 Os Osmium 190.23	77 Ir Iridium 192.217	78 Pt Platinum 195.078	79 Au Gold 196.96654	80 Hg Mercury 200.59	81 Tl Thallium 204.3833	82 Pb Lead 207.2	83 Bi Bismuth 208.98037	84 Po Polonium (209)	85 At Astatine (210)	86 Rn Radon (222)
87 Fr Francium (223)	88 Ra Radium (226)		104 Rf Rutherfordium (261)	105 Db Dubnium (262)	106 Sg Seaborgium (266)	107 Bh Bohrium (262)	108 Hs Hassium (263)	109 Mt Meitnerium (268)									

57 La Lanthanum 138.9055	58 Ce Cerium 140.116	59 Pr Praseodymium 140.90765	60 Nd Neodymium 144.24	61 Pm Promethium (145)	62 Sm Samarium 150.36	63 Eu Europium 151.964	64 Gd Gadolinium 157.25	65 Tb Terbium 158.92534	66 Dy Dysprosium 162.50	67 Ho Holmium 164.93032	68 Er Erbium 167.26	69 Tm Thulium 168.93421	70 Yb Ytterbium 173.04	71 Lu Lutetium 174.967
89 Ac Actinium (227)	90 Th Thorium 232.0381	91 Pa Protactinium 231.03588	92 U Uranium 238.0289	93 Np Neptunium (237)	94 Pu Plutonium (244)	95 Am Americium (243)	96 Cm Curium (247)	97 Bk Berkelium (247)	98 Cf Californium (251)	99 Es Einsteinium (252)	100 Fm Fermium (257)	101 Md Mendelevium (258)	102 No Nobelium (259)	103 Lr Lawrencium (262)

It is the atom that gives the rich distinctive qualities to the elements as we perceive them at our macroscopic level: gold, copper, sulfur, chromium, lead, uranium, carbon, helium, and so on. All the basic elements are now known to us, and they total a little more than a hundred. They can be arranged in the Periodic Table of Elements according to their weights. (This is how we know that all the elements in the universe have been discovered: there are no gaps or blanks in the Periodic Table.) Everything in the universe is composed of the atoms of these few elements arranged in various molecular combinations.

So, what is the quartz pebble made of? It is composed of molecules of the elements silicon and oxygen, which are composed of atoms made of protons, neutrons, and electrons.

14 Next down, things get more complicated. When the Greek philosopher Democritus first theorized that all matter was composed of atoms, he pictured little indivisible pieces of solid matter and called them "atoms," from the Greek *a-tomé*, "uncuttable." This image of the atom prevailed in scientific thinking well into the nineteenth century. Then it was discovered that the "uncuttable" atom had parts. But these parts were still thought of as tiny solid pieces of charged matter that in turn might be made up of even smaller solid pieces of charged matter, and so on, perhaps infinitely. But new discoveries soon destroyed this picture of the atom and its constituents. At the subatomic level there are no pieces of solid matter, or solid pieces of anything. The notion of "solid matter" as we know it at the experiential level ceases to exist and is replaced by points of energy and coherent force fields.

With the development of high-energy research tools it was found that the atom is nothing less than a three-ring circus with its wild-animal acts and high-wire performances all going on at the same time. The heart of the atom seemed to be an endless wellspring of quirky particles, so disparate and chaotic that, at first, they made no sense at all.

Today, after three or four decades of phenomenally successful probing, what we know is this: The nucleus of the atom is composed of protons and neutrons orbiting a nuclear center in tightly organized shells. It is spherical or distorted into the shape of a football or doorknob. Its basic particles, proton and neutron, are essentially the same particle in different energy states, bound together by a charged particle called a pion. The exchange of pions creates the strong nuclear force that binds the atomic nucleus together.

Much more has been revealed by the high-energy particle accelerators. A whole family of particles exists that are subject to the strong nuclear force, and another family subject only to the weak force. And all particles, it seems, have antiparticles; so there exist antiprotons, antielectrons (called positrons), and antineutrinos. To date more than two hundred particles have been discovered in experiments, and several hundred more have been postulated in theory but have yet to be discovered in reality.

Polymethylene crystals (magnified 37,000 times) show that nature grows both "left-handed" and "right-handed" spiral designs.

15 So, until the early 1960s chaos reigned. Then in 1964 a theory was devised that began to account for the activity in this little three-ring circus. This "quark" theory was devised to explain the behavior of all the particles in the nucleus subject to the strong force. All the hundreds of particles that have been discovered in the heart of the nucleus can be explained as combinations of

quarks and antiquarks. The proton and neutron, for instance, are made up of three quarks each. Even the pion is made up of two quarks.

At first all this was only theory. Then in 1968 the first quarks were found in accelerator experiments. By 1984 a total of six quarks had been found and their basic properties revealed.

This is **the quark level of organization.**

16 So, what is the quartz made of? It is composed of molecules of the elements silicon and oxygen, which are composed of atoms made of protons, neutrons, and electrons, which in turn are composed of various combinations of quarks. Everything in the universe can finally be explained in terms of combinations of quarks and force fields.

Is this the end of the story? No one knows. It is turning out that the quark story is not really simple after all. Each quark, it has been discovered, comes in three "brands" (physicists say three "colors"), so there are really eighteen quarks. But since each quark has an antiquark, one can think in terms of thirty-six quarks. Moreover, theorists have had to postulate the existence of eight "gluons," which carry the binding charge between quarks. The theories that have made sense of this complex world are called quantum electrodynamics (QED) and quantum chromodynamics (QCD), and both theories have been marvelously successful in bringing order out of chaos.

But intensive searching continues for ever more fundamental constituents of matter. Physicists keep hoping they will finally arrive at rock-bottom reality and know at last what the universe is made of. Maybe there is such a resting place, but in their nightmares theorists sometimes fear that the levels might continue ad infinitum, and the search for reality may never end. What can be said at present is that, although there are theories that proceed beyond quarks —the superstring theory, for instance—they are only theories with no supporting evidence.

THE DEMATERIALIZATION OF MATTER

17 "What is everything made of?" To such a question Werner Heisenberg once wrote that

> the final answer will more closely approximate the views expressed in Plato's *Timaeus* than those of the ancient materialists. . . . The elemental particles of present day physics are more closely related to the Platonic bodies than they are to the atoms of Democritus.
>
> The elemental particles of modern physics, like the regular bodies of Plato's philosophy, are defined by the requirements of mathematical symmetry. They are not eternal and unchanging, and they can hardly, therefore, strictly be termed real. Rather, they are simple expressions of fundamental mathematical constructions which one comes upon in striving to break down matter ever further, and which provide the content for the underlying laws of nature. In the beginning, therefore, for modern science, was the form, the mathematical pattern, not the material thing. And since the mathematical pattern is, in the final analysis, an intellectual concept, one can say in the words of Faust, "*Am Anfang war der Sinn*"—"In the beginning was the meaning."

Mathematics and Eternal Truths

Mathematics is, I believe, the chief source of the belief in eternal and exact truth, as well as in a supersensible intelligible world. Geometry deals with exact circles, but no sensible object is *exactly* circular; however carefully we may use our compasses, there will be some imperfections and irregularities. This suggests the view that all exact reasoning applies to ideal as opposed to sensible objects; it is natural to go further, and to argue that thought is nobler than sense, and the objects of thought more real than those of sense-perception. Mystical doctrines as to the relation of time to eternity are also reinforced by pure mathematics, for mathematical objects, such as numbers, if real at all, are eternal and not in time. Such eternal objects can be conceived as God's thoughts. Hence Plato's doctrine that God is a geometer, and Sir James Jeans' belief that He is addicted to arithmetic. Rationalistic as opposed to apocalyptic religion has been, ever since Pythagoras, and notably ever since Plato, very completely dominated by mathematics and mathematical method.

The combination of mathematics and theology, which began with Pythagoras, characterized religious philosophy in Greece, in the Middle Ages, and in modern times down to Kant. . . . I do not know of any other man [Pythagoras] who has been as influential as he was in the sphere of thought. . . . The whole conception of an eternal world, revealed to the intellect but not to the senses, is derived from him.

Bertrand Russell

18 Matter has been dematerialized, not just as a concept of the philosophically real, but now as an idea of modern physics. Matter can be analyzed down to the level of fundamental particles. But at that depth the direction of the analysis changes, and this constitutes a major conceptual surprise in the history of science. The things that for Newton typified matter—e.g., an exactly determinable state, a point shape, absolute solidity—these are now the properties electrons do not, because theoretically they cannot, have. . . .

The dematerialization of matter encountered in this century . . . has rocked mechanics at its foundations. . . . The 20th century's dematerialization of matter has made it conceptually impossible to accept a Newtonian picture of the properties of matter and still do consistent physics.

Norwood Russell Hanson

Just as Newton shattered the medieval crystal spheres, modern quantum theory has irreparably smashed Newton's clockwork. We are now certain that the world is not a deterministic mechanism.

Nick Herbert

The knowledge of science fails in the face of all ultimate questions.

Karl Jaspers

What Is the Origin of Matter?

19 In the history of ideas, certain questions have to wait before they can be asked. One such question (the most obvious of all) was so overwhelming that it was asked and immediately tucked away, never to be taken seriously again. The question: What is the origin of matter?

The problem has been ignored because it seemed insoluble; a simple creationist answer appeared the only one possible. When did the universe begin? What created matter? Or from what was matter created? "God created the

I think it is safe to say that no one understands quantum mechanics. Do not keep saying to yourself, if you can possibly avoid it, "but how can it be like that?" because you will go "down the drain" into a blind alley from which nobody has yet escaped. Nobody knows how it can be like that.

Richard Feynman

At the basis of the whole modern view of the world lies the illusion that the so-called laws of nature are the explanation of natural phenomena.
LUDWIG WITTGENSTEIN

universe and set matter in motion." And the little girl who persisted—"Then who made God?"—we brushed aside.

Her question is legitimate. Philosophers have long pointed out that the creationist answer is no answer at all. It was merely a *deus ex machina* like that employed by Greek tragedians to unravel a tangled plot. The deity dropped in from above the stage and, by divine fiat, set everything right. To say that X created Y—or G created M—*ex nihilo,* "out of nothing," is merely to define the question as being off-limits to serious inquiry.

At this early stage of inquiry into the origin of matter only a few promising lines of thought have been developed. In his "steady-state" theory of the universe, Sir Fred Hoyle assumed that matter is being created continually in space out of nothing, but he never attempted a serious explanation of how this might happen. Hoyle did little more than pose the problem.

> Matter is capable of exerting several types of influence—or fields as they are usually called. There is the nuclear field that binds together the atomic nuclei. There is the electro-magnetic field that enables atoms to absorb light. There is the gravitational field that holds the stars and galaxies together. And according to the new theory there is also a creation field that causes matter to originate.

To this last statement, Hoyle adds: "Matter originates in response to the influence of other matter."

Matter-in-motion can create other matter; for matter-in-motion is energy, and energy can be transformed into more matter. Therefore, in theory, if we can imagine the universe beginning with even a very small amount of matter—perhaps just a few atoms—in a state of acceleration, then we can logically describe how all the matter in the universe might have come into existence. Each bit of matter traveling at high speeds can be transformed into more matter.

20 Today we can **almost** create matter in our laboratories. In a phenomenon known as "pair-creation," physicists can create electrons in the vacuum of the accelerator, that is, out of nothing. They have also succeeded in creating pairs of positive and negative protons out of nothing. Weisskopf states that, in his opinion, this represents the actual creation of matter.

Electrons can also be created from photons of light. The interesting point is that light does not have mass, while electrons have. Photons (with a mass of zero) are massless energy; at the speed of light the photons can be transformed into mass according to the mass-energy transformation equation:

$$E = mc^2$$

What does all this mean? One implication seems to be that questions about the origin of matter are not wholly out of order. Nevertheless, at the present time really convincing answers are lacking. In all cases physicists began their experiments with something (not "nothing"), and they had at their disposal sophisticated scientific equipment with which they could accelerate particles into higher energy states. Theoretically, if we can imagine a universe empty of all mass but a single, lonely electron, plus some force that can push that electron into relativistic speeds, then we can logically account for all the rest of the matter in the entire universe. But what that "Prime Mover" might be still bothers us.

The best we can do at present is to hold on to the question and not be lured into thinking it has been answered. We will probably have to rephrase the question numerous times before an answer begins to come. Indeed, it might be found in some different frame of reference altogether.

✦

PYTHAGORAS

The Universe Is Made of Numbers

Pythagoras was the thinker who first proved that knowledge of the world is possible. He was a Greek philosopher . . . and mathematician, astronomer, physicist, musician, teacher, monastic, mystic, feminist, psychotherapist, seer, and cult leader . . . which indicates only that he was an unusual human being with a bright mind, a zest for life, and a passion to understand the world.

Pythagoras was born on the beautiful Aegean island of Samos about 580 BC. He was the son of Mnesarchus, an engraver of gems, probably an affluent aristocrat and landowner. Pythagoras lived at the right time and place for intellectual growth. First, he was given the finest formal education available in gymnastics, music, mathematics, and what was known of the natural sciences. Second, he lived at a geographic crossroads where ideas from the East—Mesopotamia, Persia, India, and perhaps China—were beginning to flow into the Mediterranean world. Third, a new scientific outlook was emerging in the Ionian cities, and Pythagoras was thoroughly trained to see and think as a scientist. Finally, he traveled widely in Egypt, tradition says, where he learned geometry and astronomy, and also some cultural lore from the priests; and to Phoenicia, Chaldea, Arabia, and perhaps India. All in all, Pythagoras was fortunate intellectually: he had ample experiences, observations, questions, and ideas, that are the ferment of philosophy.

Around the age of fifty he returned home from his travels and found that Samos had been usurped by the tyrant Polycrates. So Pythagoras, and probably a few followers, emigrated westward to Italy and settled at a health spa known as Crotona. There he founded one of the great schools of antiquity.

His school was an institution of learning and a sanctuary for the cultivation of the spirit. It was housed in a sprawl of buildings extensive enough to accommodate hundreds of students. Members took vows of loyalty and adhered to strict rules. They shared property, ate meals together, wore a distinctive white garb, and were known for their quiet lives, modest behavior, and solemn decorum.

Members were divided into two groups: the "outsiders" (*exoterici*), who studied "in silence" during a five-year probationary period; and the "insiders" (*esoterici*), who were admitted to the secrets of the cult and permitted to listen to the teaching of Pythagoras himself. Pythagoras was one of the first feminists. He admitted women to his school equally with men and saw to it that they were given the same basic education—philosophy, mathematics, music, and the arts; but in addition they were given vocational training in the care of the home and family.

If we can believe later historians, it is not difficult to reconstruct a day in the life of the Pythagorean community.

On awakening, members practiced memory exercises, attempting to recall exactly the events of the day before, in sequence; then the day before that, and so on. This practice was probably connected to the Pythagorean belief that all learning is recollection—that is, remembrance of truths known by the soul from previous lifetimes—and was doubtless designed to perfect the memory so that it could better apprehend the eternal truths.

Each member then went on a solitary morning walk. Members valued solitude and silence and practiced both throughout the day. This early morning stroll helped them to maintain personal harmony and to cope with the stressful demands of the world.

Members then attended classes. They studied and discussed the subjects they were taking, the doctrines of the cult, and the regulations that governed their living together. After another walk, they devoted an hour or so to health care. They would "compete at wrestling in the gardens and groves or at high-jump with leaden weights in their hands, while others would practice the art of pantomime."

They lunched on bread and honey. Afternoons were filled with more studies. Toward evening they enjoyed a promenade, two or three together walking along the streets or through the countryside. They marched in cadence, "walking in graceful rhythm together," so as to maintain harmony in all things. Supper was taken in small groups and consisted of maize, bread, raw and cooked vegetables and herbs, some meat, and a small amount of wine.

After the evening meal, libations were offered to the gods. Animal sacrifices were prohibited by the Pythagoreans, who believed that animals and humans alike share "the privilege of having a soul." The community worshiped Apollo the Life-Giver, but other gods and demons were honored, and the ceremonies included magical rites and divination.

Evening was a social time, but not for idle chatter. Members read and discussed in groups, with younger members reading what the older members chose. As the evening drew to a close more libations were offered, and one of the elders gave a short talk or homily. At bedtime, members donned "pure white night-garments" and slept in "pure white beds." "By such disciplines," a later Pythagorean wrote, they "sought to arrange their lives entirely for the purpose of following God."

Hovering over the community was the philosopher himself, a power and final authority, a felt presence, a god incarnate—a Christ-figure. Pythagoras was a tall man, always dressed immaculately in a white robe. Some of his followers were convinced that he worked magic and performed miracles. It was reported (by Aristotle) that the citizens of Crotona thought of him as a manifestation of Apollo and thought he possessed a "golden thigh," which he displayed at the Olympian games. He lived simply and ate abstemiously—little more than bread and honey, some vegetables, and a little wine. He loved mathematics, astronomy, and music, and all three became elements of his mystical religion.

Pythagoras was married, probably late in life, to a Crotonan woman named Theano. A daughter, Damo, became caretaker of her father's secret writings, and a son, Telauges, succeeded his father as head of the Pythagorean community.

✦

Above all, have respect for yourself.

After going to bed do not allow sleep to close your eyelids until you have first examined all your actions of the day, asking yourself: Wherein have I done amiss? What have I omitted that ought to have been done? If you find on reflection that you have done anything amiss, be severe with yourself; if you have done anything good, rejoice.

From the Pythagorean *Golden Verses*

[The Pythagoreans] say that at the center there is fire, the earth being in effect one of the planets, which moves in a circle about the center and thus produced night and day. They hold the theory that there is another earth, behind and facing this one, which they call the counter-earth.

ARISTOTLE

Assist a man in lifting a burden, not in laying it down.

Let no swallows nest on your roof.

Reason is immortal, all else mortal.

In Hades, [a Pythagorean philosopher] said, referring to the unseen after-world, the uninitiated will be dreadfully unhappy, for they will be constantly occupied pouring water from a leaky pitcher into a leaky sieve.

PLATO
Gorgias

By healing your soul you will thereby deliver it from all evils, from all afflictions.

[The Pythagoreans] construct the entire visible universe out of numbers—not numbers in the abstract, but spatially extended units of magnitude.

It was Pythagoras who discovered nature's *modus operandi:* mathematics. "The language of nature is mathematics," as Galileo later phrased it. This is one of humanity's great discoveries; it made possible the science of physics and the development of our technological civilization. Bertrand Russell once wrote that Pythagoras was "intellectually one of the most important men that ever lived, both when he was wise and when he was unwise."

The story is told of Pythagoras's passing by a blacksmith shop and hearing from inside the ringing of hammers pounding on the anvils. The blows produced a variety of pitches. Pythagoras went inside to watch and observed that the lower notes were produced by the heavy hammers, the higher notes by the lighter hammers. Pythagoras had already experimented with the measuring of weights and knew that the weight of any object can be broken into fractional units and described mathematically. He had probably also worked with stringed instruments and knew that harmonic intervals are determined by the length of the vibrating string and can be expressed in precise ratios with abstract numbers. Now it dawned on him that all natural objects had their own vibrations and that the entire universe of matter-in-motion had a mathematical structure. Everything in the cosmos is vibrating, he concluded, as though the world is a great orchestra and every material object is an instrument in that orchestra, giving off its own musical pitch. Anvils, bells, cymbals, and pounding drums; the tinkle of porcelain shattering; the ring of the sculptor's chisel against marble; the boom of a volcano erupting; and even the planets orbiting through the night skies—everything vibrates and makes music. Pythagoras coined the phrase "the music of the spheres" and claims to have actually heard such music.

This was an important intellectual event: the movement from singular objects/events to universal mathematical generalizations. This discovery provoked in Pythagoras a lifelong love affair with abstract mathematics and geometry and facilitated numerous discoveries. He discovered several geometrical theorems, tradition tells us, the most famous still bearing his name—the "Pythagorean Theorem": the sum of the squares of the sides of a right triangle is equal to the square of the hypotenuse. (We are told that Pythagoras was so elated by this discovery that he made an offering to the gods.) He also worked with square roots and discovered that $\sqrt{2}$ is an inexpressible number. (Its existence became one of the secrets of the Pythagorean cult, since it wasn't supposed to exist; and the records tell of the excommunication of one of its members for betraying the existence of this "irrational" number.) He was intrigued by an arrangement of ten dots in triangular form, called a *tetractys,* which became a religious symbol; those joining the community took an oath on the tetractys: "I swear by Him who reveals Himself to our minds in the tetractys, which contains the source and roots of everlasting nature"—that is, the secret of immortality. It is not impossible that Pythagoras had stumbled on a psychic symbol (called a *shri yantra* in Tibetan Buddhism), a symbol of unity and wholeness employed in meditation.

The other Ionian philosophers had sought to discover what substance the world is made of—such as water, air, fire, or something else. But Pythagoras concluded that reality is not a substance but a formal structure that can be expressed in pure numbers. "The whole of modern physics, with its mathematical theories of light, radiation, atomic structure, and so forth, is a continuation of the same line of thought and a vindication of the Pythagorean point of view" (R. G. Collingwood). The approach of modern physics is still that of Pythagoras: what the universe is "made of" is of secondary importance; what we seek is a quantification of the "vibrations" of whatever the substantial entities are.

Since these mathematical patterns of change can be apprehended by the hu-

A Pythagoras Lexicon

gnomon
tetractys
kosmos
harmonium
philosophia
mathematika
decad
hypotenuse

man mind, knowledge of the world is truly possible. This is the philosophical significance of Pythagoras's discovery.

Pythagoras was not only a scientist and mathematician; he was also a mystic and redeemer. He sought the secret of living for himself and his followers; and he seems to have developed one of history's earliest intellectually coherent "ways of liberation."

The key was *harmonium*, "harmony." Any structure is in a state of harmony if all its parts "vibrate" together. The cosmos is a harmonious whole, Pythagoras believed. "They supposed the whole heaven to be a *harmonia* and a number," wrote Aristotle. Similarly, the soul—a sort of mini-cosmos—can enjoy a state of harmony when all its parts work together. Most of the time the soul—imprisoned in the physical body, juggling an ever-changing blending of opposites—has a difficult time coordinating all its parts.

Pythagoras taught that this present lifetime is but a short interlude in a long journey of the soul. Each soul is reincarnated repeatedly into material form; and in each incarnation the body (*sôma*) again becomes the prison of the soul (*sêma*). After each lifetime the soul descends to Hades, where it undergoes a purging of its sin; then it returns to Earth and once more becomes re-incarnate in its prison house.

The goal of life is to put a stop to this round of rebirth—the "wheel of things," as Pythagoras phrased it. This can be achieved by striving for a virtuous life, which to the Pythagoreans meant a harmony of soul—a soul in tune with itself and with the cosmos. The truly harmonious soul will not be returned for rebirth but will become forever a part of the divine world-soul.

How can this harmony be achieved? First, through meditation on cosmic harmony. When we become absorbed into the cosmic vibrations and partake of its harmony, we are able to identify our soul with the cosmos. Second, by living a well-balanced life (in terms of diet, exercise, and good habits) and keeping the components of the soul properly attuned. This was the reason-for-being of the Pythagorean community: to provide a closed environment free of stress, with time for quietude, where healthful habits and routines could be practiced.

Thus, "the music of the spheres" and the harmony of the soul can become one.

Pythagoras lived to be at least eighty years old. The populace of Crotona became incensed at the political activities of the Pythagoreans, who were authoritarian in their philosophy of power, believing that those with true knowledge should rule. The Crotonans were decidedly democratic and perceived the cult as a threat. Mobs stormed the monastery, burned it, killed a large number of the community (forty, by one report), and drove away the rest.

Pythagoras was forced to flee. Chased by assailants, he came to a patch of beans, against which the Pythagoreans had a taboo. He halted, "declaring that he would let himself be killed rather than reveal the secret doctrines" of the community. They killed him. The date was about 497 BC.

The Pythagorean community endured for only about a century longer and then vanished from history.

✦

REFLECTIONS

1 Reflect on the snowflakes and other illustrations of natural objects/events throughout the chapter. What can you infer about "nature" from their common patterns?

Rationalism is an adventure in the clarification of thought.
ALFRED NORTH WHITEHEAD

No good argument for or against the existence of matter has yet been brought forward.
BERTRAND RUSSELL

2 Why was Thales's prediction of the eclipse so important that we date the beginnings of philosophy and science from this event? (Recall earlier comments about Thales on pp. 23–24.)
3 We possess two clear-cut kinds of knowledge about the real world—empirical knowledge and a priori knowledge. Clarify the working of each and then go to the question raised on pp. 484–485. Can you think of any further ways of knowing reality? Might Bergson's notion of intuitive knowledge be correct?
4 Summarize—briefly, and very carefully, in your own words—exactly what the Jovian philosopher saw and did as he watched the baseball game. In fact, did he see the baseball game at all? What is the role of memory in the construction of knowledge? Now, how does this analogy apply to our knowledge of (a) the natural world, (b) human behavior, and (c) the personality of another individual?
5 Now, when all is said and over with, isn't it true that all robins' eggs are blue? What's the hassle all about? Why make such a big deal of something that everyone knows?
6 Note the comment on p. 484: "We are still a bit puzzled as to why mathematical knowledge describes so accurately the operations of nature." What is the best answer you can give to this puzzle?
7 Whether or not you have ever studied physics or chemistry, spend some time pondering and just enjoying the Periodic Table of Elements (p. 488). This table shows how incredibly far we have come since the first philosopher-scientists began to inquire into the nature of the "world-stuff"—matter. Note the many varieties of order evident in the Periodic Table. What is your philosophic response to the varieties of relationships and patterns to be found here—that is, in "nature"? Do you think you can share Sir Fred Hoyle's feeling (see marginal quote on p. 487) about the fascination of pure matter?
8 Ponder Heisenberg's and Hanson's statements on pp. 490–491 (see also Russell's remark on this page, marginal quote). Can you restate in your words what you think they mean when they all contend that, in the twentieth century, "matter has been dematerialized"? What might be some of the philosophic consequences of this achievement?
9 Note the four known physical forces, the forces that "perform the work" of the universe by keeping "matter in motion." Besides these basic four, do you have any evidence that there are any forces at work in the universe?
10 Spend some time—perhaps a lot of time—reflecting on Zeno's paradoxes on motion. Take any one and analyze the argument to the point where you understand his logical errors (if there are any).
11 Criticize the argument that God must have created matter because the assumption that matter has existed through all eternity is an illogical assumption. Therefore, there must have been a "first cause"—which is God (pp. 491–492). Refer to the "cosmological argument" for God on pp. 586ff.
12 Have you personally speculated on the problem of the origin of matter? Are you willing to do so now? What questions can you think of to initiate inquiry? To whom might we turn for hard data that would help us phrase our questions in an intelligible fashion?

Space / Time / Motion

7-2

In answer to the perennial question, How does the world work? Einstein created a view of the universe as a vast system of elastic things with only a single absolute, the velocity of light. Everything else is variable: time, mass, volume, and even space are changelings that will be perceived differently, depending on who or what is doing the perceiving. This chapter deals with some aspects of the philosophy of the physical sciences, analyzes how the mind goes about creating physics, and discusses certain philosophical problems that still exist in the way we do physics. As of AD 2002 the universe of motion can be accounted for by three systems of physics: classical Newtonian, relativistic, and quantum mechanics. To Richard Feynman's comment that physics is the attempt to figure out "what in hell's going on out there," we now have new insights—and puzzlements.

What Physics Is and Isn't

1 The first Greek philosophers had a passion to understand the world, but they lacked—and they knew they lacked—the basic tool for accomplishing this: physics. About 525 BC the Greek mystic Pythagoras discovered that "the world is made of numbers," but he was powerless to do anything with his discovery. Then, after two more millennia had passed, a mathematician named Galileo sat in church one day watching a chandelier swing back and forth. Because Galileo was determined to understand everything, he went home and worked out the mathematics of the swinging chandelier. With that, physics was born.

Today we can describe the world using three systems of physics. **Classical physics** (or Newtonian physics) nicely describes the ordinary motions of daily experience, such as falling trees, boiling water, satellite orbits, and so on.

It is estimated there may be 135,000,000,000 stars in the Galaxy, and there may be as many as 100,000,000,000 other galaxies distributed through space. Astronomers are generally convinced that there are innumerable worlds on which life might develop.

Isaac Asimov

This galaxy in the constellation Centaurus (NGC 5128) appears to be a collision between two large galaxies; it is a source of intense radio noise.

One of our problems is trying to figure out which is up and which is down.

JOHN YOUNG
(from Apollo X spacecraft)

Relativity physics describes the motions of objects moving at high speeds such as gamma rays, neutron stars, and gravity waves. **Quantum physics** describes the motions of very small particles such as photons, electrons, and quarks. So far, it appears that all the motions in the universe can be described by one or more of these systems—almost.

It would be convenient if we could say (as of AD 2002) that classical physics is fully understood, and that only a few epistemological problems still exist in the other two systems. But this would be false. The really bothersome problems have to do with the nature of physics as a whole. The modern quip, "If you think you understand it, you need help!" applies to the very nature of physical thinking.

2 The science of physics is commonly misunderstood, even by physicists. Several points need to be clarified. First, by definition, physics deals with motion and only with motion; and it is the motion of moving objects that can be captured with mathematics and symbolic formulas, as in the equation $d = vt$, where d stands for distance, v for velocity, and t for time. With this simple equation, physicists can calculate distances traversed by every moving thing in the universe. And $d = vt$ is a paradigm for how all equations work, even the complex mathematical formulas of relativity and quantum mechanics. Because everything in the universe is in motion, physics is *the* universal science.

Let's clarify a second point. We never see motion. All we ever see are *objects that are moving.* To account for what we perceive the objects doing, we create an abstraction in our minds that we call "motion." Motion, therefore, is a mental thing, not a real thing. Movement is real, we assume, but motion is created by an observing consciousness. And because moving objects follow mathematical patterns, we can symbolize those patterns with numbers; this symbolization process is also mental. From this it should be clear that our knowledge of the physical world is entirely symbolic. As far as physics is concerned, our understanding ignores all the real objects of the universe and reduces their movements to abstract formulas.

I cannot believe that God plays dice with the cosmos.
ALBERT EINSTEIN

Let's run that one more time. Say you're sitting in your garden at sunset and you see a dove fly homeward for the night. If you're a physicist, there is but a single aspect of this scene that is of professional interest: the dove's motion. Physics has no interest in the dove as such; other scientists who specialize in anatomy, physiology, animal behavior, and so on, will focus on the dove. So if you subtract physics from this evening scenario, what do you have left? The dove! The dove and its motion are entirely different things. That is, objects are distinct from their motion. Now think of the entire universe as made up of moving objects. If you subtract physics—the science of motion—from everything, what do you have left? *You still have all the objects in the universe.* To physicists—as physicists—the objects themselves are not part of the picture. Objects as such cannot be symbolized with mathematics and therefore, as far as physics is concerned, remain out of the picture and unknown.

"After a while one begins to think that space and time are not quite real."
RICHARD BACH
"Chang," ***Jonathan Livingston Seagull***

Physics is one of humanity's great success stories. It began with the pre-Socratic Greeks, but it then lingered through the Dark Ages and was revitalized only with the advent of such men as Galileo, Newton, and Kepler, who possessed the ability to use mathematics. Still, many of today's physicists want to claim knowledge in realms that lie outside their field, forgetting that their science is limited to motion and that even then their understanding is only symbolic.

I maintain . . . that the transient now with respect to which the distinction between the past and the future of common sense and psychological time acquires meaning has no relevance at all apart from the egocentric perspectives of a conscious (human) organism and from the immediate experiences of that organism.
ADOLF GRÜNBAUM

3 The most vexing problem in physics lies in the very nature of human thinking and can be overcome only in pure imagination. One more time, please, go sit in your garden and watch the dove head home. It takes the dove *time* to fly to its nest, and it must fly through *space* to get there. The formula $d = vt$ will enable you to calculate the distance the dove will travel in a given time at a certain speed.

But there's a problem. Time and space are not "things." Time is not a real something like a river or stream that a moving object can navigate, nor is space any kind of "stuff" a dove can fly through. Despite the almost universal assumption by physicists that time is real, time is an experience and only an experience, and without living experiencers with enduring consciousnesses time would not exist. So when you watch the dove fly through the evening sky in ten seconds or so, it is your experiential time that you bring to bear on the dove's movement. It is only in your conscious mind that you perceive its flying "through time." Likewise "space" is our word for the "emptiness" that we see the dove fly through, but that emptiness is entirely without content and cannot be said to be real.

All physical thinking, therefore, combines subjective elements (time and space) with objective motion to create equations that work to quantify the universe's motion and render it comprehensible. This assembling of subject and object is therefore inescapable in physical thinking, without which the human intellect could make no sense of anything that moves—which means everything in the universe.

4 One of the goals of philosophy is to pin down the location of phenomena so we can think about them precisely, and to do this we need to be able to think about things where they are and not where they are not. If we are not clear on the "location" of an event, then it becomes impossible to think about it clearly; we attribute false connections to it and misinterpret it. If we think that time is real, then we talk about the beginning of time and the end of time, which is absurd (something can have a beginning and ending only if it endures *in time*). Likewise, if we think space is real, then we can speak of the bending of space, the contraction and expansion of space, the warping of space, and so on; and this too is absurd.

The idea that time can vary from place to place is a difficult one, but it is the idea Einstein used, and it is correct—believe it or not.
RICHARD FEYNMAN

The critical distinction between what is real and what is only experiential has been entirely obliterated in physical thinking, making it virtually impossible to honor the principle that demands that we think about objects in their true contexts and not commit the error of interpreting them in terms of false functions. I once asked a physicist to tell me how physicists deal with the subject/object problem. His reply: "They just ignore it." As they must—as physicists. The very nature of physics requires the annihilation of subject/object boundaries to get the work done.

The issue is whether causality is an ultimate principle or merely a substitute for statistical regularity.
HANS REICHENBACH

The problem, therefore, lies in being able to distinguish when to allow our minds to create pragmatic "spacetime" formulas and when to think clearly about space and time as entirely distinct and separate entities. Once we begin to think that space and time are real, we are in trouble.

CLASSICAL PHYSICS

5 Physics addresses directly the concerns of the earliest pre-Socratic philosophers who asked: What are the basic elements? Is there a universal unchanging substance that underlies the various forms of matter that we perceive? What makes the elements clump together to form the macrophysical objects of sense? What exactly is motion, and what causes it? In a word, what's really going on out there, and why?

Reality as we understand it today is composed of atoms and their particle components energized by fields of force. There seem to be only four forces in the universe—electromagnetic, the strong and weak forces, and gravity—and all have been subdued by mathematics. We also understand atoms in astounding detail and can use their individual components—protons, neutrons, electrons, and so on—in a host of experiments. Most physicists would agree that every kind of motion yet discovered in the universe, large and small, can now be accounted for mathematically with one or more of the three systems of physics.

The operations of classical physics are familiar to all of us; even if we have no formal knowledge of physics, we still make use of it when we play baseball, water the lawn, or drop a brick on our toe and are reminded that we are governed by gravity. Sir Isaac Newton laid the foundations for classical physics when he wrote: "All things being considered, it seems probable to me that God in the beginning formed matter in solid, massy, hard, impenetrable, moveable particles." Newton went on to conclude that all of nature is composed of atoms and forces that are either attractive or repulsive; chemical compounds can be

THE MESSAGE FROM PLANET X

There is no absolute time throughout the universe by which absolute simultaneity can be measured. Absolute simultaneity of distant events is a meaningless concept.

How radical this notion is can be seen by a thought experiment in which vast distances and enormous speeds are involved. Suppose that someone on Planet X, in another part of our galaxy, is trying to communicate with the earth. He sends out a radio message. This is, of course, an electromagnetic wave that travels through space with the speed of light. Assume that the earth and Planet X are ten light-years apart, which means that it takes ten years for the message to travel to the earth. Twelve years before a radio astronomer on earth receives the message, the astronomer had received a Nobel Prize. The special theory permits us to say, without qualification, that he received this prize *before* the message was sent from Planet X.

Ten minutes after receiving the message, the astronomer sneezes. The special theory also permits us to say, without qualification, and for all observers in any frame of reference, that the astronomer sneezed *after* the message was sent from Planet X.

Now suppose that sometime during the ten-year period, while the radio message was on its way to the earth (say, three years before the message was received), the astronomer fell off his radio telescope and broke a leg. The special theory does *not* permit us to say without qualification that he broke his leg before or after the sending of the message from Planet X.

The reason is this. One observer, leaving Planet X at the time the message is sent and traveling to the earth with a speed judged from the earth to be slow, will find (according to his measurements of the passing of time) that the astronomer broke his leg *after* the message was sent. Of course he will arrive on earth long after the message is received, perhaps centuries after. But when he calculates the date on which the message was sent, according to his clock, it will be earlier than the date on which the astronomer broke his leg. On the other hand, another observer, who also leaves Planet X at the time the message is sent, but who travels very close to the speed of light, will find the astronomer *broke* his leg before the message was sent. Instead of taking centuries to make the trip, he will make it in, say, only a trifle more than ten years as calculated on the earth. But because of the slowing down of time on the fast-moving spaceship, it will seem to the ship's astronaut that he made the trip in only a few months. He will be told on earth that the astronomer broke his leg a little more than three years ago. According to the astronaut's clock, the message was sent a few months ago. He will conclude that the leg was broken years before the message left Planet X.

If the astronaut traveled as fast as light (of course this is purely hypothetical; not possible in fact), his clock would stop completely. It would seem to him that he made the trip in zero time. From his point of view the two events, the sending of the message and its reception, would be simultaneous. *All* events on earth during the ten-year period would appear to him to have occurred before the message was sent. Now, according to the special theory there is no "preferred" frame of reference: no reason to prefer the point of view of one observer rather than another. The calculations made by the fast-moving astronaut are just as legitimate, just as "true," as the calculations made by the slow-moving astronaut. There is no universal, absolute time that can be appealed to for settling the differences between them.

MARTIN GARDNER
The Relativity Explosion

TIME DILATION AND SPACE TRAVEL

Speed of spaceship relative to earth in terms of the speed of light (c)	Factor by which crew's time slows down compared to Earth time	Number of years of crew time required for round-trip journey to a star 100 light-years away
0.9999	70.712	2.8
0.98	5.025	40.6
0.95	3.203	65.7
0.90	2.294	96.9
0.75	1.512	176.4
0.50	1.155	346.4
0.10	1.005	1990.0

explained as combinations of these atoms. He also recognized seemingly nonmaterial processes such as light and heat. Mass and energy are conserved no matter what physical or chemical changes they undergo. The principle of cause and effect is a universal law, unbroken and nonnegotiable. Time and space exist as absolutes of nature. In summary, then, according to Newtonian principles, everything in nature can be accounted for with fundamental concepts of matter and assumed forces, causality, and the laws of conservation. The entire universe, and everything in it, obeys these laws.

RELATIVITY PHYSICS

6 Then Einstein came along with relativity physics, and the tidy principles of classical physics became blurred and indistinct. The lyrical observation of Alexander Pope (amended by Sir John Squire) is not a bad summary of the physics story:

Nature and all her Laws lay hid in Night.
God said, "Let Newton be," and all was Light.
It could not last. The Devil, shouting "Ho!
Let Einstein be," restored the *status quo*.

The search for ultimate reality, then, is a natural and necessary part of man's being. We need to realize that this kind of concern is part of what it means to be human. We also need to realize, however, that while some kind of commitment is inevitable, a final answer to this question can never be given, for man is limited, he is finite; he can never be expected to know all. In short, he is encapsulated, and for him to know the infinite is impossible by definition.

JOSEPH ROYCE

Einstein authored two relativity theories: the special theory of 1905, which deals primarily with light, and the general theory of 1916, which focuses on gravitation. There had been two competing theories of light since the seventeenth century. Newton had argued that light is composed of tiny particles of matter, while Christiaan Huyghens had insisted that light is more likely a wave-motion. By the early nineteenth century, experiments had proven that light behaves like a wave, so that, by Einstein's time, the wave theory was far ahead of the particle theory.

A wave is an undulation or oscillation that occurs in some specific substance. Seismic waves, for example, move through rock; sound waves move through air and water. Waves are real, of course, but because they are time phenomena, our apprehension of them is an activity of perception and intellect. Toss a pebble into a pond, and waves move outward over the surface of the water. It may appear to our eyes that the water moves outward, but this is an illusion. The water remains in place while the waves move up and down on its surface. When we proceed to quantify the motion of a wave (say, from crest to crest), we are measuring pure motion, not the medium (water) that carries the motion; and such measurement is a mental activity, resulting in an abstraction.

But what is the medium that light moves through? The notion had been around since Aristotle that the universe is bathed in "aether," an invisible gas-like fluid that was thought to fill all space. So ether was resurrected to serve as the medium for the propagation of light waves. This idea worked fairly well until 1887, when two physicists, Albert Michelson and Edward Morley, performed an experiment that virtually proved the nonexistence of any such medium. The results of their elegant experiment were reluctantly accepted by physicists. Even so, the problem remained.

Einstein made two initial assumptions: that Newton's absolute space doesn't exist, and that there is no such thing as ether. So, if neither absolute space nor ether exist, then, he said, let's just assume that light is a different kind of animal that doesn't require a medium to move in. Perhaps light waves are "free waves" that can oscillate all by themselves and propagate through empty space.

Then, in his 1905 relativity paper entitled "On the Electrodynamics of Moving Bodies," Einstein made two further assumptions, both intuitive on his part but encouraged by lingering contradictions in classical mechanics. First, when two or more systems are in uniform motion relative to one another, not only will the (internal) physics of each system remain normal, but it will be impossible to tell which system is in motion and which is at rest. That is, all motion is relative, and there is no way of distinguishing between two objects in motion relative to one another. For instance, if two jetliners zoom past each other each moving at six hundred miles per hour, you could, if you wished, argue that one of the planes is at rest and the second is in motion, or that the second is at rest and the first is in motion. Which you choose to say is in motion and which is at rest is entirely arbitrary; nothing in physics selects one over the other, and the equations work either way.

Einstein's second assumption was that light, when measured, will always appear to be moving at the same speed—299,792 kilometers per second—regardless of any motion of the light's source or of the person who measures the light. Light is a constant—and the only constant in the universe.

What the first assumption means is this. Both Galileo and Newton had described not just the motion of individual objects but also the motion of *systems,* and they had concluded that the laws of motion *within* systems remain the same regardless of their speed. For example, if you are in flight on a commercial jetliner traveling at six hundred miles per hour relative to the ground, all the laws of physics (as you experienced them back on the ground) will remain unchanged. As you get up from your seat to stretch your legs and walk up and down the aisle, your motions inside the plane will be just the familiar motions you knew at home. *Within the system* (called a "coordinate system"), everything is normal. And should a second jetliner (another "coordinate system") zoom past going in the opposite direction, then, if passengers on both planes were able to look over at

There is disagreement among physicists as to the philosophic implications of such relative measurements. The problem is whether these phenomena are real — that is, whether the object actually undergoes these changes — or whether the changes are merely observational phenomena.

One school of thought holds that these phenomena take place only from the standpoint of an observer in one reference system who is watching objects in another system moving at high speeds. In other words, they are observational, and the thought experiment involving the light-clock appears to imply that they are perceptual only.

In the diagram, the light-clocks are on two spaceships moving at high speeds relative to each other, speeds not far short of the speed of light. What would a passenger on each spaceship see if he could observe the light-clock on the other spacecraft?

Light-clock A, on your ship, just sits there, blinking. The top bulb sends a beam of light down to the photoelectric cell, which in turn triggers the bottom bulb, which sends a beam of light to the cell at the top; so down and up the light-beams go.

There is an identical light-clock (B) on the other spaceship. As it passes, what would you see? You would perceive a much longer beam of light than is emitted by your own clock, which (to you) is at rest. So the light-beam on the other spaceship travels farther **in the same period of time** as your light-beam. This could have two explanations: either the light of the other light-clock is moving faster or time has slowed down. The former is impossible, according to relativity, since the speed of light is a constant; it always travels at 186,000 miles per second. Therefore, what you are witnessing is a slower movement of time on the other spaceship compared with the movement of time according to your clock.

But ask: What would the passengers on the other spaceship see as they watch your clock pass by? They would see precisely what you see, only reversed. To you, **his** time has slowed down; to him, **your** time has slowed down.

This sort of thought experiment seems to indicate that the whole matter of relativity is merely perceptual. Einstein's equations describe nothing more than

Perhaps the most majestic feature of our whole existence is that while our intelligences are powerful enough to penetrate deeply into the evolution of this quite incredible Universe, we still have not the smallest clue to our own fate.

SIR FRED HOYLE

one another, the two systems would appear normal to all observers. In other words, just one set of physical laws is sufficient to describe all motions in the universe, whether individual or in systems, even when those motions are occurring at great speeds relative to one another.

Einstein agreed that these descriptions are accurate as long as they are restricted to objects moving at relatively modest speeds. But when great speeds are involved, these equations no longer work. What actually happens is that a passenger in one of the jetliners will peer over at the passengers in the other jetliner and literally see a different set of physical laws in operation. She would see that time has slowed down, mass has increased, and the length of everything (parallel to the line of flight) has shrunk and flattened.

These two assumptions are the foundation stones of the special theory of relativity. With rigorous mathematics, Einstein proceeded to build upon them a new physics that is logically coherent and (relatively) faithful to empirical fact.

7 Several bizarre consequences follow from Einstein's relativistic equations. First, the addition and subtraction of velocities, an important principle in New-

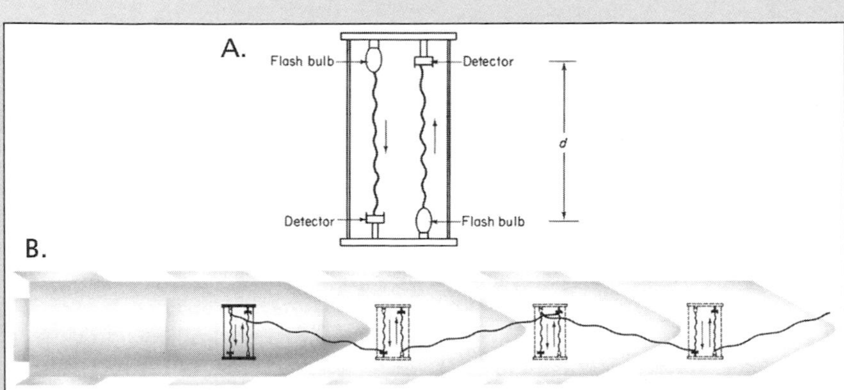

Light-clocks redrawn from David S. Saxon and William B. Fretter, *Physics for the Liberal Arts Student.*

the way we would measure things that move very fast relative to our point of observation.

But other physicists are not so sure. Some are convinced that such phenomena are not perceptual, but real, that they really happen to objects. It would seem that the increase in particle mass in the accelerators and the slowdown of decay time in the disintegration of pions is not merely a matter of measurement, but is an event that the particle actually undergoes. If this is not the case, then why the adjustments that are necessary in the magnetic fields?

The same dilemma applies to time. Saxon and Fretter candidly write that to understand relativistic phenomena, "we must realize that time dilation is a property of time itself, not of any particular clock."

At present the puzzle does not appear to be solvable.

tonian mechanics, was no longer possible. For example, if your pilot announced over the public address system that you were flying at 600 miles per hour ("ground speed") but that the plane was bucking a headwind of 50 miles per hour, then you could with assurance subtract 50 from 600 and conclude that you were actually flying at only 550 miles per hour.

But at very high speeds this simple calculation will no longer work, for time will have ceased to be a valid measuring stick. Time itself has turned out to be variable. Time ("clock time," or time as observed and measured) is "elastic" and can contract (but not expand) to different degrees, depending on the relative speed of an object in relation to an observer. Any clock that reaches a speed of 161,000 miles per second relative to an observer would be judged to have slowed down to half its normal speed.

Second, this notion of an "elastic time" annihilates the idea of "simultaneity." In relativity every individual and every system has its own private clock. At low velocities all clocks will appear synchronized, but at high speeds they will register different times. And clocks can alter their rhythms while they are in motion. This is a true relativity in which logical coherence, congruence, and

Hitherto people have looked upon the Principle of Causality as a proposition which would in the course of years admit of experimental proof with an ever-increasing exactitude.

Now Heisenberg has discovered a flaw in the proposition. . . . The principle of causality loses its significance as an empirical proposition.

Causality is thus only conceivable as a Form *of the theoretical system.*

ALBERT EINSTEIN

Zeno (c. 450 BC)

Zeno's Paradoxes

For almost 2500 years philosophers and mathematicians have had fun with—and suffered sheer anguish from—the logical paradoxes of a philosopher named Zeno. About 450 BC Zeno made a trip to Athens from his home town of Elea in Italy and presented a series of paradoxes to a gathering of eminent thinkers. Socrates was in the audience and engaged him in a discussion of some of his arguments. Zeno's aim was to show that some of our common assumptions about motion, space, and time appear to lead us into contradictions.

His most famous argument is the story of a handicap race between Achilles and a tortoise. If the tortoise begins the race some distance ahead of Achilles, then by the time Achilles reaches the point where the tortoise *was*, the tortoise, however pokey, will have moved ahead a ways. Again, when Achilles reaches the point where the tortoise *was*, the tortoise will still be ahead, though the distance between them is forever closing. Therefore Achilles can never overtake the tortoise.

Zeno argued that motion is an illusion: If an object moves, then it must move either in the place where it is or in some place where it is not. But obviously it cannot move where it is not; it should be equally obvious that it cannot move where it is. Therefore, concludes Zeno, it cannot move, and motion does not exist.

Another of his paradoxes has to do with space. If space **is**, it will be **in** something; for everything that **is** is in something; and to be in something is to be in space. Space then will be in space, which will be in another space, and so on ad infinitum. Therefore space does not exist.

(Stephen Hawking, the Cambridge cosmologist, posed a similar paradox when he entitled his best-selling book *A Brief History of Time.* By definition the word "history" refers to something that has endured for some period in time. This implies that time has endured in time, which has endured in time, which has endured in time, and so on. Which is the point Zeno was making: Time, therefore, is not real.)

simultaneity are no longer workable concepts. Every temporal perspective is true, or more properly, the judgment that a time experience is "true" or "false" is inapplicable. In special relativity, one's perspective is one's perspective, and that's an end to the matter.

A third inference is that the speed of light in a vacuum (symbolized as c) is a universal speed limit: nothing can move faster than light. Newtonian theory had held that quantities of anything can be increased indefinitely, but Einstein's equations set severe limits to increases in speed, mass, and volume. As an object approaches the speed of light, its mass will sharply increase, and at c its mass will become infinite—which is impossible. Therefore, nothing but light can move at the speed of light, and nothing in the universe can move faster than light.

8 In his last paper of 1905, Einstein wrote, "The mass of a body is a measure of its energy." He was saying that the assumptions of special relativity imply that mass and energy are not two things but one. They are equivalent. Mass can be changed into energy, and energy into mass. Energy is not a weightless something; it has mass. Mass is "crystallized" energy, and energy is "liberated" mass. The conversion of mass into energy can be precisely calculated with the for-

Another of Zeno's paradoxes involves the racetrack: A runner cannot reach the end of the raceway until he has reached the halfway mark; but he can't reach the halfway mark until he has first reached halfway to the halfway mark (the "quarterway" mark), and so on, ad infinitum. Conclusion: the runner can never even begin the race, and motion is therefore an illusion.

A similar point is made in Zeno's famous paradox of the arrow: At any instant, an arrow in flight occupies a space equal to itself, and therefore is at rest. This holds true of the arrow at any instant of its alleged flight through the air. At every instant it is at rest, and you can't derive motion from a series of rest stops, no matter how many. Therefore the arrow cannot move, and motion doesn't exist.

We may intuit or **feel** that Zeno's arguments are wrong; but achieving intellectual clarity as to where and why they are wrong may require some time. Is Zeno right, for instance, when he argues that everything that exists "exists in something"? For something to exist, does it have to exist in space? (What about ideas, pain, love, and dreams? They exist, don't they? Of course they do. But where? Answer: In my (spaceless) experience.) Moreover, what is space? Is space real? Isn't space nothing other than my mind's concept for the volume of nothingness between real objects? And what of the arrow? We know full well from experience that arrows fly through the air all the time and hit or miss their targets.

So Zeno must be setting a mind-trap or playing a word-game (and he is!); but we must persist with intellect until we see clearly what the trap is and to understand the word-game.

Zeno was one of the truly great Greek minds. He invented arguments, notes Bertrand Russell, "all immeasurably subtle and profound, to prove that motion is impossible. . . . From him to our own day, the finest intellects of each generation in turn attacked the problems, but achieved, broadly speaking, nothing." Although Zeno's paradoxes have now been solved mathematically and logically, they remain so intriguing that new volumes about them appear almost annually.

mula $E = mc^2$. Measured in ergs (a unit of energy), the energy stored in one gram of mass equals the speed of light times the speed of light, and the resulting number is mind-boggling. Thus a very small amount of mass can be converted into an enormous amount of energy. The result of this simple formula is the atomic bomb—and the Atomic Age. As far as the world is concerned, the bombs detonated over Hiroshima and Nagasaki were proof enough that Relativistic equations work.

9 In 1908 the mathematician Hermann Minkowski—whom Einstein called "my very great teacher in Zürich"—praised the special theory in an address before a meeting of scientists: "Gentlemen!" he said, "from now on, space in itself and time in itself should descend into a shadow and only a union of both should retain its independence." It was Minkowski, therefore, who performed a marriage of convenience that bound time and space together into a single concept called "space-time" (increasingly written as "spacetime"). Einstein adopted this fused entity and made it a cornerstone of his general theory.

The objective world simply is, it does not happen. Only to the gaze of consciousness, crawling upward along the life-line of my body, does a section of this world come to life as a fleeting image in space which continuously changes in time.

HERMANN WEYL

The general theory rests on the "equivalence principle," an idea that Einstein later dubbed "the happiest thought in my life." The principle states that the attraction produced by a massive body in a gravitational field is identical to

acceleration produced in a nongravitational coordinate system. We all know what gravity feels like; it plants us firmly on the ground and lets us know that every massive object will try to move or fall downward, given the chance. Einstein had become convinced that the *experience* of acceleration in outer space would be identical to the *experience* of this "pull" of gravity. An astronaut returning to Earth from a trip to the Moon will be shoved back in her seat when the thruster rockets are burned to achieve a course correction; and everything else in the module that isn't bolted down will also move to the rear of the spacecraft. So familiar will this acceleration be that, if her craft has no windows so she can look out and orient herself, she won't be able to tell the difference between her acceleration experience and the experience of gravitation back on Earth. What elated Einstein was that he believed that both situations could be described with the same equations. Acceleration and gravitation are mathematically "equivalent."

10 Einstein spent years developing the implications of the equivalence principle, all of which pushed the limits of the envelope. First, imagine a beam of light moving from one side of an accelerating spacecraft to the other. As the spacecraft reaches extreme velocities, the beam of light, as it moves across the craft in a finite amount of time, will be deflected downward and strike the opposite wall at a point lower than it would have without acceleration; for between the time the light leaves one wall and reaches the other, the craft will have moved forward, bending the light. Therefore, because acceleration bends light and because acceleration and gravitation are "equivalent," Einstein reasoned that gravitation too should bend light.

In the inescapable flux, there is something that abides; in the overwhelming permanence, there is an element that escapes into flux.
Alfred North Whitehead

And there the idea rested, without support from observation or experiment, until 1919, when two English expeditions were dispatched to Brazil and the African island of Principe to observe a solar eclipse. The hope was to find out if starlight would be bent as it passed close by the Sun's massive body; only during an eclipse could light from distant stars be seen. Measurements confirmed Einstein's calculations. Today this phenomenon is observed almost daily—or nightly—and is called "lensing"; light from distant quasars, for example, is bent by great galactic lenses that lie between us and the light sources.

From the equivalence principle, Einstein made other inferences, among them that clocks would be seen to run at different rates in different gravitational fields, and that light radiating from a massive body like the Sun or a star would lose some of its energy. Confirmation of both would have to wait for the development of more sophisticated technologies.

Does the harmony which human intelligence thinks it discovers in Nature exist apart from such intelligence? Assuredly no. A reality completely independent of the spirit that conceives it, sees it or feels it, is an impossibility. A world so external as that, even if it existed, would be forever inaccessible to us. What we call "objective reality" is, strictly speaking, that which is common to several thinking beings and might be common to all; this common part . . . can only be the harmony expressed by mathematical laws.

JULES HENRI POINCARÉ

11 But what exactly is gravity? Why do massive objects in a gravitational field behave as they do? This was the basic question; other questions were derivative. Newton's mechanics had concluded that gravity is a mysterious force that operates instantaneously over vast distances; but Einstein's special theory had proved that "instantaneity" is impossible because nothing can move faster than light.

So, to answer these questions, Einstein abandoned classical physics altogether and created a new system of thought. Gravity, he theorized, is not a force exercising a long-distance pull over massive objects. Gravity is shaped space. (Space apparently is not nothing; it is something.) It can be curved, warped, buckled, and bent, like an elastic rubber sheet; and massive objects like the Moon, the Sun, and the planets roll around on that rubber sheet, interacting as they swing past one another in their orbits. This theory allowed Einstein, in treating gravity, to focus entirely on motion rather than force.

Gravity, therefore, is a distortion of space itself that occurs in the presence of massive objects. As the cosmologist John Wheeler has put it, matter tells space how to curve, and curved space tells matter how to move. The Sun, for example, shapes the space around it in such a way that the planets must follow the geometry of bent space. At great distances from the gravity source, space is flat and clock time moves normally; but close-in to the massive source of gravity, space becomes increasingly curved, clocks slow down, and light rays are bent as they curve around the massive object that is bending the space. In the presence of gravity, time and space would be affected just as they would be at accelerated velocities.

To describe this cosmic behavior required not only extremely complex mathematics but also a new geometry, and Einstein spent years studying Riemannian (non-Euclidian) geometry to be able to describe general relativity and integrate it into special relativity.

QUANTUM MECHANICS

12 With the advent of quantum physics, our understanding of the physical world became even more blurred and indistinct. The beginning of quantum physics dates from December 14, 1900, when Max Planck read a paper to the German

Physical Society in Berlin. In it he assumed that radiation such as light is composed of discrete packets of energy that he called quanta, and he presented a mathematical formula describing their behavior. Energy had previously been thought of as continuous (wavelike); Planck reinterpreted it to be discontinuous (particle-like).

But these quanta, it was later found, have a dual nature—they are both discrete particle and continuous wave. These wave-particles ("wavicles") are so elusive that their location and speed cannot be pinned down at the same time; they can be apprehended only in terms of probabilities.

Today almost all the fundamental concepts so familiar from daily life—concepts such as cause and effect, matter, energy, and even "reality"—have been upset by quantum physics. Physics has simply revealed that, at the microphysical level, nature follows a different set of rules that seem strange and arbitrary. Scientists and philosophers have been sent back to rethink both the real and the nature of our knowledge of the real.

13 The history of quantum physics is largely the story of attempts to figure out the structure of the atom—what it's composed of and how it works. If we remind ourselves how small an atom is—the diameter of a typical atom is a hundred millionth of a centimeter, a typical nucleus one ten-trillionth of a centimeter—then scientific progress in the microphysical domain since 1900 is nothing less than miraculous.

It was Ernest Rutherford who proved that the atom is not the smallest unit of matter. He demonstrated that an atom is mostly empty space containing a very tiny, positively charged nucleus of massive protons surrounded by a negatively charged orbiting cloud of lightweight electrons. Then Rutherford's student Niels Bohr suggested that orbiting electrons could jump from one orbit to another. With each jump, an electron would either give up a discrete amount (a "quantum") of energy in the form of a photon, or absorb energy in discrete quanta if it was struck with a photon. Bohr went on to theorize that in an atom containing multiple electrons its electrons must exist in "shells," and the electrons in the outermost shell determine the chemical properties of each element.

Rutherford and Bohr's models destroyed once and for all the Democritean notion that an atom is a solid little hard billiard ball. Atoms possess structure, and as the twentieth century progressed, that structure appeared increasingly complex.

14 In 1925 Werner Heisenberg published his famous "Uncertainty Principle," which held that atomic particles can never be completely defined, for the more their motion is pinned down, the more uncertain their position becomes. What this means, before mystification, is that, at the microparticle level our observations disturb the objects that we are trying to observe so that we can never see the objects in their pristine state. When trying to assess accurately what is observed, therefore, the observer's existence must be taken into account; he or she becomes part of the equation. Whether this uncertainty is merely an artifact of observation, or whether it is in some sense built into reality itself—this question, with its weighty implications, instantly became a topic of vehement debate.

It was weighty for two reasons. First, because if this condition of uncertainty is an aspect of nature itself (an important "if"), then the principle of causality as a universal unbreakable "law of nature" collapses and must be replaced by an uncomfortable probabilism that no one wants or knows how to handle. Because the principle has so often been interpreted to mean that nature is not deterministic, it has severely altered scientific thinking and went far to create a view of the world as capricious and unpredictable, without order or meaning.

The second weighty implication is that the human mind can never precisely know reality. That the human intellect can progressively come to understand the real world has been a precious axiom of faith that can be traced as far back as Pythagoras and Plato. To find now that this dream is unfounded would be a blow to human self-confidence.

15 Since Rutherford first demonstrated that the atom has internal structure, more than two hundred particles have been found, and each particle has its own role to play in the atomic system. All the physical matter in the universe is composed of protons, neutrons, and electrons; and these in turn seem to be built up of six relatively heavy pointlike objects called quarks and six lightweight particles called leptons, operating in four fundamental kinds of force fields.

If we think of physical reality as an onion, physicists have penetrated through layer after layer into what they thought was the onion's center, only to find that there was still another layer underneath. Many physicists believe that quarks and leptons may be truly elementary. Nevertheless they persist undaunted in their attempt to peel off another layer of the onion.

16 A striking fact about quantum mechanics is that many of its creators wanted to disown it. Planck was always unhappy with the quantum way of looking at things. Schrödinger remarked, "I don't like it, and I'm sorry I ever had anything to do with it." Einstein found it repugnant: "An inner voice tells me that it is not yet the real thing." He once remarked that quantum speculation struck him as a "system of delusions of an exceedingly intelligent paranoic." "No reasonable definition of reality could be expected to permit this," he grumbled of the whole quantum affair.

"The problems of language here are really serious," complained Heisenberg the mathematician. "All the words or concepts we use to describe ordinary physical objects, such as position, velocity, color, size, and so on, become indefinite and problematic if we try to use them of elementary particles."

17 Strangeness characterizes everything about quantum physics. Just a brief listing of the more puzzling phenomena will indicate the depth of physicists' annoyance at quantum behavior. Regarding the wave-particle duality, the question persists: Is nature essentially particulate or wavelike? Should our most fundamental picture of nature be deterministic or probabilistic, particulate or fieldlike? The jury is still out. At the purely pragmatic level, this duality no longer presents a problem; physicists work with equations that apply to both phenomena at the same time. The problem is one of understanding how both phenomena can be real, or more accurately, of discovering what kind of animal would present itself to observers as two distinctly different phenomena rather than one. In the famous double-slit experiment, photons and other particles begin their journey as particles and end up as waves, and when the experimenter tries to figure out where, when, and how this sex-change occurs, he finds that the mere act of inquiring determines what the answer will be. Nature can't be in conflict

with itself, so the problem must lie in the human intellect, which doesn't yet have sufficient information to sort out what's really going on.

18 There are many other strange events embedded in quantum theory:

- Strict causality is thrown to the winds: causal event *A* may be followed by effect *B*, or it may not; an event may or may not be established as either cause or effect.
- Particles can affect one another from a distance even when no force or connection exists between them ("spooky action at a distance" was Einstein's description of it, and he fairly rejected the notion).
- A quantum particle may be in two places at once, or (by some interpretations) it can occupy two different places in time (at the same time!). (Obviously, quantum theory strains at definitions.)
- A particle's environment often determines its characteristics; in fact it is considered "not quite real" except in relation to its context. Abstracted from this idea is the larger philosophical notion that everything in the universe is related to, and gets its characteristics from, everything else.
- The concept of a detached observer vanishes in quantum physics; in theory the physicist is in dialogue with reality, together working out the way that quantum reality will reveal itself; the observer changes reality in the act of observing it.
- In some experiments (but depending on interpretations), particles from past and future seem to collide in the present and produce interference patterns.
- Reality becomes a fuzzy concept; it is often conceived to be both/and rather than either/or. For example, cats (per Schrödinger) can at the same time be both alive and dead (or neither) until observed.
- To some quantum field theorists there is no such thing as empty space. Underlying all existence is the "quantum vacuum," an unseen, immeasurable ground state thought of as a "sea of potential." Space may seem empty to the rest of us, but to a quantum physicist it is filled with potentiality, and all the objects in the universe are merely patterns of energy emerging out of this vacuum.
- Existence is evanescent; particles are considered to be not permanent objects but only fleeting manifestations of energy created out of the quantum vacuum; these transitory particles appear at random and disappear back into the vacuum.

Quantum strangeness is thus found at all levels of experiment and theory. Though it continues to challenge the brainpower of both physicists and philosophers, a kind of pragmatism has settled over the physics community. As long as the equations "work," further questions are not seriously pursued.

Still, the deepest problems persist and lie in the realm of intellect and understanding. Bohr went so far as to argue that the human mind can't comprehend the quantum world and therefore shouldn't try to. Physicists, he said, are just wasting their time worrying about resolving irresolvable contradictions. But in the eyes of most physicists this was going too far. Schrödinger accused Bohr of trying "to complement away all difficulties" by refusing to discuss them.

19 How is all this to be interpreted? What *is* real? For starters, note the depth of the problem. Heisenberg: "In light of quantum theory . . . elementary par-

ticles are no longer real in the same sense as objects of daily life, trees or stones." Bohr: "An independent reality can neither be ascribed to the phenomena or the agencies of observation." The most extreme interpretation, as always, comes from John Wheeler: "Nothing is more important about quantum physics than this: it has destroyed the concept of the world as 'sitting out there.'"

One frequent answer is that the word "real" should be reserved for what the observer sees, and if different observers see different things, then each person must resign himself to living with his own perceptions, since all perceptions are said to be equally "correct." This problem was exacerbated by Einstein when he showed that the hallowed space-time coordinate system of classical physics has no objective significance but serves only as an "elastic" framework for describing one's relative perspective on a fast-moving world.

With this, the observer became, for the first time ever, an inextricable part of what is observed. An observer sees what he sees, and what he sees may not be at all what is really out there. In other words, the real is essentially off-limits to human investigation, and we are justified in using the word "real" to refer to our subjective perceptions—a point of view that is hardly new, going back at least to the Greek skeptics and recurring with each full moon during the next two millennia.

The standard working interpretation—called the Copenhagen interpretation because it was Bohr who first developed it—holds that a quantum object has no real physical existence until it is measured, "real physical existence" being defined in terms of locatability. The properties that it *will* have can be described with probability statistics, but only when the particle is measured does it suddenly have definite space-time coordinates.

More extreme interpretations, derived from experiments like the double-slit experiment, suggest that "reality" is in some way determined by, even created by, consciousness. This may mean only that distinct qualities can never be determined until observed, or it may mean that nothing possesses distinct qualities until observed, or it may mean that nothing exists until observed. In all these interpretations, the observer is not merely a passive observer but a powerful player in determining the fundamental nature of reality.

After relativity and quantum physics, it is more than just beauty that is in the eye of the beholder.

✦

ALBERT EINSTEIN

The Second Scientific Revolution

The historian Adolph Harnack once declared, "People complain that our generation has no philosophers. Quite unjustly: it is merely that today's philosophers sit in another department, their names are Planck and Einstein."

Albert Einstein was and still is a baffling phenomenon. Biographers have tried in vain to explain how one man could accomplish so much in so short a time—in less than a year, 1905, often called Einstein's "*annus mirabilis,*" his "wonder year." At that time he was a twenty-six-year-old just-married clerk working in a Swiss patent office. He possessed no academic credentials or laboratory and was totally unknown to the scientific community. Writing in his spare time—*spare time!*—he produced five brief treatises and submitted them to the monthly journal *Annalen der Physik* in Berlin.

These five papers shook the world. In the first paper Einstein established new principles for determining the size of molecules. In the second paper he worked out the mathematics of Brownian motion, the jiggly movements of molecules that had puzzled scientists for seventy-five years. His third paper explained the photoelectric effect by postulating that light is composed of discrete packets of energy that behave as both waves and particles; for this he received the Nobel Prize. The fourth paper dealt with the special theory of relativity; in it he revised our fundamental notions of time and space by showing that light is a constant and that all measurements of time, mass, and motion are relative to the observer. The fifth and last paper stated that mass and energy are equivalent and that any particle of matter can be converted into an enormous quantity of pure energy. This idea is symbolized by the formula $E = mc^2$, and with it the Atomic Age was born.

Subsequent work on Einstein's theories gradually revealed that he had given us a bizarre *Through the Looking Glass* world that we could never have imagined, a universe that contains a fourth dimension, in which time (or our measurement of time) speeds up and slows down, where simultaneity is a nonconcept (one person's now is another person's then), where time travel (into the future, but no return) is actually possible, where accelerated objects appear to shorten or elongate; a universe that shrinks and expands like a balloon; a crazy world in which your plane doesn't land at the airport but where the airport lands at your plane.

✦

Einstein's childhood was rather ordinary. He was born in 1879 near Ulm in southwestern Germany. His father, Hermann Einstein, and mother, Pauline Koch, both spoke a soft Swabian dialect, which became Einstein's native vernacular. Hermann set up an electrical and engineering workshop, but the business failed within the year and the family moved to Munich. There the business prospered for a time, and the Einsteins were able to move into a suburban home with trees and a garden. Hermann was a hefty, happy-go-lucky man, a hard worker who enjoyed his family and spent quality time with them on outings in the countryside where he could stop at taverns to buy beer and munch on radishes and sausages.

Einstein's education began with his attending a Catholic elementary school near his home. His habit of pausing to think through questions before responding to them was interpreted by his teachers and family as a sign that he might be retarded; he was also slow in learning to speak, and his teachers judged his prospects to be unpromising. Hermann once consulted the school's principal about a possible profession for Albert. "It doesn't matter," the headmaster told the father. "He'll never make a success of anything."

Einstein attended the Catholic school for five years, then transferred to Munich's Luitpold Gymnasium when he was ten. For six years he studied Latin and Greek, history, geography, and beginning mathematics. He also found that an educational system is worse than useless when run by drill sergeants who demand rote regurgitation and punish originality. "Such treatment destroys the healthy feelings, the integrity, and self-confidence of the pupils." He left Luitpold without getting his diploma, expelled (apparently) because, as an extant notice reads, "your presence in the class is disruptive and affects the other students."

In the autumn of 1895 (at age sixteen), he sought admission to the Swiss Polytechnic Institute in Zürich. He loved the sciences and had science teachers who could inspire him, though his physics professor finally became impatient with his aloofness and suggested that he study medicine, law, or perhaps philology —anything, so long as he gave up physics: "You're a smart young man, Einstein. But you have one fault," he was told; "one can't tell you anything." Nevertheless, Einstein studied hard and devoured vast amounts of scientific material.

In June 1902 he was hired by the Patent Office in Bern and worked there for seven years. He could walk to work each morning from his one-room apartment, eat a brown-bag lunch at his desk, get his work done, and still have up to eight hours daily to think about physics. He had also begun to think about a pretty dark-haired fellow student named Mileva Marić, who had come from Zagreb to study physics. They lived near one another in the same boarding house, studied together, developed a friendship, and became lovers. They were married in January 1903. In time two sons, Hans Albert and Eduard, were born to them.

Einstein left the patent office in 1909 and turned to teaching, first at the University of Zürich and then at the University of Prague. In the spring of 1914 he accepted a professorship in physics at the University of Berlin. During the war, he remained holed up in Berlin and worked intensely on the physics of gravitation. In 1916 he published a paper entitled "The Foundation of the General Theory of Relativity." In it he literally destroyed the Newtonian notion that gravity is an attractive force by arguing that gravitation results from a distortion of space-time created by massive objects. He specified ways that his predictions could be verified, and in 1919 the Royal Society of London announced that it had been able to confirm his theories during a solar eclipse. With this confirmation he became world-famous almost overnight, a fact he accepted with genial stoicism as long as it didn't interfere with his work.

On Einstein:
Einstein's theory of relativity is probably the greatest synthetic achievement of the human intellect up to the present time.

BERTRAND RUSSELL

Madame Curie never heard the birds sing.

For the rest of my life I want to reflect on what light is.

There is such a thing as a passionate desire to understand, just as there is a passionate love for music. This passion is common with children, but it usually vanishes as they grow up.

Whoever is careless with the truth in small matters cannot be trusted with important matters.

Nationalism is an infantile disease. It is the measles of mankind.

Out yonder there was this huge world . . . which stands before us like a great eternal riddle.

The world we have made as a result of the level of thinking we have done thus far creates problems we cannot solve at the same level at which we created them.

Politics are for the moment. An equation is for eternity.

Insofar as mathematics is about reality, it is not certain; and insofar as it is certain, it is not about reality.

Reality is the real business of physics.

The whole of science is nothing more than a refinement of everyday thinking.

The most beautiful thing we can experience is the mysterious. It is the source of all art and science.

The true value of a human being is determined by the measure and the sense in which he has attained liberation from the self.

Only a life lived for others is a life worthwhile.

The Lord God is subtle, but malicious he is not.

I cannot imagine a God who rewards and punishes the objects of his creation, whose purposes are moulded after our own—a God, in short, who is but a reflection of human frailty.

Never do anything against conscience even if the state demands it.

Whoever undertakes to set himself up as a judge of Truth and Knowledge is shipwrecked by the laughter of the gods.

The unleashed power of the atom has changed everything save our modes of thinking.

His relationship to Mileva had begun to deteriorate; after the war Mileva returned to Zürich and remained there for the rest of her life. The two were formally divorced in 1919. In the summer of 1919 Einstein was married to his cousin Elsa Einstein, whom he had known since childhood. A friend wrote that "their marriage, when it took place, seemed the most obvious thing in the world to both of them." They lived quietly in Berlin with her two daughters by a previous marriage.

During these years he traveled widely, lecturing on his physical theories. He would typically arrive in some city by train (third class) with his violin under his arm. The Einsteins were in California in 1933 when Hitler rose to power. On the trip home to Berlin, Einstein was informed that the Nazi police had ransacked his summer cottage and confiscated his sailboat. When they landed in Belgium, he proceeded to the German embassy and renounced his citizenship. They settled briefly in Belgium, then sailed to England and back to the United States. Princeton, New Jersey, became their new home, and Einstein worked at the Institute for Advanced Study for the rest of his life. There he walked a mile each morning to his office, where he worked on the unified field theory; he played his violin and sailed a small sailboat on a nearby lake. He became an American citizen in 1941 but confessed that he still felt like a European.

But his ordeal had wrought a profound change. A friend wrote: "It was as if something had deadened in him. He sat in a chair at our place, twisting his white hair in his fingers and talking dreamily about everything under the sun. He was not laughing any more."

When Elsa died in 1936, he was again alone. He lived "like a bear in his cave," he said, and immersed himself in his work. His friend Leopold Infeld commented that "it seemed that the difference between life and death for Einstein consisted only in the difference between being able and not being able to do physics."

Despite a notoriety that took a toll on his time, he continued to work toward a theory that would harmonize the physics of electromagnetism with the physics of gravitation, that is, a theory that would unify new discoveries in the domains of the very large and the very small.

Life on Mercer Street in Princeton was good. Days were spent at the institute; evenings were passed with friends or in playing the piano or reading. With him was his longtime secretary, a stepdaughter named Margot, and his sister Maja. At last his health deteriorated; he developed an aneurysm. Chronic pain forced him to give up sailing his boat, smoking his pipe, and even playing his violin. He died quietly in his sleep at Princeton Hospital on April 18, 1955.

✦

Although what he thought about most of the time was physics, he was also, by default, a philosopher. "I am more a philosopher than a physicist," he once said. But he was not one of the philosophers of the traditional kind, whom he despised, for they use long words trying to express the inexpressible. He was a truth-seeking and wisdom-seeking kind of philosopher whose singular passion was to understand the world. "I am not interested in this or that phenomenon," he once remarked, "or in the spectrum of this or that element. I want to know His thoughts, the rest are details."

Einstein was always mystified by the simplicity and beauty of mathematical constructions; he stood in awe of Maxwell's field equations and even of his own physical theories. His friend Philipp Frank put it thus: "Einstein's cosmic religion has been the belief in the possibility of a symbolic system of great beauty and conceptual simplicity from which the observed facts can be logically derived. Whatever his system may look like and whatever symbols may be used does not matter."

Note carefully the words "symbolic system." Einstein's goal—in fact, the goal of all science—was to understand exactly how the human mind can discover what is really going on out there. "It is existence and reality that one wishes to comprehend," Einstein said. This is the age-old question all over again: Can the subjective mind know the objectively real? And if so, exactly how? It was critically important to Einstein that he come to a clear understanding of this problem that lay at the heart of his work.

The answer to this question is disturbing. We must first remember that Einstein was a thoroughgoing empiricist. "All knowledge of reality starts from experience and ends in it," he said. "Propositions arrived at by purely logical means are completely empty as regards reality." Pure logical thinking, without first garnering information from the senses, tells us nothing about the real world.

But once empirical patterns have been established by observation, the mind can capture and symbolize those patterns with mathematics. Mathematical symbols remove phenomena from the realm of sense perception and convert them into precise abstract equations, and Einstein believed that as long as mathematical formulations remain constant, they can be accepted not just as valid but also as objectively true.

> I am convinced that we can discover by means of purely mathematical constructions the concepts and the laws connecting them with each other, which furnish the key to the understanding of natural phenomena. . . . Experience remains, of course, the sole criterion of the physical utility of a mathematical construction. But the creative principle resides in mathematics. In a certain sense, therefore, I hold it true that pure thought can grasp reality, as the ancients dreamed.

Thus it was Einstein's belief that only through mathematics can the structure of the world be apprehended. But mathematics are not real; they do not "belong to the world"; they are concepts residing in, and created by, the human mind. *Mathematics are symbols.* Therefore it is by means of symbols, and only symbols, that the dynamic truth of the real world can be apprehended by the human intellect. When scientists "look" at reality, they're not looking at the world but only at symbols. As Niels Bohr put it, science is "a *purely symbolic procedure.*" Mathematical symbols "will *never* describe nature itself," said Sir James Jeans. "Our studies can never put us into contact with reality." Sir Arthur Eddington declared, "We have learnt that the exploration of the external world by the methods of physical science leads not to a concrete reality but to a *shadow world of symbols,* beneath which those methods are unadapted for penetrating."

Einstein was not happy with this outcome. It irritates the rational spirit; it is humiliating to find that we must deal with the world over great symbolic distances. Einstein longed to know the truth about the world, the ultimate and final truth, *His* Truth. But virtually everyone, scientist and layman alike, has given up on trying to grasp the deeper meaning of physical phenomena. Physicists can justly rejoice when they succeed in creating a mathematical formula that works. But Einstein was neither the first nor the last to feel that there must be more to the "reality" story than abstract equations.

✦

What I seek to accomplish is simply to serve with my feeble capacity truth and justice at the risk of pleasing no one.

Science without epistemology is . . . primitive and muddled.

Most of the fundamental ideas of science are essentially simple, and may, as a rule, be expressed in a language comprehensible to everyone.

The discovery of the nuclear chain reaction need not bring about the destruction of mankind any more than did the discovery of matches.

Science is the attempt to make the chaotic diversity of our sense-experience correspond to a logically uniform system of thought.

Quantum mechanics is very impressive. But . . . I am at all events convinced that He [God] does not play dice.

Reflections

1 On p. 500 you find the statement "We never see motion." Do you understand what is being said? Do you agree or disagree? Why?

2 The next time you're doing 70 miles per hour on the freeway and dozens of cars are moving along with you (or ahead of you), do physics in your mind by separating the objects from their motions. Does this exercise give you insight into thinking about everything else in the universe that is in motion?

3 Describe as precisely as you can the role of time in the creation of physical formulas.
4 What arguments can you think of both *for* the reality of time and *against* the reality of time?
5 The same for space: Can you think of any arguments for the reality of space? Does the definition of "space" on p. 501 make sense to you? Can you think of a better definition?
6 On p. 502 you find the sentence: "The critical distinction between what is real and what is only experiential has been entirely obliterated. . . ." Explain in your own words what that obliteration means and why it is inevitable.
7 If you had been a scientist named Einstein living around 1904, would you have made the two assumptions that he made about space and ether? Why or why not?
8 What is meant by calling Einstein's universe an "elastic universe"? (§7) How can time be variable? Or is this merely a mathematician's pragmatic pipe dream? Can you understand why, according to some relativity physicists, simultaneity is not a valid concept?
9 State what Einstein meant by "the equivalence principle" (§9). Does this formula strike you as a mathematical convenience or as a description of reality?
10 Quantum physics seems to suggest (§12) that at the microphysical level of reality nature follows a different set of rules. How can that be? What do you think of the statement that nature seems "strange and arbitrary"?
11 What exactly was Heisenberg trying to say with his famous uncertainty principle? Does it have philosophic implications?
12 Quantum strangeness (§13) excites physicists while at the same time puzzling them, annoying them, and giving them headaches. As you read through the list of weird events, would you like to be a quantum physicist? Could you become creatively challenged by such strange behavior?
13 After reading through this chapter, formulate some sort of answer to the age-old query about the nature of reality. Find some adjectives that would characterize it.
14 In what sense was Einstein a philosopher? Did his scientific thinking differ from his philosophic thinking? Is so, how?
15 "It is existence and reality that one wishes to comprehend," said Einstein (pp. 518–519). What was Einstein's conclusion as to whether the mind can know reality? How can it know it? What aspects of the real can the human mind apprehend? What can it *not* understand?
16 Einstein finally concluded that it is only through mathematics that the world can be apprehended (p. 519). Do you think he was right?
17 See the marginal quotation on p. 518: "Never do anything against conscience even if the state demands it." Can you understand how Einstein's experience in Germany would have led him to this ethical conviction? Do you share it?
18 Ponder Zeno's argument that space doesn't exist. Could he be right? If space does exist, does that make his argument wrong? If space doesn't exist, does that make his argument right?

COSMOS

7-3

This chapter deals with cosmology, the study of the universe as a whole. The great religious traditions all include a cosmological model of the universe. All are mythical and illustrate the human need to know where we fit into the overall scheme of things. Today's cosmologists draw on information collected from New Technology Telescopes, the Hubble Space Telescope, radioastronomy, infrared and X-ray astronomy, spectroscopy, and many other sources; they are hard at work constructing new models that (hopefully) adhere to observation. These new models continue to minister to our human need to understand ourselves and our place in the cosmos. This chapter raises questions about what it means to live in a big-bang universe, an expanding universe, a curved universe of warped space, and perhaps, a dying universe.

ANCIENT COSMOLOGIES

The Universe is not only queerer than we imagine—it is queerer than we can imagine.

J. B. S. HALDANE

1 Our humanoid ancestors lived very close to the stars. Their lives were much affected by them, especially by the steady points of light that wandered through the star fields as though they were alive. They might in fact be the bright bodies of the gods themselves, playing beneath the blue-black firmament, gods such as Jupiter, Venus, and Mars.

People felt themselves enclosed in a finite container of some sort: a box, or a valley with an inverted clay bowl arching overhead, or a flat disk under a giant crystalline dome. When thinkers tried to make sense of their cosmos they saw different things.

Egyptians thought of their flat Earth as the floor of a rectangular box. Some saw also a flat sky that extended away to the distant corners of the box; but others saw a bowl-shaped sky supported around the rim by a range of mountains surrounding the world like a great wall. The stars were burning lamps suspended high above from the roof or dome.

2 Babylonians knew their flat Earth to be a round disk of land floating in a vast sea. Beyond this sea mountains rose to support the dome holding aloft the heavens. These heavens were the dwelling place of the gods and were strictly off-limits to mortals; man's sole domain was his circular disk of Earth. He could neither visit the outer corners of Earth nor gaze upon the abode of the immortal gods.

The ancient Hebrews saw above them a gigantic bowl of beaten metal (like the "brazen heaven" of Homer's *Iliad*) that separated the lower from the upper waters. This "firmament" was shot through with small holes through which the waters could shower upon the Earth. The Sun and Moon were attached to the vaulted firmament and appeared to roll across it each day. The firmament was held up around the edge by a great range of mountains ("pillars of the sky"). An ocean of water extended around the sides of the inverted bowl and down under the Earth. High above the water dwelt God and the Host of Heaven. Beneath the flat surface on which the people lived "roots of Earth" plunged deep into the abysmal waters. Also under the Earth, near its center, there existed an enormous cavern called *sh*^{e}*ol* where (some said) the ghost-shades of men slept after death.

3 The night could be quiet, but it was the raging, blinding fireball by day that dominated the lives of people.

To Egyptians the sundisk that scorched the desert and brought green life to the meandering Nile was the god Amon-Ra, floating across the liquid sky in a barge. He passed into the Valley of the Gods at sunset and emerged from the valley at dawn.

Mesopotamians saw the eastern gates opening each morning and Shamash the sun god racing out in a great chariot drawn by wild asses. The sun was one of the chariot's burning orange-bright wheels. At sunset Shamash exited through the western gates and all through the night drove his chariot along a dark tunnel under the mountainous edge of the universe, emerging again from the eastern gates at dawn.

To early Greeks, Helios arose daily out of the eastern sea in a quadriga drawn by four white stallions. As he lifted his fiery chariot into the sky the stars were scattered and dove into the sea. In late afternoon he approached the western boundaries of the Earth, and faraway peoples living too near the edge would be singed by the heat of his chariot.

To the ancients the universe was closed, and they felt a kind of security in knowing that. There was continuous interaction among the gods, the evil spirits, and humans who wandered the flat Earth. Generally, good things went on above, bad things went on below, and man knew that his place was somewhere in the middle.

TODAY'S UNIVERSE

4 As the twenty-first century begins, what do you and I see when we look up at the stars?

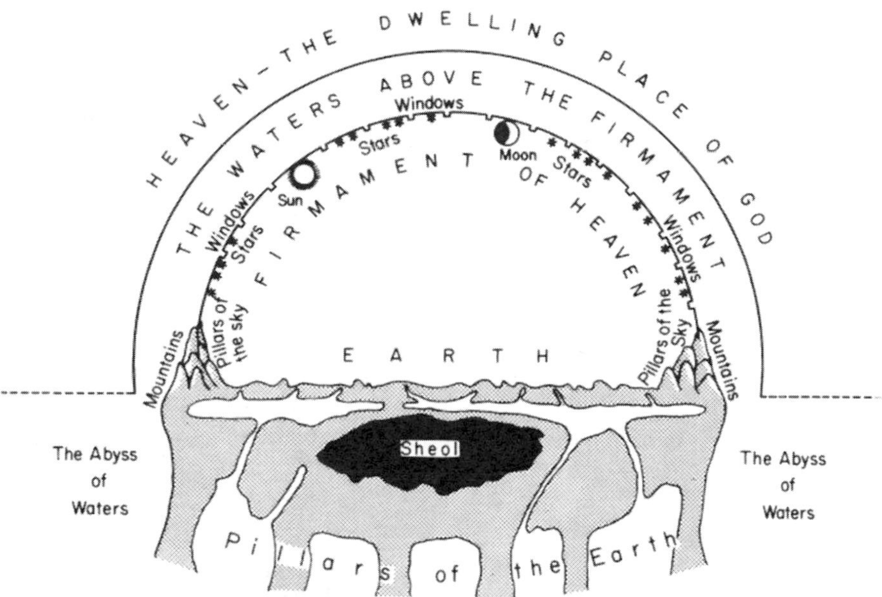

Hebrew cosmos assumed by Old Testament writers. Noteworthy in this cosmology is *sh^{e}ol,* a dank cavern beneath the surface of the flat Earth where the ghost-shades of the dead spend eternity in sleep. While this indicates the concept of an afterlife, *sh^{e}ol* is not at this stage of Hebrew thought a place of punishment; but in later Judaic cosmology, under Zoroastrian influences, *sh^{e}ol* was transmuted into the familiar hell of burning fires.

We know, first and last, that we are looking **out into space** and **back in time.** Whenever we look at any object in space we are also looking into the past: about 1¼ seconds into the past when looking at the nearest natural object (our Moon); about 9 minutes back in time to the nearest star (our Sun); about 4 years back in time to the second nearest star (Alpha Centauri); about 2 million years into the past when gazing at our nearest neighbor galaxy (Andromeda). And with the aid of telescopes we can peer into time past 12 billion years. The farther we look out in space, the farther we are looking back in time.

Egyptian cosmos showing the goddess Nut, her body dotted with stars, bending in a giant arc over the Earth, represented by a reclining figure wearing a skin of leaves. The Sun moves across the sky above the goddess in a heavenly barge.

This woodcut depicts man's restless curiosity to know what "the heavens" are really like. Here a courageous adventurer has traveled to the edge of the universe, poked his head through the firmament, and beholds the machinery that moves the heavenly bodies. Quite literally, this is what *Homo scientificus* has succeeded in doing.

Astronomers today share a unique kind of excitement because there exists a real possibility that we may be looking far enough into the past to see events that took place near the time of origins—the creation of our universe. Evidence indicates that such a beginning occurred between 12 billion and 25 billion years ago, and some of the objects we are now seeing (notably the quasars) are probably phenomena that happened shortly after that beginning.

5 Conceptualizing the size of the universe as we know it today strains our imaginations. Indeed, one may have to live with incredible concepts for a time before they can become believable.

Our solar system is composed of our star/sun and nine orbiting planets, plus assorted planetoids, asteroids, and comets. If we take the orbit of the planet Pluto as the outside limit of our solar system, then the solar system is 7.5 billion miles (or 11 light-hours) in diameter. This local system is our home, our "front yard," incredibly small on a cosmic scale. The nearest star to our sun is a little more than 4 light-years away (26 trillion miles). Our Milky Way galaxy is 100,000 light-years across, and our solar system moves within one spiral arm of our galaxy, 30,000 light-years from its center. We are really quite far out and not even in the central plane.

I always felt that man is a stranger on this planet, a total stranger. I always played with the fancy: maybe a contagion from outer space is the seed of man. Hence, our prior occupation with heaven—with the sky, with the stars, the gods—somewhere out there in outer space. It is a kind of homing impulse. We are drawn to where we come from.

Eric Hoffer

Furthermore, our galaxy is a part of a larger system. Some two dozen galaxies move together in what is known as the "local group." These include the Andromeda galaxies and the Magellanic clouds.

Photographs taken with very long exposures through giant telescopes reveal billions of galaxies extending in all directions. Many are spiral-shaped like our Milky Way, but they also come in many other shapes and sizes. Sometimes as many as several hundred galaxies appear together on a single photographic plate spanning but a few minutes of arc across the sky. The largest radiotelescopes now reach out more than 10 billion light-years—and the galaxies keep on going.

It is not impossible that we may be part of a "metagalaxy," a cluster of hundreds or thousands of galaxies spiraling together in what might look like our own Milky Way magnified a million times.

The Expanding Universe

6 Modern cosmology is based on a single discovery made by Dr. Edwin Hubble in 1929. That discovery was that the universe is expanding. With refined photographic equipment we can see literally billions of galaxies—"island universes"—and judging from the "red shift" (the Doppler effect) in their spectra, they all appear to be moving away from us at constant speeds. This expansion is the fundamental fact that any and all cosmological theories are obliged to explain.

In your mind's eye draw an imaginary sphere one mile in diameter and fill it with quarters and half-dollars floating about a foot apart. These coin-disks are the galaxies of our perceptual universe. If we locate ourselves at the center of this imaginary sphere, then what we observe is that all these coin-galaxies are receding from us. Those nearer to us are moving slower; the farther away they are the greater their speed of recession from us. Out near the edge of the sphere their velocities are nearing the speed of light. When, all around the inside surface of the sphere, the galaxies reach that speed, they become invisible. Each galaxy emitting light in our direction at 186,000 miles per second, but moving away from us at 186,000 mps, would cross over the threshold of perception. Light would require infinite time to reach us; hence, it becomes invisible. This is the edge of our "perceptual universe." All galaxies reaching the speed of light would vanish from sight.

These perceptual limits we must accept, but we can't avoid wondering what lies beyond perception. If we exist in a pulsating universe, then we wonder how far the galaxies continue beyond that perceptual threshold before they begin their long journey back to the center. How much of the pulsating bubble can we actually see? Are there other bubble-universes? If so, how many? Could they possibly extend to infinity? How much space exists between the bubble-universes?

The Big-Bang Model

7 At present we can do little more than develop models that are coherent extensions of our theories about the closer parts of the universe that lie within our range of perception.

The big-bang theory holds that all of the matter in the universe was pulled together by gravity into one huge, hot ball—a "primordial atom"—several hundreds of light-years in diameter. As gravitational forces increased, the ball became ever more condensed. Pressure and temperature reached enormous levels. As contraction continued, there occurred a gravitational collapse amounting to an implosion. The outer layers rushed inward until they reached a critical point at which the massive cosmic ball exploded. This is the "big bang."

Matter was flung outward in all directions. Great clouds of gases and dust formed. Stars condensed from the dust clouds and pulled one another closer into clusters; great accumulations of matter began swirling as galaxies. This vast hodge-podge of exploded matter continued—and still continues—to journey outward from the scene of the explosion.

According to this picture, there was but a single explosion and since that time the universe has been "running down." From the time of the explosion the second law of thermodynamics (entropy) operates to dissipate energy. Living things exist only during this interim period while the fires are still burning. After that all the galaxies, stars, and planets will grow cold and die; they will float outward forever into the distance reaches of space. There will be no more heat and no more light.

The Pulsating Model

8 The pulsating model concurs with the big-bang model that matter was shot outward in all directions by a cosmic explosion. However, the total gravitational attraction of all the mass in the universe is so great that the universe cannot "escape from itself." That is, the gravitational pull of the universe's mass is greater than the force of the explosion. Galaxies traveling outward will gradually slow down—as though there were an elastic net around the entire universe—and reverse their direction, moving back toward the center from which they were exploded. As all mass converges, it becomes again a primordial hot ball. The dynamics repeat themselves and another big bang sends matter on its way through space. Calculations indicate that explosions occur at intervals of 80 billion years. After each explosion galaxies, stars, and planets are born and life emerges, perhaps throughout the universe. But ultimately the stars grow old, life dies, and all matter contracts again into a hot ball.

Thus, the universe "pulsates," from explosion to explosion. A pulsating universe is anything but dead; it is a live, eternal universe, building up energy and dissipating it randomly only to build up energy again, losing nothing. Its perpetual processes are inherent and irrevocable.

We are now at a point in time 14 billion years after the last big bang. The universe is still rapidly expanding. Twenty billion years from now most of the galaxies will have stopped receding and begun their return journey. In 60 billion years another explosion will start the cycle again, and, perhaps, 80 billion years hence, countless living beings will look up at the stars at night and wonder what it's all about.

> ***"One ought not to grumble at Heaven that things happen according to its Way (Tao). . . . When stars fall or the sacred tree groans, the people of the whole state are afraid. They ask, "Why is it?" I answer: There is no reason. This is due to a modification of Heaven and Earth, to the mutation of Yin and Yang. . . . If people pray for rain and get rain, why is that? I answer: There is no reason for it. If people do not pray for rain, it will nevertheless rain."***
>
> Hsün Tzu (c. 250 BC)

9 It is interesting how closely the pulsating-cosmos theory resembles the teleocosmologies of some of mankind's religions. According to Hindu mythology, the god Shiva spins out the universe while he dances; when the Lord of the Dance tires, his creative activity wanes, the universe runs down, all life vanishes, and there is quiescence until Shiva revives and begins dancing again. This cosmic cycle, billions of years long, repeats itself eternally.

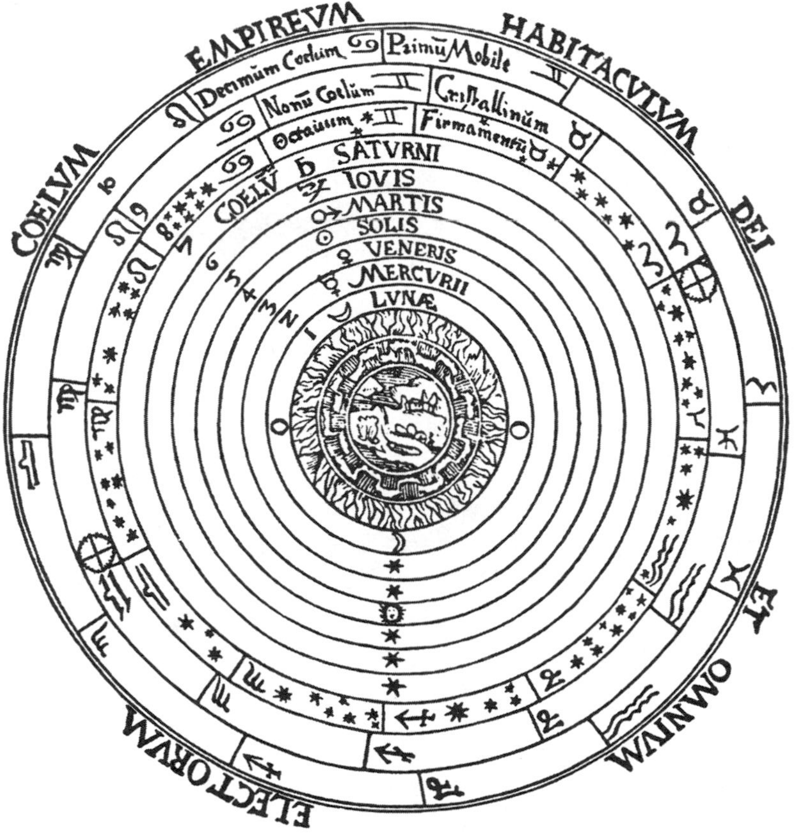

A medieval diagram of the geocentric (Ptolemaic) universe. With Earth at the center, the other members of the solar system move in concentric orbits. Diagram from Peter Appian's *Cosmographia* (1539).

Next pages: In contrast to the fanciful ancient cosmologies, here is the universe as we know it today. These dust clouds, stars, star clusters, and much more are merely a fraction of our own Milky Way galaxy. The smaller, dark globules in the photograph are dense masses of gas and dust contracting into stars; that is, new stars are continually being born out of such interstellar matter. This is a photograph of the Star Queen (or Eagle) nebula (M16) in the constellation Serpens.

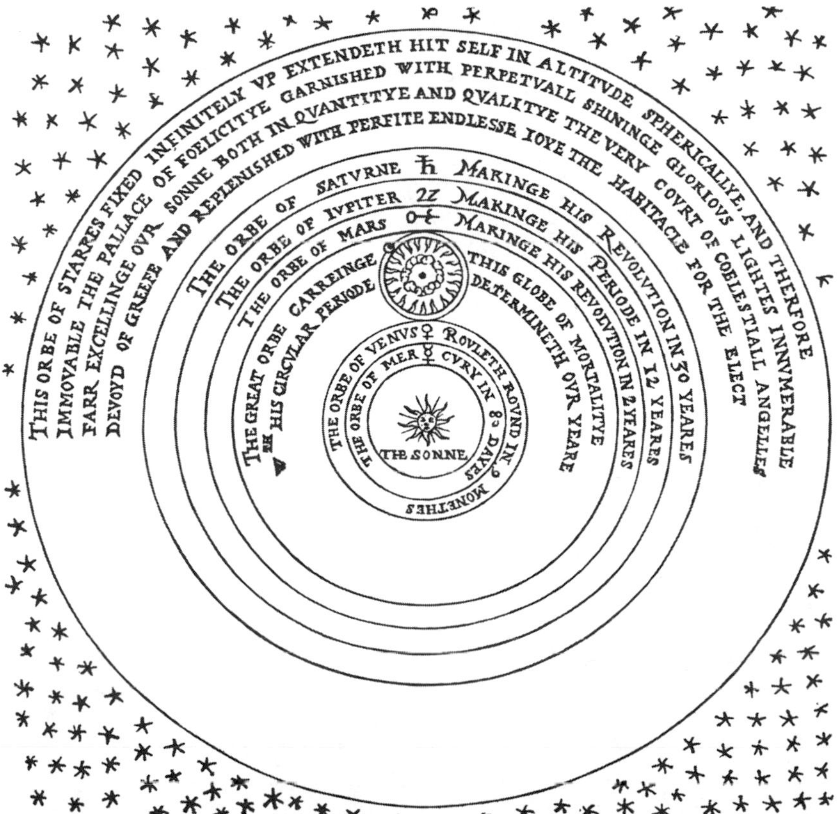

The heliocentric (Copernican) cosmos as drawn by Thomas Digges in 1576. In the center of the system is "the sonne," and the other heavenly bodies — though, surprisingly, not the stars — revolve in circular orbits around the Sun. Notice, however, that the Moon revolves around the Earth.

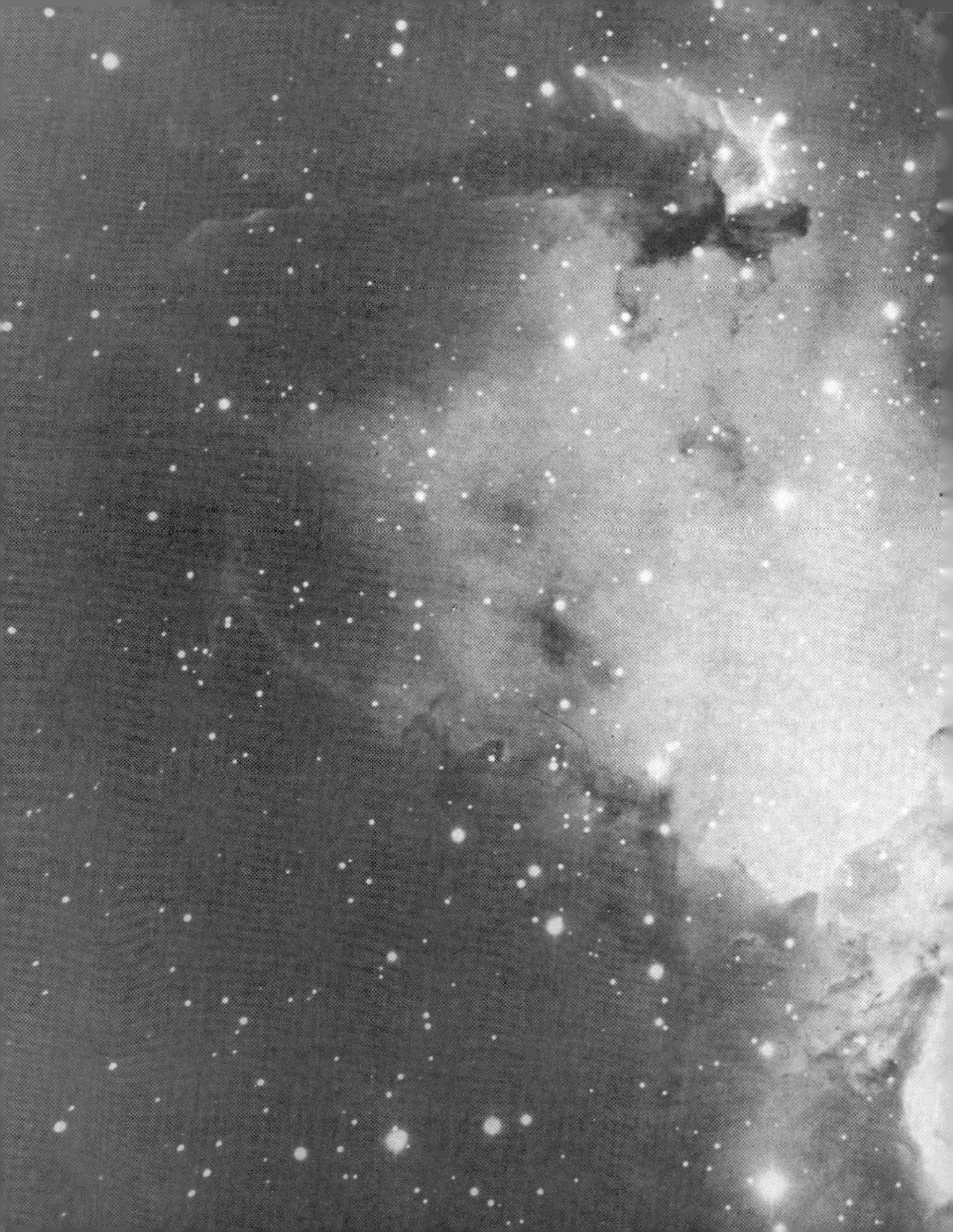

Photograph taken by the Hubble space telescope of a region in the Eagle Nebula in the constellation Serpens, 7,000 light years from Earth. These great columns of hydrogen gas and dust are giving birth to new stars. The tallest column is about 1 light year from top to bottom. Photo courtesy Jeff Hester and Paul Scowen (Arizona State University), and NASA.

Similar also is the Norse cycle, which ends in the Doom of the Gods (the *Götterdämmerung*), when the forces of chaos will inaugurate the final battle. In stunning contrast to most religious teleocosmologies, the battle will be fought in vain. The valiant warriors of Valhalla, and even the gods themselves, will be crushed, and all life will be extinguished. Earth and cosmos will be consumed by fire. Then, after a long while, a new Earth will be born, and order will be restored by the sons of Odin and Thor. Mankind too will be generated again from a human couple who will have survived the conflagration. Thus, after a fiery end, the cycle of life begins again.

And Then What Happened?

There is an amusing short tale by the Irish writer Lord Dunsany (in his book *The Man Who Ate the Phoenix*) in which Atlas explains to Dunsany what happened on the day when science made it no longer possible for mortals to believe in the old Greek model of the universe. Atlas admits that he had found his task rather dull and unpleasant. He was cold, because he had the earth's South Pole on the back of his neck, and his hands were always wet from the two oceans. But he remained at his task as long as people believed in him.

Then the world, Atlas says sadly, began to get "too scientific." He decided he was no longer needed. So he just put down the world and walked away.

"Yes," Atlas says. "Not without reflection, not without considerable reflection. But when I did it, I must say I was profoundly astonished; utterly astonished at what happened."

"And what did happen?"

"Simply nothing. Simply nothing at all."

Martin Gardner
The Relativity Explosion

A Multibubble Universe—?

10 Recent cosmologists are beginning to envision the possibility that the universe may consist not merely of a single pulsating bubble, but several bubbles or perhaps an infinite number. All that we can perceive is a portion of our own bubble-universe, but if there is one pulsating bubble, then why not more? If matter should extend infinitely, then the dynamics of pulsation must operate everywhere in similar fashion.

This multibubble universe is more gigantic than anything the human mind has heretofore tried to comprehend. Yet the more knowledge we obtain the more credible a multibubble cosmology becomes. The fact of the matter is that there is a feeling of aristocentrism about the notion that there is but a single bubble-universe—namely ours.

When you understand all about the sun . . . and all about the rotation of the earth you may still miss the radiance of the sunset.

Alfred North Whitehead

For myself, I find it hard to accept the big-bang theory. I would like to reject it. How can I believe such a naive theory that says there was a finite time only twice as long as the age of our earth, [when] the universe was vastly different from its present state—a red hot ball? I much prefer Mr. Hoyle's more subtle steady-state. But I have to face the facts, as a working physicist. The evidence mounts up, experiments after experiment, [and] at least suggests that the clear predictions of the most naive theory—the big-bang—are coming true.

Philip Morrison

Do We Live in a Curved Universe?

11 One aspect of the theory of relativity is that space is "curved" and that therefore we live in a "curved universe." Einstein suggested that the total gravitational force of all mass produces a universe that must be understood in terms of "curved space geometry." All objects moving in such a universe—from massive pulsars to massless photons—would follow curved trajectories. Whether the universe is curved positively or negatively (or not curved at all) has not yet been established. If negatively curved, it is an "open" universe; mass moving along gravitational lines of force would exit from our universe and vanish. But if positively curved—and there seems to be increasing direct evidence that it

> ***Everything indeed, everything visible in nature or established in theory, suggests that the universe is implacably progressing toward final darkness and decay.***
>
> LINCOLN BARNETT

is—then it is a "closed" universe curving back on itself. Mass (and photons of light) would curve in great circles through the gestalt gravitational fields.

If positive curvature is real, then visual displacement of distant objects may be far greater than we have thought. Nothing in the heavens would be where we presently "see" it. Light emitted by objects will have been bent in its journey to us. Out near the edge of our perceptual universe, where galaxies are receding from us at great speeds, the objects we observe may now exist in some other part of the universe altogether; indeed, they may not now exist at all. Moreover, the speeds we observe may represent their velocities billions of years ago. Where such objects are located now, and what their velocities are, we cannot be sure. We find ourselves caught in a frustrating but exciting quandary.

We are beginning to get an idea of our place in the cosmic picture, but undoubtedly some shattering discoveries—always the unexpected—are still in store for us.

GALILEO GALILEI

"The Noblest Eye Is Darkened"

Galileo became the founder of modern physics because he possessed one rare and simple gift: he could see.

He lived in an era when reality was prescribed, not perceived. Descriptions of the real world were supplied by Great Authorities, and when you looked at the world you were required to see what you were told was there to be seen; no more, no less.

Galileo protested in anger, saying in effect: "I will do my own seeing! I will see for myself whatever exists to be seen."

This stance might be called the "Galileian Principle"—the declaration that we will allow no intervention in our interpretation of our own experience. But such arrogance—the conviction that we can see for ourselves—was quite enough to threaten the Great Authorities and ignite the flames of the Inquisition.

Galileo's father, Vincenzio Galilei, was a well-educated Florentine musician who sought to grace his son with all the qualities of a Renaissance man; he tutored him in Latin and Greek, mathematics and music (lute and organ), drawing and painting. His mother, Giulia Ammannati, was intelligent and educated but touchy and difficult; she bequeathed obstinacy and competitiveness to her offspring. Galileo, born in 1564, was the first of their seven children.

At ten he entered the monastery school of Vallombrosa; for five years he was immersed in Latin classes and Italian literature. At seventeen he enrolled at the University of Pisa. He displayed an aptitude for the sciences but he had a passion for mathematics, which remained the first love of his life.

One day he went to meditate in the cathedral of Pisa. A large oil-burning chandelier had been pulled over to one side for lighting, and once lit had been released to swing back and forth. Galileo observed that each swing took precisely the same amount of time, no matter how wide the arc of the swing. To make sure of this he timed the swings by his own pulsebeat. He then went home, constructed two pendulums of the same length, set them swinging in various arcs, and timed them. However wide the arc, the swings took the same time. Galileo had discovered "isochronism," which he proceeded to quantify and describe with mathematics.

The book of Nature is written in the language of mathematics.

I do not feel obliged to believe that the same God who has endowed us with sense, reason, and intellect has intended us to forgo their use.

We must deal with the real world, and not one on paper.

Without mathematics, one wanders about in a dark labyrinth.

On Galileo (by his friend Castelli when he heard of Galileo's blindness):
The noblest eye is darkened which nature ever made, an eye that had seen more than the eyes of all that are gone and that had opened the eyes of all men to come.

On Galileo:
"To give us the science of motion God and Nature have joined hands and created the intellect of Galileo."

PAOLO SARPI

They who in proof of any assertion rely simply on the weight of authority, without adducing any argument in support of it, act very absurdly.

This was a quiet beginning for the science of physics—the study of (in Newtonian terms) matter-in-motion.

While at Pisa Galileo developed a reputation for articulate dissent. He made a perfect nuisance of himself by challenging his teachers' authoritarian pronouncements and arguing incessantly with them, for which he was nicknamed "the wrangler." It is not surprising that he left the university without a degree.

In 1592 he was appointed to the University of Padua, where for eighteen years he taught mathematics and geometry, mechanics (physics), and astronomy. His spacious home accommodated boarders; his doors were open to friends and a steady flow of visitors. He shared his innovative ideas with all who would converse with him. All things mechanical intrigued him, and he loved to putter around and make gadgets in his well-stocked workshop.

Galileo was a man of medium stature, heavy set, not unattractive. He could be charming or abrasive, depending on mood more than circumstance. He possessed a rare intellect (estimated IQ 185) and a razor-sharp tongue, which he used to cajole friends, awe students, entertain public audiences, season conversations with wit, and make fools of detractors. He was a gifted writer. Without his enormous literary talent we would not have masterworks from his pen—and neither would he have been in constant trouble.

Early in July 1609 Galileo heard rumors about a magnifying instrument developed by a Dutch lensmaker. The few people who had seen it considered it merely a novelty, but with characteristic insight Galileo obtained the instrument and converted what was regarded as a toy into a major instrument for the acquisition of scientific knowledge.

In January 1610, shivering in the wintry cold, Galileo turned his telescope on Jupiter and saw "three little stars, small but very bright" on either side of the planet. Three nights later he recognized what they were: orbiting moons. "What we are seeing with our own eyes are four starlets which revolve around Jupiter, just as the Moon revolves around the Earth, and all of them together trace out a grand revolution around the Sun in the period of twelve years."

What Galileo had seen, rightly interpreted, would demolish the entire geocentric world-view, and the tyranny of the Aristotelian/Ptolemaic dogma would be broken. He published his discoveries in a small Latin pamphlet, which he called *Sidereus Nuncius*—Message from the Stars. It immediately produced a swell of both accolades and anger. A copy was sent to the great German astronomer Johannes Kepler, who hailed it as epoch-making. Galileo was invited to Rome, where he was wined and dined. There he won the respect, if not the affection, of the Jesuit astronomers and was inducted into a prestigious academy of science.

But his enemies also increased in number and fervor. Books and articles appeared branding his discoveries the fantasies of a heretic. In 1613 he published three letters on sunspots and again offended the Aristotelian scientists, who knew that the sun, being perfect, could not have "spots." In the same year he also wrote a letter setting forth his opinions on the proper relationship of religion and science; it was circulated among faculty members at the University of Pisa. Within a few months this letter had found its way to those heading the Inquisition in Rome and was being scrutinized for heretical opinions. The pope appointed a special commission to investigate the matter, and on March 5, 1616, the Holy Office published its official position:

> The view that the sun stands motionless at the center of the universe is foolish, philosophically false, and utterly heretical, because contrary to Holy Scripture. The view that the earth is not the center of the universe and even has a daily rotation is philosophically false, and at least an erroneous belief.

Galileo had been working for some years on a monumental book comparing the two worldviews, and it was published in 1632 with the title *Dialogue Concerning the Two Great World Systems—Ptolemaic and Copernican.* It took him five years to write it, but it was the culmination of a lifetime of insightful seeing and brilliant theorizing—a masterpiece.

Galileo had discovered that the world of matter-in-motion is a simple system that can be described with mathematics. He discovered this through his own experiments—by timing a swinging chandelier, by dropping cannonballs from the Tower of Pisa, for instance.

Moreover, he saw—as did the ancient Greeks—that just a few observations give us universal knowledge. Just a few demonstrations of uniform acceleration give us knowledge of all falling objects in the whole universe. Picture him: Galileo working in his laboratory in Padua, developing formulas for understanding the most distant reaches of the cosmos. Terrestrial dynamics and cosmic dynamics are one. This was a disturbing discovery because cosmic knowledge had heretofore been held in protective custody within the sanctuary of sacred theology.

Galileo belonged to his time, of course. He was not an agnostic; he never questioned the existence of God. He believed that God had created the world on a mathematical model. But what delighted Galileo and dismayed the theologians was the claim that our human knowledge is the same as God's knowledge. Mathematical understanding is perfect understanding, Galileo had seen, whether found in God's mind or ours. What all this comes down to is that God reveals himself in two ways: through scripture **and** through nature. And while scriptural revelation is obscure, ambiguous, even cryptic—just listen to the theologians argue ad infinitum over its interpretation—nature's revelation has the clarity and certainty of mathematical precision and is, therefore, a superior kind of knowledge. When Galileo took the next logical step and said that Holy Writ should be corrected by natural knowledge, that his reasoning was dangerous became only too clear. This position was Galileo's own "protestant" revolt against the tyranny of arbitrary authority.

Galileo's greatest contribution to science was in method. With rare insight he studied the dynamic motions of worldly as well as heavenly objects, attempting to quantify them—to express all his observations mathematically. This was the true beginning of the science of physics as we know it today.

Galileo's philosophical importance is that he separated two different worlds of reality and began to write an "instruction manual" for one of them: the real world, the world-out-there, the beautifully ordered cosmos of matter-in-motion, which operates according to mathematical principles. Such qualities as number, motion, figure, magnitude, position—the so-called primary qualities—all belong to this real world. The "instruction manual" for the operation of this world is the textbook of physics.

The other world—the human world, the world-in-here—is composed of colors, tastes, sounds, odors—the so-called secondary qualities—as well as feelings, opinions, values, spiritual events, and other experiences. Galileo considered this experiential world to be so chaotic that no "instruction manual" could be written for it.

In August 1632 the office of the Inquisition banned sale of the *Dialogue*, and existing copies were confiscated. Galileo was ordered to Rome to stand trial. The warrior's strength was gone, but he was still stubborn. On April 12, when examined by the Dominican inquisitor, he stated that his book had been properly licensed by the authorities and that he had held and discussed the Copernican view as theory and not fact, as he had been directed in 1616.

The pope personally ordered strong action against Galileo—that he be further questioned under threat of torture, that if he still remained recalcitrant he was to be interrogated before a plenary session of the Holy Inquisition, and that he be imprisoned or silenced.

On Galileo:
"It is probably to Galileo's inherent capacity to observe that modern science owes its inception; . . . His desire was to see precisely what things happen and how they happen, rather than to explain why they happen so."
STILLMAN DRAKE

(Before the Inquisition, June 22, 1633) *I, Galileo Galilei . . . arraigned personally before this tribunal and kneeling before you . . . abjure, curse, and detest [my] errors and heresies . . . and I swear that in the future I will never again say or assert . . . anything that might furnish occasion for a similar suspicion against me.*

(Written about 1637 as Galileo was going blind) *These heavens, this earth, which by wonderful observation I had enlarged a thousand times . . . are henceforth dwindled into the narrow space which I myself occupy.*

On June 21, 1633, Galileo stood before the Inquisition. The judges implored him to confess honestly his true views. His devious reply was that he had never been a Copernican. The threat of torture was used, but he continued to hold that, ever since he had been warned nineteen years earlier, he had considered the Copernican view to be false. He was lying, of course; they knew he was lying. He was ushered back to his room.

The following day, June 22, 1633, he was returned to the great hall of the Inquisition. The judges and cardinals were present in full regalia. He was sentenced to life imprisonment according to the pleasure of the Holy Office. He was handed a written formula of confession, forced to kneel and recite:

> I, Galileo Galilei . . . arraigned personally before this tribunal and kneeling before you . . . swear that I have always believed, do now believe, and by God's help will for the future believe, all that is held, preached and taught by the holy Catholic and Apostolic Roman Church. But whereas . . . after an injunction had been judicially intimated to me by this Holy Office, to the effect that I must altogether abandon the false opinion that the sun is the centre of the world and moves . . . I wrote and printed a book in which I discuss this doctrine already condemned. . . .
>
> Therefore . . . I abjure, curse, and detest the aforesaid errors and heresies, . . . and I swear that in the future I will never again say or assert, verbally or in writing, anything that might furnish occasion for a similar suspicion against me. . . .

After the trial Galileo was eventually allowed to return to his villa near Florence, where he remained for the rest of his life, under house arrest. He could wander in his garden, study, receive friends, and teach his students; but he could not leave the premises. His favorite daughter, Maria Celeste, came to live with him and, for a few months, helped to restore life. But his health continued to fail and was severely aggravated by his daughter's death in 1634.

In 1637 came the final irony—the loss of his eyesight. In despair he cried, "These heavens, this earth, this universe, which by wonderful observation I had enlarged a thousand times . . . are henceforth dwindled into the narrow space which I myself occupy." When his old friend Castelli heard of his blindness, he wrote: "The noblest eye is darkened which nature ever made, an eye that had seen more than the eyes of all that are gone and that had opened the eyes of all men to come."

Even then the fire was not entirely gone. Though forbidden to publish, he completed a giant opus entitled *Dialogues Concerning Two New Sciences*, which laid the philosophical foundations of modern physics. Friends smuggled it out to Holland, where it was published in 1638. The Dutch government awarded him a gold chain to honor his many contributions, but the Inquisition denied him permission to accept it.

By November 1641 his strength was gone, at last. Always a faithful Catholic, he received the last sacraments of the church. He died on January 8, 1642, at four o'clock in the morning, in the arms of his disciples.

Reflections

The deflation of some of our more common conceits is one of the practical applications of astronomy.

Carl Sagan

1 There is one single idea which, if we could assimilate it deep into our consciousness, can change the way we perceive the universe. When looking at all heavenly objects, "we know, first and last, that we are looking **out into space** and **back in time.**" Next time you have a clear sky and a little time, recall this fact as you gaze at each star or planet with new space/time eyes.

2 Reflect on, and just appreciate, the ancient cosmologies. In general, what do you think of the accomplishments of these prescientific minds in ordering their perceptions of their universe?

3 Browse through the pages of this and the following chapter and gaze empathetically into the photographs of the stars, galaxies, and other deep-space objects that populate our universe. Move **into** the pictures . . . and **out into** the universe. Can you comprehend its vastness? What do you feel as you ponder a universe of such dimensions?

4 "Modern cosmology is based on a single discovery"—that we live in an expanding universe (p. 525). What does that mean? What is expanding? Where are we located in this expanding model?

5 Review each of the cosmologies currently considered viable. Do you understand the general dynamics of the big-bang and pulsating theories? Do you understand what kind of evidence astronomers are now seeking that would make possible a final determination of which theory is correct?

6 As you think of the cosmologies most widely held by scientists today, which would you prefer to believe in? Or live in? Which would be the most comforting and secure?

7 If we are living in a pulsating universe, then the probability is very high that life develops throughout the universe and exists for lengthy durations after each big bang. What does this possibility do to your thinking about the nature of life? about God? and the universe? about yourself? about the purpose of life?

8 What is meant by Einstein's phrase that "space is curved"? If, by definition, space is "nothing," then how can "nothing" be curved? (See pp. 531–532.)

9 Martin Gardner's account (from Lord Dunsany) of how Atlas "just put down the world and walked away" is a charming parable; and, as with all parables, the meaning remains implicit. Make explicit what the story says to you.

I think the universe is slowing down. In fact, it is slowing down so fast that sometime in the future the expansion of galaxies will cease and contraction begin. . . . The galaxies will coalesce with one another and finally merge once again into a primeval fireball.

ALLEN SANDAGE

BIOCOSMOS

7-4

"The cosmos revealed to us by the new advances in astronomy and biology is far grander and more awesome than the tidy world of our ancestors" (Carl Sagan). Our perception of the universe has gradually expanded to include other solar systems and the possibility that they may harbor intelligent beings. The search for a "cosmic context," as revealed in our religious mythologies, is a deep human need, and it has just begun. This chapter asks what it might mean if we are not alone in the universe. What if other intelligent beings exist, and what if they are very advanced in thought and awareness? The search for intelligent life in the universe could bring about a revolution in our self-perception, our ethics, our religions, and our philosophies.

WE ARE NOT ALONE

1 Only a few years ago the attitude of the scientific community toward the existence of life on other worlds was an unyielding skepticism, and any scientist entertaining the notion that "we are not alone" was considered fashionably incorrect and unprofessional. In 1934 the British astrophysicist Sir Arthur Eddington summarized the scientific consensus by saying that there may exist "other globes that are or have been inhabited by beings as highly developed as Man; but we do not think they are at all common," and "present indications seem to be that it is very long odds against a particular star undergoing the kind of accident which gave birth to the solar system."

Sometimes I think we're alone. Sometimes I think we're not. In either case, the thought is staggering.
BUCKMINSTER FULLER

All this has changed during the last two or three decades. The scientific community now accepts the idea that planets are a commonplace occurrence; more than that, several dozen planets have now been detected orbiting nearby stars. The notion that the creation of our solar system was a once-in-a-billion accident has passed from the scene. The prevailing theory today is that solar systems condense from the same nebula of gas and dust that gave birth to the parent stars; and planetary systems similar to our own are assumed to be scattered through the universe, orbiting their home stars in the same way that Sol's nine planets swirl around their Sun. Some of those planets will undoubtedly be blessed with just the right conditions for creating and sustaining life.

2 One of the first modern scientists brave enough to argue for the existence of extraterrestrial life was Harlow Shapley, the American astronomer who discovered the true nature of the Milky Way galaxy. In 1957 Shapley wrote that "sentient organisms, the product of biochemical evolution, must be a common occurrence in the universe." Given the nature of planetary origins, the mixing of chemical compounds on a planet's surface, and the mechanisms of organic evolution, it is virtually certain that at least a hundred million "high life" habitats exist, "and the number is probably more like a hundred trillion." He speculated that half of these suitable planets have evolved high-life forms comparable to, or more advanced than, those on Earth. Thus, "we have decided that *we are not alone* in this universe."

Harlow Shapley (1885–1972)

3 Since Shapley's early thoughts on the matter, the idea that extraterrestrial life forms really exist has become commonplace, both among scientists and with the world's general populace—at least those who have access to movies and television. Thanks to *Star Trek, Star Wars, Close Encounters of the Third Kind,* and endless late reruns of old sci-fi movies, we all have lodged in our subpsyches (and nightmares) endless parades of very real extraterrestrials. Who would dare argue that Vulcans and Klingons, Yoda and ET are mere figments? Popular consciousness of possible existence of extraterrestrials has so completely changed that "alien abductions" and "body snatching" seem like everyday affairs.

4 Life cannot exist on stars, of course, because of their high temperatures and violently roiling surfaces; so life would most likely develop on planets situated in stable, near-circular orbits around the stars where temperatures would permit the growth of cell structures. Requisite also would be some sort of atmosphere and free water. Within these broad parameters for tolerable conditions, it would seem quite possible that some form of living organism would eventually develop.

The earth is the cradle of mankind, but one cannot live in the cradle forever.

TSIOLKOVSKY

The trouble with living on a small planet is that it tends to make most of the inhabitants think small.

LARRY NIVEN

Shapley made the conservative guess that perhaps one star in a thousand has a planetary system; and that perhaps one in a thousand systems has a planet with just the right temperature tolerances for life; then of these planets perhaps only one in a thousand has sufficient quantities of air and water to transform organic molecules into protoplasm. Using these figures Shapley estimated that only one star in a trillion has a planet that meets all the requirements. Still, if the total number of stars in the universe is about a hundred billion billion, then the number of planets with suitable conditions for life comes out to be a hundred million. "This is a minimum," Shapley concluded: "Personally I would recommend . . . its multiplication by at least a thousand times, possibly a million."

5 Since Shapley made his calculations an enormous amount of careful thought has been given to the possible actuality of alien life-forms. Frank Drake and Carl Sagan developed a plausible formula for calculating the number of communicating civilizations that may exist in our Milky Way galaxy at the present

In our time this search [for extraterrestrial life] will eventually change our laws, our religions, our philosophies, our arts, our recreations, as well as our sciences. Space, the mirror, waits for life to come look for itself there.

RAY BRADBURY

moment in time. In their equation—$N = R_* f_p n_e f_l f_i f_c L$—the number of such advanced civilizations N is assumed to be the function of seven variables:

- $R_* =$ the number of stars that are born each year in our Milky Way galaxy (a good estimate: ten per year)
- $f_p =$ the average number of planets orbiting each star (on average: about one)
- $n_e =$ the number of such planets that have a life-sustaining environment (again, probably about one per planetary system)
- $f_l =$ the number of such congenial planets on which life actually evolves (again, probably one. The consensus among biologists is that life will eventually evolve in just about any congenial site, given enough time.)
- $f_i =$ the number of these life-bearing planets that evolve intelligent life (the probability number: one. The reasoning is the same as for f_l: given sufficient time, intelligence will almost always evolve.)
- $f_c =$ the number of intelligent life-forms that develop a communications technology (a conservative guess: perhaps 1 percent)
- $L =$ the average lifetime of such a communicating civilization. (Here we're stumped and can make only feeble guesstimates. We know of only one such civilization—our own. If *we* make it through the next couple of centuries, how long will *our* "communicating civilization" last?)

If we establish contact with extraterrestrial life it will reveal to us our true place in the universe, and with that will come the beginning of wisdom.

ISAAC ASIMOV

Substituting figures for the symbols in the Drake/Sagan formula, we get:

$$N = 10 \times 1 \times 1 \times 1 \times 1 \times 1/100 \times L$$
$$\text{or} \quad N = 1/10 \times L$$

The conclusion, therefore, is that the number of civilizations in our galaxy with whom we could communicate at the present time is one-tenth the mean lifetime of such a technological civilization. If scientific societies such as ours last, say, two hundred years after they reach the technological stage, then one-tenth of two hundred is twenty. There are only twenty possible contacts in our galaxy of over a hundred billion stars. We might as well give up hope of finding other intelligent life in the biocosmos and learn to live with our loneliness and fantasies.

But *if* civilizations survive their crisis transition and then continue on for millions of years—and a reasonable argument can be made that, having survived a technological infancy (rather like a three-year-old child playing with a hand grenade), civilizations continue to exist almost forever—then there exist thousands or millions of extraterrestrial societies right now. The figure could be one-tenth of a million or one-tenth of a billion; but in any case, our attempt to make contact across the light-years of space would not be undertaken in vain.

What is clear is that the human species has reached a point in our relationship to the biocosmos from which there can be no turning back. A logician, Peter Angeles, makes the point: "If extraterrestrial intelligence is never found at any time in the universe, the quest will still go on; there will always remain a possibility in an infinite universe that extraterrestrial intelligence exists *somewhere,* or did exist *somewhere,* or will come into existence *somewhere.* In an infinite universe the biocosmic belief cannot be eradicated."

A Cosmic Context for Mankind

6 Carl Sagan reminds us that all human societies, like human infants, begin their lives in an egocentric condition. "A human infant begins to achieve maturity by the experimental discovery that he is not the whole of the universe. The same is true of societies engaged in the exploration of their surroundings." Maturity must include the continuing reassessment of oneself in relation to one's world and to the component parts of that world. The need to understand our place in the scheme of things has taken on a special meaning because of humankind's problematic future on this world and the probable existence of life on other worlds. In the words of Nobel laureate George Wald, "We need some widely shared view of the place of Man in the Universe."

The universe is old, the race of man young. There may be . . . must be . . . other races out there—or even closer to home.

Roger Zelazny

The search for extraterrestrial life should be seen as a natural, normal next step in the "reality adjustments" we make in our relationships. Such adjustments continue on all fronts: in man's relationship to man, in our ecological ties with other fauna and flora that share our planet, and with the life-sustaining physical elements of our environment. We live in times of change; vital information about ourselves and our world is acquired faster than we can process it. We urgently need to know where we stand so that we can make sound survival judgments and behave appropriately.

"There is today," notes Sagan, "—in a time when old beliefs are withering—a kind of philosophic hunger, a need to know who we are and how we got here. There is an ongoing search, often unconscious, for a cosmic perspective for humanity."

A one-planet deity has for me little appeal.

Harlow Shapley

From the time of their joint beginnings, philosophy and science have worked together to achieve a more realistic picture of humankind—of our origins, our nature, and our destiny.

Sagan: "We are aware of our deep connection, both in form and in matter, with the rest of the universe. The cosmos revealed to us by the new advances in astronomy and biology is far grander and more awesome than the tidy world of our ancestors. And we are becoming a part of it, the cosmos as it is, not the cosmos of our desires."

Our religious myths reveal that we humans want desperately to be participants in a meaningful biocosmic program. The chances are strong that we are in fact participants, and always have been. Hopefully, in the not too distant future, we may at last discover that we belong to a true biocosmos.

Our Expanding Consciousness

7 Isaac Asimov has drawn up a short history of cosmic measurements showing "the successive enlargement of man's picture of the universe."

I have declared infinite worlds to exist beside this our earth. It would not be worthy of God to manifest Himself in less than an infinite universe.
Giordano Bruno (1548–1600)

500 BC: **5,000 miles** (the distance across the known universe: a flat disk-shaped Earth with a vaulted dome. The calculator: Hecataeus of Miletus)
225 BC: **8,000 miles** in diameter (a spherical Earth. The calculator: Eratosthenes of Cyrene)
150 BC: **48,000 miles** (an imaginary sphere including the Moon. The calculator: Hipparchus of Nicaea)
1671: **1,800,000 miles** (the diameter of the known universe: the solar system as far out as Saturn. The calculator: Giovanni Cassini)
1704: **6 million miles** (diameter of the known universe derived from the orbit of Halley's Comet. The calculator: Edmund Halley)
1840: **320 trillion miles** or 54 light-years (diameter based on the known distance to the star Vega. The calculator: Friedrich von Struve)
1906: **55,000 light-years** (diameter of hypothetical disk-like galaxy. The calculator: Jacobus Kapteyn)
1920: **330,000 light-years** (diameter of Milky Way galaxy. The calculator: Harlow Shapley)
1923: **5.4 million light-years** (a spherical universe including the newly recognized Andromeda galaxy. The calculator: Edwin Hubble)
1940: **400 million light-years** (the known universe including galaxies observed to be 200 million light-years away from us. The calculator: Milton Humason)
1963: **2 billion light-years** (after discovery of the first quasar by Maarten Schmidt)
1973: **24 billion light-years** (based on measurement of the most distant object observed in the universe as of this date, a quasar known as OH471)
2002: **25 billion light-years** (based on a distant red galaxy photographed by the Hubble Space Telescope's Advanced Camera for Surveys that appears to be 12.5 billion light-years from the Earth)

This list is more than a compendium of figures. It is a metaphor for the expansion of our consciousness. As our worldview has grown so has our perception of the parts—ethical, religious, esthetic, epistemological—that make up that worldview.

The science-fiction writer Larry Niven reminds us that planet dwellers riding along on a cosmic pinpoint tend to think small. We can't deny our history: tunnel-vision has plagued our perceptions. Today we are challenged **to see** the universe as it really is. This gigantic bubble-cosmos is there and it undoubtedly contains all forms of life, and when we discover our cosmic context then our primitive worldviews will turn into new visions.

Consequences

8 What will it mean if we establish contact with extraterrestrial intelligences (ETs)? Since we have misgivings about our own future on Earth, perhaps the realization that **they exist** will itself be the most significant message. The astronomer George Abell suggests that we should be jubilant if we "discover even *one* other civilization that has endured for tens of thousands of years; at least if those fellows made it, perhaps there is hope for us!"

The impact upon how we think of ourselves will be deep. From an evolutionary standpoint it was probably inevitable that one single species would win out over all others on Earth in the survival game; the capacity for abstract reason probably gave us humans the decisive edge. But it's lonely at the top!—far lonelier than we now admit to ourselves—and this ontological loneliness is surely the motivating drive behind much human behavior for which we commonly give other facile explanations: the destructive competition within our own species (wouldn't this competitive animosity be redirected if we were forced to relate with several kinds of peer-intelligent life-forms?); our cruelty to other forms of life (that is, our general lack of empathy and respect for other living things); our preoccupation with the noise of communication (words, speeches, dialogues, and other silence breakers) as compared with communication itself; and a variety of problems in our relationships with one another (for instance, individual alienation and the resulting pressures we place on others to end our loneliness). If we were forced to relate to peers or superiors—forced to understand, empathize, tolerate, respect—then our individual and collective self-images would probably undergo rapid change.

The APCD predicts no smog again tomorrow . . . Birmingham, Alabama, has had an air pollution crisis this week . . . The planet Mars today had a violent dust storm, and it'll take at least 10 days to clear . . . On the moon the low tonight will drop to 307 degrees below zero, and tomorrow it'll climb all the way up to an afternoon high of 273 degrees above zero . . . The astronauts will stir up some more dust tomorrow cruising around in the moon buggy, so there'll be light to moderate eye irritation on the moon.

KELLY LANGE ***(KNBC News)***

9 Religious ideas would also undergo change. In a biocosmos of populated planets with varied rotation times ("days") and revolution periods ("years"), severe strain would be placed on doctrines and dogmas that tie Ultimate Reality to Earth functions. For instance: **sacred space** (geography: "holy ground," holy cities [Mecca, Jerusalem, Benares], holy temples, shrines, the "Holy of Holies"); **sacred time** (sabbaths, Holy Days, Holy Weeks, sacred festivals); **sacred languages** (Sanskrit, Arabic, Hebrew, or "King James English"); **sacred foods** (corn in the Eleusinian and Osirian mysteries, Eucharistic bread and wine, "kosher" foods); **sacred teleocosmic dramas** that depend upon Earth history ("Adam and Eve and the Snake," Faithful Remnants and Chosen People, the New Jerusalem, the "End of the World"); and our **anthropomorphic images** of the deities (note Michelangelo's frescoes on the ceiling of the Sistine Chapel).

10 Our ethical and esthetic notions will be threatened. We will be forced into asking new kinds of questions. Would ETs be "persons" or "selves"? Would they have a serious "right to life"? On what criteria might they be defined as worthy of our moral concern? (Could one **not** be morally concerned with ET or Yoda?) What is the role of empathy in moral considerations? Could we empathize with alien beings? What if—because of **their** appearance—we could not empathize with them? Or what if—because of **our** appearance—they couldn't empathize with us? (Is empathy learned or is it inherent?)

Imagine ETs engaging in behavior that, to our way of thinking, is clearly immoral: ritual flagellation of themselves to develop "moral qualities"; indiscriminate sex with countless variations on a theme by de Sade; the practice of "emotional violence" to maintain "survival readiness"; and so on. The more humanoid they appeared to us, the more easily we would become offended by behavior that, if **we** indulged in it, would be defined and felt as lewd, obscene, disgusting, immoral.

11 Given such situations, what are our capacities for rapid redefinition of "right" and "wrong" and "beauty" and "ugliness"? What might be their capacities for rapid redefinition? Could we develop a calculus of "minimal reaction" that would guide human behavior toward ETs so that, as with other life-forms

Astronaut Ed Mitchell: You develop an instant global consciousness, a people orientation, an intense dissatisfaction with the state of the world and a compulsion to do something about it.
Astronaut Rusty Schweickart: I'm not the same man. None of us are.

I think there is no question that we live in an inhabited universe that has life all over it.

GEORGE WALD

For the first time in the history of our species, we have devised tools—unmanned space vehicles and large radio telescopes—to search for extraterrestrial life. I would be very ashamed of my civilization, if, with these tools at hand, we turned away from the cosmos.

CARL SAGAN

on Earth, we would inflict the least possible harm? Could we communicate such a calculus to them? Would a biocosmic perspective serve to clarify the pragmatic character of moral and esthetic codes? How might humans respond to a truly advanced morality? (What is "a truly advanced morality"?)

On one point there is universal agreement among speculators: whatever ETs look like, they will **not** look like us. They will not be humanoid. "The biology on other planets is of course expected to be different from our own because of the statistical nature of the evolutionary process and the adaptability of life." This conclusion, written by Frank Drake and Carl Sagan, opens the door to every plausible organismic configuration imaginable to the human mind.

In hundreds of his stories, Ray Bradbury has described scenarios in which humans and ETs confront each other and find themselves caught in sundry dilemmas. These sci-fi settings can serve as thought experiments that prevision the ethical and esthetic problems of actual encounter.

In a *Life* magazine article Bradbury painted verbal pictures of how extraterrestrials might appear. Among the beings that he conjured were creatures that live in very thick atmospheres and have extremely small bodily openings to cut down on intake; and creatures that live in very thin atmospheres and have "mouths and nose vents like barn doors."

Bradbury warns:

> To the lonely space man, an alien woman with the above features would hardly be attractive. Right here, the entire field of esthetics looms before us. Astronautical history may depend on those concepts of beauty and utility our men take along as unacknowledged cargo to the stars. Countless books will have to be written under the general title: *Esthetics and Etiquette for Other Worlds.* Otherwise, we are in danger of mistaking a rough skin for a rough mind, a third eye for an evil eye, a cold hand for a cold and hostile heart.

THE HUMAN PRESERVE

12 What is mankind's place in the cosmos? As a better understanding of our universe has been growing, old perspectives have become obsolete. New answers are more realistic, but they are sometimes more painful.

We humans, historically, have undergone three agonizing decentralizations. We have waged a steady struggle **against** decentralization, but at the same time—paradoxically—our accumulating knowledge has gradually forced us to abandon all illusions about our centrality.

The **cosmological decentralization** was the first painful reassessment of Man's place in the scheme of things. In the 1540s Nicholas Copernicus revived the ancient theory that the Earth orbits the Sun, a literally Earthshaking notion that our home planet is not the center of all Creation as people had hoped and religion had held. Then early in the seventeenth century the Copernican theory gained ground with the observations of Galileo and the mathematical calculations of Kepler and Brahe. The battle raged between those who would defend Man's right to be the center of the cosmos and those who, consenting to fact, were beginning to see that the heliocentric theory was empirically true. But as evidence mounted, bitterness increased.

It seems always great to me when God's world gets a little bigger and when I get a somewhat more true view of my place and my smallness in that universe. The growing awareness of cosmic cohabitation is enormously important to me, and it fits well into a growing knowledge of God's world.

KRISTER STENDAHL

It was Galileo Galilei, a teacher of geometry and astronomy at the University of Padua, who suffered most from resistance to heliocentrism. With naive optimism, Galileo published his theories and invited scholars and churchmen to check his evidence supporting the heliocentric theory. He didn't forsee the hostile reaction he would receive. When he invited a certain professor of philosophy to look through his telescope and see for himself the moons of Jupiter, the professor merely laughed and declined. He knew, from logic alone, that Jupiter could not have moons, and he knew on theological grounds that the Earth was the center of the universe.

A similar argument was put forth by a Florentine astronomer named Francesco Sizzi. In a famous polemical passage he reasoned:

> There are seven windows in the head: two nostrils, two eyes, two ears, and a mouth. So also in the heavens there are two favorable stars, two unfavorable, two luminaries, and Mercury alone undecided and indifferent. From all this, and from other such natural phenomena, such as the seven metals, etc., all too pointless to enumerate, we can conclude that the number of planets is necessarily seven.
>
> Furthermore, the [alleged] satellites [of Jupiter] are invisible to the naked eye, and therefore can have no influence on the earth, and therefore would be useless, and therefore do not exist.
>
> Besides all this, the Jews and other ancient peoples as well as modern Europeans have always divided the week into seven days and have named them after the seven planets. Now if we [like Galileo] increase the number of planets, this whole and beautiful system falls to the ground.

Consider the question of whether earth is the only haven for intelligent life in the universe. It is very unlikely that such is the case. On the contrary, the number of planets in the universe capable of sustaining life is believed to be enormous, perhaps as many as 10^{22}, which is about a million times greater than the total number of individual cells in the human body.

SAXON AND FRETTER

13 Following this first cosmological displacement, two other cosmic shifts have taken place. The first occurred early in this century when it was discovered by astronomers that our solar system is not central to our Milky Way galaxy. Rather, it is located in a spiral arm, and this is indeed the periphery—the "south forty"—of our island universe.

The second cosmic displacement took place during the 1930s when it was established that the Milky Way galaxy is only one of many island universes. We are but one of a local cluster of some two dozen galaxies; and we are an infinitesimal part of a universe composed of billions of galaxies. Our Milky Way is not central in any way that we can see, except to us.

In theory there could be a fourth cosmological displacement: the discovery that our bubble-universe is only one of many. While much can be said for the theory, whether other pulsating universes exist would seem to be quite beyond our knowing. However, there appears to be no good reason **not** to believe (provisionally) that there are pulsating bubbles scattered in all directions through the universe. To cling to the belief that there is but a single bubble-universe rings now like another aristocentric claim. Cosmologically, we are part of the universe, which undoubtedly extends farther than we can ever know.

14 Humanity has also undergone a **biological decentralization.** We have considered ourselves superior to all other living creatures and believed we possess a divine mandate to conquer, domesticate, or kill the "lower" animals. (Darwin warned us against such hierarchical semantics: "Never say higher or lower," he said.) Moreover, there was a qualitative difference between man and the animals: the former had a soul, while the latter did not.

Charles Darwin brought the simmer to a boil. Shortly after his publication in 1859 of *The Origin of Species,* the battle lines were drawn. The notion that man was not created as man—in distinctive Homo sapient form—and placed

What is the ultimate truth about ourselves? Various answers suggest themselves. We are a bit of stellar matter gone wrong. We are physical machinery—puppets that strut and talk and laugh and die as the hand of time pulls the strings beneath. But there is one elementary inescapable answer. We are that which asks the question. Whatever else there may be in our nature, responsibility towards truth is one of its attributes.

SIR ARTHUR EDDINGTON

Once the human species has initiated the search for other life in the universe, the search can never end; for until we find it, there will always be the possibility that it exists; and the search will never end until we find it.

PETER ANGELES

in the Garden by God himself; the idea that humans might have developed over great spans of time from primitive animal creatures that were distinctly unhuman—this was an insult comparable to the cosmological decentralization.

The climax of the battle might be thought of as the "monkey trial" in Dayton, Tennessee, in 1925. The young science teacher, John Scopes, was indicted in a test case for teaching evolution in the high school. By the time defense attorney Clarence Darrow had shown the fallacy of the arguments against evolution and had placed William Jennings Bryan, the prosecuting attorney, on the stand, the trial had become a worldwide spectacle. Darrow lost the case legally; but time has shown that the principle of intellectual freedom was the real victor. Since the Scopes trial we have been less disturbed that our remote ancestors might have been something other than "human."

We are now undergoing another phase of the biological decentralization through a reassessment of our ecological status. Although our pride seems less involved in this process, we are realizing that man is but part of a system. By some criteria, we can claim to be a superior part of the system, but we are having to come to terms with the fact that we can't exist without the system. Nor can we proceed to do whatever we wish to the fauna and flora around us. To survive we must bow to the balancing mechanisms at work within the ecosystem. Man is not the system; we did not **make** the system. We **belong** to it.

15 Humans are also undergoing a **psychological decentralization,** and, more than likely, it is just beginning.

Until the present time nothing has challenged man's **intellectual** superiority as evident in our capacities for abstract reasoning, communicating, knowledge-storage, mental flexibility, and cultural evolution. In the evolutionary niches where humans struggled to survive, these qualities were clearly supreme. But if man must confront other intelligent forms of life, this could turn out to be the most painful "right of passage" the human species has had to face. (The only greater ego-shock I can imagine would be the shattering realization that the human race is irrevocably bound for extinction.)

There is some likelihood that we are nearing such a confrontation just because we are beginning to consider the possibility that other forms of intelligent life may exist on Earth. Higher primates, we are finding, have greater intellectual skills than we thought—dolphins, gorillas, and Bonobo chimps come to mind. They may possess an intelligence as great as humans but so different that we underestimate it because we don't understand it.

The most severe reassessment of who and what we are will come if we confront extraterrestrial intelligence. Almost inevitably, **they** will contact **us,** which means that, in some ways, they will be far advanced beyond us. Their intelligence may be superior to man's—perhaps an IQ of 250 is merely bright normal to them. By comparison—however much it may traumatize us—the only appropriate stance for us humans may be one of humility adjustment.

16 The *Pioneer* and *Voyager* planetary probes, humankind's first interstellar travelers, carry plaques and records indicating the planet of origin and bearing pictures of the beings that inhabit it. The striking fact is **the explicit assumption** that other intelligent creatures might someday intercept the probe and wonder who sent it hurtling through space.

All these decentralizing crises that humans have experienced, or will experience, are religious in nature, for they deal with the ultimate questions of Man's place in the universe and our relationships within it.

It has heretofore been a role of Western religion to affirm human worth. The preservation by religious institutions of the convictions that Man is only just lower than the angels and that we are, in fact, children of God has been both comforting and healing. Humankind might not have survived the struggle without the sense of worth and purpose such beliefs have given us.

Nevertheless, as a child grows he realizes that he must compromise his egocentered nature if he is to live in the world of adult human beings. Mankind's decentralizations are part of our growth as a cultured species; it is a part of our **human**ization. To face realistically one's place in the scheme of existence offers us yet another chance to adjust to the world as it is. For some, accepting realities is more fulfilling than defending beliefs, no matter how therapeutic those beliefs may be. We can feel better about ourselves and others when we no longer have a need for aristocentric myth.

✦

The receipt of an interstellar message would be one of the major events in human history, and the beginning of the deprovincialization of our planet.

CARL SAGAN

CARL SAGAN

The Encyclopaedia Galactica

The cosmos is all there is or ever was or ever will be.

In the deepest sense, the search for extraterrestrial intelligence is a search for who we are.

Whether we are alone in the cosmos is something I dearly want to know.

Something like the processes that on earth led to man must have happened billions of other times in the history of our galaxy. There must be other starfolk.

I

He stands on a rocky cliff by the sea. Waves churn below and seagulls skim the breakers. He wears an orange windbreaker.

"The Cosmos is all there is or ever was or ever will be. Our feeblest contemplations of the Cosmos stir us . . . we know we are approaching the greatest of mysteries."

He plucks a dandelion seed from a crevice in the rock and lets it dance away in the wind.

"Come with me," he beckons.

For years to come, Carl Sagan will be known as the eloquent tour guide who lectured us and dreamed us through the light-years of space and time in his thirteen-part television series *Cosmos.* The dandelion seed is transformed into "the spaceship of the imagination," and Sagan, backed by a gifted team of filmmakers and scientists, and with dazzling special effects, shows us the wonders of the universe.

"In the last few millennia we have made the most astonishing and unexpected discoveries about the Cosmos and our place within it."

Sagan invites us to share his knowledge and excitement, and this "personal voyage" becomes the grandest of adventures. Before it is over he shows us supernovas, pulsars, black holes, star clusters, exploding galaxies, the big bang, other worlds where intelligent life might be found—and countless other cosmic and historical events.

"They remind us that humans have evolved to wonder, that understanding is a joy, that knowledge is prerequisite to survival."

II

Sagan leans against a stop sign, watching a police officer give out a ticket, listening to railcars roaring past. He wears the same orange windbreaker.

"I lived here . . . in Brooklyn. . . . I knew my immediate neighborhood intimately—every candy store, front stoop, backyard, empty lot, and wall for playing Chinese handball. It was my whole world."

In winter, he recalls, he could see the stars. "I looked up at them and wondered what they were." His friends told him "they were lights in the sky." Since he already knew that, he went to the library and found a book on stars. "I opened the book breathlessly right there in the library and the book said something astonishing—a very big thought. Stars, it said, were suns, but very far away. The sun was a star, but close up."

"I was ignorant . . . but I could tell that if the stars were suns they had to be awfully far away, farther away than 86th street, farther away than Manhattan, farther away, probably, than New Jersey.

"This just blew my mind. Until then, my universe had been my neighborhood. Now I tried to imagine how far away I'd have to move the sun to make it as faint as a star. I got my first sense of the immensity of the universe. I was hooked."

Sagan decided then and there that he would become an astronomer.

"But," his worried grandfather asked, "how will you make a living?"

Carl Sagan was born in Brooklyn in 1934, of an American-born mother and an emigrant Russian father, a cloth cutter in the garment industry. His parents expected their son to follow the family vocation, but they had the wisdom to support his own gifts and intellectual interests. "As a child it was my immense good fortune to have parents and a few good teachers who encouraged my curiosity." So he grew up under the city lights, playing handball, devouring science fiction, and dreaming of other worlds "fabulously unlike Brooklyn."

After high school, Sagan headed directly for a career in science. In 1951, at sixteen, he entered the University of Chicago on a scholarship. Ten years later he emerged with four degrees in science, including a Ph.D. in astronomy and astrophysics. He was twenty-six.

While in graduate school at Berkeley and Stanford, Sagan sensed the far-ranging implications of the work of the biochemists. At twenty-two he wrote his first technical paper on "Radiation and the Origin of the Gene"; this was followed by more than three hundred articles and a dozen books, most of them related to the biochemistry of life-origins. Sagan was preeminently an exobiologist.

"Science is a joy," he said, "and it belongs to everyone. It is not just something for an isolated, remote elite. It is our birthright."

III

In tropical southern India, inside a temple dedicated to Shiva, Sagan walks among some very old bronze statues of Hindu gods.

"The most elegant and sublime of these bronzes is a representation of the creation of the universe at the beginning of each cosmic cycle, a motif known as the Cosmic Dance of Shiva."

Sagan describes the blackened-bronze figure standing in a circle of flame: Shiva as Nataraja, dancing the Cosmic Dance of creation and destruction. Shiva's right hand holds a drum, symbolizing creation; his left hand holds a torch of flame, representing the conflagration that will finally destroy the universe. "Creation and Destruction."

Sagan emerges from the dark interior of the temple and sits in the warm sun. In a niche in the temple wall above him is a gray stone statue of the ever-popular Ganesha, the elephant-headed god of prosperity and enlightenment.

"The most sophisticated cosmological ideas came from Asia, and particularly from India," Sagan ponders aloud. "Most cultures imagine the world to be only a few hundred generations old. Hardly anyone guessed that the cosmos might be far older. But the ancient Hindus did." The Hindu cosmic cycle of 8.64 billion years—about half the actual age of our universe—is "a kind of premonition of modern astronomical ideas"—especially the theory of the oscillating universe.

Music from a village festival drifts through the palm trees.

"The big bang," he notes, "is modern scientific myth. It comes from the same human need to solve the cosmological question."

The philosophic enterprise that Sagan is conducting is a part of what he calls "cosmic consciousness-raising." For our

Encyclopaedia Galactica:
Entry World: 806.4615.0110
Civilization Type: 1.0 J.
Society Code: 4G4, "Humanity."
Star: G2V, $r = 9.844$ ***kpc,***
$\theta = 00°05'24''$,
$\phi = 206°28'49''$.
Planet: third,
$a = 1.5 \times 10^{13}$ cm,
$M = 6 \times 10^{27}$ g,
$R = 6.4 \times 10^{8}$ cm,
$p = 8.6 \times 10^{4}$ s,
$P = 3.2 \times 10^{7}$ s.
Extraplanetary colonies: none
Planet age: 1.45×10^{17} ***s.***
First locally initiated contact: 1.21×19^{9} ***s ago.***
Receipt first galactic nested code: application pending.
Biology: C, N, O, S, H_2O, PO_4.
Deoxyribonucleic acid.
No genetic prosthesis.
Mobile heterotrophs, symbionts with photosynthetic autotrophs. Surface dwellers, monospecific, polychromatic O_2 ***breathers.***
Fe-chelated tetrapyroles in circulatory fluid.
Sexual mammals.
$m \approx 7 \times 10^{4}$ g,
$t \approx 2 \times 10^{9}$ s.
Genomes: 4×10^{9}.
Technology: exponentiating/fossil fuels/nuclear weapons/organized warfare/environmental pollution.
Culture: ~200 nation states, ~6 global powers; cultural and technological homogeneity underway.
Prepartum/postpartum: 0.21 [18],
Individual/communal: 0.31 [17],
Artistic/technological: 0.14 [11]
Probability of survival: (per 100 yr): 40%.

I believe that a thousand years from now our descendants will look back on our time and marvel that in so critical, confused, and dangerous an age we were able to avoid self-destruction and take decisive steps to understand that vast cosmic ocean of which we are a tiny part.

We live in an age where the fundamental questions—about the nature of matter, the origin of life and consciousness and intelligence, the beginnings and ends of worlds and universes—are being approached rigorously and scientifically. We have an opportunity to satisfy that passion to know.

We have always watched the stars and mused about whether there are other beings who think and wonder. In a cosmic setting vast and old beyond ordinary human understanding, we are a little lonely.

It may be that we are very much like the inhabitants of, let's say, isolated valleys in New Guinea, who communicate with their neighbors by runner and drum, and who are completely unaware of a vast international radio and cable traffic over them, around them, and through them.

era, science—or more exactly, the scientific way of thinking—is the source of the fundamental data of consciousness. It alone can give us an understanding of the realities of our universe. After millennia of mythology, it is now possible for the human mind to enter realistically into the fabric of the universe and to involve itself, in a liberating way, with the events of the cosmos.

Intelligibility becomes a function of the interaction between the self and the world. In his work, Sagan is facilitating this interaction of selves with a newly discovered cosmos. He is guiding us through an odyssey that can resurrect all our rationalities and all our sentiments. "In *Cosmos,* we have tried to speak not just to the mind but also to the heart." From physics and chemistry to the music of the spheres and the poetry of our souls, *nothing is to be left out.* Our total humanness is to be expressed and reaffirmed.

IV

Sagan walks to the helm of "the spaceship of the imagination." At the console he reaches upper left and punches up a monitor showing the Milky Way galaxy; at upper right is a readout screen for displaying information on each world and its life-forms.

"Advanced technological civilizations would know about many worlds," he explains. A great blue-white spiral galaxy comes up on the screen at the front of the spaceship.

"Perhaps they would share their finds, assembling some vast repository of the knowledge of countless worlds. They might compile an Encyclopaedia Galactica.

"Perhaps someday there will be an entry in the Encyclopaedia Galactica for our planet or perhaps, even now, there exists a planetary dossier . . . a listing for 'Earth.' What do they know about us?"

World: 806.4615.0110
Civilization Type: 1.0 J
Society Code: 4G4, "Humanity" . . .
  Technology: Exponentiating
  Fossil fuels/nuclear weapons
  Organized warfare
  Environmental pollution . . .
Probability of survival (per 100 yr): 40%

The Encyclopaedia Galactica is Sagan's way of imaging "a cosmic context for mankind." We have an essential longing to know where we fit into the scheme of things.

Meanwhile, until such evidence is obtained, we must think in cosmic terms. The truth, notes Sagan, is that we have moved in a cosmic perspective since our presapient beginnings. "The deepest cosmological questions are embedded in human folklore and myth, superstition and religion." We have *assumed* that a relationship with heavenly beings exists.

"We have always watched the stars and mused about whether there are other beings who think and wonder. In a cosmic setting vast and old beyond ordinary human understanding, we are a little lonely."

The search for a cosmic context for mankind has begun and cannot end until that context is known.

"In the deepest sense," writes Sagan, "the search for extraterrestrial intelligence is a search for who we are."

✦

In memoriam: December 20, 1996

REFLECTIONS

1 In only a couple of decades scientists have done a remarkable about-face on the question of the existence of life on other planets. Carl Sagan has written extensively on the human need for, and search for, a "cosmic context" within which we could better understand ourselves. Are you in essential

agreement with Sagan's assessment of this "philosophic" need? Do you share it?

2 What do you think of Larry Niven's sagelike comment (p. 539) that the trouble with people who live on small planets is that they "tend to think small"? Is this a truism, or an adage you could store for later use?

3 The Florentine philosopher Francesco Sizzi has become famous (or infamous) for his reply to Galileo. After your first chuckle, what did you think of his stand and the way he rationalized it?

4 What do you think of the intent of the Drake/Sagan formula? Although some of the quantities are not yet known with any precision, what is the general message of the equation itself? On reflection, what do you think of "the L-factor"?

5 Reflect on the impact upon our thinking and feeling of the discovery of the existence of extraterrestrial life and intelligence. What is your evaluation of the implications suggested in this chapter? Can you think of other eventual changes in the way we think and feel when such an event occurs?

6 Phrase in your own way your response to the question, "What is humankind's place in the cosmos?" (Maybe you can be specific by focusing on Man's relationships to component elements of the universe, such as our Earth, other human beings, other living creatures, hypothetical aliens, and so on.)

7 Put into your own words the three decentralizations that humankind has experienced. If taken seriously, how do you think these new perspectives would affect (1) our self-image as individuals? and (2) mankind's collective image of itself (if there is such a thing)?

8 Note the statement on p. 547: "All these decentralizing crises that humans have experienced, or will experience, are religious in nature." Is this meaningful? Do you agree? Why or why not?

9 What do you think of the afterthoughts by Astronauts Mitchell and Schweickart on how their space voyages changed their lives (see marginal quote on p. 544)?

10 What do you think of the proverblike saying by Tsiolkovsky (marginal quote on p. 539)?

Of Ultimate Concern

We have seen the highest circle of spiraling powers. We have named this circle God. We might have given it any other name we wished: Abyss, Mystery, Absolute Darkness, Absolute Light, Matter, Spirit, Ultimate Hope, Ultimate Despair, Silence.

Nikos Kazantzakis

We are all children in a vast kindergarten trying to spell God's name with the wrong alphabet blocks.

Tennessee Williams

Of Ultimate Concern

8-1

This chapter deals with the philosophy of religion. The psychology of religion has placed religion in its evolutionary context and clarified some of its functions. This chapter suggests definitions and ponders several aspects of religious thinking: anthropomorphic spirits, spirit possession, the function of myth, and teleocosmic dramas. It deals with apocalyptic interpretations of history, the battlefield cosmology, the final eschaton, and some of the messianic figures who will return to initiate the final act of the great drama. Then some gentle spirits suggest that at the heart of religion can be found a "perennial philosophy" that binds humanity together in a single momentous vision.

Greek Tragedy

1 Religion is universal. It is found in every culture, in every age, in every place where humans have lit their fires, suffered loss of loved ones, and wondered about the meaning of life. Religion can be understood, therefore, only as we come to understand ourselves, only as we understand who we are, what we are, and what this need is.

We humans have been emerging for some five or six million years, and during this formative period virtually everything about us has changed and evolved. Over this span of time we have grown taller and developed a gracile skeletal frame, a delicate face, a bony chin, and a skull that rides securely atop a vertical column of vertebrae. But while these attributes all point in the direction of *Homo sapiens*, one characteristic alone identifies us as truly human: a big brain. It is this anatomical breakthrough that allows us to think abstractly, develop self-awareness, project ethical values—and create religion.

There are many paths to God, my son. I hope yours will not be too difficult.

Lew Wallace
Ben-Hur

CAN RELIGION BE DEFINED?

Religion is one's attitude toward whatever he considers to be the determiner of destiny.

JAMES BISSETT PRATT

Religion is man's ultimate concern for the Ultimate.

PAUL TILLICH

Religion is the ritual cultivation of socially accepted values.

JOHN FISCHER

Religion, as a minimum, is the belief in spiritual beings.

E. B. TYLOR

Religion is a propitiation of, and dependency on, superior powers which are believed to control and direct the course of nature and human life.

SIR JAMES G. FRAZER

Religion is *concern* about experiences which are regarded as of supreme value; *devotion* towards a power or powers believed to originate, increase, and conserve these values; and some *suitable expression* of this concern and devotion, whether through symbolic rites or through other individual and social conduct.

EDGAR S. BRIGHTMAN

Religion consists in the perception of the infinite under such manifestations as are able to influence the moral character of man.

MAX MÜLLER

Let the one who puts a jinx on the village die. Let him die, he who thought evil thoughts against us. Also give us fish.

Wapokomo prayer

2 Using this big brain, we have gradually discovered the true nature of the human condition, and what we have found is totally unacceptable. We have discovered that the human situation fails utterly to provide the basic essentials necessary for the fulfillment of our human capacities and the realization of hopes and dreams. We come into this world prepared to love, to grow, to create, and to be happy; but what we find is a debilitating environment waiting to crush our humanness.

Human life, at its very core, is Greek tragedy. The Buddha was blunt in his assessment of it: To exist *is* to suffer. In this condition the best we can hope for is to achieve a semblance of nobility in our suffering. But this is monstrously unsatisfactory.

For a million years evolution has labored to produce a creature with intelligent awareness. Now this creature, using that intelligent awareness, finds that

A religion, on its doctrinal sides, can thus be described as a system of general truths which have the effect of transforming character when they are sincerely held and vividly apprehended.

ALFRED NORTH WHITEHEAD

Religion is a belief in an ultimate meaning of the universe.

ALFRED R. WALLACE

Religion is a theory of man's relation to the universe.

S. P. HAYNES

Religion is our feeling about the highest forces that govern human destiny.

JOHN MORELY

Religion is a sense of the sacred.

SIR JULIAN HUXLEY

Religion is (subjectively regarded) the organization of all duties as divine commands.

IMMANUEL KANT

The essence of religion is the feeling of utter dependence upon the infinite reality, that is, upon God.

F. SCHLEIERMACHER

Any activity pursued in behalf of an ideal and against obstacles and in spite of threats of personal loss because of conviction of its general and enduring value is religious in quality.

JOHN DEWEY

In a maritime community depending on the products of the sea there is never magic connected with the collecting of shellfish or with fishing by poison, weirs, and fish traps, so long as these are completely reliable. On the other hand, any dangerous, hazardous, and uncertain type of fishing is surrounded by ritual. . . . Coastal sailing as long as it is perfectly safe and easy commands no magic. Overseas expeditions are invariably bound up with ceremonies and ritual.

E. B. TYLOR

he is trapped in a user-*un*friendly predicament—an ontological Prison from which there seems to be no escape.

The AMA [American Medical Association] urges you to let the faith that nourishes you grow strong, for faith is a physician.

TV commercial

TRANSFORMATION

3 Religion is humankind's profoundly human response to this unacceptable condition. It is in religion that the bitter truth of human existence is confronted by the human spirit, mind, and heart. Like all our creations, religion is a mechanism of survival, and without it the human species might not have survived. Religion translates an impossible situation into possibilities; it creates a worldview within which we can live a life worthy of our natures and aspirations.

"O, Great Motage, Protector of humble men, Descendant of the Great Fish, Father of the most Terrible Volcano and Devourer of all enemies, we humbly beg your leave to join with the Methodists."

What is it exactly that we can't live with? The field of study called psychology of religion has clarified some of the adaptive functions performed by religious thought. It has found that there are seven elemental conditions that characterize the collective experience of the human race.

1. We are helpless in the face of natural catastrophes such as earthquakes, tornadoes, tsunamis, and hurricanes; biological misfortunes like genetic diseases, viruses, and aging; and man-made devastations like terrorism and war. But religion assures that we are not helpless; divine assistance is immanently available. We can call upon God for help. Because He created the world and is in charge of events, He can alter their occurrence. Failing that, He is there to give us strength to face whatever happens to us.

2. We have discovered that **the universe is uncaring.** We humans may think we're important, but there is *nothing* in nature that is friendly or suppor-

PRAYER

In the year 204 BC Scipio Africanus sailed from Sicily to attack Hannibal's forces at Carthage. Just before the great expedition sailed, Scipio stood on his flagship at dawn and, after the herald had ordered silence, offered his prayer.

> Ye gods and goddesses, who inhabit the seas and the lands, I supplicate and beseech you that whatever has been done under my command, or is being done, or will later be done, may turn out to my advantage and to the advantage of the people and the commons of Rome, the allies, and the Latins who by land or sea or on rivers follow me, [accepting] the leadership, the authority, and the auspices of the Roman people; that you will support them and aid them with your help; that you will grant that, preserved in safety and victorious over the enemy, arrayed in body and laden with spoils, you will bring them back with me in triumph to our homes; that you will grant us the power to take revenge upon our enemies and foes; and that you will grant to me and the Roman people the power to enforce upon the Carthaginians what they have planned to do against our city, as an example of [divine] punishment.

Was Scipio's prayer answered? He shortly destroyed two great armies of Carthaginians and Numidians and went on to decisively defeat Hannibal in a battle near Zama on October 19, 202 BC. There was a tradition that Scipio was a favorite of the gods and was therefore in intimate communication with them. How does one determine whether prayers are answered if not in terms of results?

O millet, thou hast grown well for us; we thank thee, we eat thee.

Ainu prayer

tive of our humanness; on the contrary the forces of nature are aggressively hostile and destructive. Religion has responded by assuring us that this picture is false. Caring *does* exist. God watches over us with loving care and notices even the falling sparrow. Likewise the celestial Buddha sends savior-beings called bodhisattvas who are eternally available to walk at our side as we move along the path of suffering. Every religion assures that there exists a Cosmic Consciousness or other celestial beings who observe us empathetically and care about the quality of our lives.

"The priest—he used to read from the Moslem Quran, *and the Hindu* Gita, *moving from one to the other as if it mattered not which was being read as long as God was being worshipped."*

***Gandhi* (the motion picture)**

3. It follows that **the universe is unjust** or, better, that our human passion for justice is not a characteristic to be found in the real world. However precious the concept of justice is to us, nature knows nothing of it. When a flood drowns a village or disease strikes a family, it terminates the good and the bad with democratic disregard. To this travesty, religion has responded by revealing to us a cosmic system that is absolutely just. God sees into our hearts, judges our true selves, and treats us accordingly with unerring fairness. In our human systems justice may be rare or nonexistent, but in a cosmic perspective justice always prevails—if not in this world, then assuredly in the next. Heaven awaits good souls, and hell will welcome the bad ones. Or, in some Eastern traditions, individuals who have accumulated good karma will attain eternal bliss while those with bad karma will return to this world as animals, insects, or demons. The system never fails in its weighing of merit.

"Captain Pike has his illusions, and you, Captain Kirk, have your realities. May you find your way as pleasant."

"THE MENAGERIE"
Star Trek

The priest smiled. "What man who has lived for more than a score of years desires justice, warrior? For my part, I find mercy infinitely more attractive. Give me a forgiving deity any day."

ROGER ZELAZNY

4. **We are mortal.** We live out our all-too-brief lifetimes; then we die. But not before getting sick, growing old, and burying loves ones. Countering this insult, our religions flatly deny mortality; the denial of death is a central

We have art that we do not die of the truth.
Friedrich Nietzsche

News item: This is the first step in the investigation into the bridge disaster. A public hearing will be held . . . next week. The cause may never be learned, but as Assemblyman "Smith" put it, "This bridge collapse was not an act of God. Someone is responsible."
KNBC News

Spirit of this place, we give thee tobacco; so help us, save us from the enemy, bring us wealth, bring us back safely.
Iroquois prayer

Great Quahootze! Let me live, not be sick, find the enemy, not be afraid of him, find him asleep, and kill many of him.
Nootka Indian prayer

tenet of every religion. The soul is immortal, they tell us; it lives on in a spiritual state, experiencing the familiar pleasures in a Heaven, a Garden, Elysian Fields, or a Western Paradise. For good people, or persons of faith, the soul never dies but lives on into an afterlife.

5. **The universe is capricious.** The world of physical objects/events is largely a collection of random, disconnected occurrences, without pattern or significance. The human brain, however, has evolved to crave order, and disorder is deeply felt as destructive entropy. Religion has responded by assuring us that physical events do not happen randomly. They are willed by God, and no events are outside God's sphere of control. When seemingly fortuitous events impact our lives, they reveal God's investment in humanity, for they are sent to test us and offer us opportunities for spiritual growth. Natural events are not the chaotic happenings we perceive them to be but are components of a planned economy.

6. That **the universe is meaningless** is a discovery of the empirical sciences. Only gradually during the last four centuries has it become clear that physics and chemistry have nothing to say about human values. To a creature that thrives on meaning, this too is an insult. We humans cannot live without meaning, but nature and cosmos give us no help whatever in meeting this need. By contrast, religion informs us that we are participants in a cosmic drama that is unfolding above and beyond the plane of mundane history, and this drama is driven by a plot supervised by a playwright/director. Far from being meaningless, we belong to a universe in which every event has meaning and carries a message—providing we are wise enough to decipher it.

7. As for the future, **there are no grounds for hope.** Physical events are subject to the second law of thermodynamics; the universe is running down. Human history is going nowhere. Civilizations disintegrate, individuals pass from the scene, and death, finally, is victorious over all. But this dismal prognosis is transmogrified by the religious vision. Every major religion assures devotees that both history and cosmos are following a predetermined path to a goal—a telos. In the fullness of time a savior-being—a Christ figure or Paraclete, a Mahdi, a Maitreya, a Soshyans, a Kalki—will return to Earth and usher in an epoch of prosperity and peace. In China the Golden Age that was anciently lost will be recovered, after which harmony will again prevail between Heaven and Earth. Visions of the "end of time" vary greatly, yet they are all the same: there is no cause for despair, because grounds for a hopeful future are underwritten by no less than God and Cosmos.

4 We humans are stubborn, rebellious, and creative; and we are survivors. We refuse to accept the unacceptable. Not having been given a place to live, we proceed to create a place where human life will be honored. In terms of function, therefore, religion is the alteration of our perception of the human condition in order that we may live. This is the grandest creative achievement of the human spirit.

To summarize, our religions have created a world where there is no death, where someone or something is in charge of events, where there is a plan for the world, a plan for human history, a plan for each of us; where our lives are given value and significance; where justice prevails (now or later); where our individual selves are of ultimate worth; where we are loved and supported, empathized

πνεῦμα, *ατος, τό,* (πνέω) *a blowing,* **πνεύματα ἀνέμων** Hdt., Aesch.: alone, *a wind, blast,* Trag., etc. **2.** metaph., **θαλερωτέρῳ πν.** with more genial *breeze* or *influence,* Aesch.; **λύσσης πν. μάργῳ** Id.; **πν. ταὐτὸν οὔποτ' ἐν ἄνδρασιν φίλοις βέβηκεν** *the wind* is constantly changing even among friends, Soph. **II.** like Lat. *spiritus* or *anima, breathed air, breath,* Aesch.; **πν. βίου** *the breath* of life, Id.; **πν. ἀθροίζειν** to collect *breath,* Eur.; **πν. ἀφιέναι, ἀνιέναι, μεθιέναι** to give up *the ghost,* Id.; **πνεύματος διαρροαί** the wind-pipe, Id. **2.** *that is breathed forth, odour, scent,* Id. **III.** *spirit,* Lat. *afflatus,* Anth.: *inspiration,* N.T. **IV.** *the spirit* of man, Ib. **V.** *a spirit;* in N.T. of *the Holy Spirit,* **τὸ Πνεῦμα, Πν. ἅγιον**:—also of *angels,* Ib.:—of *evil spirits,* Ib. Hence

πνευμᾰτικός, *ή, όν, of spirit, spiritual,* N.T.

πνεύμων, in later Att. **πλεύμων,** *ονος, ὁ,* (πνέω) *the organ of* breathing, *the lungs,* Lat. *pulmo,* Il., Plat.: mostly in pl., Trag.; **πνεῦμ' ἀνεὶς ἐκ πλευμόνων** Eur.

πνεῦν, Dor. poët. for **ἔπνεον,** impf. of **πνέω.**

πνευστιάω, *to breathe hard, pant,* Arist.; Ep. part. **πνευστιόων,** Anth.

ΠΝΕ΄Ω, Ep. **πνείω,** Ion. impf. **πνείεσκον**: f. **πνεύσομαι,** Dor. **πνευσοῦμαι**: aor. 1 **ἔπνευσα**: pf. **πέπνευκα**:—Like other dissyll. Verbs in **-έω,** this Verb only contracts **εε, εει**:—*to blow,* of wind and air, Od., Hdt., Att.; **ἡ πνέουσα** (sc. **αὔρα**) *the breeze,* N.T. **II.** *to breathe, send forth an odour,* Od.:—c. gen. *to breathe* or *smell of* a thing, Anth. **III.** of animals, *to breathe hard, pant, gasp,* Il., Aesch. **IV.** generally, *to draw breath, breathe,* and so *to live,* Hom.; **οἱ πνέοντες = οἱ ζῶντες,** Soph. **V.** metaph., c. acc. cogn. *to breathe forth, breathe,* **μένεα πνείοντες** *breathing* spirit, of warriors, Il.; so, **πῦρ πν.** Hes.; **φόνον, κότον' Ἄρη** Aesch.; so, **πνέοντας δόρυ καὶ λόγχας** Ar.; **Ἀλφειὸν πνέων,** of a swift runner, Id. **2.** **μέγα πνεῖν** *to be of* a high *spirit, give oneself airs,* Eur.; **τόσονδ' ἔπνευσας** Id.:—also, with a nom., as if it were the wind, **μέγας πνέων** Id.; **πολὺς ἔπνει καὶ λαμπρὸς ἦν** Dem.

Note the variety of different, but associated, meanings attached to the Greek word *pneuma* and its related forms.

with, known, and understood; where we can dream and know that our dreams are not in vain.

5 This, then, is a brief phenomenological overview of humankind's religion. Note that it is solely an analysis of experience. It does not involve a description of reality or make value judgments about what is true or false or which religion is "the best" religion. All religion is true for those who believe, and false for those who don't.

What we need is well-informed blind belief.
"Professor Harry Wolper"
Creator

But this description is only half the story. The purpose of life is to live, and once we possess a worldview that is consonant with our humanness, we then proceed to enjoy a quality of life denied to us by the Prison. In the final analysis, therefore, religion exists in order to transform human experience. In fact, not a few scholars define religion as the dimension of human existence that enables us to transcend everyday consciousness. We often ask about "the meaning of life," to which Joseph Campbell responds that we're asking the wrong question. What we are actually seeking, he says, is not "the meaning of life" but the experience of being alive. The Hindus insist that in us all there exists

The world is now without mysteries.
Pierre Berthelot (1885)

We would be a lot safer if the Government would take its money out of science and put it into astrology and the reading of palms. I used to think that science would save us. But only in superstition is there hope. I beg you to believe in the most ridiculous superstition of all: that humanity is at the center of the universe, the fulfiller or the frustrater of the grandest dreams of God Almighty. If you can believe that and make others believe it, human beings might stop treating each other like garbage.

Kurt Vonnegut, Jr.

an intuition that ordinary consciousness is not enough: "There has to be more than this," they say. And every religious tradition has taught that the spiritual life enables the human psyche to tap into higher levels of consciousness. Carl Jung, the Swiss psychologist, wrote, "No matter what the world thinks about religious experience, the one who has it possesses the great treasure of a thing that has provided him with a source of life, meaning and beauty and that has given a new splendor to the world and to mankind." "By once seeing God," declared Ramakrishna Paramahamsa, "man is no longer bound down by the fetters of the world. He attains freedom from all worldly cares and anxieties, and nothing can ever bind him again."

The ultimate transformation of consciousness is that of the mystic, and testimony to mystical experiences comes from every tradition, from the elemental to the most sophisticated. A typical mystical consciousness was described by no less than Alfred Tennyson: "All at once, out of the intensity of the consciousness of individuality, the individuality itself seemed to dissolve and fade away into boundless being, and this is not a confused state, but the clearest of the clearest, utterly beyond words, where death was an almost laughable impossibility, the loss of personality (if so it were) seemed no extinction, but the only true life."

Religious mystics often describe an experience that they say feels like "waking up." Siddhartha's experience while meditating under the bo-tree is typical: "There arose within him the eye to perceive the noble truths, the wisdom that lights the true path, the light that expels darkness. . . ." Similarly, Baha'u'llah, the founder of the Baha'i faith, recalled: "I was but a man like others, asleep upon my couch, when lo, the breezes of the All-Glorious were wafted over Me, and taught Me the knowledge of all that hath been." In the minds of Christians the mystical moment described by Saint Paul on the Damascus road stands out as a paradigm: "Suddenly there shone from heaven a great light round about me. . . . We shall all be changed in a moment, in the twinkling of an eye."

The lonelier I am, the more of a recluse I become, the greater is my love of myths.

Aristotle

6 Religion should not be confused with various forms of rational thought that follow upon religious experience. As time passes and people find that they share similar convictions, doctrines develop. A **doctrine** is a formal, abstract interpretation of religious experience. Its purpose is to crystallize and preserve the fundamental elements of an experience and to make it possible for those within the group to communicate concerning the nature of the experience. A doctrine is a social phenomenon. Those with similar beliefs are saying they belong together as part of the believing group; more than that, they are attempting to resurrect and participate in the religious experience that the doctrine refers to.

Faith brings us to truth; philosophy makes us grasp it; ethics makes us practice it; and ritual makes us one with it.

Jagmanderlal Jaini

"It Was a Good Play. . . ."

Finding Dr. Faustus in his study, Mephistopheles recounted to him the story of creation.

The endless praises of the choirs of angels had begun to grow wearisome; for, after all, did he not deserve their praise? Had he not given them endless joy? Would it not be more amusing to obtain undeserved praise, to be worshipped by beings whom he tortured? He smiled inwardly, and resolved that the great drama should be performed.

For countless ages the hot nebula whirled aimlessly through space. At length it began to take shape, the central mass threw off planets, the planets cooled, boiling seas and burning mountains heaved and tossed, from black masses of cloud hot sheets of rain deluged the barely solid crust. And now the first germ of life grew in the depths of the ocean, and developed rapidly in the fructifying warmth into vast forest trees, huge ferns springing from the damp mould, sea monsters breeding, fighting, devouring, and passing away. And from the monsters, as the play unfolded itself, Man was born, with the power of thought, the knowledge of good and evil, and the cruel thirst for worship. And Man saw that all is passing in this mad monstrous world, that all is struggling to snatch, at any cost, a few brief moments of life before Death's inexorable decree. And man said: "There is a hidden purpose, could we but fathom it, and the purpose is good; for we must reverence something, and in the visible world there is nothing worthy of reverence." And Man stood aside from the struggle, resolving that God intended harmony to come out of chaos by human efforts. And when he followed the instincts which God has transmitted to him from his ancestry of beasts of prey, he called it Sin, and asked God to forgive him. But he doubted whether he could be justly forgiven, until he invented a divine Plan by which God's wrath was to have been appeased. And seeing the present was bad, he made it yet worse, that thereby the future might be better. And he gave God thanks for the strength that enabled him to forgo even the joys that were possible. And God smiled; and when he saw that Man had become perfect in renunciation and worship, he sent another sun through the sky, which crashed into Man's sun; and all returned again to nebula.

"Yes," he murmured, "it was a good play; I will have it performed again."

From Bertrand Russell's *Mysticism and Logic* (Doubleday Anchor, 1957), pp. 44 – 45.

As a religious institution develops, leaders emerge who are empowered to distinguish between true and false doctrines. Thus, they proclaim dogmas. A **dogma** is a doctrine that is supposed to have universal acceptance by all believers. It is a closed issue. It must be accepted as true if the benefits offered by the religion are to be attained.

A **creed** also is a formalization of elemental religious experience. The term is from the Latin word *credo*, "I believe." A creed thus functions to distinguish believers from nonbelievers. Creeds in the form of short, capsule statements of essential beliefs are often used as passwords and symbols of membership.

Lastly, **theology** is the intellectualization of the totality of one's religion. Traditionally, the theologian belongs to a particular religion. He is not a philosopher of religion who, with an eye to objectivity, studies the religious experience of all mankind. Rather he is a believer who stands within the "circle of

faith," attempting to update and reinterpret the meaning of the faith for the people of his own time. Thus a Muslim theologian speaks to Muslims, a Catholic theologian speaks to Catholics, and so on.

This traditional role, however, is at present undergoing revision. Today's theologians commonly make statements of ultimate concern that apply to all human beings and not merely to the members of a limited circle of faith.

Imagine how the Christian conscience would react to the idea that, behind the scenes, God and the Devil were the closest friends but had taken opposite sides in order to stage a great cosmic game. Yet this is rather much how things stood when the Book of Job was written, for here Satan is simply the counsel for the prosecution in the court of Heaven, as faithful a servant of the court as the advocatus diaboli at the Vatican.

Alan Watts

The Role of Myth

7 Religion is expressed in myth. A **myth** is a story involving the supernatural that is accepted by members of a social group—a clan, a tribe, an ethnic group, a religious community large or small, a nation—that explains the origin, significance, or meaning of an event. When that story is believed, it becomes true; and when it becomes true through belief, it is then called religion.

Believers are usually committed to the myths of a single tradition. However, the goal of philosophy of religion is to achieve a synoptic overview of the human race's entire mythic experience; stories from many traditions are studied together to discover insights not revealed from the study of a single heritage.

Since the time of the ancient Greeks the word "myth" has been a technical term and does not carry the implication that a story is "merely imagination" and therefore does not correspond to reality. This negative use of the term functions primarily to derogate others' beliefs and has no place in critical philosophy. "Myth" derives from the Greek *muthos* (or Latin *mythos*) and refers to the story embodied in the spoken part of a religious ritual, as distinct from the *dromenon*, the acted-out part of the ritual. Religious drama generally contains both story and action. What goes on in the action part you could know only if you were present to see it played out; but the spoken story can be told and retold down through the ages, quite apart from the drama and its religious meaning.

Throughout the twentieth century a picture of the role of myth gradually emerged. E. B. Tylor (*Primitive Culture*) and Sir James Frazer (*The Golden Bough*) were among the first to discern recurring ideas and themes. Both came to believe that myths reveal universal patterns or "laws" through which the human psyche manifests itself. Sigmund Freud (*Totem and Taboo*) and Carl Jung

(*Man and His Symbols*) added to our understanding of subconscious materials that express themselves in symbols, images, motifs, and themes.

The greatest illumination of myth came from the scholarship of Joseph Campbell (*Hero with a Thousand Faces, The Masks of God* in four volumes). Campbell opened three doors into the world of mythology:

1. Myths play a vital role in the collective life of mankind. They are not just classical folktales or delightful stories. Myths nourish mankind's collective spiritual life, and the society that loses its capacity for myth is without soul.
2. Campbell also showed that it is in our myths that we can discover humankind's most penetrating assessment of the human condition. Myths vividly reveal why the human condition is intolerable and why we are compelled to alter our perception of it.
3. Campbell documented the one great theme that dominates all mythology: the hero's journey. This is the master myth, and every mythic story illustrates one or more stages of this odyssey, which is a symbolic account of the psychic journey made by each human being in his or her lonely passage from birth to death and beyond.

An admirable piece of work infinitely more complex than the usual feminist novel. Gail Godwin gives the devil his due, and he turns out to be, at least half the time, female.

JANET GARDNER
(from a book review of *Violet Clay*)

8 The story of Demeter and Persephone is a classic example of myth and illustrates its symbolic nature. The story of the Eleusinian mystery has come down to us in an epic poem called the *Homeric Hymn to Demeter.* This drama was one of the favorite religious stories of the Greek world, and for more than a thousand years the little town of Eleusis, fourteen miles west of Athens, gave worshipers a very personal drama of salvation.

Every person acquires the stature of the enemy he wrestles with.

NIKOS KAZANTZAKIS

The story is told that the beautiful Persephone, daughter of Demeter and Zeus, was gathering flowers in the meadow one spring day—"roses and crocuses and beautiful violets, irises also and hyacinths and narcissi." As she reached to pick an especially beautiful flower, the earth suddenly opened and from the nether world sprang Pluto, riding in a chariot. The "wide-pathed earth yawned," and the god of Hades "caught her up reluctant in his golden car and bore her away lamenting" into the dark world of the dead.

From a distance her mother heard her cries, but nowhere could Persephone be found. For nine days Demeter wandered over the earth, searching. Then

A FEELING OF THE SACRED

The most beautiful thing we can experience is the mysterious. It is the source of all true art and science. He to whom this emotion is a stranger, who can no longer pause to wonder and stand rapt in awe, is as good as dead: his eyes are closed. This insight into the mystery of life, coupled though it be with fear, has also given rise to religion. To know that what is impenetrable to us really exists, manifesting itself as the highest wisdom and the most radiant beauty which our dull faculties can comprehend only in their most primitive form—this knowledge, this feeling, is at the center of true religiousness. In this sense, and in this sense only, I belong in the ranks of devoutly religious men.

ALBERT EINSTEIN

Ekam sat, vipra bahudha vadanti. *"Truth is One; sages call it by various names."*

Vedic text

Helios revealed to her what had happened. Furious that Zeus had conspired in her daughter's captivity, Demeter left the home of the gods on Olympus and wandered in the world of man. At the town of Eleusis she was treated with love, even though she was in disguise; so it was there that she decided to settle.

Eventually she revealed to the Eleusinians her true identity and asked that they build her a temple. When it was finished, she enclosed herself in her new home; then she set out to seek revenge on Zeus. She decreed a "most dreadful and cruel year for mankind over the all-nourished earth," and "in the fields the oxen drew many a curved plough in vain, and much white barley was cast upon the land without avail." One by one the gods entreated her to return nourishment to the Earth, but she vowed not to relent until she had her daughter with her again.

Finally Zeus commanded the Keeper of the Dead to return Persephone to the land of the living. But crafty Pluto "secretly gave her sweet pomegranate seed to eat" before allowing her to return to the bright world of sunlight. Therefore part of her belonged to the nether world, and she was obliged to spend a third part of every year there with her husband, Pluto, reigning as queen of Hades; the other two-thirds she could spend with her mother and the gods and men. So Demeter, with divine justice, allowed the earth to come alive for two-thirds of each year and allowed it to die for a third season.

Before returning to Olympus, Demeter taught her divine mysteries to the people of Eleusis—"awful mysteries which no one may in any way transgress or pry into or utter." All who were willing to study, purify themselves, and go through the sacred rites could share in her divine mysteries.

Annual ceremonies began with an elaborate parade from Athens and continued for nine days at Eleusis. Devotees participated around the clock in moving rituals and plays. They drank a sacred drink and thereby infused into their mortal bodies the immortality promised by the divine mythos. They became actors, each one of them, as the solemn story was gradually revealed and reenacted and as the gods were brought to life again in the religious drama.

Myths like the Eleusinian perform numerous functions. They explain natural events, provide a feeling of control over the uncontrollable, and reduce the

Better Off Without Them

For the most part the immortal gods were of little use to human beings and often they were quite the reverse of useful: Zeus a dangerous lover for mortal maidens and completely incalculable in his use of the terrible thunderbolt; Ares the maker of war and a general pest; Hera with no idea of justice when she was jealous as she perpetually was; Athena also a war maker, and wielding the lightning's sharp lance quite as irresponsibly as Zeus did; Aphrodite using her power chiefly to ensnare and betray. They were a beautiful, radiant company, to be sure, and their adventures made excellent stories; but when they were not positively harmful, they were capricious and undependable and in general mortals got on best without them.

Edith Hamilton

threat of the unknown. They provide social coherence and cultural continuity, and when recounted in drama, song, dance, and around the campfire, they make for lively communal entertainment.

At one level the Eleusinian myth accounts for the cycle of the seasons. Spring is the time of fertility when crops grow and meadows again turn green; but summer and fall soon follow, and the cold winter kills all. Why? Because Persephone, the bringer of life energy, must for a season die to this world. The myth puts death in perspective: there can be no spring without winter, no day without night, no birth without death.

Persephone's descent into Hades is symbolic death, but she is rescued to live again in an eternally recurring spring. This theme is universal. In Mesopotamia the god Tammuz dies but is sought and found in the underworld by Ishtar, who loved him. A similar story is told of Adonis, who is found by Aphrodite; of Osiris and his resurrection by Isis; of the Shinto goddess Izanami, who is pursued into the nether regions by her husband, Izanagi. In every case the hero is persistently sought by someone who loved him, and this love ensures that the hero is not lost to death but will return to life. Persephone's annual death in Hades is a sacrifice (analogous to Christ's death on the cross); because she dies and returns, all life will be renewed.

One who has experienced this will understand something of it; it cannot be more clearly expressed, since all that comes to pass in this state is so obscure. I can only say that the soul feels close to God and that there abides within it such a certainty that it cannot possibly do other than believe.

SAINT THERESA OF AVILA

9 A myth is mostly a social phenomenon. However, if a story performs similar functions for a single individual, then the word "myth" remains valid.

Viktor Frankl, a psychiatrist who survived the horrors of Nazi concentration camps, remembers a conversation he once had with a rabbi.

> He had lost his first wife and their six children in the concentration camp of Auschwitz where they were gassed, and now it turned out that his second wife was sterile. I observed that procreation is not the only meaning of life, for then life in itself would become meaningless, and something that in itself is meaningless cannot be rendered meaningful merely by its perpetuation. However, the rabbi evaluated his plight as an orthodox Jew in terms of despair that there was no son of his own who would ever say *Kaddish* [prayer for the dead] for him after his death.
>
> But I would not give up. I made a last attempt to help him by inquiring whether he did not hope to see his children again in Heaven. However, my question was followed by an outburst of tears, and now the true reason of his despair came to the fore: he explained that his children, since they died as innocent martyrs, were found worthy of the highest place in Heaven, but as for himself he could not expect, as an old sinful man, to be assigned the same place. I did not give up but retorted, "Is it not conceivable, Rabbi, that precisely this was the meaning of your surviving your children; that you may be purified through these years of suffering, so that finally you, too, though not innocent like your children, may become worthy of joining them in Heaven? Is it not written in the Psalms that God preserves all your tears? So, perhaps none of your sufferings were in vain." For the first time in many years he found relief from his suffering, through the new point of view that I was able to open up to him.

THE ANTHROPOMORPHIC SPIRITS

10 Early human beings lived out their lives in a world of aggressive natural forces: rainstorms, floods, forest and veld fires, locusts and famine, illness, pain, and death. Most of these forces were hostile—they were "evil." But there were

Indeed, I do not forget that my voice is but one voice, my experience a mere drop in the sea, my knowledge no greater than the visual field in a microscope, my mind's eye a mirror that reflects a small corner of the world, and my ideas—a subjective confession.

Carl G. Jung

friendly forces too: rain for crops, life-generating energies that brought new lambs to flocks and new children to families and clans, sun to make their corn grow, good winds to push outriggers, good conditions that filled their nets with fish. These were uncontrollable forces; storms, floods, and forest fires came whether humans liked it or not.

What are the energies behind the raging hurricane or the burning disease? The universe about us is conceived within the limits of our own experience. We cannot negotiate with unseen forces; we cannot think about the inconceivable. Yet conceive them we must, and negotiate we must. Therefore we think of them as consciousnesses with minds, wills, appetites, and emotions—like us. We call them "spirits," and they come in many guises: demons, ancestral ghosts, angels, gods and goddesses, kami, jinn, and on and on.

The spirits are like us, and we can talk with them. We can cajole, threaten, complain to, pray to, and bargain with them. We can understand why at times they behave with consistency (which we do) or become capricious and unpredictable (which we also do). We can bribe them into doing us favors; we can offer them gifts of varying worth. More sophisticated spirits are believed to respond to subtler forms of sacrifice: the sacrifice of one's will, of earthly goods, of pleasures, or of one's ego.

These processes arise from man's need to survive the onslaught of aggressive forces from nature and society. During peaceful times these personified forces can help humans achieve fulfilling goals; they enable us to "grow in spirit" and become more stable, confident, and loving—at peace with one's self.

Religion functions to work out a "saving" relationship. In Judeo-Christian terms this relationship is called justification—getting into a "right relationship with God." But this relationship can be generalized: getting into a right relationship with Shiva, with Allah, with Isis, with Christ, with Mithras, with Amitabha Buddha; all these symbolic relationships move us toward the desired goal—"salvation."

11 If the spirits live for a long while, they frequently become part of a "theological complex," a system so grandiose that they are no longer accessible to the masses of people and cannot meet their daily needs. In the Greek and Roman religions the gods became so engrossed with the affairs of state that they were no longer of any concern to the common person. During the time of the Roman Empire the great gods of the Roman pantheon were functionaries of state ceremonies, to be worshiped by emperors and other dignitaries. So distant had they become that the farmer and the merchant had long since forgotten them.

And so, the great gods were replaced by godlets, by the lares and penates who still had time to take care of the mortals' mundane affairs. Pomona would look after their fruit trees, Melona their beehives, Epona their horses, Juventa their children; and two-faced Janus still had time to act as sentinel over doors, looking after all who went in or came out of their houses.

This is a common development. Whenever the deities become too great, too important—too distant in their transcendent glory—to take care of humans' immediate interests, then lesser spirits inevitably replace them and carry on their ministrations. They may be called angels, guardian spirits, genii, lares and penates, saints, bodhisattvas, or avatars. But in all cases, they remain responsive and available in time of need.

Spirit Possession

Without God, we cannot.
Without us, God will not.
Saint Augustine

12 Spirits "possess" or "inhabit" people. We humans have been quite sure of this, since we intuit ourselves to be a spirit inside a body. If one's own being is a dualism of essence and matter—soul and body—then it is only reasonable that other spirits, too, might be able to inhabit our physical bodies.

This phenomenon—"spirit possession"—has been a universal means of accounting for the complexities of human behavior. Possession can explain the strange aberrations that we observe in others, such as epileptic seizures; and it nicely accounts for feelings we find inside ourselves: dizziness, fevers, convulsions. Most of the "altered states" of religious consciousness—ecstatic trances, visions, conversions, speaking in tongues, oracular prophecies—can be thus explained. Negatively, if possessed by a bad spirit (by a demon, a witch, a jinn, or a reified entity such as "sin"), we can point to the cause of the evil things we do and place blame accordingly. On the other hand, when possessed by congenial spirits, then we can do good things and even accomplish feats that otherwise would have been beyond our capability.

From earliest times special techniques have been used for exorcising unwanted spirits and for inducing visitations by good spirits. To be possessed by the Holy Spirit is the most valued of human experiences, according to Zoroastrians, Christians, and Muslims. In some circles this blessing would be validated by intense emotion (like the "strange warming of the heart" reported by John Wesley), by glossolalia (among Pentecostals), or by an egoless consciousness (among Catholic mystics).

13 People have experiences they invest with special significance and that effect drastic changes in their lives. We preserve the essence of such episodes by reflecting on them and interpreting them. Interpretations usually draw upon familiar theological concepts and linguistic tools. What the experience "means" is therefore, to some extent, culturally conditioned.

When attempting to understand a religious experience, two interpretations should be taken into account. One, of course, is the interpretation of the event given by the experiencer herself. This point of view will develop within the framework of the person's religious beliefs, and it is this interpretation that gives the experience meaning and affects her life.

Another interpretation can be made by an objective observer who can explain the experience in terms of motivations, emotional needs, or altered states in body chemistry. Although the objective account does not pretend to include the meaning that the experience holds for the experiencer, it can provide a valuable perspective for understanding the larger context of the event.

Teleocosmic Dramas

14 People have rarely been able to shake the feeling that they are participants in a sweeping drama or some kind of a teleological movement and that their lives are a vital part of its program. Our search for meaning is so deep that we are willing to be cast in whatever teleocosmic dramas are available.

When hope is taken away from a people, moral degeneration quickly follows.

Pearl S. Buck

Teleocosmic programs are a part of every religious tradition, from the simplest to the most sophisticated, and they have been embroidered in infinite detail by theologians and philosophers. Because our need to interpret is irrepressible, our interpretations commonly take on a teleological structure. Somewhere we will find the basis for a storyline, a plot, a plan, a goal-directed scheme, even a conspiracy—recall the *Book of Job,* for instance, in which God and Satan conspire to do a number on hapless Job.

We have been cast in the play just by being born. Our roles are to be taken seriously, for how well we perform our given roles affects the quality of our lives and determines our destiny. Little wonder, then, that we commit time and energy to the clarification of the teleocosmic plot so that we can better understand and play our roles.

Apocalyptic Dramas

15 We saw in an earlier chapter (5-1) that the metaphor of the drama has been used by philosophers of history to try to interpret the meaning and the goal of human history. Just as a drama may move from the opening curtain through three or four acts that are subdivided into scenes, and with a named dramatis personae who move the suspenseful plot through its tangles to a resolution of the plot, and a final curtain, this way of interpreting history provides a living storyline in which we humans can participate individually and collectively.

It's not surprising, Sir. Sharing an orbit with God is no small experience.

"Counselor Troi"
Star Trek / The Next Generation

The interpretation of history as drama has been developed to its highest point in the Western family of religions—Zoroastrianism, Judaism, Christianity, and Islam. The metaphor called for a moment in time for the opening curtain such as 4004 BC (Archbishop Ussher's famous calculation) or 5737 BCE (the Judaic calculation)—and a set moment for the descent of the final curtain—AC 156, 732, 1946, 1984, or 2026. Various elements of the plot have been mapped so that one's role in the drama should, in principle, be knowable; and if we can understand the plot, determine which scene is currently playing, and read "the signs of the times," then we can know what is expected of us by the Playwright. With a correct reading of the plot (especially if we have a script), we'll know when the dénouement is destined to occur.

These are personal linear-historical dramas, directed from above. They are apocalyptic dramas, given that much of the program—backdrop, props, stagehands, as well as the Director—are offstage, above space and time, supervising the drama, while we humans are in space and time, moving along from scene to scene, playing out the story.

16 The teleocosmic drama held in common by the Western family of religions had its origins in the worldview of the parent religion, Zoroastrianism. Here the battlefield metaphor was first developed by the founder Zoroaster (circa 660 BC), and the drama—not unlike *Macbeth* or *Richard III*—is the account of a great battle. When this world was created by the Divine Mind, hosts of heavenly creatures of light also came into being: a Holy Spirit through whom the God of Light works his will, plus the Amesha Spentas (Immortal Holy Ones) and Yazatas (Angels), all led by Ahura Mazda, the Creator and Wise Lord of this world and the final judge and redeemer of history.

The evil counterparts are the daevas led by the supreme evil spirit, Angra Mainyu, the Lord of Darkness. Human history is a battlefield confrontation of evil forces and heavenly forces, led by the "military generals" Spenta Mainyu and Angra Mainyu. In this aeons-long struggle, humans are caught up in a cosmic conflagration and must decide, of our own free will, on which side we will take a stand.

For humans, just as for the spiritual forces, the war is essentially a moral struggle. The individual has but one lifetime during which to determine his or her destiny. Professor Robert Smith describes the cosmic scenario:

> The cardinal Zoroastrian moral principle that each man's soul is the seat of the war between good and evil sets the stage for man's plight. This war in the breast is of critical importance as the supreme Ahura Mazda is not unopposed in creation. Over against Asha (the Truth) is Druj (the Lie). Truth is confronted with Falsehood, Life with Death. The Good Spirit is opposed by the Bad Spirit. On this earthly battlefield, Angra Mainyu is set over against Spenta Mainyu in dualistic fashion. One must feel that they are co-equals in this earthly battle. However, the capacity of Angra Mainyu for mischief is boundless and the evil power he possesses is many times multiplied by the demons he creates to assist him. Without man's active participation on the side of Ahura Mazda, the world will not be a "brighter place to live" and man will not "be like God." Consequently, even in the working out of the Zoroastrian doctrine that the ultimate victory will be Ahura Mazda's, the first duty of every right-thinking man is to oppose and win the battle here and now.

The battle rages down through human history, a human's only weapons being Truth and Righteousness, assisted by Good Thoughts, Good Words, and Good Deeds—all very real personified spirits. Each person must "fight all the enemies of Good Mind as though they were his own enemies and as if he were the only warrior upon the battlefield."

But all battles come to an end when victors vanquish the losers. Entire armies win and lose battles, but armies are really composed only of individual soldiers. So prior to a battle's final outcome, each soldier carries on his own personal life or death struggle. So also for Zoroaster's spiritual warriors of light against darkness.

For the first time in world religion we have the drama of individual judgment in the eschatological context of a great cosmic battle. If a warrior falls in battle, then his judgment takes place on the fourth day after his death. For three nights the soul of the deceased sits at the head of its former body, meditating on its past thoughts, words, and deeds. During this time the soul is comforted (if it has been a righteous soul) by good angels or tormented (if it has been wicked) by demons.

On the fourth day the soul makes its way to the Chinvat Bridge. Before crossing, the soul must hold the scales for the final weighing of its merits and demerits. When judgment is rendered and sentence passed, the soul walks onto the bridge. The Zoroastrian text called the *Bundahishn* describes what takes place in the center of the bridge.

> There is a sharp edge which stands like a sword; . . . and Hell is below the Bridge. Then the soul is carried to where stands the sharp edge. Then, if it be righteous, the sharp edge presents its broad side. . . . If the soul be wicked, that sharp edge

> continues to stand edgewise, and does not give a passage. . . . With three steps which it (the soul) takes forward (evil thoughts, evil words, evil deeds) it is cut down from the head of the Bridge, and falls headlong into Hell.
>
> When (the righteous soul) takes a step over the Chinvat Bridge, there comes to it a fragrant wind from Paradise, which smells of musk and ambergris, and that fragrance is more pleasant to it than any other pleasure.
>
> When it reaches the middle of the Bridge, it beholds an apparition of such beauty that it hath never seen a figure of greater beauty. . . . And when the apparition appears to the soul, (the soul) speaks thus: "Who art thou with such beauty that a figure of greater beauty I have never seen?" The apparition speaks (thus): "I am thine own good actions. I myself was good, but thine actions have made me better."
>
> And the apparition embraces the soul, and they both depart with complete joy and ease into Paradise.
>
> But if the soul be that of a wicked man . . . there blows to him an exceedingly foul wind from Hell [and] it sees an apparition of such extreme ugliness and frightfulness that it hath never seen one uglier and more unseemly. . . .
>
> She speaks (thus): "I am thine own bad actions. I myself was ugly, and thou madest me worse day after day, and now thou hast thrown me and thine own self into misery and damnation, and we shall suffer punishment till the day of Resurrection."
>
> And the apparition embraces it, and both fall headlong from the middle of the Chinvat Bridge and descend to Hell.

17 The cosmological structure of the Zoroastrian drama was adopted by its offspring Judaism, Christianity, and Islam. Some elements were revised, but most remained intact. In late Judaic religion, the archangels and angels fought on behalf of Yahweh/God and constituted the Forces of Light, while demons and evil spirits led by Satan made up the Forces of Darkness.

Before being conflated with Zoroastrian elements, Hebrew religion had its own heritage, which (after the sixth century BCE) was combined with the battlefield metaphor.

The Judaic teleocosmology began in the Garden of Eden. This was paradise, and the tenants were perfect, companions to one another and children of God. This is the opening scene of the drama, and the final scene is a return to Eden—to paradise and perfection. By the time the vision had been filled out with details, the Hebrews had ceased to be a wandering tribe and had become a nation. The final scene of the plot was therefore envisioned as a "messianic age" in which the nation Israel, or at least a faithful Remnant, would reign supreme over all the earth. Truly it would be a paradise, for peace would last forever and prosperity would surpass all expectation. As one fragment of late Jewish literature put it, every grapevine would bear a thousand clusters, every cluster would bear a thousand grapes, and every grape would yield a gallon of wine.

Between these opening and closing scenes lies human history as we know it, with suffering and death. Although this is the only condition that evolutionary man has ever known, we find great satisfaction in the conviction that there was a time when everything was right and that we can anticipate a future setting in which all will be made right again.

Being a child of Judaism and a grandchild of Zoroastrianism, Christianity adopted the same beginning to the teleocosmic drama—the garden paradise of Eden—and developed further the metaphor of the cosmic battlefield. Christians, however, added a new element. Along the timeline of human existence, there came a moment when life was suddenly given meaning by the intervention of the Creator deity himself. Until the advent of the redeemer god, human suffering had been pointless; it counted for nothing. But after his appearance, human suffering became a "trial by fire" to create spiritually worthy souls who, collectively, would compose a "communion of saints" to bear witness until they could join together in the Kingdom of God. Nevertheless, human suffering will continue until the final act of the drama, when the Reign of God begins with the Parousia, the Return of the Messiah: "For the Lord himself, at the summons, when the archangel calls and God's trumpet sounds, will come down from heaven, and first those who died in union with Christ will rise; then those of us who are still living will be caught up with them on clouds into the air to meet the Lord, and so we shall be with the Lord forever" (I Thess. 4:16f.).

For early Christians (and adventist groups of any century), this is the joyous fulfillment of God's plan. With a climactic crescendo—full orchestra and chorus—it closes out the tragic drama and begins the Reign of God.

The Eschaton—End of Drama

18 In linear historical plots, we find that believers almost universally conclude that they are living near the end of the play—an event called the eschaton. They hope that the dramatic last scene will be acted out during their lifetime. Deep in our marrow we want to know that the bloody history of man's agony is nearly over; that peace, justice, and goodwill are about to prevail; that in our own ephemeral lifetimes we will be able to enjoy a modicum of happiness. To live prior to the dénouement of the drama leaves one in a suspended state—like leaving a motion picture before the ending.

Man is a creature of hope, and his teleocosmic dreams almost always foresee a future time when life will be good again and there will be no more fear, pain, loneliness, and death. But it is here that we humans reveal our pessimism. We intuit that we cannot bring about such conditions by ourselves, so we envision supernatural beings who will appear on Earth at their appointed times to call a drum roll for the last act of the great drama.

Judaism looks forward to the coming of the **Messiah** ("Anointed One"). According to one interpretation, the nation Israel will be established by Yahweh/God as a Chosen Light to the Gentiles to rule over them forever. According to another interpretation, the Son of Man will appear to usher in a spiritual Messianic Age.

Christians came to believe that **Jesus the Christ** (again, the Anointed One) will return and supervise the Last Judgment, the separation of the righteous from the wicked. He will represent God himself when the Reign of God begins.

In Buddhism, **Maitreya** is at present a Buddha-in-the-making, waiting to come to Earth in due time to inaugurate the final age and bring peace. In Hinduism, a messiah named **Kalki** will make his appearance on a white horse and brandishing a flaming sword. This savior, the tenth avatar of Vishnu, will save the righteous and destroy the wicked at the end of the fourth hopelessly depraved world period.

In Zoroastrianism, a messiah called **Soshyans** will appear in the final days and preside over a general resurrection. A flood of molten metal will pour across the Earth, purging the wicked of their evil but bathing the righteous in soothing balm. Ahura Mazda will hurl the Evil One, Ahriman, into a lake of fire, and the saved will then dwell together in a new Heaven and a new Earth, enjoying eternal peace. (Incidentally, in this particular drama, adults will remain forever at the age of forty and children at fifteen.)

In Shi'ite Islam, devotees await a messianic figure entitled the **Mahdi** to complete the task, begun by Muhammad, of carrying the message of salvation to all mankind. This "Divinely Guided One" will usher in a period of peace before the end of the world and the onset of the Last Judgment.

All Religion Is One

19 There is a minority report within man's religions that contends that all religions are one. Most have said this because they wanted it to be so, but some of these assertions are the result of personal experience with many religious faiths.

With appropriate definition, perhaps we can say that religion is one thing. But differences are only too obvious. The various gods are thought to possess different characteristics; they behave differently and demand different responses from their devotees.

Yet when individuals plunge very deep into their faith, they commonly emerge with a feeling of oneness. It could be that our most profound experiences are similar but become differentiated in the process of interpretation. It might be that certain universal psychophysical processes—alpha rhythms, visions, out-of-body mechanisms—operate to produce similar experiences.

It may also be that we find what we're looking for. If one wishes to find the differences in the many religions of the human species, they can be found; but if one searches for similarities underlying the varied religious approaches to the Riddle of Life, they too are there and can be found.

20 One of the more successful attempts to clarify "the highest common factors" contained in the great religions has been called the Perennial Philosophy. Aldous Huxley described four such elements from which we might infer that, however varied the paths we travel, humanity's religious quest is quintessentially One.

1. This world as we conceptualize and experience it is a manifestation of a greater reality, a "Divine Ground of Being." All the realities of experience, both mental and material, are merely "bits and fragments" of that Ultimate Reality. They constitute only limited, angular glimpses of that Divine Ground.
2. Human beings can acquire knowledge *about* that Divine Ground, but such knowledge is relatively unimportant. Of greater significance is the fact that we can enter into a direct intuitive knowledge of it, a knowledge involving our whole being and not merely our conceptualizing intellects. This is a mystical knowing that unites the knower with the Known, or the known with the Knower.

3. In his very nature, man is a duality. We are composed of ephemeral elements (body, ego-self, data bits, memory) and eternal essence (soul, atman, "divine spark"). The ephemeral elements are temporal and temporary, but the eternal essence can become One with the Divine Ground of Being.
4. The singular goal of human existence on Earth is for each individual to come to know the eternal essence of his being and to identify it more and more closely with the Divine Ground of all Being.

Huxley considered the Perennial Philosophy to be one of the great insights in the history of human understanding, and his judgment is shared by some present-day philosophers of religion. Huxley's previsions are clear and strong:

> In existing circumstances there is not the slightest chance that any of the traditional religions will obtain universal acceptance. Europeans and Americans will see no reason for being converted to Hinduism, say, or Buddhism. And the people of Asia can hardly be expected to renounce their own traditions for the Christianity professed, often sincerely, by the imperialists who, for four hundred years and more, have been systematically attacking, exploiting and oppressing, and are now trying to finish off the work of destruction by "educating" them. But happily there is the Highest Common Factor of all religions, the Perennial Philosophy which has always and everywhere been the metaphysical system of the prophets, saints and sages. It is perfectly possible for people to remain good Christians, Hindus, Buddhists or Moslems and yet to be united in full agreement on the basic doctrines of the Perennial Philosophy.

21 There was a man who worshiped Shiva but hated all other deities. One day Shiva appeared to him and said, "I shall not be pleased with thee so long as thou hatest the other gods." The man was inexorable. After a few days Shiva again appeared to him and said, "I shall never be pleased with thee so long as thou hatest." The man kept silent. After a few days Shiva again appeared to him. This time he appeared as Hari-har, namely, one side of his body was that of Shiva, and the other side that of Vishnu. The man was half pleased and half displeased. He laid his offerings on the side representing Shiva and did not offer anything to the side representing Vishnu. Then Shiva said, "Thy bigotry is unconquerable. I, by assuming this dual aspect, tried to convince thee that all gods and goddesses are but various aspects of the one Absolute Brahman."

22 The Muslim mystic Ibn Arabi is quoted as saying:

> There was a time when I took it amiss in my companion if his religion was not like mine, but now my heart admits every form. It is a pasture of gazelles, a cloister for monks, a temple for idols, a Ka'bah the pilgrim, the tables of the Law, and the sacred book of the Qur'an. Love alone is my religion, and whithersoever man's camels turn, it is *my* religion and *my* faith.

✦

Joseph Campbell

The Hero with a Thousand Faces

It's the same story, over and over again: wherever two or more members of the human species have lit their fires and shared their fears and dreams, there emerges, out of the psychic depths, the fabulous stories that reveal what it means to be human. These stories always arrive in the shape of myth, for myth is the only form of symbolic expression available to the unconscious mind. Myths, therefore—provided their cryptic language can be decoded—can be seen as the precious treasure-trove of secrets that reveal the deepest layers of the evolving, emerging human psyche.

This is the life-message of Joseph Campbell, author of the enormously popular *The Hero with a Thousand Faces.* Campbell devoted his professional life to studying and deciphering the myths of the world's cultural traditions. What he found was that "the fundamental themes of mythological thought have remained constant and universal, not only throughout history, but also over the whole extent of mankind's occupation of the earth." In other words, having looked at thousands of the mythical stories embedded in humankind's storehouse of tradition, he discovered that a few themes occur repeatedly, and that within these few themes exists a great "monomyth," a single mythical plot-line that reveals what is of ultimate importance to the human race. Campbell spent virtually his entire life clarifying and elaborating on that one momentous vision quest—the life-journey of the World Hero. This singular heroic odyssey is, in its essence, the life-story of each person as well as the collective story of the journey of the human race.

Long before he died in 1987 Joseph Campbell was aware that his own life had become a classic example of the hero's journey. He was born in New York City in 1904, the first child of Josephine and Charles Campbell. Their religious heritage was Roman Catholic, and until he was about fifteen he attended a Catholic day school. ("I was a little altar boy.") This heritage gave him a rich ground of knowledge and understanding of the spiritual yearnings of human beings.

By the age of twelve he had begun to read voraciously, a habit he followed for another seven decades. At fifteen he attended a Catholic prep school and there, one day, he was given a copy of the life of Leonardo da Vinci, a book, he said, that helped him "discover his ignorance." "My whole world shifted with that book." He had already begun to study the lore of the American Indians and the romances of the Celtic tradition.

Then he was "grabbed" by James Joyce's *A Portrait of the Artist as a Young Man,* in which the lead character Stephen Dedalus was wrestling with the problem Campbell was facing. "And the problem is when you're deeply built into the system of the church and you're losing your faith"—what do you do? "It's no fun. I mean, it started when I was studying biology. There's absolutely no relationship between the biological evolution of the human species, the animal and plant world, and what you get in the Book of Genesis. . . . And how can you go through life with that?" His problem was to find a way to salvage the spirituality of faith, with all its magnificent symbols, and yet stay open to the accumulation of empirical knowledge of the modern age. "Joyce helped release me into an understanding of the universal sense of these symbols." But what ultimately saved him, Campbell recalls, were insights from the Hindu Upanishads. "Already in the ninth century B.C. the Hindus realized that all of the deities are projections of psychological powers, and they are within you, not out there."

At seventeen he attended classes at Dartmouth, but felt alienated; he was already becoming a free spirit, restive under restraints and experts telling him what he had to read. "In respect to the world of the intellect I was never interested in small, specialized studies. I think they tend to dehumanize you. In his wonderful, majestic translation of everything into human values, Leonardo da Vinci seemed to me to represent what I was looking for."

So at eighteen he transferred to Columbia University. More at home there, he participated in athletics (he was a track star), music (he earned money playing the saxophone in jazz bands), and earned bachelor's and master's degrees in medieval literature. Columbia awarded him a traveling fellowship, so at twenty-three he left for Paris where he studied medieval languages and Arthurian legends —*"and the whole world opened up."* There he discovered modern art (Klee, Picasso, and Brancusi) and new writers (Yeats, Eliot, and more of Joyce with *Ulysses,* which, he said, was "all protein" and no fat).

The next year (1928) he proceeded to Munich, where he began to devour the works of Goethe, Mann, Freud, and Jung. He took up Sanskrit, which opened up the world of Indian literature —"an awakening you can't imagine." All his earlier knowledge of Arthurian legend, Celtic myth, and American Indian folklore began to link together into "the same motifs." He was following in the footsteps of Jung, Joyce, and Mann: "this is what everyone is working on who is trying to retain the positive values that are in this heritage, and at the same time move into a global period of life where we don't isolate ourselves and say everybody else is worshiping devils."

He was not the same man at twenty-four that he was at eighteen when he first enrolled at Columbia; when he returned to the University after his European adventure and was told to take up where he left off, the free spirit rebelled. He dropped the doctoral program and retired to the woods of Woodstock in northeastern Connecticut where, with his sister, he rented a cabin for $20 a year. For five years he "just read, and read, and read, and read."

After the Woodstock years Campbell wasn't sure that he ever wanted to get a job; he just wanted to read. Still he had sent out lots of résumés, and eventually an offer came for a teaching position at the all-girls Sarah Lawrence College. "When I saw all the pretty girls I said, yes, I want a job." Martha Graham was teaching dance at Sarah Lawrence, and one of her students, Jean Erdman, decided to take Campbell's individual study course

Life is not a problem to be solved but a mystery to be lived.

People say that what we're all seeking is a meaning for life. I don't think that's what we're really seeking. I think what we're seeking is the experience of being alive.

Indeed, the first and most essential service of a mythology is this one of opening the mind and heart to the utter wonder of all being.

On Joseph Campbell: The moments of synchronicity . . . that highlighted his life confirmed his deep belief that devotion to one's own inner work is the beam that keeps you on the path.

PHIL COUSINEAU

For it is a basic idea of practically every war mythology that the enemy is a monster and that in killing him one is protecting the only truly valuable order of human life on earth, which is that, of course, of one's own people.

Privation and suffering alone open the mind of a man to all that is hidden to others.

Mythologies and their deities are productions and projections of the psyche. What gods are there, what gods have there ever been, that were not from man's imagination?

Where the moralist would be filled with indignation and the tragic poet with pity and terror, mythology breaks the whole of life into a vast, horrendous Divine Comedy.

What is important about a lightbulb is not the filament or the glass but the light which these bulbs are to render.

If a person isn't willing to paddle his own canoe he's not going to get across the river.

***There's something rather . . . exhilarating about putting yourself on the side of* life, *instead of on the side of protective* ideas.**

I follow philosophers up to the point where their feet leave the ground.

A woman in one of Campbell's courses once asked "What about the woman?" [He answered] "The woman's the mother of the hero; she's the goal of the hero's achieving; she's the protectress of the hero; she is this, she is that. What more do you want?" The woman said, "I want to be the hero."

in esthetics. Later when Jean left on a world tour, he gave her a copy of Spengler's *The Decline of the West*—assigned reading, apparently, requiring a personal report when she returned. He recalls that he was hooked, and he hoped she was too. She was. They were married in 1938, and for fifty years the Campbells pursued their own careers, separately and together. Joseph read, wrote, and lectured; Jean, who was from Hawaii, did "what we all do here, which is dance." Evenings were often spent with the Campbells' listening to each other: Joe would read his day's writing to Jean, and she would share with Joe her reflections on the philosophy of dance and details of her dance creations. Lecturing was as natural to Joseph Campbell as reading, writing, and breathing. He had begun to lecture widely in the 1960s, mostly on college campuses; during the 1970s and 1980s he lectured worldwide. His essential message was that myths affect the way we live our lives. He was seen everywhere as "the wise old man, the rarest of archetypes in a land of eternal youth."

During this time he continued to read and write, almost ceaselessly. *The Hero with a Thousand Faces* was published in the Bollingen series in 1949 (it had earlier suffered the usual rejections from publishers). In 1968 his twenty-one-year labor of love on world mythology was published as *The Masks of God,* in four volumes. A collection of his popular lectures was published in 1972 as *Myths to Live By. The Inner Reaches of Outer Space* came out in 1986. The final volume of the five-volume *The Historical Atlas of World Mythology* was published posthumously in 1988.

His eightieth birthday was celebrated in 1984 at the Palace of Fine Arts in San Francisco, with a thousand admirers in attendence, including numerous celebrities who had been influenced by his work. A specially made film of his life and work, *The Hero's Journey: The World of Joseph Campbell,* premiered at the Museum of Modern Art in New York in 1986, followed soon by the six-part PBS series *The Power of Myth,* which was produced and guided by Bill Moyers. Only a few months later, on October 30, Joseph Campbell died quietly in Honolulu. He was 83.

Mankind's myths are always believed by devoted believers to be historical and to describe, in some sense, real events; without such belief ("faith") they could not perform their task. But the supposed events depicted in myth are not historical. There never was a Garden of Eden with talking snake, or an awakened Buddha hunkering under the hood of a giant cobra; there was no Jain Tirthankara three thousand feet tall, or Olympian deity transmorphing into a bull, or a gentle Bodhisattva looking down from Tushita heaven, or kami-spirits guarding the rice paddies.

So "who invents these impossible tales?" Campbell asked himself. "And why—though obviously absurd—are they everywhere so reverently believed?"

Campbell came to believe, early on, that by comparing the mythical stories of all the world's traditions "one might arrive at an understanding of their force, their source and possible sense." So for more than half a century he delved into mankind's mythologies and religions—Eastern, Western, ancient, modern, and primitive. He found that the Vedas were right: "Truth is one, the sages speak of it by many names." "Myths are the 'masks of God' through which men everywhere have sought to relate themselves to the wonders of existence." They illuminate the inner life of the collective human psyche, the spiritual wellsprings of human experience. Out of the archetypes of this spiritual realm we create the personifications whom we call gods.

> [Myths] speak, therefore, not of outside events but of themes of the imagination. And since they exhibit features that are actually universal, they must in some way represent features of our general racial imagination, permanent features of the human spirit—or, as we say today, of the

psyche. They are telling us, therefore, of matters fundamental to ourselves, enduring essential principles about which it would be good for us to know; about which, in fact, it will be necessary for us to know if our conscious minds are to be kept in touch with our own most secret, motivating depths. In short, these holy tales and their images are messages to the conscious mind from quarters of the spirit unknown to normal daylight consciousness.

What is it that drives our mythologies? Above all else, writes Campbell, there has dawned in "this wonderful human brain of ours" a special awareness denied (apparently) to all other living creatures: Each of us knows he will die. "The recognition of mortality and the requirement to transcend it is the first great impulse to mythology." Man beholds the truth of his own finality; and he finds it so horrendous, so terrifying, so totally unacceptable that, in order to continue to live, he is driven to find a solution; and this solution can be found only in myth. Man also knows that he is a part of a larger social body; we are mortal as individuals but immortal as a continuing society. The individual achieves an immortality by identifying with his society's ongoing cycle of generations.

✦

"Long long ago, when wishing still could lead to something. . . ."—thus Campbell, quoting *Grimm's Fairy Tales*, begins his narration of the monomyth of the hero's journey. Of all the myths that together reveal the secrets of the human adventure, the universal Hero's Journey is the deepest and most compelling.

There is a single formula, a single plot, to the hero's "universal adventure." Restive under the shadows of his mundane life, the hero leaves his familiar world and ventures out into the unknown. There he confronts dragons (both real and spiritual), wrestles with the forces of evil, and wins a decisive victory; he returns to the daylight world to bestow the results of his achievement on his fellow human beings. Mustering all his resources he has faced the bright realities of human existence, and in the process has been transformed. He has died to the world and been reborn; he is ready to perform creative acts that, if accepted, will bestow a higher consciousness on his fellow men. Everywhere, hero myths show that "the really creative acts are represented as those deriving from some sort of dying to the world."

The hero, by definition, is "someone who has given his or her life to something bigger than oneself." Becoming worthy of that challenge, becoming up to it, requires enormous growth; and growth comes only with wrestling and suffering; and because the hero possesses the right qualities, he must plunge ahead; growth is therefore inevitable. During the bitter trials he discovers what was lacking in his previous existence, and his consciousness is transformed. Now he **sees** what he did not previously see. He now experiences life where before he knew only death. He has matured; the narrow, infantile ego-self has died; the new adult self is up to the challenge, whatever it may be. Courage is the prime requisite at every stage of the journey, but a special courage is often demanded when the Hero returns to the world and finds that the boon that he has to offer is not wanted, or is misunderstood, or **can't be** understood. He has to accept that those who have never left home cannot **see** what he has seen. ("There are some teachers," Campbell notes, "who decide they won't teach at all because of what society will do with what they've found.")

But no matter. The hero's journey is primarily a quest to discover the inner thing that we already are; we ourselves are the mystery that we are seeking to know. And it is precisely this that is the universal odyssey. The outer world constantly changes from year to year and generation to generation; but "the inward life of man is exactly the same." Quite apart from whether the world recognizes what we achieve, the vision quest is its own re-

You don't ask what a dance means, you enjoy it. You don't ask what the world means, you enjoy it. You don't ask what you mean, you enjoy yourself.

What's the meaning of a flower?

If you don't get it here, you won't get it anywhere.

All the heavens, all the gods are within us.

I will participate in the game. It's a wonderful, wonderful opera. Except that it hurts. That wonderful Irish saying, you know, "Is this a private fight, or can anybody get into it?"

The virtues of the past are the vices of today. And many of what we thought to be the vices of the past are the necessities of today.

I think of mythology as the homeland of the muses, the inspirers of art, the inspirers of poetry. To see life as a poem and yourself participating in a poem is what myth does for you.

What's running the show is what's coming up from way down below.

ward; for "we're not going on our journey to save the world but to save ourselves."

✦

Joseph Campbell was gifted with a marvelous memory for capturing the myriad details of mankind's mythic tradition, and he possessed a mind that insisted on marshalling those details into a singular vision: he was driven, always, toward the Big Picture. At the same time that he was a voracious reader, he was a thinker; and it is his vision of the whole of human reality created by these passionate gifts that earns him a place in the history of philosophy. He transformed the **multi**verse of pleasant folk stories into a **uni**verse of insight. Though he disdained the irrelevance of the staid and stuffy philosophic tradition, he was at heart a synoptic philosopher who chose mythology as the window through which he would peer at the world, and, in the grand tradition, seek the truth about the human enterprise and the plight of modern humanity.

Joseph Campbell worked through to an unqualified affirmation of the world and life. Like us all, he had in his own lifetime witnessed the full range of joy and sorrow that flesh is heir to, and he had relived humankind's agony and bliss through myths. But despite these truths—the same truths that led the Buddha to teach that all life is sorrow and Schopenhauer to suggest that life should never have been—Campbell insisted on seeing the glass half full. The first step lies in "the recognition of the monstrous nature of life" and "the realization that this is just how it is and that it cannot and will not be changed. . . . So if you really want to help this world, what you will have to teach is how to live in it. And that no one can do who has not himself learned how to live in it in the joyful sorrow and sorrowful joy of the knowledge of life as it is."

> People ask me, "Do you have optimism about the world?" And I say, "Yes, it's great just the way it is. And you are not going to fix it up. Nobody has ever made it any better. It is never going to be any better. This is it, so take it or leave it. You are not going to correct or improve it."
>
> It is joyful just as it is. I don't believe there was anybody who intended it, but this is the way it is. James Joyce has a memorable line: "History is a nightmare from which I am trying to awake." And the way to awake from it is not to be afraid, and to recognize that all of this, as it is, is a manifestation of the horrendous power that is of all creation. The ends of things are always painful. But pain is part of there being a world at all.

✦

Reflections

1 In what sense might "religion" (a big abstraction) be considered an evolutionary development? That is, in terms of survival, in what ways does religion help us survive? (In that sentence, what does "us" refer to—to our bodies? our ideas? our skills? our emotions?)

2 In §2 you find the sentence: "Human life at its very core is Greek tragedy." What exactly is meant by calling it a Greek tragedy? Do you agree?

3 It has often been held (as in §3) that the purpose of religion is transformation. The transformation of what from what to what? Do you think it's true that we humans long for transformation? Would "salvation" or "redemption" or "transcendence" be a better word for it? Put into your own words what you think is meant by "transformation."

4 Can you identify with the statement in §5 that religion is often experienced as a sort of waking up? What would such an experience be like for you? Do you know someone who claims to have had such a waking-up or enlightenment experience?

5 What is meant by thc phrasc "tclcocosmic drama"? How does an apocalyptic drama differ from the more general teleocosmic dramas? List some of the human needs that are met by teleocosmic dramas.

6 Judaism, Christianity, and Islam all adopted the battlefield cosmology as the primary structure of its worldview. Is the battlefield concept familiar to you? Is it congenial? Who is the winner in the battlefield drama? Necessarily? Why so?

7 After reflecting on the suggested definitions of religion, develop the best definition you can as you personally understand it. Can you defend, rationally and empirically, each part of your definition?

8 Note the anthropologist Tylor's observation of the use of ceremonies and rituals by maritime communities (see marginal note on p. 557). What inference can you make from such practice?

9 How would you respond to the question asked in the box on p. 559: "How does one determine whether prayers are answered if not in terms of results?" Was Scipio's prayer answered?

10 Study the varied meanings attached to the Greek word *pneuma* in ancient times (see box on p. 561). What can you conclude from a comparison of the multiple English translations of this word?

11 Understanding the more technical usage of the word "myth" is important. What psychological and epistemic function does myth satisfy? What about the beliefs held by the rabbi described by Frankl—would you call these beliefs myths? If so, what exactly are you saying about his beliefs?

12 What are your thoughts and second thoughts after reading the list of future saviors (pp. 573–574)?

13 After your first startled reaction to Kurt Vonnegut's plea on p. 562 (see marginal quote), can you bring yourself to agree with him? Can you at least build a hypothetical case for what he is saying?

ULTIMATE REALITY

8-2

This chapter continues the attempt to understand the phenomenon of religion. It notes our habit of anthropomorphic thinking and raises the problem of "divine knowledge." The existence of God has been, for almost two millennia, one of the troubling subjects for Western philosophers and theologians. This chapter deals with the three classic attempts to prove that God exists: the cosmological, ontological, and teleological arguments. Nietzsche's powerful pronouncement that "God is dead" had an impact on Christian theology during the first half of the twentieth century. Then Thomas Merton suggests that there is always another side of the mountain . . .

ULTIMATE QUESTIONS

1 The Ethiopians make their gods black-skinned and snub-nosed; the Thracians say theirs have blue eyes and red hair. If oxen and horses had hands and could draw with their hands and make works of art just as men do, then horses would draw their gods to look like horses, and oxen like oxen—each would make their bodies in the image of their own.

XENOPHANES

2 The questions that we ask about Ultimate Reality are always phrased in terms of our own particular worldview, of course; and the questions that have meaning to a Hindu or Buddhist may be meaningless to a Christian or Muslim. Problems about Ultimate Reality cannot be made intelligible apart from the thought framework within which they are posed.

"Non ridere, non lugere, neque detestari, sed intelligere." ***"Not to laugh, not to lament, not to curse, but to understand."***

BARUCH SPINOZA

The questions we in the West ask are deceptively simple: Does God exist? What is he like? How can we know what he wants of us?

In Eastern religion, the Hindu might ask: What is the true nature of the Ultimate Reality that lies beyond the gods? Is the world of physical matter merely illusion? How can I attain liberation from the round of rebirths? The Buddhist might ask: Is it really true, as the Buddha claimed, that to exist is to suffer? If so, how can I escape suffering and attain enlightenment?

Other, Far Eastern worshipers might ask: What is the true way of life—the Tao? How can I best seek the Tao so that my life may be peaceful and full? What does Heaven want of me?

Most intellectual people do not believe in God, but they fear him just the same.
WILHELM REICH

3 Philosophy is neither theology—which attempts to make religion intellectually meaningful—nor evangelism—which attempts to persuade others to believe. Rather, philosophy's concerns are primarily metaphysical and epistemological. Metaphysical: What is Ultimate Reality? How many orders of reality exist? Is there a supernatural order of reality? Do deities and spirits exist? Does God exist? In fact, what exactly is meant by such terms? Epistemological: Can we humans who belong to the natural order know that which belongs to the supernatural order? If so, how? Does God (or do the gods) "reveal"? Does he reveal a person (as some Christian theologians claim) or a data content? How can we be sure about the source of supernatural fact-claims mediated through human beings?

If only God would give me some clear sign! Like making a large deposit in my name at a Swiss bank.
WOODY ALLEN

THE PROBLEM OF DIVINE KNOWLEDGE

4 The images of deity that men hold are largely the product of particular circumstances of time and place. Western religions of Near Eastern origin conceive deity as male. We ask if he exists and we speak of a father-god. The majority of men, however, have imagined their deities to be feminine, and to these goddesses they have prayed for intercession, tender care, love, and life-generating energies.

The Judeo-Christian God is necessarily masculine since our god-concepts originated in the Bedouin sheikdoms that wandered out of the Arabian desert into the Fertile Crescent. The gods of these nomadic clans were modeled after the sheik chieftain. They were strongly masculine deities, associated with the aggressive forces of nature—volcanoes, earthquakes, storms—and with intertribal battles. Rarely, if ever, does the concept of a female deity evolve in a Bedouin society with patriarchal dominance. The early Hebrew god Yahweh exhibits the characteristics of the sheik chieftain. He is authoritarian in monitoring the loyalty pledged to him by his followers. He is stern, demanding, and quick to punish backsliding. He is a "jealous God" who will tolerate no competition from other gods. This early Hebraic world was patriarchal and the survival qualities necessary in a deity were authority and firmness; he must be quick to anger and of mighty power in battle. The blood covenant binding the deity to his tribe (Exodus 24:4–8) is basically Bedouin: he will be their leader and protector as long as they obey and "keep the covenant."

By contrast, where sprawling vineyards cover the hillsides and the valleys shelter fields of grain and fruit trees, here we are more likely to find the goddesses and their consorts. In gentler climes and social settings, the qualities

associated with feminine roles—love, fertility, nurturance—are more valued than the fearsome, bellicose qualities of the desert deities. These female deities are at once Earth Mothers, fertility goddesses, and sacred virgins. As Earth Mothers they generate the life-giving forces that underlie the birth and growth of all living things. As fertility goddesses they symbolize conception, and by means of mystery rites, temple prostitution, and spring festivals, they can be persuaded to stimulate fertility in man's clans, flocks, and crops. As eternal virgin goddesses their primary purpose is to symbolize purity and to merit the devotion of mortal men.

5 When deities are considered to be male, then they frequently mate with mortal women. Zeus was forever entangled in amorous affairs, and the shepherd-god Krishna spent much of his time in the company of beautiful milkmaids. In Zoroastrian myth, the seed of Zoroaster, preserved for thousands of years in a crystal-pure lake, will impregnate three virgins who are to appear at intervals of three thousand years; they will give birth to the savior gods for each period of human history, the last being Soshyans, who will inaugurate the Last Judgment.

In Buddhist myth, a male bodhisattva (savior-being) placed his reflection in the womb of Queen Maya. In her tenth month of pregnancy she gave birth to the Buddha from her right side. Her case was both a virgin conception and a virgin birth. We can follow the sequence of historical development by inverting this order of thinking: Buddhist apologists began with the undeniable facts of the Buddha's existence and his birth from a mortal mother. Since the Buddha's paternity was known (from doctrinal tradition) to have been divine, the supernatural parent must, of course, be male. This is a rather obvious line of logic. In similar fashion, the Holy Spirit that impregnated the Virgin Mary must be conceived in human minds as an aspect of the masculine Father-God.

This enigma—the virgin conception by Mary—has produced more doctrines and convened more councils than any other event in Western history. The idea of a male deity mating with a mortal maiden to produce what would logically be a God-man—half God, half man—is a common enough motif in man's religions, but the soteriological complexities of the Christian version required centuries of analysis and debate. Is this "son of God" himself man or God or both? Throughout the first four centuries of Christianity there were churchmen who held that he was solely God or solely man, but the doctrine that he was both God and man finally prevailed. This conclusion, however, merely posed further problems. If he was both, then how did his divine nature relate to his human nature? And what was the relationship of the divine nature in Jesus to the divine nature in the Father? (The Council of Nicea settled these questions in AD 325; the churchmen reaffirmed his dual nature and concluded that the divine nature in the Son and the Father were "in essence" the same.) What about will? If he was both God and man, did he have two distinct wills? (This problem—the "monothelite" controversy—was settled at a council in Constantinople in 681: Jesus has two wills, the divine and the human, but the human will was subservient in all things to his divine will.) And what of Mary? If Jesus was wholly God as well as wholly man, does this not mean that Mary was the mother of God? (The Council of Ephesus in 431 answered yes. She is properly designated Theotokos, "the bearer of God.") (Saint Jerome, who is best known for his translation of the Scriptures into Latin [the Vulgate], had a friend named Paula whose daughter Eustochium took the vows of a nun and thus became "a bride of Christ." Jerome considered Mary to be the Mother of God, and he habitually addressed Paula as the mother-in-law of God. This is not the only case, however, where a god had a mother-in-law. Demeter, for instance, was Pluto's mother-in-law after Persephone became the bride of the king of Hades.)

The most beautiful and most profound emotion we can experience is the sensation of the mystical. It is the sower of all true science. He to whom this emotion is a stranger, who can no longer stand rapt in awe, is as good as dead. That deeply emotional conviction of the presence of a superior reasoning power, which is revealed in the incomprehensible universe, forms my idea of God.

ALBERT EINSTEIN

It both is and is not; neither is, nor is not.

THE BUDDHA

Not female, nor yet male is it, neither is it neuter. Whatever body it assumes, through that body it is served.

The Upanishads

6 When we find ourselves theologically entangled in mundane human relationships such as these, it is easy to lose our philosophical perspective. But if we can survive the subtleties of such debates, we may feel that our anthropomorphizing has gone too far. Xenophanes observed very early that "mortals suppose that the gods have been born, that they have voices and bodies and wear clothing like men"; he complained that "Homer and Hesiod attributed to the gods all sorts of actions that when done by men are disreputable and deserving of blame—such lawless deeds as theft, adultery, and mutual deception."

The supernatural figures of our great living religions may be ethically and spiritually nobler, but their anthropomorphic qualities are just as human as those shared by the Olympian gods and goddesses.

7 Much thought has been given to the problem of divine knowledge by other Western philosophers who were aware of our anthropomorphic manner of thinking.

The rash assertion that "God made man in His own image" is ticking like a time bomb at the foundations of many faiths, and as the hierarchy of the universe is disclosed to us, we may have to recognize this chilling truth: if there are any gods whose chief concern is man, they cannot be very important gods.

Arthur C. Clarke

Philo of Alexandria (fl. c. AD 40) contended that no qualities conceivable by the human mind can be attributed to God. God, that is, cannot be thought about. Whenever we think we are thinking about God, we are merely "deifying" human qualities. All we can do, Philo concluded, is to say what God is not.

Around the year AD 500 an anonymous writer called Pseudo-Dionysius (his writings were for a time attributed to a certain Dionysius mentioned by Saint Paul) decided that there are two ways of knowing God. Following the positive way, we can collect the qualitative concepts that we apply to man—man is good, wise, loving, alive, and so forth—and attribute these qualities in their ultimate form to the divine nature. That is, God is perfect goodness, wisdom, love, being, and so on. Since God is perfect, we can be sure that we are correct in attributing perfect qualities to God even though we cannot ourselves conceive these perfect qualities. (What exactly is "perfect wisdom" or "perfect being"?) But there is a second way of knowing—the negative way. We can collect in our minds all the qualities that we are sure God cannot possess: God is not corporeal matter; he is not evil; he cannot hate, cheat, deceive, and so on. By a process of "remotion" all these qualities are removed from our thinking about God. Thus, as we proceed to subtract all qualities that God cannot possess, we are left with an increasingly accurate nonconcept of God. By the "darkness of unknowing" we can arrive at a mystical notion of what God in fact is.

There is no Hindu and there is no Muslim.

Guru Nanak

Arguments for the Existence of God

8 **The Cosmological Argument** In our Western philosophical tradition, there have been several attempts to prove, rationally or empirically, that God exists. At least three are noteworthy. These are the cosmological, ontological, and teleological arguments for the existence of God.

The cosmological argument was first stated by Aristotle and further developed by Thomas Aquinas (1225–1274). The argument attempts to prove logically that there must be an "unmoved mover" and that such a force is in fact what we have thought of as God.

We live in a world of matter-in-motion. This is an obvious empirical fact. Aquinas observed that if an object is at rest, then it is not in motion; but any object at rest is potentially in motion. Motion is the actualized potential of a particular object. All objects at rest are potentially in motion, but no object will be activated into motion unless it is caused to move by something that is actually moving. No object at rest can be activated by another object at rest, nor can an object at rest set itself in motion. This means simply that every object in motion was set in motion by something else; but that something else must have been set in motion by something before it, and so on. Therefore we are confronted with an infinite series of objects, each of which actualizes the potential motion of the next in the series. But if we attempt to account for motion by going back in our minds in an infinite regression, we find ourselves in a logical contradiction—a dead end. Something must start the series, and this something, from a purely logical standpoint, must be something without an antecedent activator. Such an activator must necessarily be pure actuality and not potential. Whatever this pure actuality is, it is the "unmoved mover" that, writes Thomas, "everyone understands to be God."

Every saint has a past and every sinner a future.
OSCAR WILDE

9 **THE ONTOLOGICAL ARGUMENT** The ontological argument was developed by Anselm of Canterbury (1033–1109). Anselm is sometimes called the father of Scholastic philosophy, that movement of the twelfth and thirteenth centuries that rekindled intellectual activity in the West after the Dark Ages. Saint Anselm was a devoutly religious Benedictine monk whose writings, debates, and pastoral leadership greatly influenced his time.

While Thomas's cosmological argument for God is founded upon an empirical observation of matter-in-motion, Anselm's argument has no such empirical referent. It attempts to prove God's existence from the nature of thought alone. For several weeks Anselm had been convinced that such a proof might be possible. He devoted much thought and prayer to it and finally, late one night during vigils, his proof of God's existence stood clearly before his mind. Anselm was sure that he knew, by thought alone, that God exists—indeed, that God has to exist. Here is his argument:

The mind has a concept of a Being than which nothing greater can be conceived. This Being, than which nothing greater can be conceived, must exist in reality as well as in thought. For if it existed only in thought (subjectively), then it would be possible for the mind to conceive of an even greater being who exists in reality (objectively) as well as in thought, and this being would be greater. But this is impossible. Therefore, this Being, than which nothing greater can be conceived, must exist in reality as well as in thought. And this Being is God.

Faith is best defined as expecting the best until the worst has been proved.
GERALD ENSLEY

Anselm was elated that he could prove rationally what he already knew to be true. To his proof, he appended a thankful prayer to God "because through your divine illumination I now so understand that which, through your generous gift, I formerly believed. . . ." He continued: "So truly dost thou exist, O Lord God, both in thought and in fact, that it is impossible for the minds of Thy creatures not to know of Thine existence."

10 **THE TELEOLOGICAL ARGUMENT** The teleological argument for the existence of God is based on the apparent order and design of nature and cosmos, and on the purposive nature of evolution.

From earliest times man has wondered about the cyclical motions of the stars and planets, the endless rounds of days and seasons, the consistency of nature's operations, and the rhythmic patterns of order in the world about him. Greek thinkers used the word *logos* (literally, "word") to account for this order. This logos might be thought of as a kind of "world reason," an organizing force, possibly emanating from a divine mind, that binds all the dynamic elements of nature into a working order.

Today, of course, we know that the cosmos has more order than the ancients could have imagined, an order that can be described in terms of mathematical equations, physical and chemical formulas, and psychobiological processes. Living organisms have distinctive metabolic and life-cycle rhythms, largely determined for each by an incredibly complicated DNA code. Subatomic studies have revealed the complex configurations of energy patterns. We also know that cosmic processes—involving suns, galaxies, and perhaps even the pulsating universe itself—run through ordered sequences resembling birth, life, and death.

The question: Can all this beautiful harmony exist apart from an ordering intelligence, a mind that would be the creator and sustainer of this order? The Stoics, among others, drew a simple analogy. The human mind is fundamentally an organizer: it orders, systematizes, labels, and stores bits of experience for later use. Our minds order our experiences of reality. Likewise, there must be a Cosmic Mind pervading reality itself and operating toward similar ends. The ordered world as we know it cannot be accounted for apart from the ordering of a Cosmic Intelligence.

The teleological argument—as the word "teleology" indicates—has to do with direction or destiny; and it was the development of life and the movement of evolution that seemed to demonstrate most clearly the possibility of a directive intelligence.

This argument was given careful scrutiny by the biologist Lecomte du Noüy in his book *Human Destiny.* Du Noüy calculated that according to the laws of probability the emergence of living organisms from inorganic molecules would have been less than one in a hundred billion. He concludes that life could only begin through an act of a purposive intelligence, and that the movement of evolution is, in his word, "telefinalistic."

> Telefinality orients the march of evolution as a whole and has acted, ever since the appearance of life on earth, as a distant directing force tending to develop a being endowed with a conscience, a spiritually and morally perfect being. To attain its goal, this force acts on the laws of the inorganized world in such a way that the normal play of the second law of thermodynamics is always deflected in the same direction, a direction forbidden to inert matter and leading to ever greater dissymmetries, ever more "improbable" states.

The Death(s) of God(s)

11 Is God dead? Friedrich Nietzsche thought so.

> Have you not heard of that madman who lit a lantern in the bright morning hours, ran to the market place, and cried incessantly, "I seek God! I seek God!" As many of those who do not believe in God were standing around just then, he provoked

much laughter. Why, did he get lost? said one. Did he lose his way like a child? said another. Or is he hiding? Is he afraid of us? Has he gone on a voyage? or emigrated? Thus they yelled and laughed. The madman jumped into their midst and pierced them with his glances.

"Whither is God" he cried. "I shall tell you. We have killed him—you and I. All of us are his murderers. . . . God is dead. God remains dead. And we have killed him. How shall we, the murderers of all murderers, comfort ourselves? What was holiest and most powerful of all that the world has yet owned has bled to death under our knives. Who will wipe this blood off us? What water is there for us to clean ourselves? What festivals of atonement, what sacred games shall we have to invent? Is not the greatness of this deed too great for us? Must not we ourselves become gods simply to seem worthy of it? There has never been a greater deed; and whoever will be born after us—for the sake of this deed he will be part of a higher history than all history hitherto."

Even for a god there is a point of no return.
Star Trek, NBC-TV

Here the madman fell silent and looked again at his listeners; and they too were silent and stared at him in astonishment. At last he threw his lantern on the ground, and it broke and went out. "I come too early," he said then; "my time has not come yet. This tremendous event is still on its way, still wandering—it has not yet reached the ears of man. . . ."

It has been related further that on that same day the madman entered divers churches and there sang his *requiem aeternam deo*. Led out and called to account, he is said to have replied each time, "What are these churches now if they are not the tombs and sepulchers of God?"

Almost all philosophers have confused ideas of things. They speak of material things in spiritual terms, and of spiritual things in material terms.
BLAISE PASCAL

12 Nietzsche and others have presaged the death of God. But what does such a statement mean? A modern death-of-God theologian, William Hamilton, rhetorically asks, "Is there really an event properly called 'the death of God'? Or is the current chatter enveloping the phrase simply another of the many non-events afflicting our time?" He answers: "No. The death of God has happened. To those of us with gods, and to those without. To the indifferent, the cynical and the fanatical. God is dead, whatever that means."

To Nietzsche it meant that the very concept of God as traditionally conceived in Western thought no longer has the power, as it once did, to transform human life. Belief in a God is still held by individuals, and countless others pay lip service to god doctrines. But these beliefs no longer do what beliefs are supposed to do: to grip one's very existence with ultimate truths; to establish one firmly in a meaningful teleocosmic plan; to transform character and hence the quality of one's whole life; to make one feel special and of infinite worth; to provide secure and final answers to questions about living and dying.

Worldviews have changed. Spirits and demons have died: we now account for human behavior in terms of operant conditioning and motivation. The Devil has died: a "devil" is nothing more than a mental abstraction that we have personified and objectified. And a capricious, all-too-human deity can no longer command our devotion. We have seen too many gods; our anthropomorphic habits are too obvious to be brushed aside. God, too, is dead.

13 If we scan the pantheon of man's divinities, we discover deicides without end. Sooner or later, it seems, all the gods of men die.

There was a time when Egyptian *fellahin* knew that King Osiris weighed the hearts of men before they could enter into his kingdom, and Isis the Queen was a benefactor to all—revealing laws, rendering justice, calming the sea, timing the harvests, and persuading men and women to love each other.

"Clearly I Miss Him . . ."

"But if I live later, I will try to live in such a way, doing no harm to any one, that it will be forgiven."

"By whom?"

"Who knows? Since we do not have God here any more, neither His Son nor the Holy Ghost, who forgives? I do not know."

"You have not God any more?"

"No. Man. Certainly not. If there were God, never would He have permitted what I have seen with my eyes. Let them have God."

"They claim Him."

"Clearly I miss Him, having been brought up in religion. But now a man must be responsible to himself."

"Then it is thyself who will forgive thee for killing."

"I believe so," Anselmo said.

Ernest Hemingway
For Whom the Bell Tolls

Politics and religion are obsolete; the time has come for science and spirituality.
Vinobe Bhave

The sky god Varuna was able to see into the hearts of his Aryan worshipers and cast away their sins. The redeemer god Balder returned each spring to the snow-laden northland and brought with him light and warmth. The mystery gods Dionysus, Orpheus, and Mithras promised immortality to all who pledged their loyalty and performed the proper rites. From his temple on the slopes of Mount Parnassus the bright sun-god Apollo offered divine wisdom and worldly counsel to faithful pilgrims.

The beautiful virgin goddess Artemis protected wandering children and assuaged the pain of women in childbirth. Persephone brought health and prosperity to her devotees, then led them down to the nether realm where she was queen. The virgin Athena, proud and protective, was close to the hearts of her Athenian worshipers, who turned to her in peace for health and in war for courage.

Now that Starglider has effectively destroyed all traditional religions, we can at last pay serious attention to the concept of God.
"Dr. Choam Goldberg"
in Arthur C. Clarke's
The Fountains of Paradise

The virgin-born Quetzalcoatl, who, in Nahuatl mysteries, was a man become god, presented himself as an example of man's purest aspiration, having burned himself in a fire to purge away his sin. Lord Mazda proffered aid and eternal life to righteous Zoroastrians who believed in Spenta Mainyu (the Holy Spirit) and in the Amesha Spentas (the Immortal Ones—angellike beings and divine messengers).

As long as there were followers who believed in them, all these gods and goddesses could transform lives. But when, with the passing of the centuries, there were no longer any believers, then no more lives were transformed, no more guilt forgiven, no more souls saved.

In the pantheon of deceased gods and goddesses are enshrined the most awesome names ever uttered by the suppliant voices of mortal men and women: Adonis, Aphrodite, Apollo, Aton, Bacchus, Balder, Cybele, Demeter, Diana, Dionysus, El, Fortuna, Gaia, Hel, Hercules, Indra, Ishtar, Isis, Janus, Jupiter, Marduk, Mars, Nanna, Orpheus, Osiris, Persephone, Quetzalcoatl, Rudra, Sa-

Belief and Freedom

Religions cannot be inculcated by force. There is no such thing as a belief that is not held voluntarily through a genuinely spontaneous inner conviction. Different people's convictions will differ, because Absolute Reality is a mystery of which no more than a fraction has ever yet been penetrated by—or been revealed to—any human mind. 'The heart of so great a mystery cannot be reached by following one road only.' [Symmachus] However strong and confident may be my conviction that my own approach to the mystery is a right one, I ought to be aware that my field of spiritual vision is so narrow that I cannot know that there is no virtue in other approaches. In theistic terms this is to say that I cannot know that other people's visions may not also be revelations from God—and these perhaps fuller and more illuminating revelations than the one that I believe that I myself have received from Him.

Arnold Toynbee

turnus, Shamash, Tammuz, Thor, Uranus, Varuna, Venus, Wotan, Xochipilli, Zagreus, Zeus. . . .

14 One of the tasks of a theologian is to update the faith and make it intelligible to his contemporaries. Numerous attempts have been made to deal with the problem of God-knowledge in modern terms. A notable example is that of Dr. Paul Tillich.

Tillich contended that we cannot know anything about God, but this limitation does not prevent God's working in our lives. Knowing about him and experiencing him are hardly the same. God is "the ground of our being." We exist, and objects exist; but "existence" is a human category of thought, and God is beyond existence. He is pure being itself.

But, Tillich notes, we are caught in a human predicament that we had best accept. It is true that we cannot conceive the inconceivable or speak the unspeakable. But if we think or speak at all, then we must think in concepts and speak with language symbols. Therefore, we must continue to do just this, but with the full understanding that our thoughts and words refer to nothing whatever that is real. There is nothing to be gained by fighting our predicament, says Tillich. Rather, we must accept it and live within its confines. Let's continue to speak of God as "he" (or in other traditions as "she" or "it"); we can continue to think of God as "knowing," "seeing," "hearing," "loving," and so on. These are pragmatic modes of thinking and feeling. Man is a symbolic creature, and we can live with our condition providing we don't confuse symbol and reality. Such words as God and he are indispensable as symbols, but we must never mistake them for realities.

The only "God" that "exists" is beyond the gods of man. Since all our thinking ultimately is symbolic, Christians can continue to think of the Christ as the "new man" described by Paul, the whole man whose existence and essence have become one. He symbolizes the ultimate possibilities for each of us. It is only by accepting these symbols for what they truly are—as ontological aspects of

We must be brave enough to declare that every culture must create its own God idea rather than rely upon outworn tradition.

Joshua Loth Liebman

Cause me to pass from the unreal to the real, from darkness to light, from death to immortality.

Brihadaranyaka I.3/28

the human condition—that we can come to terms with our existence and express our "ultimate concern for the Ultimate."

15 Religious experience is absolute. It is indisputable. You can only say that you have never had such an experience and your opponent will say: "Sorry, I have." And there your discussion will come to an end. No matter what the world thinks about religious experience, the one who has it possesses the great treasure of a thing that has provided him with a source of life, meaning and beauty and that has given a new splendor to the world and to mankind. He had pistis [faith] and peace. Where is the criterium by which you could say that such a life is not legitimate, that such experience is not valid and that such pistis is mere illusion? Is there, as a matter of fact, any better truth about ultimate things than the one that helps you to live?

Carl G. Jung

✦

Carl Gustav Jung (1875–1961)

Thomas Merton

The Other Side of Kanchenjunga

On October 15, 1968, Thomas Merton, an American Catholic monk from a Trappist monastery in Kentucky, began a spiritual journey. "I am going home," he wrote in his journal, "to a home where I have never been in this body."

In actual fact, he was sitting in a Pan Am jet on the runway of the San Francisco International Airport waiting for takeoff. Destination: Southeast Asia. It was early morning, with the taxiing planes performing a "slow ballet of big tail fins in the sun."

> The moment of take-off was ecstatic. . . . We left the ground—I with Christian mantras and a great sense of destiny, of being at last on my true way after years of waiting and wondering and fooling around. May I not come back without having settled the great affair.

This trip would carry him—while still "in the body"—through unscheduled adventures in India, Sri Lanka, and Thailand. In Bangkok the great affair would be settled.

The world first knew of Thomas Merton in 1948 when his autobiographical novel, *The Seven Storey Mountain,* revealed who he was and how he became a Trappist.

"In a year of a great war and down in the shadow of some French mountains on the border of Spain, I came into the world"—1915. "That world was the picture of Hell, full of men like myself, loving God and yet hating Him; born to love Him, living instead in fear and hopeless self-contradictory hungers."

His parents were artists—strong-willed, independent, avant-garde—and they shaped their son's inner world before their early deaths, his mother when he was six, his father when he was fifteen. From both came a Dionysian drive "for work and vision and enjoyment of expression." His mother was filled with "insatiable dreams" and a "great ambition after perfection"; she was "worried, precise, quick, critical of me, her son," and intellectually demanding. She kept a detailed diary in which she chronicled her son's every move.

Merton's youth was disturbed and unhappy. Out of a loneliness that was to haunt him all his life he very early began to write down his thoughts and feelings.

No one is so wrong as the man who knows all the answers.

What is important is not liberation from the body but liberation from the mind. We are not entangled in our own body but entangled in our own mind.

Our real journey in life is interior; it is a matter of growth, deepening, and of an ever greater surrender to the creative action of love and grace in our hearts.

Every moment and every event of every man's life on earth plants something in his soul. . . . Most of these unnumbered seeds perish and are lost, because men are not prepared to receive them.

By the time he was eight he had written three "novels."

His late teens took an Augustinian turn: wild revelries and continual affairs. While he was attending Cambridge a young woman bore him a son; Merton abandoned both, and they were later killed in an air raid in London. He contributed bawdy sketches to school papers and once became a barker for a sleazy sideshow.

By his early twenties Merton's psyche was a raging fire. Driven by enormous guilt, confusion, and loneliness, fueled by boundless energies, creative urges, and an intense longing for love, beauty, and perfection, Merton had arrived at the classical spiritual condition for "the making of a monk." Although he converted to Catholicism at twenty-three, much of the next two years seems to have been spent in confession. Still, the love affairs and wild parties and miserable hangovers continued.

The turning point came in December 1941—the week the world exploded at Pearl Harbor. Thomas Merton renounced that world and entered the Trappist Abbey of Our Lady of Gethsemani.

The Trappists were (and still are) one of the world's most severely ascetic communities. They are a reform branch of the Cistercian Order (a reform branch of the Benedictines), founded at La Trappe in France in 1664. The monks of Gethsemani call themselves the Order of Cistercians of the Strict Observance (they sign "OCSO" after their names) and have developed a lifestyle more austere even than that of their forefathers.

Their days are lived in terms of prayer, work, and silence. They arise at 2 AM for prayer, meditate or read till 5:30, offer more prayers at 7:45 and 11:00, observe vespers at 4:30, listen to a reading at 6:10, and retreat to bed at 7:00 PM. They subsist on a meager vegetarian diet. Labor consists of hoeing, cutting, and threshing in the monastery's orchards and fields; tending livestock; and making repairs. They live in silence; all communication is managed with four hundred basic gestures in sign language.

Merton's first years at Gethsemani were relatively happy, even though the physical labor, fasting, and scanty diet often left him weak. Separated from the world, his spirit found a modicum of peace, and he began the long process of healing. He was allowed to live in a "hermit hatch" a half-mile from the monastery.

He wrote continually and passionately, and in his seventh year as a monk he published *The Seven Storey Mountain.* To everyone's surprise, it soared upward on the best-seller lists, and the author was hailed as a new Augustine—"the most significant spiritual leader in America" —and more. Overnight fame and admiration came from the world to this world-renouncing monk. Soul-mates, would-be disciples, and notables made their way to the hermit hatch, and Merton's solitude was lost. Still, he continued producing poetry, essays, and novels and carried on a voluminous correspondence. His writings would eventually be collected into more than forty volumes.

In the summer of 1968, Merton was invited to attend an interfaith conference in Bangkok, Thailand. For a decade he had been studying Eastern literature and religion and had long felt a kinship with other "contemplatives" who had withdrawn from the world to give their spiritual lives highest priority. (It was a Hindu monk who first persuaded him to read St. Augustine's *Confessions.*) He corresponded with Theravada monks, Tibetan *rimpoches* ("spiritual masters"), Hindu *swamis,* and Taoist and Confucian priests. He developed a warm friendship with Daisetz Suzuki, the famed Zen master, and felt especially close to Zen. In 1965 he published *The Way of Chuang Tzu,* an interpretation of the Chinese sage whose teachings struck a responsive chord in Merton. Chuang-Tzu had written: "The effect of life in society is to complicate and confuse our existence, making us to forget who we really are by causing us to become obsessed with what we are not." To that Merton had responded: "I think I may be pardoned for consorting with a Chinese recluse who shares the climate and peace of my own kind of solitude, and who is my own kind of person."

His flight from San Francisco carried him first to Bangkok, where he experienced firsthand the "other world" he knew so well from books and letters, and then to Calcutta—"the big, beat-up, teeming, incredible city. People!" The next stop was Dharamsala to meet with the Dalai Lama, the Tibetan leader in exile. Merton held long conversations with a teacher of Tantric Buddhism, who urged him to find a guru to pursue enlightenment. Merton wrote in his journal: "At least he asked me if I were willing to risk it and I said why not? . . . I would like to learn something by experience and it does seem that the Tibetan Buddhists are the only ones who at present have a really large number of people who have attained to extraordinary heights in meditation and contemplation." His time with the Dalai Lama was immensely rewarding; of special value was their exchange of ideas on methods of meditation. Easily and naturally Merton moved into the Buddhist experience. The Dalai Lama called him a *geshe,* a "learned lama."

Merton traveled next to Darjeeling in northeastern India, overshadowed to the north by the breathtaking Himalayan range and the peak of Kanchenjunga. On the way he visited with a Buddhist teacher, Chatral Rimpoche, and discussed meditation and the difficulty of attaining "perfect emptiness." Merton recalled:

> The unspoken or half-spoken message of the talk was our complete understanding of each other as people who were somehow on the edge of a great realization and knew it and were trying, somehow or other, to go out and get lost in it—and that it was a grace for us to meet one another. . . . He told me, seriously, that perhaps he and I would attain to complete Buddhahood in our next lives, perhaps even in this life, and the parting note was a kind of compact that we would both do our best to make it in this life. . . . He was surprised at getting on so well with a Christian and at one point laughed and said, "There must be something wrong here!"

In Sri Lanka Merton talked with hermits living in caves near Kandy, then journeyed to Polonnaruwa. Here, at last, there was a gathering together of all the scattered pieces in the spiritual vision of this Western trespasser. In a natural grassy amphitheater, a massive outcropping of granite has been carved into four great statues of the Buddha. "The whole thing is very much a Zen garden . . . and the great figures, motionless, yet with the lines of full movement, waves of vesture and bodily form, a beautiful and holy vision." What these figures meant is not easily expressed either by a Western poet or for Western readers. "Polonnaruwa was such an experience that I could not write hastily of it and cannot write now, or not at all adequately."

> I am able to approach the Buddhas barefoot and undisturbed, my feet in wet grass, wet sand. Then the silence of the extraordinary faces . . . questioning nothing, knowing everything, rejecting nothing, the peace . . . that has seen through every question without establishing some other argument. For the doctrinaire, the mind that needs well-established positions, such peace, such silence, can be frightening. . . . I don't know when in my life I have ever had such a sense of beauty and spiritual validity running together in one aesthetic illumination. . . . I know and have seen what I was obscurely looking for. I don't know what else remains, but I have now seen and have pierced through the surface and have got beyond the shadow and the disguise.

We can help one another to find out the meaning of life, no doubt. But in the last analysis the individual person is responsible for living his own life and for "finding himself."

Others can give you a name or a number, but they can never tell you who you really are. That is something you yourself can only discover from within.

Thomas Merton represents for the modern world a new stage of maturity in religious understanding—a new spirit in dialogue and a new way of listening. It is worth noting that he did not arrive at this stage from an assumption that "all religions are One" (he thought that cliché rather useless) or through an intellectual comparison of doctrinal similarities.

> It is characteristic of Merton's approach to Eastern thought that he did not so much reach out for contact with other traditions, but rather went so deeply into his own that he could not help discovering the common roots. A strange journey indeed: the traveler, instead of going abroad, digs into the ground on which he stands, but digs so deep that he comes out in China.
>
> David Steindl-Rast

What Merton gradually came to see is not an uncommon realization for seekers: that experience opens the avenues of communication, whereas belief closes them off; that experience encourages dialogue, whereas belief encourages pronouncement; and that whereas experience leads to empathy and appreciation, commitment to doctrinal formulas produces antipathy and disparagement.

Merton found that those who enter into a "dialogue of experience" can share and learn from one another.

> This inclusive view made it impossible for him to deny any authentic scripture or any man of faith. Indeed, he discovered new aspects of truth in Hinduism and Buddhism, in Zen, and in Sufi mysticism. His lifelong search for meditative silence and prayer was found not only in his monastic experience but also in his late Tibetan inspiration.
>
> Amiya Chakravarty
> In the Preface to *The Asian Journal*, vii

In just this way, Merton pondered the stone Buddhas of Polonnaruwa. His spiritual security could allow these new symbols to produce fresh illuminations. From Sri Lanka Merton flew back to Bangkok. On the morning of December 10, 1968, he spoke to a gathering of monks and clerics on "Marxism and Monastic Perspectives." He spoke casually and with humor, noting that both monk and Marxist believe that "the claims of the world are fraudulent," and his speech concluded with a call for empathy for other religions and an openness to the "painfulness of inner change."

Shortly after lunch Merton returned to his guest cottage to rest. When he failed to reappear, his friends went to his cottage and found him lying on the floor, with an electric fan, still spinning, across his chest. He had been accidentally electrocuted.

A few weeks earlier, during a visit to the forested tea country of Assam, Merton had stood looking at the snow-covered peak of Kanchenjunga. He wrote in his journal: "Last night I had a curious dream about Kanchenjunga. I was looking at the mountain and it was pure white, absolutely white, especially the peaks that lie to the west. And I saw the pure beauty of their shape and outline, all in white. And I heard a voice saying—or got the clear idea of: 'There is another side to the mountain.'"

Thomas Merton had climbed the peak alone, as all must. The seeker—whether he be Buddhist, Christian, Hindu, Jew, Muslim, Jain—must find his own path. It takes enormous courage and, perhaps, a special grace to see that there is another side. "There is another side of Kanchenjunga and of every mountain."

✦

Reflections

1 How do philosophical concerns with religion differ from theological and evangelical concerns (pp. 582–583)?

2 We could analyze ad infinitum "the problem of divine knowledge" and the way we anthropomorphize our deities. We have created literally millions of gods and goddesses "in the image of man" (and woman). No thinker has expressed the problem better than the Greek philosopher Xenophanes (p. 582). Is the human habit of anthropomorphizing a new insight for you, or have you previously worked through the problem? Do you still accept a deity image with anthropomorphic qualities? If you answer Yes, then how do you reconcile your imagery with our anthropomorphic predicament?

3 Analyze critically the cosmological argument developed by Aristotle and Aquinas (pp. 586–587). What are the basic assumptions upon which the argument rests? What are its logical fallacies, if any? After analysis, does it remain to you a persuasive argument for the existence of God?

4 Analyze critically the ontological argument of Saint Anselm (p. 587). What implicit assumptions are behind the argument? What are its major fallacies? In the final analysis, what is its persuasion power to you personally?

5 Analyze critically the teleological argument for God's existence (pp. 587–588). What fallacies are involved in this argument, if any? Where would you go for hard data to help clarify the question and to answer it? Is the argument convincing?

6 On the subject of "the death of God," read again pp. 588–591. What are the death-of-God theologians saying to us? (Try to avoid easy, simplistic answers.) Are they correct, in your opinion? How could you check their fact-claims or value judgments to decide if they are correct?

7 What is your assessment of the conviction of Carl Jung, the Swiss depth-psychologist (p. 592), that "religious experience is absolute. It is indisputable. . . ."?

8 To the best of your knowledge, and after pondering this chapter, what is the nature of Ultimate Reality? Can it be described in mere human words? Is it material? Is it natural but nonmaterial? Is it personal (that is, personlike)? Does it take the form of deity? If so, do you think this deity has particular characteristics such as masculinity or femininity? What kinds of human experiences might be interpreted as indicators of the existence and/or nature of this Ultimate Reality? (Take care, all along the way, to offer rational arguments or empirical evidence in support of your ideas; or, if this is not possible, then label carefully which ideas are personal beliefs.)

Death
Immortality

8-3

This chapter raises philosophic issues about the meaning of death. Each and every religious tradition prescribes ways to ameliorate the death event and help us accept it. But why exactly do we fear the nonbeing of death? Why do humans universally deny it? Various concepts of immortality are suggested, and arguments given for and against the immortality of the soul. The chapter includes Elizabeth Kübler-Ross's now-famous analysis of the human response to the impending death event, and Robert Heinlein poignantly ponders the painful moments that personal immortality might involve.

All Graves Are Wrong

1 "You been up to the grave yet?" asked the hunter, as if he knew I would answer yes.

"No," I said.

That really surprised him. He tried not to show it.

"They all go up to the grave," he said.

"Not this one."

He explored around in his mind for a polite way of asking. "I mean . . . " he said, "Why not?"

"Because it's the wrong grave," I said.

"All graves are wrong graves when you come down to it," he said.

"No," I said. "There are right graves and wrong ones, just as there are good times to die and bad times."

He nodded at this. I had come back to something he knew, or at least smelled was right.

"Sure, I knew men," he said, "died just perfect. You always felt, yes, that was good. One man I knew, sitting at the table waiting for supper, his wife in the kitchen, when she came in with a big bowl of soup there he was sitting dead and neat at the table. Bad for her, but, I mean, wasn't that a good way for him? No sickness. No noth-

O great Nzambi, what thou hast made is good, but thou hast brought a great sorrow to us with death. Thou shouldst have planned in some way that we would not be subject to death. O Nzambi, we are afflicted with great sadness.

Congo funeral chant

ing but sitting there waiting for supper to come and never knowing if it came or not. Like another friend. Had an old dog. Fourteen years old. Dog was going blind and tired. Decided at last to take the dog to the pound and have him put to sleep. Loaded the old blind tired dog on the front seat of his car. The dog licked his hand, once. The man felt awful. He drove toward the pound. On the way there, with not one sound, the dog passed away, died on the front seat, as if he knew and, knowing, picked the better way, just handed over his ghost, and there you are. That's what you're talking about, right?"

I nodded.

"So you think that grave up on the hill is a wrong grave for a right man, do you?"

"That's about it," I said.

"You think there are all kinds of graves along the road for all of us?"

"Could be," I said.

"And if we could see our life one way or another, we'd choose better? At the end, looking back," said the hunter, "we'd say, hell, that was the year and the place, not the other year and the other place, but that one year, that one place. Would we say that?"

"Since we have to choose or be pushed finally," I said, "yes."

"That's a nice idea," said the hunter. "But how many of us have that much sense? Most of us don't have brains enough to leave a party when the gin runs out. We hang around."

"We hang around," I said, "and what a shame."

We ordered some more beer.

Ray Bradbury
"The Kilimanjaro Device"

2 Our feelings about death are the subtlest of all motivators, but also the strongest. No problem in the human condition has been subject to man's creative imagination more than the prospect of one's own cessation. Ernest Becker writes that "the idea of death, the fear of it, haunts the human animal like nothing else; it is the mainspring of human activity—activity designed largely to avoid the fatality of death, to overcome it by denying in some way that it is the final destiny for man."

Millions long for immortality who do not know what to do with themselves on a rainy Sunday afternoon.
Susan Ertz

There is no experience that so forces even the most unphilosophic among us into philosophizing. Plato viewed the philosophic life as a rehearsal for death.

While I thought I was learning how to live, I was learning how to die.
Leonardo da Vinci

"To philosophize," wrote Montaigne, "is to learn to die." Schopenhauer summarized it all: "Death is the true inspiring genius, or the muse of philosophy. . . . Indeed, without death men could scarcely philosophize at all."

There is significant variation in how far each of us will go to avoid facing the fact that we must die. The evidence for postmortem consciousness is ambiguous, which only adds to our need to relieve anxiety about nonexistence and to mitigate the agony we associate with dying. Our minds create elaborate myths to allay our anguish over this event. Yet it is a universal event and a basic function of the cosmos.

3 It is difficult to define "death" except in arbitrary terms. "A person is dead when his heart stops"—we have long believed. But this age-old criterion is obsolete now that medical science can sustain a body's physical processes, including a beating heart, for months or years by artificial means. If the machines are shut down, the heart stops. Was the individual alive while the heart was beating?

Brainwaves are a better indicator, for to exist as a human person is to have a mind. Without the possibility of consciousness, there is no person; there exists only a physical organism that has lost its potential as a person. Therefore, when all the brainwaves are flat on the electroencephalograph, we conclude that the person is dead.

Yet even this is not accurate. Cases are known in which brain waves were nonexistent for many hours (that is, the person potential apparently ceased to exist), but the individuals were ultimately restored to full health, physically and mentally.

Another test of life/death is the brain's use of oxygen. If no oxygen is being used, brain cells are dying. When sufficient cells die (and this occurs within minutes of the onset of oxygen deprivation), then the brain reaches a point of irreversibility. At that point in time the person can be pronounced "dead."

How arbitrary and loose are our definitions, yet how crucial! At present, we can agree upon certain working definitions of "life" and "death" without having the foggiest notion of what **life** (and its absence, **death**) really is.

Death Is a Nonexperience

4 We cannot experience death, although in our fear and confusion we may not know this to be so. Death can never be experienced because death is the cessation of experience. Wittgenstein's pungent logic helps: "Death is not an event in life. Death is not lived through." We may be able to experience dying to some degree. If one believes he is dying and indeed he is, he may be able to experience a progression of dying events. But if one is convinced he is dying, but in fact he is not (that is, he recovers), then he has not experienced dying. One can be sure he is experiencing dying only if he dies; hence—from a strictly logical point of view—no one can ever be sure that he is having such an experience.

Spoken of John Keats: He always knew he would die young. Therefore, he saw as much beauty as he could.
Richard Janaro

Thanatologists—philosophers of the death event—make a helpful distinction between the unique inner experience—the cessation of consciousness—and the outer experience—the termination of physiological processes. The latter we obtain through observation of the death events of others. We can watch the gradual deterioration of life processes and then their actual termination, and we say this is the end of life: this is death.

Within ourselves, all we experience is the onset of the cessation of consciousness. This is often a gradual process, beginning long before the termination of our physiological processes. Most individuals subside into an unconscious state or coma at some point before death occurs, so they don't experience the later (and possibly eventful) stages leading to the death event.

I don't mind dying. I just don't want to be there when it happens.

WOODY ALLEN

5 Which of these events do we fear and so desperately try to avoid? Or do we fear both? Would we really care about the termination of our physiological processes if we could be assured that the cessation of our consciousness would not follow?

We do not fear death itself, and death—the cessation of consciousness—is nothing to be feared. Each night when we enter sleep we experience the cessation of consciousness; this is an experience that probably resembles the final cessation followed by death. Each night we die, literally. (But we awaken again. There is no wonder that sleep has become a synonym for death and that we universally picture ourselves waking from it.)

While we are reasoning concerning life, life is gone; and death, though perhaps they receive him differently, yet treats alike the fool and the philosopher.

DAVID HUME

Three distinct kinds of fear are associated with death, and one of them—fear of suffering—is realistic. One does not live for very long before learning that pain and grief are companions of death. As children we see animals in pain before they die; throughout life we witness the agony of individuals caught in war, accidents, and disease. The constant association of pain and death never ceases. It becomes difficult for us to think of death without feeling the fears we have been conditioned to associate with it.

Another kind of fear, less common, results from confusion. For instance, a teenaged girl awoke repeatedly with nightmares about death, and her terror became so intense it dominated her waking hours as well. When her ideas of death were explored with a therapist, it was discovered that what she really feared was being buried alive. That is, the body in her dreams would in fact be dead, but she was unable to separate the idea of consciousness from the buried corpse. Well-known stories by Edgar Allen Poe and others supply ideas that can grow into such nightmares. When the fallacy of identification was recognized, the girl's "fear of death" gradually diminished.

FEAR OF NONBEING

6 Another kind of death anxiety is all-pervasive. This is the universal fear: the fear of nonexistence. It is not fear of possible punishment in some hell or purgatory; nor is it merely a fear of the unknown. Rather, we experience a relentless anguish about nonexistence itself. We fear the experience of non-being, not recognizing that this is a contradiction in terms. However, a rational response to a nonrational fear is no solution.

We can remind ourselves that we already know "the experience of nonexistence." None of us were alive, say, two hundred years ago, but it didn't bother us then, nor does it concern us now. And, barring a scientific breakthrough, most of us will not be alive two hundred years hence. But this bothers

"There ain't no word in Sioux for goodbye."

"Walter Crow Horse"

Miner's Request
Find Proof of Man's Soul

PHOENIX (UPI)—An obscure Arizona miner named James Kidd was a man concerned with the human soul.

In a handwritten will dated in 1946 he said:

"After my funeral expenses have been paid and $100 (given) to some preacher of the Gospel to say farewell at my grave, sell all my property, which is all in cash and stocks and have this balance money go into a research or some scientific proof of a soul of the human body which leaves at death."

58416

Phoenix arizona
Jan 2. nd 1946
this is my first and only will
and is dated the second day in
January 1946. I have no, heirs
have not been married in my life,
an after all my funeral expenses
have been paid and $100. one hundred
dollars to some preacher of the
gospital to say fare well at my
grave sell all my property which
is all in cash and stocks with
E F Hutton Co Phoenix some in
safety box, and have this balance
money to go in a reserach or some
scientific proof of a soul of the
human body which leaves at death
I think in time their can be a
Photograph of soul leaving the
human at death,

James Kidd

(dated 2 nd January 1946)

some cash in Valley Bank some in Bank America L.A. Cal

VOL 541 PAGE 198

The last will of James Kidd, who disappeared in Arizona's Superstition Mountains. Reproduced courtesy of the Clerk of the Superior Court, Phoenix.

Kidd was last seen in 1949 when he apparently left to work on two mining claims. He was 70 and a year after his disappearance he was declared legally dead. His will was filed for probate in 1964.

He left a checking account of $4,100.66 at the time of his disappearance, and he owned stocks worth more than $100,000 which have nearly doubled because of dividends and other earnings.

A Miami man who knew Kidd said the miner had always talked about the supernatural and, despite the fact he never went to church, believed in the existence of a human soul which could be photographed as it left the body.

The court hearings on the will begin here before Maricopa County Superior Court Judge Robert L. Myers.

UPDATE: The case of the James Kidd will was closed on January 30, 1973, and the estate was awarded to the American Society for Psychical Research. Since that time ASPR research has concentrated on two hypotheses: "that some part of the human personality is capable of operating outside the living body on rare occasions"—that is, a temporary out-of-body experience (OBE); and "that it may continue to exist after the brain processes have ceased and the organism is decayed" —that is, permanent immortality.

Six OBE projects have been conducted. An OBE "fly-in" and an attempt to correlate OBEs and apparitions both supported the OBE hypothesis, but other interpretations (e.g. ESP) are possible. Perceptual experiments with OBEs and psychophysiological studies of subjects gave similar results: evidence in harmony with OBE hypothesis but other explanations possible. Instrumental recordings (i.e. photos) and a test of mediums gave negative results.

As for the second hypothesis, deathbed studies of apparitions, visions, hallucinations, etc. (reported by attending doctors and nurses) supported the conclusion that "some of the dying patients indeed appeared to be already experiencing glimpses of ecsomatic existence." But again, other interpretations can't be ruled out; so these results "should not be taken as a final balance of evidence for or against survival." Masses of data are still being processed.

ASPR Newsletter, Numbers 22, 24, and July 1976.

us. The possibility of nonexistence in the future can disturb us, while nonexistence in the past doesn't.

Why?

7 **Valhalla** (Norse): the great hall of immortality where warriors await the call of Odin to join in the final battle (the *Götterdämmerung*). **Elysium** (Greek): a place at the end of the Earth on the banks of the river Oceanus where perfect happiness rewards those favored by the gods. **Paradise** (Persian): a lush, green

Victories against Darkness

Death plays an important part in each day of my life. I have worked half in shadow, half in sun all of my life. When I put my new book *The Halloween Tree* (a history of Death in the world, really) in the mail eight weeks ago, I cried half-aloud: "There you are, Death, one up on you again!" My books are victories against darkness, if only for a small while. Each story I write is a candle lit for my own burial plot which it may take some few years to blow out. More than many writers, I have known this fact about myself since I was a child. It puts me to work each day with a special sad-sweet-happy urgency.

Ray Bradbury

We know what fear is. We live with it all of our lives. Only the dead are without fear.

The Magnificent Seven

park that serves as a temporary resting place for righteous souls awaiting the final resurrection. **Gardens of Delight** (Islamic): a place of reward for the faithful of Allah where, robed in silk and brocade, they are given all earthly delights imaginable. **Heaven** (Christian): the abode of God where the righteous dead will dwell together in perfect happiness in God's presence after the Last Judgment. **Svarga** (Vedic): a joyful place high above the world, bathed in flute song, where, for the faithful, the good things of this life will continue forever. **Isatpragbhara** (Jain): the heaven at the very top of the universe whither the pure consciousnesses of the righteous will rise and enjoy perfect bliss. **Isles of the Blest** (Orphic): the mystic Greek isles where the purified, now free from rebirth, will be rewarded with eternal happiness. **Kingdom of Osiris** (Egyptian): an oasis in

Last Flight

The following letter is by Flying Petty Officer First Class Isao Matsuo of the 701st Air Group. It was written just before he sortied for a kamikaze attack. His home was in Nagasaki Prefecture.

28 October 1944

Dear Parents:

Please congratulate me. I have been given a splendid opportunity to die. This is my last day. The destiny of our homeland hinges on the decisive battle in the seas to the south where I shall fall like a blossom from a radiant cherry tree.

I shall be a shield for His Majesty and die cleanly along with my squadron leader and other friends. I wish that I could be born seven times, each time to smite the enemy.

How I appreciate this chance to die like a man! I am grateful from the depths of my heart to the parents who have reared me with their constant prayer and tender love. And I am grateful as well to my squadron leader and superior officers who have looked after me as if I were their own son and given me such careful training.

Thank you, my parents, for the 23 years during which you have cared for me and inspired me. I hope that my present deed will in some small way repay what you have done for me. Think well of me and know that your Isao died for our country. This is my last wish, and there is nothing else that I desire.

I shall return in spirit and look forward to your visit at the Yasukuni Shrine. Please take good care of yourselves.

How glorious is the Special Attack Corps' Giretsu Unit whose Suisei bombers will attack the enemy. Movie cameramen have been here to take our pictures. It is possible that you may see us in newsreels at the theater.

We are 16 warriors manning the bombers. May our death be as sudden and clean as the shattering of crystal.

Written at Manila on the eve of our sortie.

Isao

Soaring into the sky of the southern seas, it is our glorious mission to die as the shields of His Majesty. Cherry blossoms glisten as they open and fall.

Inoguchi and Nakajima
The Divine Wind

the western desert with lush vegetation where the souls of the blessed will forever rest under spreading shade trees. **House of Song** (Zoroastrian): a place somewhere among the stars beyond the Chinvat Bridge where the righteous will enjoy perfect happiness in their companionship with one another.

Our endless contemplation of various heavens and hells reflects the conviction that we do not really die. Deep within we intuit that we are immortal. Actually, we are split by an ambivalence about the mystery of death. On the one hand, we know we will die, and as a social convention we confess this to others; but on the other hand, each of us has an instinctlike resistance: "It can't actually happen to me."

In a certain sense the whole of mythical thought may be interpreted as a constant and obstinate negation of the phenomenon of death. By virtue of this conviction of the unbroken unity and continuity of life myth has to clear away this phenomenon. Primitive religion is perhaps the strongest and most energetic affirmation of life that we find in human culture.

ERNST CASSIRER

Generally, man does not identify the self/essence with one's physical body. When we look at others, we see bodies, of course; we perceive physical organisms. But when we look into another's eyes, we see not merely the working parts of a transducer (cornea, iris, and so forth); we "see" a person. As we watch facial expressions, we "see" in others what we feel in ourselves: a self or soul that dwells in the body but that is not part of it. Our experience of consciousness feels like a "spirit" that dwells inside a "house," and various religious traditions refer to the coming and going of one's "spirit" into and out of the body. It "inhabits" a body. Indeed, several spirits may inhabit a body, simultaneously or in turn.

8 The Greeks developed the belief that the human spirit is free and of great value, while the body, quite a separate entity, is of little importance. The spirit can leave the body and wander where it wills. Some of the Greek philosophers held that the soul can be truly free only when the body-prison dies and releases it. The Greeks, therefore, had no strong feelings about mutilation or cremation. They felt concern if the corpse could not be given proper rites without which the soul could not find release; and it was especially tragic when Greek sailors were lost at sea and could never be given proper burial. Nevertheless, the body as such was of little worth.

What the hell happened to the last fifty years?

Forever Young

Our Judeo-Christian psyche-ology ("soul-ology") has been less dualistic. Jews and Christians distinguished between spirit and body, but they could never think of them as separable entities; therefore, after death reassembly of bodily materials is necessary for survival. The Hebrew could not imagine spirit wandering about without a body. For the Hebrew, as for the Egyptians, Sumerians, and others, mutilation of the body is a tragic misfortune, for we must carry into the next life whatever scars we acquire in this life.

Jesus uttered words to the effect that if your eye or hand causes you to sin, then destroy it, for "it is better for you to get into the Kingdom of God with but one eye than to be thrown into Gehenna with both eyes . . . " (Mark 9:47). These words were not meant symbolically; they reflect the late Judaic notion that we take into the next life whatever scars we sustain in this one. When Jesus reappeared to his disciples after the discovery of the empty tomb, he was seen to bear on his spirit-body the wounds of the crucifixion.

Fresco on wall of the tomb of a nobleman, Menena, at Royal Thebes. The fresco retains its vivid colors after 3,500 years. Note that the faces and parts of the bodies of Menena and his family have been chiseled away, thus ensuring that the soul of each would enter the next life faceless and maimed, a misfortune for an Egyptian who believed that we carry into the next life the scars acquired in this one.

In the Egyptian tomb of Menena, some culprit regained entrance to the burial chamber of this nobleman and mutilated the freshly painted frescoes. The faces of Menena and his family were chiseled away to ensure that they would go faceless into the next life.

Each of us should write our own epitaph, so that we will state to ourselves simply how it is we want to be remembered.

Roy Menninger

The Denial of Death

9 In Western thought we have strong religious reassurance that we will survive physical death. Orthodox doctrine denies that we die. The recorded fact-claim that Jesus awakened after physical death and promised us that we shall do the same is part of our Western theology of history. We have inherited a specific interpretation of the death event: there is no death of the self, and physical death is merely an event in a continuing drama.

Since these various antideath concepts are part of our own teleocosmic worldview, it is easy to avoid the feeling of certainty that death, in fact, awaits each of us. The idea of total oblivion has not been widely held or seriously faced.

We come from a dark abyss, we end in a dark abyss, and we call the luminous interval life.

Nikos Kazantzakis

10 Our difficulty in accepting the finality of death can be seen in a simple analysis of our linguistic utterances. Our talk about death generally occurs in two ways: we speak of our own death as "my death" and of the death of others as "your death." As I sit behind my typewriter thinking about death, it is rather easy to contemplate "your death." I read about the death of others in the morning newspaper; I saw it on the late news on television; it was vividly portrayed in a recent film I saw. Occasionally I see the death of others on the highway as I hurriedly drive by on the other side of the road. Perhaps I am one of those rare persons who has been with someone who died. In such an instant I observe "your death" as the cessation of respiration and heartbeat, in short, the termination of bodily process. But "my death" is a completely different matter. Not only is it impossible for me to observe, I have great difficulty thinking about it and imagining what it is like. How does one contemplate one's own nonbeing? It was this question that led Freud to postulate that every person, in his unconscious mind, is convinced of his own immortality. In observing his patients Freud discovered that denial functions as a coping mechanism enabling patients to handle their anxiety about their own death. Every time we attempt to contemplate our own death, Freud noted, we do so as spectators, that is, we are unable to think about or imagine our own nonbeing. What Freud described clinically was the overwhelming difficulty we have in thinking about death as a personal experience, death in its interiority.

O my soul, do not aspire to immortal life, but exhaust the limits of the possible.

Pindar

The starting point is to investigate the nature of our experience as we think about and attempt to contemplate our own death. What is involved in my own experience (and I assume your own experience as well)? The first thing I am aware of is ambiguity. When I recognize my own mortality and finitude and the fact that my death is a reality, I feel helpless, even frustrated, that I can do nothing about it. I feel trapped by some power, some force I do not fully understand and cannot avoid. In her clinical experience Elisabeth Kübler-Ross has found that many of her terminally ill patients think of death as an uncontrollable, powerful force that comes upon them and about which they can do nothing. One patient said, "Right now I feel strong and well, but I know I have something growing inside of me that is beyond my control." It is this sense of "no exit," no way out of an existence in which death is the end, that gives rise to the basic ambiguity regarding the human condition.

Beauty is what death is all about

Robert Badra

Richard Doss

11 When attempting to face the fact of death, the ever-present television screen is no help. It blurs the distinction between the living and the dead by holding before us an illusion of immortality. Television has been called "the great immortalizer." Each day we watch innumerable figures who, we have been told, are no longer alive. Yet obviously they live. They are alive before our eyes. The (alleged) fact that some physical organism no longer exists in space/time seems to make little difference.

Consider how that past ages of eternal time before our birth were no concern of ours. This is a mirror which nature holds up to us of future time after our death.

Lucretius

From the time we enter formal education the great men of history live on in our books and our minds. They are as alive as others we read about who may or may not be alive. We don't (and can't) make any clear distinction between the living and the no-longer living. Is George Washington dead? Not to millions of schoolchildren. Is Martin Luther King, Jr., dead? John Kennedy? Clark Gable? Mother Theresa? Jimmy Stewart? Marilyn Monroe? John Wayne? They all return on television, again and again, to renew the living personalities that we want to remember. Over and over we see Robert Kennedy's victory speech at the Ambassador Hotel, and Princess Diana's final exit from the hotel toward the black Mercedes.

12 For those who can't believe in the true survival of consciousness, the human mind has rationalized a variety of comforting alternatives. They allow us to retain the feeling that something of us is left after we cease to exist.

When one has lived as long as I have, it's a serious matter to die. Every year one puts out new roots.

David Lindsay
Voyage to Arcturus

Biological immortality stresses the continuity of germ plasm from parent to offspring. **Social immortality** reminds us that we will linger in the memories of others for the good we do. **Moral immortality** holds that while we may be forgotten, we can add our small contribution to the continuing moral development of the human species. **Life-cycle immortality** suggests that energy is never lost but is conserved in other living things: from life to dust and to life again.

In the genre of science fiction, we can comfort ourselves with quasi-immortal states such as **cryonic suspension** ("freeze now, thaw later" or, in Alan Harrington's phrase, "freeze-wait-reanimate") or **total transplants** whereby a continually renewed physical organism can sustain indefinitely an individual consciousness. Scientists are also researching the mechanics of **regeneration,** which operate so well for some lower creatures such as starfish and lobsters.

It's a Train Trip

Life is so short. The only thing you really have, that is really precious, is your time, is life itself. If you recognize that, if you really enjoy life, as I have, the hours and the days are the most special, precious thing in the world. There's nothing I could urge anybody to do that would make more sense than to live your life every day at a time and really savor it and enjoy it. And even though I've always had that view, I was running like everybody else. We all do it. We think in terms of destinations and accomplishing things, and et cetera, and the destination is what?—death. It's a train trip. And the train is moving very fast, and you look out the window and you don't see anything. You ought to get off the train and walk around.

Hugh Hefner

But all such notions are consolation prizes rather than immortalities. They are designed to ease the pain of loss—the loss of conviction that consciousness survives death.

Does true immortality—the survival of a conscious self—really exist? Is there any conceivable way that there could be a continuity of conscious experience after the termination of our physical processes? What arguments—rational or empirical—might convince us that such continuity does indeed take place?

Arguments for Immortality

13 The strongest **rational argument for immortality** is based on belief in the goodness of God. This is an "if . . . then" kind of argument: If God exists and if he is good, then immortality must necessarily exist.

According to this reasoning, it is unthinkable that God would create purposive beings who dream dreams and have the capacity for unlimited growth, only to let all this come to nothing. Could a good God not make provision for the fulfillment of these dreams and the actualization of this potential? The fact is that man barely begins to understand life and to grow during his short lifetime. Most of us just begin to touch our dreams and solve some problems—and it's over. This would surely be an agonizing joke for a compassionate God to play on his children.

Therefore, there must exist an afterlife where man's self/essence can continue to grow. How great such a growth potential would be, especially if released from the impediments of the physical body, we can only imagine.

The American Personalist philosopher, Edgar Brightman, considered this to be the strongest argument for immortality. To his way of thinking there is no strong argument for immortality apart from the existence of God; but granting God's existence, then there exists no weighty argument against immortality.

Belief in immortality secures a bond of union between the living and the dead, which is a fact of immense importance for the continuity of culture and for the safe keeping of tradition.

Ashley Montagu

Judgment scene before King Osiris. The dog-headed god Anubis is weighing the heart of the deceased Princess Entiuny against a symbol for truth; if judged worthy, her spirit will be allowed to pass on into the Kingdom of Osiris, a desert paradise somewhere toward the setting Sun. The goddess Isis, sister of Osiris and compassionate interceder, stands behind the princess.

The Heart of Hellas
Epitaphs

My name is—What does it matter?—My
Country was—Why speak of it?—I
Was of noble birth—Indeed? And if
You had been the lowest?—Moreover, my life
Was decorous—And if it had not been so,
What then?
                    and I lie here now beneath you—
Who are you that speak?
To whom do you speak?

PAULUS SILENTIARIUS

Epitaph of an Abstainer

Remember Euboulos the sober, you who pass by,
And drink: there is one Hadês for all men.

LEONIDAS OF TARENTUM

Epitaph of a Slave

Alive, this man was Manês the slave: but dead,
He is the peer of Dareios, that great King.

ANYTE

Epitaph of a Young Man

Hail me Diogenês underground, O stranger, and pass by:
Go where you will, and fairest fortune go with you.
In my nineteenth year the darkness drew me down—
And ah, the sweet sun!

ANONYMOUS

Epitaph of a Sailor

Tomorrow the wind will have fallen
Tomorrow I shall be safe in harbor
Tomorrow
        I said:
                    and Death
Spoke in that little word:
The sea was Death.
                              O Stranger
This is the Némesis of the spoken word:
Bite back the daring tongue that would say
        Tomorrow!

ANTIPHILOS OF BYZANTIUM

DUDLEY FITTS (translator)
Poems from the Greek Anthology

14 The strongest **empirical evidence for immortality**—and it may seem strange to some—is from seances during which contact is allegedly established with discarnate spirits.

It would not be far wrong to say that "special effects" and/or hypnosis is involved in 95 percent of all mediumistic activity; and therefore perhaps 5 percent of seances are free of fraud and demonstrate authentic phenomena. Now, within this 5 percent, the great majority of happenings can be accounted for with known psychological principles or telepathic hypotheses. This leaves only a small part of 1 percent that necessitate hypotheses assuming something like discarnate spirits. Within this very small percentage of cases, interesting but problematic events occur. For instance, the "discarnate spirits" frequently reveal information that no one present could possibly know. It has been suggested that there is a "collective subconscious" or a "superconsciousness" that is tapped by the mind of the medium; and while such a theory is not beyond the realm of possibility, the hypothesis of the existence of discarnate spirits seems at present a simpler and better explanation.

It is somewhere within this small percentage of spiritualistic phenomena that empirical data might be found to support the idea of a continued consciousness after physical death. At present we have no verified data in this area, and much more research is needed.

You bury only my body, not me.

SOCRATES

Arguments Against Immortality

15 The strongest **rational argument against immortality** derives from empirical observations that man has a profound "instinct" to stay alive. We are terrorized by this final unknown, this "great Perhaps," as Rabelais put it; and along with this ultimate fear goes man's incredible power of imagination. We can create an endless variety of concepts to meet our emotional needs. Therefore, with a simple formula—man's intense need plus his and her ever-fertile imagination—we may be able to explain to our satisfaction all of man's dreams of immortality: subtle imagery of blissful spirits, teleocosmic schemes of reincarnation, myths without end about heavens and hells and how we can get there, or stay out. As one surveys the range of man's fantasies about postmortem life, it seems that they just might be our most lavish creative productions. Man dreams of a paradise, but this life is anything but a paradise. There must be a paradise somewhere. . . . This is a rational argument, but it is founded upon empirical observation and possesses considerable coherence; while it proves nothing, as an inductive hypothesis it is formidable.

16 The strongest **empirical evidence against immortality** is the observation—apparently without exception—that the termination of physical processes is soon followed by the cessation of consciousness as measured on EEGs and other instruments. That is, our bodies die and we have no evidence—unless the "discarnate spirits" are real—that consciousness continues in any form. We have no scientific knowledge at present that would be compatible with the continuation of consciousness; just the reverse, in fact: our best scientific knowledge is only compatible with the cessation of consciousness.

The bullfight is a miniature of life. Death is a part of life, and it is an integral part of the bullfight. As in life, death hovers; it is inevitable, if not for the man, certainly for the bull. And in life, each of us must eventually die. One of the things the matador is saying when he fights bravely is that the way we die is important, or, that what is really important is how we live.

JOSEPH ROYCE

This is the great error of our day in the treatment of the human body that physicians separate the soul from the body.

Plato

We could argue that, from the cessation of brainwaves on an electroencephalograph, we cannot validly infer that consciousness ceases. This is strictly true. Yet no alternative inference seems better. We can think of such things as "organized electromagnetic fields" or "vibration patterns" that somehow sustain themselves without underlying physical systems, but do we have any dependable evidence at present that would lead us to believe such concepts refer to anything real? Since there appears to be a one-to-one causal relationship between brainwaves and consciousness, there is logical justification for inferring the end of experience from the termination of the brain's electrical activity.

The Future of Death

17 How we perceive "the problem of death" depends partly upon the attitude options open to us at any particular time and place. Mankind's general stance toward death has wavered between a stubborn denial and a grudging submission. Our religious myths deny the death of the personal self while confirming the intolerable anxiety and pain of physical death.

If I were given the choice of how long I should like to live with my present physical and mental equipment, I should decide on a good deal more than seventy years. But I doubt whether I should be wise to decide on more than three-hundred years. Already I am very much aware of my own limitations, and I think that three-hundred years is as long as I should like to put up with them.

Sir Fred Hoyle

Western man has long attempted to see death in new ways, and, thanks to recent investigations, death is now perceived as the terribly complex and ambiguous event that it is. From the nihilistic angle, the shriek of Ivan Ilytch paints the horror of facing one's own death at the end of a meaningless life. But Albert Camus goes further: "Because of death, human existence has no meaning. All the crimes that man could commit are nothing in comparison with that fundamental crime which is death."

By contrast, a more positive feeling is expressed by those who see death as the singular event that puts one's life in perspective and acts as the ultimate source of its meaning. Without death, they contend, our lives would be meaningless. The length of one's lifetime is irrelevant. If one lives a life filled with good experiences, then fifty years of meaningfulness is a full measure; but if one's life is meaningless, then five hundred years would be hell.

18 A brand new kind of vision has recently emerged: a prolongation of life that borders on immortality. For as long as we humans defined ourselves as "mortal

men" condemned to a death condition with "no exit," it was impossible for us to dream of alternatives. We could not allow ourselves to think that there might be an "exit." When we want very, very much something that is wholly beyond our reach, it is too painful to dream of possessing it; but given the remotest chance of grasping it, then we dream. More life—in quality perhaps, but certainly in quantity—may be (**may** be) within reach.

Science has extended the life expectancy of an individual in the Western world by about twenty-five years during the last century, and there is every reason to expect this trend to continue. How long might a lifetime become if we could solve the secret of aging? Or if we could learn how to transplant all human vital organs or replace them with synthetic surrogates? Or discover a chemistry that will prevent senility and loss of memory? Or develop a eugenics technology that would pair genetic factors that sharply increase human longevity? Recent trends in microbiology and related fields enable us to take some of these possibilities seriously for the first time.

Je m'en vay chercher un grand Peut-être. ***(I am going to seek a great Perhaps.)***

Rabelais
(from his deathbed)

A blunt defiance of death is now coming from some quarters. Alan Harrington, author of *The Immortalist,* takes an unequivocal stand: "Death is an imposition on the human race, and no longer acceptable. Man has all but lost his ability to accommodate himself to personal extinction; he must now proceed physically to overcome it. In short, to kill death: to put an end to his own mortality as a certain consequence of being born."

19 Current reassessment of man's place in a biocosmos of living creatures is another helpful perspective. Whether or not we succeed in the near future in making contact with extraterrestrial intelligences (ETIs), this "cosmic context for man" has become a coherent world-view within which we can rethink the nature and destiny of man. In this perspective we are faced with a new kind of question about death.

> Suppose we should discover that ETIs actually exist who enjoy life spans of three hundred years, or five hundred years, or a thousand. Might we then come to feel that man's life span of three score years and ten is wholly intolerable?
>
> How might we humans feel if ETIs are enabled to fulfill their plans and dreams to a degree that has heretofore seemed unthinkable to us? Could we continue to accept docilely the early and frustrating curtailment of our dreams?
>
> In terms of our self-esteem, could we continue to tolerate a seventy- to eighty-year life span? Wouldn't all our deaths then be viewed as premature?
>
> How long might we want to live under present conditions if we discover that some ETIs live for hundreds or thousands of our Earth years?
>
> What grounds do we have for assuming that death events as we know them are cosmic universals? Perhaps our notions are based solely on local and contingent examples.
>
> Is it remotely conceivable that there may be forms of "process termination" other than death as we know it?
>
> Wouldn't higher life-forms at least attempt to establish control over both the time and the conditions of life termination?
>
> Wouldn't such control in fact be merely an extension of scientific and medical goals now on our human drawing boards?
>
> If such control could be accomplished by man, how might it affect the whole intent and meaning of human existence?

From a ninety-year-old woman: "I'm looking forward so much to the next life. If it weren't for that I'd have nothing at all to look forward to."

Anne Christian

If we could live for two thousand years, would our present profound need for immortality be assuaged? What would we want **then?**

20 In a science-fiction classic, *Time Enough for Love,* Robert Heinlein captures the painful contrast between the near-immortal members of the Howard families and the short-lived "ephemerals"—that is, us. The Howards are normal Earthlings who find that they live for centuries as a result of a natural genetic mutation. The oldest member of the clan, Lazarus Long, reminisces about one short period of his long life, a very happy time spent with a short-lived ephemeral, Dora.

Death does not carry a passport.

Anwar Sadat

My death does not belong to me—it is the outer limit of my consciousness, the last of my possibles. The meaninglessness of death for me is summed up in the phrase that "my death is the one moment of my life which I do not have to live." My death is not for me but for others; it is not my concern, but the concern of others who will notice it and need to deal with it.

Joseph Mihalich

When my time comes, I hope no one drains my veins of their sustaining fluid and fills them with formaldehyde, then wastes me by putting me in a concrete box in the ground for eternity. Rather, just a simple pine box with an acorn on top of it. Find a place where a tree is needed and return me to nature. When the acorn grows, I can nourish it and give back in some measure what I've taken. Maybe someday kids can crawl in my branches or a raccoon might curl up in my trunk or the larks can sing out from my leaves. At any rate, I would rather let an oak tree be my epitaph than a marble slab be my tombstone.

Mike Royko

Dora is the only woman I ever loved unreservedly. I don't know that I can explain why. I did not love her that way when I married her; she had not had a chance as yet to teach me what love can be. Oh, I did love her, but it was the love of a doting father for a favorite child or somewhat like the love one can lavish on a pet.

I decided to marry her not through love in any deepest sense but simply because this adorable child who had given me so many hours of happiness wanted something very badly—my child—and there was only one way I could give her what she wanted and still please my own self-love. So, almost coldly, I calculated the cost and decided that the price was low enough that I could let her have what she wanted. It could not cost me much; she was an ephemeral. Fifty, sixty, seventy, at the most eighty years, and she would be dead. I could afford to spend that trivial amount of time to make my adopted daughter's pitifully short life happy—that's how I figured it. It wasn't much, and I could afford it. So be it.

✦

I decided that the husband of an ephemeral had to be an ephemeral, in every way possible to him. The corollaries to that decision caused us to wind up in Happy Valley.

Happy Valley—The happiest of all my lives. The longer I was privileged to live with Dora, the more I loved her. She taught me to love by loving me, and I learned—rather slowly; I wasn't too good a pupil, being set in my ways and lacking her natural talent. But I did learn. Learned that supreme happiness lies in wanting to keep another person safe and warm and happy, and being privileged to try.

And saddest, too. The more thoroughly I learned this—through living day on day with Dora—the happier I was . . . and the more I ached in one corner of my mind with certain knowledge that this could be only a brief time too soon over—and when it *was* over, I did not marry again for almost a hundred years. Then I did, for Dora taught me to face up to death, too. She was as aware of her own death, of the certain briefness of her life, as I was. But she taught me to live *now,* not to let anything sully *today* . . . until at last I got over the sadness of being condemned to live.

Death versus Life

21 Clearly, **how** one dies is very important—while one is still alive. We want assurance that our death will be dignified; that the conditions of termination will be surrounded by respect and honor; that it will not be degrading to ourselves or loved ones; that it will not be an unplanned, messy kind of death. We want to feel sure that it will not result from ignominious causes: from cowardice, foolish anger, or stupidity. And certainly not least, we want the assurance that our

last experience of consciousness will not be dominated by physical pain or emotional anguish.

There are two central questions involved in facing our own death: the questions of what we can leave behind and what we can take with us. It has been written that we must develop convictions and feelings about each of these questions if we are to face our own cessation with any sense of peace.

But some say that the better question is: What can I do with the days I have left to make life really worthwhile?

✦

Fruit must fall from the tree.

JERRY HUNTER

There are many forms of life in space. Many forms of death, too.

Space: 1999

Omar Khayyam

"One Thing at Least Is Certain—This Life Flies"

"In the city of Balkh, on the street of the slave-sellers, in the house of Amir Abu Sa'd" —so the story goes, and the storyteller is Nizam of Samarkand—"I had joined the crowd of happy guests. In the course of our friendly conversations, I heard Omar say, 'My grave will be in a spot where the trees will shed their blossoms on me twice in each year.'

"Which seemed to me impossible—for there is but one springtime. Still, I knew that he never spoke idle words.

"Then, in the year 530—it being some years since the great man had veiled his countenance in the dust—I came to Nishapur; and I went to visit his grave on the eve of Friday, taking with me a guide to lead me to the tomb. He brought me to the Hira cemetery. I turned to the left and his tomb lay at the foot of a garden wall, over which hung the flowering branches of pear-trees and peach-trees. On his grave had fallen so many flower-petals that his dust was covered beneath them.

"Then I remembered what he had said in the city of Balkh, and I fell to weeping. Because, on the face of the whole Earth, I had found no one to compare with him.

"May Allah have mercy upon him!"

Omar Khayyam was a mathematician, astronomer, and poet born at Nishapur in the extreme northeastern corner of Persia. He lived from about AD 1038 (AH 432 by the Moslem calendar) to AD 1123 (AH 517). The word *khayyam,* which means "tentmaker," was the profession of his father, Ibrahim, and possibly his also by inheritance. He was apparently schooled in his home city and was recognized for his talents from his earliest years. He became court astronomer to King Malikshah, who placed him in charge of an observatory—"House of the Stars"—and gave him a royal stipend in gold. For decades, free of material worries, he labored lovingly on his star charts (he reformed the calendar), geometry (he wrote a commentary on Euclid), and mathematics (his works include *Treatise on Algebra*); and he composed elegant poetry. He was respected by his fellow scientists, esteemed by the king, worshiped by his devoted followers, and hated by religious leaders.

This is virtually all we know about Omar Khayyam's life. Of Omar's mind and heart we know considerably more. By common consent he was the greatest thinker of his time, possessing an extraordinary mind that soared high above those of his contemporaries. What is remarkable is that Omar was both a brilliant mathematician ("left brain") and a brilliant poet ("right brain"); it is unusual to find the analytical intellect living in harmony with the romantic intuitions of the poet.

He spent his life, says his translator Edward FitzGerald, "busied in winning knowledge of every kind." Al-Qazwini says that Omar was "versed in all kinds of philosophy and mathematics." He studied Greek philosophy and expounded it; he pondered Avicenna's thought system and criticized it. He experimented with algebraic equations and geometric constructions five hundred years ahead of his time. He had a superb memory: he once reproduced a book almost word for word after reading it through seven times.

Omar's clear intellect brought him into direct conflict with the entrenched religious establishment. Despite the influx of Greek ideas and the rational ferment created by an impending enlightenment, Shi'ite orthodoxy remained extremely repressive. New ideas were fought down, often violently, and the variety of politicoreligious sects emerging were at one another's throats.

Such repression was intolerable to Omar, who proceeded to speak his mind fearlessly. He criticized bigotry, superstition, and mindless adherence to custom. As a scientist, he was offended when narrow-minded individuals held to beliefs that contradicted the simplest rational observations. He abrasively carried on running battles with an ignorant clergy who refused to consider any idea not sanctioned by scripture or tradition. As a result, he was denounced as the "arch-freethinker" of his time and warned to "bridle his tongue."

Omar's outspokenness brought criticism and reprisal. He was challenged by the Sufis and marked by the Assassins. The Sufi Razi derides him as "an unhappy philosopher, atheist, and materialist," citing two of his verses to prove the extent of his "confusion and error." He was disliked by al-Ghazzali and deplored by al-Qifti for his rationalism, whose "inward meanings are to the Law stinging serpents," filled with malice. The great poet Jalalu'd-Din Rumi complained that many had turned to Greek philosophy because of Omar: "How long [will you study] this philosophy of the Greeks? Study instead the philosophy of the Faithful!" Al-Qazwini tells of a certain theologian who came to Omar privately in the early morning for lessons in philosophy but in the evening denounced him from the pulpit as a "freethinker and atheist."

In Persia Omar's claim to fame has always been his achievements in mathematics and astronomy, but in the West he is loved for his poetry. In it he confided his passion and his pain.

In *The Rubaiyat of Omar Khayyam* each *rubaiyah* is a self-contained epigram expressing a complete thought. Its lines follow the rhyme scheme aaba, the third line lending a suspense that is resolved with the finality of the last line. Rubaiyat were written by everyone who could hold a pen, from toddlers to the most exquisite laureates. Over a thousand have been attributed to Omar, though a majority of these were probably penned by other poets.

In twelfth-century Persia these rubaiyat served a special purpose: freedom of expression. Since one might pay a dear price for such expression, the rubaiyat, with their veiled allusions, offered protection from inquisitors. While other verse forms might tell stories or embody religious ideas, the rubaiyat contained the more authentic feelings and ideas of its author and thus became a very personal medium of expression. The most unorthodox ideas could be given innocuous interpretations so as to offend no one.

What we find in Omar's rubaiyat, which were not written for publication, is the thought of a vigorous "freethinker"

The Wine of Life keeps oozing drop by drop,
The leaves of Life keep falling one by one.

Ah, make the most of what we yet may spend,
Before we too into the Dust descend . . .

"While you live,
Drink! for, once dead, you never shall return."

Into this Universe, and Why not knowing
Nor Whence, like Water willy-nilly flowing;
And out of it, as Wind along the Waste,
I know not Whither, willy-nilly blowing.

Ah, my Beloved, fill the Cup that clears
TO-DAY of past Regrets and future Fears:
To-morrow! —Why, To-morrow I may be
Myself with Yesterday's Sev'n thousand Years.

Come, fill the Cup, and in the fire of Spring
Your Winter-garment of Repentance fling:
The Bird of Time has but a little way
To flutter—and the Bird is on the Wing.

A Book of Verses underneath the Bough,
A Jug of Wine, a Loaf of Bread—and Thou
Beside me singing in the Wilderness—
Oh, Wilderness were Paradise enow!

Not one returns to tell us of the Road,
Which to discover we must travel too.

I sent my Soul through the Invisible,
Some letter of that After-life to spell:
And by and by my Soul return'd to me,
And answer'd "I Myself am Heav'n and Hell."

The Moving Finger writes; and having writ,
Moves on: nor all your Piety nor Wit
Shall lure it back to cancel half a Line,
Nor all your Tears wash out a Word of it.

who is fighting stupidity and hypocrisy. They are the outpourings of a soul undergoing great personal struggle. Further, they express outrage toward Time and Fate and the absurd futility of the human dream. Omar's cry of agony comes from the fact that his mind clearly sees that religion's preachments about life and death are wrong; but, try as he will, he cannot drive through to any comforting solution of his own. His lines are bitterest when he sees Fate canceling all that he has cherished: the splendor of marble palaces, the beauty of the rose, the laughter and the love of a lover. He rages, he ridicules, he tries to celebrate; but in the end, he despairs. In this life, while "the Moving Finger writes," there can be no peace.

Omar is in love with life—an emotion that most religions strongly discourage. His mind is filled with images of beautiful things: fields of golden grain, red roses and purple hyacinths, flowing water, wind, snow in the desert, caravans, books, merriment with friends, music and song, lips he has kissed and tresses caressed, a jug of wine, a potter thumping his clay, a *muezzin* chanting from the minaret.

But a shadow darkens the splendor of all he sees. A rose is a rose, Omar reminds himself; the moon is the moon; his lover is his lover. But he utterly fails, for a rose is not a rose but a loveliness that blossoms today, then wilts tomorrow and dries into dust. And his lover, beside him now "singing in the wilderness"—tomorrow his lover, too, will be dust beneath the rose bush. And the moon—

> Yon rising Moon that looks for us again—
> How oft hereafter will she wax and wane
> How oft hereafter rising look for us
> Through this same Garden—and for one in vain!

A rose is not a rose for Omar; it is a rose-in-time. **Time** is the enemy. He rages at it for what it does to us—bringing us life and beauty and dreams, then coldly quenching that beauty and killing the dreams. Time brings, and it takes away. Time destroys all, in time. Like a pre-Einsteinian relativist, he knows that realities exist only in a four-dimensional space-time equation. He can't perceive a rose as just a rose, though Heaven knows he tries. He **is** a realist.

> The Wine of Life keeps oozing drop by drop,
> The Leaves of Life keep falling one by one.

Omar therefore tries to fall back hard upon the present—

> Ah, my Beloved, fill the Cup that clears
> TO-DAY of past Regrets and future Fears . . .

But this doesn't work very well. "Live for today—it's all we have." It's a bit like saying forget the world, go lie on the beach, and hear only the joyous sounds of the sea—while your heart is breaking. True, you may long with all your heart to accomplish it, to pretend that what is isn't so, to convince yourself that in a few days, or weeks, or years, time will have taken care of it all and the hurt will be gone—which it will, and you know this. But as often as your mind whispers the wish, the rest of your being cries out that what is is what is. And the pain lingers.

This is what it means to be human: to know that all you have is the present moment, the Now; but to be aware during all your Nows that the time will come, too soon, when the Now is over—and then?

> Oh, threats of Hell and Hopes of Paradise!
> One thing at least is certain—This Life flies,
> One thing is certain and the rest is Lies;
> The Flower that once has blown for ever dies.

One begins to sense a refreshing candor reading through Omar's quatrains. He states simply what many of us have wanted to say. He reproves the cosmos and whatever runs it. "I won't capitulate. . . . No self-respecting human soul would live life as it is Given. It humiliates our hopes and devastates our dreams." This is blunt thinking, and we may prefer our philosophers to be more ambiguous. Sometimes Omar is ambiguous, sometimes he isn't.

In the final analysis, Omar Khayyam came to terms with death—specifically his own death—on his own terms. His religious traditions supplied him with a full set of assumptions preparing a believer for death and the afterlife. But these assumptions didn't satisfy Omar, who proceeded to work out his own realities about death, in his own way, with courage and candor. Omar blasphemes because he must, but he blasphemes on our behalf.

The analytic philosopher may want to argue that there is something wrong with Omar's questions; his assumptions are faulty and his logic is flawed. Were he a biologist or physicist, and not a poet, he might have thought in terms of chemical processes and sequences of causal events. But in the last analysis, Omar may be right: he speaks our pain for us, crying out against the Tyranny of Time.

Not a few scholars have suggested that Omar's ideas should be heard with common sense: that our picture of him must not be one of an unkempt drunkard by the wayside but rather of a quiet sage living his daily rounds, watching the stars, drawing circles with his compass, drinking with his friends. Not that his pain was not deep; his quatrains are certainly not cold equations. But for Omar, as for the rest of us, life must still be lived hourly, and with whatever gusto an old "freethinker" can muster.

It is pleasant to believe that Omar's despair might have been eased by a modicum of wit—which we know he possessed, for we are told that Omar one day came upon some bricklayers repairing the academy of Nishapur. They were having trouble with a donkey, loaded down with bricks, that was refusing to enter the building, despite kicking and prodding. Omar laughed, and going up to the donkey, whispered in its ear:

> O lost and now returned, *'yet more astray'*
> Thy name from men's remembrance passed away,
> Thy nails have now combined to form thy hoofs,
> Thy tail's a beard turned round the other way!

Without further ado, the donkey trotted into the building, and the workmen asked Omar how he had persuaded the stubborn animal to move. He replied that in a previous life the donkey had been a lecturer at this very academy, and that, until it was recognized and acknowledged, it was unwilling to visit his old friends.

And if **you** saw a donkey acting like a jackass, could you resist the temptation to walk up to it and say **something** in its ear? Omar's laughter echoes through the centuries, though early writers, who had misplaced their sense of humor, missed Omar's delight and invested the account with weighty implications of strange powers and doctrines of reincarnation.

Today the grave of Omar Khayyam is known or visited by few. It is to be found four miles southeast of the town of Nishapur, adjacent to a mosque. Visitors, it is certain, would be welcome: should we in our joyous rounds reach the spot where he is dust, we are invited to have one on him, and "turn down an empty Glass!"

Dedicated to Dr. Robert W. Smith.

THE LAST RITE OF PASSAGE

In 1969 Dr. Elisabeth Kübler-Ross, a Swiss-born psychiatrist, published a book entitled *On Death and Dying.* Having spent years listening to terminally ill patients, she had discovered that an individual facing death typically undergoes a five-stage sequence of adjustments, beginning when first told that the end is near. Dr. Ross's discovery became famous almost overnight, partly because it has the ring of truth and partly because it is a powerful, redemptive interpretation of an event that all of us will face. The heart of her discovery is revealed in the title of her later anthology (1975), *Death: The Final Stage of Growth.*

Dr. Ross found that her patients' first reaction is **denial.** This is an unavoidable first response, and it is very important and necessary when one begins to face the inevitability of one's own death. The second reaction is also inevitable: **anger and rage.** Being alive is a familiar condition, and one resents having to give it up while others continue to live. If one is religious, then turning this anger on God, the supposed bringer of good things—but now this, the ultimate evil—is a healthy response.

Then the individual begins to **bargain** for time, promising to be good or to do good deeds in return for God's granting an extension of life for a day, a month, or a year. When Martin Luther thought he was dying, he promised God that he would enter the priesthood. When Nikos Kazantzakis became terminally ill, he imagined going into the streets and begging fifteen minutes of life/time from passersby.

Then **depression** comes with the realization that bargaining is hopeless, that there is no escape, that one is totally and absolutely helpless to do anything whatever to avoid the end of bodily processes and the cessation of consciousness. Kübler-Ross calls this depression a "preparatory grief," and this stage too is inevitable and necessary. Now the patient becomes quiet and usually wants to be alone. It is a time for reflecting on one's past life and taking stock of one's accomplishments and failures.

Finally comes **acceptance.** The patient acknowledges that the time has come, and it's all right. Although this final stage may appear outwardly as a depressive resignation, it is far more than that; it is at this time that consolidation and growth can take place.

This five-stage pattern has become a convenient mnemonic device repeated ad infinitum in textbooks, lectures, and pop treatises on death. But Dr. Ross spends considerable time emphasizing what it means. First, she points out that this fivefold sequence is familiar to all of us because we experience something like it whenever deep, significant events impact our lives, events such as serious illness, loss of someone close, abandonment, divorce, retirement, loss of a job or vocation, even a religious conversion. Any one of these traumatic events can initiate a responsive sequence that includes denial, anger, bargaining, and so on.

Second, this pattern of experience is—or can be—a blessing. The anticipation of death can be the creative force that leads to growth. Kübler-Ross states that this is the goal of her life's work: to help mortal humans see that life does not have to end in anguish and despair. She writes, "I hope to convey one important message to my readers: namely, that death does not have to be a catastrophic, destructive thing; indeed, it can be viewed as one of the most constructive, positive, and creative elements of culture and life."

These five stages are not absolute. Death is as individual an event as life itself, and one may not go through every stage in the order given. Personal choice plays a major role in determining how we experience each stage. It is not uncommon for a dying person to become fixated on denial, anger, or remorse and fail to find acceptance and resolution.

But if one has learned how to live, then growth—the search for the authentic self—has already become the elemental goal of one's life, and these five stages constitute the final rite of passage of personal growth toward humanness. Often, writes Kübler-Ross, "we must learn to die in order that we may learn to live, that growing to be who you truly are requires sometimes that you die to the life chosen for you by society, that each new step of growth involves a throwing off of more of the shackles restraining you." It is when we stand at the threshold of death that we receive the final opportunity for growth. But we need not wait for death. We can learn to die to the world with every deep change in our lives. A growing human doesn't wait for death but embraces every opportunity for growth that life provides.

This, says Dr. Ross, is the greatest lesson we can learn by listening to our patients: *"LIVE, so you do not have to look back and say: 'God, how I have wasted my life.'"*

✦

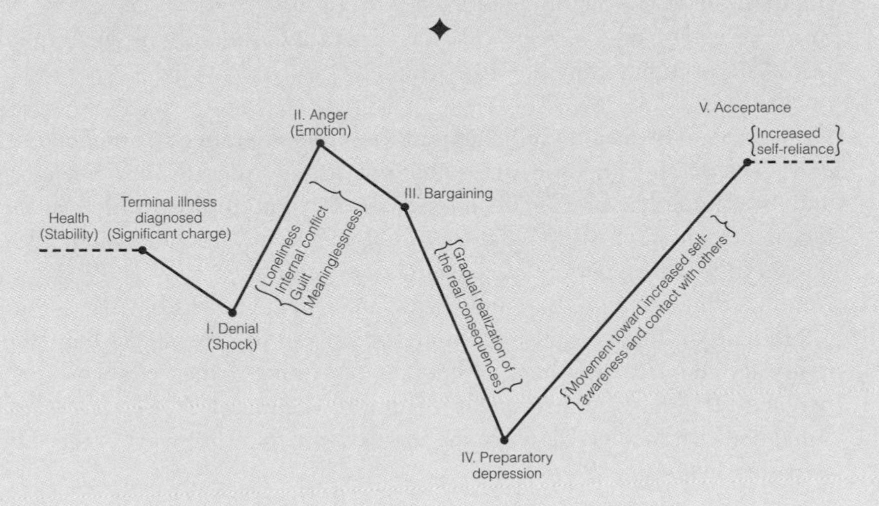

Reflections

1 "All graves are wrong when you come right down to it" (pp. 598–599). How do you respond to the point Bradbury is making?

2 How would you answer the question: "Would we really care about the termination of our physiological processes if we could be assured that the cessation of our consciousness would not follow?" (p. 601).

3 "The possibility of nonexistence in the future can disturb us, while non-existence in the past doesn't." Why?

4 This "fear of nonexistence" is widely dealt with in existential literature, and many philosophers are convinced that this fear is one of the powerful driving forces behind much human behavior. So, what exactly is meant by the "fear of nonexistence" (or "nonbeing")? Is the concept meaningful to you personally?

5 Three kinds of fear commonly associated with death are described on p. 601 of this chapter. Are these descriptions accurate, in your judgment? Have any of these fears (or others) been a significant part of your experience? How have you dealt with them?
6 Think a while about the James Kidd will (pp. 602–603). Do you think there is any empirical evidence for the existence of a "soul"? Do you think there could be? If so, what kind of evidence? How would you go about gathering evidence? That is, what path might you follow if you really wanted to "show cause" why you should receive the James Kidd estate?
7 Review and clarify in your own mind the empirical and rational arguments presented in this chapter for and against immortality (pp. 609–612). Which of these arguments are most persuasive? On the basis of these four arguments, what is your conclusion regarding the existence of personal immortality?
8 Answer the following question as precisely as you can, but first give careful attention to the definition of each term in the question: "Where do you think we will go after we die?" (If you think that fallacious or meaningless words are used here, then rephrase the question until you get it to produce results.)
9 Evidence would seem to indicate that the preponderance of human beings can't face death without myth. Myths that attend upon death, its meaning, and its aftermath are legion in all religions. In your opinion, could mankind face death without myth? (What is meant by myth in such a question?) What do you think the experiential consequences might be?
10 Note the diagram on p. 620 and review the stages that Kübler-Ross found a terminally ill patient must go through. Can you feel the stages empathetically and identify with them? What is the meaning of the five stages to you personally? What do these stages mean philosophically?
11 What does Dr. Kübler-Ross say she learned from her discovery of these five sequential steps?

Meaning
Existence

8-4

This chapter returns to the question of ultimate meaning in our lives—the problem of the World Riddle, the heart of which is, What do we *really* want? What, in the final analysis, drives us and guides us? What end—if anything—are we striving to accomplish? Do we truly want what society tells us we want (in our society it has to be some form of consumerism)? Are fulfillment goals for each of us genetically established? Or do we have true freedom in choosing "the path with a heart" that would be right for us? Amidst the profusion of alternatives that the world stands ready to offer us, it often seems that the right choice must be vigorously sought, recognized, and fought for. As Jean-Paul Sartre says, "You are free, therefore choose."

The Knowledge That Hurts Most

1 Once there lived in the ancient city of Afkar two learned men who hated and belittled each other's learning. For one of them denied the existence of the gods and the other was a believer.

One day the two met in the market-place, and amidst their followers they began to dispute and to argue about the existence or the non-existence of the gods. And after hours of contention they parted.

That evening the unbeliever went to the temple and prostrated himself before the altar and prayed the gods to forgive his wayward past.

And the same hour the other learned man, he who had upheld the gods, burned his sacred books. For he had become an unbeliever.

Kahlil Gibran

Philosophy is the highest music.

Plato

". . . in New Orleans. On Bourbon Street."
"No, that's your dream. It's not mine."
"Well, then, what is yours?"
"I have no dream."

2 The Don Juan of the Mind: no philosopher or poet has yet discovered him. What he lacks is the love of the things he knows, what he possesses is *esprit*, the itch and

"How terrible for you!"
Tennessee Williams
This Property Is Condemned

delight in the chase and intrigue of knowledge—knowledge as far and high as the most distant stars. Until in the end there is nothing left for him to chase except the knowledge which hurts most, just as a drunkard in the end drinks absinthe and methylated spirits. And in the very end he craves for Hell—it is the only knowledge which can still seduce him. Perhaps it too will disappoint, as everything that he knows. And if so, he will have to stand transfixed through all eternity, nailed to disillusion, having himself become the Guest of Stone, longing for a last supper of knowledge which he will never receive. For in the whole world of things there is nothing left to feed his hunger.

Friedrich Nietzsche

What *Did* I Want?

3 New Zealand, maybe. The Herald-Trib had had the usual headlines, only more so. It looked as if the boys (just big playful boys!) who run this planet were about to hold that major war, the one with ICBMs and H-bombs, any time now.

We shall not cease from exploration
And the end of all our exploring
Will be to arrive where we started
And know the place for the first time.
T. S. Eliot
Four Quartets

If a man went as far south as New Zealand there might be something left after the fallout fell out.

New Zealand is supposed to be very pretty and they say that a fisherman there regards a five-pound trout as too small to take home.

I had caught a two-pound trout once.

About then I made a horrible discovery. I didn't want to go back to school, win, lose, or draw. I no longer gave a damn about three-car garages and swimming pools, nor any other status symbol or "security." There was no security in this world and only damn fools and mice thought there could be.

Somewhere back in the jungle I had shucked off all ambition of that sort. I had been shot at too many times and had lost interest in supermarkets and exurban subdivisions and tonight is the PTA supper don't forget dear you promised.

Oh, I wasn't about to hole up in a monastery. I still wanted—

What *did* I want?

I wanted a Roc's egg. I wanted a harem loaded with lovely odalisques less than the dust beneath my chariot wheels, the rust that never stained my sword. I wanted raw red gold in nuggets the size of your fist and feed that lousy claim jumper to the huskies! I wanted to get up feeling brisk and go out and break some lances, then pick a likely wench for my *droit du seigneur*—I wanted to stand up to the Baron and dare him to touch my wench. I wanted to hear the purple water chuckling against the skin of the Nancy Lee in the cool of the morning watch and not another sound, nor any movement save the slow tilting of the wings of the albatross that had been pacing us the last thousand miles.

May you find your path and follow it!
The Buddha

I wanted the hurtling moons of Barsoom. I wanted Storisende and Poictesme, and Holmes shaking me awake to tell me, "The game's afoot!" I wanted to float down the Mississippi on a raft and elude a mob in company with the Duke of Bilgewater and the Lost Dauphin.

"I've traveled so far, and all I've done is come back home."
***Gandhi* (the motion picture)**

I wanted Prester John, and Excalibur held by a moon-white arm out of a silent lake. I wanted to sail with Ulysses and with Tros of Samothrace and eat the lotus in a land that seemed always afternoon. I wanted the feeling of romance and the sense of wonder I had known as a kid. I wanted the world to be what they had promised me it was going to be—instead of the tawdry, lousy, fouled-up mess it is . . . .

Maybe one chance is all you ever get.

Robert Heinlein
Glory Road

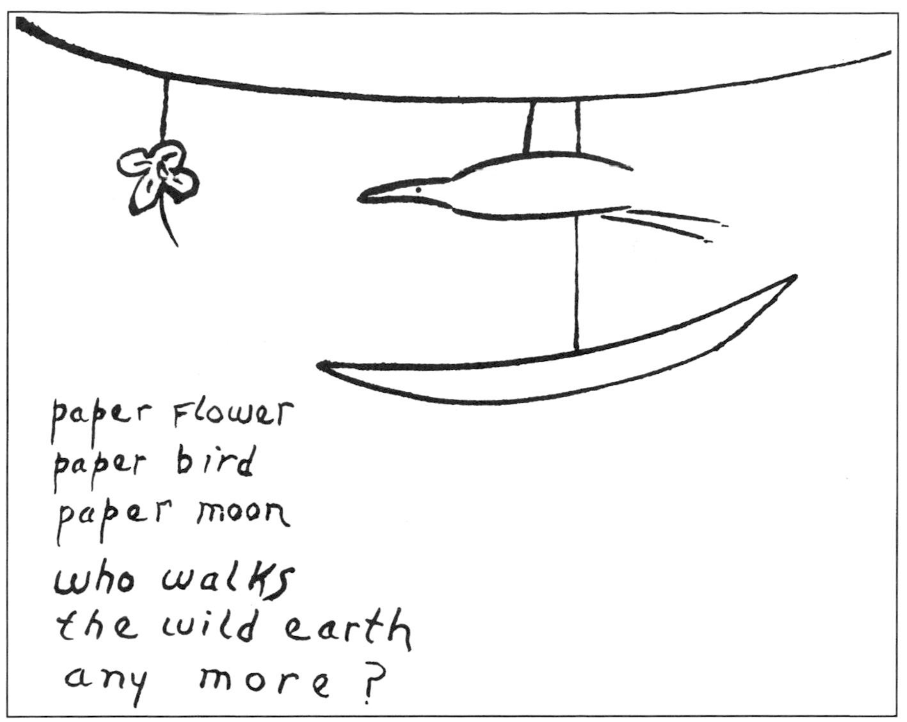

paper Flower
paper bird
paper moon
who walks
the wild earth
any more ?

4 Has any one of us not asked, sometime or perhaps often, "What am I doing here?" But what is the answer?

Ever look at a male lion in a zoo? Fresh meat on time, females supplied, no hunter to worry about—he's got it made, hasn't he? Then why does he look bored?

ROBERT HEINLEIN
Glory Road

Socrates believed that we are here to be happy and that the path of happiness is through knowledge, which leads to virtue, which leads to happiness. **Epicurus** taught that we are here to cultivate the pleasures of the mind—wisdom and understanding—but the Cyrenaic philosopher **Aristippus** became famous for teaching that we are here to cultivate pleasures, and the more the merrier (and those of the mind only as a last resort). A prophet from Nazareth, **Yeshua bar Yoseph,** suggested we are here to learn the qualities of faith and love toward one another so that we will merit membership in the Reign of God when it begins. Shortly after that, **Paul of Tarsus** preached that we are here to have faith in the Messiah so that our original sin could be washed away and we would be ready for the return of the Christ.

If I had my life to live over again, I would have made it a rule to read some poetry and listen to some music at least every week. . . . The loss of these tastes is a loss of happiness, and may possibly be injurious to the intellect, and more probably to the moral character, by enfeebling the emotional part of our nature.

CHARLES DARWIN

Lao-tzu apparently believed that we are here to seek the Tao and know the inner harmony of Nature's Way; but **Confucius** disagreed, declaring that we are here to discover the proper way to behave in our relationships with each other. **The Buddha** taught that we are here to transcend *tanha*—the selfish craving that is the cause of human suffering—and enter the state of *nirvana.* **Shankara,** a Hindu mystic, was convinced that we are here to discover that this world is only *maya* ("illusion") and to realize that each of us is already one with Ultimate Reality.

Muhammad believed that we are here to render faithful obedience to Allah as revealed in the Quran. **John Calvin** told the Genevans that we are here solely to love God and so live a life of faith and discipline that we will "enjoy

You missed life

Him forever." But **Hegel,** being a philosopher on the rational side, wrote to persuade us that we are here to develop our capacity for reason and, in so doing, manifest the logic of the Absolute Mind in the movement of human (especially German) history.

Existence and the Real: Persistent Confusion

The true biologist deals with life, with teeming boisterous life, and learns something from it, learns that the first rule of life is living. The dry-balls cannot possibly know a thing every starfish knows in the core of his soul and in the vesicles between his rays.

John Steinbeck

5 It is impossible to define the purpose of life in a general way. "Life" does not mean something vague, but something very real and concrete, just as life's tasks are very real and concrete. They form man's destiny, which is different and unique for each individual. No situation repeats itself and each situation calls for a different response. Sometimes the situation in which a man finds himself may require him to shape his own destiny by action. Sometimes a man may be required simply to accept fate, to bear his cross.

When a man finds that it is his destiny to suffer, he will have to accept suffering as his task; his single and unique task. He will have to struggle for the realization that even in suffering he is unique and alone in the universe. No man can relieve him of his suffering, or suffer in his place. His unique opportunity lies in the way in which he bears his burden.

Viktor Frankl

6 The central character of *Nausea,* Antoine Roquentin, enunciates Jean-Paul Sartre's reflections on the meaning of human existence.

> Prior to these past few days, I had really never felt what it means "to exist." . . . Ordinarily, existence hides itself. It is here, round about us, within us: we are it, and we cannot speak two words without speaking of it, but in the end we never grasp it. . . . Existence is not something which can be thought from a distance: it overwhelms you brusquely. . . .

[Existence means nothing more than] to be here; existents appear, they are encountered, but they can never be inferentially deduced. I believe there are people who have understood this, but they have been trying to overcome this contingency by inventing a Necessary Being who causes himself (a *causa sui*). No Necessary Being, however, can explain existence. . . . There is not the least reason for our "being-there." . . . And I, too, am "*de trop*" [superfluous, unnecessary, absurd]. And yet people are trying to hide themselves behind the idea of law and necessity. In vain: every existent is born without reason, prolongs its existence owing to the weakness of inertia, and dies fortuitously.

JEAN-PAUL SARTRE

Does the grass bend when the wind blows upon it?

CONFUCIUS

7 That Man is the product of causes which had no prevision of the end they were achieving; that his origin, his growth, his hopes and fears, his loves and his beliefs, are but the outcome of accidental collocations of atoms; that no fire, no heroism, no intensity of thought and feeling, can preserve an individual life beyond the grave; that all the labours of the ages, all the devotion, all the inspiration, all the noonday brightness of human genius, are destined to extinction in the vast death of the solar system, and that the whole temple of Man's achievement must inevitably be buried beneath the debris of a universe in ruins—all these things, if not quite beyond dispute, are yet so nearly certain, that no philosophy which rejects them can hope to stand. Only within the scaffolding of these truths, only on the firm foundation of unyielding despair, can the soul's habitation henceforth be safely built.

BERTRAND RUSSELL

If a patient [should ask] Frankl, "What is the meaning of life for me?" he is likely to get a Socratic answer: "What is the best chess move?"

AARON UNGERSMA

Those who have suffered much become very bitter or very gentle.

WILL DURANT

LESSONS

Charles Beard (1874–1948) was a renowned historian and economist. His colleague, George Counts, tells of a conversation they had in the autumn of 1931.

> He and I were motoring over the hills of Connecticut in the vicinity of New Milford. Having been profoundly impressed by the vast range of his knowledge and thought, a range that seemed to embrace the entire human record from ancient times, I asked how long it would take him to tell all he had learned from his lifetime study of history. After contemplating the question a few moments he replied that he "thought" he could do it in "about a week." We drove on a short distance in silence. Whereupon he said he could probably do it in a day. After another brief pause, he reduced the time to half an hour. Finally, bringing his hand down on his knee, he said: "I can tell you all I have learned in a lifetime of study in just three laws of history. And here they are:
>
> "First, whom the gods would destroy they first make mad."
>
> "Second, the mills of the gods grind slowly, yet they grind exceedingly fine."
>
> "Third, the bee fertilizes the flower that it robs."
>
> About ten days later we took a stroll along Riverside Drive in New York City. Evidently he had been giving further thought to my question. At any rate, he said he would like to add a fourth law to his laws of history:
>
> "When it gets dark enough you can see the stars."

GEORGE S. COUNTS
"Charles Beard, The Public Man,"
in Howard K. Beale (ed.)
Charles A. Beard: An Appraisal

Trivialities

8 But wherein do such pronouncements about the absurdity of existence become statements about the real world? Are they not more on the order of reflexive value judgments that betray the inner world of the individuals who make them? After all, to say the world is meaningless is merely to say, "I find no meaning in it." Value judgments are personal responses, not scientific descriptions.

Much modern Western philosophy has contended that there are no real values and that, by a sort of hopeless tour de force, each of us must inject meaning into his own life. Existentialists such as Heidegger and Sartre have held that only a personal confrontation with death itself puts our lives in perspective but that this "flash of authenticity" cannot be made a part of our everyday consciousness. But this is questionable, for "there are states of consciousness that are not 'everyday consciousness' and which are not 'transcendental' either. These produce a definite sense of values and purpose." In saying this, perhaps Colin Wilson is closer to the truth, and he goes on:

> "Peak experiences" all seem to have the same "content": that the chief mistake of human beings is to pay too much attention to everyday trivialities. We are strangely inefficient machines, utilizing only a fraction of our powers, and the reason for this

If you are creating, how can you not feel alive?
Lori Villamil

The Creations of My Mind

1. With clarity and quiet, I look upon the world and say: All that I see, hear, taste, smell, and touch are the creations of my mind.

2. The sun comes up and the sun goes down in my skull. Out of one of my temples the sun rises, and into the other the sun sets.

3. The stars shine in my brain; ideas, men, animals browse in my temporal head; songs and weeping fill the twisted shells of my ears and storm the air for a moment.

4. My brain blots out, and all, the heavens and the earth, vanish.

5. The mind shouts: "Only I exist!

6. "Deep in my subterranean cells my five senses labor; they weave and unweave space and time, joy and sorrow, matter and spirit. . . .

10. "I impose order on disorder and give a face—my face—to chaos.

11. "I do not know whether behind appearances there lives and moves a secret essence superior to me. Nor do I ask; I do not care. I create phenomena in swarms, and paint with a full palette a gigantic and gaudy curtain before the abyss. Do not say, 'Draw the curtain that I may see the painting.' The curtain is the painting. . . .

13. "I am the worker of the abyss. I am the spectator of the abyss. I am both theory and practice. I am the law. Nothing beyond me exists."

Nikos Kazantzakis
The Saviors of God

is our short sightedness. Koestler's "mystical" insight made him feel that even the threat of death was a triviality that should be ignored; "So what? . . . Have you nothing more serious to worry about?" Greene's whisky priest: "It seemed to him, at that moment, that it would have been quite easy to be a saint." Death reveals to us that our lives have been one long miscalculation, based on a triviality.

A painter who is painting a large canvas has to work with his nose to the canvas, but periodically he stands back to see the effect of the whole. These over-all glimpses renew his sense of purpose.

Man's evolution depends upon a renewal of the sense of over-all purpose. For several centuries now, the direction of our culture has been a concentration upon the minute, the particular. In the field of science, this has produced our present high level of technological achievement. In the field of culture, we have less reason for self-congratulation, for the concentration upon the particular—to the exclusion of wider meanings—has led us into a cul de sac. Yeats described the result as "fish gasping on the strand"—a minute realism that has lost all drive and purpose.

I have the key to happiness: remember to be profoundly, totally conscious that you are.
I myself, sorry to say, hardly ever use this key. I keep losing it.

Eugene Ionesco

Work, Work . . . to Kill the Flowers

9 In subjecting these views to the critical questioning that constitutes one important side of the philosophical task, we are, therefore, engaging in an experiment that is both very personal and at the same time "vicarious." We are not only taking the personal risk of having our views exposed as inadequate, but, since most of our views are also those of the vast majority of the rest of the people in our culture, it is the intellectual outlook of our whole culture that is here being put to the test. If we should suffer the collapse of some of our cherished beliefs (and the loss of a cherished belief does involve a painful sort of suffering), then it is not only for ourselves that we suffer, but for those many others in our culture who share those beliefs. It is only through such suffering, however, that human thought progresses.

But human thought does progress, and this is what makes the enterprise worthwhile. Many people must have suffered the kind of intellectual agony of which we

In shallow ponds, even little fish can stir up a commotion. In the oceans, the largest whales make hardly a ripple.

Hindu proverb

Grown-Ups Are Very Strange

When you can measure what you are speaking about, and express it in numbers, you know something about it; but when you cannot measure it, when you cannot express it in numbers, your knowledge is of a meager and unsatisfactory kind: it may be the beginning of knowledge, but you have scarcely, in your thoughts, advanced to the stage of science.

William Thomson, Lord Kelvin
Popular Lectures and Addresses

Grown-ups love figures. When you tell them that you have made a new friend, they never ask you any questions about essential matters. They never say to you, "What does his voice sound like? What games does he love best? Does he collect butterflies?" Instead they demand: "How old is he? How many brothers has he? How much does he weigh? How much money does his father make?" Only from these figures do they think they have learned anything about him.

Antoine de Saint-Exupéry
The Little Prince

have been speaking, during the long interval of time that separates us from our primitive ancestors; but there can be little doubt that our way of looking at the world—our world-view—is closer to the truth than the superstitious, animistic, magical views that they are known to have held. If our view is not the whole truth—and it would surely be presumptuous to say that it is—then let us press on toward that elusive goal as best we can. It is the lure of beliefs that are closer to the truth that beckons us on and leaves us dissatisfied with beliefs that are obviously short of that goal.

William Halverson

10 Just when a humanlike consciousness—in the form of self-awareness—began, we cannot at present tell. Perhaps two million years ago, perhaps fourteen million, perhaps more. But the question is academic. The significant thing is that we are giving birth to, developing, flowering, a seed planted ages ago; and that this is a glorious flowering, whatever the pain we must pay for the seeds of such flowering. After flowering, most flowers die, though most plants do not die but continue to live and grow. This inevitable flowering of man's awareness is totally unavoidable, and like a flower that has gradually, slowly, grown from bud to its moment of opening to the world, there is no turning back; it is flower, or die.

Many a time I have wanted to stop talking and find out what I really believed.

Walter Lippmann

11 Now the cello has stopped. All that can be heard is the ironic funeral march from the first symphony of Mahler. The girl is walking across the desert towards a hill, the only feature in the otherwise gently sloping terrain, apart from a black plume of smoke which is rising distantly in the air. As she gets nearer to this oily cloud of smoke, scurrying human activity can be seen on the ground beneath. Occasionally a gout of bright flame bursts along the ground, and more smoke is added to the cloud rising swiftly in the air. Now the camera, in a tracking shot, reveals a close-up of the girl's face as she walks along. At first lines of concentration furrow her forehead as she tries to make out what is going on, then the concentration is replaced by bewilderment, and then, a little later, by anger. Now the camera is static, and we see the whole scene as the girl walks up.

"My soul, your voyages have been your native land!"

Nikos Kazantzakis
"Odysseus" *The Odyssey*

Men in shirt sleeves are rushing about, their faces grimy and shining with sweat. They look bewildered and panic-stricken, but this is obviously their normal state of mind. On their backs they carry the large chemical tanks of flamethrowers, and the straps have rubbed into their shoulders for so long that they are obviously in great pain. All around the ground is seared and black. It appears that nothing could possibly grow in such a devastated place, but straggly vegetation is visibly thrusting itself up through the soil. Every moment one of the strange plants is beginning to bloom. . . . A bud appears, almost instantaneously, and begins to open. Lush, coloured petals are visible, promising future beauty. But as soon as one of the men sees this he moves up and immerses the plant in a bath of flame from the nozzle of the weapon he is carrying. All that is left when the fire dies away is charred black soil. But after only a few seconds, pushing up through this inhospitable earth, can be seen a new plant.

The girl clearly doesn't like this place, but when one of the men comes close to her, a fevered expression on his face, she lightly touches his arm.

GIRL: What is this? What are you doing?
MAN: Killing them.
GIRL: But—why?
MAN: To stop them from growing. (The man turns away to spread a carpet of flame, and then turns back to the girl.) The only way is to kill them. If we weren't doing this good work they'd be spreading all over the desert.
GIRL: But why do you want to stop them?
MAN: We don't want these—these filthy blossoms all over the desert. For one thing they'd encourage laxness—all our men would be too lazy to do any useful work, like they're doing now.
GIRL: But the only reason they're working is to kill the flowers.
MAN: And besides which, we're used to the desert. When I see those disgusting petals coming out I feel a strange—tension inside me. What would happen if I gave way to that, and watched them evolving all the way? And anyway, why are you so interested? I don't like the kind of talk you're giving me.
GIRL: It's just that I can't understand you. You're killing something that's beautiful and alive, something that can grow and give you pleasure. . . .

The man looks at the girl with a disgusted expression on his face, and quite deliberately spits at the ground by her feet. Then he turns back to his work. But just before his face goes out of frame his expression can be seen to change from one of disgust to an infinite sadness. The music fades.

Langdon Jones
The Eye of the Lens

Wer immer streben sich bemüht,
Den können wir erlösen.
(Who strives always to the utmost, him can we save.)
Johann Wolfgang von Goethe

The World-Riddle

12 Each man tries in his personal, and perhaps desperate, way to make this short life/time meaningful. We identify with the things of our universe that are comparatively timeless—with the rock-ribbed mountains, the washing oceans, the stars, with evolution, with life itself—to appropriate a little part of their time spans, their seeming immortality. Or we alleviate nonbeing by losing our selves within great causes and great principles and great people; or by becoming a part of the teleocosmic drama of our society and our religion.

Behind all this is the burden of our consciousness of death. We must attempt to be immortal, to be God, and to ease the dread of nonexistence.

Earthrise. Photo of the blue-and-white planet Earth by the first terran space travelers, December 1968. Taken by the crew of Apollo VIII when they were 240,000 miles from home. Photo courtesy of NASA.

But to strive to feel one with the stars—what is this but to die? Stars die. Earth's light will go out; life may dim and vanish, here. No matter: we are a part, an ever-so-tiny part, of the infinite program of the universe. I do not deceive myself into thinking I am buying time by longing for the suns or immersing myself in life. I am one with the stars. I am one with life. I identify, rightly, with all birth and all death of all time. And when I die, I shall not need to feel as though I never was at all; but rather that I was, and that is enough. I was a part of it all. I remain a part of all past and all future. I am a moment within the energy systems of motion and life and purpose.

Does this ease my loneliness? Yes. All this follows naturally from the constantly expanding boundaries of my conscious relatedness: the finite self within the context of the infinite.

13 What is the meaning of existence?

> For an answer which cannot be expressed the question too cannot be expressed. The riddle does not exist. If a question can be put at all, then it can also be answered. . . . For doubt can only exist where there is a question; a question only where there is an answer, and this only where something can be said. We feel that even if all possible

scientific questions be answered, the problems of life have still not been touched at all. Of course there is then no question left, and just this is the answer. The solution of the problem of life is seen in the vanishing of this problem. (Is not this the reason why men to whom after long doubting the sense of life became clear, could not then say wherein this sense consisted?)

LUDWIG WITTGENSTEIN

14 The whole world is a circus if you look at it the right way. Every time you watch a rainbow and feel wonder in your heart. Every time you pick up a handful of dust and see not the dust but a mystery, a marvel there in your hand. Every time you stop to think "I'm alive! and being alive is fantastic!" Every time such a thing happens, you're a part of the circus of Dr. Lao.

The Seven Faces of Dr. Lao

Nikos Kazantzakis

"I Know Not If I Shall Ever Anchor"

Now the day's work is done. "I collect my tools: sight, smell, touch, taste, hearing, intellect. Night has fallen. . . . I return like a mole to my home, the ground. Not because I am tired and cannot work. I am not tired. But the sun has set." With these words Nikos Kazantzakis begins the story of his life, an adventure of the mind and spirit, an odyssey—an ascent.

Three thousand years ago the Greek poet Homer narrated the story of Odysseus the seafarer who left his homeland, fought great battles, sailed the Aegean isles, drank, loved, and returned home to betrayal and boredom, then set sail again to see and conquer a larger world that dreamers never know.

In 1938 Kazantzakis created a sequel to Homer's epic poem, beginning where Homer left off. Odysseus is still the hero; he returns home, slays his wife's paramours, regains his place of authority, fathers dull offspring, and becomes thoroughly bored with it all. So he gathers his followers, builds a boat, and sails away on a final great journey. No map, no itinerary, no plan: an unscheduled voyage of freedom to explore the known world and to die in triumph, finally, in the Antarctic.

Does Odysseus find what he is seeking? No. Does he save his soul? No. Nor does it matter. Through the search itself he achieves a noble spirit. It matters not in the end that he is not delivered; he has battled through the seven levels of the soul to achieve himself. His God has been the search for God. "My soul," Odysseus cries out, "your voyages have been your native land!"

Nikos Kazantzakis was born into the passionate peasantry of Crete and raised with fishermen, farmers, and shepherds. His father, Michaeles, was a burly patriot who grew a long black beard to mourn the loss of Cretan freedom to the Turks.

Nikos later wrote that he never felt any tenderness or love from, or for, his father—only fear. "The fear he called forth in me was so great that all the rest—love, respect, intimacy—vanished." "An oak he was, with a hard trunk, rough leaves, bitter fruit, and no flowers. . . . He ate up all the strength around him; in his shade every other tree withered. I withered. . . . He it was who reduced my blood to ink."

Nikos early displayed the qualities of the scholar he would become—observant, questioning, shy, creative, nonconforming; and Michaeles, bewildered, from afar watched his son grow. "My father was wild and uneducated, but he never denied me anything when it was a question of my intellectual development. Once I overheard him say to a friend when he was in a good mood, 'Who cares about the bloody vineyards, or the raisins, wine, and olive oil! Let the whole harvest turn into paper and ink for my son! I have faith in him.'"

By contrast Nikos's relationship with his mother, Marghi, was one of secure silence. Always a mysterious shadow, she told him of her home village, their ancestors, and sailing ships. "I had never seen my mother laugh; she simply smiled and regarded everyone with deep-set eyes filled with patience and kindness. She came and went in the house like a kindly sprite, anticipating our every need without noise or effort. . . ." Her world was composed of knitting socks, cleaning vegetables, talking with neighbors, caring for the children, and greeting her husband at the door.

"Both of my parents circulate in my blood, the one fierce, hard, and morose, the other tender, kind, and saintly. I have carried them all my days; neither has died. As long as I live they too will live inside me and battle in their antithetical ways to govern my thoughts and actions. My lifelong effort is to reconcile them so that the one may give me his strength, the other her tenderness; to make the discord between them, which breaks out incessantly within me, turn to harmony inside their son's heart."

His childhood was passed in the spartan villages and the bustling streets of Herakleion. At the age of five his mother placed a golden baptismal cross around his neck and his father marched him off—"like a small sacrificial victim"—to the local school run by Greek Orthodox priests. "You're going to learn to read and write here so you can become a man," his father explained. "Cross yourself."

Between switchings, he learned about geography, history, politics, Turks, Greeks, and Greek grammar; but religious history fascinated him above all. It was a marvelous fairy tale "with serpents who talked, floods and rainbows, thefts and murders. Brother killed brother, father wanted to slaughter his only son, God intervened every two minutes and did His share of killing, people crossed the sea without wetting their feet."

How all these marvelous things could have happened, "we did not understand. We asked the teacher, and he coughed, raised his switch angrily and shouted, 'Stop this impertinence! How many times do I have to tell you—no talking!'

"'But we don't understand, sir,' we whined.

"'These are God's doings,' the teacher answered. 'We're not supposed to understand. It's a sin!'

"We shrank into our desks and did not utter a sound."

Hatred between Greek and Turk flamed into bloodshed, and Michaeles sailed with his family to the island of Naxos, where Nikos was enrolled in a school run by French Catholics. "Until this time Crete and Greece had been the confined arena in which my struggling soul was jammed; now the world broadened, the divisions of humanity multiplied, and my adolescent breast creaked in an effort to contain them all. Before this moment I had divined but had never known with such positiveness that the world is extremely large and that suffering and toil are the companions and fellow warriors not only of the Cretan, but of every man. . . ."

After the successful uprising of the Cretans against the Turks in 1897, Michaeles brought his son home to a free Crete and a passionate summer of freedom. His education continued, disrupted now only by the turbulent onset of adolescence. There awakened in him two clamoring beasts: that leopard, the flesh—relentless, hungry—and that eagle, the mind—insatiable and thirsty for understanding. For the moment, however, the

All my life I struggled to stretch my mind to the breaking point, until it began to creak, in order to create a great thought which might be able to give a new meaning to life, a new meaning to death, and to console mankind.

I force my body to obey my soul, and thus I never tire.

God sits waiting at the end of every road.

I said to the almond tree, "Sister, speak to me of God." And the almond tree blossomed.

"The soul of man is an arrow: it darts as high as it can toward heaven but always falls back down again to earth. Life on earth means shedding one's wings."

[**Jesus in *The Last Temptation of Christ***]

I see no reason why my grocer should be immortal. Or why I should. But I do see a reason why great souls should not die when they depart the flesh.

All of life is struggle.

Our lifetime is a brief flash, but sufficient.

We sing even though we know that no ear exists to hear us; we toil though there is no employer to pay us our wages when night falls.

As I watched the seagulls, I thought: "That's the road to take; find the absolute rhythm and follow it with absolute trust."

Each morning the world rediscovers its virginity.

mind soared ahead of the flesh. "I kept asking myself, How can people sing, how is it their hearts are not throbbing to learn what God's nature is, and where we come from, and where we are going."

Nikos completed his secondary education at the gymnasium in Herakleion, then sailed to Athens and spent a dismal four years pursuing a law degree at the university. But all his law courses failed utterly to nourish the needs of his mind or heart. He reminisces, sadly: "My heart breaks when I bring to mind those years I spent as a university student in Athens. Though I looked, I saw nothing. . . . In Crete I had risen in revolt against my destiny. I had given myself over to wine for one moment, touched the Irish girl for another moment. But this was not my road. . . ."

After university Nikos returned to Crete for a summer, and there he wandered the countryside, alone except for his books and notebooks. He had begun to feel the luminous satisfactions of writing. "Here is my road, here is duty." He was struggling with the ultimate themes of life and death. "Each man acquires the stature of the enemy with whom he wrestles. It pleased me, even if it meant my destruction, to wrestle with God."

In the prologue to his autobiography *Report to Greco,* Kazantzakis wrote that there are three kinds of souls: One kind of soul says "I am a bow in your hands, Lord. Draw me, lest I rot." A second kind says "Do not overdraw me, Lord. I shall break." But a third kind says "Overdraw me, Lord, and who cares if I break!"

Kazantzakis, of course, was a soul of the third kind.

These are the questions that haunted Kazantzakis's mind and heart for a lifetime: Who/What is God? What is Man's place in the world? What is the ultimate destiny of Mankind?

During his time in Paris, he had become acquainted with the ideas of two of the great Western philosophers, Nietzsche and Bergson. He was not merely influenced by them; he was overwhelmed and devastated. He wrote:

> Indignation had overcome me in those early years. I remember that I could not bear the pyrotechnics of human existence: how life ignited for an instant, burst in the air in a myriad of color flares, then all at once vanished. Who ignited it? Who gave it such fascination and beauty, then suddenly, pitilessly, snuffed it out? "No," I shouted, "I will not accept this, will not subscribe; I shall find some way to keep life from expiring."

Kazantzakis fell under the spell of Nietzsche and made a pilgrimage to all the towns in Germany where the poet/philosopher had lived. Nietzsche's Dionysian vision of man shaping himself into the superman by sheer force of will and courage captured Kazantzakis's imagination and taught him that the only way one can be free is to struggle—to lose oneself in a cause, to fight fiercely for that cause without recoil, without fear, and without hope of reward.

But as the struggle continued, it was Bergson who was finally able to heal. Early on Kazantzakis had abandoned as too materialistic the anthropomorphic imagery of Christian tradition. Now he was moved by Bergson's Apollonian concept of an *élan vital*—a life-force that can manipulate and organize matter. Under Bergson's guidance, he came to think of God not as a person or a persona but as an elemental force field of living nature working to effect more complex organizations of matter, moving relentlessly and opportunistically to produce higher forms of life. God is not matter; and the World/Cosmos is not (pantheistically) the "body of God." God, rather, is the antientropic life-force that organizes elemental matter into systems that can manifest ever more subtle and advanced forms of being and consciousness. We humans have our place as golden links in the chain of being that leads on toward forms of life yet undreamed of. Our lives develop meaning as we realize our selves as links in that chain.

> Our duty is to try to find the rhythm of God's progression, and when we find it to adjust, as much as we can, the rhythms of our small and ephemeral life with his. Only thus may we mortals manage to achieve something immortal. . . . We all ascend together, swept up by a mysterious and invisible Urge. Where are we going? No one knows. Don't ask, mount higher! Perhaps we are going nowhere, perhaps there is no one to pay us the rewarding wages of our lives. So much the better! For thus may we conquer the last, the greatest of all temptations—that of Hope. We fight because that is how we want it. . . . We sing even though we know that no ear exists to hear us; we toil though there is no employer to pay us our wages when night falls.

Nietzsche showed Kazantzakis how to frame the question; Bergson pointed the way toward an answer. "My heart's calmness always returned when I went to hear Bergson's magical voice. . . . His words were a bewitching spell that opened a small door in the bowels of necessity and allowed light to pour in."

In the search for God, where does Kazantzakis come out? Not as a true believer. Not as a Marxist prophet. Certainly not as a saint. Not as a Christ redeemed by the cross or a Buddha delivered from the world of pain. And not as a lover of women or father to a family. None of these things matter: his kingdom is not of this world. Does it matter in the end that—following in the wake of his mentor Odysseus—he does not **become** something, that he does not **arrive,** that he is not **transmogrified into spirit?** No. It matters not.

Homer's Odysseus went in search of his homeland; Kazantzakis' Odysseus sought God. "The first found his Ithaca, the second became the slayer of gods, searching for the true God." In the end, Kazantzakis knows that he is Odysseus but knows not if he will ever anchor in Ithaca—"unless Ithaca is the voyage itself."

Nikos looked the way an ascetic Greek scholar should: tall, thin, angular, with piercing eyes and shaggy brows. He dressed simply in black suit and sailor's sweater. He ate sparingly, often working through days and nights and forgetting to eat. Each morning he rose at six o'clock and took a two-hour walk before breakfast.

He worked unceasingly. The last decade of his life was marked by an easing of inner conflicts and prolific writing. From 1948 to 1957 he produced eight books. By the age of 70 his novels had been translated into thirty languages, and he was famed throughout Europe and America, mostly in the latter from the movie version of *Zorba the Greek.*

He loved his solitude. His inner life was intensely emotional, but outwardly he appeared serene, as though he were occupied with higher tensions parallel to, but quite above, the human drama. He possessed "a spiritual and mental energy," a psychologist once told him, "quite beyond the normal." He loved the sea, music, the rain, and traveling. He was honest, simple, direct, and without guile.

In 1953 Kazantzakis developed leukemia, but it had little immediate effect upon the pace of his life and work. He knew he had not finished his work; he had volumes to write; he needed more time. "I feel like doing what Bergson says—going to the street corner and holding out my hand to start begging from passers-by: 'Alms, brothers! A quarter of an hour from each of you.' Oh, for a little time, just enough to let me finish my work. Afterwards, let Charon come."

In 1957 he visited China on invitation of the government; against his doctor's advice he made the journey, wanting to see what changes had taken place since his visit two decades earlier. In Canton he received a smallpox vaccination to which he had an allergic reaction. He flew home via Tokyo, Alaska, and over the Pole to Denmark, and finally to Freiburg, Germany. Infection, temperature of 105°, flu, complications. He was visited in the University Clinic by Albert Schweitzer, the one man in all the world he most admired. Then, with his wife at his side, he "slept away, lovingly, beautifully, kindly, without complaint." He died October 26, 1957, four months before his 75th birthday.

Charon came at last.

Nikos Kazantzakis was inevitably controversial. Few understood him; passionate Greeks flew into a rage before attempting to understand. His thoughts were too subtle, his phrases too erudite, his allusions veiled, his words undefined (or redefined), his philosophical framework too ethereal for the popular reader. Not being understood, he was misrepresented. Like Nietzsche he was attacked for what he had never said.

He was first accused of atheism by the Greek Orthodox Church in 1939 and a trial date was set, but he was never summoned. In 1953 the church fathers tried again, outraged by his imaginative treatment of Jesus in *The Last Temptation of Christ.* In 1954 the book was placed on the Index of forbidden books by the Roman Catholic Church. Kazantzakis telegraphed the Committee of the Index a line (in Latin) saying he would go "over their heads" and let the Lord himself be his judge. To the leaders of the Greek Church he wrote (in Greek): "Holy Fathers, you gave me a curse, but I give you a blessing. May your conscience be as pure as mine, and may you be as moral and as religious as I."

After Kazantzakis's death the archbishop of Athens refused to allow his body to lie in state (as was customary for renowned sons of Hellas) or to celebrate a funeral mass for him. At home in Crete he was given a Christian burial and his body was laid to rest by the great wall of the city where he was born.

On his tombstone in Herakleion are engraved the words: "I do not hope for anything. I do not fear anything. I am free."

Reflections

1. Assuming that you have just read through this chapter—text, marginal quotations, vignettes, illustrations, and all—then your responses must be numerous, mixed, and fragmented. Without forcing coherence at this point, what are some of the most luminous meaning-events that linger in your mind? Ask yourself why each item is meaningful.
2. Ponder the quotation from Robert Heinlein (see marginal quote on p. 625). How would you answer his question, "Then why does he look so bored?"
3. What do you think of the point that Viktor Frankl is making on p. 626?
4. On pp. 628–629, Colin Wilson scores a point that, for many of us, is quite meaningful. What does it say to you?
5. When you compare the statements by Lord Kelvin and Saint-Exupéry (p. 629, Box), what is your first (and most authentic?) response? Can these two points of view be reconciled? Is there room in your life for both?
6. Reflect at length, and with leisure, on the passage from Langdon Jones's "Eye of the Lens." Among several possible meanings, what do you think the author is saying?
7. Kazantzakis comes to a very clear conclusion about the meaning of life. State his conviction in your own words. Are you in essential agreement or is his conclusion a copout?
8. Having arrived at this point—assuming that you have read through the entire textbook—how would you proceed now to answer such a question as "What is the meaning of life?" or "Why are we here?" Are such questions still meaningful questions? If you still feel a bit stymied by such a question, then study carefully, and with a good deal of time and reflection, just the marginal quotations in this final chapter—then return and attempt to answer the question again. Do this several times, if necessary. If no answer emerges, proceed to Postlude.

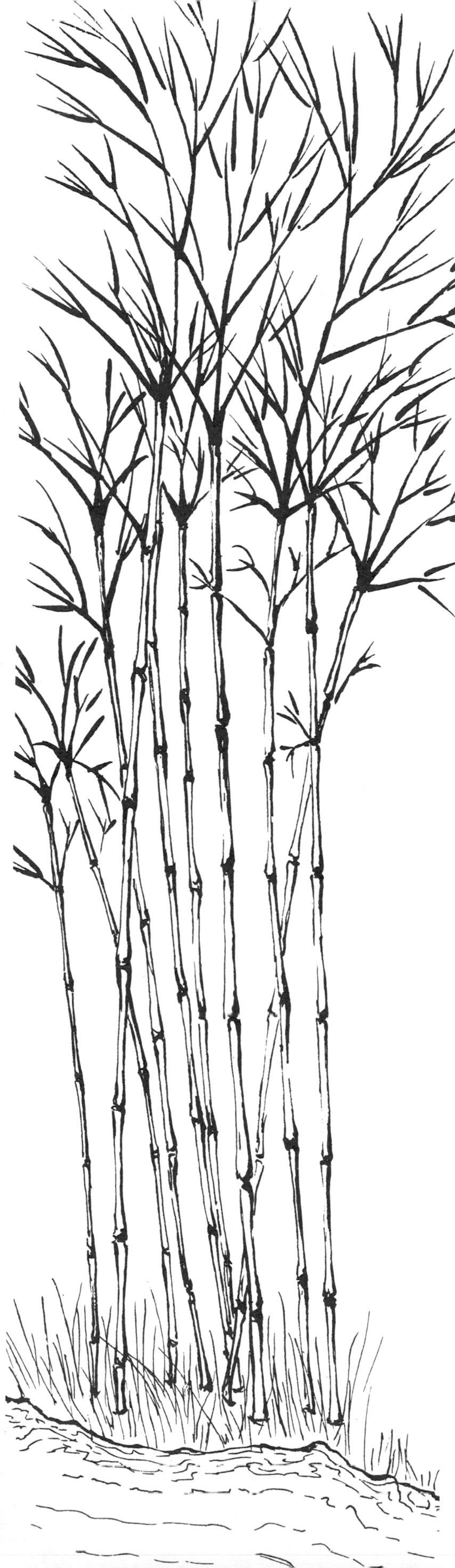

POSTLUDE

The Mahayanas tell the story of a sage
who once stood on a riverbank
looking across at the opposite shore.
Although the far side
was but dimly visible
through the river mists,
he could see that it was
unspeakably beautiful.
The hills were green
and the trees were all in blossom.

So he said to himself,
"I want to go there."
There was a raft tied
at the river's edge.
He untied the raft
and began to paddle
toward the distant shore.

The journey was long and hazardous
for the currents in midstream were swift.
The raging rapids tossed and turned the raft,
and he had to work with all his strength
to maintain his balance.
From the center of the river
both shores were lost from view,
and there were times when he was not sure
which way he was drifting.
But he continued paddling,
and in due time
he reached the far shore.

He got out of the raft and said,
"Ah, at last I am here.
It was a perilous journey,
but now I have reached nirvana."
He looked about him.
The hills were green
and the trees were all in blossom.

Then he turned around and looked back.
He could not see the opposite shore
whence he came.
Nor was there any river to be seen.
And there was no raft.

Glossary

When making use of the following brief definitions of terms, note again what a definition is. Definitions are only predictions of possible meanings that words may be given in living contexts based on past usage. Exact meanings can never be known apart from the concrete situation in which they are used. Therefore, think of the following definitions merely as openers.

absolute A concept of something that is assumed to be free of all qualifications. Whatever is absolute would be underived, complete, perfect, and unconditioned; as such, it could not be modified or changed in any way.

abstraction A concept, created by the mind, that takes into account only selected characteristics of a set of objects which are thought of as belonging to the same class. Once the mind has created a generalized abstraction (not **this** painting by Gauguin but painting-in-general), the mind is freed from having to deal with particular objects.

agnosticism In epistemology, a term (coined by Thomas Huxley) referring to the deliberate suspension of speculation and judgment about things that cannot be known (e.g., the afterlife or the supernatural). The word can be used to mean "I don't know" or "It cannot be known."

ambiguous Refers to a word or other symbol that has different meanings in different contexts. To say that a word is ambiguous often means that one is at a loss to interpret it correctly because one doesn't know the original context in which it was used. Some ancient philosophers (notably Heracleitus) used ambiguity deliberately to challenge his listeners.

analytic (1) A twentieth-century philosophic movement whose main concerns are the logical analysis of language and the process of reasoning. (2) In epistemology, a particular kind of statement in which the predicate merely spells out what the subject implies (e.g., "A triangle has three angles"). An analytic statement says nothing about the real world.

anthropomorphic Literally, "in the form of man." The projection of human qualities onto nonhuman objects (e.g., nature, animals, deities). For instance, the Greek gods and goddesses were anthropomorphic, possessing all the physical, mental, and emotional characteristics of mortals.

antinomian Literally, "against the law." In the widest sense, refers to those who deliberately choose to exist outside the accepted BTF-patterns of their society. In Western religion, the word is often used to refer to religious groups that, considering themselves saved by their faith or special knowledge, hold that they are then above all laws and restrictions.

apocalyptic A specific movement in Western religious thought and literature purporting to reveal the (heretofore hidden) divine plan of history. In the four great Western religions (Zoroastrianism, Judaism, Christianity, and Islam), apocalyptic literature moves within the framework of a cosmic battle taking place between the forces of Good and the forces of Evil, detailing dramatic events in the struggle, and revealing the future progress of the conflict to the eschaton or end-time. See TELEOCOSMOS.

a priori (or apriori) In epistemology, a kind of knowledge not derived from, or dependent upon, experience. Rather, it is a universal and necessary knowledge, such as $7 + 5 = 12$. Kant held that time, too, is a priori; the mind brings time to its experience of objects/events and does not derive its notion of time from experience of anything in the real world. Time, that is to say, is prior to experience. (Don't confuse a priori knowledge with the notion of "innate ideas," which we are supposedly born with.)

argument, philosophical A sort of dialectical conversation, carried on with others or oneself, by which one attempts to clarify his thinking, especially to clarify the validity of the fact-claims used to support ideas or statements. A philosophical argument is not an ego-argument.

aristocentric Refers to an inordinate claim to a position of superiority, for oneself or one's group. From the Greek aristos (superlative of agathos, "good") meaning "the best of its kind" or "the most to be valued." **Aristocentric claims** are most often made in behalf of one's ethnic group or "race," one's tribe or nation, or one's religion.

atheism A denial of theism (a-theism); the explicit conclusion that God or gods do not exist. Often a positive statement that the hypothesis of supernatural beings is not required to account for anything observed in human experience.

authoritarianism The claim on the part of an individual or institution to be a special source of trustworthy knowledge. In epistemology, the position that our most dependable information derives from, or is validated by, some particular authority. Contrasts with the position that knowledge is best validated by personal experience.

authority In epistemology, one of the four basic sources of knowledge. Knowledge we accept on the authority of others.

autonomy The capacity for self-determination; the freedom to operate in terms of one's own volition. Also, functioning harmoniously as an integrated self rather than merely responding inconsistently to disparate environmental stimuli. "Autonomy means the capacity of the individual to make valid choices of his behavior in the light of his needs" (Gail and Snell Putney, *The Adjusted American*).

axiology A branch of philosophy concerned with the study of values, their origin and nature.

belief (Unthinking) acceptance of an idea or system of ideas—that is, "blind belief." As in "I believe it. Don't confuse me with the facts!" Contrasts with faith.

biocosmos The conception of a universe that would include life as inherent and natural; that is, a cosmos in which life-forms are an integral factor in the overall process of cosmic evolution.

biogenesis The general term for the study of the origin of life. There have been numerous biogenetic theories. ARCHEBIOSIS (chemical evolution) is the theory that life develops from inorganic compounds whenever conditions permit it, both on the Earth and (probably) throughout the cosmos. PANSPERMIA (or transmission) suggests that life drifted to Earth from some other world, perhaps in meteorites. SPONTANEOUS GENERATION suggests that fully developed species are produced from nonliving matter. HYLOZOISM is the theory that all matter is alive. CREATIONISM is the theory that life originates only through an act of the supernatural.

Brahman In Hindu thought the absolute and supreme Reality, as compared with the unreal and illusory nature of this world; Ultimate Reality itself; pure being.

BTF-patterns An abbreviation for behavior, thought, and feeling patterns, the basic elements which together constitute selves and societies.

causality An assumption that certain events cause or produce subsequent events. This is an axiomatic assumption of naturalism and a working assumption of science: that nothing happens without prior cause and that the cause-effect principle applies universally.

coherence test A truth-test stating that any fact-claim that coheres with previously accepted facts can be considered to be true.

concept A mental construct containing all the objects/events that one has classed together according to selected common properties; an abstraction. Contrast with PERCEPT: we have percepts of particular objects/events (this seashell, this panda, this orbit), while a concept is a generalized notion to which the singular object/events belong (seashell, panda, orbit). Most common nouns are employed as concepts.

contextualism In ethics, the school of thought that holds that relevant ethical decisions can be made only within the context of a particular ethical problem where the unique factors of the situation can be taken into account. Contrast with ethical FORMALISM.

contingent In epistemology, a hypothesis or conclusion that is not necessarily true. A conclusion that, being derived from empirical observation, is only probably true. All robins' eggs are probably blue, but they are not necessarily blue. Contrast with necessary knowledge. See DEDUCTION.

correspondence test A truth-test (developed primarily by Bertrand Russell) that can be used whenever empirical observation is possible. It states that if there is a high degree of correspondence between a (subjective) idea or statement and an (objective) object/event, then the concept can be considered true.

cosmological argument An argument for the existence of God, first proposed by Aristotle and further developed by Aquinas. The argument is based on the assumption that causality is absolute and real. Every event must be preceded by another event which is its cause. But it is impossible to think of an infinite regress of causal events. Therefore, there must have been a first cause, an Uncaused Cause which started off this domino-chain of events; this First Cause is defined as God.

cosmology The study of the nature and structure of the universe. Sometimes used to refer to the study of the origin of the universe, though more correctly this is termed cosmogony.

cosmos From the Greek *kosmos,* "the world" or "the ordered universe." Refers to the entire universe considered as a single, harmonious order; a Gestalt world-system.

creationism The theory that life originated through an act of the supernatural; carries the implication that life cannot originate through other means. (Theory is not limited to any particular account of life-origins, such as the Hindu, Hebrew, Norse, et al.).

deduction In logic, the process of drawing out (explicating, making explicit) the implications of one or more premises or statements. Deductive conclusions necessarily follow from the premises. (All bitter fruit is poisonous. Manzanillas are bitter fruit. Therefore, manzanillas are necessarily poisonous.) In deductive logic, the conclusion can be valid (if it has been correctly inferred) and yet be false because the starting premises were false. But if the premises are true and the conclusion is correctly inferred, then the conclusion must be both valid and true.

determinism The assumption or doctrine that every event in the universe has a prior cause and that all effects are at least theoretically predictable if all the causes are known.

dialectic From the Greek *dialektike,* "to converse." The attempt to clarify thought and arrive at facts through a back-and-forth sort of conversation. See ARGUMENT. Also, a thought-process (associated with and propounded by Hegel) wherein ideas attempt to grow and complete themselves through a three-beat rhythm of thesis, antithesis, and synthesis; a back-and-forth progressive movement of thought.

doubt, methodical A philosophical method of deliberately disbelieving any idea in order to force it to prove its truth-value with empirical facts and/or rational argument. A way of making fact-claims prove their credentials and of preventing them from being accepted uncritically. Methodical doubt is a helpful corrective to our tendency to take ideas for granted.

dualism The view that there exist two related entities, neither of which can be reduced to or identified with the other. In psychology, dualism implies that mind and body are separate entities, different in kind, and that neither can be explained in terms of the other. Metaphysical dualism is the position that there are two orders of reality (usually assumed to be the natural and supernatural), each of which is a distinct and irreducible order.

ecstasy Greek *ek-stasis,* "standing outside" (oneself). A mystical mode of consciousness found in almost every religion in which the self is considered to have been displaced by a possessing spirit (usually a good spirit) which brings about a trance or frenzied condition considered to have ultimate religious significance.

egocentric illusion An epistemological condition: the fact that each of us perceives himself to be the hub and center of the cosmos, though in reality none of us is such a center. From a perceptual standpoint, the universe would appear to revolve around every perceiving creature, human and nonhuman alike.

egocentric predicament A term coined by the American philosopher Ralph Barton Perry to describe the epistemological fact that each of us is limited to our own perceptual world and cannot move beyond perception to know what the real world is like as it exists apart from perception. Some extreme idealists (e.g., Berkeley) assess this predicament and proceed to the conclusion that the inexperiencible world doesn't exist. Realists usually accept the predicament as a nuisance but proceed to develop a structure of probable facts about the real world which (they assume) lies beyond direct perception.

élan vital Literally, "vital impulse." Term used by Henri Bergson to refer to the impulse-to-life, which, he theorized, directs evolution upward toward the development of higher, more complex forms of life.

empathy The capacity on the part of any creature—man or animal—to assess correctly what another creature is experiencing but without itself sharing the experience. Empathy implies understanding of, but not participation in, another's inner world.

empirical In philosophy, the word "empirical" is used in at least two distinct ways. (1) It refers to knowledge acquired by our senses only. Any other knowledge (facts derived by reason, for instance) is not empirical. An "empiricist" would be one who tends to trust the senses (over reason) as our basic source of trustworthy information. In science, there is frequently the added implication that the sense data must be "public facts," that is, subject to repeated experiment and verification. (2) "Empirical" is often used to refer to any knowledge gained by any human experience (not merely sense experience). This wider definition would include dreams, emotions, religious experiences, and so on; any knowledge derived from these experiences would be called empirical.

epistemic naivety The condition of one who accepts uncritically his own vast accumulation of data, not yet having come to terms with the contradictions, fictions, and fallacies found in any large accumulation of disparate fact claims.

epistemic Shortened form of epistemological.

epistemology Branch of philosophy which studies human knowledge. It analyzes the sources of knowledge, processes of thought, truth-tests, fact-claims, value-judgments, etc. A study of what we truly know and don't know.

eschatology Literally, the doctrine of "last things." One's ideas regarding the final events at the "end of time." The Western Zoroastrian-Judaic family of religions holds that history will end through the intervention of supernatural forces. See TELEOCOSMOS and APOCALYPTIC.

ESP Extrasensory perception. See PSI.

essence The qualities without which any particular object/event would not exist or would be a distinctly different kind of object/event. The qualities necessary for anything to be what it is. (Existentialists are especially concerned to point out that objects may have essences, but that man does not.)

ethnocentrism A sociological term referring to the universal tendency of social groups—tribes, nations, races, cultures, religions—to take their own superiority for granted. See ARISTOCENTRISM.

ethics Branch of philosophy that analyzes notions of right and wrong in human relationships. Normative ethics attempts to establish ideals for intent and behavior. The field of ethics is theoretical, in contrast to morality, which refers to one's actual behavior relative to standards by which such behavior is judged to be right and wrong.

etiology, etiological The study of the origins of things or the study of their causes.

existence In existentialism, the word "existence" refers to one's experience of vivid, concrete reality in the living present. Often it carries the connotation of being profoundly aware that one is; that to exist is living in, emphasizing, experiencing fully, being intensely involved in the conscious present.

existentialism School of philosophy emerging from the dehumanizing conditions of World War II, but having deep historical roots, especially in the writings of Søren Kierkegaard (1813–1855). Existentialism emphasizes the uniqueness and freedom of the individual person and argues that each person must take full responsibility for his own existence and to "create himself." Most existentialists hold that existence can have meaning only as one participates fully in life. A central motif in existential thought is "the individual versus the crowd."

fact An idea or statement about which one can feel a high degree of certainty because, having been doubted and then subjected to logical and empirical analysis, it still stands.

fact-claim Any idea submitted as a candidate for consideration as an item of human knowledge. In epistemology, a fact-claim becomes a fact only after it has been carefully checked with the truth-tests and logical analysis and has passed muster; only then does it deserve to be called a "fact."

faith In philosophical usage, the capacity which enables one to act upon the best facts that he possesses, although they are incomplete and there is no signed guarantee of satisfactory results. In a general sense, faith is the courage to proceed to live—to exist as fully as possible—in terms of possibilities and probabilities rather than absolutes and certainties. Contrast with BELIEF.

fallacy An error in reasoning. In logic, a conclusion arrived at by means of inaccurate reasoning. A logical mistake.

fatalism The doctrine that every event of our lives is predetermined and that no amount of effort on our part can change anything or make any difference. The source of the predetermination is usually attributed to some vaguely conceived notion of natural causation, though it can be attributed to divine causes. (Originally "fatalism" was inflicted by the three Greek Fates or goddesses of destiny.) Fatalism can be both a mood and a rationalization for submission to conditions over which one feels he has no control.

finite Limited, having definite boundaries. In theology, a limited deity; one that is not omnipotent.

formalism In ethics, the position that there are universal ethical standards that apply to all men; such "laws" are often believed to have been revealed by a deity. Formalistic ethics contrasts with both RELATIVISM and CONTEXTUALISM, which hold that no such universal laws exist.

free will The theory that man's will is free to make authentic choices that are not predetermined; an affirmation that man's feeling of freedom is accurate and that our choices made between options are genuine decisions. Free will is the doctrine that, somehow, the human consciousness is not subject to the same causal principles which the scientist assumes to operate in the rest of the physical world. Some solution to the controversy over free will versus determinism is a precondition to any discussion of ethics and responsibility.

God Roughly synonymous with Ultimate Reality or Ultimate Being. In philosophy the existence of a deity would be a hypothesis developed to account for empirical data or to be supported by rational arguments. It would not be, as in religious systems, the object of uncritical belief.

hedonism In ethics, the doctrine that pleasure is the ultimate goal of life which does and should determine our behavior. Philosophical hedonists (e.g., Bentham and Mill) held that man labors under "two sovereign masters": pleasure and pain. Life should be devoted to the avoidance of pain and the augmentation of pleasure, for self and others.

hominid (*Hominidae*) Scientific classification of the evolutionary branch that includes the three great apes (chimpanzees, gorillas, orangutans) and humans. In taxonomy the Hominidae constitute a family.

hominoid (*Hominoidae*) Scientific classification of the evolutionary branch that includes the great apes (hominids plus gibbons) and humans. In taxonomy the Hominoidae are a superfamily.

hylozoism Theory held by the earliest Greek philosophers that all matter is alive or in some way possesses life.

idealism Idealism is the theory that reality is primarily mental rather than material; it consists of mind (or Mind), minds, ideas, or selves. There are numerous brands of idealism, no two quite alike. Plato was an idealist since he believed that "ideas" exist in the cosmos quite apart from brains. Christians are similarly idealistic if they believe that "ideas" or "eternal verities" exist in the mind of God. George Berkeley was an idealist since he believed that only minds (God's and ours) exist. G. W. F. Hegel was an idealist because he believed the Absolute Mind (a superlogical God of sorts) permeates human activity and that we can "think God's thoughts." Mary Baker Eddy, the founder of Christian Science, was an idealist because she believed that we all exist within the Mind of God, the only Reality. Eastern religions such as Hinduism and Buddhism are idealisms since they hold that life's true purpose (for instance, Zen satori, "awareness," or the trance-state of nirvana) is achieved only through an odyssey of the mind. Shankara's teaching that this world is maya ("illusion"), "comparable to foam, a mirage, a dream," makes this interpretation of Vedanta the Eastern world's most extreme philosophical idealism.

imply To make statements from which logical inferences can be drawn, but without explicitly stating them. The process of drawing out implications is termed INFERENCE. In everyday usage there is much confusion between infer and imply. See LOGIC.

induction In logic, the process of developing generalized explanations, hypotheses, or laws from a collection of facts. Induction is the commonest of our daily procedures for gathering knowledge. It includes the hasty generalizations we are prone to make based upon very limited experience (that is, an inadequate collection of related facts). Inductive conclusions are never necessary (as are deductive conclusions), but only probable. See DEDUCTION, CONTINGENT.

inference An idea that the mind is forced to create after having seen the implications of certain propositions. One infers—draws out, makes explicit—what is implied in a set of premises. The branch of philosophy called logic studies the rules by which we can infer ideas correctly from given premises.

intuition (1) A source of knowledge—ideas, remembered facts, hypotheses, solutions to problems—which seem to emerge from the subconscious mind, apparently produced through activity of the subconscious before appearing in the light of consciousness. (2) Term used by Henri Bergson to describe the only method he believed could give us an accurate understanding of reality; a process of "intellectual empathy" through which we can understand the duration or unbroken continuum which in fact constitutes physical reality.

invalid (in·val′id, not in′va·lid) Refers to an idea that has not been inferred correctly; a fallacious conclusion produced by faulty reasoning.

logic Branch of philosophy defined as the study of valid inference; systematic analysis of the correct and incorrect processes of reasoning.

macrocosm Refers to man's particular vantage point as he views, and attempts to comprehend, the universe. The macrocosm is man's experiential level of reality as he looks up and down, so to speak: up at cosmic realities (cosmos) and down at microscopic realities (microcosm). Without the aid of instruments man is caught at the macrocosmic level since neither cosmos nor microcosm is directly perceivable.

materialism The doctrine that everything in the universe is nothing other than various manifestations of matter-in-motion, and, in theory, can be reduced to, and explained by, principles of causality. All the objects/events for which we have such diverse labels—matter, mind, energy, life, and perhaps spirit—are only variant forms of matter-in-motion.

maya The Hindu doctrine that this world is unreal; it is mere illusion. All we know are the illusory surface appearances of things. If the material world is unreal, only Brahman or Ultimate Reality is truly real.

metaphysics A branch of philosophy concerned with what actually exists, that is, with what the true nature of things really is. Traditionally, metaphysics has been divided into two subbranches: ONTOLOGY, the study of being, and COSMOLOGY, the study of the cosmos (cosmology is now generally thought of as a branch of astronomy). See ONTOLOGY.

monism Any worldview that purports to reduce all existence to a single order of reality; the doctrine that there is but one order of reality, whether it be mind (which would be called "psychical monism") or matter-in-motion ("naturalistic monism"), or some other kind of reality.

moral Refers to the way one overtly behaves in his relationships with others. In the most general sense, moral behavior is intended to produce, somewhere, somehow, constructive results; immoral behavior is intended to produce destructive results. Contrast with ETHICS, which is the theoretical study of ideal (normative) relationships.

mystic One who seeks or one who experiences dissolution of ego-self and separateness and feels that his being has merged or become united with Deity, Ultimate Reality, or Nature.

mysticism The school of religion that values the mode of consciousness in which the ego-self is lost and an experience of oneness with Ultimate Reality is attained. Epistemologically, the mystic commonly claims that only through a mystical experience—as opposed to rational or empirical inquiry—can reality be known.

myth A story or account, by definition involving some element of the supernatural, that is accepted by a community as a satisfactory answer to, or explanation of, some meaningful question or experience. Historically, myths are held collectively by religious communities, tribes, nations, or the like; but a story can perform the same function for an individual, in which case use of the term myth is justifiable.

naive realism The uncritical acceptance of one's sense data as representing accurately the nature of the real world; a sort of "blind faith" in what one's senses seem to tell him.

naturalism The worldview that holds that there is but a single order of reality, that of matter-in-motion. Naturalism, by definition, excludes the existence of a "supernatural" order of reality.

nihilism In epistemology, the doctrine that nothing is knowable, or is worth knowing; the contention that all knowledge is illusory, relative, and meaningless. Similarly, in ethics, nihilism is the doctrine that all moral judgments are irrational, relative, and, finally, meaningless. In a word, nihilism is the belief that there is no knowledge, no value, and no meaning that is of any real worth to man.

nirvana A mode of consciousness valued by the Buddhist and Hindu as the supreme goal of human existence. Literally, "extinction of consciousness," but better conceived as a state of consciousness described as an experience of wholeness, peace, and joy. In Hindu and Buddhist doctrine this mode of consciousness will continue after death for one who has reached the point of liberation (*moksha*) from the Wheel of Karma—the "round of rebirths."

objective Refers to whatever exists in the real world apart from our perception of it. Having to do with the perceived object as opposed to the perceiving subject. See SUBJECTIVE.

Occam's razor (Also called the Principle of Parsimony.) One of the fundamental principles of scientific method. It states that, all else being equal, the simplest explanation is the best. That is, in developing inductive hypotheses, the simplest hypothesis that accounts for all relevant data is most likely to be true. Named after the scholastic philosopher William of Occam, who phrased it: "The number of entities should not be needlessly increased."

ontological argument A logical argument for the existence of God developed by Saint Anselm of Canterbury (1033–1109). Anselm attempted to prove the existence of God from the nature of thought alone.

ontology From the Greek *ontos*, "being," and *logos*, "study of." Branch of philosophy that studies the nature of reality or being, especially as applied to living things. The term "ontological" is commonly used to emphasize the fact that some specific quality is an inescapable aspect of life itself. The fear of death, for instance, is said to be ontological since there is no way—short of the extinction of consciousness—to escape the fear. We could repress it, but the fear would remain a part of our being, buried precariously in the unconscious, where it can become a powerful but unrecognized cause of puzzling behavior.

panpsychism The doctrine that everything is composed of, or contains, mind or "soul" (*psyche*). Some Western thinkers have speculated that the binding forces within atoms might be, in some way, the operations of mind.

panspermia The biogenetic theory that life may have developed on Earth after having been transferred from other worlds, perhaps by meteorites. See BIOGENESIS.

pantheism The doctrine that God is All. Pantheists usually hold that God is in all matter or that the totality of all matter is "the body of God."

paradox A condition where two mutually exclusive ideas or statements appear to be true; and until the arrival of further data or some sort of resolution, both ideas or statements must be accepted and acted upon.

parsimony, principle of See OCCAM'S RAZOR.

percept The first-stage result of the mind's organization of sense data. The mind perceives a concrete object—this coin or this car—which remains in consciousness as an unnamed, singular object. A percept (or perception) is what is given in consciousness, the object of cognition. Contrast with CONCEPT, in which objects are mentally classed with other objects, and the mind henceforth thinks of the class rather than the object. Contrast also with SENSE DATUM, a raw, unorganized sense-response.

philosophy The love of wisdom. From Greek *philein* ("to love") and *sophia* ("wisdom"). Philosophy comprises several distinct disciplines or methods that have in common the goal of improving upon the condition of human knowledge and our knowledge of the human condition.

pluralism The worldview holding that there exist more than two orders of reality, each of which is distinct and irreducible. For instance, if one believes that the universe is composed of matter, mind, spirit, and divine-essence, then he would be a pluralist. Compare with MONISM and DUALISM.

pragmatic test The truth-test (developed primarily by William James) stating that if an idea or statement "works"—that is, brings about desirable results—then the idea or statement can be considered true. James held that the truth-value of any idea is to be judged in terms of the results it can produce.

pragmatic paradox A human condition in which an idea must be believed to be true in terms of correspondence—that is, one must be convinced that some object/event exists as a real entity—before the idea can be considered to be true on the pragmatic-test. For example, one must believe that immortality exists as a real event (which, one must believe, could be empirically checked, under the right conditions, with the correspondence-test) before the belief in immortality can produce positive results in his life. If he believed it to be true solely on the pragmatic test, it would in fact not be true because it wouldn't "work."

pragmatism An American school of philosophy associated mainly with William James and John Dewey. One of its central themes is that philosophy should be put to work solving the more pressing human problems instead of preoccupying itself in metaphysical speculations. According to the pragmatists, truth is tentative and forever changing; truth is the quality of whatever ideas "work" at the present time.

precognition Having knowledge of an event supposedly before it happens. See PSI.

predestination A theological term referring to divine predeterminism. The doctrine that God has already determined (at least) whether each human soul will be saved or lost, or (at most) that every singular event of existence will occur as planned. A "hard" predestination logically excludes the possibility of free will.

predicament A problem condition to which, by definition, there is no solution; a situation that must be accepted. One may be able to deal productively with problems arising from a predicament (e.g., fear of nonbeing), but not with the predicament itself (that each of us faces nonbeing).

premise In logic, an idea or statement that, along with other ideas or statements, can lead to a conclusion. In reasoning, a premise is a starting statement, an opener.

primal freedom Freedom from subjective limitations, thereby enabling one to make authentic choices; freedom from primal limitations.

primary qualities In epistemology, the qualities, according to John Locke, that inhere in real objects: e.g., weight, motion, shape, extension. Compare with SECONDARY QUALITIES.

PSI Refers to all parapsychological or "paranormal" experiences. Among them: TELEPATHY, the sending of messages (ideas and/or feelings) from one mind to another; CLAIRVOYANCE, the mind's "seeing" an object/event at a distance; PSYCHOKINESIS (PK), "mind over matter," the power of the mind to influence the behavior of objects; PRECOGNITION, knowledge of an event (supposedly) before it takes place. ESP (extrasensory perception) is a rough synonym for PSI, though we do not know at present whether such experiences (if they do in fact occur) are truly extrasensory.

psyche Greek word meaning "soul"; usually thought of as a substantialized, objectified form of the self, though in earlier times and other places the word has been given a bewildering variety of meanings.

psychokinesis The power of the mind to influence directly the behavior of objects/events. See PSI.

rational Roughly synonymous with "reasonable"; having the capacity to engage in reasoned inquiry.

rationalism In epistemology, a philosophical tradition that holds that our most dependable information derives from reason rather than from empirical observation. A rationalist is one who trusts reason more than the deceptive "rabble of the senses."

rationalize The process of developing reasons ("rationales") for holding certain beliefs or performing certain actions—reasons which are not the true reasons but which are more acceptable than the true reasons. One who is subjectively naive will thus delude himself as well as others; one who is subjectively aware may reserve his rationales only for others. By definition, a rationalization is a fallacy engaged in out of need to defend one's thoughts, feelings, or actions. (Don't confuse with RATIONALISM.)

real, realism Among the most important terms in philosophy. To be real is to exist apart from perception. If I state that the teakwood figurine of the Buddha on my desk is "real," then I am stating the belief that the figurine exists as a "thing-in-itself" quite apart from my perception of it; if I were not perceiving it in any way whatsoever, it would still exist. (This position is material realism, and modern use of the term is often restricted to this meaning, real therefore refers to material objects or the physical world in general.) If I should go further and claim that the Cosmic Buddha exists, quite apart from my perception of him (or It), then this is a theological realism. If I claim that beauty exists in the orchid or rainbow, apart from my perception (that is, I close my eyes but I am convinced that "beauty" still remains in the rainbow), then I am an esthetic realist. Lastly, if I claim that right and wrong (or Good and Evil) actually exist in the real world, then I am a value realist or an ethical realist.

In common parlance we speak of dreams, headaches, fears, bad vibrations, etc. as "real." "They are my realities," we contend. "Don't tell me my head doesn't hurt. My headache is real!" But the headache is not real, as the term is used in philosophy; the headache certainly does not exist apart from your perception of it.

reality In epistemology, the totality of all things that exist apart from perception. The real world. See REAL, REALISM. In social science, a fabric of BTF-patterns shared by members of a particular society; all that is considered to be real by that social group.

reason One of many kinds of thinking (others being remembering, daydreaming, intuiting, dreaming, etc.). The mental process of using known facts to arrive at new facts. In logic, the activity of inferring conclusions from premises.

relativism In ethics, the belief, based on empirical observation, that what is considered to be right and wrong differs from one society to another and from one person to another. The term usually implies that there are no universal codes of right and wrong. Contrast with FORMALISM. (Don't confuse with Einstein's RELATIVITY.)

relativity In physics, Albert Einstein's theories of special (1905) and general (1916) relativity. Roughly, a system of mathematics and physics predicting the behavior of matter-in-motion at high speeds. (Don't confuse with ethical RELATIVISM.)

samadhi Literally, "concentration"; a form of meditation. In Hinduism and Buddhism, a trancelike mode of consciousness wherein the mind achieves a blissful, contentless, transpersonal state; the attainment of *atman*, or authentic self-essence.

satori In Zen Buddhism, the "moment of awakening" when a mediator realizes the illusory nature of self and separateness; a holistic feeling of mystical oneness.

Scholasticism A movement in Western ecclesiastical history beginning c. AD 1100 and flowering during the thirteenth century, resulting from the recovery of the Greek classics and the revitalized use of rational inquiry following the Dark Ages. A period of renewed intellectual activity within the framework of the accepted truths of medieval Catholic religion. Among the great Scholastic philosophers (the "schoolmen") were Anselm of Canterbury, Bernard of Clairvaux, Peter Abelard, Albertus Magnus, and Thomas Aquinas.

Scholastic method Specifically, the use of reason by the Scholastic philosophers, not to discover truth but to explore, explicate, and defend known (i.e., revealed) truths. The truths themselves were not subject to doubt or inquiry.

secondary freedom The capacity to make genuine choices without being limited by external restrictions (e.g., economic, social, political). Contrast secondary limitations (which are objective) with primal limitations (which are subjective). See PRIMAL FREEDOM.

secondary qualities According to John Locke, qualities that do not inhere in objects/events but are subjective sensations (e.g., color, sound, taste) Compare with PRIMARY QUALITIES.

self The conscious subject that experiences, designated by "I" or "ego." The word has frequently been used to refer to some unknown entity that unifies the data of consciousness into a coherent, operational system. Self, however, may be better conceived as the coherent system rather than some hypothetical unifying entity. An ambiguous and problematic concept.

self-determination In psychology and ethics, the position that one's personal BTF-patterns have antecedent causes, but that such causes may reside within one-self and not in the environment. We can become "self-caused." Self-determination is a middle position between an extreme free will position, which denies determinism, and a behavioristic position, which denies free will.

semantics Broadly, the study of meaning. A study of the total response of the human organism to symbols of all sorts (words, signs, gestures, etc.). In a narrow sense, the study of words and their meanings.

sensation The immediate response of the senses to stimuli. A synonym for SENSE DATUM. (Sensation does not refer to emotional responses.)

sense data Immediate sensory responses as registered in consciousness—patches of color, bits of sound—that are synthesized by the mind into the perception of an object. Sense data (singular, datum) are the first raw materials of experience that make their way from our sense receptors to the interpretive areas of the brain, where they are organized into perceptions of particular objects.

skepticism In epistemology, an attitude of doubt; either a deliberate methodical doubt to force fact-claims to prove themselves or a general doctrine of philosophical agnosticism, a sincere doubt that accurate knowledge is possible.

solipsism The doctrine that only "I" (the solipsist, of course) exist. A logical (but quite illogical) inference from the conclusion that all we can truly know are our own experiences.

soul Roughly, a substantialized, objectified notion of the self. See PSYCHE.

subjective Refers to the subject that experiences, as opposed to the object that is experienced. The term refers to the location of events that constitute the experiencing process (subjective), as opposed to the events that belong to the real world (objective).

substance The ultimate "stuff" (Greek *physis*) of which any object is made; the underlying reality to which primary qualities adhere. The word "substance" is a label applied to the assumption that there is a continuing essence in any object that remains immutable through all ephemeral changes in its "perceivable" qualities.

summum bonum In ethics, the Ultimate Good of human existence; that is, the final goal toward which all our endeavors should be directed. Various such goals have been proposed: happiness, pleasure, self-actualization, ethical love, soul-salvation, etc.

supernatural An order of reality above and outside the natural order. In philosophy, the supernatural is not the object of religious belief; supernaturalists would contend that it is necessary to postulate such an order to account for the complex data of experience. Contrast with NATURALISM; see also MONISM, DUALISM.

sympathy Literally, "to suffer with" another. The capacity not merely to understand what another is experiencing (which is EMPATHY), but the actual duplication, so to speak, in one's own experience of what another is experiencing.

synoptic From the Greek *sun-optikos*, "seeing the whole together" or "taking a comprehensive view." The attempt to achieve an all-inclusive overview of one's subject matter and to see all its parts in relationship to one another.

Tao In Chinese religion, "The Way"; a sort of cosmic pathway that lies between or within the interactions of the energy-modes Yang and Yin. To discover the Tao is to begin to live in perfect harmony with self and cosmos. Now written **Dao.**

teleocosmos From the Greek *Telos*, "finished" or "complete" implying purposive design and goal-directed movement; and kosmos, "an ordered universe." A worldview with a program that moves with direction and purpose, and in which man plays a major role. The most noteworthy teleocosmic worldviews belong to man's religions and resemble cosmic dramas in structure, including a full cast of characters—protagonists and antagonists, gods and demons, supporting roles and bit players—and carefully designed plots leading to a dramatic climax and a dénouement. Man's role is the central element of teleocosmic dramas, though this fact may be obscured by large-scale cosmic events that occur as the drama unfolds.

teleological argument An argument for the existence of God based on the apparent purposive nature of evolutionary movement and/or the design and order of the universe. Order implies an orderer; design implies a designer. The American Personalists considered this to be the strongest empirical argument for the existence of God.

teleology From the Greek *Telos*, "finished" or "complete." The theory that deliberate purposive activity, rather than mere chance, is involved in some process. The interpretation of any series of events—such as an organism's growth, evolution, or human history—as expressions of purposeful movement; goal-directed, as though planned out and guided toward a present end or ideal.

telepathy Communication of mind with mind via supposedly extrasensory media. See PSI.

theism Belief in gods or God. Often used to mean belief in a specific Western doctrine of an omnipotent, omniscient, and personal deity. Contrast with ATHEISM, the denial that gods or God exists.

theology The rational organization of religious beliefs and practices in order to render them logically coherent and meaningful. Theology is an intellectual discipline in contrast to religion, which involves one's whole being.

time dilation A phenomenon predicted by Albert Einstein's special theory of relativity: for any object moving at great velocities (relative to the speed of light) time would slow down.

truth "Truth is the approximation of thought to reality" (Brand Blanshard). Truth is a quality possessed by ideas and statements, a quality that is of value to a philosopher only after having been carefully checked with one or more of the truth-tests. The notion of an ethereal, nonspecific (and untestable) truth is meaningless.

valid In logic, a technical term referring to a conclusion that has been correctly inferred from specific premises. Validity is the property of an idea or statement that has been correctly derived by logical inference.

vitalism The doctrine that a "life principle" must suffuse itself (or be injected) into inorganic matter before life-processes can begin. What this "vital" element might be is usually unspecified, but it is often associated with the supernatural.

worldview In a broad sense, one's philosophy of life; an all-inclusive, coherent way of looking at life and the cosmos. From the German *Weltanschauung*, a sort of unconscious, totalic fabric into which one incorporates all his experiences and through which he sees the world.

Credits

Text References

Introduction

xx Excerpt from *A Concise Introduction to Philosophy* by William Halverson, pp. 18ff. Copyright © 1981 by William Halverson. Reprinted by permission of The McGraw-Hill Companies.

Part I The Fine Art of Wondering

Chapter 1-1 The World-Riddle

4 Alexei Panshin, *Rite of Passage* (Ace SF, 1968), p. 252.
6 From *The Little Prince* by Antoine de Saint-Exupéry. Copyright © and renewed 1971 by Harcourt, Inc., and reprinted by permission of the publisher.
8 Viktor E. Frankl, *Man's Search for Meaning* (Washington Square, 1963), pp. 167ff. Copyright © 1959, 1962, 1984, 1992 by Viktor E. Frankl. Reprinted by permission of Beacon Press.
8 From *Out of My Life and Thought* by Albert Schweitzer. Translated by A. B. Lemke. Copyright © 1933, 1949 by Henry Holt & Company, Inc. Copyright © 1990 by Rhena Schweitzer Miller. Translation copyright © 1990 by Antje Bultmann Lemke. Reprinted by permission of Henry Holt and Company, Inc.
9 Abraham Maslow, reprinted from *Psychology Today,* August 1970, p. 16. Copyright © Sussex Publishers, Inc. Reprinted with permission.
10 Gordon Allport, from Frankl, *Man's Search for Meaning* (Washington Square, 1963), pp. ix–xiii. Copyright © 1959, 1962, 1984, 1992 by Viktor E. Frankl. Reprinted by permission of Beacon Press.
12 Desmond Morris, *The Naked Ape* (McGraw-Hill, 1967), pp. 187, 189, 156, 159.
12 Konrad Lorenz, excerpt from *On Aggression* by Konrad Lorenz (bantam, 1967), p. 233. Copyright © 1963 by Dr. G. Borotha Schaeler Verlag, Wien; English copyright © 1966 by Konrad Lorenz; copyright © Deutscher Taschenbuch Verlag GMBH and Co., Munich. Reprinted by permission of Harcourt, Inc.
13 Jacques Cousteau, from "The Undersea World of Jacques Cousteau: The Night of the Squid," ABC-TV, telecast April 12, 1970.
13 Abraham Maslow, *New Knowledge in Human Values* (Harper, 1959), pp. 123, 126.
14 Rene Dubois, *The Torch of Life* (Pocket Books, 1962), p. 15. Copyright © 1962 by Pocket Books, Inc. Credo Perspectives, planned and edited by Ruth Nanda Anshen. Reprinted by permission of Simon & Schuster, Inc.
14 Joseph Campbell, from "The Power of Myth (#2)," hosted by Bill Moyers, PBS-TV, 1984.
15 Program notes by E. C. Stone for the London recording of Richard Strauss's *Also Sprach Zarathustra* by the Vienna Philharmonic Orchestra, conducted by Herbert von Karajan.

Chapter 1-2 The Spirit of Inquiry

22 Socrates, Plato, *The Apology,* in *The Last Days of Socrates,* translated by Hugh Tredennick (Penguin Classics, 1954; rev. ed. 1959), pp. 49–52. Copyright © 1954, 1959, 1969 by Hugh Tredennick. Reprinted by permission of Penguin Putnam Inc. (The opening line of Socrates' defense is from the Jowett translation.)
25 Thomas: John 20:24–29; Paul: 1 Corinthians 1:20, Colossians 2:8, Galatians 3:28.
25 St. Augustine, quoted from Philip Schaff, *History of the Christian Church,* vol. 3, *Nicene and Post-Nicene Christianity* (Eerdmans, 1950 [1910]), pp. 998, 1004.
25 St. Anselm, quoted from Schaff, *History,* vol. 5: *The Middle Ages* (1949 [1907]), pp. 600ff.
25 Abelard, quoted from Schaff, *History,* vol. 5, pp. 622–624.
27 Paul Tillich, *Dynamics of Faith* (Harper, 1957), pp. 31ff.
28 René Descartes, *Meditations* 1: "Things We May Doubt."

Chapter 1-3 Critical Analysis

I am especially indebted to my colleague, Professor Robert Putman, a Socratic scholar, for his assistance with this chapter.

41 Jean Brun, *Socrates* (Walker, 1962), p. 21.

Chapter 1-4 Synoptic Synthesis

57 William Halverson, *A Concise Introduction to Philosophy,* pp. 18ff. See page xx above.

65 Brand Blanshard, "Limited Minds and Unlimited Knowledge." An address to the University Class at Bucknell University. From the *Bucknell University Bulletin.* Used by permission.

67 R. Buckminster Fuller, "Technology and the Human Environment," from Robert Disch (ed.), *The Ecological Conscience: Values for Survival,* pp. 175ff. Copyright © 1970. Reprinted by permission of Prentice Hall, a Pearson company.

Part II The Condition and the Odyssey

In Part II of this book my indebtedness to others is especially great. The concept of the egocentric illusion (Chapter 2-1) is to be found, in various contexts, throughout the writings of Arnold Toynbee; though I alone am responsible for this elaboration of the idea. Chapters 2-2, 2-3, and 2-4 were enriched by concepts and material from Barbara Taylor Christian. I have incorporated many of her observations dealing with personality and growth.

75 William Halverson, *A Concise Introduction to Philosophy,* pp. 18ff. See page xx above.

Chapter 2-1 Predicament

80 "The Prayer of the Little Ducks," from *Prayers from the Ark* by Carmen Bernos de Gasztold, translated by Rumer Godden (Viking, 1962), p. 59. Copyright © 1962 by Rumer Godden. Reprinted by permission of Penguin Putnam.

82 Paul Horton and Chester Hunt, *Sociology* (McGraw-Hill, 1964), p. 91. Copyright © 1984 by Paul Horton and Chester Hunt. Reprinted by permission of The McGraw-Hill Companies.

83 Milton Rokeach, *The Three Christs of Ypsilanti* (Knopf, 1964), pp. 4ff, 313f, 315.

86 Horton and Hunt, *Sociology,* p. 86. See p. 82 above.

87 Joseph Campbell, *The Hero with a Thousand Faces* (Meridian, 1956), pp. 44ff.

90 Camus, from the preface to "The Myth of Sisyphus," in *The Myth of Sisyphus and Other Essays,* translated by Justin O'Brien. Copyright © 1955 by Alfred A. Knopf, Inc. Reprinted by permission of Random House.

91 Camus, from the preface to "The Stranger," in *Lyrical and Critical Essays,* edited and with notes by Philip Thody and translated by Ellen Conroy Kennedy. Copyright © 1968 by Alfred A. Knopf, Inc. Copyright © 1967 by Hamish Hamilton, Ltd. and Alfred A. Knopf, Inc. Reprinted by permission of Random House.

Chapter 2-2 Self

99 Arthur W. Combs (ed.), *Perceiving, Behaving, Becoming: A New Focus for Education* (ASCD 1962 Yearbook, Washington, D.C.), p. 84. Copyright © Association for Supervision & Curriculum Development.

100 Erich Fromm, *The Art of Loving* (Bantam, 1963), pp. 49ff. Copyright © Harper & Row, Inc. Reprinted by permission of HarperCollins Publishers.

103 David Hume, *Treatise of Human Nature,* bk. 1, pt. 2, sec. 5.

106 S. I. Hayakawa, "The Fully Functioning Personality," in *Symbol, Status and Personality* (Harcourt Brace & World, n.d.), pp. 51ff.

106–107 James F. Masterson, *The Search for the Real Self* (The Free Press, 1988), quotations and paraphrases of pp. viiff., 42–46.

114 From James T. Baker, *Ayn Rand* (Twayne Publishers, 1987), p. 150.

Chapter 2-3 Growth

117 Excerpt from "The Young Monkeys" by Harry and Margaret Harlow in *Psychology Today,* September 1967. Copyright © 1976 by Sussex Publishers, Inc.

120–121 Alice Miller, *The Untouched Key* (Doubleday Anchor, 1990), pp. 167–170. Copyright © 1990 Doubleday. Reprinted by permission of Random House.

121 Rollo May, *Love and Will* (Norton, 1969), pp. 165ff.

123 Gregory Bateson, "Language and Psychotherapy," quoted from Alan Watts, *Psychotherapy East and West* (Mentor, 1961), p. 105

123–124 Desmond Morris, *The Naked Ape* (McGraw-Hill, 1967), chap. 4, "Exploration."

124 Combs, *Perceiving, Behaving, Becoming,* pp. 141ff. See page 99 above.

125 Alexei Panshin, *Rite of Passage* (Ace SF, 1968), pp. 241ff. Copyright © 1968 Alexei Panshin.

131 From *The Madman* by Kahlil Gibran. Copyright © Kahlil Gibran and renewed 1946 by the Administrators C.T.A. of Kahlil Gibran Estate and Mary G. Gibran. Reprinted by permission of Random House.

Chapter 2-4 Lifetime

137 William Shakespeare, *As You Like It* II.vii.144ff.

143 From *Developmental Psychology Today: An Introduction* (CRM Books, Del Mar, California), p. 383. Copyright © 1970.

147 Hudson Hoagland, "Some Biochemical Considerations of Time," and Roland Fischer, "Biological Time," in Dr. J. T. Fraser (ed.), *Voices of Time* (George Braziller, 1966), pp. 325 and 360, respectively. Copyright © 1966 J. T. Fraser.

154–155 Erik H. Erikson, "A Healthy Personality for Every Child," in Robert H. Anderson and Harold G. Shane (eds.), *As the Twig Is Bent* (Houghton Mifflin, 1971), pp. 136ff.

158 Leo Tolstoy, *The Death of Ivan Ilyich,* translated by Aylmer Maude (Oxford), quoted from Joseph Royce, *The Encapsulated Man* (Van Nostrand, 1964), pp. 108ff.

159 Joseph Campbell, *The Power of Myth,* with Bill Moyers, edited by Betty Sue Flowers (Doubleday, 1988), p. 139. Copyright © 1988 Doubleday. Reprinted by permission of HarperCollins.

160 *Newsweek,* January 3, 1972, p. 56.

Part III The Real World: Knowing and Unknowing

167 R. Buckminster Fuller. See page 67 above.

Chapter 3-1 Knowledge

175 J. Samuel Bois, *The Art of Awareness* (William C. Brown, 1973).

Chapter 3-2 Senses

185 Lincoln Barnett, *The Universe and Dr. Einstein* (Mentor, 1952), pp. 123ff.
192 R. Buckminster Fuller, "This is the New Invisible World," *TV Guide*, February 6–12, 1970, p. 9.
192 Quoted with permission of Professor Courland Holdgrafer.

Chapter 3-3 Mind

201–202 S. I. Hayakawa, *Language in Thought and Action* (Harcourt, 1963). Copyright © 1978 by Harcourt Brace & Company. Reprinted by permission of Harcourt, Inc. These sections on abstracting and classifying are indebted to chapters 10, 11, and 12 of Dr. Hayakawa's semantics text. The story of the village animals is a paraphrase of the account found on pp. 214ff.
204 S. I. Hayakawa, *Language in Thought and Action* (Harcourt, 1963), p. 216 (original italics removed). See p. 201–202 above.

Chapter 3-4 Truth

217 For Charles S. Peirce's original article "How to Make Our Ideas Clear," see Walter G. Muelder and Laurence Sears, *The Development of American Philosophy* (Houghton Mifflin, 1940), pp. 341ff.
218 John J. McDermott (ed.), *The Writings of William James* (Modern Library, 1968), p. xxi. The introduction to this anthology contains an excellent brief biography of James.

Part IV The Inner World/The Fantastic Journey

227 Nikos Kazantzakis, *The Saviors of God* (Simon & Schuster, 1960), pp. 47ff.

Chapter 4-1 Psyche

229 R. D. Laing, *The Politics of Experience* (Ballantine, 1967), p. 26.
231 William James, quoted from Charles T. Tart (ed.), *Altered States of Consciousness* (John Wiley, 1969), p. 21.
231 Carlos Castaneda, *The Teachings of Don Juan: A Yaqui Way of Knowledge* (Ballantine, 1969).
234–235 Milton H. Erickson, "A Special Inquiry with Aldous Huxley into the Nature and Characteristics of Various States of Consciousness," in Tart, *Altered States of Consciousness*, pp. 45–71. See page 231 above.
236 Erich Fromm, D. Suzuki, and de Martino, "Zen Buddhism and Psychoanalysis" (Allen & Unwin, 1960), quoted from Tart, *Altered States of Consciousness*, p. 490. See page 231 above.

Chapter 4-2 Time

244 R. M. MacIver, *The Challenge of Passing Years: My Encounter with Time* (Simon & Schuster, 1962), p. xxiii.
245 Excerpt from A. Cornelius Benjamin, "Ideas of Time in the History of Philosophy," in J. T. Fraser (ed.), *Voices of Time* (George Braziller, 1966), p. 4. Copyright © 1966 by J. T. Fraser. Reprinted by permission of Dr. J. T. Fraser.
245 Friedrich Waismann, "Analytic-Synthetic," in Richard M. Gale (ed.), *The Philosophy of Time* (Doubleday Anchor, 1967), pp. 55ff.
248 St. Augustine, *Confessions*, bk. 11 (any edition).
249 Jean Piaget, "Time Perception in Children."
250 Arthur C. Clarke, *Profiles of the Future* (Bantam, 1964), p. 138.
251 J. B. Priestley, *Man and Time* (Dell, 1968), pp. 205, 288.
252 Louise Robinson Heath, *The Concept of Time* (University of Chicago Press, 1936), p. 199.
252 William James, *Psychology, Briefer Course* (Holt, 1892), p. 280.
252 Paul Fraisse, *The Psychology of Time*, translated by Jennifer Leith (Harper, 1963), pp. 84ff. Copyright © 1963 by Paul Fraisse. Reprinted by permission of HarperCollins Publishers, Inc.
256 Eric Berne, *Games People Play* (Grove, 1964), p. 178
257 Carl Rogers, "Toward a Theory of Creativity," from Carl Rogers, *On Becoming a Person* (Houghton Mifflin, 1961), pp. 353ff.
260 Quoted in Friedrich Paulsen, *Immanuel Kant: His Life and Doctrine* (Frederick Ungar, 1963), p. 40f.

Chapter 4-3 Freedom

267 Carl R. Rogers and Barry Stevens, *Person to Person: The Problem of Being Human* (Real People Press, 1967), p. 47.
268 St. Paul. See Romans 7:15–24.
269 Peter L. Berger, *Invitation to Sociology: A Humanistic Perspective* (Doubleday Anchor, 1963), p. 176.
271 Bruno Bettelheim, "Joey: A Mechanical Boy," in *Frontiers of Psychological Research* (Freeman), pp. 223–229. Re-

printed from *Scientific American.* Original article dated March 1959.

272 B. F. Skinner, *Beyond Freedom and Dignity* (Knopf, 1971). For similar ideas presented in fictional form, see Skinner's *Walden Two* (Macmillan, 1948).

274 Rogers and Stevens, *Person to Person,* p. 50. See page 267 above.

275–276 Robert D. Cumming (ed.), *The Philosophy of Jean-Paul Sartre* (Modern Library, 1966), p. 233.

Chapter 4-4 Symbols

289 Edwin A. Burtt, *Man Seeks the Divine* (Harper, 1957), pp. 137ff. Copyright © 1957 Harper & Row Publishers, Inc.; copyright © 1964 Edwin Arthur Burtt. Reprinted by permission of HarperCollins.

289–290 Charles J. McDermott, "Inside Story," *Saturday Review,* May 30, 1970, p. 4, from Martin Levin's "Phoenix Nest," *Saturday Review.* Copyright © 1970 Charles J. McDermott. Used with permission.

291 Leland E. Hinsie and Robert Jean Campbell, *Psychiatric Dictionary* (Oxford, 1960).

291 Reuben Abel, *Man Is the Measure* (Macmillan, The Free Press, 1976), p. 84.

292 J. Samuel Bois, *The Art of Awareness* (William C. Brown, 1973).

Part V Delicate Coexistence: The Human Love/Hate Condition

301 Snell Putney and Gail J. Putney, *The Adjusted American: Normal Neuroses in the Individual and Society* (Harper Colophon, 1966), p. 3

301 R. D. Laing, *The Politics of Experience* (Ballantine, 1967).

Chapter 5-1 History

303 Arnold J. Toynbee, *A Study of History,* 12 vols. (Oxford University Press, 1934–1961).

308 R. G. Collingwood, *The Idea of History* (Oxford University Press, Galaxy Book, 1956), p. xii.

313 Rosalind Murray (Toynbee), "Long Centuries Grown Cold," quoted from Arnold Toynbee, *A Study of History* (Oxford University Press, 1954), vol. 10, p. 140.

314 Edward Hallett Carr, *What is History?* (Vintage, 1961).

315 Arnold J. Toynbee, *A Study of History* (Oxford University Press, 1954), vol. 10, p. 140.

Chapter 5-2 Laws/Conscience

330 Martin Luther King Jr., quoted from Milton Mayr, *On Liberty: Man v. the State* (Center for the Study of Democratic Institutions, 1969), p. 5.

330 Henry David Thoreau, quoted from Paul Kurtz (ed.), *American Thought before 1900* (Macmillan, 1966), p. 312.

330 Martin Luther, quoted from Joseph Fletcher, *Situation Ethics* (Westminster, 1966), p. 62.

330 Lewis F. Powell Jr., quoted from Milton Mayer, *On Liberty: Man v. the State,* p. 5. See pagc 330 above.

331 Immanuel Kant, quoted from Milton Mayer, *On Liberty: Man v. the State,* p. 78. See page 330 above.

332 Quoted from the television series "The Bold Ones," NBC-TV.

333 *Sicut universitatis conditor,* Ep. 1.401 (October, 1198), quoted from Henry Bettenson (ed.), *Documents of the Christian Church,* pp. 161ff., 157ff.

334 *Unam sanctam,* quoted From Henry Bettenson (ed.), *Documents of the Christian Church,* pp. 161ff., 157. See above.

335 Socrates, Plato, *Crito* in *The Last Days of Socrates,* translated by Hugh Tredennick (Penguin, 1959), pp. 89ff. See page 21 above.

336–337 "Obedience to Authority," by Stanley Milgram, in *TV Guide,* August 21, 1976. Copyright © 1976 by News America Publishing, Inc., Radnor, Pennsylvania. Reprinted with permission of *TV Guide.*

338 Joseph Klausner, *Jesus of Nazareth* (Beacon, 1964), pp. 371, 376.

339 Plato, *The Phaedo,* in *The Great Dialogues of Plato,* translated by W. H. D. Rouse (Mentor, 1956), p. 521.

Chapter 5-3 Lifestyles

345–346 Ruth Benedict, *Patterns of Culture* (Mentor, 1948), p. 2.

346–348 Narration from the television series *Primal Man,* part 2: "The Battle for Dominance," David Wolper Productions. Dialogue is from filmed experiments at Stanford University by Philip Zimbardo, "The Psychological Power and Pathology of Imprisonment," a statement prepared for the U.S. House of Representatives Committee on the Judiciary, Subcommittee No. 3: Hearings on Prison Reform, San Francisco, October 25, 1971.

350 Carlos Castaneda, *The Teachings of Don Juan: A Yaqui Way of Knowledge* (Ballantine, 1969). Originally published by the University of California Press.

350 Paul Horton and Chester Hunt, *Sociology* (McGraw-Hill, 1964), p. 88. See page 82 above.

351 Paul Kurtz (ed.), *American Thought before 1900* (Macmillan, 1966), pp. 15ff.

356–357 Henry David Thoreau, quoted from Peyton E. Richter (ed.), *Utopias: Social Ideals and Communal Experiments* (Holbrook, 1971), p. 65.

Chapter 5-4 Ethics

363 From *The Madman* by Kahlil Gibran. See page 131 above.

365 From *A Concise Introduction to Philosophy* by William Halverson, pp. 254ff. See page xx above.

368 Kahane, quoted in *Playboy,* October 1972, p. 69.

368–369 "High Chaparral," NBC-TV; David Dortort, executive producer in association with the National Broadcasting Company. Reprinted with permission.

374 For a readable account of the "Categorical Imperative," see Lewis White Beck's translation of Kant's *Critique of Pure Reason* (Bobbs-Merrill Library of Liberal Arts, 1956). For a modern formulation of ethical formalism, see Walter G. Muelder, *Moral Law in Christian Social Ethics* (John Knox, 1966).

375 For discussions of contextualism, see Joseph Fletcher's books *Situation Ethics* (Westminster, 1966) and *Moral Responsibility* (Westminster, 1967); for a critical debate on contextualism and formalism, see Harvey Cox (ed.), *The Situation Ethics Debate* (Westminster, 1968).

379–380 Albert Schweitzer, *The Teaching of Reverence for Life* (Holt, 1965).

PART VI THE PROTOPLASMIC VENTURE

382 Sheila Ostrander and Lynn Schroeder, *Psychic Discoveries Behind the Iron Curtain* (Bantam, 1971), pp. 33ff. Copyright © Sheila Ostrander and Lynn Schroeder. Published by Prentice-Hall. Inc.

CHAPTER 6-1 LIFE

396 John Keosian, *The Origins of Life* (Reinhold, 1964), p. 47.

401–402 From *Biology and the Future of Man*, Philip Handler, ed. (Oxford, 1970), p. 504. Copyright © 1970 Oxford University Press, Inc. Reprinted with permission.

402 Spencer D. Pollard, *Science News*, April 8, 1972, p. 228. Reprinted by permission of *Science News* and the correspondent.

404 Sir Julian Huxley, *Evolution in Action* (Mentor, 1957), p. 13. Copyright © 1953 Julian S. Huxley. Reprinted by permission of HarperCollins.

404–405 Rene Dubois, *The Torch of Life*, pp. 50ff. See page 14 above.

405 Philip Handler, *Biology and the Future of Man*, pp. 488ff. See page 401 above.

405 Harry Overstreet, *The Enduring Quest* (Norton, 1931), pp. 234ff.

CHAPTER 6-2 HUMANS

412–416 Sir James G. Frazer, *Folklore of the Old Testament* (Macmillan, 1923), pp. 3ff. Reprinted by permission of Trinity College, Cambridge.

417 Anne Baring and Jules Cashford, *The Myth of the Goddess: Evolution of an Image* (Viking Arkana/Penguin Books, 1991), p. 25. Copyright © 1991 Penguin Putnam.

418 Desmond Morris, *The Naked Ape* (McGraw-Hill, 1967), p. 48.

420 Philip Handler, *Biology and the Future of Man*, p. 928. See page 401 above.

422 From "Monkeys, Apes and Man," a National Geographic Special, CBS-TV, telecast October 12, 1971 (italics added). Copyright © 1971 The National Geographic Society. Printed by permission of The National Geographic Society.

423 Konrad Lorenz, *On Aggression* (Bantam, 1967), pp. 233, 230. See page 13 above.

424 Ashley Montagu, *On Being Human* (Hawthorne, 1966), pp. 101, 97, 96.

425 Sir Julian Huxley, *Evolution in Action* (Mentor, 1957), p. 9. See page 404 above.

426 Philip Handler, *Biology and the Future of Man*, p. 492 (final italics added). See page 401 above.

CHAPTER 6-3 EARTH

432 From *Out of My Life and Thought* by Albert Schweitzer. See page 8 above.

433 *Poems from the Greek Anthology*, translated by Dudley Fitts, p. 114. Copyright © 1938, 1941, 1956 by New Directions. Reprinted by permission of New Directions Publishing Company.

436–437 George S. Sessions, "Panpsychism versus Modern Materialism," paper delivered at the Conference on "The Rights of Non-Human Nature" at Pitzer College, Claremont, California, April 18, 1974. See also George S. Sessions, "Anthropocentrism and the Environment Crisis," *Humboldt Journal of Social Relations* 2 (fall/winter 1974).

438–439 "Prior Possession." Reprinted by permission of Robert Baker.

441 Philip Handler, *Biology and the Future of Man*, p. 491. See page 401 above.

442 Reprinted with permission of *The New York Times*.

446–447 Albert Schweitzer, "The Ethics of Reverence for Life," *Christendom* 1 (winter 1936), quoted from Charles R. Joy (ed.), *Albert Schweitzer: An Anthology* (Harper, 1947), p. 270.

447 Pavel Simonov, "Dostoevsky as a Social Scientist," *Psychology Today*, December 1971, p. 104.

CHAPTER 6-4 FUTURE

459–460 Alvin Toffler, *The Eco-Spasm Report* (Bantam, 1975), p. 101. Copyright © 1975 Alvin Toffler. Reprinted by permission of HarperCollins.

462–463 McHale's comment on Clarke, in John McHale, *The Future of the Future*, p. 275.

462–463 Fred Hoyle, *Encounter with the Future* (Trident, 1965), chap. 11, "The Anatomy of Doom," Credo Perspectives, planned and edited by Ruth Nanda Anshen. Copyright © 1965 Fred Hoyle. Reprinted by permission of Simon & Schuster.

463 Arthur C. Clarke, *Profiles of the Future* (Bantam, 1964), pp. 56, 207, 230.

465–466 From a conversation with Robert McCall, January 1984.

467–468 Ray Bradbury, quoted from James L. Christian (ed.), *ExtraTerrestrial Intelligence* (Prometheus, 1976), p. 12.

Poem quoted from *Why Man Explores*, a symposium held at California Institute of Technology on July 2, 1976, sponsored by NASA/Langley Research Center, televised by PBS. Poem reprinted by permission of Ray Bradbury.

469 This selection first appeared in a book edited by Robert Bundy, *Images of the Future: The Twenty-first Century and Beyond* (Prometheus, 1976), p. 232.

469 Robert Bundy (ed.), *Images of the Future*, p. 235. See above.

470 Quoted in Friedrich Paulsen, *Immanuel Kant: His Life and Doctrine* (Frederick Ungar Publishing Co., 1963), p. 40f.

Part VII
Microcosm/Macrocosm/Cosmos

479 Carl Sagan, from the television series *Cosmos.*

Chapter 7-1
Knowledge of Nature

482 Account of the baseball game taken from *The Memoirs of Professor R. Kulashto* (Ganymede Press, A.D. 2068), pp. 291ff.

486 Sir Arthur Eddington, quoted from Harry Overstreet, *The Enduring Quest* (Norton, 1931), pp. 27ff.

490 Werner Heisenberg, "From Plato to Max Planck," in *The Atlantic Monthly,* November 1959, p. 113. Copyright © 1959 The Atlantic Monthly Company, Boston, MA. Reprinted with permission of Prof. Heisenberg.

491 Bertrand Russell, *A History of Western Philosophy* (Allen & Unwin, 1946), pp. 48, 55ff.

491 Norwood Russell Hanson, "The Dematerialization of Matter," quoted from Paul R. Durbin, O.P., *Philosophy of Science: An Introduction* (McGraw-Hill, 1968), p. 103.

492 Fred Hoyle, *Frontiers of Astronomy* (Mentor, 1957), p. 303.

Chapter 7-2
Space/Time/Motion

503 Martin Gardner, *The Relativity Explosion* (Vintage, 1976), pp. 45ff. Copyright © 1976 Martin Gardner and reprinted with permission.

508 For more on Zeno's word games, see Wesley C. Salmon (ed.), *Zeno's Paradoxes* (Bobbs-Merrill Library of Liberal Arts, 1970).

Chapter 7-3 Cosmos

531 Martin Gardner, *The Relativity Explosion* (Vintage, 1976), p. 192. See page 502 above.

Chapter 7-4 Biocosmos

538 Sir Arthur Eddington, *New Pathways in Science* (University of Michigan Press, 1959), p. 309.

539 Harlow Shapley, *Of Stars and Men* (Washington Square, 1960), pp. 133ff., 67. Copyright © Harlow Shapley.

541–542 Isaac Asimov, *Of Matters Great and Small* (ACE, 1976), pp. 19–34 (final entry not in original).

544 Ray Bradbury, "The Search for Extraterrestrial Life, *Life* magazine, October 24, 1960.

545 Francesco Sizzi is quoted in Oliver Lodge, *Pioneers of Science* (1893), p. 106.

Part VIII
Of Ultimate Concern

553 Tennessee Williams, *Suddenly Last Summer.*

553 Nikos Kazantzakis, *The Saviors of God* (Simon & Schuster, 1960), p. 101.

Chapter 8-1
Of Ultimate Concern

559 Scipio's prayer, quoted from Frederick C. Grant (ed.), *Ancient Roman Religion* (Bobbs-Merrill Library of Liberal Arts, 1957), p. 159.

563 Quoted from Bertrand Russell, *Mysticism and Logic* (Doubleday Anchor, 1957), p. 44f.

567 Viktor Frankl, *Man's Search for Meaning* (Washington Square, 1963), p. 189f. See page 8 above.

571 Robert W. Smith, *Concepts of Man, Soul, and Immortality in the Gathas of Zarathustra* (1976). Reprinted by permission of the author.

571–572 *Sandor Bundahishn* 95.5–20.

574–575 Aldous Huxley, *The Perennial Philosophy* (Harper, 1945).

575 Swami Abhedananda (comp.), *The Sayings of Ramakrishna* (Vedanta Society, 1903), p. 54, quoted from John B. Noss, *Man's Religions*, 4th ed. (Macmillan, 1969), p. 226f.

575 Ibn Arabi, G. F. Moore, *The History of Religions* (Scribner's, 1919), p. 450.

578 Joseph Campbell, *Myths to Live By* (Bantam, 1973), p. 24.

Chapter 8-2
Ultimate Reality

587 This wording of St. Anselm's "Ontological Argument" follows closely the text of Philip Schaff, *History of the Christian Church,* vol. 5: *The Middle Ages* (Eerdmans, 1949 [1907]), pp. 601ff.

588 Lecomte du Nouy, *Human Destiny* (Longmans, Green, 1947), p. 87.

588–589 From *The Portable Nietzsche,* translated by Walter Kaufmann (Viking, 1954), p. 95f. Copyright © 1954, 1968, 1977 The Viking Press, Inc. Reprinted by permission of Penguin Putnam.

590 Ernest Hemingway, *For Whom the Bell Tolls* (Scribner's, 1940), p. 41.

591 Arnold J. Toynbee, *A Study of History* (Oxford University

Press, 1954), vol. 10, p. 14. Copyright © 1954 Oxford University Press. Reprinted by permission.

CHAPTER 8-3 DEATH/IMMORTALITY

598 From "The Kilimanjaro Device," in Ray Bradbury's *I Sing the Body Electric!* (Bantam, 1971), p. 3ff. Reprinted by permission of Don Congdon Associates, Inc. Copyright © 1965 Ray Bradbury.
602–603 "Miner's Request: Find Proof of Man's Soul," UPI report.
603 Ray Bradbury in a letter to the author, April 22, 1972.
605 "Last Flight," in Rikihei Inoguchi and Tadashi Nakajima with Roger Pineau, *The Divine Wind* (Bantam, 1960), p. 178f. Reprinted by permission of Roger Pineau and the United States Naval Institute.
607 Richard W. Doss, "Life and Death in the Biocosmos," quoted from James L. Christian (ed.), *ExtraTerrestrial Intelligence* (Prometheus, 1976), p. 218. Used by permission.
608 From a video biography of Hugh Hefner. Copyright ©1992 Alta Loma Productions, Inc. Used with permission.
610 *Poems from the Greek Anthology,* translated Dudley Fitts, pp. 126, 116, 106, 108, 107. See page 433 above.
613 See appendix to James L. Christian (ed.), *ExtraTerrestrial Intelligence* (Prometheus, 1976), pp. 295ff.
614 Robert Heinlein, *Time Enough for Love* (Putnam's, 1976), p. 326. Copyright © 1973 Robert A. Heinlein. Reprinted by permission of Penguin Putnam.
616–619 See *Rubaiyat of Omar Khayyam,* translated by Edward FitzGerald (any edition).

CHAPTER 8-4 MEANING/EXISTENCE

623 From *The Madman* by Kahlil Gibran. See page 131 above.
623–624 Friedrich Nietzsche, Quoted from Erich Heller, "The Modern German Mind: The Legacy of Nietzsche," in Thomas J. J. Altizer (ed.), *Toward a New Christianity: Readings in the Death of God Theology* (Harcourt, 1967), p. 103.
624 Robert Heinlein, *The Glory Road* (Berkley Medallion, 1970), pp. 34ff. Copyright © 1963 Robert Heinlein.
626 Viktor E. Frankl, *Man's Search for Meaning,* pp. 122ff. See page 8 above.
626–627 Jean-Paul Sartre, *La Nausée* (Gallimard, 1938), pp. 162ff. The English translation used here is by Kurt F. Reinhardt in his *Existentialist Revolt* (Frederick Ungar, 1952), p. 157.
627 George S. Counts, "Charles Beard, The Public Man," in Howard K. Beale (ed.), *Charles A. Beard: An Appraisal* (Octagon, 1976).
628–629 Colin Wilson, *Introduction to the New Existentialism* (Houghton Mifflin, 1966), pp. 151, 154.
628 Nikos Kazantzakis, *The Saviors of God* (Simon & Schuster, 1960), p. 47f.
629 These extracts from William Thomson and Saint-Exupéry are quoted from W. Lambert Gardiner, *Psychology: The Story of a Search* (Brooks Cole, 1970), p. 189, and the flash of insight that juxtaposed these two quotations must be credited to Professor Gardiner.
629–630 William Halverson, *A Concise Introduction to Philosophy* (Random House, 1967), p. 215f.
631 Langdon Jones, "The Eye of the Lens," in Michael Moorcock (ed.), *The Best SF Stories from New Worlds,* no. 6 (Berkley Medallion, 1971), p. 69f. Reprinted by permission.

ILLUSTRATIONS

PRELUDE

Arizona Metropolis 3000 A.D. by Robert T. McCall. Reproduced by courtesy of the artist.

INTRODUCTION

xix Owl on a silver tetradrachm of Athens, minted in the reign of Hippias, c. 516 B.C.
xxi *The Dropouts* by Howard Post. Copyright © 1969 United Features Syndicate Inc., and used with permission.
xxii *Peanuts* by Charles M. Schulz. Copyright © 1968 United Features Syndicate Inc., and used with permission.

PART I THE FINE ART OF WONDERING

Part-opening photograph by John Fry, Dallas.

CHAPTER 1-1 THE WORLD-RIDDLE

4 Auguste Rodin, *The Thinker.* Ink drawing by Charles Gottlieb, from *A Study of History,* vol. 12, by Arnold J. Toynbee (Galaxy Edition, 1964). Reprinted by permission of Oxford University Press.
6 Drawing by Abner Dean from *What Am I Doing Here?* Copyright © 1947 Abner Dean.
7 *Where Do We Come From? What Are We? Where Are We Going? (D'où venons-nous? Que sommes-nous? Où allons-nous?)* by Paul Gauguin, 1897. Oil on canvas, 139.1 × 374.6 cm ($54\frac{3}{4}$ × $147\frac{1}{2}$ in.). Museum of Fine Arts, Boston (Tompkins Collection). Photograph copyright © Museum of Fine Arts, Boston.
8 *Castle of the Pyrenees* by René Magritte, 1959. Copyright © 1985 Georgette Magritte. Reprinted by permission.
9 Abraham Maslow. Courtesy *Psychology Today* magazine.
10 Viktor Frankl. Courtesy USIU, San Diego.
10 *Calvin and Hobbes* by Bill Watterson. Copyright © 1986 by Bill Wattreson. Distributed by Universal Press Syndicate. Reprinted with permission. All rights reserved.
15 *Christina's World* by Andrew Wyeth, 1948. Museum of Modern Art, New York (purchase). Copyright © 2002 The Museum of Modern Art, New York.

Chapter 1-2 The Spirit of Inquiry

26 *The Ancient of Days* by William Blake, 1794. Copyright © The Whitworth Art Gallery, University of Manchester, England.
29 *Calvin and Hobbes* by Bill Watterson. Copyright © 1986 by Bill Watterson. Distributed by Universal Press Syndicate. Reprinted by permission. All rights reserved.

Chapter 1-3 Critical Analysis

42 Editorial cartoon by Frank Interlandi. Copyright © 1976 by *The Los Angeles Times.* Reprinted by permission.

Chapter 1-4 Synoptic Synthesis

58 Zen Garden. Rene Burri/Magnum.
61 *Frank and Ernest.* Reprinted by permission of NEA, Inc.
66 Shri Yantra reprinted from S. Vernon McCasland, Grace E. Cairns, and David C. Wu, *Religions of the World* (Random House, 1969).

Part II The Condition and the Odyssey

Part-opening photograph by John Fry, Dallas.

Chapter 2-1 Predicament

80 *The Little Ducks,* drawing by Jean Primrose. Reprinted by permission of Random House.
84 Drawing by Abner Dean from *Cave Drawings for the Future.* Copyright © 1954 Abner Dean.
86 *Soldier Joe.* Drawing copyright © 1944, renewed © 1972 Bill Mauldin. Reprinted by permission.

Chapter 2-2 Self

94 Drawing by Abner Dean from *What Am I Doing Here?* Copyright © 1947 Abner Dean.
95 Copyright © Joseph Ferris. Reprinted with permission.
97–101 Zen oxherding pictures, originally drawn by the Zen Master Kakuan (c. A.D. 1100–1200), who also wrote the verse and prose comments for each picture. These woodblock prints are by the Zen artist Tomikichiro Tokuriki, from Paul Reps, *Zen Flesh, Zen Bones* (Doubleday Anchor, n.d.), pp. 136–155. Reprinted by permission of Charles E. Tuttle, Tokyo.

Chapter 2-3 Growth

117 Courtesy of Dr. Harry Harlow and the University of Wisconsin Primate Laboratory.
117 Courtesy of the University of Wisconsin Primate Laboratory.
119 *The Scream* by Edvard Munch. Oslo Kommunes Kunstsamlinger Munch-Museet.
122 Drawing by Abner Dean from *What Am I Doing Here?* Copyright © 1947 Abner Dean.
124 *Standing Couple* by David Park, 1958. Courtesy of the Krannert Arts Museum, University of Illinois.
128 *Passing the Buck* by Dick Sargent. Reprinted by permission of *The Saturday Evening Post.* Copyright © 1954 The Curtis Publishing Company. Photo courtesy Dr. Maurice Riseling, Laguna Niguel, California.
129 *Girl Before a Mirror* by Pablo Picasso, 1932. The Museum of Modern Art, New York (gift of Mrs. Simon Guggenheim). Photograph copyright © 2002 The Museum of Modern Art.
131 *Ziggy.* Copyright © Ziggy and Friends, Inc. Distributed by Universal Press Syndicate. Reprinted with permission. All rights reserved.

Chapter 2-4 Lifetime

141 Nat Farber/*Life* magazine. Copyright © Time Inc. Reprinted with permission.
146 Copyright © Sidney Harris. Reprinted with permission.
153 Illustration by Hudson Talbott.
156 Joseph Stacey.
158 Kobal Collection.
165 Drawing by Abner Dean from *What Am I Doing Here?* Copyright © 1947 Abner Dean.

Part III The Real World: Knowing and Unknowing

Part-opening photograph by John Fry, Dallas.

Chapter 3-1 Knowledge

171 Photograph copyright © 2002 The Museum of Modern Art.
172 *Calvin and Hobbes* by Bill Watterson. Copyright © 1987 by Bill Watterson. Distributed by Universal Press Syndicate. Reprinted by permission. All rights reserved.
173 Cartoon by Boris Drucker. Copyright © 1976 *Playboy.*
174 *Peanuts* by Charles M. Schulz. Copyright © 1965 United Features Syndicate Inc. and used with permission.

Chapter 3-2 Senses

186–190 Electromagnetic spectrum diagram developed by Ronald L. Smith, former director of Tessman Planetarium, Rancho Santiago College.
193 Copyright © 1971 Henry Martin.

Chapter 3-3 Mind

201 Drawing by Abner Dean from *What Am I Doing Here?* Copyright © 1947 Abner Dean.
201 Courtesy Dr. S. I. Hayakawa.
204 Village animals redrawn from S. I. Hayakawa, *Language in Thought and Action,* p. 214. Copyright © 1963 Harcourt Brace & Company. Redrawn with permission.
205 Cartoon by Dennis Renault. Used by permission.
207 Sky maps by John Polgreen from *The Sky Observer's Guide.* Copyright © 1959, 1965 Western Publishing Company, Inc.

Chapter 3-4 Truth

215 Bertrand Russell, photo by Lotte Meitner-Graf, London.

Part IV The Inner World: The Fantastic Journey

Part-opening photograph by John Fry, Dallas.

Chapter 4-1 Psyche

230 Alinari/Art Resource, New York.

Chapter 4-2 Time

247 *The Persistence of Memory* by Salvador Dali, 1931. The Museum of Modern Art, New York (given anonymously). Photograph copyright © 2002 The Museum of Modern Art.
253 *Dennis the Menace* by Hank Ketchum. Copyright © North America Syndicate. Used by permission.
254 *Sally Forth* by Craig MacIntosh. Reprinted by permission of King Features Syndicate, Inc.
258 Monument Valley, from *Arizona Highways,* June 1972, p. 18f. Reproduced courtesy of the photographer, Dick Dietrich.

Chapter 4-3 Freedom

272 Photo courtesy B. F. Skinner.
273 Photo courtesy Dr. Carl Rogers.
276 *Calvin and Hobbes* by Bill Watterson. Copyright © 1985 by Bill Watterson. Distributed by universal Press Syndicate. Reprinted by permission. All rights reserved.

Chapter 4-4 Symbols

283 Copyright © Sidney Harris.
284 *B.C.* by Johnny Hart. Used by permission of Johnny Hart and Field Enterprises.
287 *Peanuts* by Charles M. Schulz. Copyright © 1967 United Features Syndicate Inc., used with permission.

Part V Delicate Coexistence: The Human Love/Hate Condition

Part-opening photograph by John Fry, Dallas.

Chapter 5-1 History

313 *Guernica* by Pablo Picasso, Museo del Prado, Madrid.

Chapter 5-3 Lifestyles

351 *Senecio* by Paul Klee.
356 Louis Wain Estate.

Chapter 5-4 Ethics

366 Paul Reps, *Zen Telegrams* (Charles E. Tuttle, 1959), p. 39. Reprinted by permission of Charles E. Tuttle, Tokyo.
378 *Calvin and Hobbes* by Bill Watterson. Copyright © 1987 by Bill Watterson. Distributed by Universal Press Syndicate. Reprinted by permission. All rights reserved.
379 Courtesy NASA.

Part VI The Protoplasmic Venture

Part-opening photograph by John Fry, Dallas.

Chapter 6-1 Life

392 Photos courtesy Dr. Stanley Miller.
403 Photograph by Leonard Lee Rue III/National Audubon Society/Photo Researchers.

Chapter 6-2 Humans

421 Illustration by James Bama for the cover of *The Naked Ape* by Desmond Morris. Reprinted by permission of Dell Publishing Company, Inc.
425 Paul Reps, *Zen Telegrams* (Charles E. Tuttle, 1959), p. 39. Reprinted by permission of Charles E. Tuttle, Tokyo.

Chapter 6-3 Earth

436 Paul Reps, *Zen Telegrams* (Charles E. Tuttle, 1959), p. 39. Reprinted by permission of Charles E. Tuttle, Tokyo.
439 Redrawn from a drawing by Charles W. Schwartz, from *A Sand County Almanac* by Aldo Leopold. Copyright © 1949 by Oxford University Press, Inc. Reproduced by permission.
446 *Calvin and Hobbes* by Bill Watterson. Copyright © 1985 by Bill Watterson. Distributed by Universal Press Syndicate. Reprinted by permission. All rights reserved.

Chapter 6-4 Future

459 *B.C.* by Johnny Hart. Used by permission of Johnny Hart and Field Enterprises.
464 The nuclear winter scenario. Illustrations copyright © 1983 Jon Lomberg and used by permission of the artist.
465–466 Photos courtesy Robert McCall.
467 Ray Bradbury. Photo by Thomas Victor. Reprinted by permission of Ray Bradbury.

Part VII Microcosm/ Macrocosm/Cosmos

Part-opening photograph by John Fry, Dallas.

Chapter 7-1 Knowledge of Nature

485 Particle streaks. Reproduced courtesy NAL (National Accelerator Laboratory), Batavia, Illinois.
489 Reproduced courtesy E. I. DuPont de Nemours & Co., Inc., Wilmington, Delaware. From Cyril Ponnamperuma, *The Origins of Life* (Dutton, 1972), p. 104.

Chapter 7-2 Space/Time/Motion

500 Reproduced courtesy of the Hale Observatories.
507 William B. Fretter, *Physics for the Liberal Arts Student* (Holt, 1971), p. 165. Redrawn by permission of Holt, Rinehart and Winston, Inc.
510 Chase, copyright © 1988 *The New Yorker.* Reproduced by permission of the cartoonbank.com.

Chapter 7-3 Cosmos

523 Hebrew cosmos, redrawn from S. H. Hooke, *In the Beginning,* vol. 6 of *The Clarendon Bible* (Oxford, 1947), p. 20. Redrawn by permission.
523 Egyptian cosmos, redrawn from Oliver Lodge, *Pioneers of Science* (Dover, 1960).
527 The geocentric cosmos, woodcut from John C. Brandt and Stephen P. Maran, *New Horizons in Astronomy* (Freeman, 1972), p. 82. Reprinted by permission.
527 The heliocentric cosmos, from John C. Brandt and Stephen P. Maran, *New Horizons in Astronomy* (Freeman, 1972), p. 82. Reprinted by permission.
528–529 The Star Queen Nebula (M16) in the constellation Serpens. Photo courtesy Hale Observatories.

Chapter 7-4 Biocosmos

540 Pathfinder. Photo courtesy Jet Propulsion Laboratory/ NASA.

Part VIII Of Ultimate Concern

Part-opening photograph by John Fry, Dallas.

Chapter 8-1 Of Ultimate Concern

558 Cartoon by Clayton D. Powers, *Esquire* (December 1965), p. 213. Copyright © 1965 Esquire, Inc. Reprinted by permission of *Esquire.*
562 *Frank and Ernest.* Reprinted by permission of NEA, Inc.
563 Detail of painting of Adam and Eve by Lucas Cranach the Elder. Courtauld Institute Galleries, London (Lee Collection).
564 *Calvin and Hobbes* by Bill Watterson. Copyright © 1972 by Bill Watterson. Distributed by Universal Press Syndicate. Reprinted by permission. All rights reserved.
564 Detail of mural *The Last Judgment* by Michelangelo from the Sistine Chapel, the Vatican. Photo Alinari/Art Resource, New York.

Chapter 8-2 Ultimate Reality

592 Carl Jung. © CORBIS.

CHAPTER 8-3 DEATH/IMMORTALITY

599 "The Grim Reaper," in Ingmar Bergman's motion picture *The Seventh Seal.* Copyright © 1960 Ingmar Bergman. From *Four Screenplays by Ingmar Bergman.* Reproduced by permission of Simon & Schuster, Inc.

602 James Kidd's will. Reproduced courtesy Clerk of the Superior Court, Phoenix.

604 King David weeping after having been told of the death of his son (2 Samuel 19:1); in the background, Joab, the general of David's army who killed him. Painting by Guy Rowe, from *In Our Image* by Houston Harte (Oxford, 1949). Reproduced courtesy of Houston Harte.

612 *Calvin and Hobbes* by Bill Watterson. Copyright © 1986 by Bill Watterson. Distributed by Universal Press Syndicate. Reprinted by permission. All rights reserved.

CHAPTER 8-4 MEANING/EXISTENCE

625 Paul Reps, *Zen Telegrams* (Charles E. Tuttle, 1959), p. 81. Reprinted by permission of Charles E. Tuttle, Tokyo.

626 Drawing by Abner Dean from *What Am I Doing Here?* Copyright © 1947 Abner Dean.

632 Earthrise. Photo courtesy NASA.

Index to Marginal Quotations

Name/Subject Index

Page numbers in italics refer to illustrations.